P9-APX-991

SECOND EDITION

PRINCIPLES OF MARKETING

Charles W. Lamb, Jr.
M.J. Neeley Professor of Marketing
M.J. Neeley School of Business
Texas Christian University

Joseph F. Hair, Jr.
Chairman, Department of Marketing
College of Business Administration
Louisiana State University

Carl McDaniel
Chairman, Department of Marketing
College of Business Administration
University of Texas at Arlington

COLLEGE DIVISION South-Western Publishing Co.
Cincinnati Ohio

Sponsoring Editor: Randy G. Haubner
Developmental Editor: Cinci Stowell
Production Editor: Sharon L. Smith
Production House: Del Mar Associates
Cover Designer: Ben Ross Design
Interior Designer: John Odam Design Associates
Photo Research: Kathryn A. Russell, Pix Inc.
Marketing Manager: Scott D. Person

SB61BA

Library of Congress Cataloging-in-Publication Data
Lamb, Charles W.
Principles of marketing / Charles W. Lamb, Jr., Joseph F. Hair, Jr., Carl McDaniel. — 2nd ed.
p. cm.
Includes bibliographical references and indexes.
ISBN 0-538-82982-6
1. Marketing. 2. Marketing—Management. I. Hair, Joseph F. II. McDaniel, Carl D. III. Title.
HF5415.L2624 1993
658.8—dc20 93-19613
CIP

2 3 4 5 6 7 8 9 10 VH 9 8 7 6 5 4

Printed in the United States of America

Chapter-opening credits:
1: © Mon Tresor/Panoramic Images; 2: © Chie Fukuhara/Photonica; 3: © Masahiki Kono/Photonica; 4: © Ko Chifusa/Photonica; 5: © Shin Watanabe/Photonica; 6, 21: © Takeshi Daigo/Photonica; 7: © Umon Fukushima/Photonica; 8: © Ryo Konno/Photonica; 9: © Masano Kawana/Photonica; 10: © Dominique Sarraute/The Image Bank; 11, 14: © K. Shimauchi/Photonica; 12: © Hideki Kuwajima/Photonica; 13: © Red & Blue/Photonica; 15: Mercer © 1993; 16: © Minori Kawana/Photonica; 19: © Ryo Konno/Photonica; 20: © William Thompson/Photonica; 22: © Goro Seki/Photonica.

South-Western Publishing Co. is an ITP Company. The ITP trademark is used under license.

To my daughters Christine and Jennifer Lamb
—Charles W. Lamb, Jr.

To my wife Dale and son Joey
—Joseph F. Hair, Jr.

To my children Mark, Chelley, and Maxine
—Carl McDaniel

BRIEF CONTENTS

CONTENTS

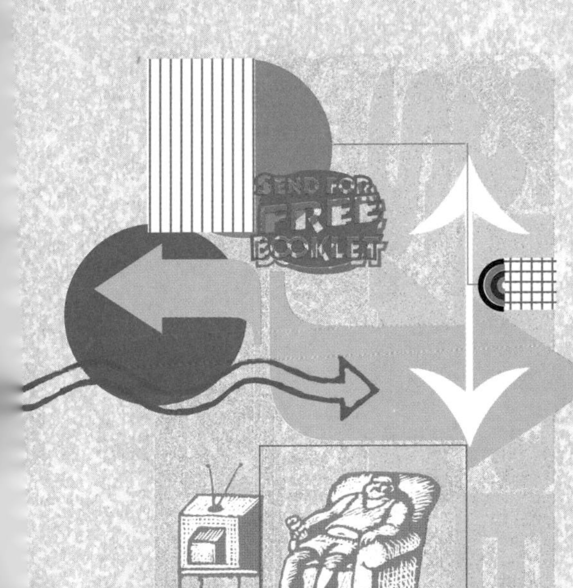
SEND FOR
FREE
BOOKLET

30¢ OFF
FARMER JOHN
PRICE
GET 1: FREE
(MAXIMUM VALUE $1.80)
ANY Campbell's
HOME COOKIN' SOUP
2 FOR 17.99

Preface

Marketing innovation is increasingly essential for organizations that want to grow and prosper. For example, Sam Walton was a great innovator. He created Wal-Mart around a vision of selling quality branded merchandise at very aggressive prices using the most sophisticated logistical and merchandising management information systems available. Wal-Mart expects sales to top $100 billion by the end of the decade.

We recognize that innovation is also critical in a textbook. Our goal is to take both the student and the instructor beyond the expected. *Principles of Marketing,* Second Edition, provides a lively, interesting, and comprehensive introduction to the field of marketing. As in the first edition, we have gone to great lengths to ensure that "lively and interesting" never means superficial or shallow. Our informal, stimulating writing style and use of thousands of current, real-world examples continues in the second edition. We did extensive research so that we could cover the latest marketing concepts and theories in a practical and contemporary manner. In summary, we have built on the strengths of the first edition to make the subject come alive for the student.

TEXTBOOK INNOVATIONS THAT GO BEYOND THE EXPECTED

A Chapter on Multicultural Marketing in the United States

The United States has become a multicultural society. We live in a country that offers a richly interwoven fabric of customs, cultures, traditions, purchasing patterns, values, and attitudes. During the 1990s, the United States will become a society characterized by three large racial and ethnic minorities. Chapter 7 explores the meaning of cultural diversity, the sociodemographic characteristics of the largest minority markets, and marketing strategies used to successfully target these markets.

An Emphasis on Global Marketing throughout the Book

Professors and accrediting associations stress the importance of international business concepts in today's world and recommend their thorough integration throughout the business curriculum. "Thinking globally" cannot be an afterthought. It must become part of every manager's tactical and strategic planning. Nor should global marketing be an afterthought in a principles of marketing textbook. Accordingly, we have moved the subject to the front of the book as Chapter 3. Global marketing is now rightfully positioned as a key component of the business environment. *Principles of Marketing,* Second Edition, stresses early the importance of developing a "global vision."

Global marketing is fully integrated throughout the book as well. Our "International Perspectives" boxes, which appear in most chapters, provide expanded global examples and concepts. Each box concludes with thought-provoking questions carefully prepared to stimulate class discussion. For example, the box in Chapter 8 describes the evolution of marketing research in the former Soviet Union and asks students to think about the unique problems a researcher would face there.

We have also added numerous international examples within the body of the text.

An icon like the one on page xxi marks key global examples for ready reference. For example, on page 129 we discuss the meanings of colors in different cultures to exemplify how cultural differences affect marketing decisions.

Finally, to give students an opportunity to analyze global issues, we have added comprehensive global marketing cases after several part divisions. Also, a number of our new video cases have a global orientation.

A Full Chapter on TQM

The philosophy and techniques of total quality management are vital to progressive organizations that want to achieve success in the competitive marketplace of the 1990s and beyond. Because marketing and TQM share a strong emphasis on customer satisfaction, marketing professionals can make a unique contribution to the implementation of TQM. Chapter 22 describes the elements of TQM and discusses the roles of management, employees, and suppliers in the TQM process. For example, we discuss how pressure from Toyota in the early 1980s resulted in an increased focus on quality by Philips Electronics Ltd., a supplier of auto headlamps. We also address the role of marketing in TQM and how marketing control and the marketing audit can help in implementing TQM.

More New In-Text Features

We have added a number of other features to *Principles of Marketing,* Second Edition, to create a richer and more meaningful learning experience. These features will broaden students' perspective and help them comprehend and retain the material they read.

- *Focus on small business:* Many students, at some point in their career, will either own or work for a small company. We have added boxes that illustrate how the material relates to small business or can be used by a small firm.
- *Focus on ethics:* In this edition we continue our emphasis on ethics by adding comprehensive ethics cases to the ends of part divisions. From the first edition, we have retained and updated the chapter on ethics and social responsibility (Chapter 20). The ethical issues boxes, complete with questions focusing on ethical decision making, have been revised and added to every chapter. Instructors will note that the popular ethical scenarios in the instructor's manual have been updated.
- *Video cases:* Each chapter now includes a video case to provoke student thinking and make the chapter concepts come alive. The authors screened hundreds of videos to find the select few that best demonstrate chapter concepts. Companies featured in the video cases include Maytag, General Tire, PepsiCo, and Colgate-Palmolive.
- *Critical thinking cases:* Our society has an enormous capacity for generating data, but our ability to use the data to make good decisions has lagged behind. Experts contend that too often we accept the data presented to us at face value instead of evaluating it critically and making the effort to understand and interpret it. In the hope of better preparing the next generation of business leaders, many educators are beginning to place greater emphasis on developing critical thinking skills. *Principles of Marketing,* Second Edition, contributes

to this effort with an integrative "Critical Thinking Case" at the end of each of the seven major parts. We have specially designed the cases to be short yet provocative. Case topics range from creating a marketing strategy for a new dry dog food to analyzing Anheuser-Busch's entry into the draft beer market.

- *Writing exercises:* College placement offices around the country inform us that  employers are demanding graduates with better written communication skills. Thus we have added two writing exercises at the end of each chapter. These exercises are marked with the icon shown here. For example, in Chapter 7 students are asked to write a letter to a fictitious newspaper, refuting the paper's assertion that people are the same everywhere and want the same things.
- *New opening vignettes that are revisited at the end of the chapter:* Each chapter begins with a new, current, real-world story about a marketing decision or situation facing a company. These vignettes have been carefully prepared to stimulate student interest in the topics to come in the chapter and can be used to begin class discussion. For this edition we have added a special section before the chapter summary called "Looking Back." This feature answers the "teaser questions" posed in the opening vignette and helps illustrate how the chapter material relates to the real world of marketing. For example, the Chapter 2 vignette presents the environmental challenges facing Taco Bell and poses intriguing questions. "Looking Back" provides closure by explaining how Taco Bell's external environment affects the company.
- *Text-integrated learning objectives:* To further aid student learning, we have fully integrated the text material with individual learning objectives listed in the chapter openers. A numbered icon like the one here ❷ precedes each learning objective. The icons then appear in the margins and summaries to mark where each objective is fulfilled. The icons also appear in all major supplements to create an integrated teaching system.
- *Margin definitions of key terms:* Prominent placement of definitions in the book's margins makes it easy for students to check their understanding of key terms. If they need a fuller explanation of any term, the discussion is right there—next to the definition.

The Features Students Liked Best from the First Edition

Feedback from students and instructors enabled us to create innovative pedagogical devices for *Principles of Marketing,* Second Edition, by adding the best features from the first edition.

- *Learning objectives:* Learning objectives appear at the beginning of each chapter. These objectives help students identify the key learning goals of each chapter before studying the material.
- *Layout:* The full-color design of the book, including about 150 carefully selected photos and 200 exhibits, complements its clear, interesting writing style.
- *Key terms:* Key terms appear in boldface in the text, with margin definitions where they first appear. A complete alphabetical list of key terms appears at the end of each chapter, with page citations for easy reference.
- *Chapter summaries:* Each chapter ends with a summary that distills the main points of the chapter. Chapter summaries are organized around the learning objectives.

- *Review and discussion questions:* End-of-chapter questions focus student attention on key concepts. Review questions can be used in class to assess students' grasp of the material. They are also helpful for students who want to test their own comprehension of important concepts. Discussion questions provide an opportunity to explore real-world applications. These questions are also designed to encourage critical thinking.
- *Cases:* Every chapter concludes with two cases, one of which is a video case. Both cases provide an opportunity for students to apply marketing knowledge in real-world situations. Longer, more comprehensive cases appear at the end of all seven textbook parts.
- *Computer software:* A stand-alone package called *Decision Assistant* has been developed to illustrate the use of twelve analytical techniques useful to marketers. Problems that can be solved with *Decision Assistant* appear at the end of selected chapters.
- *"Careers in Marketing":* Appendix A presents information on a variety of marketing careers, with job descriptions and career paths, to familiarize students with employment opportunities in marketing. This appendix also indicates what people in various marketing positions typically earn and how students should go about marketing themselves to prospective employers.
- *"Developing Interpersonal Marketing Skills":* Appendix B will help students develop influencing, negotiating, and networking skills. Any person who chooses a career in marketing, or any other area of business, must have these important interpersonal skills in order to advance. Detailed exercises to improve these skills are provided in the instructor's manual.
- *"Financial Arithmetic for Marketing" and "Tools of Marketing Control":* Marketers need to know the basic components of various financial analyses. We have presented these basics in Appendixes C and D.
- *Glossary:* A comprehensive glossary of key terms appears at the end of the book.
- *Indexes:* Two indexes—a names/companies/products index and a subject index—are included to help students quickly find text topics and examples.

STUDENT SUPPLEMENTS BEYOND THE EXPECTED

Principles of Marketing, Second Edition, provides an excellent vehicle for students to learn the fundamentals. However, to truly understand the subject, students need to apply the principles to real-life situations. We have provided a variety of supplements that give students the opportunity to apply concepts through hands-on activities.

- *A new Marketing Plan Project:* This comprehensive, term-long project gives students hands-on experience in applying marketing concepts to a realistic business scenario. The project book guides students step by step in preparing a marketing plan for a business of their choice. An accompanying instructor's manual provides all the information instructors need to administer and evaluate the project.
- *A new set of Marketing Experiential Exercises:* These short exercises send students out into the business world to discover for themselves how real companies apply marketing concepts. The exercises will expose students to issues in

globalization, small business, diversity, ethics, and TQM. This supplement contains a number of self-contained exercises from which to choose. The accompanying instructor's manual guides instructors in evaluating student responses.

- *A comprehensive Student Study Guide:* All questions in the study guide are keyed to the learning objectives by numbered icons. As students work through the study guide, they may find they need further review on some topics. They can easily find all related material in the text and study guide by simply looking for the icon. In addition to the true/false, multiple-choice, and essay questions found in the first edition, we have added application questions, many in the form of short scenarios. Study guide questions were designed to be similar in type and difficulty level to the test bank questions, so that review using the study guide will help students improve their test scores. The guide also includes chapter outlines with definitions of key terms, definitions of learning objectives, and vocabulary practice.
- *Fancy Footwork: The Marketing Program:* This computer simulation enables students to make real-world product decisions for a new line of athletic footwear through the four stages of the product life cycle. Students develop strategies for the four P's in marketing their products and receive performance feedback and suggestions for improving their marketing mix.
- *Export to Win!:* This six- to nine-hour computer simulation helps students understand exporting and international marketing while playing an interesting and challenging game. It is based on a successful commercial version developed for the U.S. Department of Commerce, which helps business professionals learn to expand markets by exporting.

INSTRUCTOR SUPPLMENTS BEYOND THE EXPECTED

The First Comprehensive and Fully Integrated Teaching System for Principles of Marketing

All major supplements that accompany *Principles of Marketing,* Second Edition, are integrated to provide you with the best-organized, easiest-to-use teaching and testing system. A complete selection of package components—from the traditional test bank and transparencies, to leading-edge videodisc technology, lecture software, and the annotated instructor's edition of the textbook—let you teach your course in your own style.

The textbook and supplements are organized around the learning objectives that appear at the beginning of each chapter. Numbered icons identify the objectives and appear next to the corresponding material throughout the textbook, as well as in the annotated instructor's edition, instructor's manual, test bank, and study guide. When your students need further review to meet a certain objective, you and they can quickly identify the material covering that objective by simply looking for the icon. A correlation table at the beginning of every chapter in the test bank enables you to create tests that fully cover every learning objective or that emphasize the objectives you feel are most important. This integrated structure creates a comprehensive teaching and testing system.

All components of our comprehensive support package have been developed to help you prepare lectures and tests as quickly and easily as possible. We provide a

wealth of information and activities beyond the text to supplement your lectures, as well as teaching aids in a variety of formats to fit your own teaching style. Changing to *Principles of Marketing,* Second Edition, will lighten your teaching load while giving your students the tools they need to master the principles of marketing.

New Lecture Presentation Manager Software

Our new *Lecture Presentation Manager* software, with graphics capabilities, gives you the ability to deliver dynamic customized lectures. This software integrates South-Western text files, graphics, and support software together with your own text files, graphics, and support software and formats them for easy and effective classroom display using any standard computer projection device.

CNBC Videos for Current, Real-World Examples

A complete array of professionally produced videos from CNBC Business News is available to supplement your presentations. These videos contain actual footage from CNBC to bring real-world examples to the classroom. The videos are updated quarterly, so they always cover the hottest topics and companies in marketing. The CNBC *Video Instructor's Manual* previews the videos for you and provides chapter correlations and discussion questions to help you integrate the videos with the text material.

Videodisc Technology to Make Lectures Come Alive

For instructors interested in multimedia presentations, our laser videodisc will excite your students with color and variety. The *Principles of Marketing,* Second Edition, videodisc contains animated illustrations, transparencies, and videos for classroom projection. The videos, transparencies, and illustrations can be viewed in any order you choose, and with an optional computer and South-Western software, you can prepare a complete video "script" of your classroom presentation ahead of time. An accompanying *Videodisc Guide* describes how to integrate this technology in your classroom. A compatible "CAV-type" videodisc player is required to use this ancillary.

Abundant Annotation in the Instructor's Edition

We have gone to great lengths to provide the most useful *Annotated Instructor's Edition* ever prepared for teaching principles of marketing. We provide all of the margin information you want most—the tips, examples, and teaching aids that enrich your course, ease your preparation, and help you connect marketing concepts to "real life" business events. Each chapter contains approximately thirty annotations, which fall into these categories:

- *Teaching Tips:* Suggestions for activities from marketing instructors around the country who have found effective ways to involve students. About half the activities are described fully in the annotations; the other half are described in more detail in *Great Ideas for Teaching Marketing,* Second Edition, edited by the textbook authors.
- *Themes:* Examples that relate text concepts to areas of current interest in marketing:

  Cross-Cultural Marketing
  Global Marketing
  Ethics in Marketing

Environmental Concerns
Service Marketing
Small Business Marketing
Nonprofit Marketing

- *Company Examples:* Examples about well-known companies that illustrate points mentioned in the text.
- *More on . . . :* Supplements to the text discussion, in the form of alternative views, insights from business experts, interesting examples, and trend analyses.
- *Transparencies:* Cues linking text discussions to the transparencies that are part of the teaching package.

The Hottest News in Marketing, Sent Every Week by Fax

Our innovative new fax service, called FACTS, will provide you with summaries of three to five current and exciting marketing articles chosen from leading publications. Articles are chosen to follow the textbook sequence throughout the term. This free service also includes information on how the article supplements the text, learning objectives for each article, discussion questions, and quiz questions with answers. FACTS will provide you with the very latest examples for your lectures and with a basis for class discussion.

A Video Instructor's Manual to Integrate Videos into Your Lectures

In addition to the twenty-two new custom video cases found at the end of each chapter of the textbook and our quarterly updated CNBC videos, we offer you sixteen more quality marketing teaching videos. Our *Video Instructor's Manual* includes video descriptions, tips on integrating each video with the textbook, teaching objectives, and multiple-choice and discussion questions for each video.

An Enhanced Instructor's Manual, the Core of an Integrated Teaching System

Each chapter of the *Instructor's Manual* begins with the learning objectives and a brief summary of the key points covered by each objective. The integrated teaching system then comes together in the detailed outlines of each chapter. Each outline, integrated with the textbook and with other supplements through the learning objectives, refers you to the support materials at the appropriate points in the lecture: transparencies with discussion suggestions, additional examples not included in the textbook, exhibits, supplemental articles, additional activities, boxed material, and review and discussion questions. These outlines assist you in organizing lectures, choosing support materials, bringing in outside examples not mentioned in the book, and taking full advantage of text discussion. Our lecture outlines are something that you can really use—not just a list of headings.

In addition to complete solutions to textbook questions and cases, the manual supplies additional cases for selected chapters, twelve ethical scenarios, summaries of current articles, class activities, and comprehensive class exercises for developing interpersonal marketing skills. Our manual is truly "one-stop shopping" for everything you need for your complete teaching system.

Comprehensive Test Bank Integrated into the System

To complete the system, our enhanced *Test Bank,* like the other supplements, is organized around the learning objectives. At the beginning of each test bank chapter

is a correlation table that classifies each question according to type, complexity, and learning objective covered. Using this table, you can create exams with the appropriate mix of question types and level of difficulty for your class. You can choose to prepare tests that cover all learning objectives or emphasize those you feel are most important.

The *Test Bank* is even more comprehensive this edition, with approximately 25 true/false, 100 multiple-choice, and 25 essay questions per chapter. We've added numerous application questions, many of which are short scenarios, to test student understanding beyond memorization. All questions have been carefully reviewed for clarity and accuracy. Questions are identified by topic and show the rationales and textbook pages where the rationales appear.

Other Outstanding Supplements

- *Transparency acetates:* More than 225 full-color transparency acetates are provided with *Principles of Marketing,* Second Edition. Most are creatively prepared visuals that do not repeat the text. Only acetates that highlight concepts central to the chapter are from the textbook. All acetates use greatly enlarged type so they can be read in the back row of a large lecture hall.
- *New Instructor's Handbook:* This helpful book was specifically designed for instructors preparing to teach their first course in principles of marketing. It provides helpful hints on developing a course outline, lecturing, testing, giving feedback, assigning projects, and using the components of the entire teaching/learning package to maximize student interest and minimize planning time.
- *New edition of Great Ideas for Teaching Marketing:* Edited by the authors of the textbook, *Great Ideas for Teaching Marketing,* Second Edition, is a collection of suggestions for improving marketing education by enhancing teaching excellence. The publication includes teaching tips and ideas submitted by over 200 marketing educators from the United States and Canada. Contributors' names, addresses, and telephone numbers are provided so they can be reached directly for additional information about their teaching techniques.
- *Computerized test bank (MicroSWAT III):* This software contains all test questions from the printed test bank, with a pull-down menu that allows you to edit, add, delete, or randomly mix questions for customized tests. The gradebook feature eases grade calculation and record keeping.
- *Decision Assistant software:* Our *Decision Assistant* program helps familiarize students with twelve basic analytical techniques used by marketing managers. Case problems that can be solved with *Decision Assistant* software appear at the end of selected chapters. For example, the King Battery Corporation case at the end of Chapter 21 teaches the student to use a Monte Carlo simulation technique for sales forecasting.
- *Two excellent instructor's manuals for simulation games:* These manuals provide concise descriptions of the two games—*Fancy Footwork* and *Export to Win!*—suggestions for getting students started using the games, game variations, sample computer output for both student and instructor, the logic used in building each simulation, and much more.

ACKNOWLEDGMENTS

Every textbook owes its content, personality, and features not just to the authors but to a team of hardworking individuals behind the scenes. We appreciate the support and encouragement we have received from our colleagues and deans at Texas Christian University, Louisiana State University, and the University of Texas at Arlington. We are especially indebted to our editor, Randy Haubner, who brought focus to the project and offered many creative suggestions and ideas. It is always a pleasure to work with someone who will settle for only the best. We also could not have done without the advice and help of Cinci Stowell and Elisa Adams, our developmental editors, as well as Jim Sitlington, Sharon Smith, and Scott Person at South-Western Publishing Company.

Our secretaries and administrative assistants, Fran Eller at TCU, RoseAnn Reddick at UTA, and Mary Jennings and Cindy Capello at LSU, typed and retyped thousands of pages of manuscript, provided important quality control, and helped keep the project (and us) on schedule. Their dedication, hard work, and support were exemplary.

We would also like to acknowledge several other colleagues who played important roles in the development of this book. Julie Baker, University of Texas at Arlington, revised Chapter 11 and contributed the TQM material in Chapter 22. Amelie Storment provided invaluable input and assistance on the revisions of several chapters. Jay Weiner, Stan Madden, Sue Cisco, Linda Catlin, and Tom White contributed interesting cases on a variety of current topics.

Thanks, too, to the following people for preparing the high-quality supplements our customers expect: Erika Matulich, Jill Kapron, Elizabeth Elam, Japhet Nkonge, Joe Alexander, Diana Haytko, Lee Meadow, Ron Taylor, and Rebecca Smith.

Finally, we are particularly indebted to our reviewers, listed on pages xxx and xxxi.

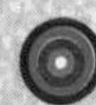

REVIEWERS OF THE FIRST EDITION

Ronald Adams
University of North Florida

Kenneth Anglin
Central Michigan University

Julie Baker
University of Texas at Arlington

Ronald J. Bauerly
Western Illinois University

Abe Biswas
Louisiana State University

Scot Burton
Louisiana State University

Daniel P., Darrow
Ferris State University

Patrick Dunne
Texas Tech University

Elizabeth L. Elam
University of Wisconsin–Madison

Gary Ernst
North Central College

Robert C. Ferrentino
Lansing Community College

Faye W. Gilbert
University of Mississippi

Ronald W. Halsac
Community College of Allegheny County–North Campus

Mark Johnston
Louisiana State University

Jill Elizabeth Kapron
University of Wisconsin–Madison

Marianne Knue
University of Cincinnati

Neil A. Kumpf
Xavier University

Ron Lennon
Barry University

Erika Matulich
University of Wisconsin–Madison

Martin Meyers
University of Wisconsin–Stevens Point

David Morris
University of New Haven

Janeen Olsen
Louisiana State University

F. Michael Sisavic
University of Portland

Bob E. Smiley
Indiana University

Robert H. Solomon
Stephen F. Austin State University

Elnora W. Stuart
Winthrop College

Robert L. Thornton
Miami University

John E. Weiss
Colorado State University

James F. Wenthe
Georgia College

James F. Wolter
Grand Valley State University

Elizabeth Wilson Woodside
Louisiana State University

Reviewers of the Second Edition

Aaron Ahuvia
University of Michigan

Larry Anderson
University of Texas–Arlington

Eric J. Arnould
California State University–Long Beach

Al Belskus
Eastern Michigan University

Jeffrey L. Bradford
Bowling Green State University

Alan Brokaw
Michigan Technological University

Donald W. Caudill
Bluefield State College

E. Wayne Chandler
Eastern Illinois University

David Collins
Webster College

Herbert Conley
Howard University

John Coyle
The Pennsylvania State University

Jane Cromartie
University of New Orleans

Geng Cui
Hampton University

Dallas G. Dearmin
Boston University

Michael Dotson
Appalachian State University

Pat Dunne
Texas Tech University

Barbara Dyer
University of Tennessee

Michael Elliott
University of Missouri–St. Louis

Margaret A. Emmelhainz
University of Dayton

David W. Finn
Texas Christian University

John Gardner
Cleveland State University

Marc H. Goldberg
Portland State University

Ronald Goldsmith
Florida State University

Kent Gourdin
University of North Carolina at Charlotte

Joyce L. Grahn
University of Minnesota–Duluth

Ward Hanson
Purdue University

Tim Hartman
Ohio University

Art Jacobson
University of Miami

J. Steven Kelly
DePaul University

Marianne Knue
University of Cincinnati

Harold W. Lucius
Rowan College

Jacob Manakkalathil
University of North Dakota

H. Lee Meadow
Northern Illinois University

Martin Meyers
University of Wisconsin–Stevens Point

Ronald E. Michaels
Indiana University

William C. Moser
Ball State University

JoNel Mundt
University of the Pacific

K. H. Padmanabhan
University of Michigan

Gillian Rice
American Graduate School of International Management

Bert Rosenbloom
Drexel University

Susan Sampson
Babson College

Ronald Savitt
University of Vermont

Martin Schwartz
Miami University

Peter B. Shaffer
Western Illinois University

Matthew D. Shank
Northern Kentucky University

Mary F. Smith
California State University–San Bernardino

Thaddeus H. Spratlen
University of Washington

E. Craig Stacey
Drexel University

Shirley Stretch
California State University–Los Angeles

Jack L. Taylor, Jr.
Portland State University

Hsin-Min Tong
Radford University

C. Burk Tower
The University of Wisconsin–Oshkosh

Donald Walli
Greenville Technical College

Rita Wheat
University of Southern California

Thomas F. White
Regis University

Alvin J. Williams
University of Southern Mississippi

Kathryn Frazer Winstead
Bentley College

Poh-Lin Yeoh
University of South Carolina

INTRODUCTION TO THE AUTHORS

Charles W. Lamb, Jr.—Texas Christian University

Charles Lamb is the M.J. Neeley Professor of Marketing, M.J. Neeley School of Business, Texas Christian University. He served as chair of the TCU marketing department from 1982 to 1988.

Lamb has authored or co-authored more than a dozen books and anthologies on marketing topics and over 100 articles that have appeared in academic journals and conference proceedings.

He is vice president for publications for Academy of Marketing Science, a member of the American Marketing Association Education Council, a member of the board of directors of the American Association for Advances in Health Care Research, and a past president of the Southwestern Marketing Association.

Lamb earned an associate degree in business administration from Sinclair Community College, a bachelor's degree from Miami University, an MBA from Wright State University, and a doctorate in business administration from Kent State University. He previously served as assistant and associate professor of marketing at Texas A&M University.

Joseph F. Hair, Jr.—Louisiana State University

Joseph Hair is William A. Copeland III Endowed Professor of Business Administration and Chairman, Department of Marketing, Louisiana State University. Previously, Hair was an associate professor of marketing and held the Phil B. Hardin Chair of Marketing at the University of Mississippi. He has taught graduate and undergraduate marketing and marketing research courses.

Hair has authored twenty-seven books, monographs, and cases and over sixty articles in scholarly journals. He also has participated on many university committees and has chaired numerous departmental task forces. He serves on the editorial review board of several journals.

He is a member of the American Marketing Association, Academy of Marketing Science, Southern Marketing Association, and Southwestern Marketing Association.

Hair holds a bachelor's degree in economics, a master's degree in marketing, and a doctorate degree in marketing, all from the University of Florida. He also serves as a marketing consultant to businesses in a variety of industries, ranging from food and retailing to financial services, health care, electronics, and the U.S. Departments of Agriculture and Interior.

Carl McDaniel—University of Texas, Arlington

Carl McDaniel is a professor of marketing at the University of Texas–Arlington, where he has been chairman of the marketing department since 1976. He has been an instructor for more than twenty years and is the recipient of several awards for outstanding teaching. McDaniel has also been a district sales manager for Southwestern Bell Telephone Company. Currently, he serves as a board member of the North Texas Higher Education Authority.

In addition to *Principles of Marketing,* McDaniel also has co-authored numerous textbooks in marketing and business. McDaniel's research has appeared in such publications as the *Journal of Marketing Research, Journal of Marketing, Journal of the Academy of Marketing Science,* and *California Management Review.*

McDaniel is a member of the American Marketing Association, Academy of Marketing Science, Southern Marketing Association, Southwestern Marketing Association, and Western Marketing Association.

Besides his academic experience, McDaniel has business experience as the co-owner of a marketing research firm. He has a bachelor's degree from the University of Arkansas and his master's and doctorate degrees from Arizona State University.

SECOND EDITION

PRINCIPLES OF MARKETING

PART ONE

THE WORLD OF MARKETING

CHAPTER 1

An Overview of Marketing

LEARNING OBJECTIVES

After studying this chapter, you should be able to

1. Define the term *marketing*.
2. Describe several reasons for studying marketing.
3. Describe several marketing management philosophies.
4. Discuss the difference between selling and marketing orientations.
5. Explain how firms implement the marketing concept.
6. Describe the marketing process, and identify the variables that make up the marketing mix.

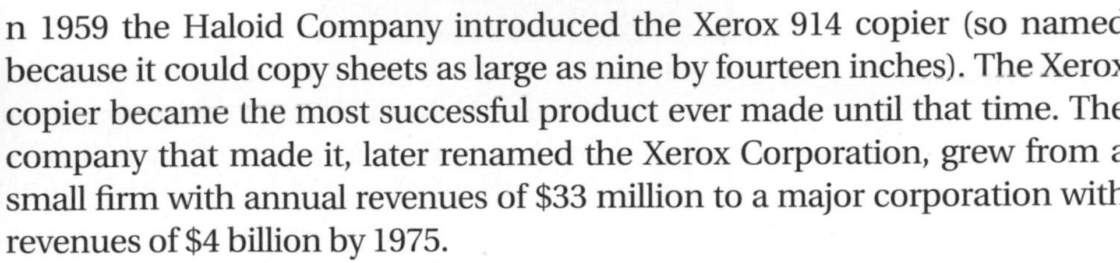

In 1959 the Haloid Company introduced the Xerox 914 copier (so named because it could copy sheets as large as nine by fourteen inches). The Xerox copier became the most successful product ever made until that time. The company that made it, later renamed the Xerox Corporation, grew from a small firm with annual revenues of $33 million to a major corporation with revenues of $4 billion by 1975.

In its early years, Xerox was protected by a patented process. Competition was weak and fragmented, while demand was growing rapidly. Inefficiencies in product development, production, marketing, and other areas could be offset by higher prices.

In the 1970s competition increased dramatically. Japanese firms began selling photocopiers at prices much lower than Xerox prices, IBM began marketing medium-priced copiers, and Kodak entered the market at the high-price end. Xerox's market share fell from nearly 100 percent in the late 1960s to less than 50 percent by 1980.

David Kearns, CEO and chairman of Xerox Corporation during that time, later said, "We were horrified to find that the Japanese were selling their small machines for what it cost us to make ours. Our costs were not only way out in left field, they weren't even in the ballpark. Let me tell you, that was scary, and it woke us up in a hurry."

Wayland R. Hicks, executive vice president for marketing and customer operations, added that the company simply "had grown arrogant." According to Hicks, "we had to re-create products to conform to customers'—not our predetermined corporate—concept of high-quality features and output."

Xerox now mails annual questionnaires to 40,000 customers worldwide to pinpoint the reasons behind their buying decisions. These questionnaires ask for customers' opinions about sales, service, administration, billing, and products.[1]

What seemed to be the management philosophy at Xerox in the 1970s? What seems to be the management philosophy today? Can you think of other organizations that have gone through similar changes in management philosophy? What caused this change? Why are these organizations and their customers better (or worse) off now than before the change in management philosophy? These issues are explored in Chapter 1.

WHAT IS MARKETING?

What does the term *marketing* mean to you? Many people think it means the same as *selling*. Others think marketing is the same as personal selling and advertising. Still others believe marketing has something to do with making products available in stores, arranging displays, and maintaining inventories of products for future sales. Actually, marketing includes all these activities and more.

Marketing has two facets. First, it is a philosophy, an attitude, a perspective, or a management orientation that stresses customer satisfaction. Second, marketing is a set of activities used to implement this philosophy. The American Marketing Association's definition encompasses both perspectives: "**Marketing** is the process of planning and executing the conception, pricing, promotion, and distribution of ideas, goods, and services to create exchanges that satisfy individual and organizational objectives."[2]

marketing
Process of planning and executing the conception, pricing, promotion, and distribution of ideas, goods, and services to create exchanges that satisfy individual and organizational objectives.

concept of exchange
Idea that people give up something to receive something one would rather have.

The Exchange Concept

Exchange is the key term in the American Marketing Association's definition of marketing. The **concept of exchange** is quite simple. It means that people give up something to receive something they would rather have. Normally we think of money as the medium of exchange. We "give up" money to "get" the goods and services we want. Exchange does not require money, however. Two persons may barter or trade such items as baseball cards or oil paintings.

Five conditions must be satisfied for any kind of exchange to take place:

- There must be at least two parties.
- Each party must have something the other party values.
- Each party must be able to communicate with the other party and delivering the goods or services that the other party desires.
- Each party must be free to accept or reject the other's offer.
- Each party must believe that it is appropriate or desirable to deal with the other party.[3]

Exchange will not necessarily take place even if all these conditions exist. They are,

Photo 1-1 a&b Marketing is a set of activities (planning, promotion, etc.) implemented to create a mutually satisfying exchange between the seller and the buyer.

Exhibit 1.1

Exchanges That Take Place Between a Public Agency and Its Citizens

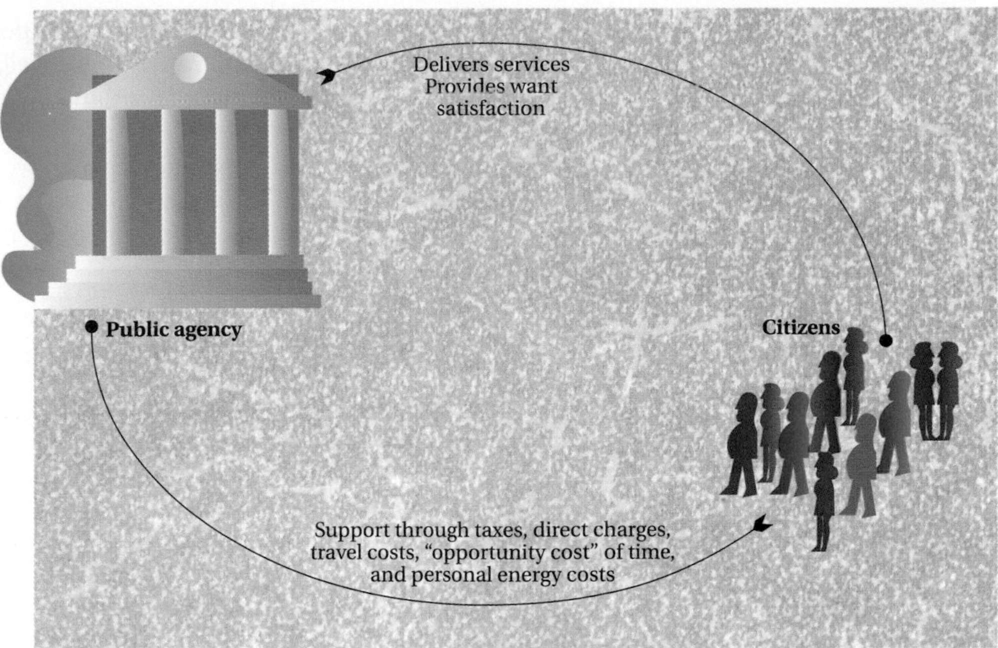

however, necessary for exchange to be possible. For example, you may place an advertisement in your local newspaper stating that your used automobile is for sale at a certain price. Several people may call you to ask about the car, some may test-drive it, and one or more may even offer you less than your asking price. All five conditions necessary for an exchange exist. But unless you reach an agreement with a buyer and actually sell the car, an exchange will not take place.

Notice that marketing can occur even if an exchange does not occur. In the example just discussed, you would have engaged in marketing even if no one bought your used automobile.

Exchange is not restricted to profit-seeking enterprises. Exhibit 1.1 illustrates the exchange relationship between a public agency and its citizens. An agency, such as a public library or a municipal recreation and parks department, delivers want-satisfying services that citizens perceive as valuable. Citizens support the agency through their payments of tax dollars, direct charges for using the services, and travel and transportation costs. Citizen support also includes the opportunity cost of not engaging in another activity while they use a service and the personal energy costs spent to use the service.

2 WHY STUDY MARKETING?

You may be asking, "What's in it for me?" or "Why should I study marketing?" These are important questions whether you are majoring in a business field other than marketing (such as accounting, finance, or management information systems) or a nonbusiness field (such as journalism, economics, or agriculture). There are several important reasons to study marketing: Marketing plays an important role in society, marketing is important to businesses, marketing offers outstanding career opportunities, and marketing affects your life every day.

Marketing Plays an Important Role in Society

The U.S. Bureau of the Census predicts that the total population of the United States will reach 268 million by the end of the 1990s. Think about how many transactions

are needed each day to feed, clothe, and shelter a population of this size. The number is huge. And yet the system works quite well, partly because the well-developed U.S. system gets the output of farms and factories to us in a convenient, economical, and sanitary way. A typical U.S. family, for example, consumes 2.5 tons of food a year. Marketing makes food available when we want it, in desired quantities, at accessible locations, and in sanitary and convenient packages and forms (such as instant and frozen foods). Food is just one of the many products that are part of our standard of living.

Marketing Is Important to Businesses

The fundamental objectives of most businesses are survival, profits, and growth. Marketing contributes directly to achieving these objectives. Marketing includes these activities, which are vital to business organizations: assessing the wants and satisfactions of present and potential customers, designing and managing product offerings, determining prices and pricing policies, developing distribution strategies, and communicating with present and potential customers.

All businesspeople, regardless of specialization or area of responsibility, need to be familiar with the terminology and fundamentals of accounting, finance, management, and marketing. People in all business areas need to be able to communicate with specialists in other areas. Therefore, a basic understanding of marketing is important to all businesspeople.

Marketing Offers Outstanding Career Opportunities

Between a fourth and a third of the entire civilian work force in the United States performs marketing activities. Marketing offers great career opportunities in such areas as professional selling, marketing research, advertising, retail buying, distribution management, product management, product development, and wholesaling. Marketing career opportunities also exist in a variety of nonbusiness organizations, including hospitals, museums, universities, the armed forces, and various government and social service agencies (see Chapter 11).

As the world marketplace becomes more challenging, U.S. companies are going to have to become better marketers. In high-tech to low-tech industries, profit and

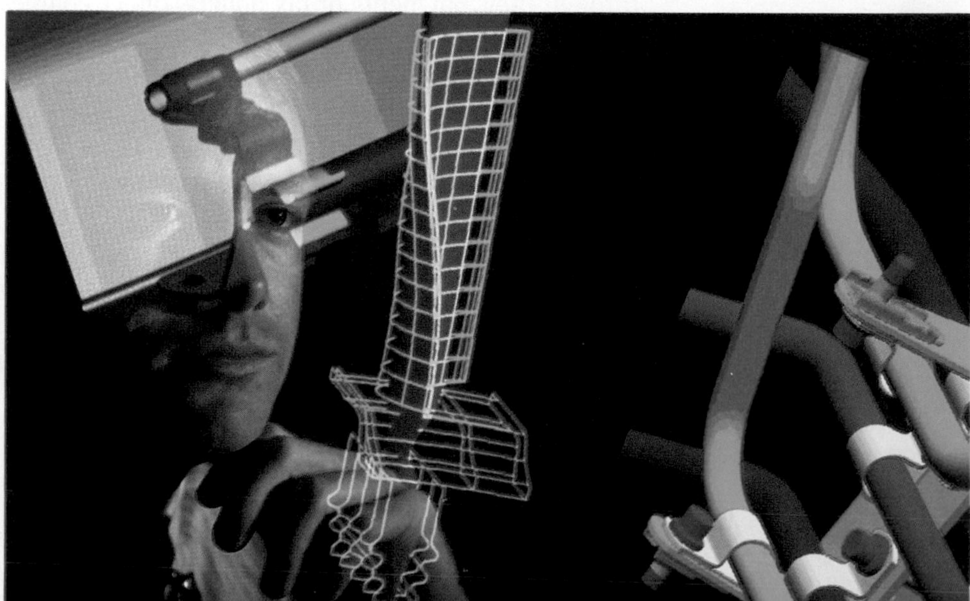

Photo 1-2 Markeing offers career opportunities in many areas, including product development: computer aided design of aircraft engines and components at Pratt & Whitney speeds up product delivery and helps identify problems at the source.

Photo by Ken Kerbs?DOT Pictures

nonprofit organizations, the demand for marketing-educated personnel is growing.

Korn/Ferry International and the Graduate School of Management at the University of California, Los Angeles, conducted a study of 1,362 senior executives from Fortune 500 firms. According to their study, marketing is the fastest route to the top in today's corporate world. When asked to predict what the fastest route will be in ten years, senior executives once again said marketing. For more detailed information about careers in marketing, see Appendix A. The American Marketing Association also publishes a book, *Careers in Marketing and the Employment Kit,* that provides extensive information about career opportunities in marketing.

Marketing Affects Your Life Every Day

Marketing plays a major role in your everyday life. You participate in the marketing process as a consumer of goods and services. About half of every dollar you spend pays for marketing costs, such as marketing research, product development, packaging, transportation, storage, advertising, and sales expenses. By developing a better understanding of marketing, you will become a better-informed consumer. You will better understand the buying process and be able to negotiate more effectively with sellers. Moreover, you will be better prepared to demand satisfaction when the goods and services you buy do not meet the standards promised by the manufacturer or the marketer.

3 MARKETING MANAGEMENT PHILOSOPHIES

Four competing philosophies strongly influence an organization's marketing activities. These philosophies are comonly referred to as production, sales, marketing, and societal marketing orientations.

Production Orientation

production orientation
Philosophy that focuses on the internal capabilities of the firm rather than on the desires and needs of the marketplace.

A **production orientation** is a philosophy that focuses on the internal capabilities of the firm rather than on the desires and needs of the marketplace. A production orientation means that management assesses its resources and asks these questions: "What can we do best?" "What can our engineers design?" "What is easy to produce given our equipment?" In the case of a service organization, managers ask, "What services are most convenient for the firm to offer?" and "Where do our talents lie?"

There is nothing wrong with assessing a firm's capabilities; in fact, such assessments are major considerations in strategic marketing planning (see Chapter 21). A production orientation falls short because it does not consider whether what the firm produces most efficiently also meets the needs of the marketplace. A production orientation does not doom a company to failure, particularly not in the short run. Sometimes what a firm can best produce is exactly what the market wants. In other situations, such as in the absence of competition in an elementary economy, or when demand exceeds supply, a production-oriented firm can survive. The story about Xerox Corporation at the beginning of this chapter illustrates what can happen to a production-oriented organization over the long run.

Sales Orientation

sales orientation
Philosophy that assumes buyers resist purchasing items that are not essential.

A **sales orientation** assumes that buyers resist purchasing items that are not essential. It is also based on the ideas that people will buy more goods and services if aggressive sales techniques are used and that high sales result in high profits.

At Dell Computer, people are considered better for production than robots because only people are flexible enough to adapt to customers' individual needs. Dell has prospered because of its ability to rapidly fulfill custom orders, a prime example of the marketing orientation.

Not only are sales to the final buyer emphasized, but intermediaries are encouraged to push manufacturers' products more aggressively. The fundamental problem with a sales orientation, as with a production orientation, is a lack of understanding of the needs and wants of the marketplace. Sales-oriented companies often find that, despite the quality of their sales force, they cannot sell goods or services if the market does not want them. The International Perspectives example at the end of this chapter illustrates the drawbacks of a sales orientation.

Marketing Orientation

marketing orientation
Philosophy that assumes responsiveness to customer wants should be the central focus of all marketing activity.

marketing concept
Idea that the social and economic justification for an organization's existence is the satisfaction of customer wants and needs while meeting organizational objectives.

A **marketing orientation,** which is the foundation of contemporary marketing philosophy, is based on an understanding that a sale does not depend on an aggressive sales force but rather on a customer's decision to purchase a product. What a business thinks it produces is not of primary importance to its success. Instead, what a customer thinks he or she is buying—the perceived value—defines a business. It also determines a business's products and its potential to prosper.

This philosophy, called the **marketing concept,** is simple and intuitively appealing. It states that the social and economic justification for an organization's existence is the satisfaction of customer wants and needs while meeting organizational objectives. The marketing concept includes the following:

1. Focusing on customer wants so the organization can distinguish its product(s) from competitors' offerings
2. Integrating all the organization's activities, including production, to satisfy these wants
3. Achieving long-term goals for the organization by satisfying customer wants and needs legally and responsibly

The following examples illustrate the three key features of the marketing concept. First, Wal-Mart Stores has become the leading discount retailer in the United States by focusing on what its customers want: everyday low prices, items always in stock, and cashiers always available. Second, at DuPont, a team of chemists, sales and marketing executives, and regulatory specialists developed a herbicide that corn growers can apply less often.[4] Third, at Dell Computer, employees from top manag-

ers to assembly workers meet weekly to carefully examine customer complaints and employee suggestions, with the goal of ensuring that customers have a "quality experience" and are "pleased, not just satisfied."[5]

Societal Marketing Orientation

societal marketing concept
Idea that an organization exists not only to satisfy customer wants and needs and to meet organizational objectives but also to preserve or enhance individuals' and society's long-term best interests.

One reason a marketing-oriented organization may choose not to deliver the benefits sought by customers is that these benefits may not be good for individuals or society. This important refinement of the marketing concept, called the **societal marketing concept**, states that an organization exists not only to satisfy customer wants and needs and to meet organizational objectives but also to preserve or enhance individuals' and society's long-term best interests. Marketing "environmentally friendly" products and containers, discussed in Chapter 20, is consistent with a societal marketing orientation. The Ethics in Marketing story that follows shows how complex societal marketing issues can be.

ETHICS IN MARKETING

Kool-Aid Man versus the Child Activists

For several years, Kraft General Foods, maker of Kool-Aid, the fruit-flavored powdered-drink mix, has wooed child consumers with its Wacky Warehouse Club, an incentive program that offers toys, T-shirts, and other items for "Kool-Aid points" found on Kool-Aid packages. But its latest offering, a thirty-minute "Wacky Zany Video," . . . has aroused criticism from consumer groups that charge the program is little more than an overlong commercial. . . .

Presented by Kool-Aid Man, the star of Kool-Aid TV commercials, the Wacky Zany video is a montage of silent-movie footage, cartoons, and other images in quick-cut MTV style. One segment parodies police dramas and calls on viewers to find the Kool-Aid Man, wanted for crashing through walls.

Activists charge that the video is a sad example of the growing commercialization of children's programming. "Kids are presumably spending money on points to get something wonderful, and all they're getting is messages about the product," says Peggy Charren, president of Action for Children's Television. "The only thing corporations are educating the prework force for is buy, buy, buy."

Is it ethical for marketers to promote products directly to children? Should marketing for children be regulated? If so, what regulations should be imposed? Who should impose and enforce them? Should marketers be allowed to use hero figures to promote products to children? Should incentive programs like Kool-Aid's "Wacky Zany Video" be allowed?

Source: Adapted from Svein L. Hwang, "When Does a Bonus Start Being a Plug?" *The Wall Street Journal*, 20 September 1991, p. B1. Reprinted by permission of *The Wall Street Journal*, ©1991 Dow Jones & Company, Inc. All Rights Reserved Worldwide.

4 CONTRASTING SALES AND MARKETING ORIENTATIONS

As noted at the beginning of this chapter, many people confuse the terms *sales* and *marketing*. These orientations are substantially different. Exhibit 1.2 compares the two orientations in terms of five characteristics.

The Organization's Focus

Most sales-oriented firms are highly bureaucratic. Personnel tend to be "inward-looking," preoccupied with employment security and conditions. They focus on satisfying their own short-term needs rather than their customers' needs.

In contrast, marketing-oriented firms recognize that customers direct the activities of the firm, and their internal organization reflects this awareness. A marketing orientation means that all departments coordinate their activities and focus on satisfying customers. As David Kearns, CEO of Xerox Corporation, has noted, "Customer satisfaction is the number one thing that drives market share. The customer is

	What is the organization's focus?	What business are you in?	To whom is the product directed?	What is your primary goal?	How do you seek to achieve your goal?
Sales orientation	Inward upon the organization's needs	Selling goods and services	Everybody	Profit through maximum sales volume	Primarily through intensive promotion
Marketing orientation	Outward upon the wants and preferences of customers	Satisfying consumer wants and needs	Specific groups of people	Profit through customer satisfaction	Through coordinated marketing activities

Exhibit 1.2

Contrasting Sales and Marketing Orientations

the reason we exist."[6] According to Leslie H. Wexner, CEO and founder of The Limited, a chain of women's apparel stores, "The common thread among retailers who really are doing it right is that they realize that the customer is the one calling the shots, not the other way around."[7]

Customer-Oriented Personnel

Employees' attitudes and actions in marketing-oriented firms must be customer-oriented. An employee may be the only contact a particular customer has with the firm. In that customer's eyes, the employee is the firm. Any person, department, or division that is not customer-oriented weakens the positive image of the entire organization. For example, what if a person answers the telephone abruptly or discourteously? The potential customer may well assume that the employee's attitude represents the whole firm. To promote the right attitude, Chrysler Corporation has begun paying dealers for high scores on customer satisfaction surveys.[8]

A study conducted by the U.S. Office of Consumer Affairs found that between 37 and 45 percent of all people unhappy with the service they receive do not complain. They simply go someplace else.[9]

The person who answers the phone is often the customer's only contact with a firm. In marketing-oriented organizations, a strong interest in satisfying customers or clients is an important characteristic of all employees—but especially of those who interact directly with the public.

The Role of Training

Leading marketers recognize the role of employee training in customer service. For example, all new employees at Disneyland and Walt Disney World must attend Disney University, a special training program for Disney employees. They must first pass Traditions 1, a day-long course focusing on the Disney philosophy and operational procedures. Then they go on to specialized or technical training.

Similarly, McDonald's has Hamburger University. At American Express's Quality University, line employees and managers learn how to treat customers. One of former American Express CEO James Robinson's favorite sayings is

"Promise only what you can deliver, and deliver more than you promise."[10] Some Japanese department stores provide elevator operators with two months' training. Because elevator operators have so much contact with customers, they must know how to respond to customers' questions.[11]

There is an extra payoff for companies like Disney, McDonald's, and American Express that train their employees to be customer-oriented. When employees make their customers happy, the employees also become happy. Companies like Metropolitan Life, American Express, and Federal Express offer employees benefits such as flexible work hours, compressed work weeks, and job sharing to make employees happier.[12] Having contented workers leads to better customer service and greater employee retention.

Empowerment

In addition to training, some marketing-oriented firms are giving employees more authority to solve customer problems on the spot. The term used to describe this delegation of authority is **empowerment.** Montgomery Ward sales clerks, for example, are now authorized to approve checks and handle merchandise return problems. Before, only store managers performed these functions.[13] Fidelity Bank in Philadelphia has raised the average annual salary of its 100 customer-service representatives 58 percent. In addition, the representatives can resolve problems involving sums up to $1,000. Until recently, they needed a supervisor's approval to resolve any problem involving money. A survey taken after Fidelity made the change revealed an increase in customer satisfaction. Over 90 percent of the bank's customers said they would recommend the bank to a friend, up from 65 percent previously.[14]

empowerment
Practice of giving employees expanded authority to solve customer problems as they arise.

The Firm's Business

As Exhibit 1.2 illustrates, a selling-oriented firm defines its business (mission) in terms of goods and services. A marketing-oriented firm defines its business in terms of benefits its customers seek. People who spend their money, time, and energy expect to receive benefits, not just goods and services. This distinction has enormous implications for the way organizations define their business.

A sales-oriented firm will probably miss opportunities to serve customers whose wants can only be met through a wide range of product offerings instead of specific products. For example, one of the primary benefits people seek from libraries is broader general knowledge. This benefit can be achieved through a wide range of products and services, including books, movies, lectures, discussion groups, trips, and so forth. Books alone are not what consumers seek; instead they want the benefit of general knowledge derived from learning. By offering additional services, libraries can reach more customers and better satisfy existing customers.

Defining a business in terms of goods and services rather than in terms of the benefits customers seek is sometimes called **marketing myopia.** In this context, the term *myopia* means narrow, short-term thinking. This orientation can threaten an organization's survival. For example, some large luxury passenger ships were threatened by competition from the airlines. Others have survived because they have recognized they are in the floating hotel business, not the transportation business. Another example is movie theater operators like American Multi-Cinema (AMC). They have learned that good movies alone will not attract customers. The same movie may be showing in five or six theaters in the same area, so AMC has made convenience a top priority. Most AMC box offices accept credit cards and phone-ahead ticket sales. Some AMC theaters offer such tasty treats as iced cappucino,

marketing myopia
Practice of defining a business in terms of goods and services rather than in terms of the benefits customers seek.

mineral water, crab cakes, salads, quiche, egg rolls, and croissant sandwiches. Many theater operators also understand that they are not just competing against other movie houses in the neighborhood. The real threat comes from other forms of entertainment—everything from going out for a steak to taking in the ballet.[15] Both these examples show how products emerge to better deliver the benefits consumers seek and what can happen when a company adapts to changing customer needs.

Answering the question "What is this firm's business?" in terms of the benefits customers seek, instead of goods and services, has at least three important advantages:

- It ensures that the firm keeps focusing on customers and avoids becoming preoccupied with goods, services, or the organization's internal needs.
- It encourages innovation and creativity by reminding people that there are many ways to satisfy customer wants.
- It stimulates an awareness of changes in customer desires and preferences so that product offerings are more likely to remain relevant.

The marketing concept and the idea of focusing on customer wants do not mean that customers will always receive the specific goods and services they want. It is not possible, for example, to profitably manufacture and market automobile tires for $25 each that will last for 100,000 miles. Furthermore, customers' preferences must be mediated by sound professional judgment as to how to deliver the benefits they seek. As one adage suggests, "People don't know what they want—they only want what they know." Consumers have a limited set of experiences. They are unlikely to request anything beyond those experiences because they are not aware of benefits they may gain from other potential offerings. For example, before the automobile, people knew they wanted transportation but could not express their need for a car.

To Whom the Product Is Directed

A selling-oriented organization targets its products at "everybody" or "the average customer." A marketing-oriented organization aims at "specific groups of people" (see Exhibit 1.2). The fallacy of developing products directed at the average user is that relatively few average users actually exist. Typically, populations are characterized by diversity. An average is simply a midpoint in some set of characteristics. Since most potential customers are not "average," they are not likely to be attracted to an average product marketed to the average customer. Consider the market for shampoo as one simple example. There are shampoos for oily hair, dry hair, and dandruff. Some shampoos remove the gray or color hair. Special shampoos are marketed for infants and elderly people. There is even shampoo for people with average or normal hair (whatever that is), but this is a fairly small portion of the total market for shampoo.

A marketing-oriented organization recognizes that different customer groups and their wants vary. It may therefore need to develop different goods, services, and promotional appeals. A marketing-oriented organization carefully analyzes the market and divides it into groups fairly similar in terms of selected characteristics. Then the organization develops marketing programs that will bring about mutually satisfying exchanges with one or more of those groups. Consider this example:

> Paying attention to the customer isn't exactly a new concept. Back in the 1920s, General Motors Corporation helped write the book on customer satisfaction by designing cars for every lifestyle and pocketbook. This was a breakthrough for an industry that had been largely driven by production needs ever since Henry Ford promised any color as long as it was black.[16]

Marketing-oriented firms seek to fulfill the wants and needs of specific groups of people, such as affluent senior citizens. This retired couple, on vacation in Cape May, New Jersey, is a prime target for firms offering leisure activities, travel, and vacations.

Chapter 6 thoroughly explores the topic of analyzing markets and selecting those that appear to be most promising to the firm.

The Firm's Primary Goal

A selling-oriented organization seeks to achieve profitability through sales volume and tries to convince potential customers to buy, even if the seller knows that the customer and product are mismatched. Selling-oriented organizations place a higher premium on making a sale than on developing a long-term relationship with a customer.

relationship marketing
Strategy of forging long-term partnerships with customers.

In contrast, the ultimate goal of most marketing-oriented organizations is to make a profit from satisfying customers. **Relationship marketing** is the name of the strategy that entails forging long-term partnerships with customers. For business-to-business marketers it means effectively becoming a part of the customer's organization and contributing to its success, not just closing a sale.

General Electric, for example, has engineers stationed full-time at Proxair, a maker of industrial gases, to help boost the productivity of GE-built electrical equipment.[17] Baxter International developed ValueLink, a computer-based inventory control system, to help its hospital customers reduce inventory costs while improving the internal distribution of supplies. Baxter takes on the time-consuming task of making sure essential items like needles, bandages, and syringes wind up in the right place in the proper numbers. With ValueLink, Baxter can often become a hospital's sole source of supplies.[18]

marketing mix
Unique blend of product, distribution, promotion, and pricing strategies designed to produce mutually satisfying exchanges with a target market.

four P's
Product decisions, distribution (or place) decisions, promotion decisions, and pricing decisions, which together make up the marketing mix.

Tools the Organization Uses to Achieve Its Goals

Selling-oriented organizations seek to generate sales volume through intensive promotional activities, mainly personal selling and advertising. In contrast, marketing-oriented organizations recognize that promotion is only one of four basic marketing tools. Together these tools comprise what is commonly called the **marketing mix,** or the **four P's**—product decisions, distribution (or place) decisions, promotion decisions, and pricing decisions. Chapters 9 through 19 focus on these topics. A marketing-oriented organization recognizes each of the four components of the marketing mix as equally important. On the other hand, selling-oriented organizations view promotion as the primary means of achieving their goals.

A Word of Caution

This comparison of selling and marketing orientations is not meant to belittle the role of promotion, especially personal selling, in the marketing mix. Promotion is the means by which organizations communicate with present and prospective customers about the merits and characteristics of their organization and products. Effective promotion is an essential part of effective marketing. Salespeople who work for marketing-oriented organizations are generally perceived by their customers to be problem solvers and important links to supply sources and new products.

Chapter 17 and Appendix A examine the nature of personal selling in more detail.

5 IMPLEMENTING THE MARKETING CONCEPT

Although the marketing concept is a simple and appealing management philosophy, firms seem to have trouble implementing it. Three difficult hurdles must be overcome: organized resistance, slow learning, and fast forgetting.[19] Organized resistance means that some departments, such as manufacturing and finance, may feel threatened if marketing is identified as the key function of all employees. Slow learning means that diffusion of the marketing concept takes a long time, even with the endorsement of top management. Fast forgetting means that successful firms sometimes forget how and why they became successful and unintentionally abandon the marketing concept.

Implementing the marketing concept is harder than it may seem. According to Thomas J. Pritzker, president of Hyatt Hotels, there's a fallacy that customer service can just be turned on: "Management has to set a tone and then constantly push, push, push."[20] To successfully implement the marketing concept, management has to enthusiastically embrace and endorse the concept and encourage its spread throughout the organization.[21]

The success of Nordstrom, the Seattle-based retailer, illustrates the result of strong management support for customer service. Employees can do almost anything to satisfy shoppers. One employee received a panic call from a regular customer who was on his way to the airport and needed some clothes. The employee chose several appropriate garments, charged them to the customer's account, and met the customer outside the store with a bagful of clothes. Another employee at the same store delivered a pair of stockings to a frantic executive's office in time for her to change for a big meeting.[22] There is even one story, which the company doesn't deny, about a customer who got his money back on a tire, even though Nordstrom doesn't sell tires. In 1993, Nordstrom received the highest overall customer satisfaction rating from 2,000 shoppers who participated in a study ranking 70 U.S. retail and department store chains on attributes such as price, convenience, and quality of offerings.[23]

Changes in Authority and Responsibility

Changing from a production or selling orientation to a marketing orientation often requires major revisions in relationships within the firm. Nonmarketing people who have been making marketing decisions, such as production managers, may suddenly lose their authority. Personnel in such areas as marketing research may find that they have gained considerable authority.

One way of winning acceptance for the marketing concept is to get everyone who will be affected by the change to participate in the planning process. During a period of change, some human relations problems are inevitable. Implementing the marketing concept slowly rather than in a revolutionary fashion normally smoothes the transition.

Sometimes companies fool themselves into thinking they've implemented the marketing concept when they really have not. Management may concentrate on some of these trappings of marketing:

- *Declarations of support from top management:* speeches, annual reports
- *Creation of a marketing organization:* appointment of a marketing head and product or market managers, transfer of the product development and service functions to marketing, reassignment of salespersons around markets, strengthening of the advertising function
- *Adoption of new administrative mechanisms:* formal marketing planning approaches, more and better sales information, reporting system restructured around markets
- *Increased marketing expenditures:* staffing, training and development, advertising, research

Although these are actions taken by firms that actually implement the marketing concept, by themselves they are not enough to change old production-focused ideas and habits. When a person or a company has been doing something a certain way for many years, change often comes very hard.

For example, the top management of Xerox Corporation, which was profiled at the beginning of this chapter, spent much of the 1970s building huge layers of bureaucracy and wasting millions of dollars developing products that never reached the marketplace. It took Xerox ten years to realize that its old strategy of throwing people at problems and raising prices as costs went up just wouldn't work. It wasn't until 1980 that Xerox finally realized how capable its Japanese counterparts were and how little Xerox knew about customer wants.[24]

Front-Line Experience for Management

Detroit Diesel Corporation requires all managers and distributors to call or visit four customers a day. At Xerox Corporation, executives spend one day a month taking complaints from customers about machines, bills, and service. At Hyatt Hotels,

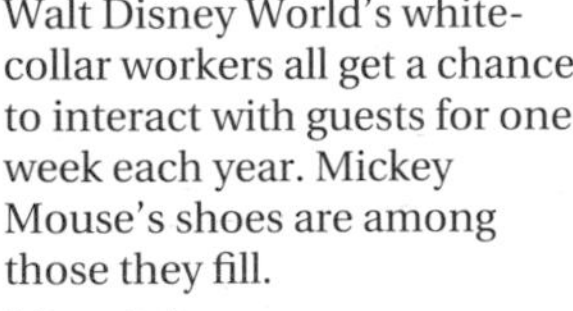
Walt Disney World's white-collar workers all get a chance to interact with guests for one week each year. Mickey Mouse's shoes are among those they fill.

senior executives, including president Thomas J. Pritzker, put in time as bellhops.[25] Walt Disney World's managers also join the "front line":

> Annually all the "white collar" types at Walt Disney World, the management if you will, undertake a week-long program called cross-utilization. In essence, it means giving up the desk, the secretary, and the white collar and donning a themed costume or an apron and heading for the front-line action. For a week the "bosses" sell tickets or popcorn, dish out ice cream or hot dogs, load and unload rides, park cars, drive the monorail or trains, or take on any of the 100 "on-stage" jobs that make the park come alive for guests.[26]

6 THE MARKETING PROCESS

Earlier in this chapter, marketing was defined as the process of planning and executing the conception, distribution, promotion, and pricing of ideas, goods, and services to create exchanges that satisfy individual and organizational objectives.

Marketing entails the following activities:

- Gathering, analyzing, and interpreting information about the environment (environmental scanning)
- Finding out what benefits people want the organization to deliver and what wants they want the organization to satisfy (market opportunity analysis)
- Setting marketing objectives
- Deciding exactly which wants, and whose wants, the organization will try to satisfy (target market strategy)
- Developing and implementing one or more appropriate mixes of marketing activities (the four P's) to satisfy the desires of selected target markets
- Periodically evaluating marketing efforts and making changes if needed

These activities and their relationships, shown in Exhibit 1.3, form the foundation on which most of the rest of the book is based.

Organization Mission

One of top management's biggest responsibilities is to formulate the organization's basic purposes and mission statement. As noted earlier, an organization's mission statement answers the question "What is this firm's business?" The mission statement is based on a careful analysis of the benefits sought by present and potential customers as well as existing and anticipated environmental conditions. This long-term vision of what the organization is or is striving to become establishes the boundaries within which objectives, strategies, and actions must be developed. The importance of carefully defining an organization's mission was forcefully stated by Thomas Watson, Jr., former chairman of the board of IBM:

> I firmly believe that any organization, in order to survive and achieve success, must have a sound set of beliefs on which it premises all its policies and actions. . . . Next, I believe that the most important single factor in corporate success is faithful adherence to those beliefs. . . . In other words, the basic philosophy, spirit, and drive of an organization have far more to do with its relative achievements than do technological or economic resources, organization structure, innovation, and timing. All of these things weigh heavily on success. But they are, I think, transcended by how strongly the people in the organization believe in its basic precepts and how faithfully they carry them out.[27]

When an organization's management ignores this advice, the enterprise suffers.

Exhibit 1.3

The Marketing Process

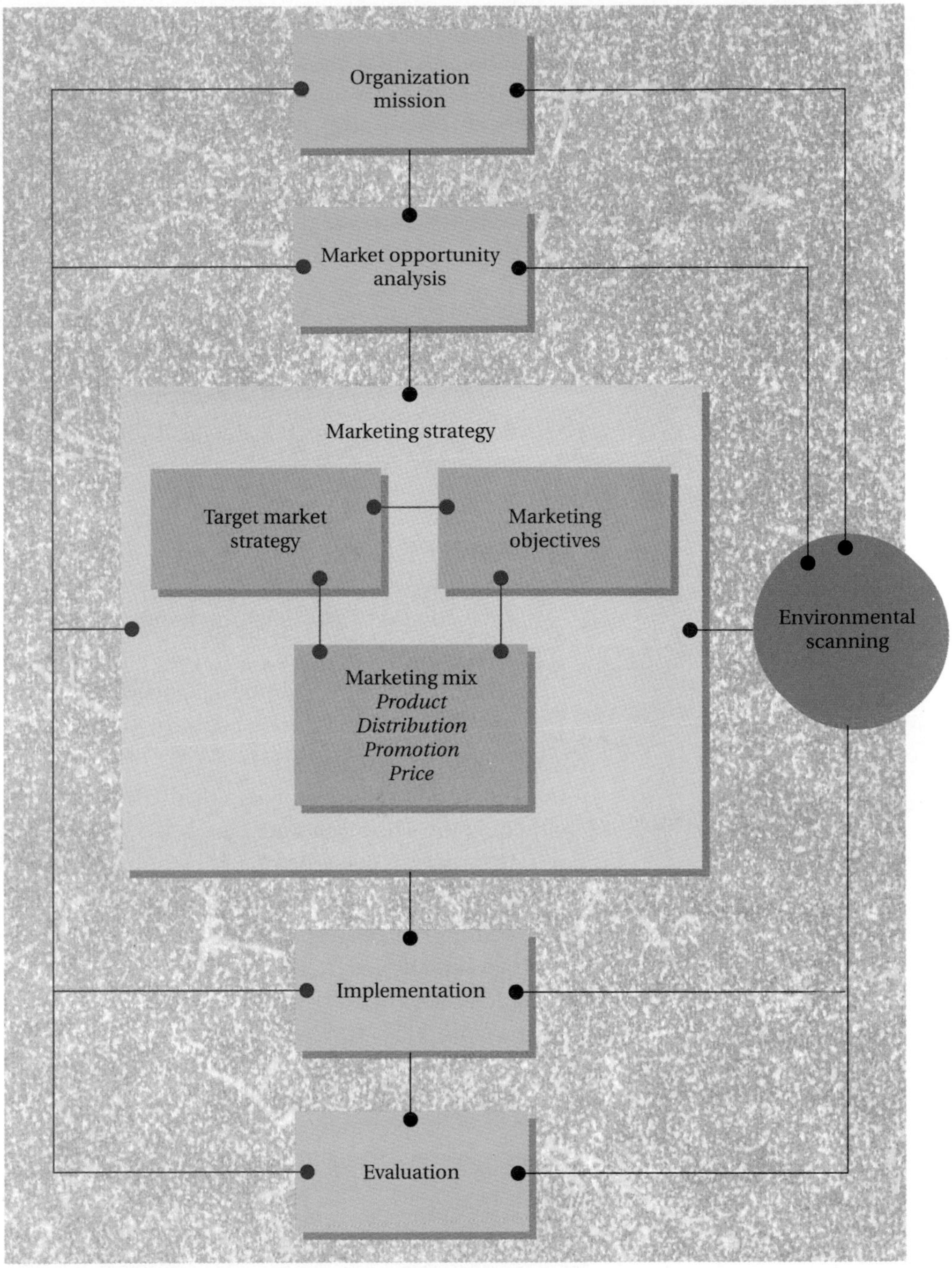

Organization mission

Market opportunity analysis

Marketing strategy

Target market strategy

Marketing objectives

Marketing mix
Product
Distribution
Promotion
Price

Environmental scanning

Implementation

Evaluation

Many formerly successful business and nonbusiness organizations have faltered because they have incorrectly answered the questions "What is our business?" and "What should it be?"

Consider the following examples from the nonprofit sector. Where would the Lung Association be if it had not revised its mission from destroying tuberculosis to controlling and preventing lung disease? What would be the YMCA's current status if it had not broadened its original mission of improving lower-class people's social conditions through religious indoctrination and educational activities? Why was YMCA's decision to include all-purpose service activities for both middle- and lower-class people so effective?

Clearly the continued success of these organizations can largely be attributed to the insight of their top management in redefining their mission. We will return to the topic of organization mission in Chapter 21.

Environmental Scanning

environmental scanning Collection and interpretation of information about forces, events, and relationships that may affect an organization.

Environmental scanning is the collection and interpretation of information about forces, events, and relationships that may affect the organization. It helps identify market opportunities and threats and provides guidelines for the marketing strategy. These sorts of data are gathered with the help of a marketing decision support system (see Chapter 8).

Chapter 2 focuses on six important forces that affect marketing decision making:

- *Social forces* such as the values of potential customers and the changing roles of families and women working outside the home
- *Demographic forces* such as the ages, birth and death rates, and locations of various groups of people
- *Economic forces* such as changing incomes, inflation, and recession
- *Technological forces* such as advanced communications and data retrieval capabilities
- *Political and legal forces* such as changes in laws and regulatory agency activities
- *Competitive forces* from domestic and foreign-based firms

Market Opportunity Analysis

market opportunity analysis Description and estimation of the size and sales potential of market segments of interest to a firm and assessment of key competitors in these market segments.

A market segment is a group of individuals or organizations that share one or more characteristics. They therefore have relatively similar product needs. A **market opportunity analysis** describes market segments of interest to the firm, estimates their size and sales potential, and assesses key competitors in these market segments.

- *Describing market segments:* Criteria commonly used to describe consumer markets are the geographic location of potential customers, their demographic characteristics, their psychological characteristics, the benefits they seek from using a product, and the amount of product they purchase or consume. Criteria commonly used to describe business markets are their geographic location, their size, the key criteria that they use in making purchase decisions, their

Marketing managers need to be on the lookout for new opportunities. One way is to keep track of what the competition is doing—for instance, by attending trade shows. The National Business Aircraft Association convention in Dallas was one of many such shows put on each year.
© Chris Sorensen/The Stock Market

market segment size
Number of potential customers in a market segment.

market segment sales potential
Maximum amount of a product that could be sold in a market segment during a specified period.

company sales potential
Amount an organization could possibly sell in all market segments in which it competes or plans to compete during a specified period.

company sales forecast
Amount a company actually expects to sell in all segments in which it competes or plans to compete during a specified period.

marketing strategy
Plan that involves selecting one or more target markets, setting marketing objectives, and developing and maintaining a marketing mix that will produce mutually satisfying exchanges with target markets.

purchasing strategies, the structure of the decision-making unit, and the personal characteristics of decision makers.

- *Estimating market segment size and sales potential:* The term **market segment size** refers to the number of potential customers in a market segment. **Market segment sales potential** is the maximum amount of a product that could be sold in a market segment during a specified period. **Company sales potential** is the amount the organization could possibly sell in all market segments in which it competes or plans to compete during a specified period. A **company sales forecast** is the amount the company actually expects to sell in all segments in which it competes or plans to compete during a specified period.
- *Analyzing key competitors:* Since a company does not normally compete on a direct basis with all firms in an industry, competitor analysis can be restricted to those firms perceived as key competitors. Key competitors are other firms that target the same markets with similar products or substitutes that meet the same need. For example, when U.S. Surgical Corporation entered the market for surgical skin closure with surgical stapling equipment, the new product represented a competitive threat to needle and suture suppliers. There were no other surgical stapler manufacturers at the time. The purposes of competitor analysis are to identify the strengths and weaknesses of key competitors, to assess their current marketing strategies, and to predict their future actions. Exhibit 1.4 shows many of the ways well-managed companies keep up with the activities of competitors.

Target Market Strategy

As Exhibit 1.3 illustrates, **marketing strategy** involves three activities: selecting one or more target markets, setting marketing objectives, and developing and maintaining a marketing mix (product, distribution, promotion, and pricing) that will produce mutually satisfying exchanges with target markets.

Chapter 6 identifies the general strategies for selecting target markets. These are the basic options: to try to appeal to the entire market with a single marketing mix, to

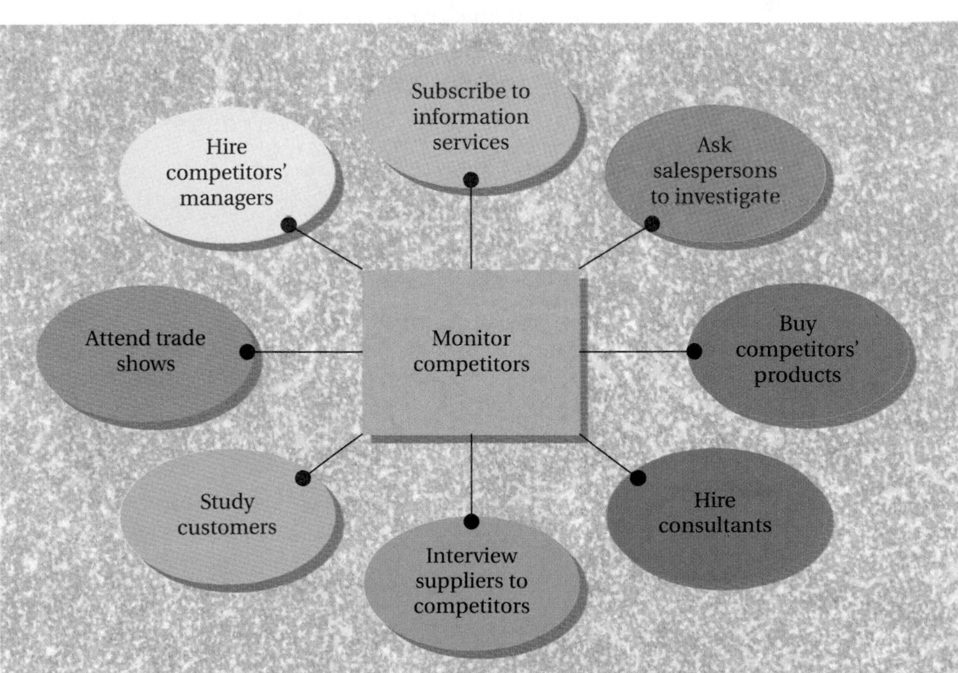

Exhibit 1.4

Sources of Information for Monitoring Competitors' Marketing Programs

concentrate on only one segment of the market, or to attempt to appeal to multiple market segments using multiple marketing mixes. The characteristics, advantages, and disadvantages of each strategic option are also examined in Chapter 6.

Marketing Objectives

marketing objective
Statement of what is to be accomplished through marketing activities.

A **marketing objective** is a statement of what is to be accomplished through marketing activities. Marketing objectives should be consistent with organization objectives and should be stated for each target market.

Carefully specifying marketing objectives offers two major benefits. First, when the objectives are attainable and challenging, they motivate those charged with achieving the objectives. They also serve as standards by which everyone in the organization can gauge their performance. Second, the process of writing specific marketing objectives forces executives to sharpen and clarify their thinking. Written objectives also allow marketing efforts to be integrated and pointed in a consistent direction.

behavioral objective
Actions that marketing managers want target consumers to take.

For marketing objectives to be realized, they must be clear, express realistic expectations, be based on adequate support for the program, and state precise behavioral objectives. **Behavioral objectives** are actions the marketing managers want target consumers to take. For example, behavioral objectives might be to get people to test-drive a new Chrysler, to fly on a new commuter airline, to drink more Minute Maid orange juice, or to buy a reformulated Tony's frozen pizza.

Recently, General Mills entered the $13 billion bread market by launching a microwave bread line under the famed Betty Crocker label. Exhibit 1.5 presents hypothetical examples of good and bad marketing objectives for Betty Crocker's Microwave Bread using the preceding criteria. The success of the new bread line depends on the trusted name of Betty Crocker, consumer awareness of Betty Crocker, and the size of the U.S. bread market.

The Marketing Mix

As noted earlier, the term *marketing mix* refers to a unique blend of product, distribution, promotion, and pricing strategies designed to produce mutually satisfying exchanges with a target market. (Distribution is sometimes referred to as place, thus giving us the "four P's" of the marketing mix—product, place, promotion, and price.)

The marketing manager can control each component of the marketing mix. A

Exhibit 1.5

Four Criteria for Marketing Objectives

Criteria	Poor goal	Good goal
Overall marketing objectives clearly stated	To get people to buy our new Betty Crocker Microwave Bread Shop products	To obtain 5 percent of fresh-baked bread market in twelve months
Behavioral objectives clearly stated	To have sales increase	To stimulate 30 percent of all U.S. households to try one loaf of Betty Crocker Microwave Bread
Expectations realistic	To obtain half the fresh-baked bread market	Given strong name of Betty Crocker in baked bread goods market and fact that Americans consume 50 lbs of bread a year, to achieve 18 percent share of fresh-baked bread market
Adequate support for program	(No mention of budget dollars in program statement, no check to make sure program meshes with corporate goals)	Given commitment by General Mills to grow in baked goods market, to budget $45 million, $41 million, and $35 million in the next three years for Betty Crocker's Microwave Bread Shop

These women are not just buying a product, a particular cosmetic. They are making a purchase decision in the context of a complete marketing mix: brand and store image, sales clerk attitude and competence, advertising, packaging, price, and many other factors.

© 1980 Ted Horowitz, Bloomingdale's, New York/The Stock Market

strategy for each component must be uniquely constructed and blended with those of the other components to achieve an optimal marketing mix. Any mix is only as good as its weakest component. For example, an excellent product with a poor distribution system will likely fail.

Successful marketing mixes have been carefully tailored to satisfy the target market(s). At first glance, McDonald's and Wendy's may appear to have roughly identical marketing mixes. After all, they are both in the fast-food business. However, McDonald's targets parents with young children. It has Ronald McDonald, special children's Happy Meals, and playgrounds. Wendy's generally targets the adult crowd. Wendy's doesn't have a playground, but it does have carpeting (for a more adult atmosphere), and it pioneered fast-food salad bars.

Variations in marketing mixes do not occur by chance. They represent fundamental marketing strategies devised by astute marketing managers attempting to gain advantages over competitors and to achieve competitive success.

Product Strategies

Typically the marketing mix begins with the product offering. It is hard to devise a distribution system or set a price without knowing the product to be marketed. Thus, the heart of the marketing mix is a firm's product offerings.

INTERNATIONAL PERSPECTIVES

How Japan Became No. 3 for P&G

After losing $200 million in Japan, Procter & Gamble has turned the country into its second-largest foreign market after Germany. . . . As chairman-CEO Edwin L. Artzt says in a talk he gives to college students, at first P&G "stormed into the Japanese market with American products, American managers, American advertising, and American sales methods and promotional strategies." . . .

The result was disastrous until P&G learned how to adapt products and marketing style to Japanese culture. For instance, product performance is a top priority with Japanese consumers, who place less importance on price than U.S. customers.

P&G introduced disposable diapers to the Japanese in 1977 and controlled the market with Pampers for four years. But when local competitors UniCharm and Kao Corp. introduced superabsorbent diapers in the early 1980s, Japanese mothers dumped Pampers in favor of the more absorbent products.

By early 1985, Pampers had only a 6 percent market share. After making Pampers thinner, more form-fitting, and more absorbent, P&G again holds the lead in the $750 million-plus category, with a 28 percent share. . . .

"You must know your customers, the trade, the culture, and your competition well enough to think and act like a Japanese company," Artzt said in his speech. "Compete with them there, for you will ultimately have to compete with them in your home market. That is one of the driving motivations to succeed in Japan."

Discuss the marketing mistakes P&G made when it first entered the Japanese market. Exhibit 1.3 provides a useful framework for your answer. What major lessons did P&G learn from this experience? Are these lessons transferable to other foreign markets?

Adapted from Laurie Freeman, "Japan Rises to P&G's No. 3 Market," *Advertising Age* (10 December 1990), p. 42. © Crain Communications Inc., 1990.

Marketers view products in a much larger context than you might imagine. A product includes not only the physical unit but also the package, warranty, service subsequent to sale, brand and company image, and many other factors. The names Yves St. Laurent and Gucci create additional value for everything from cosmetics to bath towels. We buy things not only for what they do but also for what they mean.

Distribution Strategies

Distribution strategies are concerned with making products available when and where customers want them. Wholesalers and retailers participate in what is called a marketing channel or channel of distribution. Physical distribution consists of all business activities concerned with storing and transporting products so that they arrive in usable condition at designated places when needed. Physical distribution is also part of distribution strategy.

Promotion Strategies

Promotion includes personal selling, advertising, sales promotion, and public relations. Its role is to help bring about mutually satisfying exchanges with target markets by informing, educating, persuading, and reminding them about the benefits of an organization or a product. A good promotion strategy can sometimes dramatically increase a firm's sales. Each element of promotion is coordinated and managed with the others to create a promotional blend or mix.

Pricing Strategies

Price, what a buyer must give up to receive a product, is the most flexible of the four components of the marketing mix. Marketers can raise or lower prices more frequently than they can change any other marketing mix variable. Thus price is an important competitive weapon.

MARKETING AND SMALL BUSINESS

The Importance of Good Marketing Skills

Most of you will not end up working for a major corporation. Some of you will start your own enterprise, and others will go to work for a small or moderate-size company.

Persons who start their own business are often called entrepreneurs. People are pulled toward entrepreneurship by several powerful incentives. First, the potential financial return is typically greater than one could achieve by working for someone else. Second, entrepreneurship offers freedom from supervision and the rules of bureaucratic organizations. Third, there is the freedom from routine, boring, and unchallenging jobs. On the other hand, starting and operating one's own business requires hard work, long hours, and much emotional energy. Sometimes people invest their life savings in a small business only to see it fail.

Two keys to success for America's 16 million small firms are adequate capital and good marketing skills. A general rule of thumb is to have enough start-up capital to establish the operation plus enough working capital to get through the first two years without earning a profit. Many entrepreneurs don't come close to this rule, and as a result, they fail.

Money alone, however, does not guarantee success. Entrepreneurs still need to understand and implement the marketing concept. Hundreds of thousands of small businesses have failed because they offered a good or service that no one wanted. Other small firms couldn't get adequate distribution, priced their offerings incorrectly, failed to develop a good promotional strategy, or failed to spend enough money promoting their organization and product.

LOOKING AHEAD

This book is divided into twenty-two chapters organized into seven major parts. Written from the marketing manager's perspective, each chapter begins with a brief list of learning objectives followed by an opening vignette—a short story about a marketing situation faced by a firm or industry. At the end of each vignette, several thought-provoking questions link the story to the subject addressed in the chapter. Your instructor may wish to begin chapter discussions by asking members of your class to share their views about the questions.

The examples of international marketing highlighted in most chapters will help you understand that marketing takes place all over the world, between buyers and sellers in different countries. These and other international marketing examples throughout the book, marked with the icon shown here, are intended to help you develop a global perspective on marketing.

Marketing ethics is another important topic selected for special treatment throughout the book. Many business executives and educators have noted that business education needs to focus more on ethical issues. Chapters include highlighted stories about firms or industries that have faced ethical dilemmas or have engaged in practices that some consider unethical. Questions are posed to focus your thinking on the key ethical issues raised in each story.

Entrepreneurship and small business applications are also highlighted in many chapters. This material illustrates how entrepreneurs and small businesses can use the principles and concepts discussed in the text.

Chapters conclude with a final comment on the chapter-opening vignette, a summary of the major topics examined, a listing of the key terms introduced in the chapter, review questions, discussion and writing questions (writing questions marked with an icon), and two or three cases with discussion questions. All these features are intended to help you develop a more thorough understanding of marketing and to enjoy the learning process.

The remaining chapters in Part One introduce you to the dynamic environment in which marketing decisions must be made and to global marketing. Part Two covers consumer decision making and buyer behavior; business-to-business marketing; the concepts of positioning, market segmentation, and targeting; the unique challenges of marketing to multicultural target markets; and the nature and uses of marketing research and decision support systems. Parts Three through Six examine the elements of the marketing mix—product, distribution, promotion, and pricing concepts and decisions. Part Seven focuses on marketing ethics and social responsibility, strategic planning and forecasting, and total quality management. Two appendixes—one on careers in marketing and one with experiential marketing exercises—conclude the book.

LOOKING BACK

Look back at the story about Xerox Corporation that appeared at the beginning of this chapter. You should now find the questions that appear at the end of the story to be simple and straightforward. The management philosophy at Xerox in the 1970s was clearly production-oriented, but the company is now marketing-oriented. Xerox, like many other organizations, such as the so-called Big Three automakers (General Motors, Ford, and Chrysler), became marketing-oriented only after losing significant market share to competitors that did a better job of focusing on customer wants

and delivering customer satisfaction. The Xerox story illustrates that marketing-oriented companies are rewarded by satisfied customers, who continue buying from those firms that offer the goods and services that best match their needs.

KEY TERMS

behavioral objective 22
company sales forecast 21
company sales potential 21
concept of exchange 6
empowerment 13
environmental scanning 20
four P's 15
marketing 6
marketing concept 10
marketing mix 15
marketing myopia 13
marketing objective 22
marketing orientation 10
marketing strategy 21
market opportunity analysis 20
market segment sales potential 21
market segment size 21
production orientation 9
relationship marketing 15
sales orientation 9
societal marketing concept 11

SUMMARY

1 **Define the term *marketing*.** The ultimate goal of all marketing activity is to facilitate mutually satisfying exchanges between parties. The activities of marketing include the conception, pricing, promotion, and distribution of ideas, goods, and services.

2 **Describe several reasons for studying marketing.** First, marketing affects the allocation of goods and services that influence a nation's economy and standard of living. Second, an understanding of marketing is crucial to understanding most businesses. Third, career opportunities in marketing are diverse, profitable, and expected to increase significantly during the 1990s. Fourth, understanding marketing makes consumers more informed.

3 **Describe several marketing management philosophies.** The role of marketing and the character of marketing activities within an organization are strongly influenced by its philosophy and orientation. A production-oriented organization focuses on the internal capabilities of the firm rather than on the desires and needs of the marketplace. A sales orientation is based on the beliefs that people will buy more products if aggressive sales techniques are used and that high sales volumes produce high profits. A marketing-oriented organization focuses on satisfying customer wants and needs while meeting organizational objectives. A societal marketing orientation goes beyond a marketing orientation to include the preservation or enhancement of individuals' and society's long-term best interests.

4 **Discuss the difference between selling and marketing orientations.** First, a sales-oriented firm focuses inward on its own needs; marketing-oriented firms focus outward on customers' needs and preferences. Second, sales-oriented companies consider themselves to be deliverers of goods and services, whereas marketing-oriented companies view themselves as satisfiers of customers. Third, sales-oriented firms direct their products to everyone; marketing-oriented firms aim at specific segments of the population. Fourth, although the primary goal of both types of firms is profit, sales-oriented businesses pursue maximum sales volume through intensive promotion, whereas marketing-oriented businesses pursue customer satisfaction through coordinated marketing activities.

5 **Explain how firms implement the marketing concept.** To successfully implement the marketing concept, management has to enthusiastically embrace and endorse the concept and to encourage its spread throughout the organization. Changing from a production or selling orientation to a marketing orientation often requires changes in authority and responsibility and front-line experience for management.

6 **Describe the marketing process, and identify the variables that make up the marketing mix.** The marketing process includes scanning the environment, analyzing market opportunities, setting marketing objectives, selecting a target market strategy, developing and implementing a marketing mix, and evaluating marketing efforts and making changes if needed. The marketing mix combines product, distribution, promotion, and pricing strategies in a way that creates exchanges satisfying to individual and organizational objectives.

Review Questions

1. Explain the concept of exchange. What conditions are necessary for an exchange to take place?
2. Explain how a knowledge of marketing can help you in a career.
3. How will an understanding of marketing make you a more sophisticated consumer?
4. Explain production and sales orientations. What are the major shortcomings of these marketing management philosophies?
5. Why is training an important step in implementing the marketing concept?
6. What are the variables of the marketing mix, and how do they relate to the target market?
7. Why is it important that an organization clearly define its mission?

Discussion and Writing Questions

1. In your new position as marketing manager for the nonprofit National Wildlife Federation, you have made the adoption of a marketing orientation your first goal. Write a memo to our staff explaining why you believe the organization will benefit from this new approach.
2. Donald E. Petersen, chairman of the board of Ford Motor Company, remarked, "If we aren't customer-driven, our cars won't be either." Explain how this statement reflects the marketing concept.
3. How does the concept of marketing myopia reflect the fundamental difference between sales and marketing orientations?
4. A friend of yours agrees with the adage "People don't know what they want—they only want what they know." Write your friend a letter expressing the extent to which you think marketers shape consumer wants.
5. How does direct experience serving customers help managers implement the marketing concept?
6. Can a firm be successful without adopting a marketing orientation? Why or why not?

CASES

1.1 AT&T's Universal Card

Is the credit card party over? Some banks in the credit card business make more money on credit cards than from all other sources combined. Nevertheless, new competitors in the market are finding they must offer consumers more services at a lower cost. Low or no annual fees, low interest rates, buyer protection programs, free life insurance for travelers, and discounts for long-distance calls billed to credit cards—all are incentives offered to consumers to get them to switch.

In an already crowded market, AT&T introduced its own Universal Card. In the first six months after introduction, the Universal Card became one of the forty most widely held bank cards. The Universal Card has no annual fee (average annual fee for bank cards is $18.65) and offers a 10 percent discount on long-distance telephone service. The interest rate is set at 8.9 percent above the prime lending rate and is adjusted each quarter.

The big credit card companies, like Citibank, are eagerly buying up credit card portfolios from failed banks and savings institutions. How can newcomers like Sears and AT&T hope to compete in this crowded market? Sears offered Discover cards to some of the 70 million Sears charge card holders. AT&T looked to its list of calling card holders. Both are also willing to earn less than the other credit card companies. Industry analysts predicted that AT&T wouldn't make any money in the first few years of operation but would have 35 million cards out in the first five years—making it one of the major players in the credit card business.

The major credit card banks didn't simply sit back and watch AT&T. Citibank switched $30 million of its communications business from AT&T to MCI. Citibank also asked federal regulators to look into the relationship between AT&T and Universal Bank for possible violation of federal banking and communications laws.

Another problem AT&T faces is converting customers who pay on time into customers who don't. Most calling card holders pay their phone bills on time. But credit card companies make a significant percentage of their income from interest on outstanding balances. With a low interest rate and no annual fee, however, consumers who carry balances on their credit cards are more inclined to switch to AT&T's Universal Card.

Questions

1. Why do you think AT&T has been so successful in introducing the Universal Card?

2. What business is AT&T in? Did AT&T need to redefine its mission statement when it entered the credit card industry?

3. What factors affect the adoption of credit cards? (Hint: You should consider more than just consumers in answering this question.)

Suggested Readings

"AT&T Universal Card Turns its First Profit," *American Banker,* October 23, 1992, pp. 6.

"AT&T Universal Card Wins Baldridge Award," *American Banker,* October 15, 1992, pp. 11.

"The Wrath of Paul Kahn," *American Banker,* June 9, 1992, pp.1.

Note

Here's some credit card advice: Get two cards. Get one card with no annual fee and a twenty-five- to thirty-day grace period before interest accrues. Use this card for small monthly transactions. Pay it off in full each month. Don't worry about the interest rate, because you won't be paying any. Get a second card with the lowest possible interest rate, and use it to spread out those large purchases over time.

1.2 Colgate-Palmolive

Video title: *An Introduction to Marketing at Colgate-Palmolive*

Colgate-Palmolive Company
300 Park Avenue
New York, NY 10022

SIC codes: 2841 Soaps and other detergents
2842 Specialty cleaners
2844 Perfumes and cosmetics
3991 Brooms and brushes (including toothbrushes)
2047 Dog and cat food

Number of employees: 24,100

1993 revenues: $7 billion

Major brands: Colgate toothpaste, Palmolive soaps

Largest competitors: Procter & Gamble, Lever Brothers

Background

William Colgate founded the Colgate Company in New York in 1806 to produce a bar soap. The company's chief competitor at the time was the housewife. The majority of soap produced in the early 1800s was produced at home for personal consumption. It was a tedious chore, so housewives flocked to the stores to buy the Colgate product, and the company was a success. In 1877, the company added toothpaste to its product line, first in jars and then in collapsible tubes. In 1928, Colgate merged with the Palmolive-Peet Company, forming the Colgate Palmolive-Peet Company. The Peet name was dropped in 1952. Today, Colgate-Palmolive offers a wide range of consumer products in five broad categories: oral care, personal care, surface cleaners, fabric care, and pet nutrition.

Industry

For the most part, sales of oral care and cleaning products depend on the size of the population. Any increase in domestic sales comes at the expense of the competition or from growth in population, because most households in the U.S. market are already consumers of these products. Growth in the cleaning products market is expected to average between 1 and 3 percent per year over the next ten years. Such slow growth makes the market highly competitive. In most of the product lines sold by Colgate-Palmolive, the company competes head to head with Procter & Gamble and Lever Brothers. P&G holds the largest market share for most of the oral care and cleaning products sold in the U.S. market. In the laundry detergent market, Colgate-Palmolive is a distant third in market share (P&G, 50 percent; Lever, 35 percent; Colgate-Palmolive, 10 percent).

Colgate-Palmolive

Instead of relying on sales and special promotions to increase its dominance in the U.S. market, P&G permanently reduced its selling prices. This move seems to have had little effect on Colgate-Palmolive's strategy. Colgate-Palmolive tends to focus on establishing a global market for specific products. For example, Colgate-Palmolive has decided to focus its efforts on toothpaste, and its international market share for Colgate toothpaste is 43 percent, up 14 percent from ten years ago. By June 1992, the company was halfway to meeting its five-year goal of $9 billion in sales. By focusing on its two lines with the greatest growth potential, oral care and personal care products, the company continues to increase both sales and profits.

In addition to pursuing growth through its current

product lines, Colgate-Palmolive seeks growth through acquisitions. The company's acquisition of Mennen gave it access to the Chilean market (Mennen had a plant in Chile).

In a 1992 interview, Mr. Shannahan, Colgate-Palmolive's president and chief operations officer, said that the company would consider pursuing marketing opportunities in Nigeria as well as expanding its market in Chile. According to Shannahan, the biggest problem Colgate-Palmolive faces in foreign markets is obtaining good management. For this reason, the company offers extensive help to its managers in these foreign markets.

Questions

1. Which of the marketing orientations do you think best describes Colgate-Palmolive? Give reasons to support your position.
2. Considering the information provided in this case, what would you say is Colgate-Palmolive's mission?
3. What factors might account for Colgate-Palmolive's market share abroad being larger than its domestic share?

References

Riccardo A. Davis, "Setting the Pace on Colgate's New Path," *Advertising Age,* 28 September 1992, p. 4.

Million Dollar Directory 1993 (Parsippany: NJ: Dun & Bradstreet Information Services, 1993).

Seema Nayyar, "Building on Its Strengths: Colgate Has Been Shopping for Brands That Could Open Up New Markets," *Adweek's Marketing Week,* 15 June 1992, p. 18.

Standard & Poor's Industry Surveys (New York: Standard & Poor's Corporation, October 1993).

CHAPTER 2

The Marketing Environment

LEARNING OBJECTIVES
After studying this chapter, you should be able to

1. Discuss the external environment of marketing, and explain how it affects a firm.
2. Describe the social factors that affect marketing.
3. Explain the importance of current demographic trends to marketing managers.
4. Identify consumer and marketer reactions to the state of the economy.
5. Identify the impact of technology on a firm.
6. Understand the political and legal environment of marketing.
7. Understand the basics of foreign and domestic competition.

From the late 1980s through the early 1990s, Taco Bell experienced record-breaking growth each year. The firm's major competitors experienced flat to negative growth during the same period, even while adding new outlets. Unmatched increases in revenue, customer counts, and profit made Taco Bell the fast-food industry trendsetter. It wasn't always so.

When PepsiCo bought the Taco Bell chain in 1978, customers believed that Taco Bell served excellent products at the right price, even though it wasn't an industry leader. As PepsiCo expanded the chain east, however, the customer base evaporated. Outside California, Mexican food had no broad popularity, and in comparison to hamburger chains, Taco Bell seemed expensive. Product prices climbed. A taco was 79¢. Other products cost $1.65, and some were as high as $2.99. For the next several years business stagnated. New customers were hard to attract. Taco Bell was stuck in a no-growth rut.

Things began to change in 1983, when John Martin became president of Taco Bell. The company immediately began changing the look of the stores and introducing new products. At the same time, supermarket shoppers were warming to the idea of preparing Mexican food at home. The timing was right. Sales grew about 7.5 percent overall from 1984 to 1987. Compared to the industry as a whole, the company was doing slightly better than average.

A mandate was given to top management to determine what was holding the company back and what would power future growth. Environmental scanning by Taco Bell management led to the concept of value marketing. They determined that the 1990s would be a "value decade." Futurists and trend analysts have identified a more conservative behavior trend they call "neo-traditionalism." Aging baby boomers are raising children, worrying about college, and caring for their own aging parents. The "shop till you drop" attitude of the eighties dropped. Value-consciousness is driving consumer purchase decisions like never before. Market leaders, therefore, will consistently deliver value as defined by the customer.

Taco Bell research defined its customer core as heavy fast-food users. These are people who visit a fast-food restaurant seventeen times a month, on average. Heavy fast-food users make up only about 30 percent of the customer population but account for about 70 percent of industry sales. Another common trait of Taco Bell customers is that they are in a hurry. The primary customer lives in the middle of a time famine: two jobs, two children, too many responsibilities. It's a lack of time that's driving a global search for convenience.

In addition to convenience, Taco Bell customers demand value. Value to them means fillingness ("Did I get enough to eat?"), price, service, and product quality. Taco Bell enjoyed a strong image of quality, fresh ingredients, but prices were perceived as far too high. A 1985 study found 19 percent of the respondents believing that Taco Bell was too expensive, second only to Wendy's. Taco Bell was becoming a change-of-pace fast-food option, not a mainstream occasion. By 1988, the firm was still experiencing marginal sales gains. Management determined that changing the image among heavy users was the ticket to business growth.

Further research showed that value for price was an everyday requirement. So management began to experiment with a permanent price reduction of the regular taco, the "flagship" menu item. But if the price dropped too low, it might signal a drop in quality to target customers. So the key was improving the price/value ratio without hurting Taco Bell's quality image. Marketing research pointed the way to a new "value-priced menu" that still maintained the quality image. From 1989, when the new marketing mix was created, through 1992, Taco Bell saw faster growth than any fast-food restaurant chain had ever experienced.

Changing consumer tastes and attitudes, competition, and other uncontrollable factors in the external environment have affected Taco Bell's success. Does the external environment affect the marketing mix of most companies? What other uncontrollable factors in the external environment might affect Taco Bell's future profitability? What might happen to any organization that ignores the external environment?

Adapted from speech by Art Redmond, "How Taco Bell Achieved Trend Setter Status in Fast Food Marketing," delivered at the 1992 AMA Research Conference Scottsdale, AZ.

1 THE EXTERNAL MARKETING ENVIRONMENT

As you learned in Chapter 1, managers create a marketing mix by uniquely combining product, distribution, promotion, and price strategies. The marketing mix is, of course, under the firm's control and is designed to appeal to a specific group of potential buyers. A **target market** is a defined group that managers feel is most likely to buy a firm's product.

target market
Group for which an organization designs, implements, and maintains a marketing mix intended to meet the needs of that group, resulting in mutually satisfying exchanges.

Over time, managers must alter the marketing mix because the environment in which consumers live, work, and make purchasing decisions changes. Some new consumers become part of the target market; others drop out. Those who remain may have different tastes, needs, incomes, lifestyles, and buying habits than the original target consumers.

Although managers can control the marketing mix, they cannot control elements in the external environment that continually mold and reshape the target market. Exhibit 2.1 shows that consumers and business purchasers (the target market) are influenced by both these controllable and uncontrollable variables. The right side of Exhibit 2.1 lists the uncontrollable elements that continually evolve and create changes in the target market. In contrast, the left side of Exhibit 2.1 depicts the marketing mix, those elements that managers can use to influence the target markets.

Understanding the External Environment

Unless marketing managers understand the external environment, the firm cannot intelligently plan for the future. When a team of specialists is created to continually collect and evaluate environmental information, the process is called **environmental scanning.** The goal in gathering the environmental data is to identify future market opportunities and threats.

environmental scanning
Collection and interpretation of information about forces, events, and relationships that may affect the future of an organization.

For example, during the past decade the number of affluent African-American households ($50,000 or more income) grew an astonishing 360 percent.[1] In some ways, affluent African-Americans parallel their white counterparts. Both tend to read newspapers. Both are more likely than average to own a new station wagon, to use a credit card monthly, and to make three or more annual stock transactions. Yet,

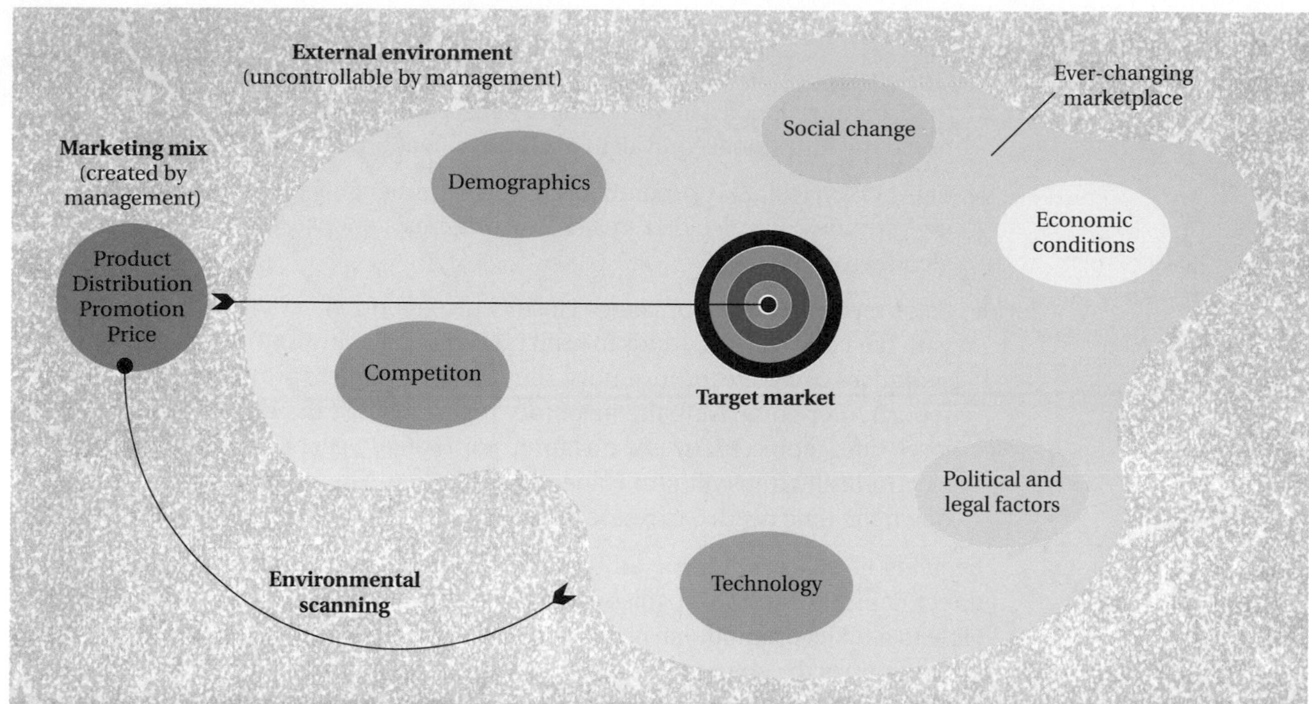

Exhibit 2.1

How Uncontrollable Factors in the External Environment Affect the Marketing Mix

affluent African-Americans are likely to watch television less often. They especially enjoy reading *Ebony, Sports Illustrated, Fortune,* and *Time.* Furthermore, they are less likely than affluent whites to join health clubs or to have spent $100 or more at a discount department store like Kmart in any given month.[2] A marketing manager for President's Health Clubs or Kmart might perceive such trends as a threat, but for *Sports Illustrated* the findings suggest a great opportunity. What does the huge increase in affluent African-American households mean to McDonald's, Chrysler Corporation, or Northwest Airlines? Marketing managers for these and countless other organizations must sift through environmental trends and decide whether they represent threats or opportunities.

The alert marketer would know that the ranks of affluent African-Americans are growing, thus increasing opportunities for firms marketing vacations and other products that have been marketed mostly to affluent whites.

© Superstock

Note how three companies responded to other environmental trends:

- DuPont, recognizing the United States' increased interest in eating healthy food, has developed a high-fiber flour substitute that can make ordinary white bread the nutritional equivalent of whole-wheat bread.[3]
- The Jackson Hole Ski Corporation, citing government health reports and changing attitudes, has decided to stop hosting races sponsored by tobacco and alcohol companies.
- Sales representatives for Hanes Hosiery use hand-held computers equipped with bar code reading wands to keep track of retailer inventories. When representatives complete the inventory, they use a lightweight printer to create a full report. After comparing the inventory report against the store's target stock level, sales representatives use a laptop computer to generate a new order and electronically transmit it to Hanes's main office. The system drastically cuts down the time needed to restock the store.

Evolving lifestyles, changing attitudes, and emerging technology—all outside the direct control of the companies—led DuPont to develop a new product, Jackson Hole to alter its promotional plans, and Hanes to improve its distribution.

Sometimes the changing environment can pose a threat. When it does, marketing managers' challenge is to convert the threat to an opportunity. Consider the following example:

> What do you do when you're in the suntan business and America decides to end its love affair with the sun? As the sale of sun blocks climbed, Coppertone was frustrated in its attempt to get its share of the emerging market. "Coppertone is for tanning, not for blocking," consumers seemed to be saying.
>
> So the company went back to its origins—a cute little girl with a dog nipping at her bathing suit and the slogan "Tan, Don't Burn." Whom do you want to protect most from the sun? Children. What's the most important quality a children's sun block should have? Waterproofing.

Coppertone called its new sun block Water Babies and featured the name on the package along with the little girl and the dog. The Coppertone sponsorship was visible but smaller. Water Babies has been an enormous success. Not only is it a new profit center, but it's also helping Coppertone keep pace with a changing lifestyle trend—sensible skin care.[4]

Environmental Management

No one business is large or powerful enough to create major external environmental change. Marketing managers are basically adapters rather than agents of change. For example, despite the huge size of General Motors, Ford, and Chrysler, they have not been able to stem the competitive push by the Japanese for ever-growing automobile market share in the United States. Competition is basically an uncontrollable element in the external environment.

This is not to say, however, that a firm is always completely at the mercy of the external environment. Sometimes a firm can influence evolving external factors. For example, extensive lobbying may help persuade Congress to pass legislation limiting Japanese automobile imports. A company may help tame an overly aggressive competitor by filing an antitrust suit. When a company implements strategies that attempt to shape the external environment within which it operates, it is engaging in **environmental management.**

environmental management Implementation of strategies that attempt to shape the external environment within which a firm operates.

Let's take a closer look at the factors within the external environment that are so

important to marketing managers: social, demographic, economic, technological, political/legal, and competitive. (See also Exhibit 2.1.)

2 SOCIAL FACTORS

Social change is perhaps the most difficult external variable for marketing managers to forecast, influence, or integrate into marketing plans. Although there are hundreds, perhaps thousands, of economic forecasters, very few firms venture into analyzing and forecasting social trends. Managers have to depend largely on their knowledge of the past and on their observations.

During the United States' first 150 years, four basic values strongly influenced attitudes and lifestyles:

- *Self-sufficiency:* Every person stood on his or her own two feet.
- *Upward mobility:* If you did the right thing, success would come.
- **Protestant work ethic:** This set of principles stressed hard work, dedication to family, and frugality.
- *Conformity:* No one wanted to stick out like a sore thumb; being different was not a desirable trait.

Protestant work ethic
A set of principles that stress hard work, dedication to family, and frugality.

Today, some of these values don't hold. Because of private pension plans and government's generosity, U.S. citizens have the lowest savings rate among industrialized nations. Also, the many government programs reduce the need for self-reliance and, instead, create a "psychology of entitlement." This notion suggests that "government owes me a good standard of living."

Yet the dream of upward mobility is more widespread than ever before. Almost two out of three Americans believe they have a good chance for advancement in the future. Moreover, 79 percent feel they are more likely to succeed than their fathers. Still, most people (59 percent) view themselves as middle class.[5]

This ad reflects one prime value of today's consumers: high quality. Timex has long stressed the reliability and durability of its watches.
Courtesy of Timex Corporation

Basic Values in the United States Today

These basic values are important to today's consumer: (1) self-respect, (2) security, (3) warm relationships with family and friends, (4) a sense of accomplishment, (5) self-fulfillment, (6) respect from others, (7) a sense of belonging, and (8) the chance to have fun and excitement.[6] A study conducted about every ten years found a number of changes from the previous decade. Self-respect, for example, ranked first in both decades, but women placed less emphasis than men did on it and security. Perhaps women who have entered the work force and achieved success have al-

ready attained these two values. In fact, women now emphasize self-fulfillment and a sense of accomplishment. Although the chance to have fun and excitement still ranks last, more consumers in all age groups, except people over 60, endorse its importance.

Values of Baby Boomers

baby boomers
Persons born between 1946 and 1964.

As the **baby boomers** (persons born between 1946 and 1964) march into their forties, with their own babies to care for, this age group also is shifting from yesterday's values of "me first" to an inevitable yearning for a better home life. This group cherishes convenience, which has resulted in a growing demand for home delivery services for items like large appliances, furniture, and groceries. In addition, the spreading culture of convenience explains the tremendous appeal of prepared take-out foods and the necessity of microwave ovens, which over 80 percent of all U.S. families now own.[7] The microwave has even revived dying products. For example, since Kraft General Foods reformulated Cheese Whiz into a microwavable hot cheese sauce, Cheese Whiz sales have soared 40 percent annually.[8]

Marketing-Oriented Values of the 1990s

Today's consumers are demanding, inquisitive, and discriminating. No longer willing to tolerate products that break down, they are insisting on high-quality goods that save time, energy, and often calories. U.S. consumers rank the characteristics of product quality as (1) reliability, (2) durability, (3) easy maintenance, (4) ease of use, (5) a trusted brand name, and (6) a low price. Shoppers are also concerned about nutrition and want to know what's in their food. In the late 1980s, barely a third of grocery shoppers read labels on the foods they bought; today half of them do.[9]

Today's shoppers are also environmentalists. Eight in ten U.S. consumers regard themselves as environmentalists, and half of those say they are strong ones.[10] Four out of five shoppers are willing to pay 5 percent more for products packaged with recyclable or biodegradable materials. Many marketers predict that by the year 2000 it will be very hard to sell a product that isn't environmentally friendly.

poverty of time
Lack of time to do anything but work, commute to work, handle family situations, do housework, shop, sleep, and eat.

In the nineties, fewer consumers say expensive cars, designer clothes, pleasure trips, and "gold cards" are necessary components of a happy life. Instead, they put value on nonmaterial accomplishments, such as having control of their lives and being able to take a day off when they want.[11] Dual-career families have a **poverty of time,** with few hours to do anything but work and commute to work, handle family situations, do housework, shop, sleep, and eat. In a recent study of 1,010 people, half said they would sacrifice a day's pay for an extra day off each week. Of those surveyed, 21 percent said they had "no time for fun anymore," 33 percent said they don't accomplish what they set out to do each day, and 38 percent reported cutting back on sleep to make up for lost time.[12] In fact, the market for devices to help us relax and sleep has been growing at about 14 percent each year since the late 1980s and should top $300 million in annual sales by 1995.[13]

It is very true that the values of today's U.S. consumers make them "tough customers." Yet this change is not just a U.S. phenomenon. The box on page 37 will introduce you to the world's toughest customers for a variety of products. The findings are based on international marketing research.

The Growth of Component Lifestyles

From preteens to older consumers, people in the United States are piecing together component lifestyles. In other words, they are choosing products and services that

INTERNATIONAL PERSPECTIVES

The World's Toughest Customers

Disposable Diapers

Toughest customers: Japanese parents insist on the thinnest diaper in the smallest possible package. Scant storage space in tiny homes makes trim packaging a necessity. Conscientious parents also change their babies frequently; they have the time, because 92 percent of mothers with children under 4 are full-time homemakers.

Other nationalities: Australian customers prefer thick diapers. Ecologically minded U.S. citizens, fretting over diminishing landfill space, have turned to slender, superabsorbent diapers tightly packed in smaller cartons. Like the Japanese, Koreans, want their children's diapers thin and tailored to fit, almost like underwear.

Electric Irons

Toughest customers: For the Japanese, everything on this small appliance—from the soleplate to the handle—must be absolutely smooth and free of defects. Nothing delights the gadget-happy Japanese more than an iron that beeps as it changes temperature.

Other nationalities: Germans want a simple, clean-looking iron of any color, as long as it's white. Every feature should be exactly where function dictates. U.S. consumers are more price-driven than others and more concerned about safety. That's why irons with an automatic shut-off are popular in the United States. Once the appliance breaks, U.S. owners rush out the same day to buy a replacement with the newest features.

Laundry Detergents

Toughest customers: Italians, Spaniards, and U.S. Hispanics. All three place great importance on the way their families look; immaculate appearance matters. They value the high-efficiency detergents that are more powerful cleaners and can readily discern differences in performance among brands.

Other nationalities: U.S. and British consumers are generally less fastidious than they used to be about laundry. Kids wear clothes with spots that don't come out. But dress shirts must be stain-free. The Japanese were the first to adopt concentrated detergents in smaller boxes with less packaging to be disposed of or recycled. Germans fret about water pollution and generally use less detergent, fabric softener, and chlorine bleach than other nationalities.

Athletic Footwear

Toughest customers: Germans avidly read the specifications and expect salespeople to prove that novel construction and materials produce a shoe that performs as well as promised.

Other nationalities: Japanese consumers are right behind the Germans in their quest for the technologically sophisticated and well-made shoe. U.S. buyers are extremely brand-conscious and demand comfort. They are more inclined to regard athletic shoes as a fashion item than as a serious piece of sports equipment. No more than 20 percent of the sneakers sold in the United States ever see heavy-duty use on a tennis court or running track.

Why do you think the toughest customers for different products come from different countries? Which country do you think would have the overall toughest customers? Why?

Adapted from "How to Deal with Tough Customers," *Fortune*, December 3, 1990, pp. 44–45.

meet diverse needs and interests rather than conform to traditional stereotypes. In the past a person's profession—for instance, banker—defined his or her lifestyle. Today a person can be a banker and also a gourmet, fitness enthusiast, dedicated single parent, and conservationist. Each of these lifestyles is associated with different goods and services and represents a target audience. For example, for the gourmet, marketers offer cooking utensils, wines, and exotic foods through magazines like *Bon Appetit* and *Gourmet*. The banker/fitness enthusiast buys Adidas equipment and special jogging outfits and reads *Runner* magazine. Component lifestyles increase the complexity of consumers' buying habits. The banker may own a BMW but change the oil himself or herself. He or she may buy fast food for lunch but French wine for dinner, own sophisticated photographic equipment and a low-priced home stereo, shop for socks at Kmart or Wal-Mart and suits or dresses at Brooks Brothers.

The changing role of women has been a major shift in the marketing environment. *(left)* In the 1950s, marketers viewed women mainly as housewives. *(right)* Today women are also viewed as career women with a complex mix of roles.

(left) H. Armstrong Roberts; *(right)* © 1991 P. Barry Levy/ProFiles West

The Changing Role of Families and Working Women

Component lifestyles have evolved because consumers can choose from a growing number of goods and services, and most have the money to exercise more options. Rising purchasing power has resulted from the growth of dual-income families. Approximately 58 percent of all females between 16 and 65 years old are now in the work force. Female participation in the labor force will grow to 63 percent by 2005.[14] This phenomenon has probably had a greater effect on marketing than any other social change.

Although dual-career families typically have greater household incomes, they have less time for family activities (poverty of time). Their purchase roles (which define what items are traditionally bought by the man or the woman) are changing, as well as their purchase patterns. Consequently, new opportunities are being created. For example, small businesses are opening daily that cater to dual-career households by offering specialized goods and services. Ice cream and yogurt parlors, cafes, and sports footwear shops have proliferated. With more women than ever working full time, there is a special demand for new household services. San Francisco Grocery Express, a warehouse operation, uses computers to take customers' telephone orders. Customers refer to a catalog listing grocery items and prices. Later, vans deliver the food to the purchasers' front doors.

Dual careers have also meant, for example, that substantially more men shop for food. Many products are being updated to appeal to these male shoppers. Kraft General Foods, for example, redesigned its Kraft salad dressing bottles and labels to look more masculine. Also, since men do not respond as well as women to conventional grocery promotions (newspaper advertising, coupons, price promotions), manufacturers and retailers face the challenge of finding ways to effectively promote products to this group.

At the same time, many traditionally male-oriented products are being modified for or promoted to women because of the growth in female purchasing power. For example, many people would say there is no more masculine product than a Smith & Wesson revolver. Yet after Smith & Wesson launched LadySmith, a line of guns specifically for women, the gunmaker's sales to women jumped from 5 percent of the company's total to nearly 18 percent. Toyota sells almost 60 percent of its cars to women. "Women have become extremely knowledgeable about the car business," says corporate marketing manager Ren Rooney. "They have some influence on 80

percent of our purchases."[15] Avis also decided to start targeting women after it noted that the number of female business travelers was growing faster than the business travel market in general. The company gave discounts to members of the National Association for Female Executives, created an ad campaign showing a woman in a car, and placed the ads in women's magazines such as *Lear's, Entrepreneurial Woman,* and *New Woman.* The tag line: "We make the road a little less lonely."

3 DEMOGRAPHIC FACTORS

demography
Study of people's vital statistics, such as their ages, births, deaths, and locations.

Demographic factors—another uncontrollable variable in the external environment—are also extremely important to marketing managers. **Demography** is the study of people's vital statistics, such as their ages, births, deaths, and locations. Demographics are significant because the basis for any market is people.

The United States in the 1990s

Although the U.S. population is growing older, it is also growing at a slower rate. The 1990 census revealed that the U.S. population rose to 250 million in 1990 from 227 million in 1980, representing an annual growth rate of less than 1 percent. But the slow rate masks an array of differences among various ethnic and age groups.

For instance, the United States is becoming more middle-aged. The number of 24- to 44-year-olds increased 30 percent between 1980 and 1990, while the number of 10- to 24-year-olds fell by 12 percent. The baby boomlet of the 1980s resulted in a modest 11 percent increase in the number of children under age 10. The population aged 65 or older has grown 23 percent since 1980, more than twice as fast as the population as a whole. The biggest spurt has come among the very old, with the number of people over 85 growing 44 percent. That group remains small, though; only 1 percent in the United States are 85 or older.[16]

The population growth rate of less than 1 percent and a rate of new household formation under 2 percent is the slowest U.S. growth rate since the Great Depression. These rates will decline even more as we move through the decade, with at least twelve states showing no growth at all. This phenomenon will profoundly affect consumer goods marketers, because they can no longer count on expanding overall markets to fuel sales increases. Consumer goods marketers will be able to prosper in the domestic market only by taking competitors' customers or tapping into specialized niches, such as the growing elderly market, before competitors do.

The mid-1990s are being characterized as a struggle for market share and profits. Several of the big consumer goods mergers—for example, R.J. Reynolds with Nabisco and Kraft with General Foods—were partially driven by demographics. In other words, these companies gained new customers by acquiring their competitors. If a marketer can't count on many new customers entering the marketplace, buying existing customers may make sense. Another approach is to ensure market share by building brand loyalty in the young.

market segmentation
Process of dividing a market into meaningful, relatively similar, identifiable segments or groups.

In the past, marketing managers could promote products nationally, heavily using network television advertising. Basically, mass promotions were aimed at a few dominant market segments. **Market segmentation**, the subject of Chapter 6, is the process of breaking a market into relatively homogeneous and identifiable groups. The purpose is to design a marketing mix to meet the needs of consumers who are attractive to the firm. The traditional favorite was the white, middle-class, full-time housewife worried about "ring around the collar." But the mass market she represented is growing much more slowly and has been fragmented by social change.

Today there are many market segments of vastly different kinds of consumers with different backgrounds, tastes, and needs. "America is no longer a melting pot—it's a mosaic," notes Joel Weiner, senior vice president of marketing at Kraft General Foods.[17]

Identifying attractive market segments and creating products to meet specific needs is a tricky task. Often it is even harder than before to reach a specific segment with a promotional message, because the media that carry the promotional messages are also fragmenting. The major television networks, for example, have been the cornerstone of national consumer goods advertising. Now, in cities with cable television, viewers can flip through an average of thirty-five additional channels. The three major networks have only 67 percent of the prime-time audience, down from 90 percent ten years ago. Yet during the decade, the price of a thirty-second commercial doubled to an average of $113,000.[18] The following article illustrates how some marketers are trying to use special promotions to reach school-aged children.

ETHICS IN MARKETING

Marketing in the Public Schools

A slowdown of U.S. population growth means that it is more important than ever to build brand loyalty at an early age. As the thinking goes, attaining a desirable level of long-range market share requires generating brand loyalty early in life and maintaining that loyalty as the consumer ages.

Because the average U.S. parents both work, children are either home alone or out at the malls for longer periods of time. They make buying decisions that their parents used to make. As a result, many marketers are making a beeline for the nation's schools. Whittle Communications, for example, created Channel One, a commercial television network for America's high schools. Coca-Cola Foods' Minute Maid publishes a summer fun guide touting the joys of selling lemonade—Minute Maid's brand, of course. Pepsi distributes a space shuttle poster to science classes that serves as a billboard for the Pepsi logo.

Procter & Gamble offered elementary schools a no-strings-attached deal: The more Jif peanut butter sold, the more P&G would contribute to each school that signed up with the company. There would be no restriction on how the schools spent their money. P&G expected to split $4 million among the schools that registered. If anything, the program was too successful. Nearly one of every three elementary schools in the United States signed up. A $4 million pot translated into just under $200 for each of the 21,600 schools enrolled—enough to buy a few basketballs.

Kellogg launched a four-week "Game of the States" promotion. The game was created after a National Geographic Society survey found U.S. students ranked nearly last in an international geographic literacy test. Not incidentally, the program touted Kellogg brands and impeded other cereals' penetration into elementary schools. Elementary schools had to schedule one additional "Kellogg's Cereal Day" for each week of the promotion, guaranteeing Kellogg products exclusivity. In return, they received posters and maps for each student. Each week, cafeteria staff distributed a sticker sheet to apply to one of four U.S. regional maps. Students had to put the right stickers in the right states. Participation levels determined the winning schools. The grand prize? A thousand dollars for trips to the state capital, where the "educator" Tony the Tiger greeted the kids.

Some programs sponsored by other corporations have won praise. Merrill Lynch created a Scholarship Builder program to inspire inner-city first-graders to aim for college. American Express set up a National Academy Foundation to provide job experiences for high school students. The Exxon Education Foundation funded an experiment on new teaching methods. Polaroid's Project Bridge helped employees switch careers to become math or science teachers.

Federal aid to education has barely kept pace with inflation, and rising school taxes have created a homeowners' revolt. Marketers have claimed that they are simply filling a vacuum left by decreased government support. Do you agree? If a student's learning is enhanced, even though there is a commercial tie-in, is that wrong? What would you say to Kellogg and Procter & Gamble about their school promotions?

Baby boomers, now middle-aged, focus on families and finances. This life insurance ad is right on target with its photo of a father and his triplet sons.

Massachusetts Mutual Life Insurance Company

Middle-Aged Consumers: Largest and Fastest-Growing U.S. Market

The Pepsi generation has matured. As the age of today's average consumer moves toward 40, average consumption patterns also change. People in their early 40s tend to focus on their families and finances. As this group grows in numbers, they will buy more furniture from manufacturers like Lazy Boy, American Martindale, Baker, and Drexel-Heritage to replace the furniture they bought early in their marriage. The demand for family counselors and wellness programs should also increase. Additionally, discount brokers like Charles Schwab and mutual funds like Fidelity and Dreyfus should profit. Because middle-aged consumers buy more reading materials than any other age group, the market for books and magazines should remain strong throughout the 1990s. People who buy magazines on the newsstand tend to be younger, so newsstand sales may falter while subscription sales take off.

During the remainder of the1990s, merchants will offer more products and services aimed at middle-aged markets. Styles will have a more conservative look, commercials will feature more middle-aged actors, and the general atmosphere of retail stores will be less youth-oriented. Already, Dayton Hudson department stores have been redecorated to reflect this changing image.

The oldest baby boomers turn 50 in 1996, and research has found that they will not accept aging gracefully. This is the market segment that spurred the health food and exercise industries. Many middle-aged consumers want to look as young as they feel. They are demanding skin treatments, hair coloring, hair transplants, and spas. Ads for Canyon Ranch Spa in Arizona and Massachusetts use middle-aged models, who claim to "age better by living younger." People in the United States spend almost $2 billion annually on cosmetic surgery.[19] The most popular procedures are nose jobs, followed by eyelid lifts and face-lifts. A third of all cosmetic surgery is performed on men. For the 66 million who are in their late 40s, the adventure of youth continues.

Older Consumers: Not Just Grandparents

Today's 50-plus consumers are wealthier, healthier, and better educated than earlier generations. Although they make up only 26 percent of the population, 50-plus

consumers buy half of all domestic cars, half of all silverware, and nearly half of all home remodeling.[20] Smart marketers are already targeting this growing segment. By 2020, over a third of the population will be 50 years old or older.[21]

Many marketers have yet to tap the full potential of the huge and lucrative senior market because of enduring misconceptions about mature adults, all based on stereotypes. Here are a few:

- *Stereotype:* Older consumers are sick or ailing. *Fact:* A full 85 percent of mature citizens report themselves to be in good or excellent health.
- *Stereotype:* Older consumers are sedentary. *Fact:* 80 percent of all travel dollars spent in the United States are spent by people over 50 years old.
- *Stereotype:* Older consumers have a poor retention rate. *Fact:* Senior citizens are readers and much less influenced by TV than younger consumers. They not only retain what they read, but they are willing to read far more copy than younger people are.
- *Stereotype:* Older consumers are interested only in price and are intolerant of change. *Fact:* Although senior citizens are as interested in price as anyone else, they are more interested in value. And a generation that has survived the better part of a century that has witnessed more technological change than any other in history can hardly be considered resistant to change.[22]

Marketers who understand the mature market are actively pursuing it. Aging consumers create some obvious opportunities. JCPenney's Easy Dressing clothes make up a catalog line of Velcro-fastened clothing for women with arthritis or other ailments who may have difficulty with zippers or buttons. Sales from the first catalog, distributed in 1991, were three times higher than expected.[23] Other retailers are adding more rest stops in stores and arranging shelving so customers needn't bend over. Grocers are considering attaching magnifying glasses to grocery carts with elastic cords. General Motors and Toyota are adding "older" features to their cars. Toyota is installing simpler audio systems with fewer gadgets in its Camry sedans. Some GM cars now offer a "head-up display" that flashes vehicle speed and other signals on the front windshield, making them easier to read.[24] On the cruise ship *Crown Odyssey,* owned by Royal Cruise Line, passengers take water aerobics classes, order broiled fish with lemon, and attend seminars on stress reduction. Are the passengers health-conscious yuppies? No, Royal is simply trying to meet the wishes of its 50-plus target market. Sales of Post Natural Bran Flakes rose rapidly when Kraft General Foods began using durable entertainers Lena Horne and Steve Allen in its advertising.

The Growing Singles Market

The 1990 census showed that about 23 million people in the United States live by themselves, a 91 percent jump for women since 1970 and a 156 percent increase for men.[25] Two trends lie behind this singles surge: Unprecedented numbers of adults are never marrying, and by some estimates, 60 percent of all couples divorce.

It's an attractive market but a tough one. Studies show singles share such traits as a tendency to spend more than married adults on travel, convenience foods, and restaurants. But this vast, fragmented group includes everyone from carefree 21-year-olds to elderly widows. They are also widely scattered geographically, although the greatest concentration of single households is in the Midwest (see Exhibit 2.2).

There is also the delicate task of getting a message across without offending. According to Jane R. Fitzgibbon, a group director of Ogilvy & Mather Advertising,

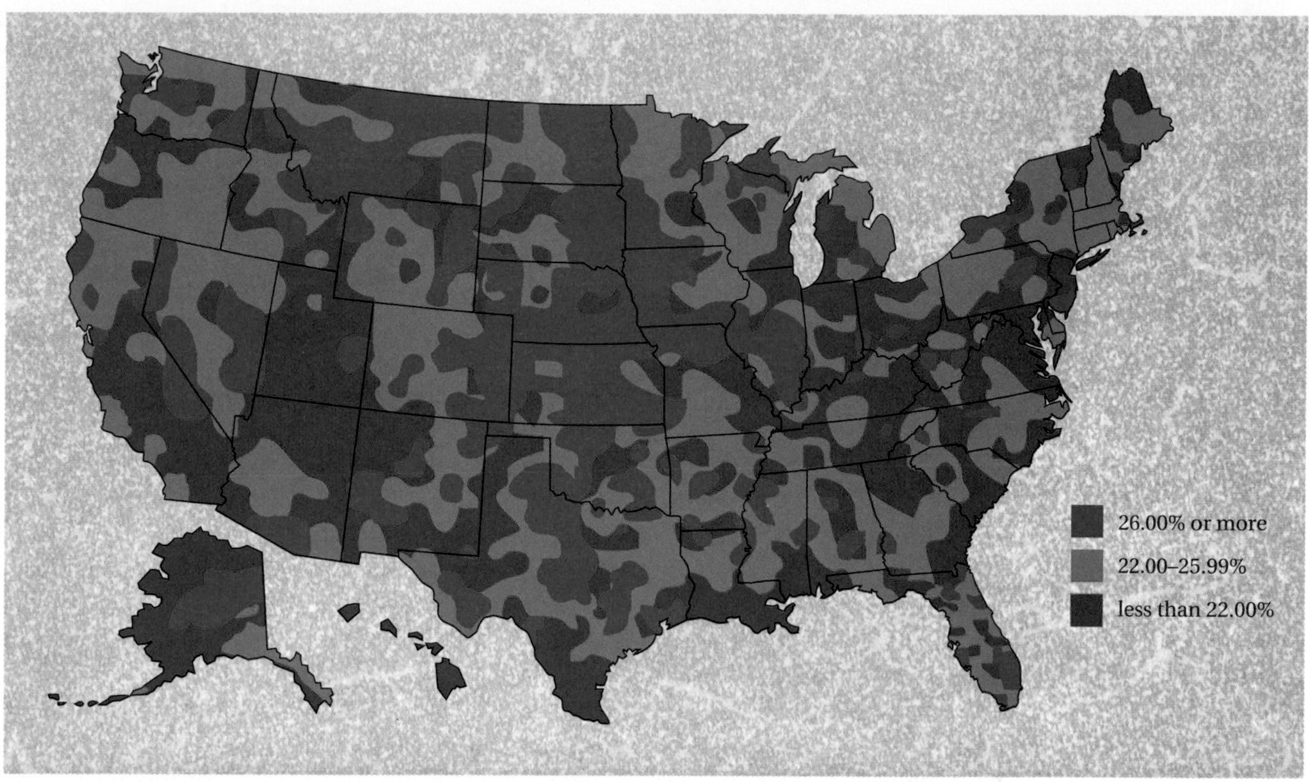

Exhibit 2.2

Where the Singles Are

Source: "The Singles Scene," *American Demographics*, July 1992, p. 18. Reprinted with permission © *American Demographics* July 1992. For subscription information, please call (800)828-1133.

too often marketers have been "treating singles as if they were just some sort of extramarital aberration."[26]

Campbell made that mistake with its Soup for One line. "Our consumers told us Soup for One is a lonely name. They are eating alone, and they don't need to be reminded," says Robert Bernstock, a vice president in the soup division.[27] In 1990, after years of mediocre sales, the Soup for One label was removed. In 1993, single-serving sizes come without the offending label, and sales have improved.

On the other hand, Procter & Gamble has been very successful with Folgers Singles, coffee in single-serve bags. Advertising uses the song "One" from the Broadway musical *A Chorus Line* to position the product as "One sensational way to wake up." Trans World Airlines, responding to research showing that 35 percent of airline travelers are single, has created a series of commercials targeting the market. One spot followed a 30-something young man traveling alone in Europe, reflecting on his father's advice to take the trip now, while he's still young.[28]

On the Move

The average U.S. citizen moves every six years.[29] Population shifts, as well as changing age patterns, open new markets. Areas experiencing a large influx of people create many new marketing opportunities for all types of businesses in those regions. Conversely, significant out-migration from a city or town may force many of its businesses to either move or close down. The greatest gains in population during the past decade were in the Far West and in the Mountain states.

4 ECONOMIC FACTORS

In addition to social and demographic factors, marketing managers must understand and react to the economic environment. The three economic areas of greatest

concern to most marketers are the distribution of consumer income, inflation, and recession.

Rising Incomes

As disposable, or after-tax, incomes rise, more families and individuals can afford the "good life." After adjustment for inflation, median incomes rose 3 percent between 1980 and 1992.[30]

Today about two-thirds of all U.S. households earn a "middle-class" income. The rough boundaries for a middle-class income are $18,000, comfortably above poverty, to about $75,000, just short of wealth. In 1993 almost half the households were in the upper end of the $18,000 to $75,000 range, as opposed to only a quarter in 1980. (The percentage of households earning above $75,000 rose from 2.6 percent to 7.4 percent of the total households.[31]) As a result, middle-class families are buying more goods and services than ever before. For example, in raising a child to age 17, a middle-class family will spend $120,000 in 1990 dollars.[32] This new level of affluence is not limited to professionals or even individuals within specific age or education brackets. Rather, it cuts across all household types, well beyond what businesses traditionally consider to be markets for high-priced goods and services. This rising affluence primarily stems from the increasing number of dual-income families.

Unfortunately, the recession of the early 1990s kept poor people from moving into the middle class. (A college education is the single most important factor in moving up in economic class.[33]) The real purchasing power of lower-income households has stagnated since 1980.

During the remainder of the 1990s, many marketing managers will focus on families with incomes over $35,000, because this group will have the most **discretionary income** (income after taxes and necessities). Some marketers will concentrate their efforts on higher-quality, higher-priced goods and services. The Lexus automobile and American Airlines' "international class" service for business-class seats on transcontinental flights are examples of this trend.

discretionary income
Income after taxes and necessities.

Inflation

inflation
General rise in prices resulting in decreased purchasing power.

Inflation is a general rise in prices resulting in decreased purchasing power. Fortunately, the United States has had a low rate of inflation for almost a decade. The early 1990s have been marked by an inflation rate under 5 percent. These economic conditions benefit marketers, because real wages, or purchasing power, go up when inflation stays down. A significant increase in inflation almost always depresses real wages. In contrast, a slowdown in inflation tends to boost purchasing power and allows people to buy more goods and services.

A number of pricing strategies to cope with inflation are discussed in Chapter 19. But in general, marketers must be aware that inflation causes consumers to react in two ways:

- *Decrease their brand loyalty:* In a recent research session, a panelist noted, "I used to use just Betty Crocker mixes, but now I think of either Betty Crocker or Duncan Hines, depending on which is on sale." Another participant said, "Pennies count now, and so I look at the whole shelf, and I read the ingredients. I don't really understand, but I can tell if it's exactly the same. So now I use this cheaper brand, and honestly, it works just as well."
- *Stock up:* Many consumers take advantage of coupons and sales to stock up.

Inflation pressures consumers to make more economical purchases. However, most consumers try hard to maintain their standard of living.

In creating marketing strategies, managers must realize that, despite what happens to the seller's cost, the buyer is not going to pay more for a product than the subjective value he or she places on it. No matter how compelling the justification might be for a 10 percent price increase, the marketer must always examine its impact on demand. Many marketers try to hold prices level as long as practical during times of inflation to avoid losing customer brand loyalty. In setting prices, marketing managers should also use the expected cost at the time of shipment or build in price escalators as inflation increases.

Recession

recession
period of economic activity when income, production, and employment tend to fall

A **recession** is a period of economic activity when income, production, and employment tend to fall—all of which reduce demand. The problems of inflation and recession go hand in hand, yet they require different strategies. The following strategies can counter the effects of reduced demand:

- Improving existing products and introducing new ones that help manufacturers reduce production hours, waste, and material costs. Recessions increase demand for goods and services that produce economy and efficiency, offer value, help organizations streamline practices and procedures, and improve customer service.
- Maintaining and expanding such customer services as sales of replacement parts. In a recession, many organizations postpone the purchase of new equipment and materials.
- Holding the line on prices, continuing to emphasize top-of-the-line products, and promoting products' value, demonstrated quality, durability, satisfaction, and capacity to save time and money. High-priced value items consistently fare well during recessions.[34]

5 TECHNOLOGY AND RESOURCES

Sometimes new technology is an effective weapon against inflation and recession. New machines that reduce production costs can be one of a firm's most valuable assets. Unfortunately, the United States isn't developing new technology nearly as well as it should be at a time when innovation has become more important than ever.

Although the United States still generates more patents than any other nation, other countries, especially Japan, are catching up. Since 1983, Japan has gained against the United States in thirty-eight of forty-eight product categories, particularly office computers, electronics, transportation equipment, and shipbuilding. U.S. spending on research and development (R&D) has been averaging about 2 percent of gross domestic product, but the Japanese have dramatically increased their spending to 3 percent.[35] Moreover, growth in R&D spending by both the U.S. government and private industry slowed during the second half of the 1980s and then began to fall.[36]

Another telling statistic is how R&D money is spent. In the early 1990s, the United States spent 16 percent more on R&D than did Japan, Germany, France, and the United Kingdom combined. Yet these four countries together spent 12 percent more than the United States on R&D not related to defense.[37]

R&D expenditures are only a rough measure of where the United States stands in terms of innovation. A look at management of the R&D process can be even more revealing. U.S. managers tend to be obsessed with short-term (one to three years) profits and minimal risk taking. The result is an infatuation with slight variations of existing products (line extensions), which tend to be low in risk and are often very profitable, instead of true innovations. Honey Nut Cheerios and Diet Cherry Coke (both line extensions) are probably not the path to world economic leadership.

To regain its world leadership, the United States must instill a culture for innovation in business and alter its capital-gains tax. The tax on capital gains, which slashes the reward for successful innovation, is higher in the United States than in virtually any other developed country. A start-up company that doubled in value over the past decade would have provided its investors with a return, after inflation and the capital-gains tax, of just over 1 percent annually.[38] Under those rules, many managers ask, "Why bother?"

Companies must also learn how to innovate, and large R&D budgets aren't the sole answer. One of the biggest R&D spenders in the United States is General Motors, yet by most standards the company is not a leading innovator. On the other hand, Corning has "relatively low" R&D budgets but is arguably one of the five most innovative companies in the world.[39] The difference is in management and corporate culture.

Again, we might take a clue from the Japanese. In Japan, a single team of engineers, scientists, marketers, and manufacturers works simultaneously at three levels of innovation. At the lowest level, they seek small improvements in an existing product. At the second, they try for a significant jump, such as Sony's move from the microcassette tape recorder to the Walkman. The third is true innovation, an entirely new product. The idea is to produce three new products to replace each present product, with the same investment of time and money. One of the three may then become the new market leader and produce the innovator's profit.[40]

Companies must also learn to foster and encourage innovation. Rubbermaid teaches its people to let ideas flow out of its so-called core competencies, the things it does best. Bud Hellman, who used to run a Rubbermaid subsidiary, was touring one of the company's picnic-cooler plants in the late 1980s when he suddenly realized he could use its plastic blow-molding technique to make a durable, lightweight, inexpensive line of office furniture. The result was the Work Manager System, which accounts for 60 percent of sales at Rubbermaid's furniture division. Toro, a Minnesota maker of mowers and other lawn equipment, fosters innovation by letting all employees know they won't be penalized for taking a risk on new ideas that fail.

To spur new ideas, Bell Atlantic started what it calls its Champion program. Any employee with a good idea gets to leave his or her job for a while at full pay and benefits and receive training in such skills as writing a business plan and organizing a development schedule. The innovator also gets money to invest in the idea. The employee becomes the idea's champion, with a strong incentive to develop it successfully. The innovator can invest 10 percent of his or her salary in the project and give up bonuses in return for 5 percent of the revenues if the product gets to market. Since the company started the program in 1989, Champion has generated two patents, with eleven more pending.[41]

Many scientists believe the world will see more innovations between 1995 and 2005 than we have seen in the previous hundred years.[42] Exhibit 2.3 forecasts where the R&D action will be for the remainder of the 1990s.

Exhibit 2.3

Top Twenty Technologies for the Remainder of the 1990s

Source: Adapted from Daniel Burrus, "A Glimpse of the Future," *Managing Your Career*, Spring 1991, pp. 6, 10. Copyright by Daniel Burrus.

1. Genetic engineering The mapping, restructuring, and remodeling of the human and animal gene code will allow us to eliminate or enhance a specific trait. Agricultural applications will include crops that are insect-proof, drought-resistant, and nitrogen-fixing. Human applications will range from predicting inherited genetic diseases to applying gene therapy to correct genetic disorders.

2. Advanced biochemistry Using genetic engineering techniques, scientists will create new drugs, such as Interleukin-2, to fight such diseases as cancer in humans and animals.

3. Bioelectricity Damaged or dysfunctioning nerves, muscles, and glands will be stimulated through bioelectricity. For example, bioelectricity is currently being used in humans to stimulate the growth of severed bones, regulate defective hearts and lungs, speed the healing rate of wounds, and act as an alternative to addictive painkillers.

4. Advanced computers The development of faster, more powerful computers will be based on evolving chip technologies. A single Sarnoff chip contains 100 or more tiny lasers, creating the first functional optoelectric integrated circuit. By the late 1990s, these chips will be used in powerful new desktop computers.

5. Multisensory robotics A new generation of robots will be able to handle duties beyond repetitive functions. In a few years, we'll see the first useful service robots, such as smart shopping carts, mobile helpers used in factories, and personal robots.

6. Artificial intelligence The continued expansion of computers will enable them to perform functions normally attributed to human intelligence, such as learning, adaptation, recognition, and self-correction.

7. Parallel processing Multiple computers attack a problem simultaneously, thus speeding the process.

8. Digital electronics The digitizing of audio, video, and film will yield better organization. Soon, companies will begin digitizing all types of information on such a large scale that any tidbit can be retrieved almost instantaneously.

9. Lasers Improvements will include the expanded use of lasers in surgery (microwave scalpels will completely replace metal scalpels) and holography (3-D imagery will become common in advertising).

10. Fiber optics Optical fibers will improve communications in the majority of U.S. households and businesses. By the end of the decade, the majority of U.S. homes will have fiber-optic connections that can carry four signals at once: telephone, TV, radio, and computer data.

11. Optical data storage Optical memory systems will expand to read and store information in digital form. Examples include all optical disks, optical film, floptical disks, and bar code readers.

12. Microwaves Currently microwaves have two major applications: sending wireless digital information (satellite dishes) and heating objects (ovens). New applications in the 1990s will range from microwave clothes dryers to cancer treatments.

13. Advanced satellites As more countries send satellites into orbit, additional and improved uses for satellite technology will emerge.

14. Photovoltaics (PV) New uses will be found for PV cells, which convert sunlight into energy. In the next few years, solar hydrogen (an economical, pollution-free energy source) will be used increasingly for rural electrification and as an alternative for automobile and jet fuel.

15. Micromechanics Micromechanics is the design and construction of tiny mechanisms able to link up with microelectronic circuits, allowing the creation of smaller, faster electronic products. The first quantum transistor, recently developed, is 100 times smaller and 1,000 times faster than current transistors. Mass-produced, these transistors will revolutionize the electronics industry.

16. Molecular design A supercomputer creates new materials built molecule by molecule, atom by atom. The first products to move out of the lab are tailor-made enzymes for industrial use.

17. New polymers The adaptation of complex chemical structures makes them lighter, stronger, more resistant to heat, and able to conduct electricity. Applications range from garbage bags and army tanks to running shoes, ball bearings, and moldable batteries.

18. High-tech ceramics New versions of ceramic materials are resistant to corrosion, wear, and high temperatures. We'll soon see ceramic auto engine parts, which yield cleaner-running engines, and a ceramic-based automotive gas turbine engine.

19. Fiber-reinforced composites Lightweight, noncorrosive composite materials will continue to develop; they often are stronger than steel. Applications include home building materials, bridges, and aircraft.

20. Superconductors Superconductors are inexpensive materials that carry electricity without any loss of energy. Near-term uses range from less expensive but more advanced magnetic imaging machines for hospitals, superconducting TV antennas, and faster computer circuits. By the 21st century, scientists hope to complete development of superconducting cables that transmit electricity and magnetically levitated trains.

6 POLITICAL AND LEGAL FACTORS

Political and legal factors are other important uncontrollable variables in the marketing environment. Business needs government regulations to protect the interests of society, protect one business from another, and protect consumers. In turn, government needs business, because the marketplace generates taxes that support public efforts to educate our youth, protect our shores, and so on. The private sector also serves as a counterweight to government. Decentralization of the power inherent in a private enterprise system supplies the limitation on government essential for the survival of a democracy.

Every aspect of the marketing mix is subject to laws and restrictions. It is the duty of marketing managers or their legal assistants to understand these laws and conform to them. It is easy for a marketing manager or sometimes a lawyer to say no to a marketing innovation. For example, a lawyer could warn that a new package design may prompt a copyright infringement suit. However, the challenge is not simply to keep the marketing department out of trouble but to help it implement creative new programs to accomplish marketing objectives.

Federal Legislation

Federal laws that affect marketing fall into several categories. First, the Sherman Act, the Clayton Act, the Federal Trade Commission Act, the Celler-Kefauver Antimerger Act, and the Hart-Scott-Rodino Act were passed to regulate the competitive environment. Second, the Robinson-Patman Act was designed to regulate pricing practices. Third, the Wheeler-Lea Act was created to control false advertising. These key pieces of legislation are summarized in Exhibit 2.4.

In addition to the major pieces of legislation outlined in Exhibit 2.4, many laws have been passed to protect the purchaser, user, and innocent third parties. A sampling of these consumer protection laws is shown in Exhibit 2.5.

Exhibit 2.4

Primary U.S. Laws That Affect Marketing

Legislation	Impact on marketing
Sherman Act of 1890	Makes trusts and conspiracies in restraint of trade illegal; makes monopolies and attempts to monopolize a misdemeanor
Clayton Act of 1914	Outlaws discrimination in prices to different buyers; prohibits tying contracts (which require the buyer of one product to also buy another item in the line); makes illegal the combining of two or more competing corporations by pooling ownership of stock
Federal Trade Commission Act of 1914	Creates the Federal Trade Commission to deal with antitrust matters; outlaws unfair methods of competition
Robinson-Patman Act of 1936	Prohibits charging different prices to different buyers of like grade and quantity merchandise; requires sellers to make any supplementary services or allowances available to all purchasers on a proportionately equal basis
Wheeler-Lea Amendment to the FTC Act of 1938	Broadens the Federal Trade Commission's power to include the prohibition of practices that might injure the public without affecting competition; outlaws false and deceptive advertising
Lanham Act of 1946	Establishes protection for trademarks
Celler-Kefauver Antimerger Act of 1950	Strengthens the Clayton Act to prevent corporate acquisitions that reduce competition
Hart-Scott-Rodino Act of 1976	Requires large companies to notify the government of their intent to merge

State Laws

State legislation that affects marketing varies. Oregon, for example, limits utility advertising to 0.5 percent of the company's net income. California has forced industry to improve consumer products and has also enacted legislation to lower the energy consumption of refrigerators, freezers, and air conditioners. Several states, including New Mexico and Kansas, are considering levying a tax on all in-state commercial advertising.

Regulatory Agencies

Consumer Product Safety Commission (CPSC) Federal agency established to protect the health and safety of consumers in and around their homes.

Federal Trade Commission (FTC) Federal agency empowered to prevent persons or corporations from using unfair methods of competition in commerce.

Although state regulatory bodies are more actively pursuing violations of their marketing statutes, federal regulators generally have the greatest clout. The Consumer Product Safety Commission, the Federal Trade Commission, and the Food and Drug Administration are the three federal agencies most directly and actively involved in marketing affairs. These agencies, plus others, are discussed throughout the book, but a brief introduction is in order at this point.

The sole purpose of the **Consumer Product Safety Commission** (CPSC) is to protect the health and safety of consumers in and around their homes. The CPSC has the power to set mandatory safety standards for almost all products consumers use (about 15,000 items). The CPSC consists of a five-member committee with about 1,100 staff members, who include technicians, lawyers, and administrative help. The commission can fine offending firms up to $500,000 and sentence their officers to up to a year in prison. It can also ban dangerous products from the marketplace.

The **Federal Trade Commission** (FTC) also consists of five members, each holding office for seven years. The Federal Trade Commission is empowered to prevent persons or corporations from using unfair methods of competition in commerce. It is authorized to investigate the practices of business combinations and to conduct

Exhibit 2.5

Examples of U.S. Legislation Designed to Protect the Consumer

Legislative action	Impact on or change in consumer environment
Mail Fraud Act, 1872	Makes it a federal crime to defraud consumers through use of the mail
Pure Food & Drug Act, 1906	Regulates interstate commerce in misbranded and adulterated foods, drinks, and drugs
Federal Food, Drug & Cosmetic Act, 1938	Strengthens the Food and Drug Act of 1906 by including cosmetics; requires predistribution clearance on any new drugs
Flammable Fabrics Act, 1953	Prohibits interstate shipment of flammable apparel or material
Automobile InformationDisclosure Act, 1958	Requires auto manufacturers to post suggested retail prices on new cars
Food Additives Amendment, 1958	Prohibits new food additives until approved by the Food and Drug Administration
Fair Packaging and Labeling Act, 1965	Regulates packaging and labeling; establishes uniform sizes
Child Safety Act, 1966	Prevents the marketing of harmful toys and dangerous products
Cigarette Label Act, 1966	Requires labels that warn about smoking hazards
Consumer Credit Protection, 1968	Requires full disclosure of annual interest rates and other financial charges on loans and revolving charges
Fair Credit Report Act, 1970	Regulates credit information reporting and use; limits consumer liability for stolen credit cards to $50
Consumer Product Safety Act, 1972	Creates the Consumer Product Safety Commission
Fair Debt Collection Practice Act, 1978	Makes it illegal to harass or abuse any person and make false statements or use unfair methods when collecting a debt

Exhibit 2.6

Powers of the Federal Trade Commission

Remedy	Procedure
Cease-and-desist order	A final order is issued to cease an illegal practice—and is often challenged in the courts.
Consent decree	Business consents to stop the questionable practice without admitting illegality.
Affirmative disclosure	An advertiser is required to provide additional information about products in advertisements.
Corrective advertising	An advertiser is required to correct the past effects of misleading advertising (for example, 25% of media budget for FTC-approved advertisements or FTC-specified advertising).
Restitution	Refunds are required to consumers misled by deceptive advertising. According to a 1975 court of appeals decision, this remedy cannot be used except for practices carried out after the issuance of a cease-and-desist order (still on appeal).
Counteradvertising	The FTC proposed that the Federal Communications Commission permit advertisements in broadcast media to counteract advertising claims (also that free time be provided under certain conditions).

hearings on antitrust matters and deceptive advertising. The FTC is not an agency "without teeth"; it has a vast array of regulatory powers (see Exhibit 2.6).

Previously, the FTC proposed to ban all advertising to children under age 8, to ban all advertising of sugared products that are most likely to cause tooth decay to children under age 12, and to require dental health and nutritional advertisements to be paid for by industry. Business reacted by lobbying to reduce the FTC's power. The two-year lobbying effort resulted in passage of the FTC Improvement Act of 1980. The major provisions of the act are as follows:

- It bans the use of unfairness as a standard for industrywide rules against advertising. All the proposals concerning children's advertising were therefore suspended, because they were based almost entirely on the unfairness standard.
- It requires oversight hearings on the FTC every six months. This congressional review is designed to keep the commission accountable. Moreover, it keeps Congress aware of one of the many regulatory agencies it has created and is responsible for monitoring.

Food and Drug Administration (FDA) Federal agency charged with enforcing regulations against selling and distributing adulterated, misbranded, or hazardous food and drug products.

The **Food and Drug Administration** (FDA), another powerful agency, is charged with enforcing regulations against selling and distributing adulterated, misbranded, or hazardous food and drug products. After decades of focusing on medications, the agency turned its attention to consumer goods companies in the 1990s. Consider, for example, Procter & Gamble's recent run-ins with the FDA:

- *Ultra Protection Crest:* Halted its national launch after the FDA said a new toothpaste with an antibacterial agent required new-drug approval
- *Crisco Corn Oil:* Dropped "no cholesterol" labels from all its food products after the FDA told vegetable oil marketers to stop using this claim
- *Metamucil:* Doing clinical research to support cholesterol-reduction claims for this fiber laxative after the FDA asked for more data

In 1992 the Food and Drug Administration imposed a moratorium on silicone-gel breast implants, which had been found to leak and cause discomfort, infection, and perhaps immune disorders. The few small companies that remained interested in the market now face stricter regulation.

Bruce Strong/Time Magazine

- *Didronel:* Awaiting FDA approval to market this prescription drug as an osteoporosis treatment, although an advisory panel has questioned some of the data
- *Olestra:* Still hasn't won FDA's go-ahead years after its 1988 petition to sell this fat substitute[43]

FDA Commissioner David Kessler claims, "The FDA should protect consumers from economic fraud by judicious enforcement of the law."[44] He has ordered the FDA to move beyond its traditional role. According to the 1990 Nutrition Labeling and Education Act, the FDA must set new food-labeling guidelines. But new labels weren't required to be on store shelves until May 1993. The guidelines are meant to regulate health claims and standardize serving sizes for some 17,000 foods. In conjunction with the FDA's new rules, the U.S. Department of Agriculture is developing guidelines for meat and poultry products.

The Impact on Marketing Management

Businesses rarely band together to create change in the legal environment as they did to pass the FTC Improvement Act. Generally, marketing managers only react to legislation, regulation, and edicts.

Although most of this discussion has focused on regulation of product, price, and promotion, note that distribution is also heavily regulated. For instance, tying contracts, which require a customer to buy something he or she does not want in order to get a full line of a firm's products, are illegal. If a manufacturer requires a dealer to carry a full line of its products, it may be in violation of the Clayton and Sherman acts. Also, if a franchise agreement allows the franchise holder to sell only to customers within an assigned sales territory, the agreement is illegal. Nor can a franchise agreement prohibit a franchise holder from carrying a competitor's products.

The rest of the book refers to the laws and federal agencies covered in this section, as well as others that affect marketing decisions. Failure to comply with regulations can have major consequences for a firm. Sometimes just sensing trends and taking corrective action before a government agency acts can help avoid regulation. For example, if marketers had toned down their hard-hitting advertisements to children, they might have avoided an FTC inquiry.

Type of competition	Number of firms	Type of product	Ease of market entry	Price control	Importance of promotion	Key marketing task
Monopoly	One	Unique (no substitute)	Blocked	Complete	Little or none	Maintain blocked entry through public relations, huge advertising expenditures, or other means
Pure competition	Numerous	Homogeneous	No barriers	None	None	Attempt to lower product and distribution costs
Oligopoly	Few	Similar	Major barriers	Some, with care	Important	Understand competition and react quickly; strive for nonprice advantage
Monopolistic competition	Numerous	Similar	Few	Some	Very important	Maintain differentiated product

Exhibit 2.7

Types of Competition

7 COMPETITION

The competitive environment refers to the number of competitors a firm must face, the relative size of the competitors, and the degree of interdependence within the industry. Management has little control over the competitive environment confronting a firm. Yet the marketing mix, particularly pricing, depends on the type and amount of competition.

The Economics of Competition

Economists recognize four basic models of competition. These models are mainly based on the number of competitors and the nature of the products produced. Exhibit 2.7 summarizes the characteristics of the four basic models of competition and the key task of the marketing manager within each competitive situation. Chapter 19 explains how prices are actually set in each competitive environment.

Monopoly

monopoly
Form of economic competition in which one firm controls the output and price of a product for which there are no close substitutes.

At one extreme of economic competition is the **monopoly**. One firm controls the output and price of a product for which there are no close substitutes. In other words, the firm is the industry; there are no direct competitors. Utility companies are the most common form of monopoly in the United States.

A patent can give a company monopoly power for a time. Xerox, for example, held the patent on the dry-paper copying process. Not until the patent expired and competitors entered the marketplace did dry-paper copiers fall significantly in price.

Pure Competition

purely competitive market
Form of economic competition characterized by a large number of sellers marketing a standardized product to a group of buyers who are well informed about the marketplace.

At the other extreme of the competitive spectrum is pure competition. A purely competitive market doesn't exist in the real world. However, some industries closely mirror the model. A **purely competitive market** is characterized by a large number of sellers marketing a standardized product to a group of buyers who are well informed about the marketplace. New competitors can easily enter the marketplace and sell their entire output at the prevailing market price. The markets most closely

In monopolistic competition, a large number of firms offer similar products. Thus no firm can raise prices much higher than the prices charged by competitors. (*top*) A service-industry example is the quick-copy and printing shop; *(bottom)* the hardware store is an example in the consumer goods market.

(bottom) © 1986 Gabe Palmer/The Stock Market

resembling pure competition are agricultural—for example, wheat, cotton, soybeans, and corn.

In a purely competitive market, it would not make sense for one firm to raise the price. A buyer would simply go elsewhere and get the same merchandise at the prevailing market price. Similarly, there would be no reason to advertise, because the pure competitor can sell its entire output at the prevailing market price without advertising.

Oligopoly

oligopoly
Form of economic competition in which a small number of firms dominate the market for a good or service.

When a relatively small number of firms dominate the market for a good or service, the industry is an **oligopoly.** Automobile, aircraft, supercomputer, and tire and rubber producers all compete in oligopolistic markets. Oligopolies can also exist at a lower competitive level. If a town in the Arizona desert had only four or five service stations, they would be competing as an oligopoly.

Because there are few competitors, the actions of one firm have a direct impact on the others. This interdependence characterizes an oligopoly. The close relationship among firms often leads to collusion and price-fixing, which are illegal under federal and state laws. Rather than fix prices, some industries simply follow a price leader. The leader is typically the dominant firm in terms of assets, market share, or geographic coverage.

Marketing managers do not have a lot of pricing flexibility in an oligopoly. They must be alert to price changes and quickly match price decreases or lose a significant amount of market share. To further secure a position in the marketplace, marketing managers should stress service, product quality, and other nonprice forms of competition.

Monopolistic Competition

monopolistic competition
Form of economic competition in which a relatively large number of suppliers offer similar but not identical products.

The term **monopolistic competition** refers a relatively large number of suppliers offering similar but not identical products. Examples include laundries, hair stylists, aspirin or gasoline producers, lawyers, and airlines in major markets. Each firm has a comparatively small percentage of the total market, so each has limited control over market price. Firms attempt to distinguish their offerings through brand names, trademarks, packaging, advertisements, and services.

With monopolistic competition, consumers prefer the products of specific firms and, *within limits,* will pay a higher price. In other words, "I like Prell shampoo because it's a little different. But if the price goes up too much, I know Prell is not that different, so I'll switch to something else." Thus the seller has some control over price, but only within a limited range. If the marketing manager raises prices too high, the company could lose its entire market.

Competing for Market Share

As population growth slows, costs rise, and available resources tighten, firms find they must work harder to maintain their profits and market share regardless of the form of the competitive market. Take, for example, the seemingly staid breakfast cereal market. An avalanche of cereal promotions descended on consumers as Kellogg and General Mills went head-to-head for a bigger share of the $7.5 billion breakfast cereal market.

Not only do the two companies price competitively, they also bash each other's products. Boxes of Total Corn Flakes from General Mills proclaim the product "more nutritious and better-tasting than Kellogg's Corn Flakes." Kellogg counters with streamers on packages of Just Right saying its "taste beats Total." (Kellogg says it has research proving that claim but declines to disclose it.)

In 1991, Kellogg spent $100 million more on promotion than it did the previous year. As a result, sales increased 11 percent.[45] The explanation for their marketing aggressiveness is simple: A single share point, or 1 percent of total sales, means $75 million in revenue. Brands can thrive on less than that. And where profit margins run 20 percent and more, small increases in sales mean large profit gains.

Smaller firms can often survive in highly competitive markets by generating products of exceptional quality or by offering goods and services that fulfill unique needs. For example, Steiger Tractor Company has become a viable competitor in an old and stable market. The company produces a big articulated tractor, which bends in the middle to make turning easier. Using all four wheels for traction enables it to pull bigger loads. An articulated tractor can cut a farmer's labor costs by as much as 33 percent per acre.

The Steiger tractor example illustrates that, with a good marketing mix, it is still possible for small firms to compete effectively against the giants. Regardless of company size, the marketing mix—product, distribution, promotion, and price—represents management's tools of competition. Steiger developed a unique product in order to compete. Lexus, AT&T, and IBM have used product quality to gain and hold market share. Coca-Cola, Frito Lay, and 7-Eleven stores use distribution to gain competitive advantage. Firms like Wal-Mart, Toys R Us, and Thrifty Car Rental use price as a primary means of competition. Some companies, like Kraft General Foods and Procter & Gamble, are superior competitors in every aspect of their marketing mix. They have an excellent research staff that enables them to bring out the right products, an efficient distribution system involving thousands of stores and institutions, aggressive pricing, and a very large promotion budget. For example, Kraft General Foods spends over $100 million a year advertising Maxwell House coffee, and Procter & Gamble does the same for Folgers.

Global Competition

Both Kraft General Foods and Procter & Gamble are savvy international competitors as well. They each conduct business in over a hundred different nations. Many foreign competitors also consider the United States to be a ripe target market. Thus a U.S. marketing manager can no longer worry about only domestic competitors. In automobiles, textiles, watches, television, steel, and many other areas, foreign competition has been strong. Global competition is discussed in much more detail in Chapter 3.

In the past, foreign firms penetrated U.S. markets by concentrating on price, but today the emphasis has switched to product quality. Nestlé, Sony, Rolls Royce, and Sandoz Pharmaceuticals are noted for quality, not cheap prices.

With the expansion of international marketing, U.S. companies often battle each other in global markets just as intensively as in the domestic market. Consider Hasbro and Mattel toy companies, which have been competing in the United States for years. Hasbro acquired Sindy, a pudgy bike-riding teenager of a doll, from a British maker in 1986. Now Sindy has been transformed into a flashy, champagne-sipping, long-haired blonde. Although Sindy is not sold in the United States, Mattel claims she is now just a pirated version of its Barbie doll. Mattel has won a number of European court orders preventing Hasbro from selling Sindy in Holland, Belgium, France, and Germany. Lawsuits are pending in five other jurisdictions, and proceedings began in the United Kingdom, Sindy's homeland, in 1993. Sindy has warded off Barbie's challenge in Greece and Spain and has an impressive following in Europe and Australia. In May 1992, a British television special even celebrated her birthday.[46]

MARKETING AND SMALL BUSINESS

The Environment Is the Key

Understanding the environment within which a small business operates is critical to its success. Large companies can often miss changes in the environment but have the financial strength to recover and adjust over time. Ford, for example, has adjusted to strong competition from the Japanese, changing attitudes toward large cars, extensive government regulations, and the like. From the outset, small businesses must understand and react to the environment with the proper strategy. They typically don't get a second chance.

Many managers of business (large as well as small) simply fail to see how changes outside their own organization will affect business success. Other times, much effort is wasted in "reacting" to things that are irrelevant to the organization's goals or in making futile attempts to change things beyond their control. An effective small business tries to be as compatible as possible with the environment. It recognizes which uncontrollable factors can affect the firm and develops a strategy accordingly.

LOOKING BACK

Looking back at the Taco Bell story that began the chapter, you should now understand that the external environment affects all firms and their marketing mixes. Changing tastes and attitudes (social factors) and competition are only some of the uncontrollable factors that could affect Taco Bell.

For example, Taco Bell has recently had legal disputes with some of its franchisees, which will be resolved within the framework of U.S. laws. New technology has enabled the firm to centralize much of its food preparation, which in turn has dramatically lowered food costs. Taco Bell pioneered value pricing, which proved very successful during the recession of the early 1990s. Taco Bell's target consumers are relatively young males and females. As the population continues to age, Taco Bell must decide how to react. Any organization that ignores changes in the external environment is doomed to failure in the long run.

KEY TERMS

baby boomers 36
Consumer Product Safety Commission (CPSC) 49
demography 39
discretionary income 44
environmental management 34
environmental scanning 32
Federal Trade Commission (FTC) 49
Food and Drug Administration (FDA) 50
inflation 44
market segmentation 39
monopolistic competition 53
monopoly 52
oligopoly 53
poverty of time 36
Protestant work ethic 34
purely competitive market 52
recession 45
target market 32

SUMMARY

1 **Discuss the external environment of marketing, and explain how it affects a firm.** The external marketing environment consists of social, demographic, economic, technological, political/legal, and competitive variables. Marketers generally cannot control the elements of the external environment. Instead, they must understand how the external environment is changing and the impact of change on the target market. Then marketing managers can create a marketing mix to effectively meet the needs of target customers.

2 **Describe the social factors that affect marketing.** Within the external environment, social factors are perhaps the most difficult for marketers to anticipate. Several major social trends are currently shaping marketing strategies. First, people of all ages have a broader range of interests, defying traditional consumer profiles. Second, changing gender roles are bringing more women into the work force and increasing the number of men who shop. Third, a greater number of dual-career families has led to a poverty of time, creating a great demand for time-saving goods and services.

3 **Explain the importance of current demographic trends to marketing managers.** Today, several basic demographic patterns are influencing marketing mixes. Because the U.S. population is growing at a slower rate, marketers can no longer rely on profits from generally expanding markets. Since the population is also growing older, marketers are offering more products that appeal to middle-aged and elderly markets. Finally, marketers are targeting the rapidly expanding singles market.

4 **Identify consumer and marketer reactions to the state of the economy.** Marketers are currently targeting the increasing number of consumers with higher discretionary income by offering quality, higher-priced goods and services. During a time of inflation, marketers generally attempt to maintain level pricing in order to avoid losing customer brand loyalty. During times of recession, many marketers maintain or reduce prices to counter the effects of decreased demand; they also concentrate on increasing production efficiency and improving customer service.

5 **Identify the impact of technology on a firm.** Monitoring new technology is essential to keeping up with competitors in today's marketing environment. For example, in the technologically more advanced United States, many companies are losing business to Japanese competitors. Japanese businesses are prospering by concentrating their efforts on developing marketable applications for the latest technological innovations. In the United States, many R&D expenditures go into developing line extensions. U.S. companies must learn to foster and encourage innovation. Without innovation, U.S. companies can't compete in global markets.

6 **Understand the political and legal environment of marketing.** All marketing activities are subject to state and federal laws and the rulings of regulatory agencies. Marketers are responsible for remaining aware of and abiding by such regulations. Some key federal laws that impact marketing are the Sherman Act, Clayton Act, Federal Trade Commission Act, Robinson-Patman Act, Wheeler-Lea Amendment to the FTC Act, Lanham Act, Celler-Kefauver Antimerger Act, and Hart-Scott-Rodino Act. The Consumer Product Safety Commission, the Federal Trade Commission, and the Food and Drug Administration are the three federal agencies most involved in regulating marketing activities.

7 **Understand the basics of foreign and domestic competition.** The four economic models of competition are monopoly, pure competition, oligopoly, and

monopolistic competition. Declining population growth, rising costs, and resource shortages have heightened domestic competition. Yet with an effective marketing mix, small firms continue to be able to compete with the giants. Meanwhile, dwindling international barriers are bringing in more foreign competitors and offering expanding opportunities for U.S. companies abroad.

Review Questions

1. What is the purpose of environmental scanning?
2. How will marketers respond to an increasingly older U.S. population during this decade?
3. Describe typical marketing strategies during a period of economic recession.
4. How will marketers respond to the affluence of America's dual-income families?
5. Why are many U.S. companies losing business to Japanese competitors?
6. What are the major federal agencies and laws that regulate marketing activities?
7. Describe the four basic models of competition.
8. What is environmental management? Cite an example from the chapter.

Discussion and Writing Questions

1. Why is adaptability a crucial aspect of marketing management? Think of an example of marketing adaptability that you have observed in a business or industry.
2. You have been asked to address a local business group on the subject of component lifestyles and the challanges they represent to marketers. Prepare an outline for your talk.
3. Explain the concept of poverty of time and how it shapes marketing strategies. Name some products not discussed in the chapter that were developed in response to poverty of time.
4. You want your firm to start using new technology to improve its production of computer components. As marketing manager of the firm, prepare a report for your boss specifying the potential economic and ecological benefits of the new technology.
5. Which tools of the marketing mix do you think are the focus of (a) McDonald's, (b) mail-order catalog businesses, (c) General Motors, (d) oil companies, and (e) the airline industry? Which environmental factors do you feel have most greatly influenced them?
6. The International Perspectives article in this chapter discussed the world's toughest customers. Evaluate the impact of environmental factors on the preferences of customers in each country mentioned in the article.

CASES

2.1 Merck-DuPont Joint Venture

The drug industry has undergone many changes in the past few years. As companies merged, the number of competitors got smaller and the size of each competitor became larger. Edgar S. Woolard, Jr., DuPont's chairman and CEO, said, "The rules are changing very fast. Because of all the recent consolidations taking place, the risk of going it alone is much, much higher than five years ago."

To maintain high profitability, pharmaceutical companies have been forced to develop breakthrough medicines that bring premium prices. The cost of developing these new drugs is astronomical. It became imperative that companies team up to reduce the increasing financial risks associated with R&D.

Merck & Company, an industry leader, needed to expand its product line faster than its R&D operation would allow. Company growth had leveled off because of the need for funds to increase R&D. Through a joint venture with DuPont, Merck gained access to DuPont's R&D team and its experimental drugs. Dr. Roy Vagelos, Merck's chairman and CEO, felt that expanded product lines would be necessary in dealing with hospitals and insurance companies in the future. If the firm has a broad product line, deeper discounts can be offered to hospitals and insurance plans that team up for larger purchases. The joint venture brought DuPont some needed capital and access to international distribution.

Dr. David W. Martin, Jr., was selected to head the

new company. Martin said that the joint venture interested him with the "breadth of technology and the long-term commitment of the venture partners." The new company, Merck-DuPont Pharmaceuticals Company, is willing to take aggressive action to maintain its growth in the drug industry.

Questions

1. Do you think the government should be concerned with the decreasing number of pharmaceutical companies? Why or why not?
2. What competitive structure would you say the pharmaceutical industry best represents? Why do you think the pharmaceutical industry represents this competitive structure?
3. Discuss the changes that would be necessary for this structure to change to another specific structure. How would this change affect consumers?
4. How do you think a merger of this sort affected prices? Why?

Suggested Readings

"Spuring Joint Venture Formation," *Mergers & Acquisitions,* July–Augst 1991, pp. 1–10.

Michael Waldholz, "Merck-DuPont Venture Certain to Stir Drug Industry," *The Wall Street Journal,* 26 July 1990, pp. B1, B3.

2.2 Maytag

Video title: *Marketing Opportunities in Europe: 1992 and Beyond*

Maytag Corporation
One Dependability Square
Newton, IA 50208

SIC codes: 3633 Laundry equipment
3631 Cooking equipment
3635 Vacuum cleaners
3632 Refrigerators/freezers
3639 Other household appliances

Number of employees: 26,000

1993 revenues: Over $3 billion

Major brands: Maytag, Jenn-Air, Hoover

Largest competitors: General Electric, Whirlpool

Background

F. L. Maytag and three partners began in 1893 by producing and marketing farm implements. The four partners soon began looking for other products to supplement the highly seasonal farm products business. In 1907, the company introduced the Pastime washing machine. This innovation included a wooden tub and a hand crank that simulated washing clothes by hand but with less effort.

By 1909, Maytag was the sole owner of the company. During the 1920s, the company pursued national expansion and quickly moved from the thirty-eighth-largest producer of washing machines to the number-one position. By 1927, the company had produced its millionth washer. The company continued to improve its washing machine designs and to effectively adapt to changes in the market.

During World War II, the company switched its production to supporting the war effort. Maytag produced a variety of parts for military equipment and was honored by the U.S. government for its participation. The company received the National Security award. Once the war ended, the company quickly resumed production of consumer appliances.

Industry

Sales of appliances depend heavily on the economy, disposable income, interest rates, new housing starts, and consumers' ability to defer purchases. For the most part, appliance sales rely on the demand for replacements, making this a highly competitive market. Most consumers buy appliances by incurring some sort of debt (taking a loan or charging to a credit card). For this reason, interest rates affect appliance sales. Consumers typically buy major appliances once or twice every ten to fifteen years. This purchase cycle is increasing as the average life expectancy of appliances increases.

In the European market, the leading manufacturer is typically a strong national company. Each local market has traditionally favored companies that manufacture appliances with unique features for that local market. Thus the larger appliance manufacturers have generally had problems marketing their products in Europe.

Maytag Corporation

Traditionally, Maytag has been a high-end competitor, offering quality appliances at the top of the market. Although Maytag has been successful in the U.S. market, it has always had trouble marketing its products overseas. During the 1980s, the company acquired Chicago Pacific Corporation, owner of the Hoover Company, to compete more effectively in Europe. This acquisition gave Maytag increased exposure in overseas markets, because Hoover was well established in Europe. But Maytag has failed to capitalize on Hoover's European success. Industry experts believe that, to successfully penetrate the unified European market, companies need to focus on cost cutting and economies of scale. This strategy is contrary to Maytag's past marketing efforts, which have featured localized styling differences at the expense of standardization. For Maytag to successfully compete in a unified European market, it will need to develop a proper balance of local and standardized features.

Questions

1. What affect do you think a unified European market is likely to have on appliance manufacturers? Why?
2. To compete in the European market, what elements of the marketing mix do you think Maytag should concentrate on? Explain your answer.
3. What elements of the external environment (see Exhibit 2.1) do you think will have the greatest impact on appliance manufacturers like Maytag in competing in Europe? What advice would you give Maytag concerning these factors?

References

Harlan S. Byrne, "Maytag Corp.," *Barron's*, 25 May 1992, p. 35.

Kevin Kelly, "Can Maytag's Repairman Get Out of This Fix?" *Business Week*, 26 October 1992, p. 54.

Million Dollar Directory 1993 (Parsippany, NJ: Dun & Bradstreet Information Services, 1993).

Standard & Poor's Industry Surveys (New York: Standard & Poor's Corporation, October 1993).

CHAPTER 3

Developing a Global Vision

LEARNING OBJECTIVES
After studying this chapter, you should be able to

1. Discuss the importance of global marketing.
2. Discuss the impact of multinationals on the world economy.
3. Explain the differences between the traditional marketing concept and the global marketing concept.
4. Describe the external environment facing global marketers.
5. Identify the various ways of entering the global marketplace.
6. List the basic elements involved in the development of a global marketing mix.

For Gillette, the leading razor maker in most parts of the world, Japan has always been a sore spot. "It's the one significant market in the world where we're not the market leader," says Bruce Cleverly, Gillette's vice president of marketing for razors and blades. The company, which averages a 65 percent market share in 70 percent of its markets, hobbles along with a 10 percent share of the razor and blade market in Japan.

What has barred the giant Gillette from growing in Japan isn't a closed market, unfair Japanese customs, or anything else Japan is often accused of. It is rival U.S. company Warner-Lambert, owner of the Schick brand name. Although the company trails Gillette in the United States, Warner-Lambert has gained 62 percent of Japan's "wet-shaving" razor and blade market by using the Japanese style of marketing.

Now the battle is heating up as both sides promote new products worldwide. Armed with its popular Sensor brand, Gillette is launching a new strategy. While Schick stresses its Japanese way of marketing, Gillette is emphasizing its "Americanness." It is airing the same ads it runs in the United States and selling Sensor in the same packages, with the brand name in bold English letters and a Japanese version of it only in tiny letters in a corner. The company vows to double market share in Japan by 1995. Previously, Gillette had TV ads made just for the Japanese market, although it did not use foreign models and sports personalities. . . .

The Sensor, which cost $200 million and took ten years to develop, mounts twin blades on tiny springs, allowing them to adjust more closely to the curve of the face. So popular is the product in the United States and Europe that the company sold 26 million of the razors in 1990, the year the Sensor was launched. . . .

Stressing the all-American image of the Sensor is key in promoting a sophisticated image in Japan, Gillette officials say. So after launching the 1,000-yen [about $8] product in Japan, it doubled its advertising spending. Images of a Western man playing sports and kissing a woman are mingled with a detailed description of the product in one TV ad. The only difference from the U.S. ad is that the narrator says "The best a man can get" in Japanese.

The popular campaign helped Gillette raise its share of razor sales in Japan to 25 percent in the first six months of the Sensor campaign, says Norman Roberts, president of Gillette's Japanese unit. "We found the foreign talent version was much more popular" than ads using Japanese models, he says.

Schick thinks otherwise. "Schick hasn't used a foreigner" in ads in the past six years, says Yoshiaki Igarashi, group product manager of Warner-Lambert's Japanese unit. . . . The Tracer TV ads show a young Japanese actor shaving before taking his dog to the beach.

Why are international markets becoming increasingly important to American companies? Is globalization the wave of the future in international marketing? When should there be significant differences between domestic and global marketing mixes? These are some of the issues addressed in Chapter 3.

Source: Adapted from Yumiko Ono, "Gillette Tries to Nick Schick in Japan," *The Wall Street Journal*, 4 February 1991, pp. B1, B4.

1 THE REWARDS OF GLOBAL MARKETING

global marketing Individuals and organizations using a global vision to effectively market goods and services across national boundaries.

global vision Ability to recognize and react to international marketing opportunities, awareness of threats from foreign competitors in all markets, and effective use of international distribution networks.

Today, global revolutions are underway in many areas of our lives: management, politics, communications, and technology. The word *global* has assumed a new meaning, referring to a boundless mobility and competition in social, business, and intellectual arenas. No longer just an option, **global marketing** (marketing to target markets throughout the world) has become an imperative for business.

U.S. managers must develop a global vision not only to recognize and react to international marketing opportunities but also to remain competitive at home. Often a U.S. firm's toughest domestic competition comes from foreign companies. Moreover, a global vision enables a manager to understand that customer and distribution networks operate worldwide, blurring geographic and political barriers and making them increasingly irrelevant to business decisions.[1] In summary, having **global vision** means recognizing and reacting to international marketing opportunities, being aware of threats from foreign competitors in all markets, and effectively using international distribution networks.

Over the past two decades, world trade has climbed from $200 billion a year to $4 trillion. Countries and companies that were never considered major players in global marketing are now important, some of them showing great skill.

Today, marketers face many challenges to their customary practices. Product development costs are rising, the life of products is getting shorter, and new technology is spreading around the world faster than ever. But marketing winners relish the pace of change instead of fearing it.

An excellent example of a company with a global vision is Whirlpool Corporation, headquartered in Benton Harbor, Michigan. Whirlpool recently purchased the remaining interest in a joint venture it had formed with the Major Appliance Division of Philips, which is headquartered in Eindhoven, Holland. The administrative offices of Whirlpool Europe are in Comerio, Italy. On the 12-person management committee sit managers from Sweden, Holland, Italy, the United States, India, South Africa, and Belgium. Managers from different cultures help companies refine their global vision.

Global vision is equally apparent at the top of the world's leading companies. For instance, IBM prides itself on having five different nationalities represented among its highest officers and three among its outside directors. Four nationalities are represented on Unilever's board; three on the board of Shell Oil. Sony America named as its president and chief operating officer Ron Sommer, who was born in Israel, was raised in Austria, and carries a German passport.

Adopting a global vision can be very lucrative for a company. Gillette, for example, gets about two-thirds of its revenue from its international division. About 70 percent of General Motors' profits come from operations outside the United States.[2] Similarly, Colgate-Palmolive's success in international markets has often helped offset its weakness in its domestic market.[3] The corporate strategies and major brands of R.J. Reynolds are also global. Lester Pullen, the CEO of R.J. Reynolds, notes, "In perhaps ten years it may be virtually impossible to rise to the top in any major American business without international experience."[4]

Global marketing is not a one-way street, whereby U.S. companies sell their wares and services throughout the world. Foreign competition in the domestic market used to be relatively rare but now is found in almost every industry. In fact, in many industries the United States has lost market share to imported products. The percentage of U.S. computers made in the United States has fallen from 94 percent to

One example of a U.S. company with a global vision is appliance maker Whirlpool. Shown here is administrative headquarters of Whirlpool International (a U.S.-Dutch joint venture) in Comerio, Italy.
Courtesy of Whirlpool Corporation

just over 60 percent in the last ten years. During the same period, the percentage of machine tools imported from other countries grew from 23 percent to 46 percent.[5] In electronics, cameras, automobiles, fine china, tractors, leather goods, and a host of other consumer and industrial products, American companies must struggle at home to maintain their market shares against foreign competitors.

The Importance of Global Marketing to the United States

Many countries depend more on international commerce than the United States does. For example, France, Great Britain, and Germany all derive more than 18 percent of their gross domestic product from world trade, compared to about 7 percent in the United States.[6] Nevertheless, the impact of international business on the U.S. economy is still impressive. The United States exports about a fifth of its industrial production and a third of its farm products.[7] One of every sixteen jobs in the United States is directly or indirectly supported by exports. U.S. businesses export over $300 billion in goods to foreign countries every year, and almost a third of U.S. corporate profits is derived from our international trade and foreign investment. The United States is the world's leading exporter of grain, selling more than $12 billion of this product a year to foreign countries, or about one-third of all agricultural exports.[8] Chemicals, office machinery and computers, automobiles, aircraft, and electrical machinery make up almost half of all nonagricultural exports.[9]

These statistics might imply that practically every business in the United States is selling its wares throughout the world, but nothing could be further from the truth. About 85 percent of all U.S. exports of manufactured goods are made by 250 companies; less than 10 percent of all manufacturing businesses, or around 25,000 companies, export their goods on a regular basis. Most small- and medium-sized firms are essentially nonparticipants in global trade and marketing. Only the very large multinational companies have seriously attempted to compete worldwide. Fortunately, more of these smaller companies now are aggressively pursuing international markets.

With the proper manufacturing processes and superior products, U.S. companies can be successful against foreign competition. One tool-making company,

Giddings and Lewis, watched as foreign competition intensified in the United States, eventually capturing nearly half of the market. To remain competitive, the company switched to a more flexible manufacturing system. It then saw its sales increase by 38 percent.[10] Another company, Fusion Systems, makes industrial equipment used to produce a variety of goods, including optical fibers, automobile parts, and semiconductor chips. The company prospered in the Japanese market, largely because it produces superior products. The Japanese, one of Fusion's managers acknowledges, are the world's most demanding consumers. But if provided with the best product, they will buy it. Donald Spero, president of Fusion, adds, "Our business is market-driven. If we are unable to sell to the leading customers, then we're not really in business."[11]

Helping the Balance of Trade Problem

The more U.S. firms export their wares, the better our balance of trade. The difference between the value of a country's exports and the value of its imports during a certain time is its **balance of trade**. A country that exports more goods than it imports is said to have a favorable balance of trade; a country that imports more than it exports is said to have an unfavorable balance of trade. When imports exceed exports, more money flows out of the country than into it.

balance of trade Difference between the value of a country's exports and the value of its imports during a certain time.

Although U.S. exports have been booming, we still import more than we export. We have had an unfavorable balance of trade throughout the past decade. In 1992 the United States had a **trade deficit** (the difference between exports and imports) of over $100 billion. As long as we continue to buy more goods from abroad than we sell abroad, we will have an unfavorable balance of trade.

trade deficit Excess of imports over exports.

The difference between a country's total payments to other countries and its total receipts from other countries is its **balance of payments**. This figure includes the balance of trade and then some. It includes imports and exports (balance of trade), long-term investments in overseas plants and equipment, government loans to and from other countries, gifts and foreign aid, military expenditures made in other countries, and money deposits in and withdrawals from foreign banks.

balance of payments Difference between a country's total payments to other countries and its total receipts from other countries.

From the beginning of this century until 1970, the United States had a favorable balance of trade. But in the other areas that make up the balance of payments, U.S. payments have long exceeded receipts, mainly because of the large U.S. military presence abroad. Hence, in almost every year since 1950, the United States has had an unfavorable balance of payments. And since 1970, both the balance of payments and the balance of trade have been unfavorable.

❷ THE MULTINATIONAL FIRM

The United States has a number of large companies that are global marketers. Many of them have been very successful. A company that is heavily engaged in international trade is called a **multinational corporation** (MNC). Multinational corporations move resources, goods, services, and skills across national boundaries without regard to the country in which the headquarters is located. The leading multinational firms in the world are listed in Exhibit 3.1.

multinational corporation (MNC) Company that moves resources, goods, services, and skills across national boundaries without regard to the country in which the headquarters is located.

A multinational corporation is more than a business entity, as the following paragraph explains:

> The multinational corporation is, among other things, a private "government," often richer in assets and more populous in stockholders and employees than are some of the nation-states in which it carries on business. It is simultaneously a "citizen" of several

Exhibit 3.1

The World's Largest Multinational Firms, by Industry

Source: Adapted from "The Global 500," *Fortune*, 27 July 1992, p. 178. © 1992 Time Inc. All rights reserved

Industry	Company	Country
Aerospace	Boeing	U.S.
Apparel	Levi Strauss Associates	U.S.
Beverages	PepsiCo	U.S.
Building materials	Saint-Gobain	France
Chemicals	E.I. du Pont de Nemours	U.S.
Computers, office equipment	IBM	U.S.
Electronics, electrical equipment	General Electric	U.S.
Food	Philip Morris	U.S.
Forest products	International Paper	U.S.
Furniture	Johnson Controls	U.S.
Industrial and farm equipment	ABB Asea Brown Boveri	Switzerland
Jewelry, watches	Seiko	Japan
Metal products	Pechiney	France
Metals	IRI	Italy
Mining, crude-oil production	Ruhrkohle	Germany
Motor vehicles and parts	General Motors	U.S.
Petroleum refining	Royal Dutch/Shell Group	Brit./Neth.
Pharmaceuticals	Johnson & Johnson	U.S.
Publishing, printing	Bertelsmann	Germany
Rubber and plastic products	Bridgestone	Japan
Scientific and photo equipment	Eastman Kodak	U.S.
Soaps, cosmetics	Procter & Gamble	U.S.
Textiles	Toray Industries	Japan
Tobacco	RJR Nabisco Holdings	U.S.
Toys, sporting goods	Yamaha	Japan
Transportation equipment	Hyundai Heavy Industries	South Korea

> nation-states, owing obedience to their laws and paying them taxes, yet having its own objectives and being responsive to a management located in a foreign nation. Small wonder that some critics see in it an irresponsible instrument of private economic power or of economic "imperialism" by its home country. Others view it as an international carrier of advanced management science and technology, an agent for the global transmission of cultures bringing closer the day when a common set of ideals will unite mankind.[12]

Many multinational corporations are enormous. For example, the sales of both Exxon and General Motors are larger than the gross domestic product of all but twenty-two nations in the world. A multinational company may have several worldwide headquarters, depending on where certain markets or technologies are. Britain's APV, a maker of food-processing equipment, has a different headquarters for each of its worldwide businesses. Hewlett-Packard recently moved the headquarters of its personal computer business to Grenoble, France. Siemens A.G., Germany's electronics giant, is relocating its medical electronics division headquarters from Germany to Chicago. Honda is planning to move the worldwide headquarters for its power-products division to Atlanta, Georgia. ABB Asea Brown Boveri, the European electrical engineering giant based in Zurich, Switzerland, groups its thousands of products and services into fifty or so business areas. Each is run by a leadership team that crafts global business strategy, sets product development priorities, and decides where to make its products. None of the teams work out of the Zurich head-

quarters; they are distributed around the world. Leadership for power transformers is based in Germany, electric drives are in Finland, process automation is in the United States.[13]

Large multinationals have advantages over other companies. For instance, multinationals can often overcome trade problems. Taiwan and South Korea have long had an embargo against Japanese cars for political reasons and to help domestic carmakers. Also, Japan observes the Arab embargo of Israel. Yet Honda USA, a Japanese-owned company based in the United States, sends Accords to Taiwan and Korea and Civic sedans to Israel. Another example is Germany's BASF, a major chemical and drug manufacturer. Its biotechnology research at home is challenged by the environmentally conscious Green movement. So BASF moved its cancer and immune-system research to Cambridge, Massachusetts.

Another advantage for multinationals is their ability to sidestep regulatory problems. U.S. drugmaker SmithKline and Britain's Beecham decided to merge in part so they could avoid licensing and regulatory hassles in their largest markets. The merged company can say it's an insider in both Europe and the United States. "When we go to Brussels, we're a member state [of the European Community]," one executive explains. "And when we go to Washington, we're an American company, too."[14]

Multinationals can often save a lot in labor costs, even in highly unionized countries. For example, Xerox started moving copier rebuilding work to Mexico, where wages are much lower. Its union in Rochester, New York, objected because it saw that members' jobs were at risk. So it agreed to change work styles and improve productivity to keep the jobs at home.

Multinationals can also shift costs from one plant to another. When European demand for a certain solvent declined, Dow Chemical shifted production of its German plant to another chemical that had been imported from Louisiana and Texas. Computer models help Dow make decisions like these so it can run its plants more efficiently and keep costs down.

Finally, multinationals can tap new technology from around the world. Xerox has introduced some eighty different office copiers in the United States that were designed and built by Fuji Xerox, its joint venture with a Japanese company. Versions of the superconcentrated detergent that Procter & Gamble first formulated in Japan in response to a rival's product are now being sold under the Ariel brand name in Europe and tested under the Cheer and Tide labels in the United States. Also consider Otis Elevator's development of the Elevonic 411, an elevator that is programmed to send more cars to floors where demand is high. It was developed by six research centers in five countries. Otis's group in Farmington, Connecticut, handled the systems integration; a Japanese group designed the special motor drives that make the elevators ride smoothly; a French group perfected the door systems; a German group handled the electronics; and a Spanish group took care of the small-geared components. Otis says the international effort saved more than $10 million in design costs and cut the process from four years to two.

3 GLOBAL MARKETING STANDARDIZATION

Traditionally, marketing-oriented multinational corporations have operated somewhat differently in each country. They use a strategy of providing different product features, packaging, advertising, and so on. However, Ted Levitt, a Harvard professor, described a trend toward what he referred to as "global marketing," with a

A McDonald's restaurant anywhere in the world has recognizable features. But it may offer some variations to suit the local market, as at this outlet in Beijing.

H. Zeng/Agence-Chine Nouvelle/SIPA-Press

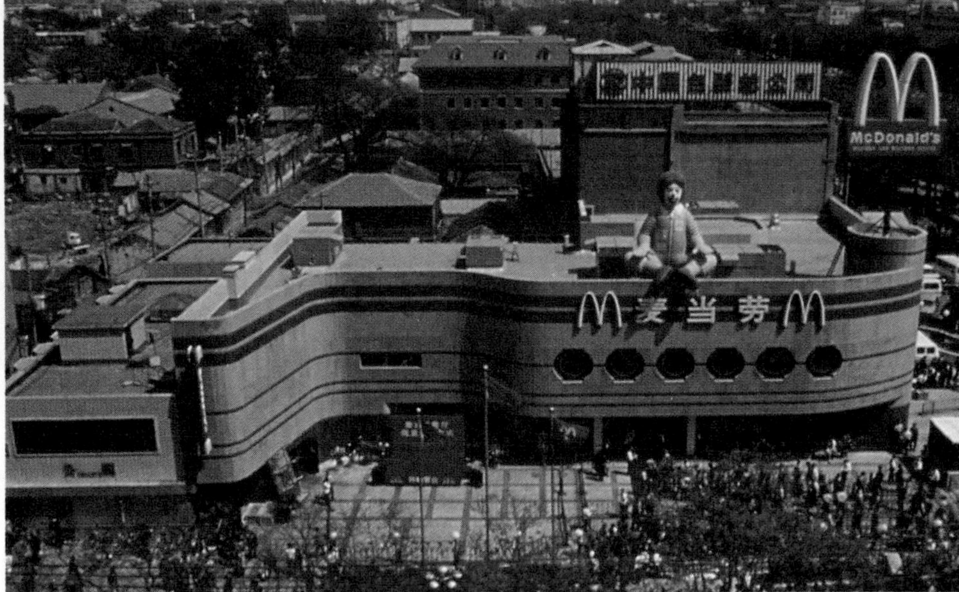

slightly different meaning.[15] He contended that communication and technology have made the world smaller, so that almost everyone everywhere wants all the things they have heard about, seen, or experienced. Thus he saw the emergence of global markets for standardized consumer products on a huge scale, as opposed to segmented foreign markets with different products. We define *global marketing* as individuals and organizations using a global vision to effectively market goods and services across national boundaries. To make the distinction, we can refer to Levitt's notion as **global marketing standardization**.

global marketing standardization
Production of uniform products that can be sold the same way all over the world.

Global marketing standardization presumes that the markets throughout the world are becoming more alike. Firms practicing global marketing standardization produce "globally standardized products" to be sold the same way all over the world. Uniform production should enable companies to lower production and marketing costs and increase profits. However, recent research indicates that superior sales and profits do not necessarily follow from global standardization.[16]

Levitt cited Coca-Cola, Colgate-Palmolive, and McDonald's as successful global marketers. However, Levitt's critics point out that these three companies' success is really based on variation, not on offering the same product everywhere. McDonald's, for example, changes its salad dressings for French tastes and sells beer and mineral water in its restaurants. It also offers different products to suit tastes in Germany (where it offers beer) as well as in Japan (where it offers sake). Also, the fact that Coca-Cola and Colgate-Palmolive sell some of their products in more than 160 countries does not signify that they have adopted a high degree of standardization for all their products globally. Only three Coca-Cola brands are standardized, and one of them, Sprite, has a different formulation in Japan. Some Colgate-Palmolive products are marketed in just a few countries. Axion paste dishwashing detergent, for example, was formulated for developing countries, and La Croix Plus detergent was custom-made for the French market. Colgate toothpaste is marketed the same way globally, although its advanced Gum Protection Formula is used in only twenty-seven nations.

As you can see, some multinational corporations are moving toward a degree of global marketing standardization. Another example is Nike, which designed a standardized global marketing plan for its Air 180 shoes. Their advanced air cushioning

system is visible through the shoe's clear midsole. For greater adaptability, the television commercials were done without spoken language. Title cards identifying Nike and promoting the Air 180's worldwide availability were used and translated into various languages. Ads use the company's "Just do it" theme. Similarly, Eastman Kodak has launched a world brand of blank tapes for videocassette recorders. Procter & Gamble calls its new philosophy "global planning." The idea is to determine which product modifications are necessary from country to country while trying to minimize those modifications. P&G has at least four products that are marketed similarly in most parts of the world: Camay soap, Crest toothpaste, Head and Shoulders shampoo, and Pampers diapers. However, the smell of Camay, the flavor of Crest, and the formula of Head and Shoulders, as well as the advertising, vary from country to country.

4 THE EXTERNAL ENVIRONMENT FACING GLOBAL MARKETERS

A global marketer or firm considering global marketing faces problems, many due to the external environment. Many of the same environmental factors that operate in the domestic market also exist internationally. They include culture, level of economic and technological development, political structure, demographic makeup, and natural resources.

Culture

Central to any society is a common set of values shared by its citizens that determine what is socially acceptable. Culture underlies the family, the educational system, religion, and the social class system. The network of social organizations generates the different overlapping roles and status positions. Swiss homemakers, for example, consider the performance of household chores central to the homemaking role and find it difficult to accept the idea of labor-saving machines or commercial products. They reject commercial appeals emphasizing the time and effort saved in performing household tasks.

Exhibit 3.2 shows how culture can influence one's view of the world. It is taken from a Japanese Airline route map. To people from the United States, our country looks upside down and backward. But the map accurately reflects the Japanese view of the world. From their viewpoint on the other side of the globe, Japan would be in the center and right side up.

Language is another important aspect of culture. Marketers must take care in translating product names, slogans, and promotional messages so as not to convey the wrong meaning. For example, when Coca-Cola reentered China in 1979, it discovered that the literal representation of Coca-Cola in Chinese characters means "bite the wax tadpole." With the help of language specialists, the company substituted new characters that sound like Coca-Cola but mean "can happy, mouth happy."[17] Likewise, a Mexican magazine promotion for a U.S.-brand shirt carried a message stating the opposite of what it was intended to communicate. Instead of reading "When I used this shirt, I felt good," the advertisement translated into "Until I used this shirt, I felt good."[18]

Each country has its own customs and traditions that determine business practices and influence negotiations with foreign customers. In many countries, personal relationships are more important than financial considerations. For instance, skipping social engagements in Mexico may lead to lost sales. Negotiations in Japan often include long evenings of dining, drinking, and entertaining, and only after a

Exhibit 3.2

The Japanese View of North America

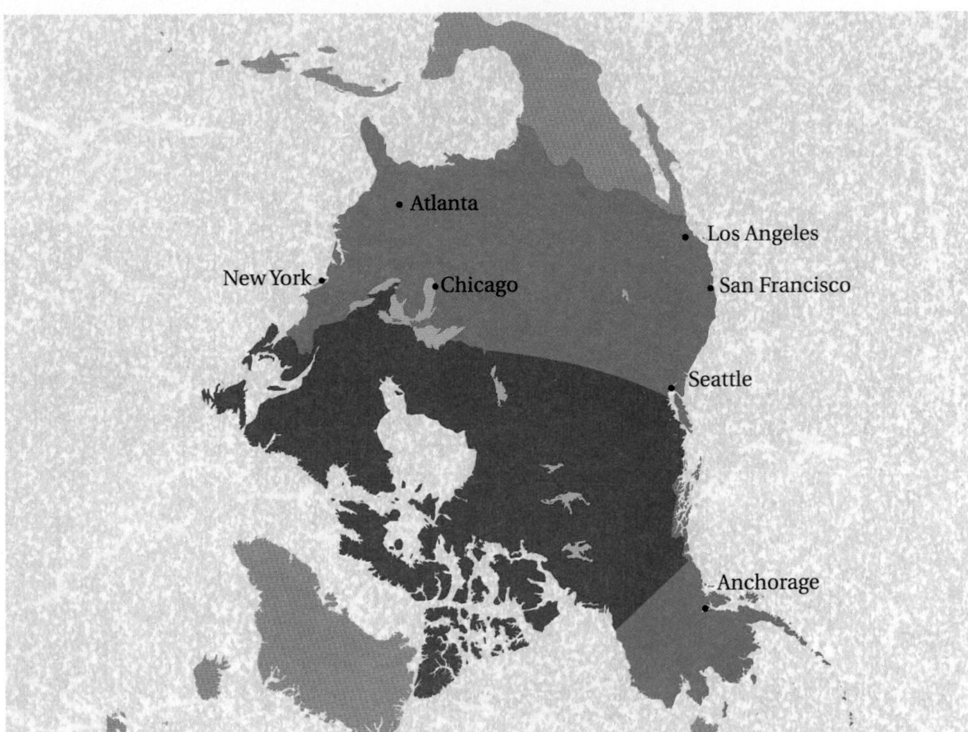

close personal relationship has been formed do business negotiations begin. The importance of punctuality also varies from culture to culture. Most U.S. businesspeople consider punctuality at meetings to be a sign of respect and are often frustrated by Latin Americans, who consider time relatively less important.

In the United States, we also prefer written contracts. If a party violates the terms of the contract, legal actions are frequently taken. However, in China, where trust is important to business dealings, oral agreements mean more. The written contract represents the beginning of a negotiation process, and many changes are to be expected.

Even if English is spoken during negotiations, communication problems still occur. For instance, Japanese may say yes or maybe when they really mean no, to avoid making their foreign counterparts lose face and feel embarrassed. When the Taiwanese shake their heads back and forth they mean yes, not no.

Businesspeople from the United States are learning that global success requires patience and cultural understanding. Consider the following:

> Recently, as finishing touches were being added to Motorola Inc.'s $400 million Silicon Harbor complex in Hong Kong, Tam Chung Ding summoned his favorite geomancer, or diviner. Tam, president of Motorola's Asia-Pacific semiconductor division, wanted the 87-year-old soothsayer to double-check the new facility's *feng shui*—literally, its wind and water—for good luck. Yes, the omens were favorable. Built on reclaimed land, the project had water—a symbol of wealth—on three sides and was ringed by mountains—a source of power. . . . "This office has about the best *feng shui* in Hong Kong," Tam boasts.[19]

Exhibit 3.3 summarizes some important cultural considerations. Several additional examples are discussed in the section on marketing mix.

Level of Economic and Technological Development

A second major factor in the external environment facing the global marketer is the level of economic development. In general, complex and sophisticated industries

Exhibit 3.3

Important Cultural Considerations in International Marketing

Differences in these cultural factors . . .	. . . Affect values and habits relating to:
Assumptions and attitudes	Time One's proper purpose in life The future This life versus the hereafter Duty, responsibility
Personal beliefs and aspirations	Right and wrong Sources of pride Sources of fear and concern Extent of one's hopes Individual versus society
Interpersonal relationships	Source of authority Care or empathy for others Importance of family obligations Objects of loyalty Tolerance for personal differences
Social structure	Interclass mobility Class or caste systems Urban-village-farm origins Determinants of status

are found in developed countries, and more basic industries are found in less-developed nations. Yet exceptions do exist. For example, a government of a less-developed nation may buy complex facilities to improve its status with the local population, even though they have neither the skills to operate the machinery nor the market to dispose of the goods.

To appreciate marketing opportunities (or lack of them), it is helpful to examine the stages of economic growth and technological development: traditional society, preindustrial society, takeoff economy, industrializing society, and fully industrialized society.

The Traditional Society

traditional society Largely agricultural society, with a social structure and value system that provide little opportunity for upward mobility.

Countries in the traditional stage are in the earliest phase of development. A **traditional society** is largely agricultural, with a social structure and value system that provide little opportunity for upward mobility. It is custom-bound, and its economy typically operates at the subsistence level because of backward or no technology. The culture may be highly stable, and economic growth may not get started without a powerful disruptive force. To introduce single units of technology into such a country is probably wasted effort. In Ghana, for instance, a tollway sixteen miles long and six lanes wide, intended to modernize distribution, does not connect to any city or village or other road. Similarly, a modern fertilizer plant in India was built but not used because the distribution system was inadequate to market the fertilizer. Clearly, these projects were not integrated into the culture.

The Preindustrial Society

preindustrial society Society characterized by economic and social change and the emergence of a rising middle class with an entrepreneurial spirit.

The second stage, the **preindustrial society,** involves economic and social change and the emergence of a middle class with an entrepreneurial spirit. Nationalism may begin to rise, along with restrictions on multinational organizations. Countries like North Korea and Uganda are in this stage. Effective marketing in these countries is very difficult because they lack the modern distribution and communication

Economic development differs in Mexico, an industrializing society (represented *left* by a street market in Oaxaca), and Canada, a fully industrialized society (represented *right* by the skyscrapers of downtown Toronto). The North American Free Trade Agreement was proposed to link both economies with that of the United States.

(left) © 1985 David Hiser/The Image Bank; *(right)* © Tony Stone Worldwide/Richard Simpson

systems that U.S. marketers often take for granted. Peru, for example, did not establish a television network until 1975.

takeoff economy
Period of transition from a developing to a developed nation, during which new industries arise.

The Takeoff Economy

The **takeoff economy** is the period of transition from a developing to a developed nation. New industries arise, and a generally healthy social and political climate emerges. Thailand, Malaysia, and India have entered the takeoff stage. For example, in recent years Thailand has had one of the fastest rates of economic growth in the world. Investors from Japan, Taiwan, and the United States are bringing capital and new technology to Thailand. Consumer markets are beginning to emerge among the more prosperous Thais, creating opportunities for foreign companies.

industrializing society
Society characterized by the spread of technology to most sectors of the economy.

The Industrializing Society

The fourth phase of economic development is the **industrializing society.** During this era, technology spreads from sectors of the economy that powered the takeoff to the rest of the nation. Mexico, Singapore, and Brazil are among the nations in this phase of development.

Countries in the industrializing stage begin to produce capital goods and consumer durable products. Demands for parts and materials create many secondary industries, such as tires for automobiles, motors for refrigerators, and electronic components. These industries also foster economic growth. As a result, a large middle class begins to emerge, and demand for luxuries and services grows. These markets become increasingly attractive to large multinational firms. The newly industrialized nations of the Pacific Rim—such as South Korea, Taiwan, Singapore, and Hong Kong—contain more than 72 million consumers who live in households with incomes exceeding $10,000. Although this is still less than half the income of the typical U.S. household, sizable consumer markets have emerged for products ranging from furniture, appliances, toilets, and televisions to dresses, shoes, and cosmetics.[20]

The Fully Industrialized Society

fully industrialized society
Society that is an exporter of manufactured products, many of which are based on advanced technology.

The **fully industrialized society,** the fifth stage of economic development, is an exporter of manufactured products, many of which are based on advanced technology. Examples include automobiles, computers, airplanes, oil exploration equipment, and telecommunications gear. Great Britain, Japan, Germany, France, Canada, and the United States fall into this category.

The wealth of the industrialized nations creates tremendous market potential. Therefore, industrialized countries trade extensively. Also, industrialized nations usually ship manufactured goods to developing countries in exchange for raw materials like petroleum, precious metals, and bauxite.

Political Structure

Political structure is a third important variable facing global marketers. Government policies run the gamut from no private ownership and minimal individual freedom to little central government and maximum personal freedom. As rights of private property increase, government-owned industries and centralized planning tend to decrease. But rarely will a political environment be at one extreme or the other. India, for instance, is a republic with elements of socialism, monopoly capitalism, and competitive capitalism in its political ideology.

Many countries are changing from a centrally planned economy to a market-oriented one. Germany is making the fastest transformation because of its reunification. Eastern European nations like Hungary and Poland have also been moving quickly with market reforms. Many of the reforms have increased foreign trade and investment. For example, in Poland, foreigners are now allowed to invest in all areas of industry, including agriculture, manufacturing, and trade. Poland even gives companies that invest in certain sectors some tax advantages.

Companies from Western Europe, Japan, and the United States have been taking advantage of the new opportunities. For example, Japan's Suzuki Motors Company has a $138 million joint venture with a consortium of nineteen Hungarian auto suppliers. General Electric has a $150 million agreement for the majority share of Tungsram, a Hungarian lighting equipment manufacturer. Although severe economic problems still must be addressed, companies willing to take a long-term view will find increasing opportunities in Eastern Europe.

Although the economy of the former Soviet Union has been unstable for the past few years, it still offers many marketing opportunities for adventurous Western companies.

The former Soviet Union is progressing more slowly than many Eastern European countries, but it also is headed in the direction of a market-oriented economy. To prepare for the changes, over 5,000 managers are currently studying abroad, and many more are studying market-oriented principles within the former Soviet Union.[21]

Changes in the Russian economy are desperately needed. Shortages of food, daily necessities, and housing are widespread. For example, shortages of wood have limited the supply of caskets, and the only people who can acquire a casket are those who can supply their own wood. Moreover, many consumer products are of poor quality. For example, the majority of Moscow's house fires are started

by faulty TV sets. The region has the ability to grow its own food. Yet its agricultural distribution system is so inefficient that up to half the food is wasted. Thus the countries of the former Soviet Union must annually buy $3.3 billion in corn, wheat, and soybeans from abroad. Despite this dire situation, the opportunity exists for companies to provide equipment to store, transport, process, and market the food that is grown.[22] RJR Nabisco is trying to process and market tomato products, hoping to save some of the 40 percent of the crop lost each year. More opportunities exist in many other inefficient industries, such as mining, oil drilling and explorations, and consumer durable goods.

Changes leading to market-oriented economies are not restricted to Eastern Europe and Russia. Many countries within Latin America are also attempting market reforms. Countries like Brazil, Argentina, and Mexico are reducing government control over many sectors of the economy. They are also selling state-owned companies to foreign and domestic investors and removing trade barriers that have protected their markets against foreign competition.[23]

Another trend in the political environment is the growth of nationalist sentiments in many nations whose citizens have strong loyalties and devotion to their country. Failure to appreciate emerging nationalist feelings can result in loss of the right to conduct business in that country. Such problems can be avoided by allowing citizens of the host country equity (ownership) participation in the operation.

Some countries have nationalized (taken ownership of) certain industries or companies, such as airlines in Italy and Volvo in Sweden, to infuse more capital into their development. Industries are also nationalized to allow domestic corporations to sell vital goods below cost. For example, for many years France has been supplying coal to users at a loss.

Legal Considerations

Closely related to and often intertwined with the political environment are legal considerations. Legal structures are designed to either encourage or limit trade. Some examples follow:

tariff
Tax levied on the goods entering a country.

- ***Tariff:*** tax levied on the goods entering a country. For example, trucks imported into the United States face a 25 percent tariff. Many goods coming from developing nations receive tariff reductions or exemptions under the Generalized System of Preferences. Since the 1930s, tariffs have tended to decrease as a barrier to trade. But they have often been replaced by nontariff barriers, such as quotas, boycotts, and other restrictions.

quota
Limit on the amount of a specific product that can enter a country.

boycott
Exclusion of all products from certain countries or companies.

exchange control
Law compelling a company earning foreign exchange from its exports to sell it to a control agency, usually a central bank.

- ***Quota:*** limit on the amount of a specific product that can enter a country. The United States has strict quotas for imported textiles, sugar, and many dairy products. Several U.S. companies have sought quotas as a means of protection from foreign competition. For example, Harley-Davidson convinced the U.S. government to place quotas on large motorcycles imported into the United States. These quotas gave the company the opportunity to improve its quality and compete with Japanese motorcycles.
- ***Boycott:*** exclusion of all products from certain countries or companies. Governments use boycotts to exclude companies from countries with whom they have a political difference. Several Arab nations boycotted Coca-Cola because it maintained distributors in Israel.
- ***Exchange control:*** law compelling a company earning foreign exchange from its exports to sell it to a control agency, usually a central bank. A company

wishing to buy goods abroad must first obtain foreign exchange from the control agency. Generally, exchange controls limit the importation of luxuries. For instance, Avon Products drastically cut back new production lines and products in the Philippines because exchange controls prevented conversion of pesos to dollars to ship back to the home office. As a result, the pesos had to be used in the Philippines. China restricts the amount of foreign currency each Chinese company is allowed to keep from its exports. Therefore, Chinese companies must usually get the government's approval to release funds before they can buy products from foreign companies.

trade agreement
Agreement to stimulate international trade.

- ***Trade agreement:*** agreement to stimulate international trade. Not all government efforts are meant to stifle imports or investment by foreign corporations. The GATT (General Agreement on Tariffs and Trade) is a good example of a structure designed to increase international trade. GATT has been successful in lowering tariffs but has had less success in reducing nontariff barriers. Negotiators from 108 nations attended a GATT meeting during 1992 in an attempt to further reduce trade barriers. The talks were unsuccessful, mostly because France and India refused to go along with the agreement.[24]

market grouping
Common trade alliance in which several countries agree to work together to form a common trade area that enhances trade opportunities.

- ***Market grouping:*** also known as a common trade alliance; occurs when several countries agree to work together to form a common trade area that enhances trade opportunities. The best-known market grouping is the European Community (EC), often called the Common Market. Its members are Belgium, France, Germany, Italy, Luxembourg, the Netherlands, Denmark, Ireland, Spain, the United Kingdom, Portugal, and Greece. The EC has been evolving for nearly four decades, yet until recently, many trade barriers existed among member nations.

The trend toward globalization has brought to the fore several specific examples of the influence of political structure and legal considerations: Japanese Keiretsu, the North American Free Trade Agreement, and United Europe.

Japanese Keiretsu

keiretsu
Japanese societies of business, which take two main forms: bank-centered keiretsu, massive industrial combines centered around a bank, and supply keiretsu, groups of companies dominated by the major manufacturer they provide with supplies.

Japanese nationalism produced the **keiretsu**, or societies of business, which take two main forms. Bank-centered keiretsu are massive industrial combines of twenty to forty-five core companies centered around a bank (see Exhibit 3.4). They enable companies to share business risk and provide a way to allocate investment to strategic industries. Supply keiretsu are groups of companies dominated by the major manufacturer they provide with supplies.

After World War II, the Japanese government actively encouraged keiretsu for two reasons. First, it assumed that interlocking ownership and close buyer-supplier relationships would help keep out foreign imports and investment. Second, the government wanted to concentrate scarce resources in industries deemed critical to Japan's long-term economic security. Groups with strong bank backing and diversified risk could more easily be directed into strategic industries.[25]

Keiretsu have indeed blocked U.S. companies, and others, from the Japanese market. The Japan Fair Trade Commission, in fact, has estimated that almost 90 percent of all domestic business transactions are "among parties involved in a long-standing relationship of some sort."[26] To see how the keiretsu block markets, consider the Matsushita keiretsu. Matsushita makes Panasonic, National, Technics, and Quasar brands. One of the world's top twenty manufacturers, Matsushita also controls a chain of about 25,000 National retail stores in Japan, which together generate more than half Matsushita's domestic sales. From batteries to refrigerators, these

Exhibit 3.4

A Japanese Keiretsu

Source: Adapted by permission of *Harvard Business Review* from Marie Anchordoguy, "A Brief History of Japan's Keiretsu," *Harvard Business Review*, July-August 1990, pp. 58–59. Copyright © 1990 by the President and Fellows of Harvard College; all rights reserved.

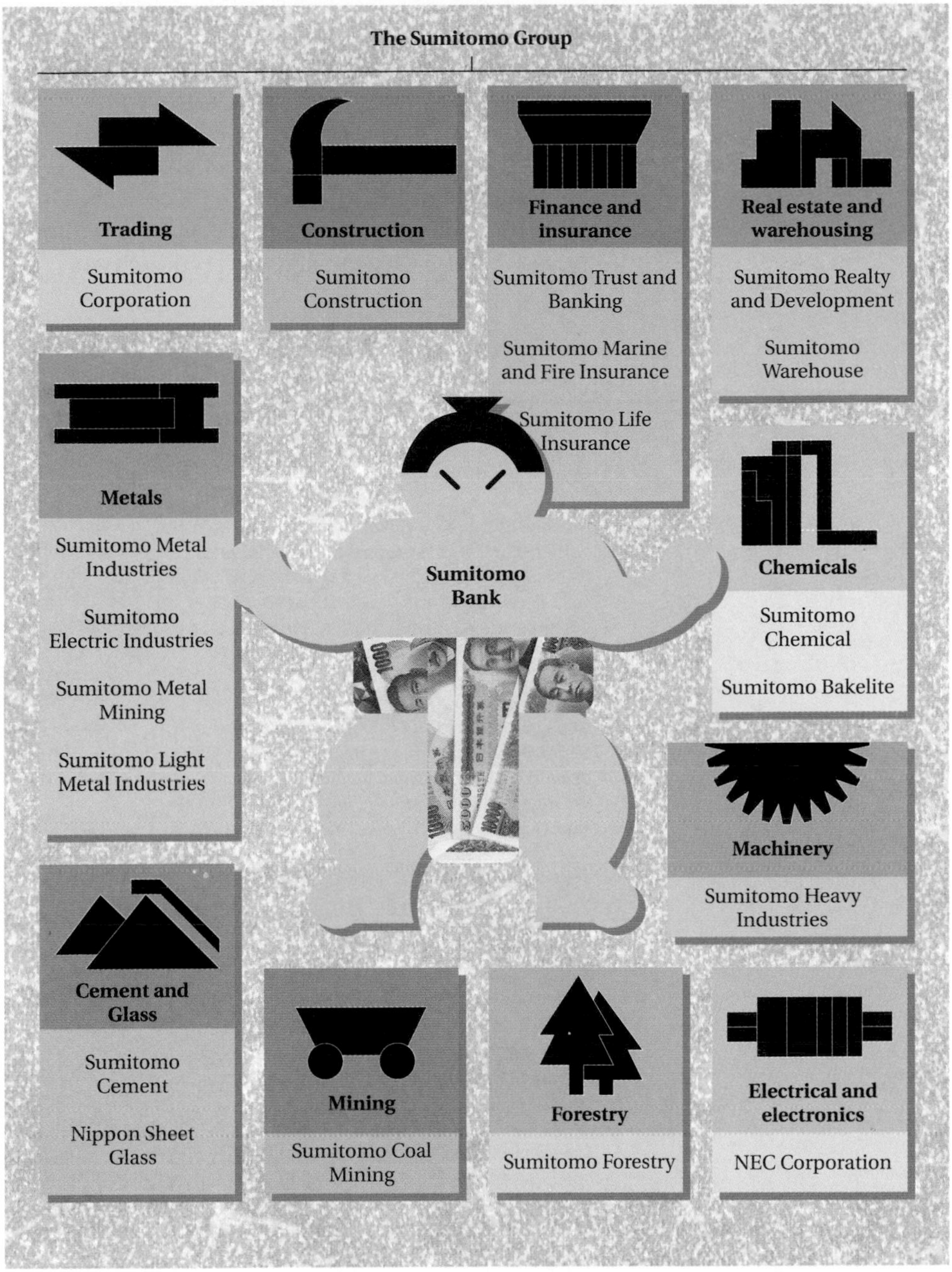

The Sumitomo Group

Trading
Sumitomo Corporation

Construction
Sumitomo Construction

Finance and insurance
Sumitomo Trust and Banking
Sumitomo Marine and Fire Insurance
Sumitomo Life Insurance

Real estate and warehousing
Sumitomo Realty and Development
Sumitomo Warehouse

Metals
Sumitomo Metal Industries
Sumitomo Electric Industries
Sumitomo Metal Mining
Sumitomo Light Metal Industries

Sumitomo Bank

Chemicals
Sumitomo Chemical
Sumitomo Bakelite

Machinery
Sumitomo Heavy Industries

Cement and Glass
Sumitomo Cement
Nippon Sheet Glass

Mining
Sumitomo Coal Mining

Forestry
Sumitomo Forestry

Electrical and electronics
NEC Corporation

shops agree to sell no other brands or, at most, few others. And the dealers agree to sell at manufacturers' recommended prices. In return, Matsushita essentially guarantees the livelihoods of the stores' owners.

Trade talks between Japan and the United States in 1992 centered on keiretsu with little success. The U.S. government demanded that the keiretsu be opened to U.S. companies. Japanese officials were reluctant to acknowledge the need to reform the keiretsu, arguing that they make the Japanese economy more efficient.[27]

North American Free Trade Agreement (NAFTA)
Treaty establishing the world's largest free-trade zone, which includes Canada, the United States, and Mexico.

North American Free Trade Agreement

In 1992, negotiators concluded the **North American Free Trade Agreement** (NAFTA), which created the world's largest free-trade zone. It includes Canada, the United States, and Mexico, with a combined population of 360 million and economy of $6 trillion.[28] The key benefits to the United States from NAFTA are summarized in

Exhibit 3.5. If the agreement is ratified by the U.S. Congress and the governments of Canada and Mexico, it will go into effect on January 1, 1994.

Canada, the largest U.S. trading partner, entered a free-trade agreement with the United States in 1988. Most of the new opportunities for U.S. business under NAFTA are thus in Mexico, America's third largest trading partner, where U.S. exports tripled from 1988 to 1992.[29] When the accord goes into effect, tariffs on about half the items traded across the Rio Grande will immediately disappear. The pact will also remove a web of Mexican licensing requirements, quotas, and tariffs that currently

Exhibit 3.5

Benefits to the United States from the North American Free Trade Agreement

Source: Kenneth Bacon, "Trade Pact Is Likely to Step Up Business Even Before Approval," *The Wall Street Journal*, 13 August 1992, p. A10. Reprinted by permission of *The Wall Street Journal*,

Elimination of Tariffs and Barriers

Approximately 65% of U.S. industrial and agricultural exports to Mexico would be eligible for duty-free treatment either immediately or within 5 years. In addition, Mexican export-performance requirements, which require U.S. companies to export as a condition of being allowed to invest in Mexico, and Mexican "local content" regulations would be eliminated. Key industries affected include:

Motor vehicle and parts: Mexican tariffs on vehicles and light trucks would be halved immediately. Within 5 years, duties on 75% of U.S. parts exports to Mexico would be eliminated. Mexican "trade balancing" and "local-content requirements" would be phased out over 10 years.

Auto rule of origin: Only autos that contain 62.5% North American content would benefit from the tariff cuts, to ensure that benefits of trade liberalization flow to North American companies.

Textile and apparel: Barriers to $250 million—approximately 20%—of U.S. exports would be eliminated immediately, with barriers to a further $700 million in U.S. exports dropped within 6 years. All North American trade restrictions would be eliminated within 10 years, with rules-of-origin provisions to ensure that benefits of liberalization accrue to North American producers.

Land transportation: U.S. trucking companies would be permitted to carry international cargo to Mexican states contiguous to the United States by 1995 and to all of Mexico by 1999. Railroads would be able to provide service to Mexico. American companies would be able to invest in and operate land-side port services in Mexico.

Telecommunications: U.S. companies would receive nondiscriminatory access to the Mexican public telephone system, and investment restrictions would be eliminated by July 1995.

Financial services: U.S. banks and securities firms would be allowed to establish wholly owned subsidiaries in Mexico. Transitional restrictions would be phased out by January 1, 2000.

Insurance: U.S. companies with existing joint ventures would be allowed to acquire full ownership by 1996; new entrants would be able to acquire majority stakes in Mexican companies by 1998. All equity and market-share restrictions would be eliminated by end of 2000.

Agriculture: Mexican import licenses, which cover about 25% of U.S. exports, would be dropped immediately, and remaining Mexican tariffs would be phased out over 10 to 15 years.

Intellectual property rights: U.S. high-technology, entertainment, and consumer goods producers would realize substantial gains in patent, trademark, and copyright protections. Compulsory licensing would be limited, resolving an important issue with Canada.

Environment/Labor Rights/Adjustment Safeguards

Environment: United States would be allowed to maintain its stringent environmental, health, and safety standards.

Worker rights: The parties assume that the benefits of the trade pact would provide Mexico with resources to enforce labor initiatives launched by the Salinas administration.

Adjustment safeguards: For import-sensitive U.S. industries, U.S. tariffs would be phased out over 10 years—15 years for some particularly vulnerable industries. U.S. workers who lose their jobs because of the trade pact would receive timely, comprehensive, and effective services and retraining through an existing or newly created program.

limit transactions in U.S. goods and services. For instance, the pact will allow U.S. and Canadian financial-services companies to own subsidiaries in Mexico for the first time in fifty years.

The first industries to benefit are likely to be autos, textiles, capital goods, financial services, construction equipment, electronics, telecommunications, and petrochemicals. Sales of companies in such industries have been rising for some time as a result of Mexico's growing economy. In 1983 Caterpillar sold only 12 pieces of heavy construction equipment to Mexico; in 1993 it shipped over 1,200. NAFTA will remove tariffs on Caterpillar equipment sold in Mexico while maintaining duties against Japanese rival Komatsu. As protections are lifted from the Mexican car industry, Rockwell International will sell more door latches, sunroofs, and window mechanisms. It already plans to build a new plant in Mexico.

Canadian companies are also eager to do business in Mexico. Magna International, Canada's largest auto parts maker, is building its first Mexican production facility near a Volkswagen assembly plant in Puebla. Another Canadian company, Northern Telecom, had only ten employees in Mexico in 1988. It plans to build sales from an estimated $200 million now to $500 million by the mid-1990s.[30] That's not an unreasonable goal, since industry experts foresee the Mexican telecommunications market expanding by 15 percent annually.

NAFTA could boost U.S. exports to Mexico by $10 billion a year, expand Canada-Mexico trade by 30 percent, and create 600,000 new jobs in Mexico.[31] Yet the NAFTA agreement may not benefit everyone equally.

ETHICS IN MARKETING

Is NAFTA Good for U.S. Workers?

Most economists agree that lowering trade barriers is good. As foreign countries sell more to the United States, they will use the revenue to buy U.S. exports. Often they will also set up shop and create jobs in the United States, as the Japanese and Germans are doing. A recent example is a BMW plant that will bring 2,000 jobs to South Carolina. Other benefits of free trade include a freer exchange of technology and managerial ideas. Although the net benefit is hard to quantify, economists project that free trade between the United States and Mexico will lift output in both countries and create tens of thousands of new U.S. jobs.

If goods trade freely, prices and production costs will equalize. To compete, countries must specialize where they have a relative edge. Low-wage countries, like Mexico, will make labor-intensive goods. Those with capital will do better with technology-intensive products. Thus, low-skilled work should flow from the United States to Mexico—or the wages of low-skilled U.S. workers must fall.

In the 1980s, factory workers whose companies competed with foreign rivals often were laid off or were forced to take wage cuts. The glut of job candidates helped hold down pay among the 64 million workers who never went beyond high school. Only the college-educated did well.

The increase in global trade bears much of the blame for unprecedented income inequality between the most- and least-educated parts of the U.S. work force. Declining pay for those at the bottom may not slow U.S. growth, since average incomes should rise as those at the top do better. But widening inequality poses other problems. The poverty rate could stay up. The tab for welfare and unemployment could mount, inflating taxes. Ultimately, resentment of the wealthy could reach a boiling point, leading to ferocious attacks on well-paid executives and even to more riots like those in 1992 in Los Angeles. "One possibility is for us to become a class society like those in Latin America," which have unequal distributions of wealth and chronically unstable governments, says Richard B. Freeman, an economist at Harvard University. "That's the direction we're headed."[32]

Should U.S. labor unions support NAFTA? In a broader sense, should the United States begin to erect trade barriers to protect lower-paying American jobs? If not, what should the federal government do, if anything, to protect or help the tens of thousands of U.S. workers who may lose their jobs because of NAFTA?

United Europe

United Europe
Agreement among members of the European Community to standardize business-related rules and reduce trade barriers.

To further enhance European trade, the EC removed many internal trade barriers on its way to what is sometimes called **United Europe**. Members standardized trade rules and taxes, and health and safety standards were coordinated. The goal was to end the need for a special product for each country—for example, a different Braun electric razor for Italy, Germany, France, and so forth. Goods marked *GEC* (goods for EC) can be traded freely, without being retested at each border.

Duties, customs procedures, and taxes were also standardized. A driver hauling cargo from Amsterdam to Lisbon can now clear four border crossings by showing a single piece of paper. Before 1992, the same driver would have carried two pounds of paper to cross the same borders.

Some economists have called United Europe the "United States of Europe." It is an attractive market, with 320 million consumers and purchasing power almost equal to that of the United States. But the EC will probably never be a "United States of Europe." In 1992 the "Maastricht treaty"—which proposed binding the EC countries together in finance, defense, economics, and foreign policy by 1999—failed when put to a vote in Denmark. In other countries, it passed narrowly. To become law, the Maastricht treaty must be approved by all twelve EC countries. Thus it must be resubmitted to the Danish people.

Many of those who voted against the Maastricht treaty were worried about local identities being submerged. For instance, French consumers feared that food safety rules dreamed up by Brussels bureaucrats might deprive them of Roquefort and other favorite cheeses. And in culturally divided Belgium, Flemish voters worried that rules granting all EC citizens the right to vote could tip the balance of power to the French-speaking community.[33]

Even in a United Europe, marketers will not be able to produce a single Europroduct for a generic Euroconsumer. With nine different languages and individual national customs, Europe will always be far more diverse than the United States. Thus product differences will continue. It will be a long time, for instance, before the French begin drinking the instant coffee that Britons enjoy. Preferences for washing machines also differ: British homemakers want front-loaders, and the French want top-loaders; Germans like lots of settings and high spin speeds; Italians like lower speeds.

Global marketer Lever Brothers has been trying, with great difficulty, to create a Europroduct fabric softener. The brand is sold in ten European countries under seven names, often with different bottles, different marketing strategies, and sometimes even different formulas. However, all the brands have a teddy bear on the label, and some of the names evoke snuggling. To compound the problem, consumers in different countries want different features in their fabric softener. Germans, for example, demand a product that's gentle on lakes and rivers, and they will pay a premium for it. Spaniards want a cheaper product that gets shirts white and soft. And Greeks want a smaller package, so they can hold down the cost of each store visit. Lever Brothers' strategy is to change the product gradually, often keeping the local brand name, and standardizing packaging and formulas bit by bit.[34]

An entirely different type of problem facing global marketers is the possibility of a protectionist movement by United Europe against outsiders. For example, European automakers have proposed holding Japanese imports at roughly their current 10 percent market share. The Irish, Danes, and Dutch don't make cars and have unrestricted home markets; they would be unhappy about limited imports of Toyotas and Datsuns. But France has a strict quota on Japanese cars to protect Renault and Peugeot. These local carmakers could be hurt if the quota is raised at all.

U.S. companies realize they have to be perceived as European or risk similar trade barriers. Their adaptation is remarkable. A number of big U.S. companies are already considered more "European" than many European companies. Coke and Kellogg are considered classic European brand names. Ford and General Motors compete for the largest share of auto sales on the continent. IBM and Digital Equipment dominate their markets. General Electric, AT&T, and Westinghouse are already strong all over Europe and have invested heavily in new manufacturing facilities throughout the continent.

Although many U.S. firms are well prepared to contend with European competition, the rivalry is perhaps more intense there than anywhere else in the world. In the long run, it is questionable whether Europe has room for eight mass-market automakers, including Ford and GM, when the United States sustains just three. Similarly, an integrated Europe probably doesn't need twelve national airlines.

Although H.J. Heinz is a huge company, it is only a sixth the size of its big European rivals Nestlé and Unilever. Heinz spent almost $1 billion modernizing its European plant and marketing. Its primary goal was to push its Weight Watchers' meals ahead of Nestlé's Lean Cuisine meals. Heinz has excellent distribution networks in Britain and Italy, but in the huge and affluent German market, Nestlé has the edge. Still, Heinz is gaining market share in Germany with Weight Watchers' beef stroganoff and apple strudel. This kind of marketing battle is likely to be waged in many European markets.

Demographic Makeup

The three most densely populated nations in the world are China, India, and Indonesia. Yet size of population can be misleading. Marketers also need to know whether the population is mostly urban or rural, because marketers may not have easy access to rural consumers. In Belgium about 90 percent of the population lives in an urban setting, whereas in Kenya almost 80 percent of the population lives in a rural setting. Belgium is thus the more attractive market.

Just as important as population is personal income within a country. The wealthiest countries in the world include Japan, the United States, Switzerland, Sweden, Canada, Germany, and several of the Arab oil-producing nations. At the other extreme are countries like Mali and Bangladesh, with a fraction of the per capita purchasing power of the United States. However, in countries with low per capita incomes, wealth is not evenly distributed. There are pockets of upper- and middle-class consumers in just about every country of the world. In some cases the number of consumers is surprisingly large. For example, India, a country with close to a billion people, has a very low per capita income. But between 10 and 20 percent of its population can be considered middle class, creating a potential market of over 100 million consumers.

The percentage of the world's population that lives in industrialized nations has been declining since 1960. Industrialized nations have grown slowly, and developing nations have grown rapidly. In this decade more than 90 percent of the world's population growth will occur in developing countries and only 10 percent in the industrialized nations. The United Nations reports that by the year 2000, 79 percent of the world's population will reside in developing countries—for example, Guinea, Bolivia, and Pakistan.

Natural Resources

A final factor in the external environment that has become more evident in the past decade is the shortage of natural resources. Petroleum shortages have created huge

amounts of wealth for oil-producing countries such as Norway, Saudi Arabia, and the United Arab Emirates. Both consumer and industrial markets have blossomed in these countries. Other countries—such as Indonesia, Mexico, and Venezuela—were able to borrow heavily against oil reserves in order to develop more rapidly. Industrial countries like Japan, the United States, and much of Western Europe experienced rampant inflation in the 1970s and an enormous transfer of wealth to the petroleum-rich nations. The petroleum-rich nations, in turn, suffered during much of the 1980s, when the price of oil fell. Many oil-producing nations were not able to service their foreign debts when their oil revenues were sharply reduced. However, Iraq's invasion of Kuwait in 1990 led to a rapid increase in the price of oil and focused attention on the dependence of the United States and other industrialized countries on foreign oil. The price of oil declined following the defeat of Iraq, but the U.S. dependence on foreign oil will likely remain high in the 1990s.

Petroleum is not the only natural resource that affects international marketing. Warm climate and lack of water mean many of Africa's countries will remain importers of foodstuffs. The United States, on the other hand, must rely on Africa for many precious metals. Japan depends heavily on the United States for timber and logs. A Minnesota company manufactures and sells a million pairs of disposable chopsticks to Japan each year. The list could go on, but the point is clear. Vast differences in natural resources create international dependencies, huge shifts of wealth, inflation and recession, export opportunities for countries with abundant resources, and even a stimulus for military intervention.

5 GLOBAL MARKETING: THE INDIVIDUAL FIRM

A company should consider entering the global marketplace only after its management has a solid grasp of the global environment. Some relevant questions are: What are our options in selling abroad? How difficult is global marketing? What are the potential risks and returns? Concrete answers to these questions would probably encourage the many U.S. firms not selling overseas to venture into the international arena. Foreign sales could be an important source of profits.

Many firms form multinational partnerships—called strategic alliances—to assist them in penetrating global markets. Strategic alliances are examined in Chapter 5. Five other methods of entering the global marketplace are, in order of risk, export, licensing, contract manufacturing, joint venture, and direct investment (see Exhibit 3.6).

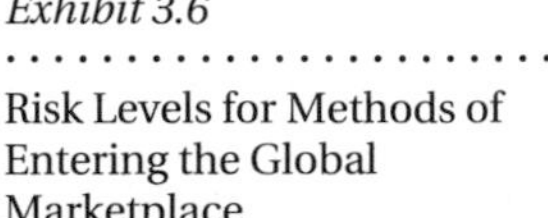

Exhibit 3.6

Risk Levels for Methods of Entering the Global Marketplace

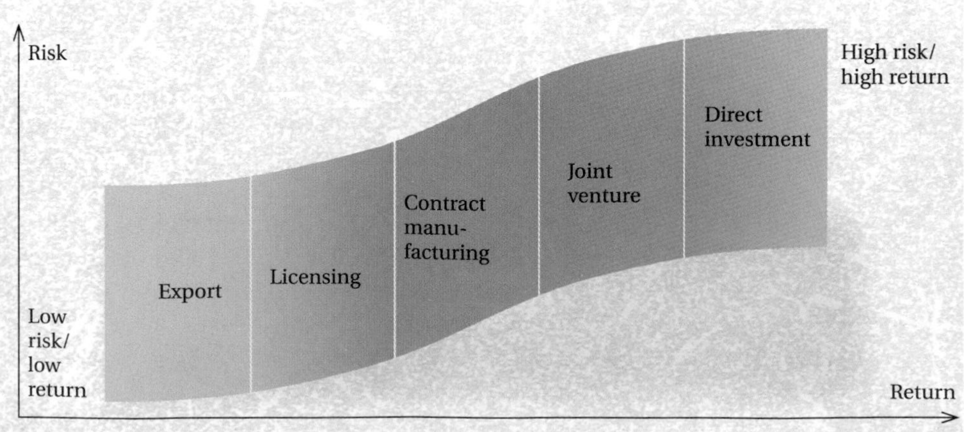

Export

When a company decides to enter the global market, exporting is usually the least complicated and least risky alternative. **Exporting** is selling domestically produced products in another country. A company deciding to export can sell directly to foreign importers or buyers, or it may decide to sell to independent exporting intermediaries located in its domestic market. Leading exports from the United States are aircraft, auto parts, and computers and computer-related products. The fifteen largest U.S. exporters are listed in Exhibit 3.7.

exporting
Practice of selling domestically produced products in another country.

buyer for export
Intermediary in the international market who assumes all ownership risks and sells internationally for its own account.

export broker
Broker who operates primarily in agriculture and raw materials.

export agent
Intermediary who either lives in a foreign country and performs the same functions as a domestic manufacturer's agent or lives in the manufacturer's country but represents foreign buyers.

The most common intermediary is the export merchant, also known as a **buyer for export**, who is usually treated like a domestic customer by the domestic manufacturer. The buyer for export assumes all risks and sells internationally for its own account. The domestic firm is involved only to the extent that its products are bought in foreign markets.

A second type of intermediary is the export agent or broker, who plays the traditional broker's role by bringing buyer and seller together. The manufacturer still retains title and assumes all the risks. **Export brokers** operate primarily in agriculture and raw materials. **Export agents**, on the other hand, consist of two types. The foreign sales agent–distributor lives in the foreign country and performs the same functions as a domestic manufacturer's agent, helping with international financing, shipping, and so on. The U.S. Department of Commerce has an agent-distributor service that helps about 5,000 U.S. companies a year find an agent or distributor in virtually any country of the world. The second category of agents resides in the manufacturer's country but represents foreign buyers. These agents act as hired purchasing agents for foreign customers operating in the exporter's home market.

Exhibit 3.7

The Fifteen Largest U.S. Exporters

Source: Adapted from "Top 50 U.S. Exporters," *Fortune*, 29 June 1992, p. 95. © 1992 Time Inc. All Rights Reserved.

Company and headquarters	Products	Exports as percentage of total sales
Boeing Seattle	Commercial and military aircraft	60.9
General Motors Detroit	Motor vehicles, parts	9.1
General Electric Fairfield, Conn	Jet engines, turbines, plastics, medical systems	14.3
International Business Machines Armonk, N.Y.	Computers, related equipment	11.8
Ford Motor Dearborn, Mich.	Motor vehicles, parts	8.3
Chrysler Highland Park, Mich.	Motor vehicles, parts	21.0
McDonnell Douglas St. Louis	Aerospace products, missiles, electronic systems	32.9
E.I. Du Pont de Nemours Wilmington, Del.	Specialty chemicals	10.0
Caterpillar Peoria, Ill.	Heavy machinery, engines, turbines	36.4
United Technologies Hartford, Conn.	Jet engines, helicopters, cooling equipment	16.9
Hewlett-Packard Palo Alto, Calif.	Measurement and computation products and systems	22.2
Philip Morris New York	Tobacco, beverages, food products	6.4
Eastman Kodak Rochester, N.Y.	Imaging, chemicals, health products	15.4
Motorola Schaumburg, Ill.	Communications equipment, cellular phones, semiconductors	25.8
Archer-Daniels-Midland Decatur, Ill.	Protein meals, vegetable oils, flour, grain	30.3

Being a successful exporter often requires patience and creativity. Consider, for example, the plight of Maine lobster fishermen who had to keep their lobsters alive while exporting them to Asia. About a quarter of the lobsters shipped to the Orient perished during the journey, even though they traveled in expensive insulated containers. Because fresh lobster brings $40 a pound in Japanese markets, the losses were significant. The solution was ingenious: Construct a rest stop in Hawaii for travel-weary lobsters. Placed in a relay pond containing fresh seawater, lobsters would have a chance to stretch their claws and absorb oxygen. The savings from increased lobster survival rates exceeded the costs to build and operate the lobster hotel.

Licensing

Another effective way for a firm to move into the global arena with relatively little risk is to sell a license to manufacture its product to someone in a foreign country. **Licensing** is the legal process whereby a licensor agrees to let another firm use its manufacturing process, trademarks, patents, trade secrets, or other proprietary knowledge. The licensee, in turn, agrees to pay the licensor a royalty or fee agreed on by both parties.

licensing
Legal process whereby a licensor agrees to let another firm use its manufacturing process, trademarks, patents, trade secrets, or other proprietary knowledge.

Because it has many advantages, U.S. companies have eagerly embraced the licensing concept. For instance, Philip Morris licensed Labatt Brewing Company to produce Miller High Life in Canada. The Spalding Company receives more than $2 million annually from license agreements on its sporting goods. Fruit-of-the-Loom manufactures nothing itself abroad but lends its name through licensing to forty-five consumer items in Japan alone, for at least 1 percent of the licensee's gross sales.

The licensor must make sure it can exercise the control over the licensee's activities needed to ensure proper quality, pricing, distribution, and so on. Licensing may also create a new competitor in the long run, if the licensee decides to void the license agreement. International law is often ineffective in stopping such actions. Two common ways of maintaining effective control over licensees are shipping one or more critical components from the United States or locally registering patents and trademarks by the U.S. firm, not by the licensee.

Franchising is one form of licensing that has grown rapidly in recent years. Over 350 U.S. franchisors operate more than 32,000 outlets in foreign countries, bringing in sales of $6 billion. Over half the international franchises are for fast-food restaurants and business services. As with other forms of licensing, maintaining control over the franchisees is important. For instance, McDonald's was forced to take legal action to buy back its Paris outlets, since the franchisee failed to maintain quality standards. McDonald's claimed the Paris franchise was dirty and provided poor service and food. Investigators found dog droppings inside one outlet, and the franchise charged extra for catsup and hid the straws from customers. Because of the damage to McDonald's reputation, the chain had only 67 outlets in all of France, compared to 270 in Great Britain and 270 in Germany. To reestablish itself, McDonald's decided to project French style and class. The first outlet to appear after McDonald's repurchased its franchise was in a handsome turn-of-the-century building on one of Paris's grand boulevards.

Contract Manufacturing

contract manufacturing
Private-label manufacturing by a foreign company.

Firms that do not want to become involved in licensing or to become heavily involved in global marketing may engage in **contract manufacturing,** which is private-label manufacturing by a foreign company. The foreign company produces

In a joint venture with Mitsubishi Corporation, KFC established over a thousand restaurants in Japan by 1993.
Courtesy of KFC

a certain volume of products to specification, with the domestic firm's brand name on the goods. The domestic company usually handles the marketing. Thus the domestic firm can broaden its global marketing base without investing in overseas plant and equipment. After establishing a solid base, the domestic firm may switch to a joint venture or direct investment.

Joint Venture

joint venture
Arrangement in which a domestic firm buys part of a foreign company or joins with a foreign company to create a new entity.

Joint ventures are quite similar to licensing agreements. In a **joint venture**, the domestic firm buys part of a foreign company or joins with a foreign company to create a new entity. A joint venture is a quick and relatively inexpensive way to "go global."

It also can be very risky. Many joint ventures fail. Others fall victim to a takeover, in which one partner buys out the other. In a survey of 150 companies involved in joint ventures that ended, three-quarters were found to have been taken over by Japanese partners. Gary Hamel, a professor at the London Business School, regards joint ventures as "a race to learn": The partner that learns fastest comes to dominate the relationship and can then rewrite its terms.[35] Thus, a joint venture becomes a new form of competition. The Japanese excel at learning from others, Hamel says. U.S. and European companies are not as good at it.

In a successful joint venture, both parties gain valuable skills from the alliance. In the General Motors–Suzuki joint venture in Canada, for example, both parties have contributed and gained. The alliance, CAMI Automotive, was formed to manufacture low-end cars for the U.S. market. The plant, run by Suzuki management, produces the Geo Metro/Suzuki Swift—the smallest, highest gas-mileage GM car sold in North America—as well as the Geo Tracker/Suzuki Sidekick sport utility vehicle. Through CAMI, Suzuki has gained access to GM's dealer network and an expanded market for parts and components. GM avoided the cost of developing low-end cars and obtained models it needed to revitalize the lower end of its product line and its average fuel economy rating. The CAMI factory may be one of the most productive plants in North America. There GM has learned how Japanese carmakers use work teams, run flexible assembly lines, and manage quality control.[36]

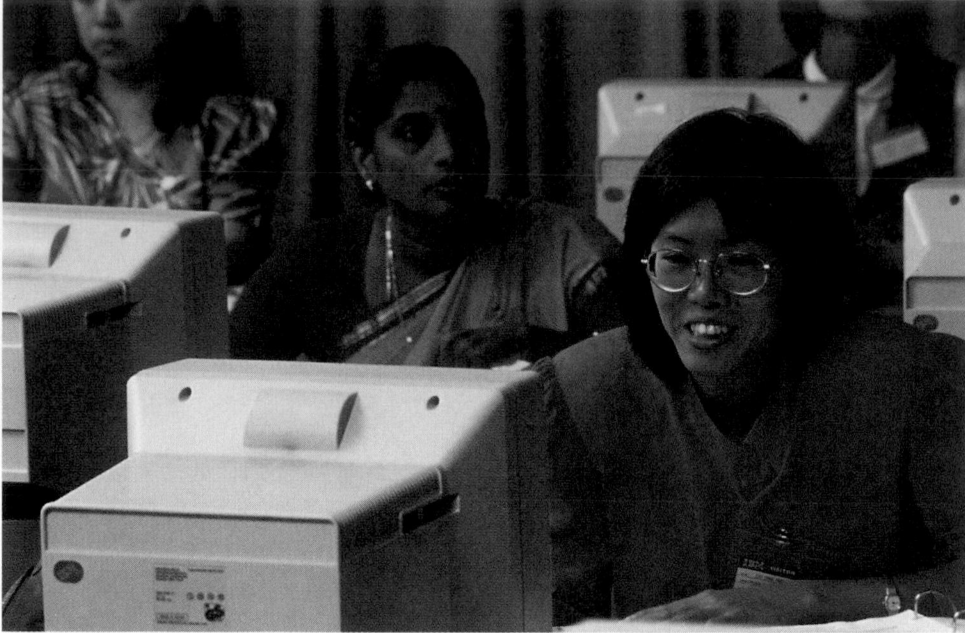

IBM pursues overseas marketing opportunities through 100 percent ownership of overseas facilities (direct foreign investment). For example, office workers receive training at IBM's Information Technology Training Center in Saigon.

Courtesy of International Business Machines Corporation

Direct Investment

direct foreign investment Active ownership of a foreign company or of overseas manufacturing or marketing facilities.

Active ownership of a foreign company or of overseas manufacturing or marketing facilities is **direct foreign investment**. Direct investors have either a controlling interest or a large minority interest in the firm. Thus they have the greatest potential reward and the greatest potential risk. Federal Express lost $1.2 billion in its attempt to build a hub in Europe.[37] It created a huge infrastructure but couldn't generate the package volume to support it. To control losses, the company fired 6,600 international employees and closed offices in over 100 European cities.

Sometimes firms make direct investments because they can find no suitable local partners. Also, direct investments avoid the communication problems and conflicts of interest that can arise with joint ventures. IBM, for instance, requires total ownership of foreign investments because it does not want to share control with local partners.

A firm may make a direct foreign investment by acquiring an interest in an existing company or by building new facilities. It might do so because it has trouble transferring some resource to a foreign operation or getting that resource locally. One important resource is personnel, especially managers. If the local labor market is tight, the firm may buy an entire foreign firm and retain all its employees instead of paying higher salaries than competitors.

The United States is a popular place for direct investment by foreign companies. In 1993 the value of foreign-owned business in the United States was over $425 billion.

6 DEVELOPING A GLOBAL MARKETING MIX

To succeed, firms seeking to enter into foreign trade must still adhere to the principles of the marketing mix. Information gathered on foreign markets through research is the basis for the four P's of global marketing strategy: product, place (distribution), promotion, and price. Marketing managers who understand the advantages and disadvantages of different ways to enter the global market and how the external environment can affect the firm's marketing mix have a better chance of reaching their goals.

The first step in creating a marketing mix is developing a thorough understanding of the global target market. Often this knowledge can be obtained through the same types of marketing research used in the domestic market (see Chapter 8). However, global marketing research is conducted in vastly different environments. Conducting a survey can be difficult in developing countries where telephone ownership is rare and mail delivery is slow or sporadic. Drawing samples based on known population parameters is often difficult because of the lack of data. In some cities in South America, Mexico, and Asia, street maps are unavailable, streets are unidentified, and houses are unnumbered. Moreover, the questions a marketer can ask may differ in other cultures. In some cultures, people tend to be more private than in the United States and do not like to respond to personal questions on surveys. For instance, in France questions about one's age and income are considered especially rude.

Product and Promotion Considerations

With the proper information, a good marketing mix can be developed. One important decision is whether to alter the product or the promotion for the global marketplace.

One Product, One Message

Some marketers adopt the strategy of global marketing standardization, which was discussed earlier. For instance, one Pepsi campaign concentrated on individuals trying to master difficult skills. A commercial featured a boy trying to conquer a spirited black horse. The commercial had no voice-over and no dialogue, but a theme song carried the message "Pepsi tastes going over the top." The lyrics linking the achievement of the individual with the taste of the product were the only element that needed to be translated for different markets.

Global media—especially satellite and cable TV networks like Cable News Network International, MTV Networks, and British Sky Broadcasting—make it possible to beam advertising to audiences unreachable a few years ago. "Eighteen-year-olds in Paris have more in common with eighteen-year-olds in New York than with their own parents," says William Roedy, director of MTV Europe, whose 200 advertisers almost all run unified, English-language campaigns in the twenty-eight nations it reaches. "They buy the same products, go to the same movies, listen to the same music, sip the same colas. Global advertising merely works on that premise.[38]

Global campaigns vary widely in scope. At one extreme were Coca-Cola's Winter Olympics sing-along commercials, beamed in twelve languages to 3.8 billion viewers in 131 countries.[39] At the other is Wolverine World Wide's recent campaign to promote a new line of outdoor apparel and footwear across Asia, Europe, and the Mideast. The ads, run in thirty countries, feature the slogan "You're only human" and compare animals in their natural garb with people in Wolverine's protective clothing. Unified themes like these not only spur short-term sales but also help build long-term product identity and save on production costs.

Even a one-product, one-message strategy may call for some changes to suit local needs, such as variations in the product's measurement units, package sizes, and labeling. Pillsbury, for example, changed the measurement unit for its cake mixes because adding "cups of" has no meaning in many developing countries. Also, in developing countries packages are often smaller so consumers with limited incomes can buy them. For instance, cigarettes, chewing gum, and razor blades may be sold individually instead of in packages.

Product Invention

In the context of global marketing, product invention can be taken to mean either creating a new product for a market or drastically changing an existing product. For the Japanese market, Nabisco had to remove the cream filling from its Oreo cookies because children there thought they were too sweet. Apple Computer had difficulty penetrating the Japanese personal computer market for many years. It refused to pay Japanese software developers to convert their programs to run on the Macintosh or to lend developers machines so they could write programs directly for Apple's computers. After Apple formed close ties with software companies, it saw sales take off.

Consumers in different countries use products differently. For example, in many countries clothing is worn much longer between washing than in the United States, so a more durable fabric must be produced and marketed. For Peru, Goodyear developed a tire that contains a higher percentage of natural rubber than tires manufactured elsewhere and has better treads in order to handle the tough driving conditions.

Adapting Messages

Another strategy is to maintain the same basic product but alter the promotional strategy. Bicycles and motorcycles are mainly pleasure vehicles in the United States. In many parts of the world, however, they are a family's major mode of transportation. Thus promotion in these countries should stress durability and efficiency. In contrast, U.S. advertising may emphasize escaping and having fun.

Global marketers often find that promotion is a daunting task in some countries. For example, commercial television time is readily available in Canada but severely restricted in Germany. Until recently, marketers in Indonesia had only a subscription channel with few viewers (120,000 out of a nation of 180 million people). Because of this limited television audience, several marketers, such as the country's main Toyota dealer, had to develop direct-mail marketing campaigns to reach their target market.

Some cultures view a product as having less value if it has to be advertised. The hard-sell tactics and sexual themes so common in U.S. advertising are taboo in many countries. Procter & Gamble's advertisements for Cheer detergents were voted least popular in Japan because they used hard-sell testimonials. The negative reaction forced P&G to withdraw Cheer from the Japanese market. In the Middle East, pictures of women in print advertisements have been covered with censor's ink. In other nations, claims that seem exaggerated by U.S. standards are commonplace. On the other hand, Germany does not permit advertisers to state that their products are "best" or "better" than those of competitors, a description commonly used in U.S. advertising.

Language barriers, translation problems, and cultural differences have generated numerous headaches for international marketing managers. Consider these examples:

- A toothpaste claiming to give users white teeth was especially inappropriate in many areas of Southeast Asia, where the well-to-do chew betel nuts and black teeth are a sign of higher social status.
- Procter & Gamble's Japanese advertising for Camay soap nearly devastated the product. In one commercial a man meeting a woman for the first time immediately compared her skin to that of a fine porcelain doll. Although the ad had worked in other Asian countries, the man came across as rude and disrespectful.

- Pepsi-Cola's slogan "Come alive with Pepsi" translated into German as "Come out of the grave with Pepsi."[40]
- Coca-Cola took out full-page ads in Greek newspapers apologizing for an earlier ad that showed the Parthenon's white marble columns tapered like a Coke bottle. Greeks have great respect for their ancient temples and were highly indignant. The general secretary of the Greek Culture Ministry said, "Whoever insults the Parthenon insults Greece."[41]

Adapting Products

Another alternative for global marketers is to alter a basic product to meet local conditions. For example, the best-selling doll in the United States is Barbie, but initially she did not sell well in Japan. Parents and children felt that the doll's breasts were too big and the legs too long. After making minor modifications and changing Barbie's eyes from blue to dark brown, Mattel sold 2 million Barbie dolls in Japan in just two years. In spite of this apparent success, Mattel still believed the sales of Barbie were not as high as they should be. Since then, the company's ongoing marketing research has shown that Japanese consumers, particularly younger ones, have become much more receptive to Western products and trends. As a result, in 1991 Mattel decided to again market the more voluptuous, blue-eyed Barbie that it sells in all its other markets.[42]

Pricing

Once marketing managers have determined a global product and promotion strategy, they can select the remainder of the marketing mix. Pricing presents some unique problems in the global sphere. Exporters must not only cover their production costs but also consider transportation costs, insurance, taxes, and tariffs. When deciding on a final price, marketers must also determine what customers are willing to spend on a particular product. Marketers also need to ensure that their foreign buyers will pay them.

Since developing nations lack mass-purchasing power, selling to them often poses special pricing problems. Sometimes a product can be simplified in order to lower the price substantially. However, the firm must not assume that low-income countries are willing to accept lower quality. Although the nomads of the Sahara are very poor, they still buy expensive fabrics to make their clothing. Their survival in harsh conditions and extreme temperatures requires this expense. Additionally, at least a small number of expensive luxury items can be sold almost anywhere.

dumping
Practice of selling products either below cost or below their sale price in their domestic market.

Some companies overproduce certain items and end up dumping them in the international market. **Dumping** occurs when products are sold either below cost or below their sale price in their domestic market. Dumping of products by foreign producers is illegal in the United States and Europe. During the 1990s, Japanese producers were charged with dumping computer chips in the U.S. market and VCRs and compact disc players in Europe.

Countertrade

countertrade
Form of trade in which all or part of the payment for goods or services is in the form of other goods or services.

Global trade does not always involve cash. Countertrade is a fast-growing way to conduct global business. In **countertrade,** all or part of the payment for goods or services is in the form of other goods or services. Countertrade is thus a form of barter (swapping goods for goods), an age-old practice whose origins have been traced back to cave dwellers. The U.S. Commerce Department says that roughly 30 percent of all global trade is countertrade.[43] In fact, both India and China have made

billion-dollar government purchasing lists, with most of the goods to be paid for by countertrade.

A common type of countertrade is straight *barter*. For example, PepsiCo sends Pepsi syrup to Russian bottling plants and in payment gets Stolichnaya vodka, which is then marketed in the West. Another form of countertrade is *compensation agreements*. Typically, a company provides technology and equipment for a plant in a developing nation and agrees to take full or partial payment in goods produced by that plant. For example, General Tire Company supplied equipment and know-how for a Rumanian truck tire plant. In turn, General Tire sold the tires it received from the plant in the United States under the Victoria brand name. Pierre Cardin gives technical advice to China in exchange for silk and cashmere. In these cases, both sides benefit even though they don't use cash.

Distribution

Solving promotional, price, and product problems does not guarantee global marketing success. The product still has to get adequate distribution. The Japanese distribution system is considered the most complicated in the world. Imported goods wind their way through layers of agents, wholesalers, and retailers. The distribution channels seem to be based on historical and traditional patterns of socially arranged tradeoffs, which Japanese officials claim are very hard for the government to change. Some marketers have tried to bypass traditional channels in Japan to ensure that their products get adequate exposure and sales support. Campbell's Soup Company, owner of Pepperidge Farm cookies, found that the cookies distributed through traditional import channels were out of date and broken by the time they reached consumers. Consequently, Campbell's began selling cookies directly to 7-Eleven stores, which are very popular in Japan. Sales immediately rose to over $16 million annually.

Retail institutions also may differ from what a company is used to in its domestic market. The terms *department store* and *supermarket* may refer to types of retail

Obtaining adequate distribution may be difficult in developing countries like Thailand, location of this citrus seller's floating market.
© 1991 Superstock

MARKETING AND SMALL BUSINESS

Opportunity for Small Businesses

Global marketing is not only the wave of the future for small firms but also the reality of the present. A small firm cannot afford to ignore foreign markets. Certain opportunities abroad are more profitable than those at home.

A small firm can be just as successful in global markets as a large business. The idea that global markets are for big business only is quite damaging to small firms' efforts to market abroad.

Exporting is the main way for a small business to enter the global market. For a better perspective on their potential for exporting, small-business owners should ask the following questions:

- What domestic forces are likely to make exporting more attractive in the future?
- At what level of commitment can the company most profitably enter exporting?
- If exporting is undertaken, what strains would be created on the company, and how can they be met?
- What domestic sales and profit opportunities exist? What costs, risks, and returns can be expected?
- What features of the product currently being sold in the United States provide a competitive edge in overseas markets?
- Is the market being sought likely to be a country or a group of buyers?
- What kind of buyers is this product likely to appeal to? How can they be identified?
- What are the consequences for the company of product modification?

outlets that are very different from those found in the United States. Japanese supermarkets, for example, are large multistory buildings that sell not only food but also clothing, furniture, and home appliances. Department stores are even larger outlets. Unlike their U.S. counterparts, however, they emphasize foodstuffs and operate a restaurant on the premises. For a variety of reasons, U.S.-type retail outlets do not exist or are impractical in developing countries. For instance, consumers may not have the storage space to keep food for several days. Refrigerators, when available, are usually small and do not allow for bulk storage.

Channels of distribution and the physical infrastructure are also inadequate in many developing nations. In China, for example, most goods are carried on poles or human backs, in wheelbarrows and handcarts, or increasingly (and this is an important advance) on bicycles. In recent years much effort has gone into extending the Chinese rail system, but many of the new lines are more strategic than commercial, and most trains are still pulled by steam locomotives.

LOOKING BACK

Look back at the story about Gillette at the beginning of the chapter. International markets often represent excellent growth opportunities for companies like Gillette. With world trade running above $4 trillion a year, companies that do not take part in global marketing are missing a great opportunity. Having a global vision and global marketing are the wave of the future. Managers possessing a global vision means that they understand target markets, economic groupings, and distribution networks on a worldwide basis.

Where it can be applied, global marketing standardization of product lines offers significant economic benefits. However, different cultures, languages, levels of economic development, and distribution channels in global markets usually require either new products or modified products. Pricing, promotion, and distribution strategies must often be altered as well.

KEY TERMS

balance of payments 64
balance of trade 64
boycott 73
buyer for export 81
contract manufacturing 82
countertrade 87
direct foreign investment 84
dumping 87
exchange control 73
export agent 81
export broker 81
exporting 81
fully industrialized society 72
global marketing 62
global marketing standardization 67
global vision 62
industrializing society 71
joint venture 83
keiretsu 74
licensing 82
market grouping 74
multinational corporation(MNC) 64
North American Free Trade Agreement (NAFTA) 75
preindustrial society 70
quota 73
takeoff economy 71
tariff 73
trade agreement 74
trade deficit 64
traditional society 70
United Europe 78

SUMMARY

1 Discuss the importance of global marketing. Businesspeople who adopt a global vision are better able to identify global marketing opportunities, understand the nature of global networks, and engage foreign competition in domestic markets. In addition, U.S. exports help us reduce the trade deficit and the balance of payments problem.

2 Discuss the impact of multinationals on the world economy. Multinational corporations are international traders that regularly operate across national borders. Because of their vast size and financial, technological, and material resources, multinational corporations have a great influence on the world economy. They have the ability to overcome trade problems, save on labor costs, and tap new technology.

3 Explain the differences between the traditional marketing concept and the global marketing concept. Multinational corporations, for the most part, have adopted a global marketing concept, which means effectively marketing goods and services across national boundaries. It may or may not mean offering a globally standardized marketing mix. In contrast, the global marketing standardization concept presumes that standardized products can be sold globally because the markets of the world are becoming more alike. In practice, global marketing standardization appears to have its limitations; "global" markets typically exist only among certain nations and often require national modifications. Thus multinational corporations that have adopted a global marketing strategy for certain products still market the majority of their goods and services regionally or locally.

4 Describe the external environment facing global marketers. Global marketers face the same environmental factors as they do domestically: culture, level of economic and technological development, political structure, demography, and natural resources. Cultural considerations include societal values, attitudes and beliefs, language, and customary business practices. A country's economic and technological status depends on its stage of industrial development: traditional society, preindustrial society, takeoff economy, industrializing society, or fully industrialized society. Political structure is shaped by political ideology and such policies as tariffs, quotas, boycotts, exchange controls, trade agreements, and market groupings. Demographic variables include population, income distribution, and growth rate.

5 Identify the various ways of entering the global marketplace. Firms use the following strategies to enter global markets, in descending order of risk and profit: direct investment, joint venture, contract manufacturing, licensing, and export.

6 List the basic elements involved in the development of a global marketing mix. A firm's major consideration is how much it will adjust the four P's—product, promotion, place (distribution), and price—within each country. One strategy is to use one product and one promotion message worldwide. A second strategy is to create new products for global markets. A third strategy is to keep the product basically the same but alter the promotional message.

Review Questions

1. Explain the difference between the balance of payments and the balance of trade.
2. Identify the environmental factors that affect the global marketing mix.
3. Explain the purpose of trade agreements. How are trade agreements different from tariffs?
4. Describe the risks and benefits of entering global markets through direct investment.
5. Briefly describe the product and promotional strategies used by global marketers.
6. Identify unique distribution problems that U.S. marketers face in other countries.

Discussion and Writing Questions

1. Why is it important that U.S. businesses become more involved in global marketing?
2. Discuss the role of multinational corporations in developing nations.
3. How viable is global marketing standardization for multinational corporations?
4. You are marketing manager for a consumer products firm that is about to undertake its first expansion abroad. Write a memo for your staff reminding them of the role culture will play in the new venture. Give examples.
5. Describe how differences in natural resources can affect the global marketing environment.
6. What is meant by "having a global vision"? Why is it important?
7. Your state senator has asked you to contribute to her constituents' newsletter a brief article that answers the question "Will there ever be a 'United States of Europe'?" Write a draft of your article, and include reasons why or why not.

CASES

3.1 Philip Morris Companies

The annual consumption of tobacco products in the United States is declining at the rate of 4 percent per year. Yet consumption is increasing abroad at about the same rate. William Campbell, CEO of Philip Morris U.S.A., is excited about the strong growth of foreign markets. The company has a 12 percent market share in Japan; its Lark brand is the number-one import in Japan. Taiwan, Thailand, Korea, and China are particularly attractive markets to tobacco manufacturers. In fact, these markets are so attractive that Philip Morris announced plans to spend $400 million in a plant expansion to meet foreign demand.

In Taiwan, 55 percent of adult men smoke, compared to less than 10 percent of women. Teenagers represent a growing market for U.S. brands. "Children have the dream to become Americanized," explains Dr. Ted Chen, professor of public health at the University of Massachusetts. "They smoke the American Dream." It is estimated that of those teens who smoke, 80 percent smoke U.S. brands.

In marketing cigarettes abroad, Philip Morris has relied on marketing techniques that are banned in the United States. In Japan the company runs cinema ads featuring actor James Coburn inviting consumers to "Speak Lark." In Malaysia, where tobacco ads on television are illegal, the company uses TV advertising to promote image, not products. RJR Nabisco tried to stage a concert in Taipei where the price of admission was five empty packs of Winstons. A local health group forced RJR Nabisco to retract its sponsorship of the concert. Models distributing free samples are not uncommon on the streets of these countries, but this practice has been banned in many U.S. cities.

Antismoking activists now have the Globallink network, a high-tech system implemented by the American Cancer Society. This network allows news and information about the tobacco control movement to travel twenty-four hours a day worldwide. Companies like Philip Morris need to worry not only about the impact of the tobacco control movement abroad but also about fallout here in the United States.

In response to Philip Morris's overseas marketing activities, a U.S. group, Stop Teenage Addiction to Tobacco, is now organizing a boycott of all products made by Philip Morris and its subsidiaries, including Kraft General Foods. Campbell responds, "We would no more insist that the laws of the United States apply in other countries than we would want the laws of other countries to apply in the United States. To do so would be paternalism at best and imperialism at worst."

Questions

1. Should companies like Philip Morris have to follow U.S. regulations when marketing products abroad? What potential problems do you see with your answer?

2. What problems does Philip Morris have in developing a global marketing strategy?

3. What cultural considerations are most important to Philip Morris?

Suggested Reading

Laura Bird, "Even Overseas, Tobacco Has Nowhere to Hide," *Adweek's Marketing Week*, 1 April 1991, pp. 4–5.

3.2 PepsiCo (A)

Video title: *The Pepsi/Soviet Partnership*

PepsiCo, Inc.
Anderson Hill Road
Purchase, NY 10517

SIC codes: 2087 Concentrates, drink
2086 Carbonated beverages
5812 Fast food restaurants
2096 Snack foods

Number of employees: 266,000

1993 revenues: Approximately $20 billion ($7 billion in soft-drink sales)

Major brands: Pepsi, Diet Pepsi, Crystal Pepsi, Mountain Dew

Largest competitors: Coca-Cola, Dr. Pepper

Background

From its beginnings in 1898, Pepsi has always battled Coca-Cola in the cola wars. Now the cola wars are spreading out across the world. In 1959, Pepsi was first introduced in the Soviet Union at the Moscow trade fair. After fourteen years of negotiations between Pepsi and the Soviet Union, in 1973, Pepsi signed a countertrade agreement with the Soviet Union. By 1985, there were twenty Pepsi-Soviet plants throughout the Soviet Union. Within five years, that number had doubled to more than forty plants. The strong partnership between the Soviets and Pepsi is based on mutual trust.

Industry

Industry experts predict that the U.S. market for soft drinks will grow 2 percent per year. Therefore, for a soft-drink producer to significantly increase its market share, it must steal customers from competing products. For years, Coca-Cola and Pepsi have battled it out in both consumer and restaurant markets. If soft-drink producers want larger sales growth potential, they will have to develop international markets. One of these growing markets is the former Soviet Union.

PepsiCo

Pepsi has the jump on Coke in the former Soviet Union. Coca-Cola announced plans in 1992 to open soft-drink operations in Moscow. Pepsi already has more than fifty bottling operations in the former Soviet Union. The strength of the partnership between Pepsi and its Russian bottling operations will continue to provide the company with a competitive advantage. In addition to assisting its bottling operators with modern production facilities, Pepsi has aided Russia in establishing quality control laboratories to help test all nonalcoholic beverages produced in the country.

The biggest problem facing Pepsi in these Soviet operations has been repatriating its profits. The Russian ruble is not a traded currency, and the government does not allow rubles to be exported. For these reasons, all Russian profits must be spend within the country. In a unique trade agreement that began in 1972, Pepsi traded its Pepsi syrup concentrate for Stolichnaya Russian Vodka and the exclusive rights to import and distribute Stoli in the United States. Although greatley modified because of the changing Russian economic landscape, this trade has allowed PepsiCo to export syrup concentrate to Russia and to supply vodka to the United States. PepsiCo profits through concentrate sales to the Russians, and this agreement has also been very beneficial to the Russian economy, because profits earned during the manufacturing process on both sides of the trade stay in Russia.

Questions

1. What problems typically plague companies like PepsiCo in taking their products overseas? How has Pepsi attempted to resolve these problems?

2. What advantages does Pepsi have in allowing the Russians to bottle and distribute its product?

3. How would you describe the arrangement between the Russians and PepsiCo? Give reasons to support your position.

References

Million Dollar Directory 1993 (Parsippany, NJ: Dun & Bradstreet Information Services, 1993).

Michael Parks, "Bloc-Buster Deal," *LA Times,* 21 July 1992, p. 1.

Standard & Poor's Industry Surveys (New York: Standard & Poor's Corporation, October 1993).

PART ONE

CRITICAL THINKING CASE

Coca-Cola

Sue Cisco

The U.S. soft-drink industry is, like all other industries, dynamic. Many forces can change business conditions. Historically, soft-drink manufacturers in the United States have been able to increase sales by placing their products in as many stores and restaurants as possible. However, fewer and fewer locations are left that don't already carry soft drinks. The result is what marketers call a "mature" market. Another problem the industry is facing is changing consumer preferences. We now prefer lighter, less sweet, and healthier drinks. Finally, the average U.S. consumer already drinks two eight-ounce glasses of carbonated drinks per day.

U.S. soft-drink manufacturers are trying strategies that they feel will enable them to maintain profits in the face of slowing population growth and changing consumer tastes. But Coke and Pepsi, which together account for about 74 percent of the total soft-drink market, are following different strategies. PepsiCo has chosen to diversify through new-product development and is also launching aggressive advertising campaigns designed to gain market share for Pepsi. Coca-Cola, on the other hand, has chosen to increase international operations and expand domestically through joint ventures.

The reunification of Germany created a once-in-a-lifetime marketing opportunity for Coke and Pepsi. The East German soft-drink market was closed to outside manufacturers for nearly forty years.

Even before removal of the Berlin Wall, Coca-Cola had approached the East German government. Although Coca-Cola was not able to begin operations in East Germany at that time, the company did collect some valuable marketing information that enabled it to pursue the market when it eventually opened up.

When the Wall came down, 17 million thirsty East German residents rushed to try the products they had seen advertised on West German television. Consumer surveys conducted at this time indicated that Coca-Cola was a name recognized by 99 percent of East Germans. Other market research indicated that East Germans were dissatisfied with the two government-produced soft drinks and were particularly interested in all Western products. Coca-Cola was also aware of its strong position in West Germany, where 11 percent of the entire company's profits had been generated in the previous year. (Coca-Cola outsells Pepsi 7 to 1 in Europe.)

Despite its advantages, Coca-Cola knew it had to act quickly to ensure success in eastern Germany. Management was aware that restaurants and small outlets would choose to serve just one cola drink, and it would likely be the first one to enter the market. Coca-Cola trucks were placed at border crossings so East Berliners, who were seeing western Germany for the first time in forty years, could be presented with cases and six-packs of free Coke. At one location, 70,000 cans were handed out in just a few hours. This goodwill gesture paved the way for Coke representatives trying to convince eastern German merchants and vendors to carry Coke products.

Coke's advertising and promotion strategy was designed to build on its strong position with restaurant owners and increase demand for Coke products. In East Berlin, sidewalk vendors began carrying signs that said "Drink Coca-Cola," and restaurants and cafes proudly displayed red-and-white umbrellas with the famous Coke logo. To reflect eastern Germans' preference for Western products, Coke used the slogan "You can't beat the feeling"—in English.

Since Coke was introduced in eastern Germany, sales have skyrocketed. Before retail sales actually began, fewer than 200,000 cases of Coke products were sold annually, and they were sold in only a few locations. From the day in mid-February 1990 when retail sales began until the end of the year, Coca-Cola sold an astonishing 126 million cases of product. Coca-Cola is anticipating that by 1995 this figure will top 600 million cases.

One of the keys to Coke's success in the eastern German soft-drink market was the proper use of market research. Another significant element was the ability to work with the local government. Unlike its competitors and many other Western companies, Coca-Cola was willing to build production facilities and distribution networks within East Germany's borders and thereby create 1,500 jobs for East German citizens. Additional jobs were provided by giving contracts for packaging, sugar, and pallet manufacturing to local suppliers. Coca-Cola endeared itself to the East German government as well as its citizens by becoming a significant corporate taxpayer and a buyer of local goods and services.

Coca-Cola can attribute its international success to many factors. According to experts, the company's strength is reacting quickly to the opportunities that arise. And by hiring local managers who understand the business and the region, Coca-Cola is able to succeed abroad.

Questions

1. Evaluate Coca-Cola's expansion into the easern Germany market by examining the conditions of the U.S. soft-drink market.
2. Compare the U.S. consumer to the consumer in unified Germany. Plan a market strategy for the German consumer.
3. Defend Coca-Cola's decision to use the U.S. slogan "You can't beat the feeling" in its lead-off campaign in the German market.
4. Predict Coca-Cola's future success in Germany. Evaluate the impact of Pepsi entering this market.
5. Judging from Coke's success in Germany, what other U.S. products do you think could be marketed there? Evaluate the threats and opportunities they will encounter.

Suggested Readings

Alison Fahey. "Thirsting for Something New," *Superbrands*, 1992, pp. 53–55.

Ferdinand Protzman. "Coke's Splash in Eastern Germany," *New York Times*, 3 May 1991, p. D6.

Patricia Sellers. "Coke Gets Off Its Can in Europe," *Fortune*, 13 August 1992, pp. 68–72.

PART ONE GLOBAL MARKETING CASE

The Düsseldorf Trade Show

Linda B. Catlin, Wayne State University
Thomas F. White, Regis University

Brown Automation Company, located in Davenport, Iowa, manufactures transfer presses* for the automotive and appliance industries. The company employs 125 people and has annual sales of $11 million. Currently, company representatives are making plans to participate in a large manufacturing trade show in Düsseldorf, Germany.

During the last three years, Brown's sales department has received numerous telephone and written requests for information about the company's products from European and Japanese firms. Several of these firms have called back after receiving the Brown sales literature and asked that a Brown representative contact the foreign firm when the representative visits Europe or Japan. Until now, Brown has never sent anyone outside North America on sales trips or to attend trade shows, although the company has sold its equipment to several Canadian firms.

Earlier this year, the company president, Jim Nelson, decided that the company should participate in the Düsseldorf trade show. His decision was based on two considerations: first, domestic sales are down 15 percent because of cutbacks in the automotive industry, and second, the increasing number of requests for information from foreign firms convinced him that there was a large potential market in Europe for Brown's products. Jim began preparing for the trade show by calling together Tom Messaic, marketing manager; John Harper, engineering manager; and Alex Carrero, controller.

This group of managers first interviewed two U.S. consultants who had worked with other U.S. companies in setting up marketing operations in Europe, including Germany, and who had contacts throughout Europe in several industries. When the Brown trade show team discussed the pros and cons of hiring one of these consultants to manage the company's participation in the Düsseldorf trade show, Tom and John were in favor, but Jim and Alex argued that the $15,000 fees were too high. As Jim said, "We've participated in many shows here in the United States, and shows can't be that much different in Germany. I know my managers can handle the Düsseldorf show on their own. Tom, I want you to take charge of this one, and John, I want you to work closely with him to cover the technical aspects related to equipment."

Tom began his preparations by calling a meeting of his staff. His marketing coordinator, Janice Beacon, suggested that they contact the local university to find someone who was familiar with German culture.

"When I studied in France during my junior year in college, I found some big differences between the way we do things here and the way the French do those same things," she said. "I think we need to be aware of how Germans conduct business differently than U.S. citizens do."

"I'm sure you're right, Janice," Tom replied, "but right now I think we need to concentrate on some of the technical details of putting together this trade show in Germany. Remember, we have only four months to figure out how to get our equipment there, what the booth will look like, and who we'll send to staff the booth. And Alex has given us a pretty small budget to do all this, so we need to be careful about how we spend the money.

"I've drawn up a list of our usual planning areas for trade shows," Tom continued. "And I've assigned each one of you to take charge of one or two of these areas. I'd like you to put together a plan for covering these at the Düsseldorf show. We'll meet again in two weeks to

* A transfer press is a customized, automated piece of industrial equipment used to move a product through two or more steps in the manufacturing process.

go over what you've done. Thanks for your input today."

Tom assigned responsibility for the following list of trade show areas to members of his staff:

- Publications, including sales and technical literature for the company's equipment, information about the firm, and business cards
- Staffing requirements for the booth and the hospitality suite at the nearby hotel
- Physical setup of the booth, including size, equipment displays, and backdrop
- Promotional items and giveaways for businesspeople visiting the booth

To the Student

Assume that you are Tom Messaic, marketing manager for Brown Automation. What issues and questions should your staff members bring up for each of the areas associated with the trade show in Düsseldorf? What are the details that need to be decided on in each area? What special considerations are necessary since this trade show is in Germany and not in the United States? Considering your answers to these questions, what will you recommend to Mr. Nelson, the company president, regarding Brown's participation in the Düsseldorf trade show this year?

PART TWO

ANALYZING MARKETING OPPORTUNITIES

55095 03010 3
VICTOR

CHAPTER 4

Consumer Decision Making

LEARNING OBJECTIVES

After studying this chapter, you should be able to

1. Explain why marketing managers should understand consumer behavior.
2. Identify the types of consumer buying decisions.
3. Analyze the components of the consumer decision-making process.
4. Explain the consumer's postpurchase evaluation process.
5. Discuss the importance of high and low involvement in buying decisions.
6. Identify and understand the individual and social factors that affect consumer buying decisions.

It's no secret that the excesses of the 1980s are out and the theme of the 1990s is back-to-basic values. These days, marketers of brands like Häagen-Dazs and BMW, which once stood for self-indulgence and conspicuous consumption, are scrambling to cope with the new values. As baby boomers have aged and had children of their own, family values have replaced the quest for self-gratification, and status symbols have become less fashionable. Consumers are now more concerned about global problems, such as the deteriorating environment and world hunger.

The shop-till-you-drop decade of excess, credit card debt, baby millionaires, and their wannabes have given way to a new age of moderation and caution. Consumers are now borrowing less, shopping carefully, and saving more. After years of working second shifts, making deals, making money, and blowing it all on Saturday night, consumers are now taking time for the simple pleasures they've been putting off, scaling back their desires, and looking for value. Gardening, for instance, is blossoming across the country as baby boomers discover the stay-at-home hobby that's inexpensive, is environmentally correct, and can increase the resale value of the home.

As a result, companies are now stressing real product attributes in their advertising instead of a fantasy-laden lifestyle. Marketers from Club Med to Häagen-Dazs are pitching to families and older individuals. Experts predict that those products with a value separate from their brand image are the ones that will flourish.

BMW, the "ultimate driving machine" in the 1980s, has cut prices on some of its existing models and has even introduced two "entry-level" models that sell for around $20,000. New ads for BMW promote the car's technical attributes, safety, and resale value rather than its place in the glamorous lifestyle. Club Med, stuck with an image of catering only to "swinging singles," is trying hard to reposition itself to married couples and families. Commercials show kids, families, and older couples at Club Med locations in beautiful tropical settings. Many of its facilities now provide full-time day care.[1]

What effect do you think consumers' values and lifestyles have on the consumer decision-making process? How do marketers respond to the constantly changing values of U.S. consumers? What other individual factors affect what consumers buy? Questions like these will be answered as you read this chapter on the consumer decision-making process and its influences.

1 UNDERSTANDING CONSUMER BEHAVIOR

Consumers' lives are in a constant state of flux. As each generation grows and matures, it may adopt values and lifestyles different from those of the previous generation. What is important also changes as consumers progress through the life cycle. Finally, consumers differ according to their demographic and social characteristics.

If a marketing manager's basic task is to create a proper marketing mix for a well-defined market, on what basis should the manager define that market? A marketer must have a thorough knowledge of consumer behavior to effectively accomplish this task. **Consumer behavior** describes the processes used to make purchase decisions, as well as to use and dispose of the purchased good or service. The study of consumer behavior also includes the analysis of factors that influence purchase decisions and product use.

consumer behavior
Processes a consumer uses to make purchase decisions, as well as to use and dispose of the purchased good or service; also includes factors that influence purchase decisions and the use of products.

The ability to create a good and to persuade the market to buy it instead of buying competitors' offerings requires insight into the consumer purchase process. Knowledge of consumer behavior reduces uncertainty when creating the marketing mix. For example, a manager can better anticipate the impact of a price increase on a product's quality image if he or she understands consumer decision-making processes. Similarly, an appreciation of culture, social class, and the role of family can help advertisers create more effective promotional campaigns.

2 TYPES OF CONSUMER DECISION BEHAVIOR

An understanding of consumer behavior begins with learning the different levels of decision making. All consumer buying decisions generally fall into three broad categories: routine response behavior, limited decision making, and extensive decision making. When buying frequently purchased, low-cost goods and services, consumers generally use **routine response behavior.** These goods and services can also be called low-involvement products, since consumers spend little search and decision time to make the purchase. Usually, buyers are familiar with several different brands in the product category but stick with one brand. A parent, for example, will not stand at the cereal shelf in the grocery store for twenty minutes thinking about which brand of cereal to buy for the children. Instead, he or she will walk by the shelf, find the family's usual brand, and put it into the cart.

routine response behavior
Type of decision making exhibited by consumers buying frequently purchased, low-cost goods and services; requires little search and decision time.

limited decision making
Type of decision making that requires a moderate amount of time for gathering information and deliberating about an unfamiliar brand in a familiar product category.

extensive decision making
Most complex type of consumer decision making, used when buying an unfamiliar, expensive product or an infrequently bought item; requires use of several criteria for evaluating options and much time for seeking information.

Suppose the children's usual brand of cereal, Kellogg's Corn Flakes, is unavailable in the grocery store. Completely out of cereal at home, the buyer now must select another brand. Getting information about an unfamiliar brand in a familiar product category is called **limited decision making**. This type of decision making requires a moderate amount of time for gathering information and deliberating. Our buyer may select several brands similar to Kellogg's Corn Flakes, such as Corn Chex or Cheerios, to compare their nutritional value and calories and to decide whether the children will like the new cereal before making a final selection. Limited decision making is also used for products bought only occasionally, such as tires, cosmetics, and books.

Consumers practice **extensive decision making** when buying an unfamiliar, expensive product or an infrequently bought item. This process is the most complex type of consumer decision making. Buyers use several criteria for evaluating their options and spend much time seeking information. Buying a home or a car requires extensive decision making.

Consumer decision making is not all alike. *(left)* The couple buying new golf clubs is using limited decision making, which requires some time for gathering information and analyzing it. *(right)* A big purchase like a car usually requires extensive decision making.

(left) © Superstock; *(right)* © 1992 Bill Bachmann/ProFiles West

The type of decision making that consumers use does not necessarily remain constant. For instance, if a routinely purchased product no longer satisfies, consumers may practice limited or extensive decision making to switch to another brand. And people who first use extensive decision making may then use limited or routine decision making for future purchases.

3 THE CONSUMER DECISION-MAKING PROCESS

consumer decision-making process Step-by-step process used by consumers when buying goods or services.

When buying products, consumers follow the **consumer decision-making process** shown in Exhibit 4.1: (1) stimulus, (2) problem recognition, (3) information search, (4) evaluation of alternatives, (5) purchase, (6) outcome, and (7) postpurchase behavior.

Note that the act of buying something is only one step in the process. Not all consumer decision making leads to an actual purchase; the consumer can end the process at any time. Keep in mind, too, that not all purchase decisions proceed through all steps of the process. Typically, people engaged in extensive decision making go through all seven steps, but those engaged in limited decision making and routine response behavior may skip some steps.

Exhibit 4.1

The Consumer Decision-Making Process

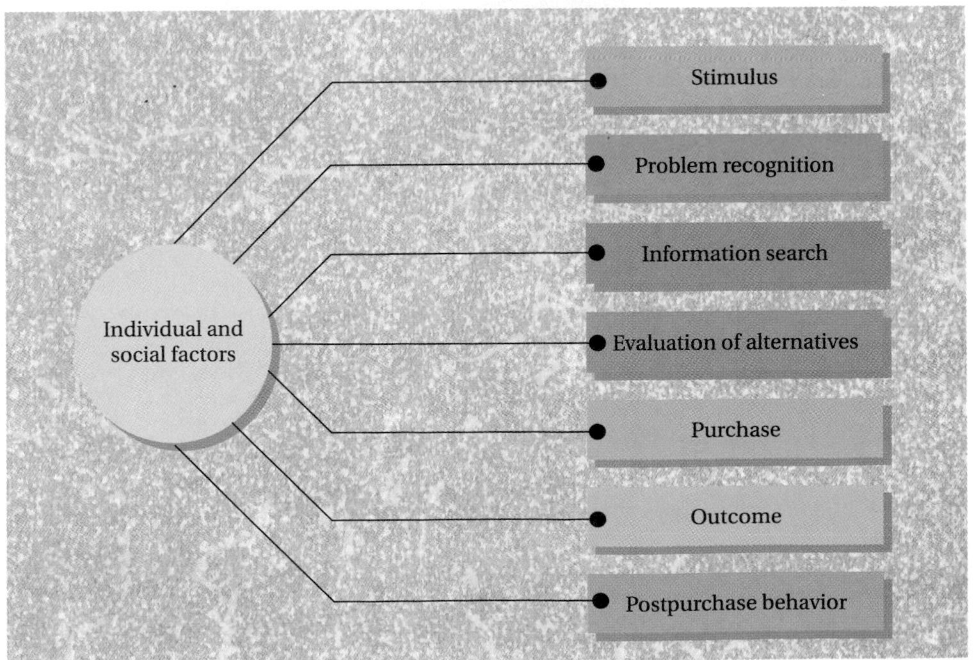

stimulus
Any unit of input affecting the five senses: sight, smell, taste, touch, hearing.

internal stimuli
Sensory input stemming from fundamental needs within the individual, such as hunger and thirst.

external stimuli
Sensory input stemming from sources outside the individual, such as packaging or advertising.

problem recognition
Result of an imbalance between actual and desired states.

need
Anything an individual depends on to function efficiently; root of all human behavior.

want
Recognition of an unfulfilled need and a product that will satisfy it.

Stimulus

Do you often feel thirsty after strenuous exercise? Has a television commercial for a new sports car ever made you wish you could buy it? Physiological thirst and TV commercials are both stimuli for consumers. A **stimulus** is any unit of input affecting the five senses: sight, smell, taste, touch, hearing. Stimuli can be either internal or external. **Internal stimuli** are a person's normal needs, such as hunger and thirst. From experience, humans have learned to respond to their internal stimuli and find the means to satisfy them, such as food or water. **External stimuli** stem from sources outside one's self. External stimuli might be the color of an automobile, the design of a package, a brand name mentioned by a friend, an advertisement on television, or cologne worn by a stranger.

The way consumers respond to external stimuli depends on how they process the content, form, complexity, and amount of information. People can perceive relatively few of the billions of stimuli in the world. The challenge for marketing managers is to produce such stimuli as advertisements, displays, and package designs that consumers will perceive and respond to.

Problem Recognition

Once a consumer has been exposed to a stimulus, the stimulus may then trigger problem recognition. An individual experiences **problem recognition** when faced with an imbalance between actual and desired states. The desired state the individual would like to achieve reflects a need or want. A **need** is anything an individual depends on to function efficiently. Needs are considered the root of all human behavior, for without needs there would be no behavior patterns.

Although marketing managers cannot create needs, they can create wants. A **want** exists when someone has an unfulfilled need and has determined that a product will satisfy it. Young children might want toys, video games, and baseball equipment. Young adults may want compact discs, fashionable sneakers, and pizza.

Lively, colorful ads are often the stimuli that draw consumers' attention. Teenagers are the target market for these hip-hop fashions. Elements of the ad respond to their wants.
© Will Crocker

A want does not necessarily have to be for a specific product; it can also be for a certain attribute or feature of a product. For instance, older consumers want goods and services that offer comfort, security, convenience, and old-fashioned values.[2] Remote-controlled appliances, home deliveries, speaker phones, and motorized carts are all designed for comfort and convenience. Likewise, a transmitter that can signal an ambulance or the police if the person wearing it has an emergency offers security for older consumers.

Marketers selling their products in overseas markets must determine the needs and wants of different consumers. In Puerto Rico, for example, Tang (an instant

orange drink) sells five times as well as it does in the United States. Kraft General Foods, manufacturer of Tang, found that Puerto Ricans want sweeter and less expensive products. Tang is both sweeter and cheaper than orange juice. Some Hispanic consumers buy in bulk for their large families, but Puerto Ricans like small containers so they can visit the store more often. Puerto Ricans are also very brand-conscious and prefer well-known brands. As a result, they are less likely to buy generic items.[3]

Consumers recognize unfulfilled wants in various ways. The two most common occur when a current product isn't performing properly and when the consumer is about to run out of something that is generally kept on hand. Consumers may also recognize unfulfilled wants if they hear about or see a product whose features make it seem superior to that currently used. Such wants are usually created by advertising and other promotional activities. For example, a teenager may develop a strong desire for a new Super Nintendo video game set after seeing it on display in a store.

Information Search

After recognizing a problem, a consumer may or may not search for more information. That decision depends on the perceived benefits of the search versus its perceived costs. The perceived benefits include finding the best price, getting the most desired model, and achieving ultimate satisfaction with the purchase decision. The perceived costs include the time and expense of undertaking the search and the psychological costs of processing information. Consumers will spend time and effort searching as long as the benefits outweigh the costs; that is, the value of more information must be greater than the cost of obtaining it.[4]

The information search should yield a group of brands, sometimes called the buyer's **evoked set** or **consideration set**, from which the buyer can further evaluate and choose. Consumers do not consider all the brands available in a product category, but they do rather seriously consider a much smaller set. For example, there are more than 30 brands of shampoos and more than 160 types of automobiles available, yet most consumers seriously contemplate only about four shampoos and two to five automobiles when faced with a purchase decision.[5]

evoked set (consideration set)
Group of brands, resulting from an information search, from which a buyer can choose.

internal information search
Process of recalling past information stored in the memory.

external information search
Process of seeking information in the outside environment.

Internal and External Information Searches

The information search can occur internally, externally, or both. An **internal information search** is the process of recalling past information stored in the memory. This stored information stems largely from previous experience with a product. For instance, perhaps while shopping you encounter a brand of cake mix that you tried some time ago. By searching your memory, you will probably be able to remember whether it tasted good, pleased guests, and was easy to prepare.

In contrast, an **external information search** seeks information in the outside environment. There are two basic types of external information sources:

Many consumers seek product information in *Consumer Reports,* a nonmarketing-controlled, public information source.

nonmarketing-controlled information source
Product information source that is not associated with advertising or promotion.

marketing-controlled information source
Product information source that originates with marketers promoting the product.

nonmarketing-controlled and marketing-controlled. A **nonmarketing-controlled information source** is not associated with marketers promoting a product. A friend, for example, might recommend an IBM personal computer because he or she bought one and likes it. Nonmarketing-controlled information sources include personal experience (trying or observing a new product), personal sources (family, friends, acquaintances, and co-workers), and public sources, such as Underwriters Laboratories, *Consumer Reports*, and other consumer-rating organizations.

A **marketing-controlled information source**, on the other hand, is biased toward specific products, since it originates with marketers promoting those products. Some examples of marketing-controlled information sources include mass-media advertising (radio, newspaper, television, and magazine advertising), sales promotion (contests, displays, premiums, and so forth), salespeople, and product labels and packaging. Many consumers are wary about the information they receive from marketing-controlled sources, arguing that most marketing campaigns stress the attributes of the product and don't mention the faults. These sentiments are highest among college graduates, people with incomes of $50,000 or more, and working parents.[6] The box on page 107 discusses the credibility of food labels, a source of marketing-controlled information.

Factors Influencing External Search

The amount of external search conducted by an individual depends on perceived risk, knowledge, prior experience, and level of interest in the good or service.[7] Generally, as perceived risk of the purchase increases, the consumer will increase the amount of search and consider more alternative brands in the evoked set. For instance, assume you want to buy a new car. The decision is a relatively risky one, mainly because of cost, so you are motivated to search for information about models, options, gas mileage, durability, passenger capacity, and so forth. You may also decide to gather information about more models, since the trouble and time it takes to find the data are less than the cost of buying the wrong car.

ETHICS IN MARKETING

To Believe or Not Believe Food Labels

Food labels are an important information source for consumers. They provide vital data about the product's nutrition content, calories, and number of servings. It's not surprising, then, that labels are also food companies' main advertising vehicle. The nutritional claims on these labels have long been one of the food industry's most powerful selling points.

Labels became even more powerful in 1987, when the Food and Drug Administration (FDA) reversed a long-standing ban on using health claims on food labels. This reversal made it legal to label a box of cereal or a can of peas as "high-fiber" or "low-fat" or "low-sodium." Sales increased in many packaged food categories. Positioned as a cancer preventive, some bran cereals were selling as much as 70 percent more within two years. Dairy companies also cashed in on the nutritional reputation of yogurt, even though many varieties are loaded with sugar, fat, and other additives.

The many highly exaggerated health claims outraged consumer groups and the FDA. In 1990, President George Bush signed into law the Nutritional Labeling and Education Act. The new law mandates labeling for all processed foods and requires the FDA to define nutritional terms like *light, low-fat,* and *reduced calories.*

Over half of U.S. consumers depend on food labels and packaging as their most useful source of nutrition information, and most feel that labels are the best place for additional information. Yet, research shows that ordinary consumers do not know much about the terms on food labels. Barely a third of those surveyed understand that the weight of ingredients determines their order on a label. Additionally, although most food shoppers understand terms like *cholesterol, calcium, preservatives, sodium, protein, calories,* and *fiber,* only one in eight understands terms like *polyunsaturated fat, hydrogenation, riboflavin, niacin,* and *potassium.*[8]

Are marketers taking advantage of consumer ignorance? How can you as a consumer protect yourself against misleading nutritional information? How heavily should food manufacturers be regulated when it comes to food labels? Should the government provide everyday consumers with more education on nutritional terms?

The more knowledgeable and better informed consumers are about a potential purchase, the less they need to search. Also, the more consumers already know, the more efficiently they search; that is, consumers will seek less information about inappropriate alternatives, and their evoked set will be smaller. A second, closely related factor is confidence in one's decision-making ability. A confident consumer not only has plenty of stored information about the product but also feels self-assured about making the right decision. People lacking this confidence will continue an information search even when they know a great deal about the product.

Consumers with prior experience in buying a certain product will have less perceived risk than inexperienced consumers. Therefore, they will spend less time searching and limit the number of products in their evoked set. Moreover, consumers who have had a positive prior experience with a product are more likely to limit their evoked set to only those items related to the positive experience. For example, many consumers are loyally devoted to Honda automobiles, which enjoy low repair rates and high customer satisfaction, and may own more than one.

Finally, the amount of interest a consumer has in a product is positively related to the amount of search undertaken. That is, a consumer who is more interested in a product will spend more time searching for information and alternatives. For example, suppose you are a dedicated runner who reads jogging and fitness magazines and catalogs. In searching for a new pair of running shoes, you may enjoy reading about the new brands available and spend more time and effort than other buyers in deciding on the right shoe.

Evaluation of Alternatives and Purchase

After getting information and constructing an evoked set of alternative products, the consumer is ready to make a decision. A consumer will use the information stored in the memory and obtained from outside sources to develop a set of criteria. These standards help the consumer evaluate and compare the alternatives. One way to begin narrowing the choices in the evoked set is to pick a product attribute and then exclude all products in the set that don't have that attribute. For instance, assume that John is thinking about buying a new compact disc player. He is interested in a remote control and the ability to hold several discs at one time (a product attribute), so he excludes all compact disc players without these features.

Another way to narrow the number of choices is to use "cutoffs," minimum or maximum levels of an attribute that an alternative must pass to be considered further.[9] Suppose John still must choose from a wide array of remote-control, multidisc players. He then names another product attribute: price. Given the amount of money he has saved, John decides he cannot spend more than $200. Therefore, he can exclude all compact disc players priced above $200. To reach a final decision, John would pick the most important attributes, weigh the merits of each, and then evaluate alternatives on those criteria.

Even when John has every intention of purchasing a new compact disc player, his purchase decision may be superseded by others' opinions as well as by unexpected situations. What if John's wife strongly opposes his decision to buy a compact disc player because she wants him to save money for their vacation? Then the chances of John's buying one are greatly reduced. Or suppose that John decides to buy a cassette player instead of a compact disc player, since cassettes are cheaper than compact discs. Unexpected situations that may also influence John's actual purchase include a change in family income, an increase in the price of disc players, or a decrease in the perceived value of the product to him.

4 Outcome and Postpurchase Behavior

Following the evaluation process, the consumer decides which product to buy (or decides not to buy at all). If the consumer does indeed buy a product, he or she expects certain outcomes of the purchase. How well these expectations are met determines whether the consumer is satisfied or dissatisfied with the purchase. Consider this example: A person who has bought a used car has somewhat low expectations of the car's actual performance. Surprisingly, the car turns out to be one of the best cars she has ever owned. Thus the buyer's satisfaction is high, because her expectations were exceeded. On the other hand, a consumer who bought a brand-new car would expect it to perform especially well. But if the car turns out to be a lemon, she will be very dissatisfied, because her high expectations have not been met.

Price often creates high expectations. One study found that higher monthly cable TV bills were associated with greater expectations of cable service. Yet, over time cable subscribers tended to drop the premium-priced cable channels, because their high expectations were not met.[10]

The degree of satisfaction or dissatisfaction with a product varies from person to person. Obviously, the more a consumer searches for information, the more satisfied he or she may be with a purchase. With increased knowledge, the buyer has more realistic expectations of the product. Also, people who feel competent in their everyday lives may also be more satisfied with their major purchases than those who feel less competent, since they tend to feel their decision was right.

One important element of any postpurchase evaluation is reducing any lingering doubts that the decision was sound. Have you ever made a major purchase and then questioned your decision? For example, suppose a consumer spends half his monthly salary on a new high-tech stereo system. Later he might start to wonder whether he should have. When people recognize inconsistency between their values or opinions and their behavior, they tend to feel an inner tension called **cognitive dissonance.** Dissonance occurs because the person knows the purchased product has some disadvantages as well as some advantages. Consumers try to reduce dissonance by justifying their decision.

cognitive dissonance Inner tension that a consumer experiences after recognizing an inconsistency between behavior and values or opinions.

Consumers can reduce cognitive dissonance by finding new information that reinforces positive ideas about the purchase, avoiding information that contradicts their decision, or revoking the original decision by returning the product. People who have just bought a new car often read more advertisements for the car they have just bought than for other cars. Dissatisfied customers sometimes rely on word of mouth to reduce cognitive dissonance, by letting friends and family know they are displeased. In some instances, people deliberately seek contrary information in order to refute it and reduce dissonance.

Understanding how consumers make purchase decisions can help marketing managers in several ways. For example, if a manager knows through research that gas mileage is the most important attribute for a certain target market, the manufacturer can redesign the product to meet that criterion. But if the firm cannot change the design in the short run, it can use promotion in an effort to change consumers' decision-making criteria. For example, the manufacturer can advertise the car's maintenance-free features and sporty European style while downplaying gas mileage.

Effective communication with purchasers aids marketing managers in reducing dissonance. Postpurchase letters sent by manufacturers and dissonance-reducing statements in instruction booklets may help customers feel at ease with their purchase. For example, a customer-service manager may slip a note inside the package congratulating the buyer on making a wise decision. Advertising that displays the

MARKETING AND SMALL BUSINESS

It Pays to Know Why

Entrepreneurs need to understand answers to questions like "Why do customers buy one product and not another?" and "Why do consumers prefer a specific good or service?" and "Why do customers patronize one store and not another?" Small-business owners who are sensitive to these questions can better understand the purchasing motivation of consumers. And knowledge of consumer buying behavior enables small-business managers to plan the offering of products more effectively and have them available when they are requested.

Consumers get much of their information from opinion leaders. A small business can enhance its own product and image by identifying with such leaders. For example, a farm-supply dealer may promote agricultural products in a community by arranging demonstrations on the farms of outstanding farmers, who are the community's opinion leaders.

Innovative entrepreneurs can use what they know about local and cultural preferences to start successful businesses. One example is Alvin Copeland, the president and founder of Popeye's Famous Fried Chicken and Biscuits, which began in New Orleans. His menu features Cajun cuisine and super-spicy fried chicken, which appeal to Louisiana consumers. Social class can be another very important consideration. Many small specialty shops have failed in large regional malls because their merchandise was aimed at lower-middle-class consumers and the mall's market was upper-middle-class or higher. In other cases, the stores had the right merchandise but the wrong decor, services, or salespeople, creating a rift with the consumers.

product's superiority over competing brands can also help relieve the dissonance of someone who has already bought the product.

5 HIGH- AND LOW-INVOLVEMENT DECISION MAKING

involvement
Amount of time and effort a buyer invests in the search, evaluation, and decision processes of consumer behavior.

high-involvement decision making
Process of deliberately searching for information about products and brands in order to evaluate them thoroughly.

low-involement decision making
Process of deciding to buy a product in which the consumer experiences little perceived risk, low identification with the product, or little personal relevance.

People usually experience cognitive dissonance only when buying high-involvement products. **Involvement** refers to the amount of time and effort a buyer invests in the search, evaluation, and decision processes of consumer behavior. The level of involvement in the purchase depends on the product's economic and social importance to the consumer. Buying a car may be more socially important to one consumer than to another. Involvement also varies according to product category and brand.

Consumers who deliberately search for information about products and brands in order to evaluate them thoroughly are most likely engaging in **high-involvement decision making.** This process resembles the model outlined in Exhibit 4.1. These consumers want to make the right decision, so they want to know as much as they can about the product category and the available brands. Goods and services that are usually high-involvement purchases are cars, TV sets, refrigerators, washing machines, home computers, insurance policies, and financial investments. Consumers usually shop around for these products, seeking information from friends, publications, manufacturers, and retailers.

On the other hand, suppose a shopper goes to the grocery store and notices a new brand of chocolate bar. The consumer thinks, "I'd really like some chocolate right now; it looks good. Why not try one?" The consumer perceives little risk if the wrong decision is made. So what if the candy bar doesn't quite meet the consumer's expectations? Low-involvement consumer decision making sharply contrasts with what goes into the purchase of a new car or home. In **low-involvement decision making**, the consumer experiences little perceived risk, low identification with the product, or little personal relevance.

This Jaguar ad recognizes that its target market is likely to be highly involved in the decision to buy one of the luxury autos. Thus it presents lots of facts.

Courtesy of Jaguar Cars Inc.

In low-involvement buying situations, consumers normally don't experience problem recognition until they are exposed to advertising or see an item displayed on a shelf. They tend to learn about low-involvement products in an almost random, spontaneous fashion. They buy first and evaluate later, whereas the reverse is true for high-involvement products. With low-involvement products, buyers seek an acceptable level of satisfaction. They tend to buy familiar brands that they expect will give them the fewest problems. For example, consumers might buy Coke because they are thirsty and want a soft drink. Although they are familiar with other brands of soft drinks, they have learned through experience that Coke quenches thirst. However, few social or financial consequences are associated with buying soft drinks, so consumers risk little in choosing Coke.

Low-involvement decision making is often habitual consumer behavior, characterized by brand loyalty. Buyers may preplan such a purchase. For example, a shopper may decide to buy Minute Maid orange juice before going to the grocery store. But the purchase decision results from experiences and evaluations that have occurred over a number of purchases. Over time, consumers build brand awareness and develop a set of simple tactics for choosing products, which permits a quick yet satisfactory decision.[11]

Factors Affecting Involvement Level

Several factors influence consumers' level of involvement in the purchase process. These factors include previous experience, interest, perceived risk of negative consequences, situation, and social visibility.

- *Previous experience:* When consumers have had previous experiences with a good or service, the level of involvement typically decreases. After repeated product trials, consumers learn to make quick choices. Because consumers are familiar with the product and know if it will satisfy their needs, they become less involved in the purchase. For example, consumers with pollen allergies typically buy the sinus medicine that has relieved their symptoms in the past.
- *Interest:* Involvement is directly related to consumer interests, such as cars, music, movies, bicycling, or electronics. Naturally, these areas of interest vary from one individual to another. Although some people have little interest in nursing homes, a person with elderly parents in poor health may be highly interested.
- *Perceived risk of negative consequences:* As the perceived risk in purchasing a product increases, so does a consumer's level of involvement. Several types of risks concern consumers. First, financial risk is exposure to loss of wealth or purchasing power. Because high risk is associated with high-priced purchases, consumers tend to become extremely involved. Therefore, price and involvement are usually directly related: As price increases, so does the level of involvement. For example, someone who is thinking of buying a home will normally spend much time and effort to find the right one. Second, consumers take social risks when they buy products that can affect people's opinions of them (for example, driving an old, beat-up car or wearing unstylish clothes). Third, buyers undergo psychological risk if they feel that making the wrong decision might cause some concern or anxiety. For example, should a working parent hire a babysitter or enroll the child in a day-care center?
- *Situation:* The circumstances of a purchase may temporarily transform a low-

involvement decision into a high-involvement one. High involvement comes into play when the consumer perceives risk in a specific situation. For example, an individual might routinely buy low-priced brands of liquor and wine. However, when the boss visits, the consumer might make a high-involvement decision and buy more prestigious brands.

- *Social visibility:* Involvement also increases as the social visibility of a product increases. Products often on social display include clothing (especially designer labels), jewelry, cars, and furniture. All these items make a statement about the purchaser and, therefore, carry a social risk.

Involvement Implications for the Marketing Manager

Marketing managers have several responsibilities when dealing with high-involvement product purchases. For one thing, promotion to the target market should be extensive and informative. A good ad gives consumers the information they need for making the purchase decision, as well as the benefits and unique advantages of owning the product. For example, Jaguar runs lengthy ads that detail technical information about these luxury cars.

Problem recognition for low-involvement purchases often does not occur until the consumer is in the store. Therefore, in-store promotion is an important tool when promoting low-involvement products. Marketing managers have to focus on package design, so the product is eye-catching and easily recognized on the shelf. Examples of products that take this approach are Campbell's soups, Tide detergent, Velveeta cheese, and Heinz catsup. In-store displays also stimulate sales of low-involvement products. A good display can explain the product's purpose and prompt recognition of a want. Displays of health and beauty-aid items in supermarkets have been known to increase sales many times above normal. Coupons, cents-off deals, and two-for-one offers also effectively promote low-involvement items.

Linking a product to a higher-involvement issue is another tactic that marketing managers can use to increase the sales of a low-involvement product. For example, many food products are no longer just nutritious but also low in fat or cholesterol. Although packaged food may normally be a low-involvement product, reference to health issues raises the involvement level. Cheerios cereal has been around for nearly fifty years. To take advantage of today's interest in health, it now advertises that it is also an excellent source of oat bran.

6 FACTORS INFLUENCING CONSUMER BEHAVIOR

The consumer decision-making process does not occur in a vacuum. On the contrary, several individual and social factors strongly influence the decision process. Exhibit 4.2 summarizes these influences. They have an effect from the time a consumer perceives a stimulus through postpurchase behavior.

Individual Factors

The individual factors that affect consumer behavior are unique to each particular person. These factors include perception; motivation; learning; values, beliefs, and attitudes; personality; self-concept; and lifestyle.

perception
Process by which people select, organize, and interpret stimuli into a meaningful and coherent picture.

Perception

The world is full of stimuli. The process by which we select, organize, and interpret these stimuli into a meaningful and coherent picture is called **perception.** In es-

Exhibit 4.2

Role of Individual and Social Factors in the Consumer Decision-Making Process

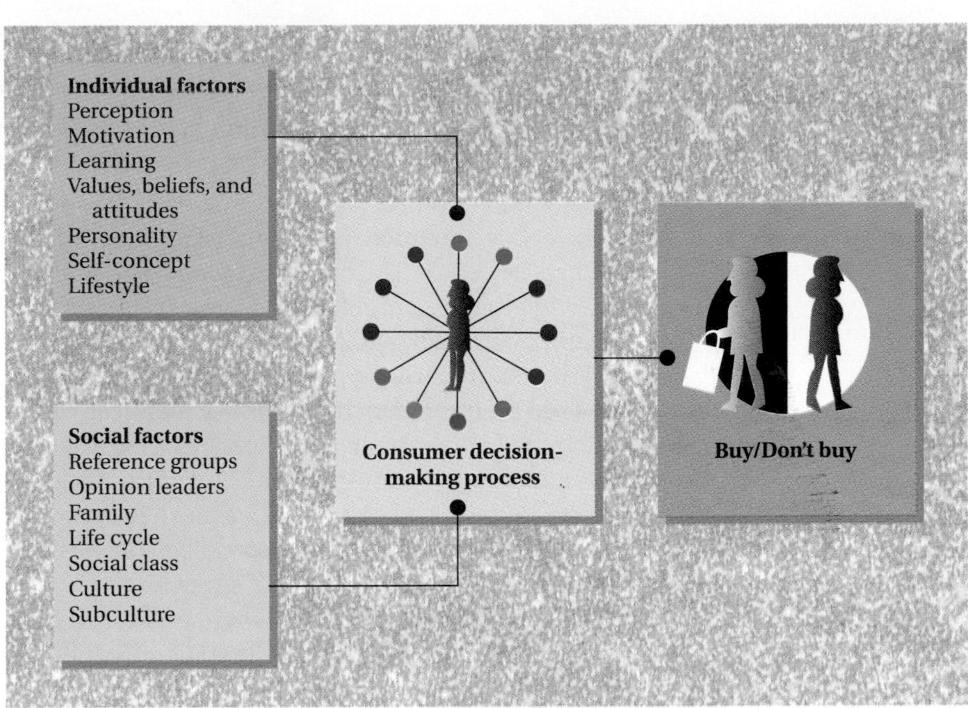

sence, perception is how we see the world around us and how we recognize we have a consumption problem.

People cannot perceive every stimulus in their environment. Therefore, they use **selective exposure** to decide which stimuli to notice and which to ignore. A typical consumer is exposed to over 150 advertising messages a day but notices only between 11 and 20.

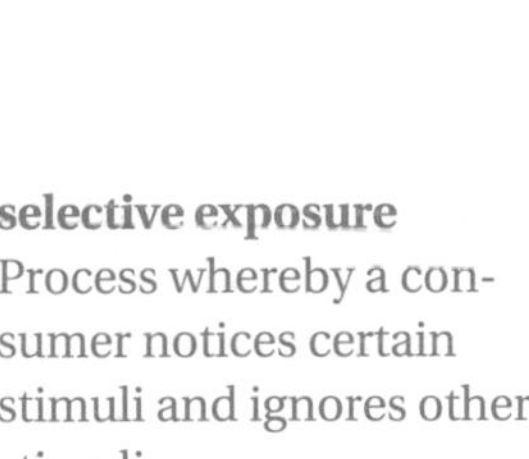

selective exposure
Process whereby a consumer notices certain stimuli and ignores other stimuli.

The familiarity of an object, contrast, movement, intensity (such as increased volume), and smell are cues that influence perception. Consumers use these cues to identify and define products and brands. Color is another cue, and it plays a key role in consumers' perceptions. One study gave college students three different "flavors" of chocolate pudding that was, in reality, vanilla pudding with food coloring added to varying degrees. Students rated the dark brown pudding as having the best chocolate flavor and the two lighter puddings as being creamier. Not one of the students indicated he or she was tasting a flavor of pudding other than chocolate. Color proved to be a critical cue for judging chocolate pudding. In fact, one might conclude that the color of the pudding was more important than its taste.[12]

What is perceived by consumers may also depend on the stimuli's vividness or shock value. Graphic warnings of the hazards associated with a product's use are perceived more readily and remembered more accurately than less vivid warnings.[13] Surveys indicate that "sexier" ads excel at attracting the attention of 18- to 25-year-old consumers. Sensuous ads from companies like Calvin Klein and Nike are considered effective at "cutting through the clutter" of competing ads and other stimuli and capturing the attention of the target audience.[14]

selective distortion
Process whereby a consumer changes or distorts information that conflicts with his or her feelings or beliefs.

Two other concepts closely related to selective exposure are selective distortion and selective retention. **Selective distortion** occurs when consumers change or distort information that conflicts with their feelings or beliefs. For example, suppose a consumer buys a Chrysler. After the purchase, if the consumer receives new information about a close alternative brand, such as a Ford, he or she may distort the information to make it more consistent with the prior view that the Chrysler is better than the Ford. Consider these other examples of selective distortion:

- Business travelers who fly often may distort or discount information about airline crashes because they must use air travel constantly in their jobs.
- People who smoke and have no plans to quit may distort information from medical reports and the Surgeon General about the link between cigarettes and lung cancer.

selective retention
Process whereby a consumer remembers only that information that supports his or her personal beliefs.

Selective retention is remembering only information that supports personal feelings or beliefs. The consumer forgets all information that may be inconsistent. After reading a pamphlet that contradicts one's political beliefs, for instance, a person may forget many of the points outlined in it.

What stimuli will be perceived often depends on the individual. People can be exposed to the same stimuli under identical conditions but perceive them very differently. For example, two people viewing a TV commercial may have two totally different interpretations of the advertising message. One person may be thoroughly engrossed by the message and become highly motivated to buy the product. Thirty seconds after the ad ends, the second person may not be able to recall the content of the message or even the product advertised.

Marketers must recognize the importance of cues in consumers' perception of products. Marketing managers first identify the important attributes that the targeted consumers want in a product and then design cues to communicate these attributes. For instance, consumers will pay more for candy wrapped in expensive-looking foil packages. But shiny labels on wine bottles signify less-expensive wines; dull labels indicate more-expensive wines.

Brand names can even send cues to consumers: the names Close-Up toothpaste, DieHard batteries, and Frigidaire refrigerators, for example, identify their qualities for consumers.[15] Consumers also perceive quality and reliability with certain brand names. The ten brand names with the highest perceived value, or *brand equity,* are Disney World, Kodak, Mercedes-Benz, CNN, Hallmark, Fisher-Price, UPS, Rolex, Levi's, and IBM.[16] Naming a product after a place can also add perceived quality and value by association. The Western names Santa Fe and Dakota elicit a sense of

These ads for Guess jeans are just some of the many that use sex appeal to attract the attention of 18- to 25-year-old consumers.
Guess by Georges Marciano

openness, freedom, and youth. On the other hand, products named after New Jersey or Detroit bring about images of pollution and crime.[17]

Marketing managers are also interested in the *threshold level* of perception: the minimum difference in a stimulus that the consumer will notice. This concept is sometimes referred to as the "just-noticeable difference." For example, how much would Sony have to drop the price of a VCR before consumers recognized it as a bargain—$25? $50? or more? One study found that the just-noticeable difference in a stimulus is about a 20 percent change in that stimulus. For example, consumers will likely notice a 20 percent price decrease more quickly than a 15 percent decrease. This marketing principle, demonstrated in pricing studies, also applies to other marketing variables as well. For example, a 20 percent increase in package size may be necessary for consumers to perceive that the product is new and better. A 20 percent louder broadcast ad may be better at getting consumers' attention. However, consumers may get so annoyed that they turn off the TV or radio.[18]

Besides changing such stimuli as price, package size, or volume, marketers can change other aspects of the product. For example, how many sports car features will General Motors have to add to a basic two-door sedan before consumers begin to perceive the model as a sports car? How many new services will a discount store like Kmart need to add before consumers perceive it as a full-service department store?

Marketing managers who intend to do business in international markets should also be aware of how foreign consumers perceive their products. For instance, in Japan, product labels are often written in English or French, even though many cannot read them. In fact, the words often do not translate into anything meaningful. But the Japanese perceive foreign words on product labels as meaning exotic, expensive, and high quality.[19] On the other hand, consumers in other countries may perceive products with foreign names as inferior or cheap.

Motivation

By studying motivation, marketers can analyze the major forces influencing consumers to buy or not buy products. When you buy a product, you usually do so to fulfill some kind of need. These needs become motives when aroused sufficiently.

The brand name by itself would conjure a strong image among potential consumers. The ad in which it appears supports that image.

Courtesy of Aramis. Photographer: Matthew Rolston

Exhibit 4.3

Maslow's Hierarchy of Needs

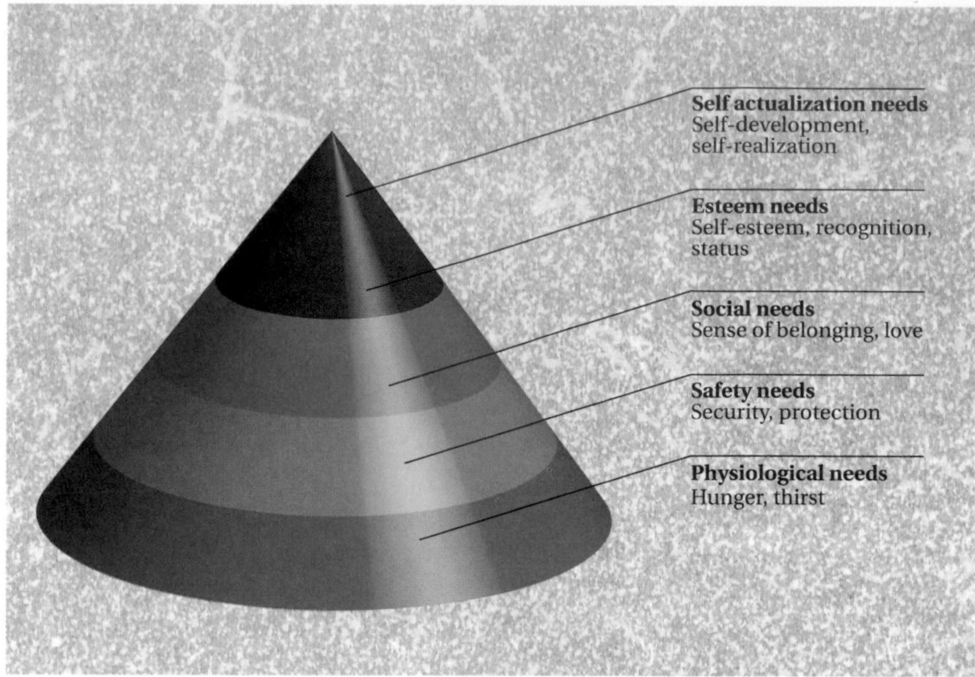

For instance, suppose this morning you were so hungry before class that you needed to eat something; you had a need for food. In response to that need, you stopped at McDonald's for an Egg McMuffin. In other words, you were motivated by hunger to stop at McDonald's. **Motives** are the driving forces that cause a person to take action to satisfy specific needs.

motive
Driving force that causes a person to take action to satisfy specific needs.

Maslow's hierarchy of needs
Method of classifying human needs and motivations into five categories in ascending order of importance: physiological, safety, social, esteem, and self-actualization.

Why are people driven by particular needs at particular times? One popular theory is **Maslow's hierarchy of needs**, shown in Exhibit 4.3, which seeks to categorize needs and explain human motivation. The hierarchy arranges needs in ascending order of importance: physiological, safety, social, esteem, and self-actualization. As a person fulfills one need, a higher-level need becomes more important.

The most basic human needs are *physiological*, needs for food, water, and shelter. Because they are essential to survival, these needs must be satisfied first. Ads showing a nice, juicy hamburger or a runner gulping down Gatorade after a marathon exemplify the use of appeals to satisfy physiological needs.

Safety needs include security and freedom from pain and discomfort. Consumers' need for safety has changed dramatically in the last few decades. Twenty years ago, automobile companies couldn't sell safety to U.S. consumers. Yet air bags are now the safety feature consumers demand most often when buying a new car, followed by antilock brakes and reinforced body construction.[20]

After physiological and safety needs have been fulfilled, *social* needs, especially love and a sense of belonging, become the focus. Love includes acceptance by one's peers, as well as sex and romantic love. Marketing managers probably appeal more to this need than to any other. Ads for clothes, cosmetics, and vacation packages suggest that buying the product can bring love.

Self-esteem needs are subdivided into two categories, one being self-respect and a sense of accomplishment, the other being prestige, fame, and recognition of one's accomplishments. Note that love is acceptance without regard to one's contribution; esteem is acceptance based on one's contribution to the group. BMW, Brooks Brothers clothiers, and Neiman-Marcus stores all appeal to self-esteem.

The highest human need is *self-actualization*. It refers to finding self-fulfillment

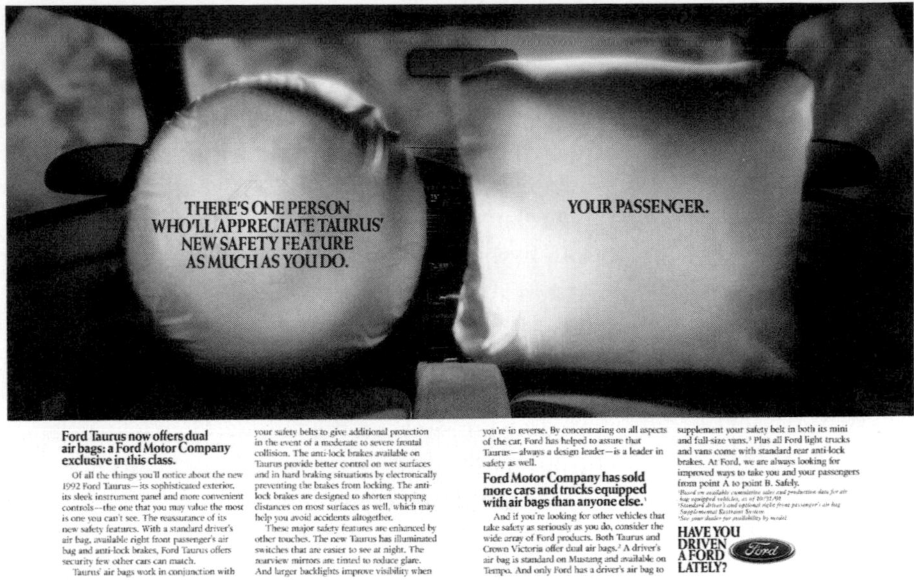

This Ford ad makes a strong appeal to consumers' safety needs.
Ford Motor Company

and self-expression, reaching the point in life at which "people are what they feel they should be." Maslow felt that very few people ever attain this level. Even so, advertisements may focus on this type of need. For example, American Express ads convey the message that acquiring its card is one of the highest attainments in life. Likewise, the U.S. Armed Forces' slogan urges young people to "be all that you can be."

Learning

learning
Process that creates changes in behavior, immediate or expected, through experience and practice.

Almost all consumer behavior results from **learning**, which is the process that creates changes in behavior through experience and practice. It is not possible to directly observe learning, but we can infer when it has occurred. Suppose you see an advertisement for a new and improved cold medicine. If you go to the store that day and buy that remedy, we infer that you have learned something.

The definition of learning says that experience can change behavior—a process called *experiential learning.* If you try the new cold medicine when you get home and it does not relieve your symptoms, you may not buy that brand again. *Conceptual learning,* which is not learned through experience, is also important. Assume, for example, that you are standing at a soft-drink machine and notice a new diet flavor sweetened with an artificial sweetener. Since diet beverages have left an aftertaste in the past, you choose a different drink. You have learned that you would not like this new diet drink without ever trying it.

People learn faster and retain the information longer when the material to be learned is important. Reinforcement and repetition also boost learning. If you see a vendor selling frozen yogurt (stimulus), buy it (response), and find the yogurt to be quite refreshing (reward), your behavior has been positively reinforced. On the other hand, if you buy a new flavor of yogurt, such as black cherry, and it does not taste good (negative reinforcement), you will not buy that flavor of yogurt again. Without positive or negative reinforcement, a person will not be motivated to repeat the behavior pattern or to avoid it. Thus if a new brand evokes neutral feelings, some marketing activity, such as a price change or an increase in promotion, may be

required to induce further consumption. Learning theory is helpful in reminding marketers that concrete and timely actions are what reinforce desired consumer behavior.

repetition
Promotional strategy in which advertising messages are spread over time, rather than clustered at one time, in order to increase learning.

Repetition is a key strategy in promotional campaigns, since it can lead to increased learning. Delta Airlines uses repetitious advertising so consumers will learn that "At Delta, we love to fly, and it shows." Generally, to heighten learning, advertising messages should be spread over time rather than clustered at one time.

stimulus generalization
Form of learning that occurs when one response is extended to a second stimulus similar to the first.

A related learning concept useful to marketing managers is **stimulus generalization.** In theory, stimulus generalization occurs when one response is extended to a second stimulus similar to the first. Marketers often use a successful, well-known brand name for a family of products because it gives consumers familiarity with and knowledge about each product in the family. Such brand-name families spur the introduction of new products and facilitate the sale of existing items. Jello frozen pudding pops rely on the familiarity of Jello gelatin; Clorox laundry detergent relies on familiarity with Clorox bleach; and Ivory shampoo relies on familiarity with Ivory soap.[21] Branding is examined in more detail in Chapter 9.

Another form of stimulus generalization occurs when retailers or wholesalers design their packages to resemble well-known manufacturers' brands. Such imitation often confuses consumers, who buy the imitator brand thinking it's the original.

U.S. manufacturers in foreign markets sometimes find little, if any, brand protection. For example, in South Korea Procter & Gamble's Ivory soap competes head-on with the Korean brand Bory, which has an almost identical logo on the package. Consumers dissatisfied with Bory may attribute their dissatisfaction to Ivory, never realizing that Bory is an imitator.[22] Counterfeit products are also produced to look exactly like the original. For example, counterfeit Levi's jeans made in China are hot items in Europe, where Levi Strauss has had trouble keeping up with demand. The knockoffs look so much like the real thing that unsuspecting consumers don't know the difference—until after a few washes, when the belt loops fall off and the rivets begin to rust.[23]

stimulus discrimination
Learned ability to differentiate among stimuli.

The opposite of stimulus generalization is **stimulus discrimination**, which means learning to differentiate among similar products. Consumers usually prefer one product as more rewarding or stimulating. For example, some consumers prefer Coca-Cola while others prefer Pepsi, and many insist they can taste a difference between the two brands.

product differentiation
Marketing tactic designed to distinguish one product from another.

With some types of products—such as aspirin, gasoline, bleach, paper towels—marketers rely on promotion to point up brand differences that consumers would otherwise not recognize. This process, called **product differentiation**, is discussed in more detail in Chapter 6. Usually product differentiation is based on superficial differences. For example, Bayer tells consumers it's the aspirin "doctors recommend most." Exxon has brought back the tiger as an advertising symbol to help differentiate its products from those of other oil companies.

Values, Beliefs, and Attitudes

value
Enduring belief that a specific mode of conduct is personally or socially preferable to another mode of conduct.

Learning helps people shape their value systems. In turn, values help determine self-concept, personality, and even lifestyle. A **value** is an enduring belief that a specific mode of conduct is personally or socially preferable to another mode of conduct. Three general types of values relate to consumer behavior: global, domain-specific, and product-specific. *Global values*—wisdom, world peace, freedom, happiness, equality—are the most generally and centrally held values. *Domain-specific values* provide guidance in certain realms, such as economics, social interaction, religion,

sports, family life, and entertainment. Consumers tend to adopt a set of values for each of these domains. For example, "Exercise is important" is a domain-specific value held by some people. Consumers also have *product-specific values* that relate to a specific class of products within a given domain. For example, "Sports equipment should be safe" is a product-specific value.

People's value systems have a great effect on their consumer behavior. Consumers with similar value systems tend to react alike to prices and other marketing-related inducements. Values also correspond to consumption patterns. People who want to protect the environment try to buy only products that don't harm it. Values can also influence consumers' TV viewing habits or the magazines they read. For instance, people who strongly object to violence avoid crime shows. Likewise, people who oppose pornography do not buy *Playboy.*

Value systems can vary quite a bit across cultures and subcultures. For example, leisure time is valued in the United States. Consumers spend a considerable amount of time and money on sporting events, movies, restaurants, vacations, and amusement parks. U.S. workers expect eight-hour days, five-day workweeks, and vacation time. Japanese workers, on the other hand, typically work twelve-hour days and often work on Saturdays as well. Only half of Japanese workers use all their vacation time. One reason most Japanese don't take more time off is that they don't want to burden their colleagues by leaving early or taking a holiday. Japanese workers also feel that their work will suffer if they put effort into other things.[24]

The personal values of target consumers may have interesting implications for marketing managers. The personal value system of today's elderly are quite different from those of previous generations. The elderly are less concerned with possessions and more interested in new experiences, personal challenges, and new adventures.[25] At the other end of the age spectrum, the "baby bust" generation, or those young adults 18 to 29 years of age, is also developing significantly different values from those of baby boomers. The baby boomers came of age during the wholesome 1950s, but today's 20-something generation grew up in a time of drugs, divorce, excessive consumption, and economic strain. As a result, they shun drugs and alcohol, postpone marriage, despise yuppies for their extravagant buying habits, and would rather hike in the Himalayas than climb the corporate ladder.[26] Like the companies described at the beginning of the chapter, many marketers are now shifting their promotions to reflect the new values of these two consumer groups. Instead of promoting individual gratification and glamorous lifestyles, they are opting for a back-to-basics approach that stresses values and personal challenges.

belief
Organized pattern of knowledge that an individual holds as true about his or her world.

Beliefs and attitudes are closely linked to values. A **belief** is an organized pattern of knowledge that an individual holds as true about his or her world. A consumer may believe that Sony's camcorder makes the best home videos, tolerates hard use, and is reasonably priced. These beliefs may be based on knowledge, faith, or hearsay. Consumers tend to develop a set of beliefs about a product's attributes and then, through these beliefs, form a *brand image*—a set of beliefs about a particular brand. In turn, the brand image shapes consumers' attitudes toward a product.

attitude
Learned tendency to respond consistently toward a given object.

Attitudes tend to be more enduring and complex than beliefs, since they consist of clusters of interrelated beliefs. An **attitude** is a learned tendency to respond consistently toward a given object, such as a brand. Attitudes also encompass an individual's value system, which represents personal standards of good and bad, right and wrong, and so forth. For instance, a motorcycle fanatic may hold the attitude that Harley-Davidson is the best bike in the world. This same consumer may also hold a deeper attitude that only U.S.-made products, such as Harley-Davidson motorcycles, should be bought by U.S. citizens.

If a good or service is meeting its profit goals, positive attitudes toward the product merely need to be reinforced. However, if the brand is not succeeding, the marketing manager must strive to change target consumers' attitudes. This change can be accomplished in three ways:

Changing beliefs about the brand's attributes

Changing the relative importance of these beliefs

Adding new beliefs

Changing beliefs about attributes: The first technique is to turn neutral or negative beliefs about product attributes into positive ones. For example, studies revealed that pork was losing sales to chicken because many consumers thought pork was fatty and unhealthy. As a result, the National Pork Producers Council launched its "Pork: The Other White Meat" campaign to reposition its product in the minds of consumers. The campaign attempts to change consumers' beliefs by telling them that today's pork is leaner, lower in calories, and lower in saturated fat than it was ten years ago. Likewise, the Beef Industry Council used the slogan "Real food for real people" to change consumers' attitudes toward its product.[27] The beef industry also actively supports such products as McDonald's McLean Deluxe as a way to change consumer beliefs that beef is high in fat.

The National Pork Producers Council uses ads to change consumers' beliefs about pork's attributes.

National Pork Producers in cooperation with the National Pork Board

Changing beliefs about a service can be more difficult, because service attributes are intangible. Convincing consumers to switch hairstylists or lawyers or to go to a mall dental clinic can be much more difficult than getting them to change brands of razor blades. Image, which is also largely intangible, significantly determines service patronage. What is a "better doctor"? How do consumers become convinced that they will get better dental care in a mall than through a family dentist? Service marketing is explored in detail in Chapter 11.

Changing the importance of beliefs: The second approach to modifying attitudes is to change the relative importance of beliefs toward an attribute. For years, consumers have known that bran cereals are high in natural fiber. The primary belief associated with this attribute is that the fiber tends to act as a mild, natural laxative. Today, however, the high fiber content of bran cereals is promoted as a possible factor in preventing certain types of cancer, vastly increasing the importance of this attribute in the minds of consumers.

Whirlpool has tried to change European consumers' beliefs about the attributes that are most important to them in a washing machine. European manufacturers believe that European consumers prefer washing machines that are narrow and load from the top. Whirlpool research, however, showed that Europeans also want a system that gets their clothes

Exhibit 4.4

Some Common Personality Traits

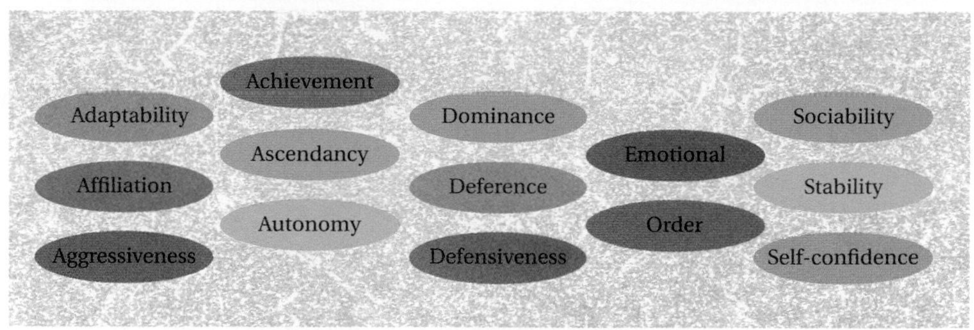

clean; that's easy to use; that doesn't use too much electricity, water, or detergent; and that has a record of trouble-free service. Whirlpool contends that if all these criteria are met, other features—such as where the machine opens and its size—become less important.[28]

Adding new beliefs: The third approach to transforming attitudes is to add new beliefs. Consumers were confused when Anheuser-Busch first introduced the beer Bud Dry, since the word *dry* is commonly used to describe wines. Many consumers have since added the new belief that beer can also be described as dry. Similarly, Kraft recently introduced fat-free mayonnaise, salad dressings, and cheeses, products traditionally known to be loaded with fat.

Personality

personality
Way of organizing and grouping the consistencies of an individual's reactions to situations.

Each consumer has a unique personality. **Personality** is a broad concept that can be thought of as a way of organizing and grouping the consistencies of an individual's reactions to situations. Thus personality combines psychological makeup and environmental forces. It includes people's underlying dispositions, especially their most dominant characteristics. Personality traits like those listed in Exhibit 4.4 may be used to describe a consumer's personality.

Some marketers believe that personality influences the types and brands of products purchased. For instance, the type of car, clothes, or jewelry a consumer buys may reflect one or more personality traits.

Self-Concept

self-concept
How a consumer perceives himself or herself in terms of attitudes, perceptions, beliefs, and self-evaluations.

ideal self-image
The way an individual would like to be.

real self-image
The way an individual actually perceives himself or herself.

Self-concept, or self-perception, is basically how consumers perceive themselves. **Self-concept** includes attitudes, perceptions, beliefs, and self-evaluations. Although self-concept may change, the change is often gradual. Through self-concept, people define their identity, which in turn provides for consistent and coherent behavior.

Self-concept combines the **ideal self-image** (the way an individual would like to be) and the **real self-image** (how an individual actually perceives himself or herself). Generally, we try to raise our real self-image toward our ideal (or at least narrow the gap). Consumers seldom buy products that jeopardize their self-image. For example, a contemporary dresser avoids clothing that doesn't project a trendy image.

Human behavior depends largely on self-concept. Because consumers want to protect their identity as individuals, the products they buy, the stores they patronize, and the credit cards they carry support their self-image.

By influencing the degree to which consumers perceive a good or service to be self-relevant, marketers can affect consumers' motivation to learn about, shop for, and buy a certain brand.[29] Marketers also consider self-concept important because it helps explain the relationship between individuals' perceptions of themselves and their consumer behavior.

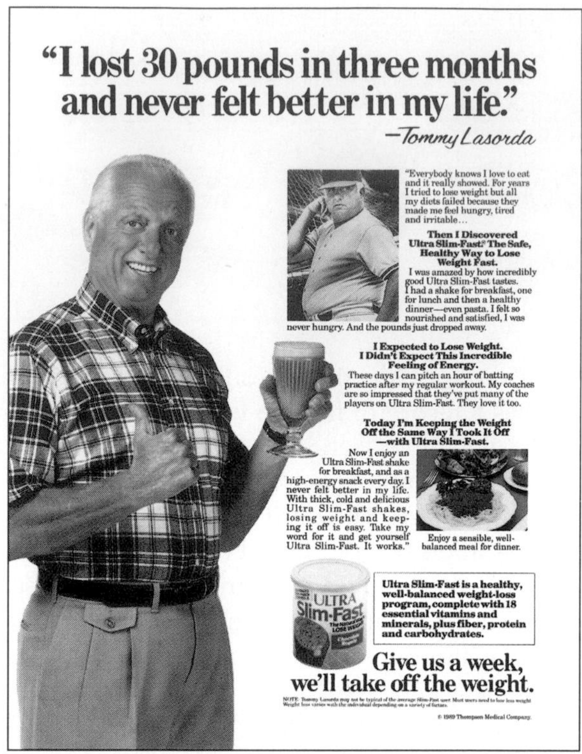

This ad for a weight-loss product relies on consumers' interest in their body image.

An important component of self-concept is *body image*, the perception of the attractiveness of one's own physical features. In one study, patients who had plastic surgery experienced significant improvements in their overall body image and self-concept.[30] Likewise, health clubs, exercise equipment manufacturers, and diet plans appeal to consumers who want to improve their self-concept by exercising and losing weight.

Lifestyle

lifestyle
Mode of living as identified by a person's activities, interests, and opinions.

psychographics
Analysis technique used to examine consumer lifestyles and to categorize consumers.

Personalities and self-concepts are reflected in lifestyles. A **lifestyle** is a mode of living as identified by a person's activities, interests, and opinions. **Psychographics** is the analysis technique used to examine consumer lifestyles and to categorize consumers.

Unlike personality characteristics, which are hard to describe and measure, lifestyle characteristics are useful in segmenting and targeting consumers. Many industries now use psychographics to better understand their market segments. For example, the auto industry has a psychographic segmentation scheme for classifying car buyers into one of six groups according to their attitudes toward cars and the driving experience. At the two extremes, "gearheads" are true car enthusiasts, who enjoy driving and working on their cars themselves, and "negatives" view cars as a necessary evil that they would just as soon do without.[31] Psychographics and lifestyle segmentation schemes are discussed in more detail in Chapter 6.

Social Factors

The second major group of factors that influence consumer decision making are social factors, which include all effects on buyer behavior that result from interactions between a consumer and the external environment. Social factors include reference groups, opinion leaders, family, life cycle, social class, culture, and subculture (refer back to Exhibit 4.2).

Exhibit 4.5

Types of Reference Groups

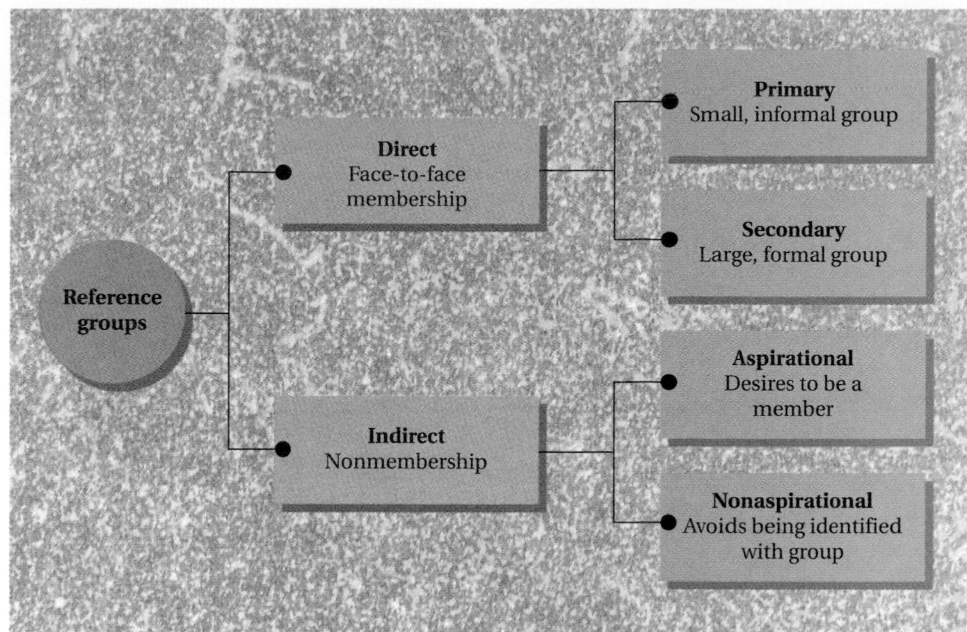

reference group
Group in society that influences an individual's purchasing behavior.

primary membership group
Reference group with which people interact regularly in an informal, face-to-face manner, such as family, friends, or fellow employees.

secondary membership group
Reference group with which people associate less consistently and more formally than a primary membership group, such as a club, professional group, or religious group.

aspirational group
Group that someone would like to join.

norm
Value or attitude deemed acceptable by a group.

nonaspirational reference group
Group with which an individual does not want to associate.

Reference Groups

All the formal and informal groups that influence the buying behavior of an individual are that person's **reference groups**. Consumers may use products or brands to identify with or become a member of a group. They learn from observing how members of reference groups solve their consumption problems and use the same solutions or criteria to make their own consumer decisions.

Reference groups can be categorized very broadly as either direct or indirect (see Exhibit 4.5). Direct reference groups are face-to-face membership groups that touch people's lives directly. They can be either primary or secondary. **Primary membership groups** include all groups with which people interact regularly in an informal, face-to-face manner, such as family, friends, and fellow co-workers. In contrast, we associate with **secondary membership groups** less consistently and more formally. These groups might include clubs, professional groups, and religious groups.

Consumers also are influenced by many indirect, nonmembership reference groups that they do not belong to. **Aspirational groups** are those that we would like to join. To join an aspirational reference group, a person must at least conform to the norms of that group. **Norms** are the values and attitudes deemed acceptable by the group. Thus a person who wants to be elected to public office may begin to dress more conservatively, like other politicians. He or she may go to many of the restaurants and social engagements that city and business leaders attend and try to play a role that is acceptable to voters and other influential people.

Nonaspirational reference groups, or dissociative groups, influence our behavior when we try to maintain distance from them. A consumer may not buy some types of clothing or cars, go to certain restaurants or stores, or even buy a home in a certain neighborhood to avoid being associated with a particular group.

The activities, values, and goals of reference groups directly influence consumer behavior. For marketers, reference groups have three important implications: They serve as information sources and influence perceptions; they affect an individual's aspiration levels; and their norms either constrain or stimulate consumer behavior. For example, aspiring young executives might check the makes of cars driven by their superiors before buying a car.

The series of Pepsi ads featuring singer Ray Charles took advantage of his credibility among consumers.
Courtesy of Pepsi Cola

Opinion Leaders

opinion leader
Individual who influences the opinions of others.

Reference groups frequently include individuals known as group leaders or **opinion leaders,** those who influence others. Obviously, it is important for marketing managers to persuade such people to purchase their goods or services.

Opinion leaders on one subject are often not opinion leaders on others. For instance, middle-aged parents who have raised three children may convince younger parents in the neighborhood to buy certain baby-care items. However, they may not be able to sway others to vacation at a particular place.

Segmenting markets by opinion leaders is a difficult task. Opinion leadership is a casual, face-to-face phenomenon and usually very inconspicuous, so locating opinion leaders can also be a challenge. Thus marketers often try to create opinion leaders. They may use high school cheerleaders to model new fall fashions or civic leaders to promote insurance, new cars, and other merchandise. On a national level, companies sometimes use sports figures and other celebrities to promote products, hoping they are appropriate opinion leaders. Research has shown that the effectiveness of celebrity endorsements depends largely on how credible and attractive the spokesperson is and how familiar people are with him or her. The endorsement is most likely to succeed if an association between the spokesperson and the product can be established.[32] For instance, Bill Cosby failed as an endorser for E.F. Hutton but succeeded with such products as Kodak cameras and Coca-Cola. Consumers could not mentally link Bill Cosby with serious investment decisions but could associate him with leisure activities and everyday consumption.

A marketing manager can also try to use opinion leaders through group sanctioning or referrals. For example, some companies sell products endorsed by the American Heart Association or the American Cancer Society. Marketers seek endorsements from schools, churches, cities, the military, and fraternal organizations as a form of group opinion leadership. Salespeople often ask to use opinion leaders' names as a means of achieving greater personal influence in a sales presentation.

Exhibit 4.6

Who Dominates Purchase Decisions in Different Product Categories

Source: Adapted from Diane Crispell, "The Brave New World of Men," *American Demographics*, January 1992, p. 40. Reprinted with permission © *American Demographics*, January 1992. For subscription information, please call (800)828-1133.

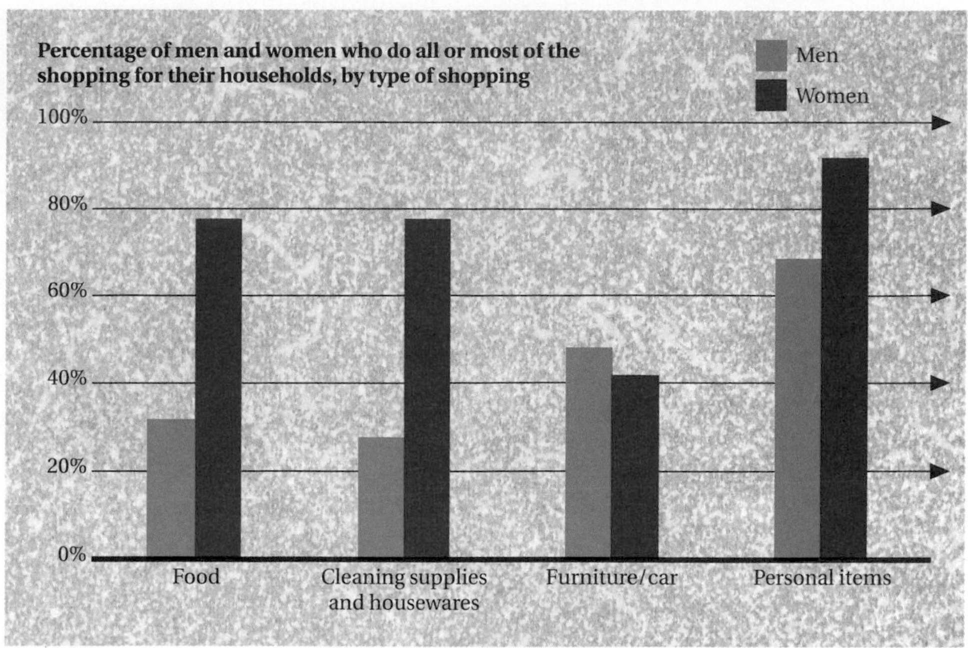

Family

The family is the most important social institution for many consumers, strongly influencing our values, attitudes, and self-concept. Moreover, the family is responsible for the **socialization process**, the passing down of cultural values and norms to children. For example, a family that strongly values good health will have a grocery list distinctly different from that of a family that views every dinner as a gourmet event. Children learn by observing their parents' consumption patterns, and so they will shop in a similar pattern.

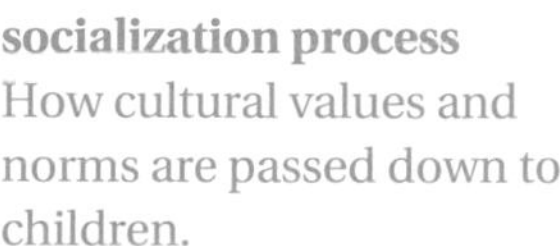

socialization process How cultural values and norms are passed down to children.

Families comprise distinct personalities, often with wide variations in age. Within a family, therefore, individual wants are unique. But because all families must operate with limited resources, many buying decisions must be based on compromise.

Decision-making roles, particularly the roles of spouses, tend to vary significantly depending on the type of item purchased. *Autonomic* decision making occurs when a husband or wife buys something independently of the other. Usually only personal products are bought independently, such as personal hygiene or hair care items. *Husband-dominant* purchases are made mostly by the husband; *wife-dominant* purchases are made mostly by the wife (see Exhibit 4.6). Husbands care more about the larger household purchases, such as furniture or cars, and may play a more dominant role than the wife when these purchases are considered. On the other hand, women typically make more of the family decisions regarding food and household items.[33] In a *syncratic* purchase situation, decisions are made jointly by husband and wife. Couples often seek balance and equity in their purchases. Recent research suggests that husbands and wives tend to compromise in an effort to be fair with each other and to avoid conflict.[34]

Changes in family structure often change the decision-making process. For example, as noted in Chapter 2, more women are now in the work force than ever before, and there are more single heads of households. Therefore, the typical family decision styles may not hold true as often as they did ten years ago. For example, although husbands have historically made decisions about insurance and financial planning, this trend may be changing. Perhaps we should not try to credit one

Children have always had a great deal of influence on families' toy purchases, but now they have input into many other purchase decisions as well.

spouse or the other with decisions of a certain type. Indeed, a single head of household has to make all types of decisions.

Family members take a variety of roles in the purchase process. *Initiators* are the ones who suggest, initiate, or plant the seed for the purchase process. The initiator can be anyone, even a stranger. You may see someone walking down the street wearing a new style of sweater and decide that you really would like a similar one. *Influencers* are those whose opinions are valued in the decision-making process. An influencer may be a friend, spouse, doctor, religious leader, lawyer, or other influential person. The *decision maker* is the person (or persons) who actually makes the decision to buy or not to buy. Finally, the *purchaser* is the one who exchanges money for goods or services, and the *consumer* is the actual user.

Children today have great influence over the purchase decisions of their parents. In many families, with both parents working full time and short of time, children may be encouraged to participate more in family decision making.[35] Children are especially influential in decisions about food. Over three-fourths of parents say their children help decide where the family goes for fast food, and over half say their kids influence the choice of a full-service restaurant. Most kids also have input into the kinds of food the family eats at home, and many even influence the specific brands their parents buy. Children are also influential in purchase decisions for toys, clothes, vacations, recreation, and automobiles, even though they are usually not the actual purchasers of such items.[36]

Life Cycle

life cycle
Orderly series of stages in which a person's attitudes and behavioral tendencies evolve, through maturity, experience, and changing income and status.

The family life cycle can also have a significant impact on consumer behavior. The **life cycle** is an orderly series of stages in which consumers' attitudes and behavioral tendencies evolve, through maturity, experience, and changing income and status.

Marketers often define their target markets in terms of the consumers' life cycle stage. For instance, families with children at home spend more of their income on food, furniture, and children's clothing and less of it on durable goods, food eaten away from home, adult clothing, and leisure activities.[37] Thus furniture stores, children's clothing retailers, and food manufacturers often target young married couples with children. The concept of life cycle, as applied to marketing, is discussed in more detail in Chapter 6.

Social Class

social class
Group of people who are considered nearly equal in status or community esteem, who regularly socialize among themselves both formally and informally, and who share behavioral norms.

The United States, like other countries and societies, does have a social class system. A **social class** is a group of people who are considered nearly equal in status or community esteem, who regularly socialize among themselves both formally and informally, and who share behavioral norms. A number of techniques and criteria have been used to measure and define social class. One contemporary view of U.S. status structure is shown in Exhibit 4.7.

Lifestyle distinctions between social classes are greater than within a given class. The most critical separation between the classes is the one between the middle and lower classes. It is here that the major shift in lifestyles appears. These are the major social classes in the United States.

- *Upper class:* The upper class consists of the capitalist class and the uppermiddle class. Upper-class individuals seem more likely to think of themselves as nice-

Exhibit 4.7

Contemporary View of U.S. Social Classes

Source: Adapted from Richard P. Coleman, "The Continuing Significance of Social Class to Marketing," *Journal of Consumer Research,* December 1983, p. 267; Dennis Gilbert and Joseph A. Kahl, *The American Class Structure: A Synthesis* (Homewood, Ill.: Dorsey Press, 1982), ch. 11.

Upper		
Capitalist class	1%	People whose investment decisions shape national economy; income mostly from assets, earned or inherited; university connections
Upper middle class	14%	Upper managers, professionals, medium businesspeople; college-educated; family income nearly twice national average
Middle		
Middle class	33%	Middle-level white-collar, top-level blue-collar; education past high school typical; income somewhat above national average
Working class	32%	Middle-level blue-collar; lower-level white-collar; income slightly below national average; education also slightly below national average
Lower		
Working poor	11–12%	Below mainstream in living standard but above poverty line; low-paid service workers and operatives; some high school education
Underclass	8–9%	People who depend primarily on welfare system for sustenance; living standard below poverty line; not regularly employed; lack schooling

looking people who are concerned with their own personal appearance. People of the upper social classes are more confident, outgoing, and culturally oriented than are people of other social classes. They also seem a bit more permissive and are willing to tolerate alternative views. The upper social classes are more likely than other classes to try to contribute something to society—for example, by publishing ideas, working voluntarily for charitable organizations, or actively participating in civic affairs.

- *Middle class:* Middle-class consumers have a much different perspective on life. Attaining goals and achieving status and prestige are important. The middle classes also have a stronger orientation outward, toward society in general and toward peers in particular, than the lower classes do. Apparently, the middle-class lifestyle is more dynamic than the relatively static lifestyle of the lower class. A distinct subclass of the middle class is the working class. The working-class person depends heavily on relatives and community for economic and emotional support. Members of this social subclass rely on relatives for tips on job opportunities, get their advice on purchases, and count on them in times of trouble. The emphasis on family ties is one sign of this group's intensely local view of the world. For instance, working-class people like the local news far more than middle-class audiences do, who show more enthusiasm for national and world coverage. Working-class people also vacation closer to home and are more likely to visit relatives.
- *Lower class:* Lower-class members typically fall at or below the poverty level. This social class has the highest unemployment rate, and many individuals or families are subsidized through the welfare system. Many are illiterate, with little formal education. Lower-class members also have poorer physical and mental health and a shorter life span than others do. Compared to more affluent consumers, lower-class consumers have poor diets and very different foods in their shopping cart (see Exhibit 4.8).[38]

Marketers are interested in social status for several reasons. First, social class often indicates which medium to put advertising in. Suppose an insurance company seeks to sell its policies to middle-class families. It might advertise on television during the local evening news, since middle-class families tend to watch more television than other classes do. If the company wants to sell more policies to upscale individuals, it might place a print ad in a business publication like *The Wall Street Journal*, which is read by a more educated and affluent class.

Second, social status may also tell marketers where certain classes of consumers shop. Wealthy, upper-class shoppers tend to frequent expensive stores, places where the lower classes might feel uncomfortable. Marketers also know that middle-class consumers regularly visit shopping malls. Therefore, marketers with products to sell to the middle class may decide to distribute their merchandise through malls.

Culture

culture
Set of values, norms, attitudes, and other meaningful symbols that shape human behavior and the artifacts, or products, of that behavior as they are transmitted from one generation to the next.

Culture is the set of values, norms, attitudes, and other meaningful symbols that shape human behavior and the artifacts, or products, of that behavior as they are transmitted from one generation to the next. Culture is environmentally oriented. The nomads of Finland have developed a culture for Arctic survival. Similarly, people who live in the Brazilian jungle have created a culture suitable for tropical living.

Human interaction creates values and prescribes acceptable behavior for each culture. By establishing common expectations, culture gives order to society. Some-

Foods bought by the poor and the affluent are out of proportion to their representation in the population. Purchases are ranked by an index with a base of 100. lists include only items bought by 10% of all households at least once in past year, not necessarily the items each group buys most.

Poor		**Affluent**	
Item	**Buying index**	**Item**	**Buying index**
Refrigerated pizza	221	Melba toast, bread sticks	192
Pork rinds	205	Frozen dinners (Italian, two foods)	191
Beef patties	187	Bottled grapefruit juice	188
Corn dogs	178	Frozen green beans	179
Frozen apple juice	174	Imported cheeses	174
Ramen noodles	187	Olive oil	171
Pizza mixes	163	Bottled water	163
Spiced lunch meat (e.g., Spam)	156	Fruit spreads	163
Hominy grits	156	Cranberry juice	162
Dried beans	156	Fresh mushrooms	158
Shortening (e.g., Crisco)	154	Liquid seasonings	156
Vienna sausage	152	Pure whipping cream	155
Powdered soft drinks (e.g., Kool-Aid)	151	Frozen carrots	151
Canned spinach	150	Nuts (cans or jars)	150
Canned peas	146	Frozen dinners (Italian, one food)	149
Canned mixed vegetables	144	Exotic fruit juices	149
Cooking sauces (e.g., for Sloppy Joes)	142	Herbal tea	146
Instant coffee	142	Fresh cranberries	146
Sugar	141	Frozen yogurt	145
Powdered creamers	141	Caviar, canned lobster or mussels	145
Per capita income less than $5,000 for family of two or more		Per capita income more than $20,000 for family of two or more	

Exhibit 4.8

Tastes in Food for the Poor and the Affluent

Source: Alix M. Freedman, "Amid Ghetto Hunger, Many More Suffer Eating Wrong Foods," *Wall Street Journal*, 12 December 1990, pp. A1, A8. Reprinted by permission of *The Wall Street Journal*, © Dow Jones & Company, Inc. All Rights Reserved Worldwide.

times these expectations are coded into laws. For example, drivers in our culture must stop at a red light.

As long as a value or belief meets the society's needs, it remains part of the culture. If it is no longer functional, it fades away. Large families were valued in the nineteenth and early twentieth centuries, when the U.S. economy was more agrarian. Children were considered an asset since they could help with the farmwork. Today, in an industrial-based economy, large families are not necessary.

Culture is dynamic. It adapts to changing needs and an evolving environment. The rapid growth of technology in this century has accelerated the rate of cultural change. TV has changed entertainment patterns and family communication and has heightened public awareness of political and other news events. Automation has increased the amount of leisure time we have and, in some ways, has changed the traditional Protestant work ethic. Cultural norms will continue to evolve because of our need for social patterns that solve problems.

Without understanding a culture, a firm has little chance of selling products in it. Colors, for example, may have different meanings in international markets than they do at home. In China, white is the color of mourning, and brides wear red; in the United States, black is for mourning, and brides wear white. Pepsi had a dominant market share in Southeast Asia, but when Pepsi-Cola changed the color of its coolers and vending equipment from deep regal blue to light ice blue, the result was catastrophic. In that part of the world, light blue is associated with death and mourning. Language is another important aspect of culture. Marketers must take care in translating product names, slogans, and promotional messages into foreign languages, so as not to convey the wrong meaning.

INTERNATIONAL PERSPECTIVES

Importing U.S. Culture to Europe

In April 1992, Euro Disney officially opened in France. The theme park and resort complex, built on sugar-beet and sunflower fields twenty miles from Paris, was one of Europe's largest construction projects.

Thousands of Europeans attended the opening festivities. They swarmed over the park, happily feasting on fast food, snapping up Disney merchandise, and gazing in wonderment. Visitors at the Buffalo Bill Wild West Show were introduced to imported live buffalo and dined on barbecued spare ribs. Disney deliberately didn't provide silverware. But the guests couldn't gnaw ribs and applaud at the same time, so Disney will provide more napkins—and teach visitors to stamp their feet.

Euro Disney is magnificent. The park's designers textured every walkway with brick and tile. Every corner is stuffed with props. In many ways, Euro Disney makes the Disney parks in Florida and California look like penny arcades. Striving not to compete with nearby medieval towns, cathedrals, and chateaux, Euro Disney's Le Chateau de la Belle au Bois Dormant—Sleeping Beauty's Castle—was designed to be more cartoonlike, with stained glass windows featuring Disney characters. Discoveryland, an updated Tomorrowland, is based on themes of Jules Verne and Leonardo da Vinci. The park also features *Visionarium,* a 360-degree movie about French culture required by the French.

Although the park was designed to appeal to Europeans, it is all-American in theme and built on traditional Disney values. Alcohol is banned, despite the French attitude that wine with a meal is proper. Research indicated that Europeans love the Prohibition era, but Disney officials decreed that images of gangsters and speakeasies were too negative for Main Street U.S.A. Although at Euro Disney it is more ornate and Victorian than Walt Disney's idealized Midwestern small town, it remains Main Street.[39]

Many French intellectuals are outraged at Euro Disney, claiming that Mickey Mouse and his friends are stifling individualism and transforming European children into consumers. Do you agree or disagree? Do you feel Disney will succeed at planting cultural values of the United States in Europe?

As more companies expand their operations globally, the need to understand the cultures of foreign countries becomes more important. Marketers should become familiar with the culture and adapt to it. Or marketers can attempt to bring their own culture to other countries, as Walt Disney did with the opening of Euro Disney in 1992.

Subculture

A culture can be divided into subcultures on the basis of demographic characteristics, geographic regions, political beliefs, religious beliefs, national and ethnic background, and the like. A **subculture** is a homogeneous group of people who share elements of the overall culture as well as unique elements of their own group. Within subcultures, there are even greater similarities in people's attitudes, values, and actions than within the broader culture. Subcultural differences may result in considerable variation in what, how, when, and where people buy goods and services.

subculture
Homogeneous group of people who share elements of the overall culture as well as unique elements of their own group.

In the United States alone, countless subcultures can be identified. The Mormon religion, for example, is common in Utah; southern Louisiana is mainly Roman Catholic. Hispanics are more predominant in those states that border Mexico; the majority of Chinese, Japanese, and Koreans are found in the Pacific region of the United States.

Many demographers predict that in the twenty-first century nonwhite racial and ethnic groups will outnumber whites in this country for the first time. Few immigrants now are of European origin. Instead, they tend to be Asian, Mexican, and Latin American. Immigrants also tend to have more children than U.S.-born citi-

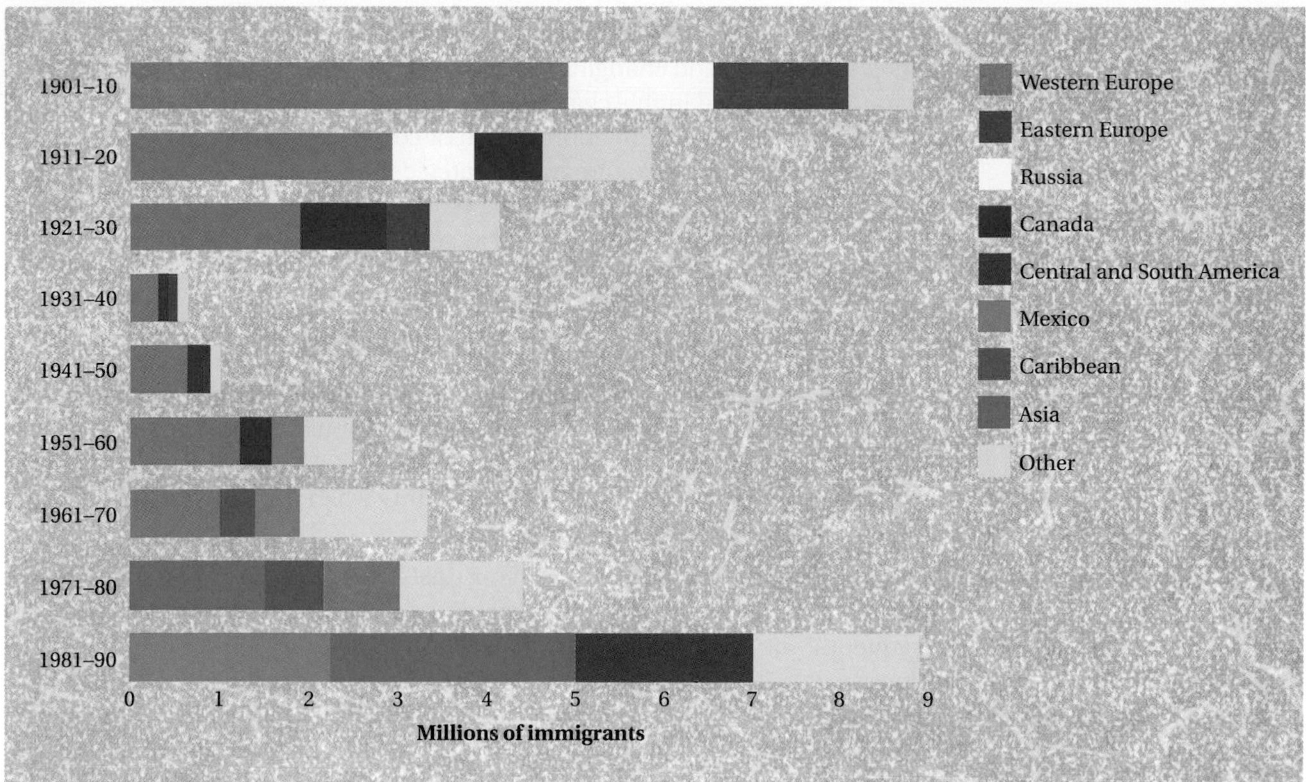

Exhibit 4.9

How Immigration to the United States Is Changing

Source: Adapted from "Let's Change the Immigration Law—Now," *Fortune*, 29 January 1990, © 1990 Time Inc. All rights reserved.

zens. Together, these two factors are boosting the share of minorities in the population.[40] Exhibit 4.9 shows how the nationalities of new immigrants have changed.

If marketers can identify subcultures, they can then design special marketing programs to serve their needs. For instance, large numbers of Latin Americans now live in southern Florida, where they speak their native language. Responding to this sizable and affluent subculture, *The Miami Herald* now publishes two versions of its daily newspaper, one in English and one in Spanish (called *El Nuevo Herald*). The newspaper appeals to its readers by emphasizing Hispanic, Cuban, and Latin American news.[41] Many marketers also use bilingual labeling and packaging in the Miami area.

Within another U.S. subculture, marketers are having a harder time promoting their products. About 7 million Asian-Americans live in the United States, according to the Census Bureau. However, the Asian-American market is composed of twenty-nine distinct ethnic groups, with no common language or culture. Marketers have to target especially carefully in their efforts to reach this group. To complicate the task further, Asian-Americans are less likely than the total population to spend time with any of the major media, to use coupons, or to shop by direct mail.[42]

LOOKING BACK

Returning to the discussion that opened this chapter, you should now be able to see how individual and social factors affect the consumer decision-making process. Many consumers have adopted back-to-basics values. These consumers no longer want expensive or high-status goods. They now desire higher-quality products at lower prices. This change in values is ultimately reflected in purchasing behavior. Companies like BMW, Häagen-Dazs, and Club Med have responded to these changing values through their advertising and product design. These companies also

KEY TERMS

aspirational group 123
attitude 119
belief 119
cognitive dissonance 108
consumer behavior 102
consumer decision-making process 103
culture 128
evoked set 105
extensive decision making 102
external information search 105
external stimuli 104
high-involvement decision making 110

closely monitor other factors that affect consumer behavior, such as perceptions, attitudes, motivation, and changing demographics.

As you've discovered in this chapter, consumer decision making is a fascinating and often intricate process. An appreciation of consumer behavior and the factors that influence it is an important part of strategic marketing planning. This understanding will help you identify target markets and design effective marketing mixes. Knowing how consumers behave, as well as why they behave the way they do, will better equip you to develop a successful marketing plan.

SUMMARY

1 Explain why marketing managers should understand consumer behavior. Consumer behavior describes how consumers make purchase decisions and how they use and dispose of the products they buy. An understanding of consumer behavior reduces marketing managers' uncertainty when they are defining a target market and designing a marketing mix.

2 Identify the types of consumer buying decisions. Consumer decision making falls into three broad categories. first, consumers exhibit routine response behavior for frequently purchased, low-cost items that require very little decision effort. Routine response behavior is typically characterized by brand loyalty. Second, consumers engage in limited decision making for occasional purchases or for unfamiliar brands in familiar product categories. Third, consumers practice extensive decision making when making unfamiliar, expensive, or infrequent purchases.

3 Analyze the components of the consumer decision-making process. The consumer decision-making process begins with a stimulus that is either internal or external. Problem recognition occurs when stimuli trigger awareness of an unfulfilled want. If additional information is required to make a purchase decision, the consumer may engage in an internal or external information search. The consumer then evaluates the additional information and establishes purchase guidelines.

4 Explain the consumer's postpurchase evaluation process. Consumer postpurchase evaluation is influenced by prepurchase expectations, the prepurchase information search, and the consumer's general level of self-confidence. Cognitive dissonance is the inner tension that a consumer experiences after recognizing a purchased product's disadvantages. When a purchase creates cognitive dissonance, consumers tend to react by seeking positive reinforcement for the purchase decision, avoiding negative information about the purchase decision, or revoking the purchase decision by returning the product.

5 Discuss the importance of high and low involvement in buying decisions. High-involvement decisions usually include an extensive information search and a thorough evaluation of alternatives. In contrast, low-involvement decisions are characterized by brand loyalty and a lack of personal identification with the product. The main factors affecting the level of consumer involvement are price, interest, perceived risk of negative consequences, situation, and social visibility.

6 Identify and understand the individual and social factors that affect consumer buying decisions. Individual factors include perception, motivation, learning, values, beliefs, attitudes, personality, self-concept, and lifestyle. Social factors include such external influences as reference groups, opinion leaders, family, life cycle, social class, culture, and subculture. Because all consumer behavior is shaped by individual and social factors, the main goal of marketing strategy is to understand and influence them.

Review Questions

1. What are the steps in the consumer decision-making process? Do all consumer decisions involve these steps?
2. Describe the role of problem recognition in consumer decision making. How do consumers recognize unfulfilled wants?
3. What factors shape the postpurchase evaluation process?
4. Which factors determine the level of consumer involvement in buying decisions?
5. What strategies can marketers use to promote high-involvement versus low-involvement products?
6. Explain the concept of a threshold level of perception.
7. Why is understanding the consumer postpurchase evaluation process important to marketers? How can marketers control cognitive dissonance?
8. Why are reference groups important to marketers?

Discussion and Writing Questions

1. Describe the three categories of consumer decision-making behavior. Name typical products for which each type of consumer behavior is used.
2. The type of decision making a consumer uses for a product does not necessarily remain constant. Why? Support your answer with an example from your own experience.
3. Considering Maslow's hierarchy of needs, give some examples of how marketers appeal to basic human motivations.
4. Recall an occasion when you experienced cognitive dissonance about a purchase. In a letter to a friend, describe the event and explain what you did about it.
5. Discuss a high-involvement purchase decision that you have made. What made it a high-involvement purchase?
6. You are a new marketing manager for a firm that wants to reach a subculture not mentioned in the chapter. For your boss, write a memo listing some products that appeal to this subculture, and recommend some marketing strategies.

CASES

4.1 Coca-Cola

The 1980s will go down in history as the decade of the cola wars. Coca-Cola and Pepsi-Cola went head-to-head in the battle to become the favorite soft drink. Soft-drink companies used many advertising ploys and catchy slogans in an attempt to convince people that a soft drink is more than carbonated sugar water; it is a lifestyle.

Blind taste tests indicated that people preferred the taste of Pepsi to Coke, but Coke was still the number-one brand. In an attempt to lure Pepsi drinkers away and to respond to the blind taste test results, Coca-Cola introduced New Coke. New Coke is a sweeter drink with less bite than the regular Coke. Loyal Coke drinkers complained loudly. They did not care that research indicated people preferred the taste of Pepsi. They wanted their old Coke back. Coca-Cola conceded and brought back the original recipe as Coca-Cola Classic. The company has kept the New Coke formula in the product line, but its sales have been a major disappointment.

Price-sensitive consumers are another problem. Sales for the soft-drink industry are currently flat. Industry experts contend that price will continue to be a major factor in consumers' decisions to buy the product. Some consumers buy whichever cola is on sale in the supermarket.

After spending the better part of a decade pitting Coke against Pepsi, Coca-Cola decided to try a new tactic. If a company has the number-three position, why not attack the number-two brand? Diet Pepsi had been around for twenty-five years, long before the introduction of NutraSweet. Diet Coke had been around for only a year. Using the new sweetener gave Diet Coke an advantage. Consumers had not yet developed as strong a taste recognition for Diet Coke as they had for Diet Pepsi. NutraSweet gives diet drinks a better taste than saccharin-based diet drinks like Diet Pepsi, which tastes bitter.

For the most part, only women were prepared to trade taste for fewer calories. Pepsi had spent most of its twenty-five years concentrating on calorie-counting women. Since Pepsi was positioned to attract them, Diet Coke was in a much better position to attract a broader audience. "Just for the taste of it" became Diet Coke's battle cry in the cola wars.

Questions

1. How can consumers prefer one brand in a blind taste test yet prefer a different soft drink in a nonblind test?
2. Do you think nondiet soft-drink consumers would switch to diet drinks? Why or why not? How would a consumer's belief structure influence this decision?
3. What recommendations would you make to Coca-Cola regarding deal-prone (price-sensitive) consumers?

Suggested Readings

"Annual Soft Drink Report [special insert]," *Beverage Industry*, March 1990.

Scott Ticer, "The Cola Superpowers' Outrageous New Arsenals," *Business Week*, 20 March 1990, pp. 162–166.

4.2 General Tire (A)

Consumer Tire Purchasing at General Tire

General Tire, Inc.
1 General Street
Akron, OH 44329

SIC code: 3011 Tires and inner tubes

Number of employees: 8,000

1993 revenues: Approximately $1.3 billion

Major brands: General Tires, Continental

Largest competitors: Michelin/Uniroyal/Goodrich, Goodyear, Bridgestone/Firestone

Background

For years, General Tire relied on the strength of its own retail operations to market its line of passenger and light truck tires. During the 1980s, the company abandoned its retail operations to focus its efforts on the production of quality tires. There are two main markets for tires in the United States: the original equipment manufacturer (OEM) market (automobile manufacturers) and the replacement market (consumers). The OEM market has always been attractive to tire manufacturers because of its high volume and nonexistent promotion cost. The high volume provides the manufacturer with a large share of the OEM tire market but at a lower profit margin. Profit margin is low because automobile manufacturers are very price-sensitive and often award the contract for tires to the lowest bidder.

Industry

During the late 1980s, a weak U.S. dollar enabled foreign manufacturers to buy U.S. tire production facilities and combine operations within their existing plants to generate greater economies of scale. For example, Michelin acquired Uniroyal and B.F. Goodrich. These acquisitions gave Michelin a 20 percent share of the tire market. Goodyear and Bridgestone/Firestone each hold a 16 percent share of the market. General Tire, which was purchased by Continental AG of Germany in 1987, is in a distant fourth place, with an 8 percent share of the market.

The tire industry is experiencing slow growth, at 1 to 2 percent per year. The slow growth is attributed mainly to new technology that enables manufacturers to produce longer-lasting tires. The single most important innovation has been the development of the steel-belted radial tire. Today, steel-belted radials account for 95 percent of all passenger car tire sales and 65 percent of all truck tire sales. Every new car built comes equipped with radial tires.

General Tire

Market research conducted by General Tire indicates that consumers have little brand loyalty when it comes to buying tires. The research suggests that consumers are more loyal to the dealer selling the tires than to the brand of tires. To some extent, consumers initially compare the original tires with other brands in the market before making a tire purchase.

One of the most attractive segments in the consumer tire market is performance tires. High-performance tires are designed to fit sports cars and performance sedans. These tires give the car better handling characteristics at higher speeds. High-performance or speed-rated tires wear faster and hence need more frequent replacement. Performance tires are premium-priced and offer a higher profit margin to the manufacturer. This segment is also one of the fastest growing in the tire market. When selecting replacement tires for their cars, consumers interested in performance tires look for a variety of product features, such as speed rating, traction, temperature rat-

ing, and appearance. General Tire competes head to head with Goodyear and Michelin in this market.

Questions

1. Describe the decision making process for buying performance tires. Use Exhibit 4.1 to explain this process.
2. What sources of information do performance tire consumers seem to use?
3. Are tires a high- or low-involvement product in general? Are performance tires different? Justify your answers.
4. What problems might General Tire have in competing with Goodyear and Michelin in the performance tire market? What does General Tire need to do to solve these problems?

References

Million Dollar Directory 1993 (Parsippany, NJ: Dun & Bradstreet Information Services, 1993).

Standard & Poor's Industry Surveys (New York: Standard & Poor's Corporation, October 1993).

Patricia Strand and Gary Levin, "Tire Makers Take Opposite Routes: Michelin Ads Rely on Brand Loyalty," *Advertising Age*, 6 February 1989, p. 34

CHAPTER 5

Business-to-Business Marketing

LEARNING OBJECTIVES
After studying this chapter, you should be able to

1. Define business-to-business marketing.
2. Identify the four major categories of business-market customers.
3. Explain the usefulness of the standard industrial classification system.
4. Explain the major differences between business-to-business and consumer markets.
5. Describe the seven types of business-to-business goods and services.
6. Discuss the unique aspects of business-to-business buying behavior.
7. Discuss the role of strategic alliances in business-to-business marketing.

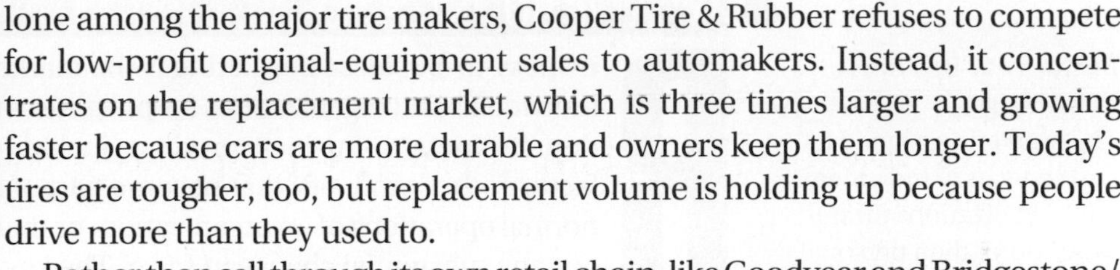

Alone among the major tire makers, Cooper Tire & Rubber refuses to compete for low-profit original-equipment sales to automakers. Instead, it concentrates on the replacement market, which is three times larger and growing faster because cars are more durable and owners keep them longer. Today's tires are tougher, too, but replacement volume is holding up because people drive more than they used to.

Rather than sell through its own retail chain, like Goodyear and Bridgestone/Firestone, Cooper distributes half its production as private-label merchandise through oil companies, large independent distributors, and such mass merchandisers as Western Auto Supply and Pep Boys. The other half goes to independent dealers, who account for 67 percent of replacement-tire sales. Those dealers love Cooper because it doesn't compete with them—unlike Goodyear, for example, which besides having its own brand just agreed to let Sears sell its brand.

Evaluate Cooper Tire & Rubber's strategy of bypassing the new-car manufacturers and instead targeting car owners who need to replace worn-out tires. What are some pros and cons for a tire maker of operating retail outlets? Why would Cooper Tire & Rubber sell as many as half the tires it produces with the brand names of customers like Western Auto and Pep Boys stamped on them?

Source: Adapted from Alex Taylor III, "New Hear This, Jack Welsh!" *Fortune*, 6 April 1992, pp. 94–95.

business-to-business marketing
The marketing of goods and services to individuals and organizations for purposes other than personal consumption.

1 WHAT IS BUSINESS-TO-BUSINESS MARKETING?

Business-to-business marketing is the marketing of goods and services to individuals and organizations for purposes other than personal consumption. Business-to-business products include those that are used to manufacture other products, that become part of another product, that aid the normal operations of an organization, or that are acquired for resale without any substantial change in form. The key characteristic distinguishing business-to-business products from consumer products is intended use, not physical characteristics. A product that is purchased for personal or family consumption or as a gift is a consumer good. If that same product, such as a microcomputer or a cellular telephone, is bought for use in a business, it is a business-to-business product.

2 BUSINESS-TO-BUSINESS CUSTOMERS

producer segment
That part of the business-to-business market consisting of individuals and organizations that buy goods and services to use in producing other products, incorporating into other products, or facilitating the organization's daily operations.

reseller market
That part of the business-to-business market consisting of retail and wholesale businesses that buy finished goods and resell them for a profit.

The business-to-business market consists of four major categories of customers: producers, resellers, governments, and institutions.

Producers

Exhibit 5.1 shows the types of firms in the **producer segment** of the business-to-business market. It includes individuals and organizations that buy goods and services for the purpose of making a profit. They use purchased goods and services to produce other products, to become part of other products, or to facilitate the daily operations of the organization. Individual producer customers often buy large quantities of goods and services. Companies like General Motors spend more than $50 billion annually—more than the gross national product of Ireland, Portugal, Turkey, or Greece—on such business products as steel, metal components, and tires. Companies like AT&T and IBM spend over $50 million daily for business goods and services, such as computer chips and parts.[1]

Resellers

The **reseller market** includes retail and wholesale businesses that buy finished goods and resell them for a profit. A retailer sells mainly to final consumers; whole

Exhibit 5.1

Components of the Producer Segment of the Business-to-Business Market

Kind of organization	Number of firms
Agriculture, forestry, fishing	559,000
Mining	280,000
Construction	1,829,000
Manufacturing	633,000
Transportation, public utilities	709,000
Finance, insurance, real estate	2,377,000
Services	6,813,000
Total	13,200,000

Aerospace and military-aircraft manufacturers sell much of their product to the U.S. government, which is the largest single market for goods and services in the world.

© Tony Stone Worldwide/Barry Lewis

salers sell mostly to retailers and other organizational customers. In 1990, over 1 million retailers and 470,000 wholesalers were operating in the United States, with combined annual sales of over $3 trillion.[2] Consumer product firms like Procter & Gamble, Kraft General Foods, and Coca-Cola sell directly to large retailers and retail chains and through wholesalers to smaller retail units. Wholesaling and retailing are explored in detail in Chapters 12 and 13.

Most retailers carry a huge number of items. For example, drugstores carry inventories of up to 12,000 items; hardware stores, from 3,000 to 25,000 items; and grocery stores, up to 20,000 different items. With so many different brands being stocked, vendors constantly struggle for retail shelf space.

Wholesalers, like retailers, carry many items. A drug wholesaler, for example, may stock up to 125,000 items; a dry-goods wholesaler, up to 250,000 items. Small producers often have difficulty getting wholesalers to carry their merchandise because of limited space and low potential profit. A wholesaler's attitude is likely to be, "I'm carrying 100,000 items. Why should I carry 100,001? I don't know you, I don't know your company, I don't know the quality of your merchandise, and I don't know whether you're dependable."

Governments

A third major segment of the business-to-business market is government. Government organizations include thousands of federal, state, and local buying units. They make up what is considered to be the largest single market for goods and services in the world.[3]

Federal Government

Name just about any good or service and chances are that someone in the federal government uses it. The U.S. federal government is the world's largest customer.

Although much of the federal government's buying is centralized, no single federal agency contracts for all the government's requirements, and no single buyer

in any agency purchases all that the agency needs. One can view the federal government as a combination of several large companies with overlapping responsibilities and thousands of small independent units.

One of the largest "companies" is the General Services Administration (GSA), which buys general-use items (like cars and desks) for all civilian agencies and military departments. A second large "company" is the Defense Logistics Agency (DLA), which buys billions of dollars worth of food, clothing, and other standard supplies for various branches of the military.

State, County, and City Government

Selling to states, counties, and cities can be less frustrating for both small and large vendors than selling to the federal government. Paperwork is typically simpler and more manageable than at the federal level. On the other hand, vendors must decide which of the over 82,000 governmental units are likely to buy their wares. State and local buying agencies include school districts, highway departments, government-operated hospitals, and housing agencies.

Nonfederal government purchasing has become more professional and standardized in recent years. Many larger cities and counties and all states use centralized purchasing, with one purchasing agent for each department of a jurisdiction. Standard specifications apply to most items purchased.

States exchange information on buying procedures and specifications through associations like the National Association of State Purchasing Officials. Nonfederal governments also use cooperative purchasing to reduce costs. Under this system, several units of government—for instance, a city and surrounding suburbs—join to buy certain goods and services. The typical result is price breaks due to volume purchasing.

Bidding

Contracts for government purchases are often put out for bid. Interested vendors submit bids (usually sealed) to provide specified products during a particular time. Sometimes the lowest bidder is awarded the contract. When the lowest bidder is not awarded the contract, strong evidence must be presented to justify the decision. Grounds for rejecting the lowest bid include lack of experience, inadequate financing, or poor past performance. Bidding allows all potential suppliers a fair chance at winning government contracts and helps ensure that public funds are spent wisely. For more information about bidding, see Chapter 19.

Institutions

The fourth major segment of the business-to-business market is institutions that seek to achieve goals different from such ordinary business goals as profit, market share, and return on investment. This segment includes schools, hospitals, colleges and universities, churches, labor unions, fraternal organizations, civic clubs, foundations, and other so-called nonbusiness organizations. The institutional market includes about 6 million organizations and spends about $250 billion annually on goods and services.[4]

A key issue to marketers is the institutional market's diversity. Organizations within this segment differ substantially in their buying behavior. Many organizations in this segment also rely on donations for many of their needed goods and services.

Exhibit 5.2

Standard Industrial Classification System

Division	Industries classified	First two-digit SIC numbers
A	Agriculture, forestry, and fishing	01, 02, 07, 08, 09
B	Mining	10–14
C	Construction	15–17
D	Manufacturing	20–39
E	Transportation, communications, electric, gas, and sanitary services	40–49
F	Wholesale trade	50–51
G	Retail trade	52–59
H	Finance, insurance, and real estate	60–67
I	Services	70, 72–73, 75–76, 78–86, 88–89
J	Public administration	91–97
K	Nonclassifiable establishments	99

3 CLASSIFYING BUSINESS AND GOVERNMENT MARKETS

standard industrial classification system (SIC) Detailed numbering system developed by the U.S. government in order to classify business and government organizations by their main economic activity.

The **standard industrial classification system** (SIC) is a detailed numbering system developed by the U.S. government to classify business and government organizations by their main economic activity. The SIC system divides the economy into eleven major divisions (shown in Exhibit 5.2) and assigns two-digit numbers to major industry groups within each division. The U.S. Census Bureau publishes data on total industry sales and employment for each two-digit code. This information is further broken down by geographic region and is available for each county in the United States.

Two-digit industry categories are then further divided into three-digit and four-digit categories, which represent subindustries within the broader two-digit categories. Exhibit 5.3 shows an example of two-, three-, four-, and five-digit codes. The fifth and subsequent digits are product classifications.

Much has been published on uses of the SIC system for marketing.[5] Exhibit 5.4 shows several SIC data sources and how they may be used by business-to-business marketers.

Although SIC data are helpful for analyzing, segmenting, and targeting markets, they have important limitations. For example, the federal government assigns only one code to each organization. Therefore, the system does not accurately describe firms that engage in many different activities or that provide various types of products. Another limitation is that four-digit codes are not assigned to industries in geographic areas where two or fewer firms are located. Thus some firms are not represented in the SIC listing. Furthermore, the four-digit system is too general to adequately describe industries that are growing more sophisticated and diversified.[6]

Exhibit 5.3

SIC Breakdown for Hand Tools

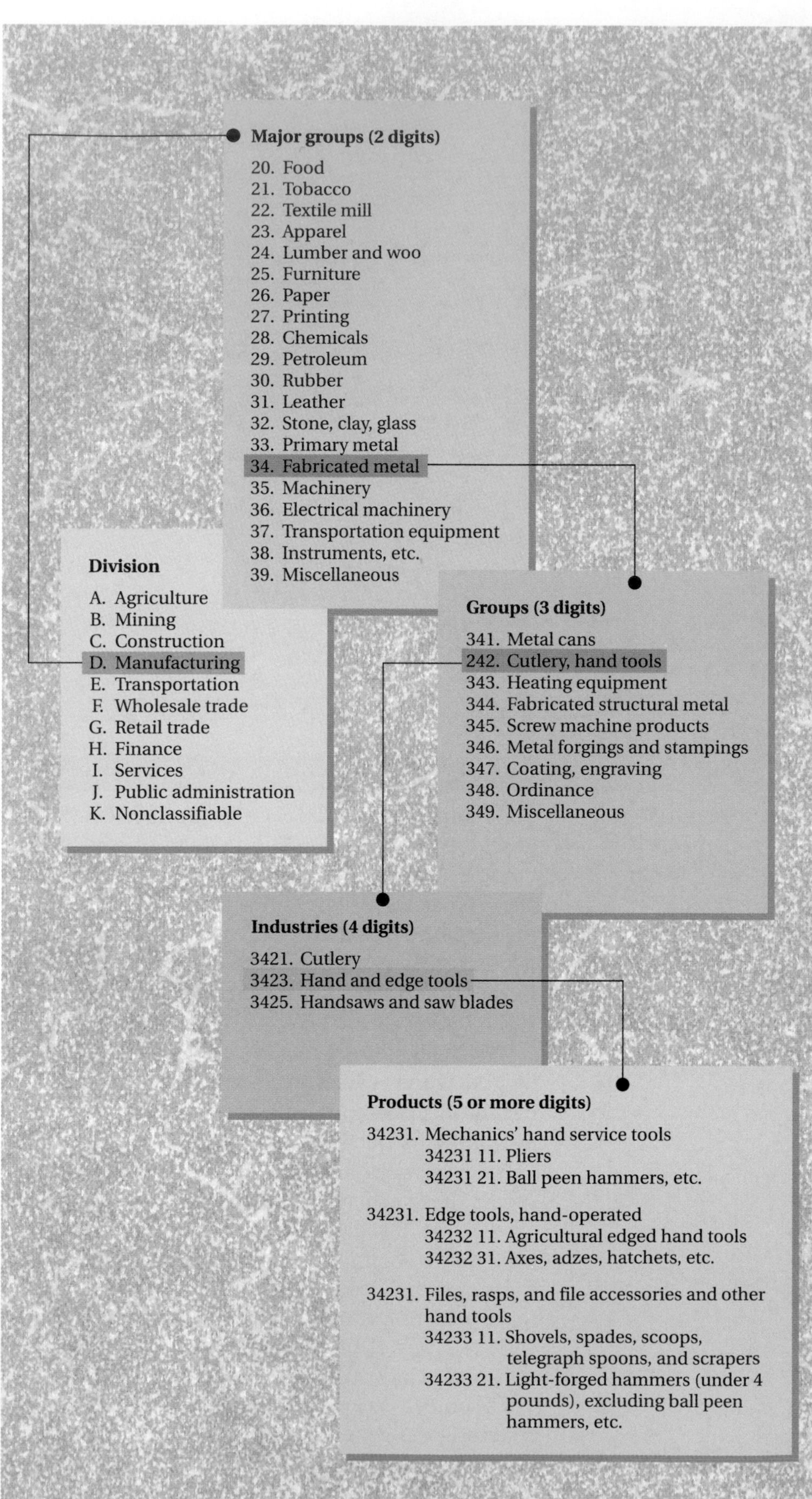

Exhibit 5.4

Selected SIC-Related Sources and Their Marketing Applications

Source: Adapted from Robert W. Haas, "SIC—A Marketing Tool in Transition," *Business*, April–June 1990, pp. 15–22.

SIC source	Possible applications to marketing
SIC Manual	Determining target markets and segments in terms of SIC codes
U.S. Census of Manufacturers	Determining market size, growth, areas of geographic concentration, number of firms; published every 5 years
Survey of Manufacturers	Determining market size, growth, areas of geographic concentration, number of firms; published annually
U.S. Industrial Outlook	Determining number of firms, areas of geographic concentration, past industry trends, projected industry forecasts
Sales & Marketing Management's "Survey of Industrial & Commercial Buying Power"	Determining number of firms by county, number of large firms, value of shipments for total United States and by state and county
County Business Patterns	Determining number of firms by county, number of employees
Dun's *Census of American Business*	Determining number of firms by employee size, sales volume, and state and county
Predicasts	Determining market size, annual growth rates; from short- and long-term forecasts by SIC in article abstracts
Private industrial directories, such as *Million Dollar Directory, Poor's Register*	Determining company names, addresses, secondary SIC codes, products produced, sales volumes, and names of key executives; on a national basis
State and county industrial directories	Similar to private industrial directories, but by individual state or county
Data bases, such as Dun & Bradstreet, Trinet, Thomas	Determining company names, addresses, sales volumes, products, number of employees, names of key executives, market share, consumption of products
Mailing-list companies	Determining company names and addresses; on labels, printouts, diskettes, tapes

MARKETING AND SMALL BUSINESS

Finding Gold in the Government

An excellent target market for small businesses is the government. Many small companies have been very successful in this market, and the government offers some distinct advantages over other markets. For one thing, there's no doubt that the government will pay its bills, although it may take its time. Also, as a government contractor, a new small business gains credibility that can help in selling to private customers. In addition, Uncle Sam buys nearly everything—from food to spark plugs to exotic scientific and technical equipment—and doesn't usually subject suppliers to the abrupt cancellations that, in industry, are a feature of recessions. By making progress payments as the steps of a project are completed, the government acts as a financing source for small businesses. Progress payments help small businesses buy the inventory needed to complete the contract. And, in the view of some small-business owners, the government is a more objective buyer than many companies are.

However, learning how to bid for government orders can be a major problem. It doesn't take long for the small-business manager to discover that up-and-coming bureaucrats feel more comfortable with big-company suppliers. Government bureaucrats also have a way of moving on to new assignments, leaving the small enterprise to prove itself over again to their replacement.

Small businesses that finally win federal procurement awards may encounter another set of problems. Sometimes the specifications are different from those the company originally understood. The government's time requirements for delivery may be unreasonably short, or the time the government takes to pay may be unreasonably long.

4 BUSINESS-TO-BUSINESS VERSUS CONSUMER MARKETS

The basic philosophy and practice of marketing is the same whether the customer is a business organization or a consumer. Business markets do, however, have characteristics different from consumer markets. These characteristics often generate approaches to creating mutually satisfying exchanges different from those common in consumer product marketing. Exhibit 5.5 summarizes the main differences between business-to-business and consumer markets.

Demand

Unlike consumer demand, business-to-business demand is derived, inelastic, joint, and fluctuating.

Derived Demand

derived demand
Demand that results from demand for another product.

The demand for business-to-business products is called **derived demand** because organizations buy products to be used directly or indirectly in producing consumer products. In other words, the demand for business-to-business products is derived from the demand for consumer products. For example, car and truck manufacturers account for a major share of U.S. steel, rubber, and aluminum consumption. An additional 5 billion pounds of aluminum are used annually in the production of beverage containers.[7]

Since demand is derived, business-to-business marketers must carefully monitor demand patterns and changing preferences in final consumer markets. Moreover, business-to-business marketers must also carefully monitor their customers' forecasts, because derived demand is based on expectations of future demand for those customers' products.

Some business-to-business marketers not only monitor final consumer demand and customer forecasts but also try to influence final consumer demand. For example, aluminum producers advertise on television and in magazines the convenience and recyclability of aluminum containers. The target of these ads is beverage purchasers and consumers.

Exhibit 5.5

Major Characteristics of Business-to-Business Markets Compared to Consumer Markets

Characteristic	Business-to-business market	Consumer market
Demand	Organizational	Individual
Purchase volume	Larger	Smaller
Number of customers	Fewer	Many
Location of buyers	Geographically concentrated	Dispersed
Distribution structure	More direct	More indirect
Nature of buying	More professional	More personal
Nature of buying influence	Multiple	Single
Type of negotiations	More complex	Simpler
Use of reciprocity	Yes	No
Use of leasing	Greater	Smaller
Primary promotional method	Personal selling	Advertising

inelastic demand
Demand that is not significantly affected by price changes.

Inelastic Demand

The demand for many business-to-business products is inelastic with regard to price. **Inelastic demand** means that an increase or decrease in the price of the product will not significantly affect demand for the product.

The price of a product used in the production of or as part of a final product is often a minor part of the final product's total price. Therefore, demand for the final consumer product is not affected. If the price of automobile paint or spark plugs rose significantly, say 200 percent in one year, do you think the number of new automobiles sold that year would be affected? Probably not. For a further discussion of inelastic demand, see Chapter 18.

joint demand
Demand for two or more items that are used together in a final product.

Joint Demand

Joint demand occurs when two or more items are used together in a final product. For example, a decline in the availability of memory chips will slow production of microcomputers, which will in turn reduce the demand for disk drives. Many business products, like hammer heads and hammer handles, also exemplify joint demand.

multiplier effect (or accelerator principle)
Phenomenon in which a small increase or decrease in consumer demand produces a much larger change in demand for the facilities and equipment needed to make the consumer product.

Fluctuating Demand

The demand for business-to-business products—particularly new plants and equipment—tends to be more unstable than the demand for consumer products. A small increase or decrease in consumer demand can produce a much larger change in demand for the facilities and equipment needed to make the consumer product. Economists refer to this as the **multiplier effect** or the **accelerator principle.**

Boeing Aircraft uses sophisticated surface grinders to make airplane parts. Suppose Boeing is using twenty surface grinders. Each machine lasts about ten years. Purchases have been timed so two machines will wear out and be replaced annually. If the demand for airplane parts does not change, two grinders will be bought this year. If the demand for parts declines slightly, only eighteen grinders may be needed and Boeing won't replace the worn ones. However, suppose in the next year demand returns to previous levels plus a little more. To meet the new level of demand,

Computers are made of many parts, including keyboards, circuitry boards, silicon wafers, and microprocessor chips. These components all sell well when computers are selling well—an example of joint demand.
© Grant V. Faint/The Image Bank

Boeing will need to replace the two machines that wore out in the first year, the two that wore out in the second year, plus one or more additional machines. The multiplier effect works this way in many industries, producing highly fluctuating demand for business-to-business products.

Purchase Volume

Business-to-business customers buy in much larger quantities than consumers. Just think how large an order Kellogg typically places for the wheat bran and raisins used to manufacture Raisin Bran. Imagine the number of tires that Ford buys at one time. Consider the number of boxes of cereal that Sam's Wholesale Clubs buys at one time.

Number of Customers

Business-to-business marketers usually have far fewer customers than consumer marketers. The advantage is that it is a lot easier to identify prospective buyers, monitor current customers' needs and satisfaction, and personally attend to existing customers. The main disadvantage is that each customer becomes crucial—especially for those business-to-business manufacturers that have only one customer. In many cases, this customer is the U.S. government.

Location of Buyers

Business-to-business customers tend to be much more geographically concentrated than consumers. For instance, more than half the nation's industrial buyers are located in New York, California, Pennsylvania, Illinois, Ohio, Michigan, and New Jersey. The petroleum, rubber, and steel industries are even more concentrated.

Distribution Structure

Many consumer products pass through a distribution system that includes the producer, one or more wholesalers, and a retailer. Because of many of the characteristics already mentioned, channels of distribution are typically shorter in business-to-business marketing. Direct channels, where manufacturers market directly to users, are much more common.

Nature of Buying

Unlike consumers, business buyers usually approach purchasing rather formally. Businesses use professionally trained purchasing agents or buyers who spend their entire career purchasing a limited number of items. They get to know the items and the sellers quite well. Some professional purchasers earn the designation of Certified Purchasing Manager (C.P.M.) after participating in a rigorous certification program.

Nature of Buying Influence

Typically, more people are involved in a single business purchase decision than in a consumer purchase. Experts from fields as varied as quality control, marketing, and finance, as well as professional buyers and users, may be grouped in a buying center (discussed later in this chapter).

Type of Negotiations

Consumers are used to negotiating price on automobiles and real estate. But in most cases, U.S. consumers expect sellers to set the price and other conditions of sale, such as time of delivery and credit terms. On the other hand, negotiating is common

in business-to-business marketing. Buyers and sellers negotiate product specifications, delivery dates, payment terms, and other pricing matters. Sometimes these negotiations occur during many meetings over several months. Final contracts are often very long and detailed.

Use of Reciprocity

Business purchasers often choose to buy from their own customers, a practice known as **reciprocity**. It is neither unethical nor illegal unless one party coerces the other and the result is unfair competition. Reciprocity is generally considered a reasonable business practice. If all possible suppliers sell about the same product for about the same price, doesn't it make sense to buy from those firms that buy from you?

reciprocity
Practice in which business purchasers choose to buy from their own customers.

Use of Leasing

Consumers normally buy products rather than lease them. But businesses commonly lease expensive equipment like computers, construction equipment and vehicles, and automobiles. The lessor, the firm providing the product, may be either the manufacturer or an independent firm. Leasing accounts for about a third of all new capital investment in the United States each year.[8]

Leasing allows firms to reduce capital outflow, acquire a seller's latest products, receive better services, and gain tax advantages.[9] The benefits to the lessor include greater total revenue from leasing compared to selling and a chance to do business with customers who cannot afford to buy. Leasing, however, is not without risks. When U.S. airlines slashed spending in the early 1990s, hundreds of jets owned by aircraft makers and leasing firms were idled.[10]

Primary Promotional Method

Business-to-business marketers tend to emphasize personal selling in their promotion efforts, especially for expensive items, custom-designed products, large-volume purchases, and situations requiring negotiations. The sale of many business-to-business products requires a great deal of personal contact.

Some business-to-business marketers use **team selling.** They assemble a team of experts who share the specialized knowledge of key buying influences within customer firms.

team selling
Practice of selling to business-to-business customers by assembling a team of experts who share the specialized knowledge of key buying influences within customer firms.

5 TYPES OF BUSINESS-TO-BUSINESS PRODUCTS

Business-to-business products generally fall into one of the following seven categories, depending on their use: major equipment, accessory equipment, raw materials, component parts, processed materials, supplies, and business services.

major equipment
Capital goods, such as large or expensive machines, mainframe computers, blast furnaces, generators, airplanes, and buildings.

Major Equipment

Major equipment includes such capital goods as large or expensive machines, mainframe computers, blast furnaces, generators, airplanes, and buildings. These items are also commonly called **installations.** Major equipment is depreciated over time rather than charged as an expense in the year it is purchased. In addition, major equipment is often custom-designed for each customer.

installation
Capital good, such as a large or expensive machine, mainframe computer, blast furnace, generator, airplane, or building.

Personal selling is an important part of the marketing strategy for major equipment because distribution channels are almost always direct from the producer to the business user.

Like other producers, farmers must purchase major equipment, such as corn harvesters.
© Tony Stone Worldwide/Curt Maas

Accessory Equipment

accessory equipment
Goods, such as portable tools and office equipment, that are less expensive and shorter-lived than major equipment.

Accessory equipment is generally less expensive and shorter-lived than major equipment. Examples include portable drills, power tools, word processors, and fax machines. Accessory equipment is often charged as an expense in the year it is bought rather than depreciated over its useful life. In contrast to major equipment, accessories are more often standardized and are usually bought by more customers. These customers tend to be widely dispersed. For example, all types of businesses buy word-processing equipment.

Local industrial distributors (wholesalers) play an important role in the marketing of accessory equipment because business buyers often purchase accessories from them. Advertising is a more vital promotional tool for accessory equipment than for major equipment regardless of their locations.

Raw Materials

raw material
Unprocessed extractive or agricultural product, such as mineral ore, lumber, wheat, corn, fruits, vegetables, and fish.

Raw materials are unprocessed extractive or agricultural products—for example, mineral ore, lumber, wheat, corn, fruits, vegetables, and fish. Raw materials become part of finished products. Extensive users, such as steel or lumber mills and food canners, generally buy huge quantities of raw materials. Since there is often a large number of relatively small sellers of raw materials, none can greatly influence price or supply. Thus the market tends to set the price of raw materials. Individual producers normally have little pricing flexibility. Promotion is almost always personal selling, and distribution channels are usually direct from producer to business user.

Component Parts

component part
Finished item ready for assembly or product that needs very little processing before becoming part of some other product.

Component parts are either finished items ready for assembly or products that need very little processing before becoming part of some other product. Examples include spark plugs, tires, and electric motors in automobiles. A special feature of component parts is that they often retain their identity after becoming part of the final product. For example, automobile tires are clearly recognizable as part of a car. Moreover, because component parts often wear out, they may need to be replaced several times during the life of the final product. Thus there are two important markets for many component parts: the original equipment manufacturer (OEM) market and the replacement market.

Many of the business-to-business features listed before in Exhibit 5.5 characterize the OEM market. The difference between unit costs and selling prices in the OEM market is often small, but profits can be quite substantial because of volume buying. Rarely does advertising play a key role in the promotion strategy for OEM markets. Even more rare is advertising to end users. Two exceptions to this generalization are NutraSweet, the artificial sweetener, and Intel, the semiconductor company. Intel pays personal computer manufacturers to feature its logo—"Intel inside"—in their ads. Intel's goal is to create a brand preference for the parts inside a computer.[11]

The replacement market is comprised of organizations or individuals buying component parts to replace worn-out parts. Because components often retain their identity in final products, users may choose to replace a component part with the same brand used by the manufacturer—for example, the same brand of automobile tires or battery. The replacement market operates differently from the OEM market. Whether replacement buyers are organizations or individuals, they tend to demonstrate the characteristics of consumer markets that were shown in Exhibit 5.5. Consider, for example, an automobile replacement part. Purchase volume is usually small, and there are many customers, geographically dispersed, who typically buy from car dealers or parts stores. Negotiations do not occur, and neither reciprocity nor leasing is usually an issue. Manufacturers of component parts often direct their advertising toward replacement buyers. Cooper Tire & Rubber, featured at the beginning of this chapter, makes and markets component parts—automobile and truck tires—for the replacement market only. Ford and other carmakers compete with independent firms in the market for replacement automobile parts.[12]

Processed Materials

processed material
Good used directly in manufacturing other products.

Processed materials are used directly in manufacturing other products. Unlike raw materials, they have had some processing. Examples include sheet metal, chemicals, specialty steel, lumber, corn syrup, and plastics. Unlike component parts, processed materials do not retain their identity in final products. Most processed materials are marketed to OEMs or distributors servicing the OEM market. Processed materials are generally bought according to customer specifications or to some industry standard, as is the case with steel and lumber. Price and service are important factors in choosing a vendor.

Supplies

supply
Consumable item that does not become part of the final product.

business service
Expense item obtained from an outside provider that does not become part of a final product, such as janitorial, advertising, legal, management consulting, marketing research, maintenance, and other services.

Supplies are consumable items that do not become part of the final product—for example, lubricants, detergents, paper towels, pencils, and paper. Supplies are normally standardized items that purchasing agents routinely buy. Supplies typically have relatively short lives and are inexpensive compared to other business goods. Because supplies generally fall into one of three categories—maintenance, repair, or operating—this category is often referred to as MRO items. Competition in the MRO market is intense. Bic and Paper Mate, for example, battle for business purchases of inexpensive ballpoint pens.

Business Services

Business services are expense items that do not become part of a final product. Businesses retain outside providers to perform janitorial, advertising, legal, management consulting, marketing research, maintenance, and other tasks. Hiring outside providers makes sense when it costs less than hiring or assigning an employee to perform the task and when outside providers are needed for their particular expertise.

6 BUSINESS-TO-BUSINESS BUYING BEHAVIOR

As you probably have already concluded, business buyers behave differently from consumers. Understanding how purchase decisions are made in organizations is a first step in developing a business-to-business selling strategy. Five important aspects of business-to-business buying behavior are buying centers, evaluative criteria, buying situations, the purchase process, and customer service.

Buying Centers

buying center
Group within an organization consisting of all those who are involved in the purchase decision.

A **buying center** includes all those persons in an organization who become involved in the purchase decision. Membership and influence vary from company to company. For instance, in engineering-dominated firms like Bell Helicopter and General Dynamics, the buying center may consist almost entirely of engineers. In marketing-oriented firms like Toyota and IBM, marketing and engineering have almost equal authority. In consumer goods firms like Procter & Gamble, product managers and other marketing decision makers may dominate the buying center. In a small manufacturing company, almost everyone may be a member.

A firm's buying center will not appear on the formal organization chart. For example, even though a formal committee may have been set up to choose a new plant site, it is only part of the buying center. Other people, like the company president, often play informal yet powerful roles. In a lengthy decision-making process like finding a new plant location, some members may drop out of the buying center when they can no longer play a useful role. Others whose talents are needed then become part of the center. No formal announcement of "who is in" and "who is out" is ever made.

Roles in the Buying Center

As in consumer purchasing, different people play roles in the purchasing process:

- *Initiator:* the person who first suggests making a purchase.
- *Influencers/evaluators:* people who influence the buying decision. They often help define specifications and provide information for evaluating options. Technical personnel are especially important as influencers.
- *Gatekeepers:* group members who regulate the flow of information. Frequently, the purchasing agent views the gatekeeping role as a source of his or her power. A secretary may also act as a gatekeeper by determining which vendors get an appointment with a buyer.
- *Decider:* the person who has the formal or informal power to choose or approve the selection of the supplier or brand. In complex situations, it is often difficult to determine who makes the final decision.
- *Purchaser:* the person who actually negotiates the purchase. It could be anyone from the president of the company to the purchasing agent, depending on the importance of the decision.
- *Users:* members of the organization who will actually use the product. Users often initiate the buying process and help define product specifications.

Examples of these basic roles are shown in Exhibit 5.6.

Implications of Buying Centers for the Marketing Manager

Vendors realize the importance of identifying and interacting with the true decision makers. Alcoa claims that every hour its sales engineers contact key design engi-

Exhibit 5.6

Buying Center Roles for Personal Computer Purchases

Role	Illustration
Initiator	Division general manager proposes to replace company's personal computer network.
Influencers/evaluators	Corporate controller's office and vice president of data processing have important say about which system and vendor company will deal with.
Gatekeepers	Corporate departments for purchasing and data processing analyze company's needs and recommend likely matches with potential vendors.
Decider	Vice president of administration, with influence from others, selects vendor the company will deal with and system it will buy.
Purchaser	Purchasing agent negotiates terms of sale.
Users	All division employees use personal computers.

neers and managers in Detroit and in the aerospace business. As a result, the aluminum industry has made inroads in what was the steel industry's market for car and airplane parts.

In reviewing a customer's buying center, a marketing manager must ask three basic questions:

- *Who is in the decision-making unit?* Define the players in the decision-making process.
- *What is each member's relative influence in the decision?* Determine where the sales efforts should be concentrated. A good sales presentation can change a neutral buying center member into an advocate.
- *What are each member's evaluative criteria, and how does he or she rate each prospective supplier on these criteria?* Decide how to make the right presentation to key decision makers. If a decision maker is concerned about on-time deliveries, then the ability to provide efficient on-time service should be stressed in the sales presentation.

Consider the following example:

The American Hospital Supply Corporation sells nonwoven disposable surgical gowns to hospitals. It tries to identify the hospital personnel who participate in this buying decision. The decision-making participants usually include the vice-president of purchasing, the operating-room administrator, and the surgeons. Each party plays a different role. The vice-president of purchasing analyzes whether the hospital should buy disposable gowns or reusable gowns. If the findings favor disposable gowns, then the operating-room administrator compares various competitors' products and prices and makes a choice. This administrator considers the gown's absorbency, antiseptic quality, design, and cost and normally buys the brand that meets the functional requirements at the lowest cost. Finally, surgeons influence the decision retroactively by reporting their satisfaction with the particular brand.[13]

Evaluative Criteria

Business buyers evaluate products and suppliers against three important criteria: quality, service, and price—in that order.

- *Quality:* Quality refers to technical suitability. A superior tool can do a better job in the production process, and a superior package can increase dealer and consumer acceptance of a brand. Evaluation of quality also applies to the salesperson and the salesperson's firm. Business buyers want to deal with reputable salespeople and companies that are financially responsible.
- *Service:* Almost as much as they want satisfactory products, business buyers want satisfactory service. A purchase offers several opportunities for service. Suppose a vendor is selling heavy equipment. Prepurchase service could be a survey of the buyer's needs. After thorough analysis of the survey findings, the vendor could prepare a report and recommendations, which constitute a purchasing proposal. If a purchase results, postpurchase service might consist of installing the equipment and training those who will be using it. Postsale services could also include maintenance and repairs. Another feature of service that business buyers seek is dependability of supply. They must be able to count on delivery of exactly what was ordered when it is scheduled to be delivered. Buyers also welcome services that help them sell their finished products. Services of this sort are especially appropriate when the seller's product is an identifiable part of the buyer's end product.
- *Price:* Business buyers want to buy at low prices—at the lowest prices, under most circumstances. However, a buyer who pressures a supplier to cut prices to a point where the supplier loses money on the sale almost forces shortcuts on quality. The buyer also may, in effect, force the supplier to quit selling to him or her. Then a new source of supply will have to be found.

Many international business buyers use similar evaluative criteria. One study of South African buyers of high-tech laboratory instruments found that they use the following evaluative criteria, in descending order: technical service, perceived product reliability, after-sales support, supplier's reputation, ease of maintenance, ease of operation, price, confidence in the sales representative, and product flexibility.[14]

Buying Situations

Often business firms, especially manufacturers, must decide whether to make something or buy it from an outside supplier. The decision is essentially one of economics. Can an item of similar quality be bought at a lower price elsewhere? If not, is manufacturing it in-house the best use of limited company resources? For example, Briggs & Stratton, a major manufacturer of four-cycle engines, might be able to save $150,000 annually on outside purchases by spending $500,000 on the equipment needed to produce gas throttles internally. Yet Briggs & Stratton could also use that $500,000 to upgrade its carburetor assembly line, which would save $225,000 annually.

If a firm does decide to buy a product, instead of making it, the purchase will be a new buy, modified rebuy, or straight rebuy.

new buy
Situation requiring the purchase of a product for the first time.

New Buy

A **new buy** is a situation requiring the purchase of a product for the first time. For example, suppose a law firm decides to replace word-processing machinery with microcomputers. This situation represents the greatest opportunity for new ven-

When Time Warner established its emergency day-care center for employees, it put play equipment and toys on its new-buy list.
James Keyser/ *Time* Magazine

dors. No long-term relationship has been established (at least for this product), specifications may be somewhat fluid, and buyers are generally more open to new vendors.

If the new item is a raw material or a critical component part, the buyer cannot afford to run out of supply. The seller must be able to convince the buyer that the seller's firm can consistently deliver a high-quality product on time.

value engineering
Systematic search for less expensive substitute goods or services.

New-buy situations often result from value engineering. **Value engineering** (also called value analysis) is the systematic search for less expensive substitutes. The goal is to identify goods and services that perform a given function at a lower total cost than those currently used. There is a growing tendency for buyers and potential suppliers to do value engineering studies. The vendor who can show the results of such studies will benefit during the negotiation process.

Modified Rebuy

modified rebuy
Situation in which the purchaser wants some change in the original good or service.

A **modified rebuy** is normally less critical and less time-consuming than a new buy. In a modified-rebuy situation, the purchaser wants some change in the original good or service. It may be a new color, greater tensile strength in a component part, more respondents in a marketing research study, or additional services in a janitorial contract.

Since the two parties are familiar with each other and credibility has been established, buyer and seller can concentrate on the specifics of the modification. But in some cases, modified rebuys are open to outside bidders. The purchaser uses this strategy to ensure that the new terms are competitive. If Boeing, for example, decides it needs additional tensile strength in an airfoil for a cargo jet, it may open the bidding to examine the price-quality offerings of several metal fabricators.

Straight Rebuy

straight rebuy
Situation in which the purchaser reorders the same goods and/or services without looking for new information or investigating other suppliers.

A **straight rebuy** is a situation vendors relish. The purchaser is not looking for new information or other suppliers. An order is placed, and the product is provided as in previous orders. Usually a straight rebuy is routine, since the terms of the purchase have been hammered out in earlier negotiations.

purchasing contract
Agreement in which a business buyer promises to purchase a given amount of a product within a specified period.

One common technique used in straight-rebuy situations is the **purchasing contract.** Purchasing contracts are used with products that are bought often and in

high volume. In essence, the purchasing contract makes the buyer's decision on a particular product routine and promises the salesperson a sure sale. The advantage to the buyer is a quick, confident decision and, to the salesperson, reduced or eliminated competition.

annual purchasing contract
Type of purchasing contract that provides a discount schedule for purchases over the period of the contract.

blanket purchasing contract
Type of purchasing contract that requires the supplier to provide a certain amount of product at the same price each month during the course of a year.

forward buying
Practice of purchasing in advance of needs to take advantage of promotional discounts offered by suppliers.

There are two common forms of purchasing contracts. The **annual purchasing contract** provides a discount schedule for purchases over the period of the contract. The more the company buys throughout the year, the greater the discount it receives. Electronic Data Systems won a landmark annual contract to supply personal computers and training to General Electric worldwide. The four-year contract was estimated to be worth $400 million to $500 million for Electronic Data Systems.[15]

The **blanket purchasing contract,** on the other hand, obliges the supplier to provide a certain amount of product each month during the year at one set price. Each year the contract and the price are renegotiated. Personal computer supplies like print wheels, ribbon cartridges, and tractor-feed paper commonly fall under blanket purchasing contracts.

Some firms use forward buying for products that fall into the straight-rebuy category. **Forward buying** is purchasing in advance of needs to take advantage of promotional discounts offered by suppliers.

Suppliers must remember not to take straight-rebuy relationships for granted. Retaining existing customers is much easier than attracting new ones.

The Purchase Process

The business-to-business purchase process is traced in Exhibit 5.7. It begins with recognition of a need. For example, a firm may realize that it must replace old machinery or expand its facilities.

The next step in the purchase sequence is a tentative decision on the type of product needed. Sometimes the buying firm then drafts product specifications. More often, though, members of the buying center select several potential sources of supply and begin negotiations. Purchasing agents may even keep lists of approved suppliers for various types of products. Negotiations begin with a discussion of the product needed, the time frame within which it is needed, and the terms of delivery. Negotiations often end when each of the potential suppliers submits a proposal with a bid, or price to be charged for the product. The buyer then analyzes the proposals and either selects the best one or asks suppliers for clarification.

Vendor Analysis

vendor analysis
Practice of comparing alternative suppliers in terms of attributes that the buying center views as important.

Buying centers, particularly in new-buy situations, use vendor rating systems, called **vendor analysis,** to compare suppliers on attributes the buying center views as important. Exhibit 5.8 illustrates the use of vendor analysis to compare personal computer suppliers. The buying center has identified the six attributes in the left column as most important. Each vendor is then rated on each attribute on a scale ranging from 0 (unacceptable) to 4 (excellent). A potential vendor's score is determined by adding all the ratings and dividing by the total number of attributes. A more sophisticated approach weights each attribute according to its importance (for example, 1 for somewhat important, 2 for moderately important, and 3 for very important), multiplies importance ratings by rating scores, and sums these to yield a total vendor score.

Completing the Transaction

After analyzing vendors, selecting a source of supply, and negotiating the terms of the purchase, the buying firm issues a purchase order, making the transaction

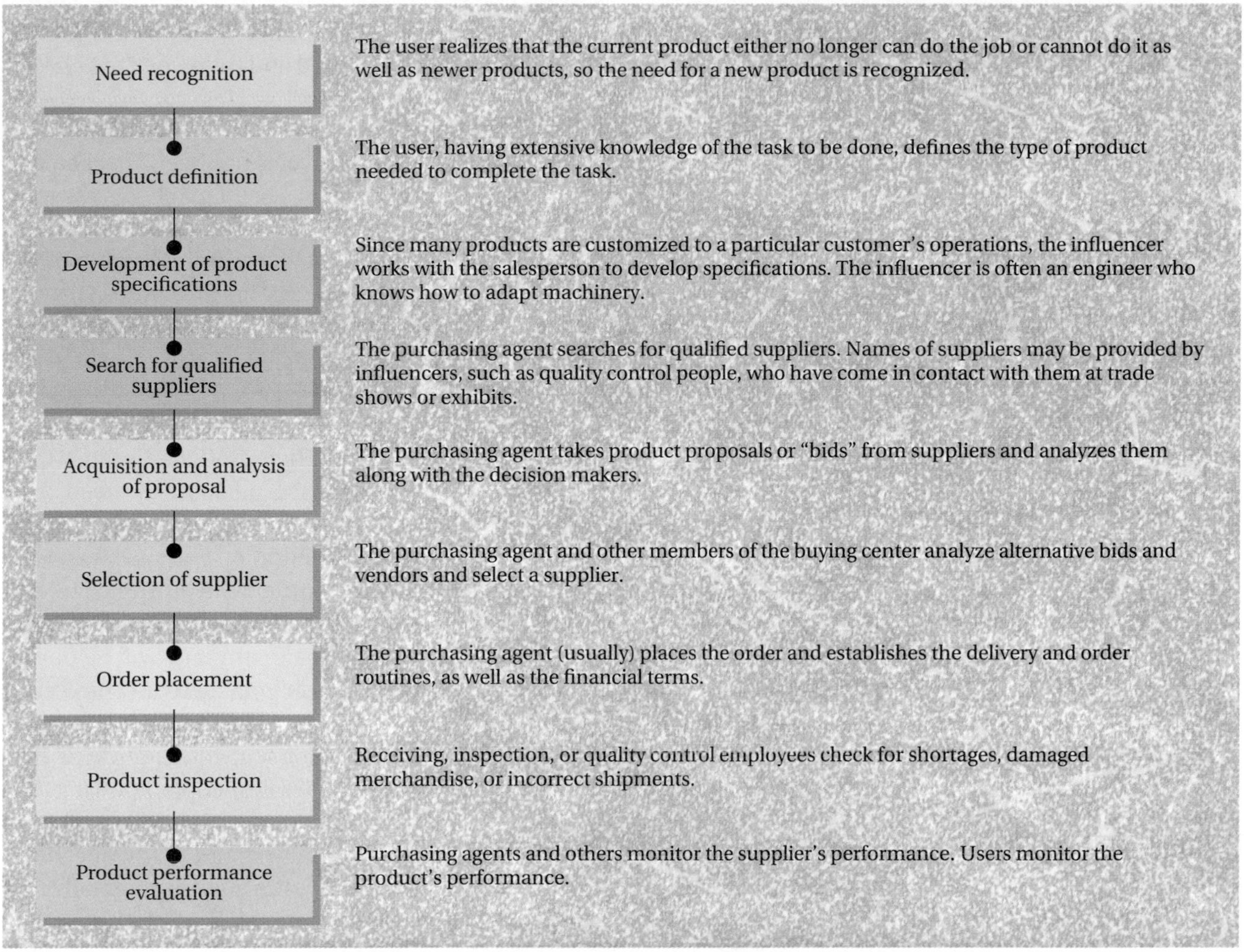

Need recognition	The user realizes that the current product either no longer can do the job or cannot do it as well as newer products, so the need for a new product is recognized.
Product definition	The user, having extensive knowledge of the task to be done, defines the type of product needed to complete the task.
Development of product specifications	Since many products are customized to a particular customer's operations, the influencer works with the salesperson to develop specifications. The influencer is often an engineer who knows how to adapt machinery.
Search for qualified suppliers	The purchasing agent searches for qualified suppliers. Names of suppliers may be provided by influencers, such as quality control people, who have come in contact with them at trade shows or exhibits.
Acquisition and analysis of proposal	The purchasing agent takes product proposals or "bids" from suppliers and analyzes them along with the decision makers.
Selection of supplier	The purchasing agent and other members of the buying center analyze alternative bids and vendors and select a supplier.
Order placement	The purchasing agent (usually) places the order and establishes the delivery and order routines, as well as the financial terms.
Product inspection	Receiving, inspection, or quality control employees check for shortages, damaged merchandise, or incorrect shipments.
Product performance evaluation	Purchasing agents and others monitor the supplier's performance. Users monitor the product's performance.

Exhibit 5.7 (above)

Business-to-Business Purchase Process

Exhibit 5.8

Example of Vendor Analysis in a Personal-Computer Buying Situation

Note: This vendor is strong except on two attributes. The purchasing agent has to decide how important the two weaknesses are. The analysis could be redone using importance weights for the five attributes.

	Rating scale				
Attributes	**Unacceptable (0)**	**Poor (1)**	**Fair (2)**	**Good (3)**	**Excellent (4)**
Compatibility					X
Affordability			X		
Reliability					X
Product line depth			X		
Service/support					X
Flexibility				X	

Total score: 4 + 2 + 4 + 2 + 4 + 3 = 19

Average score: 19 ÷ 6 = 3.17

official. Purchase orders often include such details as product identification code or description, quantity and quality to be delivered, method and frequency of delivery, and payment terms.

When products are received, they are inspected for correctness, quantity, and quality and checked into inventory. When the seller's invoice has been checked and found in order, payment is authorized. Once payment has been made, the transaction is complete.

Although the transaction is complete at this point, the buyer will take note of the product and the supplier's performance through periodic evaluations. These evaluations will help the buyer determine whether to make future purchases from this supplier.

The Salesperson's Role

The salesperson plays a very important role throughout the purchase process. Salespeople often are the first to recognize that buyers need their product. Because they are the ones recognizing the need, they are in a position to influence the product's definition and specifications.

A good salesperson serves as a link between producer and end user, so that products can be developed to meet existing wants and needs.

Salespeople who emphasize the need to the buyer are usually guaranteed that their company will be one of the suppliers considered. (The Ethics in Marketing story on page 157 provides an unusual illustration of this point.) Good salespeople, knowing that at this point they have an "in" with this particular buyer, should ask questions to determine the buyer's potential budget for this purchase. With this type of information, the salesperson can prepare a bid within the buyer's price range. The salesperson's company will have a competitive edge.

If the sale is made, the salesperson should verify that the product is packaged and ready to be delivered on time and is received in good working condition, with all parts included. Finally, throughout their follow-up service, salespeople should ensure that the customer is fully satisfied with the product and that the seller has fulfilled all presale promises.

Customer Service

More business-to-business marketers are recognizing the benefits of developing a formal system of monitoring customer opinions and perceptions of the quality of customer service.[16] Companies like Honda, Apple, and Merck build their strategies not only around products but also around deep knowledge of a few highly developed core service skills.[17]

IBM Canada saw that business customers weren't always getting the service they wanted and started a new program called "customer obsession." It began with a two-day workshop for senior managers in information and marketing services.[18] The goal was to reassess and

ETHICS IN MARKETING

Symposium or Sales Presentation?

A young doctor listened intently to a panel of distinguished physicians discuss advances in hypertension treatment at the annual meeting of the American Academy of Family Physicians. By the end of the three-hour presentation, he was thinking about switching some of his hypertension patients to a drug called a calcium channel blocker, which was much discussed at the presentation. The seminar was sponsored by the pharmaceutical company G.D. Searle, as the young physician knew. But he didn't realize that Searle—which was then running a promotional campaign for Calan, one of several calcium channel blockers—had carefully picked speakers who were well-known advocates of this class of drugs. . . .

The drug industry's public position is that it supports medical education out of concern for the safe and appropriate use of its products and for the professional advancement of its customers, physicians.

Do you think the drug industry's position is ethical? Do you think it was ethical for Searle to sponsor the seminar on calcium channel blockers? Searle didn't hide its sponsorship of the seminar. Should the company have also announced that the speakers had been carefully selected and were well-known advocates of calcium channel blockers?

Source: Adapted from "Pushing Drugs to Doctors," © 1992 by Consumers Union of U.S., Inc., Yonkers, NY 10703-1057. Reprinted by permission from *Consumer Reports*, February 1992, pp. 89–94.

redefine the firm's customer-service strategy. After the workshop, participating executives shared their new plans with all 11,000 employees, regardless of whether these employees dealt directly with customers.

Safety-Kleen, a successful marketer of automotive parts, cleaning equipment, and solvents, also focuses on customers' service needs. The firm's earnings grew by at least 20 percent for eighteen years in a row.[19] Customer service is explored in more detail in Chapter 22.

7 STRATEGIC ALLIANCES

strategic alliance
Cooperative agreement between business firms, taking the form of a licensing or distribution agreement, joint venture, research and development consortium, or partnership.

A **strategic alliance** is a cooperative agreement between business firms. Strategic alliances can take the form of licensing or distribution agreements, joint ventures, research and development consortia, and partnerships. For example, Citibank and Ford Motor Co. have introduced the Ford Citibank Visa and MasterCard. The card offers customers an opportunity to earn substantial rebates on the purchase or lease of new Ford, Lincoln, and Mercury automobiles.[20]

Companies form strategic alliances for a variety of reasons. Some are formed to share research and development costs, some because capital is needed, some to share production expertise or capacity, and some to help a company penetrate a global market. Some are even formed to reduce the threat of competition.[21]

Many strategic alliances fail to produce the benefits expected by the partners. Some fail miserably. Three general problems have been identified:

- Partners are often organized quite differently, complicating marketing and design decisions and creating problems in coordinating actions and establishing trust.
- Partners that work together well in one country may be poorly equipped to support each other in other countries, leading to problems in global alliances.
- Because of the quick pace of technological change, the most attractive partner today may not be the most attractive partner tomorrow, leading to problems in maintaining alliances over time.[22]

The two key features of successful strategic alliances are carefully chosen partners and a situation in which both parties benefit from the relationship.

Strategic alliances often involve multinational partnerships. In Japan, IBM has a strategic alliance with Ricoh to distribute low-end computers and with Fuji Bank to market financial systems. IBM has similar links with other Japanese firms. The international perspectives story below is another example of a multinational strategic alliance.

INTERNATIONAL PERSPECTIVES

A Global Strategic Alliance That Works

In 1979, Ford Motor Co. acquired 25 percent of Mazda Motors. For Ford, the acquisition was perceived as an opportunity to learn more about Mazda's technology and to possibly gain access to the huge Japanese automobile market. For Mazda, the alliance meant an infusion of cash at a time when the firm was facing a financial crisis.

The alliance partners have experienced strained relations at times. In 1993, for example, Ford, Chrysler, and General Motors considered filing a sweeping charge accusing Japanese automakers of dumping cars in the United States at unfairly low prices. When asked about the charge, one Japanese auto company official said, "They've asked us to be partners with them, and then they literally turn around and put a stick in your heart."[23]

On the positive side, Ford and Mazda have learned to cooperate on new vehicle development and to capitalize on the expertise that each has to offer the other. Ford has shared its expertise in international marketing and finance while learning new manufacturing and product development techniques from Mazda.

For Ford, the payoff has come partly in the form of sales. Ford is now the best-selling foreign nameplate in Japan, with more than 72,000 cars and trucks sold each year through the dealer network it jointly owns with Mazda.[24] Ford is also learning lessons from Mazda that it is applying elsewhere in its business. When Ford built its plant in Hermosillo, Mexico, it used Mazda's super-efficient Hofu factory in Japan as a blueprint. The Hermosillo plant quickly became one of Ford's top plants for quality and a model for renovating other facilities.

Identify some benefits you would expect Ford to gain from this strategic alliance. What benefits might Mazda gain? What are some potential problems? Can other industries expect similar benefits and problems from similar relationships?

LOOKING BACK

Look back at the story about Cooper Tire & Rubber at the beginning of this chapter. By bypassing the new-car manufacturers and instead targeting car owners who need to replace worn-out tires, Cooper avoids the intense low-profit competition in the original equipment manufacturer market. By concentrating on the much larger and faster-growing replacement market, Cooper has developed brand loyalty among consumers and distributors. Among tire manufacturers, the company ranks ninth in size but first in performance.

Although tire manufacturers like Goodyear and Firestone can exercise great control over the products marketed through company-owned stores, they give up some support from independent distributors, who are forced to compete with their suppliers.

Private-label branding allows Cooper to use excess production capacity without having to build more consumer demand. The private-label customers, such as Pep Boys and Western Auto, assume responsibility for stimulating demand in their stores for products that carry their own brand names.

KEY TERMS

accelerator principle 145
accessory equipment 148
annual purchasing contract 154
blanket purchasing contract 154
business service 149
business-to-business marketing 138
buying center 150
component part 148
derived demand 144
forward buying 154
inelastic demand 145
installation 147
joint demand 145
major equipment 147
modified rebuy 153
multiplier effect 145
new buy 152
processed materials 149
producer segment 138
purchasing contract 153
raw material 148
reciprocity 147
reseller market 138
standard industrial classification system 141
straight rebuy 153
strategic alliance 157
supply 149
team selling 147
value engineering 153
vendor analysis 154

SUMMARY

1 Define business-to-business marketing. Business-to-business marketing provides goods and services that are bought for use in business rather than for personal consumption. Intended use, not physical characteristics, distinguishes a business-to-business product from a consumer product.

2 Identify the four major categories of business-market customers. Producer markets consist of individuals and organizations that buy products for the purpose of making a profit by using them to produce other products, to become components of other products, or to facilitate business operations. Reseller markets consist of wholesalers and retailers that buy finished products to resell for profit. Government markets include federal, state, county, and city governments that buy goods and services to support their own operations and serve the needs of citizens. Institutional markets consist of very diverse nonbusiness institutions whose main goals do not include profit.

3 Explain the usefulness of the standard industrial classification system. The standard industrial classification (SIC) system provides a way to identify, analyze, segment, and target business-to-business and government markets. Organizations can be identified and compared by a numeric code indicating type of economic activity (at the broadest level), industry, geographic region, subindustry, and product classification. Unfortunately, SIC codes are inadequate for identifying organizations that engage in many different activities or that provide a variety of products.

4 Explain the major differences between business-to-business and consumer markets. In business-to-business markets, demand is derived, price inelastic, joint, and fluctuating. Purchase volume is much larger. Customers are fewer in number and more geographically concentrated. Distribution channels are more direct. Buying is approached more formally, using professional purchasing agents. More people are involved in the buying process, and negotiation is more complex. Reciprocity and leasing are more common. And finally, selling strategy normally focuses on personal contact rather than on advertising.

5 Describe the seven types of business-to-business goods and services. Major equipment includes capital goods, such as heavy machinery. Accessory equipment is typically less expensive and shorter-lived than major equipment. Raw materials are extractive or agricultural products that have not been processed. Component parts are finished or near-finished items to be used as parts of other products. Processed materials are used to manufacture other products. Supplies are consumable and not used as part of a final product. Business services are intangible products that many companies use in their operations.

6 Discuss the unique aspects of business-to-business buying behavior. Business-to-business buying behavior is distinguished by five fundamental characteristics. First, buying is normally undertaken by a buying center consisting of many people who range widely in authority level. Second, business buyers typically evaluate alternative products and suppliers based on quality, service, and price—in that order. Third, business-to-business buying falls into three general categories: new buys, modified rebuys, and straight rebuys. Fourth, business-to-business purchasing is a process that involves several steps, including developing product specifications, choosing a supplier, and evaluating supplier performance. Fifth, customer service before, during, and after the sale plays a big role in business-to-business purchase decisions.

7 Discuss the role of strategic alliances in business-to-business marketing. Companies form strategic alliances for a variety of reasons. Some fail miserably. The keys to success appear to be choosing a partner carefully and creating conditions where both parties benefit.

Review Questions

1. What are the two types of resellers? How are they different?
2. What is the standard industrial classification system (SIC), and how is it used by marketers?
3. Describe the characteristics of demand in business-to-business markets.
4. Discuss the significance of buying centers from a marketing manager's perspective.
5. Describe the role of the salesperson in the business-to-business purchase process.
6. Why is it important that business-to-business marketing managers closely monitor consumer-market demand?

Discussion and Writing Questions

1. A friend is interested in a career in business-to-business marketing. List examples of each type of business-to-business market, other than those in the chapter.
2. List three examples of joint-demand products.
3. Choose a business-to-business service not mentioned in the chapter. Assume you are the marketing manager for the firm, and list your customers.
4. Name some component products not mentioned in the chapter. What are the primary markets for these component parts?
5. Identify each type of business-to-business buying situation. For each, list an example not discussed in the chapter.

CASES

5.1 Arlington Chamber of Commerce

The Arlington Chamber of Commerce has been serving businesses and individuals in Arlington, Texas, for the past forty-five years. Established to foster economic development, the Arlington Chamber tries to bring employment opportunities to the city. The Chamber also focuses on enhancing and diversifying the tax base in Arlington. Additional taxes and continued diversification of businesses help fuel Arlington's growth. The chamber is always looking for ways to provide a progressive business environment for new and existing businesses. It has 1,700 members.

Arlington is one of the fastest-growing cities in the United States. In the early 1990s, Arlington ranked as the second fastest-growing city among cities with populations over 150,000. This rapid growth makes Arlington an attractive city for business. Rapid growth usually brings a large resource of both skilled and unskilled labor.

A survey conducted by the Arlington Chamber of Commerce indicated that 80 percent of its companies are locally owned and operated. Of the 6,795 companies sent the questionnaire, 635 responded. The main goals for this survey were to collect information about the business climate in Arlington and to help plan the future direction of the Chamber.

Among the results of the survey were the following:

- Over a quarter of the businesses are owned by women or minorities.
- More than 40 percent of the respondents have gone into business since 1990.
- Over 80 percent of the respondents employ twenty-five or fewer employees.
- Over 10 percent of the respondents export products outside the United States.
- About 38 percent of the city's manufacturers are exporters.
- About 14 percent rate Arlington an "excellent" business climate (58 percent rate it as "good").

The Chamber was excited about the results, claiming Arlington is a "hotbed" for entrepreneurs. But there was some concern that Arlington companies are not more active in exporting. The Chamber plans to provide more information to help encourage greater exports. There was also some concern that the minority- and women-owned businesses are merely figurehead companies vying for minority contracts.

Questions

1. How much credibility would you place in the results of this survey? Why?

2. What is the nonresponse problem? How would you address the nonresponse problem?

3. As a result of this survey's findings, would you move to Arlington, Texas, to start a new business? What other information would you want? Where would you go to find this information?

Suggested Reading

Lou Chapman, "Survey Reveals Arlington as Entrepreneurial Hotbed," *Fort Worth Star Telegram,* 21 November 1990, sec. 4, pp. 1–2.

5.2 General Tire (B)

Video title: *Business-to-Business Marketing at General Tire*

General Tire, Inc.
1 General Street
Akron, OH 44329

SIC code: 3011 Tires and inner tubes

Number of employees: 8,000

1993 revenues: Approximately $1.3 billion

Major brands: General Tires, Continental

Largest competitors: Michelin/Uniroyal/Goodrich, Goodyear, Bridgestone/Firestone

Background

The trucking industry is a highly competitive business. Not only do trucking transport companies compete with one another, but they also compete with air and rail transport companies for long-haul shipments. To remain competitive with other modes of transportation and to increase profits, trucking companies are always looking for ways to cut the costs of operating their fleets. One major expense that concerns the trucking industry is the cost of tires. Environmentalists are also interested in how long truck tires last. One of the problems facing us today is how to dispose of all the used tires.

General Tire

Most companies retread truck tires to prolong their life. Typically, the process works like this: Trucking companies buy a new tire and use it on the front axle (steering axle of the truck), because this is the most critical location for a quality tire. When the tread becomes worn, the company retreads the tire and moves it to the rear axle (drive axle) of the truck. When the tread becomes worn again, the tire can be retread one more time and used on the truck trailer.

Two things have to happen for the tire to last through two retreads and over 300,000 miles of travel. First, the casing (the rubber components that hold the tire on the rim and hold the tread in place) must be manufactured to stand up to this kind of use. Second, the trucking company must keep the wheels aligned and the tires properly inflated. General Tire has a distinct advantage in the truck tire market because its tires have among the most rigorous specifications in the industry. The company relies on its high-tech manufacturing process and state-of-the-art production equipment to produce a high-integrity tire casing (which means that all the components used to produce the tire casing are designed to work together as an integrated package). By designing the casing to accept multiple retreads, General can offer its customers a money-saving product and keep the tire out of the scrap pile longer, which pleases environmentalists.

General also provides its customers with a visual-inspection alignment system. This system allows General's customers to spot alignment problems early. Thus trucking companies can correct problems before a tire becomes unserviceable. Other services offered by General Tire, like scrap pile analysis (looking through customers' scrap piles to identify common problems with used tires), help the company provide better support for its customers.

Questions

1. Using Exhibit 5.7, discuss how General Tire helps facilitate the purchase of its products.

2. Explain how the decision to buy tires is different for consumers (Case 4.2) than for truck fleet owners.

3. Discuss the nature of demand for truck tires.

CHAPTER 6

Segmenting and Targeting Markets

LEARNING OBJECTIVES

After studying this chapter, you should be able to

1. Describe the characteristics of markets and market segments.
2. Explain the importance of market segmentation.
3. Discuss criteria for successful market segmentation.
4. Describe bases commonly used to segment consumer markets.
5. Describe the bases for segmenting business markets.
6. List the steps involved in segmenting markets.
7. Discuss alternative strategies for selecting target markets.
8. Explain how and why firms implement positioning strategies and how product differentiation plays a role.
9. Discuss global market segmentation and targeting issues.

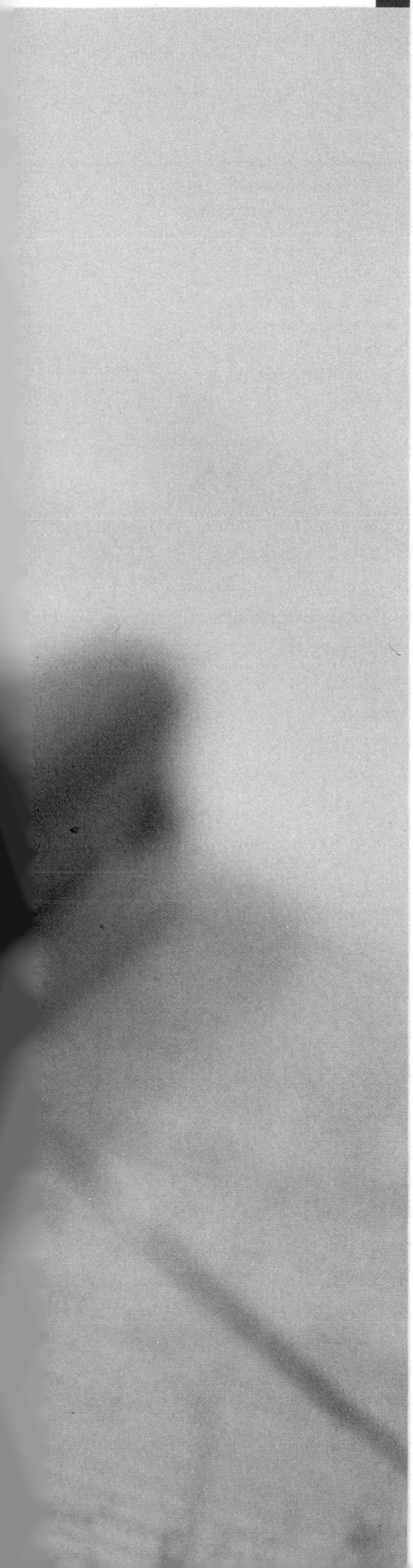

These days, consumer product companies are concluding it isn't enough to focus on a region or a state or even a city. Increasingly, the target is narrowing to a bull's-eye no bigger than an individual neighborhood or a single store. . . .

The trend is possible thanks to new insights provided by the spread of checkout scanners, which are generating more sophisticated data on consumers and buying habits. . . . "The real key here is the ability to go out and locate those folks on a store-by-store basis that are the right customers for a product," says Doug Anderson, a vice president of Spectra Marketing Systems, Inc., a Chicago consulting concern.

Using a network of food brokers and store surveyors, Market Metrics of Lancaster, Pennsylvania, collects statistics on the guts of 30,000 supermarkets around the country. In addition to compiling economic, social, and ethnic shopper profiles for each store, Market Metrics tracks traffic patterns, per capita expenditures, and neighborhood population density, as well as store size, sales volume, and even exact measurements of space devoted to health and beauty products and dairy, meat, and other departments.

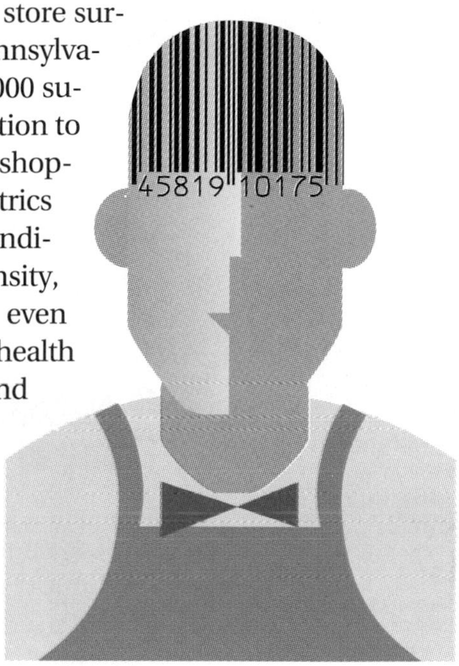

Combining these statistics with consumption pattern studies—the demographic profiles of people who buy any of 1,300 packaged goods—Market Metrics can rank specific stores based on how well they sell everything from strained baby food to upscale pasta sauce. Exhibit 6.1 illustrates some of the information that firms like Spectra Marketing Systems provide their customers. . . . Micromarketers can now target a product's heaviest users and the stores where they're most likely to shop.

How would you define the terms *micromarketing* and *heavy user*? What other bases or dimensions can you name that would help describe who buys what? Think of three specific brands of products; how would you describe them in the way shown in Exhibit 6.1?

Source: Adapted from Michael J. McCarthy, "Marketers Zero In on Their Customers," *The Wall Street Journal*, 18 March 1991, pp. B1, B5. Reprinted by permission of *The Wall Street Journal*, © Dow Jones & Company, Inc. All Rights Reserved Worldwide.

Brand	Heavy-user profile	Lifestyle and media profile	Top three target stores
Peter Pan Peanut Butter	Households with kids, headed by 18- to 5- year-olds, in suburban and rural areas	Heavy video renters Theme park visitors Below-average TV viewers Above-average radio listeners	Goodtown Super Market 3350 Hempstead Turnpike, Levittown, NY Pathmark Supermarket 3635 Hempstead Turnpike, Levittown, NY King Kullen Market 598 Stewart Ave., Bethpage, NY
Stouffers Red Box Frozen Entrees	Households headed by people 55 and older and upscale suburban households headed by 35- to 54-year-olds	Gambling casino visitors Party givers People involved in public activities Heavy newspaper readers Above-average TV viewers	Dan's Supreme Super Market 69-62 188th St., Flushing, NY Food Emporium Madison Ave. & 74th St., NYC Waldbaum Super Market 196-35 Horace Harding Blvd., Flushing, NY
Coors Light Beer	Heads of household, 21–34, middle to upper income, suburban and urban	Health club members Rock music buyers Plane travelers People who give parties and cookouts Video renters Heavy TV sports viewers	Food Emporium 1498 York Ave., NYC Food Emporium First Ave. & 72nd St., NYC Gristedes Supermarket 350 E. 86th St., NYC

Exhibit 6.1

Target Markets for Three Products

Source: From Spectra Marketing Systems, with data from Information Resources Inc., Simmons Market Research Bureau, Claritas Corp., and Progressive Grocer. Reported in Michael J. McCarthy, "Marketers Zero In on Their Customers," *The Wall Street Journal*, 18 March 1991, p. B1.

1 MARKET SEGMENTATION

The term *market* means different things to different people. We are all familiar with terms like supermarket, stock market, labor market, fish market, and flea market. All these types of markets share several characteristics. First, they are composed of people (consumer markets) or organizations (business markets). Second, these people or organizations have wants and needs that can be satisfied by particular product categories. Third, they have the ability to buy the products they seek. Fourth, they are willing to exchange their resources, usually money or credit, for desired products. In sum, a **market** is (1) people or organizations, (2) with needs or wants, (3) and with the ability, (4) and the willingness to buy. A group of people that lacks any one of these characteristics is not a market.

market
People or organizations with needs or wants and with the ability, and the willingness, to buy.

Within a market, a **market segment** is a subgroup of people or organizations sharing one or more characteristics that cause them to have similar product needs. At one extreme, we can define every person and every organization in the world as a market segment, since each is unique. At the other extreme, we can define the entire consumer market as one large market segment and the business-to-business market as another large segment. All people have some similar characteristics and needs, as do all organizations.

market segment
Subgroup of people or organizations sharing one or more characteristics that cause them to have similar product needs.

From a marketing perspective, it normally makes sense to describe market segments somewhere between the two extremes. The process of dividing a market into meaningful, relatively similar, and identifiable segments or groups is called **market segmentation.** The purpose of market segmentation is to enable the marketer to tailor marketing mixes to meet the needs of one or more specific segments. The example at the beginning of this chapter cited bases (heavy-user profile, lifestyle, and media profile) that some food and beverage marketers use to segment markets and develop marketing mixes to appeal to a brand's best customers.

market segmentation
Process of dividing a market into meaningful, relatively similar, and identifiable segments or groups.

Exhibit 6.2 illustrates the concept of market segmentation. Each circle represents a market consisting of seven persons. This market might vary as follows: one homo-

No market segmentation

Fully segmented market

Market segmentation
by gender: M,F

Market segmentation
age group: 1,2,3

Market segmentation
by gender and age group

Exhibit 6.2

The Concept of Market Segmentation

geneous market of seven people, a market consisting of seven individual segments, a market composed of two segments based on gender, a market composed of three age segments, or a market composed of five age and gender market segments. Age and gender and many other bases for segmenting markets are examined later in this chapter.

2 The Rationale for Market Segmentation

Until the 1960s, few firms practiced market segmentation. When they did, it was more likely a haphazard effort than a formal marketing strategy. Before 1960, for example, the Coca-Cola Company produced only one beverage and aimed it at the entire soft-drink market. Today Coca-Cola offers over a dozen different products to market segments based on diverse consumer preferences: choice of flavors, diet or nondiet, caffeinated or decaffeinated, and traditional soft drink or "energy drink" (such as Power Ade).[1]

Today market segmentation plays a key role in the marketing strategy of almost all successful organizations.[2] Market segmentation is a powerful marketing tool for

several reasons. Most important, nearly all markets include groups of people or organizations with different product needs and preferences. Market segmentation helps marketers define customer needs and wants more precisely.

The rapidly changing character of many markets, such as the college student market, dictates that firms not only employ market segmentation but also think of segmentation as a continuous process. Marketers should regularly identify new market opportunities, assess the strengths and weaknesses of their segmentation strategies, and update market information. Too often, managers rely on the results of five-year-old market segmentation studies, although they are usually obsolete. Many executives in a wide range of industries—such as transportation, telecommunications, computers, automobiles, clothing, and snack products—believe that market segmentation studies more than a year old have little value and may, in fact, provide misleading information.

American Express offers an interesting example of market segmentation in a service industry. AmEx has kept its share of the highly competitive credit card business by expanding from its traditional market of upper-middle-class male executives to female executives, senior citizens, small-business owners, and even students. "They have segmented the card business the way Procter & Gamble has segmented the toothpaste market," says John Love, publisher of *Credit Card News*.[3] AmEx cardholders have been grouped into fifteen distinct segments, each of which can be targeted very precisely. Since market segments differ in size and potential, segmentation helps decision makers more accurately define marketing objectives and better allocate resources. In turn, performance can be better evaluated when objectives are more precise. AmEx develops specific objectives for each of its fifteen market segments and regularly monitors them.

3 Criteria for Successful Segmentation

Marketers segment markets for three important reasons. First, segmentation enables marketers to identify groups of customers with similar needs and analyze the characteristics and buying behavior of these groups. Second, segmentation provides marketers with information to help them design marketing mixes specifically matched with the characteristics and desires of one or more segments. Third, segmentation is consistent with the marketing concept: satisfying customer wants and needs while meeting the organization's objectives.

To be useful, a segmentation scheme must produce segments that meet four basic criteria:

- *Substantiality:* A segment must be large enough to warrant developing and maintaining a special marketing mix. This criterion does not necessarily mean that a segment must have many potential customers. Marketers of custom-designed homes and business buildings, commercial airplanes, and large computer systems typically develop marketing programs tailored to each potential customer's needs. In most cases, however, a market segment needs many potential customers to make commercial sense.
- *Identifiability and measurability:* Segments must be identifiable and their size measurable. Data about the population within geographic boundaries, the number of people in various age categories, and other social and demographic characteristics are often easy to get, and they provide fairly concrete measures of segment size. Say that a social service agency wants to identify segments by their readiness to participate in a drug and alcohol program or prenatal care. Unless the agency can measure how many people are willing, indifferent, or

unwilling to participate, it will have trouble gauging whether there are enough people to justify setting up the service.

- *Accessibility:* The firm must be able to reach members of targeted segments with customized marketing mixes. Some market segments are hard to reach—for example, senior citizens (especially those with reading or hearing disabilities), those who don't speak English, and the illiterate.
- *Responsiveness:* As Exhibit 6.2 illustrates, markets can be segmented using any criteria that seem logical. However, unless one market segment responds to a marketing mix differently from other segments, that segment need not be treated separately. For instance, if all customers are equally price-conscious about a product, there is no need to offer high-, medium-, and low-priced versions.

4 BASES FOR SEGMENTING CONSUMER MARKETS

segmentation base (variable)
Characteristic of individuals, groups, or organizations used as a basis for dividing a market into segments.

Marketers use **segmentation bases** or **variables**—characteristics of individuals, groups, or organizations—to divide a total market into segments. Consumer goods marketers commonly use one or more of the following characteristics to segment markets: geography, demographics, psychographics, benefits sought, and usage rate. A more detailed description of these characteristics follows. Note that these bases are only examples. Marketers use many other characteristics to segment consumer markets. For example, social class or socioeconomic status is frequently used to segment consumer markets. This basis was examined in Chapter 4.

The choice of segmentation bases is crucial, since an inappropriate segmentation strategy may lead to lost sales and missed profit opportunities. The key is to identify bases that will produce substantial, measurable, and accessible segments that exhibit different response patterns to marketing mixes.

Geographic Segmentation

geographic segmentation
Method of dividing markets based on region of the country or world, market size, market density, or climate.

Geographic segmentation refers to segmenting markets by region of the country or world, market size, market density, or climate. *Market density* means the number of people within a unit of land, such as a census tract. Climate is commonly used for geographic segmentation because of its dramatic impact on residents' needs and purchasing behavior. Snow blowers, water and snow skis, clothing, and air-conditioning and heating systems are products with varying appeal, depending on climate.

Consumer goods companies take a regional approach to marketing for four reasons.[4] First, many firms need to find new ways to generate sales because of sluggish and intensely competitive markets. Second, computerized checkout stations with scanners enable retailers to accurately assess which brands sell best in their region. Third, many packaged-goods manufacturers are introducing new regional brands intended to appeal to local preferences. Fourth, a more regional approach allows consumer goods companies to react more quickly to competition.

Coca-Cola USA, for example, developed a special marketing campaign for Texas. The campaign included a geographic theme, "Coca-Cola Texas—home of the real thing," and participation in the state's "Don't Mess with Texas" antilitter effort.[5] Coca-Cola USA and its Texas bottlers contributed 50,000 trash bags to the voluntary cleanup effort, provided recycling bins for aluminum cans, and supplied a million schoolbook covers and half a million auto litterbags bearing antilitter messages.[6]

The box at the top of page 168 provides an interesting contrast to Coca-Cola

INTERNATIONAL PERSPECTIVES

In Search of the Euroconsumer

Claus Lippmann, aided by a cuddly teddy bear, is trying to build a new Europe. While politicians work to unite Europe politically and create the Eurocitizen, Mr. Lippmann, who markets fabric softener for Lever Europe, is looking for a related person to emerge from the single market: the Euroconsumer.

Mr. Lippmann is in charge of a fabric softener known within Lever under two different code names, Snuggle and Teddy Bear. The brand is sold in ten European countries under seven names, often with different bottles, different marketing strategies, and sometimes even different formulas. All the brands have a teddy bear on the label, and some of the names evoke snuggling.

That dizzying diversity is the legacy of what once seemed an astute policy at Lever and at many other European companies. Heavily decentralized, Lever left most product, manufacturing, and marketing decisions to powerful managers in each host country. They chose names that sounded appealing in the local language, designed packages to fit local tastes, produced products in local factories, and sometimes tinkered with formulas.

The decentralized strategy seemed to be based on a belief that European consumers represented a number of different market segments. Evaluate Lippmann's strategy of standardizing brand names, packages, formulas, and appeals. If you were the decision maker, would you treat the ten European countries where Lever's fabric softener is sold as one market, ten markets, or some number in between? What information would you like to have to help you make this decision?

Source: Adapted from E. S. Browning, "In Pursuit of the Elusive Euroconsumer," *The Wall Street Journal*, 23 April 1992, pp. B1, B3. Reprinted by permission of *The Wall Street Journal*, © 1990 Dow Jones & Company, Inc. All Rights Reserved Worldwide.

USA's strategy. Lever Europe traditionally used different marketing strategies in different European countries. But then it decided to try to develop marketing programs that will appeal to "Euroconsumers."

demographic segmentation
Method of dividing markets based on demographic variables, such as age, gender, income, ethnic background, and family life cycle.

Demographic Segmentation

As noted in Chapter 2, marketers use demographic information to segment markets because it is widely available and often related to consumers' buying and consuming behavior. Some common bases of **demographic segmentation** are age, gender, income, ethnic background, and family life cycle. Segmentation on the basis of ethnic background is discussed in Chapter 7. Since the impact of demographic factors on marketing decisions was examined in Chapter 2, the discussion of demographic segmentation here focuses on applications and illustrations.

The preteen segment spends a billion dollars a year on toys like skateboards.

© 1992 Uniphoto Inc.

Age Segmentation

Children 4 to 12 years old spend or influence the spending of over $130 billion a year.[7] Preteens spend over $1 billion annually on such play items as toys, bikes, and roller blades; $3.2 billion on food and beverages; about $800 million on movies and spectator sports; over $500 million on consumer electronics; and $620 million at the video arcade.[8] The teen market spends or influences the spending of nearly $250 billion per year.[9] Children and teens also play an important role in deciding how

$120 billion is spent on brands that wind up on the kitchen table.[10] These age segments are therefore very attractive for a variety of product categories.

Other age segments are appealing targets for a wide range of marketers. As we noted in Chapter 2, the U.S. population is growing older. People between 35 and 44 are likely to have school-aged children at home and to outspend all other age groups on food at home, housing, clothing, and alcohol. Those between 45 and 54 spend more than any other group on food away from home, transportation, entertainment, education, personal insurance, and pensions. People from 55 to 64 spend less than those 45 to 54 on almost everything except health care.[11]

Gender Segmentation

Marketers of products like clothing, cosmetics, personal care items, magazines, jewelry, and footwear commonly segment markets by gender. Gillette, for example, is one of the world's best-known marketers of personal care products for men and has been much less successful marketing to women.[12] But other marketers that have traditionally focused on men—such as Smith & Wesson, the gun manufacturer, and Anheuser-Busch, the beer marketer—have reported success in marketing to women.[13]

Income Segmentation

Income is a popular demographic variable for segmenting markets because income level influences consumers' wants and determines their buying power. Many markets are segmented by income, including housing, clothing, automobiles, and alcoholic beverages. Budget Gourmet frozen dinners are targeted to lower-income groups, whereas the Le Menu line is aimed at higher-income consumers. In Asia, Citibank targets the top 30 to 50 percent income bracket of the population, to whom the bank markets itself as a status symbol and a leader in service.[14]

The low-income segment of the market has great potential. Almost half of U.S. households have incomes of $25,000 or less. Still, this group spends heavily on education, prescription drugs, and tobacco.[15] The so-called "downscale market" is often ignored by businesses, and competition for customers is much less intense here than in other income segments.

Family Life Cycle Segmentation

family life cycle (FLC)
Series of life stages determined by a combination of age, marital status, and the presence or absence of children.

The demographic factors of gender, age, and family status often do not sufficiently explain why consumer buying behavior varies. Frequently, differences in consumption patterns among people of the same age and gender result from their being in different stages of the family life cycle. The **family life cycle** (FLC) is a series of stages determined by a combination of age, marital status, and the presence or absence of children. It is a valuable basis for segmenting markets.

Exhibit 6.3 illustrates both traditional and contemporary family life cycle patterns and shows how families' needs, incomes, resources, and expenditures differ at each stage. The horizontal flow (the lavender boxes) shows the traditional family life cycle. The lower part of the exhibit gives some of the characteristics and purchase patterns of families in each stage of the traditional life cycle. The exhibit also acknowledges that about half of all first marriages end in divorce. When young marrieds move into the young divorced stage, their consumption patterns often revert back to those of the young single stage of the cycle. About four of five divorced persons remarry by middle age and reenter the traditional life cycle, as indicated by the "recycled flow" in the exhibit.

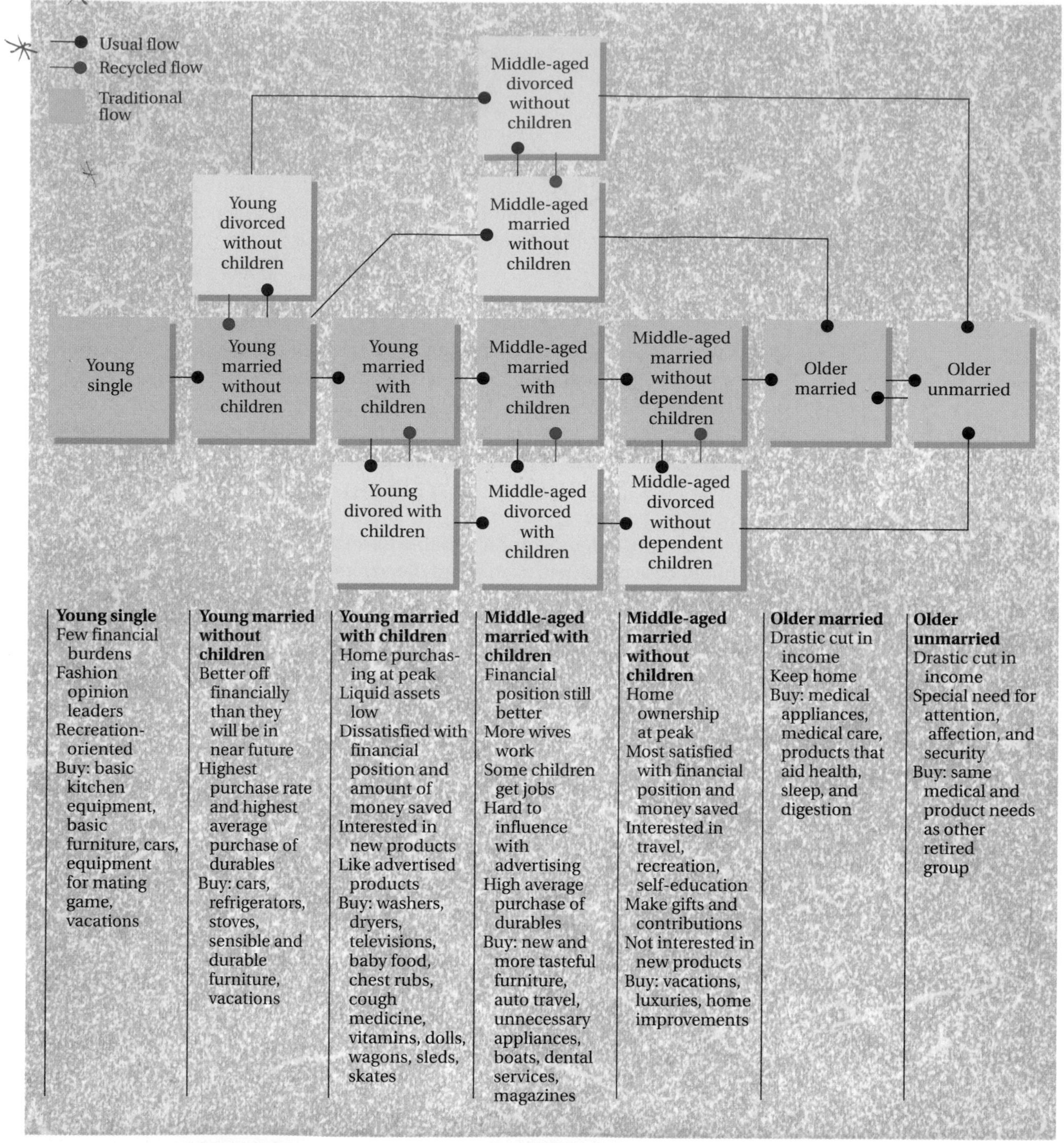

Usual flow
Recycled flow
Traditional flow

Middle-aged divorced without children

Young divorced without children

Middle-aged married without children

Young single

Young married without children

Young married with children

Middle-aged married with children

Middle-aged married without dependent children

Older married

Older unmarried

Young divored with children

Middle-aged divorced with children

Middle-aged divorced without dependent children

Young single
Few financial burdens
Fashion opinion leaders
Recreation-oriented
Buy: basic kitchen equipment, basic furniture, cars, equipment for mating game, vacations

Young married without children
Better off financially than they will be in near future
Highest purchase rate and highest average purchase of durables
Buy: cars, refrigerators, stoves, sensible and durable furniture, vacations

Young married with children
Home purchasing at peak
Liquid assets low
Dissatisfied with financial position and amount of money saved
Interested in new products
Like advertised products
Buy: washers, dryers, televisions, baby food, chest rubs, cough medicine, vitamins, dolls, wagons, sleds, skates

Middle-aged married with children
Financial position still better
More wives work
Some children get jobs
Hard to influence with advertising
High average purchase of durables
Buy: new and more tasteful furniture, auto travel, unnecessary appliances, boats, dental services, magazines

Middle-aged married without children
Home ownership at peak
Most satisfied with financial position and money saved
Interested in travel, recreation, self-education
Make gifts and contributions
Not interested in new products
Buy: vacations, luxuries, home improvements

Older married
Drastic cut in income
Keep home
Buy: medical appliances, medical care, products that aid health, sleep, and digestion

Older unmarried
Drastic cut in income
Special need for attention, affection, and security
Buy: same medical and product needs as other retired group

Exhibit 6.3

The Family Life Cycle

psychographic segmentation
Method of dividing markets based on personality, motives, lifestyle, and geodemographics.

Psychographic Segmentation

Age, gender, income, ethnicity, family life cycle stage, and other demographic variables are usually helpful in developing segmentation strategies, but often they don't paint the entire picture. Demographics provides the skeleton, but psychographics adds meat to the bones. **Psychographic segmentation** is market segmentation by personality, motives, lifestyle, and geodemographics. Psychographic variables themselves can either be used to segment markets or be combined with other variables to provide more detailed descriptions of market segments.

In its ads and its clothing, Banana Republic appeals to a lifestyle segment characterized as "free souls."
© Banana Republic Advertising

Personality

Personality characteristics reflect a person's traits, attitudes, and habits. Schlitz beer is targeted toward a personality segment described as "macho men," who feel that since the pleasures in their lives are few and far between, they want something more. The theme "You only go around once in life, so you might as well reach for the gusto" was developed to appeal to this personality segment. Cherry 7-Up is aimed at a personality segment described as "cool" teenagers. Ads show "cool" young people coping with everyday situations and use the slogan "Isn't it cool in pink?"

Motives

Marketers of baby products and life insurance appeal to consumers' emotional motives—namely, to care for their loved ones. Using appeals like economy, reliability, and dependability, carmakers like Subaru and Suzuki target customers with rational motives. Carmakers like Mercedes-Benz, Jaguar, and Cadillac appeal to status-related motives.

Lifestyles

Lifestyle segmentation divides people into groups according to the way they spend their time, the importance of the things around them, their beliefs, and socioeconomic characteristics like income and education. For example, NPD Market Research identified the following five "eating lifestyles": meat-and-potato eaters; families with kids whose diets feature soda pop and sweetened cereal; dieters; natural-food eaters; and sophisticates—high-income urban families whose diets feature alcohol, Swiss cheese, and rye and pumpernickel breads.

geodemographic segmentation
Method of dividing markets based on neighborhood lifestyle categories.

micromarketing
Marketing program tailored to prospective buyers who live in small geographic regions, such as neighborhoods, or who have very specific lifestyle and demographic characteristics.

Geodemographics

Geodemographic segmentation clusters potential customers into neighborhood lifestyle categories. It combines geographic, demographic, and lifestyle segmentations.

Geodemographic segmentation helps marketers practice micromarketing. **Micromarketing** is developing marketing programs tailored to prospective buyers

Exhibit 6.4

The VALS 2 Categories

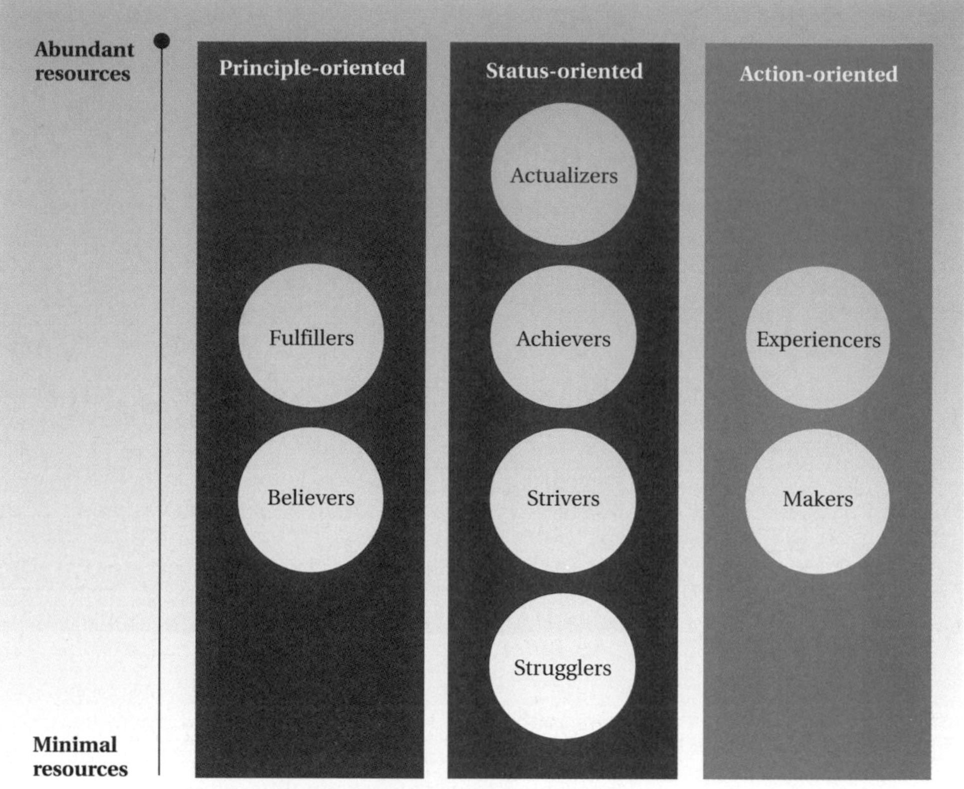

who live in small geographic regions, such as neighborhoods, or who have very specific lifestyle and demographic characteristics. Exhibit 6.1, at the beginning of this chapter, shows how consumer product companies use micromarketing. Frito-Lay uses micromarketing to enhance sales of salty snack foods.[16] When Buick introduced its new Roadmaster station wagon, it bought ads in national magazines but only for those editions mailed to 4,940 of the country's more than 40,000 ZIP codes.[17] Philip Morris has developed a data base of millions of smokers and their addresses and uses direct mail to reach them with coupons and samples.[18] Micromarketing is explored in more detail in Chapter 8.

The VALS Approach

Values and Lifestyles program (VALS)
Consumer psychographic segmentation tool, developed by SRI International, that categorizes U.S. consumers by their values, beliefs, and lifestyles.

In 1978, SRI International introduced the **Values and Lifestyles program** (VALS), a consumer psychographic segmentation tool. VALS categorizes U.S. consumers by their values, beliefs, and lifestyles rather than by traditional demographic segmentation variables. Many advertising agencies have used VALS segmentation to create effective promotion campaigns.

In 1988 SRI introduced a new psychographic segmentation tool called VALS 2.[19] As Exhibit 6.4 shows, the segments in VALS 2 are arranged vertically by their resources and horizontally by their self-orientation.[20]

Resources include education, income, self-confidence, health, eagerness to buy, intelligence, and energy level. The resources dimension is a continuum ranging from minimal to abundant. Resources generally increase from adolescence through middle age and decrease with extreme age, depression, financial reverses, and physical or psychological impairment.

The self-orientation dimension classifies three different ways of buying. Beliefs or principles—rather than feelings, events, or desire for approval—guide principle-

Exhibit 6.5

The Eight VALS Psychographic Segments

Actualizers are successful, sophisticated, active, "take-charge" people with high self-esteem and abundant resources. They are interested in growth and seek to develop, explore, and express themselves in a variety of ways. Their possessions and recreation reflect a cultivated taste for the finer things in life.

Fulfillers are mature, satisfied, comfortable, reflective people who value order, knowledge, and responsibility. Most are well educated, well informed about world events, and professionally employed. Fulfillers are conservative, practical consumers; they are concerned about value and durability in the products they buy.

Believers are conservative, conventional people with concrete beliefs and strong attachments to traditional institutions—family, church, community, and the nation. As consumers they are conservative and predictable, favoring U.S. products and established brands.

Achievers are successful career- and work-oriented people who like to, and generally do, feel in control of their lives. Achievers live conventional lives, are politically conservative, and respect authority and the status quo. As consumers they favor established goods and services that demonstrate success to peers.

Strivers seek motivation, self-definition, and approval from the world around them. They are easily bored and impulsive. Money defines success for strivers, who lack enough of it. They emulate those who own more impressive possessions, but what they wish to obtain is generally beyond their reach.

Experiencers are young, vital, enthusiastic, and impulsive. They seek variety and excitement and combine an abstract disdain for conformity and authority with an outsider's awe of others' wealth, prestige, and power. Experiencers are avid consumers and spend much of their income on clothing, fast food, music, movies, and video.

Makers are practical people who value self-sufficiency. They live within a traditional context of family, practical work, and physical recreation and have little interest in what lies outside that context. They are unimpressed by material possessions other than those with a practical or functional purpose (for example, tools, pickup trucks, or fishing equipment).

Strugglers have lives that are constricted—chronically poor, ill educated, and low skilled. They lack strong social bonds; aging strugglers are concerned about their health; they are focused on meeting the urgent needs of the present moment. Strugglers are cautious consumers who represent a very modest market for most goods and services but are loyal to favorite brands.

oriented consumers in their choices. Other people's actions, approval, and opinions strongly influence status-oriented consumers. Action-oriented consumers are prompted by a desire for social or physical activity, variety, and risk.

Exhibit 6.5 describes the eight VALS psychographic segments. Using two key dimensions, resources and self-orientation, VALS defines adult consumers with different attitudes and distinctive behavior and decision-making patterns.

Benefit Segmentation

benefit segmentation Method of dividing markets based on the benefits customers seek from the product.

Benefit segmentation is the process of grouping customers into market segments according to the benefits they seek from the product. Most types of market segmentation are based on the assumption that there is a relationship between the variable and customers' needs. Benefit segmentation is different because it groups potential customers on the basis of their needs or wants rather than some other characteristic, such as age or gender. The snack food market, for example, can be divided into six benefit segments, as shown in Exhibit 6.6.

Customer profiles can be developed by examining demographic information associated with people seeking certain benefits. This information can be used to match specific media with selected target markets. Sometimes the matching pro-

	Nutritional snackers	Weight watchers	Guilty snackers	Party snackers	Indiscriminate snackers	Economical snackers
% of snackers	22%	14%	9%	15%	15%	18%
Lifestyle characteristics	Self-assured Controlled	Outdoorsy Influential Venturesome	Highly anxious Isolated	Sociable	Hedonistic	Self-assured Price-oriented
Benefits sought	Nutritious Without artificial ingredients Natural	Low calorie Quick energy	Low calorie Good tasting	Good to serve guests Served with pride Goes well with beverage	Good tasting Satisfies hunger	Low in price Best value
Consumption level of snacks	Light	Light	Heavy	Average	Heavy	Average
Type of snacks usually eaten	Fruits Vegetables Cheese	Yogurt Vegetables	Yogurt Cookies Crackers Candy	Nuts Potato chips Crackers Pretzels	Candy Ice cream Cookies Potato chips Pretzels Popcorn	No specific products
Demographics	Better educated Have younger children	Younger Single	Younger or older Female Lower socio-economic status	Middle-aged Nonurban	Teenage	Have larger family Better educated

Exhibit 6.6

Lifestyle Segmentation of the Snack Food Market

cess is fairly simple. Procter & Gamble, for example, buys ad time on health-related TV shows to trumpet the benefits of its low-saturated fat Puritan oil.[21]

Usage Rate Segmentation

usage rate segmentation
Method of dividing markets based on the amount of product bought or consumed.

Usage rate segmentation divides a market by the amount of product bought or consumed. Categories vary with the product, but they are likely to include some combination of the following: nonusers, former users, potential users, first-time users, light or irregular users, medium users, and heavy users. Segmenting by usage rate enables marketers to focus their efforts on heavy users or to develop multiple marketing mixes aimed at different segments. Since heavy users often account for a sizable portion of all product sales, some marketers focus on the heavy-user segment. For example, parents with children aged 2 to 11 are twice as likely as the general population to spend $200 or more each year for children's toys and games.[22] Therefore, they are an attractive target market.

80/20 principle
Idea that 20 percent of all customers generate 80 percent of the demand.

The **80/20 principle** holds that 20 percent of all customers generate 80 percent of the demand. Although the percentages are not usually exact, the general idea often holds true. The alcoholic beverage market illustrates this point clearly. The top 20 percent of bourbon drinkers consume 79 percent of all bourbon, and the top 26 percent of scotch drinkers consume 80 percent of all scotch sold in the United States.[23]

Campbell Soup Company recently completed a study called "The Value of a Customer." Consumers were segmented by how loyal they are, how frequently they buy a specific brand, and how consistently they use it. Using these criteria, Campbell identified the four categories of customers shown in Exhibit 6.7: most profitable, profitable, borderline, and avoid. The most profitable group—loyal, frequent, consistent customers—was found to be three times more profitable than the borderline group. The study also showed that one-tenth of all users account for almost one-quarter of sales. But for two-thirds of users, the return on marketing effort isn't worth the cost.[24]

Exhibit 6.7

Usage Rate Segmentation by Campbell Soup Company, 1991

Source: Data from Campbell Soup Company, Camden, NJ.

Customer category	Percentage of brand users	Percentage of sales volume	Return on $1 marketing investment
Most profitable	4%	15%	$3.38
Profitable	6	9	1.43
Borderline	25	25	1.00
Avoid	65	51	0.38

Single-Variable or Multiple-Variable Segmentation

Markets can be segmented using a single variable, such as age group, or several variables, such as age group, gender, and education. Although it is less precise, single-variable segmentation has the advantage of being simpler and easier than multiple-variable segmentation. Conversely, the current trend is toward using more rather than fewer variables to segment most markets.

The disadvantages of multiple-variable segmentation are that it is often harder to use than single-variable segmentation; usable secondary data are less likely to be available; and, as the number of segmentation bases increases, the size of individual segments decreases. Still, multiple-variable segmentation is clearly more precise than single-variable segmentation.

5 BASES FOR SEGMENTING BUSINESS MARKETS

The business market consists of four broad segments: producers, resellers, institutions, and government. (For a detailed discussion of the characteristics of these segments, see Chapter 5.) Whether marketers focus on only one or all four of these segments, they are likely to find diversity among potential customers. Market segmentation offers just as many benefits to business marketers as it does to consumer product marketers.

Business market segmentation variables can be classified into two major categories: macrosegmentation variables and microsegmentation variables.

Macrosegmentation

macrosegmentation
Method of dividing business markets based on such general characteristics as geographic location, type of organization, customer size, and product use.

Macrosegmentation variables are used to divide business markets into segments according to such general characteristics as geographic location, customer type, customer size, and product use.

Geographic Location

The demand for some business products varies considerably from one region to another. For instance, many computer hardware and software companies are located in the Silicon Valley region of California. Similarly, 50,000 people work for 500 companies in the telecommunications industry in Richardson, Texas. In nearby Austin, 450 companies in the computer industry employ 55,000 workers. In Philadelphia, about 166,000 people work for 500 biotechnology and medical firms.[25]

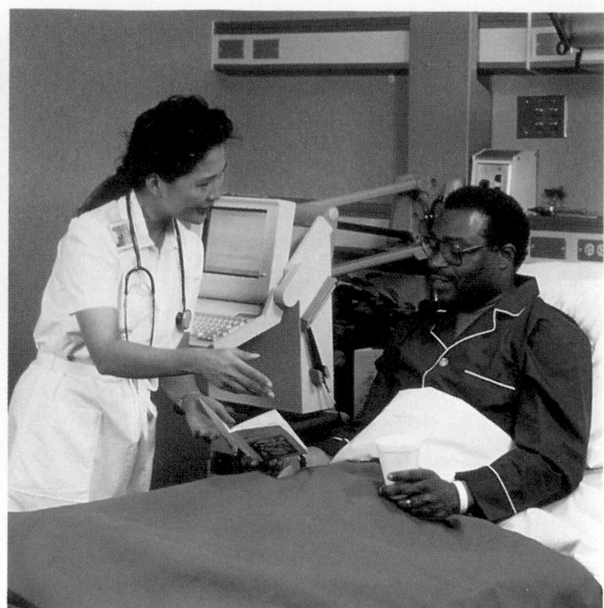

Drug companies use different marketing mixes—different promotion plans, distribution strategies, and pricing structures—*(left)* for pharmacies and *(right)* for hospitals.

(left) Laima Druskis/Stock Boston; *(right)* courtesy of International Business Machines Corporation

Some markets tend to be regional because buyers perceive all producers' offerings to be similar. Buyers prefer to purchase from local suppliers, and distant suppliers often have difficulty competing in terms of price and service. Firms that sell to geographically concentrated industries therefore benefit by locating operations close to the market.

Other markets are regional because certain products are used only in a limited area—for example, lobster traps and offshore oil rigs.

Customer Type

Segmenting by customer type allows business marketers to tailor their marketing mixes to the unique needs of particular types of organizations or industries. Many pharmaceutical firms, for example, adopt different marketing mixes for physicians, pharmacies, health care institutions, and other drug producers. Each of these organization types is concerned about different product features, uses different distribution channels, and is charged different prices.

Marketers targeting government buyers face bureaucratic structures and rules that typically do not exist in nongovernment organizations. Proposals, bids, and contracts have to be prepared according to government specifications.

Because the buying behavior of their various markets may differ, some computer and business machine marketers segment by customer type. Different sales forces are specifically trained to deal with these different customers. For example, one sales force may be trained to market to the financial services industry. Others may specialize in educational institutions, health care organizations, or government.

Customer Size

An organization's size may affect its purchasing procedures, the types and quantities of products it needs, and its responses to different marketing mixes. Banks frequently offer different services, lines of credit, and overall attention to commercial customers based on their size. American Express has also segmented the corporate credit card market based on company size. AmEx prepares different print ads for small, midsize, and large companies.[26] Volume of purchase—heavy, moderate, and light—is a commonly used business-to-business segmentation basis.

Often customer size determines a firm's selling strategies. For instance, a firm may make weekly calls to large customers and visit medium-size customers only monthly. A salesperson might not ever contact small customers, but instead a telemarketing sales force may serve them. Burlington Northern Railroad, for example, markets transportation services using different selling strategies based on customer size.

Product Use

Many products—especially raw materials like steel, wood, and petroleum—have diverse applications. How customers use a product may influence the amount they buy, their buying criteria, and their selection of vendors. Many industrial firms use the SIC system (discussed in Chapter 5) to identify end-use segments.

A producer of springs may have customers that use the product in making machine tools, bicycles, surgical devices, office equipment, telephones, and missile systems. Each of these end-use market segments has different needs, motives, and purchase criteria. The springs marketer can choose to target any one end-use segment or develop unique marketing mixes for multiple segments. However, one marketing mix probably cannot be developed that will appeal to all six end-use market segments.

Microsegmentation

Macrosegmentation often produces market segments that are too diverse for targeted marketing strategies. Thus marketers often find it useful to divide macrosegments based on such variables as customer size or product use into smaller microsegments. **Microsegmentation** is the process of dividing business markets into segments based on the characteristics of decision-making units within a macrosegment. Microsegmentation enables the marketer to more clearly define market segments and more precisely define target markets. The marketer can then design marketing mixes that more closely match the desires of target markets. Macrosegmentation can often be done using previously collected data, but microsegmentation usually depends on marketing research to gather the needed information.

microsegmentation
Method of dividing business markets based on the characteristics of decision-making units within a macrosegment.

Exhibit 6.8 lists several microsegmentation variables, which are discussed in the following paragraphs.[27]

Exhibit 6.8

Selected Microsegmentation Variables

Source: Table from *Business Marketing Management: A Strategic View of Industrial and Organizational Markets*, Fourth Edition, by Michael D. Hutt and Thomas W. Speh, copyright © 1992 by Dryden Press, reproduced by permission of the publisher.

Variables	Illustrative breakdowns
Key purchasing criteria	Quality, delivery, supplier reputation
Purchasing strategies	Optimizer, satisfier
Importance of purchase	High . . . low
Personal characteristics	
Demographics	Age, educational background
Decision style	Normative, conservative, mixed mode
Risk	Risk taker, risk avoider
Confidence	High . . . low
Job responsibility	Purchasing, production, engineering

For some business customers, the key criterion in choosing a supplier is prompt and reliable delivery. Marketers that wish to target that segment need to highlight their delivery services.

© 1992 George Disario/The Stock Market

Key Purchasing Criteria

Marketers can segment some business markets by ranking purchasing criteria, such as product quality, prompt and reliable delivery, technical support, and price. For example, Atlas Corporation developed a commanding position in the industrial door market by providing customized products in just four weeks, much faster than the industry average of twelve to fifteen weeks. Atlas's primary market is companies with an immediate need for customized doors.

Sophisticated marketers try to gain access to decision makers early in the product selection process. In some cases, marketers can influence the selection of key decision criteria and the weighting or ranking of these criteria to favor their own products.

Purchasing Strategies

The purchasing strategies of buying organizations can shape microsegments. Two purchasing profiles that have been identified are satisficers and optimizers. **Satisficers** contact familiar suppliers and place the order with the first to satisfy product and delivery requirements. **Optimizers** consider numerous suppliers, both familiar and unfamiliar, solicit bids, and study all proposals carefully before selecting one. Recognizing satisficers and optimizers is quite easy. A few key questions during a sales call, such as "Why do you buy product X from vendor A," usually produce answers that identify purchaser profiles.

satisficer
Type of business customer that places an order with the first familiar supplier to satisfy product and delivery requirements.

optimizer
Type of business customer that considers numerous suppliers, both familiar and unfamiliar, solicits bids, and studies all proposals carefully before selecting one.

Purchasing strategies have many implications. A supplier entering the market would be more likely to sell to a decision-making unit composed of optimizers than a unit consisting of satisficers relying on familiar suppliers.

Importance of Purchase

Classifying business customers according to the significance they attach to the purchase of a product is especially appropriate when customers use the product differently. This approach is also appropriate when the purchase is considered routine by some customers but very important for others. For instance, a small entrepreneur would consider a laser printer a major purchase, but a large office would find it a normal expense.

Personal Characteristics

The personal characteristics of purchase decision makers (their demographics, job responsibilities, and psychological makeup) influence their buying behavior and offer a viable basis for segmenting some business markets. IBM computer buyers, for example, are sometimes characterized as being more risk averse than buyers of less expensive "clones" that perform essentially the same functions. In advertising, IBM stresses its reputation for high quality and reliability.

6 STEPS IN SEGMENTING A MARKET

The purpose of market segmentation is to identify marketing opportunities for existing or potential products. Exhibit 6.9 traces the steps in segmenting a market. These steps apply when segmenting both consumer and business markets. Note that steps 5 and 6 are actually marketing activities that follow market segmentation (steps 1 through 4).

1. *Select a market or product category for study:* Define the overall market or product category to be studied—one in which the firm already competes, a new but related market or product category, or a totally new one. For instance, Anheuser-Busch closely examined the beer market before introducing Michelob Light and Bud Light. Anheuser-Busch also carefully studied the market for salty snacks before introducing the Eagle brand.
2. *Choose a basis or bases for segmenting the market:* This step requires managerial insight, creativity, and market knowledge. There are no scientific procedures for selecting segmentation variables. The number of possible segmentation bases is limited only by decision makers' imagination and creativity. Note,

Exhibit 6.9

Steps in Segmenting a Market and Subsequent Activities

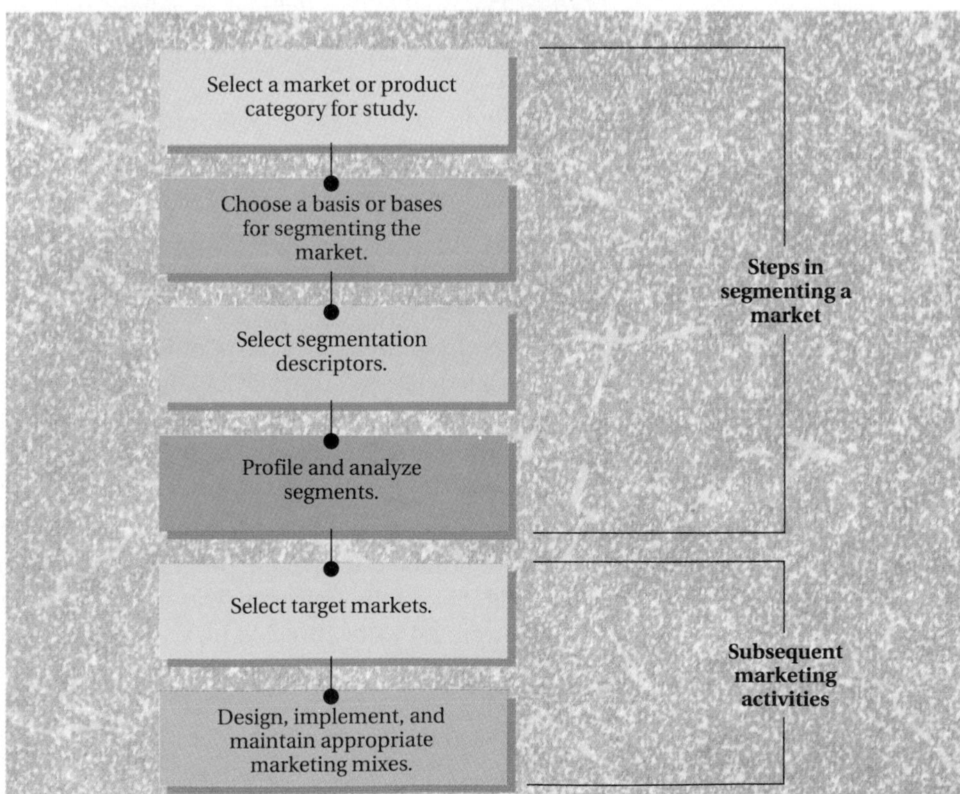

however, that a successful segmentation scheme must produce segments that meet the four basic criteria discussed earlier in this chapter.

3. *Select segmentation descriptors:* After choosing one or more bases, the marketer must select the segmentation descriptors. Descriptors identify the specific segmentation variables to use. For example, if a company selects demographics as a basis of segmentation, it may use age, occupation, and income as descriptors.
4. *Profile and analyze segments:* The profile should include segments' size, expected growth, purchase frequency, current brand usage, brand loyalty, and long-term sales and profit potential. This information can then be used to rank potential market segments by profit opportunity, risk, consistency with organizational mission and objectives, and other factors important to the firm.
5. *Select target markets:* Selecting target markets is not a part of but a natural outcome of the segmentation process. It is a major decision that influences and often directly determines the firm's marketing mix. This topic is examined in greater detail later in this chapter.
6. *Design, implement, and maintain appropriate marketing mixes:* The marketing mix has been described as product, distribution, promotion, and pricing strategies intended to bring about mutually satisfying exchange relationships with target markets. Chapters 9 through 19 explore these topics in detail.

Here's an example of market segmentation: Researchers at Texas Christian University wanted to better understand what attracted students to TCU. A study was undertaken to help admissions officers, enrollment managers, and institutional marketing representatives identify benefit segments of the college-bound student market. These are the steps that were taken:

1. *Market:* The market was defined as college-bound high school seniors. The study focused on students who had applied to TCU and been admitted to the freshman class.
2. *Segmentation basis:* The segmentation basis selected was benefits sought in a college experience.
3. *Segmentation descriptors:* Forty-three benefit descriptors derived from previous studies and group interviews were selected. The first five were size of school, quality of faculty, attractiveness of campus, distance from home, and student/faculty ratio.
4. *Segment profile and analysis:* A random sample of 1,600 accepted applicants were sent a letter requesting participation in the study, a questionnaire, and a postage-paid return envelope. Subjects were instructed to list their first three college choices and then to rate each school on the forty-three segmentation descriptors.

Analysis of the responses revealed five benefit segments. Members of the first segment were attracted to specific programs, such as business or journalism. The religious affiliation of the university was also important to this group. Members of the second segment were attracted by academic excellence. Members of the third segment sought both specific programs and academic excellence. Members of the fourth segment were attracted by religious affiliation, and members of the fifth segment focused on financial considerations. The decision makers also analyzed such information as the size of each segment and the proportion that ultimately enrolled at TCU.

Recommendations of the study were to choose one or more target markets from the segments that were identified, to develop survey materials that could be used to identify which segment applicants are in, and to develop marketing mixes tailored to the benefits sought by the target market segments.

7 STRATEGIES FOR SELECTING TARGET MARKETS

target market
Group of people or organizations for which an organization designs, implements, and maintains a marketing mix intended to meet the needs of that group or groups, resulting in mutually satisfying exchanges.

So far this chapter has focused on the market segmentation process. The next task is to choose one or more target markets. A **target market** is a group of people or organizations for which an organization designs, implements, and maintains a marketing mix intended to meet the needs of that group or groups, resulting in mutually satisfying exchanges. The three general strategies for selecting target markets—undifferentiated, concentrated, and multisegment targeting—are illustrated in Exhibit 6.10.

Undifferentiated Targeting

undifferentiated targeting strategy
Marketing approach based on the assumption that the market has no individual segments and thus requires a single marketing mix.

A firm using an **undifferentiated targeting strategy** essentially adopts a mass-market philosophy, viewing the market as one big market with no individual segments. The firm uses one marketing mix for the entire market. A firm that adopts an undifferentiated targeting strategy assumes that individual customers have similar needs that can be met with a common marketing mix.

The first firm in an industry sometimes uses an undifferentiated targeting strategy. With no competition, the firm may not need to tailor marketing mixes to the preferences of market segments. Henry Ford's famous quote about the Model T is a classic example of an undifferentiated targeting strategy: "They can have their car in any color they want, as long as it's black." At one time, Coca-Cola used this strategy with a single product and a single size of its familiar green bottle. Similarly, the Hershey Company marketed one candy bar for everyone, and the Dentyne Company sold only one size package of Dentyne gum. Marketers of commodity products, such as flour and sugar, are also likely to use an undifferentiated targeting strategy.

Exhibit 6.10

Three Strategies for Selecting Target Markets

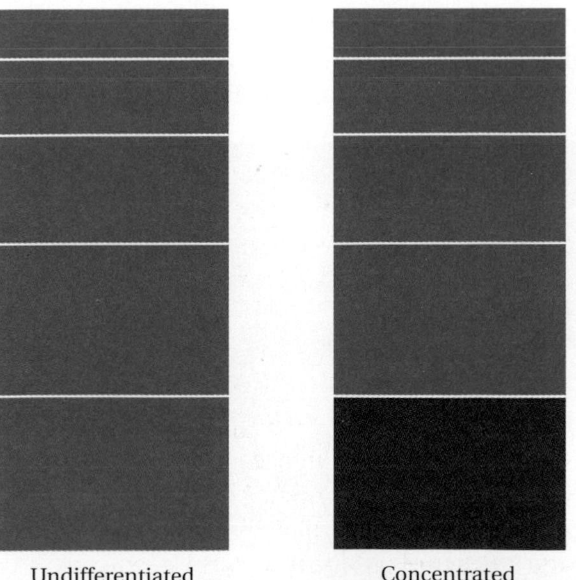

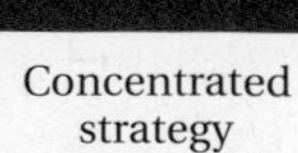

One advantage of undifferentiated marketing is the potential for saving a lot on production and marketing. Since only one item is produced, the firm should be able to achieve economies of mass production. Also, marketing costs may be lower when there is only one product to promote and a single channel of distribution.

Too often, however, an undifferentiated strategy emerges by default rather than by design, reflecting a failure to consider the advantages of a segmented approach. The result is often sterile, unimaginative product offerings that have little appeal to anyone.

Another problem associated with undifferentiated targeting is that it makes the company very susceptible to competitive inroads. Hershey lost a big share of the candy market to Mars and other candy companies before it changed to a multisegment targeting strategy. Coca-Cola forfeited its position as the leading seller of cola drinks in supermarkets to Pepsi-Cola in the late 1950s, when Pepsi began offering several sizes of containers. Coke lagged in following Pepsi's multisegment targeting strategy.

You might think a firm producing an unexciting product like toilet tissue would adopt an undifferentiated strategy. However, there are industrial segments and consumer segments in this market. Industrial buyers want an economical, single-ply product sold in boxes of a hundred rolls. The consumer market demands a more versatile product in smaller quantities. Within the consumer market, the product is differentiated as colored or white, designer-print or no-print, cushioned or noncushioned, and economy-priced or luxury-priced. Fort Howard Corporation, the market share leader in industrial toilet paper, does not even sell to the consumer market.

Concentrated Targeting

concentrated targeting strategy (or niche targeting strategy) Marketing approach based on appealing to a single segment of a market.

With a **concentrated targeting strategy** (sometimes called a **niche targeting strategy**), a firm selects one segment of a market for targeting its marketing efforts. Because the firm is appealing to a single segment, it can concentrate on understanding the needs, motives, and satisfactions of that segment's members and on developing and maintaining a highly specialized marketing mix. Some firms find that concentrating resources and doing a better job of meeting the needs of a narrowly defined market segment is more profitable than spreading resources over several different segments.

For example, 1st Business Bank targets midsize companies with annual sales

Concentrated or niche targeting involves choosing a single segment of a market, such as upscale car buyers who prefer sporty cars.

between $3 million and $100 million. The bank accepts only ten to fifteen new accounts each month, and these are carefully screened before they are accepted. With this concentrated targeting strategy, the bank has been extremely profitable, and it has had almost no loan losses in ten years.[28] Another example is Nucor Steel, which is small compared to the largest U.S. steel firms. But it concentrates its efforts on the steel joist segment of the steel market, and there it leads the industry.

Small firms often adopt a concentrated targeting strategy to compete effectively with much larger firms. For example, Nucor Steel is tiny compared to the largest U.S. steel firms. Tiny G.E.C. Holding Corp. was created with a $150,000 investment by its owners. The firm produces and markets a product that keeps people off elevator tops. Riding the tops—a game known as "elevator chicken," "elevator surfing," and "elevator action"—has led to several serious injuries and deaths among juvenile and college-aged daredevils. G.E.C. is the only firm that competes in the small market for these anti-intrusion devices, although the elevator manufacturing and servicing markets are dominated by huge firms like Otis Elevator. G.E.C. hopes to earn millions of dollars in the next few years from its anti-intrusion device.[29]

Some firms use a concentrated strategy to establish a strong position in a desirable market segment. Porsche, for instance, targets a very upscale automobile market—"class appeal, not mass appeal."

Concentrated targeting violates the old adage "Don't put all your eggs in one basket." If the chosen segment is too small or if it shrinks because of environmental changes, the firm may suffer negative or even disastrous consequences. Many oil-field supply companies in Texas learned this lesson the hard way in the 1980s, when oil prices dropped and domestic drilling activity declined.

A concentrated strategy can also be disastrous for a firm that is not successful in its narrowly defined target market. Before Procter & Gamble introduced Head and Shoulders shampoo several years ago, several small firms were already selling dandruff shampoos. Head and Shoulders was introduced with a large promotional campaign, and the new brand captured over half the market immediately. Within a year, several of the firms that had been concentrating on this market segment went out of business.

Multisegment Targeting

A firm that chooses to serve two or more well-defined market segments and develops a distinct marketing mix for each has a **multisegment targeting strategy**. Stouffer's, for example, offers gourmet entrees for one segment of the frozen-dinner market and Lean Cuisine for another. Hershey Chocolate Company, a division of Hershey Foods Corporation, has dozens of different confections aimed at various segments. For instance, it offers premium candies like Golden Almond chocolate bars, packaged in gold foil and marketed to an adult audience. A new chocolate bar called RSVP was targeted toward consumers who crave the taste of Godiva chocolates at the price of a Hershey bar.[30] Cosmetics companies seek to increase sales and market share by targeting multiple age and ethnic groups. Maybelline and Cover Girl, for example, market different lines to teenage women, young adult women, older women, and African-American women.[31] Jeans marketers like Levi's, Wrangler, and Lee also target multiple age, gender, and ethnic segments.[32] Carnival Cruise Lines recently introduced Fiesta Marina Cruises, the first cruise line specifically designed for Hispanics.[33]

multisegment targeting strategy
Marketing approach based on serving two or more well-defined market segments, with a distinct marketing mix for each.

Sometimes organizations use different promotional appeals, rather than complete marketing mixes, as the basis for a multisegment strategy. For example, different target markets are likely to be attracted to physical fitness programs called Keep

ETHICS IN MARKETING

A Remedy for Every Cold

As she rubs her temples, the woman in a new television commercial for Dristan Sinus formula describes her headache as nothing less than crushing, pounding agony. Her one hope for relief: "Only Dristan Sinus combines the leading decongestant with the modern pain reliever ibuprofen."

Not quite. The maker of Dristan Sinus also sells CoAdvil, which combines the *same* active ingredients in the *same* doses. "In terms of chemicals, they're identical," concedes a spokeswoman for American Home Products Corp., maker of both drugs.

To keep sales growing, marketers have become more aggressive in pitching similar products targeted at different ailments. Dristan Sinus targets sufferers of sinusitis; CoAdvil is billed as a therapy for the common cold.

What's the difference, for example, between Tylenol Cold formula and Tylenol Cold & Flu formula, both made by Johnson & Johnson? Although flu symptoms are generally more severe than cold symptoms, a quick glance at the labels shows the recommended dose of each medication contains precisely the same active ingredients.

The distinction is all in the form of delivery, according to a spokesman for Johnson & Johnson. Tylenol Cold comes in tablets and caplets, while the flu medication is formulated as a powder that consumers brew with hot water.

The difference between Drixoral Plus and Drixoral Sinus, both made by Schering-Plough, is even more puzzling. Both products contain a decongestant, an antihistamine, and a nonaspirin pain reliever—in identical doses. Yet the Drixoral Sinus box boldly proclaims its contents to be "The ONLY 12-Hour Sinus Medicine." In fact, the only difference between the two products is that Drixoral Sinus pills are yellow, while Drixoral Plus tablets are a vivid green. "It's market segmentation," says a spokesman for Schering-Plough.

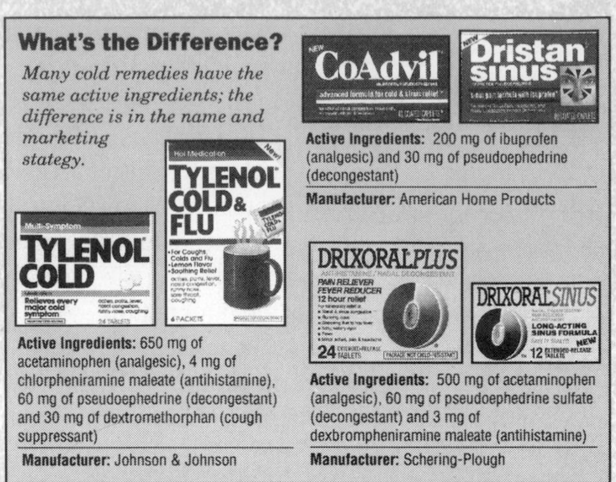

Is it ethical for a pharmaceutical firm to market essentially the same product using different brand names? Is this practice any different from tire and clothing manufacturers selling the same product using different brand names? Does the fact that the pharmaceutical firms claim the products treat different ailments have any effect on your judgment of the ethics of this behavior? Should pharmaceutical firms be prohibited from marketing chemically identical products using different brand names and claiming they relieve different symptoms?

Source: Illustration from and text adapted from Kathleen Deveny, "Copycat Cold Medicines Proliferate, Creating Confusion among Consumers," *The Wall Street Journal*, 1 February 1991, pp. B1, B3. Reprinted by permission of *The Wall Street Journal*, © 1991 Dow Jones & Company. All Rights Reserved Worldwide.

Fit, Conditioning, Fitness Training, Slimnastics, Aerobics, Aerobic Dance, Health Club, Figure Control, Jazzercise, or Revitalize. Although the basic program content may be similar, the names are designed to meet different wants. As the illustration above shows, this practice is sometimes perceived as unethical.

Public agencies, as well as private organizations, can often benefit from a multisegment strategy. Consider government efforts to persuade citizens to convert to the metric system, which has succeeded in Canada. It is highly desirable that everyone adapt to the metric system at the same time.

> It is still possible, and more efficient, to work harder with some groups than with others and to work on some segments earlier than others. Age might well be a factor because the young may easily adopt the metric system, while many people over forty will resist the change. Certain manufacturers and industries may be willing to begin using the metric system now. However, others will not change before they have to, and the

cooperation of tool makers should be enlisted early. And because reading and viewing habits of citizens differ, it will prove virtually impossible to put together a communications effort that reaches all citizens equally well.[34]

Multisegment targeting offers many potential benefits to firms, including greater sales volume, higher profits, larger market share, and economies of scale in manufacturing and marketing. Yet it also involves costs. Before deciding to use this strategy, firms should compare the benefits and costs of multisegment targeting to those of undifferentiated and concentrated targeting. The following list details the costs:

- *Product design costs:* A multisegment targeting strategy sometimes results in different products for different market segments. It may involve nothing more than a package or labeling change, or it may require a complete redesign of the product itself. An example of a slight modification is packaging Coca-Cola in various sizes and types of containers, such as twelve-ounce cans and two-liter bottles. In contrast, Compaq Computer Corporation incurred major costs in developing both desktop and laptop computers. Creating different products with unique features sought by different segments of the market can be very expensive.
- *Production costs:* Total production costs mount as a firm develops and markets different products for different market segments. Each manufacturing run may require a retooling of production equipment, during which time production lines are idle. The result is higher costs for the manufacturer.
- *Promotion costs:* Whether or not a firm produces a different product for each market segment, it normally must develop separate promotional strategies. Significant expenditures of human and financial resources are required. A firm normally must create different advertisements for each segment, and different media may be necessary for the ads.
- *Inventory costs:* The more market segments a firm tries to serve, the higher the inventory costs are likely to be. With inventory costs averaging between 20 and 30 percent of inventory sales value, a multisegment targeting strategy can be very expensive.
- *Marketing research costs:* An effective market segmentation strategy relies on accurate, detailed market information about consumer demographics; consumer reaction to various product designs or promotional appeals; consumer interests, attitudes, opinions; and so on. Gathering this information can be a time-consuming and expensive process. For example, the Kroger supermarket chain conducts more than 250,000 consumer interviews each year to determine changing consumer wants.
- *Management costs:* A multisegment targeting strategy requires extra management time. As the number of segments increases, so does the number of decisions. The firm must coordinate the marketing mix for each targeted market segment.
- *Cannibalization:* **Cannibalization** occurs when sales of a new product cut into sales of a firm's existing products. For example, in mid-1990 Coors Brewing Company discovered that 70 percent of the test market sales of Bud Dry came from other Anheuser-Busch brands. This cannibalization effect prompted Coors to place its own dry beer plans on hold. Anheuser-Busch management estimated that, after the first couple of months of test marketing, cannibalization dropped to about 40 percent, with remaining sales coming from Coors

cannibalization
Phenomenon in which sales of a new product cut into sales of a firm's existing products.

Light and Miller Genuine Draft. Industry observers had mixed views about the long-run effect of Bud Dry on sales of other Anheuser-Busch brands.[35]

8 POSITIONING

Chapter 1 examined the relationship between an organization's target market strategy and the marketing mix it uses to produce mutually satisfying exchanges with members of one or more target markets. The term **positioning** refers to developing a specific marketing mix to influence potential customers' overall perception of a brand, product line, or organization in general. Positioning assumes that consumers view competing products along dimensions relevant to their purchase and consumption behavior. **Position** refers to the place a product, brand, or group of products occupies in consumers' minds relative to competing offerings.

positioning
Developing a specific marketing mix to influence potential customers' overall perception of a brand, product line, or organization in general.

position
Place that a product, brand, or group of products occupies in consumers' minds relative to competing offerings.

product differentiation
Marketing tactic designed to distinguish one firm's products from those of competitors.

Product Differentiation

Product differentiation is a positioning strategy that some firms use to distinguish their products from those of competitors. The distinctions can be either real or perceived. Tandem Computer designed machines with two central processing units and two memories for systems that can never afford to be down or lose their data base (for example, an airline reservation system). Tandem used product differentiation to create a product with very real advantages for the target market.

AMC, the movie theater chain, has spent millions of dollars upgrading its theaters to differentiate them from the competition. Some have even expanded the concession stand beyond the standard popcorn, cola, and candy to include such culinary delights as iced cappuccino and coconut macaroons. At AMC's Santa Monica theater, moviegoers can visit the Critic's Corner Café for crab cakes, salads, gourmet pizzas, quiche, croissant sandwiches, and egg rolls.[36]

At the other extreme, bleaches, aspirin, unleaded regular gasoline, and some soaps are differentiated by trivial means such as brand names, packaging, color, smell, or "secret" additives. The marketer attempts to convince consumers that a particular brand is distinctive and that they should therefore demand it over com-

This McDonald's restaurant differentiates itself from the many other options available to city dwellers by offering live background music.
© Ken Kerbs/Dot

peting brands. If a seller can persuade a substantial number of people to demand the brand, the seller can usually raise its price above the general market level.

An interesting recent trend in marketing food products, ranging from cookies to mustard to beer, is kosher labeling as a product differentiation strategy.[37] Kosher labeling generally requires little more than compliance with certain hygienic processing standards, but it signifies product purity to many consumers regardless of their religious affiliation.

perceptual mapping — Means of displaying or graphing, in two or more dimensions, the location of products, brands, or groups of products in customers' minds.

Perceptual Mapping

Perceptual mapping is a means of displaying or graphing, in two or more dimensions, the location of products, brands, or groups of products in customers' minds. Exhibit 6.11 shows four perceptual maps for General Motors automobile divisions. Consumer perceptions and desired consumer perceptions are plotted on two axes. The horizontal axis ranges from conservative and family-oriented at one extreme to expressive and personal at the other. The vertical axis is used to rate price perceptions, and it ranges from high to low.

Effective positioning requires assessing the positions occupied by competing products, determining the important dimensions underlying these positions, and

Exhibit 6.11

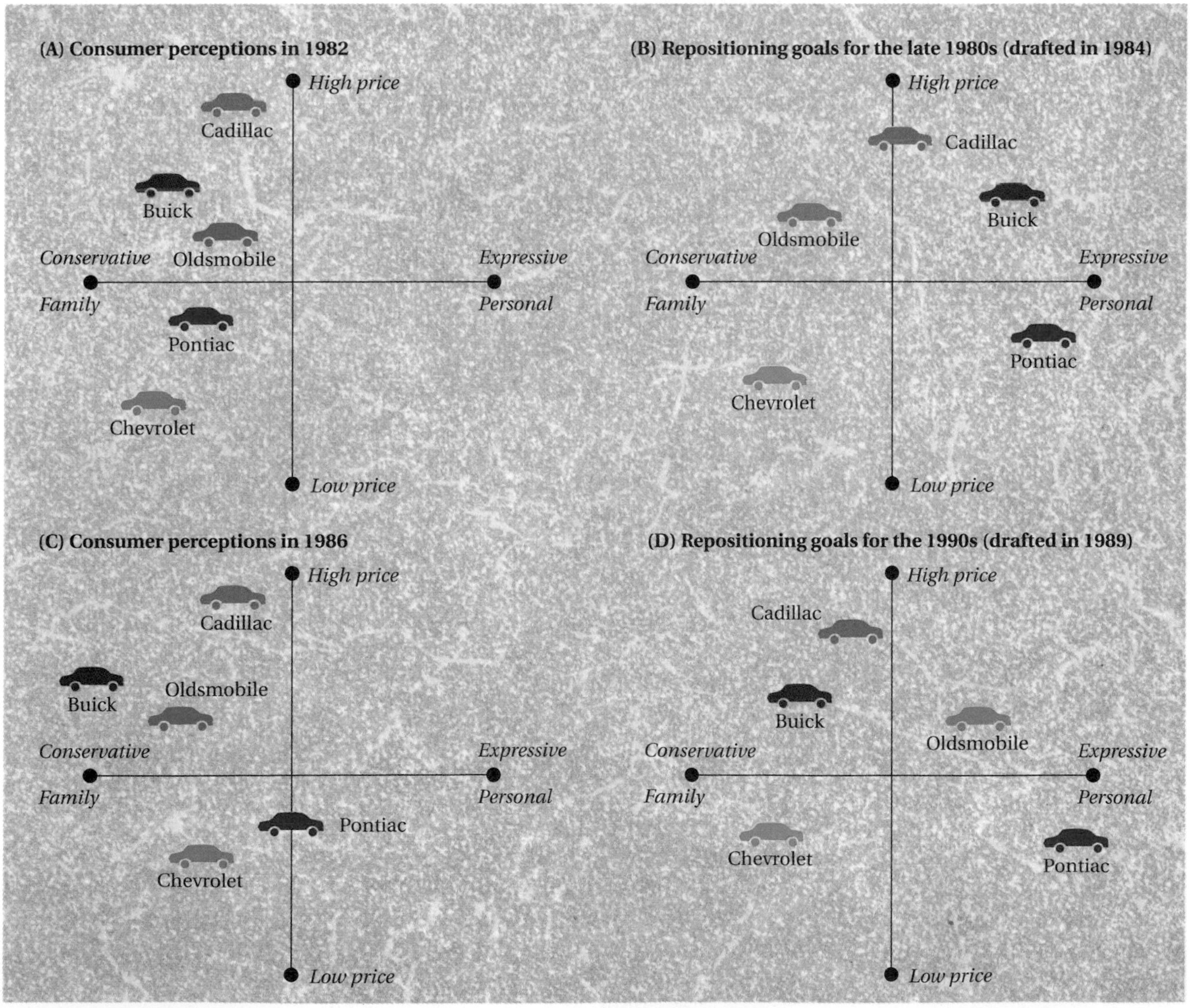

Perceptual Maps and Positioning Strategies for General Motors Passenger Cars

choosing a position in the market where the organization's marketing efforts will have the greatest impact. The French have an expression that sums up the positioning concept rather neatly: *cherchez le creneau*, or "look for the gap." To find a *creneau* you must think in reverse, go against the grain. If everyone else is going east, see if you can find your *creneau* by going west.[38] If everyone else is making large, five-passenger automobiles that appeal to luxury, why not build small economy cars? If major competitors are all stressing low price, why not introduce a prestige brand? If your major competitors are colas, perhaps stress that your product is an "un-cola."

A Positioning Example

In 1982 General Motors measured consumers' perceptions of the five GM automobile divisions: Buick, Cadillac, Chevrolet, Oldsmobile, and Pontiac. The findings are shown on the perceptual map in Exhibit 6.11A. The map shows consumer perceptions in 1982 in terms of price and "expressiveness," or family use versus personal use. Note that the various divisions are not especially distinctive. Consumers didn't clearly distinguish one brand from another, especially on the conservative/family versus expressive/personal dimension.

In 1984 the company was reorganized to reduce overlap and duplication among divisions and to produce fewer, more distinctive models.[39] The map in Exhibit 6.11B shows GM's plans for **repositioning,** or changing consumers' perceptions of the various models in customers' minds by the late 1980s. As Exhibit 6.11C shows, consumer perceptions changed very little between 1982 and 1986.

repositioning
Changing consumers' perceptions of a brand in relation to competing brands.

In 1989 General Motors introduced a new overall theme called "Putting quality on the road" that was supported by a $40 million advertising campaign. Exhibit 6.11D illustrates GM's repositioning goals for the 1990s. The following themes were selected to differentiate the divisions from one another:[40]

Buick:	Premium American Motorcar
Cadillac:	Standard Luxury Worldwide
Chevrolet:	Customer Expectations Exceeded
Oldsmobile:	Innovative Technology
Pontiac:	Performance Oriented to Young People

Positioning Bases

Firms use a variety of bases for positioning, including the following:[41]

- *Attribute:* A product is associated with an attribute, product feature, or customer benefit. For example, a promotion for Viva paper towels stressed durability, using product demonstrations. Total toothpaste, a new Colgate-Palmolive brand planned to be introduced around the world, will be positioned as an all-in-one toothpaste to fight gum disease, cavities, plaque, and tartar.[42]
- *Price and quality:* This positioning base may stress high price as a signal of quality or emphasize low price as an indication of value. Neiman-Marcus uses the high-priced strategy; Kmart has successfully followed the price and value strategy. However, Kmart has been trying to gain a more upscale image by using national brands and higher-quality Kmart brands.
- *Use or application:* During the past few years, AT&T telephone service advertising has emphasized communicating with loved ones using the "Reach out and touch someone" campaign. Stressing uses or applications can be an effective means of positioning a product with buyers. The advertising slogan "Orange juice isn't just for breakfast anymore" is an effort to reposition the

product in terms of time and place of use as an all-occasion beverage.

- *Product user:* This positioning base focuses on a personality or type of user—for instance, Revlon's introductory positioning of the Charlie cosmetic line, associating it with the lifestyle profile of the liberated woman.
- *Product class:* The objective here is to position the product as being associated with a particular category of products—for example, positioning a margarine brand with respect to butter.
- *Competitor:* Positioning against competitors is part of any positioning strategy. The Avis rental car positioning as No. 2 exemplifies positioning against specific competitors.

It is not unusual for a marketer to use more than one of these bases. The AT&T "Reach out and touch someone" campaign that stressed use also emphasized the relatively low cost of long-distance calling. Chrysler positioned its 1993 LHS sedan as an automobile for buyers in their mid-40s, from $100,000-plus-income households, that prefer expensive imports but think it's foolish to pay over $40,000 for a car.[43]

9 GLOBAL ISSUES IN MARKET SEGMENTATION AND TARGETING

Chapter 3 discussed the trend toward global market standardization, which enables firms like Coca-Cola, Colgate-Palmolive, McDonald's, and Nike to market similar products using similar marketing strategies in many different countries. The International Perspectives example in this chapter described Lever Europe's plan to appeal to "Euroconsumers." This chapter also discussed the trend toward targeting smaller, more precisely defined markets. Interestingly, both these trends—toward globalization and micromarketing—are occurring at the same time.

The tasks involved in segmenting markets, selecting target markets, and designing, implementing, and maintaining appropriate marketing mixes (described in Exhibit 6.9) are the same whether the marketer has a local perspective or a global vision. The main difference is the segmentation variables commonly used. Countries of the world are commonly grouped using such variables as per capita gross national product, geography, religion, culture, or political system.

Some have tried to group countries of the world or customer segments around the world using lifestyle or psychographic variables. So-called "Asian yuppies"—in countries like Singapore, Hong Kong, Japan, and South Korea—have substantial spending power and exhibit purchase and consumption behavior similar to those of their better-known counterparts in the United States.

LOOKING BACK

In the story at the beginning of this chapter, micromarketing was described as tailoring marketing programs for buyers who live in small geographic regions, such as neighborhoods, or who have particular lifestyle or demographic characteristics. Heavy users account for a disproportionate share of a product's sales.

The chapter examined several bases for segmenting consumer markets (such as geographic, demographic, psychographics, benefits sought, and usage rate) and several bases commonly used to segment business markets (geographic location, type of organization, customer size, purchase criteria, and importance of purchase). All these bases can be used to help describe who buys what.

KEY TERMS

benefit segmentation 173
cannibalization 185
concentrated targeting strategy 182
demographic segmentation 168
80/20 principle 174
family life cycle 169
geodemographic segmentation 171
geographic segmentation 167
macrosegmentation 175
market 164
market segment 164
market segmentation 164
micromarketing 171
microsegmentation 177
multisegment targeting strategy 183
niche targeting strategy 182
optimizer 178
perceptual mapping 187
position 186
positioning 186
product differentiation 186
psychographic segmentation 170
repositioning 188
satisficer 178
segmentation base (variable) 167
target market 181
undifferentiated targeting strategy 181
usage rate segmentation 174
Values and Lifestyles program 172

SUMMARY

1 **Describe the characteristics of markets and market segments.** A market is composed of individuals or organizations with the ability and willingness to make purchases to fulfill their needs or wants. A market segment is a group of individuals or organizations with similar product needs as a result of one or more common characteristics.

2 **Explain the importance of market segmentation.** Before the 1960s, few businesses targeted specific market segments. Today, segmentation is a crucial marketing strategy for nearly all successful organizations. Market segmentation enables marketers to tailor marketing mixes to meet the needs of particular population segments. Segmentation helps marketers identify consumer needs and preferences, areas of declining demand, and new marketing opportunities.

3 **Discuss criteria in successful market segmentation.** Successful market segmentation depends on four basic criteria. First, a market segment must be substantial—it must have enough potential customers to be viable. Second, a market segment must be identifiable and measurable. Third, members of a market segment must be accessible to marketing efforts. Fourth, a market segment must respond to particular marketing efforts in a way that distinguishes it from other segments.

4 **Describe bases commonly used to segment consumer markets.** There are five commonly used bases for segmenting consumer markets. Geographic segmentation is based on region, size, density, and climate characteristics. Demographic segmentation consists of age, gender, income level, ethnicity, and family life cycle characteristics. Psychographic segmentation includes personality, motives, and lifestyle characteristics. Benefits sought is a type of segmentation that identifies customers according to the benefits they seek in a product. Finally, usage segmentation divides a market by the amount of product purchased or consumed.

5 **Describe the bases for segmenting business markets.** Business markets can be segmented on two bases. First, macrosegmentation divides markets according to general characteristics, such as location and customer type. Second, microsegmentation focuses on the decision-making units within macrosegments.

6 **List the steps involved in segmenting markets.** Six steps are involved when segmenting markets: (1) Select a market or product category for study, (2) choose a basis or bases for segmenting the market, (3) select segmentation descriptors, (4) profile and analyze segments, (5) select target markets, and (6) design, implement, and maintain appropriate marketing mixes.

7 **Discuss alternative strategies for selecting target markets.** Marketers select target markets using three different strategies: undifferentiated targeting, concentrated targeting, and multisegment targeting. An undifferentiated targeting strategy assumes that all members of a market have similar needs that can be met with a single marketing mix. A concentrated targeting strategy focuses all marketing efforts on a single market segment. Multisegment targeting is a strategy that uses two or more marketing mixes to target two or more market segments.

8 **Explain how and why firms implement positioning strategies and how product differentiation plays a role.** Positioning is used to influence consumer perceptions of a particular brand, product line, or organization in relation to competitors. The term *position* refers to the place that the offering occupies in consumers' minds. To establish a unique position, firms use product differentiation—emphasizing the real or perceived differences between competing offerings. Products may be differentiated on the basis of attribute, price and quality, use or application, product user, product class, or competitor.

9 Discuss global market segmentation and targeting issues. The key tasks in market segmentation, targeting, and positioning are the same regardless of whether the target market is local, regional, national, or multinational. The main differences are the variables used by marketers in analyzing markets and assessing opportunities and the resources needed to implement strategies.

Review Questions

1. Explain the difference between markets and market segments.
2. What are the major benefits of a market segmentation strategy? What is the major difficulty of such a strategy?
3. Explain the concept of responsiveness as a criterion for successful market segmentation.
4. What are some common demographic variables for selecting market segments? Name some products that appeal to particular segments within a demographic category.
5. What is the purpose of microsegmentation? Describe three microsegmentation variables.
6. Outline the steps in the market segmentation process.
7. Explain the relationship between market segmentation and targeting.
8. Compare and contrast domestic market segmentation and international segmentation.

Discussion and Writing Questions

1. Describe market segmentation in terms of the historical evolution of marketing.
2. List some market segments not discussed in the chapter that are inaccessible to marketing efforts. What makes them hard to reach?
3. Which VALS psychographic segment(s) most accurately reflects your personality and consumer behavior? In several sentences, explain why.
4. Select a product category and brand that are familiar to you. Using Exhibit 6.9, prepare a market segmentation report and describe a targeting plan.
5. Explain multisegment targeting. Describe an example of a company not mentioned in the chapter that uses a multisegment targeting strategy.
6. You want your firm to adopt a product differentiation strategy. Write a memo to the president describing how three companies not mentioned in the chapter use product differentiation strategies.
7. Distinguish three positioning strategies, and identify firms that use them.
8. Select a group of people in your community with an unmet consumer need. Do you consider this a viable market segment? Why or why not?

CASES

6.1 B&Q Hardware

Companies that long thought of aging consumers as being in poor health, not interested in product features, and not wanting to spend a lot of time thinking about purchase decisions are finding out otherwise. Many companies that introduced specific products for the older consumer—Johnson & Johnson's Affinity shampoo for aging hair, Kellogg's 40-Plus bran cereal, and Gerber's Singles line of pureed foods for denture wearers—have achieved limited sales. Older consumers don't wish to be treated as older consumers.

People over 50 constitute 25 percent of the U.S. market. By 2025, they could make up almost 40 percent of the U.S. market. This growing market segment wants to enjoy life. Its members have paid their dues and are now ready to live. Discounts are great, but marketers have to find other ways of attracting these aging consumers.

On senior citizens' discount day at B&Q, a do-it-yourself hardware store, the aisles are lined with gray-haired people. Not only are the customers older, but so are the employees. B&Q is one of the few stores that is staffed entirely by people over 50. Customers in the store claim they get more satisfaction from the sales clerks because "they know what they are talking about." The chain went to a lot of extra effort in recruiting and training these employees but had a hard time breaking the stereotype. Thinking that older employees would have trouble with the training, B&Q provided an extra month's training for its older employees. It also offered a special course on proper lifting techniques to reduce the likelihood of on-the-job injuries.

The chain intends to continue staffing all its stores entirely with employees over 50. Mike Harris, a store manager at B&Q, still likes to hire younger-looking people. "I don't want the store to look like a bunch of old-age pensioners," he says. The chain's CEO disagrees. He suggests that Harris's successor may be a grand old man of 60.

Questions

1. Is the older consumer a valid market segment? Use the four criteria for successful segmentation to answer this question.

2. What can companies do to better market their products to this target segment?

3. Why do you think B&Q has succeeded in reaching this market segment?

Suggested Readings

"Paying Heed to Seniors," *Pets Supplies Marketing,* May 1992, p. 6.

Casey Gilmore, "Bankers Learn to Find Gold in Them Thar Silver Hairs," *The Kansas City Business Journal,* 22 May, 1992, p.1.

"Senior Citizens: An Untapped Niche," *Discount Store News,* 18 May 1992, p. 114.

6.2 Frito-Lay

Video Title: **Interview with a Snack Food Consumer**

Frito-Lay, Inc.
7701 Legacy Drive
Plano, TX 75024

SIC codes:	
2906	Potato chips, corn chips, and similar snacks
5812	Eating and drinking places
6794	Patent owners
2086	Bottled and canned soft drinks

Number of employees: 26,000

1993 revenues: $3.33 billion

Major brands: Fritos, Lays, Sun Chips

Largest competitors: General Foods, Borden

Background

Snack food manufacturers have always targeted heavy snackers and baby boomers. But now that interest in maintaining a healthy lifestyle is growing, especially among baby boomers, many snack food manufacturers have begun to wonder about the long-term profitability of snack foods. These companies have a big interest in the nutritional value of their products.

In 1976, after two years of product testing, Frito-Lay introduced Prontos. Prontos were Frito-Lay's early multigrain snack product, a healthier alternative to traditional salty snack foods. After two years of disappointing sales and manufacturing problems, the company pulled Prontos from the market. Throughout the early 1980s, Frito-Lay wondered if aging baby boomers would continue to eat salty snack foods, and so the company continued to test multigrain products as an insurance policy against declining demand for salty snacks. By the end of the decade, Frito-Lay was ready to give the multigrain chip another try.

Sun Chips

Early in 1991, Frito-Lay began taking Sun Chips national. Three key factors contributed to the company's decision to roll out the multigrain product nationally. First, the company believed that growth comes through innovative new products. Second, the test market results for the Sun Chip product were extremely successful. Finally, the sales force was behind the product because they believed the product would sell well in the market. Dwight Risky, Frito-Lay marketing vice president, said that if the company had not pushed the product, the sales force would have. The company committed $30 million to the national rollout.

By the end of the first year, Sun Chips had reached almost $100 million in sales. According to Risky, very few new food products achieve even a $40 million sales level in the first year. Given the outstanding success of the product, Frito-Lay decided to spend a record $20 million for advertising and direct mail for Sun Chips' second year.

Market research indicates that Sun Chips have the highest repeat purchase rate of any Frito-Lay product. For this reason the company has been focusing its promotion on creating awareness of the brand. The company expects Sun Chips to be its sixth core product within five years, along with potato and corn chips.

Questions

1. Do you think snack food consumers care about the nutritional benefits of snack foods? Why or why not?
2. Define the target market for Sun Chips.
3. Is Fran part of this market segment? Why or why not?

References

Jennifer Lawrence, "The Sunchip Also Rises," *Advertising Age*, 27 April 1992, pp. S2, S6.

Million Dollar Directory 1992 (Parsippany, NJ: Dun & Bradstreet Information Services).

Standard & Poor's Industry Surveys (New York: Standard & Poor's Corporation, October 1992).

CHAPTER 7
Multicultural Marketing in the United States

LEARNING OBJECTIVES

After studying this chapter, you should be able to

1. Understand the growing importance of multicultural marketing.
2. Appreciate and understand the increasing cultural diversity of the United States.
3. Identify key characteristics of the African-American market and some elements of an effective marketing mix for this group.
4. Identify key characteristics of the U.S. Hispanic market and some elements of an effective marketing mix for this group.
5. Identify key characteristics of the Asian-American market and some elements of an effective marketing mix for this group.
6. Identify key characteristics of the Native American market.

When Estee Lauder Cosmetics subsidiary Prescriptives launched All Skins makeup, print ads featured the faces of black, white, Asian, and Hispanic women. Those ads represent the growing U.S. racial diversity and marketers' realization that they can no longer afford to dismiss the ethnic/cultural market. "Marketers have to pay attention to anything if it represents one out of four people," said Peter Francese, publisher of *American Demographics.* "Projections are minorities will represent one of three people in this country" in twenty years, he added. Since an obvious difference among ethnic consumers is skin tone, cosmetics companies are leading the way in responding to this demographic shift.

Estee Lauder is restaging its Prescriptives Exact Color line, adding 46 new makeup shades and grouping them under the All Skins banner, with a total of 115 shades. "We are placing more effort . . . in the 'coloring of America,'" said Dan Brestle, president of Prescriptives USA. "There are more and more dark-skinned consumers" and more Asian consumers. "The census should have opened the industry's eyes to the fact the country's changing," he said.

Revlon's Almay unit, which specializes in hypoallergenic skin care, has launched Darker Tones of Almay, a line of foundations, powders, concealers, and blush.

Newcomers are also entering the market. Max Factor & Co. veteran Michael Ghafouri formed Kayla Cosmetics to market an upscale makeup line to Asians via direct-response TV advertising.

The tactics of the largest cosmetic firms are examples of ethnic and cultural market segmentation and targeting. How do you think ethnic markets are changing in the United States? Are they homogeneous or diverse? How can these markets be successfully reached?

Source: Adapted with permission from Christy Fisher, "Ethnics Gain Market Clout," *Advertising Age,* 5 August 1991, pp. 3, 12.

❶ THE UNITED STATES AS A MULTICULTURAL SOCIETY

The United States is undergoing a new demographic transition: It is becoming a multicultural society. During the 1990s, it will shift from a society dominated by whites and rooted in Western culture to a society characterized by three large racial and ethnic minorities. All three minorities will grow in size and in share of population, while the white majority declines as a percentage of the total population.

The 1990 census found that eight in ten people in the United States are white, down from nine in ten in 1960. During the 1980s, 6 million legal immigrants came to the United States, 70 percent of whom were either Asian or Hispanic. Immigrants tend to have more children than the native-born population, as do Hispanic-Americans and African-Americans. Together, these factors are boosting the share of minorities in the population.[1]

The Changing Marketplace

The U.S. population has grown from 226 million in 1980 to 253 million in 1993. Much of that growth has taken place in minority markets. Asians are the nation's fastest-growing minority group, increasing 108 percent in the 1980s, to 7.3 million. The Hispanic population grew 53 percent, to 22.3 million; with 7.7 million new members, it had the biggest numerical gain of any minority group. African-Americans, who remain the largest minority, saw their numbers increase during the past decade by 13 percent, to 30 million. In contrast, the number of non-Hispanic whites grew by 4.4 percent.[2] In 1993, about a quarter of the U.S. population were members of minority groups.

Demographic shifts will be even more pronounced in the future. Exhibit 7.1 compares the 1993 population mix and the forecasted population mix for 2023. Note that Hispanics will be the fastest-growing segment of the population. The diversity of the U.S. population is projected to stabilize around 2023 as the birthrate among minorities levels off.

Exhibit 7.1

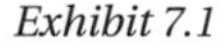

Multicultural Makeup of the United States

Source: U.S. Department of Labor, Bureau of the Census Projections.

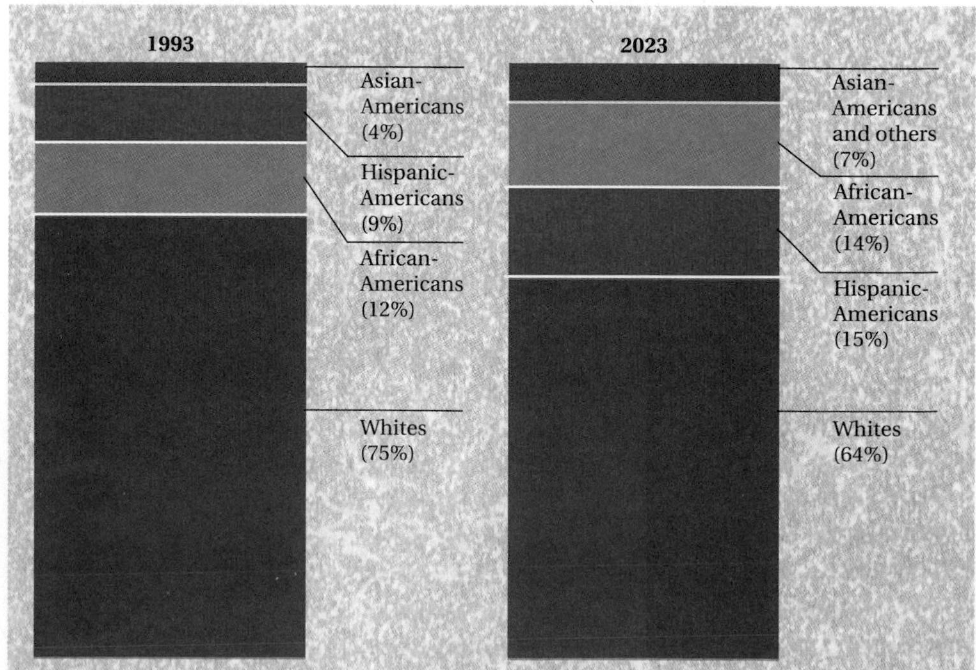

The United States is in the midst of a major demographic transition, its population becoming more diverse racially, ethnically, and culturally.

© Barbara Campbell/Liaison International

The Impact of Immigration

During the last decade, 8.7 million people immigrated to the United States. Many who were already here resented these immigrants, because unemployment was high and social services were strained. A 1992 survey found that 68 percent believed immigration was bad for the country.[3]

Unlike past waves of immigration, the new immigrants have been mainly from Asia and Latin America. Just like the existing work force, these immigrants have been split between the highly skilled and well educated and those with minimal skills and little education. On balance, the economic benefits of being an open-door society far outweigh the costs. For example, the United States is reaping a bonanza of highly educated foreigners. In the 1980s, 1.5 million college-educated immigrants joined the U.S. work force. High-tech industries, from semiconductors to biotechnology, are depending on immigrant scientists, engineers, and entrepreneurs to remain competitive. And the immigrants' links to their old countries are boosting U.S. exports to such fast-growing regions as Asia and Latin America.

Even immigrants with less education are contributing to the economy as workers, consumers, business owners, and taxpayers. Some 11 million immigrants are working, and they earn at least $240 billion a year. They're paying more than $90 billion in taxes—a lot more than the estimated $5 billion immigrants receive in welfare.[4] Immigrant entrepreneurs, from the corner grocer to the local builder, are creating jobs for other immigrants and those born here. Vibrant immigrant communities are revitalizing cities and older suburbs that would otherwise be suffering from a shrinking tax base.

Legislation passed in 1990, called the Immigration Act of 1990 (IMMACT 1990), has increased the diversity among immigrants—especially at the upper end of the socioeconomic scale. The law allows people who have no family in the United States to immigrate if they have highly prized work skills or are ready to make a significant business investment. The law nearly tripled the number of visas (to 140,000 a year) for engineers and scientists, multinational executives and managers, and other people with skills in demand. Investor immigrants, who will each put at least $1 million into the economy, account for 10,000 of those visas.

About 40 percent of the 200 researchers in the Communications Sciences Research wing at AT&T Bell Laboratories were born outside the United States. In Silicon Valley, California, much of the technical work force is foreign-born. At Du Pont Merck Pharmaceutical, a joint venture based in Delaware, a new anti-hypertensive drug was invented by a team that included two immigrants from Hong Kong and a scientist whose parents immigrated from Lithuania.

The next generation of scientists and engineers at high-tech companies in the United States will be dominated by immigrants. The number of native-born citizens getting science Ph.D.s has remained about the same, but the number of foreign-born students receiving science doctorates more than doubled between 1981 and 1991, to 37 percent of the total.[5]

Regardless of their educational level, immigrants tend to join their peers, and their peers tend to live in large coastal cities. California, New York, Texas, Florida, Illinois, and New Jersey are expected to be home to three of every four new immigrants, who will be joining already-large minority populations in those states. In California, non-Hispanic whites will become a minority within the next two decades.[6]

multiculturalism
Phenomenon that occurs when all ethnic groups in an area are roughly equally represented.

2 Ethnic and Cultural Diversity by Region

Multiculturalism occurs when all ethnic groups in an area are roughly equally represented, such as in a city, county, or census tract. It has not occurred equally across the United States. Exhibit 7.2 depicts levels of multiculturalism by county. Four of New York City's five boroughs are among the ten most ethnically diverse

Exhibit 7.2

Levels of Ethnic Diversity in the United States, by County

Source: James Allen and Eugene Turner, "Where Diversity Reigns," *American Demographics*, August 1990, p. 37. © *American Demographics*. For subscription information, please call (800)828-1133.

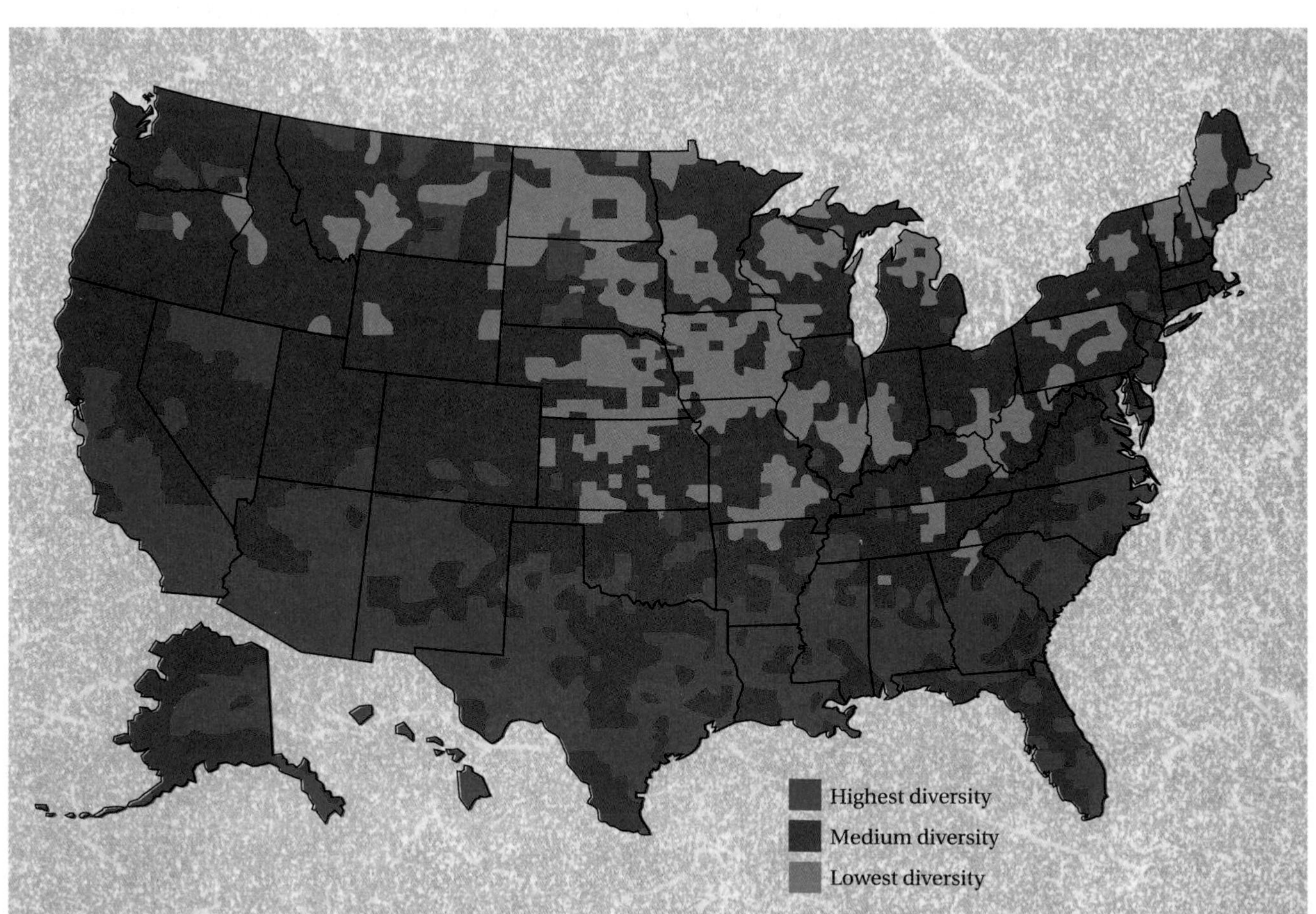

counties in the country.[7] San Francisco County is the most diverse in the nation. The proportions of major ethnic groups are closer to being equal there than anywhere else. People of many ancestries have long been attracted to the area.

The least multicultural region is a broad swath stretching from northern New England through the Midwest and into Montana. These counties have few people other than whites. The counties with the very lowest level of diversity are found in the agricultural heartland: Nebraska and Iowa.

Entrepreneurship and Ethnic Groups

The ethnic diversity of a region depends on the employment and entrepreneurial opportunities. Today, minorities own about a tenth of the nation's 14 million firms.[8] During the past decade, every large minority group increased the number of businesses owned and rates of business ownership. But some minority groups have much higher rates of business ownership than others.

The number of firms owned by Asians grew 89 percent during the past decade, not far behind the rate of Asian population growth. The number of firms owned by Hispanics grew 81 percent. Business growth was only 38 percent among businesses owned by African-Americans. But that growth rate was still faster than the 13 percent rate of this group's population growth between 1980 and 1990.[9]

The high rate of business ownership among Asians is due to several factors. First is their high level of educational attainment. In 1990, about 40 percent of adult Asian-Americans had completed college, compared with only 23 percent of whites.[10] Asian-Americans also have rather high incomes, so they have more capital to launch small businesses. Finally, a large share of Asian-Americans are recent immigrants, many of whom came to the United States specifically to go into business.

Examples of successful immigrants abound. Paul Yuan, for example, left Taiwan with his wife in 1975, seven days after their marriage. They eventually settled in Seattle with several thousand dollars in life savings and no work visas. Yuan was a college graduate, but for two years he worked in Chinese restaurants. In 1978 he became a legal resident and opened his own travel agency while working nights as a

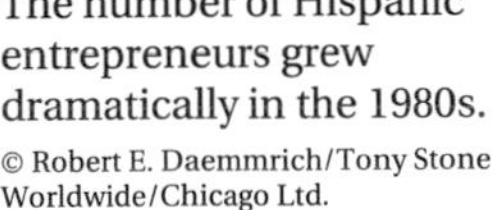
The number of Hispanic entrepreneurs grew dramatically in the 1980s.

© Robert E. Daemmrich/Tony Stone Worldwide/Chicago Ltd.

hotel dishwasher. By 1993, at 44 years of age, Yuan owned a thriving Seattle travel business, and he and his family lived in a $4 million house.

In 1965, 21-year-old Humberto Galvez left Mexico City for Los Angeles. He started pumping gas and busing tables, working his way up the ladder, with a lot of bumps along the way. After starting and selling a chain of nineteen El Pollo Loco charbroiled chicken restaurants in the Los Angeles area, he now owns six Pescado Mojado ("wet fish") seafood diners, employing 100 workers.

Taken together, minority groups are rapidly becoming a larger portion of America's business owners. They generate more income and employment in the U.S. economy as money is spent and respent.

Social Implications of Multiculturalism

Multiculturalism will have a profound impact on society as a whole. If we count men and women as separate groups, all of us are now members of at least one minority group.[11] Without fully realizing it, we have left the time when the nonwhite, non-Western part of our population could be expected to assimilate to the dominant majority. In the future, everyone will have to do some assimilation.

As minority groups grow, no single group will have the political power to dictate solutions. Agreement on how to resolve almost any public issue is likely to be hard to obtain. Reaching a consensus will require more cooperation than it has in the past.

The U.S. economy continues to move away from manufacturing and jobs requiring physical skills toward services and jobs requiring knowledge skills. More than ever, a college education will be the way for minorities to gain broader opportunities in U.S. society. But relative to rates for whites, college enrollment rates for African-Americans and Hispanics actually declined during the 1980s.[12]

As educational attainment becomes more important for individual success, differences in educational attainment will produce sharply different socioeconomic profiles for different racial and ethnic groups. This trend could create a population polarized by both race and economic opportunity. Whites and Asian-Americans could increasingly dominate high-income, high-status occupations, leaving African-Americans and Hispanics with low-income, low-status occupations. Even if job discrimination suddenly disappeared, lower educational attainment would keep many minorities from entering newly opened doors.

Marketing Implications of Multiculturalism

The marketer's task is made far more challenging by ethnic and cultural differences in educational level and demand for goods and services. First, marketing managers must realize that ethnic markets are not homogeneous. There is not an African-American market or a Hispanic market, any more than there is a white market. Yet there are many niches within ethnic markets that require micromarketing strategies.

For example, African Eye, which offers women's designer fashions from Africa, recently attracted a thousand women to a fashion show at Prince Georges Plaza near Washington, D.C. The show featured the latest creations by Alfadi, a high-fashion Nigerian designer, who also hosted the show. African Eye's dresses and outfits blend African and Western influences and are priced at $50 to $600. Says Mozella Perry Ademiluyi, the president and co-founder of African Eye: "Our customer is professional, 30 to 65, has an income level of $30,000-plus and often is well-traveled. They don't just want to wear something that is African. They want something that is well-tailored, unique, and creative as well."[13]

The Ringling Brothers Circus has several acts that appeal to different cultural groups. The Espanas, for instance, perform on the Globe of Death.
Ringling Brothers Circus

An alternative to the niche strategy used by large marketers is to maintain a brand's core identity while straddling different languages, cultures, ages, and incomes with different promotional campaigns. Levi Strauss, for example, publishes *501 Button-Fly Report* for 14- to 24-year-olds. It has Spike Lee interviewing spelunkers, roadies, cemetery tour guides, and others on what they do in their jeans. For men ages 25 and up, Levi's runs separate ads on sports programs and in magazines, showing adults in pursuits like touch football and outings with the kids. A Hispanic campaign, in TV and outdoor advertising, follows two men through their day, from working to teaching a boy to play softball. *"Levi's siempre quedan bien"*—"Levi's always fit well"—is the theme.[14]

stitching niches Combining ethnic, age, income, and lifestyle markets on some common basis to form a mass market.

A third strategy for multicultural marketing is to seek common interests, motivations, or needs across ethnic groups. This strategy is sometimes called **stitching niches,** which means stitching ethnic, age, income, and lifestyle markets back together, on some common basis, to form a large market. The result may be a cross-cultural product, such as a frozen pizza-flavored eggroll. Or it may be a product that serves several ethnic markets simultaneously. Ringling Brothers and Barnum and Bailey Circus showcases acts that appeal to many ethnic groups. It has recently broadened its appeal to Asian-Americans by adding the "Mysterious Oriental Art of Hair Hanging." Marguerite Michelle, known as the "ravishing Rapunzel," is suspended in the air on a wire attached to her waist-length hair. When the circus comes to town, the Mexican-born Michelle also goes on Spanish-language radio shows to build recognition for Ringling in the Hispanic market. The circus is promoted as *"El Espectaculo Mas Grande del Mundo."*[15]

3 THE AFRICAN-AMERICAN MARKET

African-Americans, numbering 31 million in 1993, are the largest minority group in the United States. The proportion of the population that is African-American will continue to grow well into the next century, because the birthrate for African-Americans is 22.1 births per 1,000 persons, versus 14.8 for whites. Also, the death rate among African-Americans is lower than among the general population because their average age is younger.

The immigration of African-Americans from abroad is minimal compared with the large numbers of immigrants from Latin America and Asia. Immigration accounted for nearly 30 percent of total U.S. population growth during the 1980s, but it produced only 15 percent of the increase in the African-American population.

At the beginning of the twentieth century, over 90 percent of all African-Americans lived in the South. The growing industrial base in the North and lack of economic opportunity in the South started a massive movement of African-Americans out of the rural South, with the Northeast and the Midwest becoming the chief beneficiaries. In the 1970s, African-Americans began to migrate back to the South and West from declining northern industrial cities. Today, 53 percent of all African-Americans live in the South, 19 percent each in the Midwest and Northeast, and 9 percent in the West.[16] African-American population concentration by county is shown in Exhibit 7.3.

The largest concentration of African-Americans in a metropolitan area occurs in New York City (see Exhibit 7.4). The areas of greatest population growth among African-Americans are outer suburbs surrounding central metropolitan areas. The African-American population of Gwinnett County, Georgia, north of Atlanta, increased 344 percent, for example, during the 1980s. In contrast, Gwinnett County's total population only doubled. Although the majority of both African-Americans and whites live in metropolitan areas, they tend to live in different communities. Half of whites, compared with just over a quarter of African-Americans, lived in suburban areas in 1990.

The African-American population is younger than the U.S. population as a whole.

Exhibit 7.3

Percentage of African-Americans in U.S. Counties, 1990

Source: Kathy Bodovitz, "Black America," *American Demographics* (American Diversity). Desk Reference Series no. 1, July 1991, p. 6. © *American Demographics.* For subscription information, please call (800)828-1133.

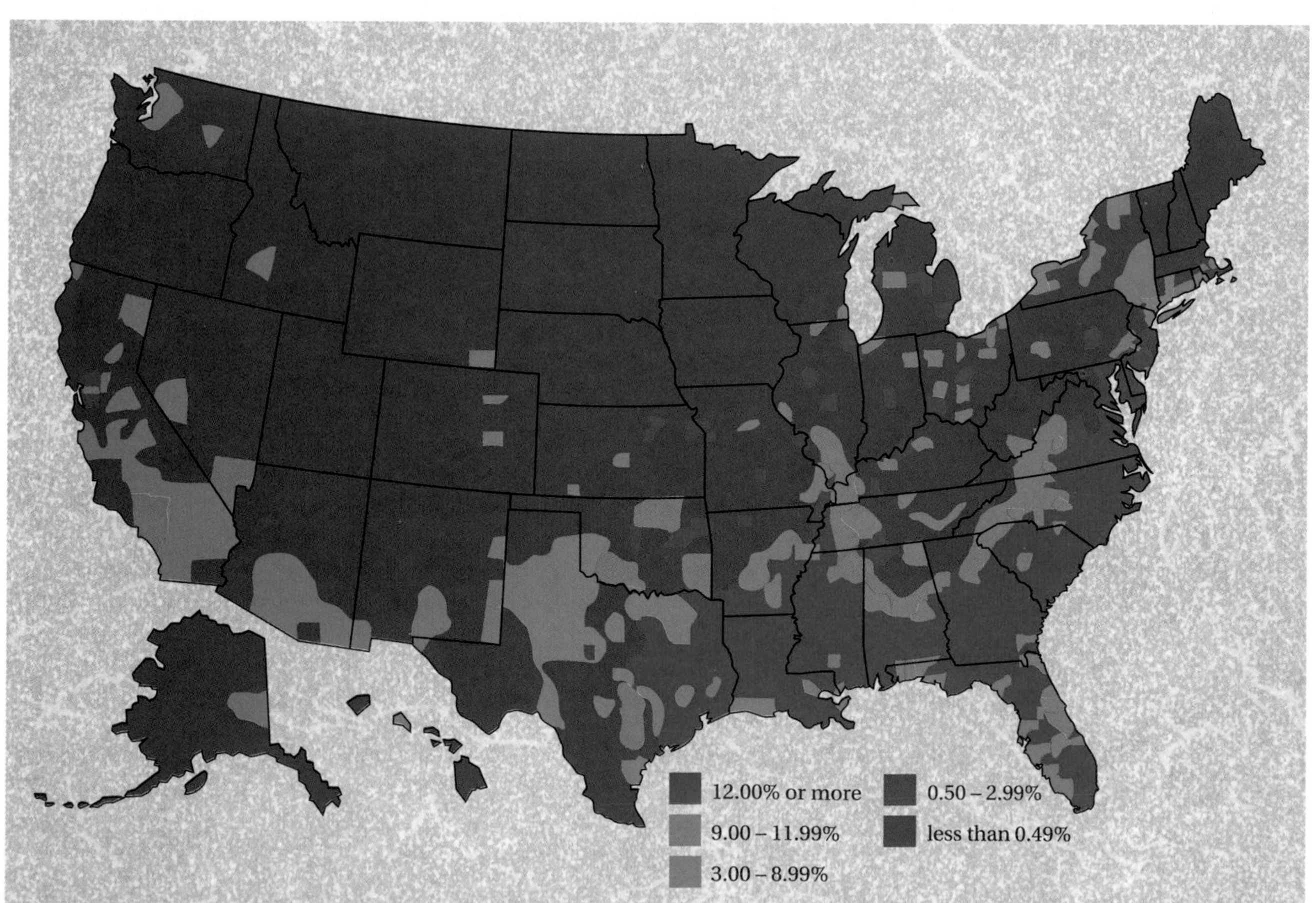

Rank	Metropolitan area	African-American population	Total population	Percentage of population that is African-American
1	New York, NY	2,250,026	17,953,372	12.53%
2	Chicago, IL	1,332,919	8,065,633	16.53
3	Washington, D.C.–MD–VA	1,041,934	3,923,574	26.56
4	Los Angeles–Long Beach, CA	992,974	14,531,529	6.83
5	Detroit, MI	943,479	4,665,236	20.22
6	Philadelphia, PA–NJ	929,907	5,899,345	15.76
7	Atlanta, GA	736,153	2,833,511	25.98
8	Baltimore, MD	616,065	2,382,172	25.86
9	Houston, TX	611,243	3,711,043	16.47
10	New Orleans, LA	430,470	1,238,816	34.75
11	St. Louis, MO–IL	423,185	2,444,099	17.31
12	Newark, NJ	422,802	723,274	58.46
13	Dallas, TX	410,766	3,885,415	10.57
14	Memphis, TN–AR–MS	399,011	981,747	40.64
15	Norfolk–Virginia Beach–Newport News, VA	398,093	1,396,107	28.51

Exhibit 7.4

Metropolitan Areas with the Largest African-American Population, 1990

Source: 1990 U.S. Census.

The median age of this group was 28.1 years in 1993, nearly five years younger than the median for all citizens. But, like the total population, the African-American population is aging. Between 1980 and 1993, the share of African-Americans 65 and older increased from 7.8 to 8.4 percent, and the median age rose by nearly three years.[17]

Income and Consumption Patterns of African-Americans

A substantial and growing African-American middle class has been overshadowed by the image of the low-income African-American. The concentration of poor African-Americans in densely populated urban areas makes them highly visible. They represent fewer than 30 percent of the U.S. poor, but they make up more than 40 percent of the poor in central cities.[18]

It is a myth that African-Americans have little discretionary income. Total expenditures by this group currently top $270 billion a year. Increasingly, marketers are finding the market segment very rewarding. The median income of dual-income African-American families is over $35,000, and about 13 percent of African-American families have incomes over $50,000.[19] Who are these affluent consumers? Like affluent whites, they tend to be well educated (32 percent college graduates), homeowners (77 percent), in the prime earning ages (66 percent between 35 and 55), married (79 percent), and suburbanites.[20]

Consumption patterns of affluent African-Americans are somewhat different from those of other wealthy Americans. Claritas Corporation of Virginia, a marketing research firm, developed the following profiles of high-income African-Americans (those with family incomes over $50,000 a year):

> This group is far more likely than average to drink scotch, to buy classical music, to smoke menthol cigarettes, to own a satellite dish, to belong to a book club, and to travel by rail. Wealthy African Americans are far less likely than the average adult to go power

boating or water skiing, or take a cruise, or to go swimming frequently. They also are unlikely to buy country music, a pickup truck, or camping equipment.

Wealthy African American adults spend heavily on dress shirts, overcoats, slacks, and sweaters, and they are more likely than average to remodel their bathrooms, and to have two or more telephone lines to their home. But they are much less likely than average to install their own carpeting or car parts, or to own power garden tools like chainsaws or rototillers. They don't clip coupons, and they don't shop at Sears; they like to go first class and charge it on an American Express Gold Card.

Like most well-educated groups, the black achievers read magazines and newspapers at rates well above average. They are especially fond of *Ebony, Sports Illustrated, Better Homes and Gardens, Fortune*, and *Time*. Although blacks in general watch more television than whites, affluent African American adults are less likely than the average person to be heavy viewers of television.

Affluent blacks will respond to marketers who affirm both their social status and their heritage. Because so few affluent African Americans have inherited wealth, they are also concerned with their financial security. On average, readers of the business magazine *Black Enterprise* set aside a startling 17 percent of their incomes for savings and investment last year, more than three times the national average. Yet 82 percent say they are still not satisfied with their current financial situation.[21]

Creating a Marketing Mix for the African-American Market

The size and purchasing power of the African-American market makes it an attractive target for the largest companies as well as for countless smaller ones. Effectively penetrating the market, however, often requires a unique and distinctive marketing mix. Thomas Burrell, president of Burrell Communications Group, which specializes in marketing to African-Americans, notes, "Marketers must realize that black people are not dark-skinned white people."[22] African-Americans have unique desires, hopes, and preferences that require a specialized marketing mix.

Product

As noted in the opening story, many firms are creating new and different products for the African-American market. Many times entrepreneurial African-Americans are the first to realize unique product opportunities. For example, Olmec Corp. is a New York–based toy manufacturer created by Yla Eason when she couldn't find an African-American superhero doll to buy her son. Her $2 million company markets more than sixty kinds of African-American and Hispanic dolls. Eason has a distribution partnership with Hasbro.

Today, both Mattel and Tyco Industries market dolls that are more than Barbies in darker plastic. Tyco just introduced Kenya, who wears beads to adorn her cornrows. Like a Mattel doll called Shani, Kenya comes in a choice of three complexions: light, medium, and dark. Shani also has a new boyfriend named Jamal.

In health and beauty aids, manufacturers owned by African-Americans—such as Soft Sheen, M&M, Johnson, and ProLine—target the African-American market. Huge corporations like Revlon, Gillette, and Alberto-Culver have either divisions or major product lines for the African-American market. Alberto-Culver, for example, has a hair care line for this segment with seventy-five products. In fact, hair care items are the largest single category within the African-American health and beauty aid category. "Let's face it—lipstick is lipstick, and nail polish is nail polish, although there are differences in shades and bases," says Jim Normandin, senior buyer for Beauty Enterprises of Connecticut. Beauty Enterprises is the largest ethnic distributor of health and beauty aids in the United States, and hair care makes up the bulk of its business. "But black [people's] hair is unique because it's coarser [than white

Among those capitalizing on renewed interest in Afrocentric products are Audrey and John Bolling III, owners of A.L.L. International Clothing Co. Their imports from Gambia and Senegal are carried in many JCPenney stores.
David Buffington Photographer

people's hair], and it's often ultra-curly; to style it certain ways you need to relax or straighten it first," says Normandin. Despite representing only 12 percent of the U.S. population, African-Americans buy 34 percent of all hair care products.[23]

Other entrepreneurs are capitalizing on "Afrocentric products" that stress African heritage and culture. Afrocentric products include art objects, books, jewelry, and clothing. "There's going to be a sustained demand for it," says Mohamed Diop, owner of Intercontinental Business Network, a New York importer of African cloth. "The interest now is much more of an intellectual interest, whereas in the '60s it was more of an emotional interest." More vendors also are marketing Afrocentric merchandise at two-day trade shows staged nationwide by Black Expo USA. In 1992 the New York show drew about 75,000 people and 350 vendors, 90 of whom sold Afrocentric products at a specially designed African village.[24]

About a third of the nation's largest African-American–owned firms cater to the African-American market (see Exhibit 7.5). Food processing, computer software, and construction are the three main industries in the twenty-five largest African-American–owned companies.

Exhibit 7.5

Largest African-American–Owned Businesses in the United States

Source: Adapted from Leon Wynter, "Who's on Top," *The Wall Street Journal–Black Entrepreneurship*, 3 April 1992, p. R11. Reprinted by permission of *The Wall Street Journal*, © 1992 Dow Jones & Companty, Inc. All Rights Reserved Worldwide.

Rank	Company and business	1991 sales (in millions)
1	TLC Beatrice International Holdings Incorporated (international food processing and distribution)	$1,500
2	Johnson Publishing Company (*Ebony* and *Jet* magazines, health and beauty aids)	252
3	Philadelphia Coca-Cola Bottling Co. (soft drinks)	250
4	H.T. Russell and Company (construction, real estate development and management)	143
5	Soft Sheen Products (health and beauty aids)	92
6	Barden Communications (cable television franchises)	86
7	Jones Transfer Company (trucking)	75
8	Garden State Cablevision Inc. (cable television franchises)	74
9	Stop Shop and Save Group (supermarkets)	6.5
10	Bing Steel Company (milled steel)	6.1

Not to be outdone by entrepreneurial firms, large companies are jumping on the bandwagon. In 1992, Dallas-based JCPenney added two clothing sections to more than 100 stores, one called the African Collection (authentic African clothing) and the other called Africa 1992 (U.S.-styled clothing made of African fabrics). It also issued a specialty catalog that offers many of the same clothes by mail.

Macy's flagship store in Manhattan is selling Cross Colours, a line of brightly colored clothing that its tags describe as ethnically inspired. Nike and Converse began selling jogging suits and other exercise wear that feature African prints. Speedo, the California swimsuit company, had the same idea. Many small stores in big cities have started selling clothes, suspenders, and sunglasses with African prints. Todd

ETHICS IN MARKETING

Hurting African-American Consumers

In 1990, R.J. Reynolds canceled its test marketing of Uptown cigarettes. The brand was developed based on research that showed a significant percentage of African-American smokers were switching from RJR's Salem to brands like Lorillard's Newport, with lighter menthol flavoring. Uptown was developed for the "taste preferences of black smokers," according to RJR. But two weeks before its planned introduction, the cigarette was attacked by the African-American community and health officials, including U.S. Secretary of Health and Human Services Louis Sullivan. R.J. Reynolds dropped the product.

Another controversial product category aimed mainly at African-Americans is malt liquor, a product much like beer but containing up to 6 percent alcohol, versus 3.5 percent for most beer. "The growth in the industry has been fastest in ethnic markets in major cities," says John Derolito, president of United Beers of Brooklyn. "We're going where the market is." United Beers, which markets the Midnight Dragon brand, was preparing to launch another malt liquor tentatively called Crazy Horse.

The mom-and-pop stores that dot inner cities have become the main sellers of the malt liquors, which seldom appear in well-to-do areas. Corner groceries are more accessible to underage drinkers than liquor stores. At the Riden Supermarket in Harlem, tall cans of Olde English 800, forty-ounce bottles of St. Ides, and sixty-four-ounce bottles of Midnight Dragon crowd the cooler. A young man who calls himself Mitch grabs a tall can of Olde English. Within two hours, he's back for another. It's a ritual that's repeated every day, says owner David Annisafi, who estimates that he sells up to twenty cases of malt each week, compared with just three cases of beer.

"It's status," says Lumumba Bandele, 20 years old, who works as a youth counselor with Manhattan Valley Youth Program. "The attitude is, 'You're a man if you've got a 40 in your hand.'" Forty-ounce cans of malt liquor sell for about $1.50.

Today, the $500 million malt liquor market is being revitalized by higher alcohol levels, lower prices, and rap heroes like Ice Cube and the Geto Boys, which are luring a new generation of drinkers. Most liquor makers preach moderation, but some malt marketers imply that their products are a cheap drunk. In one commercial, no longer airing, rapper Ice Cube boasted that he "grabbed me a 40 just to get my buzz on, 'cause I needed just a little more kick."

The most aggressive malt liquor marketer is the small brewer McKenzie River, with its St. Ides brand. The St. Ides message has been quantity, with ads routinely presenting a forty-ounce bottle as a single serving. In one commercial, rap singer King Tee said, "I usually drink it when I'm out just clowning, me and the home boys, you know, be like downing it. Cause it's stronger but the taste is more smooth. I grab me a 40 when I want to act a fool." McKenzie River has also pitched the beer as enhancing sexual performance. McKenzie River's other promotional tactics were even more controversial among regulators and inner-city community activists. The company's sales representatives routinely put stickers on containers of St. Ides warning consumers "Caution: Most powerful malt" or touted it as "No. 1 strongest malt"—a violation of federal rules. They stopped doing so in 1991.[25]

Are companies like R.J. Reynolds, McKenzie River, Anheuser-Busch, and Miller Brewing just "going where the market is"? Doesn't the marketing concept say "give the consumer what he or she wants"? Or do marketers need to draw the line and say, "This is not good for society"? If the latter is true, shouldn't R.J. Reynolds quit selling all cigarettes and Anheuser-Busch quit selling beer? Where do we draw the line?

Oldham, Mark McNairy, Antoinette Linn, and a few other major fashion designers have used African-print fabrics in their collections.[26]

African-American consumers tend to be heavy users of certain product categories that are not specifically produced for the African-American market. For example, they buy more than their share of VCRs, compact disc players, answering machines, home furnishings, major appliances, jewelry, watches, computers, candy bars, nondairy cream substitutes, corn, syrup, and tomato sauce.[27] The African-American market also represents one of the fastest-growing segments of the tourism, financial planning, and health care industries.[28]

Not all products created for the African-American market have been viewed in a positive manner. In fact, as the box on page 206 explains, some products have drawn such a negative reaction that they were withdrawn from the market immediately.

Promotion

About 3 percent of all promotional dollars spent in the United States are specifically targeted toward African-Americans.[29] But the dollar figure is growing rapidly, in part because African-Americans viewing advertisements in black media (media targeted toward African-Americans) as opposed to white media have higher personal identification with the brand.[30]

One company that reaches out to African-Americans is McDonald's, which bases its target spending on "share of stomach." African-Americans account for 15 percent of its business, or "share of stomach," so the group gets 15 percent of the marketing and advertising effort. Marketing professionals even sing the praises of one McDonald's "breakfast club" campaign, which features buppies (black urban professionals) talking like African-Americans instead of whites.

In general, the companies that are effective in reaching the African-American market include soft-drink, fast-food, automobile, tobacco, and liquor companies and, to a lesser extent, packaged-goods companies. But even within these more progressive industries there are laggards. Jeff Burns, vice president of Johnson Publishing, publisher of *Ebony*, singles out BMW and Volvo. "Blacks buy 20% of the Volvos bought in this country and yet Volvo does no marketing to the black community," he charges.[31]

To win the praise of African-American consumers today, marketers must do more than use African-American models or run ethnic ads. They must run sensitive, effective ads, which often means working with African-American ad agencies. Some believe that, all things being equal, African-American ad professionals are more effective than whites at targeting African-Americans. "The truth is that general market agencies are not prepared by inclination or background to speak to the black community," says Byron Lewis, chairman and CEO of UniWorld Group/New York. "These general market agencies have an ivory tower approach to marketing to blacks."[32] African-American agencies also claim they can help companies avoid inadvertent stereotyping, such as a Westin Hotels & Resorts ad that featured an African-American woman as director of housekeeping or a car ad from Toyota (generally considered a progressive company) that said, "Car red. Knuckles white."[33]

An example of a company that is trying to create ethnically sensitive promotions is Pillsbury. Pillsbury marketing executives had never gauged African-Americans' response to the white lumberjack character who promoted their Hungry Jacks pancake and biscuit products. When they did, they discovered that "there were blacks using our products, but they weren't using them to the same level as the general population," says Amy Hilliard-Jones, Pillsbury's director of advertising.[34] So

Pillsbury banished the lumberjack in test ads for African-American consumers by UniWorld agency. Instead, the ads run a colorfully printed slogan, "You look Hungry Jack," and feature an African-American family eating together.

Advertising agencies are also creating public service announcements against racism. For example, the Smith/Greenland agency developed a campaign on racial tolerance. The ads feature no pictures, only copy (see Exhibit 7.6). The American Association of Advertising Agencies' Ad Council is creating an antidiscrimination campaign expected to last ten years. One of the ads opens with a shot of babies of various races in side-by-side cribs in a hospital nursery. The spot then whips through a montage of harsh scenes of violence and prejudice that take place from childhood to old age, closing on a graveyard. As the babies play, a voice-over says, "Here's one time it doesn't matter who your neighbor is," and when the cemetery is shown, "Here's the other." The final tag is "Life's too short. Stop the hate."[35]

Distribution

Many of the nation's largest retailers target African-Americans. Kmart's "Looking Good" advertising campaign emphasizes the store's clothing. To better reach African-American consumers, the company appointed minority-owned agency Burrell Inc. to develop special advertising. Kmart's minority-targeted campaign was designed to reach African-American women between 18 and 49. The ads appear in such national ethnic magazines as *Ebony, Essence,* and *Class* and in African-American local newspapers and on radio stations in ten markets.[36]

Toys R Us hired minority ad agency The Mingo Group to create a comprehensive

Exhibit 7.6

An Example of a Public Service Announcement Stressing Racial Tolerance

Source: Smith/Greenland Incorporated Advertising.

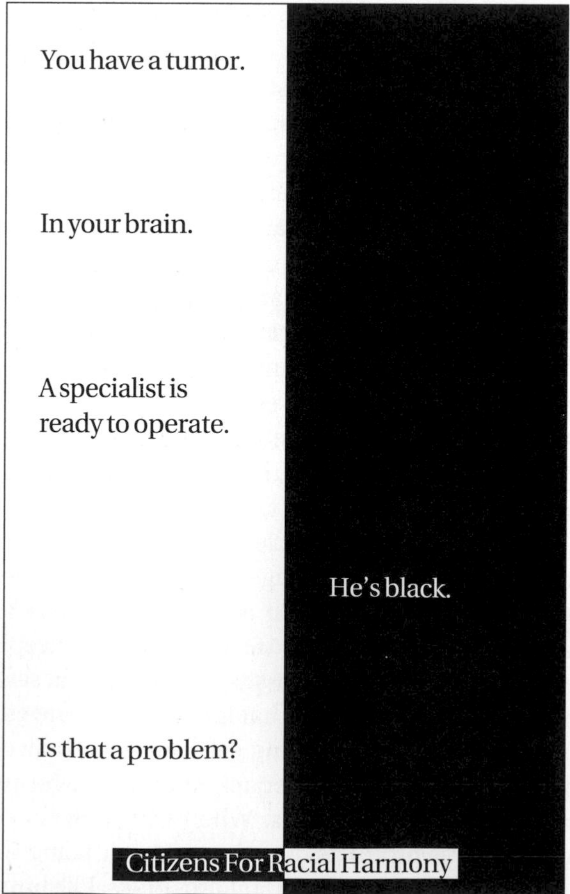

marketing and communications program targeting African-American consumers.

Spiegel, the large catalog retailer, joined with the publisher of *Ebony* to develop a fashion line and catalog aimed at African-American women. Spiegel maintains that this group spends 6.5 percent of family income on apparel, compared with an average of 5 percent for all women. This catalog, to be called *E Style*, features clothes designed especially for African-American women. Its first issue was mailed to 1.5 million African-American women, including *Ebony* subscribers and current Spiegel customers.[37]

Pizza Hut, a PepsiCo subsidiary, is making minority franchises a priority. Pizza Hut is estimated to have about 300 minority-owned stores and now includes the nation's largest African-American–owned fast-food franchise company. Larry Lundy, until recently the chain's vice president of restaurant development, bought thirty-one stores in the New Orleans area for a price estimated at $15.5 million.[38]

Shopping malls are also being developed for the African-American market. Researchers have found that African-Americans, on an average trip to a mall, spend $51.21, or 5.1 percent more than whites.[39] On the eastern edge of Atlanta, bordered on one side by palatial homes and on the other by public housing, the South DeKalb Mall restyled itself as an "Afrocentric retail center." It boosted both the share of African-American–owned stores—to 25 percent in 1992 from 15 percent in 1990—and the number of African-American store managers—to 85 percent from 65 percent. It increased the number of carts run by minorities and doubled the number of cultural shows. Almost all the mall's advertising is now aimed at African-Americans. Several mall retailers tailor their goods to blacks. Camelot Music more than doubled its selection of gospel, jazz, and rhythm-and-blues music. Foot Locker stocks styles that sell well in African-American markets, such as suede and black athletic shoes and baseball shirts from the "Negro League" of the 1930s.

For many local residents, the mall has become a focal point for racial pride. People shop there out of loyalty to the neighborhood; they delight in seeing signs of African-American culture. Edward Price, an associate manager at Southern Bell, spent nearly $800 on Christmas gifts at South DeKalb. "We need something to rally around," he says. "I want to drop as much money into that mall as possible."[40]

But many upper-income African-Americans who live near the mall drive twenty minutes to shop elsewhere. They say the mall's selection is too limited, and they scoff at the notion of fashions aimed at them. Emerson Bryan, an official with the Atlanta Regional Commission, lives less than two miles from the mall, but other than buying toothpaste and filling prescriptions, he says, "I don't do my major shopping there." He says South DeKalb sells "ethnic variety" clothes that he couldn't wear to work. "When the stores see an area that's all black, they assume we're all the same," he says. "They assume we're all rappers. We're not."[41]

Price

Product pricing is the one element of the marketing mix least affected by multicultural marketing. Unique specialty items are usually relatively expensive regardless of the ethnic market they are produced for. In contrast, consumer products in intensively competitive markets, such as hair care items, are priced very competitively.

One controversial aspect of pricing is whether the poor pay more. U.S. Census Bureau data show that very often the poor are members of a minority group. In his 1964 book, *The Poor Pay More*, David Caplovitz reported the results of a study of consumer behavior among low-income families in four New York City public housing projects. Caplovitz was interested in what durable goods poor consumers own, where they shop, how much they pay, what method of payment they use, and how secure their finances are in general. He concluded that "society now virtually presents the very poor risks with twin options: of forgoing major purchases or of being exploited."[42]

A more recent study by the Department of Consumer Affairs in New York City showed that Caplovitz's findings are still relevant. An investigation of food prices and cleanliness of stores in poor, middle-income, and affluent New York City neighborhoods revealed that consumers in poor neighborhoods pay 8.8 percent more for the same groceries than consumers in middle-class neighborhoods do.[43]

The problem faced by the poor is illustrated by Jean Shelby, a Chicago inner-city resident:

> Jean Shelby receives Fingerhut catalogs, where the boldfaced price isn't the total cost but the amount per month. One recent offer: "TV/VCR combination, $59.64 per month." The deal appealed to Ms. Shelby, who supports herself and four children on $597 a month from her part-time receptionist's job, food stamps and $422 in Supplemental Security Income for one child. She bought the set, committing herself to 19 monthly payments. . . . The total she will pay, including finance charges at a 24.9% annual rate: $1,133.16. The same set can be found in the suburbs for as little as $499. Why not save up and buy the set outright? "I want things right away," Ms. Shelby says.
>
> Fingerhut's chairman, Theodore Deikel, acknowledges that much of the merchandise could be bought elsewhere for less, but he says Fingerhut provides a real value by extending credit to people most big companies wouldn't touch and by delivering name-brand merchandize to their homes. "We're trying to give them something they don't otherwise get," says Deikel.
>
> But to cover its higher credit risks, Fingerhut charges annual interest rates of up to 24.9%. That means people like Ms. Shelby may pay nearly seven percentage points more than the average rate banks charge the more-affluent on credit-card purchases. Officials of the Minnetonka, Minn., company note that finance fees can be avoided by paying the full cash price listed in its catalogs, but they say only 30% of orders are handled that way.
>
> The discount stores, outlet malls and warehouse clubs that have redefined suburbia's idea of a bargain have largely bypassed inner-city neighborhoods like Ms. Shelby's. These retailers see bigger opportunities in serving the more-affluent middle class. The inner city is "a much harder market to make money in" because of higher costs for insurance and security and larger losses to theft, says Carl Steidtmann, chief economist at the Management Horizons retail consulting unit of Price Waterhouse.[44]

In summary, firms that target the low-income market admit prices are higher than in higher-income areas. The higher prices are justified, they say, because the costs of doing business in low-income areas are greater. Moreover, they note, if the disadvantaged consumer did not pay more, the retailers simply wouldn't serve the market.

4 THE HISPANIC MARKET

By the end of 1994, the Hispanic population will approach 24 million people, and the year 2000 should see a Hispanic population of nearly 30 million. Hispanics are one of the fastest-growing minority groups.

Four states now have more than a million Hispanic residents: California, Texas, New York, and Florida. By 2000, two more states will join this club: Illinois and New Jersey (see Exhibit 7.7). Twenty states had at least 100,000 Hispanics in 1990.[45]

Exhibit 7.7

States with the Greatest Hispanic Population, in Thousands

Source: Woods & Poole Economics, Inc.

Rank	State	1990	2000
1	California	7,737	10,144
2	Texas	4,358	5,979
3	New York	2,216	2,681
4	Florida	1,585	2,412
5	Illinois	905	1,193
6	New Jersey	740	952
7	Arizona	691	1,073
8	New Mexico	581	825
9	Colorado	425	594
10	Massachusetts	288	378
	Total U.S.	22,449	31,066

The greatest metropolitan concentration of Hispanics is in Los Angeles County, where over 3 million Hispanics live. Dade County (Miami) is a distant second, with more than 950,000 Hispanics. Cook County (Chicago) ranks third, with almost 700,000 Hispanics. About two-thirds of all Hispanics live in just twenty-five metropolitan areas. Today, the number of Hispanics in California, Texas, New York, and Florida is greater than the entire U.S. Hispanic population of 1980. The 1990 census showed that 70 percent of the Hispanic population is still concentrated in those four states. However, future censuses will show a greater dispersion of the Hispanic population.

Hispanic Submarkets

The concept of multiculturalism is nowhere more evident than in the Hispanic culture. Mexican-Americans make up 60 percent of U.S. Hispanics and are highly concentrated in the Southwest. Puerto Rican–Americans are the second-largest Hispanic subgroup, at just 12 percent, but they dominate the Hispanic population of New York City. Cuban-Americans are the majority of Hispanics in South Florida, although they are just 5 percent of all U.S. Hispanics. The remaining 23 percent of Hispanics trace their lineage to Spain, South America, or Central America.[46]

Mexican-Americans are the youngest Hispanic subgroup, with a median age of just 24, according to the Current Population Survey. Cuban-Americans are the oldest, with a median age of 39. Cuban-Americans are also the best educated: 20 percent of them who are 25 or older have attended at least four years of college. This college-educated share slips to 15 percent for "other" Hispanics, 10 percent for Puerto Rican–Americans, and 5 percent for Mexican-Americans.[47]

Advertising to Hispanic-Americans often means choosing between the English and Spanish languages. It's a difficult decision, because researchers disagree on which language is appropriate for different kinds of advertising. One study of language use found that most Hispanics think and speak in Spanish in common situations. In other words, Mexican-Americans who are having fun at a party, singing in the shower, praying, thinking, or watching television are likely to choose Spanish, according to Market Development in San Diego. But 80 percent of Mexican-born permanent residents speak at least some English, and 90 percent of first-generation, U.S.-born Mexican-Americans speak English well. A growing number of

The growing population of U.S. Hispanics is an appealing market for many retailers. To serve this group, marketers must be aware of the distinct preferences of the dominant submarkets, which are based on national origin: Cuban, Mexican, Puerto Rican.
Courtesy Maclean Hunter Media

upwardly mobile, assimilated Hispanics use English in their business and professional lives.[48]

Marketers cannot assume that they can simply use Spanish instead of English to promote to Hispanics. They must take other steps to make sure their message will be understood and be relevant. First, the translation must be correct. Coors beer blundered in converting the slogan "Get loose with Coors" into Spanish; it translated as "Get the runs with Coors."[49] Advertisers who are ignorant of subtle dialect differences among Hispanic groups frequently run into trouble. In its early marketing efforts, Tang, the instant breakfast drink, billed itself as *jugo de china*, which is a Puerto Rican term for orange juice. But to all other Hispanics, the phrase is meaningless; *jugo de naranja*—juice of oranges—would be a better choice. Another Hispanic subsegment was puzzled by a phrase that translated as "low asphalt" and wondered why it would be an attractive feature for a cigarette.[50]

Today, marketing managers are carefully targeting major segments of the Hispanic market. Some Campbell Soup ads, for instance, all feature a woman cooking but differ in such details as the character's age, the setting, and the music. In the version for Cuban-Americans, a grandmother cooks in a plant-filled kitchen to the sounds of salsa and merengue music. In contrast, the Mexican-American ad shows a young wife preparing food in a brightly colored "Southwestern-style" kitchen, with pop music playing in the background.

Hispanic Income Distribution

The total purchasing power of the Hispanic market in the United States is over $170 billion annually. Median family income for Hispanics in 1991 was $28,890, compared with $33,000 for the general population. Twenty-one percent of all Hispanic households have incomes over $35,000, and 8 percent have incomes over $50,000. Some Hispanic communities are quite affluent. In Miami, over 33 percent of the Hispanic households have incomes greater than $35,000, which is higher than the national average.[51]

Incomes are not equally distributed among Hispanic subcultures. According to the 1990 census, the median income of Cuban-Americans was $31,300, the highest of any Hispanic group. The comparative figures for Mexican-Americans and Puerto Rican–Americans, according to the U.S. Census Bureau, were $22,200 and $19,900,

respectively.[52] Puerto Rican–Americans living in New York City unfortunately have a poverty rate of 41 percent, compared with the national average of 14 percent.[53]

Miami has the second-highest total of Hispanic-owned businesses, according to Census Bureau figures—trailing only Los Angeles. But Miami's Hispanic businesses reported $500 million more in revenues than those in Los Angeles. Analysts attribute the higher revenue per business to Miami's established Cuban-American community.[54]

Creating a Marketing Mix for the Hispanic Market

The diversity of the Hispanic population and the language differences create many challenges for those trying to target this market.

Product

Hispanics, especially recent immigrants, often prefer products from their native country. Therefore, many retailers along the southern U.S. border import goods from Mexico. In New York City, more than 6,000 bodegas (grocery stores) sell such items as plantains, chorizo (pork sausage), and religious candles to Puerto Rican–Americans. They also serve as neighborhood social centers. Fresh produce is usually very important to Hispanic groups, because of their tradition of shopping every day at open-air produce markets in their native country. Many Hispanics are loyal to brands found in their homeland. If these are not available, Hispanics will choose brands that reflect their native values and culture. Research shows that Hispanics often are not aware of many mainstream American brands.[55]

Procter & Gamble noted that many retailers in Southern California were importing its Ariel detergent from Mexico. Ariel is offered in more than fifty countries and is one of the world's leading detergents. P&G is now trying to get Hispanics to switch to a new, U.S.-made version of Ariel called Ariel Ultra. Although the product has several key benefits over the imported Ariel, sales are slow. Ariel Ultra is selling well to white consumers, but Mexican-Americans prefer the original version. Tradition seems to be the main motivation.

Using a different tactic, Pepsi is importing Mirinda, its popular Mexican soft-drink line, into California. Mirinda—which comes in orange, apple, strawberry, and grapefruit flavors—could be expanded to other U.S. markets if it does well in California. Cadbury Beverages is evaluating options for its flavored mineral water called Peñafiel, which sells well in Mexico but has limited distribution in California.

Unique services have also been created for the Hispanic market. For example, La Rosa del Monte moves families back and forth between the islands of Puerto Rico and Santo Domingo and to eight sites in the United States with large Hispanic populations. These include Miami, Orlando, and Chicago. La Rosa makes moving more affordable by doubling up customers' possessions in large containers. "If we don't have enough freight to fill a container, the customer may have to wait a month or two" for delivery, La Rosa says. But the wait cuts costs by two-thirds, to an average of $1,500 for the typical household.

Promotion

Most promotional dollars targeting the Hispanic market are spent in an attempt to get them to buy mainstream goods and services. For example, Hispanics are 27 percent more likely than non-Hispanics to buy contact lenses (probably because of the relative youth of the Hispanic market). There is, of course, no such thing as a Hispanic contact lens. But Pearle Vision Centers advertise in Spanish.

Financial institutions are also targeting the Hispanic market. Valley National

Bank, which is headquartered in Phoenix and claims a 40 percent share of the Hispanic market in Arizona, formed a Hispanic market committee to develop a program called Spanish Customer Assistance. One of the most popular elements of the program, the bank says, is the *El Centro de Informacion en Español*, a twenty-four-hour telephone hotline that provides bank information and services in Spanish. To make Hispanic customers feel at home, bank employees are attending Spanish-language classes after working hours. Branch signs and promotional materials are being displayed in Spanish as well as English.[56] The bank airs commercials on Hispanic TV stations and runs print ads developed specifically for Spanish-language publications. It also is sponsoring events like the Tucson International Mariachi Conference and the Hispanic Women's Conference, making public service announcements, and providing financial advice on talk shows. Financial assistance is being provided to a summer library outreach program and a Hispanic Leadership Conference.

Media preferences among Hispanics vary widely from market to market. A survey of 5,000 households in ten markets in the continental United States, conducted by San Antonio–based Hispanic Marketing Research & Communications, found that

- 60 percent of the Hispanic market listens to Spanish-language radio, at least once in a while. In McAllen, Texas, 70 percent listen exclusively to Spanish radio; in San Antonio, only 25 percent do.
- 40 percent of the nation's Hispanics watch Spanish-language television, and between 14 percent (San Antonio) and 50 percent (Los Angeles) watch only Spanish-language television. Hispanics tend to switch to English-language television as soon as they understand enough English, but they keep listening to the music of their heritage on Hispanic radio stations.
- Spanish-language newspapers are read by 20 percent of the nation's Hispanics. In Miami, which has two daily Spanish-language newspapers and dozens of weeklies, 35 percent of the Hispanic market reads them exclusively. But markets like San Antonio and Houston have no Spanish-language dailies at all.[57]

The number of Spanish-language media outlets in the United States increased steadily during the past decade. TV stations carrying Spanish programs increased from 46 in 1983 to 111 in 1992, newspapers increased from 94 to 161, magazines increased from 121 to 220, and radio stations increased from 371 to 665.[58] The second most popular radio station in Los Angeles is KWKW, *"La Mexicana."*

There are three Spanish-language television networks: Univision, Telemundo, and Galavision. Galavision targets the Mexican-American viewer, with all its programming produced in Mexico. As a group, the three networks reach all Spanish-speaking communities in the United States. The two top Spanish-language newspapers are *La Opinion* in Los Angeles and *El Nuevo Herald* in Miami, both of which have a circulation of over 100,000.[59]

In 1993, advertisers spent over $800 million on promotions aimed specifically at Hispanics. That amount is large and growing, but it is still less than 1 percent of all U.S. advertising spending. In 1991, General Motors spent an estimated $1.5 billion on advertising. But only $3.2 million was aimed at Hispanics, who buy over 8 percent of the nation's new cars.[60] This imbalance is expected to change as marketers become more familiar with the Hispanic market.

Coca-Cola is one of the largest Hispanic promoters in the United States. Its *"El Super Concurso de el Magnate"* sweepstakes for Coca-Cola Classic generated more than half a million responses from its Hispanic viewers. The new *"Sabor para siempre"*

("Taste for always") tagline was also introduced during the sweepstakes. Commercials for Coke's promotion were aired exclusively on the twenty-three Telemundo network affiliates. They featured Andres Garcia, the popular star of Telemundo's *"El Magnate" novella* (Spanish soap opera). Retail displays offering sweepstakes coupons were available in nineteen markets. The grand prize winner received a new Ferrari and appeared on *"El Magnate,"* and eighteen other winners were given free trips to Miami and $1,000 each. The contest was one of the largest media merchandising promotions ever directed at Hispanic consumers. Coca-Cola also recently sponsored other national promotions for Hispanics, including a tie-in with "MTV *Internacional*." Diet Coke ran a Hispanic version of its "Crack the Code" promotion.[61]

Distribution

The most visible distribution channel to Hispanics consists of retail grocery stores. In general, says Gloria Alvarez, director of operations for the Mexican-American Grocers Association, retailers have become much more sophisticated in how they merchandise to Hispanics.[62] They offer more full-service meat counters, better produce, and bilingual signs.

Developing a retailing mix for Hispanics is becoming more difficult. One reason is that immigration from Latin American countries is increasing. As a result, supermarkets have to cater to more people with different product preferences. In the Los Angeles area, although 80 percent of the Hispanics are from Mexico, many other countries are now represented. A second complicating factor for retailers is acculturation. Their customers may be immigrants, but they may also be second- and third-generation Hispanics whose buying habits have moved closer to those of whites.

Different merchandising approaches are used by both chains and independents. Some operate Mexican-oriented stores, such as Vons with its Tianguis stores and Quality Foods with Viva, both in the Los Angeles area. Others, such as Ralph's or Lucky, use the same name as their other units.

Vons formed a separate eight-person management team to develop the Tianguis format. Its customer was pictured as an unacculturated Hispanic who had been in the United States for less than two years and couldn't speak English. When the first Tianguis store opened, it had a fiestalike atmosphere. Stands served Mexican foods, walls were splashed with bright colors, shoppers were serenaded with live mariachi bands, and shelves were stocked with empanadas, handmade tortillas, and other items usually found only in specialty shops. Making the extra effort to cater to prospective customers' needs paid off. In less than three years, Tianguis became one of the most profitable chains in the crowded and competitive Los Angeles grocery retail market.[63]

Sedano's Supermarkets, with twenty-one South Florida stores and annual sales of more than $200 million, dominates the Hispanic grocery business in Miami. Varadero Supermarkets, Sedano's chief Hispanic competitor, will do $100 million worth of business this year with only six Miami stores.

Specialty wholesalers are also being created to serve the Hispanic supermarkets. Midway Importing, for example, sells health and beauty aids produced in Mexico to Tianguis, Ralph's, Albertson's, Alpha Beta, and other grocery store chains. Chris Hartmen, president of Midway, notes:

> Many of these products have been up here for the last 20–25 years. But they've always come through black market groups' picking them up and distributing them—never

> with an organized approach—mainly in southern California, Chicago, and Texas. . . . The products have been way overpriced, because they've gone through several layers of distribution. No one has ever worked with these products in an organized fashion. It has always just been, "Let's get it over here, and it will sell." We're trying to make the marketplace more efficient and effective.[64]

More efficient distribution has brought down prices.

Mainstream retailers are also actively targeting the Hispanic market. Kmart, Montgomery Ward, Wal-Mart, and Mervyn's have hired ethnic specialists or tested ethnic promotional campaigns. Those moves have spurred retailers like JCPenney and Sears to boost ethnic ad budgets. JCPenney spent about $6 million on Hispanic marketing in 1991, for Spanish-language TV commercials, ad brochures and credit applications in Spanish, and Hispanic fashion shows.

Shopping malls are also trying to attract Hispanic customers. The Tucson Mall in Arizona advertises on three Spanish-language radio stations and hires a mariachi music group to help it celebrate the Mexican holiday Cinco de Mayo. Half the mall's staff is bilingual.

5 THE ASIAN-AMERICAN MARKET

By the end of 1993 there were almost 8 million Asian-Americans. During the past decade, the Asian-American population growth rate was 108 percent, twice that of Hispanics, six times that of African-Americans, and twenty times that of whites.[65] Like Hispanic-Americans, Asian-Americans are a diverse group, with thirteen submarkets. The five largest are Chinese (1.6 million), Filipino (1.4 million), Japanese (848,000), Asian Indians (815,000), and Koreans (799,000).

Immigration accounted for nearly three-fourths of the increase in the Asian-American population during the 1980s.[66] Of the two major streams of immigrants, one consists of people from Asian countries from which large numbers of people had already immigrated to the United States (for example, China, Korea, and the Philippines). This group tends to have an education and to be ready to move quickly into the mainstream of U.S. society. The other group comprises immigrants and refugees from some of the war-torn countries of Southeast Asia: Vietnam, Laos, and Cambodia. Many in this group began their lives in the United States on welfare and lack the education and skills to move out of poverty.

Asian-Americans are the most affluent ethnic group in the United States, in part because of the importance they place on education.

Fully 56 percent of Asians live in the West, compared with 21 percent of all people in the United States. Eighteen percent live in the Northeast, 14 percent in the South, and 12 percent in the Midwest. Twelve states (California, Hawaii, New York, Illinois, New Jersey, Texas, Massachusetts, Pennsylvania, Virginia, Florida, Michigan, and Washington) each have over 100,000

Asian-Americans, five more states than in 1980. Nearly four out of ten Asian-Americans live in California, and about one out of ten lives in Hawaii.[67]

Asian-Americans are highly urbanized, with 93 percent living in a metropolitan area—half in central cities and half in suburbs. In contrast, whites are twice as likely to live in suburbs as in central cities.

The high level of Asian immigration to the United States has created a youthful population. The average age of Asian-Americans is just 30, compared with 36 for whites. As Asian-Americans enter their peak earning years, their relatively high incomes will increase further.

Asian-American Income and Education

Asian-American households are more affluent than those of any other racial or ethnic group, including whites. Their median household income was about $38,000 in 1993; 32 percent of Asian-American households have incomes of $50,000 or more, compared with only 29 percent of white households.[68] The high household incomes of Asian-Americans may be due in part to their concentration in Los Angeles, San Francisco, and Honolulu, where salaries are high to compensate for the cost of living.

Another reason for high household incomes is Asian-Americans' high level of education. Among adults 25 or older, 14 percent have been to college for five or more years, compared with only 9 percent of the total population. An additional 21 percent of Asian-Americans have completed four years of college, versus only 13 percent of the total population.

A third reason for the lofty household incomes of Asian-Americans is their lifestyle. Seventy-four percent live in married-couple households, versus 72 percent of whites and 43 percent of African-Americans.[69] Married-couple households typically have two or more earners, which boosts income.

A final reason for higher incomes is the high rate of business ownership among Asian-Americans. During the past decade, they have created new businesses faster than any other U.S. population group.[70] Different groups tend to gravitate toward different specialties. The Chinese, for instance, are often found in retail, wholesale, and financial enterprises but rarely in construction or transportation. The Japanese prefer construction and transportation to retail and service establishments. Retail-oriented Korean-Americans have become a major force in food marketing.

Why does the Asian-American community start so many new businesses? A key factor is the Asian immigrants' tradition of self-employment. They turn to their fellow immigrants for help in raising money to start businesses. Asian-Americans pool their money in a ***keh,*** or cooperative, typically made up of about twenty members. Members contribute a fixed sum (usually $100 to $1,000) every month, and the total is awarded in full to a different member each month. Once the monthly payout cycle has been completed, the *keh* disbands. *Kehs* are a source of interest-free venture capital as well as a forum for exchanging business tips. There is little chance that a member would dare to stop contributing to the pot after getting his or her share. Reneging on a financial pledge to others violates Asian concepts of personal and family honor.

keh
Asian-American cooperative of about twenty people who combine their money and award it to one member each month; when everyone has participated in the payout cycle, the *keh* disbands.

Asian businesses are typically family owned and operated. During start-up, when money is scarce, they often draw on unpaid workers from the extended family. Extended kinship networks also enable immigrant households to share rents or

mortgages, provide free child care, and ensure economic security against loss of employment by other household members.

Many of the businesses serve internal markets in the Asian-American community. Business owners tend to employ people from their own subgroup. In San Francisco's Chinese community, a dollar turns over five or six times before it leaves.[71]

Creating a Marketing Mix for the Asian-American Market

Because Asian-Americans are younger and better educated and have higher incomes than average, they are sometimes called a "marketer's dream."

Product

Asian-Americans are more comfortable with technology than the general population. They are far more likely to use automated teller machines, and many more of them own VCRs, compact disc players, microwave ovens, home computers, and telephone answering machines.[72]

A recent study found that Asian-American subgroups often have dramatically different preferences:

> Most Asian-Americans drink plenty of soda. Koreans are the exception, and only 52.1% of this group reported drinking soda in the previous three months. At the same time, Koreans drink more 7-Up than any other soda, a big difference from Asian-Americans in general, whose top soda preferences are Coke (55%) and Pepsi (18%).
>
> Bud's the king of beers for Asian-Americans, too, and it was the preferred brand of 44.2% of respondents. Coors (15.3%) was No. 2 and Miller (11.4%) No. 3. Light beer was preferred by 46.8%. Scotch is the preferred liquor, named by 28.7% of Asian-Americans. Johnnie Walker (18.8%) and Chivas Regal (14.6%) were the top two brands.
>
> Asian Indians were the biggest perfume users, and 68.1% had used some kind of fragrance in the previous three months. Filipinos were close behind, at 67.5%. The Japanese, at 35.7%, used perfume the least. Overall, Chanel (20.4%) was the preferred brand.
>
> Considering the state of the U.S. auto market, it would be natural to assume that Asian-Americans prefer Asian cars. The survey indicated otherwise. In fact, Ford was the auto of choice for 28.7% of respondents. The second choice was Toyota, at 21.9%. Only 9.1% owned Hondas.
>
> Asian-American consumers show no reluctance to purchase American products, even when Asian or other foreign alternatives are available.[73]

A number of products have been developed specifically for the Asian-American market. For example, Kayla Beverly Hills salon draws Asian-American consumers because the firm offers cosmetics formulated for them. Anheuser-Busch's agricultural products division sells rice to Asian-Americans, who are rice connoisseurs. The company developed eight varieties of California-grown rice, each with a different label, to cover a range of nationalities and tastes. Its "Taste the Tradition" ads, devised by multiethnic Los Angeles agency Muse Cordero Chen, played up similarities to Asian-grown rice, which is stickier than the kind most Westerners eat. The ads captured such nuances as the differences in Chinese, Japanese, and Korean rice bowls. Sales of Anheuser-Busch's Asian rice brands are now growing more than 10 percent a year.[74]

Promotion

Cultural diversity within the Asian-American market complicates promotional efforts. Although Asian-Americans embrace the values of the larger U.S. population, they also hold on to the cultural values of their particular subgroup. Consider language. Many Asian-Americans speak their native tongue at home, particularly Koreans and Chinese. Filipinos are far less likely to do so. Or consider big-ticket purchases. In Japanese-American homes, the husband alone makes the decision on such purchases nearly half the time, compared with the wife making the decision about 6 percent of the time. In Filipino families, however, wives make these decisions a little more often than their husbands do, although by far the most decisions are made by husbands and wives jointly or with the input of other family members.[75]

Misunderstanding the cultural differences among Asian-Americans can lead to some embarrassing gaffes. Metropolitan Life Insurance angered potential customers when it ran an ad in a Korean magazine showing a family in traditional dress—Chinese dress, that is. During Chinese New Year, Coors got complaints for reinforcing sexual stereotypes in an ad showing an exotic-looking woman wrapped in the folds of a silk dragon. A spokesperson says the brewer's advertising has since gotten away from "women and dragons."[76] In another case, a company placed a Chinese-language ad to wish the community a happy new year but ran the Chinese characters upside down. Advertising agencies like Lee Liu and Tong Inc. of New York City, which specializes in the Asian-American market, are attracting mainstream advertisers who want to avoid such problems. In 1991, the agency's revenue doubled.[77]

The main medium for reaching Asian-Americans is ethnic newspapers. In contrast, Hispanic-Americans prefer radio.[78] Both groups can also be reached with television, but usually it is less cost-effective. Several Asian-language national newspapers are published in cities with large Asian populations. These include the *Korean Times* (Los Angeles, New York, Chicago, San Francisco, Seattle, Toronto, Houston, Las Vegas, and Washington, D.C.), *Chinese Daily News* (New York, Los Angeles, San Francisco, Chicago, Houston, Toronto, Vancouver, Boston, Atlanta, Honolulu, and Washington, D.C.), and *Philippine News* (Los Angeles, San Francisco, and New York).

The most effective promotions stress the basic values that are important to Asian-Americans. In rank order, they are family security, self-respect, freedom, happiness, and true friendship.[79] An effective promotional campaign should show how a good or service will enhance the Asian-American's chances of achieving these important values.

Distribution

Asian-Americans spend over $38 billion a year on retail purchases.[80] Many of these dollars flow to other Asian-Americans who operate flower shops, grocery stores, appliance stores, and other small businesses.[81] At first glance, the Ha Nam supermarket in Los Angeles's Koreatown might be any other grocery store. But next to the Kraft American singles and the State Fair corn dogs are jars of whole cabbage kimchi. A snack bar in another part of the store cooks up aromatic mung cakes, and an entire aisle is devoted to dried seafood. In most U.S. supermarkets, bags near the checkout counter are filled with charcoal. Here, they are filled with rice.

Asian-Americans are also creating their own retail chains. One thriving chain is called 99:

> The number nine represents good fortune to the Chinese—the company operates eleven supermarkets in southern California. The chain operates two types of stores—99 Price for smaller stores in neighborhoods with close-up competition from other Oriental stores, and 99 Ranch for larger, more modern-style superstores.
>
> The 99 Ranch market in Anaheim carries 30,000 different packaged products with

Specialized retail centers catering to specific Asian-American submarkets are an important element in distribution plans for products targeted to those submarkets.

© Superstock

> only about 15 percent comprised of American branded grocery, frozen food, and dairy products. The vast majority of 99's merchandise is provided by "literally hundreds" of import suppliers, many specializing in food from individual countries.
>
> A stroll up and down the seemingly endless aisles creates three distinct impressions. The first is the feeling of walking in and out of the United States, with shelves on one side housing familiar national brands, and those on the other packed with Oriental specialties. The second is the constant feeling of having "seen those items before" in other sections . . . and that's because you have. Innumerable teas and herb drinks, myriad fruit juice combinations and coffees, canned pigeon and quail eggs, bags of dried, seasoned and pickled vegetables, bottled beverages and sauces and endless grain products loom before the shopper in numerous locations of the store. The brands may be different, but the products are the same . . . or are they?
>
> "Not to the Chinese, Japanese, Korean or Vietnamese customer," says the store manager. "They all have distinct preferences based on their own cultures and customs, and they demand exactly the right items, and in the particular brands they have always known." This fierce brand loyalty extends to American products as well.
>
> The third dominant impression is service and selection in the perishables departments. Seafood and meat offerings are mind-boggling; a fully-staffed [counter] about 200 feet along the back of the store is devoted to an almost incredible selection, and this does not include several large cases of self-service and frozen seafood, meats and poultry in other locations of the store. Fish and shellfish are displayed live, already cleaned and trimmed or whole in the case, and in water-filled, serve-yourself bins, and varieties range up to 60 on a given day.[82]

Because Asian-Americans have a tendency to live in neighborhoods of people with the same ethnic background, specialized retail centers have naturally evolved. In suburban Orange County, Vietnamese immigrants have improved a once-barren area. The signs at the strip mall are almost exclusively in Vietnamese. An indoor mall, called Asia Garden, is packed on Sunday mornings. About 50,000 weekend shoppers patronize the 800 shops and restaurants, buying herbal medicine and dining on snail-tomato-rice-noodle soup. In the mornings, people may attend Buddhist ceremonies in makeshift temples; in the evenings they can applaud Elvis Phuong, complete with skintight pants and sneer.

Some entrepreneurs are building large enclosed malls that cater to Asian consumers. At the Aberdeen Centre near Vancouver, British Columbia, nearly 80 percent of the merchants are Chinese-Canadians, as are 80 percent of the customers. The mall offers fashions made in Hong Kong, a shop for traditional Chinese medicines, and a theater showing Chinese movies. Kung fu martial-arts demonstrations and Chinese folk dances are held in the mall on weekends.

6 THE NATIVE-AMERICAN MARKET

Asian-, Hispanic-, and African-Americans have been discussed in some detail because they are the largest ethnic minority groups in the United States. But consumers from South America, Australia, the former Soviet Union, and Eastern and Western Europe also help create the rich interwoven fabric that is the United States. Moreover, each group can be targeted with a unique marketing mix to meet its needs and desires.

Another group that must be singled out because of its role in U.S. history is the Native Americans. The strong bonds that American Indians still feel to their native culture are renewing Indian communities. They have not yet erased the poverty and other ills that affect many Indians. But many Indians living on and off the reservations have made educational and economic progress. A college-educated middle class has emerged, Native American business ownership has increased, and some tribes are creating good jobs for their members.

The census counted nearly 1.9 million Native Americans in 1990, up from fewer than 1.4 million in 1980. This 38 percent leap exceeds the growth rate for most other minority groups.

American Indian businesses have some important competitive advantages because of the "sovereignty" afforded reservations. Many local, state, and federal laws do not apply on the reservations. They have no sales or property taxes, so cigarettes, gasoline, and other items can be sold for low prices. Reservations can also offer lucrative activities not permitted off the reservation, such as gambling.[83]

LOOKING BACK

Like the cosmetics firm at the beginning of the chapter, more and more consumer goods companies are creating specific marketing mixes for ethnic and cultural submarkets. The reason for this new targeting effort is the rapid growth of ethnic markets in terms of both population and income. Marketers have found that subcultures often respond best to their own products and promotion.

The three major ethnic groups—African-American, Hispanic-American, and Asian-American—are quite distinct from one another. There is also significant diversity within the Hispanic and Asian markets. Diversity demands either unique marketing mixes or "stitching niches" together to form a mass market. A company that doesn't consider the multicultural nature of U.S. society will find itself at a disadvantage in the marketplace.

KEY TERMS

stitching niches 201
keh 217
multiculturalism 199

SUMMARY

❶ **Understand the growing importance of multicultural marketing.** The multicultural nature of the United States means that no longer can various ethnic groups be expected to assimilate into white,Western culture. In the future, no single ethnic group will be large enough to dictate political policy. As the United States continues to become a service-dominated economy, education will be the means for minorities to fully participate.

From a marketing perspective, multiculturalism increases the complexity of the marketing function. Demand for goods and services is often culture-driven. Within the large ethnic markets, the marketing mix is further complicated by the many submarkets. Marketers who want to reach these submarkets have to either follow a niche strategy or try to maintain a brand's core identity while straddling different languages, cultures, ages, and incomes. A third strategy is to seek common interests, motivations, or needs across ethnic groups, which is called "stitching niches."

❷ **Appreciate and understand the increasing cultural diversity of the United States.** Much of the growth in the U.S. population from 1980 through 1993 occurred in minority markets. In 1993, about 25 percent of the U.S. population consisted of minorities. That figure should reach 36 percent by 2023, with the Hispanic-Americans growing most rapidly in number. Immigration has also served as a major source of growth in minority markets. Immigrants are a boon to the economy. Some 11 million immigrants pay over $90 billion in taxes but receive only $5 billion in welfare payments. The Immigration Act of 1990 will further encourage the immigration of wealthy and highly educated persons to the United States.

❸ **Identify key characteristics of the African-American market and some elements of an effective marketing mix for this group.** In 1993, the 31 million African-Americans were the largest minority group. The proportion of the population that is African-American will continue to grow into the twenty-first century. Today, 53 percent of all African-Americans live in the South, 19 percent each in the Midwest and Northeast, and 9 percent in the West. The African-American population is younger than the U.S. population as a whole, with a median age of 27.9. Within this group is a substantial and growing middle class. Expenditures by African-Americans now top $270 billion annually.

In the marketing mix, the product element may vary to reflect African-Americans' unique desires, hopes , customs, and preferences. Health and beauty aids constitute one product category that has developed special lines for African-Americans. In addition, "Afrocentric products" stress the African heritage and culture of African-Americans. Specialized promotion for this market is growing rapidly. The most effective promotions avoid racial stereotypes. As for distribution, some special stores and shopping areas have developed to cater to this market. Although pricing is relatively uniform among all U.S. ethnic groups, some are concerned that the poor pay more because of their limited options.

❹ **Identify key characteristics of the U.S. Hispanic market and some elements of an effective marketing mix for this group.** The Hispanic population is about 24 million, and it is growing much faster than the general population. The Hispanic market consists of three diverse submarkets: Mexican-American, Puerto Rican–American, and Cuban-American. The Cuban-Americans are concentrated in Florida, Puerto Rican–Americans in New York City, and Mexican-Americans in the Southwest. Mexican-Americans are the youngest, with a median age of 24; Cuban-Americans are the oldest at 39. Cuban-Americans are the most highly educated subgroup. The total purchasing power of the Hispanic market is over $170 billion per year.

Median family income for Hispanics in 1991 was $28,890, compared with $33,000 for the general population.

Marketers have found that U.S. Hispanics often prefer products from their native country, especially if they are recent immigrants. Marketers also need to be aware of the three main Hispanic submarkets when designing promotions: Mexican-Americans, Cuban-Americans, and Puerto Rican–Americans. Subtle differences in culture and language often make it necessary to design different promotional programs for these different subgroups. Spanish-language broadcasting outlets and publications are the most effective means of reaching them. In terms of distribution, special retail chains and stores have developed. For instance, the Tianguis and Viva supermarket chains target the Mexican-American community; Sedanos serves Cuban-Americans.

5 Identify key characteristics of the Asian-American market and some elements of an effective marketing mix for this group. By the end of 1993 there were almost 8 million Asian-Americans. During the past decade, the Asian-American population growth rate was 108 percent, twenty times that of whites. There are thirteen submarkets within the Asian-American community. Fifty-six percent of all Asian-Americans live in the West, compared with 21 percent of the general population. Most Asian-Americans live in a metropolitan area. The average age of Asian-Americans is 30. This group is the most affluent of any racial or ethnic group, including whites, with a median income of $38,000 in 1993. The main reason for their affluence is their high education level. Among adults, 14 percent of Asians have been to college for five or more years, compared with only 9 percent of the general population. Asian-Americans also have the highest rate of business ownership among minority groups.

Asian-Americans tend to be good customers for technologically advanced products. As with the U.S. Hispanic market, the Asian-American market is divided into subgroups based on country of origin, with definite product preferences among those subgroups. Language and cultural differences also complicate promotion, although Asian-Americans as a whole embrace traditional U.S. values. Various ethnic newspapers help marketers reach the Asian-American subgroups. Asian-Americans often establish stores and shopping areas serving their own ethnic group. For instance, in Southern California the 99 supermarket chain serves Asian-Americans, and the Asia Garden mall almost exclusively reaches Vietnamese customers.

6 Identify key characteristics of the Native American market. American Indians are simultaneously renewing some aspects of their native culture and developing a college-educated middle class (although many Native Americans still live in poverty). Competitive new businesses are developing on the reservations, which have no sales or property taxes.

Review Questions

1. What does it mean to say that the United States is becoming a multicultural society?
2. What has been the economic impact of immigrants in the past fifteen years?
3. Explain the provisions of the Immigration Act of 1990.
4. Where are the areas of high and low cultural diversity in the United States?
5. What three basic strategies can marketers use in a multicultural society?
6. Describe how marketing mixes have been created to serve the African-American market.
7. What are the three major Hispanic-American markets, and how do they differ?
8. Why is it difficult to create a national promotion campaign for Asian-Americans?

Discussion and Writing Questions

1. Suppose you have seen the following statement in the newspaper: "People are basically the same everywhere, and we all want the same things. There is no need to create a special marketing mix for ethnic groups. Everyone, for example, likes Coca-Cola." Write a letter to the editor replying to the assumptions made here.

2. Do you think the poor pay more? Do a simple market-basket survey in your own market. Pick ten items and compare prices in a poor area and an affluent one. Describe your findings and develop reasons for them.

3. The marketing concept says to meet the needs of the consumer. Your boss says, "R.J. Reynolds was just responding to the needs of the marketplace with Uptown cigarettes. The same is true of selling malt liquor in poor neighborhoods." Write a memo explaining why you agree or disagree.

4. Retailers targeting the poor often admit that, with interest charges, the poor pay two or three times the price for which a television or other appliance could be purchased at a major discount chain. The poor, they say, can't get credit at national discounters. Either they buy from us and pay a lot more, or they do without. Discuss the ethics of this statement.

5. Do you agree that, because Asian-Americans can get interest-free loans from a *keh*, they have an unfair advantage over other ethnic groups in creating new businesses? Why or why not?

6. Because Native Americans are exempt from many local, state, and federal laws, do they have an unfair advantage over other businesspeople? Why or why not?

7. Describe the ethnic mix of the U.S. population in 1993 and the projected mix for 2023. What are the implications of the changes?

8. Discuss the social implications of multiculturalism.

CASES

7.1 Ethnic Marketing at Quaker Oats

In 1992 Quaker Oats broke up its ethnic marketing group, prompting speculation that other marketers would reduce spending to reach Asian-Americans, African-Americans, and Hispanics. Instead, such spending appears to be rising. The question is, who controls the checkbook?

Ethnic marketing departments, usually run by minority executives, introduced many companies to racially targeted marketing in the 1980s. The new departments started as relatively weak advisers to brand managers but became more influential as companies gave more weight to ethnic markets. Minorities buy half of Quaker Oats' corn products, for instance, and Quaker's spending to reach minorities tripled between 1990 and 1992.

Quaker now says ethnic markets are too important to isolate in a single office. So when the company disbanded its ethnic department, it returned responsibility for ethnic markets to brand managers. "We don't want an ethnic marketing group out there as a dangling modifier to the rest of the business," says John Blair, Quaker's vice president of marketing. "We want ethnic marketing deeply embedded in every business manager in this company."

Minority suppliers fear they will lose customers without strong minority-run ethnic departments. "If brand managers could have done this job, they would have been given the responsibility in the first place," says Ken Smikle, publisher of *Target Market News*, which tracks ethnic marketing. "We're not talking about an ethnically diverse category of executive here."

Lafayette Jones, president of North Carolina's Segmented Marketing Services, says minority suppliers must learn how to deal with brand managers to survive. He notes that his firm still does work for Procter & Gamble, which took the same tack as Quaker Oats. Quaker's Blair concedes that the company's brand managers are still mostly white, but he says they must take ethnic marketing seriously—and turn to experts "to help them with the segments they don't understand. It opens up opportunities for minority vendors."[84]

Questions

1. Do you think Quaker Oats and Procter & Gamble made the right decision when they eliminated their ethnic marketing departments? Why or why not?

2. Do you agree with minority suppliers who worry about losing business without the ethnic marketing departments? Support your answer.

3. Why do you think large consumer goods companies created ethnic marketing departments originally?

Suggested Readings

"Buying Black," *Time,* 31 August 1992, pp. 52–53.
"Hispanic Affluents: The Irresistible Force," *Hispanic Business,* November 1992, pp. 56–64.

Case 7.2 Telemundo Network

Video title: *Reaching Multicultural Markets through Telemundo*

Telemundo Network, Inc.
2470 West 8th Avenue
Hialeah, FL 33010

SIC codes: 4833 Television broadcasting

Number of employees: 1,000

1993 revenues: $135 million

Product: Spanish-language television programming

Largest Hispanic competitors: Univision, Galavision

Largest English-language competitors: ABC, NBC, CBS, Fox

Background

Over 15 years ago, McDonald's recognized the benefit of advertising on Spanish-language television. Today, the Hispanic market is one of the fastest-growing market segments in the United States. The typical Hispanic family is younger and larger than most non-Hispanic families. This market segment spends over $200 billion annually, and projections indicate that this figure will more than double by the year 2000.

Some of the key similarities of the various Hispanic groups are strong family ties, strong religious affiliations, and an interest in preserving their heritage. Most Hispanic people learn to speak Spanish first and then English. As a group, they feel it is very important to preserve their native language as part of their cultural heritage. Thus Spanish-language television programming is an attractive medium for advertisers.

Industry

The TV industry has two distinct branches: network and cable. Networks pay their affiliate stations to carry network programming. In return, the affiliates give the networks time within the original programming to sell to national advertisers. The affiliates sell the remaining advertising time to local advertisers.

Cable affiliate stations pay program producers for the rights to televise the programs. These affiliates can then sell advertising space or charge cable subscribers a fee.

With the multitude of networks and cable channels available, consumers have a wide variety of programming to choose from. As a result, advertisers often have trouble reaching their target audiences.

Telemundo Network

Telemundo Network has gone head to head with Univision for a number of years. Now the company hopes to leave Univision behind.

Hispanics switch to English-language television once they understand the English language well enough. Telemundo hopes to keep its audience with new and innovative programming. To reach the Hispanic-American market, Telemundo offers Spanish-language news stories that are of interest to that group. The network also produces entertainment programs designed to captivate this growing market segment. Programming for children is designed to help educate them about the Hispanic culture and the Spanish languages.

Questions

1. Do you think advertising to the Hispanic population is better done through Telemundo or through English-language television? Explain your answer.
2. What makes the Hispanic market so attractive to marketers?

References

Million Dollar Directory 1993 (Parsippany, NJ: Dun & Bradstreet Information Services, 1993).
Standard & Poor's Industry Surveys (New York: Standard & Poor's Corporation, October 1993).

CHAPTER 8
Decision Support Systems and Marketing Research

LEARNING OBJECTIVES
After studying this chapter, you should be able to

1. Explain the difference between a marketing information system and a decision support system.
2. Discuss the nature of database marketing and micromarketing.
3. Define marketing research and its importance to marketing decision making.
4. Describe the steps involved in a marketing research project.
5. Discuss the growing importance of single-source research.
6. Explain when marketing research should and should not be conducted.

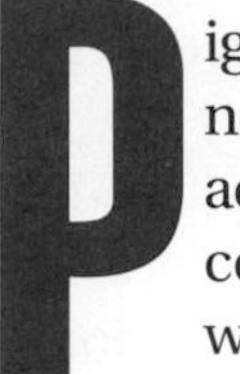

Piggyback luggage, which includes a full-size model and a carry-on model, is now the top-selling style of Samsonite's hardside luggage. This was not achieved through luck, but rather through marketing research to listen to consumer concerns, act on them, and then determine if these concerns were met.

Development of Piggyback luggage began when a study, called a *luggage exploratory,* was conducted to focus on the issues that people have when they travel. Eleven discussion groups, called focus groups, were conducted with respondents who had previously completed a screening questionnaire, so each group represented a particular lifestyle segment.

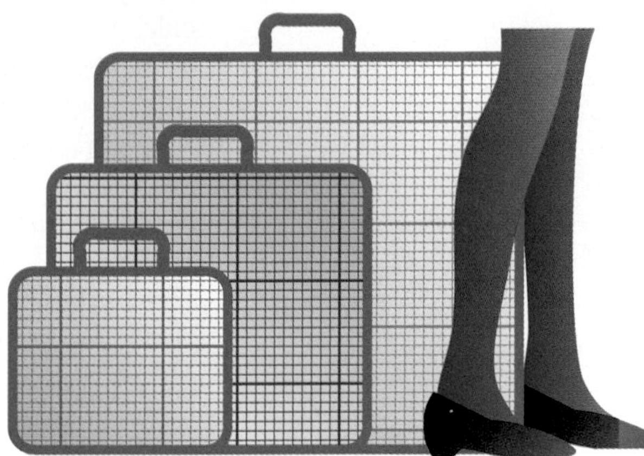

The focus groups proceeded from a general discussion of travel-related problems to a more specific discussion of travel away from home, luggage used, packing, checking or carrying on luggage, luggage image, and ideal luggage. Both men and women said that any pleasure from traveling was diminished by, among other things, transporting luggage, especially in air travel with long walks from car to gate.

Later, research was conducted to determine which direction to take in new product development. A total of 400 respondents, again prescreened and this time skewed toward women, were interviewed. Respondents viewed a series of black-and-white drawings with a brief description of each idea and then rated their interest in the ideas. One of the more appealing concepts was a "line of luggage that can be strapped together 'piggyback' fashion."

One of the designers, working in conjuction with marketing research, started development of a prototype of a revolutionary hardside case with wheels. Most full-size luggage today, be it hardside or softside, has wheels to aid in moving the case. What was so new about this luggage was that it had only two large wheels instead of the usual four, and the wheels were on the side of the luggage rather than on the bottom. . . . The designer also incorporated some untraditional ideas: a telescoping handle and a self-retracting strap. The patented handle, invisible when not in use, would incorporate a spring-loaded strap, so that other items—briefcases, handbags, other luggage, and so forth—could be loaded atop the Piggyback and secured. In essence, the Piggyback had its own luggage carrier, but without the extra weight and inconvenience of a separate piece. . . .

Another marketing research study was conducted on the Piggyback. . . . One hundred respondents were interviewed for the screening. All respondents needed to be 16 to 60 years old and had to have purchased a travel bag in the past three years and used one in the past year. All interviews were conducted on a one-on-one basis, so that any questions about operation

could be answered and noted for future reference in preparing advertising and merchandising materials.

Respondents examined a series of rough drawings, outlining the features and use of the Piggyback concept, and then rated the product, both after concept exposure and after actual use, on a four-point purchase interest scale. Although about six out of ten respondents liked the idea after concept exposure, after-use ratings increased to over seven out of ten. The study concluded that, "The purchase interest in the Piggyback case is consistently testing at a high level among the total population of luggage purchasers." . . .

Everyone loved the Piggyback. [It] was introduced using a mock-up of an obstacle course, and it received rave reviews from the attendees who gave it a "test drive." . . . In 1990, the Piggyback carryon joined the full-size Piggyback in luggage departments in stores throughout the United States. By 1992, the full Piggyback line was so successful that its sales, in effect, have been greater than those of some entire luggage companies.

Marketing research was used to create a very successful new line of luggage for Samsonite. What are some other uses of marketing research besides creating new products? What are the various techniques for conducting marketing research? How does marketing research relate to decision support systems?

Source: Adapted from Bob Bengen, "Easing Travel Restrictions," *Quirk's Marketing Research Review*, February 1992, pp. 6, 26–27.

1 GATHERING INFORMATION FOR DECISION MAKING

Accurate and timely information is the lifeblood of marketing decision making. The Piggyback luggage example illustrates how good information can help maximize sales and efficiently use scarce company resources. **Marketing intelligence** is everyday information about developments in the marketing environment that managers use to prepare and adjust marketing plans. Two systems for gathering marketing intelligence are marketing information systems and interactive decision support systems.

marketing intelligence
Everyday information about developments in the marketing environment that managers use to prepare and adjust marketing plans.

marketing information system (MIS)
System for continually gathering data from a variety of sources, synthesizing it, and funneling it to those responsible for meeting the marketplace's needs.

Marketing Information Systems

A **marketing information system** (MIS) is a system that continually gathers data from a variety of sources, synthesizes it, and funnels it to those responsible for meeting the marketplace's needs. A strong information system improves the effectiveness of marketing decision making, thus offering the firm a significant competitive advantage (see Exhibit 8.1).

An MIS presents the data in a form useful to various people within the marketing organization. For example, the Systematic Updated Retail Feedback (SURF) report is an MIS report prepared at clothing maker Liz Claiborne. The SURF report arrives weekly from sixteen stores that represent a cross section of store sizes and geographical locations. It tells Liz Claiborne managers what items consumers are buying from the racks. If retailers discover they are not ordering the best-selling clothing, they can adjust their orders.

An MIS report presents data in a general format and may therefore provide the marketing decision maker with more information than is necessary. For example, to

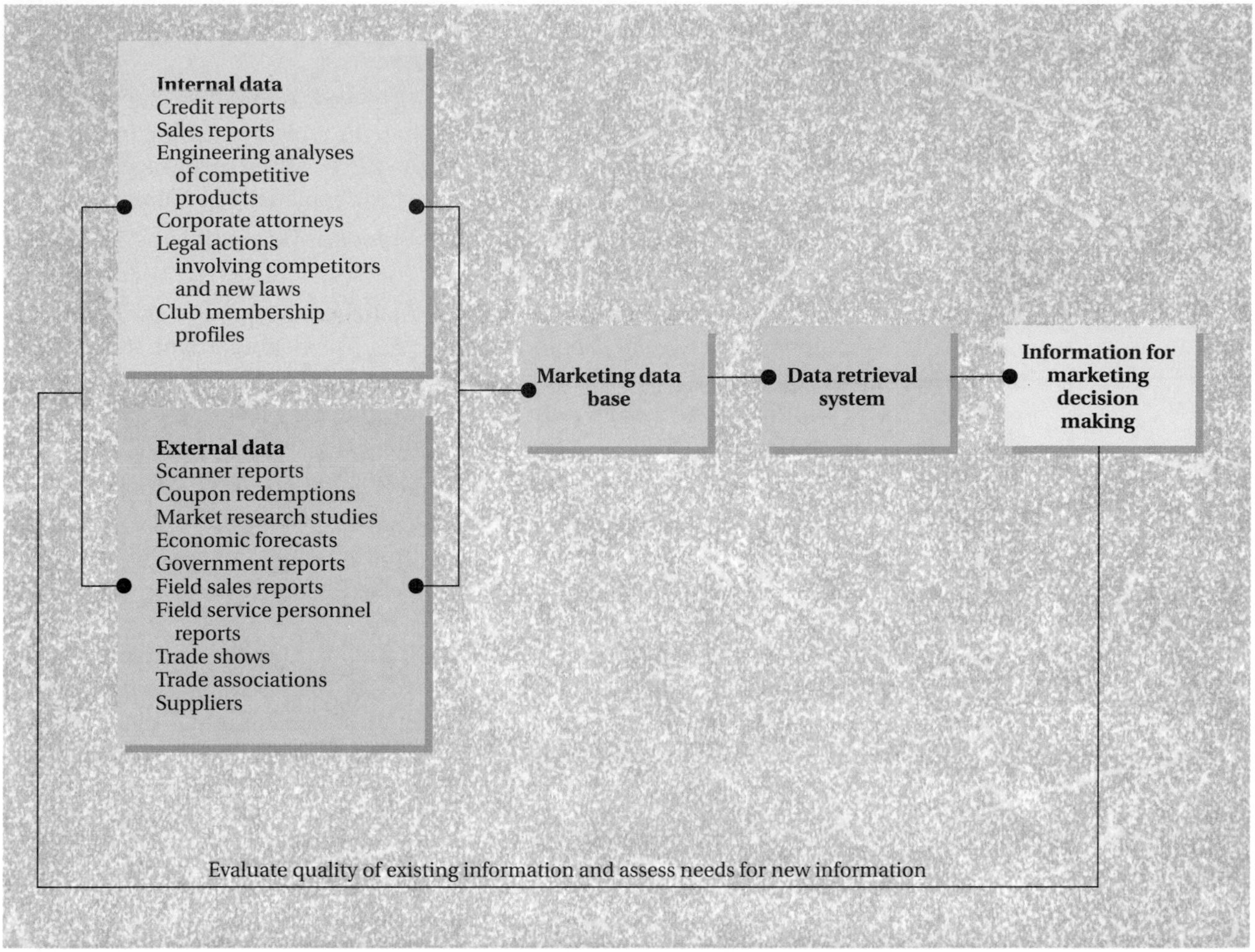

Exhibit 8.1

Structure of a Marketing Information System

get a sales forecast for Chicago, a marketing decision maker may have to scan a report that includes Chicago, Milwaukee, Detroit, and other large cities in the North Central territory. An MIS places the burden on the user to dig up and select the meaningful information and discard the rest.

In some companies, marketing specialists set up an MIS with the help of computer and data-processing specialists. Usually, however, nonmarketing personnel design and maintain the MIS. When a marketing manager decides that a new report is needed, the request may be funneled to an MIS manager. A delay in getting the necessary information may mean missed opportunities or even the need for more information. Although firms with an MIS usually have information-processing specialists available to help direct the needed information to decision makers, the system can be frustrating and time-consuming. As a result, many firms have turned to decision support systems.

Decision Support Systems

decision support system (DSS)
Interactive, flexible information system that enables managers to obtain and manipulate information as they are making decisions.

A **decision support system** (DSS) is an interactive, flexible information system that enables managers to obtain and manipulate information as they are making decisions. A DSS bypasses the information-processing specialist and gives managers access to the data from their own terminals. These are the characteristics of a true DSS system:

- *Interactive:* Managers give simple instructions and see immediate results. The process is under their direct control; no computer programmer is needed. Managers don't have to wait for scheduled reports.

- *Flexible:* DSS can sort, regroup, total, average, and manipulate the data in various ways. It will shift gears as the user changes topics, matching information to the problem at hand. For example, the CEO can see highly aggregated figures, and the marketing analyst can view very detailed breakouts.
- *Discovery-oriented:* Managers can probe for trends, isolate problems, and ask "what if" questions.
- *Accessible:* DSS is easy to learn and use by managers who aren't skilled with computers. Novice users should be able to choose a standard, or "default," method of using the system. They can bypass optional features so they can work with the basic system right away while gradually learning to apply its advanced features.

Quaker Oats' DSS contains about 2 billion facts about products, national trends, and the competition. Management credits the DSS with helping the company achieve a number-one market share in several product categories, including Quaker Oats cereals, Gatorade, Van de Camp Pork & Beans, Rice-a-Roni, and Aunt Jemima Pancakes.

More than 400 marketing professionals at Quaker Oats use the DSS daily. System use can be grouped into three major categories: reporting, tracking, and running the standard reports; marketing planning, which automates the brand planning and budgeting process by adding "what if" analysis and marketing capabilities; and eliciting people's immediate answers to spontaneous marketing questions. Consider these examples:

> Nancy Bydalek, brand manager for Quaker's Van de Camp products, uses the DSS for compiling information needed for brand planning. "By running what-if scenarios and marketing spreadsheets based on such considerations as forecasted volume, prices, and advertising spending," she says, "I get a national view of my business compared to the competition, so I can identify geographical areas that are doing well and not so well."
>
> The system also helps Quaker sharpen its promotions. "When we plan a specific promotion," explains Greg Peterson, marketing manager of the Cornmeal brand, "we go back in time and see the bottom-line effect that different promotional events had on sales. We then plug in the cost of a planned promotion and see what the final effect is going to be on the brand's volume and profit."[1]

Frito-Lay delivery people use hand-held computers to keep track of the inventory in the stores they serve. The data are transmitted to company headquarters to guide production and marketing decisions.

Other companies' successful use of DSS has resulted in its growing popularity.[2] Kmart, Northwestern Mutual Life, and 3M now find that DSS provides an invaluable competitive advantage. Companies such as Federal Express, Avis, Otis Elevator, and Frito-Lay have made it easier to gather field reports by providing their employees with hand-held computers.

Frito-Lay, for instance, has given hand-held computers to all its 10,000 delivery people. The data they collect feed a system that helps the company manage production, monitor sales, and guide promotional strategy. A de-

livery person can enter orders at each store in a minute or two, running through a programmed product list complete with prices. The machine plugs into a printer in the delivery truck to produce an itemized invoice. At day's end, it generates a sales report and, through a hookup in the local warehouse, transmits it in seconds to company headquarters in Dallas.[3]

❷ The Growing Importance of Database Marketing to Micromarketing

database marketing Creation of a large computerized file of customers' and potential customers' profiles and purchase patterns as a tool for identifying target markets.

Perhaps the fastest growing use of DSS is **database marketing**, which is the creation of a large computerized file of customers' and potential customers' profiles and purchase patterns. It is usually the key tool for successful micromarketing (see Chapter 6). Specifically, these are database marketing's capabilities:

- Identify the most profitable and least profitable customers
- Identify the most profitable market segments or individuals and target efforts with greater efficiency and effectiveness
- Aim marketing efforts to those products, services, and segments that require the most support
- Increase revenue through repackaging and repricing of products for various market segments
- Evaluate opportunities for offering new products and services
- Identify products and services that are best-sellers and most profitable

In the 1950s, network television enabled advertisers to "get the same message to everyone simultaneously." Similarly, use of a data base and micromarketing enables marketers to get a customized, individual message to everyone simultaneously through direct mail.

The size of many data bases is astounding: Ford Motor Company, 50 million names; Kraft General Foods, 25 million; Citicorp, 30 million; and Kimberly Clark (maker of Huggies diapers), 10 million new parents' names.[4] American Express can retrieve from its data base the names of all cardholders who charged purchases at golf pro shops in the past six months, attended symphony concerts, or traveled to Europe more than once in the last year. Its data base can even identify the very few people who did all three.

An increasingly popular technique for building a data base is the creation of "customer clubs." Kraft General Foods, for example, has invited children to join the Cheese & Macaroni Club. For three proofs of purchase, $2.95, and a completed membership form with the child's (and, of course, Mom's) address, Kraft General Foods will send a painter's cap, bracelet, shoelaces, book of stickers, and other goodies. Burger King is signing up 50,000 kids a day for its Kids' Club, and Coors has begun locating its loyal buyers through a Club Coors program.[5]

In 1990 Quaker Oats mailed over 5 million packages containing sixteen pages of coupons and promotional offers. Each coupon was coded with an individual household identification number. When consumers redeemed the coupons, the grocery stores' electronic scanners automatically sent detailed information about the purchase back to Quaker. Using that data, Quaker Oats could determine, for instance, who had a dog or a child. The company could then target the next round of coupons it mailed to those particular households. A Quaker Oats marketing manager noted, "Every time a coupon is redeemed, customers participate in a two-way communication."[6] Quaker planned not only to target future mailings based on demographics but also to offer more attractive incentives to resistant shoppers. After two mailings, however, the program was put on hold because of its high cost.[7]

Some experts feel that personalized database marketing will not really take off until marketers can electronically deliver their promotions to individual households—a method that is much less expensive than direct mail. Others, however, believe it can work now. George Mrkonic is president of Kmart's $7 billion specialty stores division, which includes Waldenbooks, Pace Membership Warehouses, Sports Authority, Builders Square, and Pay Less Drug Stores. He plans to increase the division's sales from 22 percent to 30 percent of company sales by 1996. The key to the success of his plan, he says, is database marketing.[8]

Marketers need to take account of consumer reaction to the growing use of data bases, however. In 1992, under pressure from New York State authorities, American Express disclosed that it was telling merchants more about its cardholders' spending habits than it had previously acknowledged. The company revealed that information about cardholders' lifestyles and spending habits was offered for joint marketing efforts with merchants. The company told cardholders that it merely provided merchants with a mailing list based on information in the initial application for the card. The New York Attorney General's office made AmEx notify more than 20 million cardholders nationwide that it compiles profiles of spending behavior and that it uses the information for "target marketing" purposes. The cardholders then had the option of having their information excluded from any future marketing efforts.[9] The following article discusses a related issue.

ETHICS IN MARKETING

Renting Internal Data Bases

Some companies rent their internal data bases to obtain extra revenue. At times, this practice can raise important ethical questions. Blockbuster Video planned to rent lists of customer rentals at its video stores in 1991. The plan was quickly dropped, however, when management found that federal law forbids video stores from disclosing information on movies that customers rent. In the summer of 1992, McDonald's began inviting customers to join the McDonald's VIP Club by filling out a form with their name, address, home phone number, sex, and birth date. Members are promised a membership card, special offers on their birthday, a newsletter, and McDonald's coupons by mail. Qualified Lists Corporation, which is compiling the internal data base for McDonald's, is offering to rent the list to outside parties. . . . [An ad in an industry publication said] lists could be broken out for "insurance, publications, catalogs and opportunity seekers." Qualified Lists planned to have 30 million names on the data base by the end of 1993. It remains to be seen if the public views access to the list as compromising privacy. Burger King doesn't rent its data base. A spokesperson for the company noted, "We were concerned that if people knew their names would be sold, it would hamper participation."

Is it unethical to rent names from internal data bases? Assume that you have an unusual hobby, such as collecting antique radios, which is noted in a data base. If a company had parts for old radios, wouldn't you want the firm to be able to reach you? Where should the line defining the right to privacy be drawn? Should Congress outlaw the sale of all internal database information?

Source: Used with permission from Scott Hume, "McD's May Be Fried by Database Rental," *Advertising Age*, 30 March 1992, pp. 1, 58. Copyright Crain Communications, Inc., 1992.

3 THE ROLE OF MARKETING RESEARCH IN DECISION MAKING

marketing research
Process of planning, collecting, and analyzing data relevant to marketing decision making.

Marketing research entails planning, collecting, and analyzing data relevant to marketing decision making. The results of this analysis are then communicated to management. Marketing research plays a key role in the marketing system. It provides decision makers with data on the effectiveness of the current marketing mix and also insights for necessary changes. Furthermore, marketing research is a main data source for both MIS and DSS.

Marketing research has three roles: descriptive, diagnostic, and predictive. First, its descriptive role includes gathering and presenting factual statements. For example, what is the historic sales trend in the industry? What are consumers' attitudes toward a product and its advertising? Second, its diagnostic role includes explaining data. For instance, what was the impact on sales when we changed the design on the package? Finally, its predictive function is to address "what if" questions. For example, how can the researcher use the descriptive and diagnostic research to predict the results of a planned marketing decision?

Differences between Marketing Research and DSS

Since marketing research is problem-oriented, managers use it when they need guidance to solve a specific problem. Marketing research, for example, has been used to find out what features consumers want in a new personal computer. It has also aided product development managers in deciding how much milk to add in a new cream sauce for frozen peas. The army has used marketing research to develop a profile of the young person most likely to be positively influenced by recruiting ads.

In contrast, the MIS and DSS continually channel information about environmental changes into the organization. This information is gathered from a variety of sources, both inside and outside the firm. One important information source is marketing research. For example, Mastic Corporation, a leading supplier of vinyl siding, asks its nationwide network of distributors and their dealers questions about product quality, Mastic's service to the distributor, the amount of vinyl the distributor sells, and the percentage used for new construction. This information then becomes part of Mastic's MIS. Other data in the MIS include new housing starts, national unemployment figures, age of housing, and changes in housing styles. Its marketing research is therefore a component or input source for its MIS.

The Importance of Marketing Research to Management

Marketing research can help managers in several ways. It improves the quality of decision making and helps managers better understand the marketplace. Most important, sound marketing research alerts managers to marketplace trends. Thus they can respond to trends early rather than react to situations that have already occurred. A discussion of these benefits follows.

Improving the Quality of Decision Making

Managers can sharpen their decision making by exploring the desirability of various marketing alternatives. For example, some years ago General Mills made a strategic decision to expand its restaurant operations into the full-service restaurant category. Marketing research indicated that Italian was the most popular ethnic food category in the United States and that interest in pasta and preference for Italian food would continue to increase. The company conducted many taste tests to find appropriate spice levels and create a menu that was sure to please target customers. These marketing research studies led to the creation of The Olive Garden Italian restaurants—the fastest-growing and most popular full-service Italian restaurant chain in the nation.

Tracing Problems

Another way managers use research is to find out why a plan backfires. Was the initial decision incorrect? Did an unforeseen change in the external environment cause the plan to fail? How can the same mistake be avoided in the future?

Samsonite's new piggyback luggage was developed in response to the findings of marketing research.
Courtesy of Samsonite Corporation

Reynolds Metals Company used marketing research to develop a new line of colored plastic food wrap in transparent shades of red, green, yellow, and blue. Test results among women showed that they loved the product. Yet after the national rollout, sales were sluggish. Again, Reynolds called on marketing research. A telephone survey found that men didn't really see the point of colored plastic wraps. Unfortunately, the purchasing staffs of most supermarkets are men. Armed with this knowledge, Reynolds crafted a simple plan. It sent samples to the buyers' homes, hoping their wives' reactions would convince them the product would sell. The strategy worked. After ten weeks, colored Reynolds plastic wraps were stocked in three-quarters of the stores nationwide, and sales exceeded expectations.

Understanding the Marketplace

Managers also use marketing research to understand the dynamics of the marketplace. Assume that you have recently gone to work for a new company that will design, produce, and market casual clothing, called Movin' Up, for college students. Perhaps one of your first concerns would be brand loyalty. That is, are college students loyal to the same brands as their parents, or will they consider new brands? You might also ask whether college students are loyal to the same brands they used in high school. The graphs in Exhibit 8.2A show responses to these questions. The data in Exhibit 8.2 are based on a marketing research study of 884 undergraduates at fifteen universities across the country.

Now suppose the company is tentatively planning to promote Movin' Up clothing through direct mail, magazines, and cable television. Management wants to know how much time college students spend each day with various media. The advertising director, Sandra Jarboe, is also interested in the magazines college students read, the cable networks they watch, and the direct-mail pieces to which they respond, as shown in Exhibit 8.2. She is also curious about which print ads college students find most appealing. Sandra believes that this information might help her design the Movin' Up advertising campaign. In addition, the promotion manager, John Gates, is considering doing a fashion show of Movin' Up clothing at various popular spring break locations. Therefore, he needs to find out where college students go for spring break. As you can see, marketing research helps managers develop the marketing mix by providing insights into lifestyles, preferences, and purchasing habits of target consumers.

proactive management
Practice of altering the marketing mix to fit newly emerging economic, social, and competitive trends.

reactive management
Practice of waiting for change to have a major impact on the firm before deciding to take action.

The Proactive Role of Marketing Research

Understanding the nature of the marketing system is required for a successful marketing orientation. By thoroughly knowing the factors that can affect the target market and the marketing mix, management can be proactive rather than reactive. **Proactive management** alters the marketing mix to fit newly emerging economic, social, and competitive trends. In contrast, **reactive management** waits for change to have a major impact on the firm before deciding to take action. The turbulent

Exhibit 8.2

A Survey of the College Market

A. A question of loyalty

Are you loyal to the same brands your parents purchase?

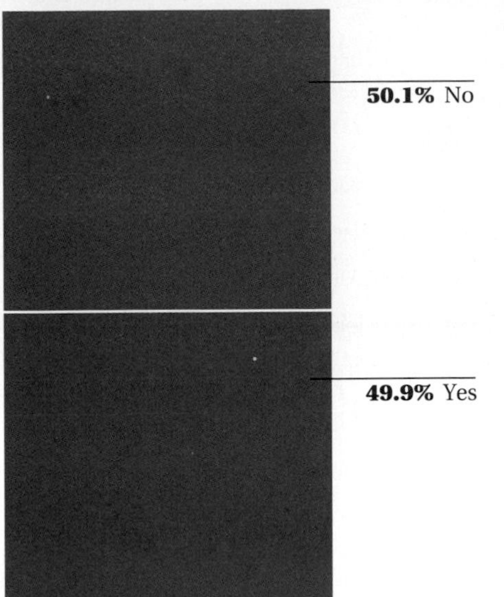

Are you loyal to the same brands that you used in high school?

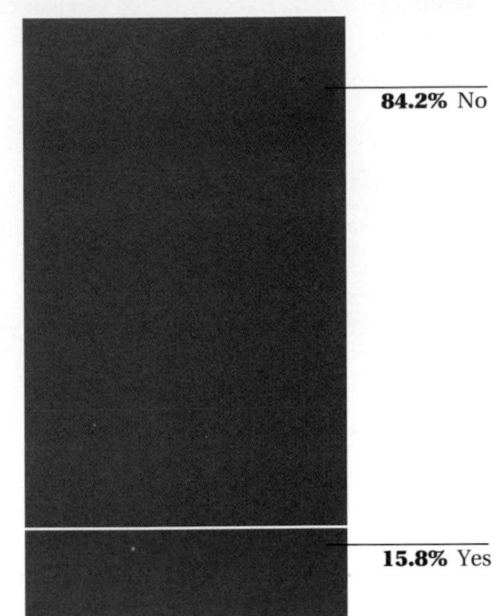

B. Media use

Average time spent per day / *Is that more or less time than spent in high school?*

Medium	Hours per day	More	Less	Same
1. Radio	2.21	55.0%	32.5%	7.9%
2. Network TV	1.57	67.2	26.1	1.8
3. Cable TV	0.98	52.7	31.4	4.4
4. Newspapers	0.81	36.4	48.4	6.7
5. Magazines	0.67	48.5	36.2	6.2

C. Top 10 favorite magazines (in order)

Magazine	Points
1. *Cosmopolitan*	424
2. *Sports Illustrated*	399
3. *Time*	325
4. *Rolling Stone*	317
5. *Glamour*	315
6. *Vogue*	261
7. *Newsweek*	199
8. *People Weekly*	190
9. *Mademoiselle*	174
10. *Elle*	168

D. Top 10 cable networks (in order)

Network	Points
1. MTV	614
2. ESPN	350
3. HBO	343
4. CNN	240
5. Showtime	78
6. Nick at Nite	74
7. Cinemax	58
8. Discovery	46
9. VH-1	45
10. TBS	42

E. What direct-mail pieces have you responded to?

Mailing	Responses
1. J. Crew	10.4%
2. Citibank Visa	10.0
3. American Express	7.1
4. L.L. Bean	6.3
5. Credit cards (nonspecific)	5.6
6. Magazine subscriptions (nonspecific)	4.8
7. Lands' End	3.7
8. MasterCard	3.3
9. Catalogs (nonspecific)	2.2
10. Publisher's Clearing House	2.2

F. Favorite print ads

Spot	Responses
1. Absolut Vodka	12.9%
2. Calvin Klein's Obsession	10.1
3. Nike	5.5
4. Calvin Klein's Eternity	2.2
5. Budweiser	2.0
6. Calvin Klein Jeans	1.8
7. Guess Jeans	1.8
8. Maxell Tapes	1.7
9. J&B Scotch	1.7
10. Benetton	1.5

G. Top 5 spring break locations

Location	Responses
1. Home	33.3%
2. Florida	17.0
3. None	9.4
4. California	5.0
5. Colorado	4.7

Exhibit 8.2

(Continued)

marketing environment can be viewed as an opportunity (a proactive stance) or a threat (a reactive stance). ConAgra, for example, used marketing research to examine the growing interest in personal health in the United States. Its research ultimately led to the creation of Healthy Choice frozen dinners, which are low in sodium and cholesterol. Marketing research plays a key role in proactive management. It helps in forecasting changes in the market and consumer desires so that goods and services can be created or modified to meet those needs.

A proactive manager not only makes short-term adjustments in the marketing mix to meet market changes but also seeks, through strategic planning, to develop a long-run marketing strategy for the firm. A strategic plan guides the long-run use of the firm's resources based on the firm's existing and projected internal capabilities and its projected changes in the external environment. For instance, Pitney Bowes'

A growing interest in personal health prompted ConAgra to conduct the marketing research that led to the development of Healthy Choice frozen dinners.

strategic plan, founded on solid marketing research, helps the firm effectively meet long-run profit and market share goals. Conversely, poor strategic planning can threaten the firm's survival. Montgomery Ward, floundering for almost a decade because of inadequate planning and poor understanding of the marketplace, had to give up its once healthy catalog sales division.

4 DEVELOPING A MARKETING RESEARCH PROJECT

Virtually all firms that have adopted the marketing concept engage in some marketing research, since it offers decision makers many benefits. Sometimes, particularly among smaller firms, limited-scale research studies are conducted informally. For example, when Eurasia restaurant, serving Eurasian cuisine, first opened along Chicago's ritzy Michigan Avenue, it drew novelty seekers. But it turned off the important business lunch crowd, and sales began to decline. The owner surveyed several hundred businesspeople working within a mile of the restaurant. He found that they were confused by Eurasia's concept and wanted more traditional Asian fare at lower prices. In response, the restaurant altered its concept; it hired a Thai chef, revamped the menu, and cut prices. The dining room was soon full again.

Whether a research project costs $200 or $2 million, the same general process should be followed. The marketing research process is a scientific approach to decision making that maximizes the chance of getting accurate and meaningful results. Exhibit 8.3 traces the steps in the research process: (1) define the marketing problem, (2) plan the research design and gather primary data, (3) specify the sampling procedures, (4) collect the data, (5) analyze the data, (6) prepare and present the report, and (7) follow up.

Exhibit 8.3

The Marketing Research Process

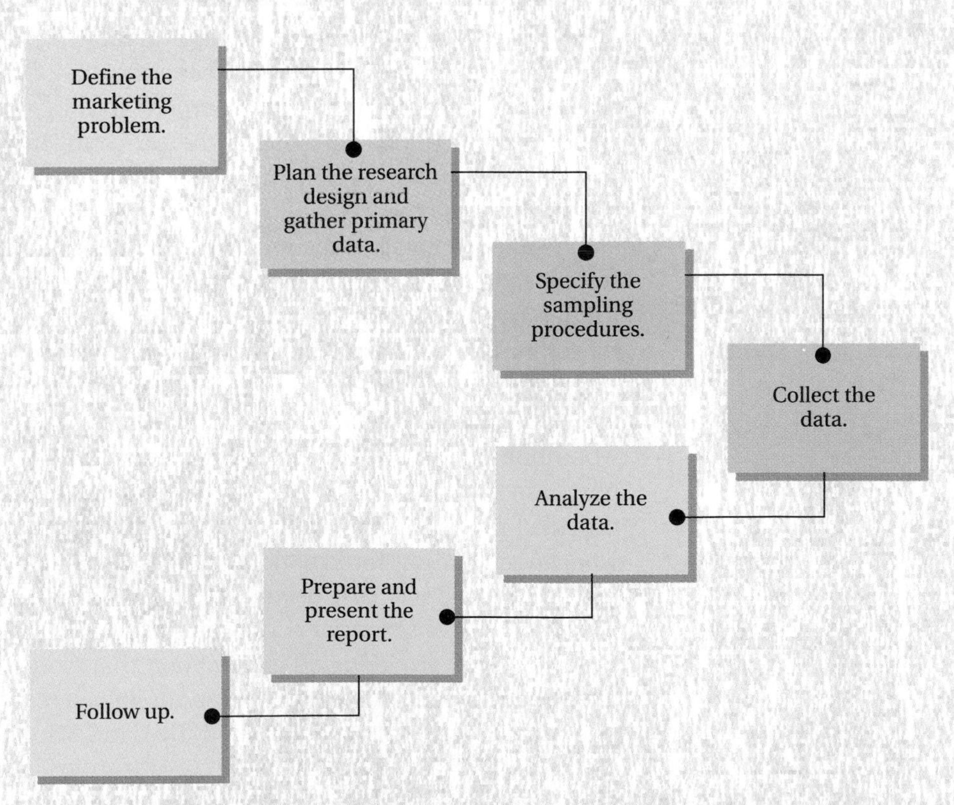

Define the Marketing Problem

The first step in the marketing research process must be to develop either a problem statement or a statement of research objectives on which the decision maker and the researcher can both agree. This step is not as easy as it sounds. But it is important, since these statements direct the rest of the study. Some situations may require only a problem statement; others lend themselves more readily to detailed research objectives.

Situation Analysis

situation analysis Extensive background investigation into a particular marketing problem.

In some cases, identifying and structuring the problem may itself become the objective of a major background investigation called a **situation analysis.** A situation analysis is especially important to the outside consultant or to any researcher dealing with a particular type of problem for the first time. Situation analysis permits the researcher to become immersed in the problem—to learn about the company, its products, its markets, its marketing history, the competition, and so forth. After gathering this background information, the researcher may need to backtrack and revise the problem statement and research objectives.

After completing a situation analysis, the researcher compiles a list of all the data required to meet the research objective and then determines the types of data required for decision making. One important type of information is secondary data.

Secondary Data

secondary data Data previously collected for any purpose other than the one at hand.

Secondary data are data previously collected for any purpose other than the one at hand. People both inside and outside the organization gather secondary data to meet their needs. Exhibit 8.4 describes major sources of secondary data. Most research efforts rely at least partly on secondary data, which can usually be obtained quickly and inexpensively. The problem is locating *relevant* secondary data.

Secondary data save time and money if they help solve the researcher's problem. Even if the problem is not solved, secondary data have other advantages. They can aid in formulating the problem statement and suggest research methods and other types of data needed for solving the problem. In addition, secondary data can pinpoint the kinds of people to approach and their locations and serve as a basis of comparison for other data.

The disadvantages of secondary data mainly stem from a mismatch between the researcher's unique problem and the secondary data already gathered, typically on a different problem. For example, a major consumer products manufacturer wanted to determine the market potential for a fireplace log made of coal rather than compressed wood by-products. The researcher found plenty of secondary data about total wood consumed as fuel, quantities consumed in each state, and types of wood burned. Secondary data were also available about consumer attitudes and purchase patterns of wood by-product fireplace logs. The wealth of secondary data provided the researcher with many insights into the artificial log market. Yet nowhere was there any information that would tell the firm whether consumers would buy such a product made of coal.

The quality of secondary data may also pose a problem. Often secondary data sources do not give detailed information that would enable a researcher to assess their quality or relevance. Whenever possible, a researcher needs to address these important questions: Who gathered the data? Why were the data obtained? What methodology was used? How were classifications (such as heavy users versus light users) developed and defined? When was the information gathered?

Exhibit 8.4

Sources and Descriptions of Secondary Data

Source	Description
Internal information	Internal company information may be helpful in solving a particular marketing problem. Examples include sales invoices, other accounting records, data from previous marketing research studies, and historical sales data.
Market research firms	Companies such as A.C. Nielsen, Arbitron, and IMS International are major sources of secondary data regarding market share for consumer products and characteristics of media audiences.
Trade associations	Many trade associations, such as the National Industrial Conference Board and the National Retail Merchants Association, collect data of interest to members.
University research bureaus, professional associations, foundations	A variety of nonprofit organizations collect and disseminate data of interest to marketing researchers.
Commercial publications	*Advertising Age, Sales Management, Product Marketing, Merchandising Week,* and many other commercial publications provide useful research data.
Government data	The federal government is a treasure trove of secondary data. Among the reports are *Census of Housing, Census of Retail Trade, Census of Services Industries, Census of Manufacturers, Statistical Abstract of the U.S., Economic Indicators,* and *U.S. Industrial Outlook.*

The New Age of Secondary Data: On-Line Data Bases

Gathering traditional secondary data is often an arduous task. Researchers write requests for government, trade association, or other reports and then wait several weeks for a reply. Frequently, they make one or more trips to the library only to find that the needed reports are checked out or missing. Today, the rapid development of on-line computerized data bases has reduced the drudgery associated with gathering secondary data. An **on-line data base** is a public information data base accessible by anyone with proper computer facilities. With over 7,000 data bases available in 1993, virtually every topic of interest to a marketing researcher is contained in some data base.

on-line data base
Public information data base accessible by anyone with proper computer facilities.

For a look at how an on-line data base can affect decision making, consider the experience of Superior, Inc. (not its actual name), a large East Coast consumer goods firm. One morning its president woke up to some unpleasant news. A competitor was rumored to be marshaling its troops for an attack on the market for one of Superior's personal care products, worth $30 million in annual sales. Later that day, concerned executives at Superior were already preparing to take a drastic step: slashing the price to defuse the competitive challenge.

Before taking that step, Superior's executives decided to do a little research. Their on-line data base told them that the competitor had been bought several years earlier by a conglomerate. Next, a check of local business newspaper data bases turned up evidence of an ad agency hiring new personnel to back up the rumored campaign. Further on-line searches revealed that the parent company had once tried to sell the unprofitable subsidiary. Another story indicated that the parent company's bonds were being downgraded and mentioned a lawsuit from a bond holder. And a business news data base revealed that a senior executive of the parent company had recently retired, with no successor named. Other stories noted that two other executives had left and hinted at turmoil at the board level.

Superior's executives decided that what at first appeared to be an aggressive threat was actually no more than a gesture by a paralyzed firm unable to take new initiatives. "If there is any gold outside," beamed one Superior executive, "it looks like they just don't have a shovel to pick it up with." Result: Superior's president decided to maintain prices and thereby preserve company profits.

On-Line Vendors

on-line database vendor Intermediary that acquires data bases from database creators.

An **on-line database vendor** is an intermediary that acquires data bases from database creators. Such vendors offer electronic mail, news, finance, sports, weather, airline schedules, software, encyclopedias, bibliographies, directories, full-text information, and numeric data bases. Thus a user can go to a single on-line vendor and gain access to a variety of data bases. Billing is simplified because a single invoice is used for all the data bases on the vendor's system. Since all vendors' data bases have a standardized search procedure, this function also is simplified. On-line vendors also provide an index to help researchers determine which data bases will most likely meet their needs.

The four most popular on-line data bases are CompuServe, a subsidiary of H&R Block; The Source, a subsidiary of Reader's Digest; Dow Jones News/Retrieval Service; and Dialog, a subsidiary of Lockheed Company. Dialog offers over 200 different data bases containing more than 100 million items of information. Exhibit 8.5 shows some of the data bases offered by the four major on-line vendors.

Exhibit 8.5

Selected Offerings of the Four Most Popular On-Line Vendors

Dow Jones	Dialog
Disclosure II (business data base)	Disclosure II (business data base)
Dow Jones News	Management Contents
Current Quotes	Standard & Poor's Corporate Description
Wall Street Journal	Books in Print
Academic American Encyclopedia	Electronic Yellow Pages
Cineman Movie Reviews	Magazine Index
AP News	AP News
Comp*U*Store	

CompuServe	The Source
Standard & Poor's General Information File	Management Contents
Washington Post	Commodity News Service
World Book Encyclopedia	Cinemax Movie Reviews
MicroQuote (stock information)	U.S. News Washington Letter
Business Information Wire	Travel Services
AP News	Employment Service
Comp*U*Store	AP News
	Comp*U*Store

On-line data bases provide several important advantages. First, the researcher can rapidly reach a much greater variety of information than ever before. Second, by efficiently using on-line search procedures, the researcher can quickly pinpoint relevant data. Third, the large in-house staffs formerly required to research and maintain files can be eliminated, reducing labor costs and increasing productivity. Finally, small firms can study the same secondary data as large organizations and do it just as efficiently.

On-line data bases have one potential disadvantage. A person unskilled at "searching" a data base may be overwhelmed with data. Researchers must carefully choose the words used to locate the right citations, abstracts, and full-text stories. Thus they must often familiarize themselves with new terminology to narrow the search. One novice researcher working for Ogilvy and Mather advertising agency in New York unintentionally punched in a command to call up all stories in their entirety. Once placed, the instruction could not be canceled. The result was a $700 bill for data and telephone time.

Computerized Database Packages

A number of companies are now offering computerized database packages for personal computers. For example, Claritas has created two packages for segmentation and demographic studies and mapping—Compass/Agency for advertising agencies and Compass/Newspapers for newspapers. Claritas recently added Arbitron radio ratings and data from Simmons Marketing Research Bureau and Mediamark on product usage to Compass/Agency. The Compass/Newspaper system contains more than 200 reports and maps. Users can also obtain data on subscribers, readership, or advertisers and display them as reports and maps or use the data in other standard software packages, such as spreadsheet, word-processing, and graphics applications.

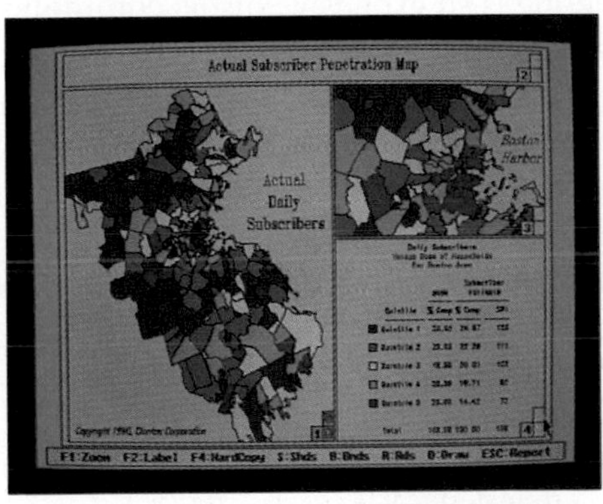

Compass/Newspapers is a computerized data base used for market segmentation, demographic studies, and mapping.
Claritas Corporation

The U.S. Department of Commerce has also made 1990 census data available for use on personal computers, including 1,300 categories based on population, education, marital status, number of children in the home, home value or monthly rent, and income. The Census Bureau also offers TIGER files, which map the location of all U.S. streets, highways, railroads, pipelines, power lines, airports, counties, municipalities, census tracts, census block groups, congressional districts, voter precincts, rivers, and lakes.[10]

Plan the Research Design and Gather Primary Data

primary data
Information collected for the first time and used to solve a particular problem.

research design
Outline of which research questions must be answered, where and when data will be gathered, and how the data will be analyzed.

Good secondary data can help researchers conduct a thorough situation analysis. With that information, researchers list their unanswered questions and rank them. Researchers must then decide the exact information required to answer the questions. Sometimes a research question can be answered by gathering more secondary data; otherwise, primary data may be needed. **Primary data,** or information collected for the first time, are used for solving a particular problem under investigation.

The **research design** specifies which research questions must be answered using primary data, how and when the data will be gathered, and how the data will be

analyzed. Typically, the project budget is finalized after the research design has been approved.

Advantages and Disadvantages of Primary Data

The main advantage of primary data is that they will answer a specific research question that secondary data cannot answer. For example, suppose Pillsbury has two new recipes for refrigerated dough for sugar cookies. Which one will consumers like better? Secondary data will not help answer this question. Instead, target consumers must try each recipe and evaluate the tastes, textures, and appearances of each cookie.

Moreover, primary data are current, and researchers know the source. Sometimes researchers gather the data themselves rather than contract projects to outside companies. Researchers also specify the methodology of the research. Secrecy can be maintained since the information is proprietary. In contrast, secondary data are available to all interested parties for relatively small fees.

On the other hand, gathering primary data is expensive. Costs can range from a few thousand dollars for a limited survey to several million for a nationwide study. For instance, a nationwide, fifteen-minute telephone interview of 1,000 adult males can cost $50,000 for everything, including a data analysis and report. Because primary data gathering is so expensive, firms commonly cut back on the number of interviews to save money.

Larger companies that conduct many research projects use another cost-saving technique. They piggyback studies, or gather data on two different projects using one questionnaire. The drawback is that answering questions about, say, dog food and gourmet coffee may be confusing to respondents. Piggybacking also requires a longer interview (sometimes a half hour or longer), which tires respondents. The quality of the answers typically declines, with people giving curt replies and thinking, "When will this end!" A lengthy interview also makes people less likely to participate in other research surveys.[11]

However, the disadvantages of primary data gathering are usually offset by the advantages. It is often the only way of solving the research problem.

Survey Research

survey research
Technique for gathering primary data in which a researcher interacts with people to obtain facts, opinions, and attitudes.

The most popular technique for gathering primary data is **survey research**, in which a researcher interacts with people to obtain facts, opinions, and attitudes. Exhibit 8.6 summarizes the characteristics of the most popular forms of survey research:

In-home interviews: Although in-home, personal interviews often provide high-quality information, they tend to be very expensive because of the interviewers' travel time and mileage. Therefore, market researchers tend to conduct fewer in-home interviews than in the past.

Nevertheless, this form of survey research has some important advantages. The respondent is interviewed at home, in a natural setting where many consumption decisions are actually made. Also, the interviewer can show the respondent items (for example, package designs) or invite the respondent to taste or use a test product. An interviewer can also probe when necessary—a technique to clarify a person's response. For example, an interviewer might ask, "What did you like best about the salad dressing you just tried?" The respondent might reply, "Taste." This answer doesn't provide a lot of information, so the interviewer could probe by saying, "Can you tell me a little bit more about taste?" The respondent then elaborates: "Yes, it's not too sweet, it has the right amount of pepper, and I love that hint of garlic."

Characteristic	In-home personal interviews	Mall intercept interviews	Telephone interviews from interviewer's home	Central-location telephone interviews	Focus groups	Self-administered and one-time mail surveys	Mail panel surveys
Cost	High	Moderate	Moderate to low	Moderate	Low	Low	Moderate
Time span	Moderate	Moderate	Fast	Fast	Fast	Slow	Relatively slow
Use of interviewer probes	Yes	Yes	Yes	Yes	Yes	No	Yes
Ability to show respondent concepts	Yes	Yes (also taste tests)	No	No	Yes	Yes	Yes
Control over interviewer	Low	Moderate	Low	High	High	n/a	n/a
General data quality	High	Moderate	Moderate to low	High to moderate	Moderate	Moderate to low	Moderate
Ability to collect large amounts of data	High	Moderate	Moderate to low	Moderate to low	Moderate	Low to moderate	Moderate
Ability to handle complex questionnaires	High	Moderate	Moderate	High if computer-aided	Low	Low	Low

Exhibit 8.6

Characteristics of Several Types of Survey Research

Mall intercept interviews: The **mall intercept interview** is conducted in the common areas of shopping malls. It is the economy version of the door-to-door interview—personal contact between interviewer and respondent, minus the interviewer's travel time and mileage costs. To conduct this type of interview, the research firm rents office space in the mall or pays a significant daily fee. One drawback is that it is hard to get a representative sample of the population.

mall intercept interview
Survey research method that involves interviewing people in the common areas of shopping malls.

Mall intercept interviews must be brief. Only the shortest ones are conducted while respondents are standing. Usually researchers invite respondents to their office for interviews, which are still rarely over fifteen minutes long. The researchers often show respondents concepts for new products or a test commercial or have them taste a new food product. The overall quality of mall intercept interviews is about the same as telephone interviews.

Telephone interviews: Compared to the personal interview, the telephone interview costs less and may provide the best sample of any survey procedure. Although it is often criticized for providing poorer-quality data than the in-home personal interview, studies have shown that this criticism may not be deserved.[12]

central-location telephone (CLT) facility
Specially designed room used for conducting telephone interviews for survey research.

Most telephone interviewing is conducted from a specially designed phone room called a **central-location telephone** (CLT) **facility.** A phone room has many phone lines, individual interviewing stations, sometimes monitoring equipment, and headsets. The use of Wide Area Telephone Service (WATS) lines permits the research firm to interview people nationwide from a single location.

computer-assisted interviewing
Interviewing method in which the interviewer reads the questions from a computer screen and enters the respondent's data directly into the computer.

Many CLT facilities offer computer-assisted interviewing. The interviewer reads the questions from a computer screen and enters the respondent's data directly into the computer. The researcher can stop the survey at any point and immediately

With computer-assisted telephone interviewing, marketing researchers can obtain a good sample of the target group, save time and money on data entry, and obtain up-to-the-second reports on survey results.

print out the survey results. Thus a researcher can get a sense of the project as it unfolds and fine-tune the research design as necessary. An on-line interviewing system can also save time and money, because data entry occurs as the response is recorded rather than as a separate process after the interview. Hallmark Cards found that an interviewer administered a questionnaire for its Shoebox Greeting cards in twenty-eight minutes. The same questionnaire administered with computer assistance took only eighteen minutes.[13]

focus group
Group of seven to ten people with desired characteristics who participate in a group discussion about a subject of interest to a marketing organization.

Focus groups: A **focus group** is a type of personal interviewing. Often recruited by random telephone screening, seven to ten people with certain desired characteristics form a focus group. These qualified consumers are usually offered an incentive (typically $30 to $50) to participate in a group discussion. The meeting place (sometimes resembling a living room, sometimes featuring a conference table) has audiotaping and perhaps videotaping equipment. It also likely has a viewing room with a one-way mirror, so that clients (manufacturers or retailers) may watch the session. During the session a moderator, hired by the research company, leads the group discussion.

Focus groups are occasionally used to brainstorm new product ideas or to screen concepts for new products. Ford Motor Company, for example, asked consumers to drive several automobile prototypes. These "test drivers" were then brought together in focus groups. During the discussions, consumers complained that they were scuffing their shoes because the rear seats lacked foot room. In response, Ford sloped the floor underneath the front seats, widened the space between the seat adjustment tracks, and made the tracks in the Taurus and Sable models out of smooth plastic instead of metal.[14]

A new system by Focus Vision Network allows client companies and advertising agencies to view live focus groups in Chicago, Dallas, Boston, and fifteen other major cities. The private satellite network lets a General Motors researcher observing a San Diego focus group control two cameras in the viewing room. The researcher can get a full group view or a close-up, zoom, or pan the participants. The researcher can also communicate directly with the moderator using an ear receiver. Ogilvy and Mather (a large New York advertising agency), StarKist Sea Foods, Seagrams, and others have installed the system.[15]

Mail surveys: Mail surveys have several benefits: relatively low cost, elimination of interviewers and field supervisors, centralized control, and actual or promised anonymity for respondents (which may draw more candid responses). Some researchers feel that mail questionnaires give the respondent a chance to reply more thoughtfully and to check records, talk to family members, and so forth. Yet mail questionnaires usually produce low response rates.

Low response rates pose a problem, since certain elements of the population tend to respond more than others. The resulting sample may not represent the surveyed population. For example, the sample may have too many retired people and too few working people. In this instance, answers to a question about attitudes toward Social Security might indicate a much more favorable view of the system than is actually the case. Another serious problem with mail surveys is that no one probes respondents to clarify or elaborate on their answers.

INTERNATIONAL PERSPECTIVES

Marketing Research in Russia

Opinion and market research in the former Soviet Union dates back to the 1960s, during a brief thaw in the political and economic climate under Khrushchev. For instance, large-scale youth surveys were conducted under the direction of Dr. Boris Grushin, then head of the Soviet Institute of Public Opinion at the *Komsomolskaya Pravda* newspaper. VNIIKS, All-Union Institute for Market Research, attached to the Ministry of Home Trade, also started doing research on issues of supply and demand around the same time. Much of VNIIKS's early work was "industrial research," in which it utilized a network of expert correspondents/informants throughout the Soviet Union.

With a few exceptions, most of the opinion surveys conducted before 1985 were designed to bolster the Party line, not to determine truth. Usually, only positive and favorable findings were published. In addition, little concern was given to proper sampling procedures and interview techniques. Most of this early research was based on self-administered questionnaires distributed at respondents' places of work, which provided respondents little faith in the promise of anonymity.

The dissolution of the Soviet Union has brought profound changes in the field of marketing research. Research organizations, reformed or newly established, sprang to life to take the public pulse, documenting social change and at the same time serving the needs of a wide variety of clients.

There are basically three types of research organizations in the former Soviet Union today. The first type conducts almost exclusively marketing research projects. It includes groups that at one time or another were affiliated with government industry and trade agencies, new joint ventures with foreign partners, such as VNIIKS (affiliated with a Finnish research institute) and INFOMARKET (owned by the Russian Ministry of Metallurgy and a Dutch research company).

The second type has a more scholarly orientation, concentrating on public opinion research and social trends. Examples are the Institute of Sociology and the Institute of Applied Social Research. Universities such as Moscow State University and the University of Vilnius have also started centers of public opinion research.

The third type of research organization seeks to combine marketing and opinion research. Their clientele is diverse, ranging from independent news agencies to various government and legislative branches, Western media, research institutes, advertising agencies, and corporations. The All Commonwealth Center for Public Opinion and Market Research and Vox Populi, headed by Boris Grushin, are typical, and two of the best known, of this kind.

Taken together, currently available research services include All Commonwealth and individual-republic surveys, consumer panels, opinion leader panels, and ad hoc studies covering a wide range of social, economic, political, and marketing or business-related topics. Data collection techniques include face-to-face interviewing, surveys by mail, and even telephone interviewing among elites or opinion leaders.

Do you think marketing research will ever be as popular in Russia as it is in the United States? What are some unique problems that a researcher would face there?

Source: Adapted from William Wilson and Xiaoyan Zhao, "Perestroika and Research: Ivan's Opinion Counts," *CASRO Journal 1992,* pp. 27–31.

Mail panels like those operated by Market Facts, National Family Opinion Research, and NPD Research offer an alternative to the one-shot mail survey. A mail panel consists of a sample of households recruited to participate by mail for a given period. Panel members often receive gifts in return for their participation. Essentially, the panel is a sample used several times. In contrast to one-time mail surveys, the response rates from mail panels are high. Rates of 70 percent (of those who agree to participate) are not uncommon.

Questionnaire Design

All forms of survey research require a questionnaire. Questionnaires ensure that all respondents will be asked the same series of questions.

open-ended question Question worded to encourage unlimited answers phrased in the respondent's own words.

Questionnaires include three basic types of questions: open-ended, closed-ended, and scaled-response (see Exhibit 8.7). An **open-ended question** encourages an answer phrased in the respondent's own words. Researchers get a rich array of information based on the respondent's frame of reference.

Exhibit 8.7

Types of Questions Found on Questionnaires from National Market Research Surveys

Open-ended	Closed-ended	Scaled-response
1. What advantages, if any, do you think ordering from a mail-order catalog company offers compared to shopping at local retail outlet? (*Probe:* What else?) 2. Why do you have one or more of your rugs or carpets professionally cleaned rather than having you or someone else in the household clean them? 3. What is there about the color of the eye shadow that makes you like it the best?	***Dichotomous*** 1. Did you heat the Danish product before serving it? Yes .... 1 No .... 2 2. The federal government doesn't care what people like me think. Agree .... 1 Disagree .... 2 ***Multiple choice*** 1. I'd like you to think back to the last footwear of any kind that you bought. I'll read you a list of descriptions and would like for you to tell me which category they fall into. (*Read list and check proper category.*) Dress and/or formal .... 1 Casual .... 2 Canvas/trainer/gym shoes ... 3 Specialized athletic shoes .... 4 Boots .... 5 2. In the last three months, have you used Noxzema Skin Cream . . . (*Check all that apply.*) As a facial wash .... 1 For moisturizing the skin ..... 2 For treating blemishes .... 3 For cleansing the skin .... 4 For treating dry skin .... 5 For softening skin .... 6 For sunburn .... 7 For making the facial skin smooth 8	Now that you have used the rug cleaner, would you say that you . . . (*Check one.*) _ Would definitely buy it _ Would probably buy it _ Might or might not buy it _ Probably would not buy it _ Definitely would not buy it

closed-ended question Question that asks the respondent to make a selection from a limited list of responses.

scaled-response question Closed-ended question designed to measure the intensity of a respondent's answer.

In contrast, a **closed-ended question** asks the respondent to make a selection from a limited list of responses. Traditionally, marketing researchers separate the two-choice question (called "dichotomous") from the many-item type (often called "multiple choice"). A **scaled-response question** is a closed-ended question designed to measure the intensity of a respondent's answer. Closed-ended and scaled-response questions are easier to tabulate than open-ended questions, because response choices are prelisted. On the other hand, if the researcher is not careful in designing the closed-ended question, an important choice might be omitted.

For example, suppose this question was asked on a food study: "What do you normally add to a taco, besides meat, that you have prepared at home?"

Avocado	1
Cheese (Monterey Jack/cheddar)	2
Guacamole	3
Lettuce	4
Mexican hot sauce	5
Olives (black/green)	6
Onions (red/white)	7
Peppers (red/green)	8
Pimento	9
Sour cream	0

The list seems very complete, doesn't it? However, consider the following responses. "I usually add a green, avocado-tasting hot sauce." "I cut up a mixture of lettuce and spinach." "I'm a vegetarian; I don't use meat at all. My taco is filled only with guacamole." How would you code these replies? As you can see, the question needs an "other" category.

A good question must also be asked clearly and concisely, and ambiguous language must be avoided. Take, for example, the question "Do you live within ten minutes of here?" The answer depends on the mode of transportation (maybe the person walks), driving speed, perceived time, and other factors. Instead, respondents should see a map with certain areas highlighted and be asked whether they live within the area.

Clarity also implies using reasonable terminology. A questionnaire is not a vocabulary test. Jargon should be avoided, and language should be geared to the target audience. A question like "State the level of efficacy of your preponderant dishwasher powder" would probably be greeted by a lot of blank stares. It would be much simpler to say "Are you (1) very satisfied, (2) somewhat satisfied, or (3) not satisfied with your current brand of dishwasher powder?"

Stating the survey's purpose at the beginning of the interview also improves clarity. The respondents should understand the study's intentions and the interviewer's expectations. Sometimes, of course, to get an unbiased response, the interviewer must disguise the true purpose of the study. If an interviewer says "We're conducting an image study for American National Bank" and then proceeds to ask a series of questions about the bank, chances are the responses will be biased. Many times respondents will try to provide answers that they believe are "correct" or that the interviewer wants to hear.

Finally, to ensure clarity, the interviewer should avoid asking two questions in one—for example, "How did you like the taste and texture of the Pepperidge Farm coffee cake?" This should be divided into two questions, one concerning taste and the other texture.

A question should not only be clear but also unbiased. A question like "Have you purchased any quality Black & Decker tools in the past six months?" biases respondents. Questions can also be leading: "Weren't you pleased with the good service you received last night at the Holiday Inn?" These examples are quite obvious; unfortunately, bias is usually more subtle. Even an interviewer's clothing or gestures can create bias.

Observation Research

observation research
Research method that relies on three types of observation: people watching people, people watching physical phenomena, and machines watching people.

In contrast to survey research, **observation research** does not rely on direct interaction with people. Three types of observation research are people watching people, people watching physical phenomena, and machines watching people.

There are two ways of *people watching people:*

- *Mystery shoppers:* Researchers posing as customers observe the quality of service offered by retailers. The largest mystery shopper company is Shop 'N Chek, an Atlanta company that employs over 16,000 anonymous shoppers nationwide. The firm evaluates salespeople's courtesy for General Motors, flight service for United Airlines, and the efficiency of hamburger ordering for Wendy's, among other clients.[16]
- *One-way mirror observations:* At the Fisher-Price Play Laboratory, children are invited to spend twelve sessions playing with toys. Toy designers watch through one-way mirrors to see how children react to Fisher-Price's and other makers' toys. Fisher-Price, for example, had difficulty designing a toy lawn mower that children would play with. A designer, observing behind the mirror, noticed the children's fascination with soap bubbles. He then created a lawn mower that spewed soap bubbles. It sold over a million units in the first year.

audit
Examination and verification of the sale of a product.

The form of observation research that features *people watching physical phenomena* is known as an audit. An **audit** is the examination and verification of the sale of a product. Audits generally fall into two categories: retail audits, which measure sales to final consumers, and wholesale audits, which determine the amount of product moved from warehouses to retailers. Wholesalers and retailers allow auditors into their stores and stockrooms and allow them to examine the company's sales and order records to verify product flows. In turn, the retailers and wholesalers receive cash compensation and basic reports about their operations from the audit firms.

Because of the availability of scanner-based data (discussed later in the chapter), physical audits at the retail level may someday all but disappear. Already the largest nonscanner-based wholesale audit company, SAMI, has gone out of business. Its client list was sold to Information Resources Incorporated, a company that specializes in providing scanner data. Nor does A.C. Nielsen, the largest retail audit organization, use auditors in grocery stores any longer. The data are entirely scanner based. Nielsen uses both auditors and scanner data for other types of retail outlets but will probably shift to scanner only when most retailers within a store category (such as hardware stores or drugstores) install scanners.

As for *machines watching people,* four types are used: traffic counters, the People Reader, Shopper-Trak, and the passive people meter.

Traffic counters are the most common and most popular form of machine-based observation research. The machines measure the flow of vehicles over a stretch of roadway. Outdoor advertisers rely on traffic counts to determine the number of exposures per day to a billboard. Retailers use the information to decide where to place a store. Convenience stores, for example, require a moderately high traffic volume to be profitable.

Observation research helps retailers learn how to get shoppers to buy more on each visit. Envirosell Inc. specializes in surreptitious filming and tracking of consumers as they travel a store's aisles.
Photograph by Chip Simons

The *People Reader* looks like a lamp. When respondents sit in front of it, they don't know that it is simultaneously recording both the reading material and the movement of their eyes. Through the use of the People Reader and specially designed hidden cameras, the Pretesting Company has been able to document typical reading habits and the impact of different-size ads:

- Nearly 40 percent of all readers either start from the back of a magazine or "fan" a magazine for interesting articles and ads. Fewer than half of the readers start from the very first page of a magazine.
- Rarely does a double-page ad provide more than 15 percent additional top-of-mind awareness (a term that refers to the first ad that comes to mind) than a single-page ad. Usually, the benefits of a double-page spread are additional feeling and communication, not top-of-mind awareness.
- In the typical magazine, nearly 35 percent of the ads get less than two seconds' worth of examination.
- The ads that produce the strongest reader involvement are three or more successive single-page ads on the right-hand side of a magazine.[17]

Shopper-Trak, another device, uses beams of infrared light to count customers as they pass through the store entrance or certain locations inside the store. In a test of the Shopper-Trak system, Kmart used it to send salespeople to crowded departments and to open more checkout lanes when lines began to get long. The retailer also wanted to be able to determine for the first time what percentage of shoppers actually make purchases. With such information, the company could perhaps convert browsers into buyers. Departments with little traffic, for instance, could be promoted more heavily with advertised specials, in-store events like the familiar "blue-light specials," and better displays at the ends of the aisles.[18]

The *passive people meter*, soon to be available, will use a cameralike device to measure the size of television audiences. The passive system, packaged to resemble a VCR and placed on top of the TV, will be programmed to recognize faces and record electronically when specific members of a family watch TV. It will note when viewers leave the room and even when they avert their eyes from the screen. Strangers would be listed simply as visitors.[19] Advertisers are demanding more proof of viewership, and the networks are under pressure to show that advertising is reaching its intended targets. Ratings are used to help set prices for commercial time.

A Nielsen executive has said that a passive system should yield "even higher quality, more accurate data because the respondents don't have to do anything" other than "be themselves." Already, however, the networks and advertisers are criticizing the passive people meter. One executive noted, "Who would want or allow one of those things in their bedroom?"[20] Others claim that the system requires bright light to operate properly. Also, the box has limited peripheral vision, so it might not sense all the people in a given room. Will the passive people meter work better than the present diary system? Only time will tell.

All observation techniques offer at least two advantages over survey research. First, bias from the interviewing process is eliminated. Second, observation doesn't rely on the respondent's willingness to provide data. Conversely, the observation technique also has two important disadvantages. First, subjective information is limited, because motivations, attitudes, and feelings are not measured. Second, data-collection costs may run high unless the observed behavior patterns occur frequently, briefly, or somewhat predictably.

Experiments

experiment
Method of gathering primary data in which one or more variables are altered to measure their relative influence on another variable.

An **experiment** is another method a researcher uses to gather primary data. The researcher alters one or more variables—price, package design, shelf space, advertising theme, advertising expenditures—while observing the effects of those alterations on another variable (usually sales). The best experiments are those in which all factors are held constant except the ones being manipulated. The researcher can then observe that changes in sales, for example, result from changes in the amount of money spent on advertising.

Holding all other factors constant in the external environment is a monumental and costly, if not impossible, task. Such factors as competitors' actions, weather, and economic conditions are beyond the researcher's control. Yet market researchers have ways to account for the ever-changing external environment. Mars, the candy company, was losing sales to other candy companies. Traditional surveys showed that the shrinking candy bar was not perceived as a good value. Mars wondered whether a bigger bar sold at the same price would increase sales enough to offset the higher ingredient costs. The company designed an experiment in which the marketing mix stayed the same in different markets but the size of the candy bar varied. The substantial increase in sales of the bigger bar quickly proved that the additional costs would be more than covered by the additional revenue. Mars increased the bar size—and its market share and profits. Consider these other successful experiments:

- *Procter & Gamble's Crest:* addition of a new stannous fluoride formulation to a toothpaste that reduces user's cavities better than the previous formulation
- *Budweiser:* better allocation of advertising dollars among geographic regions
- *Campbell's Soup Company:* more effective ads for V-8 Cocktail vegetable juice and Swanson frozen dinners

Specify the Sampling Procedures

Once the researchers decide which primary data collection technique to use, the next step in the marketing research process is to select the sampling procedures. A

sample
Subset for interviewing drawn from a larger population.

universe
Population from which a sample is drawn.

firm can seldom take a census of all possible users of a new product, nor can they all be interviewed. Therefore, a firm must sample the group to be interviewed. A **sample** is a subset from a larger population.

Several questions must be answered before a sampling plan is chosen. First, the population or **universe** of interest must be defined. This is the group from which the sample will be drawn. It should include all the people whose opinions, behavior, preferences, attitudes, and so on are of interest to the marketer. For example, in a study whose purpose is to determine the market for a new canned dog food, the universe might be defined to include all current buyers of canned dog food.

After the universe has been defined, the next question is whether the sample must be representative of the population. If the answer is yes, a probability sample is needed. Otherwise, a nonprobability sample might be considered.

probability sample
Sample drawn from a population characterized by every element having a known nonzero probability of being selected.

random sample
Type of probability sample in which every element of the population has an equal chance of being selected as part of the sample.

nonprobability sample
Any sample in which little or no attempt is made to get a representative cross section of the population.

convenience sample
Nonprobability sample that uses respondents who are convenient or readily accessible to the researcher.

measurement error
Error that occurs when there is a difference between the information desired by the researcher and the information provided by the measurement process.

sampling error
Error that occurs when a sample is not representative of the target population in some way.

frame error
Error that occurs when the sample drawn from a population differs from the target population.

Probability Samples

A **probability sample** is characterized by every element in the population having a known nonzero probability of being selected. Its desirable feature is the ability to use scientific rules to ensure that the sample represents the population.

One type of probability sample is a random sample. The **random sample** must be arranged in such a way that every element of the population has an equal chance of being selected as part of the sample. For example, suppose a university is interested in getting a cross section of student opinions on a proposed sports complex to be built using student activity fees. If the university can acquire an up-to-date list of all the enrolled students, it can draw a random sample by using random numbers from a table (found in most statistics books) to select students from the list.

Nonprobability Samples

Any sample in which little or no attempt is made to get a representative cross section of the population can be considered a **nonprobability sample.** A common form of a nonprobability sample is the convenience sample. The **convenience sample** is based on using respondents who are convenient or readily accessible to the researcher—for instance, employees, friends, or relatives.

Nonprobability samples are acceptable as long as the researcher understands the nonrepresentative nature of this type of sample. Because of their lower cost, much marketing research is based on nonprobability samples.

Types of Errors

Whenever a sample is used in marketing research, two major types of error occur: measurement error and sampling error. **Measurement error** occurs when there is a difference between the information desired by the researcher and the information provided by the measurement process. For example, people may tell an interviewer that they purchase Coors beer when they do not. Measurement error generally tends to be larger than sampling error.

Sampling error occurs when a sample somehow does not represent the target population. Sampling error can be one of several types. Nonresponse error occurs when the sample actually interviewed differs from the sample drawn. This error happens because the original people selected to be interviewed either refused to cooperate or were inaccessible. For example, people who feel embarrassed about their drinking habits may refuse to talk about them.

Frame error, another type of sampling error, arises if the sample drawn from a population differs from the target population. For instance, suppose a telephone

survey is conducted to find out Chicago beer drinkers' attitudes toward Coors. If a Chicago telephone directory is used as the frame (the device or list from which the respondents are selected), the survey will contain a frame error. Not all Chicago beer drinkers have a phone, and many phone numbers are unlisted. An ideal sample (for example, a sample with no frame error) matches all important characteristics of the target population to be surveyed.

random error
Error that occurs because the selected sample is an imperfect representation of the overall population.

Random error occurs because the selected sample is an imperfect representation of the overall population. Random error represents how accurately the chosen sample's true average (mean) value reflects the population's true average (mean) value. For example, we might take a random sample of beer drinkers in Chicago and find that 16 percent regularly drink Coors beer. The next day we might repeat the same sampling procedure and discover that 14 percent regularly drink Coors beer. The difference is due to random error.

Collect the Data

field service firm
Firm that specializes in interviewing respondents on a subcontract basis.

Marketing research field services perform most data collection. A **field service firm** specializes in interviewing respondents on a subcontract basis. Many have offices throughout the country. A typical research study involves data collection in several cities and requires working with a comparable number of field service firms. To ensure uniformity among all subcontractors, detailed field instructions should be developed for every job. Nothing should be open to chance; no interpretations of procedures should be left to the subcontractors.

Besides interviewing, field service firms provide focus group facilities, mall intercept locations, test product storage, and kitchen facilities to prepare test food products. They also conduct retail audits (counting the amount of product sold off retail shelves). After an in-home interview is completed, field service supervisors validate the survey by recontacting about 15 percent of the respondents. The supervisors verify that certain responses were recorded properly and that the person was actually interviewed.

Analyze the Data

After collecting the data, the market researcher proceeds to the next step in the research process: data analysis. The purpose of this analysis is to interpret and draw conclusions from the mass of collected data. The marketing researcher tries to organize and analyze those data by using one or more techniques common to marketing research: one-way frequency counts, cross-tabulations, and more sophisticated statistical analysis. Of these three techniques, one-way frequency counts are the simplest.

One-way frequency tables record the responses to a question. For example, the answers to the question "What brand of microwave popcorn do you buy most often?" would provide a one-way frequency distribution. One-way frequency tables are always done in data analysis, at least as a first step, because they provide the researcher with a general picture of the study's results.

cross-tabulation
Type of data analysis that relates the responses to one question to the responses to one or more other questions.

A **cross-tabulation,** or "cross-tab," lets the analyst look at the responses to one question in relation to the responses to one or more other questions. For example, what is the association between gender and the brand of microwave popcorn bought most frequently? Hypothetical answers to this question are shown in Exhibit 8.8. Although Orville Reddenbacher was popular with both males and females, it was more popular with females. Males strongly preferred Pop Rite, whereas women were more likely to buy Weight Watchers.

Exhibit 8.8

A Hypothetical Cross-Tabulation between Gender and Brand of Microwave Popcorn Purchased Most Frequently

Brand	Purchase by gender	
	Male	***Female***
Orville Reddenbacher	31%	49%
T.V. Time	12	6
Pop Rite	38	4
Act Two	7	23
Weight Watchers	4	18
Other	8	0

Researchers can use many other more powerful and sophisticated statistical techniques, such as hypothesis testing, measures of association, and regression analysis. A description of these techniques goes beyond the scope of this textbook. Their applications depend on the researchers' objectives and the nature of the data gathered.

Prepare and Present the Report

After data analysis has been completed, the researcher must prepare the report and communicate the conclusions and recommendations to management. This is a key step in the process. If the marketing researcher wants managers to carry out the recommendations, he or she must convince them that the results are credible and justified by the data collected.

Researchers are usually required to present both written and oral reports on the project. These reports should be tailored to the audience. They should begin with a clear, concise statement of the research objectives, followed by a complete, but brief and simple, explanation of the research design or methodology employed. A summary of major findings should come next. The conclusion of the report should also present recommendations for management.

Most people who enter marketing will become research users rather than research suppliers. Thus, they must know what to notice in a report. As with many other items we purchase, quality is not always readily apparent. Nor does a high price guarantee superior quality. The basis for measuring the quality of the report is the research proposal. Did the report meet the objectives established in the proposal? Was the methodology outlined in the proposal followed? Are the conclusions based on logical deductions from the data analysis? Do the recommendations seem prudent, given the conclusions?

Another criterion is the quality of the writing. Is the style crisp and lucid? It has been said that if readers are offered the slightest opportunity to misunderstand, they probably will. The report should also be as concise as possible.

Follow Up

The final step in the marketing research process is to follow up. The researcher should determine why management did or did not carry out the recommendations. Was there sufficient decision-making information? What could have been done to make the report more useful to management? A good rapport between the product

manager, or whoever authorized the project, and the market researcher is essential. Often they must work together on many studies throughout the year.

5 SINGLE-SOURCE RESEARCH

single-source research
System for gathering information from a single group of respondents by continuously monitoring the advertising, promotion, and pricing they are exposed to and the things they buy.

Single-source research is a system for gathering information from a single group of respondents by continuously monitoring the advertising, promotion, and pricing they are exposed to and the things they buy. The variables measured are advertising campaigns, coupons, displays, and product prices. The result is a huge data base of marketing efforts and consumer behavior.

E. D. Russell, director of market research services at Campbell Soup Company, claims that single-source research is bringing ever closer the holy grail of market research: an accurate, objective picture of the direct causal relationship between different kinds of marketing efforts and actual sales.[21]

Two electronic monitoring tools are used in single-source systems: television meters and laser scanners, which "read" the bar codes on products and produce instantaneous information on sales. Separately, each monitoring device provides marketers with current information about either the advertising audience or sales and inventories of products. Together, television meters and scanners measure the impact of marketing.

The two major single-source suppliers are Information Resources Incorporated (IRI) and the A.C. Nielsen Company. Each has about half the market for single-source research.[22] However, IRI is the founder of scanner-based research.

BehaviorScan
Single-source research program that tracks the purchases of 3,000 households through store scanners.

IRI's first product is called **BehaviorScan**. A household panel (a group of 3,000 long-term participants in the research project) has been recruited and maintained in each BehaviorScan town. Panel members shop with an ID card, which is presented at the checkout in scanner-equipped grocery stores and drugstores, allowing IRI to electronically track each household's purchases, item by item, over time. With such a measure of household purchasing, it is possible to manipulate marketing variables, such as TV advertising or consumer promotions, or to introduce a new product and analyze real changes in consumer buying behavior. The BehaviorScan markets are geographically dispersed cities: Pittsfield, Massachusetts; Marion, Indiana; Eau Claire, Wisconsin; Midland, Texas; Grand Junction, Colorado; and Cedar Rapids, Iowa.

InfoScan
Scanner-based, national sales-tracking service for the consumer packaged-goods industry, using data from purchases at retail stores.

IRI's most successful product, with sales of over $130 million per year, is **InfoScan.**[23] InfoScan is a scanner-based sales-tracking service for the consumer packaged-goods industry. Retail sales, detailed consumer purchasing information (including measurement of store loyalty and total grocery basket expenditures), and promotional activity by manufacturers and retailers are monitored and evaluated for all bar-coded products.

InfoScan collects daily purchase data from 2,700 supermarkets, 500 drugstores, and 250 mass merchandisers. Over time, IRI has also created a huge secondary data base. With this data base, IRI has examined 780 brands in 116 different packaged-goods product categories. The company has, in essence, what it refers to as thousands and thousands of "naturally occurring experiments"—that is, hundreds of thousands of data points relating weekly sales to price reductions and merchandising activity.

Using this data base, IRI researchers were able to look at various marketing mixes and competitive situations and determine the results of managerial decision making. For example, they looked at the weekly sales of an average brand in response to

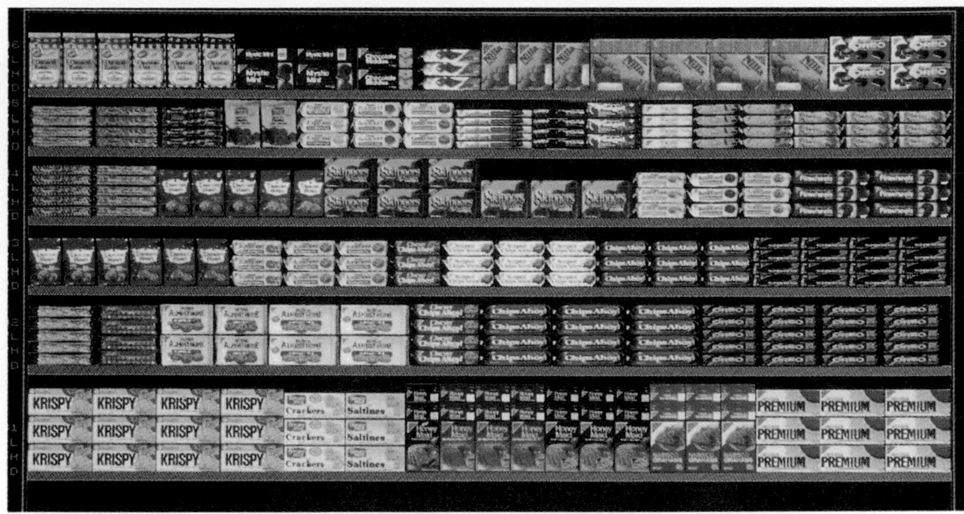

In addition to two popular scanner-based research systems, Information Resources Incorporated sells Apollo Space Management, which draws these computer-generated schematics of retail shelves.

Courtesy of Information Resources, Inc.

trade promotions. They found that a 10 percent price reduction, on average, led to a 20 percent sales increase during the week of the price reduction. A feature ad and a price reduction generated a 78 percent sales increase during the week of the promotion. An in-store display and a 10 percent price reduction doubled sales. An in-store display, a feature ad, and a 10 percent price reduction tripled sales.

Scanner Wars: IRI versus Nielsen

Like two heavyweight boxers, IRI and Nielsen are continually punching and counterpunching each other in the scanner data market. Each is seeking a competitive advantage that will sway buyers of scanner data (the most rapidly growing area of the marketing research industry). Scanner data revenues were over $200 million in 1991.[24] Kraft General foods alone spends over $300 million a year for scanner data.[25]

A major difference between IRI and Nielsen is the way the data are gathered. IRI scanner panel members present to the retailer an ID card, which has a bar code identifying the household making the purchase. Thus the data are captured at retail sites. Nielsen used a similar system consisting of 15,000 households until 1991, when Nielsen phased out its in-store panel and substituted an in-home scanner panel. The company also increased its panel size to 40,000 households in 1992. About 4,500 panel members will be connected to Nielsen's Monitor Plus TV program for tracking viewing using the People Meter. Nielsen claims its panel will measure all geographic locations. Also, by scanning at home, the system does not depend on retailers' cooperation. Nielsen's panel covers some 1,147 counties, whereas IRI covers only 30 counties. Andy Tarshis, president of NPD/Nielsen, says, "Can households in 30 counties be representative of the total United States?"[26] Tarshis also notes:

> "By increasing our panel nearly threefold, our ability to do additional analysis increases maybe tenfold," he said. "For example, warehouse clubs are becoming popular, but not everyone is a member. But by expanding our panel to 40,000, the number of households buying at the clubs may be 5,000, which is a much more usable number than we get from 15,000 households."
>
> The same is true for marketers interested in data from minorities. For example, 6 percent of the panel is Hispanic households; as the panel expands, that percentage becomes "a base large enough for us to do dramatically more analysis. We can compare Hispanic household trends on the East Coast vs. the West Coast or even look at a single market," Mr. Tarshis said. Nielsen intends to maintain at least 12 percent of the panel as black households, also enabling expanded analysis of that group.[27]

IRI's InfoScan has historically relied on cooperating supermarkets to supply scanner data. To counter Nielsen, IRI added 500 drugstores, such as Walgreens, Eckerd, and Drug Emporium. The company also added 150 mass merchandisers, including Wal-Mart, Kmart, and Target. This move was made because only 40 percent of health and beauty aid sales are realized in supermarkets. Another 40 percent are sold through drugstores, with the remaining 20 percent in mass-merchandise outlets.[28] The new IRI sample, therefore, fills out the consumer packaged goods universe.

Recently IRI provided its InfoScan panel members with a "keychain scanner," a portable, pocket-size wand to register product purchases made at nonscanner stores.[29] And so the battle continues. Some scanner data users give Nielsen the edge in data capture and IRI the software advantage.

The Future of Scanning

The next generation of scanners, to be known as Scanner Plus, will have abilities far beyond those of today's machines. These scanners will be able to communicate with personal computers in homes. One function could be to analyze an individual household's consumption based on its prior purchase patterns and offer menu projections or product use suggestions with an associated shopping list. To encourage the use of that shopping list, special offers may be made on certain listed items. These special offers could be designed for each household, rather than offered to everyone at the same time.

Scanner Plus may also keep track of each household's coupons and the other special offers received directly from advertisers. These offers will simply be entered into the household's electronic account in its personal computer as well as in its "promotion" bank in Scanner Plus.

MARKETING AND SMALL BUSINESS

Marketing Research for Small Companies

Because of the limited financial resources and expertise that most small businesses have, it is easy to jump to the conclusion that doing marketing research and creating an information system wouldn't be worth the cost. Instead, managers often rely on hunches or intuition when designing their marketing mix. They seldom receive feedback from their customers and, as a result, sometimes institute practices that customers object to. Over time, the customer base may begin to erode. Often the owners don't know why it is.

Many small-business owners who feel they are doing an outstanding job are unaware of the serious problems confronting them in the area of customer relations. For example, the owner-manager of a car dealership in a small community had this policy: "to present a high-volume, low-price dealership that has a reputation for good service." However, a random survey of customers who had used his service department showed they were dissatisfied and would no longer do business with him.

To get the most out of their marketing research dollar, small-business owners need to be frugal. Perhaps the owner and employees can do the interviewing. Or perhaps an inexpensive mail survey would be better than personal interviews.

"Turn-key" marketing research projects, where a research firm conducts the entire project and makes recommendations, tend to be expensive. A small-business owner who does everything but the interviewing, which can be assigned to a market research field service, can save a great deal of money.

Another money-saving idea is to create a simple data base from customer information cards. These can be gathered by offering a drawing for a free lunch or prize. Or use a Polk's Crisscross Directory to get the names and phone numbers of persons living nearby. Also, on-line data bases are well within the budget of most small businesses.

An example of a similar system already in use is the Vision Value card offered by Big Bear Supermarkets in Ohio. It combines scanning with the computerized equivalent of "green stamps" to provide consumers with coupons for products they actually use.[30]

6 DECIDING WHETHER TO CONDUCT MARKETING RESEARCH

When managers have several possible solutions to a problem, they should not instinctively call for marketing research. In fact, the first decision to make is whether to conduct marketing research at all.

Some companies have been conducting research in certain markets for many years. Such firms understand the characteristics of target customers and their likes and dislikes about existing products. Under these circumstances, further research would be repetitive and waste money. Procter & Gamble, for example, has extensive knowledge of the coffee market. After it conducted initial taste tests with Folger's Instant Coffee, P&G went into national distribution without further research. Consolidated Foods Kitchen of Sara Lee followed the same strategy with its frozen croissants, as did Quaker Oats with Chewy Granola Bars. This tactic, however, does not always work. P&G marketers thought they understood the pain reliever market thoroughly, so they bypassed market research for Encaprin aspirin in capsules. Because it lacked a distinct competitive advantage over existing products, the product failed and was withdrawn from the market.

Managers rarely have such great trust in their judgment that they would refuse more information if it were available and free. But they might have enough confidence that they would be unwilling to pay very much for the information or wait a long time to receive it. The willingness to acquire additional decision-making information depends on managers' perceptions of its quality, price, and timing. Of course, if perfect information were available—that is, the data conclusively showed which alternative to follow—decision makers would be willing to pay more for it than for information that still left uncertainty. In summary, research should only be undertaken when the expected value of the information is greater than the cost of obtaining it.

LOOKING BACK

Look back at the story about Piggyback luggage that appeared at the beginning of this chapter. You have seen that marketing research provides data that help managers make better decisions. Samsonite used marketing research to create the very successful line of Piggyback luggage. Marketing research can also provide clues when a marketing mix fails, as in the Reynolds Wrap example.

This chapter explained how marketing research uses a variety of survey research techniques, from focus groups to telephone surveys. Other important tools of marketing research are observation research and experiments.

Decision support systems continually gather data from a variety of sources and funnel it to decision makers, who manipulate the data to help make better decisions. One source of DSS data is marketing research information.

KEY TERMS

audit 248
BehaviorScan 254
central-location telephone facility 243
closed-ended question 247
computer-assisted interviewing 243
convenience sample 251
cross-tabulation 252
database marketing 231
decision support system 229
experiment 250
field service firm 252
focus group 244
frame error 251
InfoScan 254
mall intercept interview 243
marketing information system 228
marketing intelligence 228
marketing research 232
measurement error 251
nonprobability sample 251
observation research 248
on-line data base 239
on-line database vendor 240
open-ended question 246
primary data 241
proactive management 234
probability sample 251
random error 252
random sample 251
reactive management 234
research design 241
sample 251
sampling error 251
scaled-response question 247
secondary data 238
single-source research 254
situation analysis 238
survey research 242
universe 251

SUMMARY

1 Explain the difference between a marketing information system and a decision support system. A marketing information system gathers marketing information from various sources, synthesizes it, and puts it into a general format for use by marketing personnel. Decision support systems, on the other hand, make data instantly available to marketing managers and allow them to manipulate the data themselves to make marketing decisions. Four characteristics of decision support systems make them especially useful to marketing managers: They are interactive, flexible, discovery-oriented, and accessible. Decision support systems give managers access to information immediately and without outside assistance. They allow users to manipulate data in a variety of ways and to answer "what if" questions. And finally, they are accessible to novice computer users.

2 Discuss the nature of database marketing and micromarketing. A marketing data base is part of a decision support system composed of present and potential customers' profiles and purchasing patterns. Micromarketing is the creation of a large data base of customers' and potential customers' profiles and purchase patterns that allow targeting down to the household or even individual level. Micromarketing has several important functions. It identifies the potential profitability of specific customers and market segments. It helps determine effective packaging and pricing strategies for specific market segments. Furthermore, it provides insights into market opportunities for new products and services.

3 Define marketing research and its importance to marketing decision making. Marketing research is a process of collecting and analyzing data for the purpose of solving specific marketing problems. Marketers use marketing research to explore the profitability of marketing strategies. They can examine why particular strategies failed and analyze characteristics of specific market segments. Moreover, marketing research allows management to behave proactively rather than reactively, by identifying newly emerging patterns in society and the economy.

4 Describe the steps involved in a marketing research project. The marketing research process involves several basic steps. First, the researcher and decision maker must agree on a problem statement or set of research objectives. Sometimes this step requires a background investigation referred to as a situation analysis, usually drawn partly from secondary sources. The researcher then creates an overall research design to specify how primary data will be gathered and analyzed. Before collecting data, the researcher decides whether the group to be interviewed will be a probability or nonprobability sample. Field service firms are often hired to carry out data collection. Once data have been collected, the researcher analyzes it using statistical analysis. The researcher than prepares and presents oral and written reports, with conclusions and recommendations, to management. As a final step, the researcher determines whether the recommendations were implemented and what could have been done to make the project more successful.

5 Discuss the growing importance of single-source research. A single-source research system enables marketers to monitor a market panel's exposure and reaction to such variables as advertising, coupons, store displays, packaging, and price. By analyzing these variables in relation to the panel's subsequent buying behavior, marketers gain useful insight into sales and marketing strategies.

6 Explain when marketing research should and should not be conducted. Marketing research helps managers by providing data to make better marketing decisions. However, firms must consider whether the expected benefits of marketing research outweigh its costs. Before approving a research budget, management also should make sure adequate decision-making information doesn't already exist.

Review Questions

1. Why are decision support systems often preferred over marketing information systems?
2. List the capabilities of database marketing.
3. Describe the three functional roles of marketing research. How does marketing research relate to decision support and marketing information systems?
4. Name the pros and cons of four different types of survey research.
5. Identify some major sources of secondary data. What are the limitations of using secondary data in marketing decision making?
6. Describe the unique features of single-source research.
7. Discuss the advantages of observation research. Cite an example of a problem that could be solved using observation research.
8. Describe the differences between BehaviorScan and InfoScan.

Discussion and Writing Questions

1. One of your employees says, "Market research is too expensive, so the firm will just have to get by without it." As the manager of a small business, write a memo in reply.
2. How can market research help the manager of a service organization? List examples for a car rental agency, airline, hotel, and hospital.
3. In analyzing research findings, why is it important to know the methodology used? Provide an example.
4. What could cause a new-product failure even if the firm conducts sound marketing research?
5. As a manager, would you rather work with an MIS or DSS? Why?
6. Your firm is about to conduct a mail survey. In a memo to the marketing manager, suggest some strategies to encourage response.
7. Have you ever participated in a market research survey? Describe the experience. Would you say that the researcher was gathering high-quality information?
8. If you were a product manager, would you prefer using IRI or Nielsen for single-source data? Why?

CASES

8.1 The Missouri Lottery

You can't win if you don't play. State lotteries across the nation work hard to drive that message home to consumers. Likewise, if people don't play, the lotteries don't win—and neither do the worthwhile causes they fund.

In Missouri, where proceeds from the state lottery are earmarked for education, selecting the right scratch-off games to offer is serious business. What colors attract the most attention? How many scratch-off windows should be on the card? Is the promise of one large jackpot or many smaller prizes more appealing?

The Missouri Lottery works with Market Directions, a Kansas City–based marketing research firm, to test new games as well as monitor public attitudes toward the lottery in general. The lottery introduces a new scratch-off game every six to eight weeks and conducts three or four games simultaneously. Game concepts are tested by focus groups twice a year. "This actually is new product research," says Susan Spaulding, president of Market Directions. "Games have a very short life, so the concept must be just right coming out of the gate."

A recent example of lottery focus-group marketing research is as follows. Participants were recruited for sessions in three locations: Kansas City, St. Louis, and Moberly (in central Missouri). Random telephone recruiting sought a cross section of playing frequency—heavy players (once a week or more), infrequent (two or three times per month), and lapsed (former players who have stopped). The groups of ten were also divided by gender. The lottery's instant-ticket vendor mocked up fifteen games for use in the focus groups. Participants were asked to "shop" among the mock-ups for $30 worth of tickets.

Preferences were suprisingly similar statewide and across gender and playing frequency lines:

- *Color:* Bright colors generated the most interest.

- *Theme:* Most men preferred an action theme, while many women liked bingo. Market Directions attributes the preferences to familiarity with the themes. A horoscope theme was universally disliked because it was considered corny.
- *Windows:* Games with nine scratch-off windows won out over those with six because participants perceived a greater chance of winning.

Prize preferences, however, varied by frequency of play. Participants were asked to rank statements such as "This game has 400,000 $10 winners" and "This game gives you the opportunity to win a top prize of $50,000." Frequent players favored many small-dollar prizes, but infrequent players liked the idea of one large jackpot. Most liked the option of large jackpots being distributed monthly for life. Most participants would rather not bother with side prizes, such as dinner at a restaurant, although men were interested in an opportunity to win a car.

Source: Adapted from "Leaving Nothing to Chance," *Quirk's Marketing Research Review,* November 1992, pp. 8–9, 40.

Questions

1. What other aspects of designing a lottery game might have been covered in the focus group?
2. What other types of survey research could have been used to evaluate the lottery concepts?
3. Focus groups use a very small sample. Should focus groups always be followed by much larger surveys of some other type, such as a telephone interview?

Suggested Readings

James R. Adams, "The Validity of Qualitative Market Research," *Journal of the Market Research Society,* January 1991, p. 60.

Judith Langer, "18 Way to 'Shut Up!' " *Marketing News,* 6 January 1992, pp. 6–20.

Howard Schlossberg, "Battle Rages between Attitude and Behavior Researchers," *Marketing News,* 2 March 1992, p. 18.

Wendy Sykes, "Taking Stock: Issues from the Literature on Validity and Reliability in Qualitative Research," *Journal of the Marketing Research Society,* January 1991, pp. 3–12.

8.2 Information Resources, Inc.

Video title: *Tracking Consumer Purchases Using IRI's BehaviorScan*

Information Resources
150 N. Clinton Street
Chicago, IL 60606

SIC codes: 8732 Commercial and sociological and educational research
8742 Management consulting services

Number of employees: 2,980

1992 revenues: $276 million

Major brands: BehaviorScan, InfoScan

Largest competitors: A.C. Nielsen

Background

Companies always wonder whether their advertising campaigns are really effective. Several market research companies test advertising recall, which is the ability to remember all or part of a specific ad. Although advertising recall indicates knowledge of the ad, it does not show whether the consumer will buy the product. If you want to know the sales power of an ad, then you need to be able to test a variety of advertising messages and measure the effect of those messages on sales.

Industry

Rapid changes in technology have drastically changed the way market research data are collected and analyzed. In the past, companies relied on consumer diaries and personal interviews to collect sales data. Now, companies use data collected from the scanning of bar codes. What used to be reported monthly or quarterly can now be reported weekly or even daily with less effort and greater accuracy.

The advances in technology have created a race to build a national data base of consumers. Several marketing research firms track consumer buying habits, media usage, and other information. However, only two companies are building national single-source electronic tracking systems. These companies are Information Resources and NPD/Nielsen.

BehaviorScan

Information Resources first introduced BehaviorScan in 1979. Today the system incorporates over 20,000 panel households in eight markets. To guarantee the accuracy of its information, IRI collects data from all grocery stores in these test markets. In some cities, data are also collected from drugstores. To get the cooperation of these retailers, IRI initially installed the scanner equipment at no cost. In stores already equipped with scanners, IRI arranges to buy the sales data. The company also has the ability to control the advertising content of national magazines, newspapers, and cable television in some markets. BehaviorScan utilizes split-cable technology to send different commercials to individual households, thereby allowing advertising weight or commercial testing.

Questions

1. What concerns would you have about using scanner data to test advertising effectiveness?
2. What advantages does BehaviorScan offer to manufacturers? to retailers?

References

Million Dollar Directory 1993 (Parsippany, NJ: Dun & Bradstreet Information Services, 1993).

Howard Schlossberg "Scanning Improvements Introduced," *Marketing News*, 17 February 1992, pp. 1–2.

Standard & Poor's Industry Surveys (New York: Standard & Poor's Corporation, October 1993).

PART TWO
CRITICAL THINKING CASE

Petco Products

The pet care business in the United States exceeds $12 billion annually—almost $4 billion more than we spend on baby food. Add $4.6 billion for medical care for dogs and cats and an additional $1.7 billion for pet gear, and the total appears to be a marketer's dream. Even more astounding is the fact that these figures are most likely understated. Additional expenses for extra housecleaning and home repairs due to damage caused by pets are harder to track. For this reason these totals are not included in the total money spent on pet care.

Competitive Environment

The pet food industry is characterized as a mature and highly competitive business. Yet the dog food market continues to grow at a steady pace. There are more than 20,000 dog food vendors in the United States. Grocery stores, mass merchandisers, and discount and warehouse stores sell the majority of dog food in the United States.

There are four major types of dog food sold: dry, canned (wet), soft, and moist. Like dry dog food, soft dog food is sold in bags. Moist dog food, such as Gaines Burgers, is packaged in individually wrapped servings. Dry dog food accounts for the largest percentage of sales (see Exhibit 1).

Five large manufacturers dominate the market. These five companies account for 79 percent of the $3.3 billion dog food sales. Ralston Purina is the leader, with 47 percent of the dry dog food sold in the United States (see Exhibit 2).

Manufacturers are continually working on new dog food products. Major manufacturers traditionally spend about 3 percent of gross sales on research and development. In answer to specialty companies like Iams, many companies have added high-protein products to their lines. Premium dog foods, foods with higher protein and mineral content, are more expensive per package. This expense is offset by the fact that pet owners can feed their dogs smaller servings.

Grocery stores are always looking for something new. For the most part, the market is deal-prone; that is, consumers are price-sensitive. Dog food takes up a great deal of shelf space in the store. For these reasons,

Exhibit 1

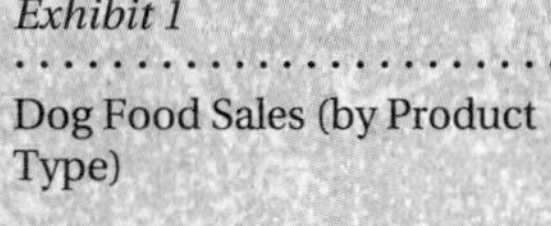

Dog Food Sales (by Product Type)

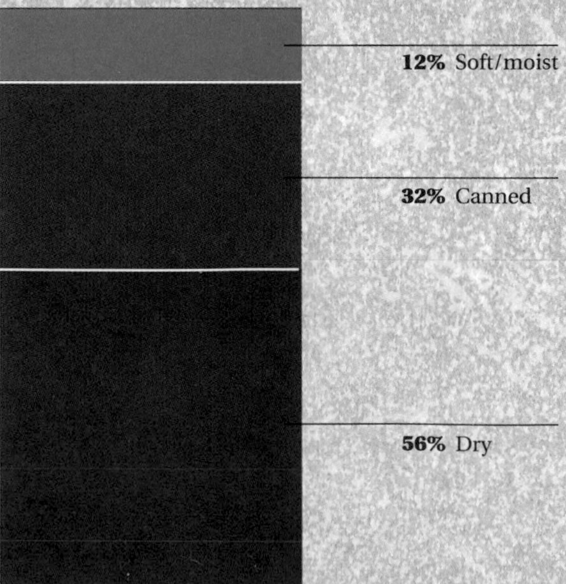

grocers like to stock fast-moving products with large advertising budgets. The premium dog food segment is the fastest-growing segment. Grocers seem to be missing out on a lot of this business unless the product is tied to a heavy coupon and advertising campaign. The bulk of this segment is being sold through specialty pet stores and veterinarians.

Profile of the Average Pet Owner

There are 35.4 million dog owners (38 percent of all households) and 31 million cat owners (33 percent of all households) in the United States. The cat population exceeds the dog population, and the percentage of households owning cats is increasing faster than that of dog owners.

The American Pet Products Manufacturers Association identifies these characteristics of pet owners:

- 23 percent of households owning pets are headed by an adult between 30 and 39 years old. Heads of households between 40 and 49 years old represent 19 percent of the market.
- 14 percent of pet owners are single and over 35 years old. Another 7 percent of pet owners are single and under 35.
- Single pet owners under 35 are more likely to consider their pets part of the family than are older pet owners.
- Single parents are more likely to agree that a pet can be a best friend than are married parents.
- 78 percent of pet owners live in houses.
- 53 percent of all pet owners make more than $30,000 annually.

First in Show 27

Petco's First in Show 27 (FIS-27) is a nutritionally complete and balanced dog food. With extra vitamin and mineral content, FIS-27 compares favorably with popular pet store dog foods. FIS-27 contains 27 percent highly digestible protein and 12 percent first-grade fats. The formula is designed to meet the high nutritional requirements of growing and active dogs. The product

Exhibit 2

Dry Dog Food (Market Share)

Note: These amounts do not include dog food sold through specialty stores and veterinarians.

Dog food sales (in millions of dollars)				
	Type of product			
Company	*Dry*	*Canned*	*Dry soft/moist*	*Total*
Ralston Purina	889	0	50	939
Grand Met	157	326	3	486
Quaker Oats	184	83	289	556
Mars	66	309	0	375
Carnation	102	158	0	260
All others	478	184	43	705
Totals	1,876	1,060	385	3,321

uses only high-grade poultry, lamb, beef, and pork, not the corn and soybean typically found in other dog food products.

Two key ingredients that set FIS-27 apart from other competitors are Odor Bloc and a garlic extract. Odor Bloc, based on an all-natural extract from the yucca plant, reduces odors associated with pet waste by up to 60 percent. It inhibits the production of ammonia, one of the main odor-causing agents in pet waste. The garlic extract is used to reduce the infestation of fleas and ticks. All-natural flavor enhancers are added to FIS-27 to make the product very flavorful.

FIS-27 is expected to be sold through grocery stores in the traditional five-, twenty-five-, and fifty-pound bags. It will be priced 40 percent below the competition.

Questions

1. Develop profiles of consumers who buy pet food from a grocery store, a specialty store, and a veterinarian. Differentiate the motives of each group.
2. Propose a multicultural approach for Petco. What type of market research will be necessary?
3. Considering the profile of a grocery store shopper and the existing competition in the dry dog food market, predict the success of FIS-27.
4. Create a plan to sell FIS-27 to a business market, consisting of kennels.
5. What changes do you think may occur in the pet food market in the next ten years? What adjustments would you recommend to Petco Products?

Suggested Readings

Robert H. Brown, "Premium Pet Foods Take Increasing Share of Market," *Food Stuffs,* 18 May 1992, p. 55.

Sue Davis, "Pet Food Processors Opt for Nurtition," *Prepared Foods,* 15 April 1992, p. 97.

PART TWO
GLOBAL MARKETING CASE

Blanchworth China

Thomas F. White, Regis University, and
Linda B. Catlin, Wayne State University

The Blanchworth China Company was founded in the British Isles in the eighteenth century and has established a worldwide reputation for premium-quality china designed and handcrafted in the United Kingdom. The china always has sold very well in the United States, and in the early 1980s, fueled by a strong dollar, it experienced an explosive growth in sales. However, as the dollar went into a long decline through the mid- and late 1980s, sales of Blanchworth china dropped by 25 percent in the United States. This decline is particularly important to Blanchworth since the U.S. market accounts for approximately 90 percent of the company's output.

The premium-quality china market is roughly divided into two segments based on price: the high segment is priced from $75 to $300 per plate, while the lower segment ranges from $25 to $75 per plate. Blanchworth has always dominated the high segment with approximately 85 percent of market share, but the company had no presence in the lower segment. Unfortunately, it was the high segment of the market that decreased 25 percent in sales dollars in the late 1980s, while the lower segment grew by 50 percent during the same period. This was clearly a worldwide trend, not only in Blanchworth's market, but also for most other discretionary income items.

In addition to the falling value of the U.S. dollar and the shrinking market for higher-priced china, several other factors helped to create a severe financial crisis for Blanchworth by the end of the 1980s. During the "good times" of the 1980s, when demand and profits were high, Blanchworth's skilled workers' union made heavy wage and work rule demands. The company's managers acceded to these demands in order to avoid any work stoppages. As a result, Blanchworth's craftsmen became some of the highest-paid skilled workers in the British Isles. Workers' salaries increased from 60 percent of the cost of product to nearly 80 percent by the late 1980s. These high labor costs, coupled with company debt incurred by the acquisition of a premium crystal manufacturer, prevented Blanchworth from lowering its prices when U.S. demand decreased.

In 1988, management was forced to propose immediate cost-reducing measures in order to save the company. Among other things, they determined to reduce their labor force by 25 percent and to purchase new equipment that would make the remaining workers more productive. After heated encounters between management and union leaders, the union finally became convinced that the labor force cuts were necessary in order to save the company. The union also agreed to rescind work rules that had worked to preclude higher worker productivity. The union made these concessions to prevent the company from declaring bankruptcy and to save most union jobs.

After a year of operation with the new equipment, Blanchworth management found that increases in productivity were offset by the larger than expected number of senior craftsmen taking advantage of the early retirement package. This package was offered as one means of reducing the labor force by the targeted 25 percent. Profits continued to slide after the work force reduction, and Blanchworth management finally decided the company would have to enter the lower segment of the premium-quality china market. While Blanchworth managers realized that there are many more competitors in this lower segment of the market than in the high-price segment, they believed the company's well-respected name and other marketing strengths would allow it to make a quick entry into this segment.

In late 1990, Blanchworth introduced a new line of products that is lighter in weight and less ornate than its original china place settings. This entire product line is produced in Eastern Europe at a fraction of the labor cost associated with the Blanchworth United Kingdom plant. Preliminary market research shows that this line has stronger appeal for the younger, first-time china buyer, who sees herself as more contemporary and value-conscious than the traditional Blanchworth customer; moreover, this younger buyer is generally less brand-loyal. Blanchworth calls its new line *Krohn China*, a name that it believes has more of a Continental sound than Blanchworth.

Krohn is carried by the same distribution channel as Blanchworth, but it has its own logo, package design, advertising agency, and display case. Management felt that the name *Blanchworth* associated with the name *Krohn* would help to establish an image of high quality, but at the same time, the name *Krohn* would differentiate the new line from traditional Blanchworth china. This name association has helped to gain the reseller support necessary in making the new line readily accessible to a large market.

As a result of Blanchworth management's decision to locate its new operations in Eastern Europe, members of the union and residents of the community in which the Blanchworth factory is located feel betrayed. Union leaders were never informed about the new product line, which could have meant the rehiring of many Blanchworth skilled workers. In addition, the move to Eastern Europe has caused ill will among many consumers throughout the United Kingdom and has resulted in some critical editorials in the local and national press.

The union contends that most U.S. customers are brand-loyal to Blanchworth because it is made by skilled workers in the United Kingdom. They argue that this loyalty stems from the fact that many U.S. citizens trace their ancestry to one or more countries in the United Kingdom. Management counters that Blanchworth has never been sold specifically as a U.K. product and that most U.S. buyers neither know nor care where their china products are made. Although there were many bitter feelings between management and the union, there were no work stoppages during 1991.

In early 1992, management announced that after the first year of sales, Krohn generated twice as much profit per plate as Blanchworth. Also, they asserted that Blanchworth employees in the United Kingdom were still not productive enough to offset the high wages these workers earned. As a result, management representatives opened discussions with union leaders about how to solve the continuing low-profit problem. Management suggested that the only solution was a further reduction in wages and benefits, as well as another major change in work rules. The union disagreed with this perspective and countered that the low level of profitability actually resulted from poor management, rather than "overpaid, unproductive workers" as suggested by management.

While they never openly stated so, union leaders suspect that management may be considering moving all Blanchworth operations to Eastern Europe. The union continues to argue that U.S. customers will not accept Blanchworth china that is not made by U.K. craftsmen. They cite the fact that 100,000 tourists tour the U.K. plant each year and that at least half of these tourists are from the United States. Many of these U.S. tourists purchase over $2,000 in china products during their visit to the plant. The union argues that the tourists who come to the plant feel a strong affinity for Blanchworth china because it is a product of the United Kingdom and that most of these on-site sales would be lost if the plant were moved to Eastern Europe. To further strengthen this argument, the union cites the U.S. Census Bureau's 1990 statistics giving the following breakdown of U.S. citizens by U.K. ancestry: England, 32.6 million; Scotland, 5.4 million; Ireland, 38.7 million; and Wales, 2.0 million.

To the Student

You are a business consultant who has been brought in to assist Blanchworth's top management with strategic decision making in several areas. During the briefing you are given additional information:

- Management is seriously considering moving all Blanchworth factory operations to Eastern Europe while keeping its other functions in the United Kingdom. They make it clear that the design and quality assurance operations would remain in the United Kingdom. There is concern about how quickly the new European plant and workers could achieve full quality production, especially if the U.K. workers shut down the British plant before the new plant is on line.
- Management is concerned about political instability in Eastern Europe. If they move both Krohn and Blanchworth, their entire production could be compromised, and there would be little chance of reopening a plant in the United Kingdom.
- Sales of Krohn in the United Kingdom are extremely sluggish but are doing well on the continent. Krohn does seem to be gaining acceptance

slowly in the United States, mostly among young couples buying it for themselves rather than receiving it as gifts from parents or other friends and relatives.

- The union and the community have threatened to discredit the firm if it moves to Eastern Europe by taking their case directly to the U.K. and U.S. customers.

Answer the following questions about this case:

1. Since management believes its foreign sales will be unaffected by moving all operations to Eastern Europe, it seems to be making the assumption that most people consider fine china to be a functional piece of household ware. Do you agree with this assumption, or would you argue that it is more a work of art with an artist and a history that are "value added" to the physical product? What research should be done before making this decision? Which research methodology do you recommend?
2. Try to anticipate the ways in which the union and the community could discredit the company name if it leaves the United Kingdom. Will U.S. consumers boycott the company *after* the move? Will U.S. consumers voice their disapproval in large numbers *before* the move? How will you get these answers?
3. What specific measures can management take to "inoculate" the firm against the union actions that you anticipated in question 2? Should the firm be proactive rather than dealing with the problem after it is a reality?
4. Should management ask for concessions in order to keep the firm in the United Kingdom? Make a list of possible concessions, and tell who should provide them (for example, union, community, national government, and so on). Concentrate on the long-term solutions when considering how a plan for a win-win solution can be reached in this case.

PART THREE
PRODUCT DECISIONS

CHAPTER 9

Product Concepts

LEARNING OBJECTIVES

After studying this chapter, you should be able to

1. Define the term *product*.
2. Classify products.
3. Define the terms *product item, product line,* and *product mix*.
4. Explain the concept of product life cycles.
5. Describe marketing uses of branding.
6. Describe marketing uses of packaging and labeling.
7. Discuss international issues in branding and packaging.
8. Identify how and why product warranties are important marketing tools.

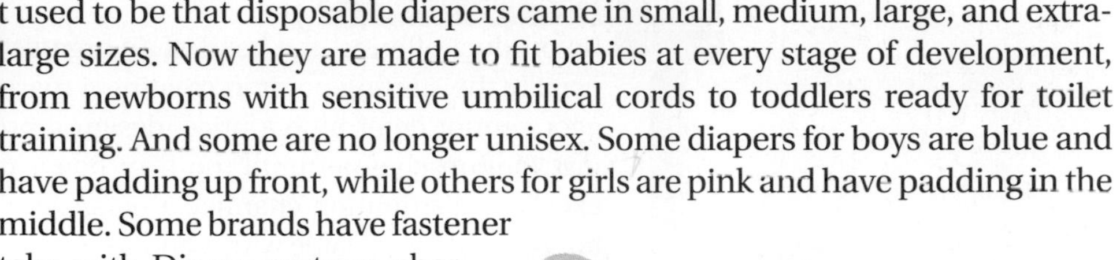

It used to be that disposable diapers came in small, medium, large, and extra-large sizes. Now they are made to fit babies at every stage of development, from newborns with sensitive umbilical cords to toddlers ready for toilet training. And some are no longer unisex. Some diapers for boys are blue and have padding up front, while others for girls are pink and have padding in the middle. Some brands have fastener tabs with Disney cartoon characters; others feature the Muppets. . . .

Procter & Gamble, which controls about 52 percent of the disposable diaper market, says these so-called "brand extensions" are simply a response to consumer demand, something it gauges through market tests. . . . Procter & Gamble now makes a dozen different kinds of Pampers and a dozen kinds of Luvs. And each kind comes in "girl" and "boy" styles and various-size packages.

Is Procter & Gamble's brand extension strategy an illustration of the marketing concept or simply an example of wasteful product proliferation? How do you think supermarket and drugstore managers feel about this strategy? Do you think consumers like or dislike having so many choices?

Source: Adapted from Gabriella Stern, "Multiple Varieties of Established Brands Muddle Consumers, Make Retailers Mad," *The Wall Street Journal*, 24 January 1992, pp. B1, B5. Reprinted by permission of *The Wall Street Journal*, © 1992 Dow Jones & Company. All Rights Reserved Worldwide.

1 WHAT IS A PRODUCT?

The product offering, the heart of an organization's marketing program, is usually the starting point in creating a marketing mix. A marketing manager cannot determine a price, design a promotion strategy, or create a distribution channel until the firm has a product to sell. Moreover, an excellent distribution channel, a persuasive promotion campaign, and a fair price have no value with a poor or inadequate product offering.

product
Everything, both favorable and unfavorable, that a person receives in an exchange—for example, a good, a service, or an idea.

A **product** may be defined as everything, both favorable and unfavorable, that a person receives in an exchange. A product may be a tangible good like a pair of shoes, a service like a haircut, an idea like obeying driving laws, or any combination of these three. Packaging, style, color, options, and size are some typical product features. Just as important are intangibles such as service, the retailer's image, the manufacturer's reputation, and the way consumers believe others will view the product.

To most people, the term *product* means a tangible good. However, note that services and ideas are also products. Services account for over 70 percent of the U.S. gross national product, and over 70 percent of the U.S. work force is employed in service industries such as lodging, food and beverage service, medicine, and law.[1] The proportion of the U.S. work force employed in service industries is increasing rapidly. Eighty-five percent of all new jobs created since 1982 have been in service industries.[2] Chapter 11 focuses specifically on unique aspects of marketing services. But the marketing process identified in Chapter 1 is the same regardless of whether the product marketed is a good, a service, an idea, or some combination.

Many products are symbolic; they help us play our roles in society. A man's tie may identify him as a white-collar worker; a pin-striped suit often denotes conservatism. The brand and model of automobile that people drive may reflect their self-concept. Many other product choices symbolize values, self-concept, and lifestyle—for example, choice of vacations, universities, and memberships in organizations.

Like other product choices, a person's choice of vacation symbolizes his or her values, self-concept, and lifestyle.
© Palmer/Kane, Inc. 1991/The Stock Market

People spend their money, time, and energy with the expectation of receiving benefits. A good or service is just a way to deliver user benefits. Charles Revson, the founder of Revlon cosmetics, stated this point clearly: "In the factory we manufacture cosmetics, but in the store we sell hope." Benefits, not products, are the objective of buying decisions. This distinction has great implications for marketing management. Marketing-oriented firms define their business in terms of the benefits customers seek. Production- and selling-oriented firms often fail because they focus on manufacturing and selling products rather than on satisfying customer wants.

Exhibit 9.1

A Classification of Consumer Products

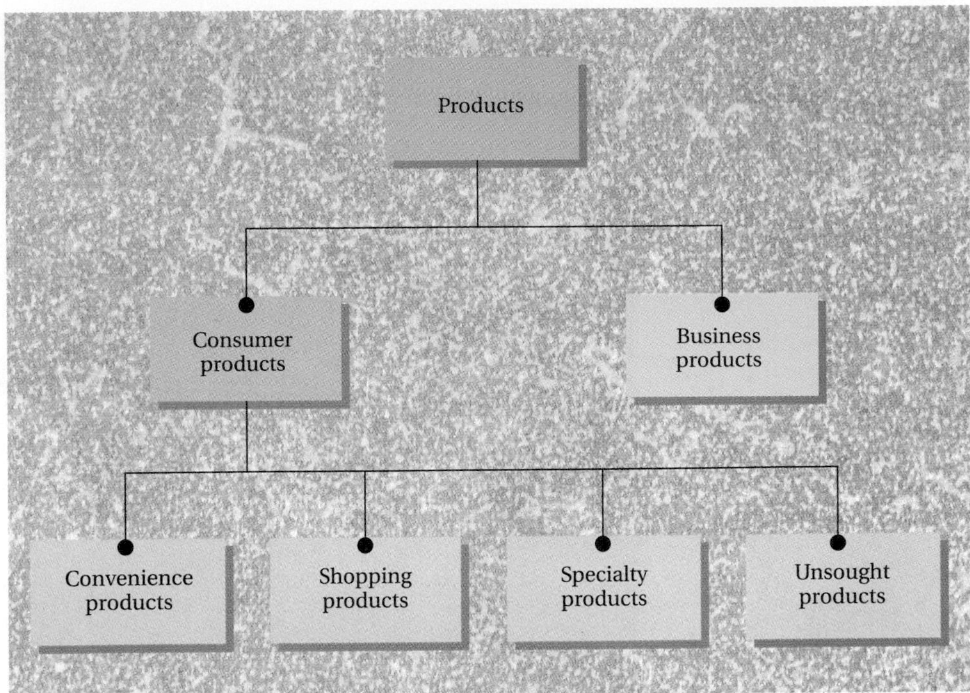

❷ CLASSIFYING PRODUCTS

Products can be classified as either business (industrial) or consumer products, depending on the buyer's intentions. Note that the key distinction between the two types of products is intended use. If the intended use is a business purpose, the product is classified as a business or industrial product. As explained in Chapter 5, a **business product** is used to manufacture other goods or services, to facilitate an organization's operations, or to resell to other customers. A **consumer product** is bought to satisfy an individual's personal wants. Sometimes the same item can be classified as either a business or a consumer product depending on its intended use. Examples include light bulbs, pencils and paper, and microcomputers.

business product – Product used to manufacture other goods or services, to facilitate an organization's operations, or to resell to other customers; also called industrial product.

consumer product – Product bought to satisfy an individual's personal wants.

We need to know about product classifications because business and consumer products are marketed differently. They are marketed to different target markets and tend to use different distribution, promotion, and pricing strategies.

Chapter 5 examined seven categories of business products: major equipment, accessory equipment, component parts, processed materials, raw materials, supplies, and services. This chapter examines an effective way of categorizing consumer products. Although there are several ways to classify them, the most popular approach includes these four categories: convenience products, shopping products, specialty products, and unsought products (see Exhibit 9.1). This approach classifies products according to how much effort is normally used in the shopping process.

Convenience Products

convenience product Relatively inexpensive item that merits little shopping effort.

A **convenience product** is a relatively inexpensive item that merits little shopping effort. That is, a consumer is unwilling to shop extensively for such an item. Candy, soft drinks, combs, aspirin, small hardware items, dry cleaning, and car washes fall into the convenience product category. For some people, a haircut is also a convenience product. Consumers buy convenience products regularly, usually without much planning. Nevertheless, consumers do know the brand names of popular convenience products, such as Coca-Cola, Bayer aspirin, and Right Guard deodor-

A home *(top)* is a shopping product; people are usually willing to buy a home only after looking at several alternatives and finding the one that best meets their needs. Antiques *(bottom)* may be a shopping product for some people. For people seeking a particular piece, however, antiques are specialty products.

(top) © 1992 David Brooks/The Stock Market; *(bottom)* © Jef Apoian/Nawrocki Stock Photo, Inc.

ant. Convenience products normally require wide distribution in order to sell sufficient quantities to meet profit goals.

Shopping Products

shopping product
Product that requires comparison shopping, because it is usually more expensive than a convenience product and found in fewer stores.

The main purpose of shopping is often to find the lowest-priced product with the required features or characteristics. A **shopping product** is usually more expensive than a convenience product and found in fewer stores. Consumers usually buy a shopping product only after comparing several brands or stores on style, practicality, price, and lifestyle compatibility. They are willing to invest some effort into this process to get the desired benefits.

Shopping products can be divided into two categories—homogeneous or heterogeneous—depending on what customers are comparing. Consumers perceive ho-

mogeneous shopping products as basically similar—for example, washers, dryers, refrigerators, and televisions.

In contrast, consumers perceive heterogeneous shopping products as essentially different—for example, furniture, clothing, housing, and universities. Consumers often have trouble comparing heterogeneous shopping products because the prices, quality, and features vary so much. The benefit of comparing heterogeneous shopping products is "finding the best product or brand for me"; this decision is often highly individual.

Specialty Products

specialty product
Product for which consumers search extensively and are very reluctant to accept substitutes.

When consumers search extensively for an item and are very reluctant to accept substitutes, that item is a **specialty product.** Fine watches, Rolls Royce automobiles, expensive stereo equipment, gourmet restaurants, and highly specialized forms of medical care are generally considered specialty products. A haircut is a specialty product for people who attach great importance to their appearance. These consumers willingly spend much time and effort to have a certain stylist cut their hair. Although many specialty items are very costly, some, like haircuts, are not.

Specialty products represent a near-perfect fit between the consumer's physical or psychological needs and the product's benefits. Brand names and quality of service are often very important. Specialty product sellers often use selective, status-conscious advertising to maintain their product's exclusive image. Distribution is often limited to one or a very few outlets in a geographic area.

Unsought Products

unsought product
Product unknown to the potential buyer or known product that the buyer does not actively seek.

A product unknown to the potential buyer or a known product that the buyer does not actively seek is referred to as an **unsought product.** New products fall into this category until advertising and distribution increase consumer awareness of them.

Some goods are always marketed as unsought items, especially needed products we do not like to think about or care to spend money on. Insurance, burial plots, encyclopedias, and similar items require aggressive personal selling and highly persuasive advertising. Salespeople actively seek leads to potential buyers. Since consumers usually do not seek out the item, the company must go directly to them through a salesperson, direct mail, or direct-response advertising.

3 PRODUCT ITEMS, LINES, AND MIXES

product item
Specific version of a product that can be designated as a distinct offering among an organization's products.

product line
Group of closely related products offered by the organization.

product mix
All the products that an organization sells.

A **product item** is a specific version of a product that can be designated as a distinct offering among an organization's products. Gillette's Trac II razor is an example of a product item (see Exhibit 9.2). A **product line** is a group of closely related products offered by the organization. For example, the column in Exhibit 9.2 titled "Blades and razors" represents one of Gillette's product lines. Different container sizes and shapes also distinguish items in a product line. Diet Coke, for example, is available in cans and various plastic containers. Each size and each container is a separate product item.

An organization's **product mix** includes all the products it sells. All Gillette's products constitute its product mix. Yet each product item in the product mix may require a separate marketing strategy. In some cases, product lines and even entire product mixes share some marketing strategy components. Pontiac Motor Division of General Motors, for example, promotes all Pontiac items and lines with its theme "We build excitement—Pontiac."

Exhibit 9.2

Gillette Company's Product Items, Product Lines, Product Mix Width, and Product Line Depth

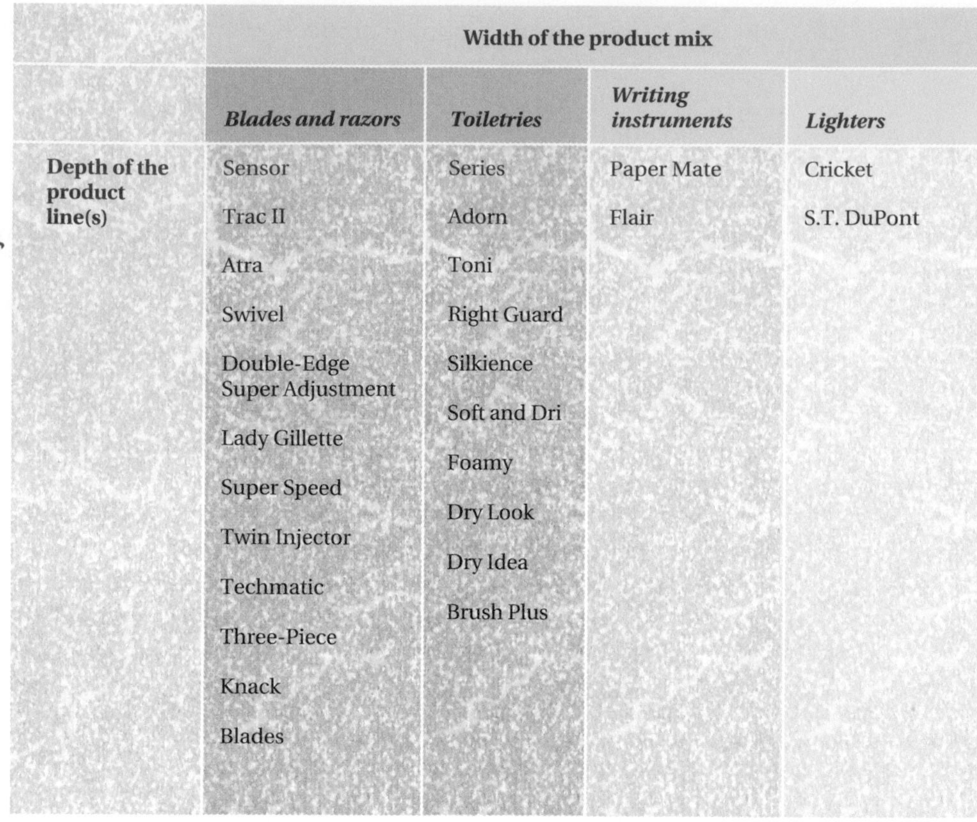

	Width of the product mix			
	Blades and razors	***Toiletries***	***Writing instruments***	***Lighters***
Depth of the product line(s)	Sensor	Series	Paper Mate	Cricket
	Trac II	Adorn	Flair	S.T. DuPont
	Atra	Toni		
	Swivel	Right Guard		
	Double-Edge Super Adjustment	Silkience		
	Lady Gillette	Soft and Dri		
	Super Speed	Foamy		
	Twin Injector	Dry Look		
	Techmatic	Dry Idea		
	Three-Piece	Brush Plus		
	Knack			
	Blades			

Organizations derive several benefits from organizing related items into product lines. Here are five examples:

- *Advertising economies:* Product lines provide economies of scale in advertising. Several products can be advertised under the umbrella of the line. Rising media costs increase the advantages of product line advertising. Campbell's Soup Company, for example, can talk about Campbell's being "m-m-good" and promote the entire line. Advertising a product line can also enhance the corporate name. For example, Heinz's 57 Varieties names both the product line and the corporation.
- *Package uniformity:* A product line allows for package uniformity. All packages in the line may have a common look and still keep their individual identities. Thus one item in the line can advertise another. Some examples include Lean Cuisine frozen dinners, Green Giant frozen vegetables, and Hermes men's toiletries.
- *Standardized components:* Product lines allow firms to standardize components, thus reducing manufacturing and inventory costs. For example, many of the components Samsonite uses in its folding tables and chairs are also used in its patio furniture. General Motors uses many parts on multiple automobile makes and models.
- *Efficient sales and distribution:* A product line enables sales personnel for companies like Procter & Gamble to provide a full range of choices to customers. Distributors and retailers are often more inclined to stock the company's products if it offers a full line. Transportation and warehousing costs are likely to be lower for a product line than for a collection of individual items.
- *Equivalent quality:* A brand name symbolizes a certain quality level to buyers.

Purchasers usually expect and believe that all products in a line are about equal in quality. Consumers expect, for example, that all Kodak films, all Campbell's soups, and all Mary Kay cosmetics will be of similar quality.

Width, Depth, and Consistency

product mix width
Number of product lines that an organization offers.

product line depth
Number of product items in a product line.

product mix consistency
Extent to which product lines are similar in terms of end use, distribution outlets used, target markets, and price range.

Product mix width refers to the number of product lines an organization offers. In Exhibit 9.2, for example, the width of the product mix is four. **Product line depth** is the number of product items in a product line. As shown in Exhibit 9.2, the blades and razors product line consists of twelve product items; the toiletries product line includes ten product items. **Product mix consistency** refers to the extent that product lines are similar in terms of end use, distribution outlets used, target markets, and price range. According to these characteristics, Gillette's product mix is generally consistent. Product line depth and product mix width and consistency are all related to marketing strategy.

Firms increase the depth of product lines to attract buyers with widely different preferences, increase sales and profits by further segmenting the market, capitalize on economies of scale in production and marketing, and even out seasonal sales patterns.

Firms increase the width of their product mix to diversify risk. To generate sales and boost profits, firms spread risk across many product lines rather than depending on only one or two. Firms also widen their product mix to capitalize on established reputations. For example, by introducing new product lines, Kodak capitalized on its image as a leader in photographic products. Kodak's product lines now include film, processing, still cameras, movie cameras, paper, and chemicals. Firms may narrow their product mix, too. Avon Products reduced the width of its product mix by selling its health care division. The company could then focus more on its main business—beauty care products.

By maintaining a consistent product mix, firms like Kodak can secure a powerful market position in a general area of specialization. They also can capitalize on

The Barbie doll product line is exceptionally deep. Barbie has a sumptuous wardrobe, lots of friends, and all the possessions a youngster might dream of.
Courtesy of Mattel

economies of scale in development, manufacturing, and marketing. The McIlhenny Company has profited from the reputation of its Tabasco brand pepper sauce by introducing a Bloody Mary mix and a picanté sauce.[3]

In contrast, some firms choose to develop inconsistent product mixes, to diversify risk and capitalize on new opportunities in unrelated areas. Neither strategy is necessarily better. What works for one firm does not necessarily work for another. The risks of developing an inconsistent product mix tend to exceed the risks of developing a consistent product mix. For example, Avis, the car rental firm, entered the quick-lube business in the late 1980s. The company has opened only 67 franchised quick-lube stations, far fewer than its goal of 200. So bitter are franchisees that many are demanding refunds, and some are filing lawsuits alleging fraud and misrepresentation.[4] Allegheny Ludlum Steel, on the other hand, markets Allegheny Steel, Jacobsen lawn mowers, True Temper tools and sporting goods, Carmet and IPM audio products, and Arnold magnetic tapes. Allegheny Ludlum's product mix is inconsistent and therefore offers few economies of scale in marketing. This strategy, however, does not necessarily pose a handicap.

Extending and Contracting Product Lines

Each product line an organization offers covers a part of the total range of products offered by the entire industry. For example, Lawnboy mowers compete in the medium-high price range of the lawn mower market. **Line extension** occurs when management decides to stretch its product line beyond its current range. A firm can extend its line up, down, or both ways to cover a larger segment of the market. A firm can also increase the depth of a product line by adding items within the current range of products.

line extension
Practice of adding products to a product line.

Downward extension entails introducing a less-expensive product, usually with fewer features or options, to a more price-sensitive segment of the market. IBM extended its product line downward when it brought out personal computers to complement its mainframe computers. The Mercedes 190 series is another example of downward extension.

downward extension
Practice of adding to a product line a less-expensive product with fewer features or options and for a more price-sensitive segment of the market.

In contrast, **upward extension** entails introducing higher-quality products, with more features and options, designed to sell at a higher price. Upward extension targets image-conscious consumers who are less price-sensitive. Toyota and Honda extended their product lines upward when they introduced the Lexus and Acura models, respectively. Dockers Authentics, introduced in 1993, are targeted toward a more upscale consumer than the original Dockers line.[5]

upward extension
Practice of adding to a product line a higher-quality product with more features and options and designed to sell at a higher price.

Downward Extension

Downward extension offers several advantages:

- The firm can tap the price-sensitive buyer.
- A company with a quality image can offer a less-expensive product to the mass market.
- The less-expensive product may discourage a new low-price competitor from entering the market.
- The firm can capitalize on economies of scale in production and distribution.

Beech Aircraft, a maker of expensive private aircraft, recently added less-expensive planes to compete with Piper Aircraft. Marriott Corporation added Marriott Courtyards to its hotel line to compete with firms like Holiday Inns and Ramada Inns in the mid-priced segment of the hotel market.

*Downward extension is not without risks. It may cannibalize sales of the higher-end (and often more profitable) product. The tactic of downward extension may also hurt the line's quality image.

Upward Extension

Upward extension is often harder than downward extension, but the rewards can be substantial. These include higher profit margins, a better growth rate, and the filling out of a product line. In the southwestern United States, several builders of mass-produced, medium-priced homes have successfully branched out into more expensive custom housing.

One of the greatest risks of upward extension is the possible inability to convince buyers of the product's quality. A medium-priced, average image is hard to overcome. Also, if current dealers carrying the company's product cater to middle-class shoppers, target customers for the higher-end (upward-extended) products may feel uncomfortable shopping in middle-class stores. JCPenney has experienced this problem with the general upward extension of its merchandise mix. Finally, higher-end competitors may be well entrenched and respond with their own lower-end brands.

Line Filling

line filling
Practice of increasing the depth of a product line by adding more items, in order to offer a complete product line.

Line filling means increasing the depth of a product line by adding more items within the present range of the product line. Potential benefits of line filling are small increases in profits and an ability to satisfy dealers complaining about lost sales because of missing items in the line. Other advantages include using excess production capacity, becoming the leading full-line firm, and plugging holes to keep competitors out.

Contracting Product Lines

Sometimes product lines become overextended. When this happens, some items in the product line need to be eliminated. What are some symptoms of product line overextension? First, some products in the line are not contributing to profit because of low sales or cannibalization from other product items. Second, manufacturing or marketing resources are being disproportionately allocated to slow-moving products. Third, items in the line have become obsolete because of new product entries in the line or by competitors. Other possible symptoms are listed in Exhibit 10.10 in Chapter 10.

Three major benefits are likely when a firm contracts overextended product lines. First, resources become concentrated on the most important products. Second, managers no longer waste resources trying to improve the sales and profits of poorly performing products. Third, new product items have a greater chance of being successful because more financial and human resources are available to manage them.

Repositioning

Repositioning is changing consumers' perceptions of a product. For example, Kentucky Fried Chicken is trying to reposition itself to attract more health-conscious customers. The strategy includes gradually changing the restaurant's name to KFC, reducing dependence on the word *fried*, and adding grilled, broiled, and baked poultry items to the menu.[6]

Changing demographics, declining sales, or competitors' actions often motivate

firms to reposition established products. For example, the changing demographics of snackers and eroding market share led Frito-Lay to reposition its top-selling brand, Fritos, after fifty-eight years of successfully targeting all ages. The repositioning effort includes making major changes in the Fritos logo and packaging, focusing on those between the ages of 9 and 18, and launching a major new radio and TV advertising campaign.[7]

Modifying Existing Products

Marketing managers must not only decide whether to add new products to their lines to extend them up or down, but they must also decide if and when to modify existing products. **Product modification** changes one or more of a product's characteristics—for example, its quality, functional characteristics, or style.

product modification
Change in one or more of a product's characteristics—for example, its quality, functional characteristics, or style.

A **quality modification** is a change in a product's dependability or durability. Reducing a product's quality may let the manufacturer lower price and appeal to target markets unable to afford the original product. Increasing quality can help the firm better compete with rival firms. Increasing quality can also result in brand loyalty, ability to raise prices, or new market segmentation opportunities. Automobile safety features such as antilock brakes and air bags are examples of quality modifications.

quality modification
Change in a product's dependability or durability.

A **functional modification** is a change in a product's versatility, effectiveness, convenience, or safety. In response to widespread consumer perceptions that aerosol propellants are harmful to the environment, Dow Chemical began offering its bathroom cleaner in a trigger-spray version. The Procter & Gamble deodorant brands Right Guard, Old Spice, and Sure Pro have also been introduced in nonaerosol trigger-spray or pump versions.[8]

functional modification
Change in a product's versatility, effectiveness, convenience, or safety.

A **style modification** is an aesthetic product change rather than a quality or functional change. Clothing manufacturers commonly use style to motivate customers to replace products before they are worn out.

style modification
Aesthetic product change rather than a quality or functional change.

Planned obsolescence is a term commonly used to describe the practice of causing products to become obsolete before they actually need replacement. Some argue that planned obsolescence is wasteful. Some claim it is unethical. Marketers respond that consumers favor style modifications because they like changes in the appearance of goods like clothing and cars. Marketers also contend that consumers, not manufacturers and marketers, decide when styles are obsolete.

planned obsolescence
Practice of changing a product's style so that it becomes outdated before it actually needs replacement.

4 PRODUCT LIFE CYCLES

The **product life cycle** is one of the most familiar concepts in marketing. Few other general concepts have been so widely discussed. Although some researchers have challenged the theoretical basis and managerial value of the product life cycle, most believe it has great potential as a marketing management tool.

product life cycle
Concept describing a product's acceptance in the marketplace over four stages: introduction, growth, maturity, and decline.

The product life cycle concept provides a way to trace the stages of a product's acceptance, from its introduction (birth) to its decline (death). As Exhibit 9.3 shows, a product progresses through four major stages: introduction, growth, maturity, and decline. (Chapter 10 examines the process of developing a new product—transforming a new-product idea into a marketable product.)

Note that the product life cycle illustrated in Exhibit 9.3 does not refer to any one brand. Rather it refers to the life cycle for a product category or product class. A **product category** includes all brands that satisfy a particular type of need—for example, passenger cars, cigarettes, soft drinks, and coffee.

product category
All brands that satisfy a particular type of need.

The time a product spends in any one stage of the life cycle may vary dramatically. Some products, such as fad items, move through the entire cycle in weeks. Others, such as electric clothes washers and dryers, stay in the maturity stage for decades. Changes in a product, its uses, its image, or its positioning can extend that product's life cycle.

The product life cycle concept does not tell managers the length of a product's life cycle or its duration in any stage. It does not dictate marketing strategy. It is simply a tool to help marketers forecast future events and suggest appropriate strategies. Exhibit 9.3 illustrates the typical life cycle for a consumer convenience good, such as a washer or dryer. Exhibit 9.4 illustrates typical life cycles for styles (such as formal, business, or casual clothing), fashions (such as miniskirts or stirrup pants), and fads (such as leopard-print clothing).

introductory stage
First stage of the product life cycle, which represents the full-scale launch of a new product into the marketplace.

Introductory Stage

The **introductory stage** of the product life cycle represents the full-scale launch of a new product into the marketplace. Information data bases for personal use, room-

Exhibit 9.3

The Four Stages of the Product Life Cycle

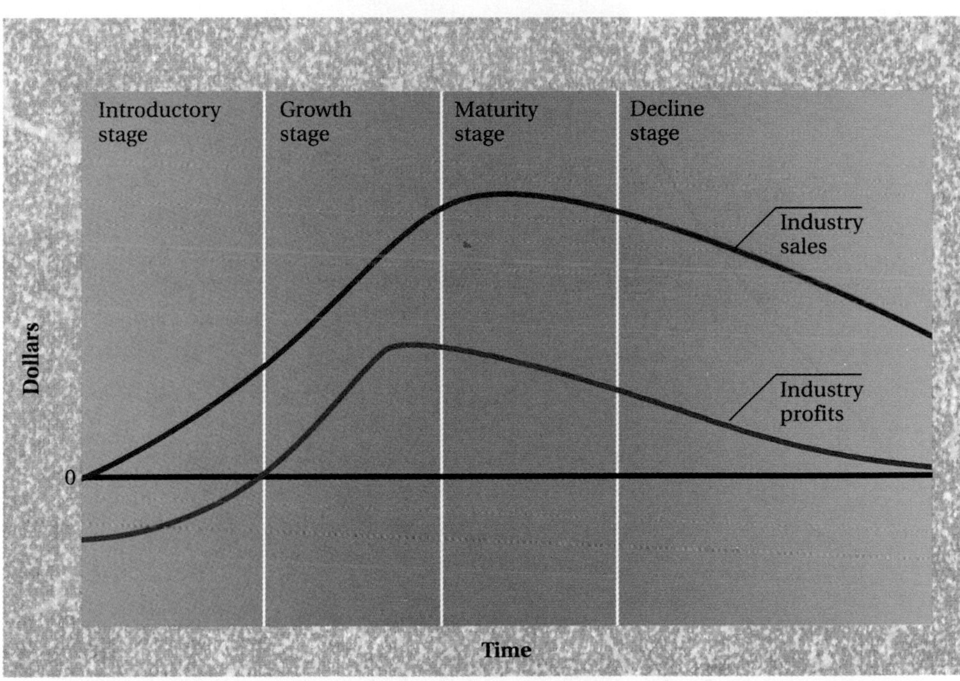

Exhibit 9.4

Style, Fashion, and Fad Life Cycles

deodorizing air conditioning filters, and wind-powered home-electric generators—all are product categories that have recently entered the product life cycle. A high failure rate, little competition, frequent product modification, and limited distribution typify the introduction stage of the product life cycle.

Marketing costs in the introductory stage are normally high. High dealer margins are often needed to obtain adequate distribution, and incentives are needed to get consumers to try the new product. Advertising expenses are typically high because of the need to educate consumers about the new product's benefits. Production costs are also often high in this stage, as product and manufacturing flaws are identified and corrected and efforts are undertaken to develop mass-production economies. As Exhibit 9.3 illustrates, sales normally increase slowly during the introductory stage. Moreover, profits are usually negative because of research and development costs, factory tooling, and high introduction costs.

Optical compact discs, used for interactive multimedia presentations and digital photography, are in the introductory stage of the product life cycle.
© Scott Morgan/Westlight

The length of the introductory phase is largely determined by product characteristics, such as the product's advantages over substitute products, the educational effort required, and management's commitment of resources to the new item. A short introductory period is usually preferred, to help reduce the impact of negative earnings and cash flow. As soon as the product gets off the ground, the financial burden should begin to diminish. Also, a short introduction helps dispel some of the uncertainty surrounding the new product.

Promotional strategy in the introductory stage focuses on developing product awareness and informing consumers about the product category's potential benefits. At this stage the communications challenge is to stimulate primary demand—demand for the product in general rather than a specific brand. Intensive personal selling is often required to gain acceptance for the product among wholesalers and retailers. Promotion of convenience products often requires heavy consumer sampling and couponing. Shopping and specialty products in this stage demand educational advertising and personal selling to the final consumer.

Growth Stage

growth stage
Second stage of the product life cycle, characterized by increasing sales, heightened competition, and healthy profits.

If a product category survives the introductory stage, it advances to the **growth stage** of the life cycle. In this stage, sales typically grow at an increasing rate, many competitors enter the market, large companies may start to acquire small pioneering firms, and profits are healthy. Emphasis switches from primary demand promotion (for example, compact disc players) to aggressive brand advertising and communication of the differences between brands (for example, Sony versus Panasonic and RCA).

Distribution becomes a major key to success during the growth stage, as well as in later stages. Manufacturers scramble to acquire dealers and distributors and to build long-term relationships. Without adequate distribution, it is impossible to establish a strong market position.

Toward the end of the growth phase, prices normally begin falling and profits peak. Price reductions result from increasing economies of scale and increased competition. Also, most firms have recovered their development costs by now, and their priority is in increasing or retaining market share and enhancing profits.

Maturity Stage

maturity stage
Third stage of the product life cycle, in which sales begin to level off and the market approaches saturation.

A period during which sales continue to increase, but at a decreasing rate, signals the beginning of the **maturity stage** of the life cycle. New users cannot be added indefinitely, and sooner or later the market approaches saturation. Normally, this is the longest stage of the product life cycle. Many major household appliances are in the maturity stage of their life cycles. For example, over half of all washer, dryer, and refrigerator purchases are replacements for worn-out products rather than purchases by new users.

For shopping products and many specialty products, annual models begin to appear during the maturity stage. Product lines are lengthened to appeal to many market segments. Service and repair assume more important roles as manufacturers strive to distinguish their products from others. Product design changes tend to become stylistic (how can the product be made different?) rather than functional (how can the product be made better?). Powdered drink mixes, electric drip coffee pots, and high-meat-content dog foods are examples of products that are in the maturity stage.

As prices and profits continue to fall, marginal competitors start dropping out of the market. Dealer margins also shrink, resulting in less shelf space for mature items, lower dealer inventories, and a general reluctance to promote the product.

Promotion to dealers often intensifies during this stage in order to retain loyalty. Heavy consumer promotion by the manufacturer is also required to maintain market share.

Consider these well-known examples of competition in the maturity stage: the so-called "cola war" featuring Coke and Pepsi, the "beer war" featuring Anheuser-Busch's Budweiser brands and Philip Morris' Miller brands, and the "burger wars" pitting leader McDonald's against challengers Burger King and Wendy's.

In the coffee product category, Kraft General Foods' Maxwell House and Procter & Gamble's Folgers brand each accounted for about 30 percent of the $3.9 billion market. After several years of sluggish sales, Maxwell House launched new, hard-hitting comparative ads claiming that consumers prefer its taste to Folgers. Folgers protested to Kraft General Foods and the major television networks, asserting that the results were wrong and the advertising was unfair. Harvey Dzodin, vice president of commercial clearance at Capital Cities/ABC, said, "We can't comment on the specifics of the challenge, but the matter is percolating through the system, and we're attempting to filter through the facts."[9]

Another characteristic of the maturity stage is the emergence of so-called "niche marketers" who target narrow, well-defined, underserved segments of a market. Starbucks Coffee, for example, targets its gourmet line at the only segment of the coffee market that is growing: new, younger, more affluent coffee drinkers.[10]

Decline Stage

decline stage
Fourth and final stage of the product life cycle, in which sales drop and falling demand forces many competitors out of the market.

A long-run drop in sales signals the beginning of the **decline stage.** The rate of decline is governed by how rapidly consumer tastes change or substitute products are adopted. Many convenience products and fad items lose their market overnight, leaving large inventories of unsold items, such as designer jeans. Others die more slowly, like citizen band (CB) radios, black-and-white console television sets, and nonelectronic wristwatches.

Falling demand forces many competitors from the market. Often a small specialty firm will buy the manufacturing rights for a product and sell it to that segment of the market still desiring the product. Two Minnesotans acquired Ipana tooth-

paste after a major packaged-goods company dropped it. Within five years the new firm had over 1.5 million loyal Ipana users.

Some firms have developed successful strategies for marketing products in the decline stage of the product life cycle. They eliminate all nonessential marketing expenses and let the brand decline at a normal rate. Cutting advertising does not hurt sales in the decline stage. S&P Company has successfully adopted this strategy. By buying has-been and never-were brands of beer and offering them at discount prices, S&P profits handsomely. S&P has become the sixth largest brewer in the United States, based on market share.[11]

Extending Product Life Cycles

Products in the maturity stage of the product life cycle do not necessarily slip directly into decline and then elimination. Sometimes product life cycles can be extended, as illustrated in Exhibit 9.5. Marketing managers use several strategies to extend product life cycles:

- *Promoting more frequent use of the product by current customers:* The Florida Orange Growers Association successfully used this strategy in its "Orange Juice Is Not Just for Breakfast" campaign. Overall juice consumption rose following TV ads reminding people that orange juice is a healthy, refreshing beverage suitable for any time of the day.
- *Finding new target markets for the product:* Johnson's Baby Shampoo was remarkably successful in adding mothers, sisters, and later fathers and brothers to their original target market of infants. The new theme, "It's mild enough to use every day," was the only change in the product's marketing strategy, yet the target market's size expanded several hundred percent.
- *Finding new uses for the product:* After decades of level sales, Arm & Hammer baking soda was promoted as a refrigerator freshener, plumbing system cleaner, litter box freshener, and even a toothpaste. Sales skyrocketed when each new suggested use appeared in print and television advertisements.
- *Pricing the product below the market:* Bic pens and Timex watches revolutionized their industries. Their competitors had not successfully introduced prod-

Exhibit 9.5

Extending the Product Life Cycle

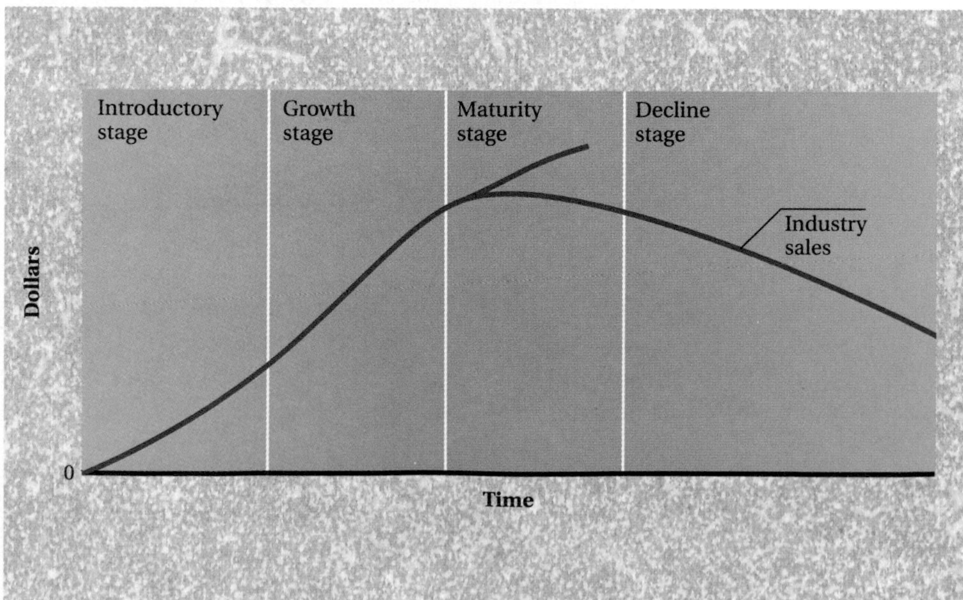

Marketing mix strategy	Product life cycle stage			
	Introduction	*Growth*	*Maturity*	*Decline*
Product strategy	Limited number of models; frequent product modifications	Expanded number of models; frequent product modifications	Large number of models	Elimination of unprofitable models and brands
Distribution strategy	Distribution usually limited, depending on product; intensive efforts and high margins often needed to attract wholesalers and retailers	Expanded number of dealers; intensive efforts to establish long-term relationships with wholesalers and retailers	Extensive number of dealers; margins declining; intensive efforts to retain distributors and shelf space	Unprofitable outlets phased out
Promotion strategy	Develop product awareness; stimulate primary demand; use intensive personal selling to distributors; use sampling and couponing for consumers	Stimulate selective demand; advertise brand aggressively	Stimulate selective demand; advertise brand aggressively; promote heavily to retain dealers and customers	Phase out all promotion
Pricing strategy	Prices are usually high to recover development costs (see Chapter 19)	Prices begin to fall toward end of growth stage as result of competitive pressure	Prices continue to fall	Prices stabilize at relatively low level; small price rises are possible if competition is negligible

Exhibit 9.6

Typical Marketing Strategies Used by Manufacturers During Stages of the Product Life Cycle

ucts of acceptable quality at low prices. The introduction of these two brands substantially changed the shape of the ballpoint pen and wristwatch product life cycles.

- *Developing new distribution channels:* For years Woolite fabric cleaner was sold only in department stores. Then American Home Products introduced the product in supermarkets and grocery stores without changing the product, the price, or the promotional appeal. Sales tripled in the first year.[12]
- *Adding new ingredients or deleting old ingredients:* The laundry detergent industry has relied on this strategy to extend the life cycles of brands, adding whiteners, brighteners, bleaches, scents, and various other ingredients and attributes. Unscented Bounce, Charmin-Free, decaffeinated beverages, and sugar-free soft drinks all are products with deleted ingredients.
- *Making a dramatic new guarantee:* Spray 'n Wash shifted from declining sales to rapidly growing sales almost immediately after offering this guarantee: "If Spray 'n Wash doesn't remove a stain from a shirt—any shirt—we'll buy you a new shirt."[13]

Implications for Marketing Management

The product life cycle concept encourages marketing managers to plan so they can take the initiative instead of reacting to past events. The product life cycle is especially useful as a predicting or forecasting tool. Since products pass through distinctive stages, it is often possible to estimate a product's location on the curve using historical data. Profits, like sales, tend to follow a predictable path over a product's life cycle. Exhibit 9.6 briefly summarizes typical marketing strategies during each stage of the product life cycle.

Mercedes-Benz has a well-known, prestigious brand mark that helps everyone identify its products on the street.

5 BRANDING

The success of any business or consumer product depends in part on the target market's ability to distinguish one product from another. Branding is the major tool marketers have to distinguish their products from the competition's.

A **brand** is a name, term, symbol, design, or combination thereof that identifies a seller's products and differentiates them from competitors' products. A **brand name** is that part of a brand that can be spoken, including letters (GM, YMCA); words (Chevrolet); and numbers (WD-40, 7-Eleven). The elements of a brand that cannot be spoken are called the **brand mark**—for example, the well-known Mercedes-Benz and Delta Airlines symbols.

brand
Name, term, symbol, design, or combination thereof that identifies a seller's products and differentiates them from competitors' products.

brand name
Part of a brand that can be spoken, including letters, words, and numbers.

brand mark
Elements of a brand that cannot be spoken, such as symbols.

brand equity
Value of successful company and brand names.

Benefits of Branding

Branding has three main purposes: identification, repeat sales, and new product sales. The most important purpose is identification. Branding allows marketers to distinguish their products from all others. Many brand names are familiar to consumers and indicate quality. Exhibit 9.7 lists, in order, the ten brand names that U.S. consumers believe signify the highest-quality products.[14]

The term **brand equity** refers to the value of company and brand names. Brand equity, not the value of the company's facilities, was the reason RJR Nabisco was bought out for the record price of $30 billion in 1988. RJR Nabisco brands with hefty brand equity include Del Monte fruits and vegetables, Ritz crackers, and Camel cigarettes.[15]

Exhibit 9.7

The Most Respected Brand Names in the United States

Source: Peg Masterson, "American Brand Names Gain Clout," *Advertising Age*, 30 March 1992, p. 47. Copyright, Crain Communications Inc., 1992.

1. Disney World/Disneyland	6. Levi's
2. Kodak	7. Mercedes-Benz
3. Hallmark	8. Arm & Hammer
4. United Parcel Service	9. AT&T
5. Fisher-Price	10. IBM

The best source of future sales is satisfied customers. Branding helps consumers identify products they wish to buy again and avoid those they do not. Two recent studies illustrate this point. One revealed that 62 percent of consumers surveyed buy only well-known brand names. The other found that 61 percent of consumers surveyed regard brand names as an assurance of quality.[16]

master brand
Brand so dominant in consumers' minds that they think of it immediately when a product category, use situation, product attribute, or customer benefit is mentioned.

brand loyalty
Consumer's consistent preference for one brand over all others in its product category.

The term **master brand** has been used to refer to a brand so dominant in consumers' minds that they think of it immediately when a product category, use situation, product attribute, or customer benefit is mentioned.[17] Exhibit 9.8 lists the master brands in several product categories. How many other brands can you name in these eleven product categories? Can you name any other product categories in which the master brands listed in Exhibit 9.8 compete? Probably not many. Campbell's means soup to consumers; it doesn't mean high-quality food products.

Brand loyalty, a consistent preference for one brand over all others, is quite high in some product categories. As Exhibit 9.9 shows, over half the users in some product categories are loyal to one brand. Brand identity is essential to developing brand loyalty.

The third main purpose of branding is to facilitate new product sales. Company and brand names like those listed in Exhibit 9.7 are extremely useful when introducing new products. Of the 6,125 new products placed on shelves in the first five months of 1991, just 5 percent bore new brand names. The rest were line extensions.[18]

Types of Brands

Firms face complex branding decisions. As Exhibit 9.10 illustrates, the first decision is whether to brand at all. Some firms actually use the lack of a brand name as a selling point. These unbranded products are called generic products. Firms that decide to brand their products may choose to follow a policy of individual branding (different brands for different products) or a policy of family branding (common names for different products). Some firms choose to market manufacturers' brands, private (distributor) brands, or both.

Exhibit 9.8

Master Brands in Selected Product Categories

Source: Peter H. Farquhar, Julia Y. Han, Paul M. Herr, and Yuji Ijiri, "Strategies for Leveraging Master Brands," *Marketing Research*, September 1992, pp. 32–43.

Product category	Master brand
Baking soda	Arm & Hammer
Adhesive bandages	Band-Aid
Rum	Bacardi
Antacids	Alka-Seltzer
Gelatin	Jell-O
Soup	Campbell's
Salt	Morton
Toy trains	Lionel
Cream cheese	Philadelphia
Crayons	Crayola
Petroleum jelly	Vaseline

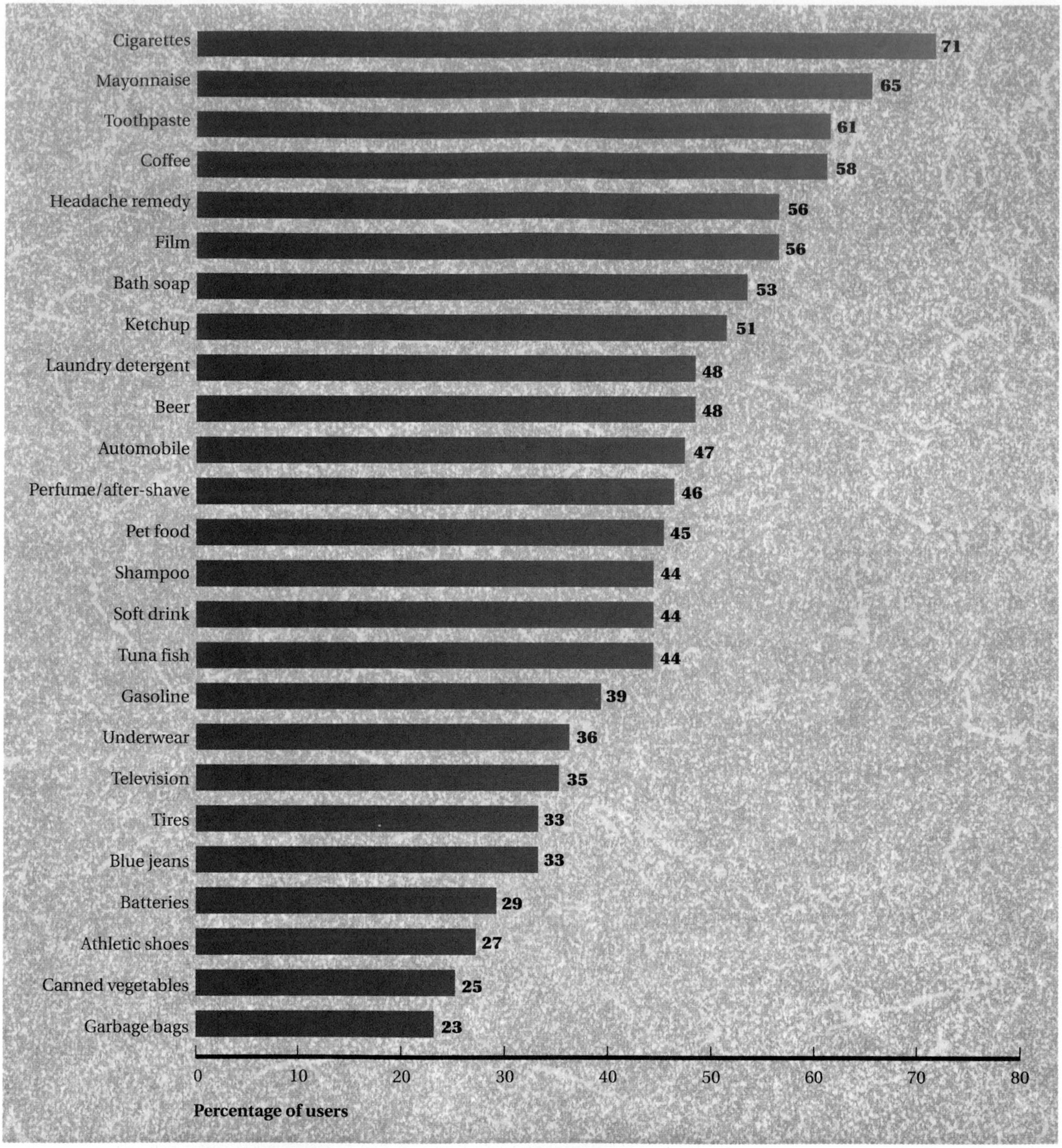

Product	Percentage of users
Cigarettes	71
Mayonnaise	65
Toothpaste	61
Coffee	58
Headache remedy	56
Film	56
Bath soap	53
Ketchup	51
Laundry detergent	48
Beer	48
Automobile	47
Perfume/after-shave	46
Pet food	45
Shampoo	44
Soft drink	44
Tuna fish	44
Gasoline	39
Underwear	36
Television	35
Tires	33
Blue jeans	33
Batteries	29
Athletic shoes	27
Canned vegetables	25
Garbage bags	23

0 10 20 30 40 50 60 70 80

Percentage of users

Exhibit 9.9

Percentage of These Products' Users Who Are Loyal to One Brand

Source: Ronald Alsop, "Brand Loyalty Is Rarely Blind Loyalty," *The Wall Street Journal*, 19 October 1989, p. B1. Reprinted by permission of *The Wall Street Journal*, © 1989 Dow Jones & Company. All Rights Reserved Worldwide.

Generic Products

A **generic product** is typically a no-frills, no–brand name, low-cost product. The concept of generic products became popular in the late 1970s. (Note that a generic product and a brand name that becomes generic, such as cellophane, are not the same thing.) Generic products have captured significant market shares in some product categories, such as canned fruits, canned vegetables, and paper products.

The main appeal of generics is their low price. Generic grocery products are usually 30 to 40 percent less expensive than manufacturers' brands in the same product category and 20 to 25 percent less expensive than retailer-owned brands.

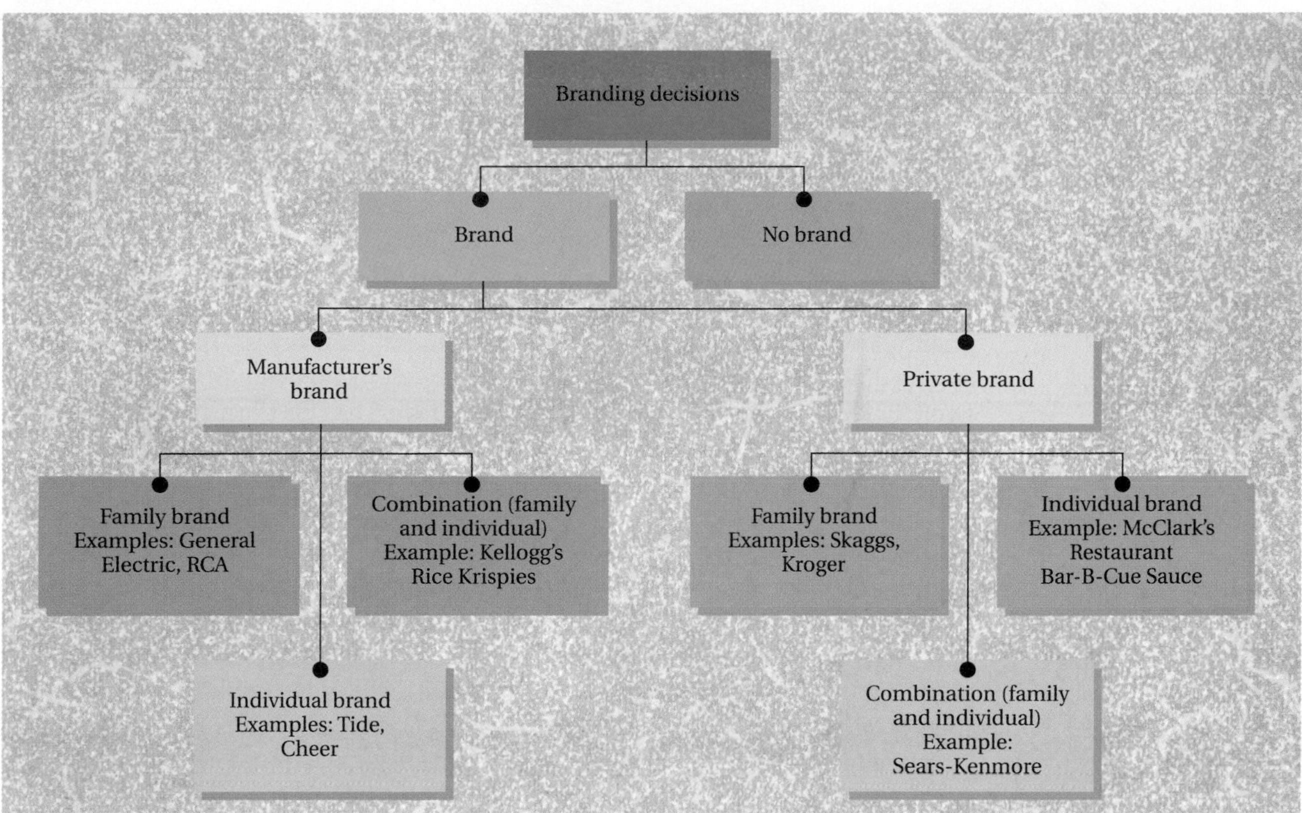

Exhibit 9.10

Major Branding Decisions

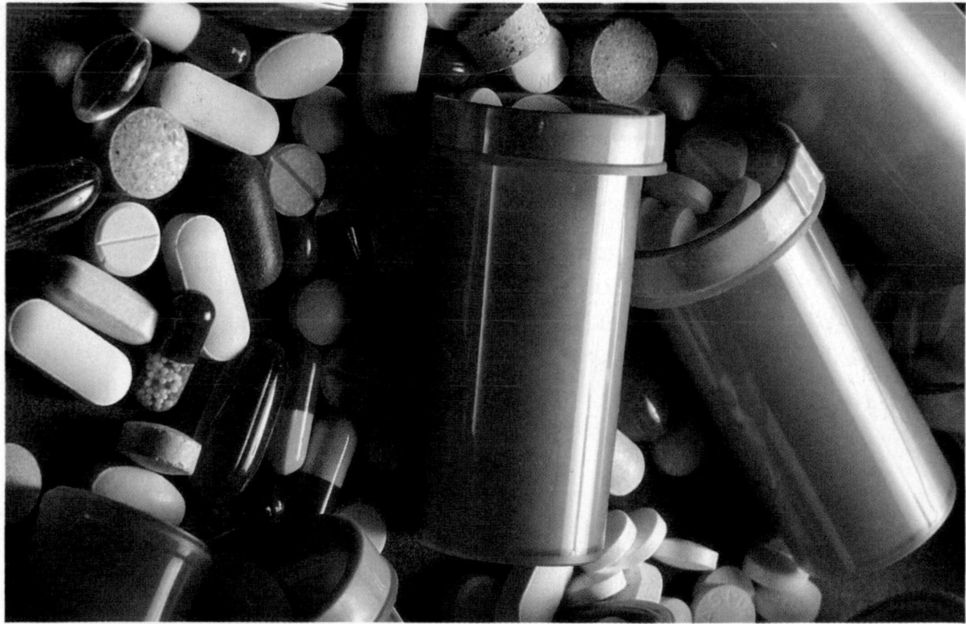

Generic pharmaceuticals have become a major factor in the drug market. They often sell for considerably less than their brand-name competitors.

generic product
No-frills, no–brand name, low-cost product.

Pharmaceuticals is another product category where generics have made inroads. When patents on successful pharmaceutical products expire, low-cost generics rapidly appear on the market. Sales of generic pharmaceuticals in the United States exceeded $3 billion in 1991. When the patent on Merck's popular antiarthritis drug Clinoril expired in 1990, sales declined by 50 percent almost immediately. To avoid a similar loss of sales, Merck introduced its own generic version when its patent on Dolobid expired in 1992.[19]

Individual Brands

individual branding
Practice of using a different brand name for each product.

Many companies use different brand names for different products; this concept is referred to as **individual branding.** Companies use individual brands when their products vary greatly in use or performance. For instance, it would not make sense to use the same brand name for a pair of dress socks and a baseball bat. Individual brands are also used when products vary greatly in quality. Holiday Inn distinguishes its upscale hotels with the name Holiday Inn Crowne Plaza. This name enables management to maintain the prestigious image of this high-quality product while fiercely competing in a less prestigious market with Holiday Inn, a lesser-quality, lower-priced brand that offers fewer amenities. Likewise, Procter & Gamble targets different segments of the laundry detergent market with Bold, Cheer, Dash, Dreft, Era, Gain, Ivory Snow, Oxydol, Solo, and Tide. The Dial Corp. markets Dial and Tone soaps, Brillo soap pads, Purex bleach and detergent, Parson's ammonia, Treet luncheon meats, and a host of other brands.[20]

Family Brands

family brand
Practice of using the same brand name to market several different products.

A company that markets several different products under the same brand name is using a **family brand.** For example, Sony's family brand includes radios, television sets, stereos, and other electronic products. Campbell's Soup Company uses family branding on its wide assortment of soups. Campbell's introduced over 200 new soup products in the late 1980s, all identified as Campbell's soups.[21]

A family brand, however, is no guarantee of success. A brand name can only be stretched so far. Such products as Bic pantyhose, Life Savers gum, and Sara Lee dinner entrees soon failed, and Dial deodorant hasn't nearly matched the success of the bar soap. Bic was an acceptable brand for lighters and pens but not wearing apparel. Johnson & Johnson was surprised when consumers didn't flock to buy its baby aspirin. Research revealed that the Johnson & Johnson name was synonymous with gentle baby products. Further research showed that parents were more concerned with quickly reducing the child's fever than with providing gentleness.

Manufacturers' Brands

manufacturer's brand
Manufacturer's name used as a brand name.

The brand name of a manufacturer—such as Kodak, Lazy Boy, and Fruit-of-the-Loom—is called a **manufacturer's brand.** Sometimes the term *national brand* is used as a synonym for manufacturer's brand. This term is not always accurate, however, since many manufacturers serve only regional markets. The term *manufacturer's brand* more precisely defines the brand's owner. Some manufacturers assign individual brand names to different products; others use family branding.

Private Brands

private brand
Brand name that a wholesaler or a retailer uses for products it sells.

A **private brand** is a brand name owned by a wholesaler or a retailer. Hunt Club (a JCPenney brand), Sam's American Choice (Wal-Mart), and IGA (Independent Grocers' Association) are all private brands. Private brands account for 18 percent of U.S. supermarket unit sales and about 14 percent of dollar sales.[22] Supermarket retailers and wholesalers generally expect the quality of private brand merchandise to improve in the future, providing customers with better value and retailers with opportunities to differentiate themselves from competitors.[23]

Using Manufacturers' and Private Brands

Most wholesalers are too small to develop their own brands and rely instead on manufacturers' brands. But as retailers and wholesalers grow, they often must decide whether to establish their own private brands or to continue selling only manufacturers' brands.

The advantages of staying with manufacturers' brands include the following:

- Heavy advertising to the consumer by manufacturers like Procter & Gamble helps develop strong consumer loyalties.
- Well-known manufacturers' brands, such as Kodak and Fisher-Price, can attract new customers and enhance the dealer's prestige.
- Many manufacturers offer rapid delivery, enabling the dealer to carry less inventory.
- If a dealer happens to sell a manufacturer's brand of poor quality, the customer may simply switch brands but remain loyal to the dealer.

The advantages of developing private brands include these:

- Manufacturers typically offer a lower gross margin (sales price minus cost of goods sold) than a dealer can earn on its own brand. In addition, because the private brand is exclusive, there is less pressure to mark the price down to meet competition.
- A manufacturer can decide to drop a brand or a dealer at any time or even to become a direct competitor to its dealers.
- A private brand ties the customer to the dealer. A person who wants a DieHard battery must go to Sears.
- Dealers have no control over the intensity of distribution of manufacturers' brands. Wal-Mart store managers don't have to worry about competing with other sellers of Sam's American Choice products or Ol' Roy dog food. They know that these brands are sold only in Wal-Mart and Sam's Wholesale Club stores.[24]

However, these advantages can be offset by some important disadvantages associated with private brands:

- Dealers must market the brand, thus cutting into the higher gross margin.
- To obtain a favorable price, dealers must often buy in large quantities. Thus dealers incur all the costs and risks, such as deterioration and obsolescence, of carrying large inventories.
- If the product is of poor quality, customers have only the dealers (wholesalers or retailers) to blame. Therefore, dealers may lose the customers.
- Some dealers, particularly discounters, have trouble promoting their own brands because consumers perceive them as lower in quality. Kmart, for example, has begun adding more manufacturers' brands in recent years.

Trademarks

trademark
Legal, exclusive right to use a product brand name or other identifying mark.

service mark
Trademark for a service.

A **trademark** is a legal term indicating the owner's exclusive right to use a brand or part of a brand. Others are prohibited from using the brand without permission. A **service mark** performs the same function for services, such as H&R Block and Weight Watchers. Parts of a brand or other product identification may qualify for trademark protection—for example:

- Shapes, such as the Jeep front grill and the Coca-Cola bottle or even buildings like Pizza Hut.
- Ornamental color or design, such as the decoration on Nike tennis shoes, the

The Green Giant started out in 1925 *(top)* as a fur-dressed muscleman hoisting the company's giant green peas. He was added to the label as an afterthought, to support the Green Giant brand name. In 1935 he turned green, got a new leaf suit, and started smiling *(bottom)*. In that guise he solidified the company's claim that Green Giant is a brand name instead of a descriptive term.

Courtesy of Pillsbury Co.

black-and-copper color combination of a Duracell battery, Levi's small tag on the left side of the rear pocket of its jeans, or the cut-off black cone on the top of Cross pens.

- Catchy phrases, such as Prudential's "Own a piece of the rock," Merrill Lynch's "We're bullish on America," and Budweiser's "This Bud's for you."
- Abbreviations, such as Bud, Coke, or The Met.

Rights to a trademark last as long as the mark is used. Normally, if the firm does not use it for two years, the trademark is considered abandoned. If a new user picks up the trademark after the owner abandons it, the new user can claim exclusive ownership of the mark.

The Lanham Act of 1946 specifies what types of marks can be protected and the remedies available for trademark violations. When an organization is convicted of trademark infringement, it faces severe penalties. For example, the injured party can sue for triple the damages actually suffered and any profits the offending firm made from the mark. Federal law also allows for the destruction of all materials bearing the infringing mark. A company whose warehouse is filled with items bearing the illegal mark could end up losing a lot.

An old law required that a trademark be used in interstate commerce before it could be registered. The Trademark Revision Act of 1988 allows organizations to register trademarks based on a bona fide intention to use the mark (normally within six months following the issuance of the trademark). Furthermore, this act allows a company to register its trademark for ten years, compared with twenty years under the old law. To renew the trademark, the company must prove it is using it.

generic product name
Name that identifies a product by class or type and cannot be trademarked.

Companies that fail to protect their trademarks face the problem of their product names becoming generic. A **generic product name** identifies a product by class or type and cannot be trademarked. Former brand names that were not sufficiently protected by their owners and were subsequently declared to be generic product names in U.S. courts include aspirin, cellophane, linoleum, thermos, kerosene, monopoly, cola, and shredded wheat.

Companies like Rolls Royce, Cross, Xerox, Levi's, Frigidaire, and McDonald's aggressively enforce their trademarks. Rolls Royce, Coca-Cola, and Xerox even run newspaper and magazine ads stating that their names are trademarks and should not be used as descriptive or generic terms. Some ads threaten lawsuits against competitors that violate trademarks. In 1992, Xerox began a year-long ad campaign throughout the Commonwealth of Independent States to combat the growing problem of trademark infringement in the former Soviet Union.[25]

Despite severe penalties for trademark violations, trademark infringement lawsuits are not uncommon. One of the major battles is over brand names that closely resemble another brand. Coors Brewing Co., for example, sued Robert Corr, who produces a line of soft drinks under the name Corr's Beverages. Hyatt Hotels has blocked Hyatt Legal Services from featuring the term *Hyatt* in its advertising.

INTERNATIONAL PERSPECTIVES

Where Trademarks Are Up for Grabs

Copycat goods and trademarks are epidemic in South Korea. Going well beyond pirated computer software and fake designer goods from struggling mom-and-pop factories and backstreet markets, copycat products are solidly in the Korean mainstream. Even the biggest companies in South Korea mimic some of the world's best-known products, and they sell their wares in the best department stores and supermarkets. . . .

In the soap section, Tie laundry detergent bears the orange box and whirlpool design of Procter & Gamble's stalwart Tide brand. However, P&G doesn't make Tie or license it. A subsidiary of the giant Lucky Goldstar group produces it.

Nearby is white bar soap packaged much like P&G's Ivory. But it's either White soap, also from Lucky, or Bory, from Dong San Fat & Oil Industry Company. Dong San, which makes Dial deodorant soap under license from a subsidiary of The Dial Corp. of the United States, faces competition from a brand called Date, which apes Dial's logo and gold package design.

Similarly, Pizza Heart, a local restaurant chain, sounds like Pizza Hut, the PepsiCo chain. And because *v*'s sound like *b*'s, Bory soap sounds much like Ivory. A spokesperson for Dong San, Bory's maker, says, "It's totally different from Ivory because it is spelled B-o-r-y and Ivory is spelled I-v-o-r-y."

In the long run, Korean companies using the copycat strategy have severely limited themselves. Although they are entrenched in the Korean market of 44 million people, the businesses can't take brands such as Tie and Juicy & Fresh into much bigger markets abroad, including the United States and much of Europe, where such trademarks are better protected.

"If they try to sell those products outside Korea, we can stop them," says William Piet, a spokesperson for Wrigley. "If they had been more creative, they'd be more competitive on the world market."

Most people would agree that it is unethical to intentionally deceive customers about the brands of products they are buying. But where do you draw the line? Should Ivory have a monopoly on soap packages with a white background and blue lettering? Is the brand Bory soap so close to Ivory that consumers will be deceived? What actions, if any, do you think the U.S. government should take to get the South Korean government to prohibit trademark infringements by South Korean companies?

Source: Adapted from Damon Darling, "Where Trademarks Are Up for Grabs," *The Wall Street Journal*, 5 December 1989, p. B-1. Reprinted by permission of *The Wall Street Journal*,

Companies must also contend with fake or unauthorized brands, such as fake Levi's, Mickey Mouse shirts, Rolex watches, and Louis Vuitton handbags. Levi Strauss & Co. has spent over $2 million on more than 600 investigations of counterfeit Levi's jeans. Other companies, including IBM and Coca-Cola, are very aggressive in trying to identify and eliminate counterfeiters.[26] The International Perspectives article above deals with protecting trademarks in some foreign countries.

6 PACKAGING

Packages have always served a practical function. That is, they hold contents together or protect goods as they move through the distribution channel. Today, however, **packaging** is also a container for protecting and promoting the product.

packaging
Container for protecting and promoting a product.

Packaging Functions

The three most important functions of packaging are to contain and protect products, promote products, and facilitate product storage, use, and convenience. A fourth function of packaging that is becoming increasingly important is to facilitate recycling and reduce environmental damage.

Containing and Protecting Products

The most obvious function of packaging is to contain products that are liquid, granular, or otherwise divisible. Packaging also enables manufacturers, wholesalers, and retailers to market products in specific quantities, such as ounces.

Physical protection is another obvious function of packaging. Most products are handled several times between the time they are manufactured, harvested, or otherwise produced and the time they are consumed or used.

Many products are shipped, stored, and inspected several times between production and consumption. Some, like milk, need to be refrigerated. Others, like beer, are sensitive to light. Still others, like medicines and bandages, need to be kept sterile. Packages protect products from breakage, evaporation, spillage, spoilage, light, heat, cold, infestation, and many other conditions. Some packages are tamper-proof or child-proof, but others are designed to be easy to open.

Promoting Products

In 1991, over 15,000 new products were introduced in U.S. supermarkets alone.[27] To get attention on such crowded shelves, marketers are relying on packaging. Thus a key role of packaging in the 1990s is product promotion.

Packaging does more than identify the brand, list ingredients, specify features, and give directions. A package differentiates a product from competing products and may associate a new product with a family of other products from the same manufacturer. A new Campbell's soup, with the familiar red label, would be a good example of association. Packages use designs, colors, shapes, and materials to try to influence consumers' perceptions and buying behavior. Packages are the last opportunity marketers have to influence buyers before they make purchase decisions.

Consumers associate colors with products. In one study, green was identified with vegetables by 92 percent of the respondents—a fact not unnoticed by Green Giant.[28] Green Giant repackaged its frozen vegetables using a "sea of green" package design. The goal was to create a strong brand identity in the freezer case. Yellow, the color of Dole's labels, is associated with canned fruit. Red and pink have long been associated with processed meats and white and blue with bread and butter products.

Packaging has a measurable effect on sales. Quaker Oats revised the package for Rice-A-Roni without making any other changes in marketing strategy and experienced a 44 percent increase in sales in one year.[29] Warner-Lambert packaged its Tracer razor in a new design that allows consumers to test the razor's flexible head without opening the package.[30]

Packages are also very important in establishing a brand's image. Coca-Cola USA recently redesigned the Fresca soft-drink bottle to appeal to upscale adults.[31] Procter & Gamble relied solely on packaging to reposition Safeguard from a male body soap to an antibacterial deodorant soap for the whole family.[32]

Some firms modify package sizes instead of raising prices. The following Ethics in Marketing example describes a practice that is sometimes called "downsizing."

Facilitating Storage, Use, and Convenience

Wholesalers and retailers prefer packages that are easy to ship, store, and stock on shelves. They also like packages that protect products, prevent spoilage or breakage, and extend the product's shelf life. The new variety in disposable diapers, described at the beginning of this chapter, has caused a storage problem for many retailers, who now must decide how many items to stock in a limited amount of space.

Consumers' requirements for convenience cover many dimensions. Consumers are constantly seeking items that are easy to handle, open, and reclose. They also want reusable and disposable packages. Surveys conducted by *Sales & Marketing Management* magazine revealed that consumers dislike—and avoid buying—leaky

ETHICS IN MARKETING

Less Product for the Same Price

For more than thirty years, StarKist Seafood put 6-1/2 ounces of tuna—the industry standard—into its regular-size can. Check a store shelf today, though, and you'll find StarKist's cans weigh 3/8 of an ounce less, for exactly the same price. The result: a nearly 5.8 percent price increase.

What StarKist did to its cans is called "downsizing"—decreasing package size while maintaining price. In a recession, manufacturers say, downsizing helps them hold the line on prices despite rising costs. But manufacturers use the practice in inflationary periods, too, as a way of keeping prices from rising beyond the psychological barrier for their products. . . .

StarKist, a unit of the H.J. Heinz Co., defends its downsizing, saying that the new can handles and stacks better and uses less steel—a boon to the environment. A company spokeswoman also argues that the smaller-size can has a higher ratio of tuna to the oil or water it's packed in, benefiting the consumer.

Critics of downsizing argue that marketers use it to raise prices without telling consumers they're paying more for less. Some argue that the practice is deceptive. What do you think? Is downsizing a deceptive practice? Do consumers notice when the weight or unit count per package is reduced? Comment on the StarKist defense for downsizing. Can you name other brands that have been downsized in recent years?

Source: Adapted from John B. Hinge, "Critics Call Cuts in Package Size Deceptive Move," *The Wall Street Journal*, 5 February 1991, pp. B1, B6.

ice cream boxes, overly heavy or fat vinegar bottles, immovable pry-up lids on glass bottles, key-opener sardine cans, and hard-to-pour cereal boxes. Such packaging innovations as zipper tear strips, hinged lids, tab slots, screw-on tops, and pour spouts were introduced to solve these and other problems. Spreckels, for example, introduced a resealable four-pound package for its sugar. The package, which looks like a milk or juice carton, overcomes consumer complaints about the traditional sugar packages breaking and not resealing well.[33]

Some firms use packaging to segment markets. For example, different-size packages appeal to heavy, moderate, and light users. Salt is sold in package sizes ranging from single serving to picnic size to giant economy size. Campbell's soup is packaged in single-serving cans aimed at the elderly and singles market segments. Beer and soft drinks are similarly marketed in various package sizes and types. Packaging convenience can increase a product's utility and, therefore, market share and profits.

Facilitating Recycling and Reducing Environmental Damage

One of the most important packaging issues in the 1990s is compatibility with the environment. A growing number of consumers are annoyed by wasteful packaging and prefer, if not demand, recyclable, biodegradable, and reusable packages.[34]

Some firms use their packaging to effectively target environmentally concerned market segments. McDonald's, for example, announced in 1990 that it would stop using styrofoam containers because paper wrappers are better for the environment. Procter & Gamble markets Sure Pro and Old Spice as "eco-friendly" pump-spray packages that do not rely on aerosol propellants. Other firms that have introduced pump sprays include S.C. Johnson (Pledge furniture polish), Reckitt & Coleman Household Products (Woolite rug cleaner), Rollout L.P. (Take 5 cleanser), and Richardson-Vicks (Vidal Sassoon hair spray).[35]

persuasive labeling
Labeling that focuses on a promotional theme or logo rather than on consumer information.

Labeling

An integral part of any package is its label. Labeling generally takes one of two forms: persuasive or informational. **Persuasive labeling** focuses on a promotional theme or logo, and consumer information is secondary. Standard promotional claims—

Heightened consumer interest in protecting the environment has led many marketers to adopt recyclable packaging.

such as "new," "improved," and "super"—have little impact on consumers' product evaluations. Consumers have been saturated with "newness" and thus discount these claims.

informational labeling Labeling designed to help consumers make a proper product selection and lower their cognitive dissonance after the purchase.

Informational labeling, on the other hand, is designed to help consumers make proper product selections and lower their cognitive dissonance after the purchase. Sears attaches a "label of confidence" tag to all its floor coverings. This label gives such product information as durability, color, features, cleanability, and care and construction standards. Most major furniture manufacturers affix labels to their wares that explain construction features, such as type of frame, number of coils, and fabric characteristics.

The Nutritional Labeling and Education Act of 1990 directed the Food and Drug Administration to provide detailed nutritional information on most food packages and to establish standards for health claims on food packaging. An important outcome of this legislation will be guidelines for using terms like *low fat, light, reduced cholesterol, low sodium, low calorie,* and *fresh.*[36]

Universal Product Codes

universal product code (UPC) Series of thick and thin vertical lines, readable by computerized optical scanners, that represent numbers used to track products; also called bar codes.

The **universal product codes** (UPC) that appear on many items in supermarkets and other high-volume outlets were first introduced in 1974. Because the numerical codes appear as a series of thick and thin vertical lines, they are often called bar codes. The lines are read by computerized optical scanners that match codes with brand names, package sizes, and prices. They also print information on cash register tapes and help retailers rapidly and accurately prepare records of customer purchase, control inventories, and track sales. The UPC system and scanners are also used in single-source research (see Chapter 8).

7 GLOBAL ISSUES IN BRANDING AND PACKAGING

As the International Perspectives article showed, brand imitations are widely available in some countries. Counterfeiting is also a major problem for some international marketers, including the makers of Levi's jeans, Rolex and Seiko watches, and Gucci and Louis Vuitton handbags. International marketers must also address some other concerns regarding branding and packaging.

Branding

When planning to enter a foreign market with an existing product, a firm has three major options for handling the brand name:

- *One brand name everywhere:* This strategy is useful when the company markets mainly one product and the brand name does not have negative connotations in any local market. The Coca-Cola Company uses a one-brand-name strategy. This strategy will not work, however, for a consumer goods marketer like Gillette, which sells over 800 products in more than 200 countries. The advantages of a one-brand-name strategy are greater identification of the product from market to market and ease of coordinating promotion from market to market.

- *Adaptations and modifications:* A one-brand-name strategy is not possible when the name cannot be pronounced in the local language, the brand name is owned by someone else, or the brand has a negative or vulgar connotation in the local language. Parker Bros. is known as Parker outside the United States because of translation problems with *Bros.* In French the brand name Pet is vulgar and the brand name Flic has a negative connotation (it refers to the police). Minor modifications made each of these brand names more suitable. Gillette's Silkience hair conditioner is called Soyance in France and Sientel in Italy. The adaptations were deemed to be more appealing in the local markets.
- *Different brand names in different markets:* Local brand names are often used when translation or pronunciation problems occur, when the marketer wants the brand to appear to be a local brand, or when regulations require localization. The British American Tobacco Company markets numerous local brands of low-priced cigarettes. Coca-Cola's Sprite brand had to be renamed Kin in Korea to satisfy a government prohibition on the unnecessary use of foreign words.

Packaging

Three aspects of packaging that are especially important in international marketing are labeling, package aesthetics, and climate considerations. The major labeling concern is properly translating ingredient, promotional, and instructional information on labels. Care must also be employed in meeting all local labeling requirements. Several years ago, an Italian judge ordered that all bottles of Coca-Cola be removed from retail shelves because the ingredients were not properly labeled. Labeling is also harder in countries like Belgium and Finland, which require bilingual labeling.

Package aesthetics may also require some attention. The key is to stay attuned to cultural traits in host countries. For example, colors may have different connotations. Red is associated with witchcraft in some countries, green may be a sign of danger, and white may be symbolic of death.

Aesthetics also influence package size. Soft drinks are not sold in six-packs in countries that lack refrigeration. Products like detergent may be bought only in small quantities because of a lack of storage space. Other products, like cigarettes, may be bought in small quantities, even single units, because of the low purchasing power of buyers.

Extreme climates and long-distance shipping necessitate sturdier and more durable packages for goods sold overseas. Spillage, spoilage, and breakage are all more important concerns when products are shipped long distances or frequently handled during shipping and storage. Packages may also have to ensure a longer product life if the time between production and consumption lengthens significantly.

warranty
Guarantee of the quality or performance of a good or service.

express warranty
Written guarantee that a good or service is fit for the purpose for which it was sold.

8 PRODUCT WARRANTIES

Just as a package is designed to protect the product, a warranty protects the buyer and gives essential information about the product. A **warranty** confirms the quality or performance of a good or service. An **express warranty** is a written guarantee. Express

warranties range from simple statements—such as "100 percent cotton" (a guarantee of quality) and "complete satisfaction guaranteed" (a statement of performance)—to extensive documents written in technical language. In contrast, an **implied warranty** is an unwritten guarantee that the good or service is fit for the purpose for which it was sold. All sales have an implied warranty under the Uniform Commercial Code.

implied warranty
Unwritten guarantee that the good or service is fit for the purpose for which it was sold.

Congress passed the Magnuson-Moss Warranty-Federal Trade Commission Improvement Act in 1975 to help consumers understand warranties and to get action from manufacturers and dealers. A manufacturer that promises a full warranty must meet certain minimum standards, including repair "within a reasonable time and without charge" of any defects and replacement of the merchandise or a full refund if the product does not work "after a reasonable number of attempts" at repair. Any warranty that does not live up to this tough prescription must be "conspicuously" promoted as a limited warranty.

LOOKING BACK

Look back at the story about Procter & Gamble disposable diapers that appeared at the beginning of this chapter. Procter & Gamble's brand extension strategy is an illustration of the marketing concept because P&G is providing products that better meet customers' needs. Many merchants would like to see a return to limited varieties of diapers. They will, however, stock the products and varieties demanded by their customers.

KEY TERMS

SUMMARY

1 Define the term *product*. A product is anything, desired or not, that a person or organization receives in an exchange. The basic goal of purchase decisions is to receive the tangible and intangible benefits associated with a product. Tangible aspects include packaging, style, color, size, and features. Intangible qualities include service, retailer's image, manufacturer's reputation, and the social status associated with a product. An organization's product offering is the crucial element in any marketing mix.

2 Classify consumer products. Consumer products are classified into four categories: convenience products, shopping products, specialty products, and unsought products. Convenience products are relatively inexpensive and require limited shopping effort. Shopping products are of two types: homogeneous and heterogeneous. Because of the similarity of homogeneous products, they are differentiated mainly by price and features. In contrast, heterogeneous products appeal to consumers because of their distinct characteristics. Specialty products possess unique benefits that are highly desirable to certain customers. Finally, unsought products are either new products or products that require aggressive selling because they are generally avoided or overlooked by consumers.

3 Define the terms *product item*, *product line*, and *product mix*. A product item is a specific version of a product that can be designated as a distinct offering among an organization's products. A product line is a group of closely related products offered by an organization. An organization's product mix includes all the products it sells. Product mix width refers to the number of product lines an organization offers. Product line depth is the number of product items in a product line. Product mix consistency is the extent to which product lines are similar. Product lines can be extended downward by introducing less-expensive items. Upward extension entails

manufacturer's brand 290
master brand 287
maturity stage 283
packaging 293
persuasive labeling 295
planned obsolescence 280
private brand 290
product 272
product category 280
product item 275
product life cycle 280
product line 275
product line depth 277
product mix 275
product mix consistency 277
product mix width 277
product modification 280
quality modification 280
service mark 291
shopping product 274
specialty product 275
style modification 280
trademark 291
universal product code 296
unsought product 275
upward extension 278
warranty 297

the introduction of more expensive items. Line filling is adding new products within the present range of the product line. Firms modify existing products by changing their quality, functional characteristics, or style.

4 **Explain the concept of product life cycles.** All products undergo a life cycle with four stages: introduction, growth, maturity, and decline. The rate at which products move through these stages varies dramatically. Marketing managers use the product life cycle concept as an analytical tool to forecast a product's future and devise effective marketing strategies.

5 **Describe marketing uses of branding.** A brand is a name, term, or symbol that identifies and differentiates a firm's products. Established brands encourage customer loyalty and help new products succeed. Types of brands include individual, family, manufacturer's, and private.

6 **Describe marketing uses of packaging and labeling.** Packaging has four functions: containing and protecting products; promoting products; facilitating product storage, use, and convenience; and facilitating recycling and reducing environmental damage. As a tool for promotion, packaging identifies the brand and its features. It also serves the critical function of differentiating a product from competitors and linking it with related products from the same manufacturer. The label is an integral part of the package, with persuasive and informational functions. In essence, the package is the marketers' last chance to influence buyers before they make a purchase decision.

7 **Discuss international issues in branding and packaging.** In addition to brand piracy, international marketers must address a variety of concerns regarding branding and packaging. These include choosing a brand name policy, translating labels and meeting host-country labeling requirements, making packages aesthetically compatible with host-country cultures, and offering the sizes of packages preferred in host countries.

8 **Identify how and why product warranties are important marketing tools.** Product warranties are important tools because they offer consumers protection and help them gauge product quality.

Review Questions

1. Discuss the function of the product in the marketing mix.
2. What are the advantages of creating product lines?
3. What are some strategies firms use to extend product life cycles?
4. Discuss individual and family branding strategies.
5. Describe each consumer product classification using specific examples.
6. How does the product life cycle concept help managers take a proactive approach to marketing?

Discussion and Writing Questions

1. Consider Charles Revson's remark: "In the factory we manufacture cosmetics, but in the store we sell hope." What does this statement imply about product benefits?
2. Imagine several specific products that your firm produces. For new sales employees, write a list of the products and their tangible and intangible benefits.
3. List some specific examples of products that have experienced quality, function, and style modifications.
4. A local business association has asked you, a manufacturer, to give a talk on what the future holds for manufacturers' brands and how they will be able to maintain their share of the market. Write an outline for your speech.

CASES

9.1 Colgate-Palmolive

Colgate-Palmolive thought it had a sure winner in the laundry detergent market when it introduced Fab 1. As a prepackaged product, Fab 1 offered convenience to users. The single-use pack was designed to supply enough detergent to wash a load of clothes and then to

act as a fabric softener in the dryer. Advertising was aimed at the market's largest consumers, large families.

Procter & Gamble and the Clorox Company were both test marketing similar products at the time. Colgate-Palmolive was so eager to beat the competition to the market that it introduced Fab 1 nationally without test marketing it.

Typical consumers of laundry detergent buy three or four different products to do the laundry. Some of the products they buy are detergent, fabric softener, and dryer sheets. Fab 1 was a product consumers could buy to fill the functions of these individual products.

Preliminary research indicated that the major problems consumers had with existing products were problems of convenience. Focus groups said that a small, lightweight, easy-to-use product would be an ideal detergent. By putting the detergent into a soft cloth, Fab 1 offered consumers a detergent and fabric softener in one convenient application-size package. All the user had to do was throw the laundry into the dryer, and the soft cloth became a dryer sheet. Ads focusing on the convenience of the product were prepared showing the typical housewife using Fab 1. It appeared that Colgate-Palmolive had developed an answer to all laundry problems.

The product may have been more successful had Colgate-Palmolive targeted the niche of consumers who rank convenience above other product attributes. College students, singles, and apartment dwellers are more concerned with convenience than traditional laundry detergent consumers are. The latter group did not like the premeasured packages because they had to use a whole package for even a small load of laundry. Also, traditional laundry detergent users were not convinced that Fab 1 was more economical to use than the standard detergents and fabric softeners.

Colgate-Palmolive failed to ask focus groups how important each attribute of the product is. Large families do more laundry than other consumers, and for them, the ability to adjust the amount of each laundry product needed for each load is far more important than convenience. If there had been a huge price benefit, these consumers may have adopted Fab 1. But without it . . .

Questions

1. What type of product is Fab 1? (See Exhibit 9.1.) What stage of the product life cycle does Fab 1 best fit in? Explain your answers.
2. How does Fab 1 fit into Colgate-Palmolive's product line?
3. Should Colgate-Palmolive kill the product, reposition the product, or leave it as a line extension?

Suggested Readings

Cara Appelbaum, "Targeting the Wrong Demographic," *Adweek's Marketing Week*, 9 November 1990, p. 20.

9.2 Underwriters Labs

Video title: *Helping Make New Products Safe for All Consumers*

Underwriters Laboratories, Inc.
333 Pfingsten Road
Northbrook, IL 60062

SIC code: 7397 Commercial testing laboratory

Number of employees: 3,900

1993 revenues: $200 million

Major brands: UL Mark, UL Safety Standards

Largest competitors: None

Background

Underwriters Laboratories was founded in 1894 by William Henry Merrill. Merrill, a crack electrical investigator, sensed a need for an independent testing facility to protect the safety of consumers. The company is a not-for-profit firm, established to test and evaluate the safety of products and materials in the interest of public safety. This independent status allows Underwriters Labs to be completely unbiased when testing manufacturers' products. More than 40,000 manufacturers rely on the testing services of Underwriters Labs, and the UL Mark is placed on more than 6 billion new products each year. For consumers, the UL Mark means that the product has been tested and is found to meet the current safety standards established by Underwriters Labs.

Underwriters Labs also publishes more than 600 safety standards each year. These standards are recognized by many government agencies and consumer safety organizations. These standards are updated regularly to incorporate changing technology. In 1992 alone, Underwriters Labs revised 88 standards and added 10 new ones to its list.

Underwriters Labs plays a major role in new product development and production for many manufacturers. The UL standards give manufacturers a set of guidelines for designing and manufacturing new products. Underwriters Labs engineers help manufacturers meet UL safety standards. Once a product receives the UL Mark,

UL field representatives make periodic, unannounced visits to the manufacturing plants to make sure the product continues to meet the UL standards.

Underwriters Labs plays two major roles in new product development. First, the company helps manufacturers produce safer products. Second, after the product enters the marketplace, the company provides assurance to consumers that the products continue to be manufactured to strict safety specifications.

Questions

1. In which stage of the product life cycle do you think Underwriters Laboratories has the greatest influence over manufacturers? Explain your answer.
2. What is the effect of the UL Mark on a product? Do you think consumers really care?
3. What are the benefits of the UL Mark to manufacturers?

References

Million Dollar Directory 1993 (Parsippany, NJ: Dun & Bradstreet Information Services, 1993).

Miscellaneous company information.

Standard & Poor's Industry Surveys (New York: Standard & Poor's Corporation, October 1993).

9.3 *Decision Assistant:* Ultra-Warmup Corporation

The Situation

The marketing manager of Ultra-Warmup Corporation is perplexed. The company recently introduced a new line of sophisticated athletic warm-up attire. Recognizing the rage for having something printed on the front of athletic attire, the company has embossed the name "Le SweatSuit" in flaming magenta on the front. Yet sales have been disappointing. The company's management thought the product would be perceived by consumers as a specialty product and cannot understand why sales have been so poor.

Management has consulted a marketing research organization that gathered some data regarding people's perceptions about the product. These perceptions are presented in Exhibit 9.11. As a market researcher for the research firm, you have been given the task of analyzing the data.

The Solution Technique

The Product Classification Matrix tool in the *Marketing Decision Assistant* can be used to evaluate this product and place it on a grid having two dimensions. The first dimension measures the economic cost of acquiring a product, and the second measures the social cost. The *Marketing Decision Assistant,* depending on the location of the product on the grid, defines the product as either a convenience, shopping, or specialty good. In addition, it suggests a marketing strategy.

Enter the average responses as prompted. Key ALT-G to display the product classification grid and ALT-D to display the computed classification scores.

What If?

Consider each of the following situations independently:

1. What if people had rated the amount of time spent looking for the product at 4.1? What implication would this rating have for product strategy?
2. What if people had said that the likelihood of positive social reaction to the use of the product was 3.2? What implications would this rating have?
3. What if people had said that the amount of time spent looking for the product was 4.1 and that the likelihood of a positive social reaction to the use of the product was 3.3? What implications would these ratings have for the marketing of the product?

Exhibit 9.11

Responses of People Concerning the Attributes of "Le SweatSuit"

The scale for each question is from 1 to 5, with 1 being low and 5 being high.
1. What is the frequency of product purchase? (1.8)
2. How much time is spent looking for the product? (2.1)
3. How expensive is the product? (1.9)
4. How likely is it that the product will perform as expected? (2.6)
5. How likely is a positive social reaction to the use of the product? (1.3)
6. How likely is it that a poor product choice will harm the consumer's ego? (3.1)

CHAPTER 10

Developing and Managing Products

LEARNING OBJECTIVES
After studying this chapter, you should be able to

1. List the six categories of new products.
2. Understand the importance of developing new products.
3. Identify the organizational groups or structures used to facilitate new product development.
4. List the steps in the new product development process.
5. Identify the main goal of product development for the global market.
6. Explain the diffusion process through which new products are adopted.
7. Explain the product management form of organization.
8. Identify the cost of sustaining weak products, and explain procedures for deciding to abandon a product.

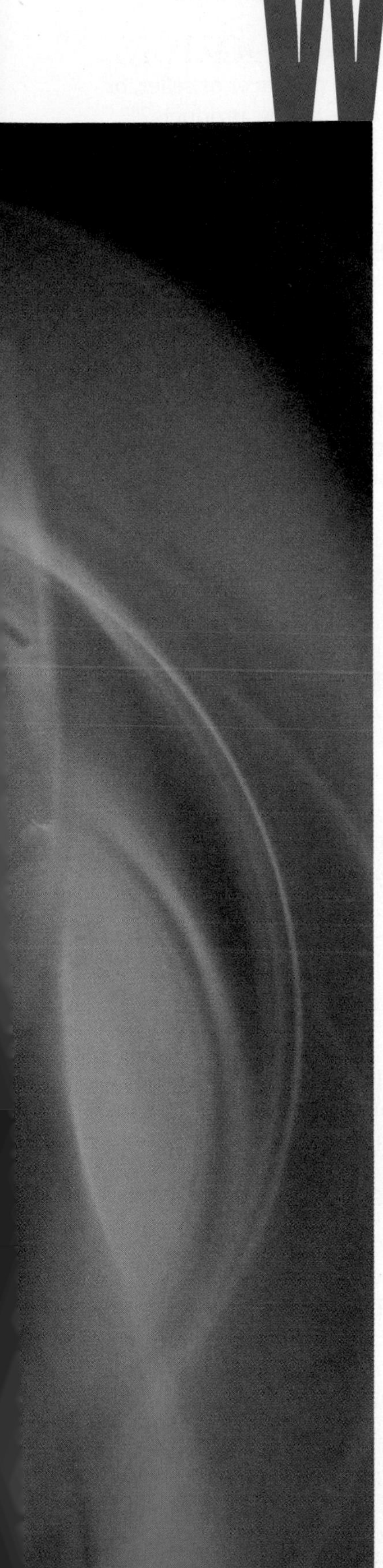

When Procter & Gamble Co. scientists invented a combination shampoo-conditioner, top management responded with a yawn. The project, dubbed BC-18, didn't even rate a new brand name. . . . Management decided to call the new product Pert Plus, linking it to low-market-share brand Pert shampoo. "Nobody paid a lot of attention to it," according to Edwin L. Artzt, P&G chairman and chief executive officer.

Now everyone in the shampoo market is paying attention. Pert Plus has become the leading brand of shampoo, with about 12 percent of the fragmented $1.4 billion U.S. market, where more than 1,100 products compete. And P&G's two-in-one formula, sold under various names in different countries, is now the world's best-selling shampoo product. Competitors are fast trying to copy it. Unilever's Chesebrough-Pond's USA unit, Revlon Group, and Helene Curtis Industries are launching their own combination products with a flurry of promotions.

Is Pert Plus really a new product? Why has it been so successful? What are some possible reasons for selling the product under different names in different countries? Is Pert Plus an example of the practice of inventing a product and then trying to create a need? Other than the laboratory, what are some good sources of new product ideas?

Source: Adapted from Alecia Swasy, "How Innovation at P&G Restored Luster to Washed-Up Pert and Made It No. 1," *The Wall Street Journal*, 6 December 1990, pp. B1, B8.

❶ NEW PRODUCTS

new product
Product new to the world, the market, the producer or seller, or some combination of these.

The term **new product** is somewhat confusing, because its meaning varies widely. Actually, there are several "correct" definitions of the term.

What Is a New Product?

A product can be new to the world, the market, the producer or seller, or some combination of these. There are six categories of new products:[1]

- *New-to-the-world products (also called discontinuous innovations):* The telephone, television, and computer are commonly cited examples of new-to-the-world products. Digital audiotapes were first introduced in the 1980s. Recordable compact discs hit the market in 1990. New-to-the-world products account for about 10 percent of all new products introduced each year.
- *New product lines:* These products, which the firm has not previously offered, allow it to enter an established market. ConAgra Frozen Foods, for example, introduced a new line of frozen pizzas targeted at the "healthy" segment of the frozen food market.[2] Williamson-Dickie Manufacturing, after specializing in the "heavy soil" segment of the work clothes market for nearly seven decades, introduced a line of fashion clothing.[3] The rationale for this strategy is to capitalize on the strong image the Dickie brand has among "working people." New product lines account for about 20 percent of all new products introduced each year.
- *Additions to existing product lines:* This category includes new products that supplement a firm's established line. American Express introduced its Platinum Card to complement its familiar green card and gold card. The annual fee for Platinum Card membership is $300. Additions to existing product lines account for about 26 percent of the new products introduced each year.
- *Improvements or revisions of existing products:* L'eggs launched its biggest marketing push ever for a new brand called Classics. The line, made with the synthetic material Lycra, is positioned as better fitting than competing products.[4] Kingsford Products, a unit of Clorox, introduced a cleaner-burning charcoal lighter fluid.[5] The Pert Plus brand of shampoo, discussed at the beginning of this chapter, is also an example of an improved or revised product. However, many "new and improved" products are revised very little. About 26 percent of all new products are improvements or revisions.
- *Repositioned products:* These are existing products targeted at new markets or market segments. Johnson & Johnson's repositioning of its baby shampoo as a product for everyone falls into this category. Repositioning represents 7 percent of all new products each year.
- *Lower-cost products:* This category refers to products that provide similar performance to competing brands at a lower cost. Reduced costs may result from technological advantages, economies of scale in production, or lower marketing costs. Wilkinson Sword introduced a new line of high-performance disposable razors to compete with Gillette's Sensor and Schick's Tracer. The new line, called Ultra-Glide, is positioned as a low-priced, high-performance disposable shaving system.[6] Kimberly-Clark's new Kleenex Premium toilet tissue is priced well below the premium lines of other tissue makers.[7] Lower-cost products account for about 11 percent of the new products each year.

Among the types of new products are new-to-the-world products like the Habitrol patch, which helps smokers kick their nicotine addiction *(left)*, and additions to existing product lines, such as American Express's Platinum Card *(right)*, which joins the older green card.
(left) © Will Crocker

❷ The Importance of New Products

The product life cycle concept reminds us that developing and introducing new products is vital to business growth and profitability. A continuing stream of new products is needed for most firms to sustain long-term growth in sales and profits.

Exhibit 10.1 illustrates this point. Profits from sales of product 1 peak during the growth stage of the product life cycle. If no new products are introduced, company profits will likely decline continuously thereafter. To sustain and perhaps increase profits, one or more new products must be introduced before product 1 advances to the maturity stage of the product life cycle.

Major consumer and industrial goods manufacturers expect new products to account for a big proportion of their total sales and profits. Each year Sony introduces 1,000 new products. About 800 of these products are improvements of existing products, but 200 are aimed at creating whole new markets.[8] Rubbermaid expects to generate 30 percent of its yearly revenue from products launched in the past five years.[9]

Exhibit 10.1

The Importance of New Products

New product 1
New product 2
Sales volume
Sales volume
Profits
Profits
Sales
+
0
−
Time

New product development is both expensive and risky. Only a small proportion of all seemingly good ideas result in new product introductions. The process of developing and testing a new product can take several years and millions of dollars. For example, Gillette spent $200 million over ten years developing the Sensor razor. McDonald's spent twelve years developing and testing salads before introducing them. McDonald's also tested pizza in a limited number of outlets three times (1984, 1986, 1989) before finding a product that consumers were willing to repurchase.

Many products that are introduced fail to meet management's (or consumers') expectations. How many of the following failures do you remember?

Vaseline Intensive Care aftershave lotion (perceived as greasy)

Pepperidge Farm Star Wars cookies (overpriced, poor quality)

Texas Instruments 99/4A computer (lacked features for the cost)

Gerber's Singles food-in-a-jar (reminded adults of baby food)

Clairol's Touch of Yogurt shampoo (considered a poor name)

3 ORGANIZING FOR NEW PRODUCT DEVELOPMENT

It is important for most firms to have a steady stream of new products. An organized structure is essential to purposefully cultivate new products. Yet in many firms top managers tend to receive new product ideas passively rather than actively soliciting them. Moreover, managers often poorly process the ideas they do receive, and chance determines whether or not these ideas are fully considered. One of the main requirements for generating new product ideas and successfully introducing new products is support from top management.

Several kinds of groups or structures within an organization can facilitate a steady stream of new products. These include new product committees, new product departments, and venture teams.

New Product Committees

new product committee Ad hoc group whose members represent various functional interests and who manage the new product development process.

A **new product committee** is an ad hoc group whose members manage the new product development process. They usually represent functional interests, such as manufacturing, research and development, finance, and marketing. Many organizations use new product committees to screen ideas.

New Product Departments

new product department Separate department that manages the new product development process on a full-time basis.

One alternative to a new product committee is a **new product department.** This separate department performs the same functions as a new product committee but on a full-time basis. Ideally, people in the product development department communicate with their peers in the operating departments. Setting up a formal department helps ensure that authority and responsibilities are well defined and delegated to specific individuals. New product departments typically recommend new product objectives and programs, plan exploratory studies, evaluate concepts and ideas for new products, and coordinate testing and direct interdepartmental teams.

As Exhibit 10.2 illustrates, the new product department can be situated in one of several places within the organization. As a separate department with authority to develop new products, it can be free from the undue influence of production, marketing, and other groups. A separate department also has the authority to accomplish its tasks. Thus the new product development manager can rely less on people outside his or her sphere of influence.

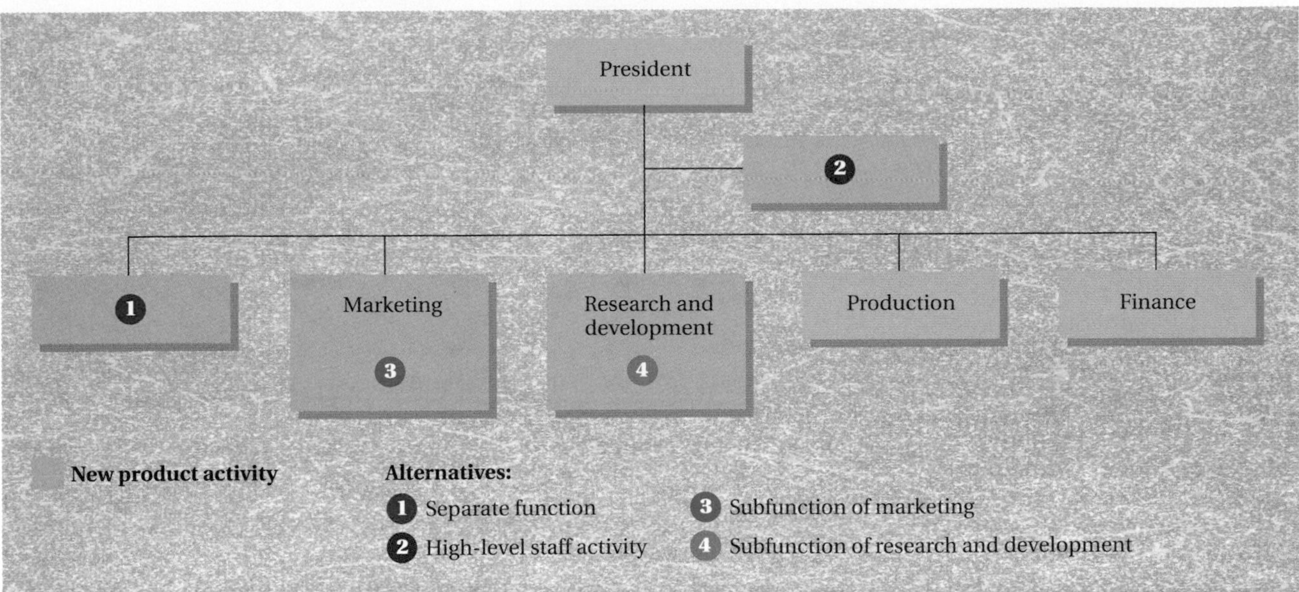

Exhibit 10.2

Situating New Product Departments within Organizations

As a high-level staff activity, new product development usually has the strong support of top management. As a staff function, however, it must depend on other functional areas to carry out various activities. For example, the department must rely on marketing to conduct marketing research, production to build prototypes or working models, and finance to develop financial statements projecting the product's profitability.

If a company is consumer-oriented, it may choose to place new product development within the marketing function. The result may be new products sharply attuned to the customers' needs. On the other hand, production and financial considerations may be skimped. For example, if production management feels excluded from the planning process, they may show little enthusiasm for estimating production runs, developing prototypes, and so forth.

The last option is to integrate the product development department into research and development. This arrangement is common in chemical, pharmaceutical, and electronics industries, where basic research is a well-funded and essential part of the organization. Grouping new product development and basic research together can offer great advantages. When the two groups work and communicate closely, product development can suggest areas in which basic research might lead to major commercial successes.

New Product Venture Teams

venture team
Entrepreneurial, market-oriented group staffed by a small number of representatives from different disciplines.

A **venture team** is an entrepreneurial, market-oriented group staffed by a small number of representatives from different disciplines. Team members from marketing, research and development, finance, and other areas focus on a single objective: planning their company's profitable entry into a new business. Venture groups are most often used to handle important business and product tasks—tasks that do not fit neatly into the existing organization, that demand more financial resources and longer times to mature than other organizational units can provide, and that require imaginative entrepreneurship neither sheltered nor inhibited by the larger organizations.

Unlike new product committees, venture teams require a full-time commitment. In contrast to new product departments, venture teams form and disband as needed instead of being stable departments within the overall organizational structure. Signode Industries, a major producer of steel and plastic strapping systems and

other industrial product lines, uses four- to six-member venture teams to generate new product ideas.

The term *intrapreneur*—for an entrepreneur working inside a large organization—is often used to describe members of venture teams. Colgate-Palmolive Company created Colgate Venture for intrapreneurs to develop specialized, small-market products, such as a deodorizing pad for cat litter boxes and a cleaning solution for teenagers' orthodontal retainers. Colgate Venture has five operating divisions and employs about seventy people.

What's New in Organizing for New Product Development?

The earlier a product is brought to market, the greater the chance that profits will be strong. Delays lead to lost sales.[10] Xerox Corporation executives were stunned to learn that Japanese competitors were developing new copier models twice as fast as Xerox and at half the cost. Xerox management recognized that it had to greatly reduce its normal four- to five-year product development cycle or continue to lose market share—and possibly its reputation as the world's leading copier manufacturer. After a major reorganization and multimillion-dollar investment, Xerox was able to cut its development time to two years.[11]

Now U.S. manufacturers of all kinds are trying to find new ways to shorten their development cycles and be the first to market new products. To do this, they are completely revising their procedures for developing new products. For example, the Big Three carmakers (General Motors, Ford, and Chrysler) all formed task forces to cut bureaucratic procedures and streamline the development process.[12]

parallel engineering (simultaneous engineering, concurrent engineering) Product development process in which all relevant functional areas and outside suppliers participate at all stages, thereby streamlining the development process and reducing its cost.

A new organizational form called **parallel engineering, simultaneous engineering,** or **concurrent engineering** has emerged to shorten the new product development process and reduce its cost. The process is fairly straightforward. All relevant functional areas and outside suppliers participate in all stages of the development process. Group members perform development tasks together, thereby avoiding, for example, the need for designers to make changes when engineers or manufacturing are unable to meet design specifications.[13] Involving key suppliers early in the development process enables them to design and develop critical component parts.

General Motors, Ford, and Chrysler have all set up parallel engineering programs. Chrysler used the approach in developing the Viper, General Motors used it in developing the Cadillac Seville, and Ford used it in revamping the Taurus.[14] GM is also using parallel engineering to design the world's first mass-market electric car.[15] And IBM used the concurrent process to develop the AS/400 midrange computer.[16]

The benefits of parallel engineering are clear. The Japanese call this process of all departments working together *wai-gaya* (loosely translated as "hub-bub"). They require only half to two-thirds the engineering hours to develop automobile products comparable to those of U.S. manufacturers.[17]

4 THE NEW PRODUCT DEVELOPMENT PROCESS

The management and technology consulting firm Booz, Allen & Hamilton has studied the new product development process for over thirty years. Analyzing five major studies during this period, the firm has concluded that the companies most likely to succeed in developing and introducing new products are those that take the following actions:

- Make the long-term commitment needed to support innovation and new product development

Exhibit 10.3

The New Product Development Process

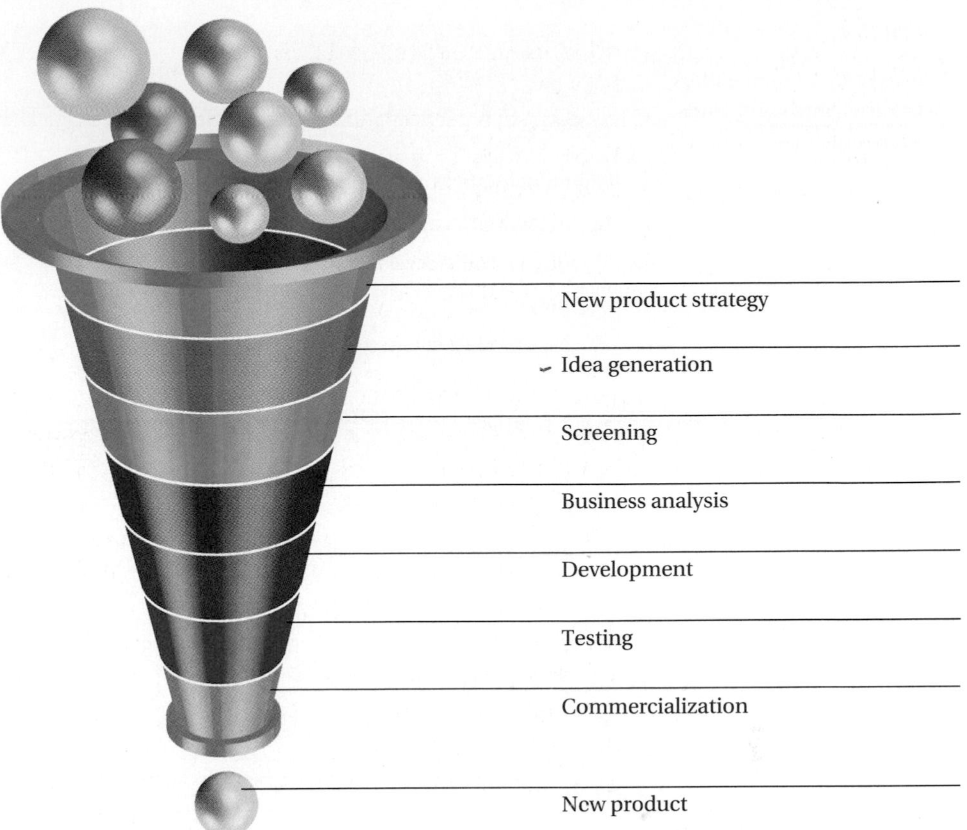

- Use a company-specific approach, driven by corporate objectives and strategies, with a well-defined new product strategy at its core
- Capitalize on experience to achieve and maintain competitive advantage
- Establish an environment—a management style, organizational structure, and degree of top-management support—conducive to achieving company-specific new product and corporate objectives[18]

Most companies follow a formal new product development process, usually starting with a new product strategy. Exhibit 10.3 traces the seven-step process, which is discussed in detail below. The funnel-shaped exhibit illustrates how each stage acts as a screen. The purpose is to filter out unworkable ideas.

New Product Strategy

new product strategy Strategy that links the new product development process with the objectives of the marketing department, the business unit, and the corporation.

A **new product strategy** links the new product development process with the objectives of the marketing department, the business unit, and the corporation. A new product strategy must be compatible with these objectives, and in turn, all three objectives must be consistent with one another.

New product strategy is a subset or part of the organization's overall marketing strategy. It sharpens the focus for idea generation. Moreover, this strategy provides general guidelines for screening and evaluating new product ideas in two ways. First, the new product strategy specifies the roles that new products must play in the organization's overall plan. Second, it describes the characteristics of products the organization wants to offer and the markets it wants to serve.[19]

Idea Generation

New product ideas come from many sources. The most important are customers, employees, distributors, competitors, research and development staff, and outside

Exhibit 10.4

Sources of New Product Ideas

Source: Adapted from Michael G. Duerr, *The Commercial Development of New Products.* Reprinted by permission of the Conference Board.

Sources	Responses		Most important	
	Number	*Percentage*	*Number*	*Percentage*
Internal sources				
Marketing	157	41	33	59
Research and development	154		41	
Employees	66	9	3	2
New product committee	50	7	4	3
Corporate planning	42	5	2	2
Total	469	62	83	66
External sources				
Customers	130	17	36	28
Acquisitions	59	8	4	3
Consultants	48	6	1	1
Inventors	43	6	2	2
Advertising agency	8	1		
Total	288	38	43	34
Total for all sources	757	100	126	100

consultants. Exhibit 10.4 shows the sources of new product ideas identified in a study of 179 companies. The "Responses" column identifies how often each source was mentioned. The "Most important" column shows how often each source was identified as most important.

Customers

The marketing concept suggests that customers' wants and needs should be the springboard for developing new products. Computer companies, for example, recognize that customers can develop software extremely valuable to other users. At IBM, the Installed User Program was set up to acquire user-developed programs that run on IBM's midsize and large computers. The Installed User Program learns of promising software developed outside the company from either the customers themselves or IBM field representatives. When IBM decides to acquire rights to a particular program, the company negotiates an agreement (basically a one-time, flat-fee payment) with the developer. Other companies also actively encourage customers' input. The International Perspectives article illustrates how S.C. Johnson & Son has used Japanese customers' input to develop new products for Japan and other markets.

Employees

Marketing personnel—advertising and marketing research employees as well as salespeople—often create new product ideas, because they analyze and are involved in the marketplace. Firms should encourage their employees to submit new product ideas and reward them if their ideas are adopted.

For example, 3M Corporation's Post-it Notes started with an employee's new product idea. In 1974 the research and development department of 3M's commercial tape division developed and patented the adhesive component of Post-it Notes.

INTERNATIONAL PERSPECTIVES

New Product Ideas from Japanese Customers

S.C. Johnson & Son has found that a "willingness to adapt and develop products to meet local needs can ease the way to success in Japan." According to president and CEO Richard M. Carpenter, "We did not immediately impose our Western ways on Japanese consumers. Instead, we studied the market and conducted extensive consumer research, subsequently modifying existing products and developing new ones for Japan."

For example, disposing of the hot oil used to cook tempura was "a problem for Japanese households. Pouring it down the drain not only clogs the plumbing but pollutes Japan's rivers and streams." So Johnson developed Tempura Oil Solidifier, which enables the oil to be disposed of as a solid waste.

Johnson also developed a special-formula grout cleaner to remove mildew in Japanese homes and Raid Fumigator, an adaptation of the familiar Raid insecticide. The oil solidifier and grout cleaner are being considered for launches in several other countries. The fumigator product has already been introduced abroad.[20]

Why has S.C. Johnson & Son successfully introduced new products in Japan while other U.S. firms have failed? What new product development and international marketing lessons can we learn from this example? Is Johnson product-, sales-, or marketing-oriented? Why?

However, no one identified a use for the adhesive until a year later. An employee of the commercial tape division sang in the church choir. He used paper clips and slips of paper to mark places in hymn books. But the paper clips damaged his books, and the slips of paper fell out. The solution, as we now all know, was to apply the adhesive to small pieces of paper and sell them in packages. The rest is history.

Distributors

A well-trained sales force routinely asks distributors about needs that are not being met. Because they are closer to end users, distributors are often more aware of customer needs than manufacturers are. The inspiration for Rubbermaid's litter-free lunch box, named Sidekick, came from a distributor. The distributor suggested that Rubbermaid place some of its plastic containers inside a lunch box and sell the box as an alternative to plastic wrap and paper bags.[21]

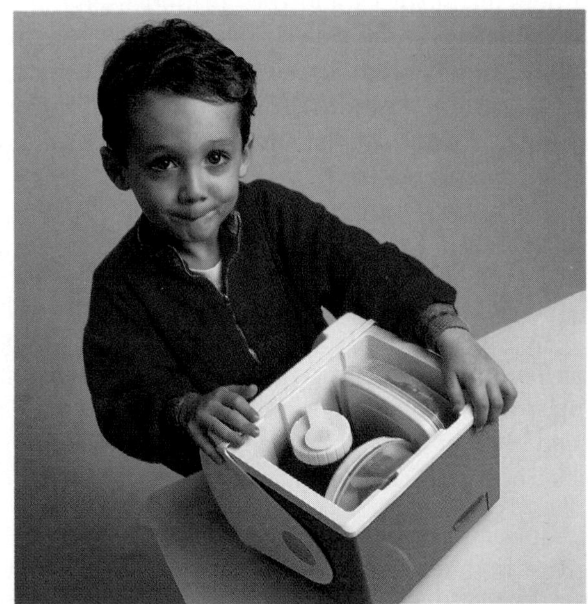

Some ideas for new products come from distributors, who may have better insights into consumers' needs than do manufacturers. Rubbermaid's litter-free lunch box set is one such idea.
Photograph by John S. Abbot

ETHICS IN MARKETING

Should Western Union Compete with Its Distributors?

In 1991 Western Union was planning to introduce a new service that would directly compete with about 2,500 firms that distribute Western Union's money-wiring service. Western Union intended to become the first national supplier of a check-cashing service. The plan was to offer the new service through a network of 500 to 1,000 outlets located mostly in cities.

A number of Western Union's distributors that are also in the check-cashing business contended that Western Union would be acting unethically by going into direct competition with them. They said that Western Union has proprietary market information about them, "such as the financial performance of specific locations."

"This is a tremendous conflict of interest," charged Jeffrey Silverman, president of M.S. Management Co. in Illinois, one of the largest check-cashing chains. "The information is extremely confidential, and now they are going to be competitors of ours. Who is to say that this confidential information isn't going to influence their future business decisions?"

James Calrano, president of Western Union's parent company, insisted that the plan would "end up benefitting all check cashers because of the heavy marketing and promotion the company plans to unleash. The company currently spends a huge $30 million annually to support its money-wiring business."[22]

Evaluate the charge that Western Union's plan to introduce a new service that will directly compete with many of its distributors is unethical. Evaluate Western Union's response to this criticism. What should Western Union do?

Competitors

No firms rely solely on internally generated ideas for new products. A big part of any organization's marketing intelligence system should be monitoring the performance of competitors' products. One purpose of competitive monitoring is to determine which, if any, of the competitors' products should be copied. Competitive monitoring may even include tracking products sold by a company's own customers. The Ethics in Marketing article is an example of this practice. It also shows how marketing channel members normally respond.

Research and Development

basic research
Scientific research aimed at discovering new technologies.

applied research
Research aimed at finding useful applications for new technologies.

product development
Process of converting applications for new technologies into marketable products.

product modification
Change in one or more of a product's characteristics—for example, its quality, functional features, or style.

Research and development (R&D) is carried out in four distinct ways. **Basic research** is scientific research aimed at discovering new technologies. **Applied research** takes these new technologies and tries to find useful applications for them. **Product development** goes one step further by converting applications into marketable products. **Product modification** makes cosmetic or functional changes in existing products. Many new product breakthroughs come from R&D activities. The story at the beginning of this chapter about Procter & Gamble scientists inventing Pert Plus illustrates the value of R&D.

Consultants

Outside consultants are always available to examine a business and recommend product ideas. Examples include the Weston Group; Booz, Allen & Hamilton; and Management Decisions. Traditionally, consultants adopt a strategic posture, assessing company product needs as well as market opportunities. They determine whether a company has a balanced portfolio of products and, if not, what new product ideas are needed to offset the imbalance. For instance, an outside consultant conceived Airwick's highly successful Carpet Fresh carpet cleaner.

Techniques for Generating New Product Ideas

Creativity is the wellspring of new product ideas. A variety of approaches and techniques have been developed to stimulate creative thinking. The two considered

The National Cancer Institute spent eleven years seeking natural substances that fight cancer. Out of over 130,000 substances tested, it found one: taxol, an extract from the bark of a yew tree that grows in America's old-growth forests. Today researchers at Bristol-Myers Squibb, a big U.S. pharmaceutical company, work with NCI to further develop a taxol cancer treatment and more accessible sources of the chemical.
Entheos

most useful for generating new product ideas are brainstorming and focus group exercises:

brainstorming
Technique for generating new product ideas in which group members propose, without criticism or limitation, ways to vary a product or solve a problem.

- *Brainstorming:* The goal of **brainstorming** is to get a group to think of unlimited ways to vary a product or solve a problem. Group members avoid criticism of an idea, no matter how ridiculous it may seem. The sheer quantity of ideas is what matters. Objective evaluation is postponed. Signode Industries is one of many companies that have used brainstorming to generate new product ideas.
- *Focus groups:* As noted in Chapter 8, an objective of focus group interviews is to assess group interaction when members are exposed to an idea or a concept. These interviews usually include seven to ten people. Sometimes focus groups generate excellent new product ideas—for example, Cycle dog food, Stick-Up room deodorizers, Dustbusters, and Wendy's salad bar. In the industrial market, machine tools, keyboard designs, aircraft interiors, and backhoe accessories have evolved from focus groups.

Screening

screening
Stage in the product development process that eliminates ideas inconsistent with the organization's new product strategy or obviously inappropriate for some other reason.

After new ideas have been generated, they pass through the first filter in the product development process. This stage, called **screening,** eliminates ideas that are inconsistent with the organization's new product strategy or are obviously inappropriate for some other reason. The new product committee, the new product department, or some other formally appointed group performs the screening review. Most new product ideas are rejected at the screening stage.

concept test
Evaluation of a new product idea, usually before any prototype has been created.

Concept tests are often used at the screening stage to rate concept (or product) alternatives. A **concept test** evaluates a new product idea, usually before any prototype has been created. Typically, researchers get consumer reactions to descriptions and visual representations of a proposed product.

Concept tests are considered fairly good predictors of early trial and repeat purchases for line extensions. They have also been relatively precise predictors of success for new products that are not copycat items, are not easily classified into existing product categories, and do not require major changes in consumer behav-

ior. Examples include Betty Crocker Tuna Helper, Cycle dog food, and Libby Fruit Float. However, concept tests are usually inaccurate in predicting the success of new products that create new consumption patterns and require major changes in consumer behavior. Examples include microwave ovens, videocassette recorders, computers, and word processors.

Business Analysis

business analysis
Stage in the product development process where demand, cost, sales, and profitability estimates are made.

New product ideas that survive the initial screening process move to the **business analysis** stage, where preliminary demand, cost, sales, and profitability estimates are made. For the first time, costs and revenues are estimated and compared. Depending on the nature of the product and the company, this process may be simple or complex.

The newness of the product, the size of the market, and the nature of competition all affect the accuracy of revenue projections.[23] In an established market like soft drinks, industry estimates of total market size are available. Forecasting market share for a new entry is a bigger challenge.

Analyzing overall economic trends and their impact on estimated sales is especially important in product categories that are sensitive to business cycle fluctuations. If consumers view the economy as uncertain and risky, they will put off buying durable goods like major home appliances, automobiles, and homes. Likewise, business buyers postpone major equipment purchases if they expect a business recession.

These questions are commonly asked during the business analysis stage:

- What is the likely demand for the product?
- What impact would the new product probably have on total sales, profits, market share, and return on investment?
- How would the introduction of this product affect existing products? Would it cannibalize existing products?
- Would current customers benefit from the product?
- Would it enhance the image of our overall product mix?
- Would it affect current employees in any way? Would it lead to hiring more people or reducing the size of the work force?
- What new facilities, if any, would be needed?
- How might competitors respond?
- What is the risk of failure? Are we willing to take the risk?

Answering these and related questions may require studies of markets, competition, costs, and technical capabilities. But at the end of this stage, management should have a good understanding of the product's market potential. Costs increase dramatically once a new product idea enters the development stage.

Development

development
Stage in the product development process when a prototype is developed and a marketing strategy is outlined.

In the early stage of **development,** the R&D or engineering department may develop a prototype of the product. During this stage, the firm should start sketching out a marketing strategy. The marketing department should decide on the packaging, branding, labeling, and so forth. In addition, it should map out preliminary promotion, price, and distribution strategies.

In the development stage, the technical feasibility of manufacturing the product at an acceptable cost is thoroughly examined. This stage can last a long time and thus be very expensive. For example, Crest toothpaste was in the development stage

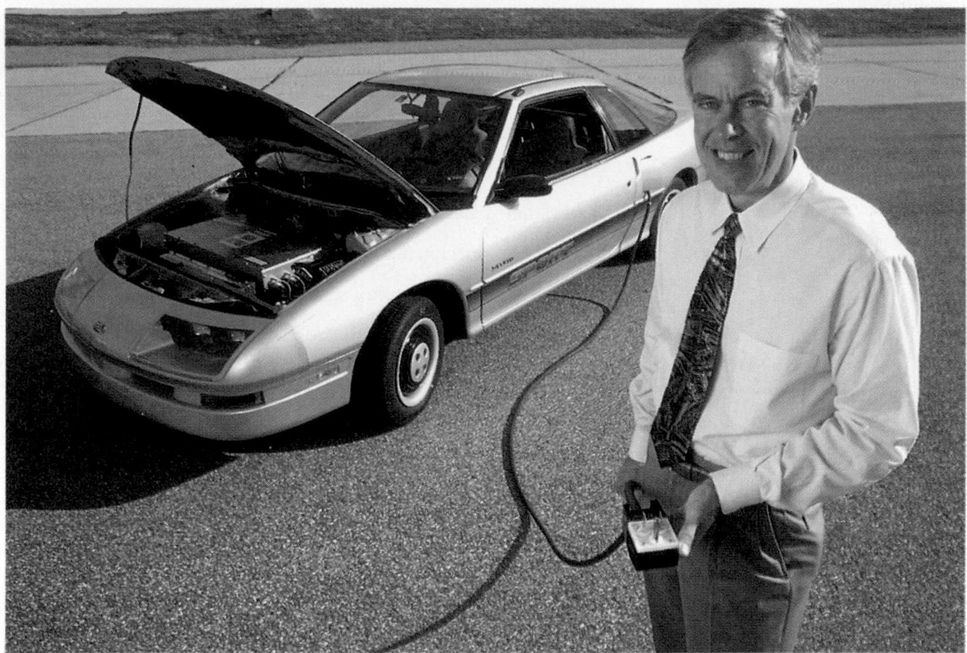

To develop its new electric car, the Impact, General Motors is using parallel engineering. Kenneth R. Baker, who heads the effort, has assembled a small team of engineers, production workers, and marketing experts to bring the product concept to reality.
© Peter Yates/SABA

for ten years. It took eighteen years to develop Minute Rice, fifteen years to develop the Polaroid Colorpack camera, fifteen years to develop the Xerox copy machine, and fifty-five years to develop television.

The development process works best when all the involved areas (R&D, marketing, engineering, production, and even suppliers) work together rather than sequentially. You may recall from earlier in this chapter that this process is called parallel engineering, simultaneous engineering, or concurrent engineering.

Laboratory and use tests are often conducted on prototype models during the development stage. Laboratory tests subject products to much more severe treatment than is expected by end users. User safety is an important aspect of laboratory testing. In fact, the Consumer Product Safety Act of 1972 requires manufacturers to conduct a "reasonable testing program" to ensure that their products conform to established safety standards.

Many products that test well in the laboratory are also tried out in homes or businesses. Examples of product categories well suited for use tests include human and pet food products, household cleaning products, and industrial chemicals and supplies. These products are all relatively inexpensive, and their performance characteristics are apparent to users.

Most products require some refinement based on the results of laboratory and use tests. A second stage of development often takes place before market testing.

Testing

After products and marketing programs have been developed, they are usually tested in the marketplace. **Test marketing** is the limited introduction of a product and a marketing program to determine the reactions of potential customers in a market situation. Test marketing allows management to evaluate alternative strategies and to assess how well the various aspects of the marketing mix fit together. Quest, Seagram's new low-calorie line of sparkling water, was test marketed for nearly a year before its national introduction in 1993.[24]

test marketing
Stage in the product development process during which a product is introduced in a limited way to determine the reactions of potential customers in a market situation.

The cities chosen as test sites should reflect market conditions in the new product's projected market area. Yet no "magic city" exists that can universally represent

Exhibit 10.5

A Checklist for Selecting Test Markets

In choosing a test market, many criteria need to be considered, especially the following:
Similarity to planned distribution outlets
Relative isolation from other cities
Availability of advertising media that will cooperate
Diversified cross section of ages, religions, cultural-societal preferences, etc.
No atypical purchasing habits
Representative population size
Typical per capita income
Good record as a test city, but not overly used
Not easily "jammed" by competitors
Stability of year-round sales
No dominant television station; multiple newspapers, magazines, and radio stations
Availability of retailers that will cooperate
Availability of research and audit services
Freedom from unusual influences, such as one industry's dominance or heavy tourism

market conditions, and a product's success in one city doesn't guarantee it will be a nationwide hit. When selecting test market cities, researchers should therefore find locations where the demographics and purchasing habits mirror the overall market. The company should also have good distribution in test cities. Moreover, test locations should be media-isolated. If the TV stations in a particular market reach a very large area outside that market, the advertising used for the test product may pull in many consumers from outside the market. The product may then appear more successful than it really is. Exhibit 10.5 provides a useful checklist of criteria for selecting test markets. Exhibit 10.6 lists the U.S. cities that are the most popular test markets.

High Costs of Test Marketing

Test marketing normally covers 1 to 3 percent of the United States, takes about twelve to eighteen months, and costs between $1 million and $3 million.[25] Some products remain in test markets even longer. Lever 2000, the deodorant soap, was test marketed for four years before it was introduced.[26] Despite the cost, many firms believe it is a lot better to fail in a test market than in a national introduction.

Because test marketing is so expensive, some companies do not test line extensions of well-known brands. For example, since the Folger's brand is well known, Procter & Gamble faced little risk in distributing its instant decaffeinated version nationally. Consolidated Foods Kitchen of Sara Lee followed the same approach with its frozen croissants. Other products introduced without being test marketed include General Foods' International Coffee, Quaker Oats' Chewy Granola bars and Granola Dipps, and Pillsbury's Milk Break Bars.

Alternatives to Test Marketing

Many firms are looking for cheaper, faster alternatives to traditional test marketing. In the early 1980s, Information Resources Incorporated pioneered one alternative: single-source research (discussed in Chapter 8). A typical supermarket scanner test costs about $300,000.

Akron, OH	Colorado Springs, CO	Greensboro, NC	Mobile, AL	Raleigh, NC
Albany, NY	Columbia, SC	Greenville, NC	Modesto, CA	Reading, PA
Albuquerque, NM	Columbus, GA	Harrisburg, PA	Monterey, CA	Reno, NV
Ann Arbor, MI	Columbus, OH	Hartford, CT	Montgomery, AL	Richmond, VA
Anniston, AL	Corpus Christi, TX	High Point, NC	Nashville, TN	Roanoke, VA
Appleton, WI	Council Bluffs, NE	Houston, TX	New Haven, CT	Rochester, NY
Asheville, NC	Dallas, TX	Huntsville, AL	New Orleans, LA	Rockford, IL
Atlanta, GA	Dayton, OH	Hutchinson, KS	New York, NY	Rome, GA
Augusta, GA	Daytona Beach, FL	Indianapolis, IN	Newport News, VA	Sacramento, CA
Austin, TX	Decatur, IL	Jacksonville, FL	Oklahoma City, OK	St. Louis, MO
Bakersfield, CA	Denver, CO	Kalamazoo, MI	Omaha, NE	St. Paul, MN
Baltimore, MD	Des Moines, IA	Kansas City, KS	Orange, TX	St. Petersburg, FL
Bangor, ME	Detroit, MI	Kansas City, MO	Orlando, FL	Salem, NC
Baton Rouge, LA	Dubuque, IA	Knoxville, TN	Pensacola, FL	Salem, OR
Battle Creek, MI	Duluth, MN	Lansing, MI	Peoria, IL	Salinas, CA
Beaumont, TX	Durham, NC	Las Vegas, NV	Philadelphia, PA	Salt Lake City, UT
Binghamton, NY	Eau Claire, WI	Lexington, KY	Phoenix, AZ	San Antonio, TX
Birmingham, AL	El Paso, TX	Lincoln, NE	Pittsburgh, PA	San Diego, CA
Boise, ID	Elkhart, IN	Little Rock, AR	Pittsfield, MA	San Francisco, CA
Boston, MA	Erie, PA	Los Angeles, CA	Poland Spring, ME	Savannah, GA
Boulder, CO	Eugene, OR	Louisville, KY	Port Arthur, TX	Schenectady, NY
Buffalo, NY	Evansville, IN	Lubbock, TX	Portland, ME	Scranton, PA
Canton, OH	Fargo, ND	Lynchburg, VA	Portland, OR	Seattle, WA
Carson City, NV	Flint, MI	Macon, GA	Poughkeepsie, NY	Shreveport, LA
Cedar Rapids, IA	Fort Collins, CO	Madison, WI	Providence, RI	Sioux Falls, SD
Champaign, IL	Fort Lauderdale, FL	Manchester, NH	Pueblo, CO	South Bend, IN
Charleston, SC	Fort Smith, AR	Marion, IN	Quad Cities: Rock Island & Moline, IL; Davenport & Bettendorf, IA (Davenport-Rock Island-Moline metro market)	Spartanburg, SC
Charleston, WV	Fort Wayne, IN	Melbourne, FL		Spokane, WA
Charlotte, NC	Fort Worth, TX	Memphis, TN		Springfield, MA
Chattanooga, TN	Fresno, CA	Miami, FL		
Chicago, IL	Grand Junction, CO	Midland, TX		
Cincinnati, OH	Grand Rapids, MI	Milwaukee, WI		
Cleveland, OH	Green Bay, WI	Minneapolis, MN		

Exhibit 10.6

The Most Often Used Test Markets in the United States

Source: "The Nation's Most Popular Test Markets," *Sales & Marketing Management*, March 1989. Reprinted by permission of Sales & Marketing Management.

simulated (laboratory) market test
Presentation of advertising and other promotional materials for several products, including a test product, to members of the product's target market.

Another alternative to traditional test marketing is **simulated (laboratory) market tests.** Advertising and other promotional materials for several products, including the test product, are shown to members of the product's target market. These people are then taken to shop at a mock or real store where their purchases are recorded. Shopper behavior, including repeat purchasing, is monitored to assess the product's likely performance under true market conditions. Research firms offer simulated market tests for $25,000 to $100,000, compared to $1 million or more for full-scale test marketing.

High cost is not the only problem associated with traditional test marketing. One unavoidable problem is that test marketing exposes the new product and its marketing mix to competitors before its introduction. Thus the element of surprise is lost. Several years ago, for example, Procter & Gamble began testing a ready-to-spread Duncan Hines frosting. General Mills took note and rushed to market its own Betty Crocker brand, which now is the best-selling brand of ready-to-spread frosting.[27]

Competitors can also sabotage or "jam" a testing program by introducing their own sales promotion, pricing, or advertising campaign. The purpose is to hide or distort the normal conditions that the testing firm might expect in the market. When PepsiCo tested Mountain Dew Sport Drink in Minneapolis in 1990, Quaker Oats counterattacked furiously with coupons and ads for Gatorade.[28]

Despite these problems, most firms still consider test marketing essential for most new products. The high price of failure simply prohibits the widespread introduction of most new products without testing. Sometimes, however, when risks of failure are low, it is better to skip test marketing and move directly from development to commercialization.

Commercialization

commercialization
Final stage in the product development process, consisting of tasks necessary to begin marketing the product.

The final stage in the new product development process is **commercialization**, the decision to market a product. The decision to commercialize sets several tasks in motion: ordering production materials and equipment, starting production, building inventories, shipping the product to field distribution points, training the sales force, announcing the new product to the trade, and advertising to potential customers.

The time from the initial commercialization decision to the product's actual introduction varies. It can range from a few weeks for simple products that use existing equipment to several years for technical products that require custom manufacturing equipment.

The total cost of development and initial introduction can be staggering. For example, it cost Gillette over $200 million to develop and start manufacturing the Sensor razor and another $110 million for first-year advertising alone![29] A grocery industry task force concluded that, on average, manufacturers pay $5.1 million to get a new product or line extension on grocery shelves nationally.[30] Forty-six percent of spending is for advertising and promotion to persuade consumers to try the product. Another 16 percent is for promotions directed at wholesalers and retailers. Research and development and market analysis costs consume 18 percent. Making the product is the least expensive step.

Why Some New Products Succeed and Others Fail

Despite the high cost and other risks of developing and testing new products, many companies—such as Rubbermaid, Campbell Soup, and Procter & Gamble—continue to develop and introduce new products. Some succeed and some fail. With so much at stake, it is no wonder that marketers have analyzed the factors involved in both success and failure.

Success Factors

The most important factor in successful new product introduction is a good match between the product and market needs—as the marketing concept would predict. Here are other factors that increase the chances of success for both consumer and business product introductions:

- Unique but superior product
- Coordinated, proficient technical and production efforts
- Large, high-need, growth market
- Avoidance of a high-priced product with no economic advantage
- Avoidance of a competitive market with satisfied customers
- Strong marketing communications and launch effort
- Market-derived idea with considerable supporting investment

Several new products introduced in the 1980s met these criteria and thus succeeded. Exhibit 10.7 lists some of them.

Failure Factors

Associations, trade publications, consultants, and statistical bureaus estimate that the new product failure rate is about 90 percent.[31] Many products fail simply because their manufacturers lack a well-developed marketing strategy. Moreover, they do not realize the importance of creating a product to meet the consumer's need rather than producing "what we know best."

Successes	Failures
IBM PC: Big Blue claimed the power to set industry standards.	Pontiac Fiero: The car looked great but was discontinued after problems with engine fires.
Microwave food: It's changing our definition of good food.	Disk camera: The pictures turned out too grainy.
Diet Coke: This was a brilliant brand extension.	RCA's Selecta Vision: Bad timing was the death blow for the videodisc player once lauded as RCA's premier product of the 1980s.
Lean Cuisine: These pricey diet entrees, launched at the height of the recession, caught the fit-but-fast wave.	Fab 1 Shot: Colgate-Palmolive premeasured laundry detergent meant consumers couldn't use just enough for a small load.
Macintosh computer: Apple Computer's new design changed the way people use these machines.	Holly Farms roasted chickens: Consumers liked these fully cooked birds, but retailers balked at their short shelf life.
Super-premium ice cream: Häagen-Dazs, Ben & Jerry's, and DoveBar are all the perfect end to low-calorie meals.	Premier cigarette: The "smokeless" cigarette couldn't be lit with matches, and consumers didn't like the taste.
Chrysler minivans: These station wagons of the 1980s created a new category of cars.	IBM PCjr: A problematic keyboard contributed to its downfall.
Tartar Control Crest: Procter & Gamble's efforts to teach consumers about nasty tooth deposits helped restore its toothpaste market share.	Yugo: The Yugoslavian minicar was billed as the cheapest new car in the United States, and it showed.
Athletic footwear: After stumbling in 1986, Nike slam-dunked rival Reebok by winning the favor of big-city kids.	LA Beer: Despite the new sobriety trend, the market for reduced-alcohol beer had little fizz.
USA Today: The colorful national daily is still mired in red ink, but it's changed the way many newspapers look and act.	Home banking: Consumers weren't ready for this complicated "service."
Swatch watches: A new look at an old product turned watches into hot fashion accessories.	
Nintendo video games: Games like Super Mario Brothers continue so strong they're zapping the rest of the toy business.	
SPF sunscreens: Do you need SPF 5 or SPF 15? High-tech sunscreens sell well to aging baby boomers.	

Exhibit 10.7

Product Successes and Failures

Failure can be a matter of degree. Absolute failure occurs when a company cannot regain its development, marketing, and production costs. The product actually loses money for the company. A relative product failure results when the product returns a profit but does not meet its profit or market share objectives. Relative failures can sometimes be repositioned or improved to become a viable part of a product line. For instance, Tony's Pizza failed until a home economist developed a crust that didn't taste like cardboard. Similarly, Pepperidge Farm's Deli's floundered until the quality of ingredients was improved.

In the long run, products fail because product characteristics poorly match consumer needs. Other important factors that tend to cause new product failure are

- Inadequate promotion
- Poor packaging
- Lack of differential advantage
- Poor timing
- Overpricing or underpricing
- Lack of or inadequate accessories
- Poor after-sale service
- Inadequate performance
- Failure to fulfill promotional claims

Several new products introduced in the 1980s that failed for one or more of these reasons are also listed in Exhibit 10.7.

MARKETING AND SMALL BUSINESS

Checklist for Evaluating New Product Concepts

If a small business is lucky enough to have stable or increasing sales, new product additions can boost profits and market share. Small-business managers must be careful, however, not to expand beyond the firm's financial capacities. A new product requires shelf space, investment in inventory, perhaps spare parts, and maybe even a new salesperson—all of which require financial commitment.

A new small business usually has only one chance "to do it right." A failure means bankruptcy and perhaps the loss of a person's life savings. Conversely, the owner of an established small business whose product is no longer in demand may suddenly find that his or her source of livelihood has evaporated. The right new product can help offset declining demand.

The product development process is generally the same for both large and small firms. However, many entrepreneurs must do most steps in the process themselves rather than rely on specialists or outside consultants.

Here's a simple checklist for evaluating new product concepts for a small business:

1. Contribution to before-tax return on investment:
   - More than 35 percent +2
   - 25–35 percent +1
   - 20–25 percent –1
   - Less than 20 percent –2
2. Estimated annual sales:
   - More than $10 million +2
   - $2 million–$10 million +1
   - $1 million–$1.99 million –1
   - Less than $1 million –2
3. Estimated growth phase of product life cycle:
   - More than three years +2
   - Two or three years +1
   - One or two years –1
   - Less than one year –2
4. Capital investment payback:
   - Less than a year +2
   - One to two years +1
   - Two to three years –1
   - More than three years –2
5. Premium-price potential:
   - Weak or no competition that makes entry easy +2
   - Mildly competitive entry conditions +1
   - Strongly competitive entry conditions –1
   - Entrenched competition that makes entry difficult –2

This checklist is by no means complete. Yet a neutral or negative total score should give entrepreneurs reason to consider dropping the product concept.

5 GLOBAL ISSUES IN NEW PRODUCT DEVELOPMENT

Increasing globalization of markets and of competition provides a reason for multinational firms to consider new product development from a worldwide perspective. A firm that starts with a global strategy is better able to develop products that are marketable worldwide.

In many multinational corporations, every product is developed for potential worldwide distribution, and unique market requirements are built in whenever possible.[32] Some global marketers design their products to meet regulations and other key requirements in their major markets and then, if necessary, meet smaller markets' requirements country by country. For example, Nissan develops lead-country car models that can, with minor changes, be sold in most markets. For the remaining markets, Nissan provides other models that can readily be adapted. With this approach, Nissan has been able to reduce the number of its basic models from forty-eight to eighteen. This approach also allows a company to introduce new products in all its markets at roughly the same time.

The main goal of the global product development process, therefore, is not to develop a standard product or product line. Rather, it is to build adaptable products that are expected to achieve worldwide appeal.

6 THE SPREAD OF NEW PRODUCTS

Marketing and product managers have a better chance of successfully guiding a product through its life cycle if they understand how consumers learn about and adopt products. The product life cycle and the adoption process go hand in hand. A person who buys a new product never before tried may ultimately become an adopter. An **adopter** is a consumer who was happy enough with his or her trial experience with a product to use it again.

adopter
Consumer who was happy enough with a trial experience with a product to use it again.

Stages in the Adoption Process

People progress through distinct stages when deciding whether to adopt or reject a product. One model that describes this process is called *AIDA*, which stands for attention, interest, desire, and action. Another model that depicts the adoption process is called the hierarchy of effects model. Both models are examined in Chapter 15.

There are two main marketing implications of the consumer adoption process. First, since adoption is a process, people must progress through the awareness, interest, and evaluation stages before proceeding to trial and adoption. Second, different people will be in different stages of the adoption process. Thus marketers face a major challenge in directing their marketing communications. They must attract the interest of some, create interest on the part of others, stimulate trial on the part of still others, and convince other consumers to adopt and continue using the product.

Diffusion of Innovation

An **innovation** is a product perceived as new by a potential adopter. It really doesn't matter whether the product is "new to the world" or simply new to the individual. **Diffusion** is the process by which the adoption of an innovation spreads. The **diffusion process** is the spread of a new idea from its source of invention or creation to its ultimate users or adopters.

innovation
Product perceived as new by a potential adopter.

diffusion
Process by which the adoption of an innovation spreads.

diffusion process
Spread of a new idea from its source of invention or creation to its ultimate users or adopters.

Five categories of adopters participate in the diffusion process:

- *Innovators:* the first 2 1/2 percent of all those who adopt. **Innovators** are eager to try new ideas and products, almost as an obsession. In addition to having higher incomes, they are more worldly and more active outside their community than noninnovators. They rely less on group norms and are more self-confident. Since they are well educated, they are more likely to get their information from scientific sources and experts. Innovators are characterized as being venturesome.
- *Early adopters:* the next 13 1/2 percent to adopt the product. Although **early adopters** are not the very first, they do adopt early in the product's life cycle. Compared to innovators, they rely much more on group norms and values. They are also more oriented to the local community, in contrast to the innovator's worldly outlook. Early adopters are most likely to be opinion leaders because of their closer affiliation to groups. The respect of others is a dominant characteristic of early adopters.
- *Early majority:* the next 34 percent to adopt. The **early majority** will weigh the pros and cons before adopting a new product. They are likely to collect more information and evaluate more brands than early adopters, therefore extending the adoption process. They rely on the group for information but are unlikely to be opinion leaders themselves. Instead, they tend to be opinion

innovator
Consumer among the small group who first adopts a new idea or product and is eager to try.

early adopter
Consumer among the second group to adopt a new idea or product; frequently an opinion leader.

early majority
Third group of consumers to adopt a new idea or product, characterized by their deliberation.

Innovators are those consumers who rush out to buy the newest product, such as the latest computer game.
Jeffrey MacMillan/*U.S. News & World Report*

leaders' friends and neighbors. The early majority is an important link in the process of diffusing new ideas, since its members are positioned between earlier and later adopters. A dominant characteristic of the early majority is deliberateness.

late majority
Fourth group of consumers to adopt a new idea or product, characterized by their reliance on group norms.

laggard
Consumer among the final group to adopt a new idea or product, characterized by ties to tradition.

- *Late majority:* the next 34 percent to adopt. The **late majority** adopt a new product because most of their friends have already adopted it. Since they also rely on group norms, their adoption stems from pressure to conform. This group tends to be older and below average in income and education. They depend mainly on word-of-mouth communication rather than the mass media. The dominant characteristic of the late majority is skepticism.
- *Laggards:* the final 16 percent to adopt. Like innovators, **laggards** do not rely on group norms. Their independence is rooted in their ties to tradition. Thus the past heavily influences their decisions. By the time laggards adopt an innovation, it has probably been outmoded and replaced by something else. For example, they may buy their first black-and-white TV set when color television is already widely owned. Laggards have the longest adoption time and the lowest socioeconomic status. They tend to be suspicious of new products and alienated from a rapidly advancing society. The dominant value of laggards is tradition. Marketers typically ignore laggards, who do not seem to be motivated by advertising or personal selling.

Exhibit 10.8 shows the relationship between the adopter categories and stages of the product life cycle. Note that the various categories of adopters first buy products in different stages of the product life cycle. Sales in the maturity and decline stages almost all represent repeat purchasing.

Exhibit 10.8

Relationship between the Diffusion Process and the Product Life Cycle

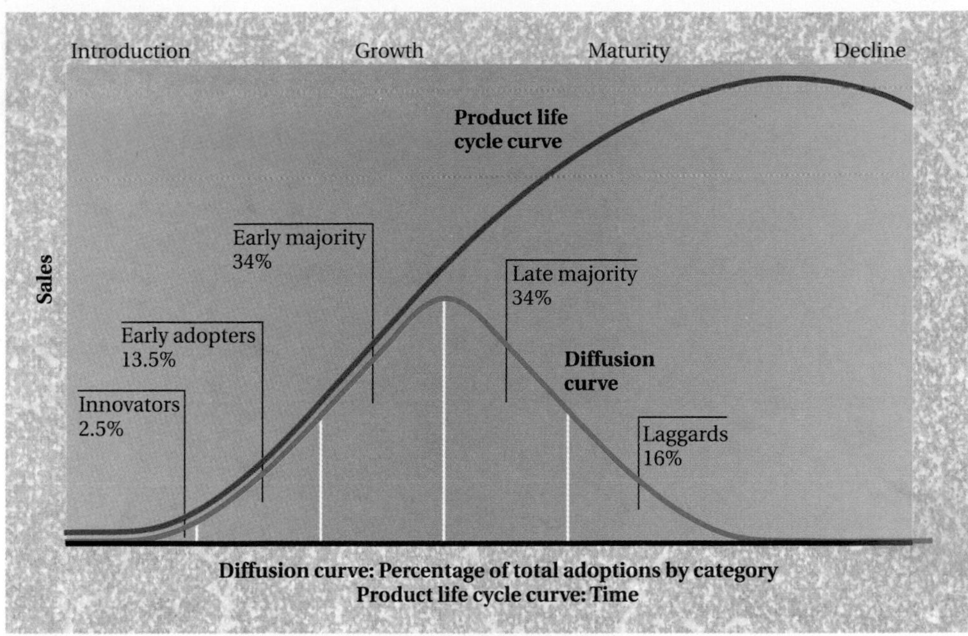

Product Characteristics and the Rate of Adoption

Five product characteristics can be used to predict and explain the rate of acceptance and diffusion of a new product:

- *Complexity:* the degree of difficulty involved in understanding and using a new product. The more complex the product, the slower its diffusion. For instance, before many of their functions were automated, 35-mm cameras were used primarily by hobbyists and professionals. They were just too complex for most people to learn to operate.
- *Compatibility:* the degree to which the new product is consistent with existing values and product knowledge, past experiences, and current needs. Incompatible products diffuse more slowly than compatible products. For example, the introduction of contraceptives is incompatible in countries where religious beliefs discourage the use of birth control techniques.
- *Relative advantage:* the degree to which a product is perceived as superior to existing substitutes. For example, because it reduces cooking time, the microwave oven has a clear relative advantage over a conventional oven.
- *Observability:* the degree to which the benefits or other results of using the product can be observed by others and communicated to target customers. For instance, fashion items and automobiles are highly visible and more observable than personal care items.
- *Trialability:* the degree to which a product can be tried on a limited basis. It is much easier to try a new toothpaste or breakfast cereal than a new automobile or microcomputer. Demonstrations in showrooms and test drives are different from in-home trial use. To stimulate trial, marketers use free sampling programs, tasting displays, and small package sizes.

Marketing Implications of the Adoption Process

Two types of communication aid the diffusion process: word-of-mouth communication among consumers and communication from marketers to consumers. Word-of-mouth communication within and across groups speeds diffusion. Opinion

leaders discuss new products with their followers and with other opinion leaders. Marketers must therefore ensure that opinion leaders have the types of information desired in the media that they use. Suppliers of some products, such as professional and health care services, rely almost solely on word-of-mouth communication for new business.

The second type of communication aiding the diffusion process is communication directly from the marketer to potential adopters. Messages directed toward early adopters should normally use different appeals than messages directed toward the early majority, the late majority, or the laggards. Early adopters are more important than innovators because they make up a larger group, are more socially active, and are usually opinion leaders.

As the focus of a promotional campaign shifts from early adopters to the early majority and the late majority, marketers should study the dominant characteristics, buying behavior, and media characteristics of these target markets. Then they should revise messages and media strategy to fit. The diffusion model helps guide marketers in developing and implementing promotion strategy.

brand manager
Person who is responsible for a single brand.

product manager
Person who is responsible for several brands within a product line or product group.

category manager
Person responsible for multiple product lines within a product category.

7 PRODUCT MANAGEMENT

Large organizations often use brand, product, or category managers to direct specific marketing efforts. Technically, a **brand manager** is responsible for a single brand. A **product manager** has responsibility for several brands within a product line or product group. A **category manager** has responsibility for multiple product lines within a product category.[33] Exhibit 10.9 shows the product responsibilities of brand, product, and category managers.

Exhibit 10.9

The Product Management Hierarchy

Product level	Management level	Responsibilities
Brand	Brand manager (product manager)	Develop marketing strategies for a new brand Recommend changes in strategy for an existing brand Position the brand Identify target segments for the brand Evaluate the effect of alternative marketing strategies on brand performance
Product line	Product manager	Evaluate products in a given line Consider extensions of the line within the product category Assess an expansion of the line to other product categories Consider candidates for deletion from the line Consider the effects of additions to and deletions from the line on the profitability of other products in the line
Product category	Top management or category manager	Evaluate existing product lines in the product category Evaluate the mix of new and existing products within the category Consider the relative emphasis on new versus existing products Consider the effects of line additions and deletions on the profitability of other lines in the category Consider the introduction of new product lines

The Original Product Manager Concept

During the 1950s and 1960s, major consumer products companies grew in sales, number of product lines, and organizational complexity. Managers developed new organizational arrangements for marketing to better cope with the dynamic nature of the marketing environment. These were the responsibilities of the product manager's job in its original form:

- Creating strategies for improving and marketing assigned product lines or brands
- Making financial and operating plans for those products
- Monitoring the results of those plans and adapting tactics to evolving conditions

The product manager's job does vary, however, and the position has been given all sorts of names—including little marketing manager, entrepreneur, information center, influence agent, integrator, little general manager, product planning and development analyst, boundary spanner, and marketing brain center.

The scope of product managers' decision-making powers and responsibilities and the people with whom they should interact have been somewhat controversial. These are some of the key issues:

- Should product managers be responsible for the profit achieved by their products?
- Should product managers act only as a source of information for their products?
- Should advertising decisions be outside the scope of the product manager's responsibilities?
- Should product managers have responsibility for marketing research decisions?

The Product Management Concept at Procter & Gamble

Procter & Gamble, originator of the product management form of organization, has fine-tuned the concept. Now individual brand managers report to a category manager, who has profit-and-loss responsibility for an entire product line. For example, a category manager for laundry detergents would have the brand managers of Tide, Cheer, Liquid Tide, and Ivory Flakes reporting to him or her.

Before P&G's reorganization, brand managers fought not only external competitors but also internal brands. Thus the brand managers of Tide and Cheer might both launch massive couponing campaigns during the same month. Both campaigns would suffer. A category manager thinks in terms of product groups and makes sure the brand managers aren't sabotaging each other. Now the brand managers can go directly to the category manager, who has the authority to make quick decisions and coordinate campaigns and other efforts. The category manager can also back them up with as much as $1 million per project.

Under the old form of organization, a brand manager would create a new concept for a product or package. The idea, usually communicated in memo form, would be sent first to engineering, then to manufacturing, and finally perhaps to people in physical distribution. Progress was slow and awkward. However, adding product supply managers has changed this sluggish procedure. For instance, the category manager for dishwashing detergent wanted a new cap for liquid Cascade. Although the cap in use was child-proof, it was also somewhat adult-proof. People from

Apple Computer is one of those firms that uses market managers instead of product managers. Market managers focus on a single segment of the target market—such as the educational market for computers—instead of on a product or product line.
Apple Computer Inc.

manufacturing, engineering, purchasing, and distribution met with the product supply manager and resolved all the cost, design, and manufacturing problems. The cap went into production without any glitches after only nine months, nearly twice as quickly as under the old system.

Market Management

Some firms, completely dissatisfied with the product manager concept, have instead created the position of market manager. A market manager focuses on a particular group of customers rather than products. For example, personal computers are used by households, educational institutions, small businesses, government institutions, and large businesses. Apple Computer has a market manager to serve each market segment. Previously, Apple had used a product manager approach, developing and marketing each product in isolation.

A market manager is responsible for annual budgets, long-range plans, sales forecasts, and profit analysis in his or her market. The market manager knows the product need in the market and thus is better able to suggest product modifications, new product ideas, and product service.

8 PRODUCT ABANDONMENT

The product life cycle concept reminds us that all products eventually decline in popularity and profitability. To maintain an effective marketing mix, firms must delete obsolete products as well as develop and introduce new ones.

A grocery industry task force found that the costs to manufacturers of deleting products—including disposal of inventory—ranged from $7,100 to $660,770.[34] Wholesalers spend only about $300 on average to drop products from their lines.

Perhaps the greatest cost of a weak product is its effect on new product ideas. While the firm struggles to maintain a weak product, it can't give new products the attention they deserve. The price for sustaining old products may be the sacrifice of new products and future profits.

Decisions to abandon a product are too important for one person to handle alone. Firms often have a **product-review committee** of high-level executives representing the marketing, production, and finance departments. Typically, the marketing executive discusses marketing strategy, customer relations, sales potential, and competitive offerings. The production executive discusses scheduling, production, and inventory problems. Finally, the finance executive discusses the company's potential profit position if the weak product were eliminated.

product-review committee
Group of high-level executives—representing the marketing, production, and finance departments—appointed to review products for elimination from a company's product line.

Product Abandonment Checklist

One of the first tasks of the product-review committee is to set a procedure for periodically evaluating the firm's products. Since many firms market a large number of products—in some cases, a thousand or more—a screening procedure helps identify weak products. Most screening procedures list product abandonment, or "early warning," criteria. Exhibit 10.10 is a sample.

After members of the product-review team agree on the screening criteria, they combine the criteria into a checklist like the one shown in Exhibit 10.11. If the product-review committee's time is limited, it can rank products just by their mean scores, from weakest to strongest. In the exhibit, the average score of 2.33 indicates that the product is in trouble. Normally the firm would want to look closely at any product with an average score of 2 or greater.

The product abandonment checklist can be as sophisticated as needed, however. For example, some criteria could be weighted more heavily than others. The purpose of this type of analysis is to pinpoint weak products and then evaluate them more intensively.

Note that a product with a bad average score should not necessarily be removed

Exhibit 10.10

Sample Product Abandonment Criteria

Product sales trend	A persistent downward trend in the sales of a product may indicate that it has reached the maturity or decline stage of its life cycle.
Price trend	A downward trend in the price of a new product may not be a big surprise, but if the trend continues when the product is better established, then it may be in trouble.
Profit trend	Declining profit, expressed as a percentage of either sales or invested capital, should raise questions about the wisdom of keeping the product on the market.
Substitute products	Many new products are improved versions of more established products. In such cases, it's a good idea to withdraw the earlier versions from the market.
Product effectiveness	If a product no longer performs its intended function, then it probably should be withdrawn from the market. For example, household bug sprays lose their effectiveness when insects develop resistance to them.
Executive time	The more time managers spend on a product, the stronger the argument for abandoning it. Sick products require constant attention; this time can be better spent elsewhere.

Exhibit 10.11

Product Abandonment Checklist

	Rating		
Early warning criteria	*Negative (3)*	*Neutral (2)*	*Positive (1)*
Product sales trend		X	
Price trend	X		
Profit trend	X		
Substitute products		X	
Product effectiveness			X
Executive time	X		
Average score: 14/6 = 2.33			

from the market. That product may complete a product line. But another product with the same score may be a good candidate for abandonment.

Timing of Product Abandonment

After deciding to abandon a product, the product-review team should decide how quickly to withdraw it. The alternatives range from dropping the product immediately to phasing it out over a period of months. This decision should be made only after reviewing current inventory levels and obligations to dealers and customers. Manufacturers of industrial products seldom drop weak products overnight. Products are normally phased out gradually to give customers time to find adequate substitutes.

LOOKING BACK

Look back at the Pert Plus example that appeared at the beginning of this chapter. Pert Plus was a new product that fit into the category labeled "improvements or revisions of existing products." It has been successful because it satisfies a need that had not been previously met: the need for a combination shampoo-conditioner.

Pert Plus had to be sold under different names in some countries because similar names were being used for other products. It violated trademarks in other countries.

The marketing of Pert Plus is not an example of inventing a product and then trying to create a need. Early test marketing clearly revealed that consumers wanted a two-in-one product.

Several sources of new product ideas were mentioned in the chapter. These include customers, employees, distributors, competitors, consultants, and internal groups, such as new product committees, new product departments, and venture teams.

KEY TERMS

adopter 321

applied research 312

basic research 312

SUMMARY

1 List the six categories of new products. New products can be classified as new-to-the-world products (discontinuous innovations), new product lines, additions to existing product lines, improvements or revisions of existing products, repositioned products, or lower-cost products.

brainstorming 313
brand manager 324
business analysis 314
category manager 324
commercialization 318
concept test 313
development 314
diffusion 321
diffusion process 321
early adopter 321
early majority 321
innovation 321
innovator 321
laggard 322
late majority 322
new product 304
new product committee 306
new product department 306
new product strategy 309
parallel (simultaneous/concurrent) engineering 308
product development 312
product manager 324
product modification 312
product-review committee 327
screening 313
simulated (laboratory) market test 317
test marketing 315
venture team 307

2 Understand the importance of developing new products. To sustain or increase profits, a firm must introduce at least one new successful product before a previous product advances to the maturity stage and profit levels begin to drop. Several factors make it more important than ever for firms to consistently introduce new products: shortened product life cycles, rapidly changing technology and consumer priorities, the high rate of new product failures, and the length of time needed to implement new product ideas.

3 Identify the organizational groups or structures used to facilitate new product development. Firms facilitate the development of new products by forming new product committees, new product departments, and venture teams. New product committees are composed of representatives of various branches of an organization and mainly play an advisory role. A new product department may be a separate department, a high-level staff function, a part of marketing, or a part of research and development. Venture team members are recruited from within an organization to work full-time on specific projects and are encouraged to take an "intrapreneurial" approach to new product development. In addition, some U.S. firms are currently adopting an organizational structure popular in Japan, called parallel engineering, in which all departments work together to develop new products.

4 List the steps in the new product development process. First a firm forms a new product strategy by outlining the characteristics and roles of future products. Then new product ideas are generated by customers, employees, distributors, competitors, and internal research and development. Once a product idea has survived initial screening by an appointed screening group, it undergoes business analysis to determine its potential profitability. If a product concept seems viable, it progresses into the development phase, in which the technical and economic feasibility of the manufacturing process is evaluated. The development phase also includes laboratory and use testing of a product for performance and safety. Following initial testing and refinement, most products are introduced in a test market to evaluate consumer response and marketing strategies. Finally, test market successes are propelled into full commercialization. The commercialization process means starting up production, building inventories, shipping to distributors, training a sales force, announcing the product to the trade, and advertising to consumers.

5 Identify the main goal of product development for the global market. A marketer with global vision seeks to develop products that can easily be adapted to suit local needs. The goal is not to develop a standard product that can be sold worldwide.

6 Explain the diffusion process through which new products are adopted. The diffusion process is the spread of a new product from its producer to ultimate adopters. Adopters in the diffusion process belong to five categories: innovators, early adopters, early majority, late majority, and laggards. Product characteristics that affect the rate of adoption include product complexity, compatibility with existing social values, relative advantage over existing substitutes, visibility, and trialability. The diffusion process is facilitated by word-of-mouth communication and communication from marketers to consumers.

7 Explain the product management form of organization. Some firms use the product management form of organization. The product manager plans product objectives and strategy, monitors progress, coordinates budget development and control, and cooperates with other departments on product cost and quality.

8 Identify the cost of sustaining weak products, and explain procedures for

deciding to abandon a product. In addition to introducing financial losses, weak products drain a firm in several ways. They demand more time from management, advertising, and sales personnel than they deserve. And they take company resources away from potentially profitable new products. Product-review committees periodically evaluate a firm's products and set criteria for product abandonment decisions. If a product meets the abandonment criteria, it is phased out immediately or gradually, depending on obligations to dealers and customers.

Review Questions

1. Name the six major new product categories.
2. What are the risks of new product development in the 1990s?
3. What is parallel engineering? What makes it an effective management strategy?
4. What management strategies help facilitate the success of new products?
5. Discuss the role of market testing in the new product development process. Why are some companies looking for alternatives to traditional methods of testing?
6. What are the categories of product failures? List some reasons products fail.
7. Describe the five categories of new product adopters.
8. Describe the basic differences among brand, product, and category managers.

Discussion and Writing Questions

1. An executive at Purex commented, "I turn down new products at least twice as often as I did a year ago. But in every case, I tell my people to go back and bring me some new product ideas." Interpret this statement in terms of today's domestic market conditions.
2. You are the new director of new product development. Describe in a memo your department's role in the organization.
3. John Luther, management consultant at Marketing Corporation of America, remarked, "People just can't shake the corporate culture's baggage. They still want to do all that market research and testing." Why is new product development often too time-consuming and complicated?
4. Describe some products whose adoption rates are or have been affected by complexity, compatibility, relative advantage, observability, and trialability.
5. What types of communication aid the product diffusion process? Identify some products you use and tell how you found out about them. Explain what influenced you to buy them.
6. Your firm is phasing out a product. Write a memo explaining why the phaseout will be gradual rather than immediate.

CASES

10.1 Cincinnati Milacron

What started out as a chat over a cup of coffee soon led to Cincinnati Milacron's best-selling machine. Bruce Kozak, a regional sales manager, bumped into Harold Faig, a product manager, one Sunday in 1985. Kozak complained to Faig that the Japanese were swamping the market for plastics machinery. Milacron had been relatively blind to the Japanese invasion. Plastics machinery sales had been increasing each year but at a rate below that of total market increases. Milacron was losing market share even though sales were increasing.

Faig and Kozak began listing specifications that a machine would have to have to beat the Japanese. Within a month, Faig called Kozak and invited him to join a venture team. The machine had been dubbed the Hafakozaki. Faig and Kozak handpicked a team to develop the new product.

Breaking down organizational walls, they selected members from marketing, engineering, and manufacturing. The initial time to develop the product, usually one year, was reduced to nine months. "If a woman can make a baby in nine months, so can we," Faig told his group. The project was renamed Project 270. The 270 days (nine months) were counted, and plans were made for company president Daniel Meyer and vice president David Noffsinger to flip the switch on that day.

The team started by visiting customers who were using plastics machinery to find out what these people look for in a product. These visits revealed that price and lead time were two critical elements involved in the purchasing decision. Milacron had always assumed that the technical features of a product and the ability to customize it were the most important features. The new goal was to reduce the cost of the product by 40 percent and to make the product "world-class," which meant standardizing it on the metric system as opposed to the U.S. measurement system. Milacron had always used the U.S. system.

The members of the group moved their offices closer together. Meetings were held each Monday so everyone could stay up to date. Instead of waiting until the weekly meeting to make decisions (which could cause delays), team members were encouraged to make decisions on the spot and then to report back on Mondays. Accounting information, usually kept secret from production and marketing people, was made available to the group. By reducing the number of parts, using cast parts instead of machined parts, and standardizing things like screw sizes, the group was able to reduce the cost of the machine by 40 percent.

The prototype of the Vista, as the new machine was later named, was introduced on December 7, 1985—Pearl Harbor day. The product was introduced to the market in the latter part of 1986. In the first full year of production, the Vista sold over twice as many machines as its predecessor had.

Questions

1. Do you think Cincinnati Milacron would have been able to introduce a product like Vista without using a venture group? Why or why not?
2. Explain why you think a company like Cincinnati Milacron ends up using over 300 different sizes of bolts in manufacturing its machines.
3. Do you think the company will be successful in competing with the Japanese? Explain your answer.

Suggested Readings

Ken Murphy, "Venture Teams Help Companies Create New Products," *Personnel Journal,* March 1992, p. 60.

10.2 Mary Kay

Video title: *New Product Development and Testing at Mary Kay*

Mary Kay
8787 N. Stemmons Freeway
Dallas, TX 75247

SIC code: 2844 Perfumes, cosmetics, and other toilet preparations

Number of employees: 1,720

1993 revenues: $450 million

Major brands: Mary Kay Cosmetics

Largest competitors: Avon, Revlon, Cover Girl, Maybelline

Background

Mary Kay began in 1963. Some thirty years later, the company's beauty consultants have over 20 million customers and sell more than $1 billion in Mary Kay products. The company strives to be a preeminent force in the distribution and marketing of beauty and health-related products.

Mary Kay relies on direct marketing for its sales. The company uses recruited beauty consultants to sell its product line directly to consumers. Each beauty consultant is treated as a small-business owner.

To support its beauty consultants, the company offers training programs in finance, marketing, distribution, and human resources. These programs cover such topics as inventory control, business record keeping, screening and planning of sales calls, and recruitment of other interested beauty consultants. The company prides itself on the support it offers consultants.

Industry

One of the biggest problems facing the cosmetics industry is the testing of new products before introducing them to the market. Historically, cosmetics companies have relied on animal testing to see if new products might be safe for human consumption. However, animal rights activists have lobbied long and hard to keep companies from using animals to test new products. It has become such an important issue that many companies now use "Never tested on animals" as part of their advertising or promotional message.

Mary Kay

Mary Kay has always been one of the industry leaders in the development and testing of new cosmetics. To test new products, the company now relies on employee volunteers instead of animals. Each product is thoroughly tested before it is ever shipped out to the beauty consultants for sale.

In addition to this type of product testing, Mary Kay beauty consultants make follow-up calls on all new clients to see how well the cosmetics are performing for them. The company wants to make sure it sells only the finest products and that consumers have no adverse reactions to the products. Follow-up calls also give beauty consultants the chance to make sure that Mary Kay products are being used properly. This sort of attention helps improve customer satisfaction.

In addition to introducing new products, Mary Kay strives to improve its product packaging. The company now uses recycled paper in its packaging and uses recycling codes to support local recycling efforts. Because of its new-product testing and recyclable packaging, Mary Kay continues to be an industry leader in the area of social responsibility.

Questions

1. How important are new products to a company like Mary Kay?
2. Do you think product safety testing is more important for companies like Mary Kay than for cosmetic companies that rely on more traditional sales outlets?
3. Do you think Mary Kay customers care about the packaging?

References

Standard & Poor's Industry Surveys (New York: Standard & Poor's Corporation, October 1993).

Million Dollar Directory 1993 (Parsippany, NJ: Dun & Bradstreet Information Services, 1993).

10.3 *Decision Assistant:* Whitley Educational Services Corporation

The Situation

Angela Douglas, director of product development for Whitley Educational Services Corporation, needs to evaluate alternatives for new products. Two choices are available: an electronic chalkboard system and a computer-based grade-recording system. Unfortunately, the firm's situation is such that it can offer only one product.

The firm has identified five criteria for deciding which products it should market: potential sales volume, level of competition, compatibility with marketing, similarity to existing products, and environmental compatibility.

Angela Douglas has asked a panel of experts to rate each of the new products on a scale of 0.00 to 1.00 and to estimate the relative importance of each attribute by assigning weights. The average ratings and weights for each product are presented in Exhibit 10.12. She has come to you for assistance in interpreting these data.

The Solution Technique

The Evaluation Matrix tool in the marketing *Decision Assistant* can be used to evaluate the potential of each of these products. Enter the data for the chalkboard system first, and key ALT-D to compute the weighted average and display the matrix. You may want to save these data (using ALT-S) before evaluating the grade-recording system.

What If?

Consider each of the following situations independently:

1. What if the demand for the electronic chalkboard system was rated 0.8? What effect would this change have on the rating of the product and on the choice of which product to produce?
2. What if the "compatibility with marketing" attribute for the computer-based grade-recording system was rated 0.2? What effect would this change have on the rating of the product and on the choice of which product to produce?
3. What if the weights of the first, third, and fourth attributes were each changed to 0.15, the second was changed to 0.30, and the fifth was changed to 0.25?

Exhibit 10.12

Product Ratings for Chalkboard and Grade-Recording Systems

Performance factors	Weight	Chalkboard	Grade System
Potential sales volume	0.23	0.4	0.8
Level of competition	0.18	0.7	0.4
Compatibility with marketing	0.26	0.3	0.8
Similarity to existing products	0.24	0.1	0.5
Environmental compatibility	0.09	0.8	0.4

CHAPTER 11
Services and Nonbusiness Marketing

LEARNING OBJECTIVES

After studying this chapter, you should be able to

1. Discuss the importance of services to the economy.
2. Discuss the unique characteristics of services marketing.
3. Explain how manufacturers become involved in services marketing.
4. Develop service marketing strategies.
5. Explain the concept of service quality.
6. Discuss relationship marketing.
7. Discuss global issues in services marketing.
8. Describe nonbusiness marketing and how it differs from profit-sector marketing.
9. Develop marketing strategies for nonbusiness organizations.

Many hospitals and hospital chains are starting to embrace marketing. In marketing a service, attention to quality is important. One component of service quality is reliability, the ability to perform the service dependably, accurately, and consistently.

Intermountain—a nonprofit chain of twenty-four hospitals in Idaho, Utah, and Wyoming—has focused on eliminating undesirable variations in health care. For example, Intermountain is trying to lower the rate of postoperative wound infections.

"In 1985, the hospital's infection rate was 1.8 percent. By using a bedside computer system to make sure that antibiotics were given to patients two hours before surgery, the hospital dropped the infection rate by half." Since postop infection adds significantly to the hospital bill, quality control helps reduce costs.

Along with cost benefits, patients realize other benefits when the reliability of health care improves. Postoperative complications can involve more pain, more time in the hospital, and—in extreme cases—even death. All these complications are likely to be reduced when hospital care becomes more reliable.

"Intermountain . . . is now focusing on . . . situations in which the wrong type or dose of medication is given, the top cause of poor care. . . . Intermountain's quality chief expects quality techniques to help eliminate up to 60 percent of such mistakes and reduce related medical costs by up to $2 million a year per hospital."

Why is quality important to the marketing of services? How do you feel about the way Intermountain is attempting to improve the quality of hospital care? What other things could Intermountain do to improve quality?

Source: Extracts from Julia Flynn Siler and Sandra Atchinson, "The RX at Work in Utah," *Business Week*, 25 October 1991, p. 113.

1 THE GROWTH AND IMPORTANCE OF SERVICES

The marketing process described in Chapter 1 and illustrated in Exhibit 1.3 is the same for all types of products and organizations. Many concepts, ideas, and strategies discussed throughout this book have been illustrated with service and nonbusiness examples. In many ways, marketing is marketing regardless of the product's characteristics or the organization. However, since services have unique characteristics that distinguish them from goods, service and nonbusiness organization marketing is unique in several ways.

The service sector substantially influences the U.S. economy. Roughly 70 percent of the U.S. work force is employed in services, and the service sector accounts for more than 60 percent of the U.S. gross national product.[1] The service sector has generated over 44 million new jobs in the past thirty years, has softened the effects of every recession since World War II, and has fueled every economic recovery.[2]

The service sector has grown dramatically since the late 1940s. After World War II, services accounted for only a third of the U.S. gross national product. In the past twenty years, 90 percent of the 36 million new jobs created in the United States have been in the service sector.[3]

Services are also important to the world economy. In many countries, the percentage of the work force employed in service industries is rising considerably. The service sector now accounts for about 60 percent of the gross national product averaged worldwide.[4]

2 HOW SERVICES DIFFER FROM GOODS

A **service** is a product in the form of an activity or a benefit provided to consumers. Services have four unique characteristics that distinguish them from goods: intangibility, inseparability, heterogeneity, and perishability.

service
Product in the form of an activity or a benefit provided to consumers, with four unique characteristics that distinguish it from a good: intangibility, inseparability, heterogeneity, and perishability.

Intangibility

The basic difference between services and goods is that services are intangible. Because of their **intangibility,** they cannot be touched, seen, tasted, heard, or felt in the same manner in which goods can be sensed. Services cannot be stored and are often easy to duplicate. Moreover, services are seldom based on any hidden technology, and no patent protection exists for services except for names. One of the favorite slogans of James Robinson, CEO of American Express, is, "Quality is the only patent protection we've got."[5]

intangibility
Characteristic of services that prevents them from being touched, seen, tasted, heard, or felt in the same manner in which goods can be sensed.

Evaluating the quality of services before or even after making a purchase is harder than evaluating the quality of goods. Compared to goods, services tend to exhibit fewer search qualities. A **search quality** is a characteristic that can be easily assessed before purchase—for instance, the color of an appliance or automobile. At the same time, services tend to exhibit more experience and credence qualities.[6] An **experience quality** is a characteristic that can be assessed only after use, such as the quality of a meal in a restaurant or a vacation. A **credence quality** is a characteristic that cannot be easily assessed even after purchase and experience. Medical and consulting services are examples of services that exhibit credence qualities.

search quality
Characteristic that can be easily assessed before purchase.

experience quality
Characteristic that can be assessed only after purchase or use.

credence quality
Characteristic that cannot easily be assessed even after purchase and experience.

These characteristics also make it harder for marketers to communicate the benefits of an intangible service than those of tangible goods. Thus marketers often rely on tangible cues to communicate a service's nature and quality. For example,

Outfitters for white-water raft trips market a service, not a good, and thus must take into account their product's intangibility (it's an experience, not a thing); inseparability (it's produced and consumed at the same time); heterogeneity (one outfitter's product is different from another's); and perishability (it cannot be stored).

the Clinton Administration's proposed health program would include "health security cards" issued to all U.S. citizens certifying their right to health care. The card is a tangible symbol of a person's enrollment in the health program.[7]

The atmosphere at facilities that customers visit or from which services are delivered is a critical part of the total service offering. These facilities should convey desired messages to potential customers. Consider this example:

> Manhattan pediatrician Laura Popper's waiting room walls are bright white trimmed with strawberry-red paint. She herself forgoes the traditional doctor's white coat for colorful clothing and always wears slacks because they are "great for crawling all over the floor with the kids." Dr. Popper states, "In starting my practice, I thought very much about my office, and that I wanted patients to be comfortable and happy there. I wanted it to represent what I am and what I hope to give people."[8]

Messages about the organization are communicated to customers through such elements as the office decor, the clutter or neatness of service areas, and the staff's manners and dress.

The Walt Disney organization is one of the best at managing tangible cues. Disneyland and Walt Disney World focus on the set (facility), the cast (personnel), and the audience. Hosts and hostesses (not employees) serve guests (not customers) at attractions and shops (not rides and stores). When cast members are hired, they are given written information about what training they will receive, when and where to report, and what to wear. They spend the first day on the job at "Disney University" learning about the Disney philosophy, management style, and history. The cast members also discover how all parts of the organization work together to provide the highest possible level of guest satisfaction. In the Magic Kingdom, the cast is just as important as the set.

Inseparability

inseparability
Characteristic of services that allows them to be produced and consumed simultaneously.

Goods are produced, sold, and then consumed. In contrast, services are often sold and then produced and consumed at the same time. In other words, their production and consumption are inseparable activities. **Inseparability** means that, since consumers must be present during the production of services like haircuts or surgery, they are actually involved in the production of the services they buy. That type

One way to overcome the intangibility of services is to use tangible cues in promotions, as Prudential Insurance Company does with its well-known rock symbol.

may also seek to stimulate positive word-of-mouth communication among present and prospective customers.

- *Creating a strong organizational image:* One way to create an image is to manage the evidence, including the physical environment of the service facility, the appearance of the service employees, and the tangible items associated with a service (like stationery, bills, and business cards). For example, the Girl Scouts updated their image to fit the growing cultural diversity in the United States and the career-mindedness of young girls. Fashion designers Bill Blass and Halston redesigned the adult uniform line, and professional women were sought to serve as troop leaders and role models. The Girl Scouts also published handbook materials in different languages.[16] Another way to create an image is through branding. Financial service firms like Fidelity Investments and Charles Schwab Discount Brokerage have established strong brand identities, or images, that help make their services tangible.[17]
- *Engaging in postpurchase communication:* Postcard surveys, telephone calls, brochures, and various other types of follow-up show customers that their feedback is sought and their patronage is appreciated.

Some professional services are subject to restrictions on advertising and other forms of promotion. For example, lawyers must warn that clients will be responsible for litigation costs and expenses if they lose their case. In addition, lawyers cannot disclose their win-loss records without including a disclaimer that past performance does not guarantee future success.[18]

Price Strategy

Several trends have changed pricing from a passive to an active part of the marketing strategy for financial services, telecommunications, transportation, and other service industries. Those trends include deregulation, intense competition, slow growth, and opportunities for firms to strengthen market position.

To maximize the number of customers, movie theaters offer reduced-price tickets to kids, a class of customer that cannot afford full-price tickets.
David Strick/ONYX

Airlines' aggressive pricing strategies illustrate both the importance of and the rapid changes in services pricing. Airline passengers today face a bewildering array of options when pricing a flight from one city to another. In fact, the lowest available fare may even differ from one ticketing agent to another. Underlying this apparent madness are competitive pricing strategies guided by computers that track travel patterns.[19] Airline price strategists can confine deep discount rates to specific cities, at off-peak times, and for only a limited number of seats.

Airlines are not the only service institutions experiencing intensive price competition following deregulation. Financial service institutions must now carefully consider the amount to charge for loans, check-writing privileges, insurance policies, brokerage services, and other services.

revenue-oriented pricing Setting prices at a level that will maximize the surplus of income over expenditures.

operations-oriented pricing Varying prices to coordinate supply and demand by encouraging maximum use of productive capacity.

patronage-oriented pricing Setting prices at a level that will maximize the number of customers using a service—for example, by pricing according to different market segments' ability to pay.

Marketers should set performance objectives when pricing each service. Three categories of pricing objectives have been suggested: revenue-oriented, operations-oriented, and patronage-oriented.[20] **Revenue-oriented pricing** focuses on maximizing the surplus of income over costs. A limitation of this approach is that for many services, determining costs can be difficult. **Operations-oriented pricing** seeks to match supply and demand by varying prices. For example, matching hotel demand to the number of available rooms can be achieved by raising prices at peak times and decreasing them during slow times. Finally, **patronage-oriented pricing** tries to maximize the number of customers using the service. Prices vary with different market segments' ability to pay, and methods of payment (such as credit) are offered that increase the likelihood of a purchase. A firm may need to use more than one type of pricing objective. In fact, all three objectives probably need to be included to some degree in pricing strategy, although the importance of each type may vary from one situation to another. For customized services (for example, legal services and construction services), customers may also have the ability to negotiate price.

5 SERVICE QUALITY

Quality is an essential part of services marketing. High quality is a big advantage in positioning a service. In addition, as shown by the example of Intermountain Health Care at the opening of this chapter, considerable cost savings are possible with higher-quality service. Business executives rank the improvement of service quality as one of the most critical challenges facing them today, according to a Gallup survey.[21] However, the quality of services is harder to define and measure than is the quality of goods, because services are intangible and inseparable. That is, quality cannot be measured before the service is delivered.

Components of Service Quality

Service quality has to be defined from the viewpoint of the customer. Five components that contribute to customers' perceptions of service quality have been identified:

- *Tangibles:* physical facilities, equipment, and appearance of personnel
- *Reliability:* ability to perform the desired service dependably, accurately, and consistently
- *Responsiveness:* willingness to provide prompt service to customers
- *Assurance:* knowledge and courtesy of employees and their ability to convey trust
- *Empathy:* caring individual attention to customers[22]

Although all these components contribute to service quality, reliability has been found to be the most important.

A service's quality is measured by comparing performance with customers' expectations (which are influenced by past experience, personal needs, and word-of-mouth communication) for each of the five components described above. Any gap between expectations and performance could be either positive or negative. For example, if a patient expects to wait twenty minutes in the doctor's office before seeing the doctor but waits only ten minutes, the positive gap increases the patient's evaluation of the responsiveness component of service quality. However, a forty-minute wait would result in a negative gap and a lower evaluation. Overall service quality is measured by combining customers' evaluations for all five components.

Poor service quality can be caused by several factors within the organization. These include top management's lack of understanding about customers' expectations; service standards or specifications that do not fit with customers' expectations; service employees' inability or unwillingness to meet the standards set by management; and advertising and other external communications to customers that create unrealistic expectations about the service.

To provide high-quality service, an organization first needs to learn about customer expectations through marketing research. Then it needs to create a strong culture that stresses the importance of quality, facilitates communication with everyone in the organization, gives employees the authority to make decisions, and rewards employees' efforts to raise the quality of service.

Several noteworthy success stories illustrate what organizations are doing to increase service quality:

- Marriott is training many of its hotel employees in "empowerment," which gives them more authority in solving guests' problems.[23]
- Alaska Airlines, voted the best U.S. airline for three years running by *Conde Nast Traveler*, spends twice the U.S. per-passenger average on meals, provides

more leg room, reduces delays due to heavy fog by using special guidance equipment, and encourages a team spirit among employees.[24]

- Humana has created Quality Action Teams that help its hospital employees in their continuous effort to improve quality.[25]
- Service-Master trains its janitorial workers in every detail of their jobs, including how to stand straight, pull a mop toward them, and trace an S-shaped pattern on the floor.[26]

Internal Marketing in Service Firms

Services are performances, so the quality of a firm's employees is an important part of service quality. Employees who like their jobs and are happy with the firm they work for are more likely to deliver high-quality service. Thus, it is critical that service firms practice **internal marketing,** which means treating employees as customers and developing systems and benefits that satisfy their needs.[27] In other words, a firm that makes its employees happy ultimately makes its customers happy.

internal marketing
Treating employees as customers and developing systems and benefits that satisfy their needs.

The activities involved in internal marketing include competing for talent, offering a vision, training employees, stressing teamwork, giving employees more freedom to make decisions, measuring and rewarding quality, and knowing employees' needs.[28] At a Seattle restaurant chain called Satisfaction Guaranteed Eateries, all employees have been given the power to do whatever it takes to please an unhappy customer, from ordering free drinks to picking up the check.[29] The Toronto-based Four Seasons Hotel interviews applicants four or five times to find those who have a friendly nature and a sense of teamwork.[30] Union Trust Bank in Connecticut accommodates mothers of young children by offering them work hours that allow them to be home when their children get out of school.[31] These examples illustrate how service firms can invest in their most important resource: their employees.

6 RELATIONSHIP MARKETING IN SERVICES

Many services involve ongoing interaction between the service organization and the customer. **Relationship marketing** is the strategy described in Chapter 1 as a means of attracting, developing, and retaining customer relationships. The idea is to develop strong customer loyalty by creating satisfied customers who will buy additional services from the firm and are unlikely to switch to a competitor. Satisfied customers are also likely to engage in positive word-of-mouth communication, thereby helping to bring in new customers.

relationship marketing
Strategy of developing strong customer loyalty by creating satisfied customers who will buy additional services from the firm.

Many businesses have found that it is more cost-effective to hang on to the customers they have than to try and attract new ones. A bank executive, for example, found that increasing customer retention by 2 percent can have the same effect on profits as reducing costs by 10 percent.[32]

It has been suggested that relationship marketing can be practiced at three levels (see Exhibit 11.2).[33] At level one, the firm uses pricing incentives to encourage customers to continue doing business with the firm. Examples include the frequent-flyer programs offered by many airlines and the free or discounted travel services given to frequent hotel guests. This level of relationship marketing is the least effective in the long term because its price-based advantage is easily imitated by other firms.

Level-two relationship marketing also uses pricing incentives but seeks to build social bonds with customers. The firm stays in touch with customers, learns about

Exhibit 11.2

The Three Levels of Relationship Marketing

Source: Reprinted with the permission of The Free Press, a Division of Macmillan, Inc., from *Marketing Services: Competing Through Quality,* by Leonard L. Berry and A. Parasuraman. Copyright ©1991 by The Free Press.

Level	Type of bond	Degree of service customization	Main element of marketing mix	Potential for long-term advantage over competitors
One	Financial	Low	Price	Low
Two	Financial and social	Medium	Personal communications	Medium
Three	Financial, social, and structural	Medium to high	Service delivery	High

their needs, and designs the service to meet those needs. For example, tellers at First Hawaiian Bank phone long-time depositors to thank them and ask how they might improve service.[34] Level-two relationship marketing has a higher potential for keeping the firm ahead of the competition than does level-one relationship marketing.

At level three, the firm again uses financial and social bonds but adds structural bonds to the formula. Structural bonds are developed by offering value-added services that are not readily available from other firms. American Airlines' AAdvantage Gold program, for instance, is offered to the top 2 to 3 percent of all American's AAdvantage (frequent-flyer) members in terms of number of miles flown. Service extras provided by AAdvantage Gold include an exclusive toll-free reservation line, the most desirable coach seats, an empty adjacent middle seat whenever possible, and first-class upgrades. Marketing programs like this have the strongest potential for sustaining long-term relationships with customers.

7 GLOBAL ISSUES IN SERVICES MARKETING

The international marketing of services is a major part of global business, and the United States has become the world's largest exporter of services. Competition in international services is increasing rapidly, however.

To be successful in the global marketplace, service firms must first determine the nature of their core product. Then the marketing mix elements (additional services, pricing, promotion, distribution) should be designed to take into account each country's cultural, technological, and political environment.

Many U.S. industries could enter the global marketplace, because of their competitive advantages. U.S. financial institutions, for example, have advantages in credit card operations, customer service, and collections management. The field of construction and engineering services offers great global potential. The United States has vast experience in this industry, so economies of scale are possible for machinery and material, personnel management, and project management. The insurance industry has substantial knowledge about underwriting, risk evaluation, and insurance operations that it can export to other countries. The leisure industry also has great potential for globalization, as the Club Med article illustrates.

INTERNATIONAL PERSPECTIVES

Club Med in Japan

Club Med is stepping up its activities in Japan's booming leisure market.

After doubling the number of accommodations at its Sahoro skiing resort two years ago, Club Mediterranee S.A. is now studying plans for a beach resort on Okinawa. Would-be Club Med vacationers can check out their intended destinations by watching videos in the company's recently opened Tokyo salon, as well as try on the Club Med brand of sports clothes.

Gone are the days when the travel industry worried that Japanese tourists, especially families, would feel uncomfortable about mixing socially with a crowd of strangers. As many as 85,000 Japanese are expected to sign up with Club Med in the year ending October 31, 1992, a 9 percent increase from a year earlier, says a spokeswoman for the company's Japanese unit. That makes Japan the fourth-largest market for the resort operator, after France, the United States, and Italy, she says.

Japanese travelers, mostly honeymooners and young families, make up as much as one-third of Club Med's resorts on Bali and Thailand's Phuket Island, the spokeswoman says. And the company is hiring Japanese-speaking entertainers for its Lindeman Island resort in Australia, hoping to attract more Japanese vacationers.

How would you describe Club Med's target market in Japan? What marketing strategies are being used to attract Japanese customers? Does it appear that Club Med has adjusted its marketing strategy to account for cultural differences between France and Japan?

Source: Adapted from Yumiko Ono, "Club Med Is Moving In on Japan in a Big Way," *The Wall Street Journal*, 20 July 1992, p. B1. Reprinted by permission of *The Wall Street Journal*, © 1992 Dow Jones & Company, Inc. All Rights Reserved Worldwide.

8 NONBUSINESS MARKETING

Few people realize that nonbusiness organizations account for over 20 percent of the economic activity in the United States. The cost of government in the United States has become the biggest single item in the family budget—more than housing, food, or health care. Together federal, state, and local governments collect revenues that amount to more than a third of the U.S. gross national product. Moreover, they employ nearly one of every five nonagricultural civilian workers.

What Is Nonbusiness Marketing?

nonbusiness marketing Marketing activities conducted by individuals and organizations to achieve some goal other than normal business goals (such as profit, market share, or return on investment).

Nonbusiness marketing includes marketing activities conducted by individuals and organizations to achieve some goal other than normal business goals (such as profit, market share, or return on investment). Nonbusiness marketing can be divided into two categories: social marketing and nonprofit organization marketing.

Social Marketing

social marketing Application of marketing methods to spread socially beneficial ideas or behaviors.

Social marketing is the application of marketing methods to spread socially beneficial ideas or behaviors.[35] Examples include efforts to get people to seek help for problems like alcohol or drug dependency, child or spouse abuse, and depression. Social marketing is also used to urge people to vote, stop smoking, get health checkups, refrain from polluting, avoid forest fires, support the American Cancer Society, and do a variety of other socially beneficial things.

Nonprofit Organization Marketing

nonprofit organization marketing Effort by public and private nonprofit organizations to bring about mutually satisfying exchanges with target markets.

Nonprofit organization marketing is the effort by public and private nonprofit organizations to bring about mutually satisfying exchanges with target markets. Those organizations include government organizations, ranging from local park

Nonprofit organizations need marketing too. For instance, the Cincinnati Zoo and Botanical Gardens developed a special celebration, the Fiesta Latina, to attract guests and developed equally special promotional materials to publicize the event.

Courtesy Mann Bukvic and Associates and The Cincinnati Zoo and Botanical Gardens

and recreation departments to the United States Army, as well as hundreds of thousands of private museums, theaters, schools, churches, and other non-government, nonprofit organizations. Although these organizations vary substantially in size and purpose and operate in different environments, most perform the following activities:

- Identify the customers they wish to serve or attract (although they usually use another term, such as *clients, patients, members*, or *sponsors*)
- Explicitly or implicitly specify objectives
- Develop, manage, and eliminate programs and services
- Decide on prices to charge (although they use other terms, such as *fees, donations, tuition, fares, fines*, or *rates*)
- Schedule events or programs and determine where they will be held or where services will be offered
- Communicate their availability through brochures, signs, public service announcements, or advertisements

Nonprofit organizations carry out these functions but often do not realize that they are engaged in marketing.

ETHICS IN MARKETING

Digging into Data Bases for Big Donors

More and more nonprofit groups, eager to tap big givers, are winnowing their files with computers to find wealthy people. They're hiring prospect researchers, skilled in the use of computer data bases, to provide detailed biographical and sometimes financial records to fund-raisers who go after potential donors.

"There's a myriad of new products and a diversity of software programs out there," says Timothy Truesdell, director of development research at Notre Dame University. And most prospect researchers figure that, as long as they find out details about prospects from public sources in legal ways, they're doing worthy work for a worthy cause.

Others are doubtful. Mary Culnan, a Georgetown University business professor and expert on privacy, told a meeting of the American Prospect Research Association . . . : "I'm somewhat appalled at what's going on. This group represents the worst fears of the privacy advocates."

Nonprofits say they have a special need to learn about the folks in their files. By knowing that a donor has $10 million in stock options from taking his company public, fund-raisers can instantly suggest a new level of giving.

Many nonprofits outdistance corporations in using computer techniques to spot the most lucrative targets. "I was amazed how much research these people do. They're way ahead of stockbrokers," says Mark C. Desmery, president of Prospex Inc., a Fishkill, New York, company that sells information about rich people.

The results can be impressive. John Gliha, who did prospect research for an Iowa State University fund-raising campaign, recalls a wealthy alumnus in California who said, "Why is it you never came to me before?" The graduate ponied up a seven-figure gift.

Do you think prospect research for the purpose of nonprofit fund-raising is ethical? Should the government regulate access to public information about individuals? What other ways could nonprofit marketers gather information about prospective donors?

Source: Adapted from Wiliam M. Bulkeley, "Nonprofits Dig into Databases for Big Donors," *The Wall Street Journal*, 8 September 1992, p. B1. Reprinted by permission of *The Wall Street Journal*, © 1992 Dow Jones & Company, Inc. All Rights Reserved Worldwide.

Often the biggest obstacle to introducing marketing into a nonbusiness organization is the word *marketing* itself. Many people think marketing is appropriate only in commercial, profit-seeking organizations. Some even consider marketing activities unprofessional, unethical, or otherwise inappropriate for nonbusiness organizations. These views clearly reflect inaccurate perceptions of marketing. "Some nonprofit people used to think that if you're doing good, somehow God will provide," says John R. Garrison, president of the National Easter Seal Society. "But almost everyone now realizes that commitment isn't enough anymore. You also have to have professionalism, or you're going to go out of business."[36]

The article above describes one way that nonprofit organizations have perhaps gone too far in adopting marketing techniques.

Benefits to Nonbusiness Managers

A commitment to understanding and enhancing marketing skills offers nonbusiness managers three major benefits. First, because marketing is a systematic process and offers a framework for decision making, relationships between actions once regarded as independent are likely to become more apparent. For example, what if a marketing problem or opportunity is seen only as a communications, price, program, or distribution need? It is unlikely to be resolved in the best way. Coordinated marketing requires that all marketing activities be resolved at the same time and that integrated action be taken.

Second, familiarity with marketing tools is likely to improve decision making. Unfortunately, some of the concepts and techniques used by marketers are unfamiliar to many nonbusiness managers. They have not been exposed to these tools in their formal training or experience.

Finally, a commitment to marketing is likely to result in more support from customers, prospective donors, foundations, regulators, legislators, and other interest groups. To the extent that marketing improves the satisfaction levels of client groups, the organization is likely to receive improved support. The municipal government of Portland, Oregon, is an example of a nonprofit organization that uses some unusual marketing techniques. The water bureau, for instance, conducts customer surveys. In the sewer department, engineers, planners, and policy makers work on projects as a team rather than independently. Performance audits evaluate whether services are effective and efficient. Police force employees go through cultural-diversity training. The goal of these programs is to make government more accountable to the public and, ultimately, to increase the city's quality of life.[37]

9 Unique Aspects of Nonbusiness Marketing Strategy

Like their counterparts in business organizations, nonbusiness managers develop marketing strategies to bring about mutually satisfying exchanges with target markets. However, marketing in nonbusiness organizations is unique in many ways—including the setting of marketing objectives, the selection of target markets, and the development of appropriate marketing mixes.

Objectives

In the private sector, the profit motive is both an objective for guiding decisions and a criterion for evaluating results. Nonbusiness organizations do not seek to make a profit for redistribution to owners or shareholders. Rather, their focus is often generating enough funds to cover expenses. For example, the Methodist Church does not gauge its success by the amount of money left in offering plates. The Museum of Science and Industry does not base its performance evaluations on the dollar value of tokens put into the turnstile.

Most nonbusiness organizations are expected to provide equitable, effective, and efficient services that respond to the wants and preferences of multiple constituencies. These include users, payers, donors, politicians, appointed officials, the media, and the general public. Nonbusiness organizations cannot measure their success or failure in strictly financial terms.

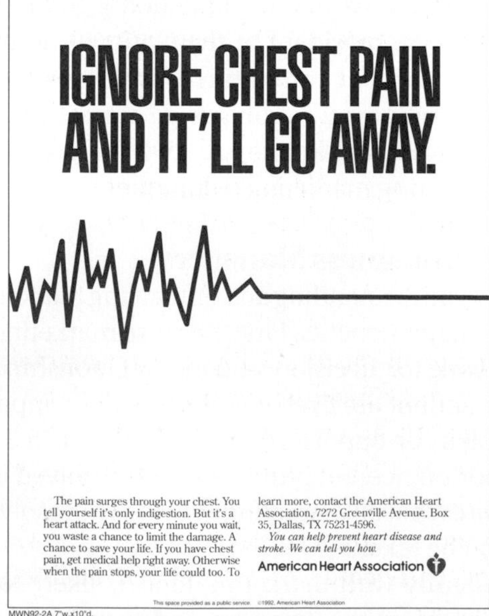

What could be harder than convincing the unwilling to think about the unpleasant? Nonbusiness marketers often face that challenge. The successful ones find ways to overcome the resistance of target markets.

The lack of a financial "bottom line" and the existence of multiple, diverse, intangible, and sometimes vague or conflicting objectives makes prioritizing objectives, making decisions, and evaluating performance hard for nonbusiness managers. They must often use approaches different from the ones commonly used in the private sector. For example, Planned Parenthood has devised a system for basing salary increases on performance:

Without clear profit and loss responsibility, how does a nonprofit pay people for performance? At Planned Parenthood, all employees must set personal objectives every year. Each goal is assigned a percentage weight to determine its importance. Managers evaluate progress against each goal, grading them from 1 for unsatisfactory to 5 for superior performance. Pay hikes are dished out based on the overall grade.[38]

Target Markets

Three issues relating to target markets are unique to nonbusiness organizations. First, instead of targeting the most receptive segments of the market, nonbusiness organizations must often target those who are apathetic or strongly opposed. Second, many nonbusiness organizations are pressured or required to adopt undifferentiated segmentation strategies (see Chapter 6). Third, nonbusiness organizations are often expected to complement, rather than compete against, private-sector organizations.

Apathetic or strongly opposed targets: Private-sector organizations usually give priority to developing those market segments that are most likely to respond to particular offerings. The need to develop marketing programs aimed at relatively unresponsive targets or people strongly opposed to receiving services like vaccinations, family planning guidance, help for problems of drug or alcohol abuse, and psychological counseling is a problem unique to nonbusiness organizations.

Given the desire or need to reach unresponsive markets, should the organization focus on the least-resistant segment, the most-resistant segment, or both? Valid arguments can be made for any of these options, depending on availability of financial resources, public health or welfare considerations, and the like.

Pressure to adopt undifferentiated segmentation strategies: Nonbusiness organizations often adopt undifferentiated strategies by default. Sometimes they fail to recognize the advantages of targeting, or an undifferentiated approach may appear to offer economies of scale and low per capita costs. In other instances, nonbusiness organizations are pressured or required to serve the maximum number of people by targeting the average user.

The problem with developing services targeted at the average user is that there are few "average" users. Therefore, such strategies typically fail to fully satisfy any market segment. Most profit-seeking firms are well aware of the need for segmenting markets and developing targeted marketing programs.

Complementary positioning: The main role of many nonbusiness organizations is to provide services, with available resources, to those who are not adequately served by private-sector organizations. As a result, the nonbusiness organization must often complement rather than compete with the efforts of others. The positioning task is to identify underserved market segments and to develop marketing programs that match their needs rather than to target the niches that may be most profitable.

Product Decisions

Nonbusiness organizations share important characteristics with private-sector service firms. Both market intangible products. Both often require the customer to be present during the production process. Both business and nonbusiness services vary greatly from producer to producer and from day to day, even from the same producer. Neither business nor nonbusiness services can be stored in the way that tangible goods can be produced, saved, and sold at a later date.

There are three specific product-related distinctions between business and nonbusiness organizations:

- *Benefit complexity:* Rather than simple product concepts, like "Fly the friendly skies" or "We earn money the old-fashioned way," nonbusiness organizations often market complex behaviors or ideas. Examples include the need to exercise or eat right, not to drink and drive, or not to smoke tobacco. The benefits that a person receives are complex, long-term, and intangible.
- *Benefit strength:* The benefit strength of many nonbusiness offerings is quite weak or indirect. What are the direct, personal benefits to you of driving fifty-five miles per hour, donating blood, or asking your neighbors to contribute money to a charity? In contrast, most private-sector service organizations can offer customers direct, personal benefits in an exchange relationship.
- *Involvement:* Many nonbusiness organizations market products that elicit very low involvement ("Prevent forest fires" or "Don't litter") or very high involvement ("Join the military" or "Stop smoking"). The typical range for private-sector goods is much narrower. Traditional promotional tools may be inadequate to motivate adoption of either low- or high-involvement products.

Distribution Decisions

The nature of services suggests that distribution channels must normally be direct from producer to consumer and that services cannot be inventoried in anticipation of demand. Nonbusiness organizations share these characteristics with profit-sector service organizations.

A nonprofit organization's capacity for distributing its service offerings to potential customer groups when and where they want them is typically a key variable in determining the success of those service offerings. For example, most state land-grant universities offer extension programs throughout their state to reach the general public. Many large universities have one or more satellite campus locations to provide easier access for students in other areas. Some educational institutions also offer classes to students at off-campus locations via video technology.

The extent to which a service depends on fixed facilities has important implications for distribution decisions. Obviously services like rail transit and lake fishing can only be delivered at specific points. Many nonbusiness services, however, do not depend on special facilities. Counseling, for example, need not take place in agency offices. It may occur wherever counselors and clients can meet. Probation services, outreach youth programs, and educational courses taught on commuter trains are other examples of deliverable services.

Soliciting funds for social marketing efforts also requires good channels of distribution. The Salvation Army places its kettles in areas with heavy foot traffic during the Christmas season. The donations then flow mostly to local units, with a small amount going to the national office. Perhaps the most sophisticated fund channel is the annual Jerry Lewis Muscular Dystrophy Telethon. Thousands of local telephone numbers are used to collect pledges at the grassroots level. Totals are then aggregated by the state or regional area, which provides the local talent and personalities for their portion of the annual program. Finally, the total gifts are reported nationally in Las Vegas, where Jerry Lewis and his staff coordinate the superstar entertainment portion of the program.

Promotion Decisions

Many nonbusiness organizations are explicitly or implicitly prohibited from advertising, thus limiting their promotion options. Most federal agencies fall into this category. Other nonbusiness organizations simply do not have the resources to

retain advertising agencies, promotion consultants, or marketing staff members. However, nonbusiness organizations sometimes have professional volunteers and donated media time or space.

Professional volunteers: Nonbusiness organizations often seek out marketing, sales, or advertising professionals to help them develop and implement promotion strategies. In some instances, an advertising agency donates its services in exchange for some potential long-term benefits. For example, one advertising agency donated its services to a major symphony because the symphony had a blue-ribbon board of directors. Donated services create goodwill, personal contacts, and general awareness of the donor's organization, reputation, and competency.

Professional associations are another possible source of assistance. For example, the Houston Chapter of the Business/Professional Advertising Association initiated an ongoing project in 1982. Its purpose is to give professional help annually to one public service project dedicated to the betterment of Houston and its citizens.

public service advertisement (PSA) Announcement that promotes programs, activities, or services of federal, state, or local governments or the programs, activities, or services of nonprofit organizations.

Public service advertising: A **public service advertisement** (PSA), also called a public service announcement, is an announcement that promotes programs, activities, or services of federal, state, or local governments or the programs, activities, or services of nonprofit organizations. Unlike a commercial advertiser, the sponsor of the PSA does not pay for the time or space. Instead, it is donated by the media.

The Advertising Council has developed PSAs that are some of the most memorable advertisements of all time. For example, Smokey the Bear reminded everyone to be careful not to start forest fires.

Price Decisions

Five key characteristics distinguish the pricing decisions of nonbusiness organizations from those of the profit sector:

- *Pricing objectives:* Revenue is the main pricing objective in the profit sector—or, more specifically, profit maximization, sales maximization, target return on sales or investment, and so on. Many nonbusiness organizations must also be concerned about revenue. However, nonbusiness organizations often seek to either partially or fully defray costs rather than achieve a profit for distribution to stockholders. Nonbusiness organizations also seek to redistribute income—for instance, through taxation and sliding-scale fees. Moreover, they strive to fairly allocate resources among individuals or households or across geographic or political boundaries.

Universities and colleges, like other nonbusiness marketers, do not seek to make a profit but only to cover their costs. Because they price their educational services below cost, they must find other sources of revenue—such as grants from the government, donations from alumni and benefactors, and fees for other types of services.
Doug Milner/© Uniphoto

- *Nonfinancial prices:* In many nonbusiness situations, consumers are not charged a monetary price but instead must absorb nonmonetary costs. The importance of those costs is illustrated by the large number of eligible citizens who do

not take advantage of so-called "free services" for the poverty-stricken. Nonparticipation rates in many public assistance programs seem to hover at around 50 percent.[39] Nonmonetary costs consist of the opportunity cost of time, embarrassment costs, and effort costs.

- *Indirect payment:* Indirect payment through taxes is common to marketers of "free" services, such as libraries, fire protection, and police protection. Indirect payment is not a common practice in the profit sector.
- *Separation between payers and users:* By design, the services of many charitable organizations are provided for those who are relatively poor and largely paid for by those who have better finances. Although examples of separation between payers and users can be found in the profit sector (such as insurance claims), the practice is much less prevalent.
- *Below-cost pricing:* An example of below-cost pricing is university tuition. Virtually all private and public colleges and universities price their services below full cost. This practice also exists in the profit sector, although it is generally an undesirable, temporary situation.

LOOKING BACK

Look back at the story about Intermountain that appeared at the beginning of this chapter. After reading this chapter, you should know the answers to the questions posed at the end of the story. Quality is important to the marketing of services for two reasons. First, quality offers service organizations a competitive edge. Second, considerable cost savings are possible with higher-quality services. Intermountain appears to be making a positive effort toward improving the quality of its health care service. Other areas that could be addressed as part of Intermountain's quality program include tangibles (for example, the hospital facilities), reliability, responsiveness, assurance, and empathy.

KEY TERMS

credence quality 336
experience quality 336
heterogeneity 338
inseparability 337
intangibility 336
internal marketing 345
nonbusiness marketing 347
nonprofit organization marketing 347
operations-oriented pricing 343
patronage-oriented pricing 343
perishability 338
public service advertisement 353
relationship marketing 345

SUMMARY

1 **Discuss the importance of services to the economy.** The service sector plays a crucial role in the U.S. economy, employing about three-quarters of the work force and accounting for more than 60 percent of the gross national product.

2 **Discuss the unique characteristics of services marketing.** Services are distinguished by four unique characteristics: intangibility, inseparability, heterogeneity, and perishability. Services are intangible in that they lack clearly identifiable physical characteristics, making it difficult for marketers to communicate their specific benefits to potential customers. The production and consumption of services is typically an inseparable process. Services are heterogeneous because their quality depends on such variables as the service provider, individual consumer, location, and so on. Finally, services are perishable in the sense that they cannot be stored or saved. As a result, synchronizing supply with demand is particularly important to service industry managers.

3 **Explain how manufacturers become involved in services marketing.** Although manufacturers are mainly marketing goods, the related services they provide often give them a competitive advantage—especially when competing goods are quite similar.

4 Develop service marketing strategies. "Product" (service) strategy issues include what is being processed (people, possessions, information), core and supplementary services, customization versus standardization, and the service mix or portfolio. Distribution decisions involve convenience, number of outlets, direct versus indirect distribution, and scheduling. Stressing tangible cues, using personal sources of information, creating strong organizational images, and engaging in postpurchase communications are effective promotion strategies. Pricing objectives for services can be revenue-oriented, operations-oriented, patronage-oriented, or any combination of the three.

5 Explain the concept of service quality. The five components of service quality, evaluated from the customer's perspective, are tangibles, reliability, responsiveness, assurance, and empathy. Service quality is measured by comparing the customer's expectations of the service with the performance of a specific service provider for each of the five quality components. Poor service quality can be caused by management's lack of understanding of customer expectations, service specifications that do not fit with customer expectations, service employees' inability or unwillingness to perform the service specifications set by management, and unrealistic customer expectations created by external communications.

Internal marketing (treating employees as customers) and relationship marketing (attracting, developing, and retaining long-term customer relationships) are both important concepts in services marketing.

6 Discuss relationship marketing. Relationship marketing involves attracting, developing, and retaining customer relationships. There are three levels of relationship marketing: Level one focuses on pricing incentives; level two uses pricing incentives and social bonds with customers; and level three uses pricing, social bonds, and structural bonds to build long-term relationships.

7 Discuss global issues in services marketing. The U.S. has become the world's largest exporter of services. While competition is keen, the U.S. has a competitive advantage in many services because of its vast experience in service industries. To be successful globally, service firms must adjust their marketing mix for the environments of each target country.

8 Describe nonbusiness marketing and how it differs from profit-sector marketing. Accounting for over 20 percent of the economic activity in the United States, nonbusiness organizations pursue goals other than profit, market share, and return on investment. Nonbusiness marketing can be divided into two categories: social marketing and nonprofit organization marketing. Social marketing fosters socially beneficial ideas or behaviors. Nonprofit organization marketing facilitates mutually satisfying exchanges between nonprofit organizations and their target markets.

9 Develop marketing strategies for nonbusiness organizations. Several unique characteristics distinguish nonbusiness marketing strategy from business marketing strategy. Public and nonprofit organizations are typically concerned with services and social behaviors rather than manufactured goods. By definition, nonprofit organizations do not seek to make a profit. Many nonprofit organizations rely on donations or tax revenues and cater to a variety of constituents. The mission of many nonprofit organizations is to seek changes in the habits and preferences of customers. Many nonprofit organizations are subject to public scrutiny and regulation. Nonprofit organizations often attract donations of money, labor, and services. Finally, politicians, volunteers, and board members often influence the activities of nonprofit organizations.

Review Questions

1. Identify the four main distinguishing characteristics of services.
2. Describe promotional strategies used by service marketers.
3. Describe the process of setting a pricing strategy for services.
4. Define the two categories of nonbusiness marketing. Give some specific examples of each type.
5. Identify the basic marketing activities of nonprofit organizations.
6. What are the benefits of a marketing approach for nonbusiness managers?
7. Identify the unique pricing policies of nonbusiness organizations.
8. Why is effective distribution such a vital part of the service marketing mix? Describe the process of setting a distribution strategy for a service firm.

Discussion and Writing Questions

1. Explain search, experience, and credence qualities. Cite examples of each not discussed in the chapter.
2. Assume you are a service provider. Write a list of implications for your firm of service intangibility.
3. You are applying for a job as a marketing manager for a service firm and have been asked how you would handle a mismatch between supply and demand. Write your answer as a memo to the vice president of marketing.
4. What are the components of service quality? Apply these components to a service experience you have had recently. Did the company's performance meet, fall below, or exceed your expectations?
5. Describe the three levels of relationship marketing, and give an example of each that is not discussed in the chapter.

CASES

11.1 American Heart Association

In the past, nonprofit organizations relied on media generosity for almost $3 billion a year in free public service ads. But free airtime for PSAs is limited, and nonprofit organizations must compete for commercial spots. Also, PSAs often run at odd times, because nonprofit organizations get the time slots that sell poorly. Who can blame the media? If they can sell the spots and make a profit, why should they give them away for free?

If the organization has little control over the time or program in which the message gets aired, tailoring the message to the target audience is almost impossible. Moreover, the target audience is unlikely to be tuned to the channel when the message is aired.

As a result, nonprofit organizations like the American Heart Association (AHA) often seek corporate sponsors to pick up the tab for advertising. A company can endorse the charity in its own ads. Or the nonprofit organization can produce the ad, credit the corporate sponsor, and let the company pay for the ad.

With corporate sponsorship, nonprofit organizations can get better advertising time slots without having to pay for them. This solution to the targeting problem raises some interesting issues.

For instance, in 1987 and 1988 the AHA ran a slice-of-life ad campaign highlighting the risk factors for strokes and heart attacks. Bristol-Myers Squibb, maker of Bufferin painkiller, paid for the advertisements. The AHA received a forty-five-second spot. Bristol-Myers then promoted Bufferin in the remaining fifteen seconds of the ad. A company spokesperson said that Bristol-Myers was happy with the association between Bufferin and the AHA.

In contrast, the AHA was displeased with this association because the AHA appeared to be endorsing the product. The organization now bans the use of product names in sponsored ads.

How can this issue be resolved? Corporations like being linked with a nonprofit organization. At the same time, nonprofit organizations need to better target their audience. To accomplish this goal, they must buy advertising. Susan Islam, broadcasting and advertising director for the American Cancer Society, says, "The only way we are going to affect behavior is by buying advertising." She is conducting a conference on corporate sponsorships. "We are all grappling with how to do it," she adds.

Questions

1. Earlier in this chapter, some distinctions between profit and nonprofit organizations were listed. Which of these distinctions are affected by the corporate sponsorship issue?
2. How would you resolve the issues raised by corporate sponsorship? Should the AHA reconsider its

stand on corporate sponsorship? Give reasons to support your opinion.

3. What responsibilities should the media have in solving these problems?

Suggested Reading

Pamela Sebastian, "IRS to Discuss Rules on Sponsorship by Corporations with Nonprofit Groups," *The Wall Street Journal,* 16 June 1992, pp. A9A, A7B.

11.2 Union Pacific

Video title: *Bulktainer Service from Union Pacific*

Union Pacific Corporation
8th and Eaton Avenues
Bethlehem, PA 18018

SIC codes: 4011 Railroads
4213 Less than truckload transport

Number of employees: 48,100

1993 revenues: $7 billion

Major service: Railway, truck, door-to-door transportation

Largest competitors: Burlington Northern, CSX Transportation, Norfolk Southern Corp.

Background

Union Pacific offers its customers one-call, one-invoice, door-to-door service. With a unique program called the Union Pacific Customer Action Team (UPCAT), Union Pacific is changing the way customers think about railroad service. Under this exciting new program, Union Pacific teams visit with the client to find out how the company's service can be improved. These teams are made up of conductors, management personnel, and sale representatives. Each member of an UPCAT team has been thoroughly trained in customer service. The teams have only one objective: improving local service to clients.

Industry

Railroads in the United States have come under heavy fire from both trucking and airline transportation companies. For years railroads believed they offered the most efficient and economical method of shipping bulk product. However, the convenience of air and truck lines has caused many railroad customers to switch. Thus railroads have had to rethink the way they provide transportation services in order to compete with the convenience of air and truck transportation.

Union Pacific's Bulktainer Service

Union Pacific's UPCAT program is causing many companies that offer bulk transportation to take notice. Union Pacific prides itself on providing the best possible service to customers, including placing railcars exactly where customers need them.

A major part of Union Pacific's services is bulktainer service. Bulktainers are specialized containers designed for the transportation of liquids. These containers can hold up to 48,000 pounds or 6,300 gallons of liquid. Lined completely with stainless steel and insulated, these containers offer potential customers the ability to ship any liquid. An internal thermometer with an external readout permits the driver to monitor the contents of each container.

Union Pacific goes the extra mile to ensure the safety of both the product and the environment from potential damage. Although the U.S. government allows chemical and food products to be shipped at different times in the same container, provided the container has been thoroughly sterilized, Union Pacific never permits food products to be shipped in containers that have been used to transport chemicals. This policy applies even to nonhazardous chemicals. Each container is equipped with a double bottom valve. If the external valve is severed in an accident, the internal valve prevents any of the liquid in the container from escaping. Finally, the company thoroughly trains each employee in the bulktainer service on the handling of liquids. This attention to detail permits Union Pacific to offer one of the finest liquid transportation services in the United States.

Questions

1. Do you think Union Pacific offers its customers a quality liquid transportation service? Why or why not?

2. How has technology changed the way Union Pacific provides its services?

3. Do you think Union Pacific should keep chemical and food containers separated, given the nature of the sterilization performed after each use? Why or why not?

References

Million Dollar Directory 1993 (Parsipanny, NJ: Dun & Bradstreet Information Services, 1993).

Standard & Poor's Industry Surveys (New York: Standard & Poor's Corporation, October 1993).

PART THREE
CRITICAL THINKING CASE

Busch Draft and the Draft Beer Wars

Total production of beer in the United States leveled off in the 1980s (see Exhibit 1). With a stable market, the brewers are fighting for precious market share. As brewers make changes in product lines and promotional strategies, they have to be concerned that they will take market share from their own products and not from competitors' brands. It has always been said that the fastest way to kill a flagship brand is to have a highly successful light beer. Coors Light, for example, far outsells Coors. Brewers are looking to attract consumers to their brands by adding dry beers and draft beers to an already overcrowded product line.

Another key factor affecting the beer industry is the political environment. Increasing legal involvement in the sales and consumption of alcoholic beverages is causing major changes in the marketing of beer. Beer producers must now put warning labels on the product. Moreover, producers are heavily promoting "designated driver" programs and social responsibility in hopes that the government will not ban beer advertising from broadcast media.

Bar sales have declined because of the "moderation movement" and anti-drunk-driving campaigns. Package sales have increased slightly. The beer industry hopes that cold-filtered bottled beer can pick up sales lost on the draft beer market.

The Beer Market

Anheuser-Busch is fast approaching the 50 percent market share level, which gives it a great advantage. It has more room than competitors to slash prices because of economies of scale.

Analysts break the market into several product types. The largest segment is the premium brands, such as Michelob and Miller High Life. The next largest segment is light beers, followed by popular brands, including Meister Brau, Busch, and Old Milwaukee. Light beer became an increasingly popular choice among U.S. consumers during the 1980s. The gains in light beer sales came at the expense of the premium brands. The pie graph in Exhibit 2 shows the 1989 market share for product type.

The graph in Exhibit 3 shows the top ten brands in 1989 and their market shares. Miller Genuine Draft made the top-ten list in 1989 for the first time. It displaced Anheuser-Busch's Michelob brand.

The Brewing Process

All beers basically follow the same brewing process until the container-handling stage. The key differences in the brewing process follow:

- *Dry beers:* A long brewing process reduces the amount of sugar and carbohydrates, leaving the beer with very little aftertaste.
- *Light beers:* Brewing with a smaller quantity of barley gives the product a lighter taste and fewer calories.
- *Draft beers:* In the United States, they must meet one of two criteria: The beer cannot be pasteurized, or it must be sold in a large container, such as a keg.

Once the product has been brewed, it is cold-filtered. If the product is to be sold as a draft beer and packaged in cans or bottles, it is tight-filtered. In the tight-filtration process, the remaining yeast can be removed from the beer to prevent additional fermenting in the package. Pasteurization is the other way of preventing the product from fermenting in the container; in the pasteurizer, heat kills the remaining yeast. According to industry experts, this heat does not significantly affect the taste of the beer.

The Draft Beer Market

The two leading brands in the draft beer segment are Miller Genuine Draft (2.4 percent market share) and Coors Extra Gold (0.6 percent market share). Anheuser-Busch test marketed its own Busch Draft. Putting a premium product, such as draft beer, in the popular price category may present some problems to the

nation's largest brewer. Anheuser-Busch has refused to admit that draft beer is a valid market segment rather than just a new method of filtering beer. Instead of taking sales away from competing draft beers, sales may be pulled from Anheuser-Busch's flagship brand, Budweiser. Miller sees the new product as a copycat of Miller Genuine Draft—"the ultimate compliment."

Consumer Profile

The draft beer segment is targeted to men, 21 to 35 years old. Research indicates that this group consumes far more beer than older drinkers. Other segments include men 35 and over, women, and ethnic markets. The 35-plus segment is fast becoming the largest segment as the median age in the United States rises. Women are a growing market for beer-based products, as are African-Americans and Hispanics.

Packaging

Corona, the Mexican import beer, has revived the long-necked glass bottle. Anheuser-Busch test marketed Busch Draft in a clear bottle. The problem with clear

Exhibit 1

Market Breakdown by Product

	Year								
Product	***1981***	***1982***	***1983***	***1984***	***1985***	***1986***	***1987***	***1988***	***1989***
Imported	5.2	5.8	6.3	7.2	7.9	8.8	9.4	9.4	8.8
Super-premium	12.7	12.8	11.5	9.1	7.6	6.0	5.4	4.8	4.5
Light	25.2	32.3	34.0	36.4	37.6	41.5	45.0	48.1	50.4
Popular	39.0	36.7	39.2	42.0	44.8	45.0	44.2	43.6	42.7
Premium	93.9	88.4	86.3	82.2	80.1	80.6	78.0	76.7	75.1
*Total**	179.2	179.0	180.1	178.0	178.5	181.6	181.3	181.9	181.8

*Including all other products

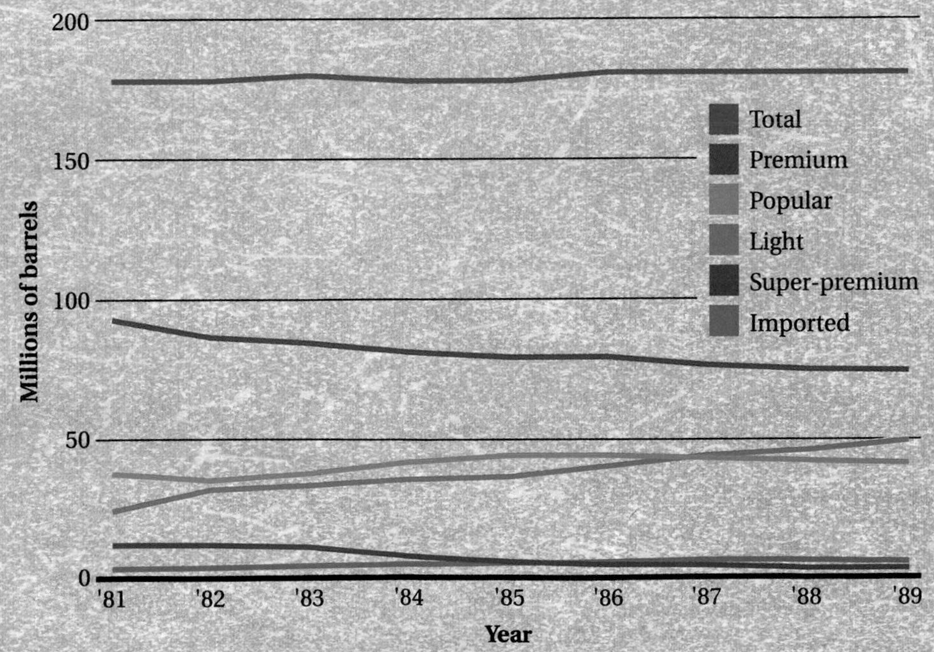

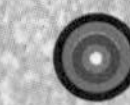

Exhibit 2

Market Share by Type

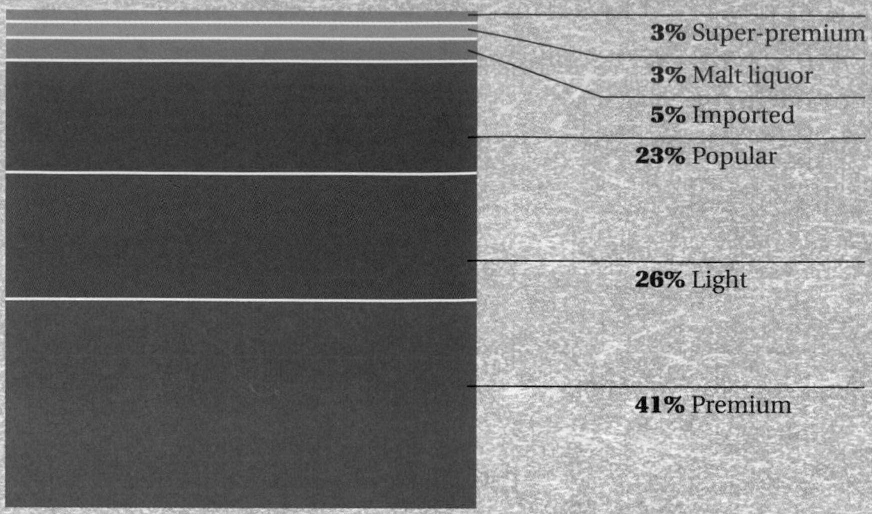

Exhibit 3

Market Share by Brand

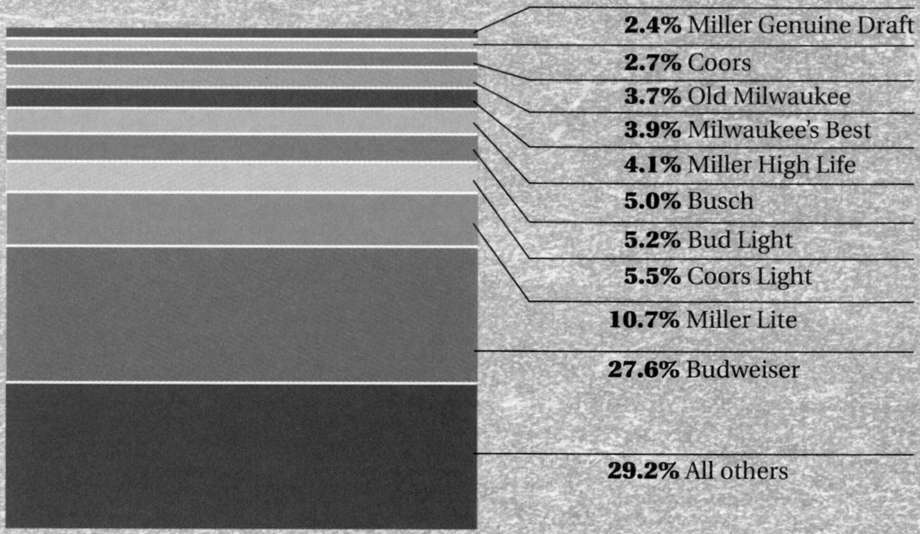

bottles is that the light tends to greatly reduce beer's shelf life. Anheuser-Busch also tested a special reflective package that shields the product from light.

Questions

1. What kind of packaging would you design for Busch Draft?
2. How would you defend Anheuser-Busch's decision to enter the draft beer market with a popular-priced beer? What would be the consequences of not entering the draft beer market?
3. What sort of target market would successfully position Busch Draft in the draft beer market?
4. What impact will Busch Draft have on Anheuser-Busch's other products?

Suggested Readings

Marj Charlier, "Bottled Draft Beers Head for Collision as Anheuser Readies Challenge to Miller," *The Wall Street Journal*, 1 May 1990, pp. B1, B4.

John C. Maxwell, Jr., "Beer '90: Special Report," *Beverage Industry*, January 1990, pp. 1, 28–36.

Al Ries and Jack Trout, "The Beer Wars," *Marketing Warfare*, 1986, pp. 137–154.

Julia Flynn Siler, "A Warning Shot from the King of Beers," *Business Week*, 18 December 1989, p. 124.

PART THREE
ETHICS CASE

The Fail-Proof Product

Beth Harmon, an employee for a large and respected marketing research firm, had been working for over four years in the area of new market analysis. It had been the custom at her firm for teams of researchers to work on projects. Beth was offered her first assignment as a team leader on a project for a large consumer packaged-goods client.

As the first step in planning the project, Beth met with her boss, Bob Luck, and a representative of the client firm, Roger Howell. They discussed how Beth and her team would design and implement research for a new type of tooth polish. It seemed strange to Beth that Bob and Roger kept stressing the importance of a strong research design that the client's top management would support. She reassured both Bob and Roger that she had studied the problem and would use a very appropriate research design. They seemed to mean something different from what she meant when they discussed research design.

- Were Bob and Roger trying to send Beth a signal, or were they just concerned that she do a good job? What might they have been trying to tell her?

Shortly after that first meeting, Beth met with her team to assign them tasks and deadlines. The research process continued, with the team collecting data and interpreting the results. They soon realized that the new product being proposed would not be accepted by the target market at all. Beth seemed disappointed that her first research project would reach such negative conclusions. But she was glad that she could save her client a lot of money in the long run by stopping the launch of a product that was destined to fail.

- Is this an appropriate outcome for a research project? How can such findings be a good investment for a firm?

The following week, while meeting with her boss, Beth alerted him to the problem with the findings for the new tooth polish. She was startled by his reaction. Bob asked her to "put a spin on the data to make it sound supportive to launching the new product." His reasoning was that Roger had already invested a great deal of time in developing the product and that Roger's career was on the line. Even if the product failed, Roger would probably not be held accountable. But if the product was shown to be a poor idea before the launch, Roger would probably lose his job. Bob explained that Roger had an excellent track record for making products successful, that the research was mostly "window dressing," and that the client was already committed to launching the product. Finally, Bob pointed out that Beth would probably have a brief career in marketing research if she discouraged the client from launching the product.

- What should Beth do and why? What are the likely consequences if she (1) discourages the product launch or (2) encourages the product launch?

After thinking long and hard about the advice her boss had given her, Beth decided to "shave the data" to make it appear at least ambivalent. In her report, she noted that although the market was not distinctly supportive of the new product, the product launch would probably be successful. Bob read her report, praised it, and asked her to reduce it to a single page and sign it.

- How is the letter different from the initial report? Should Beth sign such a letter?

While preparing the letter, Beth recalled a recent court case that had made the news: A packaged-goods manufacturer sued a major marketing research organization for advising it to launch a new product that then failed.

- What kind of risk is Beth taking? What could happen? Would you do what she did to keep your job? How might this experience affect the way Beth does her job in the future?

PART FOUR

DISTRIBUTION DECISIONS

FRAGILE
FRAGILE

CHAPTER 12
Marketing Channels and Wholesaling

LEARNING OBJECTIVES

After studying this chapter, you should be able to

1. Explain what a marketing channel is and why intermediaries are needed.
2. Describe the functions and activities that marketing channel members perform.
3. Discuss the differences between marketing channels for consumer and industrial products.
4. Describe alternative channel arrangements.
5. Discuss channel structure decisions in international markets.
6. Explain the types of firms that perform wholesaling activities and their functions.
7. Discuss the factors that influence channel choice.
8. List the steps in designing marketing channels.
9. Explain the concepts of power and conflict within marketing channels.

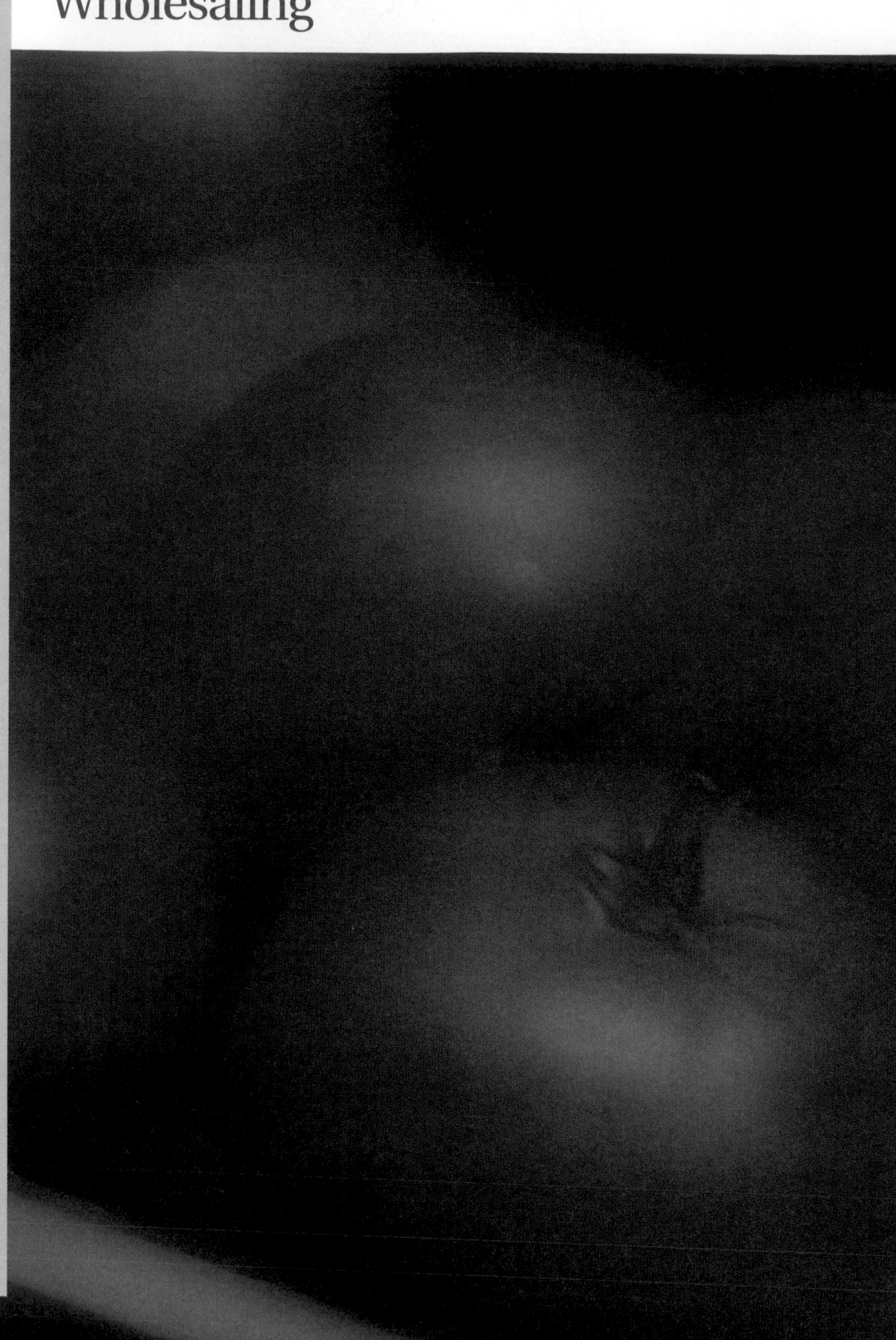

The network manager for a Denver-based environmental consulting firm was in a hurry. He needed a dozen personal computers right away—and in Alaska, no less—to help cope with the *Exxon Valdez* disaster. No major dealers were near the oil spill, and the major makers of personal computers couldn't figure out how to get machines to the site quickly. So he got on the phone to Northgate Computer Systems, a direct-mail computer retailer, and ordered the hardware. It arrived in four days.

That was back in 1989, and few companies back then would buy PCs, sight unseen, directly from the company through the mail. But now many companies routinely use direct mail to get personal computers quickly and at rock-bottom prices.

Direct-mail computer sales are booming. Although most U.S. computer makers faced stagnant revenue growth during the past few years, shipments by direct-mail marketers have jumped 35 percent. By 1995, 30 percent of all personal computers sold in the United States—about 9 million out of 30 million—may be sold via direct-mail marketing channels.

Computer buyers are also finding alternative retailers from whom to buy the latest computers and accessories: office supply outlets, department stores, warehouse clubs, and consumer electronics chains. The latest trend is computer superstores, which are cavernous, no-frills outlets with floor-to-ceiling stacks of discounted computer merchandise.

The leaders of the direct-marketing movement, Dell Computer and Gateway 2000, offer prices that are usually 30 percent or more below the list prices found in conventional computer stores. They can charge these discounted prices because they don't have the expense of running stores. Computers from reputable manufacturers, helpful salespeople, fast deliveries, and hassle-free returns are an equally attractive part of mail-order buying.

Because computer manufacturers are finding new and more direct channels for moving products from the factory to the consumer, such conventional computer stores and dealers as Computerland, Businessland, and MicroAge are hurting. In fact, in 1993 Compuadd closed all 131 of its retail computer stores.[1] Now fewer than half of all computers are bought through these channels, compared to 90 percent over a decade ago. Compaq Computers launched its own mail-order operation, called DirectPlus, to focus on small-business owners and home PC users. The operation is part of a move by Compaq to broaden sales channels beyond its base of traditional computer dealers. Many of Compaq's longtime dealers now fear their businesses will suffer, especially if Compaq broadens DirectPlus to include large corporate accounts as well.[2]

The dealer channel worked well in the 1980s, when personal computers

were relatively new and customers needed technical advice. Manufacturers insisted that dealers operate from costly storefront locations to attract walk-in business. But a marketing slump and a resulting price war forced scores of independent stores out of business. The survivors scrambled to increase profits by shifting their focus to corporate buyers, who ordered hundreds of computers at a time. Dealers hired polished sales representatives to call on the big accounts and technicians to do installations, figuring corporations would pay top dollar for such service.

The effort to boost profits by catering to giant corporations didn't work. A growing number of big customers aren't interested in paying extra for services. They like the low prices and fast delivery they can get by ordering through manufacturers' direct channels or through discount computer retailers, such as Micro Electronics and Comp USA. And most big corporations now have their own technical in-house staff to handle installations and networking.[3]

As customer needs for personal computers changed, manufacturers changed their channel strategy from using dealers to dealing directly with buyers or using other middlemen, such as discounters. What factors influenced these computer manufacturers' choice of marketing channel? How did these manufacturers determine how many intermediaries to use? What functions do intermediaries normally perform for manufacturers?

1 MARKETING CHANNELS AND CHANNEL MEMBERS

The term *channel* is derived from the Latin word *canalis,* which means canal. A marketing channel can be viewed as a large canal or pipeline with products, their ownership, communications, financing and payment, and their accompanying risk flowing through it. Formally, a **marketing channel** (also called a **channel of distribution**) is a set of interdependent organizations that ease the transfer of ownership as products move from producer to business user or consumer.

marketing channel (channel of distribution)
Set of interdependent organizations that ease the transfer of ownership as products move from producer to business user or consumer.

Many different types of organizations participate in marketing channels. Some are considered channel members (also called intermediaries, resellers, and middlemen), while others are nonmembers. Channel members negotiate and buy, sell, and facilitate the change of ownership between buyers and sellers. Nonmember channel participants, such as advertising agencies and transportation firms, do not negotiate and only support the activities of the marketing channel.

Some intermediaries take title to products and resell them. Taking title means they own the merchandise and control the terms of sale—for example, price and delivery date. Wholesalers and retailers often are examples of this type of intermediary. **Wholesalers** are firms that sell mainly to producers, resellers, governments, institutions, and retailers. In contrast, **retailers** are firms that sell mainly to consumers. Other intermediaries do not take title to the goods and services they market but do facilitate the exchange of ownership between sellers and buyers. Brokers, manufacturer's representatives, and agents are examples of this type of intermediary.

wholesalers
Firm that sells mainly to producers, resellers, governments, institutions, and retailers.

retailer
Firm that sells mainly to consumers.

Intermediaries are useful for three important reasons: specialization and division of labor, the need to overcome discrepancies, and contact efficiency.

Specialization and division of labor not only make mass production more efficient, they also make marketing channels more efficient. Intermediaries are often better equipped to distribute products to end users than manufacturers are.

Specialization and Division of Labor

Manufacturers achieve economies of scale through the use of efficient equipment capable of producing large quantities of a single product. According to the concept of specialization and division of labor, breaking down a complex task into smaller, simpler ones and allocating them to specialists will also create much greater efficiency. Economies of scale, specialization and division of labor, and professional management normally result in lower average production costs.

Marketing channels can also attain economies of scale through specialization and division of labor. Some producers lack the interest, financing, or expertise to market directly to end users or consumers. In some cases, as with most consumer convenience goods, the cost of marketing directly to millions of consumers would be prohibitive. Producers essentially hire channel members to do what the producers are not equipped to do or what these intermediaries are better prepared to do. Channel members can do some things more efficiently than producers can because they have built good relationships with their customers. Their specialized expertise enhances the overall performance of the channel.

The Need to Overcome Discrepancies

Economies of scale in production require the development of distribution channels capable of overcoming barriers to exchange. For example, assume that Betty Crocker Instant Pancake Mix can only be produced efficiently at a rate of 5,000 units in a typical day. Not even the most ardent pancake fan could consume that amount in a year, much less in a day. The quantity produced to achieve low unit costs has created a **discrepancy of quantity**, which is the difference between the amount of product produced and the amount an end user wants to buy. Marketing channels overcome quantity discrepancies by making products available in the quantities that consumers and business buyers desire.

discrepancy of quantity Difference between the amount of product produced and the amount an end user wants to buy.

discrepancy of assortment Lack of all the items needed to receive full satisfaction from a product or products.

Mass production creates not only discrepancies of quantity but also discrepancies of assortment. A **discrepancy of assortment** is the lack of all the items needed to receive full satisfaction from a product or products. For pancakes to have maximum utility, several other products are required to complete the assortment. At the very least, most people want a knife, fork, plate, butter, and syrup. Others might add

orange juice, coffee, cream, sugar, eggs, and bacon or sausage. Although it is a large consumer products company, even Pillsbury does not come close to providing the optimal assortment to go with pancakes. To overcome discrepancies of assortment, marketing channels assemble in one place the products that buyers want.

temporal discrepancy
Difference between when a product is produced and when a consumer is ready to buy it.

spatial discrepancy
Difference between the location of the producer and the location of widely scattered markets.

A **temporal discrepancy** is created when a product is produced but a consumer is not ready to buy it. Marketing channels overcome temporal discrepancies by maintaining inventories in anticipation of demand. Furthermore, since mass production requires many potential buyers, markets are usually scattered over large geographic regions, creating a **spatial discrepancy.** Often international, or at least nationwide, markets are needed to absorb the outputs of mass producers. Marketing channels overcome spatial discrepancies by making products available in locations convenient to consumers and business buyers.

Contact Efficiency

Consider your extra costs if supermarkets, department stores, and shopping centers or malls did not exist. Suppose you had to buy your milk at a dairy and your meat at a stockyard. Imagine buying your eggs and chicken at a hatchery and your fruits and vegetables at various farms. You would spend a great deal of time, money, and energy just shopping for a few groceries. Channels simplify distribution by cutting the number of transactions required to get products from manufacturers to consumers.

Consider another example, which is illustrated in Exhibit 12.1. Four students in your class want to buy a television set. Without a retail intermediary like Circuit City, Magnavox, Zenith, Sony, Toshiba, and RCA would each have to make four contacts to reach the four buyers who are in the target market, totaling twenty transactions. However, each producer only has to make one contact when Circuit City acts as an intermediary between the producer and consumer, reducing the number of trans-

Exhibit 12.1

How Intermediaries Reduce the Number of Required Transactions

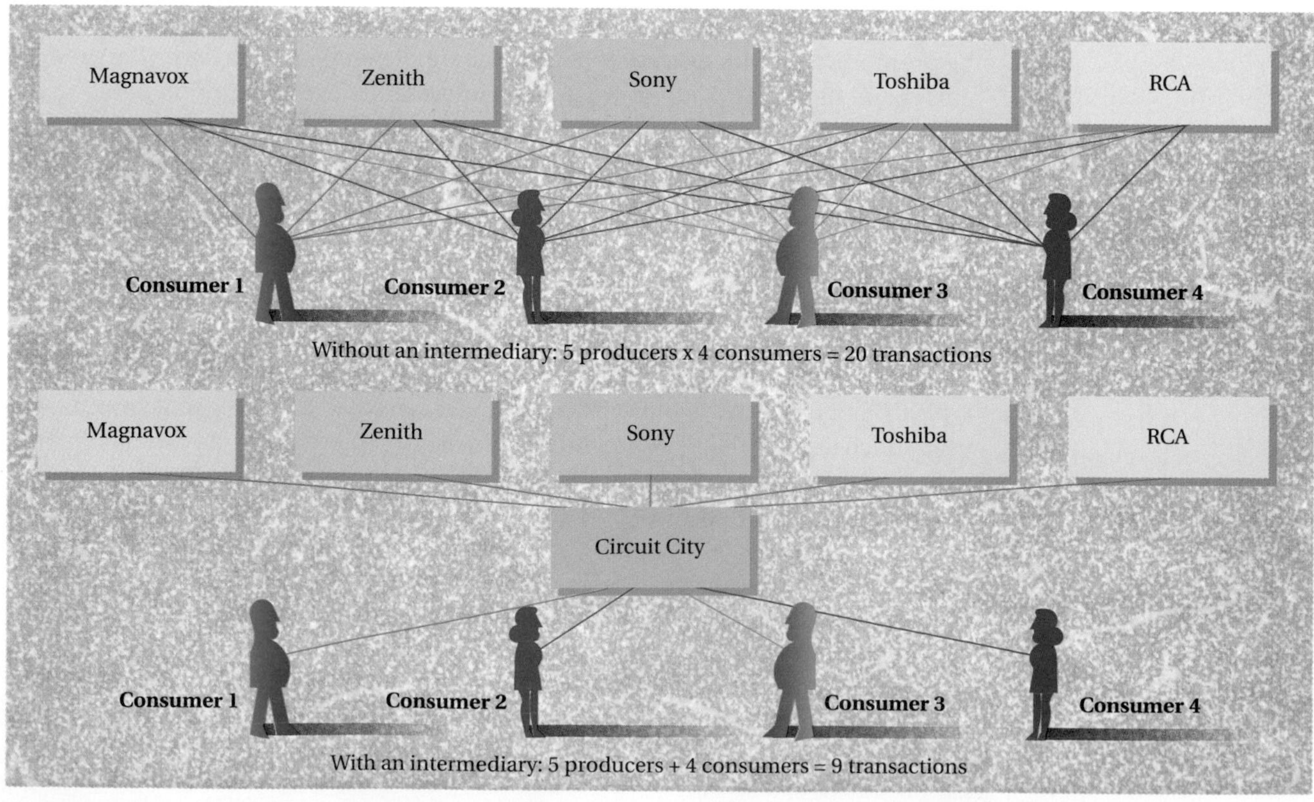

actions to nine. Each producer sells to one retailer rather than to four consumers. In turn, the consumers buy from one retailer instead of five producers.

This simple example illustrates the concept of contact efficienty. U.S. manufacturers sell to millions of individuals and families. Using channel intermediaries greatly reduces the number of required contacts. As a result, producers are able to offer their products cost-effectively and efficiently to consumers all over the world.

❷ CHANNEL FUNCTIONS

Intermediaries in marketing channels perform several essential functions that make the flow of goods between producer and buyer possible. The three basic functions that intermediaries perform are transactional, logistical, and facilitating functions (see Exhibit 12.2).[4]

At the most basic level, intermediaries perform the *transactional* functions of contacting buyers, promoting the product to be sold, negotiating the sale, and taking on the risks associated with owning and keeping a product in inventory. Producing high-quality items and offering them at fair prices do not guarantee success. Contacting and promoting make prospective buyers aware of existing products and explain their features, advantages, and benefits. Sellers and buyers must also agree on the terms of the sale, such as how much to buy and sell, which type of transportation to use to get the product to the customer, and when to deliver. They also must agree on the method and timing of payment. Sometimes buyers and sellers agree to terms covering exchanges over a specified period, such as one year. A long-term agreement eliminates the need to negotiate each transaction and may result in straight rebuy arrangements (see Chapter 5).

Intermediaries also provide the *logistical* functions of physical distribution and sorting. *Logistics* describes several activities related to the movement of goods from

Exhibit 12.2

Marketing Channel Functions Performed by Intermediaries

Type of function	Description
Transactional functions	***Contacting and promoting:*** Contacting potential customers, promoting products, and soliciting orders ***Negotiation:*** Determining how many goods or services to buy and sell, type of transportation to use, when to deliver, and method and timing of payment ***Risk taking:*** Assuming the risk of owning inventory
Logistical functions	***Physical distribution:*** Transporting and storing goods to overcome temporal and spatial discrepancies ***Sorting:*** Overcoming discrepancies of quantity and assortment by • *Sorting out:* Breaking down a heterogeneous supply into separate homogeneous stocks • *Accumulation:* Combining similar stocks into a larger homogeneous supply • *Allocation:* Breaking a homogeneous supply into smaller and smaller lots ("breaking bulk") • *Assorting:* Combining products into collections or assortments that buyers want available at one place
Facilitating functions	***Research:*** Gathering information about other channel members and consumers ***Financing:*** Extending credit and other financial services to facilitate the flow of goods through the channel to the final consumer

This barge hauling goods in Alaska is performing a logistical function for the goods' producers: physical distribution or, more specifically, transportation.
© 1989 Charles Krebs/The Stock Market

producer to consumer or end user. Transportation and storage of goods overcome temporal and spatial discrepancies. Sorting functions overcome discrepancies of quantity and assortment. These functions might include sorting out, accumulating, allocating, and assorting products into either homogeneous or heterogeneous collections. For example, grading agricultural products typifies the sorting-out process. The consolidation of many lots of grade A eggs from different sources into one lot illustrates the accumulation process. Allocating at the wholesale level—for example, breaking down a tank-car load of milk into gallon jugs—is called "breaking bulk." A buyer of case lots, in turn, sells individual units. Last, supermarkets or other retailers perform the assorting function by assembling thousands of different items that match their customers' desires.

Intermediaries also perform the *facilitating* functions of research and financing. Research provides information about channel members and consumers and asks appropriate questions: Who are the buyers? Where are they located? What are their characteristics? Why do they buy? Where do they buy? How will they respond to changes in package style, price, size, promotional appeal, or product features? Who are the major competitors, and what are their strengths and weaknesses? Financing helps producers make goods more attractive to buyers. Inventories are often financed as products flow through or are held in a channel. Manufacturers often provide credit to wholesalers and retailers who buy directly from them. Some wholesalers also furnish credit for retailers, and many retailers provide credit for final purchasers. Financial institutions may supply credit to any or all members of a channel to finance raw material purchases, operations, accounts receivable, or even purchases of major equipment. For example, a department store chain may secure credit from an insurance company to finance the construction of a new outlet.

Although individual members can be added to or deleted from a channel, someone must still perform these essential functions. They can be performed by producers, end users or consumers, channel intermediaries such as wholesalers and retailers, and sometimes nonmember channel participants. For example, if a manufacturer decides to eliminate its private fleet of trucks, it must still have a way to move the goods to the wholesaler. This task may be accomplished by the wholesaler, which may have its own fleet of trucks, or by a nonmember channel participant, such as an independent trucking firm. Nonmembers also provide many other essential functions that may have at one time been provided by a channel member. For example, research firms perform the research function; advertising agencies, the promotion function; transportation and storage firms, the physical distribution function; and banks, the financing function.

3 CHANNEL STRUCTURES

Marketing a consumer convenience good like gum or candy differs from marketing a specialty good like a Mercedes-Benz. The two products require much different distribution channels. Likewise, the appropriate channel for a major equipment supplier like Boeing Aircraft would be unsuitable for an accessory equipment producer like Black & Decker.

Channels for Consumer Products

direct channel
Distribution channel in which producers sell directly to consumers.

Exhibit 12.3 illustrates the four ways manufacturers can route products to consumers. Producers use the **direct channel** to sell directly to consumers. Direct marketing activities—including telemarketing, mail-order and catalog shopping, and forms of electronic retailing like videotex shopping and shop-at-home television networks—are a good example of this type of channel structure. For example, consumers can order L.L. Bean products directly from a catalog. There are no intermediaries the customer must go through. Producer-owned stores and factory outlet stores—like Sherwin Williams, Ralph Lauren, Oneida, and West Point Pepperel—are other examples of direct channels. Farmers' markets are also direct channels. Direct marketing and factory outlets are discussed in more detail in Chapter 13.

At the other end of the spectrum, an *agent/broker channel* involves a fairly complicated process. Agents or brokers bring manufacturers and wholesalers together

Exhibit 12.3

Marketing Channels for Consumer Products

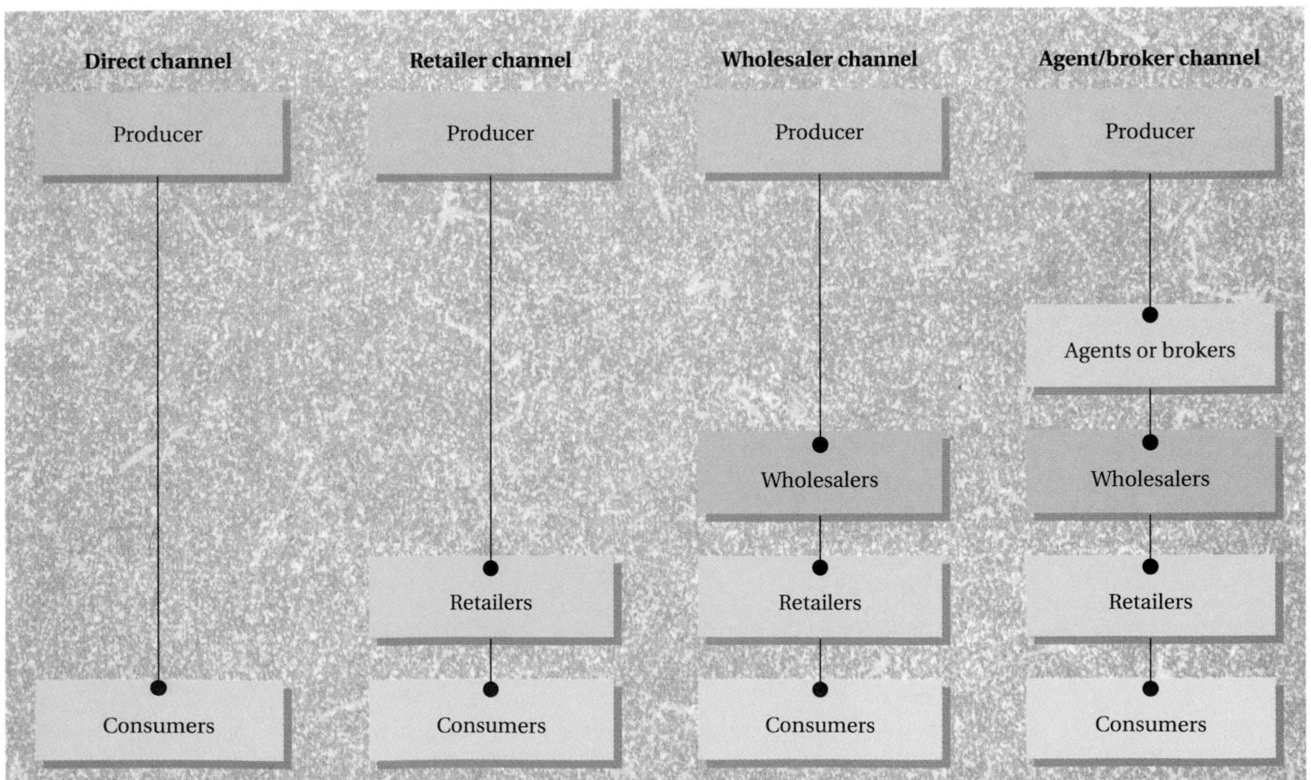

One direct channel for consumer products is the farmers' market, like this example in Boston, which puts producers in direct contact with end users.

for negotiations. Ownership passes to one or more wholesalers and then to retailers. Finally, retailers sell to the ultimate consumer of the product.

Most consumer products are sold through distribution channels similar to the *retailer channel* and the *wholesaler channel.*

Channels for Industrial Products

As Exhibit 12.4 illustrates, five channel structures are common in business-to-business markets. *Direct channels* are more typical in industrial markets than in consumer markets. For example, manufacturers buy large quantities of raw materials, major equipment, processed materials, and supplies directly from other manufacturers. Manufacturers that require suppliers to meet detailed technical specifications often

Exhibit 12.4

Major Channels for Industrial Products

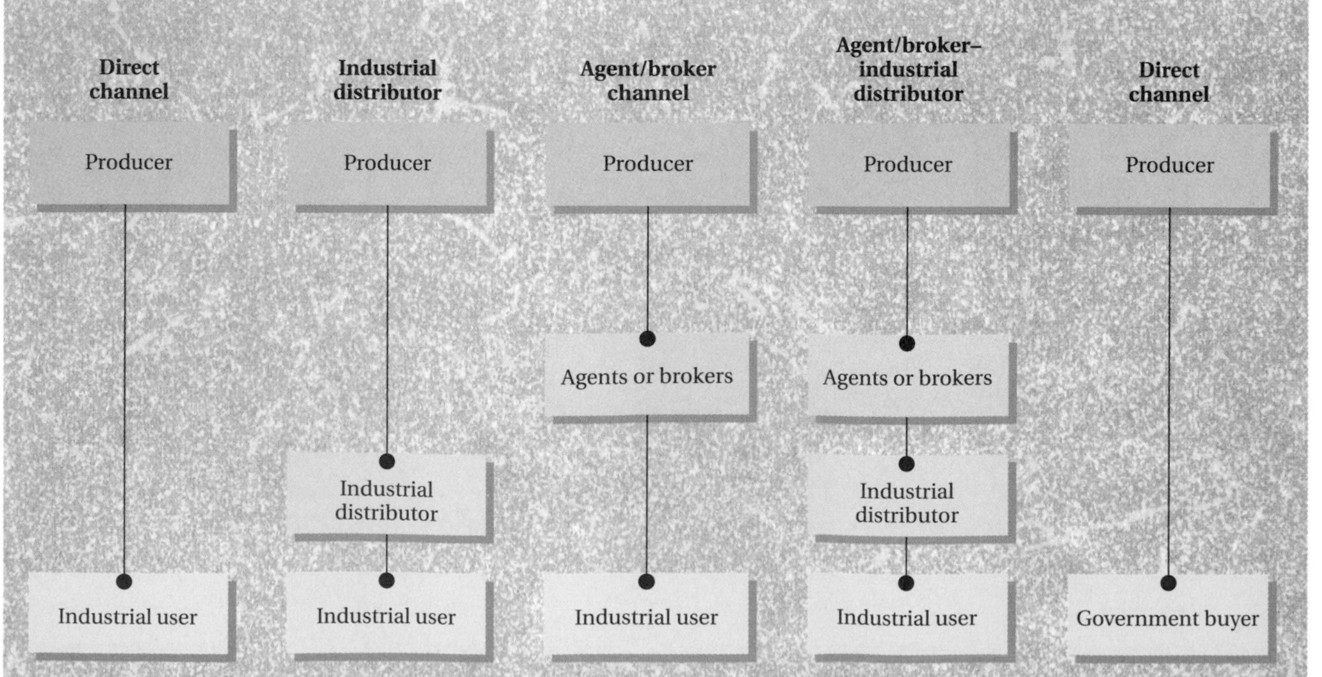

prefer direct channels. The direct communication required between Chrysler and its suppliers, for example, along with the tremendous size of the orders, makes anything but a direct channel impractical. The channel from producer to government buyers is also a direct channel. As indicated in Chapter 5, much government buying is done through bidding. Thus a direct channel is attractive.

Companies selling standardized items of moderate or low value often rely on *industrial distributors.* In many ways, an industrial distributor is like a supermarket for organizations. Industrial distributors are channel members that buy and take title to products. Moreover, they usually keep inventories of their products and sell and service them. There are over 12,000 industrial distributors in the United States.[5] Ingersoll-Rand is one of many manufacturers that uses industrial distributors to sell its line of air pressure–operated tools.

Often small manufacturers cannot afford to employ their own sales force. Instead, they rely on manufacturers' representatives or sales agents to sell to industrial distributors or organizational users. However, manufacturers' reps and selling agents are not limited to small firms. Large firms like National Semiconductor, ITT, Corning, Monsanto, Teledyne, and Mobil Oil all use manufacturers' reps.[6]

4 ALTERNATIVE CHANNEL ARRANGEMENTS

dual distribution (multiple distribution)
Use of two or more channels to distribute the same product to target markets.

Producers often devise alternative marketing channels to move their products to the end user. One such arrangement is called **dual distribution**, or **multiple distribution**, in which a producer selects two or more channels to distribute the same product to target markets. For example, Whirlpool sells its washers, dryers, and refrigerators directly to home and apartment builders and contractors, but it also sells these same appliances to retail stores that sell to consumers. Spiegel, which has traditionally used direct-mail channels, has now opened several retail stores. The company discovered that certain lines of catalog merchandise benefit from exposure in retail stores, and the stores help drive more sales through catalogs.[7]

Producers also use alternative channels for unique second brands. Hallmark, for instance, markets its Hallmark cards in department stores and its Ambassador cards in discount stores. Similarly, Burlington House area rugs are marketed through upscale retail boutiques, while its second-brand American Lifestyle rugs are sold to mass-market channels.[8]

Often nontraditional channel arrangements help differentiate a firm's product from the competitor's. For instance, Champ Products markets its premium ice cream bars at Wrigley Field and the Lincoln Park Zoo in Chicago. With that strategy, it raises the visibility of the brand and avoids the high fees that many supermarkets charge for stocking a product and giving it shelf space.[9] Similarly, Taco Bell and Pizza Hut are experimenting with selling their food products through nontraditional channels, including convenience stores.[10] Although nontraditional channels may limit a brand's coverage, they can give a small producer serving a niche market a way to gain market access and customer attention.[11]

strategic channel alliance
Producers' agreement to jointly use one's already-established channel.

More recently, producers have formed strategic channel alliances, which use another manufacturer's already-established channel. Alliances are used most often when the creation of marketing channel relationships may be expensive and time-consuming. Ocean Spray formed a strategic channel alliance with Pepsi-Cola to help increase the market presence of Ocean Spray's brands. By sharing Pepsi's distribution channels, Ocean Spray can make cans and bottles of Ocean Spray Cranberry Juice Cocktail, Cranapple, and other juice drinks available in conve-

nience stores, minimarts, and Pepsi-Cola vending machines.[12] Similarly, Rubbermaid formed a close merchandising alliance with discounter Phar-Mor to supply most of the retailer's plastic housewares. Specially designed Everything Rubbermaid departments were created in Phar-Mor stores, which showcase as many as 560 Rubbermaid items.[13]

Strategic channel alliances are also common for selling in foreign markets where cultural differences, distance, or other barriers can inhibit channel establishment. General Mills struck an alliance with Nestlé S.A. as a way to increase its presence in Europe. PepsiCo has made a strategic alliance with General Mills to combine Pepsi's snack companies in Spain, Portugal, and Greece with General Mills' operations in France, Belgium, and the Netherlands.[14] Both companies can use both marketing channels to increase distribution.

reverse channel
Distribution channel in which products move from consumer back to producer.

Reverse channels occur when products move in the opposite direction of traditional channels—from consumer back to producer. This type of channel is important for products that require repair or recycling. For example, automobile dealers generally have a service department to which consumers can bring their cars when they need repairs. Other producers of high-tech products, like Sony, have established a national network of service centers that will repair the manufacturers' brands of electronic entertainment equipment.

For many years, soft-drink and beer manufacturers have used reverse channels to collect and recycle glass bottles. They have also been big promoters of aluminum can recycling, mostly because it makes economic sense. Reverse channels for recycling have become more prevalent as producers realize the importance of limiting the solid waste that is normally dumped in landfills. Procter & Gamble is one producer that has redesigned its plastic bottles and containers to use recycled plastic materials instead of 100 percent virgin, or new, plastics. To do so, P&G had to devise a reverse channel to get discarded plastic containers for recycling. Now, in addition to its traditional channels to the consumer, P&G has contracted with channel intermediaries that collect, sort, shred, clean, and "pelletize" discarded plastic containers. The plastic pellets are then shipped back to P&G to become an ingredient in new plastic bottles and containers.[15]

Vertical Marketing Systems

Goods and services in the U.S. economy have historically been distributed through highly fragmented conventional channels (similar to those in Exhibits 12.3 and 12.4). A **conventional channel** can be described as a network of loosely aligned manufacturers, wholesalers, and retailers that bargain with each other at arm's length, negotiate aggressively over the terms of sale, and otherwise behave independently.[16] Conventional channels typically lack coordination, overall goals, interdependence, and routine procedures. They tend to be expensive and unreliable. Examples include the channels often used by small manufacturers and small retail outlets, such as independent supermarkets and shoe stores.

conventional channel
Network of loosely aligned manufacturers, wholesalers, and retailers that bargain with each other at arm's length, negotiate aggressively over the terms of sale, and otherwise behave independently.

In contrast, a **vertical marketing system** (VMS) consists of producers and intermediaries acting together. Vertical marketing systems can be described as

vertical marketing system (VMS)
Network of producers and intermediaries acting as a unified system.

> professionally managed and centrally programmed networks, preplanned to achieve operating economies and maximum market impact. In other words, these vertical marketing systems are rationalized and capital-intensive networks. They are designed to achieve technological, managerial, and promotional economies through integration, coordination, and synchronization of marketing flows from points of production to points of ultimate use.[17]

Exhibit 12.5

Comparison of a Conventional Channel and a Vertical Marketing System

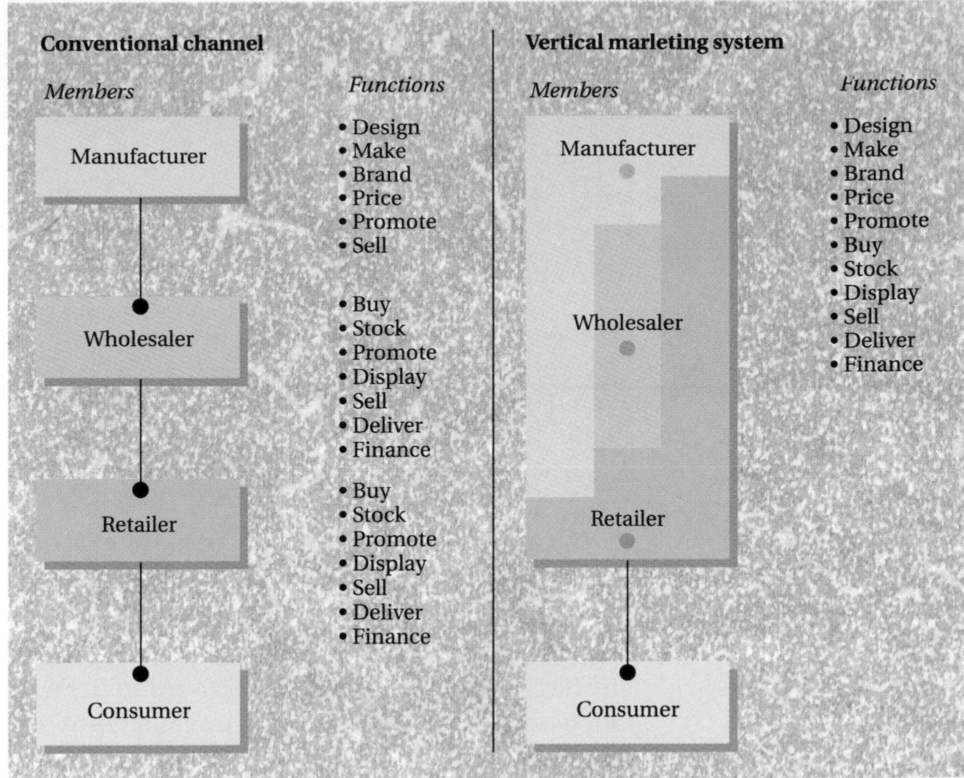

channel leader (channel captain)
Institution in a vertical marketing system that coordinates the activities of the various channel members.

corporate system
Vertical marketing system in which one firm owns successive stages in a channel of distribution.

forward integration
Manufacturer's or wholesaler's acquisition of an intermediary closer to the target market or performance of the functions of an intermediary closer to the target market.

Exhibit 12.5 illustrates the basic differences between a conventional channel and a VMS. The institution in a VMS that coordinates the activities of the various channel members is termed a **channel leader** (or **channel captain**). The three major types of vertical marketing systems are corporate, contractual, and administered.

Corporate Systems

A **corporate system**, in which one firm owns successive stages in a channel of distribution, is the ultimate in channel control. A single firm that owns the entire channel has no need to worry about intermediaries. The channel leader can be sure of supplies of raw materials, long-term contact with customers, adequate distribution, and adequate product exposure in the marketplace. Channel members' decision making is not independent or subject to major change without the channel leader's (owner's) agreement. Moreover, policies about price levels and product mixes for separate markets or heavier promotion in certain geographic regions can easily be implemented.

Corporate systems are integrated either forward or backward. **Forward integration** occurs when a manufacturer or wholesaler acquires an intermediary closer to the target market or begins performing the functions of an intermediary closer to the target market. A wholesaler could integrate forward by purchasing a retailer; examples include Sherwin-Williams, which operates over 2,000 paint stores, and Hart Schaffner and Marx, which owns over a hundred menswear clothing outlets. Or a manufacturer like Pepsi-Cola might integrate forward by buying a wholesaler. For decades, the company focused on supplying syrup and concentrate to independent bottlers. But in the early 1980s Pepsi decided it could best satisfy retailers' demands by serving them itself. After spending several billion dollars to buy out independent bottlers, Pepsi-Cola today owns bottling and distributing operations that account for half the soda in its system, compared to just 21 percent a decade ago.[18]

Pepsi-Cola's vertical marketing system is a corporate system, which means that the company owns both bottling and distribution operations.

backward integration Retailer's or wholesaler's acquisition of an intermediary closer to the manufacturing stage or performance of the functions formerly performed by an intermediary closer to the manufacturing stage.

Backward integration is just the opposite. Many large retail organizations integrate backward by developing or acquiring wholesaling and, in some cases, manufacturing operations. Large supermarkets get almost 10 percent of their stock from "captive" manufacturing facilities (those owned by the supermarket chains), many of which were acquired in the 1950s. More recently, Wal-Mart bought McLane Company, a Texas wholesaler with a reputation as one of the best specialty distributors of cigarettes, candy, and perishables in the United States. With McLane, Wal-Mart can avoid outside distributors and can lower overall costs.[19]

Contractual Systems

contractual system Vertical marketing system composed of independent firms at different channel levels (manufacturer, wholesaler, retailer) coordinating their distribution activities by contractual agreement.

A **contractual system** can be defined as a system of independent firms at different channel levels (manufacturer, wholesaler, retailer) coordinating their distribution activities by contractual agreement. Franchises like McDonald's, Arby's, Burger King, Holiday Inn, and automobile dealerships are examples of contractual systems.

A franchise system is the licensing of an entire business format. One firm (the franchisor) licenses a number of outlets (franchisees) to market a good or service and engage in a business developed by the franchisor. In turn, this licensed business uses the franchisor's trade names, trademarks, service marks, know-how, and business methods. Franchise systems are discussed in detail in Chapter 13.

Administered Systems

administered system Vertical marketing system in which a strong organization assumes a leadership position.

An **administered system** is a marketing channel in which a strong organization assumes a leadership position. The leader's strength and power may consist of sheer economic domination of other channel members. Its authority can also stem from a well-known brand name. Companies like Gillette, Hanes, Campbell, and Westinghouse are administered system leaders. An administered system leader can often influence or control the policies of other channel members without the costs and expertise required in a corporate system—perhaps by threatening to withdraw well-known brand names or by offering advertising rebates. Yet the vertically aligned companies can work as an integrated unit (an administered system) to achieve information, transportation, warehousing, promotion, and other economies. Compared to a conventional system, the net result is usually a lower overall cost, a better assortment of merchandise, faster inventory turnover, and flexibility in adjusting to changing consumer preferences.

In Japan, vertically administered systems called keiretsu are led by some of the country's largest companies, such as Toyota and Nissan. These alliances pull to-

gether government, industry, capital, and the best information on advanced technology worldwide (see Chapter 3). Toyota, for example, is the leader of an administered system of 175 primary suppliers and 4,000 secondary suppliers. In addition, leading manufacturers, like Matsushita, have distribution alliances with thousands of retailers throughout Japan.[20]

Horizontal Marketing Systems

horizontal marketing system (cooperative) Network of distribution channel members at the same level that pool their negotiating strength and achieve other economies of scale; often called a cooperative.

horizontal integration Distribution channel member's purchase of firms at the same level of the marketing channel.

A **horizontal marketing system** exists when channel members at the same level pool their negotiating strength and achieve other economies of scale. Such an organized group is often called a **cooperative.** American Hardware, with about 3,750 members, is a retail cooperative. Wholesaler-sponsored cooperatives like IGA, Spartan, and Super Valu are also examples of horizontal marketing systems.

Horizontal marketing systems often result from **horizontal integration**, which occurs when a channel member buys firms at the same level of the marketing channel. For instance, Procter & Gamble bought Noxell, the manufacturer of Noxema skin cream and Cover Girl makeup, making P&G the largest mass marketer of cosmetics in the United States. Similarly, PepsiCo acquired several restaurants—Pizza Hut, Taco Bell, and Kentucky Fried Chicken. These outlets are also retail channel members for selling Pepsi-Cola soft drinks.

5 INTERNATIONAL MARKETING CHANNELS

International marketing channels are important to U.S. corporations that export their products or manufacture abroad. Executives should recognize the unique cultural, economic, institutional, and legal aspects of each market before trying to set up marketing channels in foreign countries. They should spend a great deal of time designing the best channel strategy for each country.

Manufacturers introducing products in foreign markets face a tough decision: what type of channel structure to use. Specifically, should the product be marketed directly, mostly by company salespeople, or through independent foreign intermediaries, such as agents and distributors?[21] Using company salespeople generally provides more control and less risk than using foreign intermediaries. However, setting up a sales force in a foreign country also entails a greater commitment, both financially and managerially.

Companies wanting to sell in overseas markets are more likely to succeed with a company-controlled sales force when

- The product category is relatively new and the products within it are not standardized
- The product is closely related to the company's core business
- Product trade secrets are at risk on pending patents to protect the technology
- The product requires high service levels
- Few legal restrictions constrain direct foreign investment
- The company already has experienced salespeople who would be hard to replace with foreign agents
- The company already has an established channel of distribution in the foreign country
- Close competitors have set up their own direct distribution channels
- The foreign country's culture is very similar to U.S. culture[22]

For example, suppose a major software manufacturer wants to introduce a new software package in Europe. The software provides innovative solutions for finance-related customers, such as banks and stockbrokers, and requires specialized training and technical support after the sale. Being a veteran in the European financial software market, the company already has distribution channels and a direct sales force. Given these conditions, the manufacturer would likely use a direct channel to market its new product.

The benefits of using independent foreign intermediaries are in many cases the opposite of the conditions stated previously. For instance, if the product is fairly standardized, does not require a high level of service, is not at risk of losing patent protection, and is within a product category that does not use leading-edge technology, then independent foreign intermediaries are probably the better choice. In countries where the culture and customs are fairly different from those of the United States, inexperienced marketers may have trouble without the help of foreign middlemen. Other benefits of using foreign intermediaries include the economies of scale and scope they obtain by providing distribution services for several manufacturers. Furthermore, the manufacturers avoid having to deal with government regulations and politics in foreign countries.[23]

Firms that decide to use a foreign intermediary should take great care in choosing an overseas distributor. Since the marketer's history, trademarks, and reputation are usually unknown in the foreign market, foreign consumers will buy on the strength of the distributor's reputation.[24]

Marketers should also be aware that the channel structure abroad may not be very similar to channels in the United States. For instance, U.S. firms wishing to sell goods in Japan must frequently go through three layers of wholesalers and subwholesalers: the national or primary wholesalers, the secondary or regional wholesalers, and the local wholesalers.[25] The channel types available in foreign countries usually differ as well. The more highly developed a nation is economically, the more specialized its channel types. Therefore, a marketer wishing to sell in Germany or Japan will have several channel types to choose from. Conversely, developing countries like India, Ethiopia, and Venezuela have limited channel types available; there are typically few mail-order channels, vending machines, or specialized retailers and wholesalers.[26]

A final difficulty arises from the distance between the manufacturer and the foreign intermediary. With little or infrequent direct contact, the intermediary may be less active in promoting the manufacturer's product. Suggestions on how international marketers can motivate their foreign channel partners are discussed in the article at the top of page 379.

6 TYPES OF WHOLESALING INTERMEDIARIES

The variations in channel structures for consumer and industrial products are due to variations in the number and type of intermediaries. As mentioned earlier, intermediaries differ by whether they take title to the product (ownership rights) or simply aid the sale of a product from producer to end user. Typically, retailers and merchant wholesalers take ownership to the products, but agents and brokers do not. Exhibit 12.6 shows these two types of intermediaries, as well as manufacturer-owned intermediaries (sales offices and branches) and retailers. Retailing intermediaries are discussed in Chapter 13; for now, let's turn our focus toward the many types of wholesaling intermediaries.

INTERNATIONAL PERSPECTIVES

Motivating International Channel Partners

How does an international marketer get its foreign distributors and dealers to pay more attention to its products and promote them more aggressively? Foreign distributors and dealers, just like their U.S. counterparts, can pick and choose the products they will promote to their customers. As tough as it is for U.S. manufacturers to motivate their domestic distributors or dealers, it is even tougher in the international arena. The environment, culture, and customs affecting channel relationships can be very tricky.

The manufacturer's trickiest task is gaining channel member support in carrying out its marketing objectives. To help motivate international channel partners, marketers should find out their needs and problems, offer support, and build continuing relationships.

The needs and problems of foreign distributors and dealers can be dramatically different from those in the United States. Many foreign wholesalers and retailers—for example, those in Asia, Africa, and Latin America—are quite small by U.S. standards. When large U.S. manufacturers deal with relatively small foreign channel partners, their differing needs can cause serious communication problems. For instance, many small foreign wholesalers and retailers have little desire to grow larger and may not try very hard to promote U.S. products. Growth-oriented U.S. manufacturers may view such channel members as lazy. In fact, they may simply be operating according to their needs. Foreign channel members are also faced with limited financing, high labor costs, inefficient management, and strict government regulations.

U.S. manufacturers can provide support to their foreign intermediaries in the form of adequate profit margins, territorial protection, advertising support, financial assistance, sales and service training, business advice, and market research. For example, in Latin America Ford Motor Company's Overseas Tractor Operations trains its own and its dealers' employees in repair, maintenance, and operation of tractors and equipment. The program has paid off in good dealer relations. Training at a large Ford facility, and the foreign travel often required to attend training programs, has become a mark of prestige.

Finally, mutual commitment is needed to build successful international marketing channels. But it is hard to build such a relationship in international markets, because foreign distributors and dealers have their own business traditions, customs, and cultural norms. Therefore, the approach may have to be quite different from that taken in domestic channels. The impersonal, business-to-business relationships so common in the United States are often far less effective in other countries such as Japan and China, where more personal, participative relationships are expected. Similarly, the traditions and customs that underlie channel relationships are important. Agents and distributors in the Middle East, for example, are influenced by thousands of years of bazaar trading. Marketing to them means to wait for the customer to come to them. Financial incentives, therefore, may not motivate them to push the product aggressively.[27]

How can manufacturers and marketers best find out about the needs and problems of their foreign intermediaries? What types of help could a manufacturer give to intermediaries in developing countries? Can you think of any particular U.S. customs or business practices that could impede good channel relationships with a foreign country?

Source: Adapted from Bert Rosenbloom, "Motivating Your International Channel Partners," *Business Horizons,* March–April 1990, pp. 53–57.

merchant wholesaler
Institution that buys goods from manufacturers and resells them to businesses, government agencies, and other wholesalers or retailers; also receives and takes title to goods, stores them in its own warehouses, and later reships them.

Merchant Wholesalers

Slightly under 60 percent of all wholesale sales are conducted by merchant wholesalers, which make up 80 percent of all wholesaling establishments.[28] A **merchant wholesaler** is an institution that buys goods from manufacturers and resells them to businesses, government agencies, and other wholesalers or retailers. All merchant wholesalers take title to the goods they sell. Most merchant wholesalers operate one or more warehouses in which they receive goods, store them, and later reship them. Customers are mostly small- or moderate-size retailers, but merchant wholesalers also market to manufacturers and institutional clients.

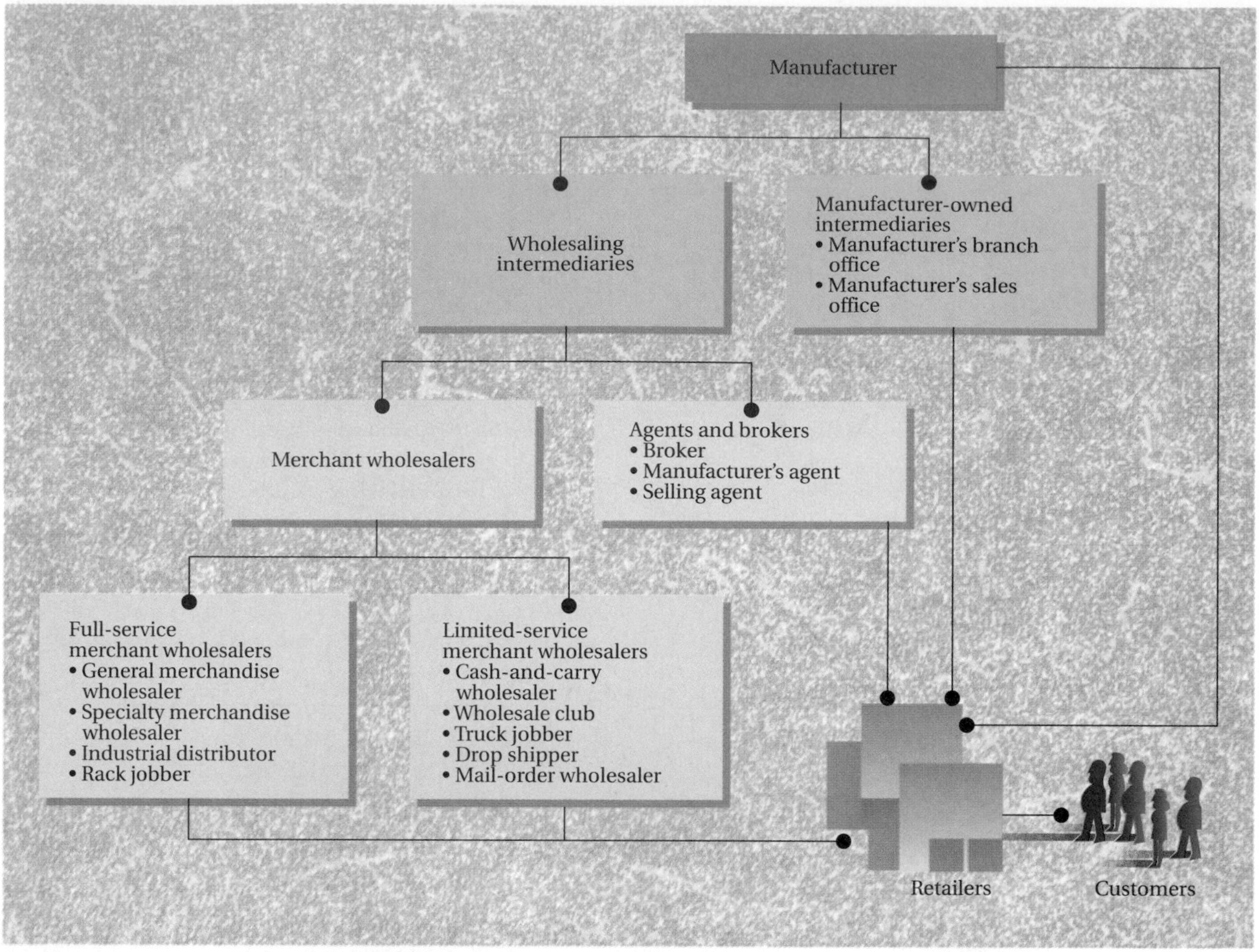

Exhibit 12.6

The Major Types of Channel Intermediaries

full-service merchant wholesaler
Wholesaler that assembles an assortment of products, provides credit for clients, offers promotional help and technical advice, maintains a sales force to contact customers, and delivers merchandise and may offer research, planning, installation, and repair.

general merchandise wholesaler (full-line wholesaler)
Wholesaler that stocks a full assortment of products within a product line.

Merchant wholesalers can be categorized as either full-service or limited-service wholesalers, depending on the number of channel functions they perform. Full-service merchant wholesalers generally perform all channel functions (refer back to Exhibit 12.2) as products flow from the producer to the final user. This classification includes general merchandise wholesalers, specialty merchandise wholesalers, industrial distributors, and rack jobbers. Limited-service merchant wholesalers include cash-and-carry wholesalers, warehouse clubs, truck jobbers, drop shippers, and mail-order wholesalers.

Full-Service Merchant Wholesalers

Full-service merchant wholesalers perform all channel functions. They assemble an assortment of products for their clients, provide credit, and offer promotional help and technical advice. In addition, they maintain a sales force to contact customers, store and deliver merchandise, and may offer research and planning support. Depending on the product line, full-service merchant wholesalers sometimes provide for installation and repair. *Full service* also means "going the extra mile" to meet special customer needs, such as offering fast delivery in emergencies.

Although they typically carry only one or two lines of merchandise, **general merchandise wholesalers** (or **full-line wholesalers**) stock a full assortment of products within the line. For instance, a hardware wholesaler will stock a full array of tools, paints, fasteners, ropes, chains, and so on. General merchandise wholesalers

SYSCO Corporation is the nation's largest full-service merchant wholesaler in the food-service distribution industry, with vast warehouses for storing goods and a large fleet of trucks for distributing them to customers.
Sysco Corporation

are common in the drug, grocery, and clothing markets in addition to the hardware market. SYSCO Corporation is the nation's largest full-line, full-service merchant wholesaler in the food-service distribution industry. The company supplies restaurants, nursing homes, hospitals, hotels, schools, colleges, and other customers with thousands of types of foods, cooking supplies, tableware, cleaning chemicals, and disposable products, ranging from caviar to chef's hats. SYSCO assembles these products from various manufacturers, stores and delivers them, and offers promotional assistance and technical advice through its sales force.

specialty merchandise wholesaler
Wholesaler that offers part of a product line to target customers but in greater depth than general merchandise wholesalers offer.

Specialty merchandise wholesalers offer part of a product line to target customers—for instance, a meat or seafood wholesaler as opposed to a grocery wholesaler. Specialty merchandise wholesalers usually offer much greater depth within the scope of the product line. For example, seafood wholesalers might carry unusual or exotic seafood. Specialty wholesalers usually have excellent product knowledge in their specialized line of merchandise, which can be very important. For example, suppose a sausage packing house needs to buy spices for a new brand of sausage and has to choose from hundreds of spices and combinations. A specialty wholesaler of spices can help make the correct choice.

industrial distributor
Full-service merchant wholesaler that sells to manufacturers rather than to retailers.

Industrial distributors can be described as full-service merchant wholesalers that sell to manufacturers rather than to retailers. Industrial wholesalers typically stock the following products:

- Maintenance, repair, and operating (MRO) supplies (such as hammers, paint, and replacement belts)
- Original equipment manufacturer (OEM) supplies (such as fasteners, power transmission components, hydraulic equipment, and small rubber parts that become part of a finished product)
- Equipment used in the operation of the business (such as hand tools, power tools, and conveyors)
- Machinery used in making raw materials and semifinished goods into finished products (such as grinders, stamping machines, and dryers)

Distributors that carry a general line or a wide assortment of industrial products are called "mill supply houses." Conversely, single-line industrial distributors offer expertise in one area, such as cutting tools or abrasives. Mill supply houses hold a larger piece of the market than single-line industrial distributors because of the economies of scale achieved by large mill supply houses. Buyers also prefer to have as few contracts for MRO supplies as possible, so they tend to choose vendors with broad product lines. Additionally, large mill supply houses can provide expertise rivaling that of single-line specialists.

rack jobber
Full-service wholesaler that performs the merchant wholesaler's functions and some usually carried out by the retailer, such as stocking shelves.

Rack jobbers perform the merchant wholesaler's functions and some usually carried out by the retailer—namely, stocking nonfood merchandise on racks or shelves. Rack jobbers serve drug, grocery, and general merchandise retailers like Kmart and Target, with such familiar products as hosiery, toys, housewares, and health and beauty aids. Rack jobbers typically sell on consignment, which means that they keep title to the goods and don't collect payment for the merchandise until it is sold. Rack jobbers hire delivery people to maintain inventory records, price the goods, and keep the merchandise fresh. In addition, they restock the racks or shelves and assemble promotional display materials.

Limited-Service Merchant Wholesalers

limited-service merchant wholesaler
Wholesaler that performs only a few of the full-service merchant wholesaler's activities.

As the name implies, **limited-service merchant wholesalers** perform only a few of the full-service merchant wholesaler's activities. Limited-service wholesalers represent just a small part of the merchant wholesaling industry.

cash-and-carry wholesaler
Limited-service merchant wholesaler that sells for cash and usually carries a limited line of fast-moving merchandise.

The **cash-and-carry wholesaler** sells for cash and usually carries a limited line of fast-moving merchandise. Customers must go to the cash-and-carry wholesaler's warehouse and then transport the goods to their retail outlets. Cash-and-carry wholesalers do not make deliveries, extend credit, or supply market information. Compared to the prices charged by full-service wholesalers, the prices of cash-and-carry wholesalers are usually lower. However, retailers' total costs may be higher, since retailers perform some wholesaling functions.

warehouse club
Limited-service merchant wholesaler that sells a limited selection of brand name appliances, household items, and groceries on a cash-and-carry basis to members, usually small businesses and groups.

Warehouse clubs are a special form of cash-and-carry wholesaler. A **warehouse club** sells a limited selection of brand name appliances, household items, and groceries on a cash-and-carry basis to members, usually small businesses and groups. Members pay an annual membership fee. Merchandise is typically sold in bulk-size cartons or in smaller containers banded or wrapped together. For example, members can buy five-pound boxes of Velveeta cheese, cartons of 1,000 ketchup "tear-packs," or shrink-wrapped packages of a dozen boxes of pencils. Warehouse clubs carry a limited assortment of merchandise—for instance, high-volume office supplies like legal pads and copier paper. Small-business members must still shop at the traditional office supply store for some of their needs. The four major warehouse club chains now operating in the United States are Price Club, Costco Wholesale, PACE Membership Warehouse (a division of Kmart), and Sam's Club (a division of Wal-Mart). Because warehouse clubs act as a wholesaler to small businesses and a retailer to group customers, this question arises: How should a warehouse club be classified? The answer is simply that it is both a wholesaling and a retailing intermediary. Retail customers generally make up the largest number of patrons, but wholesale buyers account for most of the sales.

truck jobber
Limited-service merchant wholesaler that performs the functions of salesperson and delivery person.

The **truck jobber** combines the functions of salesperson and delivery person. Normally, truck jobbers carry a very limited line of semiperishable merchandise, such as milk, bread, snack foods, beer, and candy. Truck jobbers usually sell for cash.

Their main customers are supermarkets, but they also serve hospitals, restaurants, factory refreshment shops, and hotels.

drop shipper
Limited-service merchant wholesaler that places orders for its customers with the manufacturer but does not physically handle the products it sells.

The **drop shipper** does not store or handle the products it sells. Instead, drop shippers place orders for their customers with the manufacturer, which then ships directly to the customers. Drop shippers are usually found in the bulk industries—for example, coal, lumber, bauxite, heavy equipment, and some agricultural products. Because of their weight, these items have high freight costs relative to their unit value. Direct shipment to customers thus makes sense. Like cash-and-carry wholesalers, drop shippers can offer lower prices, since they perform relatively few wholesale functions. In their case, warehousing and storage are eliminated. Drop shippers are still merchant wholesalers, even though they may never see the goods. They take title to the merchandise and therefore set the terms of the sale. Moreover, drop shippers arrange shipping and take on the risks of ownership during shipment.

mail-order wholesaler
Limited-service merchant wholesaler that sells goods by catalog to businesses, institutions, government, and other organizations.

The **mail-order wholesaler** is the counterpart to the mail-order retailer. The only difference is that the mail-order wholesaler sells goods to businesses, institutions, government, and other organizations, whereas the mail-order retailer concentrates on consumers.

Agents and Brokers

Agents and brokers represent retailers, wholesalers, or manufacturers and do not take title to the merchandise. Title reflects ownership, and ownership usually implies control. Unlike wholesalers, agents or brokers only facilitate sales and generally have little input into the terms of the sale. They do, however, get a fee or commission based on sales volume. Many perform fewer functions than limited-service merchant wholesalers.

broker
Functional intermediary that brings buyers and sellers together.

The function of a **broker** is to bring buyers and sellers together. Brokers exist in markets where these two parties would otherwise have trouble finding each other. Brokers do not usually handle the goods involved in the sale or finance either the buyer or seller. Their basic function is to represent the buyer or seller in finding another party to complete the transaction. Typically, a broker locates a potential buyer or seller (called a *principal*) and then lets the two parties resolve matters of price, quantity, delivery date, and specifications. Brokers receive a fee from the principal engaging their services.

manufacturers' agent
Functional intermediary that represents one manufacturer or several manufacturers of complementary lines and follows the terms set by the manufacturer.

Like brokers, manufacturers' agents, sometimes called manufacturers' representatives, rarely have much voice in the terms of a sales contract. A **manufacturers' agent** represents one manufacturer or several manufacturers of complementary lines and follows the terms set by the manufacturer. Agents are paid on commission and therefore must be good salespeople. They generally have excellent product knowledge and understand customer preferences within their territory.

selling agent
Intermediary used mostly by small firms on a commission basis and contracted to sell the manufacturer's entire output.

A final type of agent is a selling agent, which is used mostly by small firms. Actually, the term **selling agent** is somewhat misleading, since the agent usually assumes responsibility for the whole marketing operation of a company. In some industries, such as textiles, selling agents may even offer financial help to clients. Selling agents work on commission, usually contracting to sell the manufacturer's entire output.

Some large retailers find agents and brokers unnecessary. Sears, for instance, keeps costs down and selling practices competitive by rarely going through manufacturers' agents and brokers. Wal-Mart stirred up controversy by deciding it would deal directly with the principals of its supplying companies, rather than with their

representatives or brokers. Some representatives resented Wal-Mart's attempt to eliminate a layer of costs, specifically the 2 to 3 percent they receive in commissions. Wal-Mart claims that it wanted to improve communications and reaction time between the company and its many suppliers. Manufacturers have had mixed responses to the decision. With their already-thin profit margins, many say they cannot afford to hire a direct sales force so Wal-Mart can deal directly with them. Other manufacturers feel that, since Wal-Mart is one of their largest accounts, they should provide it with the special attention of a company account manager.[29]

manufacturers' sales branch
Manufacturer owned and controlled wholesale institution that carries inventory.

Manufacturers' Branches and Offices

As manufacturers grow, they often set up wholesale operations similar to full-service merchant wholesalers. Manufacturers manage, control, and own these wholesale institutions, called **manufacturers' sales branches**. The only distinction between manufacturers' sales offices and sales branches is that branches carry inventory and offices to not.

Manufacturers' sales branches are set up when manufacturers seek tighter control over their channels of distribution, as well as their inventory. They are common

Exhibit 12.7

Functions and Services Provided by Wholesaling Intermediaries

Wholesaler type	**Contacting and promoting** ■ Sales force ■ Advertising	**Negotiating** ■ Establishing terms of sale	**Risk taking** ■ Ownership of inventory	**Physical distribution** ■ Storage and transportation	**Sorting** ■ Sorting out ■ Accumulation ■ Allocation ■ Assorting	**Research** ■ Market information	**Financing** ■ Credit
General merchandise wholesaler	■	■	■	■	■	■	■
Specialty merchandise wholesaler	■	■	■	■	■	■	■
Industrial distributor	■	■	■	■	■	■	■
Rack jobber	■	■	■	■	■	■	■
Cash-and-carry wholesaler		■	■	Storage only	■		
Warehouse club	■		■	Storage only	■		
Truck jobber	■	■	■	■	■		
Drop shipper	■	■	■	*			■
Mail-order wholesaler	■	■	■	■	■		
Broker	■	■		*		■	
Manufacturer's agent or representative	■	■		*		■	
Selling agent	■	■		*		■	
Manufacturer's sales branch	■	■	■	■	■	■	■
Manufacturer's sales office	■	■	■		■	■	■

* Coordination of transportation only

manufacturers' sales office
Wholesale operation that performs a sales function and is owned, managed, and controlled by a manufacturer.

in the automotive, transportation equipment, electronics, lumber, millwork, and plywood industries. **Manufacturers' sales offices,** on the other hand, typically perform a sales function only and serve as an alternative to agents and brokers. Sales offices are most noticeable in the dry-goods and notions industries.

Exhibit 12.7 summarizes the functions of all the types of wholesaling intermediaries just discussed. These functions correspond to those originally described in Exhibit 12.2. Now let's turn our attention to the channel strategy decisions marketers must make.

7 CHANNEL STRATEGY DECISIONS

A marketing channel strategy requires several critical decisions. Marketing managers must decide what role distribution will play in the overall marketing strategy. In addition, they must be sure that the channel strategy they choose is consistent with product, promotion, and pricing strategies.

When determining marketing channel strategy, marketing managers face two issues: what factors will influence the choice of channel(s) and what level of distribution intensity will be appropriate.

Factors Affecting Channel Choice

Marketers must answer many questions before choosing a marketing channel. The final choice depends on analysis of several factors, which often interact. These factors can be grouped as market factors, product factors, and producer factors.

Market Factors

Among the most important market factors affecting the choice of distribution channels are target customer considerations. Specifically, marketing managers should answer the following questions: Who are the potential customers? What do they buy? Where do they buy? When do they buy? How do they buy? These questions imply that customers have preferences regarding products, sellers, time, and credit that marketing managers should be aware of. Additionally, the choice of channel depends on whether the producer is selling to consumers or to industrial customers. Industrial customers' buying habits are very different from those of consumers.

As products like computers become more common, customers require less direct support. Thus they are more willing to buy from low-frills discount stores like CompUSA.
© Mark Richards

Industrial customers tend to buy in larger quantities and require more customer service. Consumers usually buy in very small quantities and sometimes do not mind if they get no service at all, as in a discount store.

Geographic location and size of the market are also important to channel selection. As a rule, if the target market is concentrated in one or more specific areas, then direct selling through a direct sales force is appropriate. When markets are more widely dispersed, intermediaries would be less expensive. The size of the market also influences channel choice. Generally, a very large market requires more intermediaries. For instance, Procter & Gamble has to reach millions of consumers with its many brands of household goods. It needs many intermediaries, including wholesalers and retailers.

Competition in the marketplace is also a criterion for choosing a channel. Entering a channel where competition is fierce is difficult. For instance, each year thousands of new products are introduced into the marketplace. As a result, channels become crowded and difficult to enter. However, a producer may find a marketing channel that has been overlooked or avoided by its competitors. Many manufacturers have also found direct channels, such as direct mail, to be very profitable. Lifetime Automotive Products, the maker of Tripledge windshield wipers, found the direct channel to be very profitable. Selling its product through traditional retail channels required more capital than the company could raise. So the company uses a direct marketing strategy that reaches consumers through a blend of inserts in credit card bills, catalogs, print advertising, and television.[30]

Product Factors

Another rule of thumb is that products that are more complex and customized and have a high unit cost tend to use shorter and more direct marketing channels. These types of products sell better through a direct sales force. Examples include pharmaceuticals, scientific instruments, airplanes, and mainframe computer systems. On the other hand, the more standardized a product, the longer its distribution channel and the more intermediaries involved. For example, the formula for chewing gum is about the same from producer to producer, with the exception of flavor and shape. Chewing gum is also very inexpensive per unit. As a result, the distribution channel for gum tends to involve many wholesalers and retailers.

The product's life cycle is also an important factor in choosing a marketing channel. In fact, the choice of channel may change over the life of the product. For example, when photocopiers were first available, they were typically sold by a direct sales force. Now, however, photocopiers can be found in several places, including warehouse clubs, electronics superstores, and mail-order catalogs. As products become more common and less intimidating to potential users, marketing channels add less value and customers require less support. As a result, producers tend to look for alternative channels in which to move the product.[31] Häagen-Dazs, maker of super-rich ice cream, uses different marketing channels during its product's life cycle when introducing the brand in foreign countries. The strategy for whetting foreign appetites is simple: First, introduce the brand through a few high-end retailers; then build company-owned stores in high-traffic areas; and finally, roll into convenience stores and supermarkets.[32]

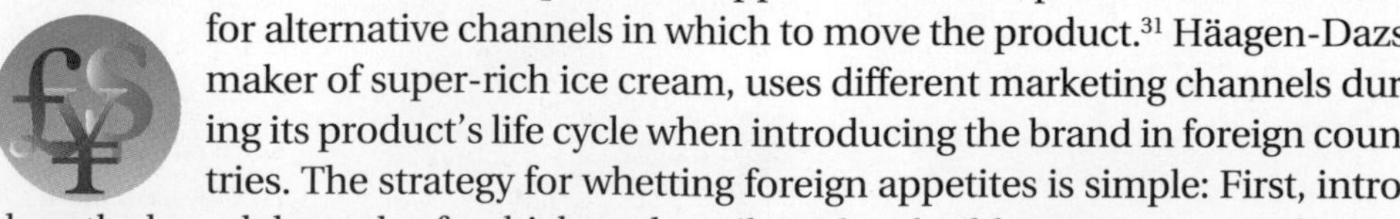

Another factor is the delicacy of the product. Perishable products like vegetables and milk have a relatively short life span. Fragile products like china and crystal require a minimum amount of handling. Therefore, both require fairly short marketing channels.

Producer Factors

Several factors pertaining to the producer itself are important to the selection of a marketing channel. In general, producers with large financial, managerial, and marketing resources are better able to use channels that require fewer intermediaries. These producers have the ability to hire and train their own sales force, warehouse their own goods, and extend credit to their customers. Weaker firms, on the other hand, must rely on intermediaries to provide these services for them.

Compared to producers with only one or two product lines, producers that sell several products in a related area are able to choose channels that are more direct. Sales expenses can be spread over more products.

A producer's desire to control pricing, positioning, brand image, and customer support also tends to influence channel selection. For instance, firms that sell products with exclusive brand images, such as designer perfumes and clothing, usually avoid channels in which discount retailers are present. Church Shoes in the United Kingdom sells its shoes only in upscale men's clothing stores that sell classic apparel. Church is concerned about image control and thus steers clear of mainstream shoe stores.[33] Many producers have opted to risk their image, however, and test sales in discount channels. Levi Strauss expanded its distribution in the early 1980s to include JCPenney and Sears. Many upscale retailers felt Levi's image had been cheapened. JCPenney is now Levi's biggest customer. More recently, OshKosh B'Gosh, purveyor of high-quality children's clothing, decided to market its lines in Sears.[34]

Levels of Distribution Intensity

Organizations have three options for intensity of distribution, or how available a product is: intensive distribution, selective distribution, or exclusive distribution.

intensive distribution
Form of distribution aimed at having a product available in every outlet where target customers might want to buy it.

Intensive Distribution

Intensive distribution is distribution aimed at maximum market coverage. The manufacturer tries to have the product available in every outlet where potential customers might want to buy it. If buyers are unwilling to search for a product (as is true of convenience goods and operating supplies), the product must be more accessible to buyers. A low-value product that is purchased frequently may require a lengthy channel. For example, candy is found in almost every type of retail store imaginable. It is typically sold to retailers in small quantities by a food or candy wholesaler. The Wrigley Company could not afford to sell its gum directly to every service station, drugstore, supermarket, and discount store. The cost would be too high.

Most manufacturers pursuing an intensive distribution strategy sell to a large percentage of the wholesalers willing to stock their products. Retailers' willingness (or unwillingness) to handle items tends to control the manufacturer's ability to achieve intensive distribution. For example, a retailer already carrying ten brands of gum may show little enthusiasm for one more brand.

Designer handbags are a type of product that is often distributed selectively. Consumers have to search to find the brand and style they want, because these handbags are available only in selected stores with a quality image.

Selective Distribution

selective distribution
Form of distribution achieved by screening dealers to eliminate all but a few in any single area.

Selective distribution is achieved by screening dealers to eliminate all but a few in any single area. Since only a few retailers are chosen, the consumer must seek out the product. Shopping goods and some specialty products are distributed selectively. Accessory equipment manufacturers in the business-to-business market usually follow a selective distribution strategy.

Several screening criteria are used to find the right dealers. An accessory equipment manufacturer like NEC may seek firms that are able to service its products properly. A television manufacturer like Zenith may look for service ability and a quality dealer image. If the manufacturer expects to move a large volume of merchandise through each dealer, it will choose only those dealers that seem able to handle such volume. As a result, many smaller retailers may not be considered.

Exclusive Distribution

exclusive distribution
Form of distribution that establishes one or a few dealers within a given area.

The most restrictive form of market coverage is **exclusive distribution**, which entails only one or a few dealers within a given area. Since buyers may have to search or travel extensively to buy the product, exclusive distribution is usually confined to consumer specialty goods, a few shopping goods, and major industrial equipment. Products distributed exclusively include Rolls Royce automobiles, Trojan yachts, Pettibone tower cranes, and Skytrak extendable boom forklifts. Sometimes exclusive territories are granted by new companies (such as franchisors) to obtain market coverage in a particular area. Limited distribution may also serve to project an exclusive image for the product.

Retailers and wholesalers may be unwilling to commit the time and investment to promote and service a product unless the manufacturer guarantees them an exclusive territory. This arrangement shields the dealer from direct competition and enables it to be the main beneficiary of the manufacturer's promotional efforts in that geographic area. With exclusive distribution, channels of communication are usually well established, since the manufacturer works with a limited number of dealers rather than many accounts.

Although exclusivity has its advantages, it also can have its pitfalls. An exclusive network may not be large enough, for instance, if demand is brisk. In addition, the producer's insistence on exclusivity might put the channel in financial jeopardy during times of weak demand. Honda's Acura division, for example, used an exclusive distribution strategy in an attempt to create a distinctive image for its high-priced cars. Unfortunately, Acura dealers have not experienced much success because of the car's small niche market, low resale demand, and ironically, infrequent need for follow-up service and repair.[35]

8 MARKETING CHANNEL DESIGN

Once a marketing manager has determined which factors influence the choice of marketing channel, then he or she is ready to design the marketing channel. Exhibit 12.8 shows the major stages in marketing channel design, along with the criteria that producers use in choosing channels and channel participants. Frequently, wholesalers and retailers can also design channels.

Identifying Channel Alternatives

The first step in marketing channel design is to determine where and how target customers want to buy the product. Market research will tell the manufacturer what

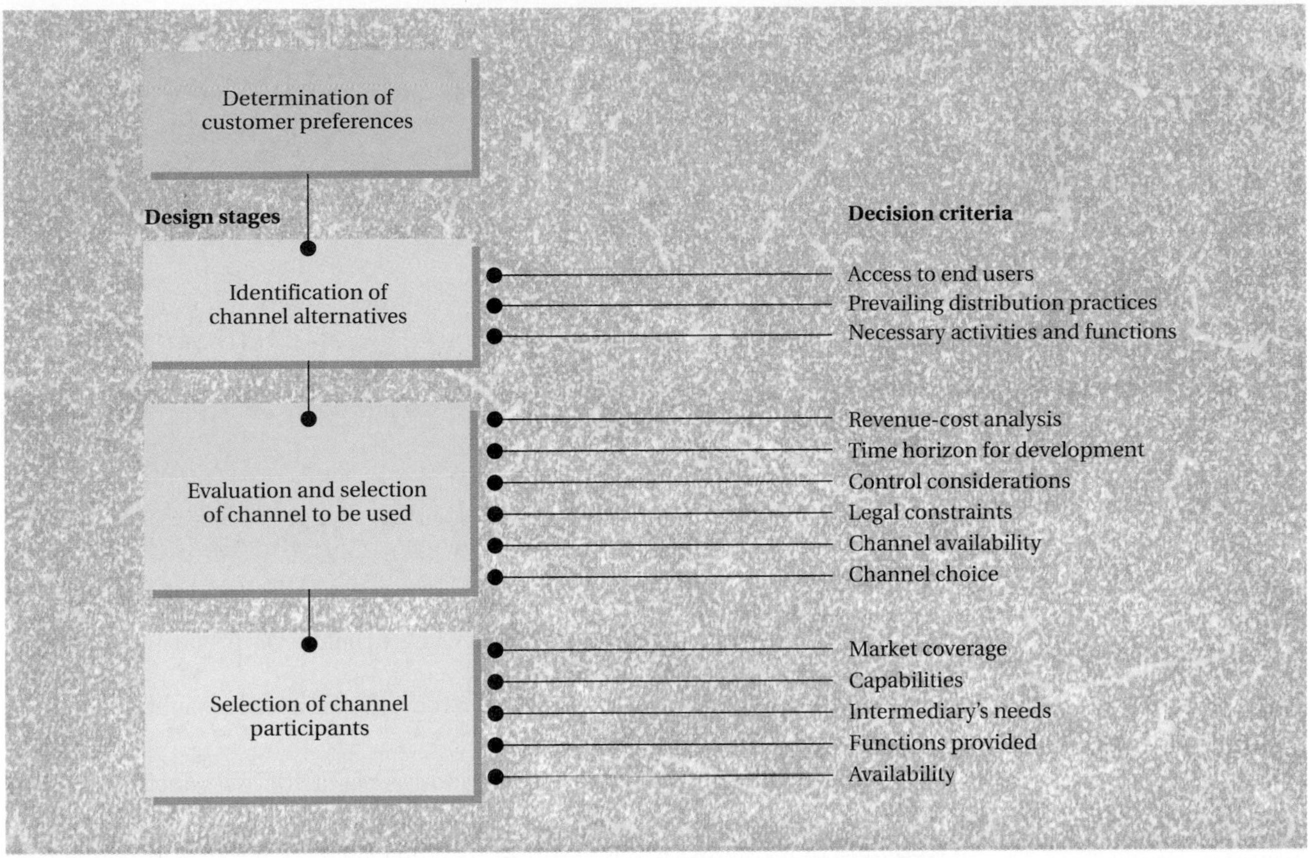

Determination of customer preferences

Design stages | **Decision criteria**

Identification of channel alternatives
- Access to end users
- Prevailing distribution practices
- Necessary activities and functions

Evaluation and selection of channel to be used
- Revenue-cost analysis
- Time horizon for development
- Control considerations
- Legal constraints
- Channel availability
- Channel choice

Selection of channel participants
- Market coverage
- Capabilities
- Intermediary's needs
- Functions provided
- Availability

Exhibit 12.8

Channel Design Decisions and Decision Criteria

type of retailing or wholesaling establishments target customers prefer, as well as how they would like to buy the product. For example, market studies might reveal that customers prefer to buy bath towels at discount stores rather than department stores. They may want to buy towels in sets that include a bath towel, a hand towel, and a face cloth. These customer preferences will provide the foundation for the manufacturer's channel strategy.

Once customer preferences have been determined, the next step is to identify the channel alternatives that match the organization's channel objectives and channel strategy. Three questions guide the identification of channel alternatives: Who has access to end users? What are the prevailing distribution practices in the industry? What activities and functions must be performed by channel members?

Access to End Users

The intermediaries that might be used to reach the target market can best be identified by working backward from the end user. Consider the following example:

> Cantel, Inc., headquartered in Toronto, Canada, was granted a license from the Canadian Department of Communications to provide a national air network for cellular mobile telephones. Management considered the following five channel alternatives:
>
> 1. *Established outlets.* One option was to create a distribution channel using established dealers and/or retailers from a broad segment of cellular-related businesses such as Sears, Canadian Tire, and Radio Shack.
> 2. *Direct sales force.* Another possibility was to sell directly to end users with a Cantel sales force. This would increase the intensity of the selling effort but would be quite expensive.
> 3. *Company-owned stores.* Cantel could also establish a network of company-owned stores to market product hardware, subscriptions, installation, and maintenance.

Because wholesalers and retailers did not want to stock its innovative product, Snap-on Tools designed a unique marketing channel. Driving clearly identified "traveling store" vans full of tools, franchised Snap-on dealers call directly on professional mechanics.

Courtesy of Snap-on Tools Corporation

4. *Franchising.* Another alternative considered was a franchise network of established companies with diverse backgrounds. Franchisees could perform both wholesaling and retailing activities.
5. *Piggybacking.* The final distribution option considered was using manufacturers of cellular equipment to market the air network.[36]

Cantel management chose the franchise option. A big factor in its decision was the fact that franchisees already had customers who were potential buyers of cellular telephones. Since Cantel was a new firm with no established reputation, management wanted to capitalize on franchisees' reputations and access to end users.

Prevailing Distribution Practices

Considering other firms' channel practices with similar products can help identify the main options. Management can gain insight by studying competitors' distribution strategies and weighing their strengths and weaknesses. Management should be careful, however, not to restrict its marketing channel options to those being used by competitors.

Cantel management examined Bell Cellular's distribution strategy, its major Canadian competition, and the distribution strategies of U.S. firms new to the industry. Others' experiences enabled Cantel managers to draw conclusions about the strengths and weaknesses of some distribution options.

Necessary Activities and Functions

Earlier, this chapter described several essential marketing channel functions (refer back to Exhibit 12.2). Producers, intermediaries, and end users must perform these functions. An important step in pinpointing feasible channel alternatives is assessing the functions and activities that need to be performed. Then management must identify which are best performed by producers and which are best performed by intermediaries. Moreover, it must determine the capabilities of different types of intermediaries under consideration. For example, Cantel recognized that a direct sales force would be very costly per customer contacted compared to other channel options. It also realized that the channel intermediaries with well-known names and favorable images could help overcome Cantel's unfamiliarity to end users. Physical distribution was discounted as an important factor in selecting a channel, since the product (use of the airwaves) did not require storage or delivery.

Evaluating and Selecting Channels

The evaluation of channel alternatives should include examining revenues and costs, the time required for channel development, control considerations, legal constraints, channel availability, and channel choice.

Revenue and Cost Analyses

A key factor in evaluating channel alternatives is the expected economic performance of each option. Intensive distribution through a variety of retail outlets may be more costly than other choices. Yet compared to selective distribution, it should generate a larger sales volume.

The ideal channel performs the needed distribution tasks at the lowest possible cost.[37] Distribution cost analysis is a useful tool for comparing the performance of existing marketing channels and estimating the revenues and costs associated with potential channels.

Channel length, channel control, and the amount of financial resources the manufacturer must invest in channel activities often are related. In general, the shorter the channel, the more control the manufacturer has and the more financial resources it must commit to channel functions and activities. Conversely, the longer the channel, the less control the manufacturer normally has and the less it must invest.[38] An important aspect of marketing channel selection is examining the tradeoffs between desired control and desired investment in channel activities.

Time for Development

Time is another significant factor in designing a marketing channel. For example, Ethan Allen spent many years developing its extensive retail network. The Limited grew from one women's specialty store to a $1 billion corporate chain over a twenty-year period. Controlled growth was perceived to be an asset rather than a liability.

Sometimes time is a critical factor. For instance, Cantel rejected the channel option of building a direct sales force. Why? Management was convinced that Cantel would not be able to hire and train representatives fast enough to beat Bell Cellular into the market. The first firm to establish a position in the market was expected to gain a big competitive advantage.

Control Considerations

The extent to which an organization wishes to control the marketing activities within a channel directly affects the channel selection process. The longer the marketing channel, the less control the manufacturer has. Furthermore, the more intensive the pattern of distribution, the less control the manufacturer has to decide how the product will be marketed. Control relationships are much clearer in vertical marketing systems than in traditional channels. Direct channels and vertical marketing systems offer the most control to the channel leader. Channel control, as well as other issues relating to channel member behavior, are examined later in this chapter.

Legal Constraints

Seven major federal laws affect marketing channel design:

Sherman Antitrust Act (1890)

Clayton Act (1914)

Federal Trade Commission Act (1914)

Robinson-Patman Act (1936)

Wheeler-Lea Amendment to the FTC Act (1938)

Celler-Kefauver Antimerger Act (1950)

Hart-Scott-Rodino Act (1976)

These acts focus on protecting and encouraging competition in the marketplace. They ban a wide range of anticompetitive behavior and address relationships between manufacturers and channel intermediaries. Exhibit 2.4 in Chapter 2 summarizes these key pieces of federal legislation.

Channel Availability

An issue often overlooked in channel design is the availability of the intermediary. Sometimes the preferred channels either have exclusive arrangements with other suppliers or for some other reason are uninterested in the supplier. Snap-on Tools had this experience nearly seventy-five years ago. The socket wrench that Snap-on developed enabled users to reduce by two-thirds the number of tools they needed. Wholesalers and retailers neither welcomed this large cutback in sales opportunity nor wanted to stock the new tools. Frustrated by lack of channel availability, Snap-on targeted professional mechanics and developed its own sales force. Essentially, the firm was forced to seek an alternative channel of distribution. Now it has over 5,000 franchised dealers worldwide who call on professional mechanics in familiar "traveling store" vans.

Channel Choice

Channel selection is a vital task because it locks in much longer commitments than do other marketing decisions. Setting up channel networks and building channel relationships often takes a great deal of time and money. Channel selection also affects decisions about other marketing mix elements.

Short channels are commonly used for expensive consumer or business products with high profit margins. Promotion strategy typically emphasizes personal selling. In contrast, long channels are commonly used for rather inexpensive consumer or business goods. Stock turnover is often high, unit margins are low, and promotion strategy emphasizes advertising.

Selecting Channel Participants

After management selects a channel structure, the next step is to evaluate prospective channel members. A useful approach is to first develop a short list of *must* requirements for each type of channel member, the functions and activities that wholesalers and retailers absolutely must perform. Next, the marketing manager develops a list of *desirable* qualities for the intermediary to possess. After compiling these two lists, prospective channel members can be ranked and evaluated according to how well they meet the criteria.

Exhibit 12.9 shows some key criteria for assessing channel candidates. Management can weight the items according to company needs and objectives, sales strength, product lines, and reputation. The firms with the highest overall scores can then be approached for membership.

After choosing the channel members, management must often recruit them. Chosen channel members are often reluctant to join the channel team. In particular, retailers may be indifferent to adding a tenth brand of gum or a fifth brand of presweetened cereal. In this case, aggressive personal selling may be needed to convince the firm to join the channel.

Exhibit 12.9

Criteria for Selecting Channel Members

1. Size of prospective channel member
   Sales
   Financial strength
2. Sales strength
   Number of sales personnel
   Sales and technical competence
3. Product lines
   Competitive products
   Compatible products
   Complementary products
   Quality of lines carried
4. Reputation
   Leadership
   Longevity
5. Market coverage
   Geographic coverage (outlets per market area)
   Industry coverage
   Call frequency or intensity of coverage
6. Sales performance
   Performance with related lines
   General sales performance
   Growth prospects
7. Management
8. Advertising and sales promotion
9. Sales compensation
10. Acceptance of training assistance
11. Transportation savings
12. Inventory
    Kind and size
    Inventory minimums (safety stocks)
    Reductions in manufacturer inventories
    Extent of postponement (speculation)
13. Warehousing
    Field locations
    Ability to handle shipments efficiently
14. Lot quantity costs
    Willingness to accept ordering policies

MARKETING AND SMALL BUSINESS

Designing a Channel

A huge organization like Westinghouse or Kraft General Foods—with an established reputation, great financial resources, many distribution channels, and quality products—has enormous channel power. Picking new channel members is rarely a problem. Small organizations are a different story.

Consider Falcon Hang Gliders, whose average output was two per month. Its market was ill defined, and the firm had virtually no financial resources. Assuming that a reasonable channel for such a company can be defined, it may have trouble entering the channel. The heart of the problem is credibility—even for small entrepreneurial manufacturers that are well financed. How does a dealer know, for example, that the manufacturer will be able to supply high-quality merchandise whenever needed over the long run?

If the channel intermediary is already handling a competing line, it is usually much less likely to accept the entrepreneurial firm. The problem of selecting the "best" channel may thus be a moot point. The question is whether anyone will handle the product. Many small manufacturers with good products have fallen into bankruptcy because they could not reach potential buyers.

Falcon Hang Glider's product was a consumer specialty good, or perhaps a shopping good, and by definition it would require only a few dealers per area. Interested parties will search for the product. But most hang glider enthusiasts live in California, and Falcon was located in Texas. Hang glider retailers have sprung up in large West Coast cities to serve the growing market. Elsewhere in the country, hang glider retailers are virtually nonexistent. As you can see, geographic customer concentration was a key market consideration for Falcon. It had a limited number of potential buyers near its manufacturing facilities.

Falcon Hang Gliders was founded by two young men just out of college with a $5,000 loan from one partner's father. Direct sales leads proved too costly, so in desperation Falcon turned to sporting-goods retailers and motorcycle shops. The company's poor financial condition meant it could not supply inventory or even a single demonstration model to the eight retailers who agreed to sell the product. Instead, pictures and brochures were used as sales aids. After using the new channel for three months, Falcon closed its doors. It had an unusual product, but it faced the distribution problems that have forced many small entrepreneurial firms out of business.

9 MARKETING CHANNEL RELATIONSHIPS

A marketing channel is more than a set of institutions linked by economic ties. Social relationships play an important role in building unity among channel members. The basic social dimensions of channels are power, control, leadership, and conflict.[39]

Channel Power, Control, and Leadership

channel power
Capacity of a particular marketing channel member to control or influence the behavior of other channel members.

channel control
Situation that occurs when one marketing channel member intentionally affects another member's behavior.

channel leadership
Marketing channel member's exercise of authority and power over other channel members.

Channel power is a channel member's capacity to control or influence the behavior of other channel members.[40] **Channel control** occurs when one channel member affects another member's behavior. To achieve control, a channel member assumes **channel leadership**, or the exercise of authority and power. A manufacturer controls new product designs and product availability. On the other hand, the retailer may wield power and control over the retail price, inventory levels, and quality of postsale service of the manufacturer's product.

Wholesaling intermediaries may also try to gain control over other channel members. When Goodyear announced plans to sell Goodyear-brand tires through Sears, hundreds of Goodyear's 2,500 independent dealers, who had been selling only the Goodyear brand, adopted other brands. Many went so far as to change their signs or consider joining with other chains.[41]

As noted earlier in this chapter, channel members rely heavily on one another. Even the most powerful manufacturers depend on dealers to sell their products. Power can take several forms:

- *Reward power:* when a channel member believes that an intermediary can help the firm achieve its goals. For example, a manufacturer may give a wholesaler a full line to sell, thereby raising the wholesaler's profit potential.
- *Coercive power:* when a channel member feels threatened—for example, a threat by a manufacturer like Compaq Computer to discontinue sales to a distributor like Businessland. Slow vehicle delivery to dealers has been used as a means of coercion in the auto industry.
- *Legitimate power:* when the channel leader has a right to make decisions. Legitimate power usually stems from the company's reputation. IBM, General Electric, and Xerox are perceived as legitimate leaders.
- *Referent power:* when one channel member identifies with another. For instance, some independent motels like to be affiliated with a motel chain. Manufacturers often enjoy seeing their brands carried at high-prestige stores, such as Neiman Marcus or Saks Fifth Avenue.
- *Expert power:* when channel members believe that another channel member's knowledge and expertise can make the system more efficient. For example, small retailers often rely on manufacturers like Procter & Gamble and Frito-Lay for advice.[42]

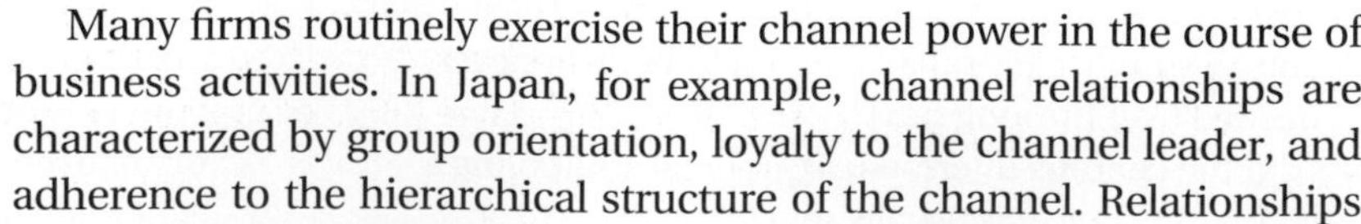

Many firms routinely exercise their channel power in the course of business activities. In Japan, for example, channel relationships are characterized by group orientation, loyalty to the channel leader, and adherence to the hierarchical structure of the channel. Relationships are for the long term, and channel members prefer to deal with partners they know well. The relationships are nurtured by personal contacts, visits, gifts, and support in hard times.[43] The Bose Corporation, manufacturer of high-quality audio speakers, discovered too late the relationship-building efforts needed to succeed in Japanese marketing channels. During the mid-1970s, the company tried to break into the Japanese market, with disastrous results. After three years of intense effort, the

company had sold fewer than 100 pairs of speakers in Japan and had no choice but to pull out of the market. Reflecting some years later on what went wrong, the company identified the key problem as failure to establish close personal relationships with its Japanese distributors.[44]

The exercise of channel power is not unique to Japan, however. In an attempt to reshape the supermarket industry, Procter & Gamble decided to institute a new price strategy in selling to wholesalers and retailers. Instead of using the price discounts and promotions that producers routinely extend to intermediaries, the company switched to everyday low pricing (EDLP): the same price at all times with no promotions or sales. This strategy ideally reduces high-cost promotions, eliminates wholesalers' binge buying of discounted products, and boosts manufacturers' earnings. Before introducing EDLP, P&G had been losing control of its costs. When the company offered a special promotion, its factories worked around the clock. Meanwhile, products bought on special deals, like coffee, could grow stale sitting around in a wholesaler's warehouse for several months. Through its strong channel position, P&G's actions may be able to restore order to the market. Unless it does, the costs of trade promotions will continue to surpass total advertising expenditures in the industry.[45]

Retailers can also develop strategies for balancing their control over manufacturers or for gaining even more control. Some actions that retailers might take to enhance their power are

- Developing expert power by obtaining information about consumers' needs and providing this information to suppliers
- Maintaining multiple sources of supply to avoid the coercive power of any single supplier
- Establishing referent power by encouraging consumers to become more loyal to the store than to a supplier's brand
- Developing a strong private brand program to avoid the coercive power of national producers
- Banding together with other retailers to buy in larger quantities and exercising reward power with suppliers[46]

Already many retailers and wholesalers have begun to balk at Procter & Gamble's new price strategy. Some chains with thousands of stores, such as Rite-Aid drugstores, A&P, and Safeway, are trimming the variety of P&G sizes they carry or eliminating marginal brands, such as Prell shampoo and Gleem toothpaste. Super Valu, the nation's largest wholesaler, is adding surcharges to some P&G products and paring back orders to compensate for profits it says it's losing under the new pricing system. Meanwhile, Certified Grocers in the Midwest has dropped about 50 of the 300 P&G varieties it stocked. And numerous chains are considering moving P&G brands from prime, eye-level space to less visible shelves. In their place the chains will stock more profitable private-label brands and competitors' varieties.[47] The article on page 396 explains the power some retailers have to charge manufacturers for shelf space.

Channel Conflict

channel conflict
Clash of goals and methods between distribution channel members.

Situations like those described in the article often lead to **channel conflict**. In a broad context, conflict may not be bad. Often it arises because staid, traditional channel members refuse to keep pace with the times. Removing an outdated intermediary may result in reduced costs for the entire system.

ETHICS IN MARKETING

Supermarket Slotting Allowances

An area in marketing that often raises ethical issues concerns the practice of "slotting allowances," often known as "street money." In this practice, fees are paid to retailers for allocating warehouse space or shelf space to manufacturers' products. . . . A number of major packaged-goods firms have reported selling 80 to 90 percent of their volume "on deal"—in other words, via specific trade promotions rather than manufacturer's list price. Much of this product volume was placed via slotting allowances paid by the manufacturer to the retailer. Slotting allowances and other trade promotion practices raise issues concerning channel efficiency and consumer welfare as well as the uses made of increased channel power by different firms in supplier-reseller networks.

One issue is the extent to which these practices are legitimate "incentives" or less savory "ransoms." Most retailers clearly view these payments as incentives for dealing with the estimated 2,000 new items and 3,000 line extensions introduced annually in grocery stores by manufacturers. Each item means purchasing, stocking, labeling, and other transaction costs incurred by the store. In effect, many retailers claim, slotting allowances and other trade promotion practices justly subsidize the retailers' costs and in effect act as a price-based . . . mechanism for allocating space. Many manufacturers, on the other hand, view such payments as ransoms demanded by an increasingly concentrated and powerful retail trade that, in fact, often does not pass on these deals to consumers in the form of lower prices.

A second issue concerns the impact of these practices on new products and smaller firms at the supplier level of the channel. For example, some stores in the New England area reportedly were requiring slotting allowances of from $15,000 to $40,000 for new-product introduction—fees required *in addition to* the more traditional trade allowances, such as cash discounts and free goods. One fifty-store chain reportedly charged a manufacturer $70,000 for one truckload's worth of new product. Many smaller packaged-goods manufacturers have argued that such practices discourage new-product introductions and innovation and, ultimately, work to suppress competition and consumer choice. Larger manufacturers, some claim, are better able to spread such costs and often can avoid paying slotting allowances. This is because retailers know those companies can back their new-product introductions with multimillion-dollar advertising campaigns.

Are retailers justified in charging slotting allowances because of the additional work required to stock the many new products introduced each year? How does this practice limit smaller companies? Why do you think that paying slotting allowances is or is not an ethical business practice?

Source: Adapted from N. Craig Smith and John A. Quelch, *Ethics in Marketing* (Homewood, IL: Richard D. Irwin, 1993), pp. 478–480. © Richard D. Irwin, Inc., 1993.

The basic sources of conflict within marketing channels can be grouped as follows:

- *Goal incompatibility:* The goal of an athletic footwear store is to sell as many shoes as possible to maximize profits, whether they be made by Adidas, Puma, or Saucony. The Adidas manufacturer wants a certain sales volume and market share in each market. Therefore, the athletic footwear store and Adidas may have conflicting goals.
- *Role incongruence:* A channel member is expected to fulfill certain roles. For instance, imagine that the owner of a McDonald's franchise insists on serving hot dogs instead of hamburgers, french fries, and shakes. The owner doesn't enforce McDonald's cleanliness standards or require employees to wear the traditional McDonald's uniform. The owner is clearly not fulfilling the expectations of the franchisor. Thus role incongruence exists.
- *Communication breakdowns:* When a manufacturer changes the marketing mix and fails to notify other channel members, conflict can result. For example, the failure to notify dealers of reduced warranty coverage from six months to three months could cause a major problem. Unaware of expired

warranties, dealers could make repairs and expect reimbursement by the manufacturer.

- *Different perceptions of reality:* A manufacturer may feel that the margins offered to the intermediaries are ample for the demands it places on retailers and wholesalers. Yet if margins seem too low, the space, service, and sales effort the intermediaries provide to the manufacturer may be minimal.
- *Ideological differences:* Sometimes channel members' values or viewpoints differ. Retailers may believe "the customer is always right" and offer a very liberal return policy. Wholesalers or manufacturers may feel that people "try to get something for nothing" or don't follow product instructions carefully. Their views of allowable returns might conflict with the retailers'.

When conflict arises within a channel, someone must take the lead to resolve the problem. Otherwise, the problem will fester, and communications and channel efficiency will decline. Conflict resolution usually employs one of the following strategies:

- *Problem solving:* Once mutual goals are set, the task is to find a solution that satisfies them.
- *Persuasion:* A powerful channel member may use persuasion to influence uncooperative channel members.
- *Bargaining:* Compromise may be used to reach new agreements.
- *Politics:* An attempt may be made to create coalitions to alter the power structure. For example, auto dealers banded together to form the National Association of Automobile Dealers to fight what they saw as the unfair practices of manufacturers.

When the issues are simple and low risk and dependence on other channel members is low, channel members usually try to use problem solving to resolve conflict. However, when the problem is more complex and the channel leader has a great deal of control, channel members often prefer to use a more political approach to conflict resolution.[48] For instance, franchisees will often band together if they feel they are not being treated fairly by the franchisor. Texas Dairy Queen franchisees took this approach when they disagreed with the national franchisor over advertising. Under a special agreement made years earlier, Texas franchisees were allowed to finance and run their own advertising campaigns. As franchise agreements were renewed, however, Dairy Queen revised the terms of the agreement so they would eventually have to adhere to the company's national advertising practices. Texas Dairy Queen franchisees took their complaints to court.[49]

LOOKING BACK

As you complete this chapter, you should be able to see how marketing channels operate and how channel members interact to move goods from the manufacturer to the final consumer. The choice of marketing channels often changes over time. Marketers respond to changing consumer preferences through channel design and the choice of intermediaries. For example, many computer manufacturers redesigned their channels as direct channels or chose discount retailers instead of upscale computer retailers, in an attempt to answer the consumer's need for convenience and low prices. You may also remember from the opening of the chapter that computer manufacturers originally had great power over retailers, dictating store

design and location. This position of power changed as the choice of channel changed. Consumer preferences can therefore transform channel design and shift channel power among intermediaries.

As you've discovered in this chapter, marketing channels and wholesalers are an important part of the marketing process. Understanding that marketing channels, wholesaling intermediaries, and channel design are important parts of strategic marketing planning will help you develop a successful marketing plan.

KEY TERMS

administered system 376
backward integration 376
broker 383
cash-and-carry wholesaler 382
channel conflict 395
channel control 394
channel leader (channel captain) 375
channel leadership 394
channel power 394
contractual system 376
conventional channel 374
corporate system 375
direct channel 371
discrepancy of assortment 367
discrepancy of quantity 367
drop shipper 383
dual distribution (multiple distribution) 373
exclusive distribution 388
forward integration 375
full-service merchant wholesaler 380
general merchandise wholesaler (full-line wholesaler) 380
horizontal integration 377
horizontal marketing system (cooperative) 377
industrial distributor 381
intensive distribution 387
limited-service merchant wholesaler 382
mail-order wholesaler 383
manufacturers' agent 383
manufacturers' sales branch 384

SUMMARY

1 Explain what a marketing channel is and why intermediaries are needed. Marketing channels are composed of members who perform negotiating functions. Some intermediaries buy and resell products; other intermediaries aid the exchange of ownership between buyers and sellers without taking title. Nonmember channel participants do not engage in negotiating activities and function as an auxillary part of the marketing channel structure.

Wholesaler and retailer intermediaries are often included in marketing channels for three important reasons: specialization and division of labor, the need to overcome discrepancies, and contact efficiency. First, the specialized expertise of intermediaries may improve the overall efficiency of marketing channels. Second, intermediaries may help overcome discrepancies by making products available in quantities and assortments desired by consumers and business buyers and at locations convenient to them. Third, intermediaries improve contact efficiency by reducing the number of transactions required to distribute goods from producers to consumers and end users.

2 Describe the functions and activities that marketing channel members perform. Marketing channel members perform three basic types of functions: transactional, logistical, and facilitating. Transactional functions include contacting and promoting, negotiating, and risk taking. Logistical functions performed by channel members include physical distribution and sorting functions. Finally, channel members perform facilitating functions, such as researching and financing.

3 Discuss the differences between marketing channels for consumer and industrial products. Marketing channels for consumer and business products vary in degree of complexity. The simplest consumer product channel involves direct selling from producers to consumers. Businesses may sell directly to business or government buyers. Marketing channels grow more complex as intermediaries become involved. Consumer product channel intermediaries include agents, brokers, wholesalers, and retailers. Business product channel intermediaries include agents, brokers, and industrial distributors.

4 Describe alternative channel arrangements. Marketers often use alternative channel arrangements to move their products to the consumer. With dual distribution or multiple distribution, they choose two or more different channels to distribute the same product. Nontraditional channels help differentiate a firm's product from the competitor's. Strategic channel alliances are arrangements that use another manufacturer's already-established channel. Finally, reverse channels exist when products move in the opposite direction of traditional channels—from consumer back to the producer. Reverse channels are often used for products that require repair or recycling.

Vertical marketing systems consist of producers and intermediaries acting as a

manufacturers' sales office 385

marketing channel (channel of distribution) 366

merchant wholesaler 379

rack jobber 382

retailer 366

reverse channel 374

selective distribution 388

selling agent 383

spatial discrepancy 368

specialty merchandise wholesaler 381

strategic channel alliance 373

temporal discrepancy 368

truck jobber 382

vertical marketing system 374

warehouse club 382

wholesaler 366

unified system and are composed of three types—corporate, contractual, and administered. Horizontal marketing systems consist of channel members at the same level that organize into groups to pool their negotiating strength.

5 Discuss channel structure decisions in international markets. International marketing channels are becoming more important to U.S. companies seeking growth abroad. Manufacturers introducing products in foreign countries must decide what type of channel structure to use—in particular, whether the product should be marketed through direct channels or through foreign intermediaries. Marketers who decide that foreign intermediaries are the right match for their products should select overseas distributors carefully. Marketers should also be aware that channel structures may be very different from those they are accustomed to in the United States.

6 Explain the types of firms that perform wholesaling activities and their functions. Wholesalers are classified into three basic categories: merchant wholesalers, agents and brokers, and manufacturers' sales branches and offices. Merchant wholesalers are independent businesses that take title to goods and assume ownership risk. Full-service merchant wholesalers perform all channel functions and include general merchandise wholesalers, specialty merchandise wholesalers, industrial distributors, and rack jobbers. As their name suggests, limited-service merchant wholesalers perform only a few of the channel functions; this classification includes cash-and-carry wholesalers, warehouse clubs, truck jobbers, drop shippers, and mail-order wholesalers. Agents and brokers facilitate sales but do not take title to goods or set sales conditions. Brokers bring buyers and sellers together, whereas agents function as salespeople for one particular manufacturer or several manufacturers of complementary product lines. Manufacturers' sales branches and offices resemble full-service merchant wholesalers but are owned and controlled by manufacturers. Manufacturers' branches are similar to offices, with one exception: Branches carry inventory and offices do not.

7 Discuss the factors that influence channel choice. When determining marketing channel strategy, the marketing manager must determine what market, product, and producer factors will influence the choice of channel. The manager must also determine the appropriate level of distribution intensity.

8 List the steps in designing marketing channels. The marketing channel design process consists of three major steps: (1) identifying channel alternatives, (2) evaluating and selecting channels, and (3) selecting channel participants. Criteria for identifying channel alternatives include access to end users, prevailing distribution practices, and necessary activities and functions. Channel evaluation and selection are based on revenue and cost analyses, development time, control considerations, legal constraints, and channel availability. Finally, considerations for selecting channel participants are market coverage, compatibilities, intermediaries' needs, functions provided, and availability factors.

9 Explain the concepts of power and conflict within marketing channels. Power, control, leadership, and conflict are the main social dimensions of marketing channel relationships. Channel power refers to the capacity of one channel member to control or influence other channel members. Channel power can be based on reward or categorized as coercive, legitimate, referent, or expert power. Channel control occurs when one channel member intentionally affects another member's behavior. Channel leadership is the exercise of authority and power. Sources of channel conflict include goal incompatibility, role incongruence, communication breakdowns, and differing perspectives and ideologies.

Review Questions

1. How do intermediaries help resolve discrepancies in quantity and assortment?
2. Describe the activities performed by channel intermediaries.
3. Identify the four major consumer product marketing channels.
4. Are intermediaries and their functions necessary aspects of marketing channels? Give reasons to support your opinion.
5. List and describe the major types of wholesaling intermediaries. What is the basic difference between merchant wholesalers and agents or brokers?
6. What is the underlying flaw of the conventional channel structure? Why are vertical marketing systems more effective?
7. Describe forward and backward integration.
8. What are the major criteria for evaluating channel alternatives?
9. Identify the major sources of channel conflict. What strategies can channel members use to resolve conflict?

Discussion and Writing Questions

1. Describe the most likely distribution channel for each of these consumer products: candy bars, Tupperware products, trade books, new automobiles, farmers' market produce, and stereo equipment.
2. List three reasons for creating new marketing channel designs. Illustrate your answer with specific examples.
3. As noted in the chapter, Procter & Gamble eliminated trade promotions to wholesalers and retailers, replacing them with everyday low pricing. What kind of channel member power was P&G exercising? Discuss the implications of P&G's action.
4. If you were a retailer, how might you respond to coercive behavior on the part of large manufacturing companies? Describe your reaction, in the form of a letter to the president of one of the offending firms.
5. Identify the types of wholesalers that would be most likely to carry the following goods: fresh produce, industrial machinery, expensive wines, lumber, and farming fertilizer. Justify your choices.
6. Describe the channel for some product you are familiar with. Explain why you think the channel is structured as you described it.
7. Describe a current example of channel conflict not discussed in the chapter. Imagine that you are one of the participants in the conflict, and write a letter to the other channel members proposing a resolution.
8. You have been hired to design a channel of distribution for a new firm specializing in the manufacturing and marketing of novelties for fraternities and sororities. In a memo to the president of the firm, describe how the channel operates.

CASES

12.1 Perrier

Perrier sparkling water had a 57 percent share of the designer water market in the United States in 1988. In February 1990 a problem in the company's filtration system caused the product to become contaminated with benzene, a minor carcinogen. The company chose to fully disclose the facts, accept full responsibility, and recall $70 million worth of product.

In April 1990 Perrier was about to resume shipping its sparkling water to the United States. Kim Jeffrey, senior vice president of marketing, expected Perrier to be in 90 percent of the U.S. market within six weeks. For each new market entered, Perrier had scheduled a two-week media blitz to announce the reintroduction of the product. The campaign was called "We're Back." Perrier also scheduled sales promotion activities to tie in with the ad campaign. Workers in Perrier Cafes wore "We're Back" apparel to pass out samples in its fifteen largest markets.

According to Jeffrey, the key to the success of the reintroduction was going to be distribution. Lost shelf space was going to have to be recaptured in the supermarkets. Perrier had never paid a retailer for shelf space for the product, a common industry practice, and did not intend to do so now. Space for the product was expected to come from space that retailers had saved for the Perrier brand by stocking it with other Perrier products.

Retailers' views on the shelf space issue were mixed. Some felt the high profit margin of the product (18 to 20 percent) would more than compensate for the shelf space needed. Others insisted that Perrier not only

would have to pay to get the shelf space back but also would have to spend a lot of money on advertising and sales promotion.

Restaurateurs were another major stumbling block for Perrier. Perrier sparkling water had about a third of the total bar and restaurant market in 1989. Some restaurants took the Perrier brand back and offered two brands of designer water to diners; others would not take Perrier brand back. In the end, consumer demand would influence restaurateurs. If they get enough requests for Perrier, restaurants will stock it.

Consumer research at the time indicated that 85 percent of Perrier customers would buy the product again. Ninety percent of consumers felt that by admitting its mistake Perrier acted responsibly. These figures led Perrier management to believe that the company could recapture 85 percent of its sales by the end of 1991. By late 1993 Perrier had managed to regain most of its distribution in supermarkets but was still struggling in restaurants, bars, and clubs. Although Perrier's comeback was slower than anticipated, prospects for the future appear bright. The company has a strong market position, bolstered by its acquisition by Nestlé, a Swiss food conglomerate, in 1992.

Questions

1. What type of advertising strategy should Perrier use to regain its market share? Why?
2. Many feel that the distribution channel contributes to the success or failure of a product. Is it important for Perrier?
3. Should Perrier pay channel members to carry the Perrier brand? What potential problems would arise from this decision?

Suggested Readings

Barbara Lippert, "Perrier Is Reformulated for a New Era," *Adweek's Marketing Week*, 7 May 1990, p. 69.

Patricia Winters, "Perrier's Back," *Advertising Age*, 23 April 1990.

12.2 Tandy

Video title: *Tandy Corporation: A Corporate Channel System*

Tandy Corporation
1800 One Tandy Center
Fort Worth, TX 76102

SIC codes:
- 5734 Personal computer stores
- 5731 Radio, TV, and consumer electronics stores
- 5061 Hi-fi stereo equipment distribution
- 3571 Electronic component manufacturing
- 3651 Household audio/video equipment manufacturing
- 3661 Telephone manufacturing

Number of employees: 40,000

1993 revenues: $5 billion

Major brands: Tandy, Grid, Radio Shack, Realistic, Memorex

Largest competitors: IBM, Apple, Packard Bell, Compaq

Background

Tandy Corporation had its beginnings in a small leather goods company named Hinkley/Tandy Leather Company, started in 1918. Radio Shack was founded in Boston in 1921 to sell high-tech products. The early Radio Shack had only one retail store and sold most of its products through the mail. In 1945, after World War II, Charles Tandy began expanding his father's business with a chain of Tandy leathercraft stores. By 1960 Tandy had 150 stores across the country. Radio Shack had only 9. Since both companies catered to the hobbyists, Charles Tandy bought Radio Shack in 1963.

Tandy has always been a leader in the electronics and computer industries. It was the first company to develop and mass-market a personal computer. The original TRS-80 was introduced in 1977 and sold over 5,000 units that year. By 1979, Tandy had a 50 percent share of the personal computer market. Today the industry is standards-driven. For a computer manufacturer to be successful, it must adhere to industry standards. Tandy prides itself on "doing it all itself" with five computer plants in Fort Worth. Tandy continues to meet or exceed industry standards.

Industry

The computer industry is plagued with decreasing sales and poor profitability. Even IBM, one of the largest computer companies, has been recording record losses. This changing profit picture has caused many computer companies to adopt new strategies for the 1990s. Many of the big players in the computer industry have slashed prices to become more competitive in the marketplace. Downsizing is another popular move. To reduce overhead costs, many companies have opted to lay off employees.

The traditional channels for computer equipment have been similar to the conventional distribution channel. Many large computer manufacturers bypass the wholesaler in order to be more selective about the types of retailers permitted to sell their products. Both Apple and IBM have traditionally sold their computer systems through authorized dealers only. Authorized dealers have included full-service computer retail stores and value-added dealers. Value-added dealers usually offer industry-specific software packages, like medical office billing systems, and bundle the hardware with the software to make the purchase easier for the ultimate consumer. Some of the smaller computer manufacturers have competed rather effectively with the larger companies by offering more economical systems through nontraditional channels, including mail order, direct sales, and mass merchants.

Tandy, like so many of its competitors, has seen declining sales as a major threat. To combat declining sales, computer companies have begun looking at other distribution channel options for selling computer equipment. IBM, Apple, and Compaq have all started selling some of their computer lines through discount computer stores. Both Compaq and IBM have also begun direct-marketing efforts with 800-number order lines.

Tandy Corporation

A key advantage that Tandy has over some of its competitors is its corporate distribution channel. By controlling the manufacturing, distribution, and retailing of its products, Tandy has enjoyed a competitive advantage. Tandy has long had an extensive mail-order business and many retail outlets. Now, with the two latest additions to its retail family, The Incredible Universe and Computer City, Tandy has moved into a new sales arena. Although Tandy has traditionally sold only Tandy products in its retail centers, these two new retail operations carry products of other manufacturers. This new approach may make Tandy a major force in the retail industry. Or it may weaken the company's share of the computer market.

Questions

1. What problems do you see in selling computer equipment through catalog or mail-order outlets?
2. Can the choice of distribution channel affect the success or failure of a computer manufacturer?
3. What advantages and disadvantages do you see for Tandy in carrying competing brands in its Incredible Universe and Computer City stores?

References

Million Dollar Directory 1993 (Parsippany, NJ: Dun & Bradstreet Information Services, 1993).

Standard & Poor's Industry Surveys (New York: Standard & Poor's Corporation, October 1993).

12.3 *Decision Assistant:* The Payton Corporation

The Situation

The marketing manager of the Payton Corporation is trying to decide whether to use its own system of manufacturer-owned wholesalers to distribute the firm's products or to use the services of a manufacturing agent. The marketing research staff believes each system of wholesalers would cover the market but at different degrees of effectiveness. The marketing research staff has developed a pessimistic, a most likely, and an optimistic sales prediction for both the wholly owned system of wholesalers and the manufacturing agent system for the six territories to be served. These data are presented in Exhibit 12.10. The marketing manager has asked you to analyze these numbers, and she wants to use a 95 percent confidence interval in making decisions.

The Solution Technique

The situation confronting the marketing manager of the Payton Corporation can best be resolved through use of the Monte Carlo simulation technique. The marketing *Decision Assistant* offers a Monte Carlo simulation predicated on triangular distributions, which assume that estimates of optimistic, most likely, and pessimistic may be skewed to the right or the left.

What If?

Consider each of the following situations independently:

1. Say that "most likely" estimates for the wholly owned system were changed to the following: Northeast, $3,945; Midwest, $6,809; Southeast, $4,915; Southwest, $7,502; Far West, $5,045; Northwest, $7,650. What effect would this change have on your decision? Justify your answer.
2. Say that "pessimistic" estimates for the manufacturing agent system were changed to the following: Northeast, $2,100; Midwest, $3,245; Southeast, $3,598; Southwest, $4,987; Far West, $2,149; Northwest, $3,305. What effect would this change have on your decision? Justify your answer.

Exhibit 12.10

Sales Estimates (in thousands of dollars)

Wholly owned system of wholesalers

Market segments	*Pessimistic forecast*	*"Most likely" forecast*	*Optimistic forecast*
Northeast	$1,980	$2,980	$6,759
Midwest	3,105	5,789	7,968
Southeast	1,696	3,897	10,950
Southwest	3,162	6,532	8,698
Far West	3,212	4,145	5,620
Northwest	2,800	7,456	7,975

Manufacturing agent system of wholesalers

Market segments	*Pessimistic forecast*	*"Most likely" forecast*	*Optimistic forecast*
Northeast	$3,175	$3,461	$4,159
Midwest	4,215	4,729	5,568
Southeast	4,636	8,193	9,051
Southwest	5,102	7,031	8,398
Far West	3,119	4,299	5,491
Northwest	4,267	6,176	7,635

LEARNING OBJECTIVES

After studying this chapter, you should be able to

1. Discuss the importance of retailing in the U.S. economy.
2. List the dimensions by which retailers can be classified.
3. Explain the wheel of retailing concept.
4. Describe the major types of retail operations.
5. List nonstore retailing techniques.
6. Describe the nature of franchising.
7. List the major tasks involved in developing a retail marketing strategy.
8. List present problems in retailing.
9. List future trends in retailing.

CHAPTER 13

Retailing

At Home Depot, the nation's largest chain of warehouse-size do-it-yourself discount specialty stores, brides-to-be can now register for socket wrenches and lawn mowers. Along with their paint and wallpaper, homeowners can get advice on matching colors from the store's interior designer. They can then have their preferences put on file for better service the next time they shop. Customers can also find greenhouses in an expanded gardening section, get special guidance on energy-saving products, or learn how to build kitchen cabinets.

These are the newest services and test programs introduced by the home improvement chain whose dedication to service has helped it shine in the otherwise troubled retailing industry. Featuring customer training, low prices, and more than 34,000 items, Home Depot has outpaced all its rivals and is currently more than twice the size of its nearest competitor, quite a feat considering that the Atlanta-based retailer is only 13 years old.

Home Depot's two guiding lights, CEO Bernard Marcus and president Arthur Blank, who founded the company with two stores in 1979, preach that it is as important to teach people how to do it themselves as it is to provide the materials. And so to a greater extent than any other home improvement retailer, the two founders have trained their salespeople to train customers. Clinics, as many as four a day, are the store's main customer aid. Such topics as how to install dry wall, put up a fence, or plan a kitchen are taught by trained sales staff or supplier representatives.

Home Depot also stresses the importance of strong employee motivation. New employees are hired not specifically for their product knowledge but for their ability to build the customer's enthusiasm about a product or a project. As incentives to hire on, salespeople are paid 20 to 25 percent more than those at rival companies. Every full-time employee is a stockholder, too, under the company's generous stock ownership plan.

As a result, Home Depot has been setting performance records in the home improvement industry, with sales increasing more than 35 percent each year over the past ten years. The company's efforts have driven sales up a hundredfold, from just $52 million to more than $5 billion. Following an already aggressive expansion plan that has put the chain in fifteen states, Home Depot now aims to triple its number of stores to about 525 by late in the decade. As part of the chain's strategy, it clusters its stores around large metropolitan areas. The chain's new-store expansion plans plus its compound sales growth cause many to liken it to Wal-Mart, the nation's largest retailer.

There are several other reasons for Home Depot's high sales growth and strong profits. Since the beginning, Home Depot has avoided the middleman or wholesaler, instead buying directly from the producer to keep prices lower

than those of the competition. Additionally, the company has always stressed cutting expenses. Since 1985, expenses as a percentage of sales have fallen to 18.1 percent, one of the retailing industry's lowest ratios. Finally, Home Depot has tried to keep its merchandise assortment current through customer testing. Says CEO Marcus, "One of the biggest lessons we learned was that we had to listen to our customers, whether they had requests on specific kinds of merchandise, needed help or counsel, or just wanted to complain."[1]

Home Depot has proved that providing customers with quality, service, and fair pricing are the keys to success in retailing. What other factors are important to the retailing mix? Home Depot has also chosen metropolitan areas as its main store locations. What factors should retailers consider in finding a location? Knowledgeable and enthusiastic sales personnel have contributed much to Home Depot's success. How does a retailer set the quality and level of service it offers?

❶ THE ROLE OF RETAILING

retailing
All activities directly related to the sale of goods and services to the ultimate consumer for personal, nonbusiness use or consumption.

Retailing—all activities directly related to the sale of goods and services to the ultimate consumer for personal, nonbusiness use—has enhanced the quality of our daily lives. When we shop for groceries, hair care, clothes, legal advice, books, and many other products and services, we are involved in retailing. The millions of goods and services provided by retailers mirror the needs and styles of U.S. society.

Retailing affects all of us directly or indirectly. The retailing industry is one of the largest employers; over 2 million U.S. retailers employ about 18 million people. By 1991, retail sales had risen to over $1.8 trillion annually.[2]

Although most retailers are quite small, a few giant organizations dominate the industry. Fewer than 10 percent of all retail establishments account for over half of total retail sales and employ about 40 percent of all retail workers. Who are these giants? Exhibit 13.1 lists the ten largest U.S. retailers.

Exhibit 13.1

The Ten Largest U.S. Retailers

Source: Adapted from "The 50 Largest Retailing Companies," *Fortune*, 1 June 1992, pp. 188–189. Retail-only data for Sears from Francine Schwadel, "Sears Terms Retail Revenue Growth Its 'No. 1 Priority,'" *The Wall Street Journal*, 3 April 1992, p. B3.

1991 Rank	Company (headquarters)	Sales (in billions)	Employees (in thousands)
1	Wal-Mart Stores (Bentonville, AR)	$44	364
2	Kmart (Troy, MI)	35	348
3	Sears, Roebuck (Chicago)	31	375
4	Kroger (Cincinnati)	21	170
5	American Stores (Salt Lake City)	20	148
6	JCPenney (Dallas)	17	185
7	Dayton-Hudson (Minneapolis)	16	157
8	Safeway Stores (Oakland, CA)	15	110
9	Great Atlantic & Pacific Tea Co. (Montvale, NJ)	11	99
10	May Department Stores (St. Louis)	11	115

❷ CLASSIFICATION OF RETAIL OPERATIONS

A retail establishment can be classified according to its ownership, level of service, product assortment, and price. Specifically, retailers use the level of service, the breadth and depth of the product assortment, and general price levels to position themselves in the competitive marketplace. These three variables can be combined in several ways to create and position distinctly different retail operations. (As noted in Chapter 6, positioning is the strategy used to influence how consumers perceive one thing in relation to all competing things.)

Specialty stores, like this shop selling Eskimo soapstone figures, carry relatively few types of products but have a good selection in those product lines.

© Robert Semeniuk/The Stock Market

Ownership

Retailers can be broadly classified by form of ownership: independent, part of a chain, or a franchise outlet. Retailers owned by a single person or partnership and not operated as part of a larger retail institution are **independent retailers**. Around the world, most retailers are independent, operating one or a few stores in their community. Local florists, shoe stores, and ethnic food markets typically fit this classification.

Chain stores are owned and operated as a group by a single organization. Under this form of ownership, many administrative tasks are handled by the home office for the entire chain. The home office also buys most of the merchandise sold in the stores.

Franchise outlets are owned and operated by individuals but are licensed by a larger supporting organization. Franchising combines the advantages of independent ownership with those of the chain store organization. Franchising is discussed in detail later in this chapter.

independent retailer
Individual or partnership that owns one or several retail establishments not part of a larger retail organization.

chain store
Retail store that is one of a group owned and operated by a single corporation with central authority.

franchise outlet
Retail store owned and operated by an individual who is a licensee of a larger supporting organization.

Level of Service

The level of service that retailers provide can be classified along a continuum, from full service to self-service. Some retailers, such as exclusive clothing stores, offer high levels of service. They provide alterations, credit, delivery, consulting, liberal return policies, layaway, gift wrapping, and personal shopping. Discount stores usually offer fewer services, and even these are often limited. Retailers like factory outlets and warehouse clubs offer virtually no services.

Product Assortment

The third basis for positioning or classifying stores is by the breadth and depth of their product line (discussed more fully in Chapter 9). Specialty stores—for example, Hallmark card stores, Lady Foot Locker, and TCBY yogurt shops—are the most concentrated in their product assortment, usually carrying single or narrow product lines but in considerable depth. Mass merchandisers (Sears and JCPenney) and department stores (Bloomingdale's, Saks, and Marshall Field's) may have a product assortment of considerable breadth but with depth in only some product lines. Discounters like Kmart, Wal-Mart, and Target carry broad assortments of merchandise with limited depth. For example, Target carries automotive supplies, household cleaning products, and pet food. However, Target may carry only four or five brands of canned dog food; a supermarket may carry as many as twenty. Other retailers, such as factory outlet stores, may carry only part of a single line. Liz Claiborne, a

Type of retailer	Level of service	Product assortment	Price	Gross margin
Department store	High	Broad	Moderate to high	Moderately high
Mass merchandiser	Moderately high	Broad	Moderate	Moderate
Specialty store	Moderately high to high	Narrow	Moderate to high	High
Supermarket	Low	Broad	Moderate	Low
Convenience store	Moderately low	Medium to narrow	Moderately high	Moderately high
Discount store	Moderate to low	Medium to broad	Moderately low	Moderately low
Off-price retailer	Low	Medium to narrow	Low	Low
Factory outlet	Low	Very narrow	Very low	Low
Warehouse club	Low	Broad	Low to very low	Low

Exhibit 13.2

Types of Stores and Their Characteristics

major manufacturer of women's clothing, sells only its own brand in its many outlet stores.

Price

Price is a fourth way to position retail stores. Some stores typically charge the full "suggested retail prices." Traditional department stores and specialty stores fall into this category. Discounters, factory outlets, and off-price retailers use low prices as a major lure for shoppers.

Gross Margin and Price

Exhibit 13.2 lists the major types of retail stores discussed in this chapter and classifies them by level of service, product assortment, and price. The last column in the table shows each type of store's typical level of gross margin. **Gross margin** shows how much the retailer makes as a percentage of sales after the cost of goods sold is subtracted.

gross margin
How much the retailer makes as a percentage of sales after the cost of goods sold is subtracted.

The level of gross margin and the price level generally match. For example, a traditional jewelry store has high prices and high gross margins. A factory outlet has low prices and low gross margins.

Supermarkets are the exception to this general rule, especially when competition is intense. Price wars among competing supermarkets, in which stores lower prices on certain items in an effort to win customers, cause gross margins to decline. When Wal-Mart entered the grocery business in a small Arkansas community, for example, a fierce price war ensued. By the time the price war was in full swing, the price of a quart of milk had plummeted to 58¢ (below the price of a pint) and a loaf of bread sold for only 9¢.[3]

3 THE WHEEL OF RETAILING

The wheel of retailing depicts the constant state of change in retailing (see Exhibit 13.3). According to this theory, new retail institutions enter a market as low-cost, low-price operations by reducing or eliminating services. As a retailer becomes

Exhibit 13.3

The Wheel of Retailing

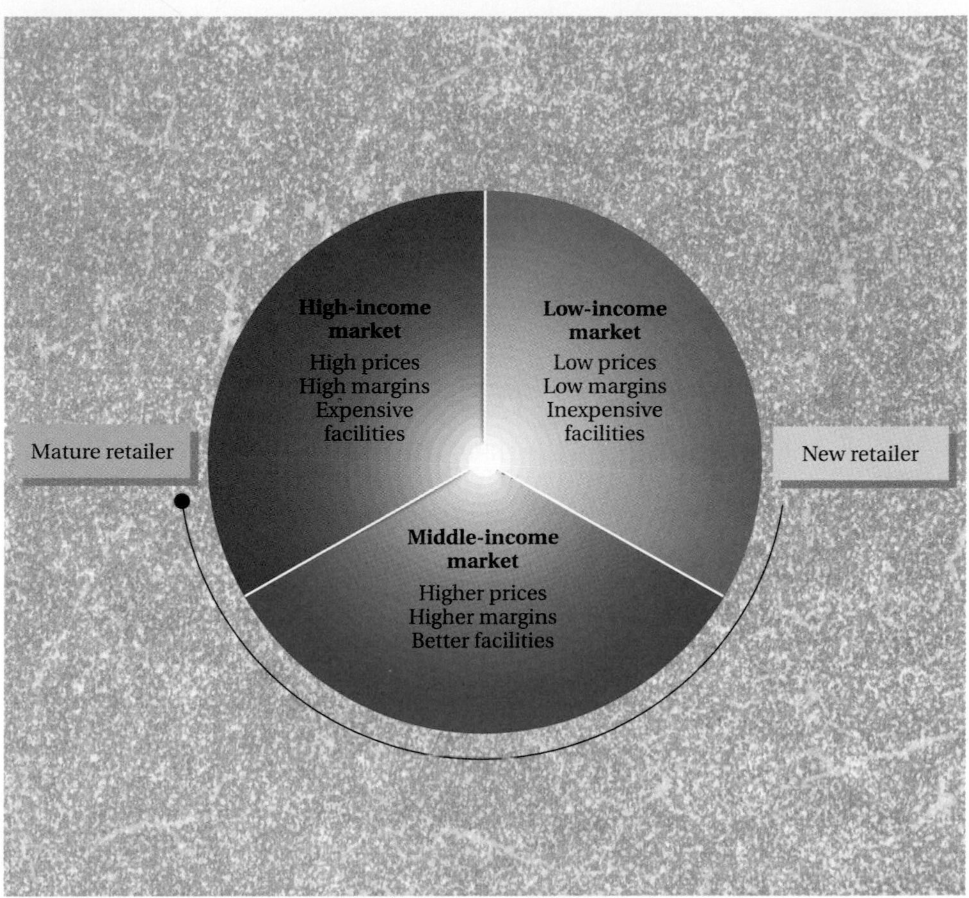

established, however, it adds services, and prices gradually increase. The retailer may then move to better locations, offer higher-quality merchandise, install better fixtures, supply even more services, and of course raise prices. As it does, it leaves a gap at the market's lower end. This vacuum is filled by new low-priced institutions that see an opportunity in this newly voided market. The reasons for retailers to upgrade over time include

- *Demographic trends:* As the standard of living increases, retailers are naturally attracted by market segments with higher levels of income.
- *Competition:* To avoid direct price competition, retailers emphasize additional services. Therefore, they need higher margins.
- *Wider assortments:* Over time, retailers tend to add higher-priced items and to stock more items.
- *Managerial evolution:* As second-generation management replaces the founders, cost-consciousness gives way to concern over store appearance and image—which pushes prices upward.[4]

Does the wheel of retailing really exist? The answer seems to be yes and no. Department stores, supermarkets, and discounters have been known to upgrade over time. New stores, however, do not always have a no-service, low-status profile. Nor does the low-cost, trading-up pattern apply to every retailing institution. The theory refers only to a single aspect of change—the price-quality continuum—and ignores other equally dynamic dimensions of retailing, such as product assortment, store size, and so on.[5] Some researchers propose that we also consider consumers' cost, including time and effort as well as product price. Theoretically, they say, what

causes the wheel to revolve are changes in time and convenience costs or value received by consumers, rather than changes in store operating costs or even the prices charged by retailers.[6]

4 MAJOR TYPES OF RETAIL OPERATIONS

There are several types of retail stores. Each offers a different product assortment and service and price level, according to its customers' shopping preferences.

Department Stores

department store
Retailer that carries a wide variety of shopping and specialty goods, including apparel, cosmetics, housewares, electronics, and sometimes furniture.

buyer
Person who selects the merchandise for retail stores and may also be responsible for promotion and for personnel.

Housing several departments under one roof, a **department store** carries a wide variety of shopping and specialty goods, including apparel, cosmetics, housewares, electronics, and sometimes furniture. Each department is treated as a separate buying center to achieve economies in promotion, buying, service, and control. A buyer usually heads each department. The **buyer** not only selects the merchandise for his or her department but may also be responsible for promotion and for personnel. For a consistent, uniform store image, central management sets broad policies about the types of merchandise carried and price ranges. Central management is also responsible for the overall advertising program, credit policies, store expansion, customer service, and so on. The buyer within each department is relatively free to operate within top management's guidelines and policies.

One Japanese retailer is following the practices of many U.S. department stores. Tobu, which opened in Tokyo in 1992, has one of the largest department stores in Asia, with over 900,000 square feet. It has buyers in each store, who select and buy the products for only that store. Like JCPenney and Mervyn's, Tobu stocks less-expensive apparel and moderately priced goods. Other Japanese department stores focus on upscale customers and expensive European designer boutiques and have a central buying staff.[7]

Because of their size and buying power, most department stores buy directly from manufacturers. Sometimes the manufacturer produces merchandise under the store's brand name (see Chapter 9). Some department stores have so much buying strength that they dominate small manufacturers, dictating manufacturers' profit margins, delivery dates, merchandise specifications, and transportation methods. This arrangement is a major shift in channel power from the manufacturer to the retailer (see Chapter 12).

A large independent department store is rare today. Most are owned by national chains. The four largest U.S. department store chains are Dayton-Hudson, May Department Stores, Federated Department Stores, and R.H. Macy. All of these operate more than one chain of retail stores, from discount chains to upscale clothiers. Sales range from about $16 billion a year for Dayton-Hudson to $6.8 billion for R.H. Macy.

Two up-and-coming department store chains are Dillard's, based in Little Rock, Arkansas, and Nordstrom, with corporate headquarters in Seattle. Until recently, both chains were family owned, but they are now listed on the New York Stock Exchange. Dillard's, with sales over $4.1 billion annually, is known for its distribution expertise. Nordstrom, with sales approaching $3.2 billion, offers innovative customer service. In the past few years, much attention has been centered on these two growing chains, and both have a very promising future as a major department store chain.

Department Store Strategies

Each year brings a dramatic new event to the department store sector of retailing. Consumers of the late 1980s witnessed the chaos of corporate takeovers, mergers, and acquisitions among the nation's largest and most widely recognized department store chains. Retail giants such as Bloomingdale's, Saks Fifth Avenue, and Marshall Field's were among the many put up for sale because of oversized debt and sluggish consumer demand. Many others were forced to cut expenses drastically to pay off debt. In the process, they became less innovative and in some cases were forced out of the business.

In the 1990s, consumers laden with debt from the previous decade's spending spree became more cost-conscious and value-oriented. Merchandise-driven power retailers like The Gap and The Limited, discounters, and even catalog outlets capitalized on the department stores' plight by offering better quality and service, at a fair price. Meanwhile, manufacturers like Liz Claiborne, Calvin Klein, and Ralph Lauren opened outlet stores of their own, taking more sales away from department stores.

To protect themselves, department store managers are learning to fight back. They are using several strategies to preserve their market share. One is to reposition department stores as specialty outlets. They are dividing departments into miniboutiques, each featuring a distinct fashion taste as specialty stores do. Department stores are also enhancing customer service to shift the focus from price. Services include complimentary alterations, longer store hours, personalized attention, after-sale follow-up, and personal wardrobe planning. Finally, department stores are expanding, remodeling, and revitalizing to show off new merchandising directions and to reflect the growth in their marketing areas.

Mass Merchandisers

Like department stores, mass merchandisers like Sears, JCPenney, and Montgomery Ward have wide product assortments. What distinguishes them from regular department store chains is their sheer size in terms of sales volume, promotional budgets, and number of stores. **Mass merchandising** is the retailing strategy of using moderate to low prices on large quantities of merchandise, coupled with big promotional budgets, to stimulate high turnover of products. The larger mass merchandisers are also vertically integrated; they own either all or part of many of the manufacturers that supply their merchandise.

mass merchandising
Retailing strategy of using moderate to low prices on most merchandise, coupled with big promotional budgets, to stimulate high turnover of products.

Because Sears and JCPenney cover most of the U.S. market geographically, network TV advertising is both feasible and economical for them. One ad broadcast on national TV reaches many of their customers. Heavy national TV exposure also gives them name identification and a strong company image. Network promotion usually centers on high-margin, dealer-brand items—for example, Diehard batteries or Sears steel-belted radial tires.

Traditional mass merchandisers like Sears are finding niche strategies attractive. The new Mainframe department targets fashion-conscious women.
© Reinhold Spiegler

During the past several years, both Sears and JCPenney have gained only slightly in sales, while their overall earnings have declined. Sears was the leading U.S. retailer until it was overtaken by Wal-Mart and Kmart in the late 1980s. Now the retail giant is struggling to regain lost ground. JCPenney also enjoyed a strong retail position in years past but has since given way to niche merchandisers

with strong target-marketing strategies. Many believe the era of the general mass merchandiser has passed, with retail growth now coming from specialty discounters and niche merchandisers. Responding to this bleak outlook, Sears and JCPenney have searched for new strategies and market niches.

A New Strategy for Sears

Reeling from its fall as the top U.S. retailer, Sears' management took perhaps the boldest move of all mass merchandisers. Sears adopted "everyday low pricing" on most products, similar to the policy at Wal-Mart. This strategy permanently marks down items from current levels and runs fewer sales promotions. Sears also expanded and revamped departments into seven separate units, called "power formats": home appliances and electronics, automotive supplies, home improvement products, home furnishings, and men's, women's, and children's apparel. Instead of being mediocre in many different businesses, Sears focused on a handful of categories in which it can compete with the best retailers. One example is Brand Central, Sears' attempt to take on appliance and electronics retailers like Circuit City. Sears has also ended the long-time practice of selling only its own Kenmore appliances and is now including brand names like General Electric, Whirlpool, and Amana.[8]

The Repositioning of JCPenney

JCPenney's strategic repositioning was another daring maneuver. To improve stagnant sales and profits, JCPenney's management redefined its target market to include more upscale consumers. The chain stopped selling hard goods like furniture, sporting goods, major appliances, and hardware and instead started concentrating on the major profit makers of department stores: clothing, jewelry, and cosmetics. Its stores now feature marble floors and fancy woodwork.[9]

Specialty Stores

specialty store
Retail store specializing in a given type of merchandise.

Specialty stores are becoming more common as retailers refine their segmentation and tailor their merchandise to specific target markets. A **specialty store** is not only a type of store but also a method of retail operations—namely, specializing in a given type of merchandise. Examples include children's clothing, men's clothing, candy, baked goods, sporting goods, and pet supplies. A typical specialty store carries a deeper but narrower assortment of merchandise in its specialty than a department store does. Generally, specialty stores' knowledgeable sales clerks offer more attentive customer service.

Consumers in specialty fashion outlets usually consider price to be secondary. Instead, the distinctive merchandise, the store's physical appearance, and the caliber of the staff determine its popularity.

Today specialty stores face many of the same opportunities and challenges that confront department stores. The format has become very powerful in the apparel market and other areas. The Limited, Limited Express, Benetton, Victoria's Secret, Foot Locker, and Crate & Barrel are several successful specialty retailers.

One of the most aggressive specialty chains is The Gap, with about 1,200 stores specializing in basic men's and women's apparel. The chain boasts sales of over $2.5 billion annually. The Gap adheres to this marketing formula: to sell well-made, inexpensive, classic clothing that doesn't render the buyer a fashion failure within a month. The Gap has turned jeans and T-shirts into fashion statements. Its advertising focuses more on the clothes and less on celebrities or gorgeous models. GapKids,

which opened its first store in 1985, appeals to parents who want good-looking, durable clothing for their children. A new line for infants and toddlers called BabyGap has joined GapKids.[10]

Supermarkets

supermarket Large, departmentalized, self-service retailer that specializes in foodstuffs and a few nonfood items.

U.S. consumers spend about 9 percent of their disposable income in supermarkets.[11] A **supermarket** is a large, departmentalized, self-service retailer that specializes in foodstuffs and a few nonfood items.

A decade ago, industry experts predicted the decline of the supermarket industry, whose slim profit margins of just 1 to 2 percent of sales left it vulnerable. Supermarkets would need an ever-growing customer base to sustain volume and compensate for low margins, they said. But annual population growth is averaging less than 1 percent a year. Population trends and a glut of supermarkets have prompted supermarket experts to look more closely at demographic and lifestyle changes. They have discovered several trends affecting their industry. For example, working couples need one-stop shopping, and the increasing number of affluent customers are willing to pay for specialty and prepared foods.

As stores seek to meet consumer demand for one-stop shopping, conventional supermarkets are being replaced by bigger superstores, which are usually twice the size of supermarkets. Superstores meet the needs of today's customers for convenience, variety, and service. Superstores offer one-stop shopping for many food and nonfood needs, as well as many services—including pharmacies, flower shops, bookstores, salad bars, takeout food sections, sit-down restaurants, juice and fruit bars, health food sections, dry cleaning services, photo processing, and banking. Some even offer family dentistry or optical shops. Offering a wide variety of nontraditional goods and services under one roof is called **scrambled merchandising.** Conventional supermarket operators have answered the superstore competition by adding upscale merchandise to their inventory and in some cases opening whole new departments, such as floral boutiques, delicatessens, and seafood departments.[12]

scrambled merchandising Practice of offering a wide variety of nontraditional goods and services in one store.

The mature supermarket industry is also facing competition from other retailers. Discounters like Wal-Mart and Kmart are carrying more food items. At the same

Today's supermarkets often compete with other types of retailers, such as superstores and discounters, by adding specialty departments.

time, supermarkets are stocking more nonfood merchandise. Warehouse clubs have added produce, meats, and bakeries; supermarkets are now stocking more club-pack products, such as twelve-roll bundles of toilet paper, twenty-four-can cases of soft drinks, and cereal multipacks. Pharmacies and photo-processing services have also become a common sight in supermarkets.[13] All are vying to become the ultimate in one-stop shopping. As the distinction between these different types of retailers blurs, price usually becomes the focal point. Double and triple coupons, everyday low pricing, and price promotions have intensified price wars among supermarkets, superstores, and combination discount and food stores.[14]

Consumers are also eating out more. Of the $500 billion or so that consumers spend on food products annually, only 54 percent is spent on food prepared at home, a decline from 70 percent in 1965. If this trend continues, spending on restaurants and takeout food will overtake the nation's grocery bill by 1996. This growth in the away-from-home food market has been driven by the entry of more women into the work force and their need for convenience and time-saving products.[15] Supermarkets have introduced specialty departments with gourmet and prepared foods.[16] Examples include seafood shops, salad bars, sandwich delis, in-store bakeries, and take-out departments.

Hypermarkets

hypermarket
Retail establishment that combines a supermarket and discount department store in one large building.

Adapted from the Europeans, the flashy **hypermarket** format combines a supermarket and discount department store in a space ranging from 200,000 to 300,000 square feet. Hypermarkets must generate huge sales volumes to compensate for steep building costs and low gross margins, usually around 7 to 8 percent. Many of these giant retailers optimistically assumed the U.S. public would accept the hypermarket. However, the concept has enjoyed little success in the United States. According to retailing executives and analysts, customers are often unwilling to shop at such mammoth stores. They feel the prices are not that much cheaper, the selection is not especially good, and long checkout lines are a hassle. Wal-Mart's Hypermart U.S.A. and Kmart's American Fare hypermart formats never got beyond the experimental stage. Both companies say they will not build any more hypermarkets.[17]

Convenience Stores

convenience store
Miniature supermarket, carrying only a limited line of high-turnover convenience goods.

In contrast, a **convenience store** can be defined as a miniature supermarket, carrying only a limited line of high-turnover convenience goods. These self-service stores are typically located near residential areas and are open twenty-four hours, seven days a week. Convenience stores thus offer exactly what their name implies: convenient location, long hours, fast service. However, prices are usually higher at a convenience store than at a supermarket. Thus the customer pays for the convenience.

From the mid-1970s to the mid-1980s, hundreds of new convenience stores opened, many with self-service gas pumps. Full-service gas stations fought back by closing service bays and opening miniature stores of their own, selling convenience items like cigarettes, sodas, and snacks. Supermarkets also wooed customers with one-stop shopping and quick checkout. To combat the gas stations' and supermarkets' competition, convenience store operators have changed their strategy. They have expanded their offerings of nonfood items with video rentals, health and beauty aids, upscale sandwich and salad lines, and more fresh produce. Some convenience stores in Texas are even test marketing Pizza Hut and Taco Bell products prepared in the store.[18]

Wal-Mart, the number-one full-line discounter, is a formidable competitor for both large chains and small retailers.

Discount Stores

discount store
Retail store that is one of a group competing on the basis of low prices, high turnover, and high volume.

A **discount store** is a retailer that competes on the basis of low prices, high turnover, and high volume. The discount industry has mushroomed into a major force in retailing, in part because of cautious spending brought about by the recession of the 1990s and changing customer demographics and priorities.[19] The discounter of the 1960s focused solely on a full line of merchandise. Discounters can now be classified into four major categories: full-line discount retailers, discount specialty retailers, membership clubs, and off-price retailers.

Full-Line Discounters

Compared to traditional department stores, full-line discount stores offer consumers very limited service and carry a much broader assortment of well-known, nationally branded "hard goods," including housewares, toys, automotive parts, hardware, sporting goods, garden items, clothing, bedding, and linens. Some even carry limited nonperishable food items, such as soft drinks, canned goods, and potato chips. As with department stores, national chains dominate the discounters.

Wal-Mart is the largest discount organization, with over $44 billion in annual sales and over 1,700 stores. In the past two decades, Wal-Mart has expanded by locating stores on the outskirts of small towns in the South and absorbing business for miles around. The chain's plans are to open around 150 new stores a year. Much of Wal-Mart's success has been attributed to its merchandising foresight, cost-consciousness, efficient communication and distribution systems, and involved, motivated employees.[20] Wal-Mart plans to move into major urban areas, such as Chicago, Los Angeles, Minneapolis, Philadelphia, and New York. It has global expansion plans for Mexico, Canada, and Puerto Rico.[21]

Kmart, the number-two discounter, has more than 4,000 stores and annual sales of over $34 billion. Wal-Mart recently surpassed Kmart in sales; Kmart is now modernizing over 2,000 stores and boosting its merchandising and advertising to improve its image.[22]

Discount Specialty Stores

Another discount niche includes the single-line specialty discount stores—for example, sporting goods stores, electronics stores, auto parts stores, office supply stores, and toy stores. These stores offer a nearly complete selection of single-line merchandise and use self-service, discount prices, high volume, and high-turnover to their advantage. These discount specialty stores are termed "category killers," since they so heavily dominate their narrow merchandise segment. Examples include Toys R Us in toys, Circuit City in electronics, Office Depot in office supplies, Home Depot in home repair supplies, and Ikea in furniture.

Ikea, the Swedish seller of furniture and housewares, sells its merchandise at a discount by shifting some of the work to the customer. For instance, a shopper who selects a bookcase must pay for it at a central location and then pick it up from a separate distribution area or from warehouse shelves. At home, the customer must assemble the bookcase but needs only one tool: an Allen wrench that comes with the purchase.[23]

With global revenues of more than $6 billion, Toys R Us is the world's largest toy seller. It operates about 500 stores worldwide. Toys R Us gained a loyal following by offering a wide selection of toys, usually over 15,000 different items per store, at prices usually 10 to 15 percent less than competitors'. Toys R Us first went international in 1984—initially in Canada, then Europe, Hong Kong, and Singapore. Breaking into the Japanese market took longer, because of the country's notorious Large-Store Law, aimed at protecting the country's politically powerful small shopkeepers. Under the law, local communities have successfully stalled big retailers for ten years or more. Finally Toys R Us opened two giant stores in Japan, with plans to open ten new stores a year from 1993 to 2000.[24] The opening of the first Japanese store attracted more than 60,000 visitors in the first three days. When the second Japanese store opened, President George Bush cut the ribbon.[25] Toys R Us also plans an aggressive expansion in Europe, with a goal of about 150 stores by the year 2000. The company has an especially strong foothold in Germany, where it is the largest toy retailer.[26]

Membership Clubs

As mentioned in Chapter 12, warehouse membership clubs like the Price Club and Costco sell a limited selection of brand-name appliances, household items, and groceries. These are usually sold in bulk from warehouse outlets on a cash-and-carry basis to members only. Individual members of warehouse clubs are charged low or no membership fees.

Warehouse stores have a major impact on supermarkets. Nearly one of every five shoppers buys some groceries at either membership clubs or other discounters. Traditional shoppers spend an average of $79 a week at the supermarket, but membership club customers spend $110 or more. This significant difference is most likely due to the bulk-purchases that consumers make in membership clubs.[27]

Off-Price Discount Retailers

off-price retailer
Retailer that sells at prices 25 percent or more below traditional department store prices because it pays cash for its stock and usually doesn't ask for return privileges.

An **off-price retailer** sells at prices 25 percent or more below traditional department store prices because it pays cash for its stock and usually doesn't ask for return privileges. Off-price retailers buy manufacturers' overruns at cost or even less. They also absorb goods from bankrupt stores, irregular merchandise, and unsold end-of-season output. Nevertheless, much off-price retailer merchandise is first-quality, current goods. Since buyers for off-price retailers purchase only what is available or what they can get a good deal on, merchandise styles and brands often change monthly. Today there are hundreds of off-price retailers, the best known being T.J. Maxx, Hit or Miss, Ross Stores, Marshall's, and Tuesday Morning. A couple of interesting variations have emerged.

Single-price stores: One new type of off-price retailer that has proliferated in the

past few years is the single-price store. For a lump sum, usually $1 per item, consumers can buy anything in the store, from shoes to shampoo. Single-price stores generally offer no frills, and customers must search through piles of merchandise. Typically, single-price chains buy their merchandise in large quantities from many sources, including wholesalers and independent vendors. Most products they buy are close-out items and discontinued products.

One Price Clothing Stores, a 400-store chain that sells women's apparel at $7 per item, opened seventy stores in 1991 and eighty more in 1992. The growing number of price-conscious consumers have become steady customers for single-price stores; One Price Clothing Stores has seen double-digit sales growth since 1987.[28]

factory outlet
Off-price retailer that is owned and operated by a manufacturer and that carries the manufacturer's own line of merchandise.

Factory outlets: A **factory outlet** is an off-price retailer that is owned and operated by a manufacturer. Thus it carries one line of merchandise—its own. Each season, from 5 percent to 10 percent of a manufacturer's output does not sell through regular distribution channels because it consists of close-outs (merchandise being discontinued), factory seconds, and canceled orders. With factory outlets, manufacturers can regulate where their surplus is sold, and they can realize higher profit margins than they would by disposing of the goods through independent wholesalers and retailers.

Today, factory outlet malls are emerging in out-of-the-way but not always rural locations. Most are situated at least thirty miles from urban or suburban shopping areas so manufacturers don't alienate their department store accounts by selling the same goods virtually next door at deep discounts. Many outlet malls are located near vacation destinations, such as Disney World and Niagara Falls, since consumers on holiday are usually in good spirits and not pressed for time.[29] Several manufacturers reaping the benefits of outlet mall popularity include Liz Claiborne, J. Crew, and Calvin Klein clothiers, West Point Pepperel textiles, Oneida silversmiths, and Dansk kitchenwares.

5 NONSTORE RETAILING

nonstore retailing
Practice of selling goods and services to the ultimate consumer without setting up a store.

The retailing methods discussed so far have been in-store methods, in which customers must physically shop at stores. In contrast, **nonstore retailing** is shopping without visiting a store. Because consumers demand convenience, nonstore retailing is currently growing faster than in-store retailing. The major forms of nonstore retailing are vending, direct retailing, and direct marketing.

Vending

vending
Form of nonstore retailing that uses vending machines to offer products for sale.

A low-profile yet important form of retailing is **vending.** U.S. consumers buy about $21 billion worth of goods annually from vending equipment. Since many vending items, like soft drinks and snacks, have traditional or relatively fixed prices, raising vending machine prices is often difficult. The key to successful management in the vending business is reducing costs and streamlining operations. Often old equipment must be replaced with new machines that have greater capacity or more selections. One trend in vending is offering different kinds of merchandise, such as personal-size pizzas, french fries, cappuccino, quick dinners, and videos. Another trend is a debit-card system for machines that have repeat customers.

Vending is very popular in Japan, where marketers have transformed the usual vending machine into a high-tech attraction. For example, new vending machines with special microchips play a tune or talk to buyers while dispensing up to twenty-four varieties of soda, sports

drinks, and ready-to-drink canned coffee and tea—hot in winter, cold in summer. Roulette-type games give lucky buyers free cans; overhead, illuminated cans advertise brand names like Coke, Suntory whiskey, and Kirin beer. One version of a Coke machine uses revolving billboards to advertise different Coke beverages.[30]

Over half the soft-drink retail sales in Japan are made through vending machines, compared with 10 percent in the United States. The Japanese market share is increasing as more women join the work force and have less time to shop in supermarkets. Vending machine sales also have a lot to do with where the machines are; most are located on city sidewalks instead of in offices and factories, as in the United States. In Japan's lawful society, machine vandalism is all but nonexistent. Therefore, a well-placed vending machine can sell as much product as a medium-size convenience store—some 10,000 cans a year.[31]

Direct Retailing

direct retailing
Form of nonstore retailing that occurs in a home setting, such as door-to-door sales and party plan selling.

In **direct retailing**, the sales transaction occurs in a home setting. This approach includes door-to-door sales and party plan selling. Companies like Avon, Mary Kay Cosmetics, Fuller Brush, Amway, and World Book Encyclopedia depend on these techniques.

The trend in direct retailing seems to be away from door-to-door canvassing and toward party plans. Party plans call for one person, the host, to gather as many prospective buyers as possible. Most parties are a combination social affair and sales demonstration.

The sales of direct retailers have suffered as women have entered the work force. Working women have little time to attend selling parties. Tupperware, which still advocates the party plan method, is betting that working women have more money to spend but are just a little harder to reach. Its sales representatives now hold parties in offices, parks, and even parking lots. They hold "stop and shops" so women can just drop in, "classes" on self-improvement, and "custom-kitchen" parties on cabinet organizing.[32] Avon is now trying to pick up sales through direct-mail efforts. The company has a toll-free number for telephone orders and will even take orders by fax.[33] Mary Kay found it tough to recruit women as sales representatives because of the better-paying jobs open to them elsewhere. But by offering competitive commissions and bonuses, Mary Kay has replenished its sales force with more part-timers, which has led to increased sales.[34]

Avon is no longer relying on door-to-door "Avon ladies" to get the word out. Slick ads and sophisticated direct-mail campaigns reach busy working women.
Avon Products, Inc.

Direct retailing is catching on in southern China, an area that has long been under communist rule. When the "Avon lady" visits factories there, women rush from the workroom to seek her advice. The average salary of these factory workers is only about $450 a year, but when Avon calls, money is no object. Avon started producing and selling cosmetics and skin cleansers in China in 1990. In the first year, sales were double the projections. Now Avon has a sales force of 8,000 Chinese women, many of whom earn more than $500 in monthly commissions. More than 60 million people live within a 100-mile radius of Avon's Guangzhou factory, so the company has plenty of potential customers. In addition, Avon advertises on Hong Kong television, so women in the area already recognize the Avon brand.[35]

Direct Marketing

direct marketing
Techniques used to get consumers to buy from their homes, including direct mail, catalogs and mail order, telemarketing, and electronic retailing.

Direct marketing, sometimes called direct-response marketing, refers to the techniques used to get consumers to buy from their homes. Those techniques include direct mail, catalogs and mail order, telemarketing, and electronic retailing. Shoppers using these methods are less bound by traditional shopping situations and perceive less risk in buying by mail or telephone. Parents with small children and those who live in rural or suburban areas are most likely to be in-home shoppers, because they value the convenience and flexibility direct marketing provides.[36]

Direct marketing strives for an immediate response from the consumer. For instance, 800 numbers advertised on cable TV stations invite shoppers to "call in now"; Ed McMahon shouts from an envelope, "You may have just won $10 million."

Direct marketing typically uses a data base of customer names. Because marketers can record the number of customers responding to a direct marketing effort, results are more accurately measured. Direct-response advertising techniques are discussed in Chapter 16.

Privacy issues have become a major concern for many consumers and politicians in light of the advances in direct marketing techniques and the use of highly specialized database marketing. Many consumers today feel that direct marketing techniques invade their privacy and pose ethical questions. Privacy will be a major issue in the 1990s, and addressing these consumer concerns will be paramount for direct marketers. The following article reflects these concerns.

ETHICS IN MARKETING

How Direct Marketers Get New Addresses

What the U.S. Postal Service does with the change-of-address labels that every household must fill out to get its mail forwarded is at the center of a controversy involving lawmakers, privacy-rights advocates, the Postal Service, and the multibillion-dollar direct-mail industry. In 1990, 26 million households moved at least once, and to get their mail to follow them, they had to fill out the form. The Postal Service then enters the information into its central data base. And that is where the controversy begins.

In the process of forwarding the mail, the Postal Service also gives the new address to twenty-three direct-mail firms, some of which sell it to other companies selling products targeted to new movers. Since 1985, the Postal Service has also given new addresses to anyone who walks into a local post office with the old address and pays $3 for the new one.

Twice a month the Postal Service gives its computer tapes from its data base to the twenty-three direct mailers who have paid the Postal Service an $80,000 initial fee and $50,000 a year for the information. The direct mailers then use the information to "clean," or update, addresses of persons whose names and old addresses they already have on their mailing lists. These same direct mailers may then use this information to create a "new movers" list, which they then resell to other direct-mail firms that want to target this market.

Many legislators and privacy advocates believe the selling of the "new movers" list violates provisions in both the Privacy Act of 1974 and the Postal Reorganization Act. The Postal Service counters that neither the agency nor the twenty-three direct-mail companies have violated the statutes. Updating addresses used by direct-mail firms is essential, they contend, to cut down on what would otherwise be millions of pieces of mail that letter carriers and mail handlers would have to resend. Direct mailers also argue that having access to new-address information is critical to the industry as it cuts down on mailing costs due to wrong addresses.

In light of the Privacy Act and other privacy laws, does the Postal Service have the right to sell names of new movers to direct-mail companies? Do you think it is justified in trying to keep mail volume down in this manner? Is the practice of selling new-movers lists to other direct mailers appropriate? Does obtaining names from anyone, not just the Postal Service, pose ethical problems?

Source: Adapted from Dana Priest, "How Direct Mailers Get New Addresses," *The Washington Post*, 15 May 1992, p. A23.

Direct Mail

Direct mail can be the most efficient or the least efficient retailing method, depending on the quality of the mailing list and the effectiveness of the mailing piece. With direct mail, marketers can precisely target their customers according to demographics, geographics, and even psychographics. Good mailing lists come from an internal data base or are available from list brokers for about $35 to $150 per 1,000 names. For example, a Los Angeles computer software manufacturer selling programs for managing medical records may buy a list of all the physicians in the area. It may then design a direct-mail piece explaining the benefits of its system and send it to each physician. Today, direct mailers are even using videocassettes in place of letters and brochures to bring their sales message to consumers.

Direct mailers are becoming more sophisticated in their targeting of the "right" customers. With a technique called predictive modeling, direct mailers can pick out those most likely to buy their products using census statistics, lifestyle and financial information, and past-purchase and credit history. American Express uses this modeling technique to target only those most likely to want its services. Before, American Express mailed millions of solicitations annually. Now, solicitations tailored to cardholders with known spending patterns are sent to no more than 500,000 people. Some are targeted to only 10,000, saving the company millions in postage while still preserving sales.[37]

New computer technology has also enabled direct-mail marketers to personalize their appeals. For example, a marketer of consumer credit cards could personalize the sales approach with these lines: "Being a May graduate of the University of Arizona, Ms. Jones, automatically qualifies you for ABC Bank's Consumer Credit Card." The university, recipient, and graduation date would change from letter to letter, giving each a personal appeal.

Rising postage and paper costs, increased competition, and possible government regulation threaten to cut into the profits of direct mailers. Direct-mail companies are now seeking alternative delivery methods—for instance, private delivery services.

Direct mailers have also suffered from the negative image of "junk mail." Consumers' mailboxes are filled daily with direct-mail solicitations, most of which are never read.

The industry is also plagued by direct-mail scams. One common scam is to notify consumers that they have won a fabulous prize or are a winner in a sweepstakes. When they try to collect their prize, they are informed that they must first make a purchase.[38]

Catalogs and Mail Order

Consumers can now buy just about anything through the mail—from a Connemara pony to a golf cart equipped with stereo and sunroof to a one-person hot-air balloon in any design wanted. Over 12 billion catalogs are mailed annually, with the average U.S. household receiving a new mail-order catalog about every five days.

Successful catalogs are usually created and designed for highly segmented markets. For example, computer manufacturers have discovered that mail order is a lucrative way to sell computers to home and small-business users. Currently, 30 percent of all microcomputers sold in the U.S. market are sold through the mail.[39] Consumers can save up to 20 percent off traditional dealer prices by buying their computers from a mail-order house. The better mail-order firms also offer free in-home repairs for a year, thirty-day money-back guarantees, and toll-free phone lines for answers to questions.[40]

L.L. Bean maintains its catalog customers' confidence by quickly and correctly shipping 99.9 percent of its orders, even during the harried Christmas season.

Improved customer service and quick delivery policies have boosted consumer confidence in mail order. L.L. Bean and Lands' End are two catalog companies known for their excellent customer service. Shoppers may order twenty-four hours a day and can return any merchandise for any reason for a full refund. Sears, whose catalog sales dropped off in the last several years, has broken up its big book and replaced it with a collection of specialty catalogs targeted to specific market segments. Other successful mail-order catalogs—including Spiegel, J. Crew, Victoria's Secret, and Tweeds—target hard-working, home-oriented baby boomers who don't have time to visit or would rather not visit a retail store.

Like their direct-mail counterpart, catalogs are suffering from rising postage rates and increased paper costs. To help cut down the costs of mailing, catalog producers are trying new delivery methods whose rates may be as much as 20 percent below the U.S. Postal Service rates. One such company, Alternative Postal Delivery, uses contractors covering 270 ZIP codes in sixteen markets to hang plastic-bagged catalogs and publications from doorknobs.[41]

U.S. catalog companies are also finding alternatives overseas, especially in Japan and Europe. Lands' End, Tweeds, L.L. Bean, Orvis, and eight others have teamed up

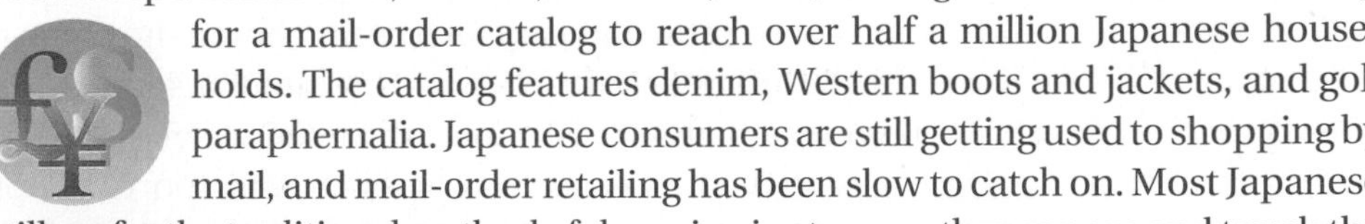

for a mail-order catalog to reach over half a million Japanese households. The catalog features denim, Western boots and jackets, and golf paraphernalia. Japanese consumers are still getting used to shopping by mail, and mail-order retailing has been slow to catch on. Most Japanese still prefer the traditional method of shopping in stores so they can see and touch the merchandise. However, signs show this resistance to mail-order shopping is beginning to ebb.[42]

Telemarketing

telemarketing
Type of personal selling conducted over the telephone.

Telemarketing is the use of the telephone in the selling process. It consists of *outbound* sales calls, usually unsolicited, and *inbound* calls—that is, orders through toll-free 800 numbers or fee-based 900 numbers. Telemarketing is different from using the phone to support field sales activities. Salespeople use the phone periodically when they need to contact clients; telemarketing is systematic and continuous.[43]

Outbound telemarketing is a profitable direct-marketing technique for reaching consumers, because of rising postage rates and decreasing long-distance phone rates. Skyrocketing field sales costs also have put pressure on marketing managers to use outbound telemarketing. Searching for ways to keep costs under control, marketing managers are discovering how to pinpoint prospects quickly, zero in on serious buyers, and keep in close touch with regular customers. Meanwhile, they are reserving expensive, time-consuming, in-person calls for closing sales.

Many consumers believe outbound telemarketing methods are intrusive. They resent persistent, obnoxious phone calls at inappropriate times by people selling everything from magazines to aluminum siding. More recently, calls have become computerized, adding to the annoyance. Although that tarnished image still lingers, outbound telemarketing has become a sophisticated, complex business. Major players include American Express, Citicorp, and General Electric. In particular, technological advances have enabled telemarketing firms to become more sophisticated in finding prospects and checking sales leads.[44]

Inbound telemarketing programs, which use 800 and 900 numbers, mainly offer order placement, lead generation, and customer service. Inbound 800 telemarketing has successfully supplemented direct-response TV, radio, and print advertising for more than twenty-five years. The recently introduced 900 numbers, in which the customer pays for the call, are gaining popularity as a cost-effective way for companies to target customers. One of the major benefits of 900 numbers is that they allow marketers to generate qualified responses. Although the charge may reduce the total volume of calls, the calls that do come through are from customers who have a true interest in the product.[45]

Electronic Retailing

Electronic retailing includes the twenty-four-hour shop-at-home television networks and videotex shopping.

Shop-at-home networks: The shop-at-home networks are specialized forms of direct-response marketing. These shows display merchandise, with the retail price, to home viewers. Viewers can phone in their orders directly on a toll-free line and shop with a credit card. The shop-at-home industry has quickly grown into a billion-dollar business with a loyal customer following. Shop-at-home networks have the capability of reaching nearly every home that has a television set. The best-known shop-at-home networks are the Home Shopping Network and the QVC (Quality, Value, Convenience) Network.

Those in the industry foresee that home shopping networks will play a major role in the future in interactive and multimedia services. Future home shopping services would essentially turn the consumer's television into a smart computer and cash register for buying pay-per-view movies, sports, shopping services, and the like.[46]

Videotex shopping: Videotex is a two-way, interactive service offered to users with personal computers. It provides customers with a variety of information, including news, weather, stock information, sports news, and shopping opportunities. Users of videotex "subscribe" to information and shopping services, usually by getting the required hardware for their personal computer and paying a monthly fee. They then "log on" to videotex services through a modem connected to their personal computer.

Prodigy, CompuServe, and GEnie are the three most popular electronic shopping and information services. Prodigy, a joint venture of IBM and Sears, has over 1.2 million subscribers who pay a monthly fee of about $13. It provides microcomputer users with the newspaper *USA Today* and advertisements from such companies as carmakers BMW and Mazda. The advertisers provide brochures, catalogs, and other information packets via the on-line service.[47] Shoppers can then ask for more information or order the product directly from their computer screen. For example, a family in the market for a child's bicycle can view a picture of the model they want on the screen and find the retailer offering the best price. Once they decide, they use their computer to send a message to the retailer and electronically transfer the proper amount of money from their bank account to the retailer's. Then a delivery service can bring the bicycle to the home.

6 FRANCHISING

franchise
The right to operate a business or to sell a product.

franchisor
Individual or business that grants operating rights to another party to sell its product.

franchisee
Individual or business that is granted the right to sell another party's product.

A **franchise** is a continuing relationship in which a **franchisor** grants business rights to operate or sell a product to a **franchisee.**[48] The franchisor originates the trade name, product, methods of operation, and so on. The franchisor also receives several types of fees from the franchisee. A franchise agreement between the two parties usually lasts for ten to twenty years. Most franchises are retail operations.

To be granted the rights to a franchise, a franchisee usually pays an initial, one-time franchise fee. The amount of this fee depends solely on the individual franchisor, but it generally ranges from $5,000 to $150,000. Besides paying this initial franchise fee, the franchisee is expected to pay royalty fees (usually 3 percent to 7 percent of gross revenues) weekly, biweekly, or monthly.[49] The franchisee may also be expected to pay advertising fees, which usually cover the cost of promotional materials and, if the franchise organization is large enough, regional or national advertising. For example, Popeye's Famous Fried Chicken and Biscuits charges new franchisees an initial $25,000 per store with a 5 percent royalty in each of the first five years, 5.5 percent in the fifth through twentieth years, and an annual advertising contribution of 3 percent of gross sales.[50]

Franchising offers the following advantages to a person who wants to own and manage a business:

- It gives the person a chance to become an independent businessperson with relatively little capital.
- The franchisee gets a product that has already been established in the marketplace.
- The franchisor provides the franchisee with technical training and managerial assistance.
- Quality-control standards enforced by the franchisor help the franchisee succeed by ensuring product uniformity throughout the franchise system.

In turn, the franchisor gets company expansion with a limited capital investment, motivated store owners, and bulk purchasing of inventory.[51] Gung Ho Stir Fry Restaurants advertises many of its franchise's benefits to potential franchisees.

Franchising is not new. General Motors has used this approach since 1898 and Rexall drugstores since 1901. Franchising is quickly becoming one of the most profitable business methods today. In 1990 there were over half a million franchised establishments in the United States, with combined sales over $750 billion. Of the $1.8 trillion in total retail sales in 1991, franchising accounted for about 35 percent.[52] Exhibit 13.4 provides some more interesting facts about franchising.

Exhibit 13.4

Franchising Facts

Source: Adapted from International Franchise Association, *Franchising Opportunities Guidebook*, Summer 1992, p. 38.

Sales	• Franchises had $757.8 billion in sales in 1991. • Franchises accounted for 35% of all retail sales. • Business format franchise sales increased 8.9%, from $213.2 billion in 1990 to $232.2 billion in 1991. • Product and trade name franchise sales increased 4.9%, from $500.7 billion in 1990 to $525.6 billion in 1991.
Jobs	• 7.2 million people were employed by franchises in more than 60 different industries. • More than 100,000 new jobs were created by franchises last year. In comparison, Fortune 500 companies lost 3.9 million jobs during the last ten years.
Growth	• A new franchise opens every 16 minutes. • More than 18,500 new businesses were created last year by franchise companies. • The total number of franchises grew from 521,215 in 1990 to 542,496 in 1991. • According to studies conducted by the U.S. Commerce Department from 1971 to 1987, less than 5% of franchises have failed or discontinued annually.
Gallup poll	• According to a recent Gallup poll, 94% of franchise business owners are successful. • 75% of franchise owners would repeat their franchise again. Only 39% of all U.S. citizens would repeat their job or business. • Average gross income before taxes was $124, 290. • Average total investment cost of a franchise was $147,570.

There are two basic forms of franchises today: product and trade name franchising, and business format franchising. In product and trade name franchising, a dealer agrees to buy or sell certain products or product lines from a supplier, either a manufacturer or a wholesaler. This approach has been used most widely in the auto and truck, soft-drink bottling, tire, and gasoline service industries. For example, a local tire retailer may hold a franchise to sell Michelin tires from his or her store. Likewise, the Coca-Cola bottler in a particular area is a product and trade name franchisee licensed to bottle and sell Coca-Cola's soft drinks.

Business format franchising is an ongoing business relationship between a franchisor and a franchisee. Typically, a franchisor "sells" a franchisee the rights to use the franchisor's format or approach to doing business. This form of franchising has rapidly expanded since the 1950s through retailing, restaurant, food-service, hotel and motel, printing, and real estate franchises.[53] Fast-food restaurants like McDonald's, Wendy's, and Burger King use this kind of franchising.

Franchisors sometimes allow franchisees to alter their business format slightly in foreign markets. For example, McDonald's, with over 800 franchise locations in Japan, is testing food items with a Japanese touch, such as steamed dumplings, curry with rice, and roast pork-cutlet burgers with melted cheese. KFC's Japanese franchisees are experimenting with grilled versions of rice balls and a fried salmon sandwich.[54]

The following article explains the advantages and disadvantages faced by small retailers, who may be franchisees or independents.

MARKETING AND SMALL BUSINESS

Retailing

There are about 1,750,000 small retailers in the United States. Retailing is one of the most popular avenues for people who want to start their own business. But there are some important advantages and disadvantages one should consider before taking the plunge.

Small retailers have several operating advantages over their larger counterparts. One is that small firms are able to react more quickly to changes in operations. Because they are usually owner-operated, they can try new product offerings and services, new methods, and new ideas without getting approval through a lengthy, elaborate process. (Endless hours spent in committee are eliminated.)

A second advantage of small business retailing is its personal touch in handling customers. Fine restaurants, high-style boutiques, and custom jewelry stores are examples of retailers that need the personal touch—and most of these are small firms.

A third advantage is that, when the market is limited, a small retailer may be able to survive. Because of the large amount of overhead usually incurred by large-scale retailers, they often cannot afford to serve small markets. Some markets would go unserved were it not for small business. By its very nature, small business is uniquely fitted to fill this void and offer a better selection of goods and services than would otherwise be available.

The smaller firm faces some definite disadvantages in the competitive arena, however. The most significant are limited managerial skill, lack of market knowledge, inadequate capital-raising capacity, and excessive government regulation. The entrepreneur is usually adept at starting firms, but the skills to manage them may be lacking. Even with partners or other shareholders, the pool of managerial skill is limited. Also, a small retailer is at a disadvantage in trying to hire qualified employees. It may be able to offer an attractive salary and fringe benefits, but it often lacks opportunities for advancement.

Many small retailers believe they lack the funds, time, and skills to get the right decision-making data. The types of information they most want are profiles of customer needs, market analyses, and sales forecasts. Secondary data from trade associations, the Chamber of Commerce, and universities are not often specialized or detailed enough to meet the needs of small retailers.

Since small retailers must compete with established firms with proven track records, adequate financing is often hard to get. The small business usually has limited equity in the business, yet a good equity base is required for loans to expand and operate. If the owner wants to maintain control of the company, selling shares to new owners is out of the question as well.

A final disadvantage is that small retailers, and small businesses in general, must cope with many government regulations. A great deal of paperwork is required to report taxes and regulated activities. The small firm cannot afford a professional staff to deal with the paperwork. Since the owner is the only one who knows what is needed, the burden of reporting falls on his or her shoulders. Thus many owners feel overworked or ignore the paperwork requirements.

7 RETAIL MARKETING STRATEGY

Retailers must develop marketing strategies based on overall goals and strategic plans. Retailing goals might include more traffic, higher sales of a specific item, a more upscale image, or heightened public awareness of the retail operation. The strategies that retailers use to obtain their goals might include a sale, an updated decor, or a new advertisement. The key tasks in strategic retailing are defining and selecting a target market and developing the six P's of the retailing mix to successfully meet the needs of the chosen target market.

retailing mix
Combination of the six P's—price, place, product, promotion, personnel, and presentation—to sell goods and services to the ultimate customer.

Retailers control the six P's of the **retailing mix**: the four P's of the marketing mix plus personnel and presentation (see Exhibit 13.5). Retailers combine these elements to come up with a single retailing method to attract the target market. The combination of the six P's also projects a store's image. Image, of course, influences consumers' perceptions. The shopper develops impressions of stores and positions one store against another. A retail marketing manager must make sure that the

Exhibit 13.5

The Retailing Mix

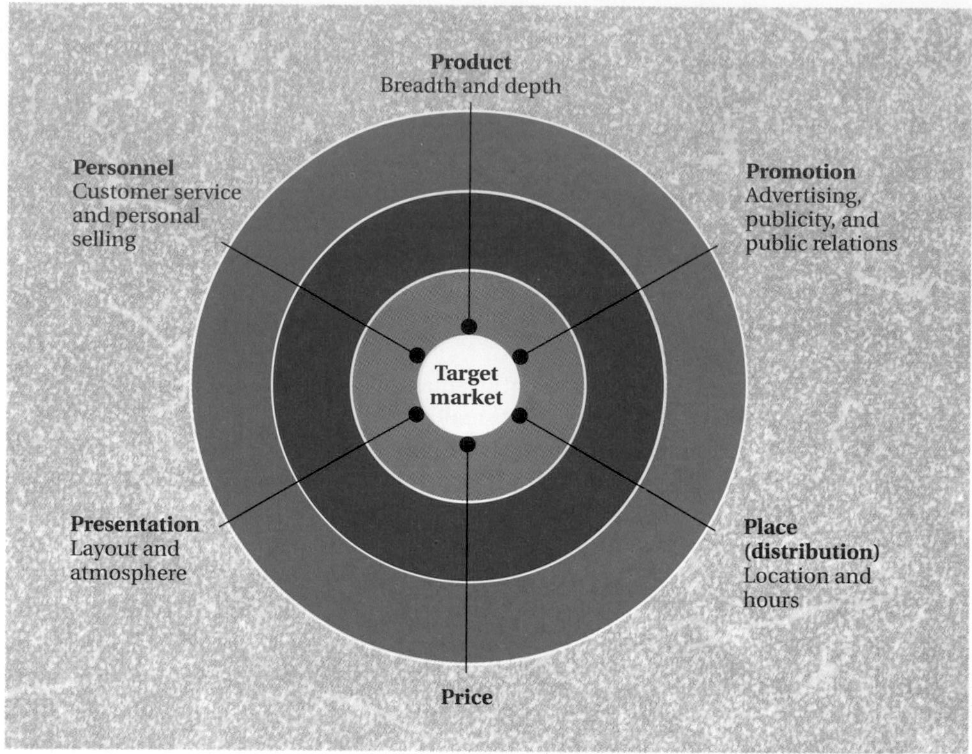

store's positioning is compatible with the target customer's expectations. As discussed at the beginning of the chapter, retail stores can be positioned on three broad dimensions: service provided by store personnel, product assortment, and price. Management should use everything else—place, presentation, and promotion—to fine-tune the basic positioning of the store.

Defining a Target Market

The first and foremost task in developing a retail strategy is to define the target market. This process begins with market segmentation, which was the topic of Chapter 6. Successful retailing has always been based on knowing the customer. Sometimes retailing chains have floundered because management lost sight of the customers the stores should be serving. In other cases, the market the firm should be serving is different from the one chosen. For example, the target market of the Hit or Miss chain was indeed a miss. It was originally positioned to appeal to teenagers seeking low-end apparel. The chain was not profitable until repositioned to reach professional women seeking values in clothing.

Target markets in retailing are often defined by demographics, geographics, and lifestyles or psychographics. A convenience store may define its main target as married men under 35 years old, in the lower income ranges, with two young children. A small local grocer might limit its target market to those living in the surrounding neighborhood. A department store may target fashion-conscious juniors, contemporaries who spend more money than other segments on quality clothing, and conservatives who want comfort and value.

Choosing the Retailing Mix

Different combinations of the elements in the retailing mix enable a retailer to carry out its particular targeting strategy. The six P's of the retailing mix are all variables that can be used in a marketing plan. Let's look at each one.

The Product Offering

The first element in the retailing mix is the product offering, also called the merchandise mix. As noted earlier, the product assortment is a key factor in classifying retail establishments.

Given their chosen target market, retailers must then decide what to sell. They can base their decision on market research, past sales, fashion trends, customer requests, and other sources. Today's retailers must know customers' buying preferences and the factors that influence them. Developing a product offering is essentially a question of width and depth of the product assortment.

After determining what products will satisfy target customers' desires, retailers must find sources of supply and evaluate the products. When the right products are found, the retail buyer negotiates a purchase contract. The buying function can either be performed in-house or be delegated to an outside firm. The goods must then be moved from the seller to the retailer, which means shipping, storing, and stocking the inventory. The trick is to manage the inventory by cutting prices to move slow goods and keeping adequate supplies of hot-selling items in stock. As in all good systems, the final step is to evaluate the entire process to seek more efficient methods and eliminate problems and bottlenecks.

One of the more efficient new methods of managing inventory is electronic data interchange, or EDI. This technology is embraced by a new retail philosophy called "quick response," which strengthens the relationship between retailer and vendor. EDI electronically connects the two partners by computer to make information about sales, stock levels, and the location of merchandise in the distribution channel readily available. The retailer can then forecast sales, automatically reorder, and balance inventory levels. For example, Dillard's department stores, one of the fastest-growing regional department store chains, has one of the most technologically advanced EDI systems in the industry.[55] Every item Dillard's sells has a bar code, so on any given day management knows how many pairs of 9 West slingback ladies shoes, for instance, have been sold. If the shoes are leaping off the shelves, Dillard's EDI system automatically orders more from the company warehouse. The warehouse, in turn, reorders automatically from the vendor. Thus, Dillard's stores are less likely than competitors' to be out of popular items or loaded up with unfashionable ones that eventually have to be marked down.[56]

In this ad, the manufacturer of Chilis shoes and the retailers Bloomingdale's and Journey's share the cost of promotion.
Chilis Footwear Inc.

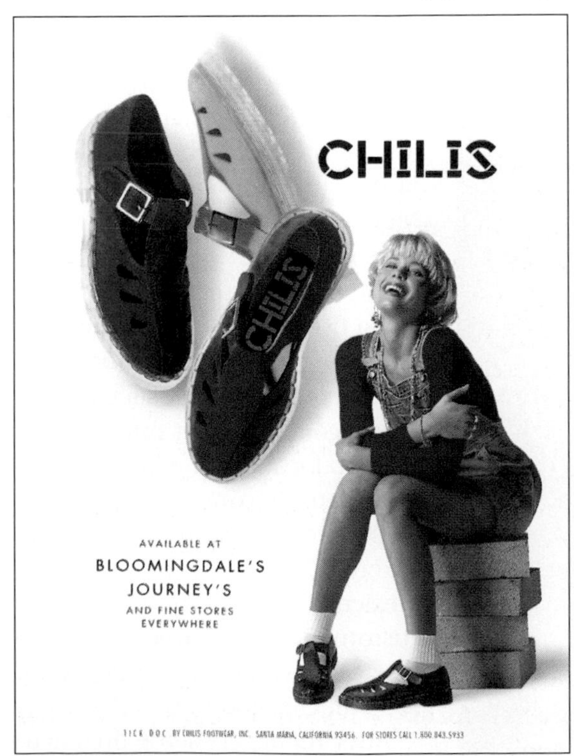

Advances in computer technology have also helped retailers spot new opportunities, such as the latest fashions. These styles can be re-created on a computer, and the designs can be transmitted electronically to manufacturers for production. New merchandise can be produced and put on store shelves in weeks rather than months. This speed gives retailers like Kmart and Dillard's a competitive advantage over other fashion retailers.

Promotional Strategy

Retail promotional strategy includes advertising, public relations and publicity, and sales promotion. The goal is to help position the store in consumers' minds. Retailers design intriguing ads, stage special events, and develop promotions aimed at their target markets. For example, today's grand open-

ings are a carefully orchestrated blend of advertising, merchandising, goodwill, and glitter. All the elements of an opening—press coverage, special events, media advertising, and store displays—are carefully planned. Sponsoring community events can also generate a lot of local publicity and may be more effective than traditional aspects of store openings, such as free giveaways and balloons.

Retailers' advertising is carried out mostly at the local level, although retail giants like Sears and JCPenney can advertise nationally. In their ads, retailers communicate information about their stores—for instance, location, merchandise, hours, prices, and special sales.

Often large retailers and well-known clothing designers or manufacturers of exclusive specialty products share the spotlight in an advertisement. For example, when Ralph Lauren and Foley's, a department store chain, team up, they let everyone know that Foley's sells the latest fashions. In turn, they enhance Ralph Lauren's prestige by associating it with a successful, distinguished fashion retailer.

The Proper Location

Another element in the retailing mix is place, or site location. Selecting a proper site is a critical decision. First, it is a large, long-term commitment of resources that can reduce a retailer's future flexibility. Whether the retailer leases or purchases, the location decision implies some degree of permanence. Second, the location will affect future growth. The chosen area should be growing economically so it can sustain the original store and any future stores. Last, the local environment may change over time. If the location's value deteriorates, the store may have to be relocated or closed.

Site location begins by choosing a community. This decision depends largely on economic growth potential and stability, the competition, political climate, and so on. Retailers like McDonald's, Target, and Kmart now follow Wal-Mart's strategy, locating in small towns instead of large metropolitan areas where the competition has grown fierce. McDonald's recently opened several new stores designed for small towns. They have about 60 percent of the square footage of a regular McDonald's. To get the needed sales volume, they serve a broader menu, including chicken, hot dogs, and a fish platter.[57] Sometimes it is not the economic profile or political climate that makes a community a good location but the geographic location of a community. For example, one of Wal-Mart's most successful stores is located in Laredo, Texas, a city bordering Mexico. The store draws not only customers from Laredo but also Mexicans who cross the border to shop for U.S. goods.[58]

Among the many other attractions at the gigantic Mall of America in Minnesota is this amusement park.

After managers settle on a geographic region or community, they must choose a specific site. In addition to growth potential, the important factors are socioeconomic characteristics of the inhabitants, traffic flows, land costs, zoning regulations, existing competition, and public transportation. Managers must also decide whether to have a freestanding unit or become a shopping mall tenant.

Freestanding stores: An isolated, freestanding location can be used by large retailers like Wal-Mart, Kmart, or Target and sellers of shopping goods like furniture and cars because they are "destination" stores. In other words, customers will seek them out. An isolated store location may have the advantages of low-site cost or rent and no nearby competitors. On the other hand, it may be hard to attract customers to a freestanding location, and no other retailers are around to share costs. One store that thrives on its isolation is the Domino's outlet near Twenty-Nine Palms, California. It is the only pizza joint on a military base that is home to 11,000 Marines and their families. Domino's sells close to 4,000 pizzas a week. Marines returning from Operation Desert Storm who wanted to satisfy their pizza cravings pushed annual sales for the store well over $1 million.[59]

Shopping centers: The tremendous boom in shopping centers began after World War II, as the U.S. population started migrating to the suburbs. The first shopping centers were strip centers, typically located along a busy street. They included a supermarket, a variety store, and perhaps a few specialty stores. Essentially unplanned business districts, these strip centers remain popular.

Next the small community shopping centers emerged, with one or two small department store branches, more specialty shops, one or two restaurants, and several apparel stores. These centers offer a broader variety of shopping, specialty, and convenience goods, provide large off-street parking lots, and usually span 75,000 to 300,000 square feet of retail space.

Finally, along came the huge regional malls. Regional malls are either entirely enclosed or roofed to allow shopping in any weather. Many are landscaped with trees, fountains, sculptures, and the like to enhance the shopping environment. They have acres of free parking. The "anchor stores" or "generator stores" (JCPenney, Sears, or major department stores) are usually located at opposite ends of the mall to create heavy foot traffic.

The largest mall in the United States opened in 1992 near St.Paul and Minneapolis, Minnesota. Covering seventy-eight acres and 4.2 million square feet of selling space, The Mall of America boasts 400-plus stores, an eighteen-hole miniature golf course, fourteen movie theaters, thirteen restaurants, two food courts, and an amusement park operated by Knott's Berry Farm. Its four anchor stores are Bloomingdale's, Macy's, Nordstrom, and Sears.[60]

Locating in a community shopping center or regional mall offers several advantages. First, the facilities are designed to attract shoppers. Second, the shopping environment, anchor stores, and "village square" activities draw customers. Third, ample parking is available. Fourth, the center or mall projects a unified image. Fifth, tenants share the expenses of the mall's common area and promotions for the whole mall. Finally, malls can target different demographic groups. For example, some malls are considered upscale; others are aimed at lower socioeconomic classes.

Locating in a shopping center or mall does have disadvantages. These include expensive leases, the chance that common promotional efforts will not attract customers to a particular store, lease restrictions on merchandise carried and hours of operation, the anchor stores' domination of the tenants' association, and the possibility of having direct competitors within the same facility.

Strip centers and small community shopping centers account for 87 percent of all retail centers and 51 percent of total shopping center retail sales. Retail analysts expect that by the year 2000, U.S. consumers will do most of their shopping at neighborhood strip shopping centers. With increasing demands on their time, they will choose speed and convenience instead of the elegance and variety offered by large regional malls.[61]

Retail Prices

Another important element in the retailing mix is price. The strategy of pricing is explained in Chapters 18 and 19. For now it is important to understand that retailing's ultimate goal is to sell products to final consumers and that the right price is critical in ensuring sales. Because retail prices are usually based on the cost of the merchandise, an essential part of pricing is efficient and timely buying.

Price is a key element in a retail store's positioning strategy and classification. Higher prices often indicate a level of quality and help reinforce the prestigious image of retailers, as they do for Lord & Taylor, Saks Fifth Avenue, Gucci, Cartier, and Neiman Marcus. On the other hand, discounters and off-price retailers offer a good value for the money.

Price is an important lure for U.S. stores on the Canadian border. The majority of Canadians live within 100 miles of the border and average two day trips per person per year into the United States, most of them to shop. Prices at U.S. border stores can run as much as 50 percent lower than prices for the same goods in Canadian stores. Canadian retailers charge higher prices because they have less competition and higher costs. U.S.-made goods sold in Canada must be labeled in French and English, which raises costs. Payrolls, too, are a bigger expense than in the United States, because the minimum wage is higher in Canada. High excise taxes, strict quotas, and stiff import tariffs make it impossible for Canadian retailers to compete with U.S. retailers selling gasoline, alcohol, tobacco, dairy and poultry products, and shoes. As a result, many Canadian retailers are closing their doors while U.S. retailers make a mad dash to the border.[62] To combat this trend, the Canadian government has instituted higher duties for Canadians bringing U.S.-bought goods back into the country. It has also removed tariffs from about twenty-five consumer products so Canadian retailers can reduce prices.[63]

Presentation of the Retail Store

The presentation of a retail store helps determine the store's image. Presentation is used to position the retail store in consumers' minds. For instance, a retailer that wants to position itself as an upscale store would use a lavish or sophisticated presentation.

atmosphere
Overall impression conveyed by a store's physical layout, decor, and surroundings.

The main element of a store's presentation is its **atmosphere**. Atmosphere refers to the overall impression conveyed by a store's physical layout, decor, and surroundings. For example, the atmosphere might create a relaxed or busy feeling, a sense of luxury, a friendly or cold attitude, or a sense of organization or of clutter. For example, the new Nike Town store in Chicago looks more like a museum than a traditional retail store. The three-story space displays products amid life-size Michael Jordan and Bo Jackson statues and glassed-in relics like baseball legend Nolan Ryan's shoes. A "History of Air" exhibit explains those pockets of air on the bottom of its shoes. A video theater plays Nike commercials

and short films featuring Nike gear.[64] These are the most influential factors in creating a store's atmosphere:

- *Employee type and density:* Employee type refers to an employee's general characteristics—for instance, neat, friendly, knowledgeable, or service-oriented. Density is the number of employees per 1,000 square feet of selling space. A discounter like Kmart has a low employee density that creates a "do-it-yourself," casual atmosphere. In contrast, Neiman Marcus's density is much higher, denoting readiness to serve the customer's every whim. Too many employees and not enough customers can convey an air of desperation and intimidate customers.
- *Merchandise type and density:* A prestigious retailer like Saks or Marshall Field's carries the best brand names and displays them in a neat, uncluttered arrangement. Discounters and off-price retailers may sell some well-known brands, but many carry seconds or out-of-season goods. Their merchandise may be stacked so high that it falls into the aisles, helping create the impression that "We've got so much stuff, we're practically giving it away."
- *Fixture type and density:* Fixtures can be elegant (rich woods), trendy (chrome and smoked glass), or old, beat-up tables. The fixtures should be consistent with the general atmosphere the store is trying to create. Retailers should beware of using too many fixtures, since they may confuse the customers about what the store is selling. By displaying its merchandise on tables and shelves rather than on traditional pipe racks, The Gap creates a relaxed and uncluttered atmosphere. The display tables also allow customers to see and touch the merchandise more easily.
- *Sound:* Sound can be pleasant or unpleasant for a customer. Classical music at a nice Italian restaurant helps create ambience, just as country-and-western music does at a truck stop. Music can also entice customers to stay in the store longer and buy more or eat quickly and leave a table for others. Music is likely to have its greatest effect when shoppers are involved in a highly emotional buying decision. For most consumers, that means buying jewelry, sportswear, cosmetics, and beer.[65] Retailers can tailor their musical atmosphere to their shoppers' demographics and the merchandise they're selling. Music can control the pace of the store traffic, create an image, and attract or direct the shopper's attention.[66]
- *Odors:* Smell can either stimulate or detract from sales. The wonderful smell of pastries and breads entices bakery customers. Conversely, bad odors can turn off customers. Examples include cigarettes, musty smells, antiseptic odors, and overly powerful room deodorizers. If a grocery store pumps in the smell of baked goods, sales in that department will increase threefold. Several department stores have tested the effects of pumping in fragrances that are pleasing to their target market.[67]
- *Visual factors:* Colors can create a mood or focus attention and therefore are an important factor in atmosphere. Shoppers are drawn to warm colors like orange and red, yet they feel more comfortable with cool colors like blue and green.[68] Some colors are better for display. For instance, diamonds appear most striking against black or blue velvet. The lighting can also have an important effect on store atmosphere. For instance, jewelry is best displayed under high-intensity spotlights and cosmetics under more natural lighting.[69]

Personnel and Customer Service

People are a unique aspect of retailing. Most retail sales involve a customer-salesperson relationship, if only briefly. When customers shop at a grocery store, the cashiers check and bag their groceries. When customers shop at a prestigious clothier, the sales clerks may help select the styles, sizes, and colors. They may also assist in the fitting process, offer alteration services, wrap purchases, and even offer a glass of champagne. Sales personnel provide their customers with the amount of service prescribed in the retail strategy of the store. For example, Bergdorf-Goodman's men's store in Manhattan is famous for its customer service, which includes sending salespeople to measure customers in their office. Home Depot salespeople—often recruited from the ranks of carpenters and electricians—are encouraged to spend all the time needed with customers, even if it's hours.[70]

Retail salespeople serve another important selling function: They persuade shoppers to buy. They must therefore be able to persuade customers that what they are selling is what the customer needs. Salespeople are trained in two common selling techniques: trading up and suggestive selling. *Trading up* means convincing customers to buy a higher-priced item than they originally intended to buy. However, to avoid selling customers something they do not need or want, salespeople should take care when practicing trading-up techniques. *Suggestive selling,* a common practice among most retailers, seeks to broaden customers' original purchases with related items. For example, McDonald's cashiers may ask customers whether they would like hot apple pie with their hamburger and fries. Suggestive selling should also be founded on helping shoppers recognize true needs rather than selling them unwanted merchandise.

As noted at the beginning of the chapter, the level of service helps in classifying and positioning retail establishments. Managers must set the level of service to be consistent with positioning objectives. The level of service refers to the types of services offered (credit, delivery) and the quality of service. Examples of quality service include fast checkout versus slow checkout and knowledgeable, helpful salespersons versus uninformed, sloppy, and inaccessible clerks. These are some of the factors managers should consider when setting the service level:

- Services offered by the competition
- Type of merchandise handled (furniture and major appliances usually require delivery)
- Socioeconomic characteristics of the target market
- Cost of providing the service
- Price image of the store (a high price usually demands a high level of service)

8 CURRENT PROBLEMS AFFECTING RETAILING

Although retailing is generally profitable, especially for the companies listed in Exhibit 13.1, the industry is not without its difficulties. Besides being in one of the most competitive industries, retailers today face several problems, including ineffective management, too many stores, "category killers," a decrease in consumer shopping, labor problems, and changing demographics.

Proactive management, efficiency, and a thorough understanding of the market are requirements for success in this fiercely competitive arena. Small businesses run by people with a good idea but little experience, training, or capital rarely last even a

year. As one seasoned executive put it, "Retailing is an industry that eats its young." Each year about 11,000 retailers go out of business.[71]

A problem plaguing retailing in general and department stores in particular is too many stores. This excess stems mainly from the overexpansion of chain retailers. The growth of retail space has consistently outstripped both population growth and consumer spending. Nationally, retail space has grown 52 percent in the past decade, to 4.5 billion square feet—18 square feet for every citizen. Meanwhile, retail sales per square foot, a key measure of productivity, has fallen by about 12 percent.[72] Thus, much more retail square footage is available than is needed to serve the population profitably.

Marketing to small, very specific segments (niche marketing) also has the potential to harm traditional department stores and mass merchandisers. The so-called "category killers" offer an enormous selection in a single product category. Financial strength, marketing skill, and reasonably priced merchandise enable them to bully their way into almost any market, however saturated, and meet their profit objectives. This practice, of course, severely squeezes the smaller chains and the few remaining independent department stores.

After the buying frenzy of the 1980s, decreases in the rates of job creation and real income growth have caused consumer spending to slacken in the United States.[73] Consumers have accumulated many goods from the last decade's shopping spree and now have curtailed spending and resumed saving. They now think twice about opening their wallets. Shopping as a form of recreation is also waning. According to a *Wall Street Journal* survey, shopping has become such a chore that more people hate browsing in stores than hate doing housework. Consumers mainly complain that retail shopping is time-consuming. Moreover, they are dissatisfied with poorly trained salespeople, lower-quality merchandise, and outrageous prices.[74]

Another potentially destructive economic trend is the shrinking pool of educated and trained workers. This is the age of computer sophistication, global marketing, and advanced technology. Unfortunately, the number of new workers with the needed skills is gradually declining. Through the 1990s, up to three-fourths of the new labor force will have limited communication skills. Retailing, the third-largest U.S. employer, hires roughly 17 percent of the nation's work force. The implications of a poorly trained work force for this labor-intensive industry are serious. Typically, entry-level sales positions are unglamorous and do not pay well. According to the U.S. Department of Agriculture, average hourly earnings of grocery store employees were just over $7 an hour. Yet retailers must vie with the glamorous high-tech industries and manufacturers for the dwindling supply of skilled labor.[75]

U.S. demographics are also working against the retailing industry. Over the last decade the number of U.S. teenagers between 14 and 17 years old dropped almost 20 percent. With its heavy reliance on young workers, as well as the increased size of many new stores, retailing could be headed for a serious labor crunch. As the president of Publix Supermarkets declared, "The single biggest challenge of the 1990s will be attracting and retaining an adequate staff of qualified workers."[76]

9 WHAT'S IN "STORE" FOR RETAILING'S FUTURE?

Predicting the future is always risky, but technological advancements, a shift in the retailer's role from distribution center to marketer, and global retailing are seen as some of the more important trends for retailing's future.

One "futuristic" device already being used in some stores is the electronic coupon dispenser.
Courtesy of Adweek Magazines

Advanced Store Technology

Several new technologies are emerging in retailing that will profoundly impact the industry. Consider this scenario:

> You enter the store and grab a shopping cart and head for Aisle 1, where the LED cart handle is telling you Tide is on special. As you stroll down the aisle a 3-D Bounty ad dangling from a light fixture catches your eye. But what clinches the sale is a 50 cents-off coupon dispensed from a machine attached to the shelf. In the background the store's own radio station plays, and you hear the adult contemporary version of a popular song fade into an ad for Coca-Cola. At the checkout counter, Headline News is on the monitor. A Snickers commercial flickers on the screen, and you snatch one from an adjacent rack. The clerk scans your purchase of a six-pack of Pepsi-Cola and a coupon machine automatically prints a coupon for Coke to be handed to you with your receipt. As you pull out your debit card to pay the bill, the cash register makes note of your purchases and sends the information to the supermarket's database. Two week's later a letter arrives—with more coupons—welcoming you to the frequent deli meat-buyer club.[77]

This scenario may sound like science fiction, but much of the technology already exists and is in stores or will be rolled out nationally over the next few years. Marketers and food manufacturers like these advanced technologies because the store is the only place where the product, the advertiser's message, and the consumer all come together in one place.

From Distribution Centers to Marketers

Supermarket retailing consultant Glen Terbeek predicts that by the year 2000 retailers, especially supermarkets, will become true marketers rather than marketers that act as distribution centers.[78] For instance, branded packaged goods and staples won't be sold in supermarkets. Instead, they will be delivered directly to consumers

INTERNATIONAL PERSPECTIVES

U.S. Retailing South of the Border

With dismal sales in the past few years, U.S. retailers are looking to Mexico as perhaps the brightest star in their expansion plans—a market that is woefully short of stores by almost any measure. Mexico has just 550 square feet of retail space per 1,000 inhabitants, compared with 19,000 square feet per 1,000 in the United States. At a time of stagnant retail growth in the United States, Mexico's retail sales have been growing at twice the rate of its economy and could soar even further with completion of the North American Free Trade Agreement. It's no wonder, then, that U.S. retailers are hailing Mexico City as one of retail's last frontiers: a city of 20 million inhabitants with only as much mall space as Toledo, Ohio.

Growth prospects have already attracted such major retail players as Kmart, Wall-Mart, and Price Company, which have recently formed joint ventures with Mexican retailers. Wal-Mart's Sam's Club store, opened under a joint venture with Mexican retailer Cifra SA, has recorded higher sales per square foot than any other Sam's outlet anywhere. U.S. franchises operating in Mexico have flourished as well, quadrupling in number to more than 100 since 1990. One Arby's restaurant franchise does $2 million a year in sales, more than any other Arby's.

The potential market in Mexico is enticing. Half of Mexico's population is under the age of 20. Although per capita income is only $2,200 a year, the richest 10 to 15 percent of the population are wealthier than most U.S. citizens. Developers of a 400-store mall in Mexico found that 12 percent of the surrounding residents had incomes above $65,000 and that 20 percent owned five to six cars.

Like pioneers anywhere, U.S. retailers entering Mexico face many problems. For instance, a franchisee opening a Pizza Inn outlet in Mexico was required to obtain seventeen permits, compared to just two in the United States. Bureaucracy isn't the only obstacle. Real estate prices in Mexico City rival those of New York's Fifth Avenue. Marketing information hardly exists. Thousands of sidewalk and street markets pose fierce competition while incurring no overhead. And Mexico's retailing culture—where U.S. fast food is fare for the wealthy and supermarkets sell everything from milk and eggs to office furniture—still has many U.S. retailers baffled.

Most U.S. retailers entering Mexico have teamed up with local partners for help in targeting potential customers. For example, Dallas's Page Boy Maternity started five Mexican clothing shops through a licensing agreement with a local investor. The retailer has learned through talking with Mexican customers that most are housewives rather than the professional group Page Boy targets in the United States. As a result, Page Boy outlets in Mexico feature sportier styles than those sold in U.S. Page Boy stores.

A new retailing success south of the border is one of the first U.S. department stores in Mexico: Sears, Roebuck & Company. Opened in 1947, Sears de Mexico has flourished in the past few years in large part because of an aggressive management team. They have transformed the fading retailer into a fashionable department store for Mexico's growing professional class. At the end of the 1980s, however, Sears wasn't living up to its Mexican customers' expectations. Sears had to choose between getting serious about Mexico or getting out of the market. Sears got serious. It targeted the affluent top tenth of the Mexican population by upgrading its stores with marble floors and tastefully subdued lighting. Sears de Mexico stores now sell styles by Nina Ricci, fragrances by Guerlain, and shoes by Bally.[79]

at home, within fifteen minutes of an order's placement, freeing shoppers to visit stores for things they enjoy buying—fresh produce, meats, or the fixings for a dinner party. Consumers who need staples would use hand scanners to record products' bar codes and update electronic shopping lists. Magazine ads would also carry bar codes so consumers could scan pages to put new products on their lists.

With the boring parts of grocery shopping taken care of almost automatically, consumers should then focus on the part of shopping that is fun. Supermarkets would sell solutions rather than ingredients. For instance, the products for a spaghetti dinner would all be grouped in one part of the store. Other possible solutions would be the categories "kids' lunch," "diet," "bridge club," "tight budget," or "new and exciting." Several merchants in the Netherlands already follow this practice. A poultry shop, for instance, will sell all the ingredients needed to cook a complete meal.

The explosion of warehouse clubs already shows that consumers want a more convenient way to do the shopping they don't enjoy. Other industries have already taken steps to improve convenience. Automatic teller machines have made visiting the bank unnecessary. Pizza delivery service has eliminated the need to go to the pizzeria. Mail-order pharmacies have grown into a billion-dollar business, with some 70 percent of all prescriptions now being refilled by mail. It's just a matter of time before supermarkets follow.

Global Retailing

Retailing is becoming more global. Major retailers are expanding their operations into Western Europe, Eastern Europe, Russia, Mexico, and Japan. Global expansion is becoming easier and more appealing. For example, retailers see attractive opportunities in a United Europe and in the newly capitalistic societies of Eastern Europe and Russia.

Franchises are also seeking new growth abroad, especially in emerging nations like Mexico, Turkey, and Venezuela. In fact, the U.S. government is making it easier to open franchises in developing countries by guaranteeing 50 percent of foreign loans for foreign franchise locations.[80] Franchising is popular in Eastern European countries, too. Pizza Hut recently opened its first franchise in Hungary and regularly has as many as 150 customers lined up outside. Fifteen more Pizza Huts will open in Hungary, as well as twenty-two KFC and forty Dunkin' Donuts outlets.[81]

In Asia, China and Japan are also relaxing trade and retailing restrictions, making their countries likely targets for U.S. retailers. The first McDonald's franchise outlet in China was an overnight success, and Domino's Pizza plans to open outlets in the Guangdong region near Hong Kong.[82] As mentioned earlier, Japan has recently relaxed retail laws, making it easier for large retailers like Toys R Us to locate among the traditional mom-and-pop stores.

LOOKING BACK

Think back now to the opening story about Home Depot. What are the elements of its retailing strategy? You will probably be quick to point out Home Depot's broad assortment of home improvement products, from paint and nails to greenhouses and lawn mowers, presented in a "help yourself" environment. Low prices are another part of its retail strategy. Also readily apparent is its commitment to customer service, as seen in the training classes and advice it provides. Finally, the chain clusters store locations around large cities. Given your understanding of retailing, you can now probably quickly list the retail strategies of many other successful retailers, such as Nordstrom, Wal-Mart, Toys R Us, and Food Lion.

KEY TERMS

atmosphere 430
buyer 410
chain store 407
convenience store 414
department store 410

SUMMARY

1 Discuss the importance of retailing in the U.S. economy. Retailing plays a vital role in the U.S. economy for two main reasons. First, retail businesses contribute to our high standard of living by providing a vast number and diversity of goods and services. Second, retailing employs a large part of the U.S. working population—over 18 million people.

direct marketing 419
direct retailing 418
discount store 415
factory outlet 407
franchise 423
franchisee 423
franchise outlet 417
franchisor 423
gross margin 408
hypermarket 414
independent retailer 407
mass merchandising 411
nonstore retailing 417
off-price retailer 416
retailing 406
retailing mix 425
scrambled merchandising 413
specialty store 412
supermarket 413
telemarketing 421
vending 417

❷ **List the dimensions by which retailers can be classified.** Many different kinds of retailers exist. They can be differentiated on the basis of ownership, level of service, product assortment, and general price levels.

❸ **Explain the wheel of retailing concept.** The wheel of retailing concept illustrates a common pattern in the retail industry. A retailer that begins as a low-cost, low-price operator eventually upgrades and increases prices. The resulting gap in the market's lower end is filled by new retailers that perpetuate the cycle. Although the theory helps to explain the patterns of change in retailing, it does not apply to all retailers or to all aspects of retailing.

❹ **Describe the major types of retail operations.** The major types of retail stores are department store, mass merchandiser, specialty store, supermarket, and discount store. Department stores carry a wide assortment of shopping and specialty goods, are organized into relatively independent departments, and offset higher prices by emphasizing customer service and decor. Mass-merchandising shopping chains resemble department stores but have a faster turnover of merchandise, lower prices, and less customer service. Specialty retailers typically carry a narrower but deeper assortment of merchandise, emphasizing distinctive products and a high level of customer service. Supermarkets are large self-service retailers that offer a wide variety of food products and some nonfood items. Two variations of supermarkets are hypermarkets, which combine a supermarket with a discount department store, and convenience stores, which carry a limited line of high-turnover convenience goods. Finally, discount stores offer low-priced general merchandise and consist of four types: full-line discounters, discount specialty retailers, membership clubs, and off-price retailers.

❺ **List nonstore retailing techniques.** Nonstore retailing, which is shopping outside a store setting, has three major categories: vending; direct retailing; and direct marketing, which includes direct mail, catalog and mail order, telemarketing, and electronic retailing.

❻ **Describe the nature of franchising.** Modern franchising takes two basic forms: product and trade name franchising and business format franchising. In product and trade name franchising, a dealer agrees to buy or sell certain products or product lines from a particular manufacturer or wholesaler. Business format franchising is an ongoing business relationship in which a franchisee uses a franchisor's name, format, or method of business in return for several types of fees.

❼ **List the major tasks involved in developing a retail marketing strategy.** Retail management begins with defining the target market, typically on the basis of demographic, geographic, or psychographic characteristics. After determining the target market, retail managers must develop the six variables of the retailing mix: product, promotion, place, price, presentation, and personnel.

❽ **List present problems in retailing.** Problems plaguing the retailing industry are ineffective management, too many stores, "category killers," a decrease in consumer shopping, labor problems, and changing demographics.

❾ **List future trends in retailing.** Future trends in retailing include technological advances in in-store promotions, a shift of retailers from distribution centers to marketers, and increased global retailing.

Review Questions

1. Describe the general characteristics used to classify retail operations. Cite examples of the types of retailers that have these characteristics.
2. According to the wheel of retailing concept, many retailers eventually upgrade. What factors influence retailers to upgrade?
3. What strategies are department stores implementing to compete in the 1990s?
4. Describe the advantages of franchising from the perspectives of the franchisee and the franchisor.
5. What are the pros and cons of freestanding locations and shopping center and mall locations for retail stores?
6. What market conditions have made retailing one of today's most competitive industries?

Discussion and Writing Questions

1. Explain the function of warehouse clubs. Why are they classified as both wholesalers and retailers?
2. You want to convince your boss, the owner of a retail store, of the importance of store atmosphere. Write a memo citing specific examples of how store atmosphere affects your own shopping behavior.
3. Identify a successful retail business in your community. What marketing strategies have led to its success?
4. Why is retailing said to be "an industry that eats its young"?
5. You have been asked to write a brief article about the way consumer demand for convenience is influencing the future of retailing. Write the outline for your article.
6. Discuss the potential challenges of international retailing.

CASES

13.1 Ann Taylor Stores

Once considered the mecca for sophisticated, urban career women, Ann Taylor Stores has stumbled on some bad times. The Ann Taylor chain became a fixture in upscale malls around the country in the 1980s, thanks to its shrewd targeting of urban working women. The specialty clothier experienced astonishing growth during the eighties. In 1989, same-store sales (sales at stores open at least one year) grew over 14 percent. Then the company unraveled. In 1990, same-store sales inched ahead only 2 percent, and the following year same-store sales dropped almost 6 percent. For its fiscal year ending in February 1992, the company reported a net loss of $15.8 million on sales of $437.7 million.

In part, Ann Taylor's troubles reflect the demise of the dress-for-success uniform insisted on by businesswomen in the 1980s. Back then, a boxy suit, silk blouse, and pearls were standard workday dress for businesswomen. But in the 1990s, working women wear just about anything from walking shorts to print dresses. Ann Taylor's management failed to recognize this trend soon enough and continued manufacturing merchandise that doesn't fit in with the working woman's new relaxed style.

Ann Taylor compounded its problems with a series of financial and marketing missteps. To pay down its heavy debt load, the company resorted to a maneuver that would prove disastrous: Suppliers were told to produce goods more cheaply, and stores were told to sell them at a higher markup. The standard markup on the company's apparel increased from 45 percent to as high as 65 percent. An astounding number of loyal Ann Taylor customers noticed the higher prices and the second-rate merchandise and complained to the company. Many abandoned the specialty retailer altogether, finding plenty of other options available.

Ann Taylor stores also embarked on a costly and overly ambitious expansion strategy. Between 1989 and 1991, Ann Taylor grew from 139 stores to 200 stores. The drastic growth in such a short time added greatly to Ann Taylor's already overloaded debt.

In 1992, Ann Taylor appointed a new chairman and CEO, who launched a major new strategy to mend the chain's torn image. Through a joint manufacturing venture, Ann Taylor is starting to produce higher-quality goods at a lower cost. The store's inventory of mostly private-label merchandise now comes in finer wools, silks, and cottons—replacing the rayons and polyester blends that had become the standard. To entice today's more casually attired working women, Ann Taylor now devotes a third of its merchandise to weekend wear. Prices have also been cut across the

board. For instance, a wool and cashmere blazer now goes for $178, down from $198 in 1992; silk blouses are $78, down from $98. The chain has also curbed its empire building. Instead, it will focus on improving existing stores, with many outlets being enlarged to accommodate the retailer's expanded array of merchandise.

Although it remains to be seen whether these changes will turn Ann Taylor around, the chain has committed itself to getting back to the basics of selling quality merchandise. The main challenge for Ann Taylor now is to woo back the thousands of customers who have written off the chain.

Questions

1. Reversing sales declines will be less painful for Ann Taylor in newer locations, where customers are less likely to have had bad experiences. Courting former customers will take time. If you were Ann Taylor's new CEO, what would be your message to once-loyal Ann Taylor customers to get them to reconsider the chain?
2. To regain consumer confidence, analysts believe Ann Taylor will be forced to announce its changes with heavy advertising. The company has traditionally done little advertising, however, relying more on catalogs and direct mail to the million or so Ann Taylor charge-account customers. As CEO, how would you promote the changes at Ann Taylor? Defend your answer.
3. Ann Taylor made a serious fashion blunder by failing to recognize the needs and wants of its target market. Write a detailed description of who you think Ann Taylor's target market is. Include demographic, sociological, and psychological descriptors, if possible.
4. Given the target market description you developed for question 3, draft a marketing plan describing a new retail strategy in terms of product, price, promotion, place, presentation, and personnel.

Suggested Reading

Teri Agins, "Ann Taylor Aims to Resew Torn Image," *The Wall Street Journal*, 14 September 1992, pp. B1, B5.

13.2 Subway

Video title: *The Subway Franchising System*

Subway
325 Bic Drive
Milford, CT 06460

SIC code: 5812 Submarine sandwich shops

Number of outlets: Over 7,000

Franchise fee: $7,500 ($40,000 total investment required, with financing available)

Major brands: Subway sandwiches

Largest competitors: McDonald's, Burger King, PepsiCo (Pizza Hut, Taco Bell, Kentucky Fried Chicken)

Background

Subway was founded in 1965 and began franchising operations in 1974. Subway is one of the fastest-growing franchise operations in the United States. The secret to this rapid growth is the low franchise fee, low required investment, and ease of store operations. The only equipment needed to open a Subway franchise is bread-baking equipment, two freezers, and a soda-dispensing machine. This equipment can all fit in a relatively small space, and so store overhead is very low. In addition, Subway offers its franchisees one of the most attractive franchise packages around. Each new franchise owner receives a two-week training program in store operations, personnel management, and marketing.

Industry

Restaurant spending is increasing at the rate of about 5 percent per year. Some of this growth can be attributed to the value focus of many restaurants. Most of the big fast-food restaurants now feature lower-priced value items. Supermarkets are also trying to tap into the prepared-food takeout market by offering salad bars and expanded deli services.

Demographic trends in the United States are likely to have a major impact on the restaurant business. Two significant factors are the aging population and the rising birth rate. As consumers age, they move away from fast-food restaurants toward midscale restaurants. These aging consumers also have an interest in eating healthful foods. Larger family size means that families are more likely to eat at home.

Subway

Sandwich shops have the unique advantage of being able to vary their product line without changing their identity or making extensive capital investments. Also, in today's health-conscious world, sandwiches offer a light and healthy alternative to the more traditional offerings of other fast-food outlets.

The key problem facing sandwich shops like Subway is attracting the non-lunch customer. Typically, people see Subway as a good place for lunch, not dinner. By promoting hot sandwiches, like the meatball sub, these stores hope to bring in dinner business. The company is also exploring some breakfast items. Another good marketing opportunity for submarine sandwich outlets has always been catering. What could possibly be better for a large informal party than a gigantic submarine sandwich?

Adapting the menu to local markets is another strength at Subway. Subway allows its franchisees the opportunity to add up to two sandwiches to the corporate list. These sandwiches are tailored to local tastes. For example, Subway outlets in Alaska have added caribou sandwiches to the menu. Stores in Bahrain offer lamb to their customers. By allowing franchisees to meet the local market demand, Subway continues to be one of the fastest-growing franchises in the world.

Questions

1. Discuss the advantages that Subway offers its franchisees. What advantages does Subway gain through having these franchisees?
2. What can Subway do to more effectively compete with the larger fast-food companies, such as McDonald's and Burger King?

References

Carol Casper, "Sub and Sandwich Market Segment Report," *Restaurant Business,* 10 December 1991, p. 121.

Susan Boyles Martin (ed.), *Worldwide Franchise Directory* (Detroit: Gale Research, 1991).

Standard & Poor's Industry Surveys (New York: Standard & Poor's Corporation, October 1993).

13.3 *Decision Assistant:* Bonita Corporation

The Situation

The president of the Bonita Corporation is trying to decide how much to emphasize the various types of retail stores that make up the channel used to distribute its products. It uses small specialty shops, traditional department stores, and discount department stores.

Bonita's president has found that each type of store seems to do better under different economic conditions. For example, when the economy is growing, specialty stores sell the most merchandise, followed by department stores and discount department stores. When the economy is declining, discount department stores sell the most merchandise, followed by traditional department stores and then specialty shops. When the economy is steady, traditional department stores do best, followed by specialty stores and then discount department stores.

Since the productive capacity of the Bonita Corporation is limited, it is important for the president to choose how to distribute the product line so as to maximize profit. The president has prepared Exhibit 13.6, which lists the estimated profits that each option will generate given a particular economic condition.

The president also estimates, based on an interpretation of the economic forecasts, that the probability of the economy growing next year is 40 percent, the probability of it declining is 35 percent, and the probability of it staying even is 25 percent. Your task is to demonstrate which stores should receive the most emphasis in the coming year.

The Solution Technique

Since the president needs to choose one of several options, and since the president has estimated the probability of the three economic states, the appropriate technique to use is decision theory. Use the Decision Tree tool in the marketing *Decision Assistant* to aid you. Key ALT-D for a table of expected outcomes under each option, or key ALT-G for a tree that graphically shows the same information.

Exhibit 13.6

Expected Profits under Different Economic States

Strategy options	Economic growth	Economic stability	Economic decline
Emphasize specialty stores	$370,000	$315,000	$220,000
Emphasize department stores	330,000	340,000	250,000
Emphasize discount stores	290,000	305,000	275,000

What If?

Consider each of the following situations independently:

1. What decision should be made if the likelihood of the three economic conditions was changed to 50 percent for growth, 40 percent for stability, and 10 percent for decline?

2. What decision should be made if expected sales, given an emphasis on specialty shops, were changed to $350,000 under conditions of growth, $335,000 under conditions of stability, and $235,000 under conditions of decline?

3. What changes in the probabilities or payoffs would make the discount store the best option?

CHAPTER 14

Physical Distribution Management

LEARNING OBJECTIVES

After studying this chapter, you should be able to

1. Explain the importance of physical distribution.
2. Discuss the concept of balancing physical distribution service and costs.
3. Describe the parts of the physical distribution system.
4. Identify the special problems and opportunities associated with physical distribution in service organizations.
5. Discuss new technology and emerging trends in physical distribution.

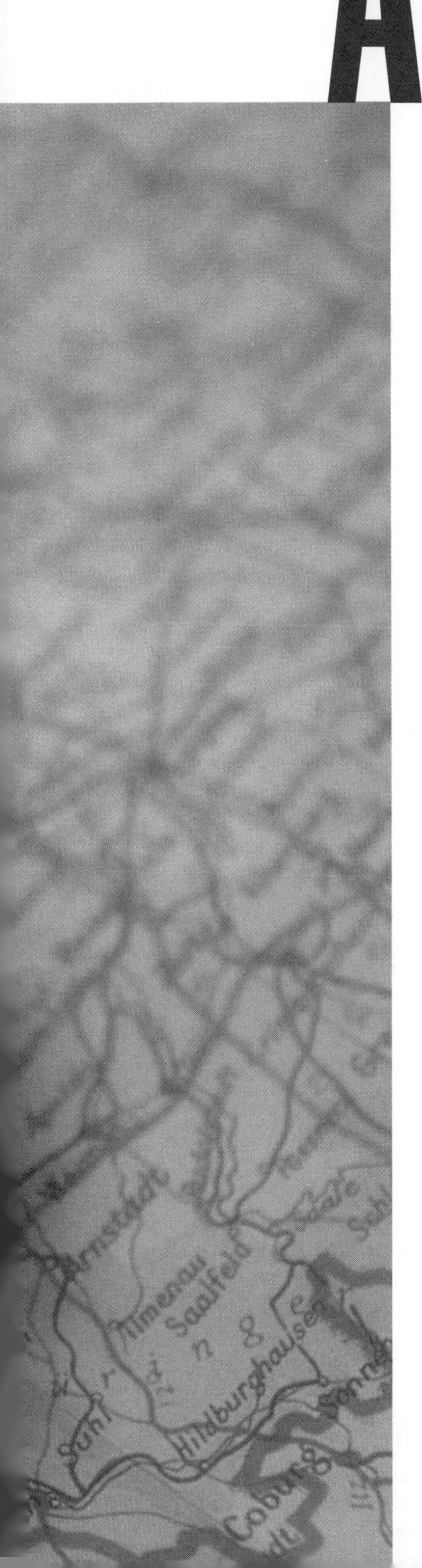

As distribution challenges go, shipping live lobsters ranks right up there. Yet in Halifax, Nova Scotia, capital of Canadian lobster exports, they have it down to a science. A thoroughly planned, tightly coordinated distribution system—stretching from Halifax to air freight gateways in Canada, the United States, Europe, and the Far East—makes it possible for discriminating diners in Tokyo or Paris to feast on crustaceans that were caught less than forty-eight hours before.

Lobster fishermen rely heavily on both domestic and international airlines to help them service the marketplace, wherever it may be. Lobster buyers want 8 a.m. delivery so they can get the lobsters to restaurants in time for lunch and dinner. Air Canada is one airline that has developed expertise in the handling of this delicate product. The airline provides cooler facilities, fast turnaround at destination, and other services that put it a cut above some of its competitors. For example, Air Canada has the quickest turnaround at London's Heathrow Airport, a major transshipment point for lobsters destined for European plates. On Air Canada flights, the crustaceans can clear customs and be made available to customers just over one hour after the plane lands—versus four to six hours for other airlines.

About 80 percent of Canada's lobster harvest is shipped south to the United States. But while the U.S. price per pound for lobster is at its lowest in thirty years, the international market for lobster, where margins are higher, is growing briskly. The market in the Far East tripled in the last five years, while the European market has doubled. The development of a reliable distribution infrastructure that enables shippers to get lobster to overseas customers therefore plays a significant role. To do this requires exacting procedures on the part of both the lobster merchants and their air freight partners. Lobsters must arrive alive at their final destination. A lobster will typically survive thirty to forty hours outside of water but is very sensitive to heat and wind. This sensitivity to its environment, therefore, puts a premium on effective packaging.

For shipments across the North Atlantic, lobsters are packed into waxed corrugated boxes with styrofoam liners and are kept cool with wet newspapers and frozen gel packs. Air Canada then adjusts the temperature on the upper deck of its freighter to the thirty-eight degrees that lobsters seem to favor. For shipments to Japan, Air Canada flies the lobster to either Los Angeles or San Francisco, where the cargo is handed over to Japan Air Lines for the final leg of the trip. For these longer flights (travel time to Japan from Halifax is about thirty hours) temperature control is critical, so lobsters often travel in style: insulated containers that have a separate compartment for dry ice (CO_2). As the dry ice melts, the cool air is pumped into the lobsters' compartment, and the CO_2 is pumped out of the container. Once the lobsters hit the ground in Japan, they are rushed back into holding tanks to await delivery to Japanese restaurants.

Cooperation between the shipper and the carrier is important to the smooth distribution of such time-sensitive goods as lobsters. Is cooperation just as important in shipping goods that aren't time-sensitive? What other goods can you think of that require special handling during distribution? How do distribution managers decide which method of transportation is best?

Source: Adapted from Jay Gordon, "The Logistics of Lobster," *Distribution*, October 1991, pp. 38–40.

1 THE IMPORTANCE OF PHYSICAL DISTRIBUTION

physical distribution
Ingredient in the marketing mix that describes how products are moved and stored.

logistics
Procurement and management of raw materials for production.

logistics management
Overseeing the movement of raw materials and finished products to intermediaries or end consumers.

Physical distribution is the ingredient in the marketing mix that describes how products are moved and stored. Physical distribution consists of all business activities concerned with stocking and transporting raw materials or finished inventory so they arrive at the right place when needed and in usable condition.

A broader term that encompasses physical distribution is **logistics**, which also includes the procurement and management of raw materials for production. **Logistics management** includes these activities:

- Managing the movement and storage of raw materials and parts from their sources to production site
- Managing the movement of raw materials, semimanufactured products, and finished products within and among plants, warehouses, and distribution centers
- Planning and coordinating the physical distribution of finished goods to intermediaries and final buyers

In summary, logistics managers are responsible for directing raw materials to the production department and the finished or semifinished product through warehouses and eventually to the intermediary or end user. Exhibit 14.1 depicts the logistics process. Most of this chapter is about the distribution of goods within warehouses and to final users.

Physical Distribution and the Marketing Concept

Because it can decrease costs and increase customer satisfaction, physical distribution is a central part of the marketing concept. It creates the time and place utility so important to consumers; they value receiving the products they want, when they want them, and where they want them. Physical distribution also broadens the variety of goods available to consumers. Few people would own a Volkswagen if they had to go to Germany to buy one. Similarly, consumers can buy a Lands' End sweater for the same price anywhere in the United States, even though the sweaters are shipped from Wisconsin. Physical distribution not only provides a greater variety of goods but also broadens the area of competition.

Logistics and physical distribution are becoming more important in marketing strategies for both changing markets and existing markets. Instead of differentiating themselves from rivals on price or product superiority, organizations are achieving

The most successful companies invest in quality distribution systems, to make sure the product gets to the right places in a timely manner. Shown here is The Gap's new high-tech distribution center outside Baltimore, which channels the chain's clothing to East Coast stores.

Exhibit 14.1

The Logistics Process

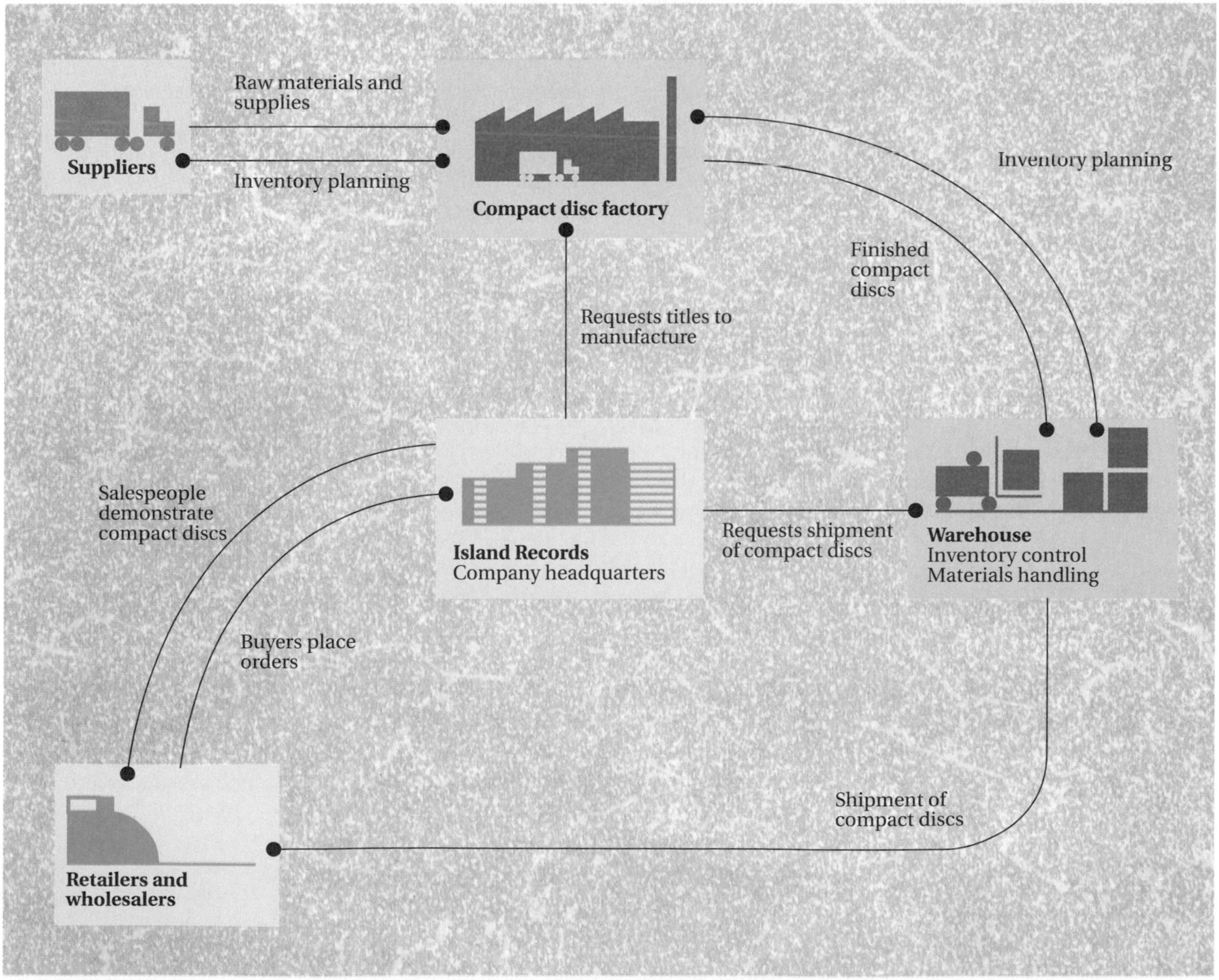

Suppliers

Raw materials and supplies

Inventory planning

Compact disc factory

Inventory planning

Finished compact discs

Requests titles to manufacture

Salespeople demonstrate compact discs

Island Records
Company headquarters

Requests shipment of compact discs

Warehouse
Inventory control
Materials handling

Buyers place orders

Shipment of compact discs

Retailers and wholesalers

an advantage through more effective physical distribution, especially in markets with standardized products. They can enhance physical distribution by shortening the time needed for storage, handling, and transportation of products.

Distribution planning is crucial. Companies often find out too late about the obstacles that may hinder the distribution of their products. The article at the bottom of this page reveals the distribution problems experienced by Merck when it tried to provide drugs to those inflicted with a debilitating disease.

The Role of the Physical Distribution Manager

The need for better service and cost control in a competitive environment underscores the importance of distribution. Physical distribution managers' scope of authority and responsibility has broadened to meet the challenge. Distribution managers do periodic strategy audits to strengthen their departments. The issues that concern them include the levels of service expected by customers, service levels achieved by competitors, warehouse and plant location, and technological and regulatory developments.

INTERNATIONAL PERSPECTIVES

A Distribution Challenge for Merck

In 1987, Merck shocked the pharmaceutical industry with a promise to give away millions of doses of a drug to treat a Third World disease called "river blindness." The announcement got great publicity, but the pharmaceutical giant soon discovered that giving away the medicine was an even tougher challenge than selling it. By 1992, the drug had only reached about 5 percent of the more than 100 million people who either had or were at risk for the disease. What hampered the giveaway was an inadequate distribution infrastructure and rough terrain in the Third World countries targeted to receive the drug.

River blindness is caused by a parasite carried by black flies. It afflicts 17 million people and threatens 90 million more, mostly in Central and West Africa and in limited areas of Central and South America. The disease causes a slow deterioration of eyesight that eventually becomes total blindness. In addition to its destructive effects on humans, the disease has taken a social and economic toll. Entire communities must flee fertile lands near rivers to escape black-fly infestation.

Although Merck's drug was originally formulated to treat parasites in animals, scientists discovered that it could be a formidable foe against river blindness. Merck then faced the daunting task of getting the drug to people who live in some of the world's poorest regions without the means to buy it at any price. Merck's solution was to donate the drug. But first, the company had to figure out how to transport the medicine to the remote villages where the disease had hit hardest. Many of these villages were accessible only on foot. Trucks couldn't be sent until laborers cleared the brush for crude roads. Without bridges, medical workers often had to cross fast-flowing rivers in primitive boats. These efforts were costly as well as dangerous for workers involved in the distribution.

Although Merck is giving the drug away free of charge, some countries still can't afford to distribute it to those in need simply because they don't have workers, vehicles, or fuel. Those that do have the money to hire workers and buy trucks to deliver the medicine are still hindered by primitive roads or no roads at all. They have the same problems with diseases like yellow fever (although the vaccine is very cheap), which kill many people because of the difficulties in distributing treatments into the bush and jungle.[1]

Can you think of any other methods of transportation that Merck might use to distribute its medicine to those in need? What distribution planning do you suppose Merck performed prior to its giveaway? Should Merck continue the giveaway despite the obstacles it has encountered?

② THE BALANCE BETWEEN SERVICE AND COSTS

Physical distribution encompasses many activities, but only recently have all these activities been combined in a single department. As distribution departments have evolved, their emphasis has changed from getting the lowest transportation rates to the broader issue of minimizing total distribution costs. Those costs are both explicit (for example, actual costs associated with distribution) and implicit (for example, missed opportunities, such as lost sales due to slow delivery systems).

The main goal of physical distribution is getting the right goods to the right place at the right time for the least cost. Unfortunately, few physical distribution systems can both maximize customer service and minimize distribution costs. The best customer service requires large inventories and rapid transportation, which drive up costs. Although reduced inventories and slower transportation may lower distribution costs, they can also result in customer dissatisfaction. Distribution managers, therefore, strive for a reasonable balance between customer service and total distribution costs.

Physical Distribution Service

physical distribution service
Interrelated activities performed by a supplier to ensure that the right product is in the right place at the right time.

Physical distribution service is the package of activities performed by a supplier to ensure that the right product is in the right place at the right time. Customers are rarely interested in the activities themselves; instead, they are interested in the results or the benefits they receive from those activities—namely, efficient distribution. Specifically, customers are concerned with how long it takes to receive an order and how consistent delivery is, how much effort it takes to place an order, and what condition the product is in when it is finally received. Order processing, order assembly, and delivery are of no consequence to the buyer. What matter most are the quality and timeliness of the supplier's performance.[2]

When setting service levels, physical distribution managers must be sensitive to their customers' needs. At the most basic level, customers demand product availability, timeliness in order processing and delivery, and acceptable distribution quality. *Availability* is the proportion or percentage of orders that can be completely filled right away. Unavailable goods must be back ordered, causing time delays and extra costs, or the customer can simply cancel the order. *Timeliness* in physical distribution service is, for the buyer, minimal time elapsed between placing the order and receiving it. *Quality* is a low incidence of in-transit damage, shipment of incorrect items, and incorrect shipment quantity.[3]

How does a distribution manager actually set the level of service? There are four possible strategies. With the first, a firm might decide to cut costs to the bone and eliminate service entirely. In this case, the distribution manager's main concern is storing, handling, and transporting the product at the least cost possible. Second, a firm may offer maximum service at any cost. Because this strategy is so expensive, it is very seldom followed.

The third strategy determines the level of service as the point at which the sum of the costs of being out of stock and carrying inventory is at its lowest point. This approach assumes that service is synonymous with inventory levels and that customers become dissatisfied when a product is not in stock. The cost of being out of stock (**stockout cost**) includes direct costs due to lost sales and indirect costs due to the loss of dissatisfied customers. The graph in Exhibit 14.2 illustrates this concept. As you can see, stockout costs are highest when inventory levels are kept at a minimum. Conversely, when excess inventory is maintained, then inventory carrying costs are high.

stockout cost
Cost of being out of stock, which includes direct costs due to lost sales and indirect costs due to the loss of dissatisfied customers.

Exhibit 14.2

How to Set the Service Level at the Least Cost

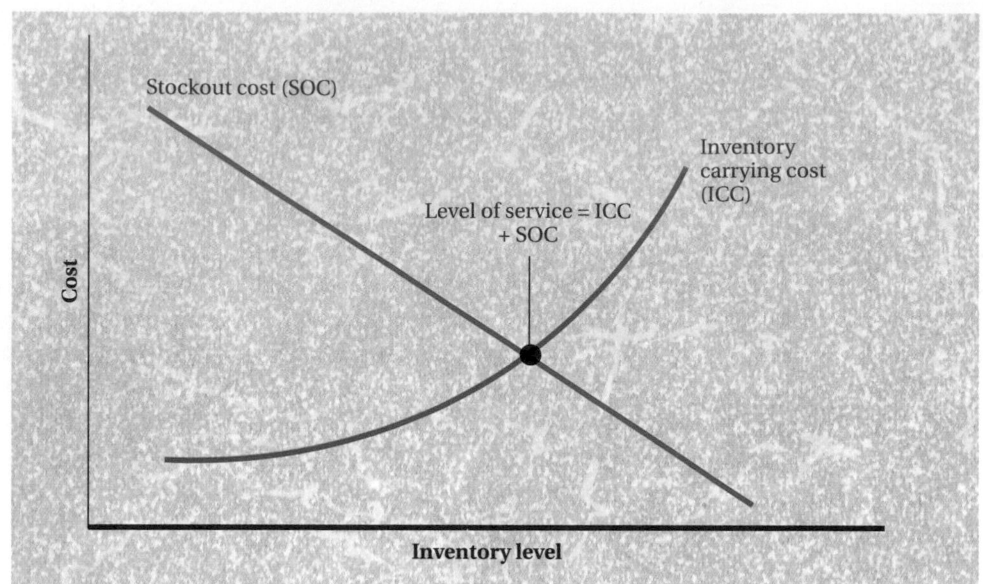

The fourth strategy is to seek a competitive advantage. The firm sets physical distribution service at a level just slightly higher than the competition's. Whirlpool's Quality Express product delivery system is an excellent example of how time-sensitive logistics can help establish or maintain a competitive advantage. Whirlpool, KitchenAid, Roper, and Estate brand household appliances are delivered to 90 percent of the company's dealer and builder customers within twenty-four hours and to the other 10 percent within forty-eight hours. The Quality Express philosophy is to deliver products to customers when, where, and how they want them. Delivery drivers unload the appliances from the trucks and put them exactly where the customer wants them. The service also offers uncrating, customizing, and installation services. Appliance dealers don't have to tie up as much capital in inventory since the product can be delivered within one day of the order. Builders don't have to worry about theft or damage since the appliances are delivered at preset times.[4]

What is the most important factor in physical distribution service? A survey of shippers showed that on-time delivery and pickup are most important. Late deliveries often translate into lost revenues. Someone is listening: On-time deliveries increased from 81 percent in 1985 to 92 percent in 1990.[5]

Total Distribution Costs

Most distribution managers try to set their service level goals at a point that maximizes service yet minimizes cost. For maximum customer service to be achieved at the lowest cost, the total cost of all parts of the physical distribution system—warehousing, materials management, inventory, order processing, and transportation—must be examined using the total cost approach. The basic idea is to examine the relationship of such factors as number of warehouses, finished-goods inventory, and transportation expenses. Of course, the cost of any single element should also be examined in relation to the level of customer service. Thus the physical distribution system is viewed as a whole, not as a series of unrelated activities.

Often the high cost of air transportation can be justified under the total cost approach. Rapid delivery may drastically reduce the number of warehouses required at distant locations. Therefore, the higher cost of using air freight may be more than justified by the savings in inventory and warehouse expenses, as shown in Exhibit 14.3.

Exhibit 14.3

How Air Freight Lowers Distribution Costs under the Total Cost Approach

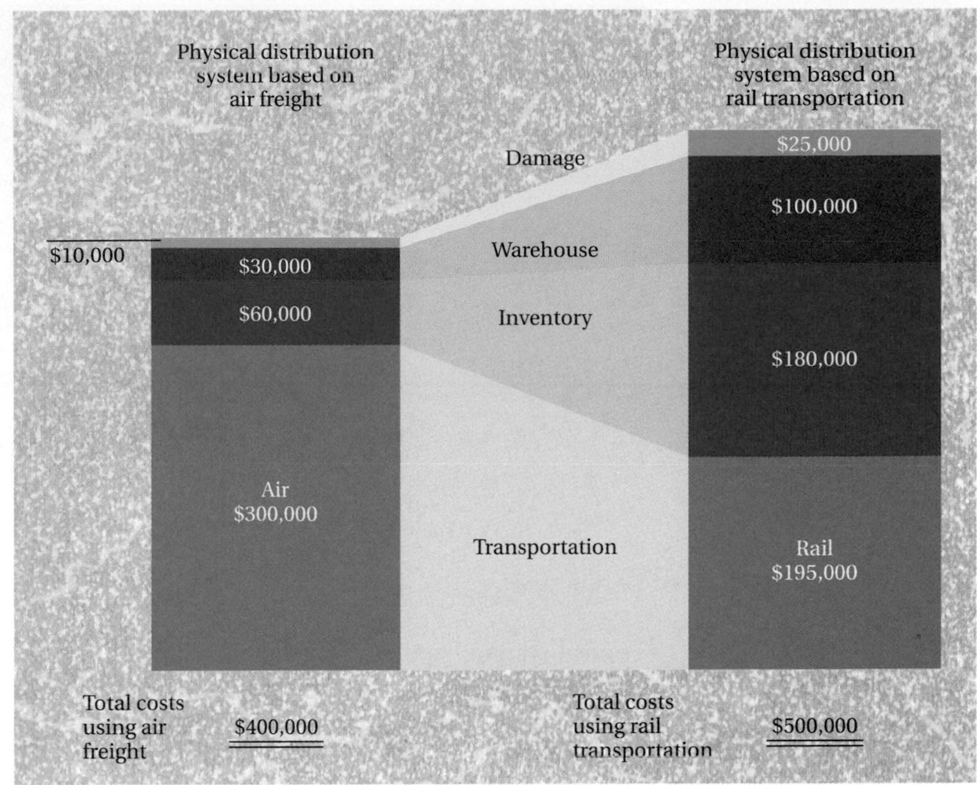

Implementing the total cost approach requires trade-offs. For example, a supplier that wants to provide next-day delivery to its customers and also minimize transportation costs must make a trade-off between the desired level of service (expensive next-day delivery) and the transportation goal (minimal costs). Setting a new service standard of delivery, perhaps two-day delivery instead of next-day, or accepting the high cost of delivery are the options available.

Ideally, the distribution manager would like to optimize overall distribution performance—that is, to balance distribution activities so that overall distribution costs are minimized while the desired level of physical distribution service is maintained. If attempts to minimize costs and maximize service don't work, the result is *suboptimization.* The problem may be a conflict between physical distribution components. For instance, the transportation people may want to provide customers with same-day delivery, but the order-processing people may take two to three days to process an order.

Suboptimization often occurs in physical distribution because in most cases different managers oversee the distribution functions. For example, inventory management may be under production, and order processing may be assigned to accounting. More than likely, these managers have different goals for customer service and costs. The only cure is for top management to recognize the role of logistics and physical distribution in helping the firm reach its overall objectives and to build better coordination into the organizational structure.

❸ PHYSICAL DISTRIBUTION SUBSYSTEMS

The physical distribution system consists of five distinct subsystems that serve several key functions: deciding on warehouse location, number, size, and type; setting up a materials-handling and packaging system; maintaining an inventory

Exhibit 14.4

The Subsystems of Physical Distribution

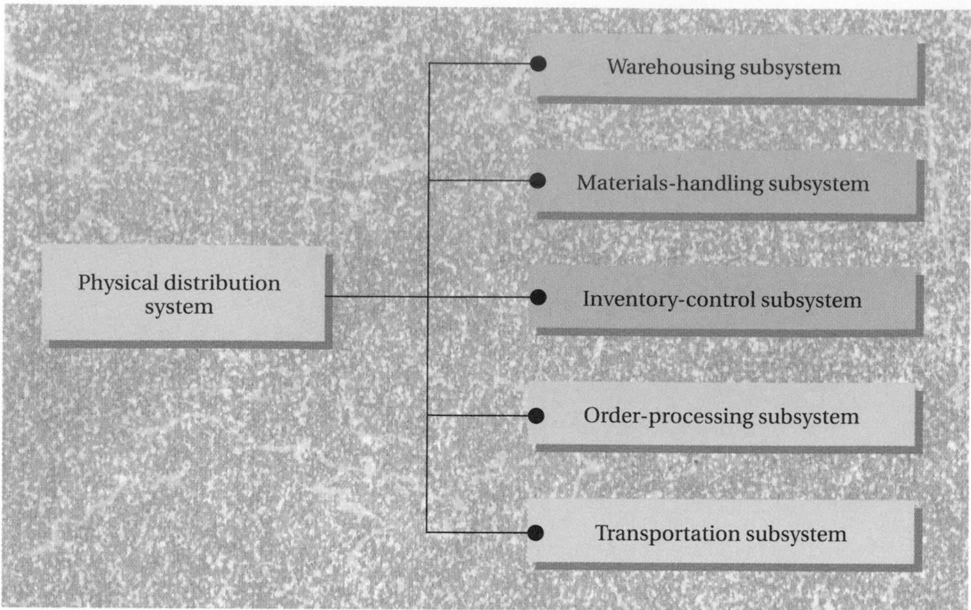

control system; setting procedures for processing orders; and selecting modes of transportation. These subsystems are shown in Exhibit 14.4. Although these subsystems are discussed here separately, they are, of course, highly interdependent.

Warehousing

Distribution management oversees the constant flow of goods from the manufacturer to the ultimate consumer. However, the final user may not need or want the goods at the same time the manufacturer produces and wants to sell them. Products like grain and corn are produced seasonally, but consumers demand them year-round. Other products, such as Christmas ornaments and turkeys, are produced year-round, but consumers do not want them until autumn or winter. Therefore, management must have a storage system to hold these products until they are shipped.

Storage is what helps manufacturers manage supply and demand, or production and consumption. It provides time utility to buyers and sellers, which means that the seller stores the product until the buyer wants or needs it. Even when products are used regularly, not seasonally, many manufacturers store excess products in case the demand surpasses the amount produced. Storing additional product does have disadvantages, however, including the costs of insurance on the stored product, taxes, obsolescence or spoilage, theft, and warehouse operating costs. Another drawback is opportunity costs—that is, the lost opportunities of using the money tied up in stored product.

If a product does require storage, the manufacturer needs somewhere to house it. Warehouses are places for holding a product until it is demanded by consumers. Distribution managers must make several key decisions about warehousing: Where are the best locations? How many warehouses are needed? What size is needed? What type of warehouse should be used?

Warehouse Location

Warehouse locations are chosen to be near the markets to be served and the production facilities. In general, if markets are near the plant, then storage facilities are usually nearby, too. Sometimes markets are widely dispersed. For instance, when

the manufacturer distributes nationally or globally, then warehouses may be located in each regional or national market served.

Other important considerations affecting warehouse location are the quality and versatility of transportation, the quantity and quality of labor, the cost and quality of industrial land, taxes, local government regulations, and local utility costs.

Warehouse Number and Size

The number of warehouses needed and their size depend mainly on the level of customer service required. A supplier that wishes to provide next-day delivery anywhere in the country may need many warehouses, located in each major region of the country. A supplier that promises to never be out of stock may need a larger warehouse to store surplus product.

More, larger, and more widely dispersed warehouses are needed when supply sources and markets are widely separated and when customer service is important. Fewer, smaller, or closer warehouses may be warranted when suppliers and markets are located near each other and service is kept at a minimum.

Types of Warehouses

There are also several types of warehouses: private warehouses, public warehouses, and distribution centers.

private warehouse
Storage facility either leased or owned by a company that needs to store a large amount of its own merchandise.

public warehouse
Independently owned storage facility that stores merchandise for others; may specialize in certain types of products, such as furniture, refrigerated foods, or household goods.

Private warehouse: A **private warehouse** is either leased or owned by companies that need to store large amounts of merchandise. Whether to own a warehouse or use a public warehouse is mainly a financial issue. Ownership entails expenses for land, building, insurance, and taxes. Although private warehouses can represent a significant investment, the firm can design them to its exact specifications and have complete control over their operation.

Public warehouse: A **public warehouse** is independently owned (not owned by the firms storing goods there). It often specializes in certain types of products, such as furniture, refrigerated foods, or household goods. Using public warehouses, a producer can place inventories close to key customers for quick delivery without the cost of building private facilities. Public warehouses also offer specialized services, such as inventory level maintenance, local delivery, materials handling and packaging, price marking, marketing information systems, and office and display space.

A warehouse may be partly or entirely vacant in lean economic times. If it is a private warehouse, the company still must maintain it and pay insurance and real estate taxes, among many other costs. But a company using public warehouses can expand its storage and distribution network during an economic upswing or reduce inventory space during slow periods without causing a cash-flow problem. When the company enters new markets, using public warehouses may reduce distribution risks and increase flexibility. It can also more effectively meet seasonal demand.

Often the best approach is to use private warehouses to meet basic storage needs and to rely on public warehouses for seasonal overflows and special situations. This dual system combines the advantages of ownership with the flexibility of the public warehouses.

contract warehousing
Agreement between a manufacturer and a public warehouse facility to provide storage space for a specified period.

Most manufacturers use public warehouses for short-term needs, usually for thirty days. Manufacturers that need longer-term storage space may enter into a contract arrangement with the warehouse. Under **contract warehousing,** both the manufacturer and the warehouse are legally committed in a business relationship for a specified period. Contract warehousing is most appropriate when the manufacturer asks the warehouse to make a major investment in facilities, equipment, or

Exhibit 14.5

The Distribution Center Concept

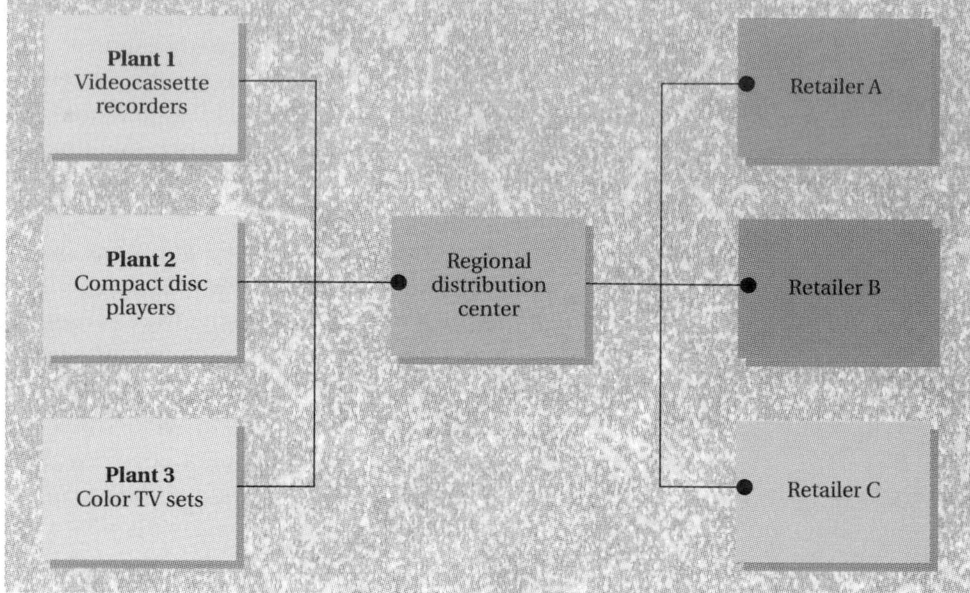

people. For example, a stored product may require extra care in handling or may be so large that additional storage space must be constructed or allocated. A long-term warehousing contract may also allow the manufacturer to lock in favorable rates.[6]

distribution center
Type of warehouse that specializes in making bulk or breaking bulk and strives for rapid inventory turnover.

Distribution center: Many corporations use distribution centers to efficiently move products to market. A **distribution center** is a special form of warehouse that specializes in making bulk (consolidating shipments) or breaking bulk (breaking up shipments that will leave the distribution center in smaller quantities). A distribution center strives for rapid inventory turnover, as opposed to long-term storage. Exhibit 14.5 illustrates the concept of a distribution center.

A distribution center differs from a warehouse in many ways. Specifically, a distribution center is a centralized warehousing operation, usually serving a regional market, that processes and regroups products. Most distribution centers are highly computerized, and they may use automated materials-handling equipment, rather than physical labor, to place and pick items. Distribution centers also improve customer service by cutting delivery time and ensuring product availability.

Materials Handling

materials-handling system
Method of moving inventory into, within, and out of the warehouse.

A **materials-handling system** moves inventory into, within, and out of the warehouse. Materials handling includes these functions:

- Receiving goods into the warehouse or distribution center
- Identifying, sorting, and labeling the goods
- Dispatching the goods to a temporary storage area
- Recalling, selecting, or picking the goods for shipment (may include packaging the product in a protective container for shipping)

The goal of the materials-handling system is to move items quickly with minimal handling. A product is typically handled sixteen times.[7] Each time it is handled, the cost and risk of damaging it increase; each lifting of a product stresses its package. Pro Fasteners, which supplies electronic component fasteners to computer manufacturers, reduced product handling quite a bit when it installed a highly automated materials-handling system. As goods are received into the warehouse, labels on each product are scanned, and lot number, quantity, and part number are auto-

matically entered in Pro Fasteners' computer system. If there is an unfilled order for the incoming product, the system automatically diverts the right amount of the product to the packing station. Thus there is no need to physically stock the product and take it right off the shelf again. If there are no outstanding orders for the incoming product, it moves directly to its proper place.[8]

Packaging

Packaging the product for shipment is a major concern of materials management. Packaging in physical distribution means protecting transported materials against breakage, spoilage, insects, and dirt. Protection is accomplished through well-designed packaging that restricts the material's movement. Waterford/Wedgwood, the distributor of Ireland's famed Waterford crystal, uses an adhesive-coated bubble wrap that sticks to the glass to cut down handling time and reduce product damage. Larger products, like furniture or computer equipment, may require shipping vehicles that are themselves padded for protection.

Automatic Identification and Bar Coding

Materials handling, like many other areas in physical distribution, is being driven by the need for fast, accurate information. **Automatic identification**, or **auto ID**, is the use of identification technology to mark and read products as they enter and leave the supplier's warehouse or as they are received by a manufacturer or retailer. Voice identification, radio frequencies, and magnetic strips can all be used, but bar coding is the chief method of auto ID.[9]

automatic identification (auto ID) Use of identification technology to mark and read products as they enter and leave the supplier's warehouse or as they are received by a manufacturer or retailer.

Bar coding is the marking of the good or its packaging with a computer-readable bar pattern. Ordinary bar codes—like the ones found on grocery products—store information in a pattern of parallel black and white lines. These bar codes can hold up to twenty or thirty characters per inch, or enough to spell out the universal product code, which is fed to a computer that tells the cash register how much to ring up. New technology, however, has increased the amount of information that can be held in bar codes, and they are no longer limited to just identifying the product. The new high-density bar codes can also tell where the product came from, where it's supposed to go, and how to handle it in transit.[10]

Another advance in bar code technology is long-range laser scanning, which can read bar codes more than fifteen feet away. Laser scanning is valuable anywhere a bar code might be hard to reach. One company that uses long-range scanners is Adolph Coors Company in Golden, Colorado. The beer brewer is using the scanner in a system designed to get beer moving faster from the warehouse to the customer. Thanks to the long range of the scanners, materials handlers don't need to be hoisted up to scan the bar code, saving time and reducing injuries. The system also saves money by making sure outgoing beer gets on the right truck. Beer shipped to the wrong place often must be discarded by the time it's retrieved, because of Coors's legendary freshness standards.[11]

unitization Increasing the efficiency of handling small packages by grouping boxes on a pallet or skid for movement from one place to another.

containerization Putting large quantities of goods in sturdy containers that can be moved from ship to truck to airplane to train without repacking.

Unitization and Containerization

Two important elements of modern materials handling are unitization and containerization. **Unitization,** or unitizing, is a technique for handling small packages more efficiently. It means grouping boxes on a pallet or skid, which is then moved mechanically, by a forklift, truck, or conveyor system.

Containerization is the process of putting large quantities of goods in sturdy

Containerization has revolutionized the shipping industry.
© Uniphoto, Inc.

containers that can be moved from ship to truck to airplane to train without repacking. The containers are sealed until delivery, thereby reducing damage and theft. They are essentially minimobile warehouses that travel from manufacturing plant to receiving dock. A container, often a special form of truck trailer body, can be reused repeatedly. The average container lasts ten years and can be repaired if damaged.

Inventory Control

inventory control system
Method of developing and maintaining an adequate assortment of products to meet customers' demands.

Another important function of physical distribution is establishing an inventory control system. An **inventory control system** develops and maintains an adequate assortment of products to meet customers' demands.

Inventory decisions have a big impact on physical distribution costs and the level of physical distribution service provided. If too many products are kept in inventory, costs increase—as do risks of obsolescence, theft, and damage. If too few products are kept on hand, then the company risks product shortages and angry customers. The goal of inventory management, therefore, is to keep inventory levels as low as possible while maintaining an adequate supply of goods to meet customer demand.

Two major decisions managers must make regarding inventory are when to buy (order timing) and how much to buy (order quantity).

Order Timing

reorder point
Inventory level that signals when more inventory should be ordered.

order lead time
Expected time between the date an order is placed and the date the goods are received and made ready for resale to customers.

usage rate
Rate at which a product is sold or consumed.

safety stock
Extra merchandise kept on hand to protect against running out of stock.

The **reorder point** is the inventory level that signals when more inventory should be ordered. Three factors determine the reorder point. First, the **order lead time** is the expected time between the date an order is placed and the date the goods are received and made ready for resale to customers. Second, the **usage rate** specifies the rate at which a product is sold or consumed. Third, the quantity of **safety stock** needed is the amount of extra merchandise kept on hand to protect against running out of stock. If safety stocks are inadequate, unpredictable usage or unreliable deliveries may cause lost sales.

The reorder point is calculated by first multiplying the order lead time by the usage rate. This figure tells an inventory manager the level of basic stock to have. To avoid stockouts, the manager would then add the quantity of safety stock to this figure to arrive at a final reorder point quantity. The computation is

$$\text{Reorder point quantity} = (\text{Order lead time} \times \text{Usage rate}) + \text{Safety stock quantity}$$

Say that a container company uses aluminum sheets to make soft-drink cans. Suppose the company uses 100 sheets per week (20 per day), and it takes two weeks after ordering for the sheets to arrive. The company also needs at least two days' worth of safety stock. The computation would look like this:

$$(2 \times 100) + 40 = 240$$

The container manufacturer would need to reorder aluminum sheets when its inventory dropped to 240 sheets.

Order Quantity

The amount to order or the level of inventory that should be ordered at any one time is guided by the economic order quantity (EOQ). The two basic figures needed to calculate EOQ are order processing cost and inventory carrying cost.

order processing cost
Total of operating expenses for the ordering or purchasing department, costs of required follow-up, operating expenses for the receiving department, expenses incurred in paying invoices, and the portion of data-processing costs related to purchasing and acquiring inventory.

ordering cost
Order processing cost divided by the number of orders placed per year, to arrive at an average cost per order.

inventory carrying cost
Total of all expenses involved in maintaining inventory, including the cost of capital tied up in idle merchandise, the cost of obsolescence, space charges, handling charges, insurance costs, property taxes, losses due to depreciation and deterioration, and opportunity costs.

economic order quantity (EOQ)
Order volume that minimizes order processing costs and inventory carrying costs.

Order processing cost is the total of operating expenses for the ordering or purchasing department, costs of required follow-up, operating expenses for the receiving department, expenses incurred in paying invoices, and the portion of data-processing costs related to purchasing and acquiring inventory. This sum is then divided by the number of orders placed per year, to arrive at an **ordering cost.**

Inventory carrying cost is the total of all expenses involved in maintaining inventory. These expenses include the cost of capital tied up in idle merchandise, the cost of obsolescence, space charges, handling charges, insurance costs, property taxes, losses due to depreciation, losses due to deterioration, and opportunity costs.

The **economic order quantity** (EOQ) is the order volume corresponding to the lowest sum of order processing costs and inventory carrying costs (see Exhibit 14.6). EOQ can be computed by using this formula:

$$\text{EOQ} = \sqrt{\frac{2 \times \text{Units sold (or average usage)} \times \text{Ordering cost}}{\text{Unit cost} \times \text{Inventory carrying cost (\%)}}}$$

A simple example will help explain EOQ. Assume that a software seller's average yearly sales of word-processing programs are $600 and the unit cost is $24. The ordering cost of program software is $48 per order. The cost of carrying it in the warehouse is 24 percent per year (24 percent per year, or 2 percent per month, of the unit cost is a typical figure for most businesses). For calculating EOQ, it is important that units sold and inventory carrying costs be in the same time unit, such as years. We can now compute EOQ:

Exhibit 14.6

The Economic Order Quantity (EOQ)

$$EOQ = \sqrt{\frac{2 \times 600 \times 48}{24 \times 0.24}} = 100 \text{ units (or two months' sales)}$$

The result shows that it is most economical for the software seller to order 100 copies of word-processing programs.

The application of EOQ presents many practical problems. For instance, small businesses need simple, easy-to-use, inexpensive inventory management systems keyed to current data sources and operations. Using EOQ requires continuous monitoring of inventory, and keeping EOQ values current requires frequent updating of order processing cost and inventory carrying cost. Furthermore, the computation of EOQ demands accurate knowledge of order processing cost per order and inventory carrying cost per dollar of inventory.[12]

However, with today's wide availability of low-cost computers and cost-estimating software, large and small firms alike have the opportunity to use EOQ to improve their inventory management. Archery Center International (ACI), a wholesale distributor of archery equipment, started out using a manual system for keeping track of inventory. The company grew rapidly, from $500,000 in sales its first year to over $5 million. Thus it became necessary to computerize its inventory management. Now ACI can enter orders directly into the computer, produce picking slips, track inventory in real time (no end-of-the-month tallying), generate invoices and packing slips automatically, produce valuable reports for both the business and its customers, and eliminate double-entry bookkeeping, since all records are updated automatically. ACI's computer system also helps determine which products to keep in stock. The computer system records how many times each of the 5,300 items in stock is being reordered, allowing management to decide whether any given item is worth selling. The system also tells management what margins the firm is making on the items it sells. This information helps management decide which items to carry and which ones aren't worth stocking—even though they may be selling well.[13]

just-in-time (JIT) inventory management
Redesigning and simplifying manufacturing by reducing inventory levels and delivering parts just when they are needed on the production line.

Just-in-Time Inventory Management

More and more manufacturing firms are using just-in-time inventory management systems. Borrowed from the Japanese, **just-in-time** (JIT) **inventory management** is a way to redesign and simplify manufacturing. For the manufacturer, JIT means that raw materials arrive at the assembly line in guaranteed working order "just in time" to be installed and finished products are generally shipped to the customer immediately after completion. For the supplier, JIT means supplying its customers with products in just a few days or even a few hours, rather than weeks. JIT is an innovative way of conducting business that has captured the attention of U.S. industry and transformed manufacturing into a competitive weapon.

Baxter International, the hospital products company, offers customers inventory management. At Hermann Hospital in Houston, a Baxter employee checks inventory and electronically transmits ordering data to the warehouse.

The basic assumption of JIT is that carrying excessive inventory is bad because it ties up capital. Thus the purchasing firm reduces the amount of raw materials and parts it keeps on hand by ordering more often and in smaller amounts. Production facilities are usually redesigned to position all the machines involved in a process closer together, thus reducing work time. The JIT system transports parts to the point where they are needed, just when they are needed on the production line. Hence, there are no piles of inventory waiting by each machine.

The benefits of JIT are many.[14] Foremost, firms practicing JIT reduce their inventories. Typically, about a third or more of a business's assets are tied up in inventory. Before Corning's Erwin, New York, plant implemented JIT, it warehoused large supplies of everything it needed in ten places inside the factory and in three leased warehouses. The cardboard boxes that packaged the finished ceramic parts Corning produces occupied a space as large as a football field. Today, two of the leased warehouses have been eliminated, along with two-thirds of the stock formerly warehoused at the factory. Gone also is the huge inventory of cardboard boxes. Now, every night, Corning's one cardboard supplier delivers what is needed for the next day. Corning estimates it has saved about $10 million in carrying costs since instituting JIT.[15]

lead time
Time it takes to get parts from a supplier after an order has been placed.

JIT also offers manufacturers other benefits, such as a shorter **lead time,** the time it takes to get parts from a supplier after an order has been placed. Manufacturers also enjoy better relationships with suppliers and decrease their production and storeroom costs. Since there is little safety stock, and therefore no margin for error, the manufacturer cannot afford to make a mistake. As a result, the high quality of parts is crucial. A manufacturer using JIT must be sure it receives high-quality parts from all vendors and is confident that the supplier will meet all delivery commitments. Finally, JIT may produce less paperwork for management.

Just-in-time inventory management is not without its risks, however.[16] (Exhibit 14.7 summarizes the benefits and risks of JIT.) Implementation of JIT is a process of continuous improvement and many small gains in efficiency over a long period. Many managers have tried to institute JIT too rapidly, only to be disappointed in the results. Shigeo Shingo, one of the initiators of the JIT movement, acknowledges that it took Toyota Motors twenty years to develop JIT fully. He estimates that companies wanting to implement JIT now should expect to need at least ten years for satisfac-

Exhibit 14.7

The Benefits and Risks of Just-in-Time Inventory Management

Benefits of JIT:
Reduced inventory levels
Shorter lead times
Improved supplier relations
Lower production and storeroom costs
Better-quality supplies
Less paperwork
Risks of JIT:
Implementing JIT principles too rapidly
Cutting inventory without implementing other JIT principles
Increased delivery costs
"Supplier shock"
Employee stress
Potential bottlenecks caused by supplier delays

tory results. Many companies have incorrectly assumed that JIT means slashing inventory levels only without paying attention to the other aspects of JIT, such as quality control, cleaner plant layouts, scheduled maintenance, and simpler product design. Their managers thus risk delivery delays, shortages of goods, and customer dissatisfaction.

Because of the lower inventory levels, JIT also demands smaller, more frequent, precisely timed deliveries from suppliers. As a result, manufacturers tend to pay much more for JIT deliveries.

JIT also has been known to create "supplier shock." Many suppliers have been strong-armed into cutting delivery times by manufacturers practicing JIT. In other instances, manufacturers' inventories have simply shifted from their warehouses to suppliers' warehouses. JIT can also create stress among workers. Experiences with a number of Japanese and U.S. companies show that sharp reductions in inventory may lead to a regimented work flow and increased levels of stress among production-line employees. Finally, JIT has the potential for causing disastrous bottlenecks in production due to even the slightest delays by suppliers. Consider the impact on General Motors' production if a labor strike occurred at its sole supplier of seat belts.

Order Processing

Another important activity of physical distribution is order-processing. The importance of proper order processing in providing good service cannot be overemphasized.

Flow of Goods and Information

As an order enters the system, management must monitor two flows: the flow of goods and the flow of information. Often the best-laid plans of marketers can get entangled in the order-processing system. Obviously, good communication between sales representatives, office personnel, and warehouse and shipping personnel is essential to correct order processing. Incorrect merchandise or partially filled orders can create just as much dissatisfaction as stockouts or slow deliveries. The flow of goods and information must be continually monitored so mistakes can be corrected before an invoice is prepared and the merchandise shipped.

order entry
First step in order processing in which a customer order is taken.

order handling
Second step in order processing, in which the order is transmitted to the office, usually on a standardized order form, and then to the warehouse floor.

Order processing begins with the customer's placement of an order, or **order entry.** The customer can be a final user or an intermediary, and the order can be placed directly by the customer or indirectly through a sales representative. The next step, **order handling,** transmits the order to the office, usually on a standardized order form, and then to the warehouse floor. At this point, credit approval and invoice preparation occur. When the order reaches the warehouse, inventory is checked to make sure the product is in stock. If the item is available and credit has been approved, the order can be filled. The goods are located, packaged for shipping, and scheduled for delivery. If the item requested is not in stock, the result is a back order, or an order sent to the production facility so an item can be produced to fill the order.

electronic data interchange (EDI)
Computer technique that electronically transmits data about retail inventories to warehouses so orders can be filled more quickly and accurately.

Benefits of Automation

Like inventory management, order processing is becoming more automated through the use of computer technology known as EDI—**electronic data interchange.** Companies that use EDI generally report that their orders are filled much faster and with few or no mistakes. EDI also requires less paperwork and frees up salespeople to provide better service.[17]

Retailers have become major users of EDI. Over 80 percent of the largest retailers (those with sales over $500 million) are now using or testing EDI with selected vendors.[18] EDI works hand-in-hand with retailers' "quick response" programs, which are designed to have the right product, in the right style and color, on the shelf through improved inventory, ordering, and distribution techniques. (See Chapter 13 for more discussion on retailers using quick-response techniques.)

Even small retailers are discovering the benefits of EDI. Some of the independent retailers selling Hallmark greeting cards are finding that merchandise orders via EDI are transmitted and received error-free at the company's Kansas City headquarters and are acknowledged in seconds. Small retailers also avoid stockouts or orders lost in the mail. Hallmark store managers use hand-held terminals to take inventory. Information stored in the terminals is then transferred electronically to Hallmark headquarters. Headquarters, in turn, uses EDI in buying its own supplies from graphic-arts materials vendors. Often they receive orders the same day they are placed.[19]

Transportation

Physical distribution managers must also decide which mode of transportation to use to move products from producer to buyer. This decision is, of course, related to all other physical distribution decisions. The five major modes of transportation are railroads, motor carriers, pipelines, water transportation, and airways. Exhibit 14.8 presents some statistics on these major transportation modes.

Distribution managers generally choose a mode of transportation on the basis of several criteria:

- *Cost:* the total amount a specific carrier charges to move the product from the point of origin to the destination. Cost is usually figured in ton-miles (a ton-mile is the movement of one ton, or 2,000 pounds, of freight a distance of one mile).
- *Transit time:* the total time a carrier has possession of goods, including the time required for pickup and delivery, handling, and movement between the point of origin and the destination.

Exhibit 14.8

Modes of Transportation in the United States

Mode	Annual ton-miles (in billions)	Percentage of total annual ton-miles	Typical cargo
Railroads	1,048	37%	Farm products, minerals, sand, chemicals
Motor carriers	712	25	Clothing, food, computers, paper goods
Pipelines	597	21	Oil, coal, chemicals
Water transportation (inland waterways only)	444	16	Oil, grain, sand, metallic ores, coal
Airways	9	Less than 1	Technical instruments, perishable products, documents

Exhibit 14.9

Six Criteria for Ranking Modes of Transportation

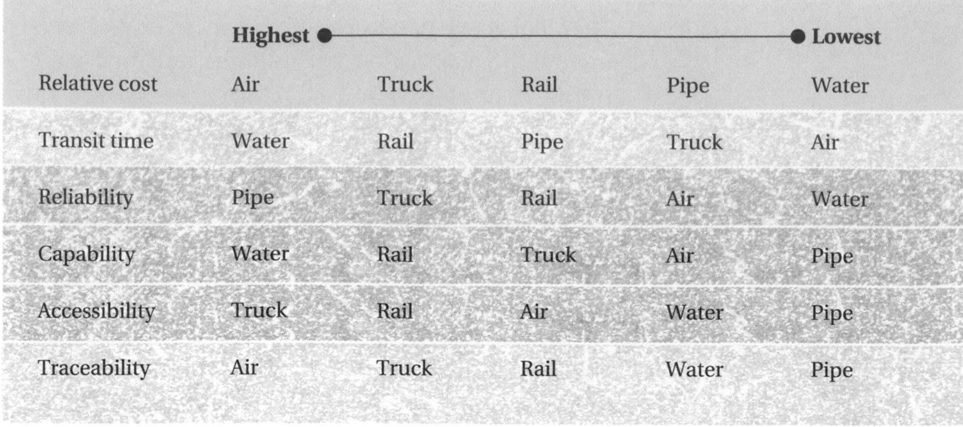

	Highest				Lowest
Relative cost	Air	Truck	Rail	Pipe	Water
Transit time	Water	Rail	Pipe	Truck	Air
Reliability	Pipe	Truck	Rail	Air	Water
Capability	Water	Rail	Truck	Air	Pipe
Accessibility	Truck	Rail	Air	Water	Pipe
Traceability	Air	Truck	Rail	Water	Pipe

- *Reliability:* the consistency with which the carrier delivers goods on time and in an acceptable condition.
- *Capability:* the ability of the carrier to provide the appropriate equipment and conditions for moving specific kinds of goods, such as those that must be transported in a controlled environment (for example, under refrigeration).
- *Accessibility:* the carrier's ability to move goods over a specific route or network.
- *Traceability:* the relative ease with which a shipment can be located and transferred.[20]

The mode of transportation used depends on the needs of the shipper. All shippers are concerned with cost, transit time, reliability, capability, accessibility, and traceability. Exhibit 14.9 ranks the basic modes of transportation on these six criteria.

Now let's examine the unique advantages and problems that these modes of transportation present to a physical distribution manager today.

Railroads

Railroads have long been the backbone of U.S. freight transportation, transporting more than a third of the total ton-miles of freight traffic. Coal is the most commonly carried rail product; over 550 million tons are carried per year, about a third of all material transported by the rail system.[21] Railroads also are the main carriers of grain and other farm products, chemicals, and raw metals and minerals.

Rail is ideal for transporting over long distances bulky items that are low in value relative to their weight. Compared to other carriers, rail is inexpensive for carload lots. Raw materials that can withstand rough handling are more suitable for rail transportation than are finished goods. A main advantage of rail over other modes is reliability, because weather rarely interrupts rail freight schedules. Most rail service, however, is relatively slow and limited.

Since their peak in the 1940s, railroads have witnessed a steady erosion in demand for their services. The construction of the nation's interstate highway system and the arrival of affordable air travel cut the industry's share of freight from about 60 percent in the late 1940s to the 37 percent share it holds today.[22] The Staggers Rail Act of 1980 deregulated the rail system, allowing the railroads more operating freedom and profoundly changing the industry. Among other changes, it brought flexible rates and the ability to contract with individual customers.

To stay competitive, railroads have responded to changing freight patterns. As commerce has broadened from local and regional trade to national and interna-

Within the transportation subsystem, railways and trucking companies compete to carry many of the same types of products.

tional markets, railroads have combined systems to offer longer single-line routes. Mergers among railroads have provided cost savings, lower capital spending requirements, and reduced labor expense, as well as a reduction in competing routes.[23] Railroad managers are emphasizing market segmentation, flexible pricing, cooperation with other transportation modes, longer-haul traffic, and long-term contracts with shippers.

Railroads would still like to capture a larger share of the freight market from motor carriers, their biggest competitor. Thus they now offer double-stack service, in which two containers are stacked on a modified rail flatcar. Double-stack transport offers about a 25 percent savings over conventional flatcar service and now accounts for about two-thirds of all rail container movements.[24]

Motor Carriers

Motor carriers are the most flexible freight-hauling mode. Almost every product used by industry or consumers moves, at some time, by truck. Over 80 percent of motor carrier freight is short-haul—that is, carried locally or under 200 miles.[25] Rates are usually economical over the short haul, and speed is better than with most other modes. Many carriers provide door-to-door service, thus reducing packing costs (since the goods are not handled as often, there is less need for protective packing materials). Unfortunately, weather can affect motor carrier service. However, minimal handling and generally smooth rides make trucking desirable for finished goods and fragile items.

Today's motor carriers emphasize service, through attention to on-time performance, claim-free shipments, shipment tracing, billing accuracy, and broad geographic coverage.[26] One service that tends to distinguish the leaders in trucking is satellite communications. Each vehicle is equipped with a transmitter tracked by satellite so headquarters and drivers can stay in constant communication. Satellite service also gives shippers the peace of mind of being able to pinpoint the location of their freight. Some systems are even able to help drivers avoid traffic congestion, which is especially valuable to shippers with time-sensitive freight, such as those using JIT inventory systems.[27]

Motor carriers play an important role in JIT programs. Manufacturers that use JIT rely on the timely delivery of raw materials directly to the assembly line, a feat achieved most successfully through the use of motor carriers. For example, an automobile manufacturing plant that has a special partnership agreement with a trucking firm will notify the trucker which models are scheduled for production during the next few days. The trucking company then takes over, picking up the needed materials from various suppliers, keeping track of where everything is in the system, and delivering the materials to the assembly line "just in time" for the operator to install it. JIT production methods have essentially redefined motor carriers, from a simple delivery service to the manufacturer's warehouse on wheels.

ETHICS IN MARKETING

The Undercharge Crisis

Across the country, companies that ship products by truck have received letters from bankruptcy trustees representing scores of failed trucking companies. The trustees are demanding reimbursement for steep price discounts once granted by the bankrupt haulers. As one shipper put it, "It's like buying a car for $3,000 less than the sticker price and two years later getting a bill for $3,000." The Interstate Commerce Commission (ICC) estimates that the so-called freight-undercharge claims could cost shippers as much as $32 billion.

The undercharge battle stems from trucking regulation dating back to 1935. Carriers file official freight rates in the form of tariffs with the ICC. They don't have to charge the official list price, but they must file any discounted prices they do charge customers. The goal of the filed-rate doctrine is to allow all shippers to know what's being charged so everyone gets fair treatment. The ICC must rely on voluntary compliance on behalf of trucking firms to file changes in rates due to lack of funds and manpower.

In 1980, Congress deregulated the trucking industry, but only partly; it eliminated barriers to new competitors but retained the requirement that rates be filed at the commission. As a result, new entrants flooded into the business, and many existing truck lines extended their reach. In the competitive fever—and, in many cases, under intense pressure from many shippers—carriers doled out discounts of as much as 50 percent or more from official rates. Sometimes they didn't bother to file the discounts with the ICC. And they often filed the discounts but used numerical codes to identify customers, a practice approved by the commission, whose officials say the codes aided computerization of rates.

Strained by the new competition, thousands of trucking companies failed. When trustees for scores of the companies discovered discounted rates had never been filed with the ICC, they began trying to collect the full rates on the ground that those rates were the only ones on file. The ICC barred the collections as an "unreasonable practice," which outraged bankruptcy trustees who claimed it was a ploy by deregulation-minded commissioners to undermine the filed-rate doctrine.

Then, in 1990, in a decision that shocked shippers, the Supreme Court decided that the unfiled rates were illegal and that the estates were entitled to the full rates. A later decision by a California judge also determined that the numerical codes used to file rates were for secret agreements and, therefore, were in violation of the filed-rate doctrine. These decisions sparked an explosion of litigation, and many of the defunct carriers have set up teams of auditors to pore over their shipping records to uncover potential undercharge claims. One trucking firm simply ceased operations without going bankrupt and sent out balance-due bills to its customers for past undercharges. Some lawyers are even using strong-arm tactics to recover claims. Stanley Works, a toolmaker, was given the ultimatum from now-defunct PIE Nationwide Inc. trustees: Settle for $90,000 now or face an audit of 32,000 old freight bills that might raise the total by $4 million.

Shippers say the trustees' demands are unethical and are driven by the millions of dollars in legal fees they will make from the undercharge suits. Lawyers for the trustees see it differently. Shippers, they say, are viewing the suits as a moral issue, whereas they are looking at it from a legal standpoint. Moreover, they say, shippers are at fault for pressuring trucking companies for discounts that drove many of them into bankruptcy in the first place.[28]

Who is really at fault in the undercharge crisis? Is it the truckers for failing to file discounted rates? The ICC for not being able to enforce rate filings? The shippers for pressuring truckers to give them discounted rates? Or are the tactics taken by the bankruptcy trustees to seek out claims unethical?

Source: Adapted from Laurie McGinley and Daniel Machalaba, "Fight over Freight: Failed Trucking Firms Are Trying to Recoup Discounts They Gave," *The Wall Street Journal*, 16 June 1992, pp. A1, A4. Reprinted by permission of *The Wall Street Journal*,

Computers are another element changing the face of trucking. For example, J.B. Hunt Transportation is testing a new IBM-designed on-board computer. The system enables truck drivers to send and receive messages and to store data on shipment status, estimated time of arrival, and customer signatures. The system also monitors driving speed and engine information, so the home office has more control over both driver safety and vehicle costs.[29]

Technology is not the only motivator of change in the trucking industry. Before 1980, carriers were bound to limited markets and rates. With passage of the Motor Carrier Act of 1980, which deregulated the industry, price became for a time the most important selection factor. Many changes and problems for the trucking industry followed. These included rate slashing, increased competition, growing demands from shippers for service and price discounts, and rising costs for insurance and equipment. As a result, many marginal trucking companies were eliminated or absorbed by larger, stronger firms. Many also went bankrupt because of competitors' aggressive pricing tactics, many of which were later found to be illegal. The article on page 462 discusses how these illegal price discounts affected the trucking industry.

Pipelines

Pipelines are quite slow as a transportation mode but offer continuous, low-cost product flow. There is no route flexibility, and route capacity is limited by the diameter of the pipe. Pipeline routes carry products in one direction, and storage terminals are required at the receiving end. Gases, liquids (oil or chemicals), and some solids (coal or watery mixtures movable in slurries) constitute the market for pipelines. Because pipelines are designed to carry only one or two products, most of them are owned by the companies that use them, such as oil and gas producers.

Despite their limited flexibility, pipelines account for almost a fourth of all intercity ton-miles.[30] Perhaps the greatest advantage of pipelines, other than low cost, is dependability. Weather and labor strikes rarely affect them. Moreover, pipelines are the lowest consumers of energy.

Water Transportation

Like rail, water transportation is ideal for shipping heavy, low-value, nonperishable goods. Examples include ore, coal, grain, sand, and petroleum products. Routes, of course, are limited, since a large cargo ship or barge can only transport its goods in oceans or deep inland channels. Because of high fixed costs, water transport requires heavy traffic from point to point in order to achieve economies of scale. Locks, channels, and ports in major industrial areas often are overused, creating costly delays. Even without the bottlenecks, service is usually slow, and in some northern areas icing problems in the winter cause further delays. Weather can also be a problem during droughts, which cut water depth and force lightening of loads. Conversely, floods and high water can also create problems.[31] Even though service is slow and weather may be a nuisance, water is still one of the cheapest means of moving raw materials and some semifinished goods regularly over long distances.

Inland waterways have made a dramatic comeback since the mid-1950s, when they hauled roughly 3 percent of the nation's freight. Today they haul about 16 percent.[32] New towboats have greatly increased the capacity of many carriers. Special barges now handle refrigerated commodities. Others contain specialized equipment for carrying asphalt, and traditional tank barges now have special linings for

The Port of Seattle is becoming busier as trade with Asia increases.

hauling chemicals. The growth of containerization and improved port facilities will mean continued expansion for transportation via inland waterways.

Not surprisingly, U.S. ocean carriers are a major player in international trade. They originate from ports along the East and West coasts and the Gulf of Mexico. Some of the largest ports, in import and export volume, are Houston, New Orleans, New York/New Jersey, Baton Rouge, Corpus Christi, and Los Angeles. The two largest U.S.-based ocean carriers are Sea-Land Services and American President Lines.

Airways

Airways are the fastest but most expensive way to move freight. Speed and limited handling of freight enable shippers to use lighter packaging. Generally, the market is confined to high-value merchandise and certain perishable items. Examples include electronic parts, fresh-cut flowers, emergency materials, and live seafood. Participants in the air freight market include the passenger airlines (which haul cargo in the holds of their passenger aircraft), all-cargo air freight carriers, and specialists in the express air delivery of small packages and shipments, such as Federal Express, United Parcel Service, and Airborne Express.

Specialized cargo planes, roll-on containerization, and efficient ground operations have helped reduce the cost of air freight. However, aircraft have a lower overall weight capacity than other modes, such as barge or rail, and so air freight will always have limitations. Weather and a lack of adequate runways in smaller communities also affect service quality and availability.

By using air transport, a manager can often eliminate costly warehouses and the inventory tied up in those warehouses. Fast service enables the shipper to provide timely and sometimes emergency service. For example, a broken $25 part has been known to shut down an entire General Motors assembly line. Shipping crucial parts by air eliminates costly production delays. Speed also tends to reduce theft, damage, and spoilage. Because air carriers offer a relatively smooth ride compared to other modes of transportation, costly packing and unpacking can be eliminated.

Air freight operators like UPS are seeking to expand overseas delivery routes as global trade increases.
United Parcel Service

Although air freight rates are the most expensive, in many instances air shipment is necessary. For example, HBO Studio Productions creates video products for cable giant Home Box Office, as well as for HBO affiliates, external advertising agencies, and other businesses. In the case of an HBO cablecast, local transportation is used to get the final edited version of the tape from the studio in Manhattan to the cable TV head end. However, projects for affiliates and outside clients—whether basketball shoe commercials for TV stations, promotional videos for the more than 200 HBO affiliates, or videos of upcoming HBO specials for television critics to review—are almost always time-sensitive. As a result, HBO uses overnight air service to deliver between 1,500 and 2,000 videos a month. If next-day delivery will be too late for a customer, HBO uses a same-day service, which will deliver the video by whatever means in a few hours.[33]

Air freight is also important in international trade. Air freight operators, especially those offering express shipments, have looked to the international arena for growth opportunities. As global markets grow, shippers need distribution systems that offer fast, guaranteed deliveries throughout the world. U.S. air freight operators have made a determined effort to build their global routes, but they have had some problems. For example, Federal Express has been far from successful in its attempt to build a full-service air express network in Europe. However, Federal Express does provide express service to sixteen European cities and overnight service from Europe to the United States. Along with UPS and Airborne, Federal Express is also expanding its efforts in Asia.[34]

intermodal transportation
Combination of two or more modes of moving freight.

piggyback (trailer on flatcar) (TOFC)
Form of intermodal transportation combining the use of truck and rail to ship containerized goods.

Intermodal Transportation

Intermodal transportation is the combination of two or more modes of moving freight. It allows a transportation buyer to exploit the advantages of each. At a growth rate at more than 5 percent per year, intermodal is the fastest-growing mode of surface transportation in the United States today.[35]

Piggyback, or trailer on flatcar (TOFC), a truck-rail combination, is the most popular form of intermodal transportation. It allows a shipper to achieve the door-to-door capabilities of a motor carrier service along with the long-haul advantages of

container on flatcar (COFC)
Form of intermodal transportation involving containers that can be transferred from rail or truck onto ship or barge.

fishyback
Form of intermodal transportation combining the use of truck, rail, and ship or barge to move containerized goods.

birdyback
Form of intermodal transportation combining the use of truck and air freight to move containerized goods.

rail. Containers can also move in a piggyback service called **container on flatcar** (COFC); they can then be transferred to ship or barge. Other popular types of intermodal transportation include **fishyback,** combining the use of truck, rail, and ship or barge to move goods, and **birdyback,** combining the use of truck and air freight to move goods.

Many experts say greater use of intermodal transportation may help relieve the congestion on major urban highways and reduce wear and tear on the nation's interstate system. Moving freight by rail, at least part of the way, is more environmentally sound than moving it by truck. Environmentalists say railroads use less fuel and create less pollution than trucks moving similar loads, without adding to road congestion and deterioration.[36]

J.B Hunt Transport Services is one trucking company that is exploiting the nation's underused rail system through intermodal transportation. Hunt has struck alliances with rail carriers to offer shippers seamless coast-to-coast service. The company has also begun converting its truck trailers into containers that can be used interchangeably on railroad flatcars or on truck flatbeds.[37] Hunt will also team up with Union Pacific Railroad to offer door-to-door intermodal service between the United States and Mexico. Hunt will feed trailers into a hub in Memphis, from which Union Pacific will ship the goods by rail to the Mexican border at Laredo, Texas. There the trailers will be transferred to Mexican motor carriers for delivery within Mexico.[38]

Supplementary Carriers

Shippers can also use several other supplementary carriers, including the U.S. Postal Service, United Parcel Service, bus services, courier express carriers, and freight forwarders.

The U.S. Postal Service and United Parcel Service specialize in handling packages under seventy pounds. UPS provides door-to-door delivery and, in many cases, next-day delivery to over 175 countries. The bus lines can also transport a large volume of packages economically. Like many passenger airlines, bus companies use excess baggage space for carrying freight from one city to another.

Usually promising overnight delivery, courier express carriers specialize in moving packages and documents quickly. Couriers typically use small trucks or vans to pick up and deliver. Federal Express, perhaps the best-known courier express carrier, handles over a million express shipments daily.

freight forwarder
Carrier that collects less-than-carload shipments from a number of shippers and consolidates them into carload lots.

A **freight forwarder** collects less-than-carload shipments from a number of shippers and consolidates them into carload lots. Forwarders charge rates equivalent to less-than-carload rates, but then they pay the lower carload rates for the consolidated shipments. Their profit comes from the difference between the two rates. Unlike express services like Federal Express, freight forwarders do not own their own long-haul equipment. Instead, they use available modes of transportation. Most offer pickup and delivery service, along with the speed and efficiency of handling carload merchandise. Historically, ground freight forwarders have handled consumer durable goods—for example, clothing, sporting equipment, and appliances.

Most small companies rely on freight forwarders to handle the details of global shipping. Faced with the major challenge of trying to track and control product distribution in an array of foreign countries, many small companies quickly turn to international freight forwarders for consolidations, shipping, and custom relations.[39]

Distribution is no less important to service organizations than it is to manufacturers. For example, putting on a symphonic concert requires sophisticated logistics planning and execution.

4 PHYSICAL DISTRIBUTION FOR SERVICES

The fastest-growing part of our economy is the service sector. The same skills, techniques, and strategies used to manage inventory can be used to manage service inventory—for instance, hospital beds, bank accounts, or airline seats. The quality of the planning and execution of distribution can have a major impact on costs and customer satisfaction.[40]

Service Industries' Distribution Opportunities

Traditional distribution means getting the right product to the right place at the right time. In the service industry, however, this narrow focus is replaced with a much broader mission: getting the right service and the right people and the right information to the right place at the right time.

One thing that sets service distribution apart from traditional manufacturing distribution is that, in a service environment, production and consumption are simultaneous. In manufacturing, a production setback can often be remedied by using safety stock or a faster mode of transportation. That is not possible with a service. The benefits of a service are also relatively intangible—that is, you can't normally see the benefits of a service, such as a doctor's physical exam. But a consumer can normally see the benefits provided by a product; for example, a vacuum cleaner removes dirt from the carpet.

Because service industries are so customer-oriented, customer service is a priority. Service distribution focuses on three main areas:

- *Minimizing wait times:* Wait times are similar to order cycle times in manufac-

turing distribution. Minimizing the amount of time customers wait in line to deposit a check, wait for their food at a restaurant, or wait in a doctor's office for an appointment is a key factor in maintaining the quality of service.

- *Managing service capacity:* This is analogous to managing inventory in a goods-producing organization. For a manufacturer, inventory acts as a buffer, enabling it to provide the product during periods of peak demand without extraordinary efforts. Service firms don't have this luxury. If they don't have the capacity to meet demand, they must either turn down some prospective customers, let service levels slip, or expand capacity. For instance, at tax time a tax preparation firm may have so many customers desiring its services that it has to either turn business away or add a temporary accountant.
- *Providing delivery through distribution channels:* Like manufacturers, service firms are now experimenting with different distribution channels for their services. These new channels can increase the time that services are available (like round-the-clock automated teller machines) or add to customer convenience (like pizza delivery or walk-in medical clinics).

Federal Express and Domino's Pizza are two firms whose innovative distribution of services has influenced their industries. Both built significant market share by focusing on the time and location of the services delivered to the customer. Federal Express satisfied an unmet need by offering guaranteed overnight delivery of packages and documents to commercial and residential customers. For Domino's, innovation meant concentrating on home delivery of pizza in thirty minutes or less.

The Functions of Physical Distribution for Services

Although service organizations provide mostly intangible benefits, they still must have supplies, raw materials, and inventory systems. Red Lobster restaurants' main service is providing customers with a sit-down seafood meal. To provide this service, the chain must have the food supplies available and ready. Red Lobster has devised an efficient physical distribution system to get fresh seafood supplies to its many restaurants. Its processing plant receives boxes of frozen shrimp that are then loaded onto a conveyor belt to be peeled, deveined, cooked, quick-frozen, and packed. Other seafood arrives at warehouses around the country and is flown fresh to Red Lobster restaurants. Red Lobster store managers prepare for each new day by predicting how many customers they will serve that day and what they will eat. Each restaurant's computer tells the manager what to expect based on what was served the same day the previous week and the same day the previous year.[41]

5 TRENDS IN PHYSICAL DISTRIBUTION

Several technological advances and trends affect the physical distribution industry today. These include automation, environmental issues, third-party contract logistics and partnerships, quality issues in transportation, and global distribution. Let's look briefly at each.

Automation

Manual handling of distribution is now outdated. Computer technology has boosted the efficiency of physical distribution dramatically—for instance, in warehousing and materials management, inventory control, and transportation. This chapter has presented many examples of how computer technology and automation have increased the efficiency of the physical distribution system. These range from satellite tracking for motor carriers to electronic data interchange, computerized inventory systems, and automatic identification techniques using bar codes.

One of the major goals of automation is to bring information to the decision maker's desk in real time. Shippers have long referred to the transportation system as the "black hole," where products and materials fall out of sight until they reappear some time later in a plant, store, or warehouse. Now carriers have systems that track freight, monitor the speed and location of carriers, and make routing decisions on the spur of the moment. The rapid exchange of information that automation brings to the distribution process helps each party plan more effectively.[42] The links among suppliers, buyers, and carriers open up opportunities for joint decision making. And as more companies compete in global markets, timely information becomes even more important.

Environmental Issues

Concern for the environment has reached new heights. A wave of new environmental laws in the United States will have a profound effect on how businesses operate. One likely effect is that logistics and distribution managers will become much more involved in environmental matters that affect their firms. Environmental rules will be directed at every stage of the supply and distribution chain. The Clean Air Act of 1990, for example, will change the way transportation and distribution are handled in the most polluted urban areas. The Clean Water Act will limit port dredging and construction, as well as the building of new distribution facilities. The Resource Conservation and Recovery Act will pressure companies to reduce the amount of toxic and hazardous waste moving through the transportation system. Customers will also begin demanding environmentally friendly service from carriers, such as minimal packaging that will still protect products during transit and recyclable and biodegradable packaging.[43]

Environmental issues are also quality issues. Most customers choose suppliers and carriers on the basis of quality. Now they will add environmental responsibility to their selection criteria.[44] Dow Chemical works closely with its contract motor carriers to ensure that the chemicals it transports are handled safely. Its program focuses on cleaning and disposing properly of the residue inside tank carriers.[45] Monsanto Chemical monitors each shipment of hazardous chemicals every mile of the way via satellite tracking. The company also holds public forums in the communities along the route to educate people about emergency procedures should an accident happen.[46]

Contract Logistics and Partnerships

Contract logistics is a rapidly growing segment of the distribution industry. In **contract logistics**, a manufacturer or supplier turns over the entire function of buying and managing transportation or another subsystem of physical distribution, such as warehousing, to an independent third party. Contract logistics allows companies to cut inventories, locate stock at fewer plants and distribution centers, and still provide the same service level or even better. The companies then can refocus investment on their core business.[47]

contract logistics
Use of an independent third party to buy and manage an entire subsystem of physical distribution, such as transportation or warehousing, for a manufacturer or supplier.

There are essentially two types of contract logistics vendors. The first are "space-based," offering services related to assets, such as trucking, warehousing, or air freight. Vendors that are "data-based" are essentially asset-free; they sell logistics management through computer systems.[48] Fashion retailer Laura Ashley, with head-

quarters in the United Kingdom, has taken advantage of both types of logistics vendors. The retailer contracted with data-based Fritz Companies, a major international forwarder. Fritz Companies provides Laura Ashley with a global information system. Laura Ashley has also delegated all its physical distribution operations to space-based Federal Express, which handles warehousing and distribution of Laura Ashley products in the United Kingdom and the United States.[49]

Not surprisingly, contract logistics often leads to exclusive partnerships between suppliers, retailers, or manufacturers, and carriers, warehousing experts, or logistics management suppliers. Many of the companies seeking partners are practicing quick-response or just-in-time inventory management principles. To put these principles into play, these companies often need sophisticated distribution systems that can deliver component parts to assembly lines or fashions to the retail shelf within tight, predefined time windows. Partnerships often provide the ability to meet delivery dates, speedily fill emergency orders, and achieve high accuracy in filling orders.

Quality in Transportation

Companies that buy transportation know that quality transport is a critical part of their success. Many shippers have developed formal quality measurement programs for the modes of transportation they use. They want carriers to deliver their products to customers on time, without loss or damage, and at competitive rates.[50] Most carriers have responded. They have improved on-time delivery and pickup, developed systems for tracing and tracking shipments, and implemented electronic communications to reduce delays and errors, shrink the amount of paperwork, and provide information every step of the way.[51]

Buyers of transportation are also using fewer carriers and demanding more from them. Shippers and carriers are developing partnerships to ensure that shippers get the quality they require. It is not unusual today to find as few as six or eight carriers handling as much as 90 percent of a shipper's transportation. Ford Motor Company's Engine Division decided it couldn't effectively use JIT with a logistics system that included hundreds of carriers. Instead, the division now relies on just one carrier, Roadway Logistics Services. Roadway was able to provide Ford with dependable deliveries so it could successfully implement its JIT strategy.[52] The advantages of forming partnerships with fewer carriers are many. Communication improves, and the carriers know they can rely on a certain level of business. Meanwhile, transportation buyers gain greater control over a central function in the distribution system.

Global Distribution

The world is indeed becoming a friendlier place for selling and buying goods and services. Russia and many countries in Eastern Europe are on their way to instituting capitalistic economies; the European Community is transforming Europe into a unified trading center; the United States, Mexico, and Canada are creating a North American trade bloc to rival the European Community; and many Third World countries are now taking a more active role in world trade. As a result, businesses will find that many of the obstacles to international trading have been removed and that the world market is more appealing.

As global trade becomes a more decisive factor in success or failure for firms of all sizes, a well-thought-out global logistics strategy becomes more important.[53] Uncertainty regarding shipping usually tops the list of reasons why companies, especially smaller ones, resist international markets. Even companies that have scored overseas successes often are vulnerable to logistical problems. Large companies have the capital to create global logistics systems, but smaller companies often must rely on the services of carriers and freight forwarders to get their products to overseas markets. One of the most critical global logistical issues for small importers is coping with customs. It is essential that the importer know what types of tariffs to expect, whether quotas restrict importation of the product, and what other regulations apply in each country it deals with.[54]

LOOKING BACK

Now that you have studied this chapter, turn back to the opening story on the distribution of lobsters. The trade-off between cost and service should now be clear. Since lobsters are highly perishable, distributors must choose a rather high-cost transportation method—air freight. This method, however, ensures that their cargo will arrive alive and fresh as far away as Asia. Although the cost is relatively high compared to other transportation modes, great value is added to the product by increased service.

SUMMARY

1 Explain the importance of physical distribution. In today's fiercely competitive environment, marketing managers are becoming aware of the importance of effective physical distribution. Rather than concentrating on product or price differentiation, many companies are developing more efficient methods of distributing goods and services to achieve a competitive advantage.

2 Discuss the concept of balancing physical distribution service and costs. Today, physical distribution service is recognized as an area in which a firm can distinguish itself from competitors. Therefore, many physical distribution managers strive to achieve an optimal balance of customer service and total distribution costs. Important aspects of service are availability of merchandise, timeliness of deliveries, and quality (condition and accuracy) of shipments. In evaluating costs, physical distribution managers examine all parts of the distribution system.

3 Describe the parts of the physical distribution system. The physical distribution system has five basic parts, or subsystems: warehousing, materials handling, inventory control, order processing, and transportation. When evaluating warehousing options, physical distribution managers must determine the number, size, and location of warehouses needed as well as the most appropriate type of warehouse—private warehouse, public warehouse, or distribution center. Important elements of materials handling are packaging, bar coding, and unitization and containerization. Inventory control systems regulate when and how much to buy (order timing and order quantity). Order processing monitors the flow of goods and information (order entry and order handling). Finally, the major modes of transportation include railroads, motor carriers, pipelines, waterways, and airways. Alternative methods of transporting goods are intermodal transportation and such supplementary carriers as freight forwarders.

4 Identify the special problems and opportunities associated with physical distribution in service organizations. Managers in service industries use the same

KEY TERMS

automatic identification (auto ID) 453
birdyback 466
containerization 453
container on flatcar 466
contract logistics 469
contract warehousing 451
distribution center 452
economic order quantity 455
electronic data interchange 458
fishyback 466
freight forwarder 466
intermodal transportation 465
inventory carrying cost 455
inventory control system 454
just-in-time inventory management 456
lead time 457
logistics 444
logistics management 444
materials-handling system 452
order entry 458
order handling 458
ordering cost 455

skills, techniques, and strategies to manage physical distribution functions as managers in goods-producing industries. Service industry physical distribution focuses on three main areas: minimizing wait times, managing service capacity, and providing delivery through distribution channels.

5 **Discuss new technology and emerging trends in physical distribution.** Several trends are emerging in today's physical distribution industry. Technology and automation are bringing physical distribution information to the decision maker's desk in real time. Technology is also linking suppliers, buyers, and carriers for joint decision making. As in many other industries today, concern for the environment is also making an impact on physical distribution. Companies are responding with programs to reduce the risk of hazardous shipments and to reduce packaging. Many companies are saving money and time by hiring third-party carriers to handle some or all aspects of the distribution process. Still another trend in distribution is the quest for quality in transportation. Carriers have improved on-time delivery and pickup, developed systems for tracking shipments, and implemented electronic communications with shippers. Finally, as the world becomes a friendlier place in which to buy and sell goods and services, the need to understand global physical distribution has assumed greater importance for many companies.

Review Questions

1. What is the role of the physical distribution manager? How is it changing?
2. What are the benefits of using public warehouses? When might a firm choose to use a private warehouse?
3. What is involved in unitization and containerization?
4. How has government deregulation affected the transportation industry?
5. Describe the criteria physical distribution managers use to choose modes of transportation.
6. What is the basic principle of just-in-time inventory management? List the benefits and risks associated with JIT.

Discussion and Writing Questions

1. Assume you are the marketing manager of a hospital. Write a report indicating the physical distribution functions that concern you. Discuss the similarities and dissimilarities of physical distribution for services and for goods.
2. Why is automation an increasingly important aspect of order processing?
3. Identify the most suitable method(s) of transporting these goods: lumber, fresh seafood, natural gas, fine china, and automobiles. Justify your choices.
4. Suppose your firm intends to use intermodal transportation to ship your product. Identify the product, and write a memo explaining why this distribution method makes good business sense.
5. Is the goal of a physical distribution system to operate at the lowest possible cost? Why or why not?
6. Which physical distribution strategy do you think is optimal? Why?

CASES

14.1 Itel Distribution Systems

Itel Distribution Systems is part of the Itel Corporation family of third-party logistics services. Logistics is the whole process of moving the product from the point of production to the ultimate consumer. *Third-party* means that companies like Itel do not take ownership of any of the products they move through the channel.

Third-party warehousing is becoming increasingly popular. As the cost of owning and operating warehouse facilities increases, businesses turn to companies like Itel. No matter what the business, Itel can offer total distribution and warehousing solutions.

Itel offers four key distribution services:

- *Freight consolidation:* Itel serves many companies. Thus shipments can be combined, reducing total shipping costs.

- *Multimodal transportation:* Itel uses many different modes of transportation, which alleviates the need to contract with separate companies for different modes of transportation.
- *Bulk transport and storage:* The company can transport and store raw materials and deliver them as needed.
- *Comprehensive inventory system:* Itel offers barcoding services, order processing, and packaging of shipments. In addition, its extensive computer system allows comprehensive information access, including the location of specific shipments.

The advantages for manufacturers of using third-party warehousing and distribution companies are twofold. First, the manufacturer can expand or contract its operations, as changes in the market or in sales levels occur, without making major capital investments. Second, companies do not have to invest in warehouse or distribution vehicles. The capital can instead be used to expand production capacity or improve products.

Using contract logistics is not without disadvantages. The main one is the loss of control. If a company turns over its warehousing and distribution functions, it loses control of the distribution process. The second disadvantage is that the company may have to sign a long-term contract with the third-party distribution company, which cancels many of the advantages.

Itel addresses the downside with its partnership focus. Itel is not just a supplier of distribution services but a partner in its customers' business. By taking total control of the customers' distribution needs, Itel lets companies focus on the specific needs of their business (concentrate on what they do best) and not worry about operating and managing distribution facilities. For example, Itel leased railway track next to one of its customer's factories to provide rail shipping directly from the plant to one of Itel's warehouse facilities.

Itel now has a total of 9 million square feet in thirty-nine distribution facilities. Through expansions and acquisitions, Itel continues to grow. To better serve its customers' needs, Itel is organized regionally (West, Central, Northeast, and Southeast). Itel's strength lies in building personal relationships within each region, not in applying the same formula in each one. Itel finds specific solutions to best meet each customer's needs. Itel wants its customers to have not only the support of a national company but also the individual attention of a local company.

Questions

1. What advantages and disadvantages come from Itel's decision to organize on a regional basis? What are the advantages and disadvantages of a national orientation?
2. Do you think Itel has done a good job in alleviating the disadvantages of using a third-party distribution company? Why or why not?
3. What advantages would Itel's customers have in using Itel? Would you recommend using a third-party distribution company?

Suggested Reading

Itel Distribution Systems company literature.

14.2 Santa Fe Railway Company

Video title: *Santa Fe Railway—A Smooth Journey*

Santa Fe Railway Company
1700 East Golf Road
Schaumberg, IL 60173

SIC codes: 4011 Railroads, line-haul operators
4111 Local and suburban transit
4213 Trucking, except local
4225 General warehousing and storage

Number of employees: 16,000

1993 revenues: $2.11 billion

Major service: Railway, truck, and door-to-door transportation

Largest competitors: Burlington Northern, Union Pacific, CSX Transportation, Norfolk Southern Corp.

Background

Rail companies have traditionally depended on the coal industry. Most products shipped by rail have a low value-to-weight ratio. For many years, the rail system has lost ground to the trucking industry for most dock-to-dock shipping. But recently, the rail companies have fought back with intermodal transport options. Santa Fe Railway offers its customers several forms of intermodal transport for quality dock-to-dock service. Piggyback rail cars can transport truck trailers more efficiently and with less environmental damage than trucks can. Double-stack cars allow Santa Fe to move twice the number of containers as before using

the same number of rail cars. These containers can be loaded onto ships for water transit or onto specially designed trailers for local truck delivery.

Industry

A series of mergers and acquisitions has made this industry highly competitive. The five largest rail and long-haul carriers now account for about 70 percent of all transport revenues. Industry experts expect the mergers to continue until there are only three big transport companies left. While the largest carriers fight for the long-haul distribution business, there is still a niche for the short-haul freight companies.

Santa Fe Railway

To maintain profitability, Santa Fe Railway is trying to reduce its dependence on the coal industry and to increase its intermodal transportation business. In the last quarter of 1992, the company's container volumes were up over 20 percent. This emphasis on intermodal transport is helping Santa Fe outpace its railway competitors.

Santa Fe Railway focuses on improving its transportation system in five key areas: technology, speed, performance, design, and service. The company relies heavily on technology to track and schedule deliveries. Advances in computer technology permit the company to offer clients single-billing options and better shipment-tracking capabilities. Its emphasis on performance and speed allow the company to offer just-in-time delivery service. Special designs in rail cars minimize damage during transit. Finally, the company's overall commitment to quality means that its customers get the best service at all times.

Questions

1. Do you think Santa Fe Railway has been successful in changing customers' attitudes about rail transportation? Why or why not?
2. What major factors contribute to damage during shipment? How has Santa Fe Railway tried to minimize these factors?
3. What factors increase the likelihood that intermodal transportation will be used? What can Santa Fe Railway do to increase its intermodal transport business?

References

Million Dollar Directory 1993 (Parsippany, NJ: Dun & Bradstreet Information Services, 1993).

Standard & Poor's Industry Surveys (New York: Standard & Poor's Corporation, October 1993).

14.3 *Decision Assistant:* Serden Corporation

The Situation

The president of Serden Corporation has recently been troubled by the increased costs of storing inventory. As a wholesaler, Serden's control over inventory costs is an important factor in its profitability. A review of the cost data by Serden's accountants reveals that the carrying cost of a unit of inventory is 12 percent of the average selling price of a product, which in this case is $9. The records also show the cost of placing an order is $800. The demand for the coming year is estimated to be 5,250,000 units.

In the past, Serden has placed only four orders per year in an effort to keep order costs low. This course of action would result in estimated total inventory costs of $711,950 for the coming year. The president has asked you, the distribution manager, to evaluate this inventory policy.

The Solution Technique

The Economic Order Quantity tool in the marketing *Decision Assistant* can be used to compute the order size that will minimize order costs. Key ALT-D to display the computations and ALT-G to display a graph of the costs.

What If?

Consider each of the following situations independently:

1. What if the carrying cost of inventory was determined to be 22 percent of the selling price? What would be the effect on the economic order quantity and order frequency?
2. What if the demand for the coming period was estimated to be 4,375,000 units? What would be the effect on the economic order quantity and order frequency?
3. What if the cost of placing an order was determined to be $2,880? What would be the effect on the economic order quantity and order frequency?

PART FOUR
CRITICAL THINKING CASE

Lumber Industries

by Marlene Kahla and Robert Solomon

Abstract
Lumber Industries grew, harvested, processed, and sold timber products, plywood, and particleboard. The company employed about 10,000 people in its operations in the southern gulf states.

Kenny Smith, export sales manager for Lumber Industries, was faced with two problems. Sales of timber products to overseas customers had been increasing at a fairly fast rate over the past few years, and the company had not altered its operating procedures or organizational structure to accommodate the nondomestic market. Kenny's department essentially operated outside the company's regular sales department. This had resulted in tension, misunderstanding, and low morale.

The other problem faced by the export sales manager was basically a procedural one. A situation had developed involving nonpayment by a Cuban customer, Mr. Heredia, who owed the company $280,000. Since Kenny Smith was relatively new at handling international transactions, he was curious as to how the customer was able to take possession of the shipment (at a foreign port) without presenting proper documentation from the bank. He also had to come up with a way to get the Cuban customer to pay the $280,000 due Lumber Industries.

There was also an ethical question facing company management. The better grades of lumber were being shipped overseas, where prices were substantially higher. This meant domestic customers were being sold an inferior product. While this practice meant higher profit for the company, there was a question as to whether domestic customers, whose patronage had helped build the company to its present position, were being treated fairly.

Source: Reprinted by permission of Southwest Case Research Association.

Lumber Industries Case Study

It was a brisk day in June. Kenny Smith, export sales manager for Lumber Industries, sat behind his desk looking out at the rolling hills of a well-manicured golf course. He thought about his current position with the company and how far he had come since his early years in Houston. As export manager for Lumber Industries he was in a more responsible position than any he had held before. He was aware, however, that his fifteen years' experience in the wholesale lumber and building supply business had taught him little about how to deal with international contractors.

As Kenny continued to stare out the window, he began mulling over his dilemma. He had just received word from the credit department that a Cuban contractor, Mr. Heredia, had not paid for a sizable shipment of plywood and had not responded to numerous inquiries concerning his account. The shipment, which Kenny had authorized, was shipped to a Puerto Rican port over six months ago. (At the time, U.S. businesses could not ship directly to Cuba.)

Company Background

Lumber Industries grew, harvested, processed, and sold timber products—primarily southern pine lumber, plywood, and particleboard. Annual sales had risen at a fairly steady rate of 2 and 3 percent for the past five years. In the most recent year, sales of all company products were approximately $300 million.

The company employed about 10,000 people in its operations in the southern gulf states. The majority of company sales (about 60 percent) were made to lumber and building supply companies (including four company-owned retail outlets), and 15 percent were to large building contractors who bought direct. Sales to overseas customers accounted for the remaining 25 percent.

Mr. Andrew Summitt was the company president. The Summitt family had founded the firm in 1923, and it was incorporated and went public in 1983. Andrew Summitt was a highly respected leader and was the motivating force behind the company's success. His current focus was on expanding lumber production, because he expected demand for pine lumber products to increase and was afraid that additional environmental restrictions might hamper future fiber conversion.

Kenny felt that because of preoccupation with activities at higher levels of the business, Mr. Summitt was not fully aware of how fast the company's exporting division was growing. In fact, Kenny had recognized for some time that exports of company products were experiencing exceptional growth and were the primary reason for the company's 3 percent sales increase the previous year. The Building Products Division would have had a somewhat disappointing year had there not been a sizable increase in export sales. The exceptional performance of the export division was due to a combination of high-quality products produced in plants located near Gulf Coast ports. This permitted ready penetration of European lumber markets. In addition, close proximity to Mexico had given the company a competitive edge in this fast-growing market.

Unfortunately for Kenny, the significance of the export division was not fully appreciated by upper-level management, since domestic and foreign sales were not recorded and reported separately in the company's financial reports (see Exhibit 1). To Mr. Summitt, sales were sales—regardless of whether they were made to domestic or foreign customers.

Organizationally, the export sales department was under the vice president of marketing, Joe Chumley. Mr. Chumley gave Kenny a free rein in operating his department as long as sales were increasing and no major problems developed. While Kenny appreciated the confidence placed in him by Joe and other company officials, he was very much aware of the responsibilities and pressures that accompanied his position.

The Current Dilemma

Kenny continued to ponder his delinquent customer. He knew that some delinquent accounts could be expected when orders were shipped without requiring advance payment. As Kenny confided to a colleague: "In the wholesale business there were always some stable ones that paid their bills. But there were others that never really 'settled up.' We used to keep a list of welshers that circulated among the wholesalers in Houston. But we later found that Robinson-Patman, or something like it, made the list illegal. I guess we made mental notes instead. Most of the wholesalers knew that not everyone was going to pay for all the lumber and supplies. When the bottom fell out of the market in Houston, we were really forced to watch who we made deals with. Now that I've gone international, it looks like I have to do the same thing. Except this time it is with those Cubans. It seems as though they take advantage of every little mistake in documentation. And since we [the United States] don't have

Exhibit 1

Building Products Sales

Product	Sales (in millions)		
	1992	*1991*	*1990*
Pine lumber	$ 69.4	$ 60.7	$ 54.7
Fiberboard	43.7	43.2	43.4
Particleboard	59.4	58.1	53.4
Plywood	40.5	29.8	25.4
Gypsum wallboard	36.6	37.0	38.0
Foam insulation	4.4	15.3	15.3
Retail distribution	37.5	37.9	30.4
Other	5.8	6.3	21.4
Total	$297.3	$288.3	$282.0

an embassy in Cuba, there is no way we can put any real pressure on the customer. For sure, there is no way to get the lumber back."

Kenny realized that exporting was a growing opportunity for the lumber industry and for the company. What bothered him was that he essentially operated outside of the company's regular sales department (see Exhibit 2). His department consisted only of himself and two telemarketing assistants. Although foreign sales depleted the supply of pine available for the domestic market, they were not coordinated with sales and supply reports or with the company's other sales representatives. Kenny commented: "When they discover that they have 25 percent less pine to sell [domestically], they will want some immediate answers. But what am I supposed to do? Exporting is hot! It is in vogue; anybody who's anybody exports—it is the thing to talk about at parties. Until two years ago, one telemarketing person handled all of our export sales—which never exceeded $13 million per year. So far this year [June] our export sales are almost $40 million."

Kenny continued to ponder some of the problems of his department: "It's tough trying to keep good relations with everyone in the sales department—and with my boss. When my department is pushing to expand export sales, supply for domestic sales suffers. One problem is the mill itself. It's difficult to explain to the forty-hour-per-week mill supervisors that I need my board feet in millimeters. They look at me like I'm from another planet when I talk metric. I am trying to market to the world when the millers just want to talk about drinking beer and fishing.

"If it's not the millers, it's the salespeople. They are mad as hell as it is. Some, like Wally Lumpkin, won't even try to understand that my telemarketers and I are just trying to do our jobs. All they see is less to sell [domestically] and unhappy customers. No attempt at coordination! We never have formal meetings to iron out our differences. On top of that, they blame me for the declining quality of their domestic lumber supply. Western Europe, the United Kingdom in particular, will pay $925 per 1,000 feet of Southern Yellow 1 (SY1) pine. The U.S. contractors will pay only $325 per 1,000 board feet. Sure, much of the SY1 pine will go to the U.K. while little, if any, gets into the domestic market. Domestic contractors, the ones that keep us in business during the off years, are not getting actual number-one-grade product. Before, they were getting a much better grade. Joe Chumley, my boss, stresses me out, too. He keeps pushing for more export sales."

Kenny's thoughts were interrupted by Doris Kemp, one of the telemarketers, who handed him a memo

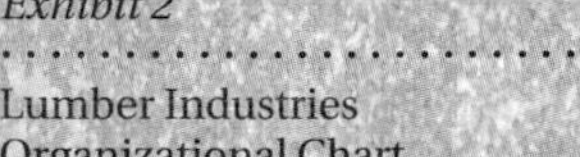

Exhibit 2

Lumber Industries Organizational Chart (Abbreviated)

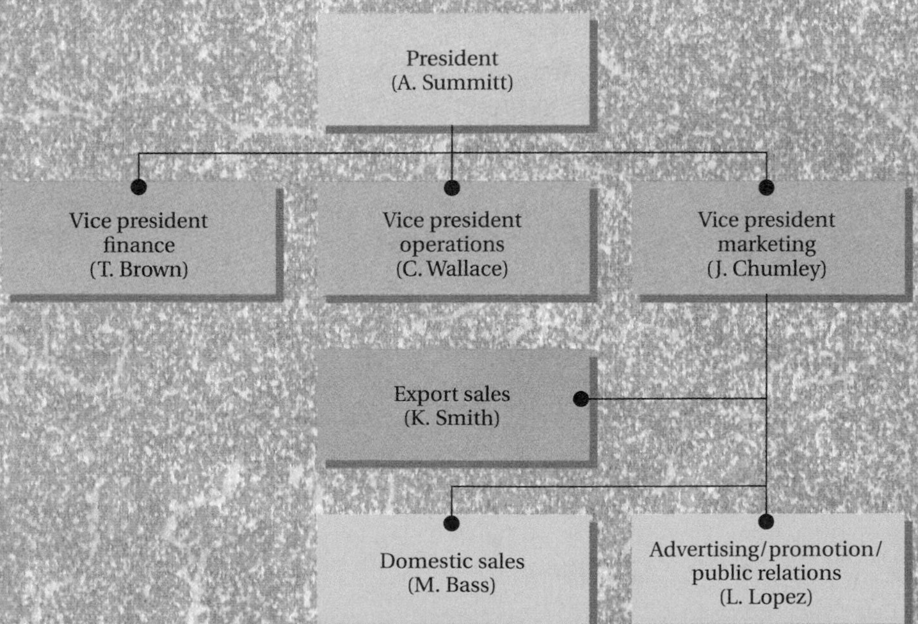

from the Puerto Rican bank. The memo indicated that Mr. Heredia had not responded to any letters or calls concerning his past-due account. Doris asked Kenny: "Why is this so important? All we have done today is work on this, this Cuban connection." Frustrated, Kenny replied: "It's just important! That's all! And don't go asking anybody questions."

Kenny swung around in his chair, looked at the golf course again, and thought: "Don't I know how to fill out papers by now? A consignee should never go to the dock and pick up the materials without stopping by the bank first. Two-hundred and eighty thousand dollars won't break the company, but it is a significant amount. This error is my responsibility. If Chumley finds out about it, I will be listening to lectures from here to retirement—if he doesn't fire me first. Shoot, what a tough call! If I can fix it, maybe he won't find out."

Because of the extended channels involved in dealing with overseas accounts, there were many opportunities for mistakes to be made. The international sale of lumber involved Lumber Industries, the foreign customer, the United States Department of Agriculture, the Export-Import Bank in New York, the bank in the country of destination (in this case, Puerto Rico), and marine and surface transportation companies. There were standard procedures for handling international shipments at each step along the way.

Obviously an error in documentation and/or procedures occurred somewhere between Kenny's desk and delivery to Mr. Heredia. In addition to the increased possibility of honest error because of the extended channel, there was also the possibility of dishonesty on the part of someone in a position to get the shipment released. Cultural, moral, and ethical standards in some countries permitted, and even encouraged, such dishonest acts as bribery and kickbacks. For whatever reason, release of the shipment without proper documentation could cost Lumber Industries $280,000.

Kenny decided to contact the Export-Import Bank (Eximbank) and ask for their assistance. He hoped they would help collect from Mr. Heredia or at least assist in finding out who failed to get the required documentation before releasing the shipment. Kenny asked Doris to get someone at the bank on the phone for him.

At this point Kenny's door opened and Mr. Chumley entered. "Well, Mr. Productive, how is the guy heading the fastest-growing department at Lumber Industries? I want you to know that your figures are surprisingly steady compared to domestic. Old Man Summitt and I are getting ready to make some capital investments and retool the mill to accommodate international standards. The revenue from your department is helping everybody."

The phone rang and Doris notified Kenny that Ms. Smart from Eximbank was on the line. Kenny realized that temperatures would soon be rising. He asked Joe if he would excuse him for a minute while he took a personal call.

Questions

1. Suggest ways the company could be reorganized to better support and coordinate activities of the domestic and foreign sales departments.
2. What might be done by Joe Chumley and Kenny Smith to ease the tension between the domestic and foreign sales divisions?
3. Why do you think the shipment to Mr. Heredia was released without proper documentation?
4. Although Mr. Heredia took possession without paying for the lumber and knows that Lumber Industries has no way of retrieving the shipment, why would it be in his best interest to pay for the lumber as agreed?
5. If the Import-Export Bank cannot, or will not, help Kenny collect from Mr. Heredia, what action should he take next?
6. What are the ethical issues involved in this case? Discuss the degree of importance of these issues and the extent to which they should influence operations.

PART FOUR
ETHICS CASE

The Generous Salesperson

Jill McCarthy, a retail buyer for a large department store, was told during her training as a buyer that the company was very sensitive to any type of inducements given buyers beyond "modest tokens of friendship." The company felt that as long as buyers were entertained or received tokens of appreciation of little or no value, their position as buyers would not be compromised.

- Why would a company feel the need for such a policy? What would constitute "a modest token of friendship"? What would be excessive?

The first year of Jill's job involved nothing that could even remotely be linked to the "bribery policy." One salesperson for a large dress manufacturer had become good friends with Jill and offered to take her to dinner so they could quietly discuss some of the emerging fashion trends that would be affecting the next season's lines. Jill was happy to go to dinner because it was a good opportunity to enjoy quiet conversation with her friend Barbara, the sales representative. The dinner went very well and was very productive for both Jill and her store.

- Does anyone feel uncomfortable accepting dinner under this policy?

Later that year Barbara invited Jill to attend an ice show with her, as a recreational activity. Jill remembered the dinner, felt that it would be very pleasant to attend anything with Barbara, and quickly accepted. On the date of the planned entertainment, Jill received four tickets and a note from Barbara saying that she was terribly sorry that she could not come to town but that she wanted Jill to invite other friends and enjoy the ice show.

- Should Jill accept the tickets? Why or why not? What are the issues in this situation?

A month later, with a note of apology, Jill received a smoked turkey and a fruitcake from Barbara in the name of Barbara's company.

- What should Jill do? Why? What harm has been done?

The following spring Barbara asked Jill to speak to the retail apparel manufacturers' trade association on the buyer's view of sales and service in retailing. Jill was very happy to receive the invitation to speak and was happier later to hear that there was an honorarium of $500 associated with the speaking engagement. She worked hard on her speech, and it was very well received. She felt she earned every penny of the $500.

- Did Jill do anything wrong by accepting? Was Barbara's involvement a problem? What danger might exist in this situation?

In late summer Barbara spent almost two days with Jill, acquainting her with some of the changes that would be made in the line and bringing her up-to-date on some new trends that were to be watched in the industry. Two weeks later Jill received a $1,000 check from Barbara's company with a notation that it was in appreciation for the time she spent advising Barbara on the needs of retailers.

- How has Jill compromised her position as a buyer? As long as she intends to be uninfluenced by the money, can she take it?

Jill realized she was in clear violation of the "bribery policy" but was not sure where she crossed the line.

- Where did Jill cross the line? Could she have continued working with Barbara after saying no to a gift or other act of friendship?

PART FIVE

PROMOTION DECISIONS

SEND FOR
FREE
BOOKLET
The Largest Selection of

CHAPTER 15

Marketing Communications and Promotion Strategy

LEARNING OBJECTIVES

After studying this chapter, you should be able to

1. Discuss the role of promotion in the marketing mix.
2. Describe the communication process.
3. Identify the goals and tasks of promotion.
4. Discuss the promotional mix and its components.
5. Analyze the role of the hierarchy of effects concept in the promotional mix.
6. Identify the factors that affect the promotional mix.
7. Explain how to create a promotional plan.

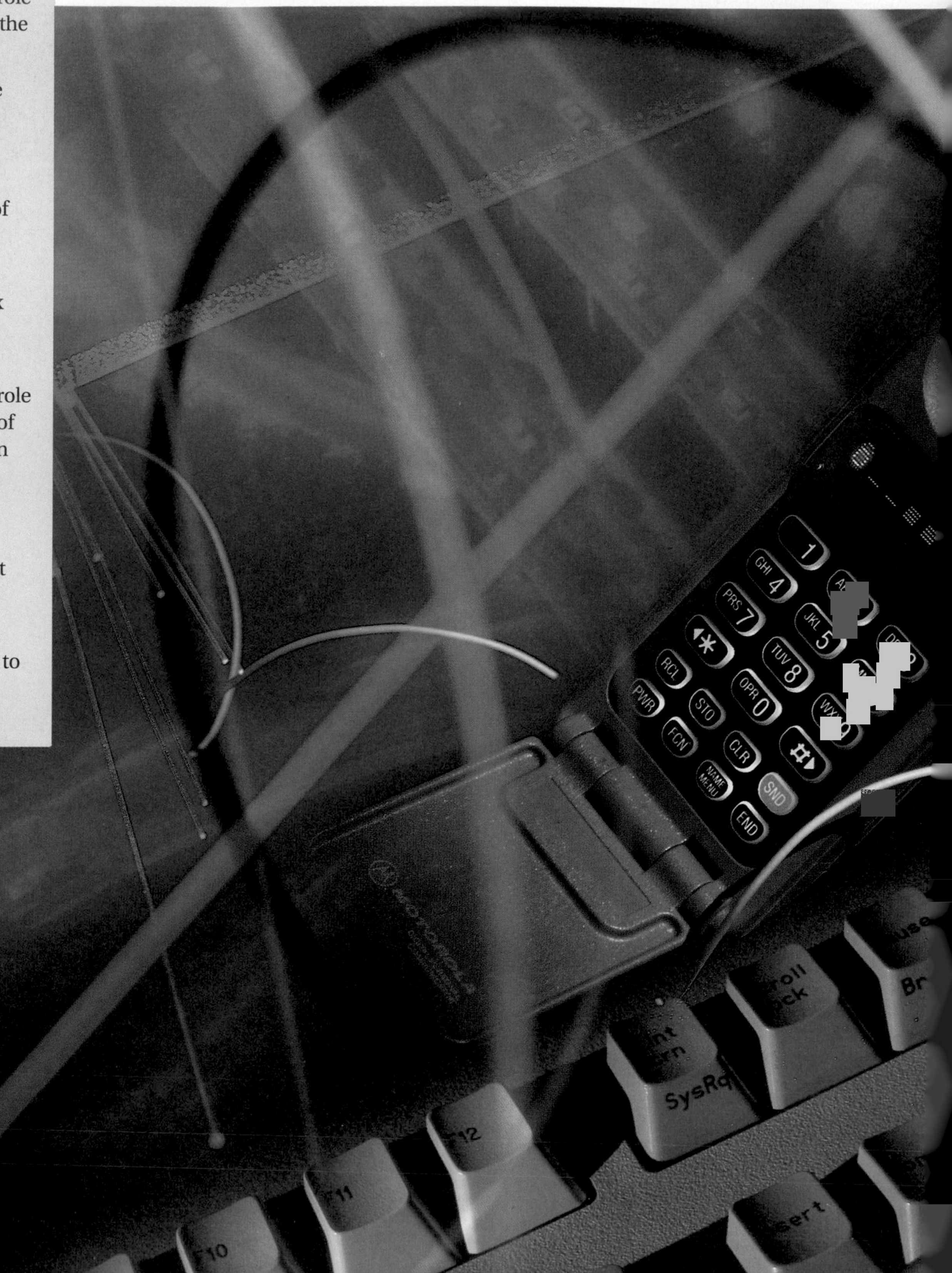

Companies use several methods to communicate sales messages to their target customers. For example, in one of the most successful product launches ever, Unilever Group's Lever 2000 three-in-one body soap became an instant hit with U.S. consumers, pushing Unilever ahead of Procter & Gamble in toilet-soap revenues for the first time in the Dutch company's long history. Heavy promotions and a $25 million advertising campaign accompanied the introduction of the new soap, positioning it as a moisturizing, deodorant, and antibacterial cleansing soap with broad family appeal. Pitches to both sexes through advertising and sampling touted Lever 2000 as the multipurpose family soap for all the "2,000 body parts." Commercials showed a couple and a baby and "some of the 2,000 body parts you can clean" by using the product. Lever 2000's advertising successfully convinced many households that they can get by with one brand of soap instead of the two or more varieties they typically buy.[1]

Another example is an award-winning promotion in which NutraSweet spotlighted the strength of its brand with a tenth-anniversary sweepstakes. The company turned the bar codes on 18,000 food and drink items into lottery numbers for a national sweepstakes. Consumers could call an 800 number and punch in the bar code from any branded good that included NutraSweet as an ingredient. A national sales promotion campaign using inserts in newspapers announced the contest, reaching over 24 million consumers. The promotion drew some 1.5 million calls during a four-week period. Over 18,000 prizes were awarded, from gumball machines to trips to any of fifty countries where NutraSweet is sold. Callers also heard messages for the branded products identified by bar code. Thus the sweepstakes not only reinforced NutraSweet's strategic positioning but cross-promoted the thousands of items using the ingredient.[2]

An effective public relations strategy and publicity helped Euro Disneyland successfully open the gates of its theme park in France in 1992. Disney sent a model of Sleeping Beauty's Palace around Europe, complete with Disney characters, to publicize the opening. Leading television stations in Britain, France, Germany, Italy, and Spain offered live broadcasts of Euro Disneyland's official opening celebration, which featured celebrities like Tina Turner, Cher, Gloria Estefan, the Temptations, and the Four Tops. Publicity on Disneyland's grand opening in Europe was featured in children's magazines, women's magazines, and the general press. Disney also publishes its own children's magazines, and they promoted Euro Disneyland extensively. As a result, grand opening attendance at the park exceeded all estimates, and European children instantly correlate Mickey Mouse with Euro Disneyland.[3]

United Parcel Service is one of the most successful shipping and delivery companies in the United States and the world. Its success can be partly credited to the great skill of its 2,500-plus sales representatives across the country. In a study by *Sales & Marketing Management,* the UPS sales force was rated as the best in its industry category. UPS scored the highest in keeping top salespeople, training salespeople, holding onto accounts, and making sure salespeople have thorough product/technical knowledge. UPS salespeople are known for their expertise in helping customers control shipping costs, work more efficiently, and gain greater information.[4]

All these companies have used a form of promotion to communicate with their target markets, whether it was advertising, sales promotion, public relations, or personal sales. What should be the role of promotion in the marketing mix of a company? How does the communication process work? What factors influence the choice of a promotional tool? How is a promotional plan created?

1 THE ROLE OF PROMOTION IN THE MARKETING MIX

promotion
Communication by marketers that informs, persuades, and reminds potential buyers of a product to influence an opinion or elicit a response.

promotional strategy
Plan for the optimal use of the elements of promotion: advertising, personal selling, sales promotion, and public relations.

differential advantage
Set of unique features of a company and its products that are perceived by the target market as significant and superior to the competition.

Few goods or services, no matter how well developed, priced, or distributed, can survive in the marketplace without effective promotion. **Promotion** is communication by marketers that informs, persuades, and reminds potential buyers of a product to influence an opinion or elicit a response. **Promotional strategy** is a plan for the optimal use of the elements of promotion: advertising, personal selling, sales promotion, and public relations. As Exhibit 15.1 shows, the marketing manager determines the goals of the company's promotional strategy in light of the firm's overall goals for the marketing mix (product, price, place, and promotion). Using these overall goals, marketers then combine the elements of the promotional strategy (the promotional mix) into a coordinated plan. The promotional plan then becomes an integral part of the marketing strategy for reaching the target market.

The main function of a marketer's promotional strategy is to convince target customers that the goods and services offered provide a differential advantage over the competition. A **differential advantage** is the set of unique features of a company and its products that are perceived by the target market as significant and superior to the competition. Such features can include high product quality, rapid delivery, low prices, and excellent service. For example, Lever 2000's differential advantage over many of its close competitors is its three-in-one formula. By properly communicating this differential advantage through effective promotion, Lever 2000 can stimulate demand for its soap over the competition. As a vital part of the marketing mix, promotion informs consumers of the product's benefits, thus positioning it in the marketplace.

2 MARKETING COMMUNICATION

communication
Process by which we exchange or share meanings through a common set of symbols.

Promotion strategy is closely related to the process of communication. As humans we assign meaning to feelings, ideas, facts, attitudes, and emotions. **Communication** is the process by which we exchange or share meanings through a common set

of symbols. When a company develops a new product, changes an old one, or simply tries to increase sales of an existing good or service, it must communicate its selling message to potential customers. Marketers communicate information to the target market and various publics about the firm and its products through its promotional programs.

interpersonal communication Direct, face-to-face communication between two or more people.

mass communication Communication to large audiences.

Communication can be divided into two major categories: interpersonal communication and mass communication. **Interpersonal communication** is direct, face-to-face communication between two or more people. When communicating face to face, people see the other person's reaction and can respond almost immediately. A salesperson speaking directly with a client is an example of marketing communication that is interpersonal. **Mass communication** refers to communicating to large audiences. A great deal of marketing communication is directed to consumers as a whole, usually through a mass medium, such as television or a newspaper. For example, when a company advertises, it generally does not know the people with whom it is trying to communicate. Furthermore, the company is unable to respond immediately to consumers' reactions to its message. Instead, the marketing manager must wait a relatively long time to see whether people are reacting positively or negatively to the mass-communicated promotion. And clutter from competitors' messages or other distractions in the environment can reduce the effectiveness of the mass communication effort.

Exhibit 15.1

The Role of Promotion in the Marketing Mix

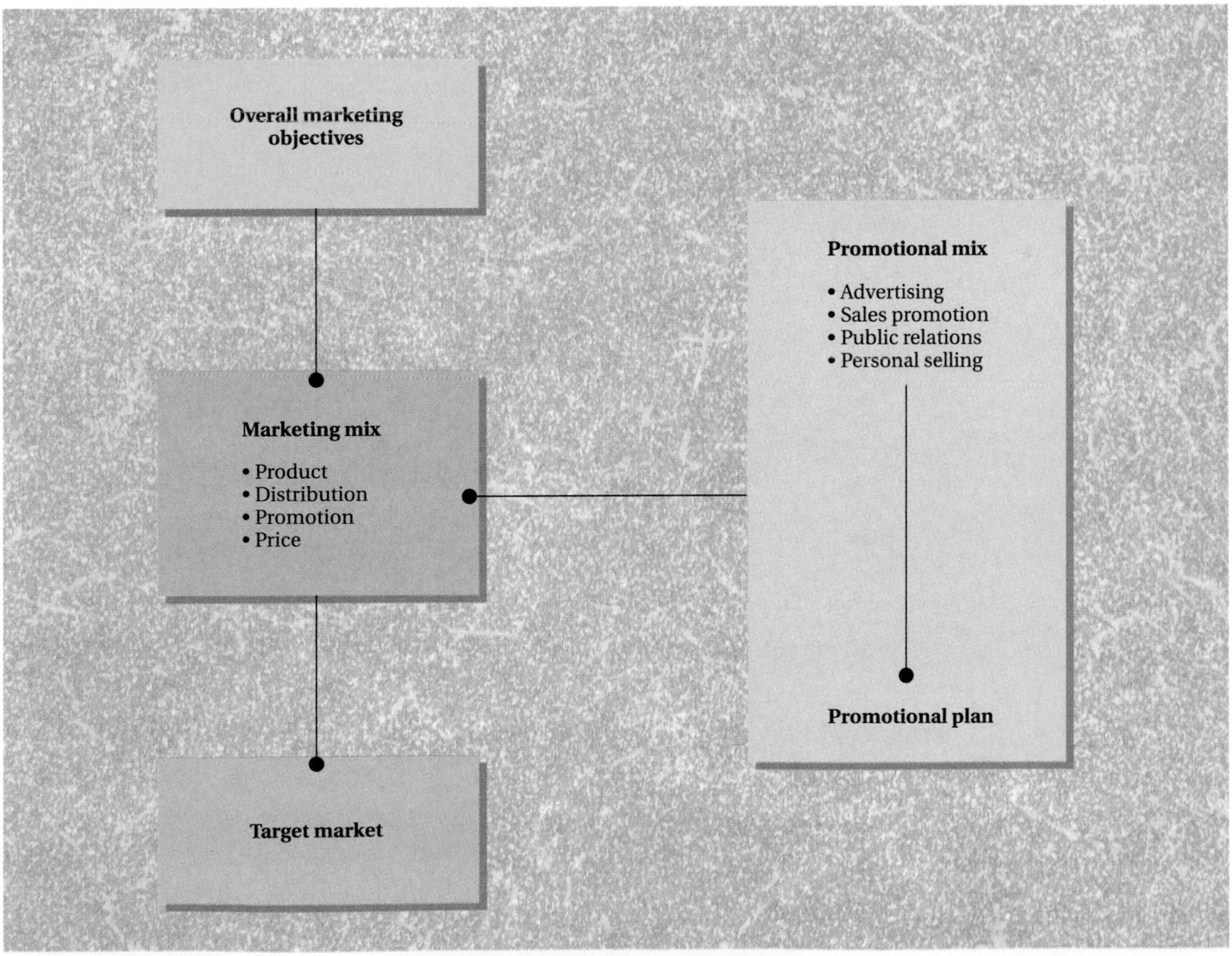

Overall marketing objectives

Marketing mix

- Product
- Distribution
- Promotion
- Price

Target market

Promotional mix

- Advertising
- Sales promotion
- Public relations
- Personal selling

Promotional plan

Barriers to Marketing Communication

Common understanding between two communicators is required for effective communication. Marketing managers must therefore ensure a proper match between the message to be conveyed and the target market's attitudes and ideas. Vividness, such as bright colors or graphics, has been shown to increase consumers' comprehension of a marketing communication, especially in product warning messages.[5] Factors that can lead to miscommunication are differences in age, social class, education, culture, and ethnicity.

Because people don't always listen or read carefully, they may misinterpret what is said or written. Researchers have found that almost one-fourth of print communication and about two-thirds of televised communication is misunderstood.[6] A classic example occurred after Lever Brothers mailed out samples of its new dishwashing liquid Sunlight, which contains real lemon juice for extra cleaning power. The package clearly stated that Sunlight was a household cleaning product. However, many people saw the word *sunlight,* the large picture of lemons, and the phrase "with real lemon juice" and thought the product was lemon juice.[7]

The Communication Process

The communication process begins when the sender has a thought or idea and wants to share it with one or more receivers. The source then encodes this message and sends it, via a transmission channel, to the receiver(s) for decoding. The sender, in turn, receives feedback from the receiver(s) as to whether the message was understood. The communication process, which we examine next, is shown in Exhibit 15.2.

Exhibit 15.2

The Communication Process

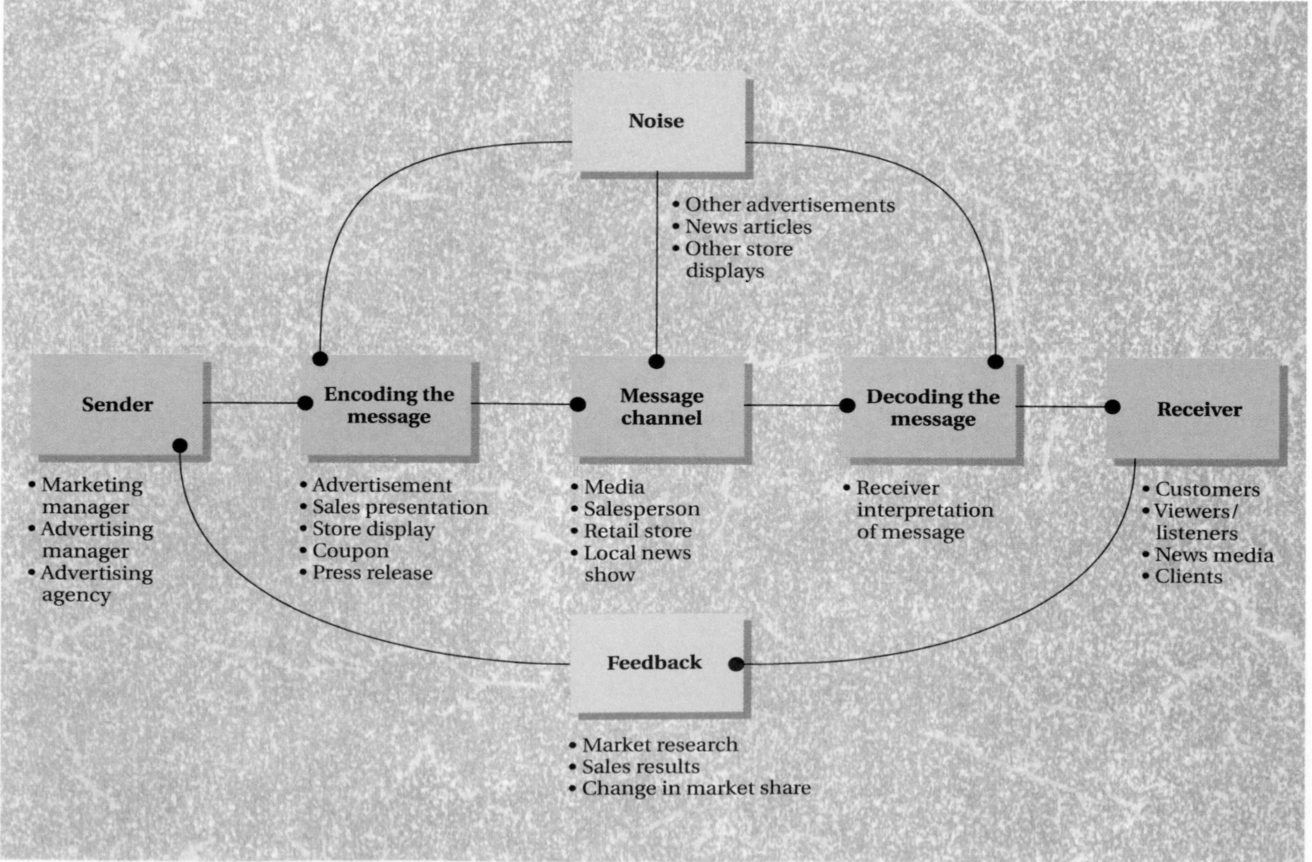

International trade requires extra effort in encoding, transmitting, and decoding messages. Language and culture differences constitute "noise" within the communication process.
© Comstock

The Sender and Encoding

sender
Originator of the message in the communication process.

The **sender** is the originator of the message in the communication process. It may be a person or an organization. In an interpersonal conversation, the sender may be a parent, a friend, or a salesperson. For an advertisement or press release, the sender is the company itself. Compaq Computer, for example, became the sender of a very important message: the introduction of its ProLinea line of low-priced personal computers.

encoding
Conversion of the sender's ideas and thoughts into a message, usually in the form of words or signs.

Encoding is the conversion of the sender's ideas and thoughts into a message, usually in the form of words or signs. In advertising, Compaq might rely on an advertising agency to encode the message. The agency encodes a promotional message that is usually concise, brief, logical, and audience-centered. The salesperson likewise encodes the promotional message as a sales presentation.

A basic principle of encoding is that what matters is not what the source says but what the receiver hears. One way of conveying a message that the receiver will hear properly is to use concrete words and pictures. For example, concrete copy like Ford's "Have you driven a Ford lately" slogan may generate a more favorable attitude and facilitate better understanding than the more abstract slogan "Get to know Geo" or Mazda's slogan "It just feels right."

Another way to ensure an effectively encoded message is to use words and phrases that the receiver will readily identify with. For example, many advertisers use slang terms in their message when they want to appeal to teenagers. Pepsi's "Chill out" commercials, which feature teens "chilling" on the beach with Pepsi, succeeded because the language makes the product appeal relevant and up to date. Similarly, McDonald's "Boys on the Block" commercial uses slang terms like *fresh*, *sup*, and *word* that are popular with today's teens.[8]

Message Transmission

channel
Medium of communication—such as a voice, radio, or newspaper—for transmitting a message.

Transmission of a message requires a **channel**—for example, a voice, radio, newspaper, or other communication medium. A facial expression or gesture can also serve as a channel. Reception occurs when the message is detected by the receiver

and enters his or her frame of reference. In a two-way conversation, such as a sales presentation given by a Compaq sales representative, reception is normally high.

In contrast, the desired receivers may or may not detect Compaq's message when it is mass-communicated, because most media are cluttered. For instance, in some media overcrowded with advertisers, such as newspapers and television, the level of reception of communication is low. Mass communication may not even reach all the right consumers. Some members of the target audience may be watching TV when the ProLinea computer is advertised, but others may not be watching then.

The Receiver and Decoding

receiver
Person who decodes a message.

decoding
Interpretation of the language and symbols sent by the source through a channel.

Compaq communicates its message to customers or **receivers**, who will decode the message. **Decoding** is the interpretation of the language and symbols sent by the source through a channel. Again, without common understanding, Compaq's message will not be understood.

Even though a message has been received, it will not necessarily be properly decoded. When people receive a message, they tend to manipulate, alter, and modify it to reflect their own biases, needs, knowledge, and culture. People from the United States, for example, often assume that Australians are just like them in their interpretations of language and gestures because they both speak English. Yet Australians often have significantly different meanings for common U.S. phrases and body language. For instance, the "thumbs up" sign in the United States means "good" or "okay," whereas to Australians it is a vulgar gesture.

Feedback

feedback
Receiver's response to a message.

In interpersonal communication, the receiver's response to a message is direct **feedback** to the source. Feedback may be verbal, as in saying "I agree," or nonverbal, as in nodding, smiling, frowning, or gesturing.

Since mass communicators like Compaq are cut off from direct feedback, they must rely on market research or analysis of sales trends for indirect feedback. Compaq might use such measurements as the percentage of radio listeners or magazine readers who recognize, recall, or state that they have been exposed to the ProLinea message. Indirect feedback enables mass communicators to decide whether to continue, modify, or drop a message.

Noise

noise
Anything that interferes with, distorts, or slows down the transmission of information.

Noise is anything that interferes with, distorts, or slows down the transmission of information. Noise can hinder any phase of the communication process. Competing computer ads can be a source of noise for Compaq's ProLinea message. Stories in a newspaper can act as noise, preventing reception of ProLinea's newspaper advertisement. Other hindrances to effective communication include situational factors, such as physical surroundings—light, sound, location, weather, and so on. Communication can also be hindered by the presence of other people or the temporary moods consumers might bring to the situation.

3 THE GOALS OF PROMOTION

People communicate with one another for many reasons. They seek amusement, ask for help, give assistance or instructions, provide information, and express ideas and thoughts. Promotion, on the other hand, seeks to modify behavior and thoughts

in some way. For example, promoters may try to persuade consumers to eat at Burger King rather than at McDonald's. Promotion also strives to reinforce existing behavior—for instance, getting consumers to continue to dine at Burger King once they have converted. The source (the seller) hopes to project a favorable image or to motivate purchase of the company's goods and services.

The Three Basic Tasks of Promotion

Promotion can perform one or more of three tasks: *inform* the target audience, *persuade* the target audience, or *remind* the target audience. Often a marketer will try to accomplish two or more of these tasks at the same time. Exhibit 15.3 lists the tasks of promotion and some examples of each.

The main thrust of this Norelco ad is to inform consumers of the electric shaver's special features and their benefits.
Norelco Consumer Products Co.

Informing

Informative promotion is generally more prevalent during the early stages of the product life cycle. It is a necessary ingredient for increasing demand for a general product category or introducing a new good or service. People typically will not buy a good or service or support a nonprofit organization until they know its purpose and benefits. Therefore, an informative ad may convert an existing need into a want or stimulate interest in a new product. Consumer advocates and social critics generally praise the

Exhibit 15.3

Possible Promotion Tasks and Examples

Informative promotions:
Increasing the awareness of a new brand or product class
Informing the market of new product attributes
Suggesting new uses for a product
Reducing consumers' anxieties
Telling the market of a price change
Describing available services
Correcting false impressions
Explaining how the product works
Building a company image
Persuasive promotions:
Building brand preference
Encouraging brand switching
Changing customers' perceptions of product attributes
Influencing customers to buy now
Persuading customers to receive a sales call
Reminder promotions:
Reminding consumers that the product may be needed in the near future
Reminding consumers where to buy the product
Keeping the product in consumers' minds during off times
Maintaining consumer awareness

informative function of promotion, since it helps the consumer make more intelligent purchase decisions.

More complex products, whether new or not, also require informative advertising. Examples include automobiles, computers, and investment services. Advertising promoting these products must detail their technical benefits. Informative advertising is also important for a "new" brand being introduced into an "old" product class—for instance, Lever 2000, discussed in the chapter opening. The new product will have to establish itself against the more mature products by explaining its benefits, initiating awareness, and positioning itself in the marketplace. The International Perspectives article that follows discusses the challenges Heinz encountered when promoting its ketchup in foreign markets.

INTERNATIONAL PERSPECTIVES

Exporting the Taste of Ketchup

To many U.S. consumers, dousing french fries in ketchup is natural. But pitching ketchup to the finicky French is like serving frog legs to kindergartners. From Stockholm to Sydney, ketchup just isn't the household staple it is in the United States, where people consume an average of three pounds of the stuff each year. Still, H.J. Heinz is trying to spread the taste of its thick red sauce to the rest of the world. With flat growth in domestic markets, foreign markets may be the Pittsburgh food company's best chance to increase earnings.

Global expansion has brought new dimensions to Heinz's promotional strategy. One of the biggest challenges has been figuring out which countries are receptive to which messages. For instance, promotional efforts in France have yielded some disappointing results. Once the market leader, Heinz was edged out by the French brand Amora ketchup, which was apparently more in tune with French tastes and trends. Amora's market research showed that youngsters were more receptive than adults to U.S. products, of which ketchup is a prime example. Amora took the number-one market position from Heinz by introducing plastic bottles resembling rocket ships and running television ads featuring kids using ketchup to paint smiling faces on fried eggs. Meanwhile, Heinz was still selling ketchup in glass bottles and running a stodgy ad featuring a cowboy on horseback in the desert lassoing a Heinz ketchup bottle. Heinz has since changed to plastic bottles and is running a youth-oriented ad featuring a sprightly teenager who places an open bottle of ketchup on the edge of a rooftop and runs downstairs in time to catch the spilling ketchup on a hot dog.

Heinz also realized that often its foreign marketing efforts are more successful when the company adapts to local cultural preferences—which often means downplaying the fact that ketchup is a typical U.S. product. In Sweden, where ketchup is served with the traditional meatballs and fishballs, Heinz deliberately avoids reminding consumers of its U.S. heritage. Instead, their ads reflect distinct Swedish concerns, such as good health. Ads emphasize that Heinz ketchup is free of preservatives and artificial coloring. In Finland, Heinz has run ads with health-related messages similar to those that aired in Sweden but reflecting the "down-to-earth" Finnish culture. Advertisements in Greece show how ketchup can be poured on pasta, eggs, and meats. Cooking lessons on how to use ketchup as an ingredient in traditional foods are offered to Japanese homemakers in Tokyo.

Typical U.S. messages still work well in Germany, where Heinz trails Kraft General Foods International's brand of ketchup. There, Kraft and Heinz are trying to outdo each other with ads featuring strong U.S. images and messages. In Heinz's latest television ad, U.S. football players in a restaurant become very angry when the twelve steaks they've ordered arrive without ketchup. Of course, the ad ends happily with plenty of Heinz ketchup to go around. Kraft's latest ad features a James Dean–style character sitting at a corner of a U.S.-style diner and arm wrestling with a bottle of Kraft ketchup. When the bottle tips over and ketchup spills out, a young blond woman sitting next to him coyly dunks a french fry into the puddle.[9]

In this ad for Nicoderm, a skin patch used to help smokers quit, the main goal is to persuade the target audience to ask their doctors for additional information.
Marion Merrell Dow Inc.

Persuading

Persuasion, the second promotional task, may have a negative meaning for many consumers. However, persuasion is simply trying to motivate a consumer to buy a product. Persuasive promotion is designed to stimulate a purchase or an action—for example, to drink more Coke or to use H&R Block tax services. Often a firm is not trying to get an immediate response but rather to create a positive image to influence long-term buyer behavior.

Persuasion normally becomes the main promotion goal when the product enters the growth stage of its life cycle. By this time, the target market should have general product awareness and some knowledge of how the product can fulfill their wants. Therefore, the promotional task switches from informing consumers about the product category to persuading them to buy the company's brand rather than the competitor's. At this time the marketing manager emphasizes the product's real and perceived differential advantages. Promotional messages used to highlight perceived differential advantages often appeal to emotional needs, such as love, belonging, self-esteem, and ego satisfaction.

Persuasion can also be an important goal for very competitive mature product categories, such as many household items, soft drinks, beer, and banking services. The marketplace is now characterized by many competitors, and often the marketing manager must encourage brand switching. Informative promotions are only moderately useful at best, since most of the target market is familiar with the brand's characteristics. The manager hopes that a persuasive campaign will convert some buyers into loyal users. For example, to persuade new customers to switch their checking accounts, a bank's marketing manager may offer a year's worth of free checks and no fees.

Persuasive promotion is not limited to profit-oriented firms. Many nonprofit organizations use persuasive advertising to solicit donations of money or service from the public. For example, the American Red Cross tries to attract blood donors. The American Cancer Society conducts antismoking campaigns. Greenpeace, the international society that protects the earth and its inhabitants, tried to discourage consumers from buying tuna. Why? While harvesting tuna, many fishing crews were killing dolphins in their nets.

Reminding

Reminder promotion is used to keep the product and brand name in the public's mind. This type of promotion prevails during the maturity stage of the life cycle. It assumes that the target market has already been persuaded of the good's or service's merits. Its purpose is simply to trigger a memory. Crest toothpaste, Coca-Cola, Miller beer, and many other consumer products use reminder promotion often.

AIDA and the Hierarchy of Effects

The ultimate goal of any promotion is to get someone to buy a good or service or, in the case of nonprofit organizations, to take some action (for instance, donate blood). A model for reaching promotional goals is called the **AIDA concept.** The acronym stands for Attention, Interest, Desire, and Action—the stages of consumer involvement with a promotional message. First, the promotion manager attracts a person's *attention* by means of a greeting and approach (in personal selling) or loud volume, unusual contrasts, bold headlines, movement, bright colors, and so on (in advertising and sales promotion). Second, a good sales presentation, demonstration, or advertisement creates *interest* in the product. Third, *desire* is created by illustrating how the product's features will satisfy the consumer's needs. Finally, a special offer or simply a strong closing sales pitch may be used to obtain purchase *action.*

AIDA concept
Model that outlines the process for achieving promotional goals in terms of stages of consumer involvement with the message; the acronym stands for Attention, Interest, Desire, and Action.

hierarchy of effects model
Model that outlines the six-stage process by which consumers make purchase decisions: awareness, knowledge, liking, preference, conviction, and purchase.

An expanded version of the AIDA concept is the **hierarchy of effects model** (see Exhibit 15.4). This model proposes that consumers' purchase decisions are the result of a six-stage process: awareness, knowledge, liking, preference, conviction, and purchase. Furthermore, the model assumes that promotion should be used to propel people along the steps in the decision process.

1. *Awareness:* The advertiser must first achieve awareness with the target market. A firm cannot sell something if the market does not know that the good or service exists. Imagine that Acme Company, a pet food manufacturer, introduced a new brand of cat food called Stripes, specially formulated for finicky cats. To increase the general awareness of its new brand, Acme heavily publicizes the introduction and places several ads on TV and in consumer magazines.
2. *Knowledge:* Simple awareness of a brand seldom leads to a sale. The next step is to inform the target market about the product's characteristics. Print ads for Stripes cat food detail the ingredients that cats love—real tuna, chicken, or turkey—as well as the product's nutritional benefits.
3. *Liking:* After the target market learns about the product, the advertiser must generate a favorable attitude. A print ad or TV commercial can't actually tell pet owners whether their cats will like Stripes. Thus Acme will compile a list of cat owners in several major metropolitan cities and send each a sample of the new cat food. Acme hopes to establish liking (by the cats as well as the owners) for their new brand.
4. *Preference:* Even though owners (and their cats) may like Stripes, they may not see any advantage over competing brands, especially if owners are brand loyal. Therefore, Acme must create brand preference by explaining why the product has a differential advantage over the competition. Acme has to convince owners that Stripes has a distinct advantage over other cat foods. Specifically, Acme has to show that cats love it and want to eat nothing else. Advertising at this stage claims that Stripes will satisfy "even the pickiest of the litter."
5. *Conviction:* Although pet owners may come to prefer Stripes to other brands, they still may not have developed the conviction (or an intention) to buy the new brand. At this stage Acme might offer the consumer additional reasons to buy Stripes, such as easy-to-open, zip-lock packaging for keeping the product fresh; additional vitamins and minerals that healthy cats need; and feline taste-test results.
6. *Purchase:* Some members of the target market may now be convinced to buy Stripes but have yet to make the purchase. Displays in grocery stores, coupons,

Exhibit 15.4

The AIDA Process and the Hierarchy of Effects Model

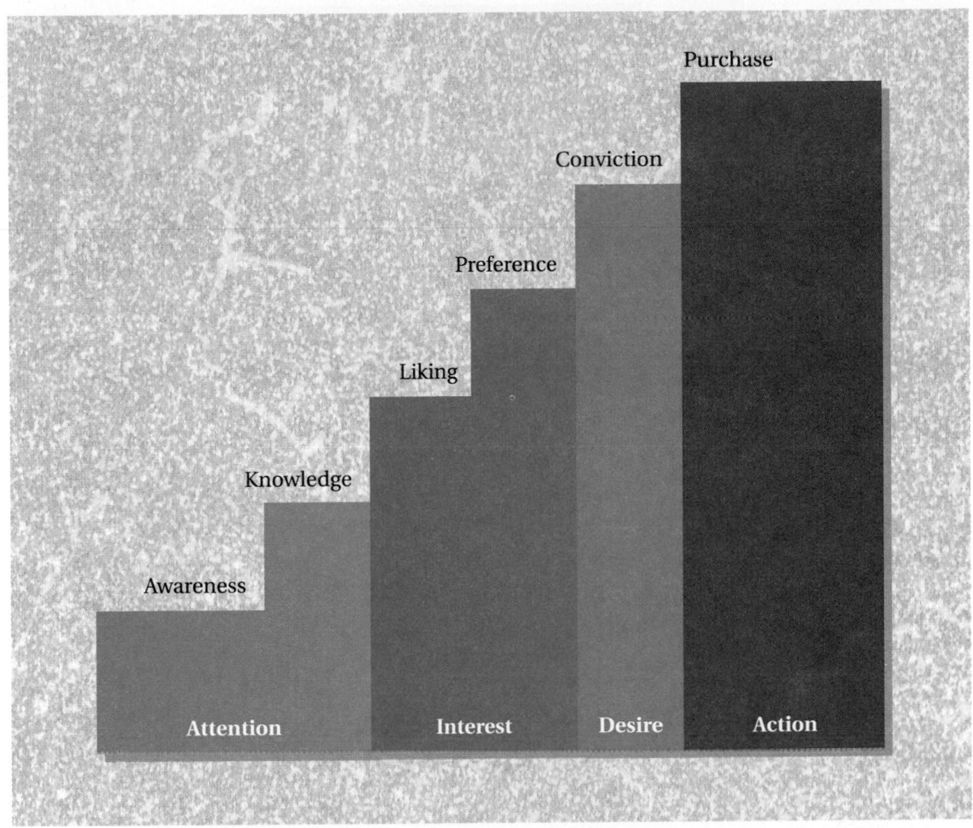

premiums, and trial-size packages can often push the complacent shopper into purchase.

Most buyers pass through the six stages of the hierarchy of effects on the way to making a purchase. The promoter's task is to determine where on the purchase ladder most of the target consumers are located and design a promotion plan to meet their needs. For instance, if Acme has determined that about half its buyers are in the preference or conviction stage but have not bought for some reason, the company may mail cents-off coupons to cat owners to prompt them to buy.

The hierarchy of effects model suggests that promotional effectiveness can be measured in terms of people progressing from one stage to the next. The order of the stages in the hierarchy of effects model has been much debated in academic literature. Certainly, conviction does not occur without knowledge or knowledge without awareness. But can purchase occur without liking or preference—for example, with a low-involvement product bought on impulse? Or can a consumer move up several steps simultaneously?[10] One study found that awareness exists before attitude change (liking and preference) and that conviction to purchase exists before purchase.[11] It was also found that consumers can move up several stages at a time and that the progression is indeed faster with low-involvement purchases.[12]

The effectiveness of promotion at various stages in the hierarchy of effects model can be directly correlated to sales. One early study failed to confirm that movement from one stage to another increases the probability of purchase.[13] However, later studies have found positive relationships between advertising recall and purchase conviction. That is, as recall for the good or service increases, so does the conviction to buy it. A positive relationship was also found between purchase conviction and actual purchase. For instance, the stronger the conviction to buy, the more likely that an actual purchase will take place.[14]

4 THE PROMOTIONAL MIX

promotional mix Combination of promotional tools—including advertising, personal selling, sales promotion, and public relations—used to reach the target market and fulfill the organization's overall goals.

advertising Impersonal, one-way mass communication about a product or organization that is paid for by a marketer.

Rarely is using a single communication resource the best way to achieve a firm's promotional goals. Instead, most promotional strategies use several ingredients—which may include advertising, personal selling, sales promotion, and public relations—to reach the target market. That combination is called the **promotional mix.** The proper promotional mix is the one that management believes will meet the needs of the target market and fulfill the organization's overall goals. The more funds allocated to each promotional ingredient and the more managerial emphasis placed on each technique, the more important that element is thought to be in the overall mix. A summary of the characteristics of the ingredients in the promotional mix is shown in Exhibit 15.5.

Advertising

Advertising is impersonal, one-way mass communication paid for by the sponsor. It can be transmitted by many different media, such as TV, radio, newspapers, magazines, books, direct mail, billboards, and transit cards (advertisements on buses and taxis and at bus stops). Since advertising lacks a means for direct feedback, it cannot adapt as easily as personal selling to the consumers' changing preferences, individual differences, and personal goals.

An advertising campaign usually has five phases: determining the advertising

Exhibit 15.5

Characteristics of the Ingredients in the Promotional Mix

	Advertising	**Personal selling**	**Sales promotion**	**Public relations**
Mode of Communication	***Indirect and impersonal***	***Direct and face-to-face***	***Usually indirect and nonpersonal***	***Usually indirect and nonpersonal***
Communicator control over situation	Low	High	Moderate to low	Moderate to low
Amount of feedback	Little	Much	Little to moderate	Little
Speed of feedback	Delayed	Immediate	Varies	Delayed
Direction of message flow	One-way	Two-way	Mostly one-way	One-way
Control over message content	Yes	Yes	Yes	No
Identification of sponsor	Yes	Yes	Yes	No
Speed in reaching large audience	Fast	Slow	Fast	Usually fast
Message flexibility	Same message to all audiences	Tailored to prospective buyer	Same message to varied target audiences	No direct control over message

objectives, setting the campaign budget, determining the message to be transmitted to the target market, selecting the message vehicle, and evaluating the campaign. Chapter 16 examines this process in detail.

Personal Selling

personal selling
Planned, face-to-face presentation to one or more prospective buyers for the purpose of making a sale.

telemarketing
Personal selling conducted over the telephone.

Personal selling is a planned, face-to-face presentation to one or more prospective buyers for the purpose of making a sale. Personal selling conducted over the telephone is called **telemarketing.**

Advertising is prevalent in the promotional mix for consumer goods, but personal selling is more prevalent for industrial goods. Because industrial products are less standardized, they often are not well suited to mass promotions. Instead, customizing is often required to fit buyers' needs and financial status. To design and sell a custom-made product, firms must secure immediate buyer feedback. Thus personal selling must be used rather than advertising. However, advertising still serves a purpose. Its role in promoting industrial goods may be to create general buyer awareness and interest through advertisements in trade media. Moreover, advertising can help locate potential customers for the sales force. For example, print media advertising often includes coupons soliciting the potential customer to "fill this out for more detailed information."

Sales Promotion

sales promotion
Marketing activities—other than personal selling, advertising, and public relations—that stimulate consumer buying and dealer effectiveness.

Sales promotion consists of marketing activities—other than personal selling, advertising, and public relations—that stimulate consumer purchasing and dealer effectiveness. Sales promotion can be aimed at end consumers, trade customers, or a company's employees. Sales promotions include free samples, contests, bonuses, trade shows, vacation giveaways, and coupons. A major promotional campaign might use several of these sales promotion tools.

Sales promotion is generally a short-run tool used to stimulate immediate increases in demand. Often marketers use sales promotion to improve the effectiveness of other ingredients in the promotional mix, especially advertising and per-

Contests are a form of sales promotion. For example, this Heinz contest is designed to stimulate short-term consumer demand for ketchup.

Courtesy of Heinz U.S.A. (a division of H.J. Heinz Co.)

sonal selling. Research shows that sales promotion complements advertising by yielding faster sales responses.

Public Relations

Concerned about how they are perceived by their target markets, organizations often spend large sums to build a positive public image. Public relations helps an organization communicate with its customers, suppliers, stockholders, government officials, employees, and the community in which it operates. Marketers use public relations not only to maintain a positive image but also to educate the public about the company's goals and objectives, introduce new products, and help support the sales effort. **Public relations** is the marketing function that evaluates public attitudes, identifies areas within the organization that the public may be interested in, and executes a program of action to earn public understanding and acceptance.

public relations
Marketing function that evaluates public attitudes, identifies areas within the organization that the public may be interested in, and executes a program of action to earn public understanding and acceptance.

publicity
Public information about a company, good, or service appearing in the mass media as a news item.

A solid public relations program can generate favorable publicity. **Publicity** is public information about a company, good, or service appearing in the mass media as a news item. Note that the organization is not generally considered the source of the information, although it often is. Although an organization does not pay for this kind of mass media exposure, publicity should not be viewed as free communication. Preparing news releases and persuading media personnel to print or broadcast them cost money. An employee or a public relations consultant performs these activities. Therefore, originating good publicity can be expensive.

Unfortunately, bad publicity comes free but can cost a company millions. Through the mass media the world learns when a firm pollutes a stream, produces a defective product, employs executives engaged in payoffs or bribes, or becomes involved in other undesirable acts. Negative consumer reactions may cost the firm plenty in lost sales. Company disasters or accidents can also hurt a company's image and sales. Many motorists avoided using Exxon products after the *Valdez* oil spill in Alaska in 1989.

5 The Hierarchy of Effects and the Promotional Mix

Exhibit 15.6 depicts the relationship between the promotional mix and the hierarchy of effects model. Advertising seems to be most effective in the awareness and knowledge stages of the hierarchy. Although advertising does have an impact in the

Exhibit 15.6

When Ingredients of the Promotional Mix Are Most Useful

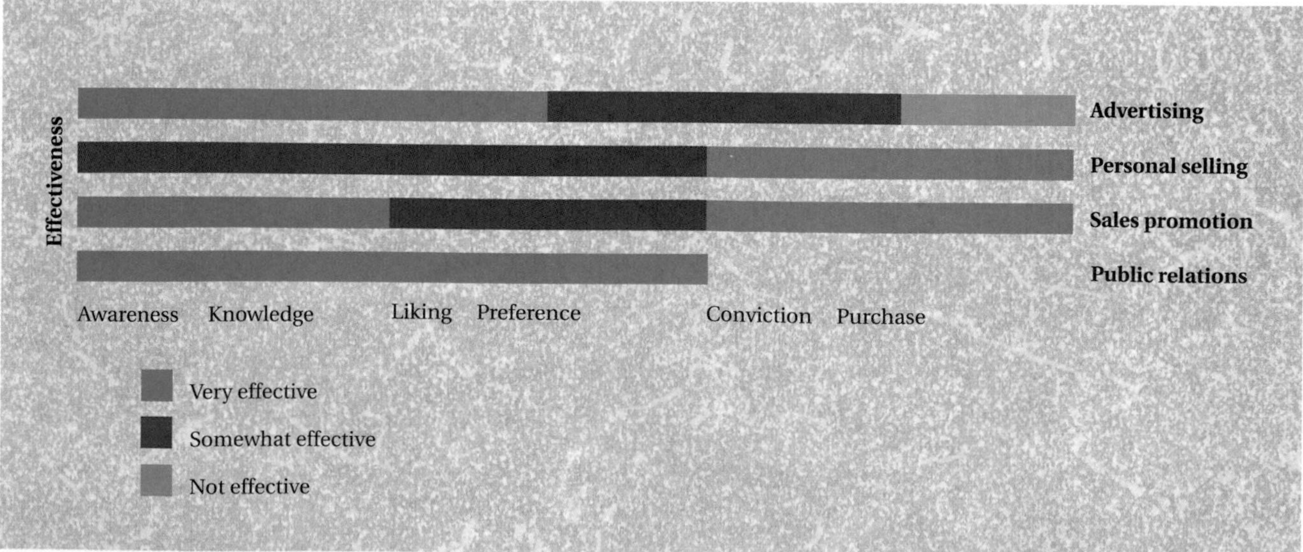

Cincinnati's annual Tall Stacks event, a celebration of the steamboating era, is sponsored by small companies that want to build awareness and big companies that want to build goodwill. Last year's official sponsors included Procter & Gamble, Chiquita Brands International, Lenscrafters, Hillshire Farm & Kahn's Company, and Cincinnati Gas & Electric Company.

The Cincinnati Enquirer/Jim Callaway

later stages, it is most useful in creating awareness and knowledge about goods or services.

In contrast, personal selling reaches fewer people at first. Salespeople are more effective at developing customer preferences for merchandise and at gaining conviction.

A good sales promotion can build awareness of a new product. Sales promotion also can stir strong purchase intent. For example, coupons and other price-off promotions are techniques used to persuade customers to buy new products. Frequent-buyer sales promotion programs, which allow consumers to accumulate points or dollars that can later be redeemed for goods, tend to increase purchase intent as well as encourage repeat purchases. Campbell Soup Company has been running the Labels for Education frequent-buyer program since the mid-1970s. Schools and public libraries collect proofs of purchase and submit them to the company each year in exchange for educational equipment from a catalog. More than 20,000 institutions participate, and Campbell's has given away more than $30 million in gifts since the program started.[15]

Public relations has its greatest impact in building awareness about a company, good, or service. Good publicity can also help develop consumer preference for a product. Many companies can attract attention and build goodwill by sponsoring community events that benefit a worthy cause, such as antidrug and antigang programs. Such sponsorships project the firm's positive image and contribute to a preference for its products in the minds of consumers and potential consumers.

Creating awareness can be difficult, especially for companies that do not sell consumer goods or services. The Ethics in Marketing article on page 498 discusses how Pharmaco, a medical research facility, created awareness through humorous, but controversial, advertisements.

ETHICS IN MARKETING

Camp Pharmaco

"The advertisements are enticing: 'Shoot Pool . . . Get Paid,' 'Watch Movies . . . Get Paid,' say two of them, illustrated with cartoons. 'Planned activities . . . meals and snacks . . . bunk beds . . . billiards . . . friendly counselors . . . just like summer camp' reads another pitch for the place, which in this ad calls itself 'Camp Pharmaco.' There is a big difference from a regular camp, the ad points out: Camp Pharmaco pays *you* up to $3,500.

"Oh, and there's another big difference: You have to take experimental drugs that haven't been proved safe for humans.

"Pharmaco is a medical research facility in Austin, Texas, and a stay here is no vacation: People who sign up take experimental drugs; undergo blood, urine, and other tests several times a day; and may suffer side effects, including headaches, nausea, and disorientation. But who would answer an ad that said all that?"

Pharmaco thinks its approach, although controversial, is much more effective. Most contract-research organizations find human subjects for testing through physician referrals or straightforward ads in the classifieds. But Pharmaco's ads—on billboards, over rock stations, and in newspapers—borrow from those for consumer products by portraying participation in drug studies as fun.

Some find Pharmaco's approach unseemly, arguing that the company's ads tend to trivialize medical research. Others, however, feel the humor in the ads gets the public's attention. A few years ago, Pharmaco used a more conventional recruiting approach, but it couldn't attract enough participants. One reason, it discovered, was the public's perception that Pharmaco was a place homeless people would go to earn money. Conventional advertising just wasn't getting the attention of potential participants. So the company decided to try humorous ads. And they seem to be working. A radio ad to attract acne sufferers featured a mock game show. Contestants who gave incorrect answers to questions about acne got a penalty of another pimple. The ad attracted 500 responses in a few days, far more than the 50 people needed to test an acne medication.

Do you think Pharmaco's humorous approach is unethical, given the very serious nature of its business? How else might Pharmaco attract the attention of potential participants?

Source: Excerpts from Elyse Tanouye, "Volunteers to Test New Drugs Are Enticed by Humorous Pitches and Handsome Pay," *The Wall Street Journal*, 1 October 1992, pp. B1, B7. Reprinted by permission of *The Wall Street Journal*,

6 FACTORS THAT AFFECT THE PROMOTIONAL MIX

Promotional mixes vary a great deal from one product and one industry to the next. Normally, advertising and personal selling are used to promote primary goods and services and are, in turn, supported and supplemented by sales promotion. Public relations helps develop a positive image for the organization and the product line. The nature of the promotional mix depends on several factors: nature of the product, stage in the product life cycle, target market characteristics, type of buying decision, available funds for promotion, and use of either a push or a pull strategy.

Nature of the Product

Characteristics of the product itself can influence the promotional mix. For instance, a product can be classified as either an industrial good or a consumer good.[16] Industrial products are normally custom-tailored to the buyer's exact specifications. Therefore, producers of most industrial goods (except supply items) rely more heavily on personal selling than on advertising. However, advertising is still frequently used for creating awareness. If advertised, industrial goods are promoted chiefly through special trade magazines. Informative personal selling is common for industrial installations, accessories, and component parts and materials. On the other hand, since consumer products are not custom-made, they do not require a company representative who can tailor them to the user's needs. Thus consumer

goods are promoted mainly through advertising to create brand familiarity. Broadcast advertising, newspapers, and various consumer-oriented magazines are used extensively to promote consumer goods, especially nondurables. Sales promotion, the brand name, and the product's packaging are about twice as important for consumer goods as for industrial goods. Persuasive personal selling is important at the retail level for shopping goods, such as automobiles and appliances.

The costs and risks associated with a product also influence the promotional mix. As a general rule, when the costs or risks of using a product increase, personal selling becomes more important. Items that are a small part of a firm's budget (supply items) or of a consumer's budget (convenience products) do not require a salesperson to close the sale. In fact, inexpensive items cannot support the cost of a salesperson's time and effort unless the potential volume is high. On the other hand, expensive and complex machinery, new buildings, cars, and new homes represent a considerable investment. A salesperson must assure buyers that they are spending their money wisely and not taking an undue social or financial risk. Many consumer goods are not products of great social importance because they do not reflect social position. People do not experience much social risk in buying a loaf of bread or a candy bar. However, buying some shopping products and many specialty products, such as jewelry and clothing, does involve a social risk. Many consumers depend on sales personnel for guidance and advice in making the "proper" choice.

Stage in the Product Life Cycle

The product's stage in its life cycle is a big factor in designing a promotional mix (see Exhibit 15.7). During the introduction stage, the basic goal of promotion is to inform the target audience that the product is available. Initially, the emphasis is on the general product class—for example, personal computer systems. This emphasis gradually changes to awareness of specific brands, such as IBM, Apple, and Compaq. Typically, both extensive advertising and public relations inform the target audience of the product class or brand and heighten awareness levels. Sales promotion encourages early trial of the product, and personal selling gets retailers to carry the product.

Exhibit 15.7

The Product Life Cycle and the Promotional Mix

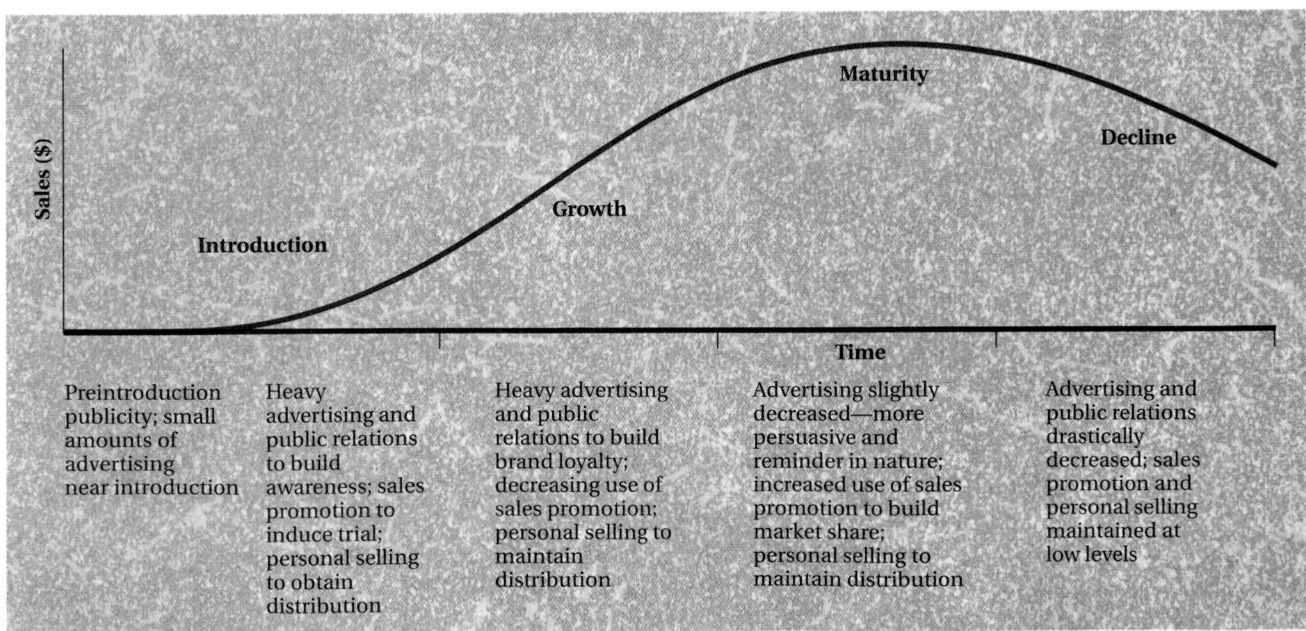

Competition is fierce in the mature market for breakfast cereals, and so advertising tends to be strongly persuasive.
© 1990 General Mills, Inc.

When the product reaches the growth stage of the life cycle, the promotion blend may shift. Often a change is necessary because different types of people are targeted. Although advertising and public relations continue to be major elements of the promotional mix, sales promotion can be reduced, since consumers need fewer incentives to purchase. The promotional strategy is to emphasize the product's differential advantage over the competition. Persuasive promotion is used to build and maintain brand loyalty to support the product during the growth stage. By this stage, personal selling has usually succeeded in getting adequate distribution for the product.

As the product reaches the maturity stage of its life cycle, competition becomes fiercer, and thus persuasive and reminder advertising are more strongly emphasized. Sales promotion comes back into focus as product sellers try to increase their market share. All promotion, especially advertising, is reduced as product sales decline, although personal selling and sales promotion efforts may be maintained.

Target Market Characteristics

Widely scattered potential customers, highly informed buyers, and brand-loyal repeat purchasers generally require a promotional mix with more advertising and sales promotion and less personal selling. However, sometimes personal selling is required even when buyers are well informed and geographically dispersed. Industrial installations and component parts may be sold to extremely competent people with extensive education and work experience. Yet salespeople must still be present to explain the product and work out the details of the purchase agreement.

Often firms sell goods and services in markets where potential customers are hard to locate. Print advertising can be used to find them. The reader is invited to call for more information or to mail in a reply card for a detailed brochure. As the calls or cards are received, salespeople are sent to visit the potential customers.

Type of Buying Decision

The promotional mix also depends on the type of buying decision—for example, a routine decision or a complex decision. For routine consumer decisions, like buying toothpaste or soft drinks, the most effective promotion calls attention to the brand or reminds the consumer about the brand. Advertising, and especially sales promotion, are the most productive promotional tools to use for routine decisions.

If the decision is neither routine nor complex, advertising and public relations help establish awareness for the good or service. For example, suppose a man is looking for a bottle of wine to serve to his dinner guests. Being a beer drinker, he is

Billboard advertising requires a clear, simple, direct message.
© 1991 Museum of Flight

not familiar with wines. Yet he has seen advertising for Sutter Home wine and has also read an article in a popular magazine about the Sutter Home winery. He may be more likely to buy this brand since he is already aware of it.

In contrast, consumers making complex buying decisions are more extensively involved. They rely on large amounts of information to help them reach a purchase decision. Personal selling is most effective in helping consumers decide. For example, consumers thinking about buying a car usually depend on a salesperson to provide the information they need to reach a decision.

Available Funds

Money, or the lack of it, may easily be the most important factor in determining the promotional mix. A small, undercapitalized manufacturer may rely heavily on free publicity if its product is unique. If the situation warrants a sales force, a financially strained firm may turn to manufacturers' agents, who work on a commission basis with no advances or expense accounts. Even well-capitalized organizations may not be able to afford the advertising rates of publications like *Better Homes and Gardens, Reader's Digest,* and *The Wall Street Journal.* The price of a single advertisement in these media could often support a salesperson for a year.

When funds are available to permit a mix of promotional elements, a firm will generally try to optimize its return on promotion dollars while minimizing the cost per contact, or the cost of reaching one member of the target market. In general, the cost per contact is very high for personal selling, public relations, and sales promotions like sampling and demonstrations. On the other hand, for the number of people national advertising reaches, it has a very low cost per contact.

Usually there is a trade-off among the funds available, the number of people in

the target market, the quality of communication needed, and the relative costs of the promotional elements. For instance, a company may have to forgo a full-page, color advertisement in *People* magazine in order to pay for a personal sales effort. Although the magazine ad will reach more people than personal selling, the high cost of the magazine space is a problem.

Push and Pull Strategies

push strategy
Marketing strategy that uses aggressive personal selling and trade advertising to convince a wholesaler or a retailer to carry and sell particular merchandise.

pull strategy
Marketing strategy that stimulates consumer demand to obtain product distribution.

Manufacturers may use aggressive personal selling and trade advertising to convince a wholesaler or a retailer to carry and sell their merchandise. This approach is known as a **push strategy** (see Exhibit 15.8). The wholesaler, in turn, must often push the merchandise forward by persuading the retailer to handle the goods. The retailer then uses advertising, displays, and other promotional forms to convince the consumer to buy the "pushed" products. This concept also applies to services. For example, the Jamaican Tourism Board targets promotions to travel agencies, which are members of their distribution channel.

At the other extreme is a **pull strategy,** which stimulates consumer demand to obtain product distribution. Rather than trying to sell to the wholesaler, the manufacturer using a pull strategy focuses its promotional efforts on end consumers. As they begin demanding the product, the retailer orders the merchandise from the wholesaler. The wholesaler, confronted with rising demand, then places an order for the "pulled" merchandise from the manufacturer. Thus, stimulating consumer demand pulls the product down through the channel of distribution (see Exhibit 15.8). Heavy sampling, introductory consumer advertising, cents-off campaigns, and couponing are part of a pull strategy. For example, using a pull strategy, the Jamai-

Exhibit 15.8

Push versus Pull Strategies

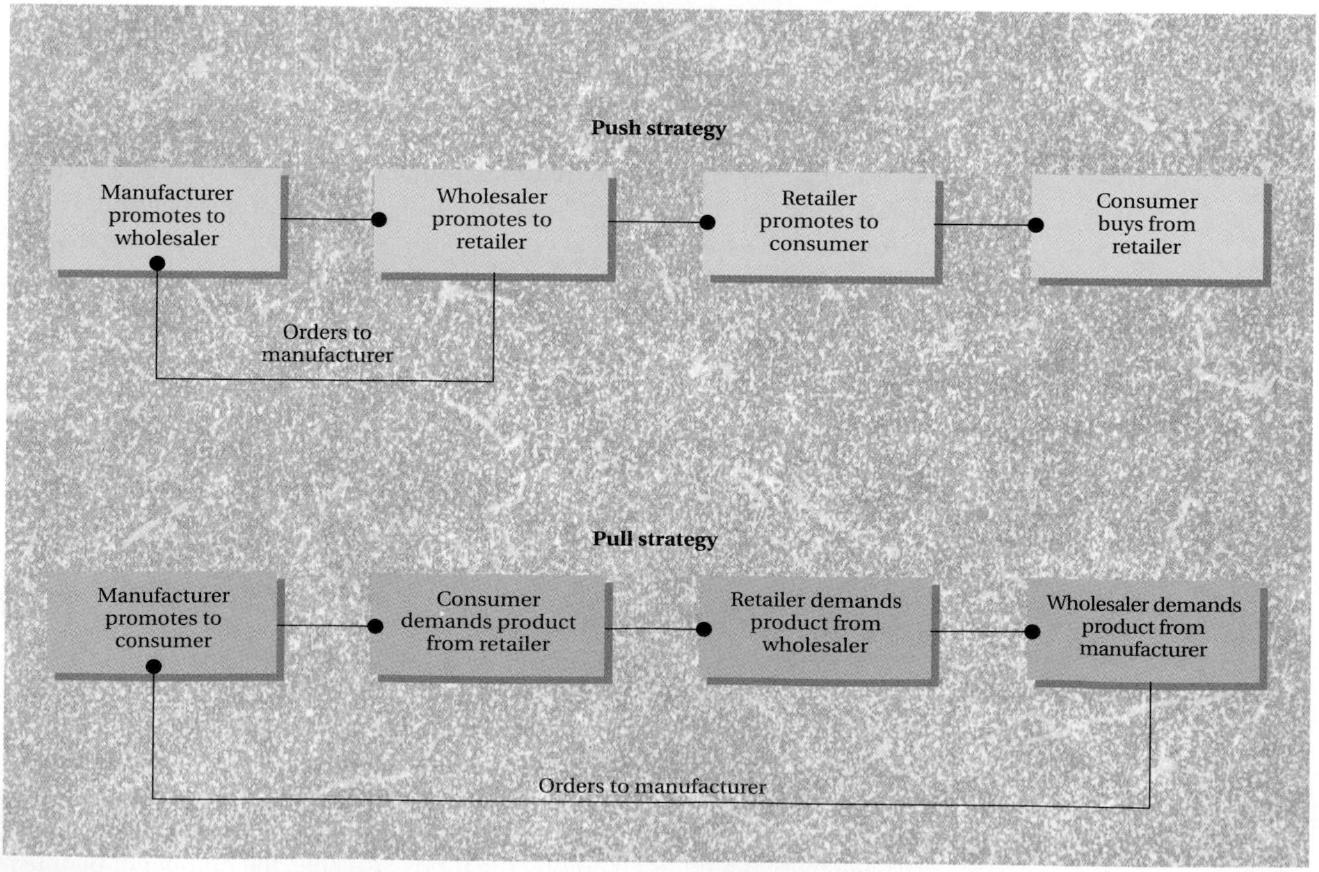

can Tourism Board may entice travelers to come to their island by offering discounts on hotels or airfare. In contrast, a push strategy relies more on extensive personal selling to channel members, on price incentives to wholesalers and retailers, and on trade advertising.

Rarely does a company use a pull or a push strategy exclusively. Instead, the mix will emphasize one of these strategies. For example, pharmaceutical company Marion Merrell Dow uses a push strategy, through personal selling and trade advertising, to promote its Nicoderm patch nicotine withdrawal therapy to physicians. Sales presentations and advertisements in medical journals give physicians the detailed information they need to prescribe the therapy to their patients who want to quit smoking. Marion Merrell Dow supplements its push promotional strategy with a pull strategy targeted directly to potential patients through advertisements in consumer magazines and on television. The advertisements illustrate the pull strategy in action: Marion Merrell Dow directs consumers to ask their doctors about the Nicoderm patch.

7 DEVELOPING THE PROMOTIONAL PLAN

promotional plan
Carefully arranged sequence of promotions designed around a common theme and geared to specific objectives.

A **promotional plan** is a carefully arranged sequence of promotions designed around a common theme that is geared to specific objectives. Because promotion is something of an art, developing a promotional plan can be a challenging task. Despite many specific policies and guidelines, creativity still plays a key role in the success of promotional planning. Effective planning can greatly stimulate sales. For example, recall the Lever 2000 promotion discussed in the chapter's opening story. In contrast, ineffective planning can waste millions of dollars and actually damage the image of the firm or its products. The promotional plan consists of several distinct steps:

1. Analyze the marketplace.
2. Identify the target market.
3. Set promotional objectives.
4. Develop a promotional budget.
5. Choose the promotional mix.

Let's look at each step more carefully.

Analyze the Marketplace

If firms truly accept the marketing concept of fulfilling consumer needs and wants, they must conduct research simply to find out what these needs and wants are. With the increasing complexity of the marketplace, proper research is necessary to ensure an effective promotional plan.

Research identifies the product's target market. Research also determines the plan's promotional objectives. As noted in Chapter 8, information can be obtained through either secondary research or primary research. Internal secondary research—using sales data, data about the effectiveness of previous advertising efforts, and the like—provides the marketing manager with valuable information for promoting a current brand. External secondary data are available through research firms that continually conduct research and sell the results to any company willing to pay. For example, national firms like A.C. Nielsen and Audits and Surveys offer data on consumer goods, such as total sales volume and market share. Using purchase

This Fuji camcorder ad effectively targets a particular market: parents.
Fuji Photo Film USA Inc.

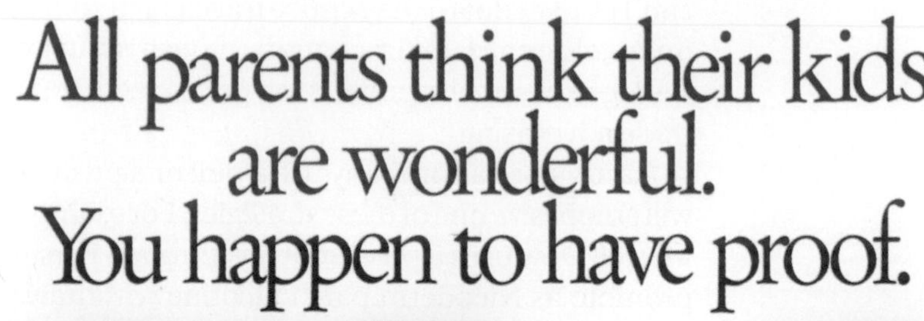

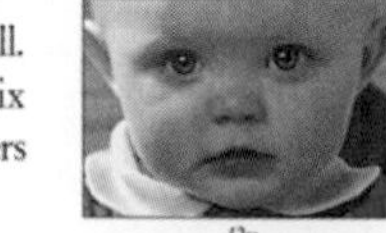

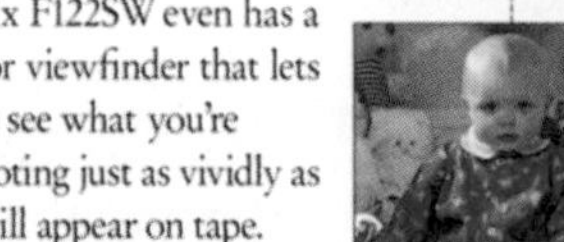

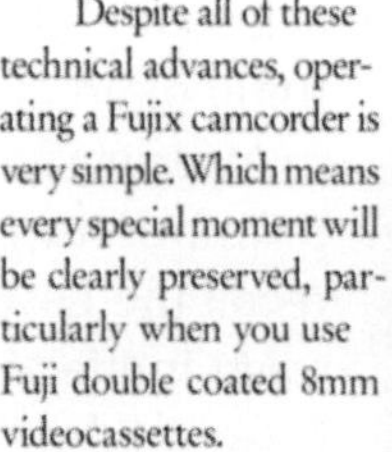

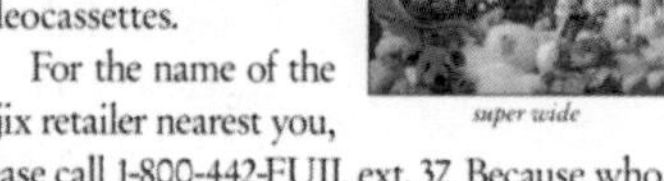

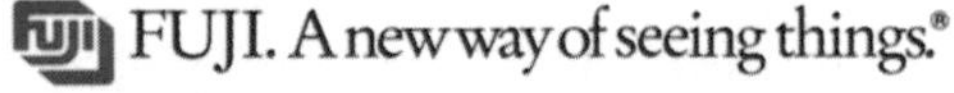

diaries kept by a panel of consumers, Market Research Corporation of America measures the flow of products into homes. And Selling Areas Marketing records the volume of goods shipped from warehouses.

In other cases, primary research, or information collected exclusively for an immediate promotion problem, is necessary for proper planning. Yet market information is usually not available for a new product or a new product category. In that case, primary research might consist of an in-home use test, test marketing, or a focus group. These methods provide valuable insights into potential buyers' characteristics and help the marketer shape the promotional plan.

Identify the Target Market

Through market research, the market segment the firm wants to reach with a given promotional plan should be explicitly defined geographically, demographically, psychographically, or behaviorally. Naturally, the target market should be those most likely to buy the product within a defined period. For example, Honda has defined its target market for the Honda Civic as young married couples with young children.

Set Promotional Objectives

awareness objective
Promotional objective that seeks to increase consumers' knowledge of a product or brand.

attitudinal objective
Promotional objective that seeks to improve or change the product's image by changing consumers' attitude toward it.

behavioral objective
Promotional objective that aims to change a buyer's behavior or prompt the buyer to take some action.

reminder objective
Promotional objective used to cue the consumer that the product is available.

recall objective
Promotional objective aimed at increasing the percentage of the target market that can recall the campaign's message and the product.

Objectives have been discussed in previous chapters, but the need to be specific and realistic requires further explanation. Objectives are the starting point for any promotional plan. Indeed, marketing managers cannot possibly plan a promotional program unless they know what goals they are trying to reach. Of course, promotional objectives should always coincide with overall marketing and corporate objectives.

To be effective, objectives should meet these four criteria:

- Objectives should be measurable and written in concrete terms.
- Objectives should be based on sound research and should identify a well-defined target audience.
- Objectives should be realistic.
- Objectives should reinforce the overall marketing plan and relate to specific marketing objectives.

For a good or service, marketing managers may pursue any combination of the four basic promotional objectives: to increase awareness, to improve or to change the consumer's attitude, to change a buyer's behavior, to remind the consumer of the product, and to increase the buyer's recall of the product. The **awareness objective** seeks to increase consumers' knowledge of a product or brand. This is an especially important objective for new products or improved brands in the introduction stage of the product life cycle. The **attitudinal objective** can also be thought of as an image objective. The goal is to improve or change the product's image by changing consumers' attitude toward it. A **behavioral objective** aims to change a buyer's behavior or prompt the buyer to take some action. The **reminder objective** is simply to cue the consumer that the product is available. Finally, the **recall objective** can only be established after the final execution of the promotional plan. It aims to increase the percentage of the target market that can recall the campaign's message and the product. Examples of some promotional objectives for Peter Pan peanut butter are shown in Exhibit 15.9.

Exhibit 15-9

Examples of Promotional Objectives

Examples of promotional objectives for Peter Pan peanut butter	
Awareness objective	To increase the awareness level for Peter Pan peanut butter from 16% to 24%
Attitudinal objective	To increase the percentage of parents who feel that Peter Pan peanut butter is the best peanut butter for their children from 22% to 35%
Behavioral objective	To increase the average number of jars of Peter Pan peanut butter sold near large residential areas each week from 120 to 135
Reminder objective	To remind consumers that Peter Pan peanut butter is the creamiest peanut butter and available at their nearest grocery and convenience stores
Recall objective	To have 25% of the market recall that Peter Pan peanut butter is the creamiest

The objective of this ad from the Beef Council is attitudinal. Consumers already know about the product, but many have turned from red meat to poultry and fish for diet reasons. The ad seeks to change their opinions about beef.

Develop a Promotional Budget

After identifying the target market and specifying the promotional goals, the marketing manager can develop a concrete budget. This is no simple task, nor is there a cookbook approach that will create an ideal promotional budget. Top marketing management usually defines the role of promotion in the marketing mix and allocates funds for it.

Theoretically, the budget needs to be set at a point where the last dollar spent on promotion equals the profits from the sales produced by that dollar. This technique is not easy to apply, however. Easier techniques for setting budgets rely on arbitrary allocation and all-you-can-afford, competitive parity, percent of sales, market share, and objective and task approaches.

arbitrary allocation
Method of setting a promotional budget that picks a dollar amount without reference to other factors.

all-you-can-afford approach
Method of setting a promotional budget that relies on determining how much the marketer can spend.

competitive parity
Method of setting a promotional budget that matches a competitor's spending.

percent of sales approach
Method of setting a promotional budget that allocates an amount equal to a certain percentage of total sales.

market share approach
Method of setting a promotional budget that allocates the amount needed to maintain or win a certain market share.

Arbitrary Allocation and All-You-Can-Afford

The easiest way to set a promotional budget is simply to pick a dollar amount; this is called **arbitrary allocation.** However, the budget allocated may or may not be enough to effectively promote the product. Nevertheless, many companies use this arbitrary method of allocation for setting their promotional budgets. A variation of the arbitrary allocation approach is for management to figure out how much it can afford to put into promotion. The **all-you-can-afford approach** is a form of arbitrary allocation, because determining what is affordable can be based on many arbitrary criteria. Perhaps the reason for the popularity of these illogical approaches to budget setting is the difficulty of measuring the effectiveness of promotion.

Competitive Parity

A second approach for setting a promotional budget is called **competitive parity**. The firm allocates enough money to meet the promotional challenge of the competition. If Competitor A spends $1 million, then management of Firm B allocates $1 million for promotion. Perhaps the biggest problem with this technique is that it ignores creativity and media effectiveness. If the money is spent in the wrong media or if the campaign is ineffective, spending even $10 million to $50 million won't be enough. One advantage of the competitive parity method is that it does force the firm to examine competitors' actions.

Percent of Sales

Another method of setting a promotional budget is to use a certain percentage of total sales. The formula for a **percent of sales approach** is

$$\text{Promotion dollars} = x\% \times \text{Previous year's total sales}$$

The percent of sales approach is not limited to total sales; it can also be based on sales by product, territory, customer group, and so on. Some firms base their promotional budget on a percentage of the sales forecast for the coming year.

The inherent weakness of this approach is that the budget becomes a consequence of sales rather than a determinant of sales. As sales decline, the promotional budget also falls. Research has shown that advertisers maintaining their promotional budgets during slow sales periods achieve better sales than those that do not. One study found that airlines that increased their advertising and promotion spending during a recession increased sales and market share; airlines that cut promotion spending lost sales and market share.[17] The percent of sales approach also bears little relationship, if any, to a firm's promotional objectives.

The appeal of the percent of sales approach is its simplicity. It is easy for managers to use and understand, since they often view costs in percentage terms. Although many companies follow this practice, studies have shown that use of the percent of sales method has declined quite a bit among organizations of all sizes.[18]

Market Share

Another approach to budgeting is to calculate how much promotion is needed to maintain or win a certain market share. This is the **market share approach.** If a firm is satisfied with its market share, it may decide to spend the dollar amount or percentage it spent to win it. If the organization plans to increase its market share, it can increase its budget to meet its goals.

Like the percent of sales approach, this method ignores quality and creativity.

Who is to say that spending $5 million this year will be more or less effective than spending $5 million last year? Moreover, the firm is letting its competition indirectly set its promotion budget. The market share approach also ignores potential new product offerings. Generally, a new product requires a heavier promotional budget to educate the target market and build product awareness. Aside from recognizing the importance of competition for market share, this approach does not greatly improve on the other methods.

Objective and Task

The most popular and most scientific approach to setting a promotion budget is the **objective and task approach.** First, management sets objectives. Second, it defines the communication tools required to achieve those objectives. Then a budget is built by adding up the costs of the planned promotional activities.

objective and task approach
Method of setting a promotional budget that begins with promotional objectives, defines the communication tools required to achieve those objectives, and then adds up the costs of the planned activities.

The objective and task approach requires that management understand the effectiveness of various promotional tools. It also assumes that achieving the objectives will be worth the costs. Anheuser-Busch uses the objective and task approach. By setting its budget to match promotional objectives, Anheuser-Busch has often been able to reduce promotion expenditures and still increase sales. The key is using promotional dollars more effectively.

Techniques Actually Used

A global survey of advertising managers found that the most popular method for setting advertising budgets was the objective and task method, followed by the percent of sales method. Interestingly, U.S. advertisers used the arbitrary allocation method more often than most of the foreign advertising managers surveyed.[19]

Another study indicated that the trend appears to be toward using the more sophisticated, data-based budgeting techniques, such as the objective and task method, instead of more traditional, judgmental approaches.[20] Several factors have contributed to this switch. First, marketing now has more influence within the organization. Thus promotional expenditures have a higher status in many firms' overall budgeting process. Second, inflation in media prices, particularly television, has consistently outstripped general inflation. Marketers must use sophisticated budgeting methods to make sure that allocating large budgets to media will achieve the desired results. Finally, as the world economy has strengthened and more companies have expanded their operations globally, worldwide media expenditures have continued to rise.[21] Out of respect for global marketing complexities, more firms have been using sophisticated budgeting, which leads to more accurate promotional spending.

Most large U.S. firms and many midsize consumer goods organizations use computerized models to set promotion budgets. These programming models are sophisticated versions of the objective and task approach. In contrast, most small businesses use rather simple procedures for setting promotional budgets, such as arbitrary allocation or the percent of sales approach.

Choose the Promotional Mix

After marketing managers allocate the budget, they select the combination of elements—advertising, sales promotion, public relations, and personal selling—that will be included in the overall promotional plan. Recall that the promotional mix depends on such factors as the type of product, its stage in the product life cycle,

MARKETING AND SMALL BUSINESS

How to Get More from Promotion Dollars

Small businesses should include all the elements of the promotional mix in their promotional plans. Compared with larger firms, the magnitude and scope of promotion for small businesses are less—but not the importance of promotion.

The National Retail Merchants Association estimates that a small business would have to close its doors at the end of three or four years if it did no promotion. The typical small business loses about 20 to 25 percent of its customers annually as people move in and out of the trade area.

For the small business, the objective and task approach to creating a budget is desirable because it is the most scientific method. However, most small businesses use either an arbitrary method or the percent of sales approach.

One method of getting more for the promotional dollar is to feature the nationally promoted products sold by the small business. Hundreds of millions of dollars are spent each year by large manufacturers promoting their products. By incorporating well-known brand names and logos into the promotion campaign, the small-business manager can capitalize on the positive image and pulling power of the national brands.

target market characteristics, type of buying decision, available funds, and push versus pull strategies.

Managers may choose several different elements for one promotional campaign. For example, public relations might be used to create a positive corporate image among target customers. Advertising could focus on developing corporate and product awareness to complement personal selling. The function of personal selling might be to interact with customers, amplify and explain the advertising messages, and design the right product to meet customers' specific needs. Personal selling might also help secure proper distribution for the product. Sales promotion may enter the picture as a special discount to prospective buyers if they purchase right away.

LOOKING BACK

Unilever did not just use advertising to launch Lever 2000, its new brand of soap. It also issued introductory coupons and gave away free samples in an effort to get customers to try the new product. Meanwhile, the company's sales force introduced the new brand to wholesalers and retailers. Public relations was also instrumental in increasing consumer awareness for Lever 2000. NutraSweet, Euro Disneyland, and UPS also use an optimal mix of advertising, personal selling, sales promotion, and public relations to communicate their promotional messages.

As you read the next two chapters on advertising, public relations, sales promotion, and personal selling, keep in mind that marketers try to choose the mix of promotional elements that will best promote their good or service. Rarely will a marketer rely on just one method of promotion.

KEY TERMS

advertising 494

AIDA concept 492

all-you-can-afford approach 507

SUMMARY

1 Discuss the role of promotion in the marketing mix. Promotion is communication by marketers that informs, persuades, and reminds potential buyers of a product in order to influence an opinion or elicit a response. Promotion strategy is the plan for using the elements of promotion—advertising, personal selling, sales

promotion, and public relations—to meet the firm's overall objectives and marketing goals. Based on these objectives, the elements of the promotional strategy become a coordinated promotional plan. The promotional plan then becomes an integral part of the total marketing strategy for reaching the target market, along with product, distribution, and price.

2 Describe the communication process. The communication process has several steps. When an individual or organization has a message it wishes to convey to a target audience, it encodes that message using language and symbols familiar to the intended receiver and sends it through a channel of communication. Reception occurs if the message falls within the receiver's frame of reference. The receiver decodes the message and usually provides feedback to the source. Normally, feedback is direct for interpersonal communication and indirect for mass communication. Noise may hinder any phase of the communication process, thereby distorting the source's intended message.

3 Identify the goals and tasks of promotion. The fundamental goals of promotion are to induce, modify, or reinforce behavior by informing, persuading, and reminding. The hierarchy of effects model outlines the six basic stages in the purchase decision-making process, which are initiated and propelled by promotional activities: (1) awareness, (2) knowledge, (3) liking, (4) preference, (5) conviction, and (6) purchase.

4 Discuss the promotional mix and its components. The promotional mix is composed of four major promotional tools: advertising, personal selling, sales promotion, and public relations. Advertising is a form of impersonal, one-way mass communication paid for by the source. Personal selling involves direct communication, in person or by telephone; the seller tries to initiate a purchase by informing and persuading one or more potential buyers. Sales promotion is typically used to back up other components of the promotional mix by motivating employees and stimulating consumer and business-customer purchasing. Finally, public relations is the function of promotion concerned with a firm's public image. Firms can't buy good publicity, but they can take steps to create a positive company image.

5 Analyze the role of the hierarchy of effects concept in the promotional mix. The hierarchy of effects model proposes that consumers' purchase decisions follow a six-stage process: awareness, knowledge, liking, preference, conviction, and purchase. The components of the promotional mix have varying levels of influence at each stage of the hierarchy of effects model.

6 Identify the factors that affect the promotional mix. Promotion managers consider many factors when creating promotional mixes. These factors include the nature of the product, product life cycle stage, target market characteristics, the type of buying decision involved, availability of funds, and feasibility of push or pull strategies.

7 Explain how to create a promotional plan. Effective promotion planning is crucial to a product's success. Promotion planning involves several distinct steps. First, promotion managers analyze the marketplace, usually by conducting research. Second, managers define the target market in terms of demographic, geographic, psychographic, or behavior variables. The third stage of promotion planning is to set specific promotional objectives. Promotion managers then determine the promotional budget and, finally, select the elements of the promotional mix.

arbitrary allocation 507
attitudinal objective 505
awareness objective 505
behavioral objective 505
channel 487
communication 484
competitive parity 507
decoding 488
differential advantage 484
encoding 487
feedback 488
hierarchy of effects model 492
interpersonal communication 485
market share approach 507
mass communication 485
noise 488
objective and task approach 508
percent of sales approach 507
personal selling 495
promotion 484
promotional mix 494
promotional plan 503
promotional strategy 484
publicity 496
public relations 496
pull strategy 502
push strategy 502
recall objective 505
receiver 488
reminder objective 505
sales promotion 495
sender 487
telemarketing 495

Review Questions

1. Describe the role of promotion in the marketing mix.
2. What is the purpose of informative promotion? When is an informative promotional strategy most appropriate?
3. What is the hierarchy of effects model? Describe its stages.
4. Describe the role of advertising in the promotional mix.
5. Identify the product-related factors that promotion managers consider when creating a promotional mix. Illustrate with examples.
6. How are promotional objectives determined in the promotional planning process?
7. Explain push and pull promotional strategies.

Discussion and Writing Questions

1. Explain the role of promotion in the marketing mix. Describe environments in which its role is lessened or heightened.
2. Why is understanding the target market a crucial aspect of the communication process?
3. With regard to promotion, why is it important for marketers to understand their target market's awareness and predisposition toward a product?
4. What types of products are promoted using persuasion? Give some examples of persuasive promotion.
5. Discuss the role of personal selling and advertising in promoting industrial products. How does it compare to consumer product promotion?
6. Assume that your firm's promotional efforts for a new product failed to meet promotional objectives. Write a report suggesting why.
7. Your company has just developed a complex electronic device that can automatically control all the appliances in a consumer's home. Write a brief promotional plan describing your market analysis efforts, target market selection, promotional objectives, and selection of a promotional mix.
8. Discuss why using the objective and task method to determine a product's promotional budget is superior to other budget-setting methods.

CASES

15.1 *Modern Maturity*

Modern Maturity, published by the American Association of Retired Persons (AARP), is the big seller in the magazine market for those over 50. *Advertising Age* picked the 50-plus market as one of the top ten magazine categories to watch.

Many changes in magazines for older readers have occurred in recent years. Magazines like *Second Wind* (targeted to older couples) and *Moxie* (targeted to older working women) were abandoned in the first year. Other magazines never even progressed beyond the testing phase. Consumers may be getting older, but that doesn't mean they are going to read magazines that remind them of that fact. One key is to never refer to age in the title of the publication.

The demographic profile of the mature reader is what attracted magazine editors to this market. People over 50 years old account for 26 percent of the population but control 50 percent of the discretionary income. The problem that arises is how to address this market segment. These consumers don't think of themselves as old. "When they look in the mirror they tend to see someone fifteen years younger," said Richard Fontana, publisher of *New Choices* magazine.

Editors are starting to rethink their strategies for reaching this market. Some editors are simply hoping to reach this market through existing magazines. Research indicates that readers from 50 to 59 years old prefer computer magazines. Readers aged 60 to 64 choose boating, women's fashion, and airline magazines.

How has *Modern Maturity* achieved success? The magazine uses three strategies. The largest single factor contributing to the success of *Modern Maturity* is the unique subscription base. The annual subscription to the magazine is only $2.40 and is part of membership in AARP. Thus the magazine is first in paid subscriptions (21.4 million) in the United States. The low subscription cost almost guarantees the magazine a large circulation.

The second strategy is to be "relentlessly upbeat." In this respect, *Modern Maturity* has set the tone for the rest of the 50-plus magazines. The publication features personality profiles and articles like a story on volunteers titled "Everyday Heroes: They're Helping Reshape America." The stories featured in *Modern Maturity* don't shy away from the age issue, but the subjects are active, optimistic, and energetic.

The final strategy concerns the advertising policy of *Modern Maturity.* "We don't put down anybody," says editor Robert Wood. The magazine turns away advertisements that have a "downer attitude." For example, *Modern Maturity* does not accept ads for crutches, wheelchairs, or other such products. Although advertising revenues would probably increase 30 percent if it did accept such ads, Wood feels that these types of ads would detract from the upbeat tone of the magazine.

Questions

1. Do you think there is a need to market magazines that target readers over 50 years old? Would it be better to reach this market through other types of publications? Give reasons to support your answer.
2. Do you agree with Robert Wood that advertising influences the reader's perception of the publication? Why or why not?
3. Does *Modern Maturity* share a frame of reference with its readers? How important is a shared frame of reference to the 50-plus market?

Suggested Reading

Patrick M. Reilly, "Older Readers Prove Elusive as Magazines Rethink Strategies for the 'Mature Market,'" *The Wall Street Journal*, 12 July 1990, pp. B1, B4.

15.2 PepsiCo (B)

Video title: *The Diet Pepsi Uh-Huh! Campaign*

PepsiCo, Inc.
Anderson Hill Road
Purchase, NY 10517

SIC codes: 2087 Concentrates, drink
2086 Carbonated beverages
5812 Fast-food restaurants
2096 Snack foods

Number of employees: 266,000

1993 revenues: Approximately $20 billion ($7 billion in soft-drink sales)

Major brands: Pepsi, Diet Pepsi, Crystal Pepsi, Mountain Dew

Largest competitors: Coca-Cola, Dr. Pepper

Background

Coca-Cola's original diet beverage was marketed under the name Tab. It was followed by Diet Pepsi. The original diet drinks used saccharine as the sweetener. Consumers found these drinks to have a bitter aftertaste but bought them for the low-calorie benefits. Then Diet Coke was introduced, with NutraSweet as the sweetener. Consumers prefer the taste of beverages sweetened with NutraSweet, and Diet Coke was a success. PepsiCo changed its recipe for Diet Pepsi in order to use the better-tasting sweetener. Now Diet Pepsi faces the challenge of convincing diet beverage drinkers (especially Diet Coke drinkers) to switch to Diet Pepsi.

Diet Pepsi

The Diet Pepsi Uh-Huh! campaign is the largest promotional campaign ever developed by PepsiCo. It has been fifteen years since Pepsi took on Coca-Cola in the Pepsi Challenge. Now the company is attacking the number-three soft drink, Diet Coke. PepsiCo kicked off its Uh-Huh! campaign by sending a million cases of Diet Pepsi to loyal Diet Coke drinkers and followed up with a heavy advertising and sales promotion campaign. The campaign features Ray Charles and the Uh-Huh! girls (three models who became instant stars).

The Uh-Huh! campaign is a unique blend of promotional efforts. To increase the effectiveness of the campaign, PepsiCo even included an Uh-Huh! update column in *USA Today.* Readers of *USA Today* were given an 800 number to call and vote on the best Uh-Huh! headlines of the week.

Questions

1. How effective do you think advertising and sales promotion are in getting people to switch soft drinks?

2. What stage(s) of the hierarchy of effects model do you think this promotional campaign is most likely to affect?

3. Using Exhibit 15.3, what type of promotion would you say the Uh-Huh! campaign is? Why?

References

Million Dollar Directory 1993 (Parsippany, NJ: Dun & Bradstreet Information Services, 1993).

Standard & Poor's Industry Surveys (New York: Standard & Poor's Corporation, October 1993).

CHAPTER 16

Advertising and Public Relations

LEARNING OBJECTIVES

After studying this chapter, you should be able to

1. Discuss the effect advertising has on market share, consumers, brand loyalty, and product attributes.
2. Identify the major types of advertising.
3. Describe the advertising campaign process.
4. Describe media evaluation and selection techniques.
5. Define the role of advertising agencies.
6. Explain the nature of advertising regulation.
7. Discuss the role of public relations in the promotional mix.

The cola wars rage every day on the television screen. As the Berlin Wall—the post–World War II symbol of the economic and psychic abyss between communism and capitalism—began to crumble in November 1989, Coca-Cola employees were there, crawling through the openings and handing out the soft drink to newly liberated East Germans. Within days, Coca-Cola vehicles were driving to East Berlin, selling Coke from the back of trucks. By the end of 1990, Coca-Cola had sold 20 million cases in a country it had been locked out of for five decades. In 1991 the company was estimated to have sold 70 million to 75 million cases there.

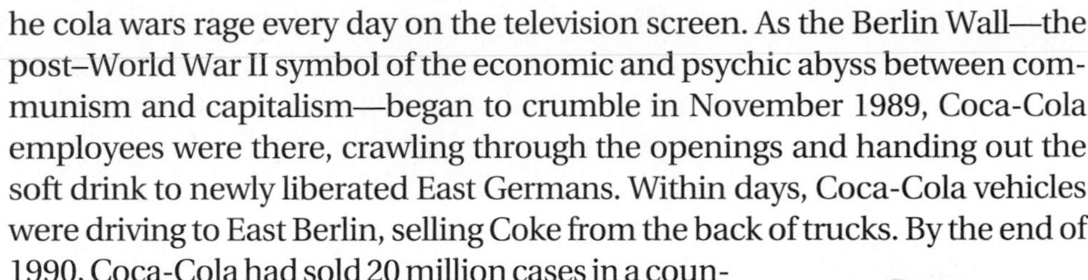

But while Coca-Cola began its ground assault, Pepsi-Cola took to the air. Within days, Pepsi had created, produced, and released a thirty-second spot called "Freedom" that aired to U.S. consumers. It delivered the image that became a symbol of the emerging democracy movement: a child handing an East German soldier a rose.

Coke seized the business at the Berlin Wall. Pepsi seized the moment. And therein lies the marketing quandary in which Coke has found itself entangled for the past few years. The two are neck and neck in domestic share of market based on supermarket sales, with Coke at 33 percent and Pepsi at 31 percent. Overseas, where Coke gets two-thirds of its revenue, it outstrips Pepsi in sales about four to one. And Coke remains the best-known brand in the world.

Yet Pepsi is winning hands down in the advertising image war that is played out on television in thirty- and sixty-second bursts. For most of the last decade, when U.S. consumers have been asked to name their favorite ad campaigns, Pepsi has either topped the list or topped Coke. Pepsi scored a painfully direct hit with a spot that featured rapper M. C. Hammer subdued into a rendition of the mellow pop tune "Feelings" when he mistakenly drinks a Coke. The Ray Charles ads for Diet Pepsi—"You got the right one, baby. Uh-huh"—gave Pepsi a number-one spot again, according to Video Storyboard Tests. Meanwhile, Coke came in sixth and Diet Coke seventeenth.

This reality brought dramatic shifts to Coca-Cola's advertising plans. Some were made in response to Pepsi; more reflect the new dynamics of a global marketplace. The soft-drink company asked its top ad agency, McCann-Erickson, to develop a new campaign and slogan for Coca-Cola Classic. Coke was eager to retire the "Can't beat the real thing" concept, which had been around with some modifications since the mid-1980s. The focus of the new campaign is the idea of "sharing," and it is more global in nature, reflecting Coca-Cola's attempt to create a coordinated worldwide ad campaign. Coke was also a major sponsor of the 1992 Olympics, in which the slogan "Coke: shared around the world" was used to solidify Coke's global image.[1]

How do companies like Coca-Cola and Pepsi create advertising campaigns? How can advertisers increase their product sales through advertising? How do they decide what type of message should be conveyed? In what medium should advertising be directed to the consumer?

❶ ADVERTISING

Advertising is defined in Chapter 15 as any form of impersonal, one-way mass communication that is paid for by the sponsor. Advertising spending increases annually, with estimated U.S. advertising expenditures now exceeding $126 billion per year.[2] Although total advertising expenditures seem large, the industry itself is very small. Only about 700,000 people are employed in the advertising departments of manufacturers, wholesalers, and retailers and in the 5,000 or so U.S. advertising agencies. This figure also includes people working in media services, such as radio and television, magazines and newspapers, and direct-mail firms.[3]

The amount of money budgeted for advertising by some U.S. firms is staggering (see Exhibit 16.1). Procter & Gamble, Philip Morris, Sears, and General Motors each spend over $1 billion annually on national advertising alone. That's over $3 million a day by each company. If sales promotion and public relations are included, this figure rises even higher. About fifty additional companies spend over $200 million each.

Different industries spend varying amounts on advertising. For example, the game and toy industry has one of the highest ratios of advertising dollars to sales. For every dollar of merchandise sold in the toy industry, about 14¢ is spent on advertising the toy to consumers. Other industries that spend heavily on advertising are health clubs and perfume and cosmetics manufacturers. Other big spenders are beverage companies like Coca-Cola and Pepsi and investment advice firms like Merrill Lynch and Dean Witter.[4]

Exhibit 16.1

Top Ten U.S. Advertisers

Source: Adapted with permission from *Advertising Age*, 4 January 1993, p. 16. © Crain Communications Inc., 1993.

Rank	Advertiser	Total annual U.S. ad spending (in millions)
1	Procter & Gamble	$2,149
2	Philip Morris	2,045
3	General Motors	1,442
4	Sears, Roebuck	1,179
5	PepsiCo	903
6	Grand Metropolitan	744
7	Johnson & Johnson	733
8	McDonald's	694
9	Ford Motor	676
10	Eastman Kodak	661

Advertising and Market Share

Today's most successful brands of consumer goods, like Ivory Soap and Coca-Cola, were built by heavy advertising and marketing investments made long ago. Their advertising dollars now are spent on maintaining brand awareness and market share.

New brands with a small market share tend to spend proportionately more for advertising and sales promotion than those with a large market share, typically for two reasons. First, beyond a certain level of spending for advertising and sales promotion, diminishing returns set in. This phenomenon, called **advertising response function**, is illustrated in Exhibit 16.2. For example, proportionately less is spent on advertising by market leader Ivory Soap than, say, a newcomer like Lever 2000. Lever 2000 will spend more in an attempt to increase awareness and market share. Ivory, on the other hand, will spend only as much as is needed to maintain its market share; anything more would reap diminishing benefits. Since Ivory has already captured the attention of the majority of the target market, it only needs to remind customers of its product.

advertising response function
Phenomenon in which spending for advertising and sales promotion increases sales or market share up to a certain level but then produces diminishing returns.

The second reason that new brands tend to require higher spending for advertising and sales promotion is that a certain minimum level of exposure is needed to measurably affect purchase habits. For example, if Lever 2000 advertised in only one or two publications and bought only one or two television spots, it certainly would not achieve the exposure needed to obtain awareness and ultimately affect consumers' purchase intentions. Instead, Lever 2000 was introduced through advertising in many different media for a sustained period.

Advertising and the Consumer

Advertising affects everyone's daily life and influences many purchases. The average U.S. citizen is exposed to about 300 advertisements a day from all types of advertising media. That's about 9,900 a month, or 109,500 per year.[5] Around 10,000 weekly and daily newspapers, 11,000 magazines, 8,500 AM-FM radio stations, 600 television stations, billions of pieces of direct mail, and thousands of billboards are sure to have an impact on consumers. Advertising affects the TV programs people watch, the content of the newspapers they read, the politicians they elect, the medicines they take, and the toys their children play with. Consequently, advertising's influ-

Exhibit 16.2

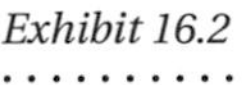

The Advertising Response Function

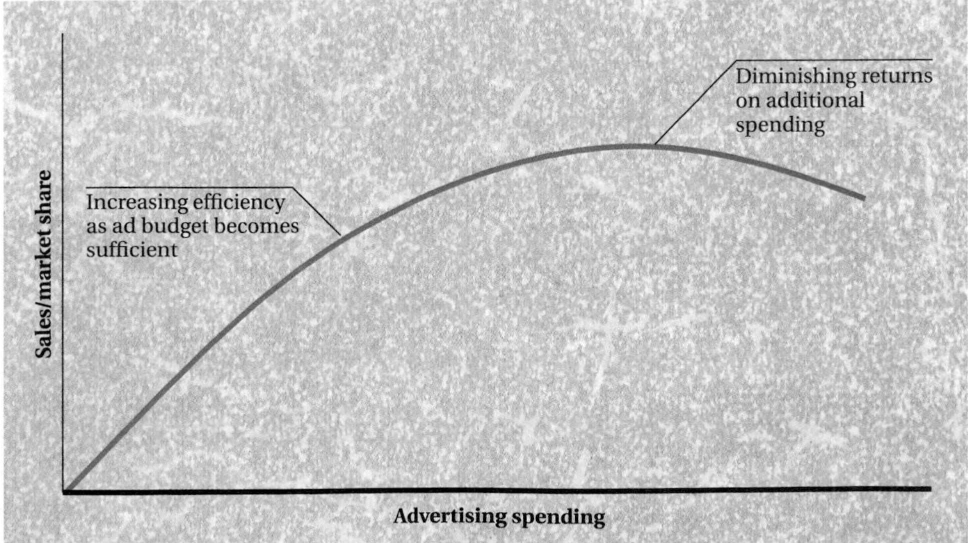

Humor in advertisements, as in this ad for Purina dog chow, is most effective with consumers who already have a positive image of the product.

ence on the U.S. socioeconomic system has been the subject of extensive debate among economists, marketers, sociologists, psychologists, politicians, professors, consumerists, and many other groups.

Attitudes and values are deeply rooted within an individual's psychological makeup. Advertising seldom succeeds in changing an attitude that stems from a person's basic value system, or moral code, and is strongly supported by his or her culture. Since advertising cannot change strongly held values, it cannot manipulate society. All the advertising in the world is not going to convince a teenage girl to buy a Barbie doll rather than clothes or makeup. However, advertising may succeed in transforming a person's negative attitude toward a product into a positive one. When prior evaluation of the brand is negative, serious or dramatic advertisements are more effective at changing consumers' attitudes. Humorous ads, on the other hand, have been shown to be more effective at changing attitudes when consumers already have a positive image of the advertised brand.[6]

Consumers' positive or negative attitudes toward an advertiser can also influence their attitudes toward the advertised product. Research has shown that when consumers feel an advertiser is trustworthy and credible, they are more likely to accept the advertised product's claim and more likely to change their attitudes and buying behavior.[7]

Advertising and Brand Loyalty

A high degree of brand loyalty is one of the advertiser's best assets, since brand value and consumer preference for the brand are the basis of market share.[8] For instance, new competitors found it hard to dislodge AT&T, "Ma Bell," after deregulation of the long-distance telephone industry. After relying on AT&T for a lifetime of service, many loyal customers have shown little response to advertising by competing companies.

Advertising can also influence product and brand selection when a neutral or favorable frame of reference already exists. When consumers are already highly loyal to a brand, they may buy more of it when advertising and promotion for that brand increase.[9]

Advertising and Product Attributes

Advertising can affect the way consumers rank a brand's attributes. When making a purchase decision, consumers can usually recall such brand attributes as color, taste, smell, and texture. For example, in the past shoppers may have selected a brand of luncheon meat based on those attributes important to them—for example, taste and variety of cuts. Today, advertising may influence consumers to choose other attributes as more important than taste and variety, specifically lower calories and fat content. Luncheon meat marketers such as Louis Rich, Oscar Mayer, and Healthy Choice now stress the amount of calories and fat when advertising their products. Automobile advertisers also have traditionally emphasized brand attributes in their advertisements. In years past, attributes such as roominess, speed, and low maintenance were considered some of the more important attributes of cars. Today,

car marketers have added safety to their list of important attributes. Safety features like antilock brakes, power door locks, and air bags are now standard messages in many carmakers' ads.

❷ THE MAJOR TYPES OF ADVERTISING

institutional advertising Form of advertising designed to enhance a company's image rather than promote a particular product.

product advertising Form of advertising that touts the benefits of a specific good or service.

The promotional plan's objectives are what determine the type of advertising used by the firm (refer back to Chapter 15). If the goal of the promotional plan is to build up the image of the company, or the industry, **institutional advertising** may be used by the advertiser. In contrast, if the advertiser wants to enhance the sales of a specific good or service, **product advertising** is used.

Institutional Advertising

Advertising in the United States has historically been product-oriented. However, modern corporations that market multiple products need a different type of advertising, the purpose of which is to promote the corporation as a whole. Institutional advertising, or corporate advertising, is designed to establish, change, or maintain the corporation's identity.[10] It usually does not ask the audience to do anything but maintain a favorable attitude toward the advertiser and its goods and services. When using institutional advertising, a corporation has four important audiences to keep in mind: the public, which includes legislators, businesspeople, and opinion leaders; the investment community, mainly stockholders; customers; and the employees of the company.

Competitive pressures and growing consumer interest in issues linked to a company's products make institutional advertising more critical than ever. Companies like Procter & Gamble and Toyota have recently launched campaigns to promote their corporate images. For instance, P&G is advertising its environmental efforts—such as recycling plastic detergent bottles and composting disposable diapers—when selling brands. In Toyota's "Investing in the Individual" campaign, the corporation is promoting Toyota-sponsored community services, such as student scholarships, rather than cars.[11]

Phillips Petroleum seeks to maintain favorable attitudes among the public by running ads like this one.

1993 Dr. Scott Nielsen/Bruce Coleman, Inc.

advocacy advertising
Form of advertising in which an organization expresses its views on controversial issues or responds to media attacks.

A unique form of institutional advertising called **advocacy advertising** is a way for corporations to express their views on controversial issues. Most firms' advocacy campaigns react to criticism or blame. Some advocacy campaigns directly respond to criticism by the media. Still other campaigns try to ward off increased regulation or damaging legislation.[12] For example, Philip Morris Company responded to legislation that would limit tobacco advertising through its advocacy advertising, sponsoring the 200th anniversary of the Bill of Rights. Philip Morris indirectly told consumers and legislators that the company had the right of free speech (implicitly protected by the Bill of Rights) and, therefore, the right to advertise cigarettes.

Product Advertising

Unlike institutional advertising, product advertising touts the benefits of a specific good or service. Product advertising can best be implemented as pioneering advertising, competitive advertising, or comparative advertising. The product's stage in its life cycle often determines which type of product advertising is used.

Pioneering Advertising

pioneering advertising
Form of advertising designed to stimulate primary demand for a new product or product category.

Pioneering advertising is intended to stimulate primary demand for a new product or product category. Heavily used during the introductory stage of the product life cycle, pioneering advertising offers consumers in-depth information about the benefits of the product class. Food companies, which introduce many new products, often use pioneering advertising. Reebok used pioneering advertising to introduce a new line of outdoor training shoes.

Competitive Advertising

competitive advertising
Form of advertising designed to influence demand for a specific brand.

Firms use competitive advertising when a product enters the growth phase of the product life cycle and other companies begin to enter the marketplace. Instead of building demand for the product category, the goal of **competitive advertising** is to influence demand for a specific brand.

Often promotion becomes less informative and more emotional during this phase. Advertisements may begin to stress subtle differences in brands, with heavy

To introduce its new line of outdoor shoes, Reebok used pioneering advertising, which presents a lot of information about the product class.
Reebok International, Ltd.

emphasis on building brand name recall and creating a favorable brand attitude. Automobile advertising has long been very competitive. Carmakers compete on factors such as quality, performance, and image. For example, Ford Motor Company stresses the theme "Quality is job one" in its advertising, and Buick's "The new symbol for quality in America" and Mercury's "All this and the quality of a Mercury" slogans also emphasize superior workmanship. The beer, soft-drink, fast-food, and long-distance telephone service industries also wage advertising "wars." Price often becomes a key promotional weapon as products begin to resemble one another.

Comparative Advertising

comparative advertising Form of advertising that compares two or more specifically named or shown competing brands on one or more specific attributes.

A controversial trend in product advertising is the growth and regulation of comparative advertising. **Comparative advertising** compares two or more specifically named or shown competing brands on one or more specific attributes. Advertisers make taste, price, and preference claims, often at the expense of the competing brand. For instance, in regional markets Coors is using a campaign claiming that 58 percent of Budweiser drinkers preferred Coors Extra Gold in taste tests. The comparative campaign's television spots, which show and mention both the competitor's product and its brand name, portray Extra Gold as tasting better than Budweiser. Sales increased 50 percent or more in markets where the comparative ads ran. Coors now plans to extend its taste claim against Miller Genuine Draft and Michelob.[13]

Before the 1970s, comparative advertising was allowed only if the competing brand was veiled and unidentified. In 1971, the Federal Trade Commission (FTC) fostered the growth of comparative advertising by saying that it provided information to the customer and that advertisers were more skillful than the government in communicating this information. Comparative ads soon flooded the marketplace. Marketers estimate that about four of every ten advertisements are comparative in some way, whether subtle or direct.[14] However, new federal rulings have prohibited advertisers from falsely describing competitors' products and may even allow competitors to sue if ads show their products or mention their brand names. This new law also applies to advertisers making false claims about their own products. For example, a federal court ordered Ralston Purina to pay several million dollars in damages to Alpo Pet Foods for making false claims about Ralston's own dog food in comparative advertising.

Is comparative advertising effective? Academic research on the subject reveals these findings:

- Direct comparative advertisements attract attention and thereby enhance purchase intentions. These ads may decrease purchase intentions for established brands by increasing consumer awareness of new ones.[15]
- Consumers perceive comparative messages as being more relevant and are able to recall more message points than if they are exposed to similar noncomparative ads.[16]
- When comparative ads are personally relevant and a brand with high credibility is the comparison product, comparative advertising for a new brand has a more positive effect on purchase intentions.[17]

The hard-sell tactics found so often in comparative ads in the United States are taboo in many countries. Germany and France do not permit advertisers to make comparative claims stating that their products are the best or better than competitors', common claims in U.S. advertising. In other nations, claims that seem exaggerated by U.S. standards are commonplace, particularly in newly capitalized countries in Eastern Europe. However, many Eastern European countries are cracking down on comparative advertising and exaggerated claims. For example, Hungary's Economic Competition Council fined Unilever the equivalent of $25,000 for running an ad claiming its brand of detergent removed stains better than "ordinary detergent." The council said the ad was unfair because the phrase "ordinary detergent" would be misunderstood by Hungarian consumers as a reference to a local detergent.[18]

3 CREATING THE ADVERTISING CAMPAIGN

advertising campaign Series of related advertisements focusing on a common theme, slogan, and set of advertising appeals.

An **advertising campaign** is a series of related advertisements focusing on a common theme, slogan, and set of advertising appeals. It is a specific advertising effort for a particular product that extends for a defined period of time. Management of advertising begins with understanding the steps in developing an advertising campaign and then making the important decisions relating to each step. Exhibit 16.3 traces the steps of the advertising campaign decision process.

The advertising campaign process is initially set in motion by the promotional plan discussed in Chapter 15. As you will remember, the promotional planning process identifies the target market, determines the overall promotional objectives, sets the promotional budget, and selects the promotional mix variables. Now advertising, along with the other promotional mix variables chosen, is used to encode a selling message to the target market. The advertisement is then conveyed to the target market, or receivers of the message, through such advertising vehicles as broadcast or print media.

Determine Campaign Objectives

advertising objective Specific communication task a campaign should accomplish for a specified target audience during a specified period.

The first step in the development of an advertising campaign is to determine the advertising objectives. An **advertising objective** is the specific communication task a campaign should accomplish for a specified target audience during a specified period of time. The DAGMAR approach (Defining Advertising Goals for Measured Advertising Results) is one method of setting objectives. According to this method,

Exhibit 16.3

The Advertising Campaign Decision Process

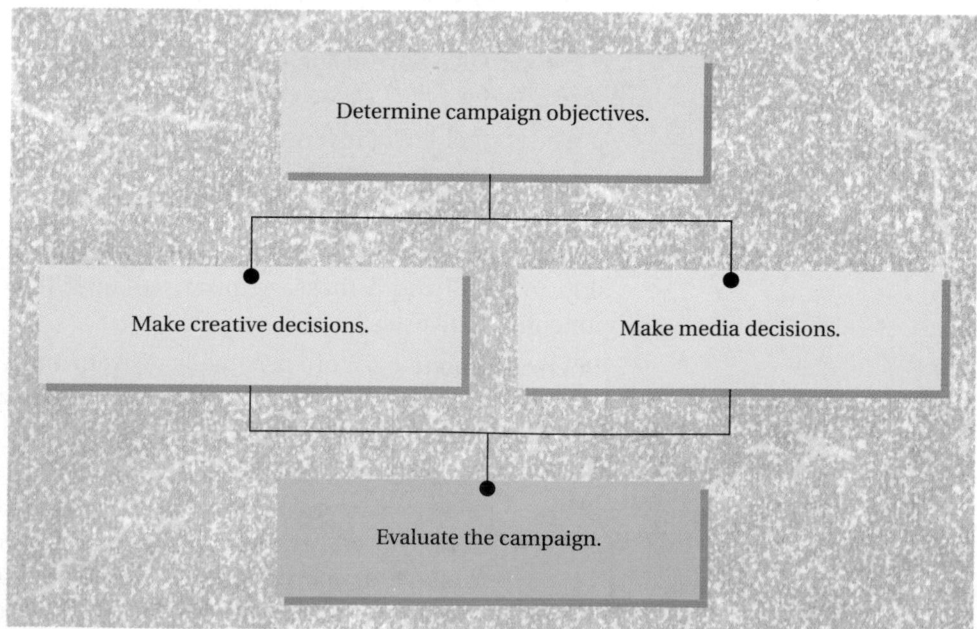

Burger King constructed an advertising campaign around the idea of BK TEEVEE and used the same character and slogan in the entire series of ads.
Courtesy Burger King Corporation

all advertising objectives should precisely define the target audience, the desired percentage change in some specified measure of effectiveness, and the time frame in which that change is to occur.

The objectives of a specific advertising campaign depend on the overall corporate objectives and the product being advertised. For example, an advertising campaign for the Toyota Camry might set this objective: to increase by 12 percent over the next two years the number of potential 25-to-30-year-old Camry buyers who are exposed to Camry ads. For BMW's introduction of new, lower-priced models, the objective might be to achieve a total of 50,000 consumer test drives within the first six months of introduction as a result of mailing video advertisements to a sample of the target audience.

Make Creative Decisions

The next step in developing an advertising campaign is to make the necessary creative and media decisions. Note in Exhibit 16.3 that both creative and media decisions are made at the same time. Creative work cannot be completed without knowing which **medium**, or message channel, will be used to convey the message to the target market. However, media decisions are addressed in this book after creative decisions.

medium
Channel used to convey a message to a target market.

In many cases, the advertising campaign objectives dictate the medium and the creative approach to be used. For example, if the objective is to demonstrate how fast a product operates, then a TV ad that shows this action may be the best medium.

Creative decisions include identifying the product's benefits, developing possible advertising appeals, evaluating the advertising appeals and selecting a unique selling proposition, and executing the advertising message. An effective advertising campaign follows the AIDA process discussed in Chapter 15.

Identifying Product Benefits

A well-known rule of thumb in the advertising industry is "Sell the sizzle, not the steak." That is, in advertising the goal is to sell the benefits of the product, not its attributes. Advertisers should know the difference between a product's attributes and its benefits. The description of a benefit tells consumers what they will receive or achieve by using the product. A benefit should answer the consumer's question, "What's in it for me?" Benefits might be such things as convenience, pleasure, savings, or relief. On the other hand, an attribute describes only a feature of the product, such as easy-open packages or a special formulation.

Marketing research and creative intuition are usually used to list the perceived benefits of a product and the relative ranking of these benefits. A quick test to determine whether you are offering attributes or benefits in your advertising is to ask "So?" Consider this example:

Attribute: "The Gillette Sensor razor has twin blades individually mounted on remarkably responsive springs to automatically adjust to the curves and contours of a man's face."

"So. . .?"

Benefit: "So, you'll get a closer, smoother, and safer shave than ever before."

Developing Advertising Appeals

advertising appeal Reason for a person to buy a product.

An **advertising appeal** identifies a reason for a person to buy a product. Developing advertising appeals, a challenging task, is typically the responsibility of the creative people in the advertising agency. Advertising campaigns can focus on one or more advertising appeals. Often the appeals are quite general, thus allowing the firm to develop a number of subthemes or minicampaigns using both advertising and sales promotion. Several possible advertising appeals are listed in Exhibit 16.4.

Choosing appeals is an important task, because the advertising appeal is part of the product's image. Beer makers have traditionally appealed to their male drinkers, the bulk of the beer-consuming market, with advertisements featuring sexy women. The Ethics in Marketing article discusses what happened when beer makers shifted their approach and targeted women.

Exhibit 16.4
Common Advertising Appeals

Profit motive	Lets consumers know whether the product will save them money, keep them from losing money, or make them money
Concern for health	Appeals to those who are body-conscious or want to be healthy
Love or romance	Is used often in selling cosmetics and perfumes
Fear	Can center around social embarrassment, growing old, or losing one's health; because of its power, requires advertiser to exercise care in execution
Admiration	Is the reason that celebrity spokespeople are used so often in advertising
Convenience	Is often used for fast-food restaurants and microwave foods
Fun and pleasure	Are the key to advertising vacations, beer, amusement parks, and more
Vanity and egotism	Are used most often for expensive or conspicuous items, such as cars and clothing

ETHICS IN MARKETING

Babe-Based Beer Ads versus Targeting to Women

The bikini-clad-blond-on-the-beach approach to beer advertising lives on. It even survived a controversy over Stroh's Swedish bikini team and a lawsuit charging that ads featuring the scantily dressed women led to sexual harassment in the workplace. Stroh's also heard outcries over the bikini team's appearance in *Playboy* magazine in various stages of undress.

Industry experts clash on whether a brand can really be hurt by advertising that portrays women as sex objects. In fact, all the publicity over the Swedish bikini team actually increased sales for Stroh's Old Milwaukee brand. But even if it doesn't result in lawsuits, boycotts, or declining sales, such advertising certainly won't win brewers any points with women, which could be a big mistake. Women make up 35 percent of the overall market for domestic beer and 45 percent of the market for light beer, the fastest-growing category.

Many beer makers believe they have no reason to change their ads, saying they're sociable and fun and are presented in a realistic manner. Most say they will continue their ads featuring what they call "healthy and vital" men and women, with an emphasis on the latter group. Coors, for instance, contends that men consume more of all Coors' brands and the company's advertising strategies are in line with these demographics. Many admit, however, that there is a heightened awareness of how women are portrayed in beer ads, due in many ways to the sexual harassment charges against Supreme Court nominee Clarence Thomas and the Stroh's bikini team dispute.

Some beer makers are now trying to target women in their advertisements. Anheuser-Busch traded in its bikinis-on-the-beach approach for the "People as genuine as the beer they drink" campaign. New ads for Budweiser featured women like Cordell Jackson, a 68-year-old Memphis grandmother who is seen on an empty stage with Stray Cats guitarist Brian Setzer, whom she emphatically tells, "You're pretty good. Not!" Another spot features a woman helping a wheelchair athlete train for a marathon. Some of the nation's largest brewers are also developing new fruit-flavored beers, which they feel will appeal more to women.

Efforts to entice women with new products and special advertising are drawing a flood of controversy, however. Health groups have begun denouncing the ads and the fruit-flavored alcohol drinks as dangerous to women. *Fetal alcohol syndrome* describes the birth defects in some babies born to mothers who drink. The new marketing efforts, the consumer and health groups say, are more likely to appeal to lower-income, poorly educated young women—the same women who least understand the risks of drinking while pregnant. The critics are especially disturbed by the fruit-flavored alcohol drinks, since women may be influenced to choose them as low-alcohol alternatives even though their liquor content is almost as high as that of most beers.[19]

Should beer makers just give up on trying to market to women altogether? If they are going to target female consumers, should they be required to put a warning on beer labels about drinking during pregnancy? How do you feel about beer being targeted to women?

Evaluating Advertising Appeals

Choosing the best appeal from those developed normally requires market research. Criteria for evaluation include desirability, exclusiveness, and believability. The appeal first must make a positive impression and be desirable to the target market. It must also be exclusive or unique; consumers must be able to distinguish the advertiser's message from competitors' messages. Most important, the appeal should be believable. An appeal that makes extravagant claims not only wastes promotional dollars but also creates ill will for the advertiser.

unique selling proposition
Desirable, exclusive, and believable advertising appeal selected as the theme for a campaign.

The advertising appeal selected for the campaign becomes what advertisers call its **unique selling proposition**. The unique selling proposition usually becomes the campaign's slogan. For example, Lever Brothers' new Lever 2000 soap carries the slogan "The deodorant soap that's better for your skin." This is also the soap's unique selling proposition.

Executing the Message

Message execution is the way the advertisement portrays its information. Any ad, whether print or broadcast, should immediately draw the reader's, viewer's, or listener's attention through visuals and sound. The advertiser must then use the message of the ad to hold consumers' interest, create desire for the good or service, and ultimately motivate a purchase. Many executional styles are available to the advertiser. Exhibit 16.5 lists some examples.

Execution styles for foreign advertising are often quite different from those we are accustomed to in the United States. Sometimes they are sex-oriented or aesthetically imaginative. For example, French advertising avoids direct-sell approaches common in U.S. ads and instead is more indirect, more symbolic, and above all more visual. For example, Perrier's wordless "Woman versus Lion" ad lends a symbolic suggestiveness to the brand.[20] In the television spot, a woman and a lion make their way through tall grass and climb opposite sides of a hill to pulsating music. At the top of the hill rests a bottle of

Exhibit 16.5

Ten Common Executional Styles for Advertising

Style	Description
Slice-of-life	Is popular when advertising household and personal products; depicts people in normal life settings, such as at dinner table.
Lifestyle	Shows how well product will fit in with consumer's lifestyle; Levi's has made concept popular with Dockers menswear commercials.
Spokesperson/ testimonial	Can feature celebrity, company official, or typical consumer making a testimonial or endorsing product: Basketball superstar Michael Jordan endorses Gatorade.
Fantasy	Creates fantasy for viewer built around the use of product: Lexus used this concept in its ads targeted to midlife consumers fantasizing about youthful dreams of growing up to be race car drivers.
Humorous	Beer makers often use humor in their ads, such as Budweiser's popular "Not!" commercial and Bud Dry's "Why Ask Why" spots.
Real/animated product symbols	Creates character that represents the product in advertisements: Energizer bunny, 7-Up red spots, and Chester Cheetah for Cheetos are all examples.
Mood or image	Builds mood or image around product, such as peace, love, or beauty: Initial ads for the introduction of Infiniti automobiles featured only serene landscapes to build a mood of luxury.
Demonstration	Many consumer products, such as bath soap and shampoos, use this technique to show consumers the expected benefits.
Musical	Conveys message of advertisement through song: Soft-drink advertisers use this technique often, as in Pepsi's "You got the right one, baby. Uh Huh!"
Scientific	Uses research or scientific evidence to give a brand superiority over competitors: Pain relievers like Advil, Bayer, and Excedrin use scientific evidence in their ads.

Perrier. As the woman reaches the bottle, the lion lets out a roar and bares his fangs. But the woman screams back ferociously and the animal retreats. The spot closes with the woman standing atop the hill drinking the Perrier while the voice-over intones in French: "Water . . . fresh air . . . life."[21]

4 Make Media Decisions

As mentioned at the beginning of the chapter, U.S. advertisers spend over $126 billion on media advertising annually. Where does all this money go? About 32 percent, or $40 billion, is spent on national advertising. The balance, or about $86 billion, goes to regional and local advertising. Exhibit 16.6 breaks down the dollar amount spent for national advertising by media type. As you can see, expenditures on TV advertising command more than half of every dollar spent on national advertising.

Media Selection Considerations

Promotional objectives and the type of advertising a company plans to use strongly affect the selection of media. Seven major criteria used in selecting media in an advertising campaign include the target market, audience selectivity, geographic selectivity, cost per contact, flexibility, noise level, and life span:

- *Target market:* Media selection is a matter of matching the advertising medium with the product's target market. If marketers are trying to reach teenage females, they might select *Seventeen* magazine. If they are trying to reach a 50-plus consumer, they may choose *Modern Maturity.* Even when market profiles match media profiles, marketing managers must also consider other factors, such as circulation and image. *Seventeen* magazine might reach part of the right market, but this might be only a small fraction of the firm's total market. Also, how do teenagers perceive *Seventeen* magazine? If teens consider it a how-to magazine and use it as a reference guide, it should enhance advertisers' credibility.

Exhibit 16.6

National Ad Spending by Medium

Source: Adapted with permission from *Advertising Age*, 4 January 1993, p. 20. © Crain Communications Inc., 1993.

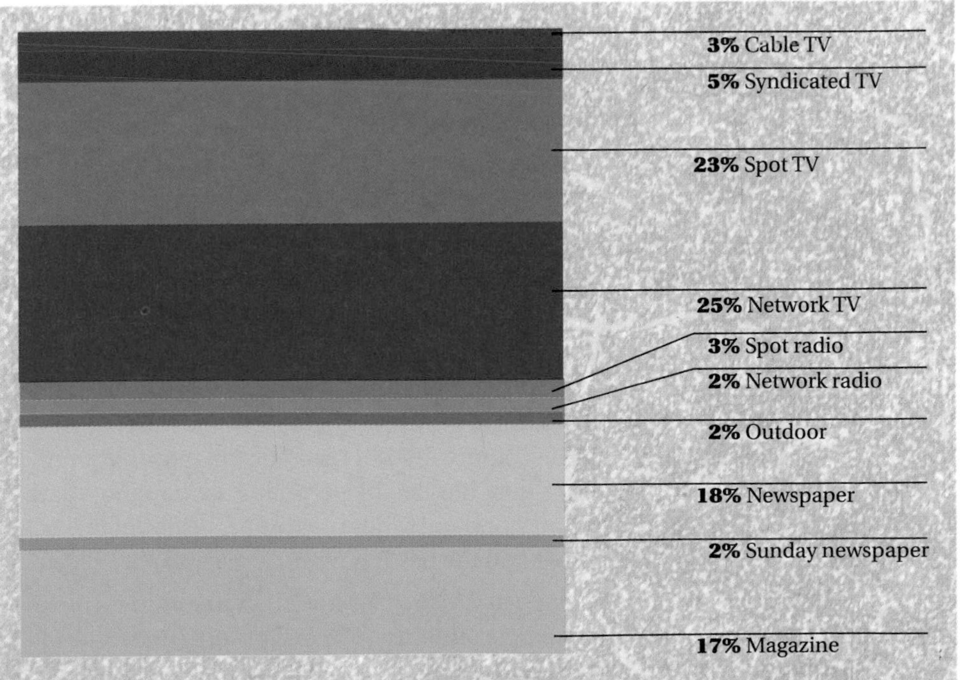

When selecting advertising media, a prime consideration is the target market. The National Federation of Coffee Growers of Colombia ran this ad for its very fine coffee in *Gourmet* magazine, which is read by sophisticated people who can appreciate the coffee's quality.

Courtesy of The National Federation of Coffee Growers of Colombia

audience selectivity
Ability of an advertising medium to reach a precisely defined market.

geographic selectivity
Ability of an advertising medium to cover a specific area.

cost per contact
Cost of reaching one member of the target market.

- *Audience selectivity:* **Audience selectivity** is the medium's ability to reach a precisely defined market. Some media vehicles, like general newspapers and network television, appeal to a wide cross section of the population. Others—such as *Bride's, Gourmet, Architectural Digest,* the Disney Channel, ESPN, and a Christian radio station—appeal to very specific groups.
- *Geographic selectivity:* **Geographic selectivity** is coverage of a specific area. For example, local radio, newspapers, and television all cover limited geographic areas. Network television and many magazines and newspapers, such as *USA Today* and *The Wall Street Journal,* offer nationwide coverage. Media like *Southern Living, Texas Monthly,* and the local evening newscast offer good coverage in limited areas.
- *Cost per contact:* **Cost per contact** is the cost of reaching one member of the target market. Naturally, as the size of the audience increases, so does the total cost. Cost evaluation of media is more thoroughly discussed later in this chapter.
- *Flexibility:* A medium's flexibility can be extremely important to an advertiser. Because of printing timetables, pasteup requirements, and so on, some magazines require final ad copy several months before publication. Thus the advertiser may not be able to adapt to changing market conditions. Radio, on the other hand, provides maximum flexibility. Usually the advertiser can change the ad on the day it is aired, if necessary.
- *Noise level:* The noise level of a medium is the level of distraction it allows for the target audience. For example, to understand a televised promotional message, viewers must watch and listen carefully. But they often watch the mes-

sage with others who contribute to the noise factor. Noise can also be created by competing ads, as when a street is lined with billboards. For example, during the three-and-a-half-hour Super Bowl XXVII game, viewers were barraged with sixty-eight commercials and promotions. Postgame research revealed there was so much ad clutter that it was almost impossible for any advertiser to break through. Over 90 percent of the viewers interviewed after the game could not even identify Frito-Lay as the official Super Bowl sponsor.[22] In contrast, direct mail is a private medium with a low noise level. No other advertising media or news stories compete for direct-mail readers' attention.

- *Life span:* Media have either a short or long life span. For example, a radio commercial may last less than a minute. Listeners can't replay the commercial unless they have recorded the program. One way advertisers overcome this problem is by repeating their ads often. In contrast, a trade magazine has a relatively long life span. A person may read several articles, put the magazine down, and pick it up a week later to continue reading. In addition, magazines and catalogs often have a high pass-along rate. That is, one person will read the publication and then give it to someone else.

Exhibit 16.7 summarizes the advantages and disadvantages of the various media.

Exhibit 16.7

Advantages and Disadvantages of Major Advertising Media

Medium	Advantages	Disadvantages
Television	Ability to reach a wide, diverse audience; creative opportunities for demonstration; immediacy of messages; entertainment carryover	Little demographic selectivity; short life of message; some consumer skepticism about claims; high cost
National	Association of prestige with programming	Long-term advertiser commitments
Local	Geographic selectivity; association with programs of local origin and appeal; can be scheduled on short notice	Lack of wide audience on independent stations; high cost for broad geographic coverage; commercial clutter
Radio	Low cost; high frequency; immediacy of message; can be scheduled on short notice; relatively no seasonal change in audience; highly portable; negotiable costs; short-term advertiser commitments; entertainment carryover	No visual treatment; short advertising life of message; background sound can distract listener; commercial clutter
Magazines	Good reproduction, especially for color; permanence of message; demographic selectivity; regional selectivity; local market selectivity; relatively long advertising life; high pass-along rate	Long-term advertiser commitments; slow audience buildup; limited demonstration capacities; lack of urgency; long lead time
Newspapers	Geographic selectivity and flexibility; short-term advertiser commitments; news value and immediacy; advertising permanence; readership not seasonal; high individual market coverage; co-op and local tie-in availability; short lead time	Little demographic selectivity; limited color capabilities; different local and national rates; low pass-along rate; may be expensive
Outdoor	Repetition; moderate cost; flexibility	Short message; lack of demographic selectivity; high "noise" level distracting audience

Evaluating and Selecting the Media Mix

media mix
Combination of media to be used for a promotional campaign.

cost per thousand (CPM)
Standard criterion for comparing media, computed by dividing the price of a single ad by the audience size in thousands.

Advertising almost always plays an important role in a promotional campaign. When advertising is used, management must evaluate and select the **media mix**, the combination of media to be used. Media decisions are typically based on cost per thousand, reach, and frequency.

Cost per thousand: The standard criterion for comparing media is **cost per thousand** (CPM). The formula for calculating cost per thousand is

$$\text{CPM} = \text{Price of a single ad} \div \text{Audience size (in thousands)}$$

For example, if the cost of an ad is $50,000 and the audience is 24 million people, the CPM is $2.08:

$$\text{CPM} = \frac{\$50{,}000}{\text{24 million people}} = \$2.08$$

CPM enables an advertiser to compare, for example, *Newsweek* with *Time.* CPM can also be used to compare the cost of different vehicles, such as television versus radio or magazine versus newspaper. An advertiser debating whether to spend local advertising dollars for TV spots or radio spots could consider the CPM of each. The advertiser might then pick the vehicle that yields the lowest CPM to maximize advertising punch.

audience duplication
Situation in which the same audience is reached by two different media vehicles.

A factor that complicates media selection is **audience duplication**—that is, the same audience being reached by two different media vehicles. For instance, assume that *Newsweek* has a circulation of 3.1 million and *Time* has a circulation of 4.6 million. If 800,000 people subscribe to both publications, the nonduplicated circulations are 2.6 million for *Newsweek* and 3.8 million for *Time.* In other words, putting an ad in both *Newsweek* and *Time* does not reach 7.7 million different consumers; it reaches 6.9 million (7.7 million – 0.8 million) different consumers. *Time* and *Newsweek* both have huge audience bases. However, their widespread popularity often creates a duplication problem with other media types. For example, an advertisement aired during the local evening news will most likely have a considerable amount of audience duplication with *Newsweek* and *Time.*

reach
Number of target consumers exposed to a commercial at least once during a specific period, usually four weeks.

Reach: The number of different target consumers who are exposed to a commercial at least once during a specific period, usually four weeks, measures a medium's **reach.** For example, if 60,000 out of 100,000 radio listeners hear a commercial for the Ford Taurus in San Antonio, Texas, at least once during a four-week period, the reach would be 60,000, or 60 percent of the total 100,000 listeners.

New product introductions or attempts at increasing brand awareness usually emphasize reach. Yet high reach levels do not necessarily mean high degrees of brand awareness or advertising recall. It is not unusual to find that a campaign achieves 90 percent reach but only 25 percent of the target audience remembers the ad. Reach is a measurement of potential. That is, a 90 percent reach means that 90 percent of an audience has an opportunity to see or hear a message. It does not measure retention.

frequency
Number of times an individual is exposed to a given message during a specific period.

Frequency: The number of times an individual is exposed to a message is the **frequency.** The average frequency is used by advertisers to measure the intensity of a specific medium's coverage. Suppose 30,000 people heard the Ford Taurus ad three times during the four-week period and 30,000 heard it five times. The computation of the average frequency is

$$\text{Average frequency} = \frac{\text{Total exposures}}{\text{Audience reach}} = \frac{(30{,}000 \times 3) + (30{,}000 \times 5)}{60{,}000} = \frac{240{,}000}{60{,}000} = 4$$

Therefore, among the 60,000 listeners reached, the average number of exposures was four.

What frequency is needed to make the advertising message effective and sell the product? Since many ads are short-lived and often only a small portion may be perceived at one time, advertisers repeat their ads so consumers will remember the message. Retention tends to peak somewhere between the third and the fifth message perceived by the receiver. Additional exposures tend to be screened out and may create a negative reaction. The ad then loses its effectiveness.

media schedule
Designation of the media, the specific publications or programs, and the insertion dates of advertising.

continuous media schedule
Media scheduling strategy, used for products in the latter stages of the product life cycle, in which advertising is run steadily throughout the advertising period.

flighted media schedule
Media scheduling strategy in which ads are run heavily every other month or every two weeks to achieve a greater impact with an increased frequency and reach at those times.

pulsing media schedule
Media scheduling strategy that uses continuous scheduling during the best sale periods and a flighted schedule at other times.

seasonal media schedule
Media scheduling strategy that runs advertising only during times of the year when the product is most likely to be used.

cooperative advertising
Arrangement in which the manufacturer and the retailer split the costs of advertising the manufacturer's brand.

The Media Schedule

After choosing the media for the advertising campaign, advertisers must schedule the ads. A **media schedule** designates the vehicles (such as magazines, television, or radio), the specific publications or programs (such as *People* magazine, "Roseanne," or the "Top 40 Countdown" radio show), and the insertion dates of the advertising.

There are three basic types of media schedules: continuous, flighted, and seasonal. Products in the latter stages of the product life cycle, which are advertised on a reminder basis, use a **continuous media schedule**. A continuous schedule allows the advertising to run steadily throughout the advertising period. Examples include Ivory soap, Coca-Cola, and Marlboro cigarettes.

With a **flighted media schedule**, the advertiser may schedule the ads heavily every other month or every two weeks to achieve a greater impact with an increased frequency and reach at those times. A variation of flighting is the **pulsing media schedule**, which combines continuous scheduling with flighting. Continuous advertising is simply heavier during the best sale periods. For instance, a retail department store may advertise on a year-round basis but place more advertising during holiday sale periods, such as Thanksgiving and Christmas.

Certain times of the year call for a **seasonal media schedule**. Products like Contac cold tablets and Coppertone suntan lotion, which are used more during certain times of the year, tend to follow a seasonal strategy.

Media Types

Advertising media are channels that advertisers use in mass communication. The basic media vehicles are newspapers, magazines, radio, television, and outdoor advertising. In recent years, however, innovative vehicles have emerged that give advertisers ways to avoid advertising clutter. These new trends are covered later in this chapter. Let's turn our attention now to the more traditional vehicles.

Newspapers: Newspaper advertising's advantages include geographic flexibility and timeliness. Since copywriters can usually prepare newspaper ads quickly and at a reasonable cost, local merchants can reach their target market almost daily. The largest source of newspaper ad revenue is local retailers, cooperative advertising, and classified ads. In **cooperative advertising**, the manufacturer and the retailer split the costs of advertising the manufacturer's brand.

Because newspapers are generally a mass-market medium, they may not be the best vehicle for marketers trying to reach a very narrow market. For example, local newspapers are not the best media vehicle for reaching purchasers of specialty steel products or even tropical fish. These target consumers make up very small, specialized markets. Newspaper advertising also encounters a lot of distractions from competing ads and news stories; thus, one company's ad may not be particularly visible.

Magazines: Compared to the cost of other media, the cost per contact in maga-

zine advertising is usually high. However, the cost per potential customer may be much lower, because magazines are often targeted to specialized audiences and thus reach more potential customers.

One of the main advantages of magazine advertising is its market selectivity. There are magazines for virtually every market segment. *PC Week* is a leading computer magazine; *Working Mother* targets one of the fastest-growing consumer segments; *Sports Illustrated* is a successful men's all-around sporting publication; *Marketing News* is a trade magazine for the marketing professional.

Radio: Radio has several strengths as an advertising vehicle: selectivity and audience segmentation, a large out-of-home audience, low unit and production costs, timeliness, and geographic flexibility. Local advertising accounts for 77 percent of radio advertising volume.[23] Like newspapers, radio also lends itself well to cooperative advertising. Radio stations and programs now are segmented on an ever-increasing variety of factors: age, race, income, lifestyle, and others. The *Spot Radio Standard Rates & Data Service* lists more than 160 radio formats, from "adult contemporary" to "young and beautiful."

Television: Television broadcasters can be divided into three basic types: network television, independent stations, and cable television. The three giants—ABC, CBS, and NBC—and a newcomer, the Fox Network, dominate network television. Independent stations are not part of national networks and often rely on viewer contributions for funds. Consumers pay to have cable television in their homes. Before the introduction of cable television, the big three networks held over 90 percent of the audience share. During the 1980s, this share dropped to around 65 percent.[24] Although they are still the dominant force in TV broadcasting, the networks have had to become more aggressive to compete with cable television and growing independent stations.

Television's largest growth market is cable television. Some 60 percent of all households subscribe to cable networks.[25] Today's cable subscribers can receive channels devoted exclusively to a particular audience—for example, women, children, African-Americans, nature lovers, senior citizens, Christians, Hispanics, sports fans, or fitness enthusiasts. Other types of special programming include news, rock and country music, culture, and health. The average cable subscriber can receive about twenty to thirty channels.

Since television reaches a wide and diverse market, it can provide an advertiser with many creative opportunities. However, television has its disadvantages. Advertising time on television can be very expensive, especially for network stations, and even more so during prime time. The cost of a thirty-second spot during NBC's "Cheers" is estimated to be about $260,000, the most expensive prime-time slot. Half-minute spots during other prime-time programs begin at about $50,000.[26] Television advertising can also involve huge production costs. A professionally produced national commercial can cost $500,000 or more to make.

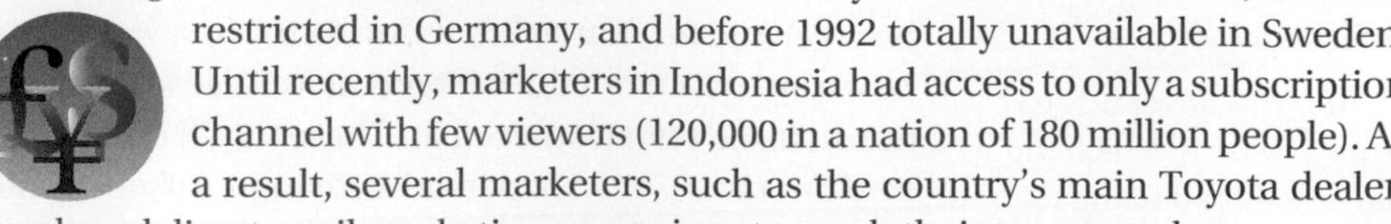

Probably the least globally standardized of all advertising media is television advertising. Commercial television time is readily available in Canada, severely restricted in Germany, and before 1992 totally unavailable in Sweden. Until recently, marketers in Indonesia had access to only a subscription channel with few viewers (120,000 in a nation of 180 million people). As a result, several marketers, such as the country's main Toyota dealer, developed direct-mail marketing campaigns to reach their target markets.

Outdoor advertising: Outdoor or out-of-home advertising is a flexible, low-cost medium that may take a variety of forms. Examples include billboards, skywriting,

In addition to billboards, outdoor advertising includes display boards on bus stop shelters, like these for The Gap.

Outdoor Advertising Association of America

giant inflatables, minibillboards in malls, lighted moving signs in bus terminals and airports, and ads painted on the sides of cars and trucks. Outdoor advertising reaches a broad and diverse market. Therefore, it is normally limited to promoting convenience products and selected shopping products.

Outdoor advertising also has the ability to be customized to local marketing needs. Advertisers usually base their billboard use on census tract data for the area. They assume that the people who are most likely to see a certain billboard will have demographic characteristics similar to those of the tract where the billboard is located. Billboards can also be targeted to the mobile or business traveler market. For instance, McDonald's recently bought about 20,000 outdoor boards in all available sizes and all available markets across the country to display the message "Great food, great value at McDonald's." The campaign allows McDonald's to use the same message nationally with a variety of products, prices, and promotions. Outdoor advertising provides McDonald's with a way to reach its customers when they're on the road.[27]

Direct-Response Advertising

direct-response advertising
Advertising that calls for consumers' immediate action, or a direct response.

Most **direct-response advertising** methods use traditional media. They also are generally targeted to the masses rather than to specific markets. However, the advertisement in some way calls for consumers' immediate action, or a direct response. Television, radio, or newspaper ads invite customers to call a toll-free number or fill out a coupon. For example, an advertisement for a consumer magazine like *People* includes an instant order form. If subscribers send in the form immediately, they can receive up to 50 percent off the newsstand price. Cable TV is also becoming popular for many types of direct-response advertising. Many people subscribe to cable, and advertising costs are lower than they are for network stations. The fastest-growing form of direct-response advertising is currently being seen in some of the country's biggest cities: direct-response billboards, a result of congested traffic and the proliferation of car phones.[28]

The twenty-four-hour shop-at-home television channels, such as the QVC (Quality, Value, Convenience) Network, are specialized forms of direct-response advertising. These shows display merchandise, with the retail price, to home shopping viewers. Viewers can then phone in their orders. Cable television has benefited the most from the success of the shop-at-home networks. However, smaller direct-response marketers, generally on the air only in brief spot ads, have felt the impact of the cable shopping networks on their total sales.

infomercial
Thirty-minute or longer advertisement that looks more like a TV talk show than a sales pitch.

A relatively new form of direct-response advertising is the **infomercial,** a thirty-minute or longer advertisement that looks more like a TV talk show than a sales pitch. Infomercials bloomed in the mid-1980s, when deregulation freed television stations and cable networks to sell entire half-hour blocks of air time for advertising, especially during the unprofitable late-night time slots. Infomercials are an attractive advertising medium for many marketers because of the cheap air time (as low as a few hundred dollars a half hour) and the relatively small amount they cost to produce, usually between $150,000 and $500,000 for thirty minutes. Although still a haven for lesser-known marketers of hair care products, juice machines, and car wax, infomercials are getting the attention of larger marketers, such as Volvo, Bell Atlantic, and The Dial Corporation. Infomercials were also a popular advertising medium for 1992 presidential candidates Bill Clinton, Ross Perot, and Jerry Brown.[29]

Cooperative Advertising

As mentioned earlier, cooperative advertising is an arrangement under which a manufacturer pays a percentage of the cost of the advertising that its customer, a retailer, places for the manufacturer's brand. About three-fourths of all cooperative advertising is newspaper advertising. The usual objective of cooperative, or co-op, advertising is to trigger short-term sales.

One reason manufacturers use cooperative advertising is the impracticality of listing all their dealers in national advertising. Also, co-op advertising encourages retailers to devote more effort to the manufacturer's lines. Sometimes co-op advertising ties retailers closer to manufacturers and aids in developing goodwill. Most important, manufacturers obtain more total promotion, since retailers share part of the expense.

Media of the Future

To cut through the clutter of traditional media vehicles, advertisers are now looking for new ways to promote their products. Some of these new media include facsimile (or fax) machines, video shopping carts, electronic "place-based" media, interactive advertising through personal computers, minibillboards, and cinema and video advertising.

Fax machines are a business communication system, but they also are being used by some marketers to deliver direct mail electronically. Fax machines are inexpensive for direct-mail use and can precisely target possible customers. Unsolicited fax advertising, however, has outraged many businesses, since they are paying for the paper, ink, and transmission of the faxed ad. Moreover, these unsolicited ads tie up fax machines whose original purpose is to speed business communication. Recent legislation will soon limit advertisers' ability to use the fax machine as a way to reach their audience.[30]

The *video shopping cart* is a new concept being tested in supermarkets nationwide. Essentially, the video shopping cart is a computerized display screen attached to the handles of an ordinary shopping cart. Strategically located sensors detect the cart as it rolls down the aisle, and the screen delivers customer-service, advertising, and sales promotion messages to the shopper. Video shopping carts can even dispense electronic "coupons": Simply push a button on the screen, and you receive the coupon discount when the product is scanned at the checkout counter.[31] Also new in grocery stores is the Checkout Channel—Cable Network News (CNN) aired to shoppers standing in line at the checkout counter. A similar in-store advertising medium is Shoppers' Video, which aspires to influence in-store purchasing deci-

Video shopping carts, which incorporate a computerized display screen, are already being tested in some supermarkets.

Courtesy Selz, Seabolt & Associates, Inc.

sions by airing programming and advertising over TV monitors suspended overhead. The service offers entertainment briefs interspersed with fifteen-second commercials for products found in the grocery store.[32]

Additional variations on *electronic "place-based" media* are now appearing in retail stores, as well as in classrooms, doctors' waiting rooms, and health clubs. For example, JCPenney is testing a program to air sports programming and advertising on TV monitors in the sportswear departments of 650 stores.[33] Channel One brings a twelve-minute daily "newscast" of current events, sprinkled with two minutes of commercials, into high school classrooms.[34]

Interactive advertising currently uses personal computers to transmit immediate, personalized advertisements to consumers. Viewers see teaser ads that instruct them to punch a key on their computer keyboard if they want more information. Viewers can then order products, conduct banking transactions, and check the stock market from their home computers. Interactive advertising will soon be available for consumers' television sets. In the near future, viewers will be able to buy equipment that will allow them to interact with TV programs and ads by pointing a joystick at the set and clicking a button. Through interactive television, consumers will be able to request information, buy products through a shopping service, check their bank accounts, and pay bills.[35]

More marketers are realizing that today's teens and college students have an enormous amount of buying power that cannot be ignored. *Minibillboards* are popping up in high school locker rooms and on college campuses across the country. These may be the new medium to reach these high-spending youths. Minibillboards, personalized to each school, feature prominent national ads next to information like study and health tips and career suggestions. A variation is wallboards for seniors, carrying news and advertisements geared to older consumers and strategically placed in senior citizen centers.[36]

Advertisers are also catching on to another new media vehicle—the *movies.* Advertisers are lining up to show their commercials to theaters full of captive, hard-to-reach young adults. About 6,800 cinemas around the country now carry ads for

sponsors like Nintendo, Diet Coke, and the U.S. Marines.[37] Another trend is the placement of advertising on rented home videos.

Evaluate the Campaign

Evaluating an advertising campaign is often the most demanding task facing an advertiser. How do advertisers know whether the campaign led to an increase in sales or market share or elevated awareness of the product? With direct-response advertising, linking the campaign to increased sales or awareness is relatively easy, since consumers are typically asked to take some action ("Don't wait—call now!"). On the other hand, since most advertising campaigns aim to create an image for the good or service instead of asking for action, their real effect is unknown. So many variables shape the effectiveness of an ad that, in many cases, advertisers must guess whether their money has been well spent. Despite this gray area, marketers spend a considerable amount of time studying advertising effectiveness and its probable impact on sales, market share, or awareness. Testing ad effectiveness can be done either before or after the campaign.

Pretests

Before a campaign is released, marketing managers use pretests to determine the best advertising appeal, layout, and media. Several common pretests are the following:

- *Consumer jury test:* The consumer jury test, or focus group interview, uses a panel of consumers from the target market. They preview several advertisements and examine the unfinished ads or storyboards. Next, panel members rank the ads by perceived effectiveness and explain their rankings and their reactions to each ad. Focus groups may also play an important role in developing the advertising appeals and determining the appropriate slogan.
- *Portfolio or unfinished-rough tests:* The purpose of the portfolio test is to evaluate print advertising. Before marketing managers select a final advertising appeal and layout, they let a sample of consumers read several dummy magazines, complete with stories and different versions of the advertisement. Next, the consumers are asked what ads they remember (unaided recall). Then they respond to questions about specific ads (aided recall). Similarly, an unfinished-rough test measures the effectiveness of proposed television commercials. An unfinished rough, or a rough videotape of a TV commercial, is shown to consumers, who are then asked to recall the message.
- *Physiological tests:* To avoid the bias sometimes encountered in other tests, some marketers have turned to physiological testing. Consumers have involuntary physical reactions to advertisements. Physiological tests measure these human responses, using galvanic skin response tests, eye movement experiments, and pupil dilation measurements as indicators of promotion awareness and interest.

Posttests

After advertisers implement a campaign, they often conduct tests to measure its effectiveness. Several monitoring techniques can be used to determine whether the campaign has met its original goals. Even if a campaign has been highly successful, advertisers still typically do a postcampaign analysis. They assess how the campaign might have been more efficient and what factors contributed to its

success. The effectiveness of a campaign is usually tested through the following:

- *Recognition tests:* The Daniel Starch Readership or Recognition Test, used to measure the effectiveness of magazine advertising, is a good example of a recognition test. Consumers are asked about their magazine ad readership and then grouped in three categories: those who noted the ad, those who can link the company name with the advertisement, and those who read at least 50 percent of the advertisement.
- *Recall tests:* A recall test can be used with ads presented through almost any medium, from television to billboards. Unlike recognition tests, recall tests do not show respondents the advertisement. Instead, to measure *unaided recall,* respondents are asked to remember the commercial or advertisement. This measure indicates how much information the target consumers learned. *Aided recall* provides cues to jog interviewees' memories. For example, consumers might respond to questions like these: What do you remember about the grocery store commercial? What did the man say to the clerk? What was the theme of the customer-clerk grocery commercial? (Exhibit 16.8 shows the results of print and television advertising awareness studies.) An implied assumption of recall tests is that higher recall ultimately changes behavior or attitudes. That is, if consumers can recall a specific product's advertisement, they are more likely to buy the product. An advertiser should not completely rely on this assumption, however. A consumer may recall the advertisement because of its style yet have no intention of ever using the product. Just because consumers can remember an ad doesn't mean they will buy the brand.
- *Attitude measures:* Often attitude measures are incorporated into recall and recognition tests. Interviewers may ask interviewees whether a promotion seems believable, convincing, dull, imaginative, informative, phony, realistic, silly, and so on. They may also ask the following multiple-choice question:

How did the advertisement affect your desire for the product?

(1) increased very much   (4) decreased somewhat
(2) increased somewhat   (5) decreased very much
(3) unaffected

Exhibit 16.8

The Most Highly Recalled Brands Advertised in Print or Television Campaigns

Source: Data from Video Storyboards, Inc., 1992; reported in Kevin Goldman, "Pizza Ads with Dash of Humor Top Pops," *The Wall Street Journal,* 9 March 1993, pp. B1, B11, and Kevin Goldman, "Risk Paid Off in 1992 Print Campaigns," *The Wall Street Journal,* 18 May 1993, p. B7. Reprinted with permission of *The Wall Street Journal,* © 1993 Dow Jones & Company. All Rights Reserved Worldwide.

Rank	Television brand awareness	Print brand awareness
1	Little Caesars Pizza	Nike
2	Pepsi/Diet Pepsi	Calvin Klein
3	Nike	Camel
4	DuPont Stainmaster	Absolut
5	McDonald's	Revlon
6	Eveready Energizer	Ford
7	Budweiser	Marlboro
8	Reebok	Lexis
9	Coca-Cola	Maybelline
10	Taster's Choice	Guess

- *Audience size measures:* Audience measures are generally made by the same research organizations that gauge advertising effectiveness. In addition to using the Starch test discussed above, marketers use the Target Group Index (TGI), which specializes in periodic magazine audience studies. Another organization, the Audit Bureau of Circulation, audits the paid circulation figures of both magazines and newspapers. The American Research Bureau (Arbitron), the largest research firm specializing in radio audience measurement, gathers information by sending consumer diaries to randomly selected households. TV audience data also are usually gathered by means of consumer diaries (journals kept by consumers detailing their television viewing habits) or through devices called telemeters. A.C. Nielsen and Arbitron dominate television measurement studies. In contrast, newspaper audience data are usually gathered through telephone or in-home interviews.

5 ADVERTISING AGENCIES

advertising agency Organization that handles the advertising and promotion functions for other organizations.

The **advertising agency,** which often handles the advertising and promotion functions for marketers, occupies a unique position in the business environment as the encoder of the marketer's promotional message. The term *advertising agency* is somewhat misleading. In reality, managers delegate the task of developing a promotional campaign, which almost always includes advertising and sales promotion, to an advertising agency. Thus an advertising agency might also be called a promotion agency. Promotion is delegated to outside organizations more often than any other business function.

Exhibit 16.9 lists the top ten advertising agencies in the United States in terms of their billings. These agencies oversee some of the largest advertising accounts in the world. For example, the Leo Burnett agencies handle the multimillion-dollar accounts of such well-known companies as Miller Brewery, Procter & Gamble, McDonald's, and Philip Morris.

Functions of an Advertising Agency

Full-service advertising agencies generally perform four functions: creative services, media services, research, and advertising planning. Creative personnel develop promotional themes and messages, write copy, design layouts, and draw illustra-

Exhibit 16.9

Top Ten Advertising Agencies in the United States

Source: Adapted with permission from *Advertising Age*, 13 April 1992, p. S-12. © Crain Communications Inc., 1992.

Rank	Agency	1991 billings (in billions)
1	Young & Rubicam, New York	$3.5
2	BBDO Worldwide, New York	2.7
3	D'Arcy Masius Benton & Bowles, New York	2.6
4	Saatchi & Saatchi, New York	2.6
5	Foote, Cone & Belding Communications, Chicago	2.5
6	DDB Needham Worldwide, New York	2.5
7	Ogilvy & Mather Worldwide, New York	2.2
8	Leo Burnett Co., Chicago	2.0
9	J. Walter Thompson Co., New York	1.9
10	Grey Advertising, New York	1.8

tions. Media service departments aid in selecting the media mix, scheduling, and controlling the media program.

Larger advertising agencies also help formulate and analyze market research studies. Often the agency aids in media research, product development research, positioning research, and so on. In almost every case, a marketing research subcontractor does most of the actual research design, data collection, and analysis.

Almost all full-service agencies work with clients in campaign design and planning. They set promotional goals, define positioning strategies, examine promotional alternatives, and create campaigns. The agency also helps develop control procedures to measure campaign effectiveness.

The account executives in an agency are responsible for maintaining a communication channel between the agency and the advertiser (the organization paying the agency). Account executives transmit objectives, concepts, and plans to the agency's creative personnel and present proposed campaigns to the advertiser. Usually, account executives are also the agency's sales force and are expected to make presentations to potential new accounts.

6 ADVERTISING REGULATION

Besides coordinating the functions of agency personnel and managing accounts, advertising agencies must also cope with the growing role and scope of advertising regulation.

Self-Regulation in the Advertising Industry

National Advertising Division (NAD)
Complaint bureau for consumers and advertisers, part of the Council of Better Business Bureaus.

National Advertising Review Board (NARB)
Appeals board for cases in which the National Advertising Division rules in favor of the complaining party.

To avoid increasing government regulation, advertising industry leaders set up procedures for self-regulation in 1971. The **National Advertising Division** (NAD) of the Council of Better Business Bureaus is a complaint bureau for consumers and advertisers. The **National Advertising Review Board** (NARB) is an appeals board should NAD rule in favor of the complaining party. After receiving a complaint about an advertisement, NAD starts investigating. It evaluates the information it collects and then decides whether the ad's claims are substantiated. If the ad is deemed unsatisfactory, NAD negotiates a change or discontinuation of the advertisement with the advertiser. If the issue reaches a deadlock or the losing party wishes to appeal, the case is referred to the NARB.

Advertising managers want to avoid having to drop or modify advertisements or commercials. This action is expensive for the following reasons: The ad must be remade; controversy can create ill will for the company; and if a substitute commercial is unavailable, the timing of the campaign may be destroyed. For instance, Procter & Gamble recently filed a truth-in-advertising complaint with NAD against the makers of Arm & Hammer baking soda toothpaste for claiming, "Two out of three dentists and hygienists recommend baking soda for healthier teeth and gums." P&G argued that there was no scientific basis for the statement. Arm & Hammer eventually agreed to change the statement to "healthy" rather than "healthier" teeth and gums.[38] Another controversy occurred after Reebok ran a shocking ad featuring its sports shoes pitted against similar Nike brand shoes. The ad depicted a pair of bungee jumpers, who leap from bridges, tethered at the ankles by elastic cords. In the commercial, the bungee jumper wearing the Nikes fell to a seemingly horrid death, leaving only his Nikes attached to the cord. After only four runs and many complaints, Reebok pulled the spot. The company thus wasted the sizable production expenses.[39]

INTERNATIONAL PERSPECTIVES

Making the Rules on Kids' Ads

Marketers trying to create one campaign for the entire European market are running into problems if they're selling to children or using children in their ads. While the ad industry hopes the European Community (EC) will allow self-regulation for children's ads, a bizarre collection of local regulations hinders pan-European efforts.

Essentially every single country in Europe has different regulations restricting television advertising to children. The local rules include, for instance, that in the Netherlands confectionery ads must not be targeted to children, air before 8 p.m., or feature children under age 14. A toothbrush must appear on the screen, either at the bottom during the entire spot or filling the whole screen for the last one and a half seconds. In Spain and Germany, war toys cannot be advertised.

Other common rules restrict the use of children in commercials or allow them to appear only if they don't endorse the product. For example, a Kellogg spot currently airing in Great Britain features a child assigning a different day to each box in a cereal variety pack. That spot couldn't run in France because children are restricted from being presenters or appearing in advertisements without adults.

But the most serious threats to advertisers are new laws in Greece and Sweden. The Greeks are trying to reinstate a 1987 law banning all toy advertising, which was struck down by the EC in 1991 for restraining trade. International toymakers claim the ban is being pushed by local toy companies to hinder foreign competition. Sweden already has a law restricting television ads from targeting children under age 12. And no commercials of any kind can air before, during, or after children's programs.

By endorsing self-regulation, members of the European Association of Advertising Agencies are trying to prevent the EC from drafting a directive on children's advertising. To do so, the organization has recently adopted a twelve-point self-regulation code. The code allows children to appear in ads but not verbally endorse a product or act as presenters. The code also does not allow children to request products or make product comparisons in ads, but children could handle or consume the product.

Although more research will need to be done before advertisers approach regulators in each country, the European Association of Advertising Agencies is diligently promoting self-regulation. Do you think self-regulation of advertising will work given the diversity of European countries? How can children be portrayed ethically in advertising?

Source: Adapted from Laurel Wentz, "Playing by the Same Rules: Harmonization of Children's Ads Sought via Self-Regulation," *Advertising Age* International Special Report, 2 December 1991, p. S-2. © Crain Communications Inc., 1991.

Self-regulation will become a test for advertisers in the European Community countries, as the International Perspectives article relates.

Federal Regulation of Advertising

When self-regulation doesn't work, in the United States the Federal Trade Commission (FTC) steps in. The FTC's main concern is with deception and misrepresentation in advertising. The FTC defines deception as "a representation, omission, or practice that is likely to mislead the consumer acting reasonably in the circumstances, to the consumer's detriment." The courts have ruled that deception can also cover what the consumer infers from the advertisement, not only what is literally said. Critics of FTC regulation point out that any message, commercial or not, has the potential for deception. Moreover, even the most honest speaker cannot control the inferences the audience will make from their statements. Studies suggest that over a fourth of the content of television ads and over a fifth of the meanings of print messages are misunderstood.[40]

corrective advertising
Advertising that amends the false impressions left by previous advertisements.

The FTC's traditional remedy for deceptive advertising is the cease-and-desist order, otherwise known as the "go and sin no more" approach. This order bans use of the advertising claims found to be false or deceptive. In some cases, the FTC requires a corrective message. **Corrective advertising** is an advertisement run to

amend the false impressions left by previous advertisements. For example, after investigating several diet-program companies for false and deceptive advertising, the FTC required them to revise their weight-loss claims to accurately reflect the programs' success in helping customers keep off the weight they lose.[41]

What are the effects of corrective advertising? Does it work? Does it really correct consumers' false impressions? In most cases, corrective ads provide useful information to consumers that may change their beliefs and modify their purchasing behavior. However, the variation on the message must be substantial to cause any effect. The overall consensus is that corrective advertising, at best, seems to work moderately well but not nearly well enough to correct the misrepresentations of deceptive advertising. Warner-Lambert had to use the following corrective statement in its ads for sixteen months: "Listerine will not help prevent colds or sore throats or lessen their severity." Nevertheless, after the sixteen months, 57 percent of regular Listerine users still believed it would prevent and reduce the likelihood of colds and sore throats.[42] Most corrective ads have little or no impact on company image or on the image of the general product category.

Often, public humiliation and bad press are all that is needed for a company to learn its lesson about deceptive advertising. A Volvo commercial showed one of its station wagons lined up alongside five other cars. Bear Foot, a souped-up pickup truck with oversized tires, drove across the line of car roofs and crushed each one—except the Volvo's. The implication was that the Volvo was extraordinarily sturdy. But the Volvo had an unfair, undisclosed advantage: Its roof was reinforced with lumber and steel. When the truth was unveiled, Volvo was forced to make a public apology. But this confession did not appease the United States Hot Rod Association, the largest sanctioning body of indoor motorsports in which Bear Foot competes. In a public exhibition, broadcast by radio and TV stations and covered by countless news journals, Bear Foot badly squashed an unreinforced Volvo with its 1,000-pound tires. The United States Hot Rod Association contends that it simply wanted to show that Bear Foot, whose reputation had been sullied by the Volvo ads, was no wimp.[43]

7 PUBLIC RELATIONS

Public relations is the element in the promotional mix that evaluates public attitudes, identifies issues that may elicit public concern, and executes programs to gain public understanding and acceptance. Like advertising and sales promotion, public relations is a vital link in a progressive company's marketing communications mix. Marketing managers plan solid public relations campaigns that fit into overall marketing plans and focus on targeted audiences. These campaigns strive to maintain a positive image of the corporation in the eyes of the public. Before launching public relations programs, managers evaluate public attitudes and company actions. Then they create programs to capitalize on the factors that enhance the firm's image and minimize the factors that could generate a negative image.

Many people associate public relations with publicity. Publicity is the effort to capture media attention—for example, through published articles or editorials in newspapers or magazines or spots on radio or television programs. Corporations usually initiate publicity through a press release that furthers their public relations plans. For instance, a company about to introduce a new product or open a new store may send press releases to the media in hopes that the story will be published or broadcast.

Managing Public Relations

The first task of public relations management is to set public relations objectives. Of course, these goals should correspond with those of the corporation's overall marketing program. In other words, public relations should be integrated with advertising, sales promotion, and other facets of marketing communications. Many public relations managers use communications research to help them set their public relations objectives, reach their targets, and evaluate the campaign. Research identifies the public's image of the company and strategies the company can take to tackle image problems.[44]

After setting the public relations objectives, the manager must then choose the most effective tools for communicating with the media. These tools include

- *Press relations:* Placing newsworthy information in the news media to attract attention to a person, good, or service
- *Product publicity:* Publicizing specific products
- *Corporate communications:* Creating internal and external communications to promote understanding of the firm or institution
- *Lobbying:* Dealing with legislators and government officials to promote or defeat legislation and regulation
- *Counseling:* Advising management about public issues and company positions and image[45]

Public relations can be directed toward ultimate consumers as well as other publics.

Ultimate Consumers

Using several methods, companies try to create good public relations with their ultimate consumers. First, they spread information about new or existing products. Many companies offer consumers information about ways to use the product, such as new recipes. Second, companies set up a system for answering consumers' questions about any matters regarding the organization. Typically, consumers write or call toll-free 800 numbers if they have any questions about the products. Procter & Gamble has established 800 numbers for many of its consumer products. Companies can then help minimize dissatisfaction by properly handling complaints. They address the reason for the complaint and make any necessary adjustments in their firms' policies, practices, or products.

Other Publics

Public relations does not center solely on the firm's customers. One important group consists of employees. Public relations personnel train company employees in ways to deal more effectively with the public. They also use internal news releases to encourage employee pride in the company and its products.

The public relations department releases information to suppliers about new products and company trends and practices. The purpose is to build a team relationship. Stockholders receive data from the public relations department about company prospects, management changes, and the firm's financial situation.

A great deal of a company's public relations effort is geared toward the community at large. Some major firms believe that educated consumers are better and more loyal customers. Educating consumers may benefit the company even if the topic doesn't have anything to do with the products it sells. For example, Coca-Cola published its first consumer education pamphlet after surveying people who had

written to the company. The pamphlet, *How to Talk to a Company and Get Action*, explained the best ways to approach any company with a complaint or request. The pamphlet itself did not promote any Coca-Cola products. In response, however, over half its readers felt more confident about the company, and 15 percent said they would buy more Coca-Cola products.[46]

Corporations can also build public awareness and loyalty by supporting their customers' favorite issues. Education, health care, and social programs get the largest share of corporate funding. In Minneapolis, Dayton Hudson's JobPlus program teaches low-income mothers the skills they need to join the work force. The retailer then gives these women work experience in its department stores.[47]

Boosting Product Introduction and Positioning

Public relations can help advertisers explain what's different about their new product by creating free news stories about it. During the introductory period, an especially innovative new product often needs more exposure than conventional, paid advertising affords.[48] Gaining exposure for new products involves planning ahead; working closely with product engineers, advertisers, and the press; and knowing who the customers and the competition are. During the introduction of Crystal Pepsi, a colorless, caffeine-free soft drink, Pepsi attributed its success in several test markets to the product's "uniqueness" and to unusual consumer awareness, generated mainly by news coverage. The successful publicity campaign prompted many consumers and retailers to ask for Crystal Pepsi before it was introduced.[49]

Public relations also helps organizations position their brands. The simplest way is to seek editorial coverage of something newsworthy about a particular brand. For instance, a product may have a new formulation that now makes it far superior to its competitors. If no new information about the product is available, public relations managers can sponsor events or community activities that are sufficiently newsworthy to achieve press coverage; at the same time, they also reinforce brand identification. As a 1992 Olympics sponsor, Bausch & Lomb handed out Ray-Ban sunglasses to every U.S. athlete, many of whom donned them at the opening ceremonies. In

Nike scores public relations points through its sponsorship of the U.S. Olympic team. News stories about the athletes put the Nike logo before the public.
© 1992 Al Tielemans/duomo

addition, all medal winners, no matter what country they came from, received a custom-made pair of Ray-Ban aviator sunglasses.[50] Sporting, music, and arts events remain the most popular choices of event sponsors, although many are now turning to more specialized events, such as tie-ins with schools, charities, and other community service organizations.

Coca-Cola is stretching its global arm to achieve worldwide brand recognition through event sponsorship. Expecting millions of people to attend a high-profile event like the Olympics, Coca-Cola was a leading sponsor of the 1992 Winter Olympics in Albertville, France, and the Summer Olympics in Barcelona, Spain. At the grand opening of EuroDisney in 1992, the company's product was the only soft drink served. Coke also showcased its product line at Expo '92, a world's fair in Seville, Spain. And to round out its global event sponsorship, Coke endorses the annual Tour de France bicycle race.[51]

"Green marketing" has also become an important way for companies to position their brands as ecologically sound and to convey concern for society. For example, in 1991 Burger King began switching its sandwich packaging from paperboard cartons to paper wrap. That one change should save about 15,000 tons of paper each year. Burger King is also using bags made from recycled newspapers for all takeout orders. In a similar effort, MasterCard teamed up with catalog merchants for its "Forests for Our Future" campaign, which plants a tree every time a MasterCard is used to make a catalog purchase. The program helps catalog merchants break the perception that the annual distribution of billions of mail-order catalogs is contributing to the destruction of the world's forests.[52]

Managing Unfavorable Publicity

Although the majority of marketers try to avoid unpleasant situations, crises do happen. Perrier, for example, faced this reality when benzene was found in some of its bottled water. In our free-press environment, publicity is not so easily managed and controlled, especially in a crisis. **Crisis management** is used by public relations managers to handle the effects of unfavorable publicity, ensuring fast and accurate communication in times of emergency.[53] A good public relations staff is perhaps more important in bad times than in good. For example, Exxon mismanaged the *Valdez* oil spill in Alaska by not preparing ahead for a crisis. A survey indicated that most respondents felt Exxon was slow to react, and many also believed the firm tried to shift the blame away from the company.[54] All public relations professionals learned a valuable lesson from this blunder: Companies must have a communication policy firmly in hand before a disaster occurs, since timing is the uncontrollable factor.[55]

crisis management
Strategy used by public relations managers to handle the effects of unfavorable publicity.

Responding rapidly to a crisis situation can generally minimize the damage to a company's image. For major image problems, marketers are urged not to waste critical time that could be spent addressing and ending the problem. Some general guidelines for handling a crisis situation follow:

- Get professional public relations help.
- Start early. The worst damage to a company's or a product's reputation tends to occur immediately after the problem becomes public knowledge.
- Avoid the "no comment" response.
- Make it a team effort. Rely on senior management, public relations professionals, attorneys, quality control experts, and manufacturing and marketing personnel.

MARKETING AND SMALL BUSINESS

How Small Businesses Spend Their Promotion Budget

Newspapers are usually a preferred form of advertising for small businesses because costs are low. Yet because coverage is not selective, much of the advertising dollar would be wasted for restaurants, stylists, and so forth with a single location in a large metropolitan area. Radio is also popular because of its low cost and ability to reach fairly specific market segments. A jewelry retailer, for example, might advertise a sale on fine watches using an easy-listening radio station with upscale demographics. Television is usually reserved for larger small businesses because of the costs involved.

Many small-business owners have found direct-response marketing—such as direct mail, telemarketing, and catalogs—to be very effective. The manager can choose the specific audience to be reached and use a personal, hometown message. Mailing lists can be compiled from charge slips, sales slips, contest entry forms, cross-referenced directories, and mailing list brokers.

Public relations for a small business can mean issuing a press release when a new store is opened or giving a speech at a local Rotary or garden club meeting. Because publicity is free, every opportunity should be taken to generate a positive image for the business. A restaurant in a small river town in Iowa, for example, received a very complimentary mention in the local newspaper after it prepared and delivered sandwiches and coffee free of charge to volunteers building a temporary floodwall to hold back the rising Mississippi River.

Small-business owners should try to measure the effectiveness of their promotion efforts. Often evaluation is a much easier task for the small firm than for the large business. Because a small business usually undertakes only one promotion project at a time, managers can easily determine whether the sales increase and resulting revenue is greater than the cost. For example, did enough customers redeem the coupons sent by direct mail to make the promotion worthwhile? Does placing a sign offering free fudge samples in the window of a small candy store increase traffic and sales enough to justify the cost? Finally, a simple yet effective way to gauge promotion is to ask, "Where did you hear about our store?" or "How did you know about our new product line?" Statements as basic as these can help target the right promotions in today's highly competitive business environment.

Note that no single approach will work for every crisis situation. Sketching out some type of crisis management plan before problems arise will help minimize the damage.

A good public relations plan and crisis management helped squash threatening rumors for both Popeye's Chicken and Reebok. In the case of Popeye's, the restaurant chain's founder and chairman was rumored to be supporting a controversial candidate in a Louisiana campaign for a U.S. Senate seat. With some seventy restaurants in the New Orleans area alone, the Popeye's chairman could ill afford any link to the politician. In Reebok's case, there were rumors that the footwear marketer was doing business in South Africa. The rumor had the potential to be especially damaging, since Reebok features African-American athletes in its commercials and has actively sought to attract African-American consumers. By confronting the rumors immediately through press conferences and advertisements, both companies were able to squelch them before their images suffered truly serious damage. Popeye's even offered a $25,000 reward for information leading to the source behind the rumors.[56]

LOOKING BACK

As you finish reading this chapter, think back to the opening story about the advertising wars between Coca-Cola and Pepsi. Both soft-drink giants spend millions on advertising campaigns each year in an attempt to increase sales and steal market share away from the other. Although their advertising messages may be quite different, both companies go through the same creative steps, from determining what appeal to use to choosing the appropriate execution style. Both companies also expend great effort in deciding which medium will be best to reach their target market. They take into account such things as audience and geographic selectivity of the medium, cost per contact, audience duplication, and reach.

KEY TERMS

advertising agency 538
advertising appeal 524
advertising campaign 522
advertising objective 522
advertising response function 517
advocacy advertising 520
audience duplication 530
audience selectivity 528
comparative advertising 521
competitive advertising 520
continuous media schedule 531
cooperative advertising 531
corrective advertising 540
cost per contact 528
cost per thousand 530
crisis management 544
direct-response advertising 533
flighted media schedule 531
frequency 530
geographic selectivity 528
infomercial 534
institutional advertising 519
media mix 530
media schedule 531
medium 523
National Advertising Division 539
National Advertising Review Board 539
pioneering advertising 520
product advertising 519
pulsing media schedule 531

SUMMARY

1 **Discuss the effect advertising has on market share, consumers, brand loyalty, and product attributes.** Advertising can increase market share, influence consumer purchases and attitudes, maintain or increase brand loyalty, and change the importance of a product's attributes. First, advertising helps marketers increase or maintain brand awareness and, subsequently, market share. New brands with a small market share tend to spend more on advertising than older brands would, to build brand awareness and market share. Brands with a large market share use advertising mainly to maintain their share of the market. Second, advertising affects consumers' daily lives as well as their purchases. Although advertising can seldom change strongly held consumer values, it may transform a consumer's negative attitude toward a product into a positive one. Third, when consumers are highly loyal to a brand, they may buy more of that brand when advertising is increased. Last, advertising can also change the importance of a brand's attributes to consumers. By emphasizing different brand attributes, advertisers can change their appeal in response to consumers' changing needs or try to achieve an advantage over competing brands.

2 **Identify the major types of advertising.** Advertising is a form of impersonal, one-way mass communication paid for by the sponsor. The two major types of advertising are institutional advertising and product advertising. Institutional advertising is not product-oriented; rather, its purpose is to foster a positive company image among the general public, investment community, customers, and employees. Product advertising is designed mainly to promote goods and services and is classified into three main categories: pioneering, competitive, and comparative. A product's place in the product life cycle is a major determinant of which type of advertising is used to promote it.

3 **Describe the advertising campaign process.** An advertising campaign is a series of related advertisements focusing on a common theme and common goals. The advertising campaign process consists of several important steps. Promotion managers first set specific campaign objectives. They then make creative decisions, often with the aid of an advertising agency, centered around developing advertising appeals. Once creative decisions have been made, media are evaluated and selected. Finally, the overall campaign is assessed through various forms of testing.

4 **Describe media evaluation and selection techniques.** Media evaluation and selection make up a crucial step in the advertising campaign process. Promotion managers choose advertising media on the basis of three main variables: characteristics of the target market, audience selectivity, and geographic selectivity. Firms typically use a combination of media called a media mix. In general, media mix decisions depend on cost per thousand (CPM), reach, and frequency factors. Major

types of advertising media include newspapers, magazines, radio, television, and outdoor advertising such as billboards and bus panels. Recent trends in advertising media include fax, video shopping carts, electronic "place-based" media, interactive advertising through personal computers, minibillboards, and cinema and video advertising.

5 **Define the role of advertising agencies.** Advertising agencies are often hired to develop promotional campaigns. Full-service advertising agencies perform four major functions: creative services, media services, research, and advertising planning.

6 **Explain the nature of advertising regulation.** Advertising practices are monitored by industry and government regulations. Industry regulation is overseen by the National Advertising Division of the Council of Better Business Bureaus and by the National Advertising Review Board. The Federal Trade Commission becomes involved in advertising regulation when industry regulation is inadequate.

7 **Discuss the role of public relations in the promotional mix.** Public relations is a vital part of a firm's promotional mix. A company fosters good publicity to enhance its image and promote its products. An equally important aspect of public relations is managing unfavorable publicity in a way that is least damaging to a firm's image.

Review Questions

1. What is institutional advertising? How does it differ from product advertising?
2. Explain the concept of the advertising response function.
3. What is cooperative advertising? Why do manufacturers find cooperative advertising useful?
4. Explain the concepts of cost per thousand (CPM), reach, and frequency. Why are these important variables to consider in selecting the media mix?
5. Explain the roles of the National Advertising Division (NAD) and the National Advertising Review Board (NARB).
6. Identify some common methods companies use to facilitate public relations.
7. Why is crisis management planning important? How should a firm respond to unfavorable publicity?

Discussion and Writing Questions

1. How can advertising, sales promotion, and publicity work together? Give an example.
2. Discuss the reasons why new brands with a smaller market share spend proportionately more on advertising and sales promotion than brands with a larger market share.
3. At what stage in a product's life cycle are pioneering, competitive, and comparative advertising most likely to occur? Give a current example of each type.
4. What is an advertising appeal? Give some examples of advertising appeals you have observed recently in the media.
5. What are the advantages of magazine advertising? Why are magazines likely to expand as an advertising medium?
6. You are the advertising manager of a sailing magazine, and one of your biggest potential advertisers has questioned your rates. Write the firm a letter explaining why you feel your audience selectivity is worth the extra expense for advertisers.
7. Do you think corrective advertising is adequate punishment for deceptive advertising? Why or why not? Is there a more effective way of discouraging deceptive advertising?
8. As the new public relations director for a cosmetics firm, you have been asked to set public relations objectives. Draft a memo outlining the objectives you propose and your reasons for them.

CASES

16.1 Borden's

After twenty years in retirement, the dependable Borden symbol Elsie the Cow is being revived as the centerpiece of an ambitious advertising campaign. According to some experts, Elsie's return may be too little, too late.

Created in 1936, Elsie was everywhere as the wholesome matriarch in Borden's dairy advertising until she was put out to pasture in the early 1970s. Borden's hopes Elsie's cuddly image will stimulate sluggish sales of its dairy brands. The company plans to put an updated version of Elsie on all its dairy products in a major television and print ad campaign. Elsie was scheduled to star in a series of TV commercials featuring an animal farm family with a talking Elsie as its mother.

Marketing experts doubt that Elsie will be an effective marketing symbol and feel that her comeback is not a guaranteed success. Several years ago, Timex, Rice-a-Roni, Campbell's Soup, and other advertisers reached back to revive old slogans and icons. For instance, Timex brought back the slogan "It takes a licking and keeps on ticking" with some success. Likewise, Campbell's "Mmm, mmm, good" slogan rekindled memories for baby boomers. But experts contend that selling Borden's products now is a quite different challenge from selling its products when Elsie was popular. Elsie may remind only an older segment of the population of the brand but not reach the younger consumers that Borden needs to attract.

Other marketing experts say that Elsie's reappearance is an act of desperation and that Borden's troubles cannot be corrected by the return of an animated cow. Borden's reported losses in 1992 indicate that its brands—from Elmer's glue to Cracker Jack popcorn—are in serious trouble. For instance, sales for Borden's processed cheese slid 11 percent while sales for the category rose 1 percent.

Borden's brands also lost their consumer appeal in part because of the company's decentralized approach in advertising. In the 1980s, Borden's acquired dozens of other food companies and kept practically all their ad agencies. By the end of the decade, the number of agencies had swelled to nineteen. Borden's has now decided to take a one-company approach to its advertising.

Despite some analysts' doubts about Elsie's return, others believe bringing her back makes sense. Even when powerful icons like Elsie aren't used for a while, they claim, they remain powerful image builders. On the strength of this theory, Borden's chairman and CEO plans to use Elsie as spokesanimal for other Borden products after she makes her comeback dairy debut. He insists that Elsie recalls a simpler era of wholesomeness and quality that even the MTV generation will relate to.

Questions

1. Describe your perception of Borden's target market, using specific demographic and psychographic descriptors.
2. Assume that you are the advertising manager for Borden's new advertising campaign featuring Elsie's return. What would be the specific objectives of your campaign in light of the target market you described in question 1?
3. Draft a statement of your creative decisions for the campaign. What will be the chief message or appeal? What will be your style of execution?
4. Do you feel that younger consumers will be able to identify with Elsie's wholesome image? What suggestions would you give Borden's chairman and CEO on his decision to bring Elsie out of retirement?

Suggested Readings

Kevin Goldman, "Experts Say Borden Has Milked Elsie the Cow for All She's Worth," *The Wall Street Journal*, 12 November 1992, p. B9.

Suein L. Hwang and Kathleen Deveny, "With Elsie as Mascot, Borden Inc. Hopes to Revitalize Its Whole Stable of Brands," *The Wall Street Journal*, 3 September 1992, pp. B1, B8.

16.2 The Wherehouse

Video title: *The Wherehouse Advertising Campaign by Foote, Cone and Belding*

Wherehouse Entertainment
19701 Hamilton Avenue
Torrance, CA 90502

SIC codes: 5735 Record and prerecorded tape stores
5731 Radio, television, and electronics stores
5734 Computer and software stores
7841 Video tape rental

Number of employees: 6,700

1993 revenues: $460 million

Major products: Prerecorded records and tapes

Largest competitors: Musicland, Camelot Music, Sound Warehouse

Background

Over 45 percent of the population bought a prerecorded tape or compact disc within the past twelve months. The typical CD or tape customer is between 25 and 44. (Of these customers, 29 percent are between the ages of 25 and 34, and 23 percent are between the ages of 35 and 44.) The majority of these consumers make over $30,000 a year. The three best-selling types of music (in order) are contemporary rock, country, and contemporary pop.

Industry

The industry is composed of many different types of retailers. Specialty record stores account for almost a quarter of all record sales in the country. The two main types of specialty record stores are the mall retailers and the stand-alone stores. The traditional mall retailers, like Camelot Music, usually have small stores in large shopping malls. These stores rely on mall traffic for customers. Other retailers, like The Wherehouse and Sound Warehouse, have stand-alone, large-format stores. These stand-alone stores must pull in customers without the draw of other stores.

The Wherehouse

The Wherehouse is one of the largest prerecorded music retailers in the United States. The company has its roots on the West Coast. To expand its sales and increase profits, the company focuses on expanding the number of stores it operates and adding other product lines. The company is gradually expanding to other parts of the country. The recently acquired Rocky Mountain Records gave the company good coverage of the Denver market. The company is always looking for other expansion options.

In addition to expanding the number of stores, The Wherehouse also seeks to expand its product lines. It added video rentals and computer software to its existing CD and tape lines. It is also expanding sales of electronics, including video game systems.

Because the company is one of the large-format, stand-alone specialty stores, it relies on its name and advertising to attract customers. The company recently hired Foote, Cone and Belding as its advertising agency. Foote, Cone and Belding's Los Angeles office developed a new advertising campaign for The Wherehouse designed to bring the target market into the stores.

Questions

1. Do you think the final ads developed by Foote, Cone and Belding meet the campaign objectives? Why or why not?
2. What media choices do you think would be best for this advertising campaign? Use Exhibit 16.7 to explain your choices.
3. What specific media vehicles would you select? Why?

References

Million Dollar Directory 1993 (Parsippany, NJ: Dun & Bradstreet Information Services, 1993).

1990 Study of Media and Markets (New York: Simmons Market Research Bureau, Inc., 1990).

Ward's Business Directory of U.S. Private and Public Companies (Detroit: Gale Research, Inc., 1992).

LEARNING OBJECTIVES

After studying this chapter, you should be able to

1. State the objectives of sales promotion.
2. List the most common forms of sales promotion.
3. Discuss the nature of selling and its importance to society.
4. Describe the advantages of personal selling over other forms of promotion.
5. Identify the different types of sales positions.
6. List the steps in the selling process.
7. Describe the functions of sales management.

CHAPTER 17

Sales Promotion and Personal Selling

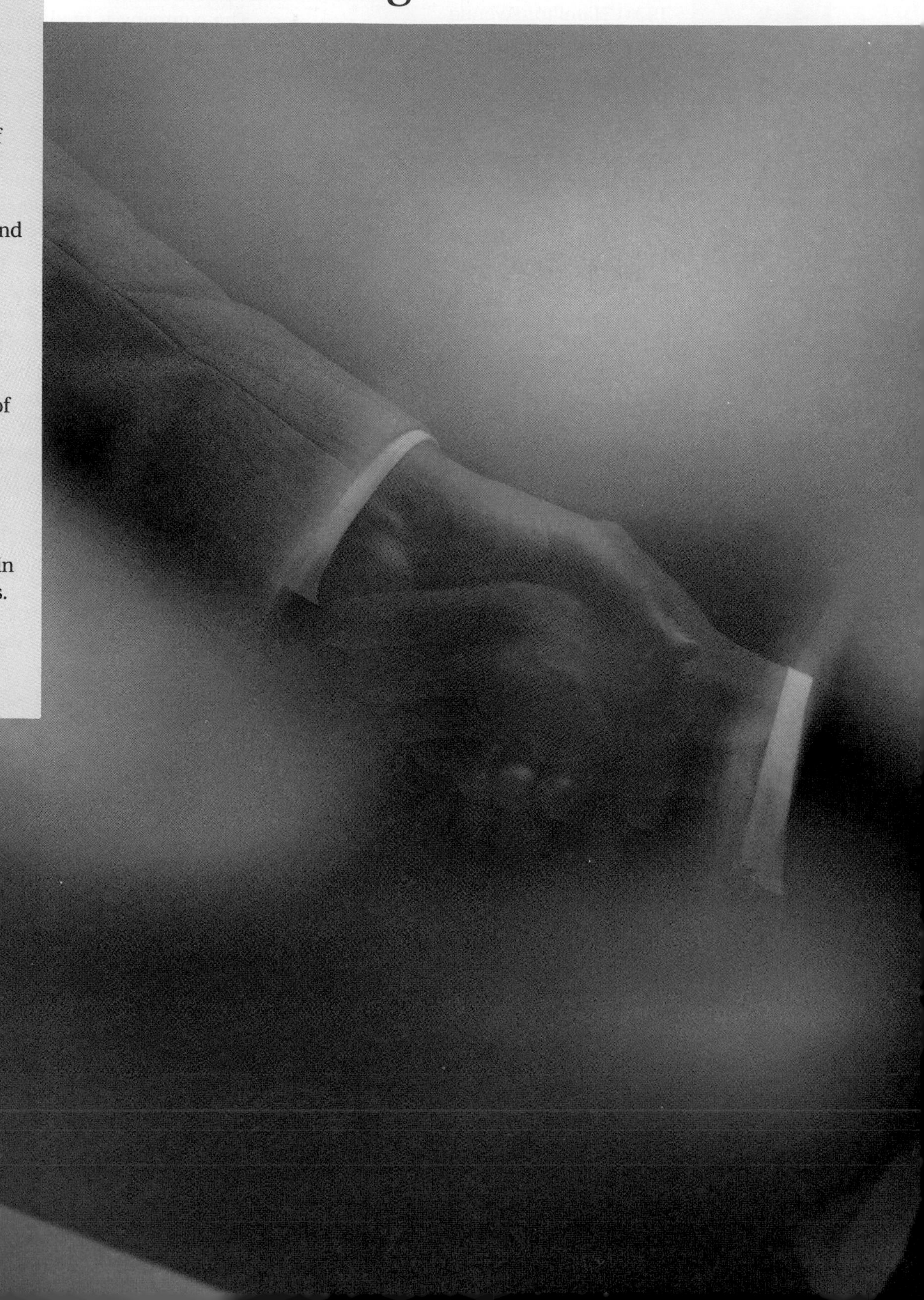

Years ago, stores handed out trading stamps to win shoppers' loyalty. The simple lure of exchanging these stamps for a toaster made S&H Green Stamps a fixture of consumer sales promotion in the 1950s and 1960s. The essence of the trading stamp idea—an incentive that is not a price cut—has now been resurrected by Loyalty Management Group and by Start, Inc.

In the United States, Canada, and Great Britain, Boston-based Loyalty Management Group launched Air Miles, a program that used the promise of free travel to win shoppers' dollars. Air Miles lined up one sponsor in each of a range of businesses and retailers in separate territories. By patronizing these sponsors, consumers enrolled in Air Miles accrued "miles" that were good on several airlines. Air Miles bought seats from the carriers at a discount bulk rate and booked members on their free flights. Air Miles got a small percentage of every transaction between an Air Miles member and a sponsor. It could also handle direct-mail campaigns that targeted the heaviest spenders from Air Miles records.

Start's frequent-buyer program is similar except that consumers' purchases are credited toward retirement savings instead of air mileage. Start places a percentage of the value of a purchase into a noninterest-bearing bank account earmarked for the customer's retirement. After a one-time fee of $25, members need only do business with any of the program's sponsors, including Spiegel, Club Med, MCI, and Eddie Bauer. The member's code is automatically recorded at the time of the transaction.

Business sponsors of Air Miles and Start pay $1 million or more to enroll and a percentage of every mile or savings dollar awarded when their product is purchased. One sponsor of Air Miles, Frito-Lay, hoped the program would help boost sales of its less popular brands. Other sponsors said the program could help draw buyers who were trying to decide where to shop. Retailers and other marketers know that today they have to promote their products harder than ever. But most promotions involve price cuts, which tend to erode a brand's image. Price cuts also encourage shoppers to switch stores and brands in search of the best deal. Frequent-buyer programs, on the other hand, reward consumers for being loyal.

Individual retailers were among the first to devise frequent-buyer programs. The Sears Best Customer program rewards active shoppers with priority repair service on home equipment, zero-percentage financing, and free specialty catalogs. Local sandwich shops often have frequent-buyer cards that give away free sandwiches to loyal diners after a certain number of sandwiches are bought. But now marketers are focusing their attention on Air Miles, Start, and other large-scale frequent-buyer incentive plans to see whether they will work. Critics say that consumers are so bombarded with promotional programs that they are losing interest. Moreover, many feel the programs are too complicated and burdensome for consumers, who must clip the proof-of-purchase codes off many of their purchases and then mail them to a processing center for mileage credit.

These critics apparently have a point. Air Miles announced in 1993 that it was halting its U.S. operations but would continue its more successful programs in Canada and Britain. The sudden failure of Air Miles left corporate sponsors wondering how to compensate customers who bought goods and services in hopes of receiving free tickets.[1]

How does a sales promotion program like Air Miles or Start build customer loyalty? Why is a frequent-buyer program better than coupons or lower prices? Do you feel today's consumers are willing to make the effort to participate in frequent-buyer programs? How should corporate sponsors of Air Miles compensate those who joined the program?

1 SALES PROMOTION

sales promotion Offer of a short-term incentive in order to induce the purchase of a particular good or service.

Besides advertising, personal selling, and public relations, marketing managers can use sales promotion to increase the effectiveness of their promotional mix. **Sales promotion** is an activity in which a short-term incentive is offered to induce the purchase of a particular good or service. Advertising offers the consumer a product with a reason to buy; sales promotion offers the product with an incentive to buy. Incentives include coupons, premiums, contests and sweepstakes, and free samples. Sales promotion is usually targeted toward either of two distinctly different markets: the ultimate consumer market or the industrial and trade market.

U.S. businesses spend about $160 billion per year on sales promotion.[2] Consumer products manufacturers spend about a quarter of their promotion budgets on consumer sales promotion, half on trade sales promotion, and the remaining quarter on media advertising.[3] Sales promotion is usually cheaper than advertising and easier to measure. A major national TV advertising campaign may cost over $2 million to create, produce, and place. In contrast, a newspaper coupon campaign or promotional contest may cost only about half as much. It is hard to figure exactly how many people buy a product as a result of seeing a TV ad. However, with sales promotion, marketers ultimately know the precise number of coupons redeemed or the number of contest entries.

The Objectives of Sales Promotion

Immediate purchase is usually the goal of sales promotion, regardless of the form it takes. Specifically, the promoter tries to increase trial of the product, boost consumer inventory, or encourage repurchase. Promotion is popular with marketers during tough economic times, when gaining a quick increase in sales is the goal.

Promotions can be effective with customers prone to brand switching. A study by the Promotion Marketing Association of America found that price promotions have a major impact on which products consumers buy: 75 percent said that a cents-off coupon had spurred them to try a different brand. Conversely, promotions can also

be an effective tool for building brand loyalty. One example is the frequent-buyer programs that reward consumers for repeat purchases.[4]

A related objective of sales promotion may be to increase the effectiveness of advertising. Often sales promotion and advertising interact to produce higher sales than an equal investment in either objective alone.

6 Selecting Sales Promotion Tools

Marketing managers must decide which sales promotion devices to use in a specific campaign. The methods chosen must suit the objectives to ensure success of the overall promotional plan.

Consumer sales promotion seeks to create new users of the product, as well as to entice current customers to buy more. When a product reaches the decline stage in its life cycle and the advertising budget is cut, consumer sales promotion may be used to show consumers new uses for the product. Consumer sales promotion is also used to support and reinforce advertising for the product. Popular consumer sales promotion tools are coupons, premiums, contests and sweepstakes, sampling, and point-of-purchase displays.

Coupons

coupon
Certificate that entitles consumers to an immediate price reduction when they buy the product.

A **coupon** is a certificate that entitles consumers to an immediate price reduction when they buy the product. Consumers receive coupons by direct mail; through the media, as in a freestanding insert in Sunday newspapers; on the product's package; through cooperative advertising, in which appears the manufacturer's coupon, redeemable only at the retailer's store; and through coupon-dispensing machines at retail stores. Coupons are a particularly good way to encourage product trial and repurchase. They are also likely to increase the amount of a product bought.

Coupon distribution has steadily increased over the years, and today's consumers are drowning in coupons. Packaged-goods marketers distribute roughly 280 billion coupons a year through print media, which equals about 3,000 per household. But shoppers redeem only about one coupon in fifty. Thus some marketers are reevaluating their use of coupons, which they feel may be less effective because of "coupon clutter." Coupons are often wasted on consumers who have no interest in the product—for example, dog food coupons that reach the petless.

The coupons inserted into the Sunday newspaper are usually combined with a full-page, glossy ad—like this coupon for Zest.

Many marketers are experimenting with directing coupons to the place where they're most likely to affect customer buying decisions: in the aisles where consumers decide which product to buy. Coupon-dispensing machines, at-

tached to the shelf below the featured product, have a 20 percent redemption rate (one person uses the coupon out of every five who take one), ten times higher than for newspaper inserts.[5] Marketers are also investigating the use of coupons dispensed at the checkout counter based on a purchase the consumer just made. Machines dispense coupons for either the product purchased or a competing brand.

Although the United States remains the world's leading coupon market, several other markets around the world are beginning to experience the same growth in couponing that occurred in the United States during the 1980s. The European Community's recent gains in political and economic freedom have given marketers more opportunity to use creative promotional techniques. The United Kingdom and Belgium are the EC's most active coupon users, and couponing has just become legal in Denmark. Other European countries have limited access to coupons. For example, in Holland and Switzerland, major retailers refuse to accept coupons. In Russia, a limited variety in advertising media and the fact that many products are unavailable make couponing impossible.[6] Coupons are not widely used in Japan because many consumers feel that using coupons may look as though they do not have much money or are being "cheap." Japanese consumers are still too embarrassed to be seen redeeming coupons.[7]

Premiums

premium
Extra item offered to the consumer, usually in exchange for some proof of purchase of the promoted product.

A **premium** is an extra item offered to the consumer, usually in exchange for some proof of purchase of the promoted product. Premiums like telephones, tote bags, and umbrellas are available when consumers buy cosmetics, magazines, bank services, rental cars, and so on. The appropriateness of the premium is crucial to its success. For example, Clinique often gives away cosmetics with a customer purchase. *Sports Illustrated* offers free videotapes of memorable sports events to new subscribers, and *The Wall Street Journal* gives away a guide to understanding money and markets. Children's toys are a popular premium in boxes of cereal.

Frequent-buyer programs are another popular premium. Frequent-flyer plans offered by airlines help build brand loyalty, and the free trips have a high retail value but a relatively low cost to the airline. Saucony, maker of athletic shoes, introduced an Extra Mile Club. Frequent buyers get running-related merchandise and rebates on future Saucony shoe purchases.[8] One study concluded that improving customer loyalty by 2 percent can boost profits as much as can cutting costs by 10 percent.[9] As a result, dozens of marketers from Waldenbooks to Volkswagen are trying variations of frequent-buyer programs and clubs to secure such loyalty.

Contests and Sweepstakes

Contests are promotions in which participants use some skill or ability to compete for prizes. A consumer contest usually requires entrants to answer questions, complete sentences, or write a paragraph about the product and submit proof of purchase. Winning a sweepstakes, on the other hand, depends on chance or luck, and participation is free.[10] Sweepstakes usually draw about ten times more entries than contests do.

When setting up contests and sweepstakes, managers must make certain that the award will appeal to the target market. For instance, a sweepstakes in a bridal magazine for an exotic honeymoon destination will definitely capture the attention of the many brides-to-be who read the magazine. Likewise, Coors's "Talkin' Can Sweepstakes," aimed at its young target market, gave away over $1 million in stereos and compact discs to those lucky enough to open one of the 300,000 "talking" cans that said "You win!"

In some cases, a contest may succeed without even giving away prizes. For example, 7-Eleven's "Sound Off" promotion asked customers to vote weekly on whimsical questions, such as "Do men drive better than women?" Customers voted by buying coffee or soft drinks in cups marked yes or no. In-store signs and local radio ads announced the weekly question and the resulting tallies. The promotion yielded a 16 percent increase in soft-drink sales and a 5 percent increase in coffee sales.[11]

Sampling

Consumers generally perceive a certain amount of risk in trying new products. Many are afraid of trying something they will not like (such as a new food item) or spending too much money and getting little reward. Sampling allows the customer to try a product risk-free. However, because of this technique's high cost, free sampling has dropped considerably in popularity among manufacturers. As a general rule, free samples of a product should only be offered when two conditions exist. First, the benefits of the new product must be clearly superior to those of existing products. Second, the item must have a unique new attribute that the consumer must experience to believe in. For example, Domino's Pizza in Royal Palm Beach, Florida, introduced its improved pizzas by dropping off free ones to customers after a rival pizza delivery driver, from Pizza Hut, pulled away. Domino's strategy was to get Pizza Hut customers to compare the two products.[12] Likewise, in testing its new Wild Bunch fruit-flavored cola drinks, Pepsi gave out free samples in Atlanta movie theaters.

Some manufacturers are turning to co-op sampling, in which several different products are delivered in the same container. The distribution costs are shared by the manufacturers. Another sampling trend is toward trial-size containers. Minibottles or cartons of a product, such as shampoo or salad dressing, are offered in stores at low prices. Retailers like this form of promotion, since the stores share the profit. Consumers also appreciate being able to buy trial-size containers since they reduce the risk of trying new products.

Sampling is one of the most effective consumer promotion tools in developing countries.[13] However, marketers who have successfully sent trial-size samples of new products to consumers in Western countries have experienced problems when using this same tactic in Eastern European countries. When Procter & Gamble introduced its Wash & Go shampoo in Poland, it mailed samples directly to people's homes—Poland's first direct-mail sampling campaign. But many of the samples never got to the intended customers. Thieves broke into mailboxes to get them, and P&G ended up paying to fix some broken mailboxes.[14]

Point-of-Purchase Displays

point-of-purchase display Promotional display set up at the retailer's location to build traffic, advertise the product, or induce impulse buying.

A **point-of-purchase display** is a promotional display set up at the retailer's location to build traffic, advertise the product, or induce impulse buying. Point-of-purchase displays include shelf "talkers" (signs attached to store shelves), shelf extenders (attachments that extend shelves so products stand out), ads on grocery carts and bags, end-aisle and floor stand displays, television monitors at supermarket checkout counters, in-store audio messages, and audiovisual displays. An in-store display can be simple—for example, a shipping crate that converts to a floor stand. What-

ever form they take, point-of-purchase displays should emphasize creativity, maintain quality, provide product information, and be entertaining.[15]

Computers are beginning to play an important role in point-of-purchase displays. Trifari, a costume jewelry manufacturer, uses interactive computers to help shoppers pick the jewelry best suited for their needs.[16] Hallmark's in-store computerized "Personalize It!" point-of-purchase displays allow consumers to personalize their greeting cards. "Personalize It!" can incorporate a nickname, shared joke, or special message into more than 200 preprogrammed cards.[17]

Point-of-purchase displays offer manufacturers a captive audience in retail stores. Point-of-purchase displays work better for impulse products, those products bought without prior decisions by the consumer, than for planned purchases like milk.[18] For example, to launch a new cheese snack called Doodle O's, Borden's decided against expensive advertising and instead created 25,000 cardboard cutouts of an orange fox wearing sunglasses. Dubbed Fox Z. Doodle, the cartoon mascot was part of a point-of-purchase display that held 200 sample-size packages of the cheese snack. The display was so effective in luring the lunchbox set that the displays often had to be refilled daily, instead of on a weekly basis as planned. Success stories like Doodle O's support the theory that shoppers may come into a store with a shopping list but are more likely to grab a product from an eye-catching display than to look for the brand on shelves.[19]

Research shows the success of point-of-purchase displays. One early study found that sales of a soft drink were almost 3 per 100 shoppers with advertising alone; sales reached almost 8 per 100 shoppers when point-of-purchase displays and advertising support were combined.[20] More recent research conducted by Information Resources Inc. uses scanner technology to record the bar code stamped on a point-of-purchase display item and notes the location of the display in the store. That information is then paired with the sales figures gathered from scanners at the store's cash registers to measure the effectiveness of the promotion. IRI research found that point-of-purchase displays could increase the sales of products like frozen dinners, laundry detergent, soft drinks, snack foods, soup, and juice by more than 100 to 200 percent.[21]

Trade Promotion

When selling to members of the distribution channel, manufacturers use many of the same sales promotion tools used in consumer promotions—for instance, sales contests, premiums, and point-of-purchase displays. There are several tools, however, that are unique to manufacturers and middlemen:

trade allowance
Price reduction offered by manufacturers to intermediaries, such as wholesalers and retailers.

- *Trade allowances:* A **trade allowance** is a price reduction offered by manufacturers to intermediaries such as wholesalers and retailers. The price reduction or rebate is given in exchange for doing something specific or buying something during special periods. For example, a local dealer could receive a special discount for running its own promotion on GE telephones.
- *Push money:* Intermediaries receive push money as a bonus for pushing the manufacturer's brand. Often the push money is directed toward a retailer's salespeople. For example, the manufacturer may offer $50 to an electronics store's sales force for every television set of its brand sold. This practice, however, may foster more loyalty to the manufacturer than to the retailer.
- *Training:* Sometimes a manufacturer will train an intermediary's personnel if the product is rather complex—as frequently occurs in the computer and communications industries. For example, if a large department store pur-

chases an NCR computerized cash register system, NCR may provide free training so the salespeople can learn how to use the new system.

- *Free merchandise:* Often a manufacturer offers retailers free merchandise in lieu of quantity discounts. For example, a breakfast cereal manufacturer may throw in one case of free cereal for every twenty cases ordered by the retailer. Occasionally, free merchandise is used as payment for trade allowances normally provided through other sales promotions. For example, instead of giving a retailer a price reduction for buying a certain quantity of merchandise, the manufacturer may throw in extra merchandise (at a cost that would equal the price reduction) "free."
- *Store demonstrations:* Manufacturers can also arrange with retailers to perform an in-store demonstration. For example, food manufacturers often send a representative to grocery stores and supermarkets to let customers sample their product while shopping. Cosmetic companies also send their representatives to department stores to perform facials and make-overs for customers to promote their beauty aids.
- *Business meetings, conventions, and trade shows:* Trade association meetings, conferences, and conventions are an important aspect of sales promotion and a growing, multibillion-dollar market. At these shows, manufacturers, distributors, and other vendors have the chance to display their products or describe their services to customers and potential customers. The cost per potential customer contacted at a show is estimated to be only 25 percent to 35 percent that of a personal sales call. Trade shows have been uniquely effective in introducing new products, which they can establish in the marketplace more quickly than can advertising, direct marketing, or sales calls. Companies participate in trade shows to attract and identify new prospects, to serve current customers, to introduce new products, to enhance corporate image, to test market response to new products, to enhance corporate morale, and to gather competitive product information.[22]

These tools help manufacturers gain new distribution for their products, obtain wholesaler and retailer support for consumer sales promotion programs, build or reduce dealer inventories, and improve trade relations.

Chapter 15 discussed pull and push promotion strategies. Consumer promotions pull a product through the distribution channel by creating demand; trade promotions push a product through the channel. Trade allowances may be offered to obtain shelf space for a new product or to induce wholesalers and retailers to buy during off-seasons. Sometimes trade deals are offered "because everyone else does it." This approach is hard to justify, since research has shown that consumer promotions are normally more effective at increasing sales than trade promotions.

Yet trade promotions have become more popular over the past several years. Advertising dropped from 43 percent of product marketers' promotion budgets in 1981 to a low of 25 percent in 1991. Trade promotion, on the other hand, has soared to about 50 percent of marketers' budgets, mostly at the expense of advertising.[23] Product discounts and pressure from retailers to pay for shelf space, especially in new-product introductions, are two of the main reasons for the increase in trade promotions. Too often, retailers don't pass on these discounts to the ultimate consumers in the form of lower prices. In some cases, retailers have even been known to resell to other retailers merchandise bought at a discount, adding on their own markup.[24]

3 PERSONAL SELLING

personal selling
Direct communication between a sales representative and one or more prospective buyers, for the purpose of making a sale.

Personal selling is direct communication between a sales representative and one or more prospective buyers, for the purpose of making a sale. Salespeople can accomplish this purpose by communicating face to face during a personal sales call or by selling over the telephone (called telemarketing).

4 Advantages of Personal Selling

Personal selling offers several advantages over other forms of promotion:

- Personal selling can be used to provide a detailed explanation or demonstration of the product. This capability is especially needed for complex or new goods and services.
- A salesperson typically has freedom to vary the message according to the motivations and interests of each prospect. Moreover, when the prospect raises objections, the salesperson is there to provide counterarguments and explanations. In contrast, advertising and sales promotion can only respond to the objections the copywriter thinks are important to customers.
- Personal selling can be directed only to qualified prospects. Other forms of promotion include some unavoidable waste because many people in the audience are not prospective customers.
- Advertising and sales promotion must often be purchased in fairly large amounts, but personal selling costs can be controlled by adjusting the size of the sales force (and resulting expenses) in one-person increments. If paying on a percentage of sales, the firm does not incur sales expense until a sale is made.
- Perhaps the most important advantage is that personal selling is considerably more effective than other forms of promotion in closing the sale and getting the customer's signature on the order form.[25]

Certain customer and product characteristics indicate that personal selling might work better than other forms of promotion. Generally speaking, personal selling becomes more important as the number of potential customers decreases, the complexity of the product increases, and the value of the product grows (see Exhibit 17.1). When there are relatively few potential customers, the time and travel costs of personally visiting a prospect are justifiable. Of course, the product or service must be of sufficient value to absorb the expense of a sales call, as is a mainframe computer, a management consulting project, or the construction of a new building. For highly complex goods, such as business jets or a private commu-

Exhibit 17.1

A Comparison of Advertising/Sales Promotion and Personal Selling

Personal selling is more important if . . .	Advertising/sales promotion is more important if . . .
The product has a high value.	The product has a low value.
It is a custom-made product.	It is a standardized product.
There are few customers.	There are many customers.
The product is technically complex.	The product is simple to understand.
Customers are concentrated.	Customers are geographically dispersed.
Examples: insurance policies, custom windows, airplane engines	Examples: soap, magazine subscriptions, cotton T-shirts

nications system, a salesperson is needed to explain the product's basic advantages and propose the exact features and accessories that will meet the prospective client's needs. Advertising and sales promotion more effectively and economically promote a product when the number of potential buyers increases, the product becomes less complex, the buyers become more dispersed, and the product decreases in value and increases in standardization (for instance, toothpaste or cereal).

5 A Career in Personal Selling

About 14 million people are employed in personal selling in the United States today.[26] This figure reflects all sorts of sales occupations, including retail sales clerks assisting in department stores, people taking orders at fast-food restaurants, and manufacturers' representatives selling to wholesalers and retailers. In addition, some engineers with M.B.A.'s design and sell large, complex production systems for major manufacturers. Compared to the advertising industry, which employs only half a million workers, personal selling employs a tremendous number of people. Chances are that students majoring in business or marketing will start their professional careers in sales. Even students in non-business majors may pursue a sales career.

Many young people get their first sales experience as retail clerks or fast-food clerks.

(top) © 1989 Bill Varie/The Image Bank; (bottom) Jan Irish/Leo de Wys, Inc.

In a sense, all businesspeople are salespeople. An individual may become a plant manager, a chemist, an engineer, or a member of any profession and yet still have to sell. To reach the top in most organizations, individuals need to sell ideas to peers, superiors, and subordinates. Most important, people must sell themselves and their ideas to just about everyone with whom they have a continuing relationship and to many other people they see only once or twice. During a job search, applicants must "sell" themselves to prospective employers in an interview.

The rewards of choosing a sales career are many. Today a top-level industrial salesperson earns an average salary of nearly $60,000 per year, while the average starting salary for a sales trainee is about $27,000.[27] Besides earning attractive salaries, skilled salespeople can rely on job security. Salespeople who reap profits for their companies are rarely laid

off. In addition, salespeople enjoy perhaps more freedom and independence than any other type of employee. Typically, salespeople are neither overly supervised nor chained to their desks. They also receive the satisfaction of seeing a direct correlation between their efforts and their achievements. The enthusiasm and positive attitude that characterize most successful salespeople tend to carry over into their personal lives.

The field of sales affords many opportunities, such as selling at the wholesale or retail level, telemarketing, selling a manufactured good, selling a service, or just strengthening sales of the good or service by performing a specific support function. In general, all sales positions can be classified into the three basic types of selling tasks: order getting, order taking, and sales supporting. However, one salesperson can, and very often does, perform all three tasks in the course of the selling job.

Order Getters

order getter
Someone who actively seeks buyers for a product.

An **order getter** is someone who actively seeks buyers for a product. An order getter's main task is to convert both prospective and present customers into buyers of the firm's products. To obtain sales, an order getter must aggressively seek prospects, inform them about the product, and then persuade them to buy it. For example, a salesperson for Hewlett-Packard would have to locate prospects, justify the reasons for buying a Hewlett-Packard computer system rather than perhaps an IBM or an Apple system, and then close the sale. Thus the order getter must thoroughly know the company's product, the competitive environment, the customer's potential use of the product, and the customer's specific needs.

An order getter can be either a member of a company's own sales force or an independent seller. Manufacturing firms often use a manufacturer's representative to sell to wholesalers, distributors, retailers, and sometimes the ultimate consumer, as with Amway products and Avon cosmetics. Telemarketers also serve as order getters. For many companies, telemarketers serve as a full-fledged selling arm for dealing with designated customer or product segments. In several industries telemarketers are even replacing field sales representatives.

inside order taker
Someone who takes orders from customers over the counter, on the sales floor, over the telephone, or by mail.

field order taker
Someone who visits existing customers regularly, checks inventory, writes up new orders, and then delivers and stocks the product for the customers.

Order Takers

Order takers do not have to go out and seek new buyers for their good or service because, in most cases, the buyer comes to them or the account is assigned to them. Order takers can be either inside order takers or field order takers. **Inside order takers** may take orders from customers over the counter, on the sales floor, over the telephone, or by mail. Examples include a cashier in a fast-food restaurant, a sales clerk in a department store, and a salesperson for a retail mail-order catalog. In contrast, **field order takers** focus on building repeat sales and accepting orders. These order takers visit their customers regularly, check inventory, write up new orders, and then deliver and stock the product for the customers. They are normally found in the beer, food, and soft-drink industries.

missionary sales representative
Someone who works for amanufacturer to stimulate goodwill within the channel of distribution and to support the company's sales efforts.

Sales Support Personnel

Sales support personnel don't actually sell a good or service. However, they do promote it through goodwill and after-the-sale customer service. Two types of support personnel are missionary sales representatives and technical specialists.

Missionary sales representatives work for manufacturers to stimulate goodwill within the channel of distribution and to support their company's sales efforts. A missionary sales representative may travel with a wholesaler's representative for a

while to reinforce the promotional effort for the product. Sometimes a missionary sales representative works with the manufacturer's new sales personnel to help them learn the territory and the accounts. Missionary sales representatives are common in consumer packaged-goods industries such as food and drug products. At the retail level, missionary sales reps may set up displays, check the stock and shelf space, and explain new product offerings to retailers. For industrial goods they usually arc a communication link between the manufacturer and key accounts. They relay any problems that arise to the manufacturer. Then new products or product applications are passed forward to the customer.

technical specialist
Salesperson with a technical background who works out the details of custom-made products and communicates directly with the potential buyer's technical staff.

Technical specialists are salespeople with backgrounds in chemistry, engineering, physics, or a similar field. They work out the details of custom-made products and communicate directly with the potential buyer's technical staff. The sales rep may make an initial presentation to a purchasing committee and then let the technical specialist take over during the question-and-answer phase. If the buyer develops an interest in the seller's product, the specialist plays a larger role, planning the product specifications and installation procedures and overseeing the installation. After making the sale, the sales representative usually relies on feedback from the technical specialist about installation dates, debugging time, and similar information.

8 STEPS IN THE SELLING PROCESS

Although personal selling may sound like a relatively simple task, completing a sale actually requires several steps. Some sales take only a few minutes, but others may take months or years to complete. Whether a salesperson spends a few minutes or a few years on a sale, these are the seven basic steps that should be used:

1. Generating sales leads
2. Qualifying sales leads
3. Making the sales approach
4. Making the sales presentation
5. Handling objections
6. Closing the sale
7. Following up

Like other forms of promotion, these seven steps of selling follow the AIDA concept (see Chapter 15). Once a salesperson has located a prospect with the authority to buy, he or she tries to get attention. An effective presentation and demonstration should generate interest. After developing the customer's initial desire (preferably during the presentation or demonstration), the salesperson properly handles objections. This step should lower cognitive dissonance and increase desire. The salesperson seeks action in the closing by trying to get an agreement to buy. Follow-up, the final step in the selling process, not only lowers cognitive dissonance but also may open up opportunities to discuss future sales. Lets look at each step of the selling process individually.

lead generation
Identification of those firms and people most likely to buy the seller's offerings.

Generating Sales Leads

Initial groundwork must precede communication between the potential buyer and the seller. **Lead generation**, or prospecting, is the identification of those firms and people most likely to buy the seller's offerings. These firms or people become "sales

Bob Clore, general sales manager of a BMW dealership in Houston, generates sales leads by asking customers for referrals. Prospects may get a videotape or even the use of a new car for a day or two. When it's time to make a deal, Clore may negotiate by fax.

leads" or "prospects." Naturally, not everyone is a prospect for a firm's good or service, nor are all prospects equally likely to buy. For example, a salesperson may have to make 125 phone calls to schedule 25 interviews. In turn, 5 presentations might result from these interviews, from which a single prospect becomes a buying customer. Sales leads are secured in several different ways: from direct mail and telemarketing programs and through various media, through cold calling, from client referrals and salesperson networking, through trade shows and conventions, and from internal company records.

Direct-mail and telemarketing programs have become quite popular as ways of generating sales leads. This type of lead generation usually starts with a list of potential clients with desirable characteristics, such as a particular occupation. For instance, if a medical equipment company is trying to sell a new piece of equipment used in heart surgery, it may start with a list of all cardiologists in the United States. With these sorts of programs, companies might send direct-mail letters or brochures, usually with a detachable coupon to be returned or an 800 number to be called for more information. Some companies employ telemarketing representatives, who use client lists to contact potential customers by telephone.

cold calling
Form of lead generation in which the salesperson approaches potential buyers without any prior knowledge of the prospects' needs or financial status.

referral
Recommendation from a customer or business associate.

networking
Finding out about potential clients from friends, business contacts, co-workers, acquaintances, and fellow members in professional and civic organizations.

Closely related to this concept are media-generated leads, for which advertisements are usually placed in business-to-business publications or in some other highly targeted media vehicle such as cable television. Again, a coupon or a toll-free number is usually provided for the prospect who would like to request more information. For example, an ad for Shure Teleconferencing Systems gives prospects the opportunity to either receive more information about the service or schedule a free demonstration.

Cold calling is a form of lead generation in which the salesperson approaches potential buyers without any prior knowledge of the prospects' needs or financial status. The salesperson may visit them but often telephones them to offset the high cost of a personal visit.

Another way to gather a lead is through a **referral**—a recommendation from a customer or business associate. **Networking** is the method of using friends, business contacts, co-workers, and acquaintances, as well as fellow members in professional

and civic organizations, to find out about potential clients. For example, Bob Clore, general manager of the BMW dealership in Houston, asks past customers for sales leads. He sends promotional videotapes to prospects, then drops off cars at potential buyers' homes for test drives.[28]

Sales representatives selling noncompeting lines and nonselling company employees are also good sources of leads. For example, Southern New England Telephone's "Catch Any Leads Lately?" program encourages employees to look for cellular phone sales leads when they're not at work. Employees can dial a twenty-four-hour hot line and give the potential customer information to operators, who then pass it along to the appropriate salesperson. For each lead employees submit—whether or not it results in a sale—they get an entry into a sweepstakes held every month that gives away such merchandise as color televisions, sweatsuits, and Ray-Ban sunglasses.[29]

Trade shows and conventions are yet another good source of leads. Since these shows and conventions are held for a specific product or industry, most leads generated are very likely to purchase. Company records of past client purchases are an excellent source of new leads, too.

Sales managers especially value lead generation because it is the main source of new business. Often, however, sales reps don't spend enough of their time prospecting. It is estimated that more than half of all leads for all products requiring a face-to-face sales interview are never followed up.[30] Yet studies have revealed that over half of the prospects who respond to direct mail or advertisements are still in the market six months later for the product they first asked about.[31] Therefore, salespeople who follow up on all leads have a competitive advantage, which should result in increased sales.

Qualifying Sales Leads

When a prospect shows interest in learning more about a product, the salesperson has the opportunity to follow up, or qualify, the lead. **Lead qualification** consists of two steps: determining which prospects have the authority to buy and assessing which can afford to pay for the good or service.

lead qualification
Determination of a sales prospect's authority to buy and ability to pay for the good or service.

To avoid wasting time and money, the salesperson needs to identify the buying authority before making a presentation. An organization chart, if available, can sometimes provide valuable clues. Asking a switchboard operator or a secretary can also lead the salesperson in the right direction. If the salesperson is still uncertain, he or she can ask a simple, direct question to qualify the prospect—for example, "Can you sign the purchase order for this product?" In some cases, purchasing authority rests with a committee. The salesperson must then identify the most influential committee members. In other situations buying authority may rest with a regional or headquarters officer located in a distant city.

Determining ability to pay is often easier than pinpointing buying authority. Information about a firm's credit standing can be obtained from Dun & Bradstreet credit ratings or other financial reporting services. For smaller concerns, a local credit bureau can provide the needed information. A salesperson should heed this advice: better to qualify ability to pay now than be left with an unpaid invoice months later.

Telemarketing and direct-mail methods not only assist in generating good leads but also help to qualify them as well. SPSS, Inc., a statistical software company in Chicago, uses telemarketers to qualify leads before passing the names along to its sales force. Telemarketers ask prospects for financial data, the best time of day for a

sales rep to call, and similar information. The company receives a smaller number of responses than it would have normally received without qualifying leads, because respondents who are not very interested rarely bother to supply more information. But those who do have a sincere interest in the product and are financially capable of buying. Qualifying leads yields a higher percentage of qualified prospects and ultimately a higher percentage of closed sales.[32]

Making the Sales Approach

An approach to a qualified prospect can take several forms. The main goal of the sales approach is either to talk to the prospect or to secure an appointment for a future time. The sales approach should always include an interest-capturing statement so the prospect has a reason for continuing the conversation. For example, the salesperson might say, "Our new robot welding arm has cut production line labor costs up to 40 percent in some installations. More important, the incidence of defective welds drops virtually to zero." An effective approach results in a face-to-face meeting with a qualified prospect. Allocating too much time on personally visiting unqualified prospects will waste valuable salesperson time and company resources.

Creating a customer profile during the approach helps salespeople optimize their time and resources. This profile is then used to help develop an intelligent analysis of the prospect's needs in preparation for the sales presentation. For example, one of the jobs of Hyatt Hotel field reps is to gather information about where the prospect stayed, how long, and what airline he or she used. Even though profiling the customer requires some extra effort, most of Hyatt's reps like having the information when the time comes to plan the next sales call or presentation.[33]

The three basic ways to get an initial interview are a letter, an unsolicited personal visit, and a telephone call. A letter is usually the least effective technique for gaining an appointment, because it is easy to ignore or turn down. An unsolicited personal visit typically means being screened by a receptionist or secretary who acts as a gatekeeper. Unsolicited visits are also often mistimed. For example, a prospect may be out of the office or otherwise unavailable. Some prospects also resent salespeople who just "drop in." A salesperson may also have to make a presentation first to a subordinate, who will then decide whether the salesperson should see the decision maker. The purpose of a telephone call is to arouse interest and introduce the sales proposition without forcing a premature decision.

Making the Sales Presentation

sales presentation
Face-to-face explanation of a product's benefits to a prospective buyer.

The **sales presentation** is the heart of the selling process. The salesperson presents the product's benefits to the prospect—in person or through tapes or videoconferencing. Videotapes, which are fast becoming quite popular, are an economical and effective way to tell prospects about a product. Carmakers were among the first to use videotapes. Although carmakers are reluctant to tie increased sales directly to a video sales pitch, they believe the videotapes are crucial in pulling consumers into dealerships for test drives.[34] Other industries have followed with their own video sales presentations. For example, Guest Quarters Suite Hotels sends free videotapes on its conference services to businesspeople planning meetings.

The quality of the sales presentation can make or break the sale. However, effective sales presentations can be expensive. The cost of face-to-face selling was about $200 per sales call in 1991.[35] This figure includes the salesperson's compensation, car and transportation costs, and entertainment costs.

The salesperson can enhance the effectiveness of the presentation by using several techniques. Allowing the prospect to touch or hold the product, using visual aids, and using words that relate important selling points of the product, such as *new, simple,* and *innovative,* can increase message retention and persuasiveness of the presentation. Practicing adaptive selling also makes the presentation more effective. **Adaptive selling** alters a presentation for each prospect in response to the nature of the sales situation.[36] Thus each presentation meets the needs of its specific audience.

adaptive selling
Altering a sales presentation for each prospect in response to the specific sales situation.

There are two basic approaches to making a presentation: stimulus-response and need-satisfaction.

Stimulus-Response Approach

stimulus-response approach
Sales pitch applying the concept that a given stimulus will produce a given response.

The **stimulus-response approach** recognizes that a given stimulus will produce a given response (see Chapter 4). When applied to a selling situation, this term means that the salesperson makes certain points (stimulus) about the good or service that ultimately lead to a sale (response).

prepared sales presentation
Structured, or canned, sales pitch.

A memorized or **prepared sales presentation** lends itself to the stimulus-response approach. Many telephone sales pitches follow this structured or "canned" format. Advantages of the canned approach are that it ensures the salesperson will tell a complete, accurate story about the product; ensures that sales points are arranged in a logical, systematic order; and usually addresses most or all potential objections. However, the canned approach also has its drawbacks. Perhaps the biggest disadvantage is that it does not allow the salesperson to adapt the presentation to the prospect. Therefore, the salesperson and presentation may seem artificial and mechanical. The canned approach is rather inflexible and discourages the prospect's participation. A salesperson may even have trouble "resuming the pitch" if interrupted by the prospect.

Need-Satisfaction Approach

need-satisfaction approach
Sales pitch that focuses on satisfying a prospective buyer's particular needs.

In contrast, the **need-satisfaction approach** emphasizes that people buy products to satisfy needs and solve problems. A salesperson employing this approach uses the prospect's need as a springboard for the sales presentation. After securing the prospect's agreement that the need exists, the salesperson offers a solution to satisfy the need. Designed more for the professional salesperson, this approach is typically used when the salesperson has a complex product line and is selling to a sophisticated audience. For example, companies like Hewlett-Packard have shifted to a need-satisfaction approach, which has required an evolution in the roles and skills of Hewlett-Packard's salespeople. They must understand customer needs, explain solutions in terms the customer can understand, and be as knowledgeable about the technology of competitors' equipment and industry standards as they are about Hewlett-Packard's own products.[37]

Many companies are expanding the boundaries of the need-satisfaction approach to emphasize long-term relationships between salespeople and clients. In this approach, the salesperson acts as a consultant. The salesperson determines a client's needs or problems, presents all possible solutions, and then recommends the solution that is in the best interest of the customer. By building a personal and professional relationship with the client, the salesperson becomes more of a partner than just another salesperson peddling some good or service. The advantages of this expanded need-satisfaction approach are increased trust between seller and buyer and a long-term selling relationship. However, this approach also requires much

The salespeople at this Hewlett-Packard outlet have shifted from a product orientation to a need-satisfaction approach, which is more customer-oriented.
Courtesy Hewlett-Packard Company

more time and considerably more skill on the part of the salesperson. Kodak is one company that uses this approach to its advantage. Kodak sales reps go through extensive training on how to think more broadly. They become partners with their retail customers, helping them run their businesses. Kodak reps routinely offer retailers a host of services, from access to Kodak's in-house experts on inventory control to training for counter clerks to guidance in running a successful promotion.[38]

The need-satisfaction approach stresses product benefits, not the physical aspects of the product. For example, people do not buy photographs; they buy memories. Women do not buy cosmetics and toiletries; they buy the expectation that they will feel younger and look more attractive. The advantage of the need-satisfaction approach is its strong marketing orientation. It is designed to meet the needs of the marketplace.

However, this approach also has two disadvantages. First, need development can be a long, drawn-out process. Second, the need-satisfaction approach requires a more sophisticated salesperson than someone making a canned presentation. The individual must be able to ask penetrating questions and to integrate the answers into an effective sales presentation focusing on how the product satisfies the customer's needs.

Handling Objections

Rarely does a prospect say "I'll buy it" right after a presentation. Often there are objections or perhaps questions about the presentation and the product. For instance, the potential buyer may complain that the price is too high, that he or she does not have enough information for making a decision, or that the good or service will not satisfy present needs. The buyer may also lack confidence in the seller's organization or product.

One of the first lessons that every salesperson learns is that objections to the product should not be taken personally. Rather, a salesperson should view objections as requests for information, not as confrontations or insults. Anticipating

specific objections, such as price, is the best way to prepare for them. A good salesperson handles objections calmly and considers them a legitimate part of the purchase decision. Suppose a prospect interrupts early in a presentation and says, "I doubt if your equipment is compatible with our existing equipment." The salesperson might reply, "That's certainly a valid concern, Ms. Jones. I think you'll see as we go along that we've anticipated that possibility and provided compatibility." The salesperson first agrees with the prospect and then goes on to refute the objection. A more direct technique is to meet the prospect's statement head-on and deny it. Some prospects appreciate this straightforward approach.

Closing the Sale

At the end of the presentation, if the prospect's objections have been met, the salesperson can try to close the sale. Closing requires courage and skill. Naturally, the salesperson wants to avoid rejection, and asking for a sale carries with it the risk of a no. A salesperson should keep an open mind when asking for the sale and be prepared for either a yes or a no.

assumptive close
Technique of ending a sales presentation that assumes the prospect is going to buy.

summative close
Technique of ending a sales presentation that summarizes the product's benefits and asks for the sale.

negotiation (extra inducement close)
Technique of withholding a special concession until the end of the selling process and using it to close a sale.

urgency close
Technique of ending a sales presentation that suggests a reason for ordering soon, such as an impending price increase.

standing-room-only close
Technique of ending a sales presention that urges customers to buy right away because the product is selling so well it may not be available later.

silent close
Technique of ending a sales presention by saying nothing and waiting for the prospect to make a response.

Customers often give signals during the presentation that they are either ready to buy or not interested. Examples include changes in facial expressions, gestures, and questions asked. The salesperson should look for these signals and respond appropriately.

Whenever the customer makes a commitment to buy, the sale closing and order processing should begin. However, if the commitment to buy is not forthcoming, a number of techniques can be used to try to close the sale. Ideally, the salesperson should be able to ask directly for the order. However, other types of closes may be more appropriate. One popular approach is the **assumptive close.** The salesperson assumes that the prospect is going to buy and says something like "Which do you want delivered, product A or product B?" or "When do you want the merchandise shipped?" A second closing technique is the **summative close,** which summarizes the product's benefits and asks for the sale. Sometimes a salesperson will withhold a special concession until the end of the selling process and use it in closing the sale; this strategy is usually called **negotiation**, or the **extra inducement close**. Examples include a price cut, free installation, free service, and a trial order. In today's economy, salespeople can use the **urgency close** in many industries. They may say, "Prices will be going up in six weeks" or "We don't anticipate being able to deliver new models for six months due to component shortages, but we have three of this year's model left. A related closing technique, called the **standing-room-only close**, urges customers to buy right away because the product is selling so well it may not be available later. A final closing method is the **silent close**, in which the salesperson says nothing at the end of the presentation and waits for the prospect to make a response.

Although some of these closing methods may sound like marketing tricks, successful salespeople avoid using deception and pressure in closing a sale and instead recognize the importance of building trust and a long-term relationship with the customer. Rarely is a sale closed on the first call. In fact, a salesperson averages about four sales contacts before a sale can be made.[39] Some salespeople may negotiate with large accounts for several years before closing a sale. As you can see, building a good relationship with the customer is very important.

More and more U.S. companies are expanding their marketing and selling efforts into global markets. A company selling in foreign markets should tailor its negotiating style to each market. For instance, in German-speaking countries—such as

Germany, Austria, and parts of Switzerland—salespeople should expect a sober, rigid business climate and negotiations that lack flexibility and compromise. Negotiations with Central and South American customers typically include a great deal of bargaining. Personal relationships are also important in Central and South America, so salespeople should make face-to-face contact with their clients. In China as well, great importance is attached to the personal relationship. Friendship means a lot, and small courtesies and follow-up presents are essential.[40] Personal relationships are also important in Japan, as discussed in the International Perspectives article.

follow-up
Final step of the selling process, in which the salesperson ensures that delivery schedules are met, that the goods or services perform as promised, and that the buyers' employees are properly trained to use the products.

Following Up

Unfortunately, many salespeople hold the attitude that making the sale is all that's important. Once the sale is made, they can forget about their customers. They are wrong. Salespeople's responsibilities do not end with making the sales and placing the orders. One of the most important aspects of their jobs is **follow-up.** They must ensure that delivery schedules are met, that the goods or services perform as promised, and that the buyers' employees are properly trained to use the products.

INTERNATIONAL PERSPECTIVES

Negotiating with Japanese Customers

Mr. Smith, the head of sales for a U.S. beverage firm, is involved in negotiations with a Japanese food company. His company plans to sell and export beer to Japan. Exploratory discussions have already been held with the U.S. representative for the Japanese company. Now Mr. Smith is flying to Tokyo to discuss the details of the sale and, if possible, secure an agreement.

In the United States, he has usually concluded similar sales deals successfully in a day or two. His habit is to get down to business as soon as possible and not spend a lot of time on preliminaries. He would like to adopt the same approach in Tokyo, so he has allowed only three days for his stay. "Business is business," he thinks, and after all, his Japanese counterparts are just as interested in the sale as he is.

Once in Tokyo, Mr. Smith takes the opportunity to begin discussions on the main points of the projected sales transaction over dinner the first night of his stay. Imagine his astonishment when he finds that his enthusiasm for discussing the sale straightaway isn't welcomed with open arms by the Japanese. Instead of definite statements, Mr. Smith hears nothing except friendly and noncommittal conversation.

The following day, at his first meeting with the heads of the Japanese company, the situation remains unchanged. In spite of several attempts by Mr. Smith to begin discussions, his Japanese counterparts say nothing about the project but instead concentrate on talking about the history, traditions, and beliefs of their company.

Mr. Smith is irritated. After all, the principle that "time is money" surely must apply to his Japanese colleagues as well. He finally loses patience when he learns that the afternoon isn't devoted to any sales discussions but has instead been reserved for sightseeing.

In despair, he turns to the Japanese businessmen with a request that they get down to business. After all, his time is limited, and he has received no indications that his Japanese counterparts are particularly interested. After a brief consultation among themselves, the Japanese finally agree to his request. However, contrary to his expectations, the negotiations don't go as anticipated. They proceed without any definite statements, let alone any promises, and no sales agreement is reached. After three days of frustration and little progress, Mr. Smith flies home without having achieved anything.

What should Mr. Smith have done differently in his sales negotiating? What types of preparations should a salesperson make before negotiating with foreign customers? What preparations do you think foreign salespeople make when calling on U.S. customers?

Source: Adapted from Sergey Frank, "Avoiding the Pitfalls of Business Abroad," *Sales & Marketing Management,* March 1992, pp. 48–52.

A basic goal of any company or professional sales department is to motivate customers to come back, again and again. Most businesses depend on repeat sales, and repeat sales depend on thorough follow-up. When customers feel abandoned, cognitive dissonance arises and repeat sales decline. Today this issue is more pertinent than ever, because customers are far less loyal to brands and vendors. Buyers are more inclined to look for the best deal, especially in the case of poor after-the-sale follow-up. More and more companies favor building a relationship with vendors.

7 SALES MANAGEMENT

There is an old adage in business that nothing happens until a sale is made. Without sales there is no need for accountants, production workers, or even a company president. Sales provide the fuel that keeps the corporate engines humming. Companies like West Point Pepperel, Dow Corning, Alcoa, and several thousand other industrial manufacturers would cease to exist without successful salespeople or manufacturers' representatives. Even companies like Procter & Gamble and Kraft General Foods that mainly sell consumer goods and use extensive advertising campaigns still rely on salespeople to move products through the channel of distribution. Thus sales management is one of marketing's most critical areas. Effective sales management stems from a highly success-oriented sales force that accomplishes its mission economically and efficiently. Poor sales management can lead to unmet profit objectives or even to the downfall of the corporation.

Just as selling is a personal relationship, so is sales management. Although the sales manager's basic job is to maximize sales at a reasonable cost while also maximizing profits, he or she also has many other important responsibilities and decisions. The tasks of sales management are to

- Set sales objectives
- Structure the sales force
- Determine the size of the sales force
- Develop the compensation plan
- Recruit the sales force
- Train the sales force
- Motivate the sales force
- Manage sales force turnover
- Evaluate the sales force

Let's look at each of these tasks.

Set Sales Objectives

Effective sales management begins with communication of sales goals and objectives. Like any marketing objective, sales goals and objectives should be stated in clear, precise, and measurable terms and should always specify a time frame for their fulfillment. Overall sales force objectives are usually stated in terms of desired dollar sales volume, market share, or profit level. For example, a life insurance company may have a volume objective to sell $50 million in life insurance policies annually (or 1,000 policies), to attain a 12 percent market share, or to achieve $1 million in profits.

quota
Statement of sales objectives, usually based on sales volume alone but sometimes including key accounts (those with greatest potential), new accounts, and specific products.

Individual salespeople are also assigned objectives in the form of quotas. A **quota**

is simply a statement of sales objectives, usually based on sales volume alone but sometimes including key accounts (those with greatest potential), new accounts, and specific products. In addition, quotas can be based on activity or financial objectives. For example, a sales representative for a cellular phone company may have the sales quota of selling $1,000 worth of equipment or five new cellular systems per week. He or she may have the objective of completing a certain number of sales calls per week. Many firms are placing more emphasis on financial objectives that require the salespeople to take into account the profit contribution of the products they sell. Those products yielding higher profits for the company will thus receive more attention.

Structure the Sales Force

Because personal selling is so costly, no sales department can afford to be disorganized. Therefore, structuring the sales department or sales force is essential. Structured departments help the sales manager organize and delegate sales duties and provide direction for salespeople. Sales departments have traditionally been organized into the four types described below: geographic, product, functional, or market. Often firms combine these types.[41]

sales territory
Particular geographic area assigned to a salesperson.

- *Geographic organization:* A common method for organizing the sales force is assigning a salesperson to a particular geographic area called a **sales territory**—for instance, a region, state, city, or other trading area. A firm like a consumer products organization that has a small number of closely related, nontechnical products might use this method. Geographically structured sales departments are most appropriate when customers are widely dispersed or when there are large regional differences in customer buying behavior. For example, sales of snow tires in southern states would not warrant the creation of separate sales territories, but they would in northern states. A simple example of this structuring method follows:

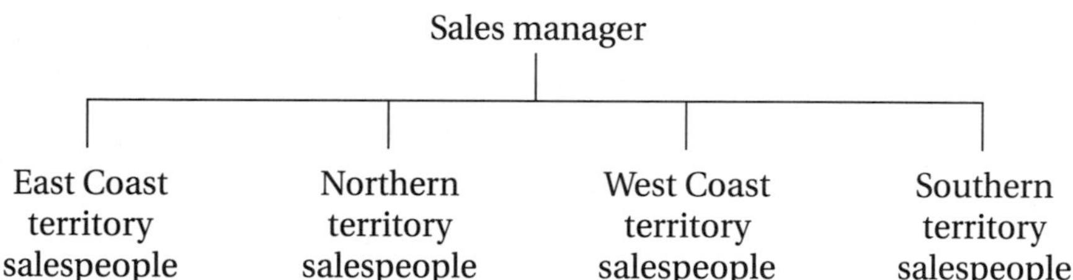

- *Product organization:* Another common method is structuring the sales organization by the product that the salesperson sells. For example, large consumer products companies may structure a sales force around brands. Structuring the sales force in this manner is most appropriate when products are complex, the differences between them are great, and the products or product groups are important enough to justify special attention. A sales force organized by product has greater knowledge of and expertise in specific product categories. Office equipment specialists are a good example of this sales structuring method:

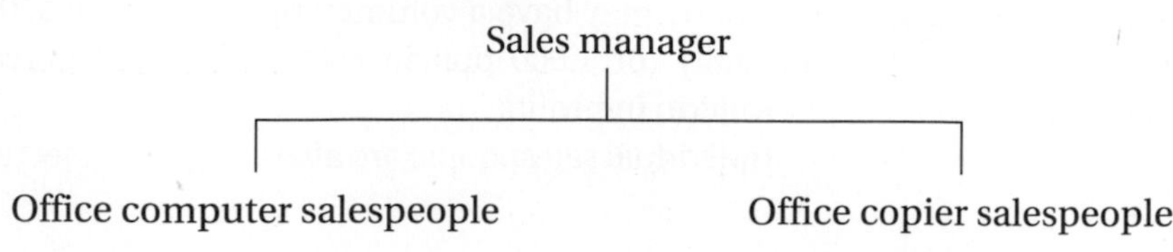

One popular way to organize the sales force is to assign a geographic territory to each sales rep. To cover the territory, the sales rep may have to travel.

- *Functional organization:* The sales department organized by function focuses on needed sales activities, such as account development or account maintenance. This structure offers specialization and efficiency in performing selling activities and is best for companies selling only a few or very similar products to relatively few target markets. Because it requires more labor, this form of organization is hard for very small firms to maintain. However, it can work well in medium-size to large firms. These firms can afford the luxury of having their salespeople perform only one task or a small number of tasks. For example, many paper makers employ representatives who work solely on selling to major clients. After the negotiations have been completed, service salespeople step in to take care of clients' postsale needs.

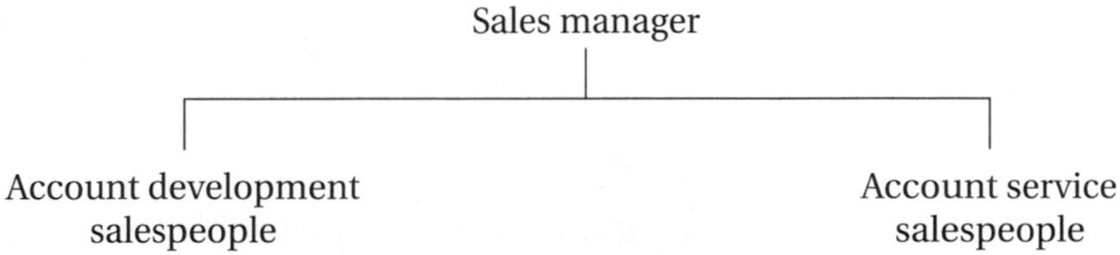

- *Market organization:* In this approach, the sales force is divided by customer groups, or target markets, and each salesperson calls on only one group. A market orientation is most appropriate when customer needs and product purchases vary considerably between target groups. This method is also used when there is a great need to identify and solve different customer problems. For example, Boeing, the aircraft manufacturer, uses a market organization for its commercial and government markets. Boeing realizes that the two markets have different needs and problems.

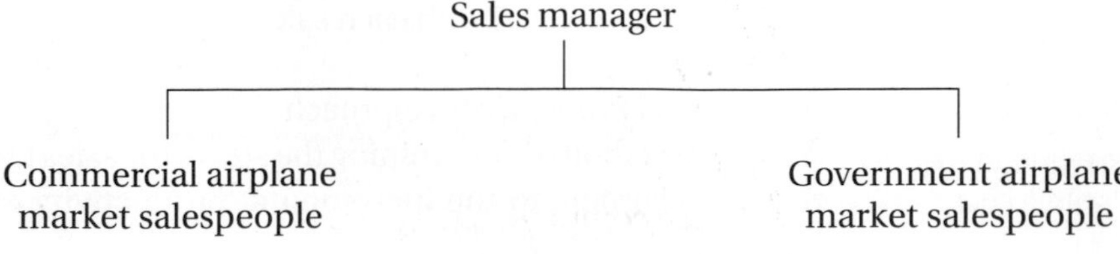

Many companies have been taking the market-oriented structure one step further, to an individual client or account level. This trend has occurred in conjunction with the increased emphasis on long-term relationships between salesperson and client. The organization typically assigns one salesperson or a team of salespeople to a client to provide better customer service. For example, Asea Brown Boveri (ABB), a Swiss-based industrial equipment manufacturer, realigned its sales force around clients after it discovered that customers were frustrated with its product-oriented sales force structure. As many as a dozen ABB salespeople called on each client at different times to sell their products. Sometimes ABB sales reps even passed each other in customers' lobbies without realizing that they were working for the same company. By reorganizing the sales force around customers, many companies hope to improve customer service, encourage collaboration with other arms of the company, and unite salespeople into customer-focused teams.[42]

Determine Sales Force Size

The ideal size of the sales force can be arrived at using several methods. Two of the most common are the workload approach and the incremental productivity approach. Sales managers rarely rely on one method to determine sales force size. Instead, they combine their own opinions on other issues—such as economic factors, industry trends, growth of the market, and the needs of customers—with these formula methods to come up with the optimal size.

Workload Approach

workload approach
Method of determining sales force size based on dividing the total time required to cover the territory by the selling time available to one salesperson.

The **workload approach** is based on the total time required to cover the territory divided by the selling time available to one salesperson. Here is the formula for using the workload approach:

$$\text{Number of salespeople} = \frac{\text{Ideal number of customers} \times \text{Frequency of calls} \times \text{Length of calls}}{\text{Selling time available from one salesperson}}$$

For example, assume that a firm has 4,000 total customers (3,000 current customers and an estimated 1,000 potential customers). Sales analysis has revealed that sales calls average 1.5 hours and that each customer should be seen seven times a year. Further examination of records has revealed that each salesperson has 2,000 hours of selling time available per year. The computation for this problem is

$$\text{Number of salespeople} = \frac{(3{,}000 + 1{,}000) \times 7 \times 1.5}{2{,}000} = \frac{42{,}000}{2{,}000} = 21$$

If the company now has eighteen people in its sales force, three new people should be hired.

The major advantage of the workload approach is its simplicity. Successful application of the technique depends on the sales manager's ability to estimate the ideal frequency of calls and the number of potential customers. However, the workload approach fails to consider either the cost of increasing the work force or the costs and profits associated with each sales call.

incremental productivity approach
Method of determining sales force size in which salespeople are added as long as the total sales increase is greater than the increase in selling cost.

Incremental Productivity Approach

A second method of determining the size of the sales force is by incremental productivity.[43] According to the **incremental productivity approach,** a manager should

increase the number of salespeople as long as the additional sales increase is greater than the additional increase in selling cost. Companies with good records know the cost of training a salesperson. This cost, plus field expenses and the salary of a new person, can be compared with the revenue generated by sales activities. Unfortunately, many companies do not have these cost data available.

Develop the Compensation Plan

Compensation planning is one of the sales manager's toughest jobs. Only good planning will ensure that compensation attracts, motivates, and retains good salespeople. Generally, companies and industries with lower levels of compensation suffer higher turnover rates. Therefore, the general compensation level needs to be competitive enough to attract and motivate the best salespeople. Many firms also take profit into account when developing their compensation plans. Instead of paying salespeople on overall volume, they pay according to the profitability achieved from selling each product. Other firms tie compensation to their quarterly, yearly, or long-range sales and marketing plan. With this method, the firm can easily encourage its salespeople to carry out the company's overall objectives, because it has created a compensation program that balances the interests of the company and of the sales force.[44] There are three basic compensation methods for salespeople: commission, salary, and combination plans.

Straight Commission System

A typical commission plan gives salespeople a specified percentage of their sales revenue. Firms with limited resources and firms selling high-priced items typically use commission plans. However, many other companies use commissions as a way to reward sales performance. If the plan is a **straight commission** system, the salesperson receives no compensation until a sale is made.

straight commission Method of compensation in which the salesperson is paid some percentage of sales.

This plan has several disadvantages. Salespeople usually must also pay their expenses from the commission. Moreover, management lacks control over the sales force since they are not paid a salary. In addition, salespeople under this compensation plan normally have little loyalty to the company, and turnover is fairly high if business conditions are slow. Also, salespeople are reluctant to perform nonselling activities that do not generate commissions.

To boost sales and upgrade service, many major retail chains have converted some of their sales departments from hourly wage to straight commission. Commission plans have always existed in department stores but have generally been reserved for high-ticket items, where the extra selling efforts that commissions encourage will pay off. Examples include furniture, electronics, and men's suits. Now some department stores are applying the plan to all departments, from linens to lingerie. However, many retailers have experienced problems with commission payment systems, as the Ethics in Marketing article describes.

Straight Salary System

As its name suggests, a **straight salary** system compensates salespeople with a stated salary regardless of their sales productivity. In some situations a straight salary plan offers maximum control but perhaps little incentive to produce. Filling out information reports, servicing accounts, calling on smaller customers, and performing other nonselling tasks are very undesirable to the commission salesperson. Yet the salaried salesperson can tolerate these tasks.

straight salary Method of compensation in which the salesperson receives a salary regardless of sales productivity.

The straight salary plan works effectively when a territory requires an extensive

amount of prospecting. In firms that use a team approach and rely on missionary sales representatives, it may be hard to tell who really closed a sale. Thus, a salary system tends to work better than a commission system in these cases.

Combination Systems

To achieve the best of both worlds, many companies have turned to a combination system, which offers a salesperson a base salary plus an incentive—usually a commission or a bonus. (Bonuses are often paid as a percentage of salary.) Combination systems have benefits for both the sales manager and the salesperson. The salary portion of the plan helps the manager control the sales force; the incentive provides

ETHICS IN MARKETING

Problems with Retail Commission Plans

The problem at Sears, Roebuck & Company's auto-service centers is the same one that retailers are grappling with all across the nation: how to motivate their sales forces. The answer many retailers found was to put their salespeople on commission plans. Retail salespeople working on commission have been growing in favor over the past several years. Among retail sales representatives, only 7 percent earned just a salary in 1990, down from 21 percent in 1981.

A sales-commission plan that works well provides benefits for the company, the sales force, and the customer. It can motivate talented salespeople, weed out the deadwood, and improve customer service as well. Commissions force salespeople to be more attentive to the customer. Commissions also help retailers control costs because salaries—considered fixed expenses—are converted to flexible costs and rise or fall depending on sales levels.

But ill-suited commission plans can backfire. Stung by declining employee morale and consumer distaste for pushy salespeople, some retailers—Sears and Dayton-Hudson Corporation among them—are scaling back aggressive commission-compensation programs. Sears recently abandoned a commission plan at its auto-service centers after California officials alleged that the centers' employees systematically recommended unnecessary repairs to customers in an attempt to boost their compensation. As a result, California officials are moving to force Sears out of the auto-repair business. Moreover, a group of Sears customers are pursuing a class-action lawsuit based on the auto-center allegations.

Dayton-Hudson also scaled back the broad commission plan it created for its sales force two years ago after employee resistance. Its sales force didn't want to give up a straight salary for a salary-plus-commission plan. Similarly, Highland Superstores, Inc., an electronics and appliance chain, also recently eliminated commissions, placing clerks on full salaries. Highland Superstores' compensation plan, which was based almost entirely on commissions, caused salespeople to become so aggressive that they alienated consumers. The plan also created a high turnover rate among clerks at the stores.

Sears and others were encouraged to move toward commissions by the growth and success of the Nordstrom Inc. department-store chain, whose sales force works almost strictly on commission. But by copying the example of Nordstrom, the other retailers failed to give their sales clerks the extensive training and the freedom to sell merchandise throughout the entire store that Nordstrom employees enjoy. Additionally, the obstacles many retailers encounter when they adopt commission formats arise because their employees have never worked for commissions and in many cases don't want the pressure. Employees at Nordstrom have always worked on commission, and it is a part of their culture.

Companies in other industries are backing away from commissions, too, as customer dissatisfaction and employee turnover rise. A case in point is the auto industry, known for its high-pressure sales tactics from salespeople on commission. In many showrooms of General Motors Corporation's new Saturn car division, for example, salespeople are paid salaries instead of commissions. The aim is to engender good customer service and teamwork among the sales force.

To what do you credit the fact that retail salespeople are not always effective on commission compensation plans? How else can retailers motivate their sales force?

Source: Adapted from Gregory A. Patterson, "Distressed Shoppers, Disaffected Workers Prompt Stores to Alter Sales Commissions, *The Wall Street Journal*, 1 July 1992, pp. B1, B5. Reprinted with permission of *The Wall Street Journal*,

motivation. For the salesperson, a combination plan offers an incentive to excel while minimizing the extremely wide swings that may occur in earnings when the economy surges or contracts too much.[45]

Progressive Corporation, a property and casualty insurance firm, compensates its salespeople using a combination plan. Although salespeople can earn bonuses tied to sales volume, bonuses are only a small part of their total compensation. Progressive wants its salespeople to spend time in the field digging up marketing intelligence and providing excellent customer service, neither of which directly results in increased sales volume. Any change in a competitor's prices or products, as well as any customer complaint, is promptly channeled back to company headquarters.[46]

Recruit the Sales Force

Sales management also has the task of recruiting and hiring the best salespeople to sell the firm's products. Sales force recruitment should be based on an accurate, detailed description of the sales task as defined by the company. Sales management should then develop the job description to match the sales force objectives. From the job description, sales management should build a profile of the ideal candidate for the job. Some of the things managers should consider in their sales candidate profile include level of education, employment background and level of experience, stability of employment history, ability to work unsupervised and to travel, knowledge of sales techniques and previous sales training, level of oral and written communication skills and organization skills, and previous compensation.[47] When Lotus Development Corporation decided to hire a direct sales force for its new Notes software, management had a clear picture of its ideal candidate—a confident go-getter accustomed to covering large territories on his or her own, experienced at making executive calls, and having about twelve to fifteen years of experience selling "solutions" in the computer field.[48]

After sales force recruiters get applications from candidates, they screen them to find the best applicants, using the profile provided by sales management. The chosen applicants are invited to a personal interview in which they may undergo some sort of testing. After initial interviews, the pool of applicants is further pared down for second and even third interviews. Finally, an applicant is chosen for the open position.

Qualities of a Good Salesperson

What traits should sales recruiters look for in applicants? What traits help ensure that the recruit will become an effective salesperson? The most important quality of top performers is that they are driven by their own goals. That is, they usually set personal goals higher than those management sets for them. Moreover, they are achievement-oriented, talk about their sales accomplishments, and are self-confident. Effective salespeople are also self-competitive; they keep close tabs on their own performance and compare it with their previous performance. They are optimistic, highly knowledgeable about the product, and assertive. They know how to listen to customers and are team players who support their co-workers. They are self-trainers who are continually engaged in upgrading their selling skills.

The way sales candidates close their employment interview suggests how they will close a sale. Do they ask the recruiter how and when they are to follow up for the position or what the next step will be? Effective salespeople always plan the next step before they leave the client's office.[49]

Recruiting Sources

Recruits may come from a number of sources: colleges and universities, other salespeople, trade journal and newspaper ads, employment agencies, and even competitors. Other sources include professional associations, women's groups, customers, former employees, and executive recruiters. Sometimes companies find that their nonselling employees are attracted to sales. The interviewer should determine how each candidate learned about the job opening. A data base can then be built to determine the best source of candidates.

Many companies offer selling internships for college students interested in their industry. Northwestern Mutual Life recruits many of its agents from college campuses, where students can participate in the company's unique intern program. At cooperating colleges, selected students undergo regular agent training and then represent Northwestern on their campus. The program introduces students to the industry and gives them a way to learn whether they would enjoy selling life insurance. The college intern program has been a great success for Northwestern: Among its leading agents nationwide, a high percentage began as college agents.[50]

Screening of Candidates

Several tools are used to screen sales candidates. Initial screening takes place when sales recruiters review the candidates' résumés. Recruiters evaluate the job applicants' qualifications, particularly their educational background and previous sales experience. For example, pharmaceutical giant Eli Lilly prefers candidates with a science or health care background. Only about a fifth of its sales force has a business-related degree.[51]

After sifting through the résumés, recruiters choose the best candidates to interview. The personal interview is by far the most helpful screening tool for selecting new salespeople, but it is also the most costly. The sales manager may use role-playing in the interviewing process to see how well the recruit would react in a variety of selling situations. Role-playing tests the candidates' knowledge of real sales situations and demonstrates their communication skills under pressure. Candidates are then compared using questions like these: How did the candidate handle interview pressures? Were the questions asked by the applicant well conceived and well stated? Does the candidate have a planned career pattern? Does the candidate have realistic goals and expectations? Can the candidate interact at multiple levels with business associates? Does the candidate show signs of being a good self-manager? Is this a major move forward for the candidate in job scope and responsibility?[52]

Women in Sales

The opportunities in sales for relatively high salaries and independence, combined with the increase in single-parent families, are prompting more women than ever before to pursue a professional sales career. Women now make up about 22 percent of the nation's sales force, with the highest percentages working in amusement/recreation services, apparel and textiles, printing/publishing, and communications (see Exhibit 17.2).

Women are making special strides selling high-tech industrial equipment, a traditionally male-dominated field. Do women perform well in industrial sales? On the whole, they perform very well. In fact, in one study women were perceived more favorably than men on a number of characteristics.[53] Successful saleswomen have a high energy level and are perceptive and effective communicators. They also seem to be more solution-oriented, avoiding the aggressive attitude of many salesmen.

Sherri Sorensen sells industrial products. Although she encounters bias because she is a woman, her positive attitude helps her overcome the "challenges" she faces.

© Alan Weiner/The Gamma Liaison Network

Exhibit 17.2

Percentages of Sales Representatives Who Are Women

Source: Adapted from "1991 Sales Manager's Budget Planner," *Sales & Marketing Management*, 17 June 1991, p. 77. Data from Dartnell Corporation, *26th Survey of Sales Force Compensation*, 1990.

Industry group	Percentage of sales reps who are female
Agriculture	7.3%
Amusement/recreation services	63.2
Apparel/other textile products	44.4
Business services	34.9
Chemicals	4.3
Communications	39.3
Construction	12.3
Electronic components	6.2
Electronics	2.4
Fabricated metals	3.6
Food products	29.7
Instruments	27.8
Insurance	14.7
Lumber/wood products	15.4
Machinery	5.3
Manufacturing	15.8
Office equipment	30.3
Paper/allied products	28.9
Primary metal products	18.9
Printing/publishing	39.7
Rubber/plastics	12.3
Wholesale (consumer)	26.2
Wholesale (industrial)	29.5
Average	22.3%

Another study found few differences between male and female salespeople in job-related attitudes and performance levels.[54]

Still, women in industrial sales are sometimes subject to stereotypes. Sherri Sorensen, industrial representative for James Clem Corporation, which sells industrial liners for use in everything from landfills to mines, still finds first meetings awkward because most of her clients expect a salesman. She also receives a lot of correspondence addressed to Mr. Sorensen. Although Sorensen generally faces

many of the same challenges other industrial saleswomen do, because she sells internationally some of her problems are entirely unique. For example, an early meeting with an important German client probably wouldn't have taken place at all if the customer had known that he was dealing with a woman. Sorensen had set up a meeting while in Zurich, and the client flew there to meet her. When he first saw her she could tell he was definitely not expecting a woman. But the meeting went well, and she eventually closed the deal. Several years later, the German client confided that if he'd known Sorensen was a woman, he would not have gone to Zurich. Sorensen doesn't let these prejudices bother her. She views them as just one more challenge to overcome.[55]

Train the Sales Force

After the recruit has been hired and given a brief orientation, training begins. A new salesperson generally receives instruction in five major areas: company policies and practices, selling techniques, product knowledge, industry and customer characteristics, and nonselling duties, such as account servicing and filling out market information reports. A good training program boosts confidence, improves morale, increases sales, and builds better customer relations. Classroom instruction may last several days for company policies and several weeks to a month for actual sales techniques. Trainees are taught everything from how to prospect to how to service the account after the sale.

Because industrial products are complex, industrial goods firms generally offer more extensive training programs than do consumer goods organizations. For example, during a year-long program, Dow Chemical trainees spend equal amounts of time in the classroom and working on related training projects. These projects might be working in Dow's customer-service center taking orders or producing in-depth marketing studies on customers or new markets. Finally, students spend time in the field selling and interacting with the company's customers and prospects.[56]

time management
Efficient allocation of time to tasks, based on their priority and urgency.

Sales trainees also learn to manage their time wisely. **Time management** is the task of efficiently allocating blocks of time to certain tasks in the selling process. Salespeople who spend their time wisely are most effective at covering their territories, tending to customer needs, seeing new prospects, generating leads, and steadily increasing both sales and profits. Exhibit 17.3 breaks down salespeople's time by function. Unfortunately, salespeople cannot distribute their time evenly among all accounts, although exceptional salespeople will make each customer feel like a preferred customer by giving sincere, personalized treatment.

Sales training is more customer-, service-, and quality-oriented than ever before. Training programs now seek to improve salespeople's listening skills and broaden product and customer knowledge to build a solid company-client partnership. In addition, training programs stress the interpersonal skills needed to become the contact person for serving customers. Since negotiation is increasingly important in closing a sale, salespeople are also trained to negotiate effectively without risking profits. Finally, many companies are teaching basic selling techniques to employees

Exhibit 17.3

How Salespeople Spend Their Time

Source: Adapted from "1992 Sales Manager's Budget Planner," *Sales & Marketing Management*, 22 June 1992, p. 85. Data from Dartnell Corporation, *26th Survey of Sales Force Compensation*, 1990.

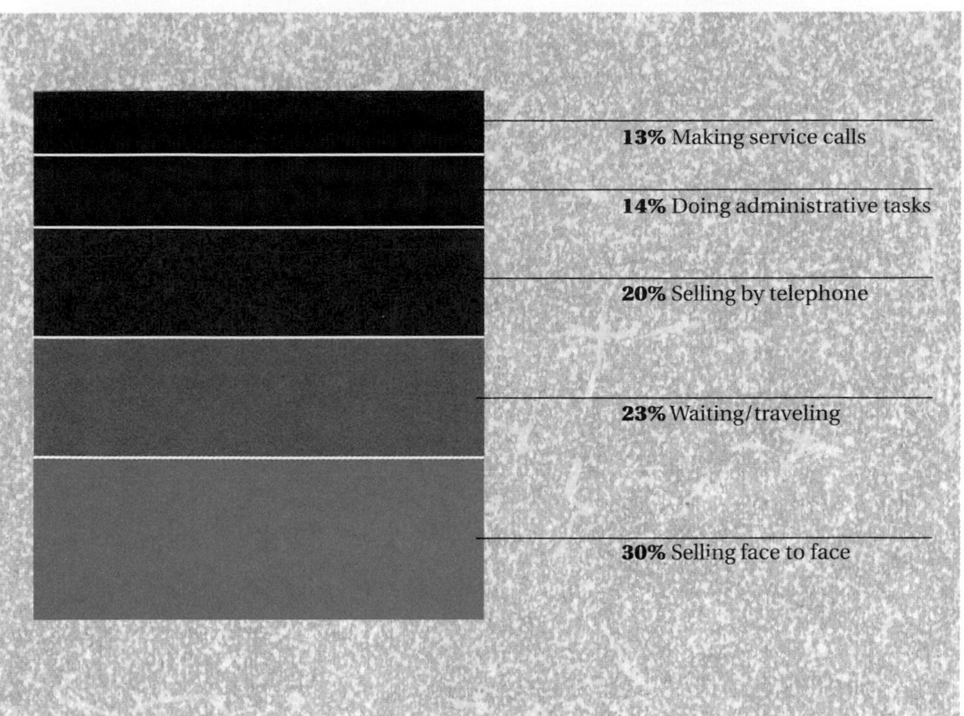

who do not sell but who are part of the selling process—for example, engineers and customer-service personnel. Exposing these nonselling personnel to the selling basics gives them a better understanding of how they can support the sales staff.[57]

Many successful companies have learned that training is not just for the newly hired. Training benefits all salespeople, regardless of their talents, experiences, or number of years on the job. For example, Norton Company, a manufacturer of industrial abrasives, annually brings in roughly a third of its more than 200 salespeople for follow-up training sessions on negotiating skills, product knowledge, and other relevant sales topics. Similarly, Hershey Chocolate USA provides continuing education for its sales force in the form of a library containing a number of videotapes and books on sales training. Hershey salespeople are encouraged to use these resources any time.[58]

Motivate the Sales Force

Training equips salespeople with the tools they need for selling. Once they have acquired these sales skills, they must be motivated to use them. Sales managers often use motivational tools or incentives to increase the sales of new products or of high-margin products that may require more effort. Motivational tools also help increase overall sales volume, add new accounts, improve morale and goodwill, move slow items, and bolster a slow selling season.[59] They can also be used to achieve short-term objectives, such as unloading overstocked inventory and meeting a monthly or quarterly sales goal. Pay, promotion, working conditions, security, recognition, and opportunities for personal growth all help motivate salespeople.

Research has shown that salespeople's performance depends on their expectations of the results of their sales efforts.[60] Salespeople who believe that they are realizing their own potential and doing something worthwhile are not only high performers in the present. They are also more likely to perform well in the future.

Two of the most important factors for building salesperson satisfaction and increasing selling motivation are sales quotas and sales incentives. Sales quotas

Sales incentives like travel motivate young salespeople.
© 1990 David Brownell/The Image Bank

provide a basis for sales planning and can be used as motivators. But setting quotas at the right level is crucial. If a quota is too easy to reach, motivation tends to decline.[61] In fact, an easy quota is less likely to be attained than a more difficult one. On the other hand, if a quota is set so high that the salespeople see little hope of ever meeting it, motivation can also decline. Sales managers should set product or sales quotas at challenging levels and attach significance to the quota. If the sales force doesn't perceive attaining quotas as important, motivation will suffer.

Sales incentives include various types of rewards, such as recognition at ceremonies, plaques, vacations, merchandise, and cash bonuses. Cash is the number-one motivational tool, with over half of all companies giving cash as an employee award.[62] In one survey, nearly 95 percent of U.S. workers ranked a cash bonus as a meaningful incentive.[63] For example, a company might reward its salespeople with a $5 bonus for each order they write, with $1,000 going to the salesperson who generates the most volume. Sales management should carefully plan the sales incentive program to make sure it will be profitable for the company as well as motivational for the sales force. There is nothing worse than realizing, after the incentive program is in full force, that it is either too generous or not generous enough. The incentive program should also be simple. Poorly planned incentive programs can end up not motivating the sales force at all.

Manage Sales Force Turnover

Sales force turnover costs the average company nearly a quarter of a million dollars each year. Not only does the company directly lose sales because of the salesperson's leaving, but it also will have to invest time and money in recruiting and training a new employee. Unfortunately, turnover is becoming one of the sales manager's biggest problems. On average, marketing managers can expect 9 percent of their sales force to leave each year.[64]

Salespeople often leave their jobs because of a lack of management support. Many salespeople are also lured to other jobs that promise to pay them more money. Interestingly, the findings of one study indicate that the longer salespeople stay with a company, the less likely they are to quit.[65]

Evaluate the Sales Force

The final task of the sales manager's job is evaluating the sales force. There are four major methods of evaluation:

- *Call-record reports:* To evaluate the sales force's performance, the sales manager needs feedback—that is, regular information from salespeople. Through call-record reports, sales managers can look at salespeople's daily activities. Although call-record reports vary from one firm to another, they generally contain information about the number of calls made and the quality of those calls. Quality is measured by such yardsticks as calls per order, sales or profits per call, or the percentage of calls that achieve specific goals. The latter may include sales of products that the firm is emphasizing. Improvement in call quality can increase total volume, change the product mix, or decrease sales cost. The sales manager can use call-record data to increase the number of profitable calls and their quality.
- *Sales force performance ranking:* A second way salespeople can be evaluated is by comparing their sales volume to that of other salespeople and then ranking them according to their performance level. This method traditionally uses overall sales volume data. However, it may be misleading because of differences in competition, customers, and territory. Instead, sales managers can rank performance by the salesperson's contribution to profit rather than overall sales volume. The highest-ranked salesperson is the one who not only sells the most (volume) but also concentrates on the most profitable products.
- *Past performance:* Salespeople can also be evaluated by their past performance. Such a comparison is especially important with new salespeople, for it will tell the sales manager of the salesperson's progress. Progress can be measured in sales and profit trends over time, as well as by number of calls made and new accounts obtained.

MARKETING AND SMALL BUSINESS

Personal Selling

Personal selling is especially critical to small businesses, because customers of small businesses usually expect more personal service. Many large retailers have switched to self-service, so the small-business owner has an opportunity to fill this void and gain a competitive advantage. Personal service and selling go hand in hand in a small retail store. A proprietor, for example, may mark a suit for tailoring while suggesting several nice shirts and ties to go with it.

Small manufacturers and wholesalers are also expected to give more personalized attention to their accounts, simply because the customers are not dealing with a large bureaucracy. The need for good personal selling skills is thus especially important for small manufacturers and wholesalers, for several reasons. First, the relationship is usually longer-term and more frequent than the relationship between a small retailer and a customer. A customer may patronize a small restaurant three or four times a year, but a wholesaler or institutional buyer may order weekly or daily from a small manufacturer. Second, the size of the transaction is larger than for a small retailer. Third, the goods provided by small manufacturers or wholesalers can have a big impact on the organizational buyer. If a small restaurant serves cold food to a patron, he or she may not come back, but otherwise there are few consequences. On the other hand, a small manufacturer that sells faulty brake drums to General Motors could be ruined.

Sales promotion is a key element in the promotional mix for many small businesses. It can be relatively inexpensive and very effective. Free samples in a candy store, sidewalk promotions, cooking classes in a gourmet accessories store, handbills in parking lots and in doors of residences, store signs, directories, point-of-purchase displays, show windows, premiums, coupons, and contests are used successfully by many small-business managers. A cabinet manufacturing shop found that sending business cards and letters of reference to area building contractors was the most effective form of sales promotion.

- *Subjective evaluation:* Finally, qualitative, or subjective, methods are used to evaluate the sales force. Examples of subjective criteria include knowledge of the company; its products, customers, and competitors; and sales tasks. The sales manager can also evaluate personal traits. These might include presentation skills, appearance, mannerisms, telemarketing skills, and temperament. This method of evaluation is open to personal biases, however, since it relies on the sales manager's observations and experiences.

LOOKING BACK

Think back now to the opening story about the Air Miles and Start frequent-buyer programs. Because the consumer receives some type of reward for buying the product over a long time, these programs build brand loyalty. This type of sales promotion technique is often better than coupons or price discounts since it enhances the value of the product to the consumer. Coupons can erode a brand's image or encourage brand switching because consumers become used to searching for the best deal. When the economy strengthens, sales promotion encouraging long-term brand loyalty becomes more important than coupons. But companies must evaluate each program carefully to reduce the risk of creating ill will, which was possible when Air Miles stopped its U.S. program barely one year after it started.

KEY TERMS

adaptive selling 565
assumptive close 567
cold calling 562
coupon 553
field order taker 560
follow-up 568
incremental productivity approach 572
inside order taker 560
lead generation 561
lead qualification 563
missionary sales representative 560
need-satisfaction approach 565
negotiation (extra inducement close) 567
networking 562
order getter 560
personal selling 558
point-of-purchase display 555
premium 554
prepared sales presentation 565
quota 569

SUMMARY

1 State the objectives of sales promotion. The main objectives of sales promotion are to increase trial purchases, consumer inventories, and repeat purchases. Sales promotion is also used to encourage brand switching and to build brand loyalty. Promotion supports advertising activities.

2 List the most common forms of sales promotion. Sales promotion includes coupons, premiums, contests and sweepstakes, sampling, and point-of-purchase displays. In addition, manufacturers and channel intermediaries use several unique promotional strategies: trade allowances, push money, training programs, free merchandise, store demonstrations, and meetings, conventions, and trade shows.

3 Discuss the nature of selling and its importance to society. Personal selling is direct communication between a sales representative and one or more prospective buyers for the purpose of making a sale. Sales is a vast and diverse industry, employing about 14 million people in the United States in jobs ranging from retail sales clerk to manufacturers' representative. Broadly speaking, all businesspeople use personal selling to promote themselves and their ideas.

4 Describe the advantages of personal selling over other forms of promotion. Personal selling offers several advantages over other forms of promotion. Personal selling allows salespeople to thoroughly explain and demonstrate a product. Salespeople have the flexibility to tailor a sales pitch to the needs and preferences of individual customers. Personal selling is more efficient than other forms of promotion because salespeople target qualified prospects and avoid wasting efforts on unlikely buyers. Personal selling affords greater managerial control over promotion costs. Finally, personal selling is the most effective method of closing a sale.

5 Identify the different types of sales positions. Sales positions are generally classified into three basic categories: order getting, order taking, and sales support.

Order getters actively seek prospective buyers and try to persuade them to buy; they may be part of a firm's sales force or independent sellers. Order takers handle either inside ordering or field ordering. Inside order takers take orders over the counter, on the sales floor, over the telephone, or by mail. In contrast, field order takers service accounts, check inventory, take new orders, and deliver and stock merchandise for customers. Sales support positions are missionary sales representative and technical specialist. Missionary sales representatives provide a variety of promotional services to support company sales efforts. Technical specialists help the sales force by describing, designing, and installing products.

6 List the steps in the selling process. The selling process is composed of seven basic steps: (1) sales lead generation, (2) sales lead qualification, (3) the sales approach, (4) the sales presentation, (5) the handling of objections, (6) the closing of the sale, and (7) follow-up.

7 Describe the functions of sales management. Sales management is a critical area of marketing that performs several important functions. Sales managers set overall company sales objectives and salespeople's individual quotas. They establish a sales force structure based on geographic, product, functional, or customer variables. Managers determine the size of the sales force, typically using either a workload approach or an incremental productivity approach. Sales management develops a compensation plan based on straight commission, straight salary, or a combination of the two. Managers recruit and train the sales force. They motivate the sales force and control turnover by providing sales quotas and sales incentives. Finally, sales managers evaluate the sales force through call-record reports, performance ranking, past performance, and personal observation.

Review Questions

1. Discuss the main objectives of sales promotion.
2. Identify the major trade promotion techniques. To what purpose do manufacturers use these methods of promotion?
3. Discuss the benefits of a career in sales.
4. When is personal selling more effective than other methods of promotion?
5. What are the two types of sales support personnel? Describe their responsibilities.
6. What are sales leads? How are they generated? Discuss the role of sales lead generation in the selling process.
7. Discuss the importance of sales force training. What types of training do salespeople typically receive?
8. What methods do sales managers use to motivate their sales force?

Discussion and Writing Questions

1. Why are some firms reducing their use of coupons as a promotional tool?
2. Discuss how different forms of sales promotion can erode or build brand loyalty. If a company's objective is to enhance customer loyalty to its products, which sales promotion technique would be most appropriate?
3. You are a new salesperson for a well-known business computer system, and one of your customers is a small business. In a memo to your sales manager, describe the sales presentation approach you will use to try to make the sale, and explain the reasons for your choice.
4. What does sales follow-up entail? Why is it an essential step in the selling process, particularly in today's marketplace? How does it relate to cognitive dissonance?
5. Explain what is meant by the familiar business adage "Nothing happens until a sale is made."
6. As the new sales manager for a firm, you have decided to adopt a compensation policy for the sales force that combines salary and commission. Write a memo to the president of the company explaining why you feel your plan will be successful.
7. Suggest some reasons why women are often more effective salespeople than men. What qualities are likely to make them successful salespeople in the market environment of the 1990s?

CASES

17.1 Coca-Cola MagiCans

On a United Airlines flight in 1990, a flight attendant opened an ordinary looking can of Coca-Cola Classic. When she tried to pour it, nothing came out, but the can had something in it. After the plane landed, the bomb squad quickly defused the can and found a ten-dollar bill inside. It was just another defective MagiCan from Coca-Cola. Although the bomb squad did not find a bomb, it became evident that Coca-Cola did. Just three short weeks after the introduction of MagiCans, Coke ceased the promotion.

This promotion created several problems for the company. Coke intended to ship 750,000 MagiCans but had only shipped 200,000. Thus the total number of prizes and the odds of winning those prizes were inaccurately advertised. The company had to look into the legal ramifications of this situation. In addition, water was placed in the cans to give them the weight of regular cans of Coke. Although the water was completely harmless, the company may also face some legal problems with consumers who drank it.

The most serious problem may be damage to the brand. Anytime a promotional activity fails, the company risks damage to the brand. Coke received nothing but bad publicity from its MagiCan promotion. Coke decided to withdraw the promotion before it received anymore bad press and serious damage occurred. This negative publicity was a serious blow to Coke's image as a premier marketer.

Coca-Cola spent two years developing the MagiCan. The promotion was test marketed in Iowa and Illinois. Test-market data indicated potential problems. For instance, curious consumers actually pried open the can to look at the mechanism. Consumers also had trouble understanding the promotion and thought that cash popping out of cans was just a metaphor not to be taken literally. Despite potential problems, Coca-Cola still launched the promotion. Caught up in the excitement of the promotion, Coke executives lost sight of how truly unusual it was. Unusual promotions require heavy advertising to provide additional explanations.

Promotions that tinker with a consumable product or its package require extreme caution. "When you are dealing with a food or beverage product, even one failure in a million is unacceptable," says John Lister, CEO of Lister Butler, Inc., a brand and corporate identity consulting firm. Coca-Cola, enamored with the promotion, is considering relaunching MagiCans. This time the company will look at every structural, chemical, and marketing aspect of the MagiCan program.

Questions

1. Do you think longer market testing should be done with promotions like MagiCans? Give reasons to support your answer.
2. Should marketers put prizes in packages that contain food products? Would your answer depend on the types of packages? Give reasons to support your answer.
3. Do you think Coca-Cola should bring back MagiCans? Why or why not?

Suggested Readings

Michael J. McCarthy, "Coca-Cola 'MagiCans' Go Poof after Just Three Weeks," *The Wall Street Journal*, 1 June 1990, pp. B1, B8.

Michael J. McCarthy, "MagiCan'ts: How Coca-Cola Stumbled," *The Wall Street Journal*, 5 June 1990, pp. B1, B8.

17.2 Packard Bell

Video title: *Packard Bell: A Company Overview*

Packard Bell Electronics, Inc.
9425 Canoga Avenue
Chatsworth, CA 91311

SIC codes: 3571 Electronic computer manufacturers
5045 Computers, peripherals, software

Number of employees: 1,630

1993 revenues: $1 billion

Major product: Packard Bell Computers

Largest competitors: IBM, Apple, Hewlet Packard, Compaq

Background

From its beginnings in 1926, Packard Bell has become one of the world's largest computer manufacturers. Although Packard Bell trails IBM and Apple, it had a 4 percent share of the U.S. market during 1992, making

it the third largest computer marketer. However, in a business where change is the rule, the company could easily lose business to other key players.

Industry

In total dollar sales, the computer and electronics business has passed the automobile and chemical industries to become the single largest industry in the United States. Personal computers make up 10.5 percent of the total computer sales; software, 8 precent; and peripherals, 25 percent. The large potential makes the computer industry a rather attractive market. In an attempt to maintain a competitive edge, companies have merged or formed strategic alliances. These partnerships are becoming much more common as new product introductions become more costly and more risky. In forming partnerships, companies are frequently looking for economies of scale or access to new channels of distribution.

Currently, most computer products are sold through computer dealers (50 percent). Value-added resellers (18 percent), direct sales (11 percent), systems integrators (5 percent), mail-order firms (5 percent), and mass merchants (4 percent) are the other key marketers of personal computer equipment. Historically, personal computer buyers have relied on the full-service computer stores. But today, because more people are familiar with the product, price has become a far more important factor in purchasing a personal computer. A novice computer user who needs advice can always call the next-door neighbor.

The two largest market segments for personal computers are the home market (36 percent) and small business (20 percent). The home market also includes home-office computer users. The balance of the market is made up of medium-size businesses (15 percent), large businesses (12 percent), educational institutions (9 percent), and the government (8 percent).

Packard Bell

Rapidly changing product designs force computer manufacturers to continually reevaluate marketing and product strategies. Today, computer systems based on the 80486 microchip dominate the marketplace. Packard Bell discontinued production of all 386-based machines to concentrate on the new technology.

The company is also investing heavily in the multimedia arena. Industry experts predict that the future of personal computing lies in multimedia systems, which are based on personal computers equipped with CD ROMs (compact disc storage devices) and sound cards. These systems are capable of reproducing video footage and sound effects on the computer. The CD ROM technology allows users to have access to about 600 megabytes of information at one time without having to load it on the hard drive. A complete set of encyclopedias fits on seven compact discs. The new technology requires faster computers, more memory, and high-quality video displays.

Multimedia systems have advantages in three of the key market segments: home, small business, and education. For the home market, this new technology has fostered more sophisticated computer games. Now, instead of shoing rough cartoons, the games almost look like motion pictures. The multimedia packages also can run an increasing assortment of educational software, benefiting both home consumers and educational markets. For small business, CD ROM technology puts large data bases of information at the user's fingertips without big investments in hard drive capacity. Packard Bell hopes that it can gain market share with its multimedia computer line. In 1986, Packard Bell decided that the mass merchants and electronics superstores were good outlets for reaching the home and small business customers.

Questions

1. Define the target market for Packard Bell multimedia computers. How would you prospect for new customers?
2. Write a sales presentation for a Packard Bell computer.
3. What objections would you expect to have to overcome during a sales presentation? How would you overcome these objections?

References

Million Dollar Directory 1993 (Parsippany, NJ: Dun & Bradstreet Information Services, 1993).

Standard & Poor's Surveys (New York: Standard & Poor's Corporation, April 1993).

PART FIVE
CRITICAL THINKING CASE

General Motors

Roger Smith was one of the most controversial chairmen of the board at General Motors (GM). When Smith took control of GM in 1981, the company was operating at a net loss. When he retired in 1990, he left one of the most profitable companies in the world. However, profits do not tell the whole story. In the past ten years, GM has lost market share in the U.S. market, its return on sales trails Ford, and its stock lags behind the Standard & Poor's 500 average. Smith may have been the best thing to happen to GM—or the worst.

Robert Stempel replaced Smith as chairman of the board at General Motors. Stempel started as a GM engineer and managed both the Chevrolet and Pontiac divisions. He also was responsible for the turnaround of GM Europe. Employees at the company think the board picked Stempel to lead GM because he's a "car guy." As an engineer, Stempel should understand the manufacturing process and what it takes to build a quality car. GM staff believe that GM should not build just pretty good cars but really superior automobiles.

To implement these changes, Stempel had to rework the company's massive bureaucracy. Ross Perot, a former GM board member, once said that trying to change GM's culture was like trying to teach an elephant to tap-dance. Stempel needed to subdue growing consumer anger toward the domestic auto industry and GM. The film *Roger & Me,* which criticized Roger Smith's decision to close GM's plant in Flint, Michigan, did little to help GM's image.

Former Procter & Gamble chairman John G. Smale took over the top spot at GM in 1993. Smale shares Stempel's vision of a leaner, more profitable organization, yet General Motors still has a long way to go to regain market share lost to the foreign car manufacturers over the past ten years. GM has undertaken a new advertising campaign to let U.S. consumers know about the high quality of GM cars and trucks. When surveyed, 92 percent of prospective car buyers said that Honda builds high-quality cars, but only 44 percent of prospective buyers consider GM vehicles first-rate. GM's "Quality on the Road" advertising campaign is designed to correct this perception, but changing consumer attitudes is a slow process. GM not only needs to promote this quality image but also needs some hit products to reinforce it.

General Motors is still plagued with manufacturing problems. The Chevy Caprice, transformed from a sedate, full-sized sedan into the futuristic bubble car, was panned by critics as one of the ugliest cars ever built. Popular car magazines referred to the Caprice as the Edsel of the 1990s. The four-door version of the Blazer, designed to compete with the Ford Explorer and Jeep Cherokee, also has had problems. *Consumer Reports* panned the Blazer, saying, among other things, that the truck had the worst paint job it had ever seen. One of GM's brightest hopes lies in the new Saturn division. Saturn, GM's first new car division in fifty-eight years, doesn't use the "Quality on the Road" advertising campaign. Instead, the division uses this slogan: "A different kind of company. A different kind of car."

The Saturn Division

Originally, Saturn was intended to be an innovative car division. GM was to invest $5 billion in completely automated manufacturing lines to build the Saturn. The price of the original subcompact models were expected to be in the $6,000 range. What first rolled off the Saturn assembly line was a compact. The car was available as a four-door sedan or a two-door coupe and sold for $10,000 to $12,000. Moreover, GM dropped the estimated production from 500,000 cars to 120,000 cars.

The Target Market

Historically, GM has drawn distinct lines between its divisions. Cadillac was the high-end division; Chevy was at the low end. Now GM has high-end Buicks competing with low-end Cadillacs. Oldsmobile is GM's experimental division, even though the most traditional Oldsmobile drivers are older women. Saturn is positioned to appeal to college-educated men and women, especially professionals. The four-door sedan is for a slightly older, more needs-driven audience. The two-door coupe is most likely to appeal to a slightly younger crowd more concerned with styling.

Saturn is targeted to pull customers from the import car market. The first models were pitted against the Honda Civic and Toyota Corolla. GM wants 80 percent of Saturn buyers to be converts from import cars. Industry experts fear the division may actually pull buyers from other GM divisions, such as Chevrolet/Geo and Pontiac. Thus Saturn may add to GM's problems, not solve them. Jack Trout, president of Trout & Reis, says that a lack of product distinction poses a major problem for GM. The Saturn resembles other GM models. Saturn's price advantage may not be enough to sway customers from buying the established car models.

Advertising

GM chose Hal Riney & Partners to develop the initial ad campaign for Saturn. One problem is that the car Riney has to pitch is not the car he thought he would be promoting. Some advertising executives offered the following recommendations to Riney:

> Saturn should be careful about wrapping itself in a country or company. Customers are buying a car, they're not buying patriotism. If it were that simple, there wouldn't be many Japanese cars on the road.
>
> *—Scott Gilbert, executive vice president and management director, Team One (advertising agency for Toyota's Lexus)*

> The advertising has to turn around a [negative] perception of the quality and reliability of domestic cars. [The theme should focus on Saturn as] a new kind of American car.
>
> *—Chuck Valentine, senior vice president and group account director, Rubin Postaer & Associates (American Honda's advertising agency)*

> [Riney should use] a value position, like at long last you don't have to spend an exorbitant amount of money for a terrific car.
>
> *—Jack Trout*

> The most important hurdle is to increase awareness. Its selling points are high value and high quality. Those tangible messages must come across.
>
> *—John Hammond, partner, J.D. Power & Associates*

The company is expected to pursue both a model-specific advertising campaign and a corporate campaign. The key issue for the corporate campaign is how to tie the Saturn division to General Motors. All the employees at Saturn are proud to be associated with GM, but they are concerned with how the GM-Saturn connection looks to consumers.

Customer Satisfaction

The Saturn division has elected to pursue a strategy of promoting customer satisfaction rather than waging a price war. Most carmakers offer cash rebates to consumers as an enticement to buy right away. Saturn offers a thirty-day, money-back guarantee. This offer, similar to an offer made by Volkswagen, allows Saturn buyers to return the car within thirty days or 1,500 miles if they are not completely satisfied.

Saturns also come with a three-year, 36,000-mile, bumper-to-bumper warranty. Owners do not have to pay a deductible for warranty repairs. GM's customary warranty is three years, 50,000 miles, with a $100 deductible for repairs.

Questions

1. Evaluate the suggestions offered by the advertising executives. Which are right for Saturn?
2. Explain why U.S. consumers may have a negative perception of U.S.-made cars. Develop advertising objectives that will change this negative image.
3. Evaluate the Saturn slogan: "A different kind of company. A different kind of car."
4. Defend Saturn's thirty-day, money-back guarantee and its warranty.
5. If you were a GM dealer, would you like to carry the Saturn line? If you were a salesperson, would you like to sell the Saturn line?

Suggested Readings

Alice Z. Cuneo, "GM's Astronomical Gamble," *Advertising Age*, 22 July 1990, p. S-6.

Kathleen Kerwin, "Saturn: GM Finally Has a Real Winner, but Success Is Bringing a Fresh Batch of Problems," *Business Week*, 17 August 1992, pp. 86–91.

"Roger Smith Reflects on Role at GM," *The Wall Street Journal*, 31 July 1990, pp. B1, B4.

Raymond Serafin, "An Open Letter to Robert Stempel," *Advertising Age*, 23 July 1990, pp. S-1, S-14.

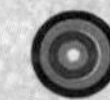

Raymond Serafin, "GM's Saturn Enters Crucial Period," *Advertising Age*, 5 March 1990, p. 16.

James B. Treece, "Here Comes GM's Saturn: More Than a Car, It Is GM's Hope for Reinventing Itself," *Business Week*, 9 April 1990, pp. 56–62.

Joseph B. White, "GM Puts Low Price on Saturn to Sell in Small-Car Field," *The Wall Street Journal*, 5 October 1990, pp. B1, B12.

Joseph B. White, "GM's New Ad Campaign Puts a Shine on Its Image—But Not Yet a Deep One," *The Wall Street Journal*, 8 October 1990, pp. B1, B7.

PART FIVE
ETHICS CASE

The Sale That Never Was

Metropolitan Power & Light was a large combined gas and electric service utility with an industrial sales force of twenty-seven people. Its major competitor was Greater Edison Utilities, which also had an industrial sales force of some eighteen salespeople. Their service territories overlapped only in regard to types of energy. For example, Metropolitan had a natural gas franchise for part of the city of Applegate, and Greater Edison served that same area with electricity. In other areas, that pattern would be reversed. In some industrial parks, both companies could provide both types of service.

Ray Houser, a sales engineer for Metropolitan, had watched with great interest as his company revised his compensation to include a substantial commission for new business. Later Metropolitan adopted a commission formula that included additional compensation when a salesperson kept an existing customer from going to a competitor. For example, a large electric motor manufacturer had been buying energy for heating from Metropolitan's electricity division. A competing utility was urging the manufacturer to build its own cogeneration plant and produce its own electric power. Ray had worked with this manufacturer to solve some of its efficiency problems and had kept it from building a separate generating plant. Because this was a documented case of his holding a large industrial customer, his commission had been enhanced by $1,800.

The managers of Metropolitan had some qualms about paying salespeople for holding business because of the difficulty of documentation. They had a fear that some salespeople would spend too much time holding customers that really were not considering leaving. Ray had sympathy for their fear but felt very strongly that salespeople's time was better spent holding large existing accounts than chasing small new accounts.

The issue was debated but left unchanged until Greater Edison adopted a similar compensation structure for its salespeople. After several months of intense competition between the two sales forces, one of the Greater Edison salespeople approached Ray at a civic club meeting and joked about conspiring to try to steal each other's accounts and improve the size of both salesperson's commissions. Ray felt uncomfortable with the joke, even though he was convinced that the competing salesman was not serious.

- When is a joke not a joke?

Several weeks later, as a recession began to take hold, some industrial customers began cutting back energy use or, in some cases, shutting down plants. Because of the commission structure, Ray's total compensation fell by about 15 percent. The salesperson from Greater Edison, Bob Mackaby, called Ray and repeated his joke, but in a much more serious way. Bob suggested that they agree on which companies to approach with competitive proposals. Those proposals would be set up so the business would not actually be lost and counterproposals could be documented. Each salesperson's paycheck would be enhanced.

- Who would be hurt by this plan? Beyond the basic issue, are there other risks?

Ray was tempted. He knew he would be able to protect his present customers if such a deal was struck, and he would at least be fully prepared for frontal assaults from his major competitor. However, he was uneasy about "throwing" his proposals for new business to the competitor.

Over time, as Ray's paycheck began to diminish further, he began to seriously reconsider Bob's offer. Finally, he agreed to do two deals with his competitor.

First, Ray and Bob were going to make serious proposals to the two largest customers of each utility company. Ray had thought a lot about what it would take to win Greater Edison's largest customer, a regional plant for one of the major carmakers. He had also wondered about the vulnerability of his largest customer, which was a turbine-manufacturing plant of national note.

- What trust relationships are involved here? How are they affected by what has happened?

Ray was extremely surprised when he found that Bob had given him proposed figures different from those Bob had given to Ray's largest customer. Ray, in fact, had come in with a poor defending proposal and had lost some 60 percent of the customer's business. When Ray approached Bob, Bob laughed and said, "You weren't really taking all that seriously, were you? Besides, who would you complain to?"

- How would you feel if you were Ray? What would you do next?

Part Six
Pricing Decisions

EXPIRES JANUARY 31, 1993
30¢ OFF
FARMER JOHN.
Fresh Roll Sausage
Regular, Hot or Premium
PRICE
39.95
EXPIRES 12/31/92
GET 1:
FREE
(MAXIMUM VALUE $1.80)
ANY Campbell's
HOME COOKIN' SOUP
03115
RETAIL PRICE PAID
(TO BE COMPLETED BY CONSUMER)
PRICE SUBJECT TO CONFIRMATION BY CAMPBELL SOUP COMPANY
5 51000 12200 9
B
2 FOR 17.99

CHAPTER 18

Pricing Concepts

LEARNING OBJECTIVES
After studying this chapter, you should be able to

1. Discuss the importance of pricing decisions to the economy and to the individual firm.
2. List and explain a variety of pricing objectives.
3. Explain the role of demand in price determination.
4. Describe cost-oriented pricing strategies.
5. Understand how the product life cycle, competition, distribution and promotion strategies, and quality perceptions can affect price.

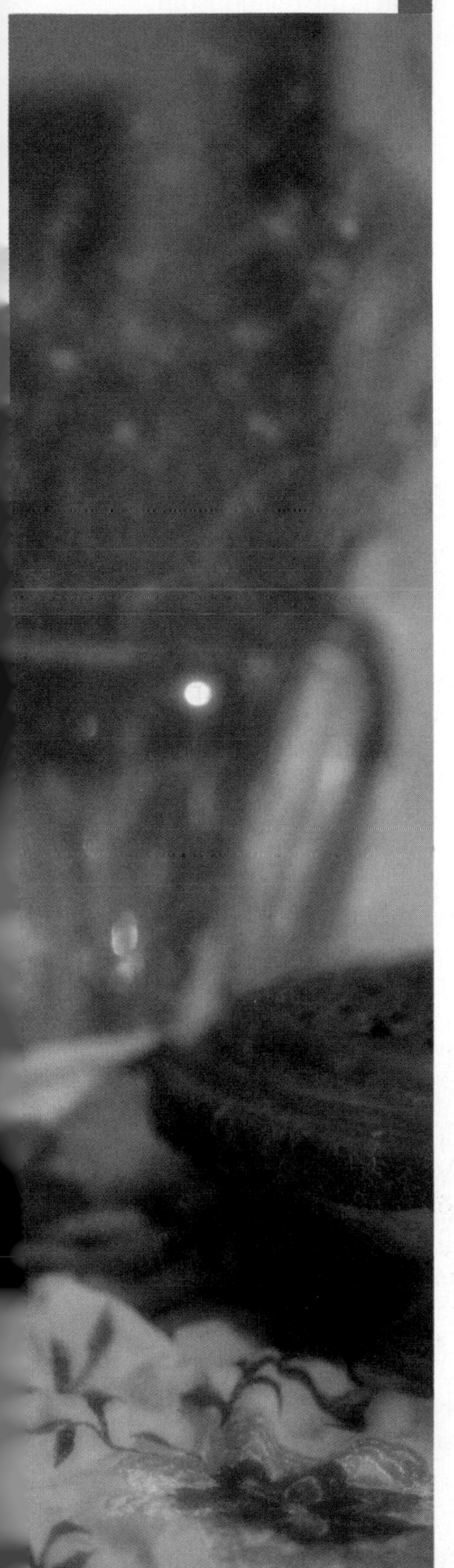

Through the 1980s and early 1990s, snack food makers were able to count on price hikes to meet their profit goals. Premium pricing by Frito-Lay formed a price umbrella for competitors to also get high prices. But those days are over.

Roger Enrico, CEO of Frito-Lay, told company managers that they are "not going to be able to achieve their profit growth targets in the mid-1990s via price. Neither the competition . . . nor consumers will allow it." Instead, Enrico is pushing to increase profits by increasing sales volume and cutting costs.

Frito-Lay went through a jarring shake-up in 1992. At the time, the company had 44 percent of the snack food market, earned a 20 percent profit, and contributed about 30 percent of parent company Pepsi's profit. In 1992, Frito-Lay dismissed 1,800 staffers, half of them at headquarters, and wrote off $91 million worth of unproductive assets to get itself ready for the new realities.

The company, which used to raise prices religiously, now seeks to expand profits by increasing its market share with less expensive offerings. In the Southeast, for instance, Frito-Lay found that dropping the price of its large bags from $2.39 to "well under" $2.00 increased unit sales by more than 10 percent and earnings by almost as much. The company introduced small 25¢ bags to complement 75¢ packages. The 25¢ bags pumped up the volume among Frito-Lay's smaller vendors. Some that formerly sold $10 to $50 in chips a week now sell $40 to $200.

Frito-Lay is also planning to make further cost cuts. In this industry the finished product is handled twice by humans: Someone packs each bag in a box, and then the route person takes the bag out of the box and puts it on a shelf. Automating box packing—one of the most difficult tasks in the packaged-goods industry—will eventually save $35 million a year. Consolidating deliveries to large customers should knock another $75 million off costs.

Competitor Borden, caught with its high prices, is stoically redesigning its own organization. Says George Waydo, the snack foods head at Borden: "The conclusion we have had to come to is that business as usual will not work." Borden is focusing on what the trade calls "up and down the street" business, the thousands of small stores and shops where the price competition isn't so intense. "Up and down" accounts for about half the industry's sales.

Like Frito-Lay, Borden is retrenching. The company has trimmed its work force by 1,000, is making its delivery system more efficient, and is offering products in small bags. The company has also reordered its marketing operation, creating specialists to sell specific sizes to specific accounts. For national chains, Borden will package and advertise some products under the Borden name and give strong regional brands new packaging to enhance their appeal. Says CEO A.S. D'Amato: "Borden will defend and grow its market position in the supermarkets. We're not going to be the first guy to blink."[1]

What type of pricing objective do you think Frito-Lay is pursuing? The company lowered prices and saw sales volume grow. What is the relationship between price and sales revenue? What is the role of cost in the pricing equation? How does competition affect price?

1 THE IMPORTANCE OF PRICE

Price means one thing to the consumer and something else to the seller. To the consumer it is the cost of something. Price to the seller is revenue—the ultimate source of profits. In the broadest sense, price allocates resources in a free-market economy. With so many ways of looking at price, it's no wonder that marketing managers find price setting a challenge. Each of these concepts is explored in more detail below.

What Is Price?

price
Perceived value of a good or service.

Price is the perceived value of a good or service. Perceived value in today's society is most commonly expressed in dollars and cents. Thus price is typically the money exchanged for a good or service. Note that *perceived value* refers to perceived value at the time of the transaction. One of the authors of this textbook bought a fancy European-designed toaster recently for about $45. The toaster's wide mouth made it possible to toast a bagel, warm a muffin, and with a special $15 attachment, make a grilled sandwich. The author felt that a toaster with all these features surely must be worth the total price of $60. But after using the device for three months and obtaining toast burned around the edges and raw in the middle every time, the disappointed buyer put the toaster in the attic. Why wasn't it returned to the retailer? The boutique had gone out of business, and no other local retailer carried the brand. Also, there was no U.S. service center. Remember, the price paid is based on the satisfaction consumers expect to receive from a product and not necessarily the satisfaction they actually receive.

Price can be anything with perceived value, not just money. When goods and services are exchanged, the trade is called barter. For example, if you exchange this book for a chemistry book at the end of the term, you have engaged in barter. The price you paid for the chemistry book was this textbook.

Price as an Allocator of Resources

mixed economy
Economy in which both the government and the private sector exercise economic control.

free enterprise
Economic system in which everyone has the right to engage in almost any business pursuit.

Let's return to the monetary notion of price. Everyone should realize that price plays a crucial role in the U.S. economic system. We live in a mixed, free-enterprise society that depends on a complex system of prices to allocate goods and services among consumers, governments, and businesses. A **mixed economy** is one in which both the government and the private sector exercise economic control. **Free enterprise** refers to an economic system in which everyone has the right to engage in almost any business pursuit.

Consumers play an important part in the allocation process through the exercise of their dollar votes. If people believe that a merchant has set a fair price for a good or

Price is the perceived value of something, based on the satisfaction the person expects to derive from that thing. For example, some people will pay a lot to go to a World Series baseball game.
© James Blank/The Stock Market

service, they vote for (buy) that product. For example, a consumer who uses Colgate toothpaste is in effect saying, "Keep producing Colgate; it meets my value expectations better than other products." Business firms that do a good job of satisfying the needs of the consumer receive more dollar votes (sales). Firms may then use the earned revenue to buy more resources to produce more goods and services. Companies that do not satisfy the consumer (and thus lack dollar votes) cannot effectively compete for resources. They must eventually switch their production to another product or go bankrupt.

The Importance of Price to Marketing Managers

Prices are the key to revenues, which are in turn the the key to profits for an organization. Price charged to customers multiplied by the number of units sold equals **revenue** for the firm. Revenue is what pays for every activity of the company: production, finance, sales, distribution, and so on. What's left over (if anything) is **profit**. Managers usually strive to charge a price that will earn a fair profit. To achieve this goal, they must choose a price that is not too high or too low. Moreover, the price must equal the perceived value to target consumers.

revenue
Price charged to customers multiplied by the number of units sold.

profit
Revenue minus expenses.

If a price is set too high in consumers' minds, the perceived value will be less than the cost, and sales opportunities will be lost. Lost sales mean lost revenue. Conversely, if a price is too low, it may be perceived as a great value for the consumer but may not meet the company's profit goals. For example, Colgate-Palmolive dropped Fab 1 Shot and Anheuser-Busch dropped LA Beer because the products missed target profit goals, not because they were losing money.

Trying to set the right price is one of the most stressful and pressure-filled tasks of the marketing manager, as trends in both the consumer and business markets attest. First, in the consumer products market, the flood of new product introductions leads potential buyers to carefully evaluate the price of a new item against the value of existing products. Second, the increased availability of bargain-priced dealer and generic brands has put downward pressure on overall prices. Third, a series of inflationary and recessionary periods have made many consumers more price-sensitive. Fourth, many firms try to maintain their large market share by cutting prices. For example, when Compaq Computer Corporation lost market share and profits, it introduced a new line of low-priced computers and dropped the suggested retail price of most of its existing machines by 32 percent.[2]

In the organizational market, ranging from hospitals and state governments to lighting equipment and computer software manufacturers, customers are becoming more price-sensitive and better informed buyers. Competitive intensity is increasing, so some installations, accessories, and component parts are being marketed like homogeneous natural resources. Computerized information systems enable the organizational buyer to compare price and performance with great ease and accuracy. Finally, improved communications and increased use of telemarketing and computer-aided selling have opened up many markets to new competitors.

2 PRICING OBJECTIVES

To survive in today's highly competitive marketplace, companies need pricing objectives that are specific, attainable, and measurable. Realistic pricing goals then require periodic monitoring to determine the effectiveness of the company's strategy. For convenience, pricing objectives can be divided into three categories: profit-oriented, sales-oriented, and status quo. Let's look at each.

Profit-Oriented Pricing Objectives

Profit-oriented objectives include profit maximization, satisfactory profits, and target return on investment. A brief discussion of each of these objectives follows.

Profit Maximization

Profit maximization means setting prices so total revenue is as large as possible relative to total costs. (A more theoretically precise definition and explanation of profit maximization appears later in the chapter.) Profit maximization does not always signify unreasonably high prices. Price and profits depend on the type of

By cutting ticket prices, airlines can sometimes maximize profits. Because of the high costs of fuel, aircraft maintenance, and flight personnel, it may make more sense to fly a plane full of reduced-fare passengers than to fly a plane with fewer full-price passengers.
American Airlines

competitive environment a firm faces, such as being in a monopoly position (being the only seller) or selling in a much more competitive situation. (See Chapter 2 for a description of the four types of competitive environments.) Also, remember that a firm cannot charge a price higher than the product's perceived value.

Many firms do not have the accounting data they need for maximizing profits. It sounds simple to say that a company should keep producing and selling goods or services as long as revenues exceed costs. Yet it is often hard to set up an accurate accounting system to determine the point of profit maximization.

Sometimes managers say that their company is trying to maximize profits—in other words, trying to make as much money as possible. Although this goal may sound impressive to stockholders, it is not good enough for planning. The statement "We want to make all the money we can" is vague and lacks focus. It gives management license to do just about anything it wants to do.

Satisfactory Profits

Satisfactory profits are a reasonable level of profits. Rather than maximizing profits, many organizations strive for profits that are satisfactory to the stockholders and management. To maximize profits, a small-business owner might have to keep his or her store open seven days a week. But the owner might not want to work that hard and might be satisfied with less profit.

Target Return on Investment

target return on investment (ROI)
Profit objective calculated by dividing a firm's net profits after taxes by its total assets.

The most common profit objective is **target return on investment** (ROI), sometimes called the firm's return on total assets. ROI measures the overall effectiveness of management in generating profits with its available assets. The higher the firm's return on investment, the better.

Return on investment is calculated as follows:

$$\text{Return on investment} = \frac{\text{Net profits after taxes}}{\text{Total assets}}$$

Assume that in 1993 Johnson Controls had assets of $4.5 million, net profits of $550,000, and a target ROI of 10 percent. This was the actual ROI:

$$\text{ROI} = \frac{550{,}000}{4{,}500{,}000}$$
$$= 12.2\%$$

As you can see, the ROI for Johnson Controls exceeded its target, which indicates the company prospered in 1993.

Comparing the 12.2 percent ROI with the industry average provides a more meaningful picture, however. Any ROI needs to be evaluated in terms of the competitive environment, risks in the industry, and economic conditions. Generally speaking, firms seek ROIs in the 10 percent to 30 percent range. For example, General Electric seeks a 25 percent ROI, whereas Alcoa, Rubbermaid, and most major pharmaceutical companies strive for a 20 percent ROI. In some industries, however, such as the grocery industry, a return of under 5 percent is common and acceptable.

A company with a target ROI can predetermine its desired level of profitability. The marketing manager can use the standard, such as 10 percent ROI, to determine whether a particular price and marketing mix are feasible. In addition, the manager must weigh the risk of a given strategy even if the return is in the acceptable range.

Company	Units sold	Unit price	Total revenue	Unit market share	Revenue market share
A	1,000	$1.00	$1,000,000	50%	25%
B	200	4.00	800,000	10	20
C	500	2.00	1,000,000	25	25
D	300	4.00	1,200,000	15	30
Total	2,000		$4,000,000		

Exhibit 18.1

Two Ways to Measure Market Share (Units and Revenue)

Target ROI is a popular method of setting pricing objectives. GE, Rubbermaid, and Alcoa are joined by companies like DuPont, General Motors, Navistar, Exxon, and Union Carbide in using a target return on investment as their main pricing goal.

Sales-Oriented Pricing Objectives

Sales-oriented pricing objectives are based either on market share or on dollar or unit sales. The effective marketing manager should also be familiar with these pricing objectives.

Market Share

market share
Company's product sales as a percentage of total sales for that industry.

Market share is a company's product sales as a percentage of total sales for that industry. Sales can be reported in dollars or in units of product. It is very important to know whether market share is expressed in revenue or units. Consider, for example, four companies competing in an industry with 2,000 total unit sales and total industry revenue of $4 million (see Exhibit 18.1). Company A has the largest unit market share at 50 percent, but it has only 25 percent of the revenue market share. In contrast, company D has only a 15 percent unit share but the largest revenue market share—30 percent. Usually, market share is expressed in terms of revenue and not units.

Many companies believe that maintaining or increasing market share is a key to the effectiveness of their marketing mix. As contrasted with a target return (on investment) strategy, market share is a demand-oriented concept. Research organizations like A.C. Nielsen and Ehrhart-Babic provide excellent market share reports for many different industries. These reports enable companies to track their performance in various product categories over time.

Conventional wisdom says that market share and return on investment are strongly related. For the most part they are; however, many companies with low market share survive and even prosper. To succeed with a low market share, companies need to compete in industries with slow growth and few product changes—for instance, industrial component parts and supplies. Otherwise, they must vie in an industry that makes frequently bought items, such as consumer convenience goods. A larger market share often boosts profitability, thanks to greater economies of scale, market power, and ability to compensate top-quality management. But the early 1990s proved that the conventional wisdom doesn't always work. Because of a general recession and extreme competition in some industries, many market leaders either did not reach their target ROI or actually lost money. The airline, personal computer, and food industries had this problem. Procter & Gamble recently switched from market share to ROI objectives after realizing that profits don't automatically follow from a large market share. PepsiCo says its new Pepsi challenge is to be No. 1 in share of industry profit, not sales volume.[3]

For over a decade, Maxwell House and Folgers, the biggest U.S. coffee brands, have been locked in a struggle to dominate the market, warring with advertising, perpetual rounds of price cutting, and millions upon millions of cents-off coupons. The aggressor recently has been Maxwell House, a unit of the Kraft General Foods division of Philip Morris. Already it has regained a few drops of market share that it had lost to Folgers, a unit of Procter & Gamble, earlier in the war. Maxwell House has introduced a shelf of new products to lure consumers with taste rather than price. Examples include ready-made coffee in refrigerator cartons and coffee syrup, both designed for consumers to pour and microwave as needed. Folgers is still the nation's best-selling coffee, although the Kraft General Foods brands, which include Yuban and Sanka, account for a 35 percent market share. P&G has 32 percent of the $3.5 billion U.S. coffee market. Kraft General Foods spends over $100 million advertising Maxwell House.

Sales Maximization

Rather than striving for market share, sometimes companies try to maximize sales. If a company is strapped for funds or faces an uncertain future, it may try to generate a maximum amount of cash in the short run. Management's task when using this objective is to calculate which price/quantity relationship generates the greatest cash revenue. Maximization of cash should never be a long-run objective, because cash maximization may mean little or no profitability. Without profits, a company cannot survive.

The objective of maximizing sales ignores profits, competition, and the marketing environment as long as sales are rising. As a short-term objective, sales maximization can be effectively used on a temporary basis to sell off excess inventory. It is not uncommon, for example, to find Christmas cards, ornaments, and so on discounted at 50 percent to 70 percent off retail prices after the holiday season. Management can also use sales maximization for year-end sales to clear out old models before introducing the new ones.

Status Quo Pricing Objectives

status quo pricing
Pricing objective that seeks to maintain existing prices or simply meet the competition.

Status quo pricing seeks to maintain the existing prices or simply meet the competition. This third category of pricing objectives has the major advantage of requiring little planning. Often firms competing in an industry with an established price leader follow the passive policy of meeting the competition. These industries typically have fewer price wars than those with direct price competition.

In other cases managers regularly shop competitors' stores to ensure that their prices are comparable. Woolworth's middle managers must visit competing Kmart stores weekly to compare prices and then make adjustments. MCI and Sprint have hammered AT&T for being "overpriced." AT&T struck back with advertisements showing their rates were essentially equal to competitors'.

3 THE DETERMINANTS OF PRICE: DEMAND

After marketing managers set pricing goals, they must set a specific price to reach these goals. The price they set depends mostly on two factors: the demand for the good or service and the cost to the seller for that good or service. When pricing goals

Exhibit 18.2

Demand Curve and Schedule for Gourmet Popcorn

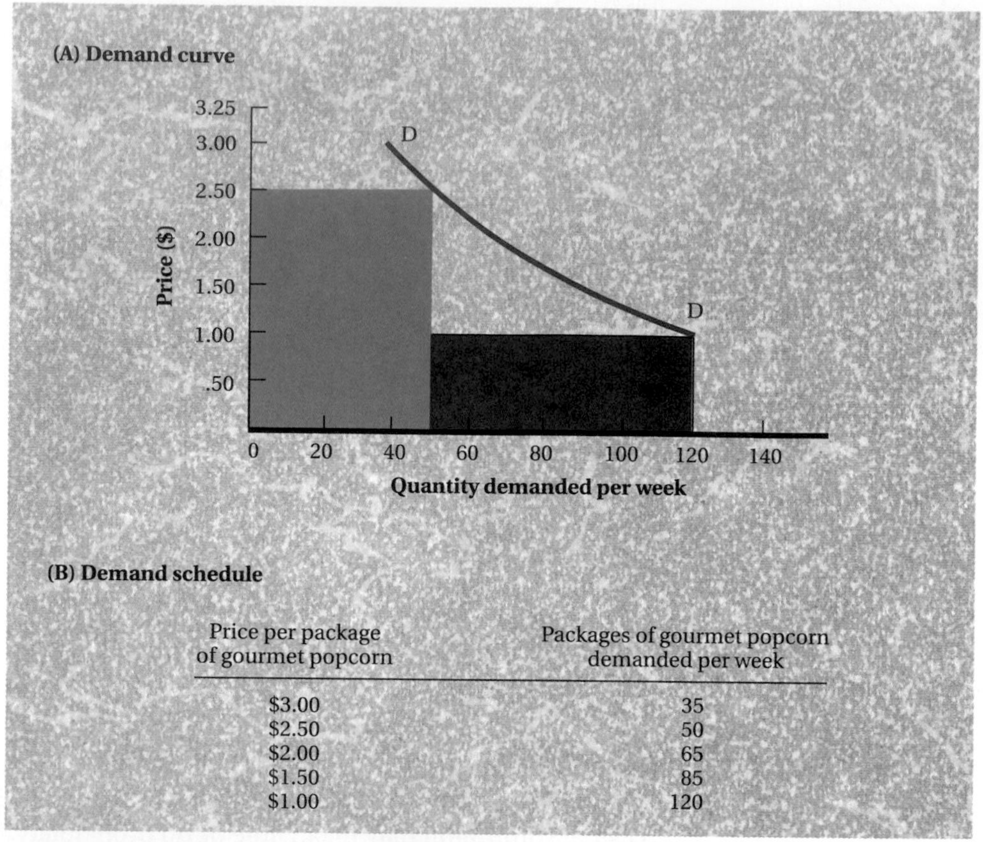

Price per package of gourmet popcorn	Packages of gourmet popcorn demanded per week
$3.00	35
$2.50	50
$2.00	65
$1.50	85
$1.00	120

are mainly sales-oriented, demand considerations usually dominate. Other factors—such as distribution and promotion strategies, perceived quality, and stage of the product life cycle—can also influence price.

The Nature of Demand

demand
Quantity of a product that will be sold in the market at various prices for a specified period.

Demand is the quantity of a product that will be sold in the market at various prices for a specified period. The quantity of a product that people will buy depends on its price. The higher the price, the fewer goods or services consumers will demand. Conversely, the lower the price, the more goods or services they will demand. This trend is illustrated in Exhibit 18.2A, which graphs the demand per week for gourmet popcorn at a local retailer at various prices. This graph is called a demand curve. The vertical axis of the graph shows different prices of gourmet popcorn, measured in dollars per package. The horizontal axis measures the quantity of gourmet popcorn that will be demanded per week at each price. For example, at a price of $2.50, 50 packages will be sold per week; at $1.00, consumers will demand 120 packages—as the demand schedule in Exhibit 18.2B shows.

The demand curve slopes downward and to the right, which indicates that more gourmet popcorn is demanded as the price is lowered. In other words, if popcorn manufacturers put a greater quantity on the market, then their hopes of selling all of it will be realized only by selling it at a lower price.

One reason why more is sold at lower prices than at higher prices is that lower prices bring in new buyers. This fact might not be so obvious with gourmet popcorn, but consider the example of steak. As the price of steak drops lower and lower, some people who are not eating steak will probably start buying it rather than hamburger. And with each reduction in price, existing customers may buy extra amounts.

Exhibit 18.3

Supply Curve and Schedule for Gourmet Popcorn

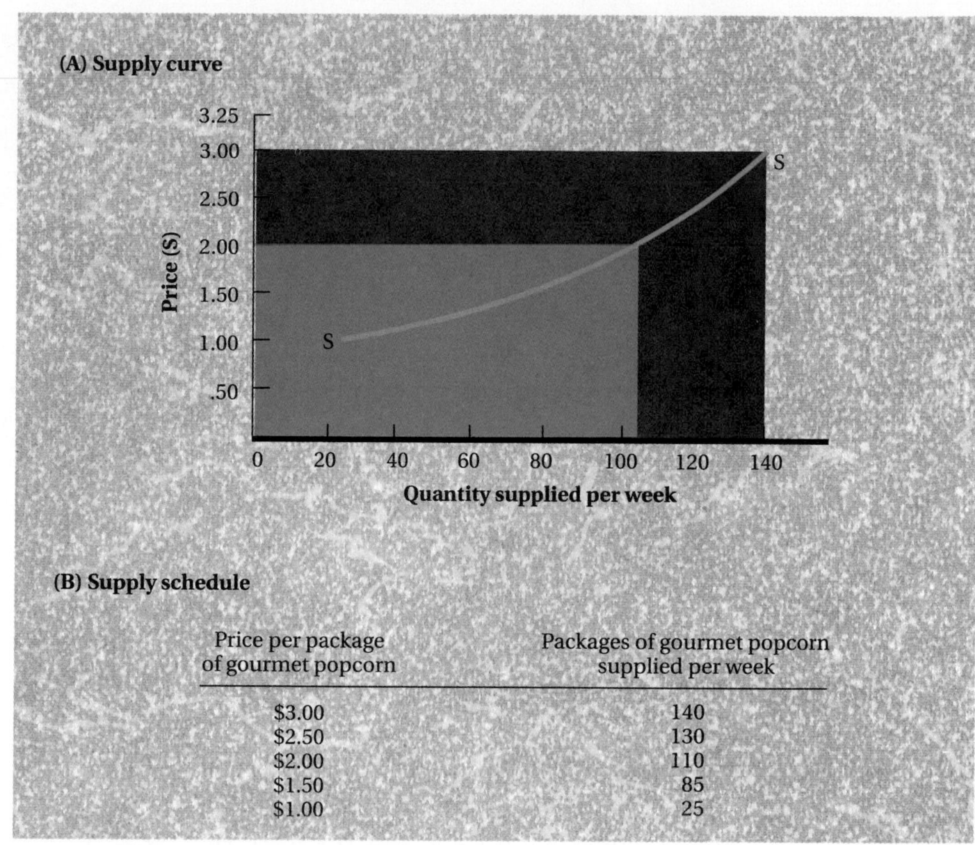

Price per package of gourmet popcorn	Packages of gourmet popcorn supplied per week
$3.00	140
$2.50	130
$2.00	110
$1.50	85
$1.00	25

Similarly, if the price of gourmet popcorn falls low enough, some people will buy more than they have bought in the past.

The Concept of Supply

supply
Quantity of a product that will be offered to the market by a supplier, or suppliers, at various prices for a specified period.

The demand schedule relates prices to the amount that customers wish to buy. **Supply** is the quantity of a product that will be offered to the market by a supplier, or suppliers, at various prices for a specified period. Exhibit 18.3 illustrates the supply schedule for gourmet popcorn and the resulting supply curve. Unlike the falling demand curve, the supply curve for gourmet popcorn slopes upward and to the right. At higher prices, gourmet popcorn manufacturers will obtain more resources (popcorn, flavorings, salt) and produce more gourmet popcorn. If the price consumers are willing to pay for gourmet popcorn increases, producers can afford to buy more ingredients. Output tends to increase at higher prices because manufacturers can sell more packages of gourmet popcorn and earn greater profits. For example, at $2 suppliers are willing to place 110 packages of gourmet popcorn on the market, but they will offer 140 packages at a price of $3.

How Demand and Supply Establish Prices

At this point, let's combine the concepts of demand and supply to see how competitive market prices are determined. So far, the premise is that if price is X amount, then consumers will purchase Y amount of gourmet popcorn. How high or low will prices actually go? How many packages of gourmet popcorn will be produced? How many packages will be consumed? The demand curve cannot predict consumption, nor can the supply curve alone forecast production. Instead, we need to look at what happens when supply and demand interact—as shown in Exhibit 18.4.

Exhibit 18.4

The Equilibrium Price for Gourmet Popcorn

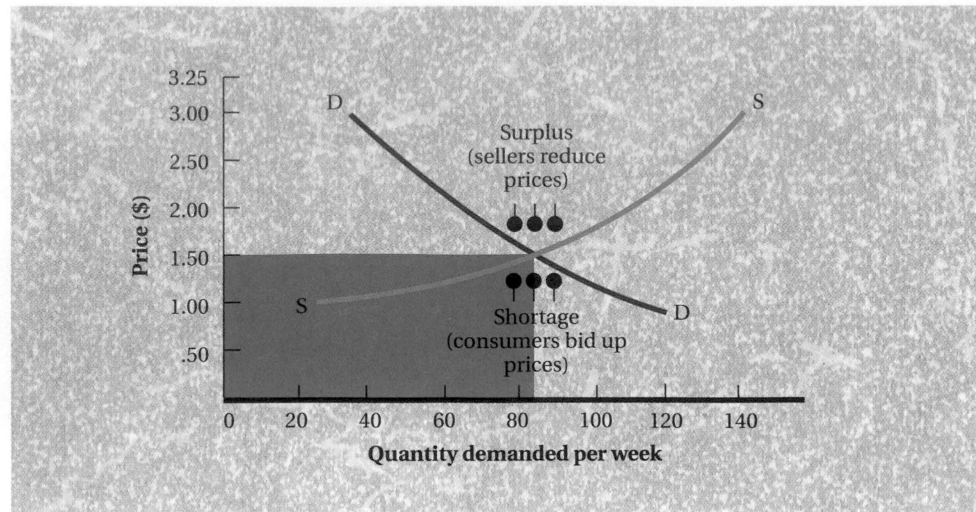

At a price of $3, the public would demand only 35 packages of gourmet popcorn. But suppliers stand ready to place 140 packages on the market at this price (data from the demand and supply schedules). If they do, they would create a surplus of 105 packages of gourmet popcorn. How does a merchant eliminate a surplus? It lowers the price.

At a price of $1, 120 packages would be demanded but only 25 would be placed on the market. A shortage of 95 units would be created. If a product is in short supply and consumers want it, how do they entice the dealer to part with one unit? They offer more money—that is, pay a higher price.

equilibrium
Price at which demand and supply are equal.

Now let's examine a price of $1.50. At this price, 85 packages are demanded and 85 are supplied. When demand and supply are equal, a state called **equilibrium** is achieved. A temporary price below equilibrium—say $1.00—results in a shortage because demand for gourmet popcorn is greater than the available supply. Shortages put upward pressure on price. As long as demand and supply remain the same, temporary price increases or decreases tend to return to equilibrium. At equilibrium there is no inclination for prices to rise or fall. However, an equilibrium price may not be reached all at once. Prices may fluctuate during a trial-and-error period as the market for a good or service moves toward equilibrium. But sooner or later demand and supply will settle into proper balance.

Elasticity of Demand

elasticity of demand
Consumers' responsiveness or sensitivity to changes in price.

elastic demand
Situation in which consumer demand is sensitive to price changes.

inelastic demand
Situation in which an increase or a decrease in price will not significantly affect demand for the product.

To appreciate demand analysis, you should understand the concept of elasticity. **Elasticity of demand** refers to consumers' responsiveness or sensitivity to changes in price. **Elastic demand** occurs when consumers are sensitive to price changes. Conversely, **inelastic demand** means that an increase or a decrease in price will not significantly affect demand for the product.

Elasticity over the range of a demand curve can be measured by using this formula:

$$\text{Elasticity (E)} = \frac{\text{Percentage change in quantity demanded of good A}}{\text{Percentage change in price of good A}}$$

If E is greater than 1, demand is elastic.

If E is less than 1, demand is inelastic.

If E is equal to 1, demand is unitary.

If the price of grocery "extras" goes up too much, this father *(top)* will stop buying them; demand is elastic. Demand for luxury goods, like this Rolls Royce *(bottom)*, is surprisingly inelastic; demand changes very little in response to price changes.

(top) © Tony Freeman/PhotoEdit; *(bottom)* © D and J Heaton/Uniphoto

Moreover, elasticity can be measured by observing these changes in total revenue:

If price goes down and revenue goes up, demand is elastic.

If price goes down and revenue goes down, demand is inelastic.

If price goes up and revenue goes up, demand is inelastic.

If price goes up and revenue goes down, demand is elastic.

If price goes up or down and revenue stays the same, elasticity is unitary.

Exhibit 18.5A shows a very elastic demand curve. Decreasing the price of a Sony VCR from \$300 to \$200 increased sales from 18,000 units to 59,000 units. Revenue increased from \$5.4 million (\$300 × 18,000) to \$11.8 million (\$200 × 59,000). The price decrease resulted in a large increase in sales and revenue.

Exhibit 18.5

Elasticity of Demand for Sony VCRs and Auto Inspection Stickers

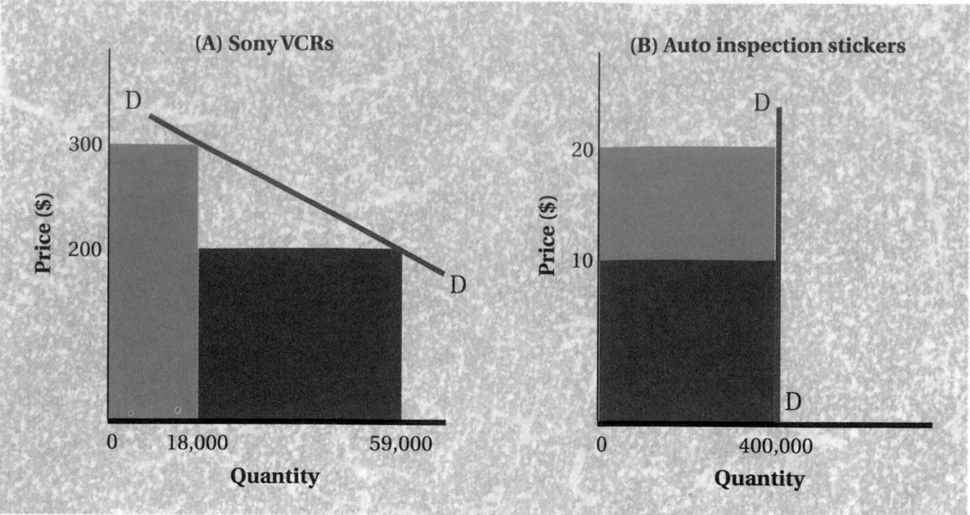

Exhibit 18.6

The Demand for Three-Ounce Bottles of Spring Break Suntan Lotion

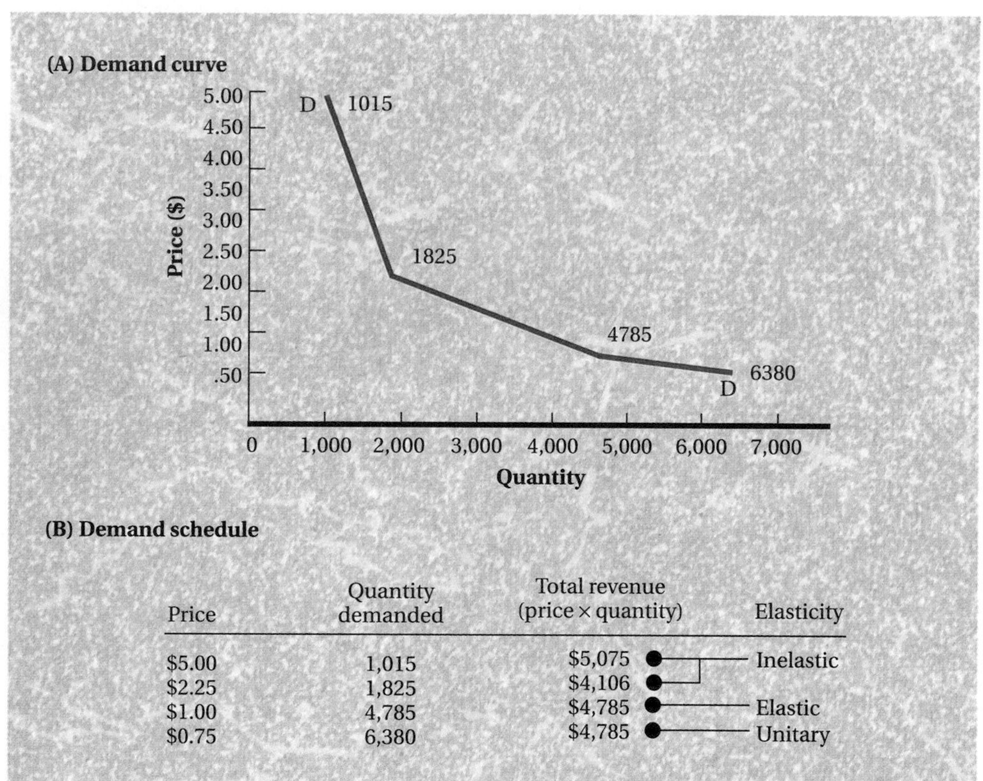

(B) Demand schedule

Price	Quantity demanded	Total revenue (price × quantity)	Elasticity
$5.00	1,015	$5,075	Inelastic
$2.25	1,825	$4,106	
$1.00	4,785	$4,785	Elastic
$0.75	6,380	$4,785	Unitary

Exhibit 18.5B shows a completely inelastic demand curve. The state of Nevada dropped its used-car vehicle inspection fee from $20 to $10. The state continued to inspect about 400,000 used cars annually. Decreasing the price (inspection fee) 50 percent did not cause people to buy more used cars. Demand is completely inelastic for inspection fees. Thus it also follows that Nevada could double the original fee to $40 and double the state's inspection revenue. People won't quit buying used cars if the inspection fee increases within a reasonable range.

Inelastic Demand

Assume that the graph in Exhibit 18.6 represents the demand for three-ounce bottles of Spring Break suntan lotion. Let's follow the demand from the highest price of $5 to the lowest of 75¢ and examine what happens to elasticity.

The initial decrease from $5.00 to $2.25 resulted in a decrease in total revenue of $969 ($5,075 – $4,106). When price and total revenue fall, demand is inelastic. The rate of decrease in price was much greater than the rate of increase in suntan lotion sales. Demand was not very flexible when the price was lowered.

Inelastic demand enables sellers to raise prices and therefore increase total revenue. For example, new life-saving drugs face an almost completely inelastic demand schedule. Some people claim that pharmaceutical manufacturers take advantage of this situation, as discussed in the Ethics in Marketing article.

Elastic Demand

In the example of Spring Break suntan lotion, when the price was dropped from $2.25 to $1.00, total revenue increased by $679 ($4,785 – $4,106). An increase in total

ETHICS IN MARKETING

Inelastic Demand for Life-Saving Drugs

One of the most conservative voices in U.S. medicine blasted Johnson & Johnson for its "unconscionable" pricing of the cancer drug levamisole, used to treat colon cancer.

Cancer expert Charles G. Moertel of the Mayo Comprehensive Cancer Center also charged that the pharmaceutical company breached its commitment to set a moderate price for the drug. Under sponsorship of the National Cancer Institute, Dr. Moertel and others tested levamisole with the staple chemotherapy drug 5-fluorouracil, commonly called 5-FU. The combination proved spectacularly effective in patients with advanced (Stage C) colon cancer, reducing recurrence by 40 percent and cutting deaths by a third.

"We were specifically promised that it would be marketed at a reasonable price," said Dr. Moertel at a recent meeting of the American Society of Clinical Oncology. Under its brand name Ergamisol, sold by J&J's Janssen unit, levamisole costs $1,250 to $1,500 for a year's supply. That's a hundredfold higher than the $14 price tag on an older veterinary version of the drug, which farmers have used for decades to treat their sheep for parasites. Among the first to protest this huge price differential was an Illinois farm woman being treated for cancer, who noticed her pills contained the same active ingredient she used to deworm her flocks.

In New Brunswick, New Jersey, a spokesperson for Johnson & Johnson said the "price of the product reflects costly research over decades to determine possible uses in humans for other diseases, including for other cancers." The spokesperson said the drug has sales of "less than $15 million a year," a relatively modest sum for a pharmaceutical product. He said that for over twenty-five years the company has partly backed over 1,400 studies involving 40,000 patients, seeking new applications of the drug in humans.

Dr. Moertel dismissed Johnson & Johnson's defense that levamisole's price boost was justified by the higher research and regulatory costs required for human consumption. "I'd think after twenty-five years of profitable marketing, they'd more than made it up," he said. "The National Cancer Institute—funded by the U.S. taxpayer—sponsored this study. The company just supplied the pills, which cost pennies." As for regulatory approval, Dr. Moertel said: "The company got a present dumped in its lap. . . . This was the quickest new-drug application in the history of U.S. medicine. We gave it to them on a silver platter." The drug received market approval from the Food and Drug Administration in 1990.

To find a new use for an old drug is a sort of windfall that doesn't justify a price surge, he said. "Just because aspirin was found to improve your risk of heart attack, should you charge more?" He added, "In this laissez-faire market, companies set the price according to what the market will bear. Unfortunately, the patient is captive." But cancer drugs are unlike other consumer products, he said. "It's not like if you can't afford a Ford, you can buy a Chevy."

If you were the marketing manager for Johnson & Johnson, would you change your price strategy for levamisole? If so, why? How would you determine the price? Do you think drug companies are simply recovering their costs, or are they taking advantage of inelastic demand?

Source: Adapted from Marilyn Chase, "Doctor Assails J&J Price Tag on Cancer Drug," *The Wall Street Journal*, 20 May 1992, pp. B1, B8. Reprinted by permission of *The Wall Street Journal*.

revenue when price falls indicates that demand is elastic. A formula can also measure elasticity. For example, if the price drops from $2.25 to $1.00, elasticity of demand is as follows:

$$E = \frac{\text{Change in quantity}/(\text{Sum of quantities}/2)}{\text{Change in price}/(\text{Sum of prices}/2)}$$

$$= \frac{(4{,}785 - 1{,}825)/[(1{,}825 + 4{,}785)/2]}{(2.25) - 1/[(2.25 + 1.00)/2]}$$

$$= \frac{2{,}960/3{,}305}{1.25/1.63}$$

$$= \frac{.896}{.767}$$

$$= 1.17$$

Since E is greater than 1, demand is elastic.

Why was demand elastic when price fell from $2.25 to $1.00? Remember that Spring Break's demand schedule does not allow it to sell 1,825 units at $2.25 and an additional 4,785 units at $1.00; instead, price is an either-or proposition. Therefore, to sell 4,785 units, Spring Break sacrificed $1.25 on 1,825 units that could have been sold at $2.25 instead of the new price of $1.00. The total sacrifice when the price was dropped from $2.25 to $1.00 was $2,281 (1,825 units × $1.25). Demand must be sensitive enough to the price change to cover the sacrificed revenue, or else total revenue will fall (demand will be inelastic). Note that Spring Break did sell an additional 2,960 units (4,785 – 1,825) when it dropped the price from $2.25 to $1.00. Thus the gross revenue gain from the price cut was $2,960 (2,960 units × $1.00). The gain of $2,960 was enough to offset the $1.25 per unit loss on the 1,825 units that could have been sold for $2.25. Therefore, by dropping the price from $2.25 to $1.00, total revenue increased $679 ($2,960 – $2,281).

Unitary Elasticity

The last price decrease was from $1.00 to 75¢. The increase in sales exactly offset the decrease in price so that total revenue remained the same. This situation is called **unitary elasticity.** Unitary elasticity is a fairly rare phenomenon. It could occur, for example, if everyone in the market for suntan lotion budgets a certain amount of money for suntan lotion and will not deviate from that figure regardless of price. When price falls, they buy more suntan lotion, and when price goes up, they buy less.

unitary elasticity
Situation in which an increase in sales exactly offsets a decrease in price so that total revenue remains the same.

Factors That Affect Elasticity

Several factors affect elasticity of demand. These include the availability of substitute goods and services, the price relative to a consumer's purchasing power, a product's durability, and a product's other uses. When many substitute products are available, the consumer can easily switch from one product to another, making demand elastic. If a price is so low that it is an inconsequential part of an individual's budget, demand will be inelastic. For example, if the price of salt doubles, consumers will not stop putting salt and pepper on their eggs, because salt is cheap anyway.

Consumers often have the option of repairing durable products like cars rather than replacing them, thus prolonging their useful life. For instance, if a person had planned to buy a new car and the prices suddenly began to rise, he or she might

One of the factors that affects elasticity of demand is the availability of substitutes. Car owners, for example, can always repair the old car instead of buying a new one. Thus the demand for new cars is elastic, or sensitive to price.

elect to fix the old car and drive it for another year. In other words, people are sensitive to the price increase, and demand is elastic.

Finally, the greater the number of product uses, the more elastic demand tends to be. If a product has only one use, as may be true of a new medicine, quantity purchased probably will not vary as price varies. A person will consume only the prescribed quantity, regardless of price. On the other hand, a product like steel has many possible applications. As its price falls, steel becomes more economically feasible to use in a wide variety of applications, thereby making demand relatively elastic.

4 THE DETERMINANTS OF PRICE: COST

Sometimes companies minimize or ignore the importance of demand and price their products largely or solely on the basis of costs. Prices determined strictly on the basis of costs may be too high for the target market, thereby reducing or eliminating sales. Or cost-based prices may be too low, causing the firm to earn a lower return than it should. In any price determination, costs generally must serve as a floor below which a good or service must not be priced in the long run.

Markup Pricing

markup pricing
Pricing method that adds to the product cost an amount for profit and expenses not previously accounted for.

mark-on
Initial markup.

gross margin
Difference between the price at which a product is actually sold and its cost.

keystoning
Practice of marking up prices by 100 percent, or to double the cost.

Markup pricing is the most popular method used by wholesalers and retailers to establish a sales price. **Markup pricing** is adding to the cost an amount for profit and expenses not previously accounted for. The total determines the selling price. When the merchandise is received, the retailer adds a certain percentage to the figure to arrive at the retail price. An item that costs $1.80 and is sold for $2.20 carries a markup of 40¢, which is a markup of 18 percent of the retail price (40¢ ÷ $2.20) or 22 percent of the cost (40¢ ÷ $1.80). (Retailers tend to calculate the markup percentage on the selling price.) The initial markup is referred to as the **mark-on.**

If the retailer had to cut the price to $2.00 before the product could be sold, the difference between the cost and the selling price would be only 20¢, or 10 percent of the actual selling price—otherwise known as the maintained markup, or **gross margin.** The gross margin reflects actual demand and is much more important than the mark-on. (See Appendix C for more information on markup pricing and the basic arithmetic of pricing.)

Markups are often based on experience. For example, many small retailers mark up merchandise 100 percent over cost (or double the cost). This tactic is called **keystoning.**

Some factors that influence markups are the merchandise's appeal to customers, past response to the markup (an implicit demand consideration), the item's promotional value, the seasonality of the goods, fashion appeal, the product's traditional selling price, and competition. Most retailers deviate widely from any set markup because of considerations such as promotional value and seasonality.

Formula Pricing

formula pricing
Pricing method in which a predetermined formula is used to set price.

A type of pricing similar to markup pricing is **formula pricing,** in which a predetermined formula is used to set price. One simple formula used by a marketing research

firm (which should know better than to ignore demand) is to charge five times the cost of the fieldwork. Since fieldwork is normally the most expensive part of a research project, this approach hopes to cover all costs and make a profit. More elaborate formulas are also used. For example, one manufacturer uses 150 percent of direct labor costs plus 200 percent of material costs plus actual shipping costs. The main advantage of this technique is its simplicity. However, like all basic cost-pricing strategies, it ignores demand.

Types of Economic Costs

variable cost
Cost that deviates with changes in the level of output.

fixed cost
Cost that does not change as output is increased or decreased.

average variable cost (AVC)
Total variable costs divided by output.

average total cost (ATC)
Total costs divided by output.

marginal cost (MC)
Change in total costs associated with a one-unit change in output.

Variable costs deviate with changes in the level of output; an example of a variable cost is the cost of materials. In contrast, a **fixed cost** does not change as output is increased or decreased. Examples include rent and executive salaries.

In order to compare the cost of production to the sales price of the goods or services, it is helpful to calculate costs per unit or average costs. **Average variable cost** (AVC) equals total variable costs divided by output. **Average total cost** (ATC) equals total costs divided by output. As plotted on the graph in Exhibit 18.7A, AVC and ATC are basically U-shaped curves. Average fixed costs (AFC) decline continually as output increases, because total fixed costs are constant. **Marginal cost** (MC) is the change in total costs associated with a one-unit change in output. For example, when output rises from seven to eight units, the change in total cost is from $640 to $750; therefore, marginal cost is $110.

All the curves illustrated in Exhibit 18.7A have a definite relationship. For example, AVC plus AFC equals ATC. Also, MC falls for a while and then turns upward with the fourth unit. Diminishing returns have set in, meaning that less output is produced for every additional dollar spent on variable input. MC intersects both AVC and ATC at their lowest possible points. When MC is less than AVC or ATC, the incremental cost will continue to pull the averages down. Conversely, when MC is greater than AVC or ATC, it pulls the averages up, and ATC and AVC begin to rise. The minimum point on the ATC curve is the least-cost point for a fixed-capacity firm, although it is not necessarily the most profitable point.

Maximizing Profits

profit maximization
Pricing method that sets price where marginal revenue equals marginal cost.

marginal revenue (MR)
Extra revenue associated with selling an extra unit of output.

Profit maximization occurs when marginal revenue equals marginal cost. **Marginal revenue** (MR) is the extra revenue associated with selling an extra unit of output. As long as the revenue of the last unit produced and sold is greater than the cost of the last unit produced and sold, the firm should continue manufacturing.

Exhibit 18.8 shows the marginal revenue and marginal costs for a hypothetical firm using the cost data from Exhibit 18.7B. The profit maximizing quantity where MR = MC is six units. You might say, "If profit is zero, why produce the sixth unit? Why not stop at five?" In fact, you would be right! The firm, however, would not know that the fifth unit would produce zero profits until it determined that profits were no longer increasing. Economists suggest producing up to the point where MR = MC. If marginal revenue is just one penny greater than marginal costs, it will still increase total profits.

The Break-Even Concept

break-even analysis
Method of determining what sales volume must be reached for a product before the company breaks even (total costs equal total revenue) and no profits are earned.

Let's take a closer look at the relationship between sales and cost. **Break-even analysis** determines what sales volume must be reached for a product before the company breaks even (its total costs equal total revenue) and no profits are earned.

The typical break-even model assumes a given fixed cost and a constant average

Exhibit 18.7

A Hypothetical Set of Cost Curves and a Cost Schedule

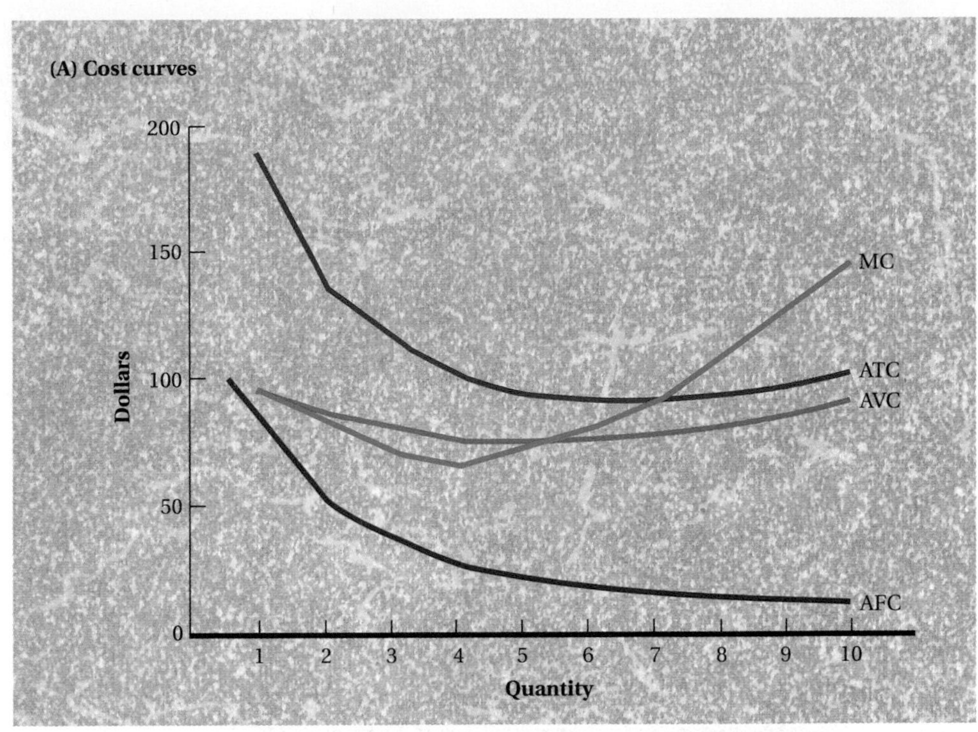

(B) Cost schedule

Total-cost data, per week				Average-cost data, per week			
1 Total product (Q)	**2 Total fixed cost** (TFC)	**3 Total vable cost** (TVC)	**4 Total cost** (TC) TC = TFC + TVC	**5 Average fixed cost** (AFC) AFC = TFC/Q	**6 Average variable cost** (AVC) AVC = TVC/Q	**7 Average total cost** (ATC) ATC = TC/Q	**8 Marginal cost** (MC) MC = Change in TC/ Change in Q
0	$100	$ 0	$ 100	—	—	—	—
1	100	90	190	$100.00	$90.00	$190.00	$90
2	100	170	270	50.00	85.00	135.00	80
3	100	240	340	33.33	80.00	113.33	70
4	100	300	400	25.00	75.00	100.00	60
5	100	370	470	20.00	74.00	94.00	70
6	100	450	550	16.67	75.00	91.67	80
7	100	540	640	14.29	77.14	91.43	90
8	100	650	750	12.50	81.25	93.75	110
9	100	780	880	11.11	86.67	97.78	130
10	100	930	1030	10.00	93.00	103.00	150

variable cost. Suppose that Universal Sportswear, a hypothetical firm, has fixed costs of $2,000 and that the cost of labor and materials for each unit produced is 50¢. Assume that it can sell up to 6,000 units of its product at $1 without having to lower its price. Exhibit 18.9 illustrates Universal Sportswear's break-even point.

Total variable costs increase by 50¢ every time a new unit is produced, and total fixed costs remain constant at $2,000 regardless of the level of output. Therefore, 4,000 units of output give Universal Sportswear $2,000 in fixed costs and $2,000 in total variable costs (4,000 units × 50¢), or $4,000 in total costs. Revenue is also $4,000 at 4,000 units (4,000 units × $1), giving a net profit of zero dollars at break-even. Notice that once the firm gets past the break-even point, the gap between total revenue and total cost gets wider and wider, since both functions are assumed to be linear.

A simple formula for calculating break-even quantities follows:

$$\begin{aligned}\text{Fixed cost contribution} &= \text{Price} - \text{AVC (average variable costs)}\\ &= \$1.00 - 50¢\\ &= 50¢\end{aligned}$$

$$\begin{aligned}\text{Break-even quantity} &= \frac{\text{Total fixed costs}}{\text{Fixed cost contribution}}\\ &= \frac{\$2,000}{50¢}\\ &= 4,000 \text{ units}\end{aligned}$$

Exhibit 18.8

Finding the Point of Profit Maximization

Quantity	Marginal revenue (MR)	Marginal cost (MC)	Total profit
0	—	—	—
1	140	90	50
2	130	80	100
3	105	70	135
4	95	60	170
5	85	70	185
*6	80	80	185
7	75	90	170
8	60	110	120
9	50	130	40
10	40	150	(70)

*Profit maximization

(A) Costs and revenues

Output	Total fixed costs	Average variable costs	Total variable costs	Average total costs	Average revenue (price)	Total revenue	Total costs	Profit or loss
500	$2,000	$0.50	$ 250	$4.50	$1.00	$ 500	$2,250	($1,750)
1,000	2,000	0.50	500	2.50	1.00	1,000	2,500	(1,500)
1,500	2,000	0.50	750	1.83	1.00	1,500	2,750	(1,250)
2,000	2,000	0.50	1,000	1.50	1.00	2,000	3,000	(1,000)
2,500	2,000	0.50	1,250	1.30	1.00	2,500	3,250	(750)
3,000	2,000	0.50	1,500	1.17	1.00	3,000	3,500	(500)
3,500	2,000	0.50	1,750	1.07	1.00	3,500	3,750	(250)
*4,000	2,000	0.50	2,000	1.00	1.00	4,000	4,000	(0)
4,500	2,000	0.50	2,250	.94	1.00	4,500	4,250	250
5,000	2,000	0.50	2,500	.90	1.00	5,000	4,500	500
5,500	2,000	0.50	2,750	.86	1.00	5,500	4,750	750
6,000	2,000	0.50	3,000	.83	1.00	6,000	5,000	1,000

*Break-even point

Exhibit 18.9

Costs, Revenues, and Break-Even Point for Universal Sportswear

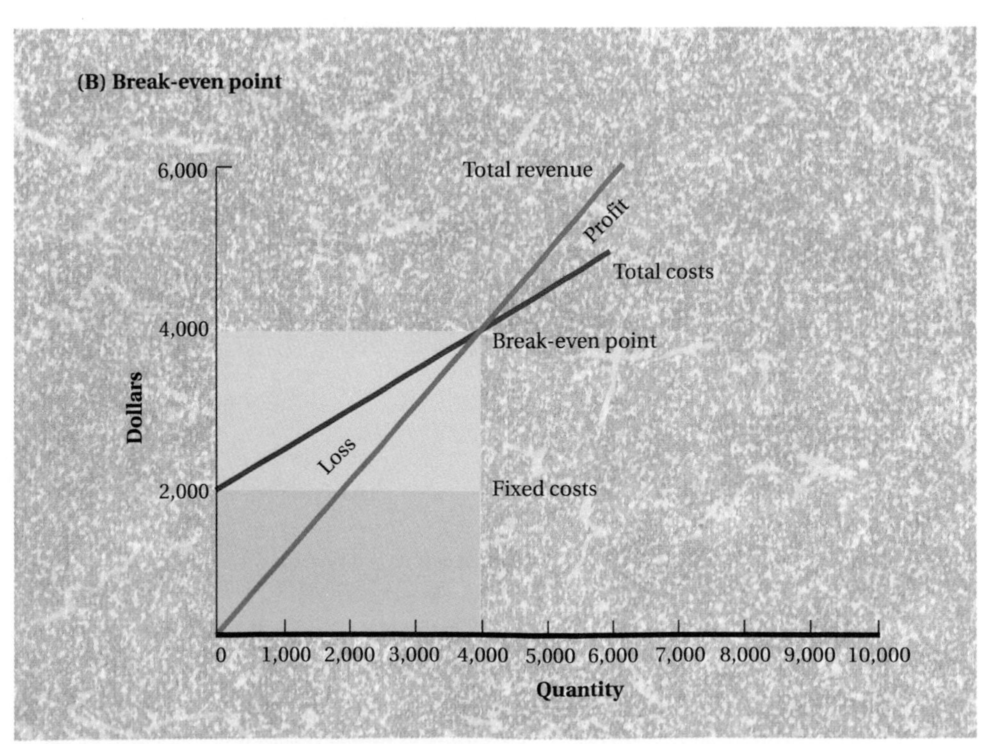

Advantages of Break-Even Analysis

The advantage of break-even analysis is that it provides a quick glance at how much the firm must sell to break even and how much profit can be earned if higher sales volume is obtained. If a firm is operating close to the break-even point, it may want to see what can be done to reduce costs or increase sales. Moreover, in a simple break-even analysis, it is not necessary to compute marginal costs and marginal revenues, because price and average cost per unit are assumed to be constant. Since accounting data for marginal cost and revenue are frequently unavailable, it is convenient not to have to depend on that information.

Disadvantages of Break-Even Analysis

Break-even analysis is not without several important limitations. Sometimes it is hard to know whether a cost is fixed or variable. For example, if labor wins a tough guaranteed-employment contract, are the resulting expenses a fixed cost? What about middle-level executives' salaries—are they fixed costs? More important than cost determination is the fact that simple break-even analysis ignores demand. For example, how does Universal Sportswear know it can sell 4,000 units at $1? Could it sell the same 4,000 units at $2 or even $5? Obviously, this information would profoundly affect the firm's break-even point.

Target Return Pricing

target return pricing
Pricing method that sets price where revenues from sales of a targeted quantity yield the target return on investment.

Target return pricing is one of the most popular methods of choosing a selling price. **Target return pricing** determines the break-even point, plus a dollar amount equal to the desired ROI (return on investment) percentage. Thus when the targeted quantity has been sold, the company will have reached its target ROI. A marketer can easily figure a target return–break-even point by treating the desired profit as an addition to fixed cost. The desired level of profit (expressed in dollars) is typically a predetermined ROI.

Assume that Johnson Controls, an industrial controls manufacturer, has just spent $1 million developing a new heat-sensing unit. The firm has a 15 percent target ROI for the new product and therefore must earn a profit of $150,000. Fixed costs allocated to the new product by the accounting department are $65,000. Average variable costs are $14, and the tentative sales price is $60 each. The following calculation applies the basic formula:

$$\text{Fixed cost contribution} = \$60 - \$14 = \$46$$

$$\text{Break-even point ROI} = \frac{\text{Total fixed cost} + \text{Total desired profit}}{\text{Fixed cost contribution per unit}} = \frac{\$65{,}000 + \$150{,}000}{\$46} = 4{,}673.9 \text{ heat-sensing units}$$

If the marketing manager has forecast sales of about 4,700 units, then the target ROI will be slightly exceeded.

By plugging different prices into the formula, the marketing manager can determine how many units must be sold to reach the target ROI. A comparison of the target ROI quantity and the sales forecast will tell the manager whether the ROI objective can be met at a given price.

5 OTHER DETERMINANTS OF PRICE

Other factors besides demand and costs can influence price. For example, the stage of the product's life cycle, the competition, product distribution, promotion strategy, and perceived product quality can all affect pricing strategy. Next we examine the impact of each.

The Stage of the Product's Life Cycle

As a product moves through its life cycle, the demand for the product and the competitive conditions tend to change. Management usually sets prices high during the introduction stage (but not always, as explained in Chapter 19) for two reasons: Demand originates in the core of the market, and management hopes to recover its development costs quickly.

The pricing strategy followed during the introduction stage of a product's life cycle often depends on elasticity of demand. If demand is relatively inelastic, management may introduce the good or service at a fairly high price—for instance, a Sony high-definition color television. On the other hand, if the target market is highly price-sensitive, management often finds it better to price the product at the market level or lower. When Kraft General Foods brought out Country Time Lemonade, it was priced like similar products in the highly competitive beverage market because the market was price-sensitive.

Prices generally begin to stabilize as the product enters the growth stage. First competitors enter the market, increasing the available supply. Then the product begins to appeal to a broader market, often lower-income groups. Finally economies of scale lead to lower costs, which can be passed on to the consumer in the form of lower prices.

Maturity usually brings further price decreases as competition increases and inefficient, high-cost firms are eliminated. Distribution channels are a significant cost factor, because of the need to offer wide product lines for highly segmented markets, extensive service requirements, and the sheer number of dealers necessary to allow high-volume production. The manufacturers that remain in the market toward the end of the maturity stage typically offer similar prices. Only the most efficient usually remain, and they have comparable costs. At this stage, price increases are usually cost-initiated, not demand-initiated. Nor do price reductions in the late phase of maturity usually stimulate much demand. Demand is limited, and similar cost structures mean that the remaining competitors will probably match price reductions.

The final stage of the life cycle, product decline, may see price decreases as the few remaining competitors try to salvage the last vestiges of demand. When only one firm is left in the market, prices begin to stabilize. In fact, they may eventually rise dramatically if the product survives and moves into the specialty good category, such as horse-drawn carriages have.

The Competition

Competition varies during the product life cycle, of course, and so at times it may strongly affect pricing decisions. For example, although a firm may not have any competition at first, the high prices it charges may eventually induce another firm to enter the market.

In the 1980s, Borden decided to make a full-scale commitment to the salty snack business. The logic was that there was only one big national competitor, Frito-Lay, which left room for a second. Also, yearly price increases by Frito-Lay kept profits rising about 20 percent annually.

Consumers may have been somewhat confused during the price war between Eagle Snacks and Frito-Lay, but they benefited from the low prices.

© 1989 P. Barry Levy/ProFiles West

The strategy worked perfectly for Borden until 1982, when Anheuser-Busch decided to expand its Eagle Snacks division from niche player to broadly distributed brand. Eagle never wanted to be a price cutter. But as it won shelf space in supermarkets, reportedly by paying retailers as much as $500 a linear foot and dropping prices, competitors fought back.[4] Says Jerry Ritter, executive vice president at Anheuser-Busch: "In the summer of 1989 we began to see the impact. By fall we knew they had knocked our socks off. So we had to become more competitive."

When Anheuser-Busch targeted Frito-Lay's Doritos tortilla chip business, the war escalated to yet another level. An observer noted, "You are attacking the family jewels. That's where they draw the line; they crush you."[5] Frito-Lay matched Anheuser-Busch on every program. Anheuser-Busch spent $15 million to $20 million in TV advertising and deep-cut price promotions. The Anheuser-Busch division won about a 4 percent market share but lost $20 million in 1992. The company could expect to make a profit in the snack business only if the price war would subside.

When a firm enters a mature market without a "price umbrella" provided by a market leader, it has three options. It can price below the market, as the Eagle Snacks division of Anheuser-Busch did. Or the new competitor can price above the market if it has a distinct competitive advantage. Lifetime Automotive Products entered the windshield wiper market with wiper blades priced at $19.95, more than three times the average price.[6] The firm's competitive advantage was a patented three-bladed wiper system that cleaned better than traditional wipers, plus a lifetime guarantee. Finally, companies entering a market at the "going market price" assume that they can reach profit and market share objectives through nonprice competition. Also, entering at the existing price level helps avoid crippling price wars.

Price wars and intense competition are not limited to the United States. As the European Community moves toward greater economic unity, price wars have begun raging in Europe—as the International Perspectives box explains.

Distribution Strategy

Adequate distribution for a new product can often be attained by offering a larger than usual profit margin to wholesalers and retailers on the item. A variation on this strategy is to give dealers a large trade allowance to help offset the costs of promotion and further stimulate demand at the retail level. An effective distribution network can often overcome other minor flaws in a marketing mix. Perhaps consumers perceive a price as being slightly higher than normal. If the good is located in a convenient retail outlet, they may buy it anyway.

Perrier carbonated mineral water has been distributed in the United States since the turn of the century, but until about 1985 sales were flat. Perrier was available only in specialty food outlets and better restaurants. Management decided to make Perrier a mass-market beverage to be sold in most grocery stores and convenience food outlets. To obtain the necessary distribution, Perrier offered major price discounts to wholesalers and retailers. Its sales topped 100 million bottles yearly before the contamination recall in 1990. Today Perrier still hasn't recovered the market share it attained in the late 1980s. Consumers found substitute brands to be equally satisfying at lower prices.

Promotion Strategy

Price is often used as a promotional tool to increase consumer interest. In the weekly grocery section of the newspaper, ads appear for many products with special low prices. These reduced prices are designed to induce consumers to shop in a particular store. Egghead Software, the largest U.S. computer software retailer, often uses price to draw crowds to its stores. For example, Egghead aggressively promoted Microsoft's MS-DOS 5 operating system with a price of $39.99, well below the $99.95 list price.[7]

Many retailers use promotional pricing for Levi's Dockers. Dockers are very popular with white-collar men ages 25 to 45—a growing and lucrative market. To attract these customers, many retailers started buying Dockers for $18 a pair and selling them for $25. Levi's intended its cheapest Dockers to retail for $35. Sensing an opportunity, Bugle Boy began a trade promotion campaign stressing higher profitability for the retailer by offering similar pants at cheaper wholesale prices. Levi's had to either lower prices or risk its $400 million annual Docker sales.[8] It ultimately lowered prices.

INTERNATIONAL PERSPECTIVES

Price Wars in Europe

"The mere hint of an economic upturn in Europe used to trigger price hikes of 5 percent or even 10 percent to fatten up corporate bottom lines. But not this time. Today's European market, swamped with goods as trade barriers drop, is doing exactly the opposite: . . . Price cuts are the order of the day. The biggest winners are Europe's consumers. . . . As shoppers walk through the GB Maxi supermarket on Boulevard Leopold III in Brussels, for example, they can grab U.S.-style coupons offering discounts worth 10 percent to 15 percent off irons and deep-fat fryers."

As Europe's markets become more open, the changes are likely to become more permanent. Increased competition will force companies to rethink their pricing. They may even find it necessary to merge with other companies in order to reduce the number of competitors. Big discount chains are also gaining ground, forcing smaller shops to cut prices.

Why do you think that price wars are occurring in Europe now and have not in the past? Will the consumer really benefit if the price wars lead to mergers and many people are laid off? If hundreds of thousands of small retailers are put out of business by giant international discounters, won't the economy be hurt? What about Europe's traditional culture?

Source: Extracts from "Price War I Is Raging in Europe," *Business Week*, 6 July 1992, pp. 44–45.

Consumers who lack good information for making a purchase decision often use the rule "you get what you pay for" to choose among competing products. A housepainter that charges higher prices than the competition may be perceived as doing higher-quality work.

Relationship of Price to Quality

Consumers tend to rely on a high price as a predictor of good quality when there is great uncertainty involved in the purchase decision. A number of studies have shown this tendency for several products. Examples include coffee, stockings, aspirin, salt, floor wax, shampoo, clothing, furniture, perfume, whiskey, and many services. Reliance on price as an indicator of quality seems to exist for all products, but it reveals itself more strongly for some items than for others.[9] Also, if the consumer obtains additional information—for instance, about the brand or the store—then reliance on price as an indicator of quality decreases.[10] In the absence of other information, people typically assume that prices are higher because the products contain better materials, more careful workmanship, or more expertise by the service professional. In other words, they assume that "you get what you pay for." One study has shown that some people believe "you get what you pay for" much more strongly than others. That is, some consumers tend to rely much more heavily on price as a quality indicator than others do.[11] Also, consumers tend to be more accurate in their price/quality assessments for nondurable goods (such as ice cream, frozen pizza, or oven cleaner) than for durable goods (such as a coffeemaker, gas grill, or ten-speed bike).[12]

Prestige pricing is charging a high price to help promote a high-quality image. A successful prestige pricing strategy requires that the retail price be reasonably consistent with consumers' attitudes toward expected prices. For example, no one goes shopping at a Gucci's in New York and expects to pay $9.95 for a pair of loafers. In fact, demand would fall drastically at the lower price. Bayer aspirin would probably lose market share over the long run if it lowered its prices. A new mustard packaged in a crockery jar was not successful until its price was doubled.

Consumers expect dealer or store brands to be cheaper than national brands.

However, if the savings over a nationally distributed manufacturer's brand is too great, consumers tend to believe the dealer brand is inferior in quality. On the other hand, if the savings aren't big enough, there is little incentive to buy the dealer brand. One scanner data study found that if the price difference between the national brand and the house brand was less than 10 percent, people tended not to buy the house brand. If the price difference was greater than 20 percent, consumers perceived the house brand to be inferior.[13]

LOOKING BACK

Look back at the Frito-Lay story that appeared at the beginning of the chapter. Frito-Lay is now pursuing a sales-oriented market share objective. Management followed the conventional wisdom that a larger market share, coupled with cost-consciousness, will lead to a larger return on investment. This was, in fact, the result at Frito-Lay.

As you learned in the chapter, the relationship between price and sales revenue depends on elasticity of demand. In Frito-Lay's case, demand was elastic: Prices were lowered and total sales revenue rose. Cost plays several key roles in the pricing equation. First, it represents a floor below which a firm cannot price its products in the long run and remain in business. Second, controlling costs can add to a firm's profitability. For any given level of revenue that exceeds total costs, a lowering of costs will increase profits. Therefore, a firm can increase profit per unit in two ways: lowering costs or increasing price.

Competition can help hold down prices in the marketplace. A firm without competition that charges a high price will soon find competitors attracted to that market. As competitors enter, prices typically fall as firms compete for market share by lowering prices.

KEY TERMS

average total cost 608
average variable cost 608
break-even analysis 608
demand 600
elastic demand 602
elasticity of demand 602
equilibrium 602
fixed cost 608
formula pricing 607
free enterprise 594
gross margin 607
inelastic demand 602
keystoning 607
marginal cost 608
marginal revenue 608
market share 598
mark-on 607

SUMMARY

1 Discuss the importance of pricing decisions to the economy and to the individual firm. Pricing plays an integral role in the U.S. economy by allocating goods and services among consumers, governments, and businesses. Pricing is essential in business because it creates revenue, which is the basis of all business activity. In setting prices, marketing managers strive to find a level high enough to produce a satisfactory profit.

2 List and explain a variety of pricing objectives. Establishing realistic and measurable pricing objectives is a critical part of any firm's marketing strategy. Pricing objectives are commonly classified into three categories: profit-oriented, sales-oriented, and status quo. Profit-oriented pricing is based on profit maximization, a satisfactory level of profit, or a target return on investment. The goal of profit maximization is to generate as much revenue as possible in relation to cost. Often a more practical approach than profit maximization is setting prices to produce profits that will satisfy management and stockholders. The most common profit-oriented strategy is pricing for a specific return on investment relative to a firm's assets. The second type of pricing objective is sales-oriented and focuses on either maintaining a percentage share of the market or maximizing dollar or unit sales. The third type of pricing objective aims to simply maintain status quo by matching competitors' prices.

3 Explain the role of demand in price determination. Demand is a key determinant of price. When establishing prices, a firm must first determine demand for its product. A typical demand schedule shows an inverse relationship between quantity demanded and price. That is, when price is lowered, sales increase; and when price is increased, the quantity demanded falls. However, for prestige products, there may be a direct relationship between demand and price. The quantity demanded will increase as price increases.

Marketing managers must also consider demand elasticity when setting prices. Elasticity of demand is the degree to which quantity demanded fluctuates with changes in price. If consumers are sensitive to changes in price, demand is elastic. If they are insensitive to price changes, demand is inelastic. Thus an increase in price will result in lower sales for an elastic product and little or no change in sales for an inelastic product.

4 Describe cost-oriented pricing strategies. The other major determinant of price is cost. Marketers use several cost-oriented pricing strategies. To cover their own expenses and obtain a profit, wholesalers and retailers commonly use markup pricing; they tack an extra amount onto the manufacturer's original price. Like markup pricing, formula pricing sets prices using a predetermined formula based on variable and fixed costs. Another pricing technique is to maximize profits by setting price where marginal revenue equals marginal cost. Still another pricing strategy determines how much a firm must sell to break even and uses this amount as a reference point for adjusting price. Finally, a popular pricing method is target return pricing. Using this strategy, a firm calculates the break-even point plus the additional amount that will equal its desired return on investment.

5 Understand how the product life cycle, competition, distribution and promotion strategies, and quality perceptions can affect price. The price of a product normally changes as it moves through the life cycle and as demand for the product and competitive conditions change. Also, management often sets a high price at the introductory stage of the life cycle and lowers it over time. High prices tend to attract competition, and competition usually drives prices down because individual competitors lower prices to gain market share.

Adequate distribution for a new product can sometimes be obtained by offering a larger-than-usual profit margin to wholesalers and retailers. Price is also used as a promotional tool to attract customers. Special low prices often attract new customers and entice existing customers to buy more.

Quality perceptions can influence pricing strategies. A firm trying to project a prestigious image often charges a premium price for a product. Consumers tend to equate high prices with high quality.

Review Questions

1. Identify current consumer market trends influencing price.
2. Describe price elasticity of demand. How does the relationship between price and revenue reflect elasticity?
3. Define variable cost, fixed cost, and average total cost.
4. Describe marginal cost and marginal revenue. How do they relate to each other?
5. What is break-even analysis? Discuss the advantages and disadvantages of using break-even analysis for pricing.
6. How does the stage of a product's life cycle affect price?
7. How do consumers "vote" for products? What do consumer "votes" mean to manufacturers?

Discussion and Writing Questions

1. Why is pricing so important to the marketing manager?
2. Your firm has based its pricing strictly on cost in the past. As the newly hired marketing manager, you believe this policy should change. Write the president a memo explaining your reasons.
3. In your opinion, has the role of price increased or decreased in importance relative to the other marketing mix variables? What developments influenced your opinion?
4. Comment on the following statement: "If the price elasticity of demand for your product is inelastic, then your price is probably too low."
5. List five products for which consumers often use price to gauge quality. Explain why you chose each product.
6. Would you buy a dealer brand that was 50 percent cheaper than a nationally advertised brand? Why or why not?

CASES

18.1 Green Tortoise Bus Line

Take a trip back in time. In the 1960s, hippie buses flourished in the United States, traveling coast to coast. The ribald behavior of passengers and cheap fares encouraged many riders to climb aboard.

Green Tortoise is a rolling remnant of the 1960s. The company owns nine antique buses whose average age is twenty years. They make regularly scheduled runs up and down the West Coast. In warmer months the company shuttles across the United States. Although most of the "gypsy" carriers have gone out of business, Green Tortoise still makes a profit. In 1981 the company bought out its last major competitor, the Grey Rabbit. It was a fitting end to the Tortoise and the Rabbit competition.

The buses have been modified to accommodate the passengers. The overhead racks have been converted into sleepers. When the seats flip down, they become sleeping platforms. The bus can sleep forty-five passengers. Roof racks for bicycles, kayaks, and canoes have been installed. The cost of renovating these buses runs $30,000. Despite their age, the company's buses are well maintained.

Creating a sense of adventure is the experience Green Tortoise provides. The driver, wearing red suspenders and sandals, greets the passengers. The back of the ticket stub says, "Know your limitations. Keep your wits about you." To this end, there is a sign on the visor warning, "If you downshift this transmission faster than 50 mph, it will blow up."

The bus even makes unusual stops. For example, on each trip between San Francisco and Seattle, the bus stops at the company's retreat off Interstate 5. The passengers are invited to participate in a communal cookout, sauna, and swim before continuing the journey. "It's adventure on the run," says Gardener Kent, owner and founder of Green Tortoise.

These bus trips are a niche business. The laid-back style of the bus line probably would appeal to only 5 percent of travelers, but 5 percent equals millions of people. Currently, Green Tortoise carries 10,000 passengers a year. Green Tortoise does not do any advertising except for handbills passed out by drivers and posted on college campuses. Demand for seats runs so strong that there is a waiting list to ride Green Tortoise.

Green Tortoise offers its passengers not only adventure but also a cheap fare. An average airline ticket between San Francisco and Seattle can cost over $400.

Greyhound charges $101 for the one-way trip, but Green Tortoise offers "the adventure" for a mere $59. The bus line charges an additional $5 to strap a bike to the roof.

"This bus," says driver Steven Spahr, "gives people a chance to act like hippies for a night and then go back to the real world the next morning. That's something Greyhound just can't do." As passengers disembark at their final destination, they frequently hug the driver and often exchange names and phone numbers with other passengers.

Questions

1. Do you think Green Tortoise fares and Greyhound fares are elastic or inelastic? Give reasons to support your opinion.
2. Do you think Gardener Kent, founder and owner of Green Tortoise, is interested in maximum profits? Why or why not?
3. What costs should Green Tortoise consider when calculating its break-even point?

Suggested Reading

Bill Richards, "Trip on the Tortoise Can Be Hair-Raising if You Aren't Hip," *The Wall Street Journal*, 14 January 1991, pp. A1, A8.

18.2 Senco Products

Video title: *Senstar: A Pricing Decision*

Senco Products, Inc.
8485 Broadwell Road
Cincinnati, OH 45244

SIC codes: 3546 Power-driven handtools
3965 Fasteners

Number of employees: 1,900

1993 revenues: $200 million

Largest competitors: Stanley-Bostich, Paslode, ITW, Duofast

Background

In 1988, Scott Allspaw, product manager at Senco, was faced with a pricing decision. The company had just developed a new machine to build pallets and needed to price it for sale. The company already supplied nail guns and nails to several of the wood pallet manufacturing companies. Nail guns were given away with the purchase of nails. To arrive at a retail price for the new machine, Allspaw looked at the competitive environment.

Industry

Pallet manufacturing is either done by hand or by machine. There are over 2,000 pallet manufacturers in the United States today. Most are located near heavy manufacturing areas. Most of the pallets sold are used for storing and shipping manufactured goods. For this reason, sales of pallets are tied to economic growth.

Most pallet manufacturers are too small to make a large capital investment in pallet manufacturing equipment. Allspaw estimates that fewer than 500 companies could afford to buy pallet assembly machinery. Buyers of Senco's new machine will have to buy nails and other supplies from Senco to keep the machine running.

There are three main types of pallets made in the United States today. Over 90 percent of all pallets are made from hardwood; plastic and metal pallets make up the balance. The main disadvantages of wood pallets are poor construction, breakage, and product damage. But wood pallets offer the advantage of lower cost ($8), design flexibility, industry acceptance, local manufacture, short lead times, and ease of handling. Wood pallets also offer the advantage of recyclability. Other wood products can be made from used and damaged pallets.

Senstar

The Senstar machine was developed to take full advantage of all the benefits associated with wood pallets and to address the main shortcomings. The machine builds highly uniform, high-quality wood pallets to customer specifications. Because all nailing is done by machine, the customer is assured of uniform quality. With the increasing use of automated storage and retrieval systems, uniformity is a key requirement of many wood pallet purchasers.

The Senstar machine can produce four pallets every two and a half minutes. When downtime is considered (time to service and to reload nails), the machine can produce over 575 pallets per day. The only other ma-

chine that can do the same thing costs over $250,000. Thus Senco has a unique position in the market.

A per-pallet cost comparison of the three production alternatives follows:

	Hand	Senstar	High-end machine
Labor	$ .92	$ .28	$ .12
Wood	4.00	4.00	4.00
Nails	.40	.40	.30
Volume	175/day	575/day	2,000/day

The labor costs are figured at $8 per hour gross wages plus $2 per hour for benefits for an average eight-hour day. It take two laborers to hand-assemble pallets and two laborers to run the Senstar machine. The high-end equipment requires three workers to operate.

Questions

1. Should Senco consider profits derived from selling supplies (like nails) for the Senstar when pricing the new machine?
2. What price would you recommend to Senco for the Senstar machine? How did you arrive at that figure?
3. Would demand for the Senstar be elastic or inelastic? Why?

References

"Exclusive Survey Reveals Pallet Purchasing Trends," *Modern Materials Handling,* February 1993, p. 12.

Million Dollar Directory 1993 (Parsippany, NJ: Dun & Bradstreet Information Services, 1993).

CHAPTER 19

Setting the Right Price

LEARNING OBJECTIVES

After studying this chapter, you should be able to

1. Describe the procedure for setting the right price.
2. Identify the three basic price policies.
3. Identify the legal constraints on pricing decisions.
4. Explain how discounts, geographic pricing, and other special pricing tactics can be used to fine-tune the base price.
5. Discuss product line pricing.
6. Explain how bidding differs from other forms of pricing.
7. Describe the role of pricing during periods of inflation and recession.
8. Discuss what the future might hold for pricing in the marketing mix.

At Quaker State Corporation's headquarters in Oil City, Pennsylvania, where executives drink coffee from mugs that look like oil cans, chief executive Jack W. Corn insists the beleaguered company has "turned the corner."

But at a Kmart auto center just four miles south of town, service manager Ed Bogert says he's seen a lot more people changing from Quaker State to Pennzoil or Valvoline. His own shop cut its use of Quaker State oil in half in the past year.

That points to problems with Quaker State's marketing. The nation's top motor oil in 1985, Quaker State already had seen its market share drop off when Mr. Corn aggravated the skid by plunging into a radical marketing change that still hasn't worked. The change in strategy began in 1988, when Mr. Corn quit the motor oil pricing war, insisting Quaker State's quality image justified higher prices.

The consequences of this refusal to match rivals' discounting have been swift and severe: Quaker State's market share, more than 22 percent in 1985, plunged to around 14 percent in 1992, putting it well behind industry leader Pennzoil and just ahead of other brands that discount their oil. According to company figures that Mr. Corn admits are "in the ballpark," Quaker State's annual volume has fallen by one-third.

As Quaker State has learned, pricing is perhaps the critical element in the success or failure of any marketing strategy. If a company seeks the high end of the market, maintaining higher prices than its rivals', then the quality edge had better be distinctive. But that isn't easy to get across in a commodity business like motor oil, where industry experts agree that even the most discriminating consumer can't detect a difference among major brands.

"To take a commodity out of the pricing fray you have to find a way to add some unique value," says Richard Winger, marketing specialist with Boston Consulting Group. "It's something that has to be built up very carefully."

Mr. Corn dismantled the company's national sales organization, turning direct sales responsibilities over to distributors, Quaker's traditional stronghold. To assist these distributors, he created a uniform pricing system that virtually eliminated bulk discounts for bigger buyers and flexible promotions for national retailers.

But Mr. Corn's cold-turkey switch from price to quality proved devastating. Mr. Corn's critics say he has turned over the company's sales responsibilities to distributors who no longer have loyalty to the brand, despite Quaker's new incentive programs. Mr. Corn boasts quality, pointing to the company's lengthy warranty and its new synthetic oil line. But to most customers—distributors in particular—oil is just a commodity, and they'll choose the cheaper brands to boost their own margins. And while Mr. Corn has reduced

costs by slashing the sales force, this also eliminates the company's ability to win and serve customers, crucial ingredients in promoting a quality image.

"There's lack of concern about market share, and market share is a pretty damn important criterion," says Earl V. Swift, Quaker State's former marketing vice president. Mr. Swift, a fourteen-year veteran and employee of the year in 1986, was dismissed by Mr. Corn.

What are the advantages and disadvantages of setting a premium price on a product? Is uniform pricing a good strategy? What role should discounts play in pricing?

Source: Adapted from Dana Milbank, "Quaker State Slips in Marketing Battle," *The Wall Street Journal*, 13 February 1991, p. B1. Reprinted by permission of *The Wall Street Journal*.

❶ HOW TO SET A PRICE ON A PRODUCT

Setting the right price on a product is a four-step process (see Exhibit 19.1):

1. Establish pricing goals
2. Estimate demand, costs, and profits
3. Choose a price policy to help determine a base price
4. Fine-tune the base price with pricing tactics

The first three steps are discussed below; the fourth step is discussed later in the chapter.

Establish Pricing Goals

The first step in setting the right price is to establish pricing goals. Recall from Chapter 18 that pricing objectives fall into three categories: profit-oriented, sales-oriented, and status quo. These goals are derived from the firm's overall objectives.

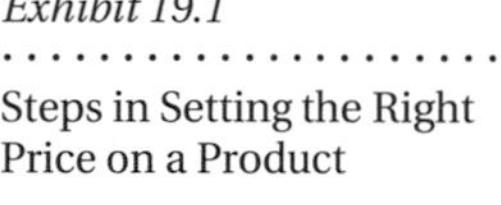

Exhibit 19.1

Steps in Setting the Right Price on a Product

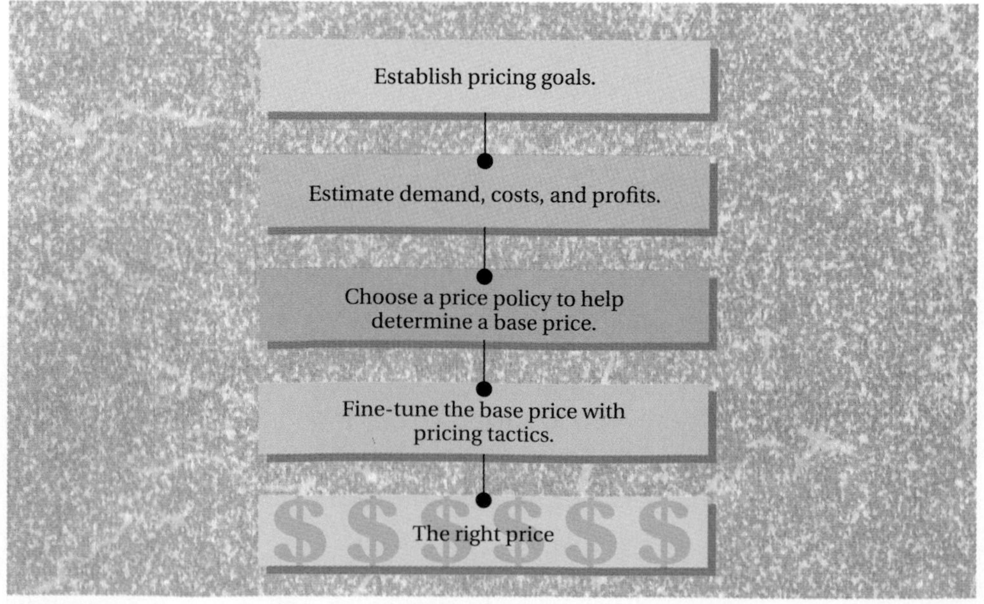

A good understanding of the marketplace and of the consumer can sometimes tell a manager very quickly whether a goal is realistic. For example, if firm A has a 20 percent target return on investment (ROI) objective and product development and implementation costs are $5 million, the manager may see that the market is too small or won't support the price required to earn a 20 percent ROI. Assume company B has an objective that all new products must reach at least 15 percent market share within three years after product introduction. A thorough study of the environment may convince the marketing manager that the competition is too strong and the market share goal can't be met.

All pricing objectives have trade-offs that managers must weigh. A profit maximization objective may require a bigger initial investment than the firm can or wants to commit. Reaching the desired market share often means sacrificing short-term profit, because without careful management, long-term profit goals may not be met. Meeting competition is the easiest goal to implement. However, can managers really afford to ignore demand and costs, the life cycle stage, and other considerations? When creating pricing objectives, managers must consider these trade-offs in light of the target customer and the environment.

Estimate Demand, Costs, and Profits

Chapter 18 explained that total revenue is a function of price and quantity demanded and that quantity demanded depends on elasticity. After establishing pricing goals, managers should estimate total revenue at a variety of prices. Next they should determine corresponding costs for each price. They are then ready to estimate how much profit, if any, and how much market share can be earned at each possible price. These data then become the heart of the developing price policy. Managers can study the options in light of revenues, costs, and profits. In turn, this information can help determine which price can best meet the firm's pricing goals.

2 Choose a Price Policy

price policy
Initial price for a product and the intended direction for price movements over the product life cycle.

The basic, long-term pricing framework for the good or service should be a logical extension of the pricing objectives. The marketing manager's chosen **price policy** defines the initial price and gives direction for price movements over the product life cycle. In addition, a price policy sets a competitive price in a specific market segment, based on a well-defined positioning strategy. For example, a carmaker would set a base price at one of the six price levels, shown in Exhibit 19.2. Changing a price level from moderate to premium may require a change in the product itself, the target customers served, promotional strategy, or distribution channels. Thus changing a price policy can require dramatic alterations in the marketing mix. A carmaker cannot successfully compete in the "super-premium" category if the car looks and drives like a Dodge Colt.

A company's freedom in pricing a new product and setting a price policy depends on the market conditions and the other elements of the marketing mix. For example, if a firm launches a new item resembling several others already on the market, its pricing freedom will be restricted. To succeed, the company will probably have to charge a price close to the average market price. In contrast, a firm that introduces a totally new product with no close substitutes will have considerable freedom.

There are three basic policies for setting a price on a good or service: price skimming, penetration pricing, and meeting the status quo pricing. A discussion of each type follows.

Exhibit 19.2

Segmenting the Automobile Market by Price

Price range	Model		
Ultra-premium *(over $100,000)*	Lamborghini Rolls Royce	 Lamborghini USA, Inc.	 By permission of Rolls-Royce Motor Cars Inc.
Super-premium *($60,000–$100,000)*	BMW 850ci Porsche 928s	 BMW of North America, Inc.	 Porche Cars North America, Inc.
Premium *($40,000–$60,000)*	Mercedes E-Class Lexus LS 400	 Mercedes Benz of North America, Inc.	 Toyota Motor Sales USA
Moderate *($15,000–$40,000)*	Cadillac Seville Mazda Miata	 Cadillac Motor Car Division	 Courtesy of Mazda
Economy *($9,000–$15,000)*	Jeep Wrangler Ford Taurus	 Chrysler Corporation	 Ford Motor Company
Basic *(under $9,000)*	Geo Metro Dodge Colt	 Chevrolet Motor Division	 Chrysler Corporation

Price Skimming

Price skimming is sometimes called a "market-plus" approach to pricing, because it denotes a high price relative to the prices of competing products. Radius Corporation produces unique oval-headed toothbrushes made of black neoprene that look like a scuba diving accessory. Radius uses a skimming policy, pricing the toothbrushes at $9.95 compared to around $2.00 for a regular toothbrush. Caterpillar sets premium prices on its construction equipment to support and capture its high perceived value. Genentech introduced TPA, a fast-acting agent to clear blood clots that cause heart attacks, at $2,200 a dose. Both Caterpillar and Genentech were also using price skimming.

price skimming
Pricing policy whereby a firm charges a high introductory price, often coupled with heavy promotion.

The term **price skimming** is derived from the phrase "skimming the cream off the top." Companies often use skimming for new products when the product is perceived by the target market as having unique advantages. As the product progresses through its life cycle, the firm may lower its price to successfully reach larger market segments. Economists have described this type of price skimming as "sliding down the demand curve." Not all companies slide down the demand curve. Genentech's TPA was still priced at $2,200 a dose four years after its introduction, despite competition from a much-lower-priced competitor.

Price skimming works best when demand is relatively inelastic in the upper ranges of the curve. If, for example, some purchasing agents feel that Caterpillar equipment is far superior to competitors' products, then premium prices can be charged successfully. Firms can also effectively use price skimming when a product is well protected legally, represents a technological breakthrough, or has in some other way blocked entry to competitors. Managers may also follow a skimming strategy when production cannot be expanded rapidly because of technological difficulties, shortages, or the skill and time required to produce a product. As long as demand is greater than supply, skimming is an attainable strategy.

A successful skimming strategy enables management to recover its product development or "educational" costs quickly. (Often consumers must be "taught" the advantages of a radically new item, such as high-definition TV.) Even if the market

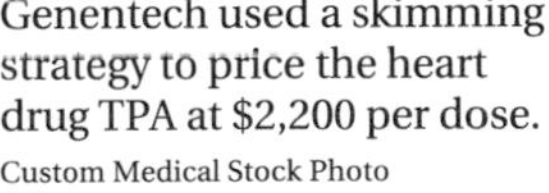
Genentech used a skimming strategy to price the heart drug TPA at $2,200 per dose.
Custom Medical Stock Photo

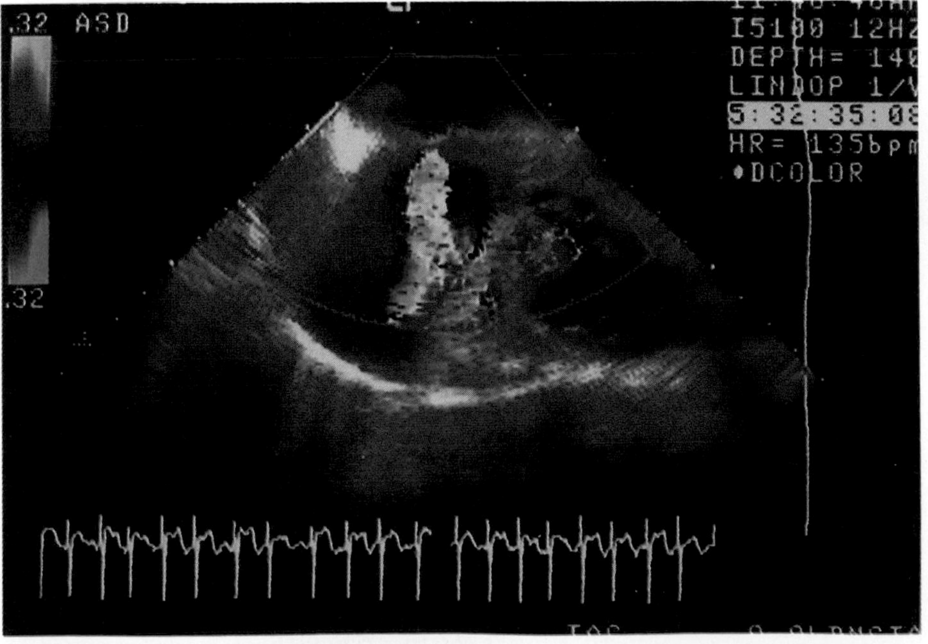

perceives an introductory price as too high, managers can easily correct the problem by lowering the price. Firms often feel it is better to test the market at a high price and then lower the price if sales are too slow. They are tacitly saying, "If there are any premium-price buyers in the market, let's reach them first and maximize our revenue per unit." Naturally, a skimming strategy will encourage competitors to enter the market.

Successful skimming policies are not limited to products. Well-known athletes, entertainers, lawyers, and hair stylists are experts at price skimming. In the overnight delivery industry, World Courier has been a price skimmer for years. It charges three to four times as much as Emory and Federal Express and still thrives. Why? It offers a unique service to a market niche that is willing to pay the price. The customer is most likely to be an international grain shipper, international lawyer, or bank or other financial institution that stands to lose hundreds or thousands of dollars with each day's delay in the delivery of its documents. The bigger shippers generally try to consolidate shipments, but World Courier uses the first available direct flight, even for one piece. Other couriers offer next-day service, but World Courier aims for 10 a.m. delivery everywhere in the world. The company will pick up as late as 8 p.m. in Europe and still guarantee delivery in New York by 9 a.m.

Penetration Pricing

penetration pricing Pricing policy whereby a firm charges a relatively low price for a product as a way to reach the mass market in the early stages of the product life cycle.

Penetration pricing is at the end of the spectrum opposite skimming. **Penetration pricing** means charging a relatively low price for a product as a way to reach the mass market. The low price is designed to capture a large share of the market, resulting in lower production costs. If a marketing manager has made obtaining a large market share the firm's pricing objective, a penetration price policy is a logical choice.

Penetration pricing does mean lower profit per unit, and it therefore requires higher volume to reach the break-even point than would a skimming policy. If reaching a high volume of sales takes a long time, then the recovery of product development costs will also be slow. As you might expect, penetration pricing tends to discourage competition.

A penetration strategy tends to be effective in a more price-sensitive market. Price should decline more rapidly when demand is elastic, since the market can be expanded through a lower price. Also, price sensitivity and greater competitive pressure should lead to a lower initial price and a relatively flat decline later.

Schlitz, founded in 1849, enjoyed a long stint as one of the premium, top-selling U.S. beers in the 1950s and 1960s. But the beer ran into trouble when it started using a quicker, more cost-effective brewing method that earned bad press and perceptions of lower quality. That change, combined with poor marketing, led to seventeen straight years of sales declines. But between 1988 and 1992, Schlitz was gradually repositioned from the premium to the popular-price segment. For many older consumers, Schlitz is still a premium beer. Yet they can buy it for $3.99 a twelve-pack, as opposed to $5.99 or $6.99 for a premium beer. Sales of Schlitz have nearly doubled since 1988—because of penetration pricing.

Shaw Industries, a billion-dollar carpet manufacturer, decided to use penetration pricing to try doubling its sales in two years. Because of its large size, Shaw can buy raw materials (over half the cost of carpet) for 15 to 30 percent less than most rivals. Shaw sells "base-grade" carpet, often found in new homes, at less than $3 a square yard. A rival's *cost* to produce "base-grade" carpet is $4 a yard.[1]

Penetration pricing is the logical choice given an elastic demand curve and low unit costs resulting from economies of mass production. A successful penetration strategy can effectively block entry into the industry. For example, say that Invista Corporation's goal is a 12 percent return on investment. Invista will reach this goal at a sales level of 80,000 units. Also assume that total market demand for the product is only 100,000 units and that any firm entering the industry would have a cost structure similar to Invista's. When Invista achieves its maximization goal by selling 80,000 units at $3.50 each, only 20,000 units of demand will remain for any potential competitor (see Exhibit 19.3). If a competitor entered the market and sold 20,000 units at $3.50 each, the competitor's average cost would be $16.00, for a total loss of $250,000 (average revenue $3.50 – average cost $16.00 = average loss per unit $12.50 × 20,000 units = $250,000 total loss). If economies of mass production are lacking, profitable entry is impossible for almost any new competitor. A well-financed organization would have to be willing to sustain big short-run losses to penetrate the market.

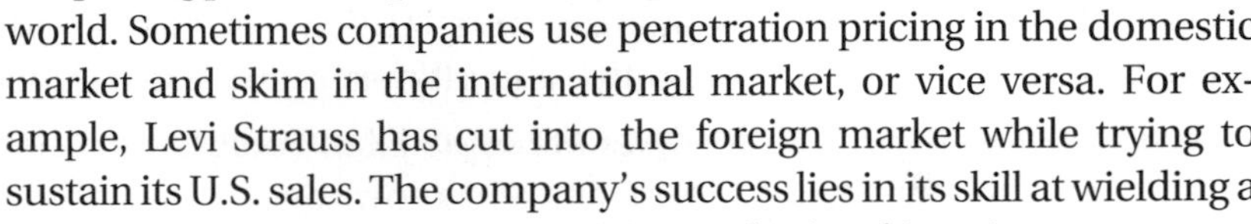

The choice of pricing policies depends on competitive conditions throughout the world. Sometimes companies use penetration pricing in the domestic market and skim in the international market, or vice versa. For example, Levi Strauss has cut into the foreign market while trying to sustain its U.S. sales. The company's success lies in its skill at wielding a double-edged pricing strategy: penetration pricing and price skimming.

Value marketing: The term *value marketing* has become very popular in the 1990s. Value marketing is related to penetration pricing to some degree, but they are not the same thing. Value marketing doesn't simply mean lowering prices or selling below the average market price. Instead, **value marketing** means offering the target market a high-quality product at a fair price and with good service. It is the notion of offering the customer a good value. Value marketing doesn't mean high quality if it's available only at high prices. It doesn't mean cheap when cheap means bare-bones service or low-quality products. Value marketing can be used to sell a $44,000

value marketing
Offering the target market a high-quality product at a fair price and with good service.

Exhibit 19.3

Average Total Cost Curve for Invista Corporation and Potential Competitors

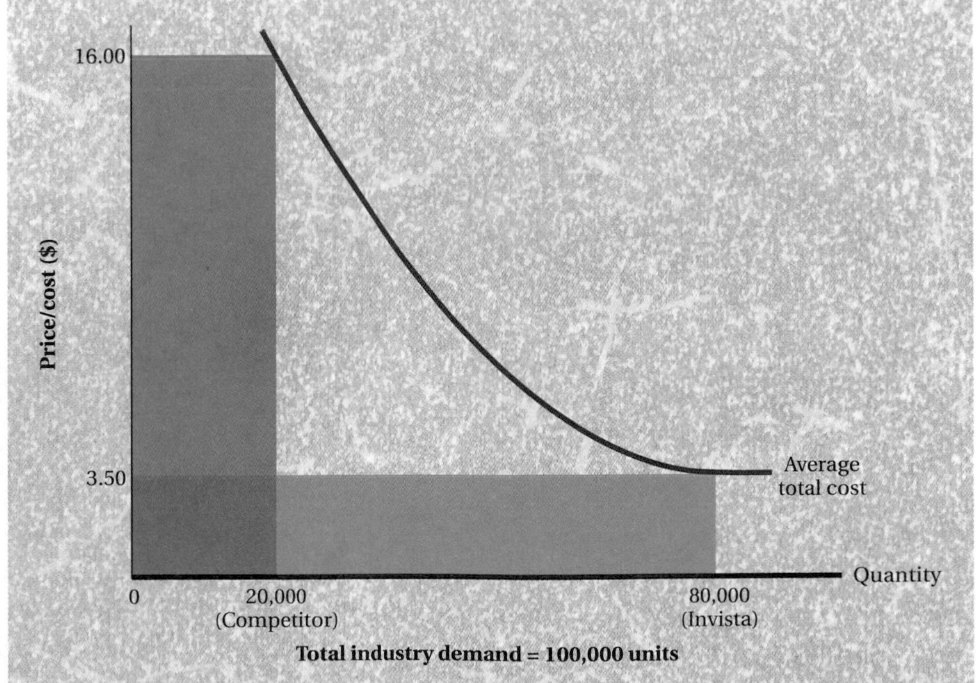

Infiniti Q45 from Nissan. Efficient manufacturing allows high-quality, well-known L'eggs hosiery to be sold at extremely competitive prices.

A value marketer does the following:

- *Offers products that perform:* This is the price of entry, because consumers have lost patience with shoddy merchandise.
- *Gives consumers more than they expect:* Soon after Toyota launched Lexus, the company had to order a recall. The weekend before the recall, dealers phoned every Lexus owner in the United States, personally making arrangements to pick up their cars and offering replacement vehicles.
- *Gives meaningful guarantees:* Chrysler offers a 70,000-mile power train warranty. Michelin recently introduced a tire warranted to last 80,000 miles.
- *Avoids unrealistic pricing:* Consumers couldn't understand why Kellogg's cereals commanded such a premium over other brands, and so Kellogg's market share fell 5 percent in the late 1980s. Compaq maintained a 35 percent price premium over other personal computer brands, even though other IBM compatibles were steadily decreasing in price. Compaq lost market share and profits, and ultimately the CEO resigned.
- *Gives the buyer facts:* Today's sophisticated consumer wants informative advertising and knowledgeable salespeople.
- *Builds long-term relationships:* American Air Lines' AAdvantage program, Hyatt's Passport Club, and Whirlpool's 800-number hot line all help build good customer relations.[2]

Status Quo Pricing

status quo pricing
Pricing objective that seeks to maintain existing prices or simply meet the competition.

The third basic price policy a firm may choose is **status quo pricing,** or meeting competition (see also Chapter 18). If it is the firm's pricing goal, the firm simply charges a price identical to or very close to the competition's price. Montgomery Ward, for example, makes sure it is charging comparable prices by sending representatives to shop at Sears stores.

Although status quo pricing has the advantage of simplicity, its disadvantage is that the strategy may ignore demand or cost or both. But sometimes meeting the competition is the safest route to long-term survival if the firm is comparatively small.

3 THE LEGALITY OF PRICE POLICIES

As we mentioned in Chapter 2, some pricing decisions are subject to government regulation. Therefore, before marketing managers establish any price policy, they should know the laws that limit the scope of their price decision making.

Unfair Trade Practices

unfair trade practice act
State law, passed in over half the states, that prohibits wholesalers and retailers from selling below cost.

In over half the states, **unfair trade practice acts** put a floor under wholesale and retail prices. Selling below cost in these states is illegal. Wholesalers and retailers must usually take a certain minimum percentage markup on their combined merchandise cost and transportation cost. The most common markup figures are 6 percent at the retail level and 2 percent at the wholesale level. If a specific wholesaler or retailer can provide "conclusive proof" that operating costs are lower than the minimum required figure, lower prices may be allowed.

The intent of unfair practice acts is to protect small local firms from giants like Wal-Mart and Target, which operate very efficiently on razor-thin profit margins. However, state enforcement of unfair practice laws has generally been lax, partly because low prices benefit local consumers.

Price Fixing

price fixing
Agreement between two or more firms on the price they will charge for a product.

Two pricing concerns that affect marketing managers are price fixing and illegal price discrimination. **Price fixing** is an agreement between two or more firms on the price they will charge for a product. For example, suppose two or more executives from competing firms meet to decide how much to charge for a product or to decide which of them will bid the lowest on a certain contract. Such practices are illegal under the Sherman Act and the Federal Trade Commission Act.

The standing legal precedent related to price fixing is the Sacony-Vacuum case.[3] The courts ruled in this case that price fixing, or even the attempt to fix prices, is illegal *per se.* That is, the reasonableness or economic impact of the fixed prices is not a defense; the conspiracy itself is illegal. This ruling has been applied to many forms of price setting by competitors. These activities are all illegal *per se:*

- Indirectly raising prices by taking an excess supply of merchandise from another channel
- Maintaining prices by distributing price lists to competitors
- Agreeing on markups or discounts
- For members of professions, like surgeons, publishing and circulating minimum fee schedules within the profession

Offenders have received fines and sometimes prison terms. Price fixing is one area where the law is quite clear, and the Justice Department's enforcement is vigorous.

The Federal Trade Commission (FTC) sought to extend the definition of illegal circumstances to contexts in which no direct illegal secret agreements occur but where market signaling is used to communicate a company's intentions about prices. In the DuPont and Ethyl Corporation case, the FTC ruled that the following

Selling below cost is not illegal if it is justified by changing market conditions.
© 1990 Peter Sibbald

practices were illegal: giving customers more than thirty days' notice of price changes, to allow competitors to know of one's intentions; and granting "most favored customer status" to a company that guarantees a price at least as low as any other, thus discouraging spot discounts.

In 1991 the FTC reached a settlement with Nintendo, the giant home video game producer, which was accused of price fixing. In this unique settlement, Nintendo agreed to issue $25 million in coupons to previous buyers of its games. The coupons could be used to buy other Nintendo products. In addition, the firm agreed to pay $4.75 million in damages and legal costs. A month earlier, Mitsubishi Electric Corporation agreed to refund $8 million to consumers to settle charges that it illegally fixed the retail price of 242,000 television sets. In earlier cases, Minolta Corporation and Panasonic Company were charged with similar antitrust violations.[4] As a result of a previous federal investigation, a class-action lawsuit was filed against the major U.S. airlines for price fixing. The case was settled by the airlines offering discount coupons worth millions of dollars to airline passengers who flew during the late 1980s. The defendants were United, American, Delta, Northwest, and USAir airlines.[5]

Recently, the FTC has dusted off an old law to fight price fixing: Section 5 of the 1914 law that created the FTC, which prohibits "unfair methods of competition" (see Chapter 2). When a company publicly announces it will raise prices, it may illegally signal others to follow suit even though no agreement exists between the firms. The FTC used Section 5 to bring its first "invitation to collude" case. It charged that representatives of Quality Trailer Products Corporation, a Texas axle manufacturer, visited a competitor, American Marine Industries, and invited it to fix prices. Before the case was settled, American Marine went out of business. Quality signed a consent agreement barring it from any future price-fixing solicitations.[6]

Although price fixing is illegal in the United States, Russia's plunge into a market economy has already found price fixing by purported competitors to be quite common, as the International Perspectives article on page 633 explains.

Price Discrimination

The Robinson-Patman Act of 1936 prohibits any firm from selling to two or more different buyers, within a reasonably short time, commodities (not services) of like grade and quality at different prices where the result would be to substantially lessen competition. The Robinson-Patman Act also makes it illegal for a seller to offer two buyers different supplementary services and for buyers to use their purchasing power to force sellers into granting discriminatory prices or services.

Six elements are needed for a violation of the Robinson-Patman Act to occur:

price discrimination
Practice of charging different prices to different customers for the same product.

- There must be **price discrimination**; that is, the seller must charge different prices to different customers for the same product.
- The transaction must occur in interstate commerce.
- The seller must discriminate by price among two or more purchasers; that is, the seller must make two or more actual sales within a reasonably short time.
- The products sold must be commodities or other tangible goods.
- The products sold must be of like grade and quality, not necessarily identical. If the goods are truly interchangeable and substitutable, then they are of like grade and quality.
- There must be significant competitive injury.

The Robinson-Patman Act provides three defenses for the seller charged with

INTERNATIONAL PERSPECTIVES

Price Fixing by Moscow's Capitalists

When Russia adopted a market economy, Vladimir Grechanik, the top financial planner of Moscow's Bread Factory No. 14, went into a panic. After seventy years of government control of everything from the cost of raw materials to salaries, the factory suddenly would be able to set its own prices. He and his fellow producers anxiously tried to calculate how much flour would cost, how much transportation might rise, and what consumers would be willing to pay.

Just before prices were freed, Mr. Grechanik and executives from Moscow's other bread factories were called to a meeting at the Moscow Bread Consortium, the de facto ministry of bread. They eyed one another nervously, suspicious that, after years of mandated equality, the system might make rivals of former comrades. The bread consortium suggested raising the free-market bread price to three-and-a-half times the old price, but not a kopeck more. The factory men were confused. In the old days, such a "suggestion" carried the full weight of a decree. But there were no certainties anymore. The new freedom was unbearable.

Left to his own devices, Mr. Grechanik returned to his office and got on the phone. For the next two days he and the other factory directors discussed their fears. Finally, they came to a decision: If the state was no longer to set prices, the factories themselves would jointly fix them—to ensure their mutual survival. "We all agreed on a single price," says Mr. Grechanik, as he walks past huge vats of flour on the factory floor. Lowering his voice, he confides, "I've heard that Bread Factory No. 26 is charging a little less, but I hope it's just a rumor."

To be sure, there are some emerging signs of free markets, as the monopolies that control prices for each segment of production start to crash against each other. The bread producers are protesting the prices set by the flour-mill conglomerate. The trade conglomerate of bakery stores is revolting against the prices set by bread producers. One store on Moscow's Kalanchovskaya Street has put up a sign over some stale bread at 3.50 rubles—well above the new fixed price—pointedly declaring its source was Factory No. 19. "We want everybody to know where it came from," says Nadeshda Verba, one of the store's employees.

There is one area where price competition seems to be emerging, ever so haltingly: the cake sector. Star Factory, notes Tamara Vlysko, deputy director of the bread consortium, sells its butter-cream *nochkas* for 54 rubles. But the following week, a rival, the Cheremushky Bread and Confectionery Plant, started offering *nochkas* for only 33 rubles. Star Factory's director flew into a rage. But rather than fight back in what might have been this city's first price war, he called Ms. Vlysko, the bureaucrat. "Why didn't you tell me what Cheremushky was charging for *nochkas*!" he sputtered. "No one's buying my cakes!" She suggested he might want to lower his price.

Do you think that plunging into a free-market economy without first educating plant managers was a good idea? Should Russia set up an equivalent of our Federal Trade Commission? Do you think Russia can really convert into a market economy? What about in the next ten years?

Source: Adapted from Laurie Hays and Adi Ignatius, "Moscow's Capitalists Decide the Best Price Is a Firmly Fixed One," *The Wall Street Journal*, 21 January 1992, pp. A1, A17. Reprinted by permission of *The Wall Street Journal*.

price discrimination, described below. In each case the burden is on the defendant to prove the defense.

- *Cost justification:* A firm can charge different prices to different customers if the prices represent manufacturing or quantity discount savings. In terms of manufacturing, however, the courts have been willing to accept only price differentials resulting from transportation efficiencies, which can easily be verified from bills of lading. The courts generally have not viewed manufacturing efficiencies as a good reason for price differentials because of the difficulty in determining exactly the cost of specified units of a mass-produced product.
- *Changing market conditions:* Price variations are justified if designed to meet fluid product or market conditions. Examples include the deterioration of perishable goods, the obsolescence of seasonal products, a distress sale under

court order, or a legitimate going-out-of-business sale. For example, a fresh produce warehouse may change its prices from one day to the next or even from one customer to the next, depending on the freshness of its fruits and vegetables. However, a shoe warehouse engaging in similar behavior might be viewed as practicing price discrimination. The courts have been rather liberal in accepting such a defense so as not to limit a firm's flexibility in responding to changing product or market conditions.

- *Meeting competition:* A reduction in price may be necessary to stay even with the competition. Specifically, if a competitor undercuts the price quoted by a seller to a buyer, the law authorizes the seller to lower the price charged to the buyer for the product in question. Since the seller may elect not to reduce the price for all customers in a competitive area, price discrimination is being practiced. The courts have been willing to accept this defense as long as the seller reduces the price to that of the competition, not less.

Predatory Pricing

predatory pricing
Practice of charging a very low price for a product with the intent of driving competitors out of business or out of a market.

Predatory pricing is the practice of charging a very low price for a product with the intent of driving competitors out of business or out of a market. Once competitors have been driven out, the firm raises its prices. This practice is illegal under the Sherman Act and the Federal Trade Commission Act.

Proving the use of this practice is difficult and expensive, however. A defendant must show that the predator, the destructive company, explicitly tried to ruin a competitor and that the predatory price was below the defendant's average cost. Consider this example:

> In 1990, the courts ordered Brown and Williamson Tobacco Company (B&W), makers of Belaire, Raleigh, Viceroy, and Kool, to pay $148.8 million to the Liggett Group Incorporated, producers of L&M, Lark, and Chesterfields, for predatory pricing. In the early 1980s, Liggett's market share had slipped to 2 percent (from 21 percent in 1950) because it had failed to realize the popularity of full-length filter cigarettes. The company had formulated plans to close down the company when it discovered generic cigarettes.
>
> By early 1984, Liggett was producing about 20 billion generic cigarettes a year, 65 percent of its volume. Thanks to these cigarettes, its market share more than doubled in three years. At the same time, demand for cigarettes in general was edging downward as the health dangers were finally sinking in. Trying to attract new smokers to B&W's brands seemed a losing proposition. The problem was how to knock out Liggett without setting off a price war that would stimulate demand for bargain smokes—and jeopardize the monopoly level profits flowing from name brands because of copycat pricing.
>
> B&W's internal planning documents take considerable shine off its corporate image by matter of factly describing a plan to put its smaller competitor in a hammerlock and then apply the pressure. Its Project G (as in Generics) involved introducing low-priced cigarettes in packs designed just like Liggett's, offering wholesalers huge rebates to purchase from B&W rather than Liggett, and then driving the financially weak Liggett from the field. It was so explicit—and repeated so often—that the judge in the case later called the documents "smoking guns" and mused that "I don't think [Liggett] could have imagined some of this stuff that's been written down."[7]

4 FINE-TUNING THE BASE PRICE WITH PRICING TACTICS

After managers understand both the legal and the marketing consequences of alternative price policies, they should set a specific price policy. The final step is to fine-

base price
General price level at which the company expects to sell the good or service.

tune the base price. The **base price** is the general price level at which the company expects to sell the good or service (recall the car example in Exhibit 19.2). The general price level, in turn, is correlated to the pricing strategy: above the market (price skimming), at the market (status quo pricing), or below the market (penetration pricing).

Fine-tuning techniques are often short-run approaches that do not change the general price level. They do, however, result in changes within a general price level. Pricing tactics allow the firm to adjust for competition in certain markets, meet ever-changing government regulations, take advantage of unique demand situations, and meet promotional and positioning goals. A discussion of several categories of fine-tuning pricing tactics—including discounts, geographic pricing, and special pricing tactics—follows.

Discounts, Allowances, and Rebates

A base price can be lowered through the use of discounts, allowances, and rebates. Discounts take a variety of forms and have several different objectives. Managers use this tactic to encourage customers to do what they would not ordinarily do—such as paying cash rather than using credit, taking delivery out of season, or performing certain functions within a distribution channel.

Cash Discounts

cash discount
Price reduction offered to a consumer, industrial user, or marketing intermediary in return for prompt payment of a bill.

A **cash discount** is a price reduction offered to a consumer, an industrial user, or a marketing intermediary in return for prompt payment of a bill. Prompt payment saves the seller carrying charges and billing expenses, and it avoids bad debt.

Quantity Discounts

quantity discount
Price reduction offered to buyers buying in multiple units or above a specified dollar amount.

Probably the most common form of discount is the quantity discount. When buyers get a lower price for buying in multiple units or above a specified dollar amount, they are receiving a **quantity discount.** In theory, the quantity discount is based on the savings in transportation and other costs realized by the seller.[8] Sellers offering quantity discounts also need to locate fewer buyers for the same number of units.

Sellers can offer quantity discounts on slow-moving items to increase their sales potential. Wholesalers can also use these discounts to discourage retailers from buying directly from the manufacturer. If the discount is close to what the retailers might receive by going directly to the manufacturer, they may continue to buy from the wholesalers.

By offering larger quantity discounts than competitors, a firm can often gain profits and market share. For example, AT&T historically relied on systemwide averaging of costs and prices. The resulting AT&T rates seldom considered differences in traffic density among long-distance routes. However, heavily used routes had much lower unit costs and were much more profitable. These were precisely the routes that MCI targeted with its Execunet long-distance service. Execunet was designed to appeal to large customers by offering deep discounts for high volume. This tactic enabled MCI to grow rapidly at the expense of AT&T.[9]

cumulative quantity discount
Deduction from list price that applies to the buyer's total purchases made during a specific period; it is intended to encourage customer loyalty.

MCI's discount on Execunet was a cumulative quantity discount. A **cumulative quantity discount** is a deduction from list price that applies to the buyer's total purchases made during a specific period; it is intended to encourage customer loyalty. The buyer's purchases are totaled at the end of the period, and the discount

received depends on the quantity (dollars or units) bought during that period. The discount percentage usually increases as the quantity purchased increases.

noncumulative quantity discount
Deduction from list price that applies to a single order rather than to the total volume of orders placed during a certain period.

In contrast, a **noncumulative quantity discount** is a deduction from list price that applies to a single order rather than to the total volume of orders placed during a certain period. It is intended to encourage orders in large quantities. The size of this discount generally increases with the size of the order. The purpose is to reward buyers whose purchase patterns help the seller reduce costs. Specifically, as the size of the buyer's order increases, the seller can ship the product in a more efficient way. For example, Coleman Products offers retailers quantity discounts on its outdoor products. The discount is substantial when a retailer orders enough merchandise to fill an entire trailer. By driving a single trailer from its Kansas plant to a retailer's warehouse, Coleman reaps big savings on transportation costs.

Functional Discounts

A third common form of discount is the functional discount. When distribution channel intermediaries, such as wholesalers or retailers, perform a service or function for the manufacturer, they must be compensated. This compensation, typically a percentage discount from the base price, is called a **functional discount** (or **trade discount**).

functional discount (trade discount)
Discount to wholesalers and retailers for performing channel functions.

Functional discounts vary greatly from channel to channel, depending on the tasks performed by the channel intermediary. A typical discount schedule is a retail list price of $500 and discounts of 45 percent and 8 percent. The retailer's cost will be $275 ($500 minus 45 percent). The wholesaler will pay $253 ($275 minus 8 percent). Note that the total discount is not 53 percent off the list price:

$$\$500 \times .53 = \$265$$

$$\$500 - \$265 = \$235$$

At 53 percent off the list price, the cost to the wholesaler would have been $235 instead of $253. Instead, discounts are figured on a chain basis from one level of the distribution channel to the next.

Trade Loading and Everyday Low Prices

trade loading
Practice of temporarily lowering the price to induce wholesalers and retailers to buy more goods than can be sold in a reasonable time.

Trade loading occurs when a manufacturer temporarily lowers the price to induce wholesalers and retailers to buy more goods than can be sold in a reasonable time. Trade loading is most common in consumer packaged goods. An estimated $100 billion in grocery products, mostly nonperishables, sit at any one time on trucks and railcars or stacked inside distribution centers, caught in gridlock due to trade loading. This idle inventory is estimated to add about $20 billion a year to the nation's $400 billion grocery bill.[10]

Assume that Procter & Gamble offers Super Valu an additional 30¢ off the normal $2.65 price per bottle of Prell. The Super Valu buyer jumps at the bargain and buys a three-month supply of Prell. Typically, Super Valu would sell Prell for $2.35 for about a month and then raise the price back to $2.65 for the last two months. It is estimated that such practices generate about 70 percent of wholesalers' profits and 40 percent of supermarkets'.[11] Wholesalers and retailers have understandably become addicted to trade-loading deals.

Trade loading ultimately costs consumers (and manufacturers) money, as shown in Exhibit 19.4. It "whipsaws" production and distribution and increases the manufacturer's costs.

Exhibit 19.4

The Costs of Trade Loading

Source: Adapted from Patricia Sellers, "The Dumbest Marketing Ploy," *Fortune*, 3 October 1992, pp. 88–89. © 1992 Time Inc. All rights reserved.

With trade loading

The manufacturer stockpiles ingredients and packaging supplies to meet peak production levels.

Plants prepare huge runs. Scheduling is chaotic, with more overtime and temporary workers.

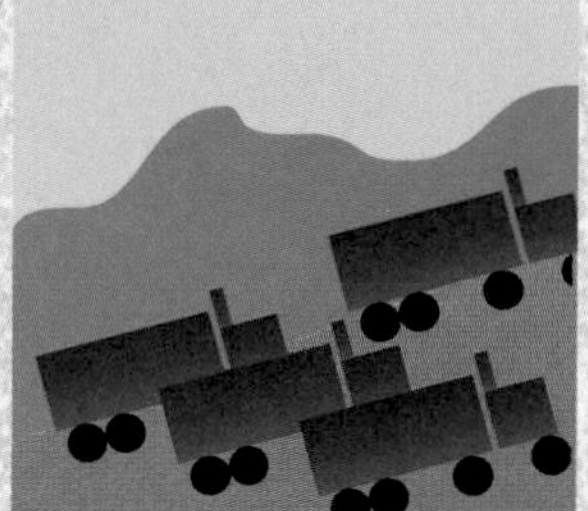

Freight companies charge premium rates for the manufacturer's periodic blow-out shipments.

Distributors overstock as they binge on short-term discounts. Cartons sit for weeks inside warehouses.

At distribution centers, the goods get overhandled. Damaged items go back to the manufacturer.

Twelve weeks after the items leave the production line, they may not be fresh for the consumer.

Without trade loading

No more panic purchases are necessary. The company cuts down on inventories, freeing up cash.

Factories run on normal shifts. The company cuts down on overtime pay and supplemental workers.

The manufacturer eliminates peak-and-valley distribution. That helps it save 5 percent in shipping costs.

Wholesalers' inventories get cut in half. That means storage and handling costs decline 17 percent.

Retailers receive undamaged products. Their perception of the manufacturer's quality improves.

The consumer gets the goods twenty-five days earlier, and—even better news—at a 6 percent lower price.

Trade discounts have more than tripled in the past decade, to around $37 billion in 1992.[12] Procter & Gamble estimates it has created over $1 billion worth of unproductive inventory that has sat in P&G's distribution pipeline. Moreover, P&G's chairman Edward Anzt notes,

> Trade loading has caused the erosion of consumer loyalty. As retailers and wholesalers buy on deals and discounts, they pass wide price swings to consumers in an unpredictable pattern, and these shoppers, no dummies, increasingly "forward buy" themselves. "People have reached the point where they won't buy unless a product is on sale. Shopping store to store for the best deal, they bulk up on whichever item—P&G's Crest or Colgate-Palmolive's Colgate, P&G's Tide or Lever Brothers' Wisk—is on promotion that week."[13]

everyday low price (EDLP)
Pricing tactic of permanently reducing prices 10 to 15 percent below the traditional levels while eliminating trade discounts that create trade loading.

P&G, the largest U.S. packaged-goods manufacturer, has decided to attack the trade-loading problem with **everyday low prices** (EDLP). EDLP is the tactic of offering lower prices (10 to 25 percent lower) and maintaining those prices while eliminating functional discounts that result in trade loading. Instead of selling, say, a case of cake mix for $10.00 most of the time and then $7.00 to load the trade, P&G will sell the case for $8.50 all the time. By 1993 the company had introduced EDLP on about half its lines, including cake mixes, liquid laundry detergents, dishwashing liquids, fabric softener sheets, toilet tissue, and automatic dishwasher detergents. List prices have fallen 8 to 25 percent on items like Mr Clean, Jif peanut butter, and Pert shampoo. P&G plans EDLP for all its products.

EDLP has sent the nation's wholesalers and retailers into shock, because it eliminates a major source of their profits. Dealers have started to fight back. Chains with thousands of stores—such as Rite-Aid drugstores, A&P, and Safeway—are pruning their variety of P&G sizes or eliminating marginal brands, such as Prell and Gleem. Super Valu, the nation's largest wholesaler, which also runs some stores, is adding surcharges to some P&G products and paring back orders to compensate for profits it says it's losing under the new pricing system. Meanwhile, Certified Grocers, a Midwestern wholesaler, has dropped about 50 of the 300 P&G varieties it stocked. Many other chains are considering moving P&G brands from prime eye-level space to less visible shelves. In P&G's place will be more profitable private-label brands and competitors' varieties.

P&G has created a pay-for-performance fee in an attempt to quell the discontent. This fee can be earned by distributors who sell a target quantity of a specific brand over a six-month period.

Will EDLP work for packaged-goods manufacturers? Quaker Oats, Duracell, and (on a limited basis) Kraft General Foods decided to find out. Others, like Ralston Purina and Colgate-Palmolive, did not change their pricing tactics. A Colgate-Palmolive spokesperson said, "We will continue to deal with customers as they wish to be dealt with."[14]

Seasonal Discounts

seasonal discount
Price reduction offered to buyers purchasing merchandise out of season.

A **seasonal discount** is a price reduction for buying merchandise out of season. It shifts the storage function to the purchaser. Seasonal discounts also enable manufacturers to maintain a steady production schedule year-round. For instance, to keep its sewing crew employed full-time, Jantzen swimwear offers seasonal discounts to retail stores in the fall and winter. One of the most familiar examples of a seasonal discount is the half-price sale on Christmas decorations that begins December 26.

It is true that sellers may not cover total costs when they offer deep seasonal

discounts. However, as long as sellers cover variable costs and make a contribution to fixed costs, the total loss will be reduced.

Promotional Allowances

promotional allowance
Payment to a dealer for promoting the manufacturer's products.

A **promotional allowance** is a payment to a dealer for promoting the manufacturer's products. It is both a pricing tool and a promotional device. As a pricing tool, a promotional allowance is like a functional discount. If, for example, a retailer runs an ad for a manufacturer's product, the manufacturer may pay half the cost. If a retailer sets up a special display, the manufacturer may include a certain quantity of free goods in the retailer's next order. For example, Kraft General Foods regularly gives Kroger and other supermarket chains free cases of food products for performing specified services.

Like other forms of discounts, promotional allowances must be made available to all buyers on essentially the same terms. The Robinson-Patman Act bans differences in promotional allowances to similar purchasers of similar goods. For instance, suppose two retailers each buy twenty cases of soap. If one receives a $50 promotional allowance and the other receives $20, the transaction is illegal.

Rebates

rebate
Cash refund given for the purchase of a product during a specific period.

A **rebate** is a cash refund given for the purchase of a product during a specific period. Rebates have become so common in the automobile industry that consumers find it unusual when a rebate is not offered.

The advantage of a rebate over a simple price reduction for stimulating demand is that a rebate is a temporary inducement that can be taken away without altering the basic price structure. A manufacturer that uses a simple price reduction for a short time may meet resistance when trying to restore the price to its original higher level. However, with rebates the price on the product remains constant, and the consumer may be less resistant to paying the regularly marked price once the rebate is discontinued.

Today manufacturers offer several different types of rebates—for example, instant rebates, product rebates, and mail-in rebates. The *instant rebate* gives the consumer a refund at the time of purchase. For example, a jar of Jif peanut butter might have a peel-off rebate coupon that says, "25¢ off this jar of Jif now." A *product rebate* gives an extra product to the consumer, usually at the time of purchase. For instance, a can of Folger's coffee may have a free package of nondairy creamer attached to it. *Mail-in rebates* offer cash to consumers as a purchase incentive. To qualify for the mail-in rebate, consumers must often collect the proof of purchase required by the rebate offer, such as a label, bar code, or cash register receipt. They mail in proof to the company within a certain time limit and then wait up to eight weeks to receive the rebate.[15]

When is a sale price really a discount from a "normal price"? That is the question that regulators across the United States are asking. Sometimes prices that seem to be discounts or rebates really aren't reduced prices at all. The Ethics in Marketing article on page 640 discusses the legal implications of offering misleading prices.

Geographic Pricing

Since many sellers ship their wares to a nationwide or even a worldwide market, the cost of freight can greatly affect the total cost of a product. Sellers may use several different geographic pricing tactics to moderate the impact of freight costs on distant customers.

ETHICS IN MARKETING

The Illusive Discount Price

In 1990 Massachusetts enacted a law that covers retailers on such matters as price comparison claims, price and quality disclosure, and the availability of merchandise advertised as marked down. Also under the rule, sales advertised in retail catalogs, which are printed months in advance, must disclose that the so-called original price is really only a reference price and not necessarily the actual former selling price.

Recently, three St. Louis furniture stores agreed to pay $352,000 in restitution to consumers under settlements negotiated by the Missouri attorney general's office. The state alleged that when advertising their sale prices, the stores had boosted the manufacturer's suggested retail price. Under the settlement, around 2,500 consumers received average refunds of $150 on furniture they had purchased earlier from the stores.

In Colorado, May Department Stores were found guilty of misleading consumers by offering sale prices for a limited time only. In reality, they offered such prices "continuously throughout most calendar periods." The state also alleged that May used preprinted price tags with inflated regular prices, which "deceptively convey the impression" that those prices were "genuine regular selling prices."

The State of New York filed a major lawsuit against Sears that charged Sears with creating "the false impression that its 'everyday low prices' represent substantial discounts from its former prices" when it "actually has offered consumers no significant savings." Sears claimed that its new prices ranged between its old "regular" and "sale" prices. Sears urged shoppers to "think of it as a sale that never ends!" But New York State contends in its suit that the ads deceived consumers because the old "sale" prices were often "the true regular prices" at which most goods were sold. The suit alleged, for example, that the retailer sold only 14 Kenmore microwave ovens at its regular price, compared with 7,576 sold at its sale price. Moreover, only 6 Kenmore canister vacuums were sold at the regular price, compared with 1,512 sold at the sale price.

What can the consumer do to determine whether the discount price is genuine? Should store managers and others responsible for deceptive pricing be sent to jail, or should the store simply be fined? What should the retailing industry do to clean up its act?

FOB Origin Pricing

FOB origin pricing
Price tactic that requires the buyer to absorb the freight costs from the shipping point.

FOB origin pricing, also called FOB factory or FOB shipping point, is a price tactic that requires the buyer to absorb the freight costs from the shipping point. It means that the goods are placed *free on board* a carrier. At that point title passes to the buyer, who pays for transportation charges. Any damage claim beyond the point of origin must be filed by the purchaser against the common carrier.

A manager using FOB origin pricing is either unconcerned about total costs varying among the firm's clients or does not view freight charges as a significant price variable. In other words, freight expenses are the buyer's problem, not the seller's.

FOB pricing treats all buyers equally. There is no geographic price discrimination. The farther buyers are from sellers, the more they pay, because transportation costs generally increase with the distance merchandise is shipped. Many industrial products, such as Lorain Hydraulic Cranes and Westinghouse auxiliary power plants, are priced FOB factory.

Uniform Delivered Pricing

uniform delivered pricing
Price tactic in which the seller pays the actual freight charges and bills every purchaser an identical, flat freight charge.

If the marketing manager wants total costs, including freight, to be equal for all purchasers of identical products, the firm will adopt uniform delivered pricing, or "postage stamp pricing." With **uniform delivered pricing,** the seller pays the actual freight charges and bills every purchaser an identical, flat freight charge. This policy equalizes the total cost for all buyers, regardless of their location.

Naturally, uniform delivered pricing discriminates in favor of buyers located far away from the seller but eliminates price competition among buyers. All buyers pay the same total price for the product. For example, although a store offering free delivery in an urban area has lower transportation costs for goods shipped to customers nearer the store than for those shipped to distant ones, customers pay the same delivered price.

Management may use this policy when a firm is trying to maintain a nationally advertised price. Uniform delivered pricing is also common when transportation charges are a minor part of total costs. The uniform delivered pricing policy is rather easy to administer and, according to the FTC, is not illegal.

Zone Pricing

zone pricing
Modification of uniform delivered pricing that divides the United States (or the total market) into segments or zones and charges a flat freight rate to all customers in a given zone.

A marketing manager who wants to equalize total costs among buyers within large geographic areas—but not necessarily all of the seller's market area—may modify the base price with a zone pricing tactic. **Zone pricing** is a modification of uniform delivered pricing. Rather than placing the entire United States (or its total market) under a uniform freight rate, the firm divides it into segments or zones (see Exhibit 19.5) and charges a flat freight rate to all customers in a given zone.

The U.S. Postal Service's parcel post rate structure is probably the best-known zone pricing system in the country. Because of increased freight costs, customers of Boston Natural Homes who are located in zone 1 might pay $500 per unit freight; those in zone 2, $1,000; and those in zone 3, $2,000. The zone pricing policy discriminates against the buyers who are closest to the seller within any given zone. A Boston Natural Homes buyer located in Indianapolis pays the same rate as a buyer in Amarillo, although the Amarillo buyer is over 900 miles farther from Boston than the Indianapolis buyer. Consequently, the Indianapolis buyer may seek another seller. Another problem of zone pricing is deciding where to place zone boundaries. A Cleveland buyer pays $500 freight, whereas the Indianapolis purchaser must pay $1,000—a 100 percent increase.

Exhibit 19.5

Zone Prices for Boston Natural Homes Delivery

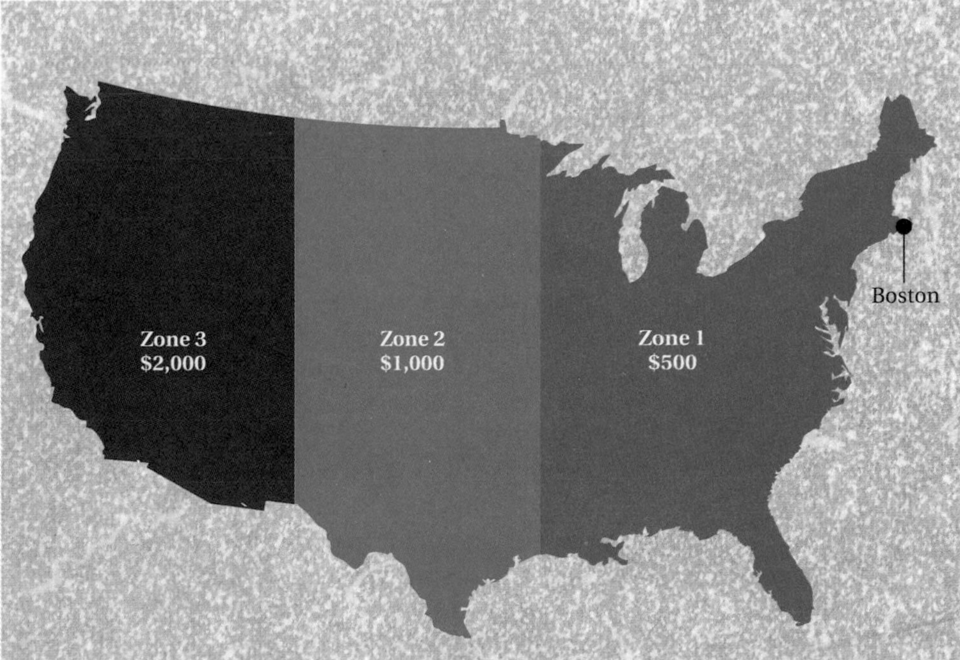

Freight Absorption Pricing

freight absorption pricing
Price tactic in which the seller pays all or part of the actual freight charges and does not pass them on to the buyer.

In **freight absorption pricing,** the seller pays all or part of the actual freight charges and does not pass them on to the buyer. The manager may use this tactic in intensely competitive areas or as a way to break into new market areas. A seller may follow this policy to achieve greater economies of scale. If the economies of scale are greater than the absorbed freight costs, the firm's total profits will increase. For example, K-Tel, the television direct marketer of golden oldies, employs this tactic.

Basing-Point Pricing

basing-point price
Price that incorporates the freight cost from a given (basing) point, regardless of the city from which the goods are shipped.

With a **basing-point price**, the seller designates a location as a basing point and charges all buyers the freight cost from that point, regardless of the city from which the goods are shipped. For instance, if Boston Overhead Cranes (BOC) used Louisville as its basing point and sold an overhead crane to a firm located in Syracuse, the buyer would pay freight charges from Louisville—even if the merchandise was shipped from BOC's Boston manufacturing facility.

Thanks to several adverse court rulings, basing-point pricing has waned in popularity. Freight fees charged when none were actually incurred, called phantom freight, have been declared illegal.

Basing-point pricing has been prevalent in the steel, cement, lead, corn oil, linseed oil, wood pulp, sugar, gypsum board, and plywood industries, as well as many others. Firms that most often adopt the basing-point system sell relatively homogeneous products and consider transportation costs an important part of total costs. Instead of a single basing point, they use multiple basing points.

Special Pricing Tactics

Unlike geographic pricing, special pricing tactics are unique and defy neat categorization. Managers use these tactics for various reasons—for example, to stimulate demand for specific products, to increase store patronage, and to offer a wider variety of merchandise at a specific price point. Special pricing tactics include a single-price tactic, flexible pricing, professional services pricing, price lining, leader pricing, bait pricing, odd-even pricing, price bundling, and two-part pricing. A brief overview of each of these tactics follows, along with a manager's reasons for using one or several tactics to change the base price.

Single-Price Tactic

single-price tactic
Policy of offering all goods and services at the same price.

A merchant using a **single-price tactic** offers all goods and services at the same price (or perhaps two or three prices). Retailers using this tactic include One Price Clothing Stores, Dre$$ to the Nine$, Your $10 Store, and Fashions $9.99. One Price Clothing Stores, for example, tend to be small—about 3,000 square feet. Their goal is to offer merchandise that would sell for at least $15 to $18 in other stores. The stores carry pants, shirts, blouses, sweaters, and shorts for juniors, misses, and large-sized women. The stores do not feature any seconds or irregular items, and everything is sold for $6.

Single-price selling removes price comparisons from the buyer's decision-making process. The consumer just looks for suitability and the highest perceived quality. The retailer enjoys the benefits of a simplified pricing system and minimal clerical errors. However, continually rising costs are a headache for retailers following this strategy. In times of inflation, they must frequently raise the selling price. The recession of the early 1990s resulted in the rapid growth of single-price chains.[16]

Stores like this one price every item the same, simplifying consumers' purchase decision. A single-price strategy has many benefits for retailers as well, although rapidly rising costs may create some headaches.

flexible pricing (variable pricing)
Price tactic in which different customers pay different prices for essentially the same merchandise bought in equal quantities.

Flexible Pricing

Flexible pricing (or **variable pricing**) means that different customers pay different prices for essentially the same merchandise bought in equal quantities. This tactic is often found in the sale of shopping goods, specialty merchandise, and most industrial goods except supply items. Car dealers, many appliance retailers, and manufacturers of industrial installations, accessories, and component parts commonly follow this practice. It allows the seller to adjust for competition by meeting another seller's price. Thus a marketing manager with a status quo pricing objective might readily adopt this tactic. Flexible pricing also enables the seller to close a sale with price-conscious consumers. If buyers show promise of becoming large-volume shoppers, flexible pricing can be used to lure their business.

The obvious disadvantages of flexible pricing are the lack of consistent profit margins, the potential ill will of high-paying purchasers, the tendency for salespeople to automatically lower the price to make a sale, and the possibility of a price war among sellers. The disadvantages of flexible pricing have led the automobile industry to experiment with one price for all buyers. Ford started offering the Cougar at one price and has seen an 80 percent increase in sales. General Motors uses a one-price tactic for the Saturn and the Buick Regal.[17]

Professional Services Pricing

Professional services pricing is used by people with lengthy experience, training, and often certification by a licensing board—for example, lawyers, physicians, and family counselors. Sometimes professional service fees are based on the solution of a problem of performance of an act (such as an eye examination) rather than on the actual time involved. A surgeon may perform a heart operation and charge a flat fee of $5,000. The operation itself may require only four hours, resulting in a hefty $1,250 hourly rate. The physician justifies the fee because of the lengthy education and internship required to learn the complex procedures of a heart operation. Lawyers also sometimes use flat-rate pricing, such as $500 for completing a divorce and $50 for handling a traffic ticket.

Those who use professional pricing have an ethical responsibility not to overcharge a customer. Because demand is sometimes highly inelastic, such as when a person requires heart surgery or a daily insulin shot to survive, there may be a temptation to charge "all the traffic will bear." Recall the Ethics in Marketing article on Johnson & Johnson's drug levamisole in Chapter 18. Drug companies claim that they charge ethical prices rather than all the traffic will bear. They say prices for new drugs need to be high to recover the research costs incurred in developing the drugs.

Price Lining

price lining
Practice of offering a product line with several items at specific price points.

When a seller establishes a series of prices for a type of merchandise, it creates a price line. **Price lining** is the practice of offering a product line with several items at specific price points. For example, Hon, an office furniture manufacturer, may offer its four-drawer file cabinets at $125, $250, and $400. The Limited may offer women's dresses at $40, $70, and $100, with no merchandise marked at prices between those figures. Instead of a normal demand curve running from $40 to $100, The Limited has three demand points (prices). Theoretically, the "curve" exists only because people would buy goods at the in-between prices if it were possible to do so. For example, a number of dresses could be sold at $60, but no sales will occur at that price because $60 is not part of the price line.

Price lining reduces confusion for both the salesperson and the consumer. The buyer may be offered a wider variety of merchandise at each established price. Price lines may also enable a seller to reach several market segments. For buyers, the question of price may be quite simple: All they have to do is find a suitable product at the predetermined price. Moreover, price lining is a valuable tactic for the marketing manager, because the firm may be able to carry a smaller total inventory than it could without price lines. The results may include fewer markdowns, simplified purchasing, and lower inventory carrying charges.

Price lines also present drawbacks, especially if costs are continually rising. Sellers can offset rising costs in three ways. First, they can begin stocking lower-quality merchandise at each price point. Second, sellers can change the prices, although frequent price line changes confuse buyers. Third, sellers can accept lower profit margins and hold quality and prices constant. This third alternative has short-run benefits, but its long-run handicaps may drive sellers out of business.

Sellers face another major problem: trying to decide where to place the prices within a line. If the prices are too close together, buyers may wonder why the price of one article is higher than another. If the price lines are too far apart, the dealer may lose a customer who is looking for a price (and quality) somewhere between the existing prices. Also, salespeople will find it difficult to "trade up" customers (persuade them to buy higher-priced merchandise) if the price lines are too far apart.

Leader Pricing

leader pricing (loss-leader pricing)
Price tactic in which a product is sold near or even below cost in the hope that shoppers will buy other items once they are in the store.

Leader pricing (or **loss-leader pricing**) is an attempt by the marketing manager to attract customers by selling a product near or even below cost, hoping that shoppers will buy other items once they are in the store. This type of pricing appears weekly in the newspaper advertising of supermarkets, specialty stores, and department stores. Leader pricing is normally used on well-known items that consumers can easily recognize as bargains at the special price. The goal is not necessarily to sell large quantities of leader items but to try to appeal to customers who might shop elsewhere.

Bait Pricing

bait pricing
Price tactic that tries to get consumers into a store through false or misleading price advertising and then uses high-pressure selling to persuade consumers to buy more expensive merchandise.

In contrast to leader pricing, which is a genuine attempt to give the consumer a reduced price, bait pricing is deceptive. **Bait pricing** tries to get the consumer into a store through false or misleading price advertising and then uses high-pressure selling to persuade the consumer to buy more expensive merchandise. You may have seen this ad or a similar one:

> REPOSSESSED . . . Singer slant-needle sewing machine . . . take over 8 payments of $5.10 per month . . . ABC Sewing Center.

This is bait. When a customer goes in to see the machine, it has just been sold, or else a salesperson shows the prospective buyer a piece of junk no one would buy. Then the salesperson says, "But I've got a really good deal on this fine new model." This is the switch that may cause a susceptible consumer to walk out with a $400 machine. The Federal Trade Commission considers bait pricing a deceptive act and has banned its use in interstate commerce. Most states also ban bait pricing, but sometimes enforcement is lax.

Odd-Even Pricing

odd-even pricing (psychological pricing)
Price tactic that uses odd-numbered prices to denote bargains and even-numbered prices to imply quality.

Odd-even pricing (or **psychological pricing**) means pricing at odd-numbered prices to denote bargains and pricing at even-numbered prices to imply quality. For years many retailers have used this pricing tactic by pricing their products at odd numbers—for example, $99.95 or $49.95—to make consumers feel they are paying a lower price for the product.

Some retailers favor odd-numbered prices, believing that $9.99 sounds much less imposing to customers than $10.00. Other retailers believe that the use of an odd-numbered price signals to consumers that the price is at the lowest level possible, thereby encouraging them to buy more units. Neither theory has ever been conclusively proved, although one study found that consumers perceive odd-priced products as being on sale.[18]

Odd-even pricing curiously affects demand. Since people buy more at odd-numbered prices (such as $49.95), demand will be relatively elastic for odd-numbered prices and then inelastic for even-numbered prices, as shown in the downward slope of the demand curve in Exhibit 19.6. Such a situation creates a sawtoothed demand curve. Odd-numbered prices stimulate demand, and even-numbered prices curtail demand.

Exhibit 19.6

The Effects of Odd-Even Pricing

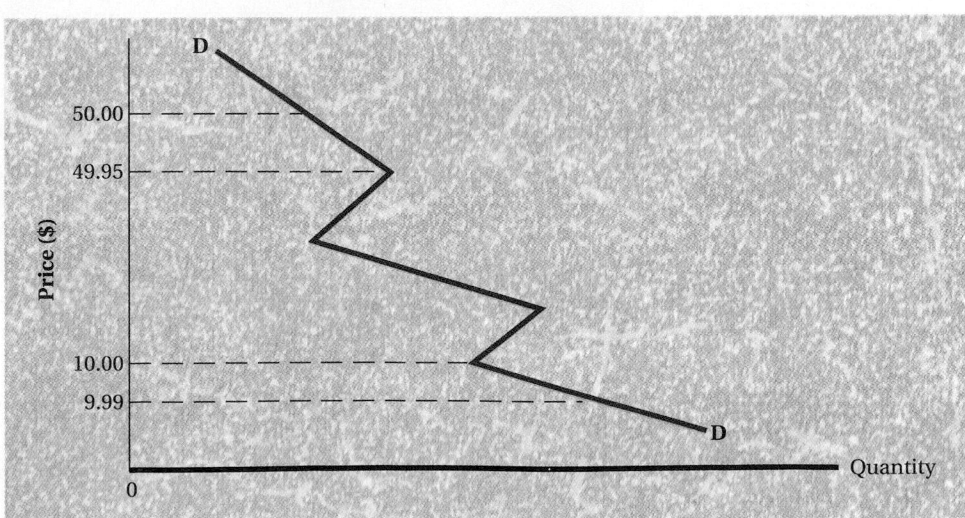

Even-numbered pricing is sometimes used to denote quality. Examples include a fine perfume at $100 a bottle, a good watch at $500, or a mink coat at $3,000. The demand curve for such items would also be sawtoothed, except that the outside edges would represent even-numbered prices and, therefore, elastic demand.

Price Bundling

price bundling
Marketing two or more products in a single package for a special price.

Price bundling is marketing two or more products in a single package for a special price. Examples include the sale of maintenance contracts with computer hardware and other office equipment, packages of stereo equipment, packages of options on cars, weekend hotel packages that include a room and several meals, and airline vacation packages. Lotus now offers "suites" of software that bundle spreadsheets, word processing, graphics, electronic mail, and groupware for networks of PCs.

Price bundling can stimulate demand for the bundled items if the target market perceives the price as a good value. Services like hotels and airlines sell a perishable commodity (hotel rooms and airline seats) with relatively constant fixed costs. Bundling can be an important income stream for these businesses because the variable cost tends to be low—for instance, the cost of cleaning a hotel room or putting one more passenger on an airplane.[19] Therefore, most of the revenue can help cover fixed costs and generate profits. The automobile industry has a different motive for bundling. People buy cars only every three to five years. Thus selling options is a somewhat rare opportunity for the car dealer. Price bundling can help the dealer sell a maximum number of options.

unbundling
Reducing the bundle of services that comes with the basic product.

Another approach is **unbundling**, or reducing the bundle of services that comes with the basic product. Rather than raise the price of hotel rooms, some hotel chains have started charging registered guests for parking. To help hold the line on costs, some department stores require customers to pay for gift wrapping.

Two-Part Pricing

two-part pricing
Price tactic that charges two separate amounts to consume a single good or service.

Two-part pricing means there are two separate charges to consume a single good or service.[20] Tennis clubs and health clubs, for example, charge a membership fee and

Many tennis clubs use two-part pricing, charging both a membership fee and a fee each time certain facilities are used.
© Bob Krist/Tony Stone Worldwide

a flat charge each time a person uses certain equipment or facilities. In other cases they charge a base rate for a certain level of usage, such as ten racquetball games per month, and a surcharge for anything over that amount.

Consumers sometimes prefer two-part pricing because they are uncertain about the number and the types of activities they might use at places like an amusement park. Also, the people who use a service most often pay a higher total price. Two-part pricing can also increase the seller's revenue by attracting consumers who would not pay a high fee even for unlimited use. For example, a health club might be able to sell only 100 memberships at $700 annually with unlimited use of facilities, for total revenue of $70,000. But perhaps it could sell 900 memberships at $200 with a guarantee of using the racquetball courts ten times a month. Every usage over ten would require the member to pay a $5 fee. Thus membership revenue would provide a base of $180,000, with some additional usage fees coming in throughout the year.

5 PRODUCT LINE PRICING

product line pricing
Setting prices for an entire line of products.

Product line pricing is setting prices for the entire line of products. Compared to setting the right price on a single product, product line pricing encompasses broader concerns. In product line pricing, the marketing manager tries to achieve maximum profits or other goals for the entire line, rather than for a single component of the line.

Relationships among Products

The manager must first determine the type of relationship that exists among the various products in the line: a complementary relationship, a substitute relationship, or a neutral relationship. If items are *complementary*, an increase in the sale of one good causes an increase in demand for the complementary product, and vice versa. For example, the sale of ski poles depends on the demand for skis, making these two items complementary.

Two products in a line can also be *substitutes* for each other. If buyers buy one item in the line, they are less likely to buy a second item in the line. For example, if someone goes to an automotive supply store and buys paste Turtle Wax for a car, it is very unlikely that he or she will buy liquid Turtle Wax in the near future.

Finally, a *neutral* relationship can exist between two products. In other words, demand for one of the products is unrelated to demand for the other. For instance, Ralston Purina sells chicken feed and Wheat Chex, but the sale of one of these products has no known impact on demand for the other.

Joint Costs

joint cost
Cost that is shared in the manufacturing and marketing of more than one product in a product line.

Joint costs are costs that are shared in the manufacturing and marketing of a product line. These costs pose a unique problem in product pricing. In oil refining, for example, fuel oil, gasoline, kerosene, naphtha, paraffin, and lubricating oils are all derived from a common production process. Another example is the production of compact discs that combine photos and music. Any assignment of joint costs must be somewhat subjective, since costs are actually shared between two or more products.

Suppose a company produces two products in a common production process, X and Y, with joint costs allocated on a weight basis. Product X weighs 1,000 pounds, and product Y weighs 500 pounds. Thus costs are allocated on the basis of $2 for X for $1 of Y. Gross margins (sales less cost of goods sold) might be as follows:

	Product X	Product Y	Total
Sales	$20,000	$6,000	$26,000
Less: cost of goods sold	15,000	7,500	22,500
Gross margin	$ 5,000	($1,500)	$ 3,500

This statement reveals a loss of $1,500 on product Y. Is that important? Yes; any loss is important. However, the firm must realize that on an overall basis, it earned a $3,500 profit on the two items in the line. Also, weight may not be the right way to allocate the joint costs. Instead, the firm might use other bases, including market value or quantity sold.

6 BIDDING: A DIFFERENT APPROACH TO PRICING

bid pricing
Process in which potential sellers are invited to state, either orally or in writing, what they will charge to provide a good or service.

No discussion of pricing would be complete without examining bidding, an important form of pricing in government and industrial markets. **Bid pricing** is a process in which potential sellers are invited to state, either orally or in writing, what they will charge to provide a good or service. The sale is awarded to one of the bidders. Bid pricing is unique, because the quantity demanded is specified in the bidding prospectus or specifications. The bid price therefore becomes a function of cost and competitors' actions. Price is usually the most important determinant of the winning bid, but other factors may enter into consideration. For example, organizational purchasers may also evaluate the bidder's past experience (especially in the area of research and development), its employees' technical competence, and the extra services provided.

Deciding Whether or Not to Bid

Let's look at the strategies a manager can use to determine whether or not the firm should bid at all. Several factors affect the analysis of a bidding opportunity: plant capacity, competition, follow-up, quantity, delivery, and profit. First, the possibility of gaining future business as a result of a successful bid will affect *plant capacity.* If a firm is operating at 50 percent capacity, it may be more eager to acquire a large job than would a firm operating at 95 percent capacity.

Second, highly competitive bidding situations are generally less attractive for each bidder than bidding situations in which there is little, if any, *competition.* Third, *follow-up* bidding opportunities are another important factor. For example, in the case of a federal government contract, a winning bid may receive a federal stock number and a high probability of repeat orders from the agency. Winning a bid also often makes other users aware of the firm's offerings. Fourth, the *quantity* desired in the bid proposal may be large enough to enable the firm to achieve economies of scale and thus make the bidding proposition more attractive.

Fifth, *delivery* is also an important consideration. A firm must be able to provide the merchandise on time to expect future business from the purchaser. Many companies will not bid on or accept a job, even if they are the low bidder, if the contracting officer believes the firm cannot deliver according to specifications. If the purchaser requires delivery of all the goods at one time, the bidder's distribution system may be taxed, and other regular customers may receive poor service during this period. The final factor is *profit* potential.

The firm should weight each of these factors according to its importance to the firm. After ranking the factors, the firm can then decide whether to bid or not to bid.

Exhibit 19.7

Expected Returns in Competitive Bidding with Expected Costs of $48,000

Our bid	Profit	Probability of success	Expected profit*
$48,500	$ 500	.96	$ 480
51,000	3,000	.82	2,460
55,000	7,000	.61	4,260
58,000	10,000	.24	2,400
62,000	14,000	.04	560
65,000	17,000	.01	170

*Expected profit = Profit × Probability of success

Deciding What Price to Bid

The higher a firm bids on a contract, the larger its returns on estimated costs will be. Also, the higher a bid, normally the lower the chances of winning the contract. Bidding therefore lends itself to applications of probability theory. By examining past success ratios and previous winning bids for a given type of good or service, a firm can construct a bidding model.

Exhibit 19.7 shows the expected returns on various bids on a project with expected costs of $48,000. The table shows that a firm wanting to maximize its expected profits should bid $55,000. A lower bid, of course, has a greater chance of acceptance but at a lower profit.

An expected-profit criterion is useful for a firm making many bids, with no single bid being crucial. According to an expected-profit criterion, the manager should choose the bid price that yields the highest expected profit. The expected-profit criterion is not a good basis for decision making if such factors as excess capacity, need to keep the assembly line running, or possible alternative uses of a new technology that will be developed under a bid must be considered.

7 PRICING DURING DIFFICULT ECONOMIC TIMES

Pricing is always an important aspect of marketing, but it is especially crucial in times of inflation and recession. The firm that does not adjust to economic trends may lose ground that it can never make up.

Inflation

When the economy is characterized by high inflation, special pricing tactics are often necessary. They can be subdivided into cost-oriented and demand-oriented tactics.

Cost-Oriented Tactics

One popular cost-oriented tactic is culling products with a low profit margin from the product line. However, this tactic may backfire for two reasons: the high volume and thus high profitability of an item with a low profit margin, and a loss of economies of scale as certain products are eliminated, which lowers the margins on other items. Also, the entire price/quality image of the line may be affected.

Any cost-oriented pricing policy that tries to maintain a fixed gross margin under all conditions can lead to a vicious circle. For example, a price increase will result in

A long time passes between bidding and completing construction of an office tower. Delayed-quotation pricing permits negotiation of the final price once construction is finished.

decreased demand, which in turn increases production costs (because of lost economies of scale). Increased production costs require a further price increase, leading to further diminished demand, and so on.

delayed-quotation pricing Pricing tactic used for industrial installations and many accessory items, in which a firm price is not set until the item is either finished or delivered.

Another popular cost-oriented tactic is **delayed-quotation pricing**, which is used for industrial installations and many accessory items. Price is not set on the product until the item is either finished or delivered. Long production lead times have forced this policy on many firms during periods of inflation. Builders of nuclear power plants, ships, airports, and office towers sometimes use delayed-quotation tactics.

escalator pricing Pricing tactic in which the final selling price reflects cost increases incurred between the times when the order is placed and delivery is made.

Escalator pricing is similar to delayed-quotation pricing in that the final selling price reflects cost increases incurred between the times when the order is placed and delivery is made. An escalator clause allows for price increases (usually across the board) based on the cost-of-living index or some other formula. As with any price increase, management's ability to implement such a policy is based on inelastic demand for the product. About a third of all industrial products manufacturers now use escalator clauses. However, many companies do not apply the clause in every sale. Often it is used only for extremely complex products that take a long time to produce or with new customers.

Demand-Oriented Tactics

Demand-oriented pricing tactics use price to reflect changing patterns of demand caused by inflation or high interest rates. Cost changes are considered, of course, but mostly in the context of how increased prices will affect demand.

price shading Use of discounts by salespeople to increase demand for one or more products in a line.

Price shading is the use of discounts by salespeople to increase demand for one or more products in a line. Often shading becomes habitual and is done routinely without much forethought. Ducommun, a metals producer, is among the major companies that have succeeded in eliminating the practice. Ducommun has told its salespeople, "We want no deviation from book price" unless authorized by management.

To make the demand for a good or service more inelastic and to create buyer dependency, a company can use several strategies:

- *Cultivate selected demand:* Marketing managers can target prosperous customers that will pay extra for convenience or service. Neiman-Marcus, for example, stresses quality. As a result, the luxury retailer is more lenient with suppliers and their price increases than is Alexander's Stores, a discounter. In cultivating close relationships with affluent organizational customers, marketing managers should avoid putting themselves at the mercy of a dominant firm. They can more easily raise prices when an account is readily replaceable. Finally, in companies where engineers exert more influence than purchasing departments, performance is favored over price. Often a preferred vendor's pricing range expands if other suppliers prove technically unsatisfactory.

- *Create unique offerings:* Marketing managers should study buyers' needs. If the seller can design distinctive goods or services uniquely fitting buyers' activities, equipment, and procedures, a mutually beneficial relationship will evolve. Buyers would incur high changeover costs in switching to another supplier. By satisfying targeted buyers in a superior way, marketing managers can make them dependent. Buyers will then tolerate higher prices—within reason.
- *Heighten buyer dependence:* Owens-Corning Fiberglas supplies an integrated insulation service (from feasibility studies to installation) that includes commercial and scientific training for distributors and seminars for end users. This practice freezes out competition and supports higher prices.

Recession

A recession is a period of reduced economic activity. Reduced demand for goods and services, along with higher rates of unemployment, is a common trait of a recession. Yet astute marketers can often find opportunity during recessions. They are an excellent time to build market share, because competitors are struggling to make ends meet.

Two effective pricing tactics to hold or build market share during a recession are value pricing and bundling. *Value pricing,* discussed earlier in the chapter, stresses to customers that they are getting a good value for their money. Revlon's Charles of the Ritz, usually known for its pricey products, introduced the Express Bar during the recession of the early 1990s. The Express Bar, a collection of affordable cosmetics and skin treatment products, sold alongside regular Ritz products in department stores. Although lower-priced products offer lower profit margins, Ritz found that volume increases can offset slimmer margins. For example, the company found that consumers will buy two to three Express Bar lipsticks at a time. "The consumer is very conscious of how she spends her income and is looking for value and quality that she can find elsewhere in department stores," said Holly Mercer, vice president of marketing for Ritz.[21]

Bundling or *unbundling* can stimulate demand in two ways during a recession. If features are added to a bundle, consumers may perceive the offering as having greater value. For example, assume that Hyatt offers a "great escape" weekend for $119. The package includes two nights' lodging and a continental breakfast. Hyatt could add a massage and a dinner for two to create more value for this price. Conversely, companies can unbundle offerings and lower base prices to stimulate demand. A furniture store, for example, could start charging separately for design consultation, delivery, credit, setup, and hauling away old furniture.

Recessions are a good time for marketing managers to study the demand for individual items in a product line and the revenue they produce. Pruning unprofitable items can save resources to be better used elsewhere. Borden's recently went through a huge restructuring of its product line. In snacks, the food processor made

about 3,200 sizes, brands, types, and flavors—but it got 95 percent of its revenues from just half of them.[22]

Prices often fall during a recession as competitors try desperately to maintain demand for their wares. Even if demand remains constant, falling prices mean lower profits or no profits. Falling prices, therefore, are a natural incentive to lower costs. During the last recession, companies implemented new technology to improve efficiency and then slashed payrolls. They also discovered that suppliers can be an excellent source of cost savings; the cost of purchased materials accounts for slightly more than half of most U.S. manufacturers' expenses.[23] General Electric's appliance division told 300 key suppliers that they must reduce prices 10 percent or risk losing GE's business. Allied Signal, Dow Chemical, United Airlines, General Motors, and DuPont have made similar demands of their suppliers. Specific strategies that companies are using with suppliers include

- *Renegotiating contracts:* Sending suppliers letters demanding price cuts of 5 percent or more; putting out for rebid the contracts of those who refuse to cut costs
- *Offering help:* Dispatching teams of experts to suppliers' plants to help reorganize and suggest other productivity-boosting changes; working with suppliers to make parts simpler and cheaper to produce
- *Keeping the pressure on:* To make sure the improvements continue, setting annual, across-the-board cost-reduction targets, often of 5 percent or more a year
- *Paring down suppliers:* To improve economies of scale, slashing the overall number of suppliers, sometimes by up to 80 percent, and boosting purchases from those that remain[24]

Tough tactics like these help keep companies afloat during economic downturns.

8 PRICING: A LOOK AT THE FUTURE

Predicting the future of anything is difficult. Nevertheless, here are a few predictions in the area of pricing:

- The increase in direct-response marketing (mail order, catalog, telephone, and computer electronic catalogs) means products will move more quickly from production lines to the consumer. Faster distribution means that fewer funds will be tied up in finished goods inventory, a cost savings to the seller that may or may not be passed on to the consumer.
- Closely related to the first prediction is that the United States is rapidly becoming an information-based society. Consumers and purchasing agents will be able to use their terminals to compare product alternatives and prices from several suppliers. The popular Prodigy information system, for example, gives detailed reports from sources like *Consumer Reports* and lists "best buys." Consumers will become more "price aware," and therefore elasticity of demand will increase—particularly for relatively homogeneous items.
- An offshoot of the information society is the "cashless society," brought forth by electronic funds transfer. Buyers may come to think of price as an accounting entry, a more abstract concept. Moreover, when consumers no longer have to write a check or count out the dollars, money management may change. Record keeping will be more accurate, thanks to the electronic recording of

transactions. On the other hand, the concept of price will be less concrete, which could lead to overspending.

- The information revolution is already aiding managers in price decisions, and it will provide more benefits in the future. Electronic data-capture techniques, such as bar codes, make data available on a real-time, on-line basis. A district manager for a supermarket like Kroger can vary prices on Kraft's mayonnaise at different stores in the district and quickly determine elasticity of demand. Similarly, a manager can analyze the impact of a 5¢-off coupon (or any other value) almost immediately. New research technologies, such as single-source marketing research (discussed in Chapter 8), accurately measure elasticity of demand. As this technology spreads, managers will become far more accurate in setting the "right price."

LOOKING BACK

Look back at the story about Quaker State oil that appeared at the beginning of the chapter. The advantages of premium pricing (skimming) are that development costs may be recovered more quickly if demand is inelastic, unit profits will be larger, and those who are willing to pay the premium price are, in fact, charged a premium price. On the other hand, premium pricing tends to attract competitors. Moreover, if a firm charges a premium price but doesn't have a distinct quality edge or other competitive advantage, sales will quickly evaporate.

Uniform pricing at first glance seems completely fair and logical. Quaker State was charging all customers the same price for a specific type of oil. There was no haggling over price, and all customers were treated the same. Yet all customers are not the same. One wholesaler may buy 2 cases of Quaker State, and another may buy 5,000 cases. Uniform pricing, without quantity discounts, doesn't consider the tremendous cost savings in a transaction for 5,000 units. More important, other oil companies did offer bulk discounts and flexible promotion allowances for national retailers. As a result, they soon attracted many of Quaker State's customers. Quantity or cash discounts encourage customers to take actions they ordinarily would not take, such as paying cash, buying larger quantities, and taking delivery out of season.

KEY TERMS

bait pricing 645

base price 635

basing-point price 642

bid pricing 648

cash discount 635

cumulative quantity discount 635

delayed-quotation pricing 650

escalator pricing 650

everyday low price 638

flexible pricing (variable pricing) 643

FOB origin pricing 640

SUMMARY

❶ **Describe the procedure for setting the right price.** Setting the right price on a product is a process with four major steps: (1) establishing pricing goals; (2) estimating demand, costs, and profits; (3) choosing a price policy to help determine a base price; and (4) fine-tuning the base price with pricing tactics.

❷ **Identify the three basic price policies.** A price policy establishes a long-term pricing framework for a good or service. The three main types of price policies are price skimming, penetration pricing, and status quo pricing. A price skimming policy charges a high introductory price, often followed by a gradual reduction. Penetration pricing offers a low introductory price to capture a large market share and attain economies of scale; value marketing, sometimes considered a subset of penetration pricing, is offering the right combination of product quality, fair price, and good service. Finally, status quo pricing strives to match competitors' prices.

❸ **Identify the legal constraints on pricing decisions.** Government regulation helps monitor four major areas of pricing: unfair trade practices, price fixing, preda-

freight absorption pricing 642
functional discount (trade discount) 636
joint cost 647
leader pricing (loss-leader pricing) 644
noncumulative quantity discount 636
odd-even pricing (psychological pricing) 645
penetration pricing 628
predatory pricing 634
price bundling 646
price discrimination 632
price fixing 631
price lining 644
price policy 625
price shading 650
price skimming 627
product line pricing 647
promotional allowance 639
quantity discount 635
rebate 639
seasonal discount 638
single-price tactic 642
status quo pricing 630
trade loading 636
two-part pricing 646
unbundling 646
unfair trade practice act 630
uniform delivered pricing 640
value marketing 629
zone pricing 641

tory pricing, and price discrimination. Enacted in many states, unfair trade practice acts protect small businesses from large firms that operate efficiently on extremely thin profit margins; these acts prohibit charging below-cost prices. The Sherman Act and the Federal Trade Commission Act prohibit both price fixing, an agreement between two or more firms on a particular price, and predatory pricing, undercutting competitors with extremely low prices to drive them out of business. Finally, the Robinson-Patman Act makes it illegal for firms to discriminate between two or more buyers in terms of price.

4 Explain how discounts, geographic pricing, and other special pricing tactics can be used to fine-tune the base price. Several pricing techniques enable marketing managers to adjust prices within a general price level in response to changes in competition, government regulation, consumer demand, and promotional and positioning goals. Techniques for fine-tuning a price can be divided into three main categories: discounts, allowances, and rebates; geographic pricing; and special pricing tactics.

The first type of tactic gives lower prices to those that pay promptly, order a large quantity, or perform some function for the manufacturer. Trade loading is a manufacturer's temporary functional discount to induce wholesalers and retailers to buy more goods than can be sold in a reasonable time. Trade loading increases inventory expenses and channel expenses and lowers the manufacturer's profits. A tactic meant to overcome these problems is "everyday low pricing," or maintaining low prices over time while eliminating the discounts that result in trade loading. Other tactics in this category include seasonal discounts, promotion allowances, and rebates (cash refunds).

Geographic pricing tactics—such as FOB origin pricing, uniform delivered pricing, zone pricing, freight absorption pricing, and basing-point pricing—are ways of moderating the impact of shipping costs on distant customers. A variety of special pricing tactics stimulate demand for certain products, increase store patronage, and offer more merchandise at specific prices.

5 Discuss product line pricing. Product line pricing maximizes profits for an entire product line. When setting product line prices, marketing managers determine what type of relationship exists among the products in the line: complementary, substitute, or neutral. Managers also consider joint (shared) costs among products of the same product line.

6 Explain how bidding differs from other forms of pricing. Bid pricing is a process in which competing sellers state what they will charge to provide a good or service. Bid pricing is unique because the quantity demanded is indicated in the bidding specifications.

7 Describe the role of pricing during periods of inflation and recession. Marketing managers employ cost-oriented and demand-oriented tactics during periods of economic inflation. Cost-oriented tactics consist of dropping products with a low profit margin, delayed-quotation pricing, and escalator pricing. Demand-oriented pricing methods include price shading and increasing demand through cultivation of selected customers, unique offerings, and systems selling.

To stimulate demand during a recession, marketers use value pricing, bundling, and unbundling. Recessions are also a good time to prune unprofitable products from product lines. Managers also strive to cut costs during recessions in order to maintain profits as revenues decline. Implementing new technology, cutting payrolls, and pressuring suppliers for reduced prices are common techniques used to cut costs.

8 Discuss what the future might hold for pricing in the marketing mix. Several trends in marketing are likely to affect pricing in the future. First, an increase in direct-response marketing is simplifying distribution and creating savings for sellers that may be passed on to consumers. Better and more accessible product information is likely to make consumers more price-sensitive. Electronic funds transfer may create a "cashless society," in which record keeping is more accurate but the concept of price more abstract. Finally, marketers' manipulation and analysis of pricing strategies are likely to become more effective with the use of new technology.

Review Questions

1. Describe the four basic steps in price setting.
2. Discuss the role of choosing a price policy in the price-setting process.
3. Identify the conditions that constitute a violation of the Robinson-Patman Act.
4. What is zone pricing? What are its drawbacks?
5. What types of relationships exist among products in a product line? Discuss how they relate in terms of demand.
6. What factors influence whether or not firms bid?
7. Compare and contrast price skimming and price penetration policies in terms of demand and competition.
8. Compare and contrast value marketing and penetration pricing.

Discussion and Writing Questions

1. You are contemplating a price change for an established product sold by your firm. Write a memo analyzing the factors you need to consider in your decision.
2. Identify several new products on the market that have followed (a) skimming, (b) penetration, and (c) status quo pricing policies. Explain why you feel each company followed its particular policy.
3. Because of the multiple channels of distribution employed by many firms, the manufacturer has little authority over the final selling price of a product; therefore, the importance of price as a marketing variable is reduced. Evaluate this statement.
4. Your firm submits a bid for an order of office furniture. List the ways you can ensure that the buyer will not overlook the high quality of your product, regardless of price.
5. How is the "information age" changing the nature of pricing?
6. Do you see everyday low prices as a solution to trade loading? Why are many manufacturers resisting EDLP?

CASES

19.1 Hudson Valley Tree

If you're looking for a Christmas tree, Hudson Valley Tree has it. The company sells a wide assortment of Christmas trees, including Douglas fir, Appalachian fir, Colorado spruce, and Vermont spruce. The company offers customers one unique advantage: No matter what kind of tree they choose, they can keep it for more than one season. Hudson Valley sells plastic trees.

Most artificial Christmas trees range in price from $99 to $149. Between 3 million and 4 million artificial trees were sold in 1993, a mere fraction of the 32 million live trees sold that year. Manufacturers expect that number to change as acceptance for artificial trees increases.

The new artificial trees are much more realistic than those of just a few years ago. The green steel trunks and lack of fresh pine aroma still give the artificial trees away. But from a distance, fake trees can pass for real. Shorter needles and more branches have replaced the old bottle brush–style limbs. Some ingenious manufacturers have even designed imperfections into the plastic trees. Bare spots and extra-tall top branches can make a fake tree look more realistic. Consumers can also shape the tree to their own specifications.

Appearance and convenience attract consumers to artificial trees. Owners can put up the tree the first week of December and keep it up through New Year's Day without worrying about pine needles all over the floor or watering the tree stand. Since artificial trees are treated with flame-retardant materials, they are not a potential fire hazard—a great advantage, especially for apartment dwellers. Many apartment land-

lords ban live Christmas trees because they're flammable. For consumers with allergies, these trees are also a blessing.

Cost is another concern. People who buy and use the tree for several years can recoup the cost in two to three years. In contrast, those consumers who go back to real trees after only one year pay an extravagant price.

The environmental issue is a toss-up. The water and soil used by live trees could be used for other crops. However, the disposal of nonbiodegradable trees is a problem. Artificial trees don't last forever.

Marketers prefer to call artificial trees lifelike or convenience trees. The areas of the country where artificial trees sell best are the Northeast and the Midwest. California is the one place where these trees haven't become popular. Unlike New England, California's climate and landscape do not match most people's image of a Christmas setting.

Questions

1. Is the price for artificial trees elastic or inelastic? Give reasons to support your answer.

2. What type of pricing strategy would you recommend to Hudson Valley? Why?

3. How do you think Hudson Valley should deal with freight costs? What implications will this decision have in the marketplace?

Suggested Reading

Jon Berry, "And You Never Need to Water It," *Adweek's Marketing Week*, 17 December 1990, p. 17.

19.2 Kentucky Fried Chicken

Video title: *Five KFC Ads: Old and New*

KFC Corp
1441 Gardner Lane
Louisville, KY 40213

SIC codes: 5812 Eating places
6794 Patent owners and lessors

Number of employees: 57,000

1993 revenues: $1.9 billion

Major product: Fried chicken

Largest competitors: McDonald's, Hardee's

Background

From Colonel Sanders's first restaurant, Kentucky Fried Chicken has taken a path of rapid growth. The secret recipe of eleven herbs and spices has become one of the world's favorite fast foods. Kentucky Fried Chicken began franchising in 1952. Since that time the company has opened franchises in fifty-eight countries, with over 4,900 U.S. locations.

The company offers franchising opportunities starting at $20,000. The average cost of opening a KFC franchise ranges from $700,000 to $1 million. Although KFC does not offer specific financing plans, it does have working relationships with certain financial institutions. Franchise contracts run twenty years.

Industry

Over $200 billion was spent in restaurants and bars in 1993, or about $500 million a day. For every dollar U.S. consumers spend in grocery stores, they spend another 52¢ in restaurants and bars. Over half of all U.S. adults are food-service patrons.

With growing competition, many restaurant businesses have begun using good-value themes to attract customers. These good-value promotions rely on low-price items (usually under $1) or combo deals (a package of items offered below the individual cost of those items).

Here is the average breakdown of costs for restaurants, as a percentage of the customer's bill:

Cost of food	33%
Labor expenses	26
Employee benefits	3
Rent/utilities	28
Advertising	5

This breakdown leaves about 5 percent of the total restaurant bill for pretax profits. This means that restaurants rely on large volumes for their profit.

Certain menu items contribute more to the bottom line than others. Drinks and desserts typically provide higher profits than entrees. By combining popular entrees with drinks and desserts, restaurants can offer consumers value and maintain their profit margins.

Questions

1. Why do you think KFC changed its advertising campaign from focusing on the product to focusing on price?
2. Do you think value-price advertising is effective in getting people to buy fast food? Why or why not?
3. What effect do you think value pricing has on total profits of fast-food restaurants like KFC?

References

Susan Boyles Martin (ed.), *Worldwide Franchise Directory* (Detroit: Gale Research, Inc., 1991).

Million Dollar Directory 1993 (Parsippany, NJ: Dun & Bradstreet Information Services, 1993).

Standard & Poor's Industry Surveys (New York: Standard & Poor's Corporation, April 1993).

19.3 *Decision Assistant:* The Machias Corporation

The Situation

Mary Machias, president of the Machias Corporation, is trying to decide whether to market a new line of sweaters. Her decision is complicated by the fact that the Machias Corporation is going to change its method of distribution. Up to this time, Machias had always sold directly to the consumer. Now, because of the expected increase in volume for the new line, the company is going to have to use wholesalers and retailers to reach the target market.

As the company's market researcher, you have determined that the selling price to the consumer can be no higher than $38.99 if the Machias Corporation is to compete with the other marketers of sweaters. The average wholesale markup in the industry is 30 percent based on the wholesale price, and the average retail markup based on the retail price is 38 percent.

The cost accountants at Machias have informed the president that the company's cost of making each sweater is $13.50 and that they need an 18 percent profit margin to meet its required rate of return. This margin is expressed as a percentage of the selling price.

The question facing the president is whether she should authorize the production and marketing of this line of sweaters. What is your advice?

The Solution Technique

Machias's problem can be resolved through use of the Markup Chain tool in the marketing *Decision Assistant.* Initially, enter Machias's cost and leave the final selling price blank. Key ALT-D for a table or ALT-G for a graph showing the required price at each level in the chain.

What If?

Consider each of the following situations independently:

1. What if the selling price to the consumer could be no higher than $37.75? What effect would this change have on the decision?
2. What if you discovered that the markup required by retailers was in fact 41 percent? What effect would this change have on the decision?
3. What if the Machias Corporation decided it required a 22 percent margin in order to meet its required rate of return?
4. Given the original selling price and margins, what is the highest cost Machias can afford to pay to manufacture the sweaters? (Hint: Enter the final selling price and leave the cost blank.)

PART SIX
CRITICAL THINKING CASE

Intel Corporation

Gordon Moore, Robert Noyce, and Andy Grove all worked for Fairchild Electronics and had doctorates in engineering. In 1957 Noyce invented one of the first two integrated circuits. The team left Fairchild and in 1968 founded Intel Corporation. The company's most notable inventions were

- The microprocessor (computer on a chip)
- DRAM (the memory found in most personal computers)
- Static RAM (used in consumer electronics)
- EPROM (erasable programmable read-only memory)

The engineers who founded Intel still run it. Gordon Campbell, president of Chips & Technologies, Intel's rival, says, "They've done so many important things in this industry it is mind-boggling."

From its beginnings, Intel has been on the cutting edge of technology. Intel invented the first microprocessor in 1971, which gave birth to the hand-held calculator. In 1974 Intel introduced the 8080 microprocessor. Since then, Intel has continued to introduce other new chips with increasingly more built-in computing power. In 1981 came the 8088 microprocessor, the chip that helped IBM bring its PC to the market. In 1984 the 80286 microprocessor gave personal computer users the same power found in mainframe computers built in the late 1970s. Introduced in 1987, the 80386 microprocessor rivals mainframes built only a few years before in terms of computing speed and memory access capacity. The 80486 chip opens a potential market for desktop mainframes.

Manufacturing Process

Microprocessors are produced by photographically developing images on a silicon surface using a chemical process. The complexity of most circuits requires that multiple exposures be done. The tolerance level between successive exposures is much smaller than one micron (0.05 percent of the diameter of a human hair). This tolerance is so small that a truck passing by the building or a person running down the corridor will vibrate the room enough to throw the superimposed image out of whack. For this reason, "clean rooms" are built on solid ground and include vibration-damping seals in the floor. A Class 1 clean room cannot vibrate any more than 200 microinches per second. When the industry hits the 0.5 micron mark, any more than half of that figure will be too much. Beyond that, the vibrations caused by employees standing on the floor will be excessive. Chips will have to be made in orbit by workers in space suits.

Clean rooms are 1,000 times cleaner than a hospital operating room. The reason for this level of sterility is that the size of the traces (circuit lines in the chips) has dropped to one micron. At two microns, a single bacterium is roughly the equivalent of a tree falling across the road. At one micron even a flu virus on the silicon's surface can render the chip useless. The air in these clean rooms is completely evacuated and filtered every few seconds. At Intel's Albuquerque plant, the air contains less than one 0.2 micron particle per cubic foot before a worker enters the room. Even the workers are too dirty to admit into the rooms without special suits.

Simply breathing emits 500 particles per minute. These suits, providing total enclosure for the worker, include a helmet that filters exhaled air.

Mainframes versus Microprocessors

To date, microprocessors have been far too slow to tap into the large computer market. A mainframe CPU (central processing unit) is a collection of high-speed logic chips chained together on a large circuit board. Thus traditional mainframe CPUs are expensive. Now, as the twenty-first century approaches, these CPUs are pushing the theoretical limits of speed. Additional performance increases will require major technological advances.

Many large computer manufacturers have decided that parallel processing is the answer. By tying together several microprocessors, large computers with more speed can be developed at a lower cost. Introduction of the 80486 makes this development more realistic. Since the lines in the 80486 are one micron wide, Intel was able to cram four times the number of transistors found in the 80386 into the new chip. This new design feature significantly reduces the distances a signal has to travel and thus accelerates the chip's speed.

RISC versus the 80486

Another increase in speed comes from reducing the number of instructions built into a single chip. These new chips are called Reduced Instruction-Set Computing (RISC). Chips capable of processing fewer instructions are faster and easier to manufacture, but they often are incompatible with existing software programs. There is some hope that software developers will modify existing programs to run under RISC systems to make better use of the speed advantage.

RISC chips are definitely faster than the 80386 microprocessor, but whether they are significantly faster than the 80486 microprocessor is unknown. For Intel, neglecting the RISC market may be a mistake.

Intel has tried for years to break into the workstation market. This high-growth market is mainly interested in speed. Both Sun Microsystems and MIPS Computer Systems are active in RISC development. Motorola has introduced its own RISC design. Although Intel feels that its 80486 chip will dominate the market because of its existing software compatibility, it is also pursuing RISC technology. Intel plans to use its RISC design for specific applications—for example, robots, automobiles, airplanes, and electronic systems.

Pricing

Intel has always used a skimming strategy in pricing new microprocessors. The 80486 is no different. The introductory price was $1,500. The first machines built using the 80486 chip sold for close to $20,000. Intel's suggested retail for the 80386SX is $65. However, because this chip is scarce, it actually sells for two times the list price. Intel continues to do well with its 80286 and 80386 chips—so well, in fact, that American Micro Devices (AMD), a rival manufacturer, sued Intel for the right to produce the 80386. AMD currently has a license to produce the 80286 but is losing sales as manufacturers switch to the newer 80386. The demand for the 80386 is so great that Intel cannot keep up with orders.

These are the selling prices of all Intel's chips:

Microprocessor	*Price*
8088-2	$ 8.00
8086	12.00
80286-12	20.00
80386SX-20	133.50
80386DX-20	245.00
80486DX-25	960.00

Questions

1. How should Intel price its line of microprocessors?

2. Are prices for each of Intel's family of microprocessors (8088, 80286, 80386, and 80486) elastic or inelastic? Give reasons to support your opinion.

3. What pricing policy would you recommend to Intel regarding future introductions and its current products? Why?

4. How would licensing other manufacturers to produce chips affect prices?

5. Predict the future of Intel Corporation in an industry where technology is changing very rapidly.

Suggested Readings

Richard Brandt, "It Takes More Than a Good Idea," *Business Week* (Special Issue, Innovation, 1989), p. 123.

Richard Brandt, Otis Port, and Robert D. Hoff, "Intel the Next Revolution," *Business Week,* 26 September 1988, pp. 74–80.

Stephen Krieder Yoder, "Rival Poised to Clone Intel Chip," *The Wall Street Journal,* 4 September 1990, pp. B1, B4.

PART SIX

GLOBAL MARKETING CASE

Pricing Exports the Hard Way

by Linda B. Catlin, Wayne State University, and Thomas F. White, Regis University

Tim Ballard looked out his office window at the mountains in the distance and thought about the phone call he had just received from Finland. One of Tim's best international customers, Olë Kulla, is a small wholesaler who travels throughout much of Scandinavia. Olë handles several lines of high-priced gifts, including the solar-powered executive gifts that Tim's company, Solar World, manufactures. Olë had called Tim today to see if Solar World would be interested in setting up a distribution network in Russia, Latvia, and Lithuania.

Tim's initial response to Olë's question was no. "Thanks for thinking of us," he told Olë, "but I don't think we're interested in trying to do business in Russia. We're too small a company to take that kind of risk, and I don't have the manufacturing capacity to extend much beyond our present markets."

However, Tim listened carefully as Olë explained that Boris Ivanov, a Moscow entrepreneur whom Olë had met a year ago in Sweden, was looking for unusual gift items to sell in Russia, Latvia, and Lithuania. Boris, according to Olë, had established a sales network in the three former Soviet republics and was always looking for new products. Olë had shown Boris some of Solar World's executive gifts, and Boris had expressed a strong interest in the products. He asked Olë to call Tim and set up a meeting or at least a telephone conference to discuss the possibility of doing business.

"Boris has been extremely successful in setting up a business, now that individuals can own businesses in the former Soviet Union. He seems to understand the free-enterprise system very well," Olë told Tim. "I think it might be worth your time to talk with him about selling Solar World products in Russia."

Tim agreed to think over what Olë had said and to let him know if he wanted to contact Boris.

"The first thing I need to do," Tim thought after this telephone conversation, "is to get out the atlas and see where Lithuania and Latvia are located! I think I know where Russia is."

The next day Tim mentioned Olë's phone call to George Stephens, Solar World's sales manager. "I'm not convinced that this is something we want to pursue," Tim said, "but isn't it interesting that even a formerly communist country might be interested in buying our executive gifts?"

"I wouldn't dismiss the Russian's inquiry completely," George replied quickly. "I happened to be talking to Ben Rodriguez over at BR, Inc., yesterday, and he's just come back from a trip to Eastern Europe and Russia. He's planning to sell some of BR's specialty advertising items to Russia.

"Ben took a consultant with him when he went to Russia," George continued. "Maybe we ought to give her a call and see what's involved in doing business over there."

Later that week Tim did talk with Nina Churkin, the business consultant whom Ben Rodriguez recommended. Nina had been born and educated in the former Soviet Union. After she emigrated to the United States, she completed an MBA at a U.S. university. She advised Tim that if he had any interest in doing business in Russia, he would have to go there in person to meet Boris Ivanov.

"It's very difficult to do business long distance with anyone in Russia. Their communication system is not as reliable and advanced as in the United States, and personal relationships are much more important in doing business there than they are here," Nina told Tim. "Also, you need to be prepared to accept payment for your product in some form other than rubles or dollars."

"I don't understand," Tim said. "The firms I sell to in Finland and in Japan give me an international letter of credit, and I receive payment through the bank. I never even have to convert from another currency."

Nina laughed. "Unfortunately, Russia and the other former communist countries don't have many hard currency reserves. They are relying heavily on countertrade for obtaining products from the West."

"Countertrade? I don't know what that is," Tim said.

"There are several forms of countertrade. The simplest is barter. That's where you trade Boris a certain number of your products in exchange for an agreed-on number of one or more products produced in Russia. An example of a Russian good he might be able to obtain for trade would be *matroyshka* dolls, those colorfully painted nesting dolls that children love. Or some companies have access to *shapka*, the distinctive fur hats many Russians wear."

"Dolls? Fur hats? What would I do with dolls or fur hats?" Tim asked. "I don't sell children's toys or clothing. That sounds like a crazy way to do business."

"Countertrade sometimes takes a different form than straight barter. I think another way of doing it is called a buy-back agreement. In this situation, you would give Boris the technical information or specialized components he needs to make the executive gifts your company produces here. Then Boris produces those gifts in Russia and gives you a specified number on a regular basis as repayment for the technical information. You can sell those Russian-made gifts to your other customers, perhaps in Europe or back here in the United States."

"You mean I would sell our technical expertise to someone in Russia? How would I protect myself in that case? What would prevent him from using it and not paying me with finished goods?"

"Only a lawyer—and one familiar with Russian law as well as U.S. law—can answer those questions. You do need to be concerned about those issues."

Tim was intrigued, although somewhat perplexed, by what Nina told him. Using a countertrade arrangement in Russia might just give him the potential to increase his production without incurring more debt. And if the finished products were already in Europe, he could eliminate the transportation costs he now had to build in when shipping from the United States.

Tim called his banker to find out more about countertrade. His banker's response was negative. "Those payment arrangements are fraught with problems," the banker said. "My advice is don't have anything to do with companies or individuals who propose countertrade. An irrevocable letter of credit is the only way you should be doing business in the international market."

Although the banker had been helpful on many occasions when Tim had needed an increase in his line of credit, Tim also realized that bankers tend to be very conservative about business transactions that eliminate the bank as a financial middleman. And since he knew that Ben Rodriguez at BR, Inc., was considering exchanging his company's finished goods for Russian-produced goods, Tim decided to regard his banker's advice as only one of many pieces to fit into what he was coming to regard as the countertrade puzzle.

Next, Tim contacted Lauren Kruph, a local attorney who was writing a comparative study of Russian and U.S. legal systems. Lauren confirmed Tim's concerns that there were a number of potential legal problems involved in doing business in Russia, especially if he decided to use countertrade.

"The problems almost certainly can be resolved," Lauren said, "but you will need to contact a Russian lawyer as well as a U.S. one. The process may be time-consuming and expensive. However, if this deal seems profitable enough in other respects, the legal expenses will be worth it."

Tim discussed the information obtained from Lauren, Nina, and the banker with his sales manager. They agreed that Tim should call Olë in Helsinki.

"I've decided to consider selling our products in Russia, Latvia, and Lithuania," Tim told Olë. "But first I want to suggest a possible deal between you and me. How about your buying the products from Solar World and then selling them to or countertrading them with Boris for some Russian products? That way, you can make a profit from this deal, too."

"I'm afraid my cash flow is not good enough for that kind of deal, Tim," replied Olë. "I already take some goods as countertrade for the Finnish and Swedish goods I sell to Boris. Possibly I could take some Russian products if Boris offers you the right ones in exchange for Solar World's products. But I can't directly buy your goods to sell or trade with Boris.

"I'm glad to know that you're anticipating the probability of a countertrade offer from Boris," Olë continued. "It's best if you're prepared to react to any of several different options he may suggest. Judging from what Boris projects he can do with the markets he wants to open up to Solar World's goods, I would guess you could eventually double your annual sales. Why don't I set up a meeting for the two of you here in Helsinki, and perhaps I can help with the negotiations?"

Olë had been Tim's first international customer and over the past six years had been a tremendous help in explaining the intricacies of doing business in Europe. Now Tim regarded Olë as a friend as well as a customer, and he appreciated Olë's offer to meet with Boris.

Tim agreed to a meeting with Boris in Helsinki and began to review Solar World's current position in preparation for his trip.

Solar World is a small firm, employing fourteen assemblers to make the company's products, including the solar-powered executive gifts that Olë sells, solar-powered flashlights and battery packs, high-tech microsolar panels (on which the company has a monopoly), and educational solar kits. The company also employs three people in office and accounting jobs, plus George, the sales manager, and Tim, the company president. Solar World's annual sales are about $1.5 million; about a fifth of the sales, or $300,000, are made in Europe and Japan.

The firm's offices and plant are in a small, one-story office building in Colorado Springs, Colorado. The rest of the building is occupied currently, so any expansion in production facilities would necessitate moving to another site.

As Tim reviewed Solar World's position, he suddenly remembered an inquiry from a German wholesaler three months ago. The German firm wanted to represent the executive gift line in all parts of Europe south of Scandinavia, where Olë had exclusive distribution rights. The German representative estimated that eventually he would be buying 10,000 units per month, perhaps as soon as six months after his first purchase. Because of the large projected volume, which was several times the amount Olë sold now, the German wanted the products at a much lower price than Solar World sold them to the Finnish distributor. The German told Tim the end-user price he needed to move the projected volume, as well as the margin he would need to handle Solar World's products. Tim used these figures to work backward when setting a price for the German. Unfortunately, he discovered that the transportation and tariff costs would not allow Solar World enough profit to do this deal with its present cost structure. Moreover, the higher volume would require a second production shift with new employees and the many costs associated with those additional employees. Tim reluctantly had turned down this potential buyer. Now, however, with the possibility of getting finished products from a factory in Russia, Tim began to rethink his options regarding sales to the German firm.

Tim developed the following list of questions that he needs to answer before meeting with Boris:

1. Define a set of alternative proposals that Boris might suggest at the Helsinki meeting; use some aspect of countertrade as the basis for each proposal.
2. What are the pros and cons of countertrade for a firm the size and complexity of Solar World?
3. If Solar World accepts one of the countertrade proposals, what are the company's resources for selling or trading the goods it receives? How would the company price these countertraded goods? How should the company price its own goods under the countertrade conditions?
4. If Tim decides to sell the technology license to the Russian firm, how should he price it?
5. Which of the alternatives identified above is the best one for Solar World? Why?

To the Student

How would you advise Tim in each area in preparation for the Helsinki meeting?

Part Seven

Contemporary Marketing Management

W
E
340 20 40 60 80 100 120 140 160 180 200 220 240 260 300 320
S
40 35 30 25 20 15 10 5 0

LEARNING OBJECTIVES

After studying this chapter, you should be able to

1. Define the meaning of business ethics.
2. Describe the nature of ethical decision making.
3. Discuss several current ethical dilemmas and global marketing ethics issues.
4. Discuss corporate social responsibility.
5. Explain the ways in which marketing meets its social responsibility.
6. Discuss consumerism.

CHAPTER 20

Ethics and Social Responsibility

Every year, some 400,000 Davis, Jennings, and Raven guns are churned out by three offshoot companies of the Jennings family. Selling for as little as $35, versus $600 for higher-quality weapons, these are the starter guns for the fearful, the criminal, and increasingly the very young. To a startling degree, they also figure disproportionately in robberies and murders, piling up an alarming toll of casualties and an unending litany of violence. Although high-power weapons dominate the headlines in fleeting moments of mass murder, these three brands of small-caliber pistols are far more lethal because of their sheer numbers, rock-bottom prices, and easy availability.

A five-month investigation by *The Wall Street Journal* followed these handguns from the factory to the middleman and ultimately to the street. Low costs and high production are key. It takes a mere three minutes to completely assemble a Raven, compared to about a half hour for more expensive guns. Unlike standard guns, which use stainless steel, the Raven and its offshoots are made from cheaper materials. As a result the Jennings family wares typically won't withstand much use compared with better-quality guns. Although Davis, Jennings, and Raven pistols all have minimal safety devices, they don't have other features that often appear on higher-quality guns that help prevent accidental discharge. Officials at the Bureau of Alcohol, Tobacco, and Firearms say the guns generally fail the "drop test" and can discharge if loaded and dropped to the floor. But that isn't a violation of any law, since, under the Gun Control Act of 1968, the test applies only to imported revolvers, not U.S.-made pistols. In fact, there are no safety requirements for U.S.-made guns, giving them the status of one of the least-regulated hazardous products in the United States.

In many ways, this is such a typical business that it's easy to lose sight of the product's main feature: It kills. The small Davis .380 derringer is especially popular among criminals, according to the Bureau of Alcohol, Tobacco, and Firearms, because of its potent firepower and ease with which it is concealed. The guns that leave the Jennings family's factories are first bought by wholesalers, who in turn sell the weapons to gun stores and pawnshops for legitimate trade. Often, though, the pistols are bought in bulk at retail by illegal dealers—particularly in states where gun laws are lax—and smuggled by bus or train to urban centers for resale. On the street, the buyer may pay more than triple the normal retail price to avoid required waiting periods, registration, and restrictions based on age and felony convictions.

Too often these buyers are inner-city youths. Like any other business, the Jennings clan target their market. The Davis, Jennings, and Raven pistols sell in all sorts of neighborhoods throughout the United States, but they sell predominantly in urban centers. Because the guns are so inexpensive and easy to obtain, they have especially gained popularity among the young, turning some neighborhoods into virtual free-firing zones. For example, a Raven gun was used by a 15-year-old to rob and murder three cocaine dealers in Brooklyn. A 14-year-old in California was suspended from school after a Jennings .22 was found in his locker. And a 5-year-old in the Bronx was found carrying a loaded Raven to kindergarten in his pocket. The Jennings family denies the idea that their guns figure predominantly in the inner city. Their customers, they say, "are just regular, everyday people who don't have the finances to buy higher-priced guns."

"We have a fire burning, and these companies are throwing gasoline on it," says Josh Sugarmann of the Violence Policy Center, which studies violence prevention. "These people know what the inner-city gun buyer wants."

The Jennings company is not under any legal obligation to control the markets it sells to, nor is it required to comply with any safety standards. But should Jennings feel some responsibility to control the violence the guns are involved in? Should the guns' safety standards be raised to avoid accidental firing? Can you give some examples of ways that U.S. corporations exercise social responsibility?

Source: Adapted from Alix M. Freedman, "A Single Family Makes Many of the Cheap Pistols That Saturate Cities," *The Wall Street Journal*, 28 February 1992, pp. A1, A6–A7. Reprinted by permission of *The Wall Street Journal*,

1 UNDERSTANDING ETHICAL BEHAVIOR

ethics
Moral principles or values that generally govern the conduct of an individual or a group.

Ethics refers to the moral principles or values that generally govern the conduct of an individual or a group. Ethics also can be viewed as the standard of behavior by which conduct is judged. Standards that are legal may not always be ethical, and vice versa. Laws are the values and standards enforceable by the courts. Ethics are personal rather than societal moral principles and values.

Defining the boundaries of ethicality and legality can often be difficult. Many times judgment is needed to determine whether an action that may be legal is indeed ethical. For example, in many states advertising liquor, tobacco, and X-rated movies in college newspapers is not illegal. But is it ethical? Likewise, it is illegal to duplicate software programs licensed for only one user, yet many businesspeople and individuals have "pirated" software on their computers.

In the following situations, judgment plays a major role in defining ethical and legal boundaries. After you read each one, try to determine whether it can be placed neatly into one of the following categories: ethical and legal, ethical and illegal, unethical and legal, unethical and illegal.

- Nicotine patches have ignited a controversy over selling prescription drugs directly to consumers. Food and Drug Administration (FDA) guidelines for prescription drug advertising require that ads making any claims at all for a product must also feature "prescribing information"—technical information about things like active ingredients and adverse reactions. These guidelines were originally created with physicians, not consumers, in mind. As a result, print ads for prescription drugs are so technical that consumers can't understand them. Many consumers simply ignore the technical jargon in print ads.

TV ads for nicotine patches try to get around the guidelines by not even mentioning that the patches are a smoking cessation device, compounding consumer confusion. Consumers also get the mistaken impression from the TV ads that nicotine patches are a quick way to break their addiction.[1]

- Under the laws of some twenty U.S. states, it is illegal for prospective adoptive parents and adoption agencies seeking birth mothers willing to give their baby up for adoption to advertise. In some states, only licensed agencies can place adoption ads. Advocates of adoption advertising say they are letting women know that the choice of adoption exists. Government adoption agencies are often slow, with some couples waiting years to be put at the top of a list for a child. The people who oppose advertising worry that prospective parents will vie for scarce healthy white infants by pitching their lifestyle as though it were a competitive product. They also believe that advertising for babies is like opening a bazaar where children are the product.[2]
- Malt liquors like St. Ides, Olde English 800, and King Cobra have become a prestige symbol among inner-city youth. Malt liquor is typically stronger than regular beer. A forty-ounce bottle is sold for as little as $1.50. Malt brewers are luring younger drinkers by featuring in their advertising popular rap stars whose rebellious lyrics exalt drinking, sexual prowess, or gang violence.[3]
- Several charities in Pennsylvania and Connecticut were charged with making fraudulent fund-raising claims, representing near-worthless goods as worth millions of dollars for children, cancer patients, and drug abusers. The charities used complex transactions to conceal the fact that most of the money raised was spent on sustaining the organizations and raising more money. One organization gave $27,232 in outdated vegetable seeds to a South Dakota Sioux reservation and claimed it had donated a $2.4 million cancer-patient aid.[4]
- A study by the New York City Department of Consumer Affairs found that grocery shoppers in poor neighborhoods paid 8.8 percent more than shoppers in middle-class areas. The discount stores, outlet malls, and warehouse clubs have largely bypassed inner-city neighborhoods to serve the more affluent middle class. Many retailers avoid the inner city because of higher insurance and security costs and larger losses due to theft. The poor also pay higher interest rates. Annual rates of 25 to 45 percent are common.[5]

As you probably noticed, few of these situations fit neatly into one category. Some situations were clearly legal but could be viewed as ethical by some consumers and unethical by others. Although others were ruled illegal, a case could be made for their legality and ethicality.

How do people develop an understanding of which types of behavior are ethical? **Morals** are the rules or habits that people develop as a result of cultural values and norms. Culture is a socializing force that dictates what is right and wrong. Moral standards may also reflect the laws and regulations that affect social and economic behavior. Thus morals can be considered a foundation of ethical behavior.

morals
Rules or habits that people develop as a result of cultural values and norms.

Morals are usually characterized as good or bad. *Good* and *bad* have different connotations, including "effective" and "ineffective." A good salesperson makes or exceeds the assigned quota. If the salesperson sells a new stereo to a disadvantaged consumer knowing full well that the person can't keep up the monthly payments, is the salesperson still a good one? What if the sale enables the salesperson to exceed his or her quota?

Business ethics reflect the values of society as a whole, which are acquired through family and through institutions like the Girl Scouts and the Boy Scouts. (*left*) Even the youngest Daisy Girl Scouts learn the importance of caring for the environment; (*right*) these Boy Scouts at a jamboree learn how to get along with one another.

(left) Girl Scouts of the United States of America; (right) © Joe Bensen/Stock Boston

Another set of connotations for *good* and *bad* are "conforming" and "deviant" behavior. A doctor who runs large ads for discounts on open-heart surgery would be considered bad or unprofessional, in the sense of not conforming to the norms of the medical profession. *Bad* and *good* are also used to express the distinction between criminal and law-abiding behavior. And finally, the terms are defined by religions, which differ markedly on what is good or bad. A Moslem who eats pork would be considered bad, as would a fundamentalist Christian who drinks whiskey.

Morality and Business Ethics

Today's business ethics are actually a subset of the values held by society as a whole. The values businesspeople use to make decisions have been acquired through family and through educational and religious institutions. Moreover, social movements, such as those against nuclear power and for women's rights, also shape businesspeople's decision making.

Ethics are very situation-specific and time-oriented. Nevertheless, everyone must have an ethical base that applies to conduct in the business world and in personal life. One approach for developing a personal set of ethics is to examine the consequences of a particular act.[6] Who is helped or hurt? How long-lasting are the consequences? What actions produce the greatest good for the greatest number of people?

A second approach stresses the importance of rules. Rules come in the form of customs, laws, professional standards, and common sense. Consider these examples:

Always treat others as you would like to be treated.

Copying copyrighted material is against the law.

It is wrong to lie, bribe, or exploit.

preconventional morality Basic level of moral development, which is childlike, calculating, self-centered, and even selfish, based on what will be immediately punished or rewarded.

conventional morality Intermediate level of moral development, which is based on loyalty and obedience to the organization's or society's expectations.

The last approach for developing a personal set of ethics emphasizes the development of moral character within individuals. Ethical development can be thought of as having three levels: preconventional morality, conventional morality, and postconventional morality.[7] **Preconventional morality**, the most basic level, is childlike. It is calculating, self-centered, and even selfish, based on what will be immediately punished or rewarded. **Conventional morality** moves from an egocentric viewpoint toward the expectations of society. Loyalty and obedience to the organi-

postconventional morality
Most advanced level of moral development, in which people are less concerned about how others might see them and more concerned about how they see and judge themselves over the long run.

zation (or society) become paramount. At the level of conventional morality, an ethical marketing decision would be concerned only with whether or not it is legal and how it will be viewed by others. **Postconventional morality** represents the morality of the mature adult. At this level, people are less concerned about how others might see them and more concerned about how they see and judge themselves over the long run. A marketing decision maker who has attained this level of morality might ask, "Even though it is legal and will increase company profits, is it right in the long run? Might it do more harm than good in the end?" Fortunately, most businesspeople have progressed beyond the self-centered and manipulative actions of preconventional morality. However, unless managers and workers take positive action, business ethics is nothing more than empty moralizing.

A businessperson with a mature set of ethical values accepts personal responsibility for decisions that affect the organization and the community. When making business decisions, he or she takes into account their effects on the needs and desires of employees. At the same time, the businessperson considers consumers who may be directly and indirectly affected by the decisions. Will these decisions create goodwill and be in consumers' best interests, too? How will these decisions affect the social structure that enables the company to exist?

2 ETHICS AND MARKETING MANAGEMENT

Many consumers perceive marketing activities as unethical and manipulative by nature. For instance, consumers often equate marketing with misleading advertisements, pushy salespeople, and high prices for poor-quality products. Indeed, some areas of marketing are particularly vulnerable to unethical behavior: product management, retailing, advertising, distribution, pricing, and personal selling. Consider the following statistics, which seem to show that those in the United States, in general, distrust businesspeople and marketers:

- A *Business Week*/Harris poll indicated that white-collar crime is thought to be very common (by 49 percent of respondents) or somewhat common (41 percent), and 46 percent of respondents believe that the ethical standards of business executives are only fair.
- A *Time* magazine study suggests that 76 percent see a lack of business ethics in business managers as contributing to the decline of U.S. moral standards.
- A Touche Ross survey reported the general feeling, even among businesspeople, that business ethics problems portrayed in the media have not been overblown or exaggerated.
- A Gallup study found that of all the various occupations, selling and advertising were judged to be at the bottom of the scale for honesty and ethical standards.[8]

Marketing managers must often weigh the needs of the business against the needs of others (for instance, customers, suppliers, or society as a whole). Objective marketing considerations can conflict with ethical standards. For example, salespeople find themselves facing conflicting wants from the customer: for high-quality products and low prices. They can feel tremendous pressure to compromise their own personal ethics for the apparent good of the business, the customer, or themselves.[9] Rigid sales or production quotas, risk of losing the sale, increased competition, lack of ethical guidelines, and greed often lead to unethical behavior in market-

Exhibit 20.1

Potential Unethical Practices by Marketing Managers

- Bribery, gift giving, and entertainment
- False or misleading advertising
- Unfair manipulation of customers
- Misrepresentation of goods, services, and company capabilities
- Lies told to customers in order to make the sale
- Price deception
- Price discrimination
- Product deception
- Unfair remarks about the competitor
- Exploitation of children and underprivileged groups in marketing strategies
- Sex-oriented advertising appeals
- Invasions of customer privacy
- Manipulation of data (falsifying or misusing statistics or information)
- Misleading product warranties
- Unsafe products
- Smaller amounts of product in same-size packages
- Stereotyped portrayals of women, minority groups, and senior citizens

ing. Some of the major ethical problems confronting marketing managers are listed in Exhibit 20.1.

Making Ethical Decisions

A marketing manager must consider the ethical implications of decision making. How do businesspeople make ethical decisions? There is no cut-and-dried answer. One study of marketing executives and marketing researchers found that three factors influenced their ethical judgments: the extent of ethical problems within the organization, top-management actions on ethics, and organizational role (executives versus researchers).[10] Marketing professionals who perceived fewer ethical problems in their organizations tended to disapprove more strongly of "unethical" or questionable practices than those who perceived more ethical problems. Apparently, the healthier the ethical environment, the greater the likelihood that marketers will take a strong stand against questionable practices. The research also showed that top managers can influence the behavior of marketing professionals by encouraging ethical behavior and discouraging unethical behavior.[11] Marketing executives expressed stronger disapproval of some questionable practices than did marketing researchers.

How can managers determine the ethicality of a decision? Using the checklist in Exhibit 20.2 will not guarantee the "rightness" of a decision, but it will improve the chances of its being ethical.

Developing Ethical Guidelines

code of ethics
Guidelines developed by a company to help its employees make ethical decisions.

Many companies have developed a **code of ethics** as a guideline to help marketing managers and other employees make better decisions. Some of the most highly praised codes of ethics are those of Boeing, GTE, Hewlett-Packard, Johnson & Johnson, and Norton Company. Creating ethics guidelines has several advantages. First, it helps employees identify what their firm recognizes as acceptable business

Exhibit 20.2

Ethics Checklist

Source: Adapted from Michael R. Hyman, Robert Skipper, and Richard Tansey, "Ethics Codes Are Not Enough," *Business Horizons*, March/April 1990, pp. 15–22.

- ☐ Does my decision treat me or my company as an exception to a common practice or convention? In other words, do I think I have the authority to break a rule?
- ☐ Would I offend customers by telling them about my decision?
- ☐ Would I offend qualified job applicants by telling them about my decision?
- ☐ Have I made this decision without input from others, so that important issues might be overlooked?
- ☐ Does my decision benefit one person or group but hurt or not benefit other individuals or groups?
- ☐ Will my decision create conflict between people or groups in the company?
- ☐ Will I have to pull rank (use coercion) to enact my decision?
- ☐ Would I prefer to avoid the consequences of this decision?
- ☐ Did I avoid truthfully answering any of the above questions by telling myself that I could get away with it?

practices. Second, a code of ethics can be an effective internal control on behavior, which is more desirable than external controls like government regulation. Third, a written code helps employees avoid confusion when determining whether their decisions are ethical. Fourth, the process of formulating the code of ethics facilitates discussion among employees about what is right and wrong and ultimately creates better decisions.[12]

Businesses, however, must be careful not to make their code of ethics too vague or too detailed. Codes that are too vague give little or no guidance to employees in their day-to-day activities. Codes that are too detailed encourage employees to substitute rules for judgment. For instance, if employees are involved in questionable behavior, they may use the absence of a written rule as a reason to continue, even though their conscience may be saying no.[13]

Aircraft manufacturer Boeing is a successful U.S. company known for its strong code of ethics.

© Matthew Neal McVay/Tony Stone Worldwide

Although many companies have issued policies on ethical behavior, marketing managers must still put the policies into effect. They must address the classic "matter of degree" issue. For example, marketing researchers must often resort to deception to obtain unbiased answers. Asking for a few minutes of a respondent's time is dishonest if the researcher knows the interview will last forty-five minutes. Should researchers conducting focus groups inform the respondents that there are observers behind a one-way mirror? Often, when respondents know they're being watched, they stop talking and interacting freely. Does a client have an ethical right to obtain questionnaires with the names and addresses of respondents from a market research firm? Many of these concerns have been addressed by the Professional Standards Committee of the American Marketing Association. A copy of the American Marketing Association's code of ethics, adopted in 1987, is shown in Exhibit 20.3.

Even the best ethics programs don't always work. Dow Corning was among the first corporations to set up a formal ethics program. Through a committee made up of company executives, Dow Corning's program sought to create a corporate culture with high ethical standards. The company audited compliance with its standards, communicated with employees about ethics, included ethics in training programs, and surveyed employees about their ethics practices twice a year. Yet the system seemingly failed. Dow Corning was accused of covering up safety problems with the silicone breast implants the company produced. Internal documents suggest that Dow Corning was aware of the safety problems for years and tried to keep the public from learning of them.[14]

3 CURRENT ETHICAL DILEMMAS

Today marketing managers face several ethical issues. Three of the major ones are tobacco and alcohol promotion, consumer privacy, and so-called "green marketing." Limited space prevents us from exploring many others, including marketing to young children, marketing that promotes sexual harassment, misleading advertising and product labels, and marketing to the disadvantaged.

Tobacco and Alcohol Promotion

Never have the tobacco and alcohol industries experienced such strong attacks as they have in the 1990s. At the heart of this controversy is R.J. Reynolds Tobacco Company's Camel brand cartoon mascot, Joe Camel. Critics claim that cigarette promotions like the Joe Camel campaign are targeted to children and teenagers in an attempt to turn them into smokers. Several studies show that this claim may have some basis. For instance, studies published in the *Journal of the American Medical Association* found that Camel ads are highly effective in reaching children. In one study, many members of a small group of 6-year-olds were nearly as familiar with Joe Camel as they were with the Disney Channel's Mickey Mouse logo.[15] Another study found that when consumers were asked to judge the age of models in cigarette ads, 17 percent of the models were perceived to be under the age of 25, an apparent violation of the tobacco industry's voluntary advertising code. Additionally, cigarette ads featuring young people were found to appear more often in magazines with younger audiences.[16]

Studies like these have prompted the U.S. Surgeon General to call for the ban of all tobacco advertising in magazines and in retail stores.[17] In California, activists have staged their own war against tobacco companies, with sophisticated advertising

Exhibit 20.3

American Marketing Association Code of Ethics

Source: American Marketing Association.

Members of the American Marketing Association (AMA) are committed to ethical professional conduct. They have joined together in subscribing to this Code of Ethics embracing the following topics:

Responsibilities of the Marketer

Marketers must accept responsibility for the consequences of their activities and make every effort to ensure that their decisions, recommendations, and actions function to identify, serve, and satisfy all relevant publics: customers, organizations, and society.

Marketers' professional conduct must be guided by:

1. The basic rule of professional ethics: not knowingly to do harm;
2. The adherence to all applicable laws and regulations;
3. The accurate representation of their education, training, and experience; and
4. The active support, practice, and promotion of this Code of Ethics.

Honesty and Fairness

Marketers shall uphold and advance the integrity, honor, and dignity of the marketing profession by:

1. Being honest in serving consumers, clients, employees, suppliers, distributors, and the public;
2. Not knowingly participating in conflict of interest without prior notice to all parties involved; and
3. Establishing equitable fee schedules including the payment or receipt of usual, customary, and/or legal compensation for marketing exchanges.

Rights and Duties of Parties in the Marketing Exchange Process

Participants in the marketing exchange process should be able to expect that:

1. Participants and services offered are safe and fit for their intended uses;
2. Communications about offered products and services are not deceptive;
3. All parties intend to discharge their obligations, financial and otherwise, in good faith; and
4. Appropriate internal methods exist for equitable adjustment and/or redress of grievances concerning purchases.

It is understood that the above would include, *but it is not limited to*, the following responsibilities of the marketers:

In the area of product development and management,

- Disclosure of all substantial risks associated with product or service usage;
- Identification of any product component substitution that might materially change the product or impact on the buyer's purchase decision;
- Identification of extra-cost added features.

In the area of promotions,

- Avoidance of false and misleading advertising;
- Rejection of high-pressure manipulations or misleading sales tactics;
- Avoidance of sales promotions that use deception or manipulation.

In the area of distribution,

- Not manipulating the availability of a product for purpose of exploitation;
- Not using coercion in the marketing channel;
- Not exerting undue influence over the reseller's choice to handle a product.

In the area of pricing,

- Not engaging in price fixing;
- Not practicing predatory pricing;
- Disclosing the full price associated with any purchase.

In the area of marketing research,

- Prohibiting selling or fund-raising under the guise of conducting research;
- Maintaining research integrity by avoiding misrepresentation and omission of pertinent research data;
- Treating outside clients and suppliers fairly.

Organizational Relationships

Marketers should be aware of how their behavior may influence or impact on the behavior of others in organizational relationships. They should not demand, encourage, or apply coercion to obtain unethical behavior in their relationships with others, such as employees, suppliers, or customers. Marketers should:

1. Apply confidentiality and anonymity in professional relationships with regard to privileged information;
2. Meet their obligations and responsibilities in contracts and mutual agreements in a timely manner;
3. Avoid taking the work of others, in whole, or in part, and represent this work as their own or directly benefit from it without compensation or consent of the originator or owner;
4. Avoid manipulation to take advantage of situations to maximize personal welfare in a way that unfairly deprives or damages their organization or others.

Any AMA member found to be in violation of any provision of this Code of Ethics may have his or her Association membership suspended or revoked.

This billboard is part of Anheuser-Busch's "Know When to Say When Campaign," designed to discourage the use of alcohol by youth.
TIME Magazine

designed to persuade the state's 7 million smokers to kick the habit, all funded by the state's cigarette tax.[18] The campaign targeted young women, teenagers, and immigrants. It was estimated to have cost the tobacco industry some $1.1 billion in lost sales in California.[19] Several big sports stadiums are eliminating tobacco ads. Although tobacco advertising is banned from TV and radio, activists claim that ads are sneaking on to the airwaves when television cameras focus on a stadium scoreboard or zoom in on an outfielder.[20] Congress is also considering some antismoking laws, including ones that would allow individual states to regulate tobacco advertising, prohibit tobacco ads that can be seen by minors, limit outdoor advertising, and end tax deductibility for tobacco products. One California bill would also ban the use of cartoons in advertising for dangerous products, especially cigarettes.[21] In addition, the U.S. Supreme Court has ruled that smokers may sue cigarette makers for hiding or distorting the health dangers of tobacco.[22]

The alcoholic beverage industry has not fared much better. Beer commercials are limited to one minute per hour during college basketball championship games. The U.S. Surgeon General has also attacked alcohol advertising, asserting that its reliance on sex and sports imagery encourages underage drinkers.[23] Congress is thinking about requiring health warnings in all alcoholic beverage ads. One bill would require alcohol ads to warn that drinking can lead to birth defects and addiction.[24] The Bureau of Alcohol, Tobacco, and Firearms has spoken out against many alcohol products that it feels are aimed at inner-city dwellers. Examples include PowerMaster, a potent malt liquor whose name had to be changed because of its connotation of strong alcoholic content, and St. Ides Premium Malt Liquor, whose commercials use rappers like Ice Cube and the Geto Boys to lure young drinkers.[25]

Many tobacco and alcohol companies are submitting to activists' pressures with new campaigns telling kids not to smoke and drink. The big tobacco companies and their trade group, the Tobacco Institute, have launched youth antismoking campaigns focusing on the peer pressure associated with smoking.[26] Anheuser-Busch spends millions annually on its "Know When to Say When" campaign. Likewise, Miller Brewing Company has tripled spending on its responsible-drinking program, which it emphasizes during holidays and spring break.[27]

Critics question the sincerity of tobacco and alcohol companies' antismoking and antidrinking ads. Many feel the ads challenge children to smoke and drink. Others believe the industries' efforts to discourage teen drinking and smoking have been drowned out by the overabundance of upbeat ads. Still others feel the ads are the industries' last effort to fend off possible regulation.[28] In fact, beer companies are not just trying to discourage regulation but are earnestly trying to keep beer ads from being banned altogether. Because the banning of alcohol and tobacco advertising could have a very big economic impact, others are also concerned. The Leadership Council on Advertising Issues estimates that

> if tobacco advertising were banned, it would send 7,904 newspaper jobs packing, while killing 165 magazines, according to a new study. If beer and wine advertising were cancelled on television, another 4,232 jobs would be lost, plus an enormous chunk of network sports programming. Without ads for hard liquor, another 84 magazines would fold, including many for blacks.[29]

Internationally as well, tobacco companies are facing tougher laws and regulations. The executive body of the European Community has recommended a ban on tobacco ads throughout the EC trade bloc. It would eliminate tobacco ads from magazines and other publications, billboards, and movie theaters and prohibit tobacco company logos on T-shirts and on the sides of racing cars. Ads would be allowed only inside tobacco shops. The EC's ban on TV tobacco advertising took effect in 1991.[30] Other countries—among them Taiwan, Australia, China, and Thailand—are also seeking to curb tobacco advertising or to stiffen regulations. For instance, Canada has some of the world's toughest antismoking regulations. Tobacco display advertising is banned from retail stores. Cigarette packages must be printed with large health warnings and must include inserts detailing the hazards of smoking. Canadian law also bans tobacco advertising in newspapers and magazines and on billboards.[31]

Consumer Privacy

Today's computer technology can collect and analyze mountains of data. Thus it is easy for companies to compile alarmingly detailed profiles of millions of their customers, with everything from salaries and home values to ages and weights of family members. Sometimes they sell the information to direct marketers. Many consumers resent the use of information acquired in business transactions to construct these detailed consumer spending profiles. In one study, almost eight in ten U.S. citizens agreed that if the Declaration of Independence were to be written today, they would probably add privacy to the list of fundamental rights—along with life, liberty, and the pursuit of happiness. The majority also believed that they have lost all control over the use of personal information.[32]

The number of marketers that have been entangled in consumer privacy issues is mounting. American Express acknowledged that information about its cardholders' lifestyles and spending habits had been offered for joint marketing efforts with merchants.[33] Blockbuster Entertainment scrapped plans to sell direct marketers information about its customers' video-renting habits after the news created controversy.[34] Equifax, the giant credit-reporting agency, with 120 million names in its

files, also gave up the practice of providing mailing lists to direct marketers after the New York State Attorney General threatened a lawsuit.[35] Even physicians and pharmacists have been found to routinely open their patient records to data collectors that sell the records to pharmaceutical companies wanting to know exactly how their products are selling. Critics of this practice say the custodians of medical records have no right to share such information with an unregulated business without patients' knowledge or consent. The practice especially alarmed patients with AIDS, mental illness, and other conditions in which a breach of privacy can have far-reaching consequences.[36]

Many companies are using the privacy issue as a marketing weapon. AT&T aired television ads attacking MCI's Friends & Family program, which offers 20 percent off some calls in exchange for customer referrals. In one AT&T ad, a woman becomes outraged when a telemarketer asks for the phone numbers of people close to her.[37] In another ad, a man returns home to be bombarded by nasty messages on his answering machine from friends whose names and numbers he gave to MCI.

Green Marketing

green marketing
Marketing of products and packages that are less toxic than normal, are more durable, contain reusable materials, or are made of recyclable materials.

Green marketing refers to the marketing of products and packages that are less toxic than normal, are more durable, contain reusable materials, or are made of recyclable materials. In short, these are products considered environmentally friendly, and their marketers are "environmentally responsible."

The vast majority of U.S. citizens are worried about the environment. Most tend to blame businesses for the environmental problems they see. One study revealed these findings:

- More than eight in ten say industrial pollution is the main reason for our environmental problems.
- Nearly three-quarters of the public say the products that businesses use in manufacturing also harm the environment.
- Six in ten blame businesses for not developing environmentally sound consumer products.[38]
- Sixty-seven percent of adults disapprove of the packaging used by fast-food businesses and consumer product manufacturers.[39]

Consumers blame themselves, too. Seventy percent say consumers are more interested in convenience than in environmentally sound products. Over half admit they are not willing to pay more for safer products.[40] Companies like Bic Corporation, which specializes in disposable products, found out that consumers are happy to pay for convenience and don't seem to mind that Bic's annual output of 4 million pens, 3 million razors, and 800,000 plastic lighters end up in landfills. In fact, the company's two refillable pens account for less than 5 percent of sales, a figure that has been steadily declining.[41]

Still, many companies are becoming environmentally sensitive. Duracell and Eveready battery companies have reduced the levels of mercury in their batteries and will eventually market mercury-free products. Sanyo sells its rechargeable batteries in a plastic tube that can be mailed back. The company then recycles both the tubes and the cadmium batteries.[42] Turtle Wax car-wash products and detergents are biodegradable and can be "digested" by waste-treatment plants. The company's plastic containers are made of recyclable plastic, and its spray products do not use propellants that damage the ozone layer in the earth's upper atmosphere.[43] Simi-

Many blame business for environmental problems around the globe, such as damage to wildlife caused by oil spills.

© 1991 John Lamar/The Stock Market

larly, L'eggs redesigned its trademark plastic egg package and replaced it with a more environmentally friendly cardboard package.[44]

Critics contend that green marketing campaigns are nothing more than an attempt to capitalize on people's concerns about the environment. One research group studied thirty-five U.S. corporations and found that many of them are using "green marketing" as a smokescreen while they continue to pollute the environment.[45]

Many companies have also been charged with making false or misleading environmental claims in their packaging or advertising. In response, many states and the Federal Trade Commission (FTC) have issued guidelines for green marketers. For instance, California's truth-in-environmental-advertising law makes it harder for companies to use the words *recycled* and *recyclable* for packaging.[46] The FTC's guidelines strongly encourage manufacturers and marketers to back up environmental claims with competent and reliable scientific evidence and to avoid overstating a product's environmental benefits.[47]

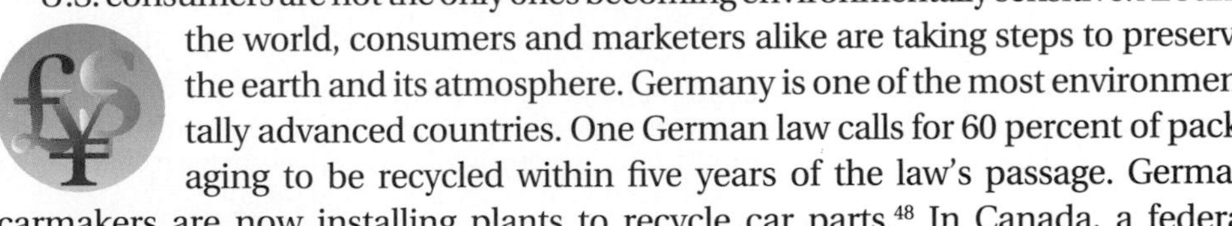

U.S. consumers are not the only ones becoming environmentally sensitive. Around the world, consumers and marketers alike are taking steps to preserve the earth and its atmosphere. Germany is one of the most environmentally advanced countries. One German law calls for 60 percent of packaging to be recycled within five years of the law's passage. German carmakers are now installing plants to recycle car parts.[48] In Canada, a federal program called Environmental Choice sets environmental standards for products claiming to be environmentally friendly. Guidelines have been introduced for thirty-four product types, and more than 600 products have been certified through the program.[49]

GLOBAL MARKETING ETHICS

There has been a strong trend in recent years toward globalization of corporations. As the number of multinational firms increases, companies and nations inevitably become more interdependent. Hence, they must learn to cooperate for their mutual benefit. However, because of cultural differences among multinational companies, increased interdependence will also heighten the potential for conflicts, many of which will involve marketing ethics.[50] In addition, developing nations may not always be able to impose their marketing, environmental, and human rights regulations on large multinational firms. Some of the major ethical issues faced by international marketers are detailed in Exhibit 20.4.

Differences in Ethics Globally

Studies have suggested that ethical beliefs vary only little from culture to culture.[51] However, certain practices, such as the use of illegal payments and bribes, are far more acceptable in some places than in others. Some countries have a dual standard concerning illegal payments. For example, German businesspeople typically treat bribes as tax-deductible business expenses.[52] In Russia, bribes and connections in the government are essential for doing business. For bureaucratic tasks, such as registering a business, bribing a public

Exhibit 20.4

Major Ethical Problems Faced by Multinational Companies

Source: Adapted from Robert W. Armstrong, "An Empirical Investigation of International Marketing Ethics: Problems Encountered by Australian Firms," *Journal of Business Ethics,* March 1992, pp. 161–171. Reprinted by permission of Kluwer Academic Publishers.

Traditional small-scale bribery: payment of a small sum of money (for example, a "grease payment" or kickback), typically to a foreign official, in exchange for his or her violation of some official duty or responsibility or in an effort to speed routine government actions

Large-scale bribery: relatively large payment (for example, a political contribution) intended to allow a violation of the law or to influence policy directly or indirectly

Gifts/favors/entertainment: lavish physical gifts, opportunities for personal travel at the company's expense, gifts received after the completion of a transaction, expensive entertainment

Pricing: unfair differential pricing, questionable invoicing (when the buyer requests a written invoice showing a price other than the actual price paid), pricing to force out local competition, dumping products at prices well below those in the home country, pricing practices that are illegal in the home country but legal in the host country (for example, price-fixing agreements)

Products/technology: products and technology that are banned for use in the home country but permitted in the host country or that appear unsuitable or inappropriate for use by the people in the host country

Tax evasion: practices used specifically to evade taxes, such as transfer pricing (adjusting the prices paid between affiliates and the parent company so as to affect profit allocation), "tax havens" (shifting profits to a low-tax jurisdiction), adjusted interest payments on intrafirm loans, questionable management and service fees charged between affiliates and the parent company

Illegal/immoral activities in the host country: practices such as polluting the environment; maintaining unsafe working conditions; copying products or technology where protection of patents, trade names, or trademarks has not been enforced; short-weighting overseas shipments so as to charge a phantom weight

Questionable commissions to channel members: unreasonably large commissions or fees paid to channel members, such as sales agents, middlemen, consultants, dealers, and importers

Cultural differences: differences between cultures involving potential misunderstandings related to the traditional requirements of the exchange process (for example, transactions regarded as bribes by one culture but acceptable in another)—including gifts, monetary payments, favors, entertainment, political contributions that are not considered part of normal business practices in one's own culture

Involvement in political affairs: marketing activities related to politics, including the exertion of political influence by multinationals, marketing activities when either the home or the host country is at war, and illegal technology transfer

official is the fastest method. It usually costs about 100,000 rubles ($500).[53] What we call bribery is a natural way of doing business in some other cultures. For global marketers, it may be best to adopt a "when in Rome do as the Romans do" mentality.[54]

In yet another example of cultural differences, the Japanese rarely enforce their antitrust laws. Everyday business practices, from retail pricing to business structuring, ignore antitrust regulations against restraint of trade, monopolies, and price discrimination. Not surprisingly, the Japanese are tolerant of scandals involving antitrust violations, favoritism, price fixing, bribery, and other activities considered unethical in the United States.[55]

Foreign Corrupt Practices Act
Legislation prohibiting U.S. corporations from making illegal payments to public officials of foreign governments in order to obtain business rights or enhance their business dealings in that country.

Concern about U.S. corporations' use of illegal payments and bribes in international business dealings led to passage of the **Foreign Corrupt Practices Act** in 1977. This act prohibits U.S. corporations from making illegal payments to public officials of foreign governments to obtain business rights or enhance their business dealings in that country. The act has been criticized for putting U.S. businesses at a competitive disadvantage. Many contend that bribery is an unpleasant but necessary part of international business.[56]

Exploitation of Developing Countries

For companies, the benefits of seeking international growth are several. A company that cannot grow further in its domestic market may reap increased economies of scale and market penetration by not only exporting its product but also by producing it abroad. A company may also wish to diversify its political and economic risk by spreading its operations across several nations.

Expanding into developing countries offers multinational companies the benefits of low-cost labor and natural resources. But many multinational firms have been criticized for exploiting developing countries. Although the firms' business practices may be legal, many business ethicists argue that they are unethical.[57] The problem is compounded by the intense competition among developing countries for industrial development. Ethical standards are often overlooked by governments hungry for jobs or tax revenues.

Take the tobacco industry, for instance. With tobacco sales decreasing and regulations stiffening in the United States and Western Europe, tobacco companies have come to believe that their future lies elsewhere: in Asia, Africa, Eastern Europe, and Russia. Despite the known health risks of their product, the large tobacco companies are pushing their way into markets that typically have few marketing or health-labeling controls. In Hungary, Marlboro cigarettes are sometimes handed out to young fans at pop concerts. Since 1987, cigarette advertising on Japanese television has soared from fortieth to second place in air time and value; it appears even during children's shows.[58]

Interestingly, at a time when smoking is being discouraged in the United States, U.S. trade representatives are talking to developing countries like China and Thailand about lowering their tariffs on foreign cigarettes. Japan, Taiwan, and South Korea have already given in to the threats.[59] Entering these developing countries, the tobacco companies and trade representatives insist, will help U.S. tobacco manufacturers make up for losses in their home market.

Environmental issues are another example. As U.S. environmental laws and regulations gain strength, many companies are moving their operations to developing countries, where it is often less expensive to operate. These countries generally enforce minimal or no clean-air and waste-disposal regulations. An increasing number of U.S. companies have located manufacturing plants, called *maquiladoras*, in

Mexico along the U.S.-Mexican border. Mexico has few pollution laws, and so *maquiladoras* have been allowed to pollute the air and water and dump hazardous wastes along the border. Many blame the *maquiladoras* for "not putting back into the border area what they have been taking out," referring to the region's inadequate sewers and water-treatment plants. Because Mexico has been eager to attract foreign employers, *maquiladoras* pay little in taxes, which would normally go toward improving the infrastructure. Ciudad Juarez, a populous and polluted *maquiladora* city bordering El Paso, Texas, generates 22 million gallons of sewage a day. It has no sewage system at all.[60]

Many fear that passage of the North American Free Trade Agreement (NAFTA) will result in further environmental problems in Mexico, as well as in Canada and the United States. NAFTA will eliminate all tariffs on trade among the three countries within fifteen years of passage, reducing the cost of thousands of products.[61] Some strenuously oppose NAFTA because of the environmental compromises that may be required.

4 CORPORATE SOCIAL RESPONSIBILITY

Ethics and social responsibility are closely intertwined. Besides questioning tobacco companies' ethics, one might ask whether they are acting in a socially responsible manner when they promote tobacco. Are companies that produce low-cost handguns socially responsible in light of the fact that these guns are used in the majority of inner-city crimes? **Corporate social responsibility** is business's concern for society's welfare. This concern is demonstrated by managers who consider both the long-range best interests of the company and the company's relationship to the society within which it operates.

corporate social responsibility
Business's concern for society's welfare, demonstrated by managers who consider both the long-range best interests of the company and the company's relationship to the society within which it operates.

The Case for Social Responsibility

Several arguments might lead a company to practice social responsibility.[62] The arguments for social responsibility include the following:

- *Changing public expectations:* Before the 1960s, the general understanding between business and society was that economic growth was the source of all progress. The mission of business, and the extent of its social responsibility, was to produce goods and services at a profit. We now recognize that economic growth sometimes has **social costs**, which are costs not directly paid for by individual consumers but borne by society as a whole. Examples include pollution, a massive underprivileged class, deteriorating cities, traffic congestion, unsafe work environments, and many other social problems. The new contract between society and business expects that business will reduce these social costs. Society now feels that business organizations must work for social as well as economic progress.

social cost
Cost not directly paid for by individual consumers but borne by society as a whole.

- *Long-run self-interest:* By helping to make the environment a better place in which to live and work, business creates conditions that are favorable for its survival and profitability. Enlightened self-interest dictates a concern for social problems. Business cannot hope to remain viable in a deteriorating society.
- *Avoidance of government regulation:* If business doesn't respond properly to societal concerns, the political system is left to address these issues. The political response is often legislation. Regulations and laws tend to restrict a company's decision-making freedom and reduce strategic options. History

As an emblem of its sense of corporate responsibility to the greater society, State Farm Insurance presents Good Neighbor Awards to people who are contributing on a local level.

Reprinted with permission of State Farm Insurance Companies

has proved that business irresponsibility has led to new regulations and, in some cases, formation of new regulatory bodies. Examples include the truth in lending and truth in packaging laws, the Environmental Protection Agency, and the Consumer Product Safety Commission.

- *Business's useful resources:* Business has the economic tools to take effective action: managerial talent, technical knowledge, and financial and physical resources to help remedy society's ills. Business is also known for its innovative and efficient use of resources. Therefore, business should be encouraged or even forced to try solving social problems.

The Case against Social Responsibility

Despite the strong case for social responsibility on the part of business, some critics don't support the concept wholeheartedly or oppose it entirely. The arguments against social responsibility include the following:

- *Business's lack of understanding:* The free-enterprise system is designed to allocate resources for the production of private goods and services. Prefer-

ences and desires for public goods and services, such as children's welfare programs and training for the hard-core unemployed, are not revealed through the marketplace. Therefore, business has no mechanism for discovering needs for social programs. Also, business success is measured by achieving tangible goals, such as attaining a certain market share or level of profitability. How would business measure the success of a social program? A firm doesn't reach profit goals in pollution control or affirmative action programs.

- *Increase of business power:* Without overall controls, guidelines, and success measures, a corporation's social actions can be arbitrary. A corporation may decide to make a grant to a museum or hire the disadvantaged solely on the basis of what management thinks is important. When managers make such decisions about social investments, they have no guidelines and are not accountable for their actions. Managers, in effect, are imposing taxes on the public by using stockholders', consumers', and employees' money for public purposes. By taking over activities traditionally in the domain of government or community agencies, business may become more powerful than it should be.
- *Dilution of responsibility to shareholders:* Theodore Levitt, a marketing philosopher, and Milton Friedman, a noted economist, argue that the social responsibility of business is to earn an adequate return for the stockholders. Levitt says that business should take care of the material aspects of welfare and government should handle the general welfare. The business of business is earning profits. Friedman says that the sole responsibility of business is to employ its resources in activities that yield profits, so long as business stays within the framework of the laws established by society. If profits are diluted too much by spending for social causes, stockholder returns will be too low to attract capital to the firm, ultimately leading to the company's downfall.
- *Creation of a disjointed effort:* Since there are no overall guidelines for business to follow in setting up social programs, companies will pursue whatever they think is important. The result will be a disjointed, unfocused, random pattern of programs. Only government can determine social priorities and then focus resources to achieve social goals.

Social Responsibility Today

Despite the arguments against social responsibility, most large corporations feel they should do more than simply earn a profit. Public opinion favors the practice of social responsibility by business. For years, however, managers have been struggling with the issue. In the beginning it was argued, in the manner of Levitt and Friedman, that businesses' first and only responsibility was to make a profit for stockholders. It became apparent, however, that this pursuit of financial gain had to take place within the laws of society. Social legislation of the 1970s made this fact clear. The result was the creation of several government bodies—including the Environmental Protection Agency, the Equal Employment Opportunity Commission, the Occupational Safety and Health Administration, and the Consumer Product Safety Commission—that recognized the environment, employees, and consumers as *stakeholders* in business. From that time on, business managers have had to learn how to balance their commitments to the corporation's owners with their obligations to a growing group of stakeholders who claim both legal and ethical rights to the corporation.[63] These corporate stakeholders include

The Equal Employment Opportunity Commission, set up by the federal government in the 1970s, helps ensure that businesses undertake their responsibility to hire qualified workers regardless of race.

Customers, clients, consumers (direct and indirect)

Debtors (financial institutions, bondholders)

Employees

Government (local, state, federal)

Managers

Organized labor

Owners (stockholders)

Public-at-large

Suppliers[64]

Earning an adequate return is still considered a firm's main social responsibility. If the company receives enough "dollar votes" for its goods and services to meet profit objectives, the firm's output is meeting society's material needs. Today, however, a firm must also develop environmental controls, provide equal employment opportunities, create a safe workplace, produce safe products, and do much more.

pyramid of corporate social responsibility
Theory that suggests corporate social responsibility is composed of economic, legal, ethical, and philanthropic responsibilities and that the firm's economic performance supports the entire structure.

One theorist suggests that four kinds of social responsibilities constitute total corporate social responsibility (or CSR): economic, legal, ethical, and philanthropic.[65] The **pyramid of corporate social responsibility** is shown in Exhibit 20.5. It portrays economic performance as the foundation for the entire structure. At the same time, business is expected to obey the law; to do what is ethically right, just, and fair; and to be a good corporate citizen. Total corporate social responsibility has four distinct components, but together they constitute the whole. Still, if the company doesn't make a profit, then the other three responsibilities are moot.

A study by Mutual Benefit Life found that 91 percent of the CEOs interviewed believed their organizations are obligated to meet the community's needs rather than leave such support to government and the not-for-profit sector.[66] Another survey asked M.B.A. students and executives of the 1,000 largest U.S. companies

Exhibit 20.5

The Pyramid of Corporate Social Responsibility

Source: Adapted from Archie B. Carroll, "The Pyramid of Corporate Responsibility: Toward the Moral Management of Organizational Stakeholders," *Business Horizons,* July/August 1991, pp. 39–48.

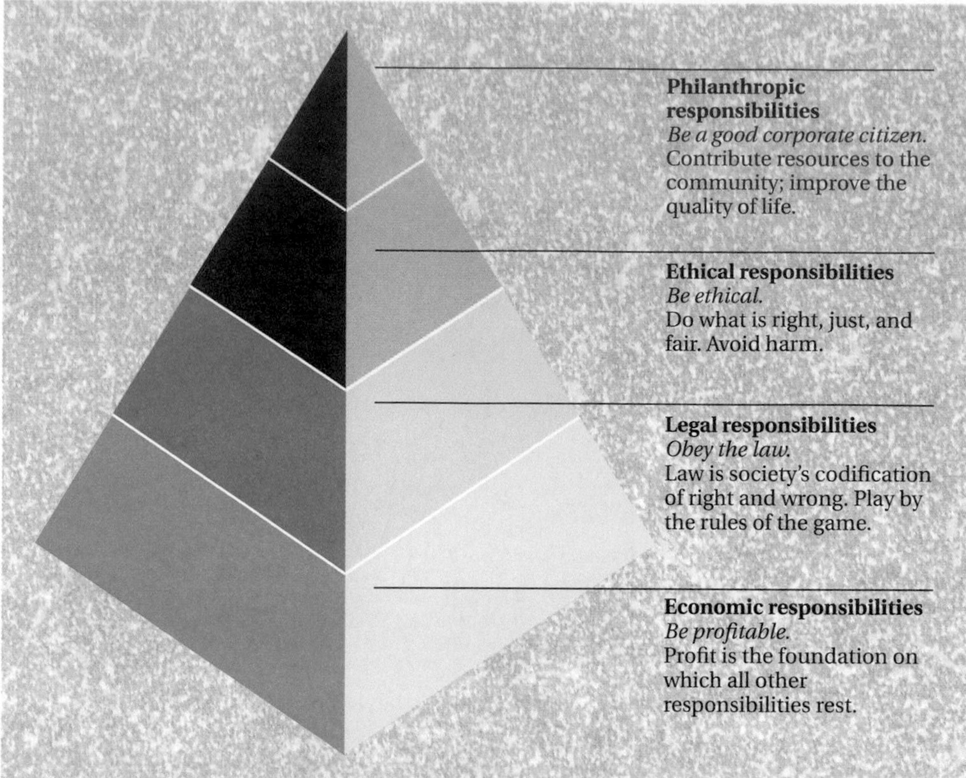

whether business should undertake more social programs. An overwhelming majority of both today's and tomorrow's leaders believe that business must become more socially responsible.[67]

Many companies are already working to make the world a better place to live. Consider these examples:

- Metropolitan Life donates over $1 million a year and Levi Strauss over $500,000 to AIDS education and support services.[68]
- Ben & Jerry's, the premium ice cream maker, sent seven workers to live with Cree Indians in Canada to see how they've been displaced by a new hydroelectric power complex.[69]
- Jantzen, the world's leading swimsuit manufacturer, makes direct grants to organizations that preserve and clean up beaches and waterways through its Clean Water campaign.[70]
- Apple Computer donates about $8 million in computer equipment and advice to U.S. schools annually.
- G.D. Searle began a program in which its representatives regularly call hypertension (high blood pressure) patients, reminding them to take their medicine.[71]

Multinational companies also have important social responsibilities. In many cases a corporation can be a dynamic force for social change in host countries. For example, multinational corporations played a major role in breaking down apartheid in South Africa, through their economic pressure on the South African government. Apartheid is the form of government that keeps the races separate. Over 300 apartheid laws were compiled over the years, based purely on the pigmentation of one's skin. Among other things, these laws forced blacks to live in the most arid regions of South Africa, banned mixed marriages, and segregated the schools. To protest apartheid, many multinational corporations closed their South African operations altogether. Other companies refused to trade with South Africa. These actions seriously impeded South Africa's economy, and by the end of the 1980s the government began making major social reforms.[72]

5 Marketing Social Responsibility

Social responsibility programs require planning and organization. They also require the efforts of the entire corporation, not just of the marketing department. However, the discussion that follows pertains only to the marketing aspects of social responsibility.

The vehicle for marketing social responsibilities in most companies is the consumer affairs department. In the past this department only handled consumer complaints and distributed consumer education materials, mostly about company products. Examples include S.C. Johnson and Sons' booklets on decorating, gift making, and antique furniture and General Mills' Betty Crocker advisory service on cooking. Other consumer affairs departments take on broader social causes, as does Seagram's campaign against drunk driving. Modern consumer affairs departments monitor company advertisements, provide input for product design, research consumer satisfaction, develop warranties and guarantees, increase product safety, oversee product packaging and labeling, choose suppliers, and improve quality control.[73]

Almost all major U.S. corporations competing in consumer markets now have a formal unit that handles consumer affairs.[74] The chief consumer affairs officer in many companies has a role in policy making and influences decisions about handling consumer inquiries, processing consumer complaints, developing consumer education programs, and researching consumer satisfaction.[75]

During the remainder of the 1990s, consumer affairs departments will broaden their influence over marketing activities. Moreover, in more firms the top consumer affairs person will report directly to the CEO. Consumer affairs department budgets will grow to meet these new and expanding responsibilities.

6 CONSUMERISM

consumerism
Political and economic struggle to increase the rights and powers of buyers in relation to sellers.

The concepts of social responsibility and consumerism go hand in hand. If every organization practiced a high level of social responsibility, the consumer movement might never have begun. **Consumerism** is a struggle for power between buyers and sellers. Specifically, it is a social movement seeking to increase the rights and powers of buyers in relation to sellers.

Sellers' rights and powers include the following:

- To introduce into the marketplace any product, in any size and style, that is not hazardous to personal health or safety, or if it is hazardous, to introduce it with the proper warnings and controls
- To price the product at any level they wish, provided they do not discriminate among similar classes of buyers
- To spend any amount of money they wish to promote the product, so long as the promotion is not defined as unfair competition
- To formulate any message they wish about the product, provided that it is not misleading or dishonest in content or execution

As Upton Sinclair described the meat-packing industry at the turn of the century, it was a hazard to workers and consumers alike.
The Bettmann Archive

- To introduce any buying incentives they wish

In contrast, these are buyers' rights and powers:

- To refuse to buy any product that is offered to them
- To expect the product to be safe
- To expect the product to be essentially as the seller represented it
- To receive adequate information about the product

The History of Consumerism

Contrary to popular opinion, consumerism is not new. The roots of this social movement can be traced to the nineteenth century.

The first consumer protection law, passed in 1872, made it a federal crime to defraud consumers through the mail. Perhaps the first general consumer outcry was heard in 1906 with the publication of Upton Sinclair's *The Jungle.* The book was a devastating exposé of the U.S. meat-packing industry. The following excerpt from *The Jungle* describes some of the horrors:

> These rats were nuisances, and the packers would put poisoned bread out for them and they would die, and then rats, bread and meat would go into the hoppers together. . . . Men, who worked in the tank rooms full of steam . . . fell into the vats; and when they were fished out, there was never enough of them to be worth exhibiting—sometimes they would be overlooked for days, till all but the bones of them had gone out to the world as Durham's Pure Leaf Lard![76]

The book helped ensure passage of the Pure Food and Drug Act of 1906 (see Chapter 2).

Throughout the late 1960s and mid-1970s, consumerism became quite influential. Inspired by the crusades of Ralph Nader and others, consumerism peaked during this period. It was less influential in the 1980s and early 1990s.

Several factors account for a decline in consumer activism. First, consumers seem more satisfied with the goods and services being placed on the market. A Gallup poll found that nearly half the respondents feel U.S. products are very high in quality, and two-thirds believe U.S. products better suit their needs than foreign

Whirlpool Corporation, headquartered in Benton Harbor, Michigan, is a prime example of a company that is responsive to consumer needs.
Courtesy of Whirlpool Corporation

made goods.[77] Second, the growing sense of social responsibility in U.S. business has heightened managers' awareness of consumer issues.[78] As a result, managers have been able to foresee and prevent problems that anger consumers. A third factor is demographics. The social unrest of the 1960s was a response partly to the U.S. role in the Vietnam conflict and partly to big increases in the proportion of 18- to 20-year-olds in the U.S. population. Rapid increases in the numbers of this specific age segment were enough to cause social and economic disharmony. Compared to previous generations, this group was more resistant to government, authority figures, and the accepted culture.[79] Today's far smaller group of 18- to 20-year-olds suggests to some demographers that interest in the consumer movement will remain unchanged for some time.

This plateau does not suggest that consumer abuse no longer exists. For instance, some companies use sham marketing research studies for fund-raising and "sugging"—selling under the guise of research. There is high-pressure selling and fraud in marketing condos, lake lots, and other things. Prospective buyers are promised wonderful gifts if they will visit the site in person. However, a "personal computer" can turn out to be a hand-held calculator; a "car phone" may actually be a toy phone shaped like a car.

Business Response to Consumerism

Only a few firms have been guilty of consumer abuse. Billions of satisfactory exchanges occur every day. Some companies enjoy an excellent reputation. Exhibit 20.6 shows the most admired U.S. corporations. To come up with the list, *Fortune* magazine asked more than 8,000 senior executives, outside directors, and financial analysts to rate the ten largest companies in their own industry on quality of management; quality of goods or services; innovativeness; long-term investment value; financial soundness; ability to attract, develop, and keep talented people; responsibility to the community and environment; and wise use of corporate assets.

Many companies are taking innovative measures to respond to consumer needs. Whirlpool spends over $500,000 a year operating a nationwide, toll-free complaint line. Pennsylvania Power and Light Company (PP&L) pioneered the utility-consumer conference. It now conducts regular meetings between PP&L departments and consumer panels.

Many consumer organizations have written codes of conduct for companies to

Exhibit 20.6

The Most-Admired U.S. Corporations

Source: Adapted from Kate Ballen, "America's Most Admired Corporations," *Fortune*, 10 February 1992, pp. 40–72.

Rank	Previous year's rank	Company (and industry)
1	1	Merck (pharmaceuticals)
2	2	Rubbermaid (rubber/plastic products)
3	4	Wal-Mart Stores (retailing)
4	10	Liz Claiborne (apparel)
5	20	Levi Strauss (apparel)
6	8	Johnson & Johnson (pharmaceuticals)
7	6	Coca-Cola (beverages)
8	6	3M (scientific and photo equipment)
9 (tie)	5	PepsiCo (beverages)
9 (tie)	3	Procter & Gamble (soaps, cosmetics)

follow. One set of guidelines comes from a coalition of environmentalists and other groups in the wake of the 1989 Alaskan oil spill, one of the worst oil spills in history. Referred to as the "Valdez Principles," after the Exxon tanker involved in the spill, this voluntary code of conduct guides companies toward higher environmental standards (see Exhibit 20.7). Companies are encouraged to sign the code and adhere to its principles.[80]

Perhaps the business world's attitude toward consumerism is best expressed by business leaders themselves:

> Every decision involves giving up something to get something. . . . The real intelligent course involves being sure that you deliver the quality the customer expects, not sacrificing quality to increase earnings. And if you make that call correctly, you may make a little less today but you're likely to make more in the future. So I think when an individual's goals or a corporation's goals are very much out of line with society's goals, they're in trouble. . . . The fact is you can't be a large, successful corporation and be working against the public will; not for long.
>
> —*Richard Hecker, Chairman and CEO, DuPont*

> The only way for a corporation to exist and capitalism to survive is to be part of the whole society. We depend upon a healthy environment to sell our products, to hire people, to have customers to sell to. . . . I really do think, particularly the large corporations, if they are going to survive as entities, the only way to do that is feel a responsibility to the communities that [they] operate in. Companies have to be concerned with the owners—the shareholders, the employees, and the customers. And the fourth is the communities [they] operate in, whether that's the country [they] operate in or a local community.
>
> —*David T. Kearns, chairman and CEO, Xerox*

> Corporations can be short-sighted and worry only about our mission, products, and competitive standing. But we do it at our peril. The day will come when corporations will discover the price we pay for our indifference. We must realize that by ignoring the needs of others, we are actually ignoring our own needs in the long run. We may need the goodwill of a neighborhood to enlarge a corner store. We may need well-funded institutions of higher learning to turn out the skilled technical employees we require. We may need adequate community health care to curb absenteeism in our plants. Or we may need fair tax treatment for an industry to be able to compete in the world economy. However small or large our enterprise, we cannot isolate our business from the society around us. Nor can we function without its goodwill.
>
> —*Robert D. Haas, president and CEO, Levi Strauss*[81]

1. Protection of the biosphere

We will minimize and strive to eliminate the release of any pollutant that may cause environmental damage to the air, water, or earth or its inhabitants. We will safeguard habitats in rivers, lakes, wetlands, coastal zones, and oceans and will minimize our contribution to the greenhouse effect, depletion of the ozone layer, acid rain, or smog.

2. Sustainable use of natural resources

We will make sustainable use of renewable natural resources, such as water, soils, and forests. We will conserve nonrenewable natural resources through efficient use and careful planning. We will protect wildlife habitat, open spaces, and wilderness while preserving biodiversity.

3. Reduction and disposal of waste

We will minimize the creation of waste, especially hazardous waste, and whenever possible recycle material. We will dispose of all waste through safe and responsible methods.

4. Wise use of energy

We will make every effort to use environmentally safe and sustainable energy sources to meet our needs. We will invest in improved energy efficiency and conservation in our operations. We will maximize the energy efficiency of products we produce and sell.

5. Risk reduction

We will minimize the environmental, health, and safety risks to our employees and the comunities in which we operate by employing safe technologies and operating procedures and by being constantly prepared for emergencies.

6. Marketing of safe products

We will sell goods or services that minimize adverse environmental impacts and that are safe as consumers commonly use them. We will inform consumers of the environmental impacts of our goods and services.

7. Damage compensation

We will take responsibility for any harm we cause to the environment by making every effort to fully restore the environment and to compensate those persons who are adversely affected.

8. Disclosure

We will disclose to our employees and to the public incidents relating to our operations that cause environmental harm or pose health or safety hazards. We will disclose potential environmental, health, or safety hazards posed by our operations and will not take any action against employees who report any condition that creates a danger to the environment or poses health and safety standards.

9. Environmental directors and managers

We will commit management resources to implement the Valdez Principles, to monitor and report upon our implementation efforts, and to sustain a process to ensure that the Board of Directors and Chief Executive Officer are kept informed of and are fully responsible for all environmental matters. We will establish a Committee of the Board of Directors with responsibility for environmental affairs. At least onc member of the Board of Directors will be a person qualified to represent environmental interests before the company.

10. Assessment and annual audit

We will conduct and make public an annual self-evaluation of our progress in implementing these Principles and in complying with all applicable laws and regulations throughout our worldwide operations. We will work toward the timely creation of independent environmental audit procedures, which we will complete annually and make available to the public.

Exhibit 20.7

The Valdez Principles

Source: Adapted from Rajib N. Sanyal and Joao S. Neves, "The Valdez Principles: Implications for Corporate Social Responsibility," *Journal of Business Ethics*, December 1991, pp. 883–890. Reprinted by permission of Kluwer Academic Publishers.

If companies across the country adopt the philosophy of these three executives, then consumerism might die for lack of issues. Such philosophies, universally adopted, would go a long way toward making U.S. firms competitive in world markets.

LOOKING BACK

In light of what you have learned in this chapter, think back now to the opening story on the marketing of handguns. You will probably agree that gunmakers should be more socially responsible in marketing their products. You may also agree that gunmakers should be more concerned with product safety instead of producing as many guns as possible for the least cost.

Although quite a few companies in the United States lack a sense of social responsibility, many others try hard to be socially responsible. For example, both Wal-Mart and McDonald's have programs to employ the disabled. Wal-Mart is also a good corporate citizen: In the 1992 presidential election the company was responsible for registering 150,000 voters.

KEY TERMS

code of ethics 672
consumerism 687
conventional morality 670
corporate social responsibility 682
ethics 668
Foreign Corrupt Practices Act 681
green marketing 678
morals 669
postconventional morality 671
preconventional morality 670
pyramid of corporate social responsibility 685
social cost 682

SUMMARY

1 Define the meaning of business ethics. *Ethics* refers to moral principles governing the conduct of an individual or group. Judgment is often needed to determine what is ethical versus what is legal. Morals are rules or habits that people develop as a result of cultural values and norms. Morals can be considered the foundation of ethical behavior.

2 Describe the nature of ethical decision making. Business ethics may be viewed as a subset of the values of society as a whole. The ethical conduct of businesspeople is shaped by societal elements, including family, education, religion, social movements, and so on. As members of society, businesspeople are morally obligated to consider the ethical implications of their decisions.

Ethical decision making is approached in three basic ways. The first approach examines the consequences of decisions. The second approach relies on rules and laws to guide decision making. The third approach is based on a theory of moral development that places individuals or groups in one of three developmental stages: preconventional morality, conventional morality, or postconventional morality.

Consumers often perceive marketing activities as unethical and manipulative. Marketers may find themselves in situations in which the needs of the business and the needs of customers, suppliers, or society as a whole are at odds. Three major factors have been found to influence the ethical behavior of marketing professionals: the extent of ethical problems within an organization, top management's actions regarding ethics, and the individual's role within an organization.

Many companies develop a code of ethics to help their employees make ethical decisions. A code of ethics can help employees identify acceptable business practices, can be an effective internal control on behavior, can help employees avoid confusion when determining the ethicality of decisions, and can facilitate discussion about what is right and wrong.

3 Discuss several current ethical dilemmas and global marketing ethics issues. Current major ethical dilemmas for marketing managers include tobacco and alcohol promotion, consumer privacy, and green marketing.

Marketing managers selling their goods or services globally should also be aware of what is considered ethical behavior in other countries. For example, bribery is often a standard business practice in other countries, although it is considered illegal and unethical in the United States. Multinational marketers must also be careful not to exploit developing countries that have unsophisticated marketing and environmental regulations.

4 Discuss corporate social responsibility. Social responsibility in business refers to a firm's concern for the way its decisions affect society. There are several arguments in support of social responsibility. First, many consumers feel business should take responsibility for the social costs of economic growth. A second argument contends that firms act in their own best interest when they help improve the environment within which they operate. Third, firms can avoid restrictive government regulation by responding willingly to societal concerns. Finally, some people argue that because firms have the resources to solve social problems, they are morally obligated to do so.

In contrast, there are critics who argue against corporate social responsibility. According to one argument, the free-enterprise system has no way to decide which social programs should have priority. A second argument contends that firms involved in social programs do not generate the profits needed to support the business's activities and earn a fair return for stockholders.

In spite of the arguments against corporate social responsibility, most businesspeople believe they should do more than pursue only profits. Although a company must consider its economic needs first, it must also operate within the law, do what is ethical and fair, and be a good corporate citizen.

5 **Explain the ways in which marketing meets its social responsibility.** Marketers have met their social responsibilities by setting up consumer affairs departments to monitor company advertising, product design, consumer satisfaction, product safety, product packaging and labeling, supplier selection, and quality control. Consumer affairs departments also handle consumer inquiries, process consumer complaints, develop consumer education programs, and create warranties and guarantees.

6 **Discuss consumerism.** Consumerism is a social movement in which buyers struggle to increase their rights and power in relation to sellers. Originating during the late nineteenth century, consumerism in the United States became an active and influential movement in the 1960s and 1970s. The decline of consumer activism in the 1980s and early 1990s is believed to be the result of several factors. First, consumers appear to be more satisfied with the goods and services provided in today's marketplace. Second, marketers have become more sensitive to consumer concerns. Finally, social unrest has declined in general because of changing demographics and the end of the Vietnam conflict.

Review Questions

1. Explain the concepts of preconventional, conventional, and postconventional levels of morality.
2. Identify the organizational factors that influence the ethical judgment of marketing professionals.
3. What is green marketing? Why is it a controversial marketing trend?
4. Describe the main arguments in favor of corporate social responsibility.
5. Explain the four levels of the pyramid of corporate social responsibility.
6. Describe the role of the contemporary consumer affairs department.
7. What are the rights and powers of sellers and buyers in contemporary business?

Discussion and Writing Questions

1. Cite examples of preconventional, conventional, and postconventional moral conduct in marketing.
2. Describe an ethical dilemma in contemporary marketing not covered in this chapter. How do you feel about the firm's solution?
3. You have been invited to debate the question of how much responsibility businesses should assume for the welfare of society and its environment. Draft notes of your position, and anticipate the response of your debating partner.
4. Why has the consumer movement faded in the 1980s and early 1990s?
5. In today's marketplace, many businesses seem to have become more responsive to consumers. Suggest possible reasons for this trend.
6. For each of the following, write a paragraph discussing the ethical dilemma described and identifying possible solutions.
   a. An insurance agent forgets to get the required signature from one of his clients who is buying an automobile insurance policy. The client acknowledges the purchase by giving the agent a signed personal check for the full amount. To avoid embarrassment and inconvenience, the agent forges the client's signature on the insurance application and sends it to the insurance company for processing.

b. A local fire alarm manufacturer relies on the door-to-door selling efforts of its sales staff. The company provides its sales force with a selling kit that includes newspaper clippings about fire victims, including photographs of badly burned children. The salespeople use the clippings to make people aware of the need for early fire detection.

CASES

20.1 Hooters, Inc.

Everyone seems to be taking sides when it comes to Hooters. The many fans of the fast-growing restaurant chain like its affordable food and drink, served up by friendly waitresses in a cheery atmosphere. Typical Hooters outlets feature rustic pine floors and tables, spicy chicken wings, and beer by the pitcher. TV monitors run nonstop sports videos, and the background music is golden oldies from the 1960s.

Critics claim the chain's appeal is blatantly sexist, from its name (slang for breasts) to the showcasing of its waitresses, called "Hooter Girls" and dressed in skimpy, revealing uniforms. Critics accuse the chain of fostering a climate in which sexual harassment can thrive. "The name should be changed because of the derogatory references to human anatomy," says the leader of a Fairfax, Virginia, group founded to protest the opening of a Hooters outlet.

Big profits can still be made from sexism, even in the 1990s. From its birth in 1983 in Clearwater, Florida, Hooters has grown into a nationwide network of 68 casual eateries in sixteen states. It expects to reach 200 restaurants by the end of 1994. Systemwide sales, in company-owned units and outlets owned by fifteen franchises, totaled $100 million in 1991. Typical Hooters restaurants serve an average of 500 customers a day, with waiting lines at lunch and dinner.

Hooters uses every opportunity to flaunt its naughty name. The chain annually sells about $5 million worth of Hooters T-shirts, hats, calendars, and other items. The controversial Hooter Girl uniform consists of running shoes, bright orange running shorts, and a cut-off T-shirt with the company's logo—an owl with two very large, saucer-shaped eyes—and the motto "More than a mouthful." (A company executive insists that the motto refers to Hooters' hamburgers.) Company officials say the chain's approach to sex is no different from that of *Sports Illustrated* magazine, which publishes an annual "swimsuit" issue. The magazine's readers "aren't checking out those girls' SAT scores," says the company's marketing vice president, adding that Hooters "doesn't cross the line of what the majority of people think is acceptable." Patrons claim the Hooter Girl uniform is no different from what you might see on someone in the mall or at the park.

All the same, at a time when national concern over men's sexual behavior has reached fever pitch, the chain's "boys-will-be-boys" attitude outrages feminists. The executive vice president of the National Organization for Women says Hooters "contributes to an atmosphere of sexual harassment." She further contends that Hooters resembles a night club or strip joint more than a neighborhood cafe.

Protests focusing on Hooters' image have picked up as the chain has begun aggressive expansion beyond its Sunbelt base. In Fairfax, Virginia, a group that included the mayor and city council members collected 200 signatures on an anti-Hooters petition. In addition to requesting that the restaurant change its name, the group said employees should be allowed to wear uniforms "reflective of a basic family atmosphere." As it turned out, the outcry and attendant publicity helped attract a standing-room-only crowd to the restaurant's opening.

Questions

1. Hooters seems to be doing quite well despite charges that it promotes sexual harassment. Why do you think this is so?
2. Should Hooters be more socially responsible in its marketing techniques? Why or why not?
3. If you were the marketing vice president of Hooters, how would you address criticism of your marketing approach?

Suggested Readings

Eugene Carlson, "Restaurant Chain Tries to Cater to Two Types of Taste," *The Wall Street Journal*, 20 March 1992, p. B2.

John P. Cortez and Ira Teinowitz, "More Trouble Brews for Stroh Bikini Team," *Advertising Age*, 9 December 1991, p. 45.

Cyndee Miller, "Babe-Based Beer Ads Likely to Flourish," *Marketing News*, 6 January 1992, pp. 1, 10.

Ira Teinowitz, "This Bud's for Her," *Advertising Age*, 28 October 1991, pp. 1, 49.

20.2 The Body Shop

Video title: *Trade Not Aid: The Body Shop's Cactus Scrub Project*

The Body Shop, Inc.
45 Horsehill Road
Cedar Knolls, NJ 07927

SIC code: 2844 Toilet preparations

Number of employees: 180

1993 revenues: $28 million

Major products: Naturally based skin and hair care products

Largest competitors: Amway, Mary Kay, Johnson & Johnson, Gillette

Background

Anita and T. Gordon Roddick opened the first Body Shop in 1976. The first store, in Brighton, England, was stocked with fifteen different products, all manufactured by third parties. The Roddicks realized that their best hope for growth was through franchising. Within one year, the company had granted franchises in England. By the end of the second year, the company had moved outside Great Britain with franchises in Brussels and Stockholm. The first U.S. franchises opened in 1988. By 1991 the company had over 700 stores around the world.

From its humble beginnings, the company has grown rapidly. It has also won many awards. Anita Roddick was chosen as Businesswoman of the Year in 1985. The Body Shop was chosen Company of the Year in 1987 and Retailer of the Year in 1989. The company also won the Queen's Award for Export in 1990.

Industry

Industry experts predict that makers of personal care products will continue to grow between 10 and 12 percent per year. These companies should expect higher profits from cost control programs, research and development, increases in selling prices, and new high-end merchandise. Some of the smaller producers will be acquired by larger manufacturers seeking to increase sales in international markets. Markets like Japan and Germany are two of the most important overseas markets. Because of changes since 1992, Europe will prove to be a major source of revenues for many of these manufacturers.

The Body Shop International

In 1983 The Body Shop began making some of its own products. Today it makes a wide line of naturally based skin and hair care products. The company makes no extravagant claims about any of its all-natural products and in fact does very little advertising. Some packages even list all the ingredients in the product. The stores offer a manual of products and their suggested uses.

The Body Shop has expanded rapidly by selling franchises. The company selects a head franchisee for each country or group of countries. This person has exclusive rights to the name and product lines within that region and is responsible for setting up subfranchisees. This method allows the company to gain the local expertise needed to sell its product lines without a big investment. The Body Shop then acts as a wholesaler to these franchisees. The franchisees offer The Body Shop ideas for new product lines.

The Body Shop's success has been built on variety. The company was one of the first to offer a large selection of products for various types of skin and hair. In 1986 the company launched its Mostly Men line of personal care products. The company continues to increase its product offerings each year. In 1991 alone, the company introduced more than fifty new products. The wide product line and continuous product innovation have kept The Body Shop at the forefront of the personal care industry.

The Body Shop has also been environment-oriented from the very beginning. Consider the company's choice of packaging: Many competitors have opted for expensive and unique packaging, but The Body Shop sticks with simple designs. Most of the products are sold in reusable bottles, and the company offers refill services on many of its high-volume product lines. The company supports recycling efforts on all packages. When it comes to environmental issues in the personal care products industry, the competition trails The Body Shop.

Questions

1. Explain the benefits of "trade not aid" to both The Body Shop and native Mexicans.
2. Do you think consumers really care about environmental issues? Explain your answer.

References

The Body Shop Annual Report, 1992.

Ward's Business Directory of U.S. Private and Public Companies (Detroit: Gale Research, Inc., 1992).

LEARNING OBJECTIVES

After studying this chapter, you should be able to

1. Describe the concept of strategic planning, and identify the steps in the strategic planning process.
2. Understand how businesses define their mission and form strategic business units.
3. Describe how businesses conduct a situation analysis, including identification of strategic windows and differential advantages.
4. Discuss the techniques for developing, evaluating, and selecting strategic alternatives.
5. Understand how firms implement strategies and alter strategies when necessary.
6. Identify several techniques to help make strategic planning effective.
7. Understand sales forecasting techniques.
8. Discuss global issues in strategic planning and forecasting.

CHAPTER 21

Strategic Planning and Forecasting

As a young couple named James Sloat and Laura Musser pledged endless love in a Maryland chapel, one wedding guest beamed especially broadly. He was Bert C. Roberts, the chairman of MCI Communications Corp.

The couple had asked him to the wedding to show their appreciation for discounts that cut their long-distance phone bills while they were courting. The MCI boss not only accepted the invitation—he swiftly turned it into a marketing weapon. The Sloats' nuptials soon were featured on two TV commercials that MCI threw into the war for long-distance market share.

That war has been running for years, of course, but this year it has risen to a new plane of intensity. When long-distance carriers' sales pitches aren't blaring from the TV or radio, their telemarketers are on the phone, often during dinner hour. In their struggle for larger chunks of what is now a $55 billion-a-year industry, American Telephone & Telegraph Co., MCI, and Sprint Corp. spent more than $4 billion on marketing in 1993. The supercharged battle is holding down their profits and making it harder for smaller players to compete.

Not only is the battle more intense, it also reflects the evolution of the industry into one offering largely a commodity product. This forces AT&T, MCI, and Sprint to strive for ways to differentiate themselves. At the same time, even as they drive for more market share, the carriers are attempting to *raise* some prices.

From 1990 through 1992, MCI raised its market share from 15 to 17 percent. The gain came primarily at the expense of AT&T, whose 1992 market share was 65 percent. Sprint, meanwhile, is spinning its wheels at about 10 percent as it struggles to keep up with its richer rivals.

MCI's market share gain has been the result of good strategic planning. What is the role of strategic planning in an organization? What is the key factor in making strategic planning work? Where does forecasting fit into strategic planning?

Adapted from John Keller, "AT&T, MCI, Sprint Raise the Intensity of Their Endless War," *The Wall Street Journal,* 20 October 1992, pp.A1, A6. Reprinted by permission of *The Wall Street Journal,*

1 THE NATURE OF STRATEGIC PLANNING

Effective decision making is based on sound planning, which is one of marketing managers' three main functions (organizing and controlling marketing activities being the other two). Specifically, marketing managers must develop both long-range (strategic) and short-range (tactical) plans. Next, they and other managers must organize the firm's resources to carry out the plans effectively and efficiently. Finally, marketing managers create a monitoring system to correct deviations from the plans or change the plans if necessary.

strategic planning
Managerial process of creating and maintaining a fit between the organization's objectives and resources and evolving market opportunities.

Strategic planning is the managerial process of creating and maintaining a fit between the organization's objectives and resources and evolving market opportunities. The goal of strategic planning is long-run profitability and growth. Thus strategic decisions require long-term commitments of resources. A strategic error can threaten the firm's survival. On the other hand, a good strategic plan can help protect a firm's resources against competitive onslaughts.[1] For instance, if the March of Dimes were still fighting polio, the organization would no longer exist. Most of us view polio as a conquered disease. The March of Dimes survived by making the strategic decision to fight birth defects instead of polio.

Strategic marketing management addresses two questions: What is the organization's main activity at a particular time? How will it reach its goals? Here are some examples of strategic decisions:

- Black & Decker's decision to buy General Electric's small consumer appliance division (a strategic success)
- Sears and IBM's joint effort to create the Prodigy on-line computer service (a billion-dollar investment; outcome unknown, but results are positive to date)
- McDonnell Douglas's decision to build the MD-11 passenger aircraft (moderate success)

Sara Lee, a big name in the food business, made the strategic decision to diversify into well-known brands of apparel. One of its acquisitions was Coach leather goods.
Coach Leatherwear

- Procter & Gamble's decision to move to everyday low pricing (implemented in 1992; outcome unknown)
- Delta Airlines' decision to acquire most of PanAm's European routes (outcome unknown, but Delta suffered huge losses in 1992)
- Sara Lee's decision to diversify out of food and to build powerful brand names in clothing (very successful acquisitions of the rights to market Hanes and Bali underwear, Coach leather goods, and Donna Karan hosiery)

All these decisions have affected or will affect the organizations' long-run course, their allocation of resources, and ultimately their financial success. In contrast, an operating decision, such as changing the package design for Post's cornflakes or altering the sweetness of a Seven Seas salad dressing, probably won't have a big impact on the long-run profitability of the company.

THE STRATEGIC PLANNING PROCESS

The strategic planning process has seven phases: (1) defining the business mission, (2) establishing strategic business units (when necessary), (3) conducting a situation analysis, (4) developing strategic alternatives, (5) selecting an alternative, (6) implementing the selected strategy, and (7) altering the selected strategy when necessary (see Exhibit 21.1). Let's look carefully at each of these phases.

2 Define the Business Mission

Perhaps the single most important aspect of strategic planning is answer the question "What business are we in and where are we going?" The answer is the firm's mission statement. The way the firm defines its mission profoundly affects long-run resource allocation, profitability, and survival.

As discussed briefly in Chapter 1, a mission statement should focus on the market or markets the organization is trying to serve rather than on the good or service offered. Otherwise, a new technology may quickly make the good or service obsolete

Exhibit 21.1

The Strategic Planning Process

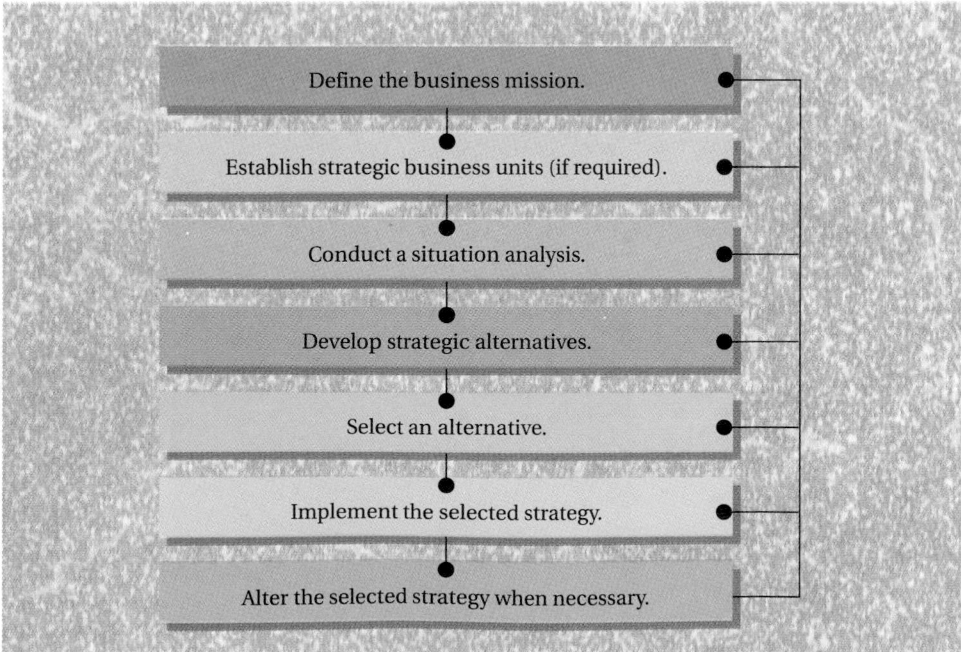

and the mission statement irrelevant to the company's functions. For example, if Frito-Lay had decided that it was in the corn chip business, it would not be an industry leader today. Frito-Lay defines its mission as being in the snack food business. Anheuser-Busch says, "Beer is and always will be our core business. However, other business complementary to beer will be developed over the long term in order to maintain Anheuser-Busch as a growth company."[2] The mission of Saturn Corporation, a subsidiary of General Motors, is "to design, manufacture, and market vehicles to compete on a global scale, as well as re-establish American technology as the standard for automotive quality."[3] Saturn sees its market as small-car consumers who have been committed to the imports.

Establish Strategic Business Units

After defining its mission, the organization may need to set up strategic business units. Small firms often have few products and serve one or two target markets. As they grow, however, they may diversify by offering different types of products. In addition, they may begin to serve different distribution channels and target markets or even enter the international market. For instance, PPG Industries, formerly Pittsburgh Plate Glass, evolved from a small plate-glass manufacturer to a $7.5 billion organization. PPG now has products ranging from chemicals to precision instruments. When companies grow this large, with different technologies and markets, they become big enough to support separate **strategic business units** (SBUs).

strategic business unit
Subgroup in a larger organization, with a distinct mission and specific target market of its own, control over its resources, its own competitors, and plans independent of the other subgroups of the total organization.

When properly created, SBUs have the following characteristics:

- A distinct mission and a specific target market
- Control over their resources
- Their own competitors
- A single business or a collection of related businesses
- Plans independent of the other businesses of the total organization

In theory, an SBU should have its own basic business functions: accounting, engineering, manufacturing, and marketing. In practice, however, because of com-

Large corporations often set up strategic business units, semi-independent businesses operating under the corporate umbrella. At Kraft General Foods, Cheez Whiz and Macaroni & Cheese are in the same SBU.
Kraft General Foods, Inc.

pany tradition, management philosophy, and the ability to achieve production and distribution economies, SBUs sometimes share manufacturing facilities, distribution channels, and even top managers.

There is no "right" number of SBUs for a firm to have. The number depends on management's willingness to delegate authority, the resources available, and the ability to identify natural and logical business units. Kraft General Foods' SBUs already include breakfast foods, desserts, pet foods, and beverages. The firm's groundbreaking work in biotechnology may lead to a new generation of intravenous fluids for critically ill patients—and yet another SBU.

❸ Conduct a Situation Analysis

After defining a mission and establishing any required SBUs, the next step in the strategic planning process is conducting a situation analysis.

SWOT Analyses

A situation analysis is sometimes referred to by the acronym SWOT, meaning that the firm should identify its internal strengths (S) and weaknesses (W) and examine external opportunities (O) and threats (T). In essence, the company is determining its present status, its current capabilities, and its future expectations. A SWOT analysis prompted dog-food maker Alpo into manufacturing cat food.

General Mills conducted a SWOT analysis and learned that large-volume cereal brands are more efficient to manufacture and promote—and thus more profitable. For cold cereals, a large volume is considered to be only 1 percent of the U.S. cold cereal market.[4] One of General Mills' strengths is its old, well-known cereal brands, such as Wheaties, Cheerios, and Kix. Management made a strategic decision to maintain the market share of its successful older cereal brands and increase the market share of the remaining older brands. Top management set this goal for General Mills brand managers: Improve a third of the existing products every year with significant changes in taste, texture, nutrition, or packaging. By 1993, the company had twelve brands with at least a 1 percent share of the market, up from seven in 1986.

Strategic Windows

One technique for examining opportunities is to seek strategic windows. A "strategic window" is a limited time during which the "fit" between the key requirements of a market and the firm's competencies are at an optimum. For instance, the air freight business was a slow-growth industry for many years. Federal Express saw a strategic window for regularly planned shipments of high-value, low-weight merchandise. The rest is history.

During the past decade, General Mills management noted that the U.S. food industry was growing at only 1 percent a year. For the company to grow faster than 1 percent a year, it had to take market share from competitors. General Mills management also realized that a strategic window was open in the restaurant business. The only national restaurant chains with great market power were in fast foods, such as Burger King and McDonald's. However, the U.S. fast-food market was not growing either. Moreover, because of growing health consciousness, consumers were demanding less beef and more chicken and seafood. The popularity of both Mexican and Italian food was mushrooming. General Mills management realized that a strategic opportunity existed for popularly priced, sit-down Italian and seafood restaurants. After extensive marketing research, General Mills created the Red Lob-

ster and Olive Garden restaurant chains. Both chains have made a major contribution to General Mills' profits.

Differential Advantage

differential advantage
One or more unique aspects of an organization that cause target consumers to patronize that firm rather than competitors.

An excellent way to examine opportunities is to seek a differential advantage over the competition. A **differential advantage** is one or more unique aspects of an organization that cause target consumers to patronize that firm rather than competitors. A differential advantage can exist solely in the firm's image; for example, frequent flyers perceive American Airlines as "the best" full-service airline. A differential advantage can also exist in any element of the marketing mix. Bang and Olufsen's differential advantage is its ability to produce ultrahigh-quality stereo systems. Kraft General Foods' differential advantage lies in its distribution system; it can reach virtually all U.S. supermarkets and fast-food stores and command adequate shelf space. Without a differential advantage, target customers don't perceive any reason to patronize an organization instead of its competitors.

There are two basic sources of differential advantage: superior skills and superior resources. *Superior skills* are managers' and workers' unique capabilities, which distinguish them from the personnel of competing firms. For example, DuPont has an exceptional competitive advantage in the production of titanium dioxide. Technicians created a production process using low-cost feedstock, giving DuPont a 20 percent cost advantage over competitors. The cheaper feedstock technology is complex and can only be accomplished by investing about $100 million and several years of testing time. Another example of superior skills is the Biltmore Resort in Phoenix, Arizona, which has consistently won Mobil's coveted five-star rating. There are fewer than twenty five-star hotel/resorts in the United States. The Biltmore management has the skills needed to maintain a commendable level of service.

Superior resources are a more tangible form of differential advantage. Examples include the scale of a manufacturing facility, a location, a distribution system, the availability of computer-aided design and manufacturing, or a family brand name. Coke is a brand name of immeasurable value. Foremost-McKesson, the huge wholesaler to drugstores and hospitals, found that its competitive advantage stemmed from customer knowledge and a superior information system.

The use of superior resources and skills secures a differential advantage for organizations like Foremost-McKesson. Differential advantage enables a firm to deliver superior customer value, attain lower relative costs, or both. Chapparal Steel, for example, is the leading low-cost U.S. steel producer because it uses only scrap iron and steel and a very efficient continuous-casting process to make new steel. In fact, Chapparal is so efficient that it is the only U.S. steel producer that ships to Japan. Similarly, Fort Howard Paper's differential advantage lies in its cost-saving manufacturing process. Fort Howard Paper uses only recycled pulp, rather than the more expensive virgin pulp, to make toilet paper and other products. The quality, however, is acceptable only to the commercial market, such as office buildings, hotels, and restaurants. Therefore, the company does not try to sell to the home market through grocery stores.

A firm can offer superior customer value in a variety of ways. It can provide superior service or superior product quality. For instance, the French cruise line Pakquey has a reputation for offering impeccable service. The brand name BMW signifies quality to many car buyers. Salomon has gained a dominant position in the ski bindings market with a stream of innovations.

INTERNATIONAL PERSPECTIVES

Differential Advantages for Germany's Midsize Giants

Germany's small and midsize companies, known as the *Mittelstand*, have a talent for export and a command of their markets that belie their small size and low profile. Companies like Krones, Korber/Hauni, Weinig,Webasto, and TetraWerke have world market shares in the range of 70 to 90 percent, and when combined, they account for the bulk of Germany's considerable trade surplus. This is an impressive feat, given that Germany was the world's largest exporter during most of the 1980s and early 1990s.

The *Mittelstand* companies are champions of global competition but have remained largely hidden for two reasons. First, most of their products—for example, labeling machines for beverages, metal filters, bookbinding textiles, and sunroofs for cars—are used in the manufacturing process or become part of the end product. These products are therefore invisible to consumers. But more important, Germany's small and midsize companies relish their obscurity. As an executive of a leading manufacturer of welding equipment said, "We are not interested in revealing our success strategies and helping those who have been inert during recent years."

Although secretive by nature, thirty-nine *Mittelstand* companies agreed to participate in a study of their strategies. The research revealed five common practices. The *Mittelstand* companies

- Combine strategic focus with geographic diversity
- Emphasize factors like customer value
- Blend technology and closeness to customers
- Rely on their own technical competence
- Create mutual interdependence between the company and its employees

The *Mittelstand* companies consistently follow a strategy that combines technical competence with worldwide marketing and sales. They focus narrowly on a particular market niche, usually one that requires technical expertise, and direct all of their resources toward maintaining the top position in that niche.

Typically, *Mittelstand* firms focus well on things that customers value. A good case in point is training. With more complex products, customers need more training in handling and maintaining the products. Many *Mittelstand* companies provide excellent service in this regard. Customers in Asia often say that they prefer German products because German technicians are superbly educated. Some companies have even set up special service subsidiaries. Festo, a leading manufacturer of hydraulic equipment, established Festo Didactic, which has become a prominent training company for engineers in hydraulics and industrial automation.

Mittelstand companies expect to meet the same high standards in foreign markets as they do at home. For this reason, they tend to create strong service networks wherever they do business. Even a good product breaks down occasionally and needs repair, and the hidden champions see no reason for compromising their service standards abroad. For example, the Japanese service network of Heidelberger Druckmaschinen, the world leader in offset printing, is as comprehensive as the network in the German home market. The head of the Heidelberger Druckmaschinen subsidiary in Tokyo noted, "How could we afford to offer an inferior service here?"

Are there *Mittelstand*-like companies in the United States? If so, give some examples. What, if anything, could the federal government do to foster the creation of *Mittelstand*-like companies? Alternatively, is their success simply a matter of corporate culture?

Source: Reprinted by permission of *Harvard Business Review*. Excerpts from Hermann Simon, "Lessons from Germany's Midsize Giants," *Harvard Business Review*, March–April 1992, pp. 115–125.

U.S. firms can boost their competitive advantage by extending the boundaries of their distribution systems to include the global market. The International Perspectives article discusses how Germany's midsize market leaders build and maintain differential advantages.

4 Develop Strategic Alternatives

To discover a strategic window or potential differential advantage, management must know how to identify and take advantage of opportunities. One method for developing alternatives is the strategic opportunity matrix (see Exhibit 21.2). Firms can explore these four options:

market penetration Marketing strategy that increases market share among existing customers.

- *Market penetration:* A firm using the **market penetration** alternative would try

Exhibit 21.2

Strategic Opportunity Matrix

	Present product	New product
Present market	Market penetration	Product development
New market	Market development	Diversification

to increase market share among existing customers. If Kraft General Foods started a major campaign for Maxwell House coffee, with aggressive advertising and cents-off coupons to existing customers, it would be following a penetration strategy. Customer data bases, discussed in Chapter 8, help managers implement this strategy.

market development
Marketing strategy that attracts new customers to existing products.

- *Market development:* **Market development** means attracting new customers to existing products. Ideally, new uses for old products stimulate additional sales among existing customers while also bringing in new buyers. McDonald's, for example, has opened restaurants in Russia, China, and Italy and is eagerly expanding into Eastern European countries. Gillette has started promoting its successful Sensor razor to women as well as men. In the nonprofit area, the growing emphasis on continuing education and executive development by colleges and universities is a market development strategy.

product development
Marketing strategy that entails the creation of new products for present markets.

- *Product development:* A **product development** strategy entails the creation of new products for present markets. The "eating healthy" craze of the early 1990s led ConAgra Corporation—maker of Banquet, Morton, Patio, and Chun King frozen dinners—to develop Healthy Choice frozen dinners, which are low in fat, cholesterol, and sodium. Kraft General Foods introduced "no cholesterol mayonnaise" and General Mills and Kellogg brought out high-fiber, low-fat, and low-sodium cereals. Managers following this strategy can rely on their extensive knowledge of the target audience. They usually have a good feel for what customers like and dislike about current products and what existing needs are not being met. In addition, managers can rely on the established distribution channels.

diversification
Marketing strategy that increases sales by introducing new products into new markets.

- *Diversification:* **Diversification** is a strategy of increasing sales by introducing new products into new markets. For example, LTV Corporation, a steel producer, diversified into the monorail business. Sony practiced a diversification strategy when it acquired Columbia Pictures. Although motion pictures are not a new product in the marketplace, they were a new product for Sony. Coca-Cola manufactures and markets water treatment and conditioning equipment, which has been a very challenging task for the traditional soft-drink company. A diversification strategy can be quite risky when a firm is entering unfamiliar markets. On the other hand, it can be very profitable when a firm is entering markets with little or no competition.

Select an Alternative

The next step in strategic decision making is to select an alternative. A corporation's philosophy and culture affect that selection. The choice also depends on the tool used to make the decision.

A diversification strategy led Sony to acquire Columbia Pictures, whose hits include the movie *Ghostbusters*.

The Role of Market Share versus Profit

Companies have a philosophy about when they expect profits. They either pursue profits right away or first seek to increase market share and then pursue profits. In the long run, market share and profitability are compatible goals.

A study of the relationship between market share and profitability reported these findings: A brand with the number-one market share had an average return on investment of 31 percent; the number-two brand, 21 percent; the number-three brand, 16 percent. Brands with the fourth-largest market share or less had a return on investment of 12 percent or less.[5] This far-reaching study found that the pattern was consistent in both the United States and Europe. It included services and manufacturers of industrial products, consumer durables, and consumer nondurable goods. Note, however, that these statistics are averages. In any specific situation, the relationship between market share and profits may not hold. Moreover, another study suggests that the effect of market share on profitability depends on the dollar value of the market share.[6] That is, having the dominant market share in a $10 million market is not the same as being the number-one firm in a $1 billion market. Apparently, market share is more likely to determine profitability at certain levels.

Many companies have long followed this credo: Build market share, and profits will surely follow. Michelin, the tire producer, consistently sacrifices short-term profits to achieve market share.[7] But attitudes may be changing. Procter & Gamble told managers that profit, not market share, is its objective. Louis Gerstner, the CEO of RJR Nabisco, has claimed, "We're not going to play the market share game, just to hold some theoretical market share. Profitability is the most important thing."[8]

The Role of Corporate Culture

Corporate culture also plays an important role in the choice of a strategic alternative. Corporate culture is the pattern of basic assumptions an organization has accepted to cope with the firm's internal environment and the changing external environment. If these assumptions have worked fairly well, management will tend to consider them valid. Therefore, new members of the organization should also consider

Corporate culture has a big influence on the way firms react to the external environment. A company like U.S. Surgical, producer of laparoscopic instruments for surgery, is a "prospector," actively looking for emerging market opportunities.
© John Madere

them the correct way to perceive, think, and feel about the firm's internal and external environments.

Internally, corporate culture is concerned with issues like worker loyalty, centralization or decentralization of decision making, promotion criteria, and problem-solving techniques. Corporate culture regarding the external environment is revealed by the way the firm reacts to problems and opportunities. Organizational response to the external environment can be categorized into four types:

- *Prospector:* focuses on identifying and capitalizing on emerging market opportunities, thus emphasizing research and communication with the market. Because of its strong external orientation, the prospector tends to build and maintain an excellent information system and product development program. A prospector prefers strategic alternatives that tap new markets or develop new goods and services. Both Ralston Purina and Philip Morris have a prospector culture. They are both leaders in bringing new consumer goods to market. United States Surgical is also a prospector. The fastest-selling surgical instruments today are those that use laparoscopes to do procedures through tiny incisions. U.S. Surgical has almost an 85 percent market share of the $3 billion laparoscopic instrument market.[9] About half of U.S. Surgical's sales come from instruments introduced within the past five years.
- *Reactor:* the opposite of the prospector. Instead of looking for opportunities, it responds to environmental pressures when forced to do so. The reactor is a follower, not a leader, and lacks a strategic focus. Emphasis is on maintaining the status quo despite environmental change. A reactor will avoid any strategic alternative that takes it out of its niche or that calls for bold, risk-taking action. Reactors include Woolworth's, Wrigley's, and Revco Drug. American Motors before its demise and AT&T before deregulation were also reactors.
- *Defender:* has a specific market domain and does not search outside that

domain for new opportunities. Instead, it tries to "defend its turf." A defender looks favorably on any strategic alternative that helps reduce operating costs. The risk, however, is that market changes might go unnoticed. Even if the defender detects such changes, it typically is unable to adjust its business practices in response. American Home Products, a defender, has probably undermined its future. Its corporate culture has emphasized strict cost controls for years. Until recently, managers had to get central management's approval for any expenditure over $500. New product development suffered as a result.

- *Analyzer:* tends to be both conservative and aggressive. It usually operates in at least one stable market and tries to defend its position in that market. An analyzer also tries to identify emerging opportunities in other markets. Unlike the prospector, the analyzer is not an aggressive risk taker. Usually "second in" to new product markets, the analyzer has the advantage of observing and learning from other firms' new-product problems. Delta Airlines, Bethlehem Steel, Aetna Insurance, and Alberto-Culver can be categorized as analyzers.

In summary, the same strategic alternative may be viewed entirely differently by firms with different corporate cultures. A highly desirable alternative for one organization may be completely unattractive to another firm.

Tools for Selecting a Strategic Alternative

Four techniques help managers choose a strategic alternative: the portfolio matrix, the market attractiveness/company strength matrix, response functions, and PIMS analysis. Let's look at each technique.

The portfolio matrix: Recall that large organizations engaged in strategic planning may create strategic business units. Each SBU has its own rate of return on investment, growth potential, and associated risk. Management must find a balance among the SBUs that yields the desired growth and profits with an acceptable level of risk. Managers must recognize that some SBUs generate large amounts of cash over and above what is required for operating expenses or for more marketing, production, or inventory. Other SBUs need cash to foster growth.

To determine the future cash contributions and cash requirements that can be expected for each SBU, managers can use the Boston Consulting Group's portfolio matrix. A matrix is a self-contained framework within which something originates and develops. The portfolio matrix classifies each SBU by its present or forecasted growth and market share. The underlying assumption is that market share is strongly linked with profitability. The market share used by the portfolio approach is relative market share, the ratio between the company's share and the share of the largest competitor. For example, if firm A has a 50 percent share and the competitor has 5 percent, the ratio is 10 to 1. If firm A has a 10 percent market share and the largest competitor has 20 percent, the ratio is 0.5 to 1.

Exhibit 21.3 is a hypothetical portfolio matrix for a large computer manufacturer. The size of the circle in each cell of the matrix represents dollar sales of the SBU relative to dollar sales of the company's other SBUs. These are the categories used in the matrix:

star
In the portfolio matrix, a business unit that is a market leader and growing fast.

- *Stars:* A **star** is a market leader and growing fast. For example, the computer manufacturer has identified the notebook model as a star. Star SBUs usually have large profits but need a lot of cash to finance rapid growth. The best marketing tactic is to protect existing market share by reinvesting earnings in

Exhibit 21.3

Portfolio Matrix for a Large Computer Manufacturer

Note: The size of the circle represents the dollar sales relative to sales of other SBUs on the matrix. 10× means sales are ten times greater than those of the next largest competitor.

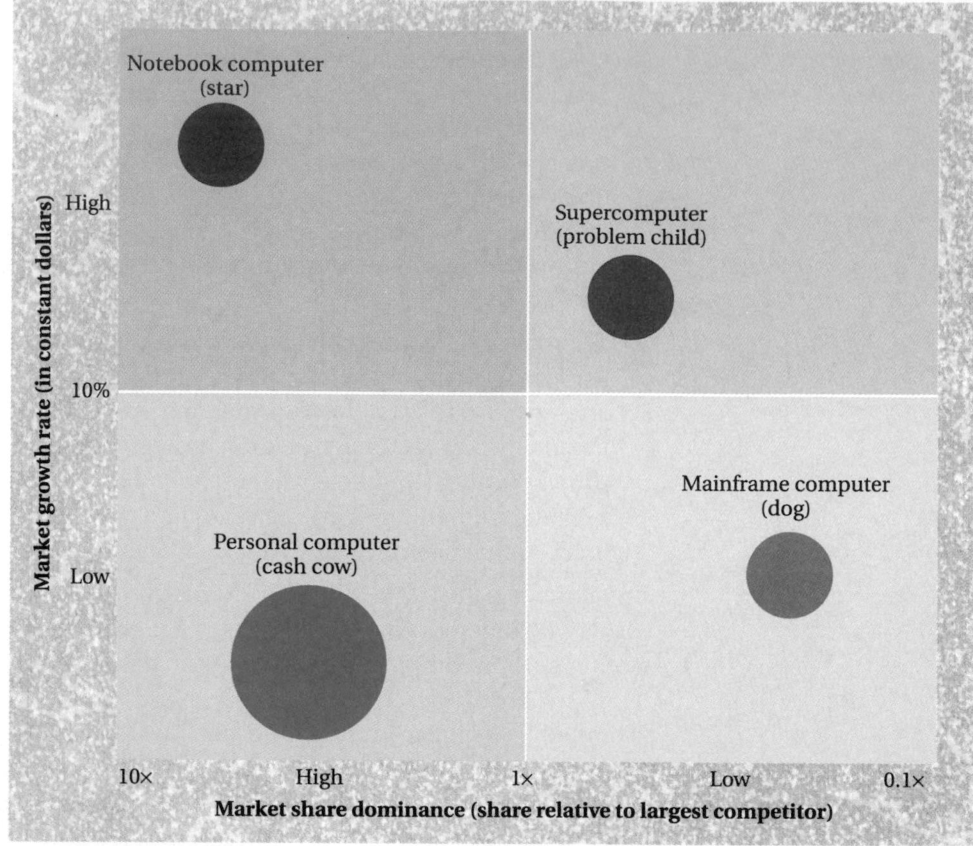

product improvement, better distribution, more promotion, and production efficiency. Management must strive to capture most of the new users as they enter the market.

cash cow
In the portfolio matrix, a business unit that generates more cash than it needs to maintain its market share.

- *Cash cows:* A **cash cow** SBU usually generates more cash than it needs to maintain its market share. It is in a low-growth market, but the product has a dominant market share. Personal computers are categorized as cash cows in Exhibit 21.3. The basic strategy for a cash cow is to maintain market dominance by being the price leader and making technological improvements in the product. Managers should resist pressure to extend the basic line unless they can dramatically increase demand. Instead, they should allocate excess cash to the product areas where growth prospects are the greatest. For instance, Clorox Corporation owns Kingsford Charcoal, Match Charcoal Lighter, Prime Choice steak sauce, Cooking Ease spray lubricant for frying foods, and a restaurant chain. Its cash cow is Clorox bleach, with a 60 percent market share in a low-growth market. Clorox Corporation was highly successful in stretching the Clorox line to include a liquid formula in addition to the original dry bleach. Another example is Heinz, which has two cash cows: catsup and Weight Watchers frozen dinners.

problem child (question mark)
In the portfolio matrix, a business unit that shows rapid growth but poor profit margins.

- *Problem children:* **Problem children,** also called **question marks,** show rapid growth but poor profit margins. They have a low market share in a high-growth industry. Problem children need a great deal of cash. Without cash support, they eventually become dogs. The strategy options are to invest heavily to gain better market share, acquire competitors to get the necessary market share, or drop the SBU. Sometimes a firm can reposition the products of the SBU to move them into the star category.

dog
In the portfolio matrix, a business unit that has low growth potential and a small market share.

- *Dogs:* A **dog** has low growth potential and a small market share. Most dogs eventually leave the marketplace. In the computer manufacturer example, the mainframe computer has become a dog. Other examples include Jack-in-the-Box shrimp dinners, Warner-Lambert's Reef mouthwash, and Campbell's Red Kettle soups. Frito-Lay produced several dogs in the late 1980s, including Stuffers cheese-filled snacks, Rumbles granola nuggets, and Toppels cheese-topped crackers—also known as Stumbles, Tumbles, and Twofers.

After classifying the company's SBUs into the matrix, the next step is to allocate future resources for each. The basic strategies are to

- *Build:* If an organization has an SBU that it believes has the potential to be a star (probably a problem child at present), building would be an appropriate goal. The organization may decide to give up short-term profits and use its financial resources to achieve this goal. Procter & Gamble built Pringles from a money loser to a record profit maker in 1993.
- *Hold:* If an SBU is a very successful cash cow, a key goal would surely be to hold or preserve market share so the organization can take advantage of the very positive cash flow. Bisquick has been a prosperous cash cow for General Mills for over two decades.
- *Harvest:* This strategy is appropriate for all SBUs except those classified as stars. The basic goal is to increase the short-term cash return without too much concern for the long-run impact. It is especially worthwhile when more cash is needed from a cash cow with long-run prospects that are unfavorable because of a low market growth rate. For instance, Lever Brothers has been harvesting Lifebuoy soap for a number of years with little promotional backing.
- *Divest:* Getting rid of SBUs with low shares of low-growth markets is often appropriate. Problem children and dogs are most suitable for this strategy. Procter & Gamble dropped Cincaprin, a coated aspirin, because of its low growth potential.

Market attractiveness/company strength matrix: A second model for selecting strategic alternatives, originally developed by General Electric, is known as the market attractiveness/company strength matrix. These dimensions are richer and more complete than the portfolio matrix but are much harder to quantify.

Exhibit 21.4 presents the market attractiveness/company strength matrix. The horizontal axis, business position, refers to how well-positioned the organization is to take advantage of market opportunities. Does the firm have the technology it needs to effectively penetrate the market? Are its financial resources adequate? Can manufacturing costs be held below those of the competition? Will the firm have bargaining power over suppliers? Can the firm cope with change? The vertical axis measures the attractiveness of a market, which is expressed both quantitatively and qualitatively. Some attributes of an attractive market are high profitability, rapid growth, a lack of government regulation, consumer insensitivity to a price increase, a lack of competition, and availability of technology. The grid is divided into three overall attractiveness zones: high, medium, and low.

Those SBUs (or markets) that have low overall attractiveness should be avoided if the organization is not already serving them. If the firm is in these markets, it should either harvest or divest the SBUs. The organization should selectively maintain markets with medium attractiveness. If attractiveness begins to slip, then the organization should withdraw from the market. Conditions that are highly attractive—an attractive market plus a strong business position—are the best candidates for

Exhibit 21.4

Market Attractiveness/ Company Strength Matrix

Note: Circle size represents dollar sales volume relative to sales of other SBUs on the matrix.

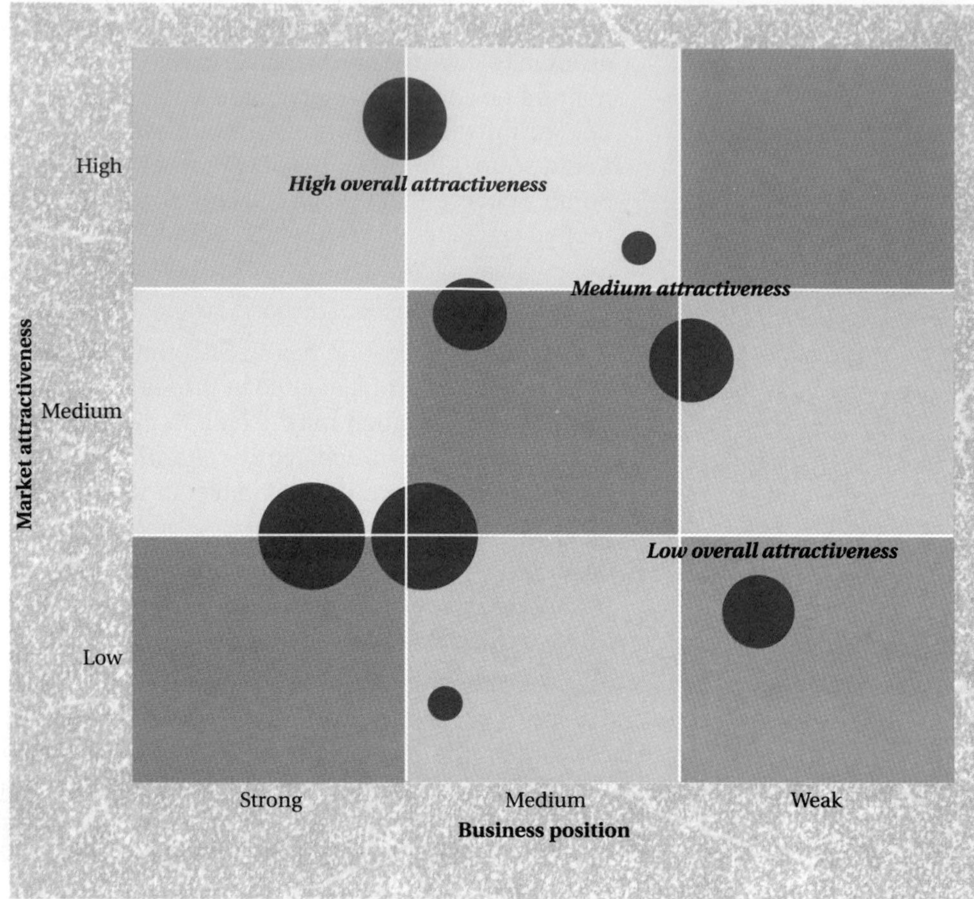

investment. For instance, Anheuser-Busch saw an attractive market for a super-premium dry beer. It created Michelob Dry with an angular, long-necked bottle to distinguish it from its other Michelobs. The beer has far exceeded Anheuser-Busch's expectations.

response function Graphed relationship between a marketing mix (or component of the mix) and sales to a specific market target.

Response functions: A third analysis technique is the use of response functions. **Response functions** are graphed relationships between a marketing mix (or component of the mix) and sales to a specific market target. Some planners substitute profits for sales when plotting response curves. The graphs in Exhibit 21.5 show how two strategic business units in the same firm might view their response functions. The exhibit shows that sales are much more responsive to changes in price for the small-car SBU (graph A) than for the large-car SBU (graph D) if other response variables for each SBU are assumed not to change.

On the other hand, personal sales effort is much more effective for large cars (graph F) than for small cars (graph C). Thus marketing management for the large-car SBU may find that the size and caliber of its sales force are critical to its success. Some sales would be generated without any personal selling, thanks to advertising and sales promotion—a phenomenon called the *market minimum.* As salespeople are added, sales begin rising at an increasing and then decreasing rate. Finally, sales peak when P_2 salespersons have been hired. This upper limit of sales that can be generated by the sales force is called the *market potential.* The difference between the market minimum and the market potential is the *marketing sensitivity of demand.* By allocating more resources to the sales staff, management can increase total revenues to S_2. Beyond that point, additional salespeople do not generate additional sales.

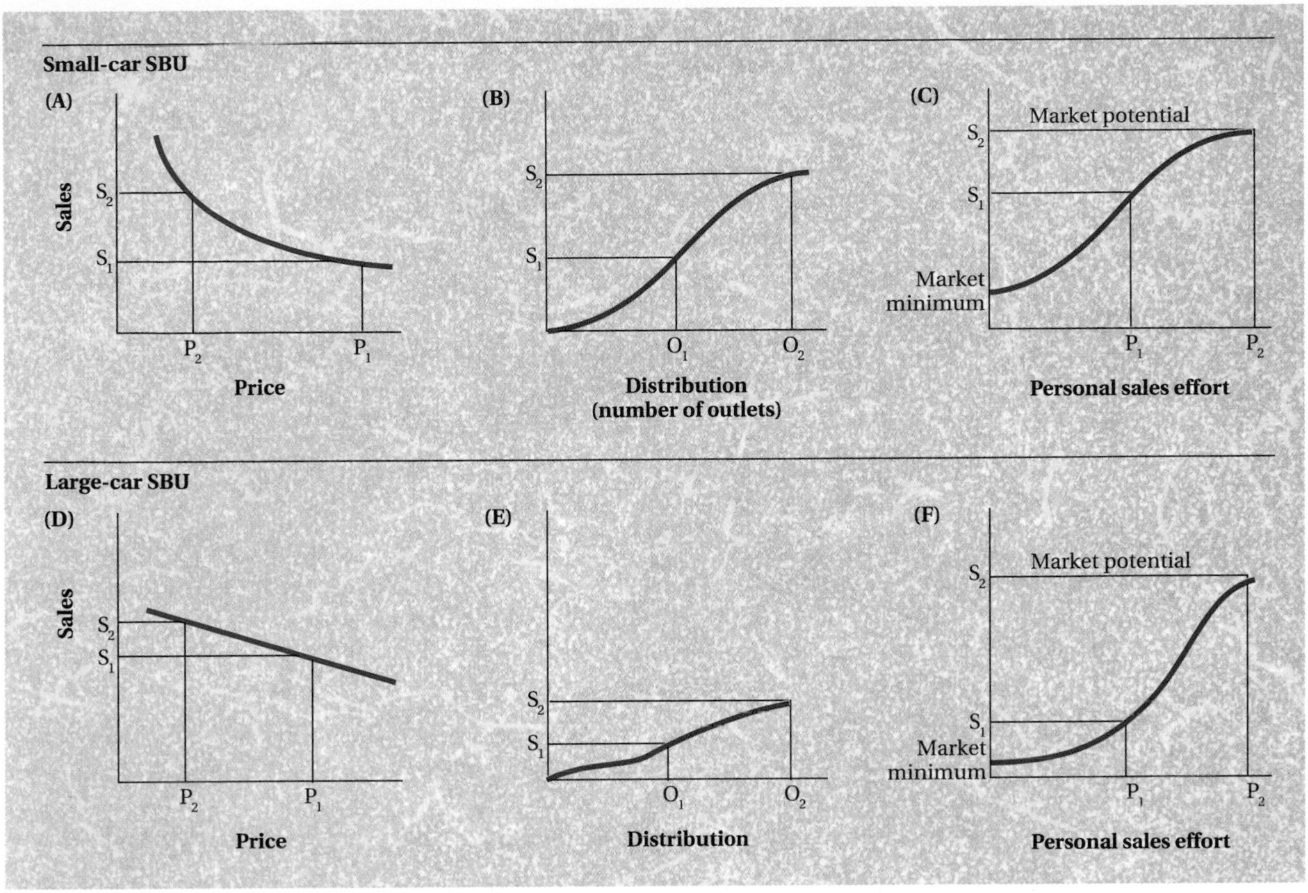

Exhibit 21.5

Hypothetical Response Functions for General Motors SBUs

Although response functions are helpful in choosing among alternatives, they have an important drawback. A response function is only as good as the assumptions behind the curve. If the assumptions are wrong, then the curve is wrong. Moreover, even if the assumptions are correct at the time an alternative is chosen, the rapidly changing external environment may change relationships among variables. Thus marketing managers must continually reevaluate alternatives. They should also periodically use past experience, marketing research, and executive judgment to reassess the shapes of the response functions.

profit impact of market strategy (PIMS)
Analyzing strategic alternatives by consulting a database program that summarizes the financial and market performance of 3,000 strategic business units of more than 450 firms.

Profit impact of market strategy (PIMS): The fourth tool for analyzing strategic alternatives is called the **profit impact of market strategy (PIMS)** program. The Strategic Planning Institute provides companies with a data base summarizing the financial and market performance of 3,000 strategic business units of more than 450 firms. PIMS focuses on the links among various factors and profitability (ROI); its data base includes successful firms and "real losers." The data base includes large and small companies; markets in North America, Europe, and elsewhere; and a wide variety of products, ranging from candy to heavy capital goods to financial services.

For each SBU, three kinds of information are presented:

- *Market conditions:* distribution channels used by the SBU, the number and size of customers, and rates of market growth and inflation
- *Competitive position:* the SBU's market share, relative product quality, prices and costs relative to the competition, and degree of vertical integration relative to the competition
- *Financial and operating performance:* annual figures over periods ranging from two to twelve years

Detailed analysis of the PIMS data base has produced some key findings:

- In the long run, the one factor that most affects an SBU's performance is the quality of its products relative to those of competitors. A quality edge boosts performance in two ways. In the short run, superior quality yields increased profits through premium prices. In the longer term, superior or improving quality is the most effective basis for growth. Quality leads to both market expansion and gains in market share.
- Market share (relative to the largest competitors) and profitability are strongly linked.
- The need to invest a lot in the SBU is a powerful drag on profitability. Investment-intensive businesses are those that use a great deal of capital per dollar of sales or per employee.
- Although market growth and relative market share are linked to cash flow, many other factors also influence performance.
- Vertical integration is a powerful strategy for some kinds of businesses but not for all. For businesses with a small market share, return on investment is highest when the degree of vertical integration is low. But for businesses with an average or above-average market share, return on investment is highest when vertical integration is either low or high and lowest when vertical integration is in the middle.
- Most of the strategic factors that boost return on investment also contribute to the long-term market value of an organization.[10]

For access to the PIMS data base, companies pay about $20,000 to $40,000 per year and agree to make their data available on a confidential basis. The data base contains successes, failures, and also-rans; data are pooled so individual businesses cannot be identified. The data provided by a business cover the market environment, competition, strategy pursued, and financial performance results, plus projections of future sales, prices, and costs. A business may obtain insights on its own strategy from PIMS results tailored to its needs.

❺ Implement the Selected Strategy

The sixth phase of the strategic planning process is implementation. Implementation requires the delegation of authority and responsibility, the determination of a time frame for completing tasks, and the allocation of resources. Sometimes a strategic plan also requires task force management.

A task force is a tightly organized unit under the direction of a manager who usually has broad authority. A task force is established to accomplish a single goal or mission and thus works against a deadline. For example, Toyota created a task force to build and market its luxury car, Lexus. AT&T assigned a task force to develop marketing plans that would protect its long-distance market from MCI and Sprint.

Implementing a plan also has another dimension: gaining acceptance. New plans mean change, and change creates resistance. One reason people resist change is that they fear they will lose something. When new-product research is taken away from marketing research and given to a new-product department, the director of marketing research will naturally resist this loss of part of his or her domain. Misunderstanding and lack of trust also create opposition to change.

Ethics should always play a central role in strategic planning and implementation. The Ethics in Marketing article explains why ethics should never be an afterthought in the strategic planning process.

ETHICS IN MARKETING

Planning for a Crisis

The keys to weathering any crisis are preventive thinking, contingency planning, quick and honest communication, and appropriate remedial measures. The company that takes these steps to manage a marketing crisis is likely not only to survive but also to prosper. Misleading ads, product recalls, improper compensation—in rueful hindsight—are crises that could have been averted. Programs that comply with legal standards and the ideals of good taste pay for themselves.

An organization should test its programs against statements of ethics from the American Marketing Association. In addition, it should have a code of conduct, a mission statement, and a statement of values. Each marketing program should be measured against these standards. If a company lacks such standards, senior management should develop them. An easy way to begin is to retain a consultant to review the firm's business and marketing practices. This review may uncover practices that might be challenged by consumer groups, the media, and regulators.

With this research as a planning aid, a crisis contingency plan can be prepared by the marketing, legal, and public relations team. That plan should include the following:

- Major areas of vulnerability
- Company spokespeople, with home and office phone numbers
- Outside resources—such as public relations firms, law firms, ethics consultants, trade associations, and government or regulatory officials—with office and home phone numbers, if possible
- Lists of business, consumer, and trade media
- A general action plan for responding to unanticipated events

Can you think of some incidents where better planning may have prevented an ethical crisis? Can a company with poor ethical policies be managed by ethical people? If a lower-level manager implements an unethical policy, should we blame the manager or the company?

Alter the Selected Strategy When Necessary

After an organization implements its strategic plan, it must track results and monitor the external environment. As mentioned in Chapter 2, the one certainty about the external environment is that it will continually change. And as it changes, managers will be pressed to adjust the strategic plan.

A key tool in evaluating the strategic plan is the marketing audit. The marketing audit uses financial and nonfinancial reports to evaluate the organization's goals, strategies, and performance. The marketing audit is discussed in more detail in Chapter 22.

Organizations, especially large ones, have much inertia. They are set up as efficient machines, and it is hard to change one part without adjusting everything else. Yet organizations can be changed through leadership, preferably in advance of a crisis. Certainly leadership helps in the midst of a crisis. A good example is the dramatic dismissal in 1992 of Robert Stempel, CEO of General Motors, and other top executives by GM's board of directors. New leadership was installed to stem the flow of red ink from GM's North American operations. The key to organizational survival is the organization's willingness to examine the changing environment and to adopt appropriate new goals and behaviors.

8 MAKING STRATEGIC PLANNING WORK

In the past decade, intense domestic and international competition led many firms into strategic planning as a faddish prescription for survival. In many companies, strategic planning became a once-a-year mechanistic process. Today, however,

Strategic planning is most successful when the whole company, starting with the management team, understands the strategic mission and concentrates on carrying it out. At Dillard's, a fast-growing department store chain, management includes William and Alexa Dillard and their five children: Bill, Mike, and Alex and Denise and Drue.

Jackson Hill/Southern Lights

strategic planning has matured and become more effective.

Effective strategic planning requires continual attention, creativity, and management commitment. First, strategic planning is not an annual exercise, in which managers go through the motions and forget about strategic planning until the next year. It should be an ongoing process, because the environment is continually changing and the firm's resources and capabilities are continually evolving. Second, sound planning is based on creativity. Managers should challenge assumptions about the firm and the environment and establish new game plans. For example, major oil companies developed the concept of the gasoline service station in an age when cars needed frequent and rather elaborate servicing. The majors held to the full-service approach, but independents were quick to respond to new realities and moved to lower-cost self-service and convenience store operations. The majors needed several decades to catch up.

Perhaps the most critical element in successful strategic planning is top management's support and participation. Most department stores struggled during the late 1980s and early 1990s; many even faced bankruptcy. The Dillard's chain, headquartered in Little Rock, Arkansas, continued to grow. From 1984 to 1992 it opened or acquired over 200 department stores. Dillard's is either No. 1 or No. 2 in every market. The chain succeeded because top management defined its strategic mission and then made sure that mission was carried out.[11] Three more examples of successful strategic planning follow.

MCI

As noted at the beginning of the chapter, MCI increased its market share in the early 1990s, chiefly at AT&T's expense. Good strategic planning has been the reason for MCI's success. After a disastrous fourth quarter in 1990, the company undertook a wrenching reorganization. The company decided to use not just a marketing discount plan but one "that structurally disadvantaged AT&T." The result was MCI Friends and Family.

The MCI Friends and Family plan gives customers 20 percent off MCI's already discounted phone rate, provided calls are made to a "circle" of people who are also on the plan. There's a catch: Customers must provide MCI with the names of candidates for their calling circles, and the names become sales leads for MCI. The discounts tend to keep customers loyal, because others in the calling circle lose the price cut when one drops out.

MCI bills customers directly, using a sophisticated billing and tracking system. AT&T has less control over its billing because most is handled by the regional Bell companies. Friends and Family capitalizes on this difference. To offer a similar plan, AT&T would have to change its billing arrangements. Tim Price, an executive at MCI who helped design this attack on AT&T, calls it "marketing jujitsu."[12]

Group Michelin

French tiremaker Michelin has a corporate culture that stresses research secrecy, loyalty, hard work, and the quest for long-term market share.[13] Although Michelin considers itself to be in the tire business, it also makes maps and restaurant guides for car drivers.

Michelin, whose taste for secrecy is legendary, once refused to let French President Charles de Gaulle visit its plants. On another occasion it let a factory burn down rather than allow firefighters inside. Yet these days Michelin admits experts from General Motors, its largest customer, which insists on being involved with suppliers in product development.

Michelin isn't simply in the tire business—it is in the radial tire business, although it no longer tries to produce radials for all market segments. To help foster quality control, Michelin insists on producing all the materials for its tires, including steel belting and synthetic rubber. It also spends heavily on research, laying out 5 percent of sales in bad times as well as good. In 1990 Michelin bought Uniroyal Goodrich Tire Company, which gave it a 20 percent global market share and sales of over $10 billion. The acquisition enabled the company to further develop market share by producing a number of brands at different prices. It now sells inexpensive nonradials produced by Uniroyal Goodrich; the Michelin brand name is reserved for quality radial tires. In 1992, Kmart began selling Michelin tires as a result of its long association with Uniroyal.

McDonald's

McDonald's accounts for nearly 40 percent of all fast-food hamburgers sold. It operates over 10,500 restaurants. Of these, more than 2,600 are located in forty-nine countries outside the United States. Its largest international markets are Japan, England, Germany, Australia, and Canada. McDonald's serves over 22 million customers per day.

All this success didn't happen by accident. McDonald's is a strong believer in planning. Its mission, derived from its strategic plan, is to be in the fast-food business with an emphasis on hamburgers. The company president, Michael Quinlan, puts it this way: "McDonald's hamburgers is what we are."[14] The strategic focus includes quality, service, cleanliness, and value—or QSCV, in company language. A director explains that McDonald's will try anything—as long as it improves Q, S, C, or V.

McDonald's strategic plan calls for increasing sales by adding restaurants, improving international profitability, and maximizing sales at existing restaurants. McDonald's accomplishes its first goal by adding over 600 restaurants each year. It plans to foster international growth by opening new restaurants (of the 600 opened per year, over 200 are international), introducing new products, and practicing more effective marketing. To better understand how McDonald's plans to increase sales of existing stores, let's examine its marketing mix.

Product

Part of McDonald's product plan relates to service and image, and the rest focuses on new products. Field inspectors check on all the stores to make sure franchisees are minding their QSCVs. McDonald's tries to add one new product about every five years. However, the company has had more and more trouble coming up with a winner that guarantees mass appeal and profits. McRib, for example, was tested in 3,500 stores. Lots of people tried McRib once but didn't like the sloppiness or the taste.

In the 1990s McDonald's will closely examine the pizza market, which is growing at about 11 percent annually. In the late 1980s it test marketed a pizza roll, called McPizza. McPizza failed miserably. To maintain QSCV, it was frozen and shipped to retail stores, but unfortunately it tasted like frozen pizza. McDonald's next effort,

To remain a leader in the fast-food business, McDonald's must have an ambitious marketing strategy. For instance, it continually evaluates new products, such as pizza and other items shown here by CEO Michael Quinlan.

© Michael L. Abramson

simply called McDonald's pizza, is already in test markets. It is freshly made using conveyer ovens that blast hot air over the top and bottom of the dish. The process leaves little room for error and produces a hot pizza in about five minutes. McDonald's is already fighting angry rivals, such as Pizza Hut, Little Caesar's Pizza, and Domino's. McDonald's must make sure that pizza doesn't cannibalize its evening sandwich sales. Although pizza looks very promising, the company is also testing breakfast burritos, a Quarter Pounder Ranchero burger, and a Western Omelet McMuffin. Its McLean burger, which appeals to health-conscious consumers, is only a very modest success.

Promotion

McDonald's spends over $1 billion a year on promotion. The company's promotion plan stresses product quality because research has shown that consumers don't seem to think much of McDonald's hamburgers, despite the billions they've eaten.

The company's advertising agencies create more than 200 distinct advertisements a year. Many stress the slogan "McDonald's . . . food, folks, and fun" and feature shots of tasty-looking products. McDonald's also targets some promotions to subsegments of its market, such as minorities and the elderly. For example, it runs over thirty different promotions annually for the Hispanic market.

McDonald's has begun testing a point-of-sale computer system that tracks individual customer spending and automatically creates bonus coupons after certain spending levels have been reached. A test store in Paramus Park, New Jersey, had 9,500 customers signed up for the Frequent Customer Club in the first ninety days.[15]

Pricing

McDonald's pricing plans for its domestic restaurants call for prices that will yield the company a 20 percent return on equity. Prices of its products are adjusted periodically to maintain the target return. Like other fast-food chains, McDonald's successfully introduced "value pricing" in the early 1990s (see Chapter 20).

A big chunk of McDonald's revenues come from franchisees. Franchisees pay 11.5 percent of sales to the corporation for rent and services.

Distribution

McDonald's is always looking for new and more efficient ways to deliver supplies to its stores. It boasts one of the most sophisticated physical distribution systems in the world. McDonald's started by building new stores in the suburbs of large cities and then spreading to smaller towns. Now the company is trying to build more restaurants in big cities. It is also cultivating semicaptive markets—toll roads, military bases, museums, and hospitals, for example, where there are a lot of people with limited dining choices. Effective strategic planning keeps the McEngine running.

7 SALES FORECASTING

A key to McDonald's successful planning is effective sales forecasts. The sales forecast for a plan is what determines its desirability. Generally, the greater the revenue potential and the lower the competitiveness of an alternative, the greater a plan's attractiveness for a company.

The Forecasting Process

sales forecast
Estimate of a firm's future sales or revenues for a specified period.

The **sales forecast** is an estimate of a firm's future sales or revenues for a specified period. One forecasting process flows downward from estimates of overall economic activity, to industry sales trends, to company revenues (see Exhibit 21.6). Company forecasts are created in a three-step process, beginning with sales and revenues for individual products, then product lines, and finally a total for the entire company. This is the complete process:

1. *Evaluate national trends:* Marketing managers often forecast sales by starting with overall estimates of economic activity and narrowing them down to a specific product. For example, a forecast might begin with a national economic forecast of the gross domestic product (GDP). GDP is the total value of all final goods and services for a specified period. Unless the company is very large, it will usually obtain GDP forecasts through secondary sources—for example, a major bank, the federal government, a consulting firm, or a university. GDP forecasts are important for most marketers, since

Exhibit 21.6

The Forecasting Process

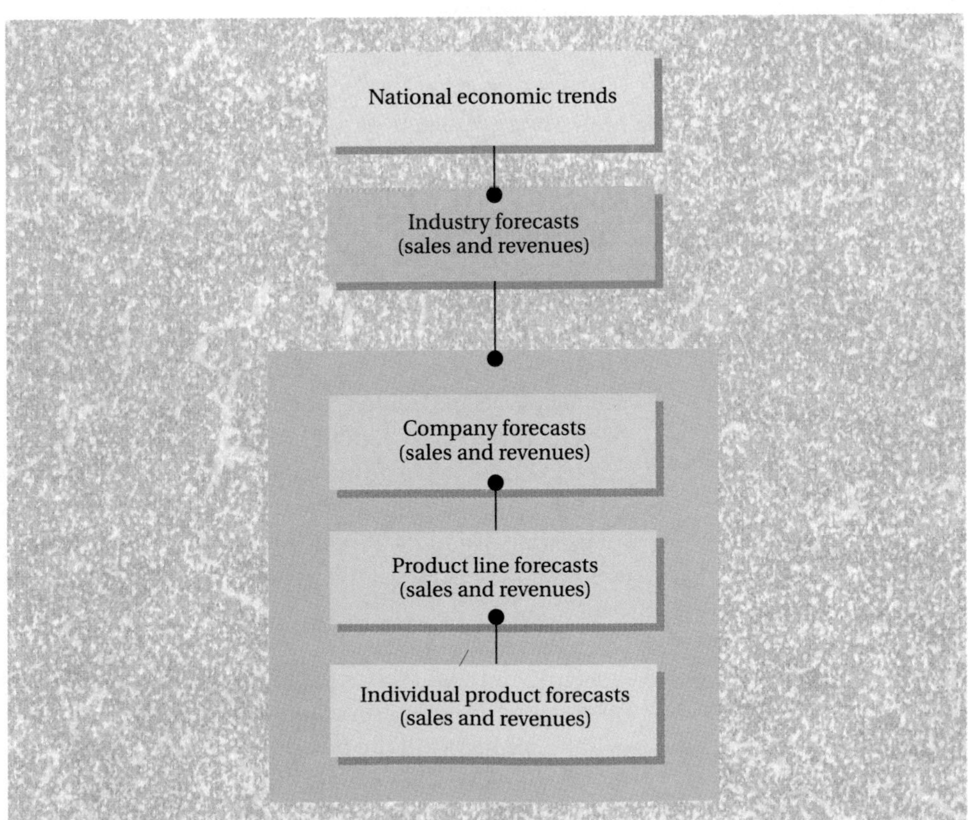

sales of most companies' goods and services tend to increase when GDP rises.

2. *Forecast industry sales:* After determining national sales trends, managers usually estimate industry sales. The overall economic health of the country usually has a major impact on individual industry sales. The first step is to determine **market sales potential**, which is the maximum amount of product that can be sold in a given industry with maximum marketing expenditures under existing marketing mixes within a specific external environment. Obviously, market sales potential changes as the environment changes. For example, the market sales potential for frozen yogurt and for low-fat and low-salt frozen dinners increased as U.S. consumers became more health-conscious.

market sales potential
Maximum amount of product that can be sold in a given industry with maximum marketing expenditures under existing marketing mixes within a specific external environment.

3. *Measure individual product sales potential:* After estimating sales for every industry in which the firm competes, managers prepare sales forecasts for individual products. Industry sales forecasts place limits on potential product sales. That is, sales for a given product cannot exceed sales of the industry in which the good is sold, unless it is sold in several industries. Also, the competitiveness of each industry has an impact on sales potential for a single product. For example, competition in the fresh-pork industry became so intense that Swift's fresh-pork sales forecasts looked dismal. Swift actually sold the division. Arco Chemical also sold assets because of intense competition in the industry.
4. *Forecast company sales:* When forecasts have been completed for each individual product, they are totaled to form a product line forecast. In larger firms these are summed together to obtain an SBU (strategic business unit) forecast. Finally, the sales forecasts for each SBU are added together to provide the firm with a company sales forecast.

Contemporary Forecasting Techniques

Marketing managers can use a number of methods to estimate sales for products, product lines, companies, and industries. These include the jury of executive opinion, sales force composite, Delphi technique, moving average, regression technique, multiple-factor index approach, and purchase intent scale.

Jury of Executive Opinion

jury of executive opinion
Sales forecasting technique that surveys a group of executive experts.

A popular method of forecasting is to use a **jury of executive opinion**, which is based on the assumption that a group of executive experts can arrive at a better forecast than statisticians using a scientific approach. A jury of executive opinion relies on the executives' past experience and intuition regarding the future. Often the technique is applied in a group meeting until everyone reaches a consensus.

Unfortunately, this simple technique is usually not very reliable. It is used mainly for existing products. When applied to new goods and services, it is usually even less accurate—especially if the product requires an unfamiliar channel of distribution.

Sales Force Composite

sales force composite
Sales forecasting technique that surveys the sales force.

A second popular technique is also subjective. The **sales force composite** uses the opinions of the sales force to create a forecast. It assumes that salespeople, who are in daily contact with the marketplace, are in the best position to project future sales. Participating in the establishment of sales estimates also is assumed to motivate salespeople to achieve their objectives.

The sales force composite, like executive judgment, is often unreliable. Some marketing managers use a historic inflator or deflator to improve the quality of the estimate. For example, if the sales force tends to underestimate actual sales by 10 percent (which makes it easier to achieve a quota), then the current estimate can be raised by the same percentage.

Delphi Technique

Delphi technique
Sales forecasting technique that asks outside experts to express an anonymous opinion, review a summary of others' opinions, and express themselves again in order to reach consensus.

The **Delphi technique** is similar to both the jury of executive opinion and the sales force composite in that it solicits opinions about the future from groups of people. The Delphi technique, however, seeks opinions of experts outside the firm, such as government or university economists or other professional futurists. Sometimes the information is sought by mail or electronic mail so opinions can be gathered conveniently from experts all over the world.

Each member of the forecasting team submits a sales estimate and the rationale behind the figure. Next someone, usually an in-house person, summarizes all the information and resubmits it to the team. This process is repeated until a consensus emerges. Team members remain anonymous so no one has to defend his or her views.

The Delphi technique is used regularly by over a hundred large companies, such as Lockheed Corporation. The major disadvantage of the technique is that it can be time-consuming and costly.

Moving Average

moving average
Sales forecasting technique that combines sales data from several of the most recent years and uses an average to obtain next year's forecast.

A **moving average** combines sales data from several of the most recent years and uses an average to obtain next year's forecast. Every year, the oldest year in the previous calculation is dropped and the year just completed is added—hence the term *moving average.*

Assume that a solar irrigation pump company sold 950 units in year 1, 525 in year 2, and 1,100 in year 3. In year 4, the company sold 1,500 units. If management uses a four-year moving average, the sales estimate for the fifth year would be as follows:

$$\text{Moving average} = \frac{950 + 525 + 1{,}100 + 1{,}500}{4}$$

$$= \frac{4{,}075}{4}$$

$$= 1{,}019 \text{ units in year 5}$$

Regression Technique

regression
Sales forecasting technique that defines a relationship between past sales (a dependent variable) and one or more independent variables.

A **regression** is an attempt to define a relationship between past sales (the dependent variable) and one or more independent variables, such as price, competitors' prices, per capita income, industry advertising expenditures, or new housing starts. Simple regression is a statistical technique that employs only one independent and one dependent variable. However, because many factors influence a product's sales, this technique has limited value to marketing managers. It would be unusual for one independent variable, such as price, to explain much more than half the total variation in a firm's sales from year to year. Therefore, marketing managers rely on multiple regression (more than one independent variable) to derive a formula that will accurately describe a relationship between sales and several independent variables.

Multiple-Factor Index Approach

Many consumer goods companies have found that sales potential can be estimated by using an index. Fisher-Price, for example, might assume that the demand for

preschool toys is directly related to the number of preschool children in the United States. If the state of New Mexico contains 1 percent of all preschool children in the country, then Fisher-Price might assume that 1 percent of all preschool toys will be sold in New Mexico. Rarely, however, is a single factor a highly reliable estimate of sales potential. Family income, location of toy store outlets, family size, education level of the head of the household, and other factors probably influence the sale of preschool toys. Therefore, it is usually best to use a multiple-factor index when trying to forecast sales.

One of the oldest and most popular multiple-factor indexes is the *Annual Survey of Buying Power,* published by *Sales & Marketing Management.* The index reflects relative consumer buying power in different regions, states, and metropolitan areas. *Sales & Marketing Management*'s index of the relative buying power of an area is given by this formula:

$$B_i = 0.5y_i + 0.3r_i + 0.2p_i$$

where

B_i = percentage of total national buying power found in area i

y_i = percentage of national disposable personal income originating in area i

r_i = percentage of national retail sales in area i

p_i = percentage of national population located in area i

For example, suppose that New Mexico has 1.11 percent of the U.S. disposable personal income, 0.96 percent of U.S. retail sales, and 0.93 percent of the U.S. population. The buying power index for New Mexico would be as follows:

$$0.5\ (1.11) + 0.3\ (0.96) + 0.2\ (0.93) = 1.02$$

Thus 1.02 percent of the nation's preschool toy sales would occur in the state of New Mexico.

The weights used in the buying power index are somewhat arbitrary. They were established for medium-priced consumer goods. Consequently, Fisher-Price would have to adjust the index to make it more meaningful for preschool toys.

Purchase Intent Scale

The purchase intent scale is typically used to forecast demand for new products (see Exhibit 21.7). In fact, it is applied throughout the new product development process. Marketing managers ask the purchase intent question during concept testing to get a rough idea of demand. They want to quickly eliminate potential "dogs," carefully look at products whose purchase intent is moderate, and push forward the projects that seem to have star potential. At this stage, investment is minimal and product modification or repositioning is easy.

Exhibit 21.7

The Purchase Intent Question for a New Coffeemaker

If this new coffeemaker sold for approximately $35 and was available in the stores where you normally shop, would you

Definitely buy the coffeemaker	1
Probably buy	2
Probably not buy	3
Definitely not buy the coffeemaker	4

As the product moves through the development process, the product itself, promotion strategy, price levels, and distribution channels become more concrete and focused. Managers evaluate purchase intent at each stage and refine demand estimates. The crucial decision for new product introduction typically follows test marketing.

Immediately before test marketing, commercial researchers use another critical stage of evaluation. Here the final, or near-final, version of the product is often placed in consumers' homes in test cities around the country. After a period of in-home use, usually two to six weeks, a follow-up survey is conducted among participants to find out their likes and dislikes. In addition, the survey asks participants how the product compares to those they already use and what price they would pay for it. The critical question, near the end of the questionnaire, is purchase intent.

The purchase intent scale is a good predictor of consumer choice for frequently purchased and durable consumer products. The scale is very easy to construct, and consumers are simply asked to judge their own likelihood of buying the new product. From past experience in the product category, a marketing manager can translate consumer responses on the scale to estimates of purchase probability. Obviously, some who claim they "definitely will buy" the product will not do so. In fact, a few who state that they "definitely will not buy" the product *will* buy it.

Assume that historical follow-up studies have told the manufacturer of a new coffeemaker the following about purchase intent for small electrical appliances:

- 63 percent of the "definitely will buy" actually buy within twelve months.
- 28 percent of the "probably will buy" actually buy within twelve months.
- 12 percent of the "probably will not buy" actually buy within twelve months.
- 3 percent of the "definitely will not buy" actually buy within twelve months.

Suppose that in-home market research for the coffeemaker resulted in these findings:

- 40 percent definitely will buy.
- 20 percent probably will buy.
- 30 percent probably will not buy.
- 10 percent definitely will not buy.

Assuming that the sample for the in-home study was representative of the target market, purchase intent can be calculated as follows:

$$(.4)(63\%) + (.2)(28\%) + (.3)(12\%) + (.1)(3\%) = 34.7\%$$

In other words, the formula shows that nearly 35 percent of the target market households will purchase the coffeemaker. The manufacturer would be deliriously happy at a sales potential figure this high for the new coffeemaker. In the world of new product development, purchase intent is very rarely this high.

What should a company do if it doesn't have historical follow-up information? A reasonable but conservative estimate would be that 70 percent of the "definitely will buy" will actually buy, 35 percent of the "probably will buy," 10 percent of the "probably will not buy," and 0 percent of the "definitely will not buy."

8 GLOBAL ISSUES IN STRATEGIC PLANNING AND FORECASTING

Chapter 3 noted that world markets are merging and many traditional market boundaries are disappearing. Progressive companies all over the world are taking advantage of the changing marketplace by developing a global vision. With a global vision come new rules of

international competition and dramatic changes in strategic planning. In industries ranging from automobiles to fast food and commodity chemicals, firms are finding that what worked in international marketing in the past may not work well today.

Strategic planners must recognize how globalization manifests itself in different industries. Many of the following patterns are usually present:

- Disappearing "national" market boundaries as competitors and customers cross traditional geographic borders to buy and to sell
- Declining numbers of competitors and increasing size of the remaining players as the smaller firms or firms with a narrow geographic focus are absorbed by the larger ones or forced out of the market
- Competing among the same group of world-class players in every national market
- Increasing interdependence among national or regional markets as developments or marketing strategies in one location affect markets elsewhere
- Growing similarity among some segments of customers worldwide as gaps in their lifestyles, tastes, and behavior narrow[16]

Recall that the third step in the strategic planning process is to conduct a situation analysis. Here are several key questions marketing managers should ask in examining global SWOT:

- What is our current competitive profile compared with local and global rivals? What unique areas of competence do we enjoy? What other strengths do we have? In what areas are we weak?
- How are we perceived by our customers or members of the trade in local markets? Is the "global" nature of our company perceived as an advantage or a disadvantage?
- Is our current global strategy in line with our competitive posture in individual markets? Is the strategy building on our strengths and shoring up our weaknesses?
- How can we turn our global scope into a differential advantage? Are there areas in which we are not exploiting the economies of scale that come with our global size? How well and how fast do we transfer innovations globally? In what areas can we improve our efficiency internally or in the marketplace?
- How does the current profile of our management compare with those of our competitors? Do we have the skills needed locally and in headquarters to implement our strategy? Is our organizational structure in line with the strategy? How can it be improved to help with implementation?[17]

Del Monte used marketing research to help marketing managers understand how its fruits and juices are perceived by customers in various countries. The research discovered that consumers use canned fruits differently—for example, with cream topping in the United Kingdom but without topping elsewhere. Although Del Monte was a known brand and had a good reputation, consumer loyalty was low and consumers were increasingly opting for value-priced private brands.

To build on high international awareness of the Del Monte brand, and also to explain why Del Monte costs more than other brands, the company created a TV advertising campaign that communicated the freshness of Del Monte's canned products without showing how they were actually used. The commercial, called "The Man from Del Monte," emphasized same-day picking and packing under the

uncompromising control of a Del Monte inspector. This highly successful commercial was shown in several countries in Europe and the Middle East, with the words translated into local languages.[18] The communication strategy proved effective because it was built on important insights from factual self-analysis.

The sales forecasting techniques discussed in this chapter can be applied in any country. The *Annual Survey of Buying Power* used in the multiple-factor index approach covers only the United States, but the U.S. Department of Commerce offers several publications that can help a global marketer in preparing a sales forecast. Updates of *Foreign Economic Trends and Their Implications for the United States* are issued semiannually for most countries in the world. The pamphlets describe economic trends in the country and analyze their implications for U.S. foreign trade. *Overseas Business Report,* published annually, deals with the basic economic structures, trade regulations, practices and policies, market potential, and investment laws in a group of countries. A similar publication is *International Marketing Handbook,* published by Gale Research Company, which provides an annual marketing profile for 142 nations.

LOOKING BACK

Look back at the story about MCI at the beginning of this chapter. The role of strategic planning at MCI, or any other organization, is to provide a long-run vision for the firm. Strategic planning thus guides the long-term commitment of resources. Managers have found that defining the mission of their organization helps them direct and focus their activities. Organizations function better as a result and become more responsive to the changing environment. Therefore, strategic planning is very important for efficiently reaching long-run goals.

The key factor in making strategic planning work is top management's commitment to the process. Top management's participation is required as well.

Forecasting, an important part of strategic planning, helps marketing managers choose a course of action. Forecasted sales, profit, and market share are among the most important criteria in choosing a strategic alternative.

KEY TERMS

cash cow 708
Delphi technique 719
differential advantage 702
diversification 704
dog 709
jury of executive opinion 718
market development 704
market penetration 703
market sales potential 718
moving average 719
problem child (question mark) 708
product development 704
profit impact of market strategy 711

SUMMARY

1 Describe the concept of strategic planning, and identify the steps in the strategic planning process. Strategic planning requires long-term planning, organization of resources to carry out the plans, and adjustment of the plans when necessary. The strategic plan affects the long-run course of the organization, its use of resources, and its long-term financial success. The steps in the strategic planning process are to define the business mission, establish strategic business units (if required), conduct a situation analysis, develop strategic alternatives, select an alternative, implement the selected strategy, and alter the selected strategy when necessary.

2 Understand how businesses define their mission and form strategic business units. A firm defines its business mission by answering the question "What business are we in?" As firms become larger and more complex, many decide to restructure into strategic business units (SBUs), with separate planning and operations for each. Each SBU should have a distinct mission and target market, control over its own resources, its own competitors, and a single business or collection of related businesses.

3 **Describe how businesses conduct a situation analysis, including identification of strategic windows and differential advantages.** A situation analysis, sometimes called a SWOT analysis, requires that management identify the firm's internal strengths (S) and weaknesses (W) and also examine external opportunities (O) and threats (T). One technique for examining opportunities is to seek strategic windows, limited times during which the "fit" between the key requirements of a market and the firm's competencies are at an optimum. A differential advantage is a unique aspect of a firm or its product offering that causes target customers to patronize the firm rather than its competitors. A firm can achieve a differential advantage through superior skills or superior resources.

4 **Discuss the techniques for developing, evaluating, and selecting strategic alternatives.** The strategic opportunity matrix can be used to help management develop strategic alternatives. The four options are market penetration, product development, market development, and diversification. Marketing managers then have four main tools for evaluating strategic alternatives. First, the portfolio matrix is a method of determining the profit potential and investment requirements of a firm's SBUs by classifying them as stars, cash cows, problem children, or dogs and then determining appropriate resource allocations for each. A more detailed alternative to the portfolio matrix is the market attractiveness/company strength matrix, which measures company and market viability. The third technique for evaluating strategic alternatives uses response functions, or graphed relationships, to analyze the impact of marketing mix variables on sales. The fourth tool, PIMS (profit impact of market strategy) analysis, uses a computer data base to compare a firm's market conditions, competitive position, and financial performance to those of other firms to forecast profitability. Corporate culture often plays an important role in selecting a strategic alternative.

5 **Understand how firms implement strategies and alter strategies when necessary.** Implementaton requires the delegation of authority and responsibility, the determination of a time frame for completing tasks, and the allocation of resources. Sometimes a strategic plan also requires task force management. A task force is established to accomplish a single goal or mission and thus works against a deadline. After an organization implements its strategic plan, it must track results and monitor the external environment. A key tool in evaluating the strategic plan is the marketing audit, which uses financial and nonfinancial reports to evaluate goals, strategies, and performance.

6 **Identify several techniques to help make strategic planning effective.** First, management must realize that strategic planning is an ongoing process and not a once-a-year exercise. Second, good strategic planning involves a high level of creativity. The last requirement is top management's support and cooperation.

7 **Understand sales forecasting techniques.** Sales forecasting is a process of estimating sales for products, product lines, companies, and industries. Contemporary forecasting employs seven techniques: jury of executive opinion, sales force composite, Delphi technique, moving average, regression technique, multiple-factor index approach, and purchase intent scale. The best tools for forecasting demand for new products are the Delphi technique, the multiple-factor index approach, and the purchase intent scale.

8 **Discuss global issues in strategic planning and forecasting.** Managers deciding to "go global" must make some dramatic changes in their strategic planning. Competitors are usually bigger, and target markets may have local quirks that

complicate marketing decisions. However, global firms often have a differential advantage, in both their home market and international markets. No matter where firms sell their products, sales forecasting techniques remain the same. Publications are available that provide economic and market data for foreign markets.

Review Questions

1. Why do firms form strategic business units (SBUs)? What characteristics make an effective SBU?
2. Describe the four strategic alternatives.
3. Discuss how different corporate cultures might respond to changes in the external environment.
4. What is the portfolio matrix? Discuss how it links SBU classification and resource allocation.
5. Identify the basic steps in sales forecasting.
6. Describe contemporary sales forecasting techniques.
7. What question should a firm ask when defining its business mission? Why?

Discussion and Writing Questions

1. Create a marketing plan to increase enrollment in your school. Write down each step, and describe the controls on the plan's implementation.
2. Why is a differential advantage critical to a firm's success?
3. Cite examples not mentioned in the chapter of specific strategies that firms use to achieve a differential advantage.
4. The former CEO of RJR Nabisco, Louis Gerstner, commented, "We're not going to play the market share game, just to hold some theoretical market share. Profitability is the most important thing." Write an analysis of the controversy over market share versus profit, referring to Gerstner's position and its pros and cons.
5. In your opinion, what type of organizational culture is best for the organization? Why?
6. How does crisis planning encourage ethical conduct? Identify critical features of a crisis contingency plan.

CASES

21.1 Fan Fare Corporation

As the story goes, Ed Barrow, manager for the New York Yankees during the 1930s, was approached by a clothing store manager with the idea of selling replica Yankee baseball caps. Barrow laughed and said, "I don't want every kid in the city running around with a Yankee cap on his head."

Some forty years later, Merle Harmon changed all that. He started his career in Denver, announcing high school sports while he was in college. Harmon joined the major leagues as a sports announcer for the Philadelphia Athletics (now in Oakland). He then moved on to the Minnesota Twins, the Milwaukee Brewers, and the New York Jets.

One year Harmon received a replica of a New York Jets football helmet as a Christmas present. Friends visiting Harmon's home asked where they could buy one. Because of their interest, Harmon decided that there was a market for sports replica items. In 1976 he opened his first Fan Fare store in Milwaukee. He sold pens, pencils, waste cans, napkins, cups, and so on. He could find little sports replica clothing to sell. For the most part, major league sports teams guarded their logo and uniform designs. Harmon became a pioneer in the sports replica marketing business.

This is how the sports clothing business works: The major league teams copyright their logos and charge manufacturers 8 to 9 percent of the sales price to manufacture the clothing. The individual teams all share equally in the proceeds from the sale of these articles, regardless of how well each individual team's items sell.

The team's success is a good predictor of how well its items will sell. Some items, however, do well regardless of the team's success. For example, the Cleveland Indians baseball cap is always a big seller, even though the team hasn't won a pennant in almost forty years. "It's a pretty cap," says Harmon.

Harmon now operates 144 Fan Fare franchise stores nationwide. Fan Fare's sales total about $45 million annually. The total market for sports replica items is a staggering $3 billion. There is even a good market for replicas of college uniforms and hats. The advantage of this business is that advertising is unnecessary. The teams do their own advertising every time they play a game. In addition, many celebrities wearing athletic apparel create high awareness without advertising. For example, Tom Selleck has often been seen with his Detroit Tigers' baseball cap. A good, visible location is all that a sports replica store needs to sell products.

For the sports replica retailers, the big selling season is Christmas. The Super Bowl offers these stores an extension of Christmas, as fans pick up their favorite teams' shirts and caps. Geography is no longer a factor. The local teams are still most popular, but the other teams have their supporters.

Questions

1. How would you define the mission statement for Fan Fare Corporation?
2. What differential advantages, if any, does Fan Fare have over the other sports replica retailers?
3. If you had to recommend a diversification strategy, what suggestions would you make? How would you redefine the mission statement?

Suggested Reading

Dan Piller, "Lookin' Sporty," *Fort Worth Star Telegram*, 13 January 1991, pp. F1, F8.

21.2 Saturn Corporation

Video title: *Saturn: A Different Kind of Car Company*

Saturn Corporation
1420 Stephenson Highway
Troy, MI 48007

SIC code: 3711 Motor vehicles and car bodies

Number of employees: 8,013

1993 revenues: $1.1 billion

Major brands: Saturn automobiles

Primary competitors: Honda, Toyota, Nissan

Background

The Saturn project was developed to bring import-car buyers back to U.S.-produced cars. The company spent five years interviewing owners of Japanese cars to find areas for improvement in the car-ownership experience. This interviewing process identified the shopping and buying experience as one of the most dreaded chores new-car buyers face. Saturn executives went to work to make buying a Saturn a pleasant experience.

Negotiating the price of a Saturn vehicle is not a policy at Saturn retail facilities (note that the outlet is called a "retail facility," completely removing the "deal" connotation). The price of each car is clearly noted on the window of the car. There is no negotiating or traditional sales pressure to make a deal right away. The company sought key retail facilities to develop hiring, training, and salary policies to match Saturn's philosophy. The result is the third-highest customer satisfaction rating in the business.

Instead of relying on traditional cash incentives, the company uses a thirty-day money-back guarantee. If the customer is not completely satisfied with the car, he or she may return it within thirty days or 1,500 miles for a refund. Among other benefits, this return policy allows the company to do a little market research. If a customer returns a car, the company can find out what is wrong and try to fix the problems.

To help retailers sell Saturns, each retailer is awarded a larger geographical area to develop—called marketing areas. One retailer is assigned to a marketing area and is responsible for building the adequate number of facilities. Customers can't "go down the street" for a better deal on the same car.

Industry

The automobile industry is expected to grow at 1 percent per year at best, making the competition for new sales fierce. Also most car manufacturers have too much production capacity. These manufacturers have a great incentive to increase sales to make better use of their production lines. The Big Three automobile manufacturers have closed some production facilities to help streamline manufacturing and reduce excess plant capacity. In addition, most car manufacturers rely on incentives like cash-back rebates and value-option packages to entice new-car buyers. Both of these tactics help sell cars, but they erode profit margins.

Competition in the small, "entry level" segment of the U.S. car market has been especially intense. Many observers questioned whether a U.S.–based company could win buyers from the inroads made by Toyota, Honda, Nissan, Mazda, and others. Given the high costs of capital, marketing, labor, and other factors, doing so at a profit presents an even greater challenge.

Saturn Corporation

Production began at the Spring Hill plant on July 30, 1990. The first Saturn was introduced in October of that year. Saturn reported profitable operations for the month of May 1993, the corporation's first profitable month since it began manufacturing cars. The goal is to break even in 1993. The company has sold 100 percent of its production every year and continues to increase production to meet consumer demands.

Saturn is positioned to appeal to college-educated men and women, especially professionals. The four-door models appeal to the slightly older, more needs-oriented segment of this market; the two-door coupe appeals to the younger, more style-oriented crowd.

Saturn was started by General Motors, but GM has intentionally distanced itself from Saturn. Saturn does not appear in any GM ads, nor does GM appear in any Saturn ads. GM didn't want any possible existing perceptions to interfere with the brand image Saturn is trying to create. This strategy may help Saturn, and successful ideas and innovations may be able to be transferred back to GM.

Questions

1. How would you define Saturn's mission?
2. What differential advantages does Saturn have over the other automobile manufacturers?
3. In what cell of the Boston Consulting Group portfolio matrix would you put Saturn? Why?

References

Million Dollar Directory 1993 (Parsippany, NJ: Dun & Bradstreet Information Services).

Kathleen Morris, "Autos: A Global Report," *Financial World,* 14 April 1992, p. 48.

Standard & Poor's Industry Surveys (New York: Standard & Poor's Corporation, April 1993).

21.3 *Decision Assistant:* King Battery Corporation

The Situation

Alan Klein, marketing manager of King Battery Corporation, must decide whether to put a new type of battery on the market. He has identified six independent market segments for the battery and has requested an estimate of the potential overall demand for this product. The sales manager is very optimistic about sales in each market. The advertising manager is negative about the possibilities. The marketing research director, whose predictions typically turn out to be the most accurate, has a different perspective. Each person's estimates are presented in Exhibit 21.8.

Klein knows that the perspectives of the advertising manager, marketing research director, and sales manager must be incorporated into his sales forecast. Furthermore, he wants to be 95 percent confident that his estimated sales forecast is accurate. The cost accounting department manager has determined that the company must have sales of $26 million to reach the profit target. Being unsure about how to proceed, Klein has come to you for help.

The Solution Technique

The situation confronting Alan Klein can best be resolved through use of the Monte Carlo simulation technique. The marketing *Decision Assistant* offers a Monte Carlo simulation predicated on triangular distributions, which assume that the optimistic, most likely, and pessimistic estimates may be skewed to either the right or the left. Use at least 200 iterations of the simulation and a standard deviation range of 2.

What If?

Consider each of the following situations independently:

1. What if the marketing manager was comfortable with a 68 percent confidence interval (standard deviation range of 1)? Would your analysis change?
2. After reading a new market research report on watch and hearing-aid batteries, the managers now agree more on their market potential. The forecast for watch batteries now ranges (in thousands) from $3,900 to $5,500, with a likely forecast of $4,200. Hearing-aid battery sales would likely be $8,800, with a range of $8,000 to $9,000 predicted. How does your analysis change?

Exhibit 21.8

Sales Estimates, in Thousands of Dollars

Market segments	Advertising manager	Marketing research director	Sales manager
Radio batteries	$2,500	$3,100	$ 8,000
Flashlight batteries	2,100	6,000	7,900
Watch batteries	2,600	4,890	11,400
Hearing-aid batteries	3,100	8,300	9,100
Portable TV batteries	1,800	2,100	5,600
Hobbyist batteries	1,800	7,300	7,500

CHAPTER 22

Total Quality Management and Control

LEARNING OBJECTIVES

After studying this chapter, you should be able to

1. Discuss the nature and importance of total quality management.
2. Describe the elements of total quality management.
3. Describe the roles of management, employees, and suppliers in total quality management.
4. Explain the role of marketing in total quality management.
5. Describe the Malcolm Baldrige National Quality Award.
6. Describe the concepts of marketing control and the marketing audit.

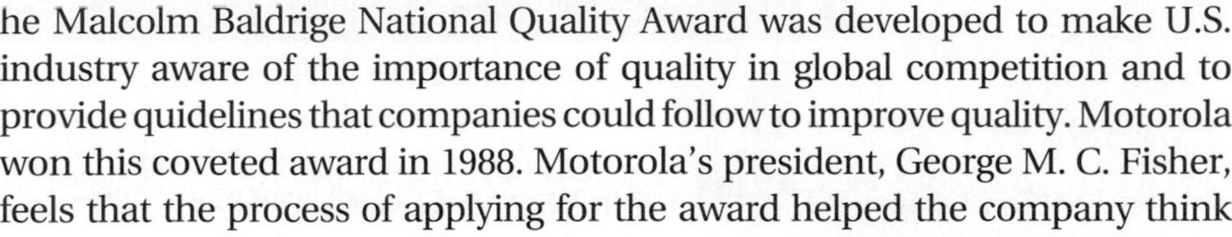

The Malcolm Baldrige National Quality Award was developed to make U.S. industry aware of the importance of quality in global competition and to provide quidelines that companies could follow to improve quality. Motorola won this coveted award in 1988. Motorola's president, George M. C. Fisher, feels that the process of applying for the award helped the company think about and address new issues, such as how to encourage a closer working relationship between factory personnel and product designers.

"Few U.S. companies can match Motorola's devotion to quality. In 1987 it set this five-year goal: reach virtual perfection in manufacturing by slashing component defects to what's known in the quality game as the six-sigma level. That's 3.4 defects per million components. Motorola has now expanded the goal to all its processes, from closing the books to applying for patents."

Applying the six-sigma standard to nonmanufacturing functions is a challenge, however, because they can't be broken into separate tasks and steps. Nevertheless, Motorola is making progress. For example, the corporate finance department now closes the monthly books in four days, compared to the twelve days needed in 1987. The process was streamlined by using clearer directions on forms and developing a simpler format for computer screens. These changes save the company $20 million per year.

Motorola learned about the importance of quality in the early 1980s. At that time, products like semiconductors and cellular phones were produced better and cheaper by Japanese competitors. Innovative new products (such as a pocket-size cellular phone), along with aggressive marketing and pricing techniques, have greatly improved the success of the company. "The ultimate aim," says Fisher, "is 'total customer satisfaction'—providing innovative products before customers even know they want them. . . . Motorola is pursuing nearly a dozen groundbreaking projects, including a car-navigation system and a global satellite-based telephone network."

Why is total quality managment important to U.S. firms? Motorola insists that its suppliers apply for the Baldrige Award. Why do you suppose it does? Should Motorola drop suppliers if they don't win the award?

Source: Extracts from Lois Therrien, "Going for the Glory," *Business Week*, 25 October 1991, pp. 60–61

❶ WHAT IS TOTAL QUALITY MANAGEMENT?

total quality management (TQM)
Coordination, throughout the entire organization, of efforts to provide high-quality products, processes, and services in order to ensure customer satisfaction.

You may recall from Chapter 1 that a central idea of the marketing concept is the satisfaction of customer wants and needs. **Total quality management** (TQM) is an organizational philosophy that provides a basis for achieving customer satisfaction. TQM is the coordination, throughout the entire organization, of efforts to provide high-quality products, processes, and services in order to ensure customer satisfaction.

Key to the TQM philosophy is the idea that quality is important at every step of the production process. Early efforts at quality control relied on inspection of the finished product. TQM strives to eliminate defects from the beginning. A product is inspected at the design stage, and the manufacturing process is engineered to be stable and reliable. Good design and good process result in a high-quality product. Service quality (discussed in detail in Chapter 11) is also an important part of TQM.

TQM is not just the responsibility of white-collar managers or of one department in an organization. It requires commitment from every employee. Unless all employees in the firm do their jobs right every single time, TQM is likely to fail.

TQM programs—like the marketing concept—are based on the need to understand customer requirements; thus marketing plays an important role in TQM. Traditional marketing techniques are used to support the quality focus in many TQM companies. For example, marketers know how to create ongoing dialogue with customers using such techniques as focus groups and customer surveys. TQM focuses on quality, on customer requirements, and on value.

A Focus on Quality

The TQM philosophy, which has been practiced by Japanese businesses for forty years, is becoming more and more important to U.S. organizations. The major reasons are the financial and production benefits of TQM and the need for U.S. firms to remain competitive in the international marketplace.

Until recently, many managers were convinced that higher quality costs more. The experience of the Japanese, however, taught that it costs more to do things poorly and then pay to fix problems than it does to do things right the first time. In addition, greater productivity can result from doing things better. In a firm that relies on product inspection for quality control, more than half of all workers are involved in finding and reworking defective products, with total investment in this process accounting for 20 to 50 percent of production costs.[1] Companies that use a TQM approach, however, have an advantage of up to 10¢ on every sales dollar over competitors. Cabot Corporation, for example, saved $1 million a year and freed new production capacity by reducing defects at one of its carbon-black plants by 90 percent over a two-year period.[2] Electrolux, a Swedish appliance maker, was able to reduce field-service repairs by 40 percent as a result of changes in design methods and other work processes.[3]

Surviving global competition is a strong motivation for companies to embrace TQM. As trade barriers come down, international competition increases. Companies that offer quality have the best chance of staying in business and prospering.

One indication of the commitment to quality among international firms was creation of the ISO 9000 series of quality standards in the late 1980s by the International Organization for Standardization. A set of five technical standards offers a uniform way to determine whether companies are using sound quality procedures.

With an eye toward improving quality, Saturn designed its assembly line in Spring Hill, Tennessee, to accommodate worker suggestions. For instance, workers ride down the line on wooden pallets with the cars, instead of trotting alongside on less comfortable concrete floors.

© Kevin Horan

Companies that want ISO certification must undergo a detailed third-party audit of their manufacturing and customer-service processes. More than fifty countries, including the United States and those in the European Community, have endorsed the standards. The regulations apply to companies making goods and to the manufacturers that supply parts or materials to those companies.[4]

Throughout the 1980s, U.S. firms steadily lost market share to higher-quality producers in Europe and Asia. The result was a growing U.S. trade deficit, especially in products like cameras, copiers, automobiles, and steel.[5] TQM was first adopted in the United States by large manufacturing companies that faced heavy competition from Japanese companies. For example, spurred by competition from Japanese carmakers during the 1980s, General Motors' Cadillac division improved quality in its cars and service so much that it won a prestigious Baldrige Award.[6] As the TQM concept became better known, U.S. firms of all sizes turned to it as a way to more effectively satisfy customers and thereby preserve their local, national, and worldwide competitiveness.

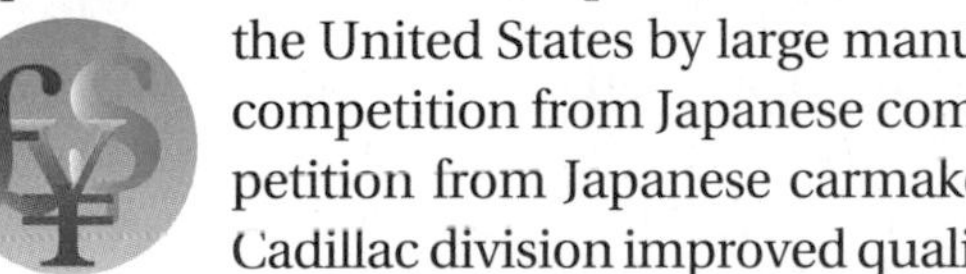

A Focus on Customers

The heart of TQM is its focus on the customer, because quality is defined from the customer's perspective. TQM's "customers" include both external customers, who are the final buyers of goods and services, and internal customers, who are an organization's employees. Because internal marketing was discussed in Chapter 11, this section discusses external customers—although some of the ideas can also be applied to internal customers. Making a total commitment to the customer means determining customer requirements and expectations, managing customer relations, setting customer service standards, resolving complaints for quality improvements, and determining customer satisfaction.[7]

Because customer expectations are the basis of TQM, identifying those expectations is the first step. The expectations of the customers in a firm's target market can be determined by answering these questions:

What product characteristics do customers want?

A key to TQM is a focus on customer satisfaction. Quality-conscious banks give customers what they want: friendly tellers and no waiting lines.
© Jay Fries/The Image Bank

What performance level is needed to satisfy their expectations?

What is the relative importance of each characteristic?

How satisfied are customers with current performance?[8]

It is important to note that management may not have a clear idea of customer expectations. U.S. auto companies, for example, have focused on producing stylish, defect-free cars, but customers perceive quality in terms of the level of service they get from dealerships.[9] Thus, customers should be approached directly, using customer surveys, focus groups, or any of the other methods covered in Chapter 8. Forum Corp., a service-quality consulting firm in Boston, worked with a bank whose customers said they simply wanted friendly service. Through focus group interviews, Forum discovered that what was most important to customers was that in especially busy periods every available bank official was helping at the service windows.[10]

Once customer expectations have been determined, the level of performance on important characteristics can be measured and compared to expectations. This way, companies can monitor customer satisfaction. GTE Telephone Operations conducts continual satisfaction research, collecting data six days a week, making 250,000 calls to customers each year.[11]

It is also important that customers' suggestions be heeded. Rolls Royce, as you will see later in the chapter, implemented customers' suggestions to add slots for glasses in the picnic table that drops from the rear of the car's front seat.

A Focus on Value

value
Relationship between what customers get and what they give up in exchange.

If customers are asked what they want, many of them will probably say they want value. **Value** is the relationship between what customers get and what they give up in exchange. What customers get includes product features, some level of quality, service, warranties, and so on. Customers give up money, time, and effort. One way to define value is to say that it means getting goods and services faster, better, and cheaper from one supplier than from another.[12] The point is that both goods quality and service quality are important in judging value.

Exhibit 22.1 combines the dimensions of service quality that were identified in Chapter 11 with dimensions of goods quality.[13] Those dimensions fall into two categories: **deliverables** (what goods and service attributes are provided) and **interactions** (how customers experience the service process). Companies can use this framework to identify customer expectations regarding value and to identify improvement opportunities. For example, the framework could be used for developing a worksheet to help firms evaluate their business. Which characteristics differentiate them from competitors? Which ones are the firm's strengths—or weaknesses? Which ones are most important to the customers the firm serves?

deliverable
Goods and services provided to the customer.

interaction
Customer experience of the service process.

Marketing must be part of the system for delivering value to the customer. Delivering value includes offering better guarantees, longer warranties, improved service, and "environmentally friendly" packaging. It also includes activities that build customer loyalty, such as 800 numbers or frequent-buyer plans—all at a reasonable price. The L'eggs brand of women's hosiery, for example, has a 54 percent market share because the combination of a strong product and a low price (almost no price increases for ten years) gives customers superior value.[14]

2 ELEMENTS OF TQM

Several elements of the TQM approach distinguish it from traditional ways of doing business. These elements include quality function deployment, continuous improvement, reduced cycle time, and analysis of process problems.

quality function deployment (QFD)
Technique that helps companies translate customer requirements into product specifications by using a quality matrix that relates what customers want with how products will be designed.

Quality Function Deployment

Quality function deployment (QFD) is a technique that helps companies translate customer requirements into product specifications. It is a way for companies to take customer demands into account during the product design stage, which is where the TQM process starts.

Exhibit 22.1

Quality Characteristics

Source: Adapted from Arthur R. Tenner and Irving J. DeToro, *Total Quality Management*, © 1992 by Addison-Wesley Publishing Company, Inc. Reprinted with permission of the publisher.

	Deliverables	Interactions
Faster	Availability Convenience	Responsiveness Accessibility
Better	Performance Features Reliability Conformance Serviceability Aesthetics Perceived quality	Reliability Security Competence Credibility Empathy Communications Style
Cheaper	Price	

QFD uses a quality chart, or matrix, that relates what customers want with how products will be designed and produced to satisfy those wants. An example of a QFD matrix for Writesharp, a pencil maker, is shown in Exhibit 22.2. Down the top left-hand side of the chart are listed all the customer expectations that have been identified through research, ranked in order of importance. Across the top of the chart are listed, first, product characteristics. At each place on the chart where expectation items and product characteristics intersect, product designers have assigned a value that represents how closely the product meets customer expectations. This section of the QFD chart gives designers guidelines for developing the best product.

benchmarking
Rating a product against the world's best products of all types.

Along with the QFD dimensions, the matrix also incorporates **benchmarking**, which is rating a company's products against the best in the world, including those in other industries. "The best" includes both functional product characteristics and customer satisfaction ratings. Benchmarking allows a firm to set performance targets and continuously reach toward those targets. In our example, the functional characteristics of Writesharp pencils (pencil length, time between sharpenings, lead dust, and hexagonality) are benchmarked (on the bottom left-hand side of the matrix), against those characteristics in competitor X's and competitor Y's pencils. Similarly, customer satisfaction benchmarks (easy to hold, does not smear, point lasts, does not roll) are ranked at the top right-hand side of the matrix. Looking at both sets of benchmarks and the inner grid that compares functional characteristics

Exhibit 22.2

Quality Function Deployment Matrix

Source: Adapted from Robert Neff, "No. 1—and Trying Harder," *Business Week*, 25 October 1991, p. 23. Reprinted from October 25, 1991 issue of *Business Week* by special permission, copyright © 1991 by McGraw-Hill, Inc.

		Functional characteristics					Customer satisfaction			
		Pencil length (inches)	Time between sharpenings (written lines)	Lead dust (particles per line)	Hexagonality	Importance rating (5 = highest)	Writesharp (now)	Competitor X (now)	Competitor Y (now)	Writesharp (target)
Customer demands	Easy to hold	●			●	3	4	3	3	4
	Does not smear		●	●		4	5	4	5	5
	Point lasts	●	●	●		5	4	5	3	5
	Does not roll	●			●	2	3	3	3	4
Benchmarks	Writesharp (now)	5%	56%	10%	70%					
	Competitor X (now)	5	84	12	80					
	Competitor Y (now)	4	41	10	60					
	Writesharp (target)	5.5	100	6	80					

● Strong correlation
● Some correlation
● Possible correlation

Customer satisfaction scale: 1 to 5 (5 = best)

with customer demands, decision makers can see that the product improvement with the biggest potential is a better-quality lead that lasts longer and generates less dust.[15]

Continuous Improvement

continuous improvement Commitment to constantly do things better.

Companies that embrace TQM know continuous improvement is necessary for maintaining quality. **Continuous improvement** is a commitment to constantly doing things better. Management tries to prevent problems and systematically improve key processes instead of troubleshooting problems as they occur. Other goals are finding ways to reduce the time between when a product is first conceived and when it is available for purchase, looking for innovation, and continually measuring performance. TQM is a never-ending journey rather than a destination.

One of the first steps in implementing continuous improvement is identifying the organization's key processes. Xerox, for example, has defined ten key processes, which include both direct line functions (customer marketing, order fulfillment, billing and collection) and supporting functions (financial management, information technology application, human resource management). Exhibit 22.3 shows the ten process areas identified by Xerox.

poka-yoke Japanese concept that means finding ways to minimize human error by changing the design.

Designing processes to reduce the potential for mistakes is another form of continuous improvement. ***Poka-yoke,*** a Japanese concept, means finding ways to minimize human error by changing the design. United Electric Controls, a producer of industrial sensors and controls, has added beveled edges to its parts so they can be assembled only the correct way. The company has been able to slash delivery times from twelve weeks to three weeks.[16]

Reduced Cycle Time

cycle time Time between product inception and delivery.

lead time Time that the customer has to wait before an order is filled.

One of the most effective ways to improve the quality of both goods and services is to reduce **cycle time,** the time from product inception to delivery. Companies that have faster cycle times than their competitors can earn profits faster and can also dramatically increase growth. For example, some manufacturing companies claim to need twenty to forty weeks of **lead time**—time that the customer has to wait before an order is filled—for delivery of parts that can be made in only eight to ten hours. Reducing these lead times improves customer service, increases quality (because parts are handled less), and results in higher profits.[17]

DuPont's Kalrez, a rubbery plastic, had a 90 percent market share in 1988, but Japanese competitors gained ground by offering better customer service. DuPont retaliated by shortening the time that it took to make its product from seventy days to sixteen, cutting its order-filling lead times from forty days to sixteen and increasing on-time deliveries from 70 percent to 100 percent. By 1991, DuPont's Kalrez sales had gone up 22 percent.[18] Motorola Lighting (a subsidiary of Motorola that produces

Exhibit 22.3

Xerox's Ten Key Business Process Areas

Source: Adapted from Arthur R. Tenner and Irving J. DeToro, *Total Quality Management,* © 1992 by Addison-Wesley Publishing Company, Inc. Reprinted with permission of the publisher.

Direct line functions	Supporting functions
Customer marketing	Financial management
Customer engagement	Physical asset management
Order fulfillment	Business management
Product maintenance	Information technology application
Billing and collection	Human resource management

electronic lighting ballasts) cut redesign work that typically takes three weeks down to two days because production and design staff now work together to solve any problem that comes up.[19]

Analysis of Process Problems

statistical quality control (SQC)
Method of analyzing deviations in manufactured materials, parts, and products.

Pareto analysis
Method for identifying a company's biggest problems that uses a bar chart to rank causes of variation in production or service processes by the degree of their impact on quality.

fishbone diagram
Visual tool resembling the skeleton of a fish that helps managers organize cause-and-effect relationships for problems.

Systematic improvement of processes requires methods for identifying the causes of manufacturing and service problems. Three tools that can be used for this are the following:

- *Statistical quality control:* a method of analyzing deviations in manufactured materials, parts, and products. **Statistical quality control** (SQC) was pioneered by Dr. W. Edwards Deming, a leader in the TQM movement in Japan, who believed that it is "the statistical understanding of systems that allows accurate diagnosis and solution of problems."[20] Data such as output per hour, percentages of defects, and the time each function takes are gathered and analyzed so improvements can be made.[21] SQC enables engineers to determine which errors are avoidable and which are not and to find the causes of the controllable problems.
- *Pareto analysis:* a method for identifying a company's biggest problems. The chief tool of **Pareto analysis** is a bar chart that ranks the causes of variation in production or service processes by their impact on quality. Most companies find that the worst problems occur again and again. Thus the most frequent problems can have the most negative impact on quality. The Pareto principle, espoused by Joseph M. Juran, another leader in the quality movement, is that 80 percent of the problems are due to 20 percent of the causes.[22] Pareto analysis allows management to concentrate on the biggest problems first. Then the next-most-frequent problems can be addressed, and so on, in a continuous attempt to improve quality. Exhibit 22.4 is an example of a Pareto chart for a package delivery company.
- *Fishbone diagram:* Once critical problems have been identified, management can determine their root causes. A **fishbone diagram**—so named because it resembles the skeleton of a fish—is a visual tool that helps managers organize cause-and-effect relationships for each problem. Exhibit 22.5 is a simplified

Exhibit 22.4

Pareto Chart Showing Elements That Affect Customer Satisfaction for a Package Delivery Company

Source: Data from Donald L. Weintraub, "Implementing Total Quality Management," *Prism* (Cambridge, MA: Arthur D. Little, Inc.), First Quarter 1991, p. 32.

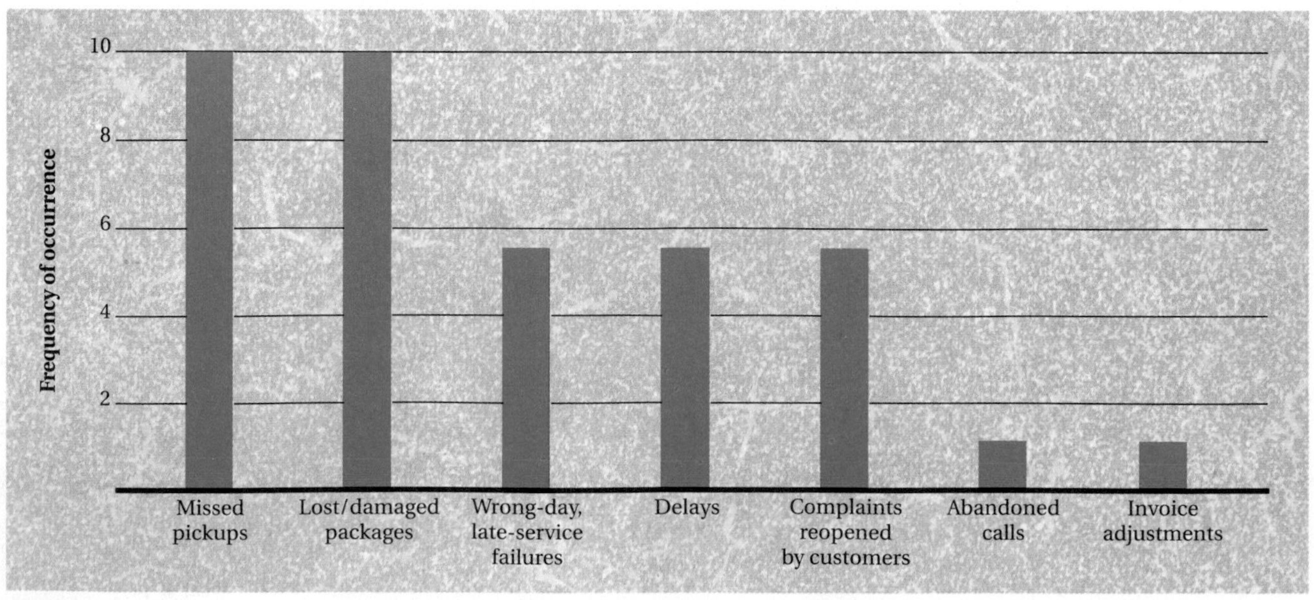

Exhibit 22.5

Fishbone Diagram Identifying Factors That Affect Order Lead Time

Source: Tamara J. Erickson, "Beyond the Quality Revolution: Linking Quality to Corporate Strategy," *Prism* (Cambridge, MA: Arthur D. Little, Inc.), First Quarter 1991, p. 18.

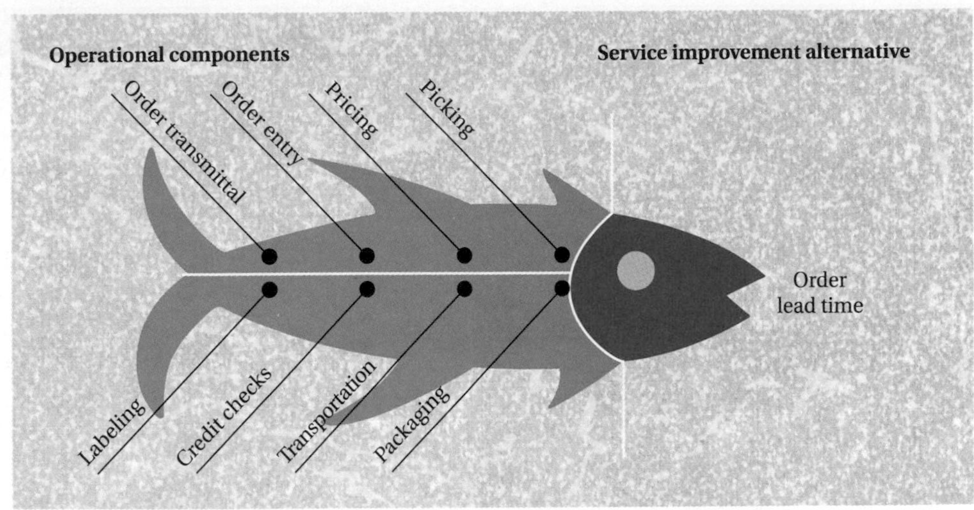

version of a fishbone diagram. The problem, or effect, identified by this diagram is order lead time. Its potential causes are such operations as labeling, order entry, pricing, and packaging. Information provided by the fishbone diagram can be used by management to identify areas where quality improvements need to be made.

All three of these tools help pinpoint problems and their causes. When the problems have been identified, they can systematically be attacked.

3 WHO IS INVOLVED IN TQM?

If TQM is to be successful, all divisions in a company and all employees must support and participate in quality control. Top and middle management, manufacturing and service employees, and suppliers all have an important role in making TQM work.

TQM at the Top

The vision and strategy of TQM are built by top management. Without top management's strong and visible commitment to TQM, other managers will be unlikely to make the changes needed to successfully implement the TQM philosophy.

W. Edwards Deming, whose ideas on statistical quality control were first embraced by Japanese manufacturers, has had a great influence on the TQM movement.

Top management's commitment to TQM must be more than just lip service. Systems have to be put into place to implement quality efforts. Philips Electronics, a company that produces auto headlamps, found this out the hard way. After starting a big push to adopt TQM, top management left implementation to lower levels in the organization. Unfortunately, top management failed to monitor the results of the program. For example, the company had no systematic way to measure customer satisfaction. Philips finally installed worldwide complaint-handling procedures and customer satisfaction surveys.[23]

Home Depot, which offers customers lots of advice on home-improvement projects, intensively trains its salespeople. They learn about every product on their aisle and the two adjacent aisles, in some cases via internal TV classes.
Ken Kerbs/DOT

One way to gain top management's support for TQM is to provide compensation or benefits tied to TQM goals. Allen-Bradley Co. and Corning are two manufacturers that have included quality objectives in the bonus plans of top management.[24]

Employee Empowerment

Empowerment, which was described in Chapter 1 as management's delegation of decision-making authority to employees, is a critical component of TQM. Empowering the work force encourages more positive attitudes toward the job, helps to reduce cycle time, and frees management to spend more time formulating strategy.

For empowerment to be successful, three factors should be in place.[25] First, all employees need to know the organization's mission, values, policies, objectives, and methodologies so the framework for making decisions is consistent across the organization. Second, employees must have the ability, skills, knowledge, and needed resources to perform their jobs. Finally, empowerment works only in an atmosphere of mutual trust between management and employees.

Ten years ago, at a Hewlett-Packard factory, 4 of every 1,000 soldered connections were defective. Engineers cut that rate in half by modifying the production process. But after the company turned the problem over to its workers, defects were reduced to under 2 of every 1 million—a thousandfold improvement.[26] At a Deere & Co. combine plant in Illinois, a worker, not a manager, arranges to fix defective parts delivered by suppliers.[27]

Teamwork

Teamwork is achieved when people work together to reach a common goal. In TQM companies, teamwork means sharing both responsibility and decision making. Instead of competing with each other, as is common in many companies, employees

work together. Mercedes-Benz found that organizing assemblers into self-directed teams helped reduce defects by 50 percent.[28]

Eastman Kodak has established a "patent process improvement team" that consists of inventors, laboratory managers, and attorneys. Lawyers now meet with scientists during the experimental stage to discuss ways of increasing the chances of yielding a patentable product or process, rather than serving as "patent gatekeepers" at the end of the process. The result has been a 60 percent increase in patent submissions and a doubling of patents issued to the company each year.[29]

Training for Quality

Training employees in quality techniques is a central part of TQM. Many of the philosophies and strategies used in TQM are very different from those to which employees in many U.S. companies have been accustomed. Training helps employees understand the corporate mission, their jobs, and their place in the organization. More specifically, employees need to know about TQM principles like teamwork and empowerment and need to learn statistical and other measurement tools. Wal-Mart Stores has become successful in part because the company invests heavily in training its employees to be friendly and knowledgeable.[30]

Even small businesses have begun large-scale training programs. Marlow Industries, a Dallas firm that makes custom thermoelectric coolers, was the 1991 small-business winner of the Baldrige Award. The average Marlow employee spent almost fifty hours in training in 1991. Thomas Interior Systems, a small Chicago-area firm that designs and resells office furnishings, spends an amount equal to 2.5 percent of its total annual payroll costs on education and training. Each Thomas employee is required to spend forty hours per year in training. This training takes place during employees' normal work schedules, and employees are paid their normal wage or salary for participating.[31]

TQM's Effect on Suppliers

Companies that adopt TQM tend to pressure suppliers to start quality programs of their own. When one company is trying to produce defect-free output, it cannot tolerate defects in the materials and parts it buys from suppliers. Many firms are moving toward long-term contracts with fewer suppliers but are requiring better quality.[32]

Philips Electronics, the auto headlamp company mentioned earlier, began its quality focus after it started supplying Toyota in the early 1980s. Pressure from Toyota forced Philips to change to a more exacting method for measuring quality than it had been using. This pressure led to packaging, manufacturing, and transportation improvements and vast savings in wasted material. In addition, defect levels dropped dramatically. By 1990, Philips had captured 60 percent of the Japanese market.[33] At the General Motors plant that makes the Buick LeSabre, managers and workers conduct weekly reviews of problem suppliers. About eighty suppliers have been dropped, many for not meeting LeSabre's quality goals.[34] Wilson Oxygen, a regional company in Austin, Texas, sells industrial products like welding supplies, beverage dispensing systems, and industrial gases. Wilson has a quality evaluation team that works with suppliers to reduce costs by eliminating errors and improving service.[35]

The concept of just-in-time (JIT) inventory management, introduced in Chapter 14, is also an example of how TQM has motivated closer cooperation between manufacturers and their suppliers. Quality is critical for suppliers of companies that

use JIT, because poor-quality parts and supplies may not be detected if delivered at the last minute.

4 THE ROLE OF MARKETING IN TQM

Marketing's philosophical link with TQM is the focus on customer satisfaction. In putting this philosophy into practice, marketing has three important roles. First, marketing personnel need to help define customers' quality expectations and translate these expectations into quality performance standards. Second, marketing professionals must apply the quality process to marketing operations. Third, marketing management can use the high quality of goods and services that result from TQM efforts to gain competitive advantage.

Determining Customers' Quality Expectations

The success of a firm's TQM efforts depends heavily on the entire organization's understanding of and response to customers' quality requirements. Thus marketing's expertise and links to the customer are needed. Identification and analysis of market segments, for example, are essential to identifying buyers' needs. Marketers can also transform customers' quality expectations into quality measures that help everyone in the firm implement TQM.

Suppose that one important quality criterion for buyers of washing machines is frequency of repair (durability). A manufacturer like Maytag must identify the business processes and results that contribute to a repair-free performance, which involves determining the product and service characteristics that reduce the need for washer repairs. Consumer surveys, analysis of repairs, appliance endurance testing, and evaluation of competitors' washing machines may all help. In addition, supporting marketing services, such as operating instructions and dealer training, may help reduce repairs. The analysis tools discussed in this chapter can be used to gather this information.

Applying TQM in Marketing

TQM concepts and methods can also be used to improve the quality of the marketing process. Quality assurance applies to planning new products, before-service marketing, sales, and after-service marketing.

Marketing's quality performance goals should take into account not only how the firm serves its outside customers but also how it serves its internal customers. Many people in an organization rely on marketing information, forecasts, materials, and sales distribution data to do their jobs well. If marketing's sales forecasts are not accurate, for example, the production side of the firm will not be able to order the proper amount of resources.[36]

Using Quality for a Marketing Advantage

High-quality products and supporting services give firms a strong competitive advantage. Quality is the appeal in an increasing number of advertising and sales promotion messages, for companies selling consumer and industrial products. Quality must be real, of course, and not just a promise.

Many industrial buyers demand quality certification from their suppliers to ensure that they are buying products of an acceptable quality. Certification shows that the supplier has statistical evidence of its compliance with accepted quality standards. Sales and marketing professionals often use certification to favorably posi-

These days, quality is marketable. Ford is one of many companies that tells potential customers, through advertising, about its achievements in the quest for quality.
Ford Motor Company

Roberta J. Nichols, Ph.D
Ford Environmental Engineer

"Environmental responsibility fuels our research."

At Ford Motor Company, responsibility for the environment goes hand in hand with building quality cars and trucks. That's why we're already building vehicles that meet California's strict emission standards for the late 90's.* It's also why we're the first U.S. manufacturer to build a car with CFC-free air conditioning and why we'll soon have a fleet of electric vehicles on the road. At Ford Motor Company, we take our responsibilities seriously.

Ford
Ford • Lincoln • Mercury • Ford Trucks

QUALITY IS JOB 1.℠ IT'S WORKING.

Buckle up–Together we can save lives.
*1993 TLEV 1.9L Ford Escort and Mercury Tracer...Available In California.
Always insist on genuine Ford Motor Company collision repair parts

tion their products against competing brands. Xerox, for example, uses the slogan "Leadership Through Quality" to project an image of quality to its customers and employees.[37]

5 THE MALCOLM BALDRIGE NATIONAL QUALITY AWARD

The Malcolm Baldrige National Quality Award was established by the U.S. Congress in 1987. It was named for the late former Secretary of Commerce.[38] The Baldrige Award is administered by the U.S. Department of Commerce's National Institute of Standards and Technology. The award program was inspired by Japan's Deming Prize for quality (named after U.S. quality expert W. Edwards Deming). The Baldrige Award recognizes U.S. companies that offer world-class quality in their goods and services. The award also promotes awareness of quality and transfers information about quality to others in the community.

The Baldrige Award examination board is made up of professionals from business and industry, universities, health care organizations, and government agencies. The most important criterion of the Baldrige Award is whether the firm meets customer expectations. The customer must be No. 1. Examiners evaluate organizations in seven categories, which are described in Exhibit 22.6. To qualify, a company must also show continuous improvement. Company leaders and employees must participate actively, and they must respond quickly to data and analysis.

Companies that have received the Baldrige Award include Xerox Business Products and Systems, IBM, Federal Express, and the Nuclear Fuel Division of Westinghouse. As many as two awards can be given each year in each category of the competition—large manufacturers, large service organizations, and small businesses—but so far the board has never issued more than five awards in one year.

Exhibit 22.6

Criteria for the Malcolm Baldrige National Quality Award

Source: Adapted from application guidelines for the Malcolm Baldrige National Quality Award, U.S. Department of Commerce, National Institute for Standards and Technology, Gaithersburg, MD.

Criterion	Maximum points	Indicators
Customer satisfaction	300	Commitment to customers, customer relationships, methods of resolving complaints, customer satisfaction results, and so on
Quality results	150	Supplier relationships, objective measures of quality, quality improvement, total quality picture
Human resource utilization	150	Training, employee involvement, performance evaluation, and staff well-being (at all levels of the work force, including upper and middle management)
Quality assurance of products and services	140	Process quality, continuous improvement, and systematic approaches to assuring a quality product
Leadership	100	How senior management sets and maintains its goals and communicates them throughout the organization, social responsibility, and values-driven management
Information and analysis	70	Data collection and analysis, quality of the data collected, and how the company uses data to prevent problems
Strategic quality planning	60	How quality-related goals are set and how the company plans to meet them, in both the short term (1–2 years) and the longer term (3 years or more)

INTERNATIONAL PERSPECTIVES

Rolls Royce Sees the Future

Unlike most car manufacturers, Rolls Royce makes its cars almost entirely by hand. This level of craftsmanship shows in the prices charged: The base price is $114,100 for the sporty Bentley and $140,200 for a Rolls Silver Spirit II.

Worried about competition from luxury carmakers like Daimler-Benz and BMW, as well as from the Japanese carmakers that are shifting to luxury cars, Rolls is increasing its efforts to build in quality. For example, the company has spent $9 million over three years training employees to use a new system that makes sure 80,000 parts are continually coordinated with the detailed assembly process, so less work must be redone.

"Rolls is slow to adopt new technology. It added antiskid brakes five years after most other luxury carmakers did, in part to refine the system so the car wouldn't lose its distinctive ultra-sensitive brake pedal. The software for a microprocessor-controlled suspension system installed in the 1990 models took Rolls and a German supplier four years to develop."

According to Rolls, about 60 percent of all models built since the company's 1904 founding are still on the road. Traditional quality control processes have contributed to the long life of the cars. These processes include things like "cleaning and treating the body shell for four days before paint is applied, or assembling some hydraulic components in oil to prevent contamination by dirt. . . . Furthermore, customers' suggestions are heeded: They resulted in the wood-veneer covers that slide over sun visors."

Rolls Royce cannot hope to fight competition on technology. Its competitive advantages are handcrafting and its "Old World cachet." These characteristics, along with some degree of innovation, will help ensure Rolls's position in the luxury-car marketplace.

Does Rolls Royce appear to use total quality management? If so, what TQM principles do you think the company uses? If not, do you think this company would benefit from adopting TQM principles?

Source: Extracts from Richard A. Melcher, "Rolls-Royce Sees the Future—and It's Still Handmade," *Business Week*, 22 October 1990, p. 96.

6 CONTROLLING MARKETING PROGRAMS

An effective TQM process depends on control. Control provides the mechanisms for evaluating marketing results in light of TQM program goals and for correcting actions that do not help the organization reach those goals within budget guidelines. Even if a firm is lucky enough to reach its goals without good controls, the chances are that some resources will have been wasted.

Unfortunately, although companies of all sizes have made great strides in implementing marketing controls, they often have not finished the process. For example, many firms have inadequate controls in the areas of product deletion, marketing cost allocations by functions or product lines, promotion effectiveness, and customer service.

formal control
Written, management-initiated mechanism that influences the probability that employees and systems will function in ways that support the stated marketing objectives.

informal control
Unwritten, typically worker-initiated mechanism that influences individual or group behavior.

Formal versus Informal Control

There are two broad classes of control within marketing organizations: formal and informal. A **formal control** is a written, management-initiated mechanism that influences the probability that employees and systems will function in ways that support the stated marketing objectives.[39] An **informal control** is an unwritten, typically worker-initiated mechanism that influences individual or group behavior. Informal control has three subsets: self-control, social control, and cultural control.

Self-control is when a person sets personal objectives, monitors their attainment, and adjusts behavior if they are off course. For example, say that Sandra Kerr, an account executive with a large New York advertising agency, has a chance to bid on a $50 million advertising budget for a division of Chrysler. The presentation must be

ready within a month. Sandra exercises self-control by working nights and weekends to prepare the proposal.

Social control, also called small group control, occurs when the marketing work unit sets standards (norms), monitors conformity with the standards, and takes action when a member deviates from them. Since the group has no formal authority, the action usually is ostracizing the person. Salespeople, for example, might set norms for expenses, sales volume, or filing dates for paperwork.

Cultural control evolves over time. Culture, in this context, consists of the values and prescribed patterns that guide worker behavior within an entire organization. Cultural control stems from the slow accumulation of organizational stories, rituals, legends, and norms of social interaction. For instance, Procter & Gamble has tried to create what it calls a culture of "total quality" and the notion that workers should go the extra mile to ensure that quality. The company's Hatboro, Pennsylvania, plant was gearing up to launch a new children's NyQuil cough syrup in time for the winter cold season. Just days before the production line was to start rolling, the factory received from a supplier 3 million NyQuil boxes printed upside down. If the faulty boxes had been run through the machine that inserts the bottles, the tops of the bottles would have ended up at the bottom of the boxes. The packages would not have stood up on the store shelves. There was not enough time to bring in engineers to design new parts. Instead, two mechanics worked around the clock for three days, and even missed the plant's annual picnic, to develop a system of springs and brushes that turned the boxes around and kept them open so NyQuil bottles could be inserted properly.[40]

Informal controls can back up formal controls to make the entire operation more efficient. Because informal controls, by definition, are not under management's direct control, the focus here is formal control systems.

How Control Works

A formal control system should make events conform to plans. The flowchart in Exhibit 22.7 traces the steps of a basic control system. The control process starts while planning is taking place. After managers set goals, they must develop standards to measure performance. When standards have been set, managers can then put the plan into action. Next, managers measure performance to make sure standards have been met. If they have been, actions continue. Otherwise, managers study deviations from standards to determine whether they fall within acceptable boundaries. If the deviations are not significant, actions continue with minor changes. When the deviations are major, the plan is halted. To revise the plan or perhaps scrap it, managers analyze cause-and-effect relationships.

Assume that Jane French, the sales manager of Joy Manufacturing, a producer of heavy industrial equipment, decides that key accounts (customers with over $500,000 sales potential per year) are not getting the attention they deserve from the sales force. The sales manager's goal is to increase the calls made to key accounts. She decides that instead of demanding a key account quota from the sales force, she will use positive motivation. She develops a new commission scheme that provides a 2-percent-of-net-sales bonus on key account sales, or $1,500—whichever is greater. She then sends a letter to each salesperson with a list of key accounts in the territory. The standard she sets is a minimum average increase in calls on key accounts of 25 percent per month over the same period a year ago. By studying summary data from individual call-record sheets, she will measure performance.

Exhibit 22.7

A Basic Control System

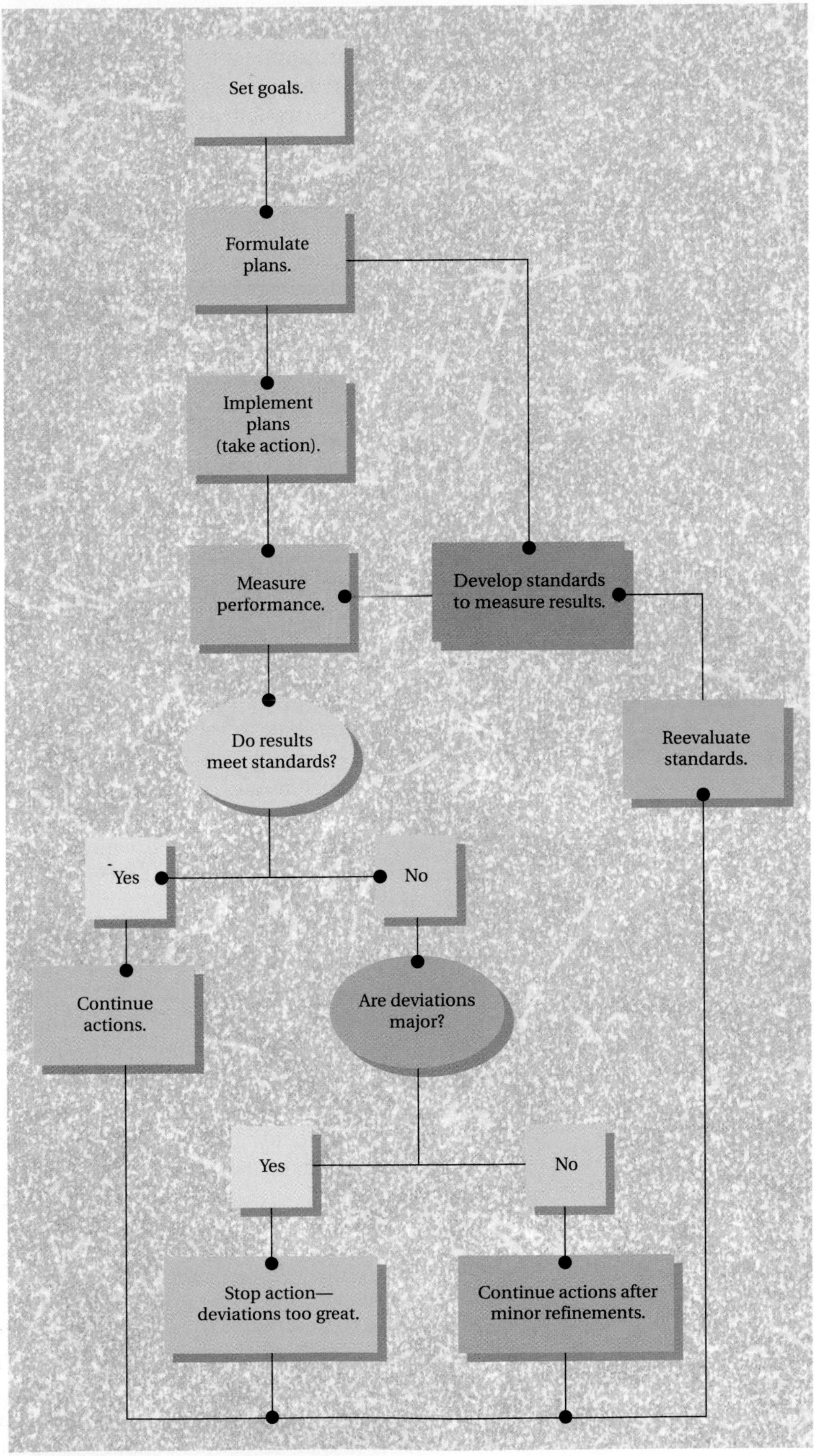

During the first six months after the new system was installed, calls on key accounts increased on average by 31 percent, and key account sales rose 43 percent over the same period a year ago. The plan was conforming to the sales manager's standards. During the seventh month, however, the percentage increase slipped to 26 percent and then fell to 22 percent. Although French was concerned about deviation from the standard, she didn't consider it a major problem. Yet the general trend was disturbing, so she asked the eight regional managers to discuss it with the sales force and to report back within a week. All reports reflected the same situation. Key accounts were now being visited so often (an average of three times per month) that many sales calls were unproductive. The sales force then began to call on other accounts and prospects where sales potential was better.

After studying the reports, French was satisfied that the key accounts were getting enough attention and that diverting time to other accounts might be more productive. The key account plan was kept in force to provide incentives to call on key accounts, but the standard was lowered to an average increase of 15 percent over the previous year. In this example, the general goals were being met, but the control system required a refinement in the standards.

TOOLS OF MARKETING CONTROL

Three useful tools of marketing control are sales analysis, cost analysis, and the marketing audit. Sales analysis and cost analysis are explained in Appendix D.

Strategic Control: The Marketing Audit

marketing audit
Thorough, systematic, periodic evaluation of the goals, strategies, structure, and performance of the marketing organization.

Perhaps the broadest control device available to marketing managers is the marketing audit. A **marketing audit** is a thorough, systematic, periodic evaluation of the goals, strategies, structure, and performance of the marketing organization. A marketing audit helps management allocate marketing resources efficiently. This tool, incorporating both financial and nonfinancial reporting, is mainly futuristic and strategic; it is not preoccupied with past performance but instead looks to the future allocation of marketing resources.

Marketing audits are not solely for firms having trouble meeting their marketing objectives. All companies should use such audits to uncover potential weaknesses and identify cost-cutting opportunities. One survey of marketing organizations found that 28 percent conducted one form of marketing audit or another.[41] The survey also showed that the marketing audit is not restricted to any single form of organization. Small and large organizations, service firms, and manufacturers all rely on the marketing audit. As strategic planning becomes more popular, the use of the marketing audit should increase.

The marketing audit has four characteristics:

- *Comprehensive:* The marketing audit covers all the major marketing issues facing an organization and not just trouble spots.
- *Systematic:* The marketing audit takes place in an orderly sequence and covers the organization's marketing environment, internal marketing system, and specific marketing activities. The diagnosis is followed by an action plan with both short-run and long-run proposals for improving overall marketing effectiveness.
- *Independent:* The marketing audit is normally conducted by an inside or outside party who is independent enough to have top management's confidence and to be objective.

- *Periodic:* The marketing audit should be carried out on a regular schedule instead of only in a crisis. Whether it seems successful or is in deep trouble, any organization can benefit greatly from such an audit.[42]

Although the main purpose of the audit is to develop a full profile of the organization's marketing effort and to provide a basis for developing and revising the marketing plan, it is also an excellent way to improve communication and raise the level of marketing consciousness within the organization. That is, it is a useful vehicle for marketing the philosophy and techniques of marketing.

Marketing Audit Procedure

Administration of an audit requires three important and related decisions: the scope of the audit, the methods by which data are to be collected, and the selection of an auditor.[43]

Scope of the audit: The audit is an information-gathering process. If it is to fully evaluate a firm's overall marketing operation, the audit should collect as much information as possible given the firm's resources. For example, a small firm may find that a limited audit is most useful, since the firm may lack the resources to both collect detailed information and implement a large number of the suggestions that may emerge from the audit.

Although there is no "best" format for all organizations, the major areas usually addressed in an audit are identified in Appendix D. This outline includes many specific questions that may serve as a checklist.

Data collection: Data are compiled from three main sources: internal interviews, external interviews, and secondary sources. Internal interviews, with key individuals in the organization, seek to get information on all aspects of the organization's operations, competencies, and constraints. The internal interviews should be supplemented by interviews with key members of the organization's external publics, such as customers, suppliers, competitors, and stockholders. The audit should also tap all pertinent secondary sources of data available in files or in literature. However, secondary sources do not provide reliable information unless they have been compiled with marketing audits in mind. Furthermore, these data must be carefully evaluated to make sure they are relevant. Together, these three sources of information offer a broad base for assessing an organization's marketing operations. The number of sources consulted and the amount of data collected depend on the scope of the audit.

Selection of an auditor: Marketing audits may be conducted by someone from within or from outside the firm. In a firm with severely limited resources, a high-ranking staff member or companywide auditing committee may conduct the audit. However, self-audits lack the objectivity of independent audits by outsiders. Self-audits are less likely to get at "sacred cows," since it is hard for people to objectively critique decisions made or influenced by them or their close colleagues. A third party, with whom people can talk openly without feeling any threat toward their position in the organization, can report insights that might not be offered as candidly to someone from within the organization.

Postaudit Tasks

After the audit has been completed, three tasks remain. First, the audit should profile existing weaknesses and inhibiting factors, as well as the firm's strengths and new opportunities available to it. Recommendations have to be judged and prioritized so that those with the potential to contribute most to improved marketing performance can be implemented first. The usefulness of the data also depends on the auditor's skill in interpreting and presenting the data so decision makers can quickly grasp the major points.

The second task is to ensure that the role of the audit has been clearly communicated. It is unlikely that the suggestions will require radical change in the way the firm operates. The audit's main role is to address the question "Where are we now?" and to suggest ways to improve what the firm already does.

The final postaudit task is to make someone accountable for implementing recommendations. All too often, reports are presented, applauded, and filed away to gather dust. The person made accountable should be someone who is committed to the project and who has the managerial power to make things happen.

LOOKING BACK

Look back at the story about Motorola that appeared at the beginning of this chapter. TQM is important to U.S. firms because it offers financial and production benefits and because it offers U.S. firms a way to remain competitive in the international marketplace. Motorola insists that its suppliers apply for the Baldrige Award to pressure them to start their own quality programs. Because Motorola is trying to produce defect-free products, it cannot tolerate defects in the materials and parts it buys from suppliers. Suppliers who successfully make improvements in quality as a result of applying for the Baldrige Award should not be dropped, even if they do not win.

KEY TERMS

benchmarking 734
continuous improvement 735
cycle time 735
deliverable 733
fishbone diagram 736
formal control 743
informal control 743
interaction 733
lead time 735
marketing audit 746
Pareto analysis 736
poka-yoke 735
quality function deployment 733
statistical quality control 736
total quality management 730
value 732

SUMMARY

1 Discuss the nature and importance of total quality management. TQM is the coordination, throughout the entire organization, of efforts to provide high-quality products, processes, and services in order to ensure customer satisfaction. The TQM philosophy includes the elimination of defects from the beginning of the production process and the involvement of everyone in the organization. TQM is important to firms of all sizes for two reasons: It offers financial and production benefits, and it offers a way for companies to remain competitive in global markets.

2 Describe the elements of total quality management. There are four elements of total quality management. *Quality function deployment* (QFD) is a technique that uses a quality chart to relate the product characteristics customers want to the way products will be designed and produced. QFD also includes benchmarking, which is rating a company's products against the best in the world. A second element is *continuous improvement,* a commitment to constantly do things better. Management adopts the perspective of prevention and systematic improvement of key processes instead of troubleshooting problems as they occur. A third element of TQM is *reduced cycle time,* which means reducing the time between product inception and delivery. Companies with faster cycle times than their competitors can earn profits faster and can also dramatically increase growth. The final TQM element is *analysis of process problems,* which can be accomplished with one or more of the following tools: statistical quality control (SQC), a method of analyzing deviations in manufactured materials, parts, and products; Pareto analysis, which uses a bar chart to rank causes of variation in production and service in order to identify a company's biggest problems; and fishbone diagrams, visual tools that help managers organize what they know about cause-and-effect relationships for each problem.

3 Describe the roles of management, employees, and suppliers in total quality management. TQM involves everyone in the organization. Top management must strongly and visibly commit to TQM, both with words and with actions. Employee empowerment (giving employees the authority to make decisions), teamwork, and training are critical to the success of TQM. Suppliers to TQM companies must also adopt quality practices, because when one company is trying to produce defect-free output, it cannot tolerate defects in the materials and parts it buys from suppliers.

4 Explain the role of marketing in total quality management. Marketing has three important roles in TQM. First, marketing personnel need to help determine customers' quality expectations and participate in translating those expectations into quality performance standards. Second, marketing professionals must themselves use TQM to improve the quality of marketing operations. Third, marketing management can use the high quality of goods and services to gain competitive advantage.

5 Describe the Malcolm Baldrige National Quality Award. The Baldrige Award was established by Congress in 1987 to recognize U.S. companies that offer world-class-quality goods and services. The award also promotes awareness of quality and transfers information about quality to others in the community.

6 Describe the concepts of marketing control and the marketing audit. A marketing control system ensures that marketing goals are achieved within guidelines. Controls are either formal (instituted by management) or informal (unwritten and typically initiated by workers). The control process begins during planning. Managers develop standards to measure performance. If measured performance does not meet standards, deviations are examined and action may be halted.

The marketing audit is the process of evaluating the goals, strategies, structure, and performance of the marketing organization. The marketing audit should be comprehensive, systematic, independent, and periodic. Administration of an audit requires decisions about the scope of the audit, data collection methods, and selection of an auditor. Postaudit tasks include interpreting the data, communicating the results, and implementing the recommendations.

Review Questions

1. Define total quality management and explain why it is important to companies.
2. How can the expectations of customers in a firm's target market be determined and translated into product specifications?
3. What is value, and how can firms provide value to customers?
4. Describe continuous improvement as a TQM strategy, and discuss one way firms can improve their performance over time.
5. What are three tools that can be used to identify the causes of manufacturing and service problems?
6. What are the roles of management, employees, and suppliers in implementing TQM?
7. What is the role of marketing in TQM?
8. Differentiate between formal and informal controls. Why are they critical to TQM implementation?
9. Describe the function of the marketing audit.

Discussion and Writing Questions

1. Use the "faster, better, cheaper" framework to describe your expectations when you buy a car, a haircut, and a meal in a restaurant.
2. Choose a product category with several competing brands that you are familiar with. For one of the brands, construct a QFD matrix using your expectations and your perceptions of how that brand meets your expectations. If you can, also include benchmarking evaluations based on your knowledge of competing brands.
3. Discuss how cycle time and the tools for identifying process problems affect continuous improvement.
4. Why are marketing personnel likely to be more qualified than personnel in other functions (such as accounting, finance, and operations) to play a large role in implementing TQM?
5. What is the relationship between TQM and control, as you see it?

6. Discuss the four characteristics of a marketing audit.
7. Choose a company (real or hypothetical) and write some specific guidelines for that company to use in conducting a marketing audit.

CASES

22.1 Weyerhaeuser Company

The disposable diaper market was saturated, but Weyerhaeuser Company thought it had found a niche. Weyerhaeuser, the leading manufacturer of store-brand disposable diapers in the United States, had a 10 percent share of the market. Rivals Procter & Gamble and Kimberly-Clark controlled 49 percent and 33 percent, respectively.

Then Weyerhaeuser decided to introduce a premium store-brand diaper. By teaming up with Unicharm, a leading Japanese diaper manufacturer, the company hoped to market the store brand UltraSofts. This product would include some of the same features found in Pampers, Luvs, and Huggies but would sell for less. Nonetheless, market analysts predicted the company wouldn't take a large market share.

The new product offered some distinct advantages for retailers. Wegmans Food Markets thought the new product would sell well. In its stores the product was sold as Wegmans UltraSofts. The company gave the product a prime place on the shelves and was even sharing the cost of promoting the new diapers. Wegmans sent out 50,000 free samples and coupons to consumers in the Rochester, New York, area. Daniel R. Wegman, president of the grocery store chain, was happy to add this product to store shelves. The product sold for less than the discount price for the nationally advertised brands and offered a higher profit margin.

The product had many of the upscale features found in the national brands—for example, a soft waistband and superabsorbent pulp. The UltraSoft diaper's unique clothlike back sheet replaced the usual plastic cover found on most diapers. The diaper didn't leak because the waterproof layers were woven under the back sheet. The diaper was based on Weyerhaeuser's own technology—advances from Unicharm and patents acquired from Johnson & Johnson when J&J abandoned its diaper business.

Ten months after UltraSoft's introduction, Weyerhaeuser abandoned its dream of marketing the diaper nationwide. The company had miscalculated the production cost and faced serious problems with the production line. As a result, Weyerhaeuser to raise the price it charged by 22 percent. Because of this increase, stores were unable to offer many promotions for the product. In addition, the system that sprayed the superabsorbent material into the pad worked ineffectively. Too much material missed the pad and corroded the production line's equipment. Bobby Abraham, president of Weyerhaeuser's personal care products division, said, "We've got about twenty problems" in the manufacturing process.

Weyerhaeuser may decide to return the product to the market. If so, Weyerhaeuser may have to raise the price charged to retailers or delete some of the product's features and lower the price. Weyerhaeuser will probably conduct the second try on a much larger scale. If the company can offer suppliers long-term contracts, it can ensure adequate supply and consistent prices for materials. Weyerhaeuser could then pass along these savings to the dealers. However, the company may have trouble winning back the dealers. Since shelf space in grocery stores is a precious commodity, no grocer wants to tie up shelf space for unprofitable products.

Questions

1. Although Weyerhaeuser's diapers offered distinct advantages to retailers, does it appear that the expectations of final customers were taken into acount before the product was developed? Why did you answer the way you did?
2. What TQM principles were apparently missed by Weyerhaeuser in developing and manufacturing its disposable diapers?
3. How could marketing play a role in bringing the TQM philosophy to Weyerhaeuser if the company decides to return the product to the market?

Suggested Readings

Alecia Swasy, "Diaper's Failure Shows How Poor Plans, Unexpected Woes Can Kill New Products," *The Wall Street Journal*, 9 October 1990, pp. B1, B2.

Alecia Swasy, "Weyerhaeuser Unveils Hybrid Diaper Brand," *The Wall Street Journal*, 26 January 1990, p. B1, B4.

22.2 Xerox Corporation

Video title: *The Xerox Hi-Rockers' Quest for Total Quality*

Xerox Corporation
800 Long Ridge
Stamford, CT 06902

SIC codes: 3579 Office machines
3577 Computer peripheral equipment
7629 Electronic and electronic repair shops
7378 Computer maintenance and repair
5111 Printing and writing paper

Number of employees: 111,000

1993 revenues: $18 billion

Major brand: Xerox

Largest competitors: Pitney Bowes, Toshiba, Olivetti Office

Background

In the late 1970s, Xerox found itself losing ground to the low-volume Japanese copier manufacturers. The industry leader was losing market share so fast that turning the company around would have taken a considerable effort on the part of every employee in the company. Xerox began its quest for excellence with a leadership-through-quality program in the early 1980s. This program began with extensive employee involvement. Every level of the organization became involved.

The company's quest for total quality focused on the external customer. Xerox defines quality as total customer satisfaction. This new focus won the company quality awards in Great Britain, France, Holland, Germany, and Japan, but the most prestigious award came in 1989, when Xerox won the Malcolm Baldrige National Quality Award. Only a handful of U.S. companies have won it. The award spurred Xerox to redouble its efforts to achieve excellence.

Industry

The document-processing business has three main segments. The low-volume segment is mainly small-business consumers. The core business is in the midrange copier segment, which is composed of large companies that rely on duplicating to support company efforts. The high-end segment is chiefly service companies that rely on the equipment to provide copying and printing services to their customers. This high-end segment is driven by two major factors: name recognition and technological advances. Name recognition comes through having a high market share in the midrange segment. Technological advances in the manufacture of high-speed copiers have enabled these companies to take business away from offset printing companies. Other technological advances include color printing and copying equipment.

The Xerox Hi-Rockers

At Xerox, quality is a competitive weapon. If the company can improve the quality of its service, it can increase its market share and profitability. Much of Xerox's profitability in the high-end copier business comes from the sale of consumables. Keeping the machines running properly helps improve customer relations, increases the likelihood of repeat purchase, and increases the sales of Xerox consumable products.

The Xerox Hi-Rockers have joined the Xerox quest for total quality. This group services Xerox high-volume copy machines in the Little Rock, Arkansas, area. The Hi-Rockers approached existing customers to find out how service might be improved. The team achieved total customer satisfaction in less than two years.

Questions

1. How successful were the Xerox Hi-Rockers in achieving total quality management? Use the customer comments to justify your answer.
2. Did the Hi-Rockers' quest for total quality require changes in the management style of the Hi-Rockers' supervisors?
3. What did customers have to give up to get improved service from Xerox?

References

Million Dollar Directory 1993 (Parsippany, NJ: Dun & Bradstreet Information Services, 1993).

Standard & Poor's Industry Surveys (New York: Standard & Poor's Corporation, October 1993).

Ward's Business Directory of U.S. Private and Public Companies (Detroit: Gale Research, Inc., 1992).

PART SEVEN
CRITICAL THINKING CASE

Levi Strauss and Company

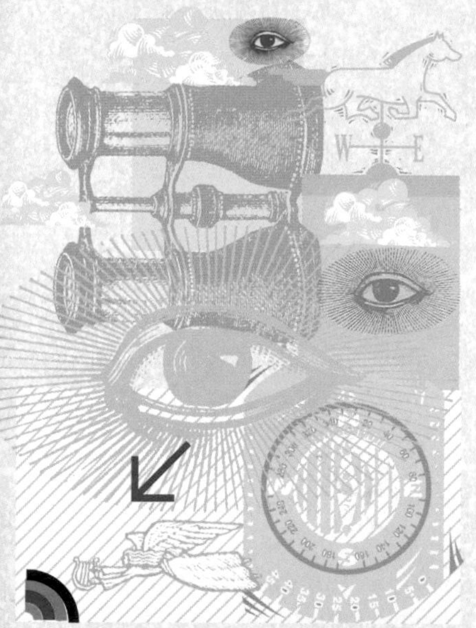

Levi Strauss began his business venture in the late 1800s in San Francisco, stitching surplus tent canvas into work pants for gold prospectors. Today the company has cornered a 22 percent market share of the $6 billion jeans market. Trailing directly behind Levi Strauss are Wrangler (13 percent), Lee (11 percent), and Gitano (5 percent). These four jeans manufacturers control over 50 percent of the market. Another 20 to 25 percent of the market is composed of the private-label jeans of stores like JCPenney, The Gap, and Sears. Blue denims are the biggest-selling jeans (70 percent of market), followed by colored denims (20 percent). Acid-washed, stone-washed, oversized, and distressed-denim jeans are some of the most popular looks today.

Target Market for Blue Jeans

In 1989 the industry sold 350 million pairs of jeans, more than enough for every person in the United States to have a new pair. Still, the market for jeans has declined quite a bit since its peak in 1981, when the industry sold 520 million pairs. The main problem is the shrinking population of 14-to-24-year-olds, the key market segment for jeans. Baby boomers have always been one of the major market segments. However, as these consumers enter midlife, they buy fewer pairs of jeans and begin looking for different products. They continue to wear blue jeans but mostly on weekends. They simply do not wear them out as fast.

Each of the four major jeans manufacturers has taken a different approach to segmenting the market. In the past, Gitano used sultry models to promote its jeans. This sort of image advertising appealed to young women. The company then realized that many of its loyal customers were older and had children of their own. In an effort to expand its market, the company broadened its appeal. Gitano's "spirit of family" campaign is aimed at mom and her teenage daughters.

Lee competes in all market segments but has directed its TV advertising to women. The company chose to focus on women for two reasons: Women constitute about 40 percent of the market, and they buy most of the children's clothes. The company emphasizes the product benefits—comfort and fit. Lee adopted the slogan "Nobody fits your body . . . or the way you live . . . better than Lee." The company targets the male market through the use of print advertising trying to maintain a "family brand" image.

Wrangler, the official jeans of the Pro Rodeo Association, concentrates on the blue-collar male market. Long associated with its hard-core cowboy positioning, the company is broadening its market to include consumers who might imitate the cowboy look. To reach this new market, Wrangler hired Texas Rangers' pitcher Nolan Ryan as a spokesperson for its products.

Levi Strauss has segmented the market not only by age but also by region and ethnic group. The company hired Spike Lee to direct a series of documentary-style ads for its 501 brand. Spike Lee has tremendous appeal with the 14-to-24-year-olds. The company targets the market of 7-to-11-year-olds with the "wild creatures" campaign featured on Saturday morning television. In the West and Southwest, the company hits the Hispanic market with the appeal that jeans are appropriate for all occasions. This group wears jeans mostly for work only.

Product Line Adaptation

Levi Strauss produces a wide range of products. In addition to its denim jeans, the company makes a complete line of clothing. The company has never lost sight of the changing marketplace. As baby boomers age, their demand for traditional denim jeans declines. Levi Strauss was one of the first companies to adapt its product line to the changing lifestyle of aging consumers. In 1978, market research indicated that older men preferred dress slacks to jeans. Levi Strauss introduced Action Slacks—comfortable, easy-to-clean slacks with an expandable waistband. Levi Strauss made middle-aged adults feel good about their older bodies. No matter how much exercise people get as they age, their bodies just don't maintain their youthful figures. By 1985 Action Slacks brought the company over $100 million in sales.

The company has another product hit with the Dockers line of clothing. Levi Strauss identified a new consumer who wanted something between jeans and Dad's pressed slacks. The Dockers line is not new to Levi Strauss. The company had marketed a line of loose-fitting chino pants under the name Dockers in both Japan and Argentina with little success. The key to the product's success in the United States is that the slacks are available in a multitude of colors. With a line of coordinated shirts and a massive promotional campaign, Dockers has become a major product category that did not previously exist. Even stores like Sears and JCPenney have created special Dockers departments. Without merchandising support from Levi Strauss, many of these stores would have missed this Dockers market segment.

LeviLink Computer Network

Making jeans is mostly a manual job. Workers hand-sew almost every seam and button on a pair of jeans.

In an industry with rapid changes in fashions and fads, retailers seldom stock large quantities of any specific size or style. Lower inventories reduce the risk to retailers when a specific style falls out of fashion but increase the risk of lost sales due to stock outages. This problem is even more severe for large retail chain stores. These stores often handwrite all orders and then send them to a central purchasing department where they are processed. Restocking an item can take as long as three weeks. LeviLink, Levi Strauss's new computer system, is streamlining these procedures.

Each store is connected directly to Levi Strauss by computer terminal. After the orders are entered into the terminal, the store receives the shipment within six days. The faster turnaround time offers two key advantages. First, it eliminates a lot of lost sales due to stock outages. Second, the system helps reduce the risk of stocking huge inventories in a constantly changing fashion business. The company estimates that for the retailers using LeviLink, sales have increased 20 to 30 percent.

The ultimate goal of Levi Strauss is to bring the equivalent of just-in-time manufacturing to the apparel business. When an order for a pair of jeans is entered into the system, the system can request that another pair of jeans be made. The company is also using the system to adjust the quantities of materials it orders from suppliers. By tying the production system closer to product sales, Levi Strauss has eliminated the need for large inventories of fabrics in warehouses next to manufacturing facilities.

Questions

1. Propose a business mission for Levi Strauss for now and the future?
2. Compare Levi Strauss to its competitors in today's market. Predict which competitors may challenge Levi Strauss's leadership in the jeans market.
3. Examine Levi Strauss's competitive advantage. Propose a plan for Levi Strauss to maintain this advantage.
4. Prepare a situation analysis for Levi Strauss. Predict possible threats and weaknesses that might hamper growth at Levi Strauss.
5. Evaluate the corporate culture of Levi Strauss. Is this the type of company you would like to work for?

Suggested Readings

Brian Bagot, "Slow Fade," *Marketing & Media Decisions*, October 1990, pp. 61–66.

Jeff Ostroff, "Targeting the Prime-Life Consumer," *American Demographics*, January 1991, pp. 30–34, 52–53.

Brenton R. Schlender, "How Levi Strauss Did an LBO Right," *Fortune*, 7 May 1990, pp. 105–107.

Part Seven
Ethics Case

The Inflatable Résumé

Each year, several million people are hired based on information obtained during an interview or listed on their résumé. Each year, some significant number of people get a job by falsifying their résumé. Bill Myer, a graduating senior at a major Midwestern university, had read articles about people fired years later for having lied on their résumés. He was determined to tell the truth on his until he was confronted with a statement by one of his fraternity brothers: "If you believe in yourself, you need to give the interviewer something to believe in as well." "What do you mean when you say 'Give them something to believe in'?" asked Bill. "I mean expand your job descriptions and experience so they fully understand that you are an experienced and capable worker," replied his friend.

Bill gave some thought to his friend's specific suggestions:

1. Expand your description of each job and your work history so they show your managerial capability, even though you may not have served in a management position.
2. If you have not had the chance to hold office in student organizations, describe the jobs you have done for those organizations with significant titles that you have given yourself. For example, if you parked cars at the fraternity spring formal, you would give yourself the title of Director of Logistics Committee.
3. Round up your grade point average or simply pick out the courses that you have done well in and report only the grade point average for them.

- What are the risks involved in doing the things that Bill's friend suggested? Do you think interviewers have seen these things done before?

Bill's friend made some other suggestions:

4. Make summer jobs sound more important by giving yourself a job title whether you had one or not.
5. Cite references of very important people at the university whether they know you well or not, because no one ever checks résumé references.
6. Add courses to your résumé that will make you appear to be more outstanding, whether you took them or not, because no one ever checks transcripts.

- Are the temporary advantages gained by this level of résumé deception worth the risk? How might interviewers check your character by checking résumé items?

The final advice given by Bill's fraternity brother involved the following:

7. Drop some experience anecdotes into a job interview that do not appear on the résumé and then apologize for forgetting to add them. Leave the impression that there may be a number of other great experiences that you did not bother to put on your résumé.
8. In the interview, mention the names of others who could have been references that the interviewer will recognize. The names will leave a good impression, and again, no one ever checks.

- Do interviewers check references, transcripts, and other such background material? What is the risk of doing what Bill's friend suggests?

Bill asked himself whether his résumé would look competitive with other résumés if he was completely truthful. He felt that some interviewers would not be as willing to talk with him without an inflated résumé but that others would probably find it refreshing that he had not tried to inflate his background.

- Do you agree with Bill's perceptions? What advantages would there be to being completely honest on a résumé?

APPENDIX A
Careers in Marketing

You can use many of the basic concepts of marketing introduced in this book to get the career you want by marketing yourself. The purpose of marketing is to create exchanges that satisfy individuals as well as organizational objectives, and a career is certainly an exchange situation for both you and an organization. The purpose of this appendix is to help you market yourself to prospective employers by providing some helpful tools and information.

AVAILABLE CAREERS

Marketing careers have a bright outlook for the 1990s. The U.S. Bureau of Labor Statistics estimates that employment in marketing fields will grow 30 percent by the year 2000. Many of these increases will be in the areas of sales, public relations, retailing, advertising, marketing research, and product management.

Sales

There are more opportunities in sales than in any other area of marketing. Sales positions vary greatly among companies. Some selling positions focus more on providing information; others emphasize locating potential customers and closing the sale. Compensation, often salary plus commission, sets few limits on the amount of money a person can make and therefore offers great potential. Sales positions can be found in many organizations, including manufacturing, wholesaling, retailing, insurance, real estate, financial services, and many other service businesses.

Public Relations

Public relations firms help create an image or message for an individual or organization and communicate it effectively to the desired audience. All types of firms, profit and nonprofit organizations, individuals, and even countries employ public relations specialists. Communication skills, both written and oral, are critical for success in public relations.

Retailing

Retail careers require many skills. Retail personnel may manage the sales force and other personnel, select and order merchandise, and be responsible for promotional activities, inventory control, store security, and accounting. Large retail stores have a variety of positions, including store or department manager, buyer, display designer, and catalog manager.

Advertising

Many organizations employ advertising specialists. Advertising agencies are the largest employers; however, manufacturers, retailers, banks, radio and television stations, hospitals, and insurance agencies all have advertising departments. Creativity, artistic talent, and communication skills are a few of the attributes needed for a successful career in advertising.

Marketing Research

The most rapid growth in marketing careers is in marketing research. Marketing research firms, advertising agencies, universities, private firms, nonprofit organizations, and governments provide growing opportunities in marketing research. Researchers conduct industry research, advertising research, pricing and packaging research, new product testing, and test marketing. Researchers are involved in one or more stages of the research process, depending on the size of the organization conducting the research. Marketing research requires knowledge of statistics, data processing and analysis, psychology, and communication.

Product Management

Product managers coordinate all the activities required to market a product. Thus they need a general knowledge of all the aspects of marketing. Product managers are responsible for the successes and failures of a product and are compensated well for this responsibility. Most product managers have previous sales experience and skills in communication. The position of product manager is a major step in the career path of top-level marketing executives.

WHERE TO LOOK

Not many people are fortunate enough to have a job fall into their lap when they graduate. It is your responsibility to find a career that satisfies both your needs and the needs of the employer.

So, where do you look? Several resources help narrow the search. Some of the obvious places to check are parents, friends, family members, career planning and placement centers, career counselors, and the companies themselves. A list of not-so-obvious resources is shown in Exhibit A.1.

Exhibit A.1

Selected Sources for Finding Out about Marketing Careers

Source: Adapted from *Occupational Outlook Handbook, 1991–92 Edition* (Washington, DC: U.S. Department of Labor, Bureau of Labor Statistics, 1992), p. 44.

Advertising Career Directory
(Hawthorn, NJ: Career Press)

American Marketing Association, *Careers in Marketing*
(Chicago)

Business Week Careers

Changing Times Annual Survey: Jobs For New College Grads

Chemical Marketing Research Association, *Careers in Industrial Marketing Research*
(New York)

College Placement Council, *CPC Annual*

Dow Jones & Co., *Managing Your Career*
(published twice a year)

Lebhar-Friedman, Inc., *Careers in Retailing*
(published annually)

Magazine Publishers Association, *Guide to Business Careers in Magazine Publishing*
(New York)

National Employment Business Weekly

Peterson's Business & Management Jobs
(published annually)

U.S. Department of Labor, *Occupational Outlook Handbook*
(Washington, DC: published biennially)

COMPENSATION

Many college graduates want to know how much they will get paid in their new career. Although this is a topic that should be considered in your selection of a company, it should not be the only one. It is up to you to decide which criteria are most important in choosing a job.

Exhibit A.2 shows the average compensation range for various marketing positions. These ranges vary depending on your education and preference for geographic location. In addition to salary, marketing positions may include a company car, bonuses, or expense accounts, forms of compensation that are not common in other professions.

Exhibit A.2

Compensation for Selected Marketing Positions

Position	Compensation
Advertising	
Advertising media planner	\$15,000–\$35,000
Assistant account executive	\$18,000–\$40,000
Account executive	\$25,000–\$60,000
Account supervisor	\$40,000–\$70,000
Marketing research	
Analyst	\$22,000–\$35,000
Project director	\$40,000–\$60,000
Research director	\$70,000–\$100,000
Product management	
Market analyst	\$15,000–\$30,000
Assistant product manager	\$17,000–\$35,000
Group manager	\$37,000–\$75,000
Group product manager	\$40,000–\$100,000
Retailing	
Trainee	\$17,000–\$25,000
Chain store manager	\$18,000–\$90,000
Buyer	\$20,000–\$60,000
Department store manager	\$30,000–\$100,000
Sales	
Trainee	\$15,000–\$30,000
Real estate agent	\$15,000–\$100,000
Insurance agent	\$17,000–\$100,000
Manufacturer's representative	\$20,000–\$80,000
Field salesperson	\$23,000–\$45,000
Sales manager	\$31,000–\$75,000
Securities salesperson	\$35,000–\$200,000

GETTING THE JOB

Before you begin to look for a job, you need to make a self-assessment and develop your résumé and a cover letter.

Self-Assessment

When it is time to look for a job, it is important that you have a good idea of your personal needs, capabilities, characteristics, strengths, and weaknesses. The idea is to prepare so you will be able to market yourself the best you can.

The following questions will help you analyze what is important to you in choosing the kind of work you will do and the kind of employer for whom you will work:

1. What do I do best? Are these activities related to people, things, or data?
2. Do I communicate better orally or in writing?
3. Do I consider myself a leader of a team or a group?
   a. Do I see myself as an active participant in a team or group?
   b. Do I prefer to work by myself?
   c. Do I prefer working under supervision?
4. Do I work well under pressure?
5. Do I like taking responsibility? Or would I rather follow directions?
6. Do I enjoy new products and activities? Or would I rather follow a regular routine?
7. When I am working, which of the following things are most important?
   a. Working for a regular salary?
   b. Working for a commission?
   c. Working for a combination of both?
8. Do I prefer to work a regular 9 a.m. to 5 p.m. schedule?
9. Will I be willing to travel more than half the time?
10. What kind of work environment do I prefer?
    a. Indoors or outdoors?
    b. Urban setting (population over a million)?
    c. Rural community?
11. Would I prefer to work for a large organization?
12. Am I willing to move?
13. Where do I want to be in three years? Five years? Ten years?

The FAB Student Model

The FAB matrix is a device adapted from personal selling that can help you market yourself to potential employers. FAB, which stands for Features-Advantages-Benefits, relates your skills to an employer's needs by citing the specific benefits you can bring to that company.[1] People want benefits, whether they are buying a car or hiring a marketing graduate to fill a job vacancy. An employer needs information that indicates how hiring you will specifically benefit the firm.

Exhibit A.3 is a model of FAB for students. The first step in FAB is as critical for you as it is for the salesperson: determining what the customer needs. In the case of the employer, needs are what the job requires or the problems to be solved. These needs should be listed in priority order, starting with the most important. Step 2 matches each need with a particular feature of the applicant (skill, ability, personality characteristic, educational attainment). In step 3, you arrange the needs and features in a FAB matrix where they become information points that you can use to construct a cover letter, résumé, or interview presentation.

You must approach a prospective employer with complete knowledge of that employer's features and job needs. Using the FAB matrix, you can match features with needs in a systematic, complete, and concise way.

Résumé and Cover Letter

When developing a résumé, you need to capture on paper your abilities, education, background, training, work experience, and personal qualifications. Many of these

Exhibit A.3

The FAB Matrix

Need of employer *"This job requires . . ."*	Feature of job applicant *"I have . . ."*	Advantage of feature *"This feature means . . ."*	Benefit to employer *"You will . . ."*
Frequent sales presentations to individuals and groups	Taken 10 classes that required presentations	I require limited or no training in making presentations	Save on the cost of training and have employee with ability and confidence to be productive early
Knowledge of personal computers, software, and applications	Taken a personal computer course and used Lotus in most upper-level classes	I can already use Word 5.0, Lotus, dBase, and other software	Save time and money on training
Person with management potential	Been president of student marketing group and social fraternity president for 2 years	I have experience leading people	Save time because I am capable of stepping into leadership position as needed

points can be developed from the FAB matrix or other self-assessment techniques. Your résumé should also be brief, usually no more than one page. The goal is to communicate your qualifications in a way that will obtain a positive response—an interview—from potential employers.

The cover letter is, in some ways, more important than the résumé. It must be persuasive, professional, and interesting. Ideally, it should set you above and apart from the other candidates for the position. Each letter should look and sound original, tailored to the specific organization you are contacting. It should describe the position you are applying for and arouse interest, describe your qualifications, and indicate how you can be contacted. Whenever possible, cover letters should be addressed to the individual, not the title. Sample résumés and cover letters can be found in your local library or student placement center. Follow up the letter and résumé with a telephone call.

THE INTERVIEW

The interview is the most important part of the job search process. An interview often decides whether or not you get the job. Here are some suggestions for before, during, and after an interview, as well as some questions interviewers frequently ask and some good questions you may want to ask them:

Before the interview:

- Interviewers have varied styles: to name a few, the "Let's get to know each other" style, the quasi-interrogation style (question after question), and the tough, probing why, why, why style. Be ready for anything.
- Practice being interviewed with a friend, and ask for a critique.
- Prepare at least five good questions whose answers are not readily available in company literature. (Obtain and read this literature, such as brochures, advertisements, catalogs, and annual reports, beforehand.)

- Anticipate possible interview questions, and frame suitable answers.
- Avoid "back to back" interviews, as they can be exhausting.
- Dress for the interview in a conservative style rather than in the height of fashion.
- Plan to arrive about ten minutes early to collect your thoughts before being called.
- Review the main points you intend to cover.
- Try to relax.

During the interview:

- Give a firm handshake in greeting the interviewer. Introduce yourself using the same form the interviewer has used (that is, use first names only if the interviewer does so first). Make a good initial impression.
- Maintain enthusiasm throughout the interview.
- Good eye contact, good posture, and distinct speech are musts. Don't clasp your hands or fiddle with jewelry, hair, or anything else. Sit comfortably in your chair. Do not smoke, even if given permission.
- Bring extra copies of your résumé with you.
- Know your "story" in detail. Present your selling points. Answer questions directly. Avoid one-word answers, but don't be wordy.
- Let the interviewer take the initiative often, but don't be passive. Find a way to direct the conversation to those things you want the interviewer to hear.
- The best time to make your most important points is toward the end of the interview, in order to leave on a high note.
- Don't be afraid to "close" the interview. You might say, "I'm very interested in the position, and I have enjoyed this interview."

After the interview:

- Upon leaving, make a note of any key points. Be sure you know who is to follow up on the interview and when a decision is to be made.
- Objectively analyze your performance during the interview.
- Send a thank-you letter that mentions any additional points of information you may have left out.

Questions frequently asked by employers:

- What are your long- and short-range goals and objectives, when and why did you establish them, and how are you preparing yourself to achieve them?
- What do you see yourself doing five years from now?
- What do you really want to do in life?
- How do you plan to achieve your career goals?
- What do you expect to be earning in five years?
- Why should I hire you?
- What do you think it takes to be successful in a company like ours?
- In what ways do you think you can make a contribution to our company?

- What qualities should a successful manager have?
- What do you know about our company?
- Do you think your grades are a good indicator of your academic achievement?
- What college subjects did you like most? Least? Why?
- What have you learned from your mistakes?
- How would you describe the ideal job for you following graduation?[2]

Questions to ask employers:

- What are the opportunities at this company for personal growth?
- Identify typical career paths based on past records. What is a realistic time frame for advancement?
- How is an employee evaluated and promoted?
- Describe a typical first-year assignment.
- Tell me about your initial and advanced training programs.
- How would you describe our company's personality and management style?
- What are your expectations for new hires?
- What are the characteristics of a successful person at your company?
- What are the company's plans for future growth, and how will they affect me?[3]

FOLLOW-UP

The in-company interview can run from a few hours to a whole day. Your interest, maturity, enthusiasm, assertiveness, logic, and knowledge of the company and the position you seek will all be under scrutiny. But you also need to ask questions that are important to you. Find out about the environment, job role, responsibilities, opportunities, and any current issues that may be of interest. To avoid future embarrassment, try to remember the names of the people you have met. If all goes well, you may be working for this firm in the near future. Good luck!

APPENDIX B
Developing Interpersonal Marketing Skills

As you study marketing, you may wonder, "How will I apply this knowledge?" The answer is that whether you major in marketing or some other area, you will be marketing throughout your professional career. Whether you work for a business firm or go into business for yourself, you will be satisfying your customers' needs while trying to make a profit. To do this, you need marketing knowledge. You also need skills.

This conclusion is supported by the American Assembly of Collegiate Schools of Business and the American Society for Training and Development. Analyzing extensive studies, both groups have concluded that students need business knowledge *and* skills. Pace University surveys of corporate recruiters and business students have also confirmed these findings.

The material presented in this appendix will help you develop skills through influencing and negotiating exercises and an actual networking experience. These skills will help you

Market goods and services to customers

Get money and other resources from managers

Get cooperation from your peers

Get dedicated support from your subordinates

Resolve conflicts

Manage your career in business

Establish mutually beneficial networks of well-informed people

INFLUENCING

You exercise influence when you want someone or some group to do something and you do not have authority over them or you prefer not to use your authority. For example, you might use influence if you want your boss to buy a more powerful computer for your personal use. Another example would be if you are a sales representative and you are trying to persuade a prospect to buy your product.

These are the steps involved in influencing (see also Exhibit B.1):

1. *Establish credibility:* You establish credibility by showing your competence in the subject, your good intentions, your good character, and your pleasing personality. Establishing credibility is a long-term activity and may require several meetings with the people you seek to influence.
2. *Appeal to reason:* The key is to show to the other party that your proposal will help solve an important problem or attain an important objective. To start, you establish rapport by commenting favorably on something that might be important to the other party. Examples include office decor, a painting, a photograph, or a trophy. This compliment will increase the individual's comfort with you and will make him or her more willing to grant you some time.

   The next step is to discover any problems or unsatisfied (or poorly satisfied)

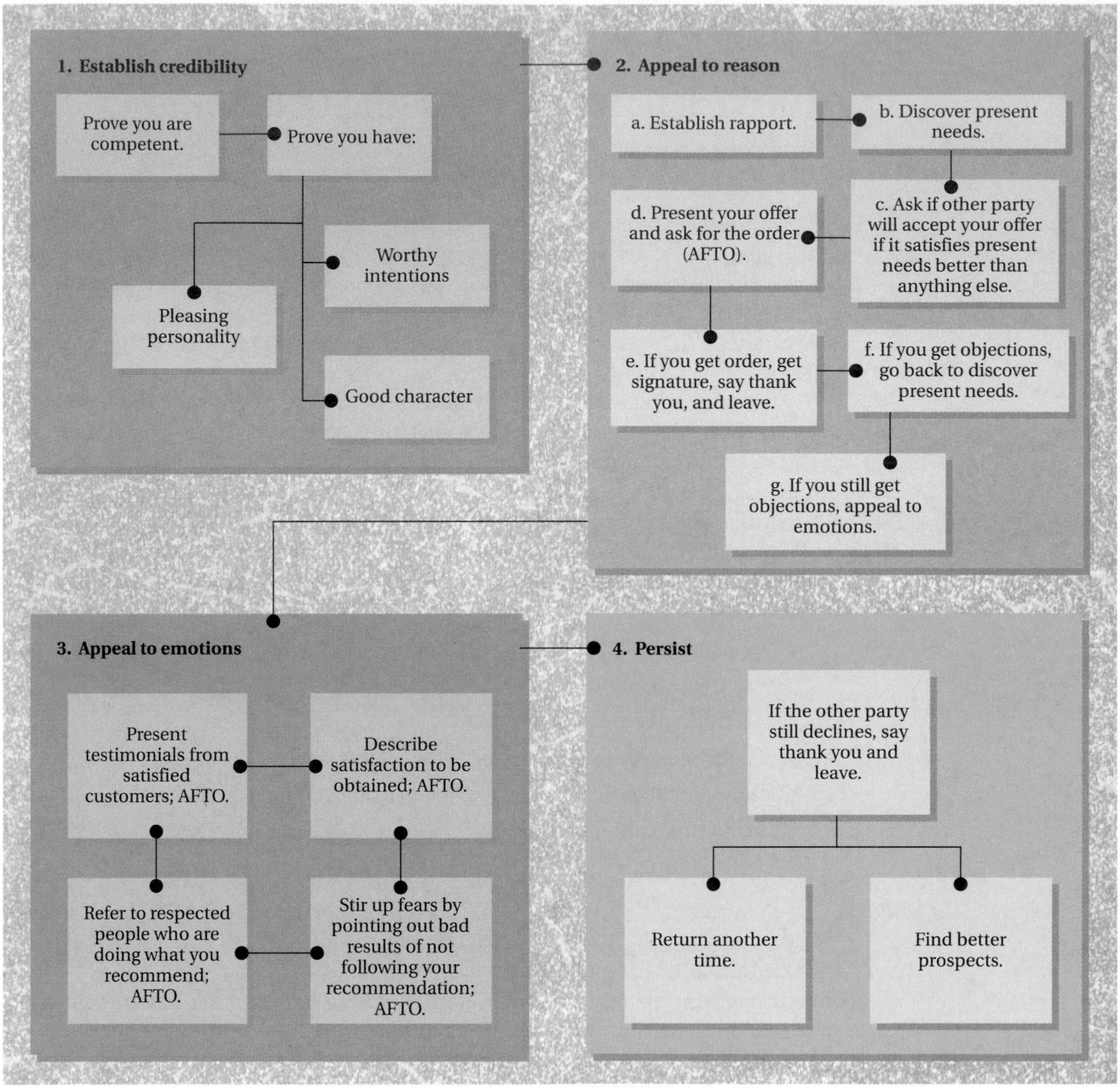

1. Establish credibility

Prove you are competent.

Prove you have:

Worthy intentions

Pleasing personality

Good character

2. Appeal to reason

a. Establish rapport.

b. Discover present needs.

c. Ask if other party will accept your offer if it satisfies present needs better than anything else.

d. Present your offer and ask for the order (AFTO).

e. If you get order, get signature, say thank you, and leave.

f. If you get objections, go back to discover present needs.

g. If you still get objections, appeal to emotions.

3. Appeal to emotions

Present testimonials from satisfied customers; AFTO.

Describe satisfaction to be obtained; AFTO.

Refer to respected people who are doing what you recommend; AFTO.

Stir up fears by pointing out bad results of not following your recommendation; AFTO.

4. Persist

If the other party still declines, say thank you and leave.

Return another time.

Find better prospects.

Exhibit B.1

Influencing

needs the other party has in an area that relates to your proposal. Ask questions and listen carefully to the answers. Encourage discussion of problems. When you feel you have enough information to make a credible proposal, ask conditionally for the order. (The word *order* is borrowed from the practice of selling. It is used here as a simple way of saying "acceptance of your offer" or "granting of your request.") For example, you might ask, "If I show you a way of reducing downtime on your assembly line, will you order my machinery?" Or "If I show you a business suit that always looks freshly pressed, will you buy it?" Or "If I show you a way of increasing the productivity of your department, would you be interested?" If you are addressing one of the person's important problems or objectives, you should get a yes answer.

Following this step, present your offer and ask for the order. If you get the order, complete the transaction, thank the individual, and leave. If you do not get the order, ask questions to understand the person's needs better, present a modified offer that responds to the objections, and then ask for the order (AFTO). If you get the order, complete the transaction, thank the individual, and leave.

3. *Appeal to emotions:* If you still do not get the order and you feel that a return to discovering needs will not be productive, show the person testimonials from satisfied customers, if possible, and then ask for the order. If that still does not work, describe the satisfaction to be obtained from your offer and then ask for the order. Refer to respected people who are doing what you recommend, and then ask for the order. Make the person aware of the negative results of not following your recommendation, and then ask for the order. You must ask for the order after you appeal to reason, after you explore objections and revise your offer to meet those objections, and after each step in appealing to the person's emotions. The moment he or she gives you the order, complete the transaction, thank the person, and leave.
4. *Persist:* If in spite of your efforts the individual declines to order, thank him or her, leave—and come back another time or find a better prospective customer or do both. In other words, persist *and* look for better prospects.

Two role-playing scenarios for practicing influencing are included in the instructor's manual that accompanies this textbook. These scenarios will help you develop your skills in exercising influence. Your instructor can provide these scenarios to you on request.

NEGOTIATING

You negotiate when you confer with someone or some group to settle a conflict. Negotiation is useful when two sides share an important goal, have a conflict, and can trade things they value. For example, you might negotiate if you want to buy a car from someone. Assume that the owner wants to sell the car (shared goal) but there is disagreement about the price (conflict). At the negotiating conference, you might discuss price, terms of payment, and items like audio equipment, special wheels, and so on. The objective is to reach a compromise acceptable to both sides. In business organizations, negotiation is used routinely. It is sometimes called conflict resolution.

These are the steps to take in negotiating (see Exhibit B.2):

1. *Prepare thoroughly:* Start by defining your goals, the other party's goals, and the goals you mutually share. Next, think about your best alternative to negotiated agreement (BATNA), or what happens if you do not reach agreement. Your eagerness to reach an agreement depends on how satisfied you are with the BATNA. If the alternative outcome makes you anxious to settle, consider whether the other party also might be feeling pressure to settle.
2. *Prepare to trade:* Identify the things you have that the other party wants and that you may be willing to give up. Also identify what the other party has that you want. Sharpen your preparation for the negotiating conference by role-playing alternative scenarios with friends or associates.
3. *Use conference tactics:* When you are in a negotiation conference, begin by stating the shared objectives. Make your opening offer as favorable to yourself as possible. If you are selling, start with a high price. If you are buying, start with

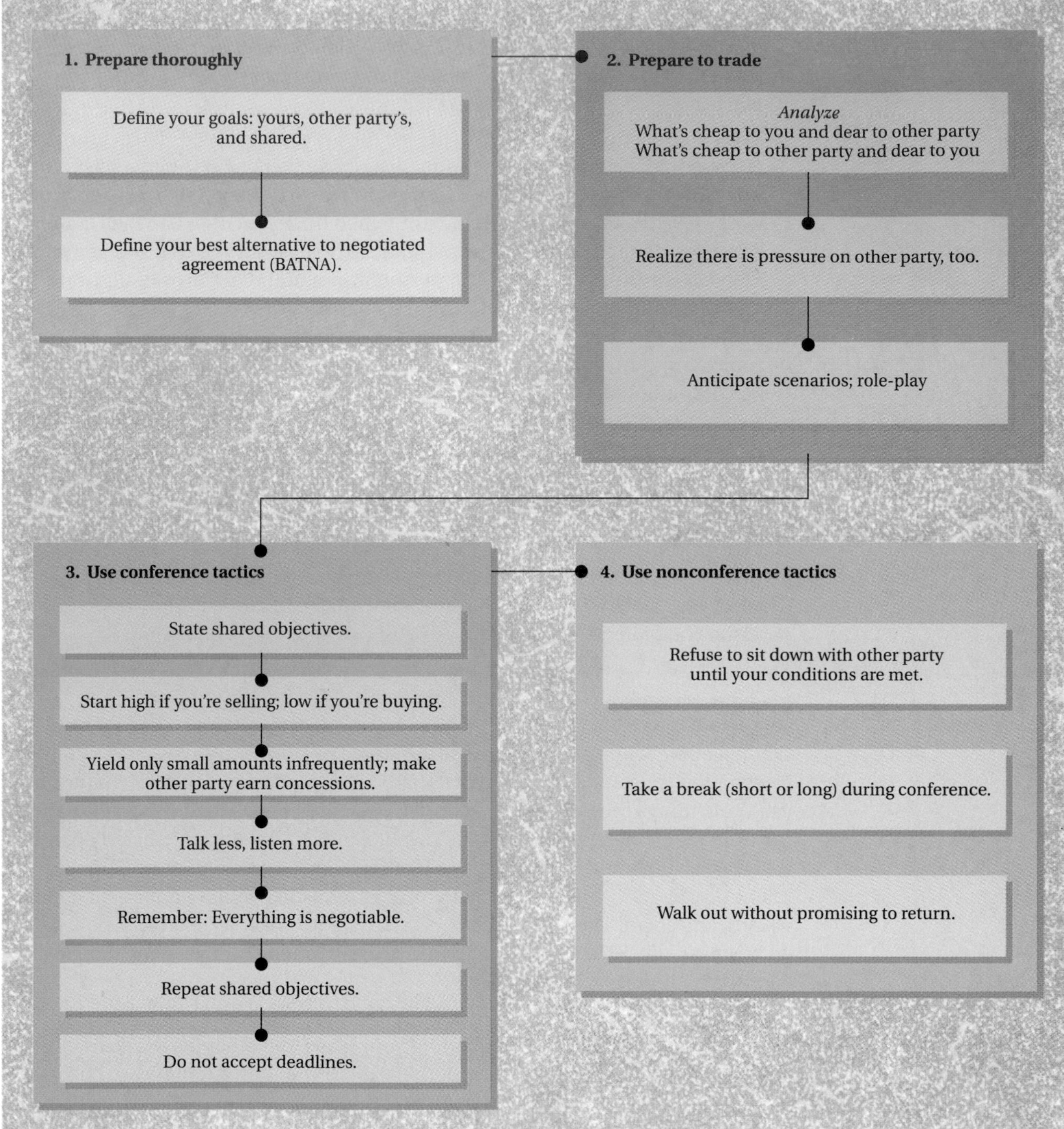

Exhibit B.2

Negotiating

a low bid. Yield only small amounts infrequently. Do not make any early concessions. Make the other side earn anything it gets from you.

Offer to keep the written record of what is said. Talk less and listen more. You can't give anything away when you are quiet. Remember that everything is negotiable, and settlement does not have to be reached at the first conference. In fact, depending on your BATNA, negotiated settlement may not even be that important to you. To keep the discussion going, repeat the shared objectives.

4. *Use nonconference tactics:* In difficult situations, consider using nonconference tactics. For example, you might refuse to attend a conference until the other side meets certain conditions. During a conference, if you feel that the other side is

not being flexible enough, take a break for a few minutes or longer. If the other party is really inflexible and you do not feel a strong need to reach a settlement, walk out without giving any promise that you will ever return. The other party may come running after you or get in touch with you by mail or telephone. On the other hand, you may decide to get in touch with the other party.

Negotiating is a complex art. You can always learn from your actions and experiences, as well as those of the other side. Review what happened. What could you have done to achieve a better outcome? What mistakes did the other party make?

Two role-playing scenarios are included in the instructor's manual that accompanies this textbook. These scenarios will help you develop your negotiating skills. Your instructor can provide these scenarios to you on request.

NETWORKING

The basic concept of networking is simple. You make contacts and exchange information. You establish relationships and possibly do some personal selling. Think of networking, then, as exchanging information with another person in the expectation that both parties will gain from this exchange.

The objective of the networking experience described here is to help you gain experience in performing three marketing activities:

- Market research to learn about the market for your services
- Public relations to make people aware of you and your good qualities
- Personal selling (influencing) to land a good job or a promotion if the opportunity arises

Exhibit B.3 outlines the steps in the exercise.

1. *Define career goals and interests:* In what kind of occupation do you see yourself? What are your strengths and weaknesses? What type of employment will make the best use of your strengths? Ask your friends and relatives for their opinions regarding these questions. Read career planning books, and try to gain some additional insights about your goals and interests. Visit your school's career planning office and have yourself evaluated objectively. Inquire about conducting "information interviews" with corporate recruiters. Have business cards printed for your networking contacts.
2. *Join professional organizations:* Identify organizations that might help you advance your goals and interests. Consult with at least three teachers in your major. Locate lists of professional organizations in the library and the yellow pages of the telephone directory. Ask friends, relatives, fellow students, alumni, and administrators for their suggestions.

   After you have identified several organizations, attend their meetings and join the ones that appear promising. Introduce yourself to other members, and casually ask them what they do and what their interests are. Casually tell them what you do and what your interests are. Exchange business cards with them. Later, note on their cards the most important things they said to you. File these cards to help you develop and maintain your network.

   Keep your objectives in mind: to learn about the market for your services, to make people aware of your good qualities, and possibly to land a great job, get a promotion, get a big increase in pay, or start a new business. All of these things have happened to students who try the networking experience.

   If some of the people you meet have accomplished what you wish to accom-

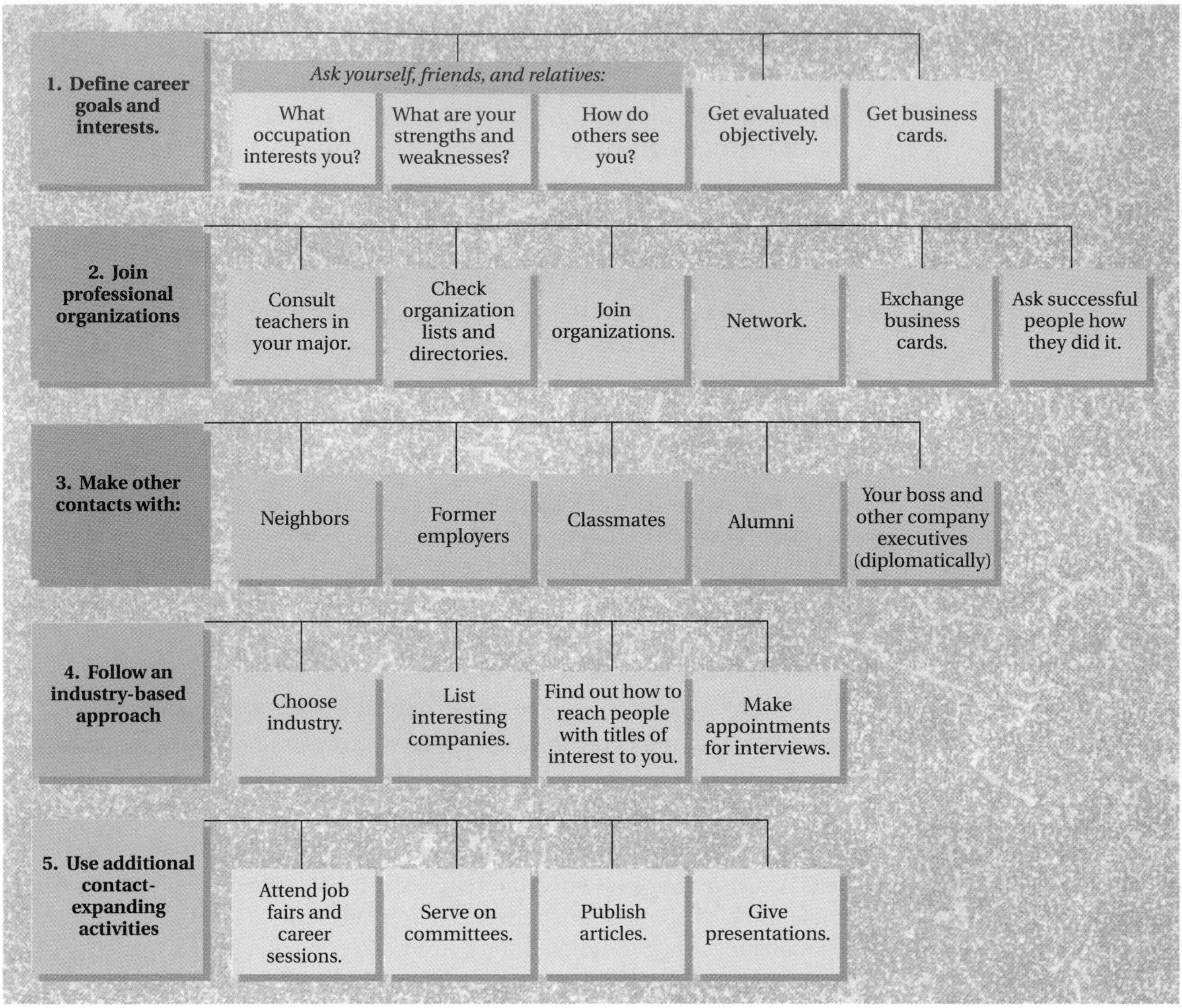

1. Define career goals and interests.
- *Ask yourself, friends, and relatives:*
  - What occupation interests you?
  - What are your strengths and weaknesses?
  - How do others see you?
- Get evaluated objectively.
- Get business cards.

2. Join professional organizations
- Consult teachers in your major.
- Check organization lists and directories.
- Join organizations.
- Network.
- Exchange business cards.
- Ask successful people how they did it.

3. Make other contacts with:
- Neighbors
- Former employers
- Classmates
- Alumni
- Your boss and other company executives (diplomatically)

4. Follow an industry-based approach
- Choose industry.
- List interesting companies.
- Find out how to reach people with titles of interest to you.
- Make appointments for interviews.

5. Use additional contact-expanding activities
- Attend job fairs and career sessions.
- Serve on committees.
- Publish articles.
- Give presentations.

Exhibit B.3

Networking

plish, ask them how they did it. Most people will be glad to tell you. Get them to focus on the strategies and tactics they used and the results they got. Ask them also about the obstacles they encountered and how they dealt with them.

Contact officers of the organizations you join, and offer to serve on committees. Focus on activities that will maximize your contacts. Do a great, enthusiastic job.

3. *Make other contacts:* Make business and professional contacts in every way possible, and then network. Introduce yourself to seat neighbors on train and airplane trips. Call former employers, teachers, and classmates. Contact alumni of the school. Call businesspeople mentioned in newspapers as having received promotions. Diplomatically, interview your boss and other people in your company about prospects for advancement. Do not upset anyone.
4. *Follow an industry-based approach:* Choose an industry you find attractive. Make a list of companies that are especially interesting. Determine the titles of people you want to meet. Find out the names of the people with the required titles by calling the switchboard and asking. Call for an appointment. Prepare a list of topics to be discussed, and conduct the interviews.

5. *Use additional contact-expanding activities:* Attend appropriate job fairs, networking meetings, and career guidance sessions. Serve on committees and task forces of business and professional groups. Get copies of professional association newsletters, and submit articles or letters to the editor. Submit articles to other publications.

   Give presentations at professional group meetings. Identify target groups of interest to you. Choose topics that will enable you to make a good impression and will interest the group. Inform the program chairperson that you would like to address the group. Prepare an outstanding presentation. Give your presentation, if invited. Give handouts. Encourage the audience to contact you for additional information. Have business cards with you at all times.

When you've finished your networking experience, write a summary. Follow this outline:

1. Your objectives for the networking experience
2. What you did to achieve these objectives
3. What results you obtained
4. Your evaluation of the usefulness of the experience to you
5. How your networking experience helped you learn about and understand market research, public relations, and personal selling
6. Your plans for future networking
7. Your suggestions for increasing the usefulness of this type of experience

Hand in your written report, and give a ten-minute presentation on your experience to your class.

Although this experience is a school assignment, you truly are marketing your services at the same time. Remember that networking is not an imposition on anyone. The people with whom you network are just as interested in networking as you are. Develop your networking skills and you will not only profit from networking but also enjoy it.

Networking is extremely useful for entering or expanding a career. However, networking is a powerful technique for many other purposes as well. For example:

- You have landed a desirable job, and your boss gives you a task that has many new aspects. Networking with experienced people may help you discover ways to save time and improve the quality of your work.
- Some time later you need to hire a competent assistant. Networking may help you to locate one. Think of yourself as being in the role of the people with whom you networked for this assignment.
- Your career is in good shape; you do not have any new, challenging assignments; and you have no need for more assistants. This might be a good time for you to think about expanding your responsibilities. Networking with people outside your usual circle of acquaintances may reveal some new activities or techniques that are not well known in your company or industry. You may discover practices in other fields that will help you or your company.

The advantages of networking continue as long as you are active. The future is unpredictable, but you will be ready for whatever happens as long as you are an active networker. Maximize your opportunities and defend against the possible threats. Make networking a way of life!

APPENDIX C

Financial Arithmetic for Marketing

Marketing arithmetic plays an important role in managing a business and setting price strategies. Marketing managers must decide when to add or drop products and know how to evaluate the performance of products, product lines, and even divisions. These decisions require a basic understanding of accounting concepts. In this appendix you will learn about income statements; the relationships between costs, stock turnover, and profits; several techniques for evaluating an investment; and the way to calculate markups.

THE INCOME STATEMENT

The income statement (also called the operating statement or profit-and-loss statement) summarizes the financial results of a firm's operations for a specific period, usually a month, quarter, or year. The ultimate objective of preparing the statement is to determine whether the organization earned a profit or suffered a loss.

The statement is divided into two sections: heading and body. The heading reveals the company name and the period covered by the statement. Note that the company in Exhibit C.1 is Malibu Surfboards, a surfboard retailer, and the income

Exhibit C.1

Malibu Surfboards Income Statement for the Year Ended December 31, 1993

Revenues				
Gross sales				$227,880
Less: Sales returns			$ 1,570	
Sales discounts			4,360	5,930
Net sales				$221,950
Costs				
Cost of goods sold				
Beginning inventory, 1/1 at cost			$41,800	
Add: Purchases at billed cost		$91,720		
Freight-in		1,970		
		$93,690		
Less: Purchase returns and allowances	$ 970			
Purchase discounts	1,750	2,720		
Net purchases at cost			90.970	
Cost of goods available for sale			132,770	
Less: Ending inventory at cost 12/31			31,500	
Cost of goods sold				101,270
Gross profit				$120,680
Operating expenses				
Marketing expenses				
Salaries of salespeople		$39,590		
Promotion costs		5,200		
Delivery and shipment		4,500	$49,290	
General and administrative expenses				
Salaries of office workers		$12,500		
Rent		16,100		
Insurance		4,280		
Office supplies		1,818		
Utilities		3,627	38,326	
Total operating expenses				$ 87,615
Net profit before taxes				**$ 33,065**

statement is for the calendar year 1993. The statement's body contains an itemized listing of revenues and expenses. The left side of the body shows that there are three key elements: revenues, costs, and in this case a net profit. The profit results from revenues being greater than the costs. Let's examine each component in greater detail.

Revenues

Gross sales are the total amount billed to customers during the year. *Sales returns* occur because not all customers are satisfied with their purchases. Perhaps a surfboard was bought as a gift for a person who doesn't like the ocean. A board may have been defective.

Malibu offers a ninety-day payment plan without charging interest. A buyer can put a third of the purchase price down and pay the balance within ninety days. Malibu management, however, prefers that buyers pay cash and offers a 3 percent discount for immediate full payment. The *sales discounts* row reflects the dollar amount of cash discounts given to purchasers during 1993.

Net sales are gross sales minus sales returns and discounts. The income statement for Malibu shows net sales of $221,950.

Costs

Malibu incurs various expenses in the process of selling surfboards. A major cost is the cost of the surfboards sold to customers during 1993, called *cost of goods sold.* The cost of goods sold depends on three items: beginning inventory, net purchases, and ending inventory.

Malibu starts each year with a certain amount of merchandise on hand for sale to customers, called *beginning inventory.* During the year, the stock of inventory on hand is supplemented by purchases from surfboard manufacturers, which are called *purchases at billed cost.* Freight charges for new surfboards are called *freight-in.*

Sometimes the purchase of goods for inventory involves returns and allowances. These are caused by goods arriving in damaged condition, late delivery, and goods sent by the manufacturer in error. *Purchase returns and allowances* represent credit given by manufacturers to Malibu for one of these three reasons. *Purchase discounts* are discounts given by surfboard manufacturers when Malibu pays promptly.

By adding purchases during the year and freight-in expenses to the beginning inventory and then subtracting Malibu's purchase returns and allowances as well as purchase discounts, we arrive at the *net purchase at cost.* Then by adding the beginning inventory and the net purchases at cost, we have the *cost of goods available for sale* during 1993. If we now subtract Malibu's *ending inventory at cost* on December 31, we can determine the *cost of goods sold* during the year, as shown in Exhibit C.1. The cost of goods sold is $101,270.

Gross profit (gross margin) is the money left to cover the expenses of selling the surfboards and operating the business. It is determined by subtracting the cost of goods sold from net sales:

Net sales	$221,950
Less: Cost of goods sold	101,270
Gross profit	$120,680

Operating expenses consist of marketing expenses and general and administrative expenses. These expenses arise from marketing activities and the running of the business. *Marketing expenses* include *salespeople's salaries, promotion costs* (such as brochures and advertising), and *delivery and shipment costs* of phone and mail orders for surfboards. *General and administrative expenses* are for such items as *salaries of office workers; rent* for the building; *insurance* of various types; *office supplies* such as paper, pencils, order forms, and computer ribbons; and *utilities*, including water, telephone, and electricity bills. Operating expenses for Malibu total $87,615.

Net profit before taxes represents the amount Malibu earned in 1993. It is what's left after subtracting the cost of goods sold and operating expenses from sales revenues. Note that net sales and net profits are not the same thing. A company may have large sales and little or no profits.

A condensed income statement for Malibu would be

Revenue	
Net sales	$221,950
Costs	
Cost of goods sold	101,270
Gross profit	$120,680
Less: Expenses	87,615
Net profit before taxes	$ 33,065

COSTS, STOCK TURNOVER, AND PROFITS

A very important relationship exists among costs, sales, stock turnover, and profit. *Stock turnover* refers to the number of times during a period (usually a year) that the average amount of goods on hand are sold. Stock turnover rate is a measure of the number of times the average inventory is sold per year. The higher the turnover, the more quickly the inventory is moving.

Stock turnover can be calculated on the basis of retail price or on cost. Malibu's income statement reflects inventory valued on a cost basis, so we will use the following formula:

$$\text{Stock turnover rate} = \frac{\text{Cost of goods sold}}{\text{Average inventory at cost}}$$

The average dollar amount of inventory at cost is calculated as follows:

$$\begin{aligned}\text{Average inventory at cost} &= \frac{\text{Beginning inventory} + \text{Ending inventory}}{2}\\ &= \frac{41{,}800 + 31{,}500}{2}\\ &= 36{,}650\end{aligned}$$

$$\begin{aligned}\text{Stock turnover rate at cost} &= \frac{101{,}270}{36{,}650}\\ &= 2.8\end{aligned}$$

There is no exact measure of a "good" stock turnover. The rate varies by industry. Supermarkets, for example, often have a stock turnover rate of about 20, whereas an appliance retailer may have a rate of 3 or 4. Rapid stock turnover may mean limited investment in inventory, less need for storage space, newer merchandise, or fewer markdowns. Generally speaking, high stock turnovers lead to higher profits. There

are exceptions to this rule, however. Assume, for example, that a dealer reduces its stock and holds sales constant (resulting in an increase in turnover). Buying in small quantities may mean the loss of quantity discounts; higher expenditures for receiving, checking, and marketing merchandise; and greater correspondence and clerical costs. In this situation, profits fall.

RETURN ON INVESTMENT

Return on investment (ROI) can be used as a yardstick to discover which investment opportunities offer the highest returns. It is the ratio of net profit after taxes to the investment used to make the net profit, multiplied by 100. Investment is not shown on the income statement, but it is on the balance sheet (statement of financial condition). The balance sheet, the other basic financial statement of a company, details assets, liabilities, and net worth.

Return on investment is often calculated by manufacturers for various new product opportunities to determine which, if any, the company should pursue. These are then compared with the cost of capital for the firm. *Cost of capital* is the weighted average of the various types of funds the company uses, such as bonds and common stock. The ROI formula is as follows:

$$\text{Percentage return on investment} = \frac{\text{Average earnings after taxes and depreciation}}{\text{Average investment}}$$

If product X has average earnings of $15,000 per year and an average investment of $105,000, then estimated ROI is $15,000 ÷ $105,000, or 14.3 percent. ROI calculations can vary greatly depending on the depreciation and tax criteria used. Obviously, the same policies must be in force when comparing two new product alternatives, or the comparison will be "apples and oranges" instead of "two apples."

Return on investment requires that costs and revenues be projected for the estimated life of the product. To avoid too much long-range guessing, some marketing managers calculate ROI for fixed periods—for example, at the end of the first, third, and fifth years. The major problem with this simple formula is that it does not account for the time value of money. Two products may have identical rates of return but different investment and cash-flow periods. One product may have a high initial investment and become profitable eight years after introduction. A second product with the same ROI may have a moderate initial investment and profitability the first year. The second product would certainly be more desirable because of the lower initial outlay and faster dollar returns. These dollars can then be reinvested or used in the business again.

Net Present Value

Let's carry the evaluation of new products one step further using the net present value approach. *Net present value* accounts for the time value of money. Assume one product would return $1 million tomorrow and another product would return $1 million five years from now. If everything else is the same, the first product is more desirable. Would you rather have $1,000 today or twenty years from now? If you took that $1,000 today and invested it at 18 percent per year, the compounded value would be $27,393 at the end of twenty years! The longer it takes to receive money in the future, the less it is worth today. This is the notion of present value, usually called discounting.

Assume that we have two products, M and N, and each has a five-year life span.

	Product M			Product N		
Year	Net cash flow	(If) (14%)	Present value of cash flow	Net cash flow	(If) (14%)	Present value of cash flow
1	$ 50,000	.88	$ 44,000	$ 10,000	.88	$ 8,800
2	40,000	.77	30,800	20,000	.77	15,400
3	30,000	.71	21,300	30,000	.71	21,300
4	10,000	.64	6,400	40,000	.64	25,600
5	5,000	.57	2,850	50,000	.57	28,500
	$135,000			$150,000		
Present value			$105,350			$ 99,600
Less cost			−10,000			−10,000
Net present value			$ 95,350			$ 89,600

Exhibit C.2

Calculating the Net Present Value of Products M and N with $10,000 Cost

The cost of both projects is $10,000, and the cost of capital to the firm is 14 percent. The expected cash flows and present values are shown in Exhibit C.2. The actual dollar cash flows for products M and N are $135,000 and $150,000, respectively. Without considering the time value of money, the firm should go with product N. However, Exhibit C.2 shows that product M's largest cash flows occur soon after the product is launched and that product N's major cash flows occur later in the life cycle. The net present value of product M is $5,750 greater than product N. Why? Again, $1 received and reinvested today is worth more than $1 received and re-invested tomorrow.

Payback

The payback period is the number of years it takes the firm to recover its original investment by net returns before depreciation but after taxes. Assume that a company is considering two new products and that each has a developmental cost of $300,000. Net returns forecasted for each product are as follows:

Year	*Product A*	*Product B*
1	$150,000	$ 40,000
2	105,000	60,000
3	55,000	80,000
4	25,000	120,000
5	5,000	200,000

As you can see, product A has the quickest payback—three years. It pays back half the original investment the first year, another $105,000 the second year, and the remainder in the third year. The shorter the payback period, the more quickly the firm recovers its original investment. Product B has a payback of four years, taking a year longer to recoup the original new product investment. If payback were the only criterion, the firm would choose product A. As you can see, however, this decision could be a mistake.

Payback ignores the cash flows after the break-even point is reached. Product A, a faddish item, has a very short life cycle. Product B, on the other hand, reveals continued growth from the first year. Projects with longer payback periods traditionally are part of long-range planning, for many new products do not yield their highest returns for a number of years. Payback also ignores the magnitude of the original cost. Note, for example, that both products had developmental expenses of

\$300,000. But what if product A's development cost had been \$25,000 and product B's had been \$4 million? The firm may have selected product A simply because it lacked funds or was unwilling to risk \$4 million.

Payback does have some good points. It can be argued that paybacks of three or four years or longer are so uncertain that it is better not to consider them at all. In our simple example, we assumed that each year's cash flow was equally likely to materialize. Also, a company that has limited development funds must concentrate on products that offer a quick return.

MARKUP PRICING

Assume that a retailer determines from past records that operating costs are 32 percent of sales and profit is 7 percent. It can mark up its merchandise by 39 percent and still cover costs and earn a profit. However, if 7 percent is considered an unsatisfactory profit, the merchant will have to add more than 39 percent to the merchandise costs. There also will be some markdowns, thefts, and employee discounts. If these three factors amount to an additional 5 percent of sales, the retailer will have to use a mark-on of 41.9 percent to earn a 7 percent profit. The formula is

$$\text{Mark-on} = \frac{\text{Gross margin (39\%)} + \text{Retail reduction (5\%)}}{100\% + \text{Retail reduction (5\%)}}$$

$$= \frac{44\%}{105\%}$$

$$= 41.9\%$$

To achieve a *maintained margin* of 39 percent, we must use an initial mark-on of 41.9 percent.

Sometimes retailers must establish a retail price based on a predetermined maintained margin and the unit cost. Suppose a merchant wants a gross margin of 41.9 percent (on retail) and an item cost of \$3.46. The formula for determining the retail price is

$$\text{Retail price} = \frac{\text{Cost (\$3.46)}}{100\% - \text{Mark-on (41.9\%)}} \times 100$$

$$= \frac{\$3.46}{58.1} \times 100$$

$$= \$5.96$$

If no markdowns are taken, a selling price of \$5.96 will provide the merchant with the desired gross margin on retail.

APPENDIX D
Tools of Marketing Control

Two important tools of marketing control in the financial area are sales analysis and marketing cost analysis. Moreover, as the importance of service and quality have increased, more companies have started using the marketing audit, a tool for strategic control. An examination of these techniques follows.

SALES ANALYSIS

All marketing plans of profit-oriented firms and many nonprofit firms involve sales of a good or service. Therefore, most organizations have revenue-related goals. *Sales analysis* refers to the general effort to evaluate the firm's success in the marketplace. Sales volume analysis and market share analysis are two of the most commonly used tools for this purpose.

Sales Volume Analysis

Sales volume analysis is the detailed examination of sales volume data for the purpose of appraising a marketing plan. It is the simplest, most common type of sales analysis performed by marketing management. It reflects the target market's reactions to the firm's offerings and the organization's achievement of goals.

Macrosales analysis is the analysis of the total or aggregate market performance. Microsales analysis subdivides total sales volume by some other basis, such as territory or product, for a more in-depth examination of sales. By examining total sales performance, the marketing manager can determine trends in total sales activity. Usually company sales are compared to those of the industry to see how well the firm or strategic business unit (SBU) is performing relative to the competition.

Exhibit D.1 shows that total sales for Jones Pump Company increased $2.5 mil-

Exhibit D.1

Sales of Jones Pump Company

Year	Company sales volume (in millions)	Increase	Company sales forecast (in millions)	Difference (in millions)
1993	$22.4	15%	$24.0	$ –1.6
1992	19.5	25	19.4	+0.1
1991	15.6	25	15.6	—
1990	12.5	25	12.0	+0.5
1989	10.0	—	9.5	+0.5

Year	Industry sales volume (in millions)	Increase	Estimated market share	Actual market share	Difference
1993	$158.3	25.0%	16.0%	14.2%	–1.8%
1992	126.6	15.5	15.0	15.4	+0.4
1991	109.6	21.0	14.0	14.2	+0.2
1990	90.0	30.0	14.0	13.9	–0.1
1989	69.1	—	13.0	14.5	–1.5

Exhibit D.2

Jones Pump Company Sales by Territory

Territory	Estimated sales (in millions)	Actual sales (in millions)	Sales difference (in millions)
1	$ 8.0	$10.0	$ +2.0
2	12.0	8.4	–3.6
3	4.0	4.0	—
Total	$24.0	$22.4	

lion from 1989 to 1990. Sales grew at an annual rate of 25 percent from 1990 through 1992, but the increase for 1993 was only 15 percent. Further insight can be gained by looking at the industry volume section, which shows the rate of growth for the industry during the same periods. Jones Pump Company outperformed the industry in 1991 and 1992 but fell behind in 1993. In fact, 1993 seems to have been a problem year. Sales were $1.6 million, or 7 percent, below Jones's forecast. Similarly, the firm achieved only 89 percent of its forecasted market share—14.2 percent actual market share versus 16.0 percent estimated market share. This kind of macrosales analysis provides warning signals that further analysis is necessary. Something went wrong in 1993, and Jones needs to uncover the cause.

The shortfall in 1993 of $1.6 million in Jones's sales can be further examined by allocating sales volume by territory and product. Exhibit D.2 shows that the sales staff met the forecast in territory 3 and went 25 percent over the company estimate in territory 1. Territory 2 achieved only 70 percent of its estimate. Thus the problem seems to lie in territory 2.

The next step is to analyze sales in territory 2 by product line (see Exhibit D.3). The culprit is the sludge pump product line. Jones manufactures specialty pumps used by the construction and petroleum industries and by municipal water systems. Territory 2 encompasses the West Coast and the southwestern states. Further inquiry by top management reveals that a San Francisco manufacturer is selling an imported pump designed for the same market Jones serves. The imported pump has a better service record, develops more horsepower per unit of energy, and costs 30 percent less than the Jones model. Since the model is so specialized, the San Francisco manufacturer's representative knows all potential buyers west of the Mississippi River. Although Jones has many loyal customers, they cannot pass up a better pump at a much lower price.

Market Share Analysis

Sales volume analysis measures performance in absolute terms but does not measure the company's activities relative to the overall market. Nor does it take the

Exhibit D.3

Jones Pump Company Sales by Product Line, Territory 2

Product line	Estimated sales (in millions)	Actual sales (in millions)	Sales difference (in millions)
Municipal water system pumps	$ 3.5	$3.6	$ +0.1
Oil field pumps	4.9	4.8	–0.1
Sludge pumps	3.6	0.0	–3.6
Total	$12.0	$8.4	

competition into account. An increase in market share usually indicates that the firm's marketing mix is more effective than that of its competitors. A declining market share may indicate a need to investigate potential problem areas.

Like sales volume analysis, market share analysis is generally most meaningful when data are broken down by sales territory, customer type, and product category. A marketing manager may find, for example, that an overall increase in market share is due to increased sales to a particular type of customer.

MARKETING COST ANALYSIS

A basic concept in accounting is the matching concept: the matching of revenues and the costs incurred in generating those revenues. As noted, sales revenue may indicate marketing success. What role do costs play? Cost analysis is one of the most important techniques for maintaining marketing control. Marketing cost analysis is based on the allocation of marketing costs by product, customer, distribution channel, or territory to measure the efficiency of the firm's marketing mix. The marketing mix is a basis for the allocation of direct costs of many types—for example, advertising costs, test market expenses, and sales force expenses. In turn, marketing costs play an important role in determining the profitability of a product or product line.

Accounting information has become more readily available in recent years for two reasons: more sophisticated accounting systems and more common use of the computer. For accounting information to be useful for marketing cost analysis, it must be reallocated twice. The first reallocation is from natural to functional accounts, and the second is from functional accounts to market segments. These reallocations provide a basis for both marketing cost analysis and profit analysis.

Natural Accounts to Functional Accounts

Natural accounts are accounts that carry the name of the category for which the expenditure was made. Examples include rent, salaries, office supplies, insurance, and equipment. *Functional accounts*, on the other hand, are classified according to marketing activity. The number and names of the accounts vary from firm to firm. Functional accounts often include personal selling, advertising, storage, packaging, shipping, order filling, billing, market research, and delivery. Most marketing expenditures are made to accomplish a specific task—for instance, to develop a specific product, to promote a specific product, or to deliver a specific product. Marketing management needs to know whether or not such activities are increasing or decreasing the profitability of the firm.

To determine the profitability of specific marketing activities, funds must be reallocated from natural to functional accounts. Consider this example. Assume that J.J. Uniform Supply, a small uniform supply company, had a net profit of $8,500, as shown in Exhibit D.4. The first step is to allocate the expenditures from natural accounts to functional accounts, as shown in Exhibit D.5. Note the breakdown of salary expenses: $8,000 (the majority) for a commissioned salesperson; $2,000 for a free-lance artist doing advertising layouts, $1,500 for a warehouse stock person, and $1,500 for a delivery person who works after school. Half the office supplies were consumed in the sales effort, and the remainder were used for advertising, record keeping, and delivery. Since storage takes up more than half the building, it is charged with over half the rent ($2,000), and the rest is allocated using the same principle. The storage facility insurance costs $1,000 annually; drafting equipment

Exhibit D.4

J.J. Uniform Supply Income Statement

Sales	$ 75,000	
Cost of goods sold	−44,000	
		$ 31,000
Expenses:		
Salaries	$ 13,000	
Office supplies	4,000	
Rent	3,500	
Insurance	2,000	
Total expenses		−22,500
Net profit		$ 8,500

		Functional accounts			
		Personal selling	*Advertising*	*Storage*	*Delivery and installation*
Natural accounts					
Salaries	$13,000	$ 8,000	$2,000	$1,500	$1,500
Office supplies	4,000	2,000	1,000	500	500
Rent	3,500	—	1,000	2,000	500
Insurance	2,000	—	500	1,000	500
Total	$22,500	$10,000	$4,500	$5,000	$3,000

Exhibit D.5

Reallocation of Costs from Natural to Functional Accounts

and tables used to prepare advertisements are insured for $500 and the delivery vehicle for $500.

Functional Accounts to Market Segments

Assume that Joe and Jane, owners of J.J. Uniform Supply, are concerned that the three markets they serve may not all be profitable. Jane decides to continue the analysis by allocating the functional costs to customer type (see Exhibit D.6). Since 67 percent of the sales are made to industrial customers, this percentage of cost of goods sold is allocated to the industrial market ($29,333). The same process is followed for the retail and institutional markets. The sales representative spent 70 percent of his time calling on industrial accounts, 25 percent calling on retailers, and 5 percent calling on institutional customers. Advertising is strictly direct mail, and Jane's files reveal that 623 pieces were sent to industrial customers, 222 to retailers, and 455 to institutional customers for a total of 1,300 advertising pieces. Thus $2,157 of advertising expenses was allocated to the industrial customers (623 ÷ 1,300 = 0.4792 × $4,500 = $2,157). Storage and delivery costs were distributed using the percentage of sales accounted for by each market.

Using the allocation procedure, Joe and Jane find that their firm is earning a 12 percent profit in the industrial market, 14 percent in the retail market, and losing money in the institutional area. What action should Joe and Jane take at this point? They have several options:

- They could drop out of the institutional market. Since the market is currently unprofitable, the company could avoid serving institutional customers.
- The advertising expenditures-to-sales ratio is very high in the institutional

		Marketing segment—Customer type		
		Industrial	Retail	Institutional
Sales	$75,000	$50,000	$20,000	$5,000
Cost of goods sold	–44,000	–29,333	–11,733	–2,934
Gross margin	$31,000	$20,667	$ 8,267	$2,066
Expenses (functional):				
Personal selling	$10,000	$ 7,000	$2,500	$ 500
Advertising	4,500	2,157	768	1,575
Storage	5,000	3,333	1,333	334
Delivery	3,000	2,000	800	200
Total expenses	$22,500	$14,490	$5,401	$2,609
Net profit	$ 8,500	$ 6,177	$2,866	($ 543)

Exhibit D.6

J.J. Uniform Supply Reallocated Income Statement

market. Joe and Jane could examine their promotional program and try to raise institutional advertising effectiveness.

- Only 5 percent of the sales effort is being devoted to the institutional market. A stronger sales effort coupled with a more effective promotion program might make the institutional market profitable.

Although J.J. Uniform Supply is a profitable company as a whole, only the industrial and retail markets are generating profits. Servicing institutional accounts actually lowers overall profitability. Before Joe and Jane take any action, however, they should consider future trends in the institutional market. If, for example, the number of competitors is expected to decrease and the average size of an institutional account to increase, they may decide to stay in the market.

A MARKETING AUDIT OUTLINE

A marketing audit is a comprehensive review of a profit-oriented or nonprofit organization's marketing activities. As the following outline explains, the audit embraces the organization's marketing orientation, planning, target market strategies, distribution decisions, product strategies, pricing strategies, and promotion strategies.

I. Orientation

1. Has the firm established a marketing orientation? That is, has the firm identified the benefits that particular customers seek and developed programs based on this input?
2. Are personnel efforts focused on satisfying the wants of actual or potential customers, rather than on programs, rules and regulations, or their own personal well-being?
3. Does the firm define its business in terms of benefits its customers want rather than in terms of products and services?
4. Does the firm try to direct its products only to specific groups of people or to everybody?

5. Is the firm's main goal to maximize customer satisfaction or to get as many customers as possible?
6. Does the firm seek to achieve its goal chiefly through coordinated use of marketing activities (promotion, product, pricing, and distribution) or only through intensive promotion?
7. Does the firm have a mission statement, and is it translated into operational terms regarding the firm's objectives?

II. Marketing Planning

A. *The External Environment*

1. Social: What major social and lifestyle trends will have an impact on the firm? What action has the firm been taking in response to these trends?
2. Demographics: What impact will forecasted trends in the size, age, profile, and distribution of population have on the firm? How will the changing nature of the family, the increase in the proportion of women in the work force, and changes in ethnic composition of the population affect the firm? What action has the firm taken in response to these developments and trends? Has the firm reevaluated its traditional products and expanded the range of specialized offerings to respond to these changes?
3. Economic: What major trends in taxation and in income sources will have an impact on the firm? What action has the firm taken in response to these trends?
4. Political, Legal, and Financial: What laws are now being proposed at federal, state, and local levels that could affect marketing strategy and tactics? What recent changes in regulations and court decisions affect the firm? What political changes at each government level are taking place? What action has the firm taken in response to these legal and political changes?
5. Competition: Which organizations are competing with us directly by offering a similar product? Which organizations are competing with us indirectly by securing our prime prospects' time, money, energy, or commitment? What new competitive trends seem likely to emerge? How effective is the competition? What benefits do our competitors offer that we do not? Is it appropriate for us to compete? Could we more usefully withdraw from some areas in which there are alternative suppliers and use our resources to serve new, unserved customer groups?
6. Technological: What major technological changes are occurring that affect the firm?
7. Ecological: What is the outlook for the cost and availability of natural resources and energy needed by the firm?

B. *Needs Assessments*

1. Are needs assessments undertaken?
2. Have secondary data been used in the needs assessments? If so, is the information current? Classified in a useful manner? Impartial? Reliable? Valid?

3. What does the firm want to learn from the needs assessments?
4. Are surveys used in the needs assessment process? If so, is each and every question necessary? Can the firm determine what will be done with the information from every question? Do the respondents have the ability to answer the questions accurately? Will respondents provide the information? Are the questions threatening or too personal? Are the questions worded simply enough to be understood by individuals with a low education level? Is the sample size appropriate?
5. How have we used the information we have generated about the firm's markets and other publics for improving products?
6. What are the evolving needs and satisfactions being sought by the firm's customers?
7. Who buys the firm's products? How does a potential customer find out about the organization? When and how does a person become a customer?
8. What are the major objections given by consumers as to why they do not buy the firm's products?
9. How do customers find out about and decide to buy the organization's products? When and where?
10. Are evaluative reports written on the needs assessment studies? If so, are the needs assessment reports too long or too technical? Do they provide a summary of the high points that are of most interest to the reader?

C. *Objectives and Mission*

1. What is the mission of the firm? What business is it in? How well is its mission understood throughout the organization? Five years from now, what business does it wish to be in?
2. What are the stated objectives of the organization? Are they formally written down? Do they lead logically to clearly stated marketing objectives?
3. Are the organization's marketing objectives stated in hierarchical order? Are they specific so that progress toward achievement can be measured? Are the objectives reasonable in light of the organization's resources? Are the objectives ambiguous? Do the objectives specify a time frame? Are the objectives that are concerned with effectiveness benefit-oriented?
4. Does the firm have both long-term and short-term plans? Do the short-term plans contribute to achievement of the long-term plan?
5. Are the objectives and roles of each element of the marketing mix clearly specified?
6. What policies inhibit the achievement of our objectives with respect to organization, allocation of resources, operations, hiring and training, products, pricing, and promotion?
7. Should the firm seek to expand, contract, or change the emphasis of its offerings or selected target markets? If so, in which product areas and target markets, and how vigorously?

D. *Marketing Planning and Evaluation*

1. Does the organization have a marketing planning and evaluation system?
2. Does the marketing planning and evaluation system include an annual program evaluation as well as a longer-term, firmwide evaluation?
3. Is this firmwide evaluation (marketing audit) conducted every five years or less to assess the overall status of all the firm's products and marketing activities? Does the audit describe the current marketing situation as well as speculate about the relevant future?
4. Is someone in the firm held accountable for ensuring that the recommendations of the marketing audit are implemented?
5. Are annual marketing plans developed, implemented, and used as the basis for evaluation?
6. Does the organization carry out periodic reviews of its programs and evaluations of its resource allocation decisions? How and with what results?
7. Is the long-term marketing audit a summation, synthesis, and integration of annual evaluations?
8. Are the short-term evaluation procedures (monthly, quarterly, and so on) adequate to ensure that our long-term objectives are being achieved?
9. Should the firm enter, expand, contract, or withdraw from any existing segments?
10. What should be the short- and long-term cost and revenue consequences of these changes?
11. Does it seem that the firm is trying to do too much or not enough?
12. What are the core marketing strategies for achieving the agreed objectives? Are they sound?
13. Are the stated objectives being met, and are these objectives appropriate?
14. Are enough resources (or too many resources) budgeted to accomplish the marketing objectives?
15. Are the marketing resources allocated optimally to prime market segments and products of the organization?
16. Does the firm offer the intended benefits to customers? Are customers satisfied with these benefits?
17. In which particular areas should the firm make special efforts to improve its effectiveness?
18. Do any programs seem to have excessive costs? Are these costs valid? Can cost-reducing steps be taken?
19. Do forms and procedures make it hard or easy for someone to do business with us? Is more information asked for than is necessary? How are the data used?
20. What is done with negative feedback about staff from customers? How are complaints handled?

21. What is the firm's reputation among its various shareholders?
22. What are the organization's major strengths and weaknesses?

III. Target Market Strategies

A. *Target Markets*

1. Are the members of each product's target markets homogeneous or heterogeneous with respect to geographic, sociodemographic, and behavioral characteristics?
2. What are the size, growth rate, and national and regional trends for each of the organization's market segments?
3. Is the size of each market segment sufficiently large or important to develop a unique marketing mix for it?
4. Are the market segments measurable and accessible? That is, are the market segments accessible to distribution and communication efforts?
5. Which are the high-opportunity and low-opportunity segments?
6. What are the evolving needs and satisfactions being sought by target markets?
7. What benefits does the organization offer to each segment? How do these benefits compare with the benefits offered by competitors?
8. Is the firm offering products to people who are not adequately served by other organizations?
9. Is the firm positioning itself with a unique product? Is it needed?
10. Is the firm targeting any unresponsive markets? If so, what contributes to their unresponsiveness?
11. How much of our business is repeat versus new business? What percentage of the public can be classified as nonusers, light users, and heavy users?
12. How do current target markets rate the firm and its competitors, particularly with respect to reputation, quality, and price?
13. What is the firm's image with the specific market segments it seeks to serve?
14. Has the firm been efficient and effective in meeting customers' needs?

B. *Other Publics*

1. What publics other than target markets (financial, media, government, citizen, local, general, and internal) represent opportunities or problems for the firm?
2. What steps has the firm taken to deal effectively with key publics?
3. What does each public seek from the firm (that is, what's in it for them)?

IV. Distribution Decisions

A. *Strategic Distribution Decisions*

1. Has there been a recent evaluation of the firm's existing distribution pattern?
2. Is there a written statement of distribution objectives?
3. Should the firm try to deliver its offerings directly to customers, or can we better deliver selected offerings by involving other organizations?

4. Are members of the target market willing and able to travel some distance to buy the product?
5. How good is access to facilities? Can it be improved? Which facilities need priority attention in these areas?
6. How are facility locations chosen? Is the site accessible to the target markets? Is it visible to the target markets?
7. When are products made available to users (season of year, day of week, time of day)? Are these times most appropriate?
8. Are timing decisions based on analysis of customers' preferences? To what extent do the choices reflect employee convenience? Inertia from the past?

V. Product Strategies

A. *Product Management*

1. What are the major products offered by the firm? Do they complement each other, or is there unnecessary duplication?
2. Where is the firm and each major product in its life cycle (calculated by using market share or sales)?
3. Are the development of new products, termination of old products, and allocation of resources correctly prioritized according to each product's life cycle?
4. Is the type of management used at each stage of the life cycle appropriate?
5. What are the pressures among various target markets to increase or decrease the range and quality of products?
6. What are the major weaknesses in each product area? What are the major complaints? What goes wrong most often?
7. Does the physical appearance of the facility create an environment that complements and enhances the product itself? Does it aid in the customer's satisfaction? Is the environment relaxing and comfortable?
8. Is the product name easy to pronounce? Spell? Recall? Is it descriptive, and does it communicate the benefits the product offers? Does the name distinguish the firm or product from all others?

B. *New Product Development*

1. Have new-product committees been established? Do they keep senior management involved and informed?
2. What major new products are in the planning stages?
3. Is the firm sufficiently organized to gather, generate, and screen new product ideas?
4. Has a feasibility analysis been conducted to examine the costs and benefits of the proposal? Has the firm set criteria regarding feasibility?
5. Does the firm carry out small-scale tests with major new products before launching them?
6. Are there sufficient personnel resources to effectively evaluate and launch new products? Do our personnel have appropriate expertise?
7. Are promotional efforts for new products adequate?

C. *Diffusion of New Products*

1. Has the firm identified opinion leaders to help speed the rate of diffusion of products?
2. Are the opinion leaders also facilitating the extent of diffusion?

D. *Product Retrenchment*

1. Are the firm's managerial resources spread too thin?
2. What can the firm do to manage effectively with reduced resources?
3. What products are being, or should be, phased out?
4. How does the organization determine which products are to be terminated?
5. Is there a regular review process to identify candidates for termination?
6. Could the resources allocated to particular products generate greater total benefits if they were reallocated?
7. Is the firm assigning the highest-caliber people to the highest-priority products?
8. What strategies are used for terminating products so customer dissatisfaction and internal opposition are minimized?
9. Is retrenchment being implemented as part of the firm's overall plan so all concerned know why it is taking place and are aware of its implications?

VI. Pricing Strategies

A. *Pricing Objectives and Policies*

1. What are the firm's objectives in pricing each product?
2. Is there a current written pricing policy statement?
3. Is the statement specific enough to give guidance to pricing decisions?
4. Does the pricing policy address all functions or objectives of price?
5. What mechanisms does the firm have to ensure that the prices charged are acceptable to customers?
6. If a proposed price increase or decrease is implemented, how will the number of customers change? Will total revenue increase or decrease?

B. *Price Setting*

1. What are the procedures for establishing and reviewing pricing policy?
2. Are prices reviewed at least annually?
3. Which method is used for establishing a price: going rate, demand-oriented, or cost-based?
4. What discounts are offered and with what rationale?
5. Can the firm identify, classify, and equitably allocate the costs associated with each product?
6. What is the going rate price of similar products?
7. Has the firm considered psychological dimensions of price in its initial price decisions as well as in its price revision decisions?
8. Are price increases keeping pace with cost increases or general inflation levels?

9. Does the firm use price promotions effectively?
10. Are there any opportunities for interested prospects to sample products at an introductory price?
11. What methods of payment are accepted? Is it in the firm's best interest to use these various payment methods?

VII. Promotion Strategies

A. *Strategic Promotion Decisions*

1. Are there clear objectives for each element of the communication mix? How are promotion activities related to these objectives?
2. How does a typical customer find out about the firm's products? Word of mouth? Personal selling? Advertising? Publicity?
3. Does the message the firm delivers gain the attention of the intended target audience? Does it address the wants of the potential target market, and does it suggest a means for satisfying these wants? Is the message appropriately positioned?
4. Is the firm getting adequate feedback from its promotional efforts?
5. Is the firm's promotion effort effectively informing, persuading, educating, and reminding customers about its products?
6. On what basis does the organization measure the effectiveness of its various communication programs?
7. Does the firm have a tendency to overpromise?
8. How is the budget for each promotional element determined? Does it appear to be at the appropriate level? How does the organization decide on which products or markets to concentrate promotion?
9. Is promotion expenditure regarded as a cost or as an investment?

B. *Advertising and Publicity*

1. Is there a well-conceived publicity program?
2. How is public relations normally handled by the firm? By whom?
3. Is the publicity effort directed at all the firm's key publics or restricted only to potential customers?
4. What does the advertising/publicity budget permit? If a greater amount were spent on this activity, would there be a proportionately greater benefit to the firm and its customers?
5. Have close working relationships been established and nurtured between those responsible for publicity and reporters and editors in each of the media outlets?
6. Is an effort made to understand each of the sought publicity outlets' needs and to provide them with the types of stories that will appeal to their audiences in forms they can readily use?
7. Which of the following media are currently being used: daily newspapers, articles and letters to the editor, weekly newspapers, weekly news magazines, monthly magazines, telephone directories, television, news and talk shows, radio spots, guest appearances, exhibitions, billboards, catalogs, posters, fliers, newsletters?
8. Has the firm chosen the type of media that will best reach target markets?

9. Are the types of media used the most cost-effective, and do they contribute positively to the firm's image?
10. Are the dates and times the advertisements will appear the most appropriate?
11. Does the organization use an outside advertising agency? What functions does the ad agency perform for the organization?
12. Is the firm using all available public relations avenues?
13. Has the firm prepared several versions of its advertisements?
14. What system is used to handle consumer inquiries resulting from advertising and promotion? What follow-up is done?
15. Are news clippings or records kept for evaluating the firm's ability to get accurate and favorable media coverage?
16. How are the advertising and public relations programs evaluated? How often?
17. What does the annual report say about the firm and its products? Who is being effectively reached by this vehicle? Does the benefit of this publication justify the cost?

C. *Personal Selling*

1. How much of a typical salesperson's time is spent soliciting new customers as compared to serving existing customers?
2. How is it determined which prospect will be called on and by whom? How is the frequency of contacts determined?
3. What incentive does the sales staff have for encouraging more business?
4. How is the sales force organized and managed?
5. Has the firm prepared an approach tailored to each prospect? Does this approach emphasize benefits to potential customers rather than benefits to the firm? Does the firm address the question "What's in it for them?"
6. Has the firm matched its sales personnel with the type of buyer characteristic of the target market?
7. Do the firm's sales representatives generate enthusiasm for the firm's products?
8. Is there appropriate follow-up to the initial personal selling effort? Are customers kept informed on the status of their orders? Are they made to feel appreciated?

D. *Sales Promotion*

1. What is the specific purpose of each sales promotion activity? Why is it offered? What does it try to achieve?
2. What categories of sales promotion are being used? Promotional pricing? Free offers? Contests?
3. How is their effectiveness evaluated?

GLOSSARY

A

accessory equipment Goods, such as portable tools and office equipment, that are less expensive and shorter-lived than major equipment.

adaptive selling Altering a sales presentation for each prospect in response to the specific sales situation.

administered system Vertical marketing system in which a strong organization assumes a leadership position.

adopter Consumer who was happy enough with a trial experience with a product to use it again.

advertising Impersonal, one-way mass communication about a product or organization that is paid for by a marketer.

advertising agency Organization that handles the advertising and promotion functions for other organizations.

advertising appeal Reason for a person to buy a product.

advertising campaign Series of related advertisements focusing on a common theme, slogan, and set of advertising appeals.

advertising objective Specific communication task a campaign should accomplish for a specified target audience during a specified period.

advertising response function Phenomenon in which spending for advertising and sales promotion increases sales or market share up to a certain level but then produces diminishing returns.

advocacy advertising Form of advertising in which an organization expresses its views on controversial issues or responds to media attacks.

AIDA concept Model that outlines the process for achieving promotional goals in terms of stages of consumer involvement with the message; the acronym stands for Attention, Interest, Desire, and Action.

all-you-can-afford approach Method of setting a promotional budget that relies on determining how much the marketer can spend.

annual purchasing contract Type of purchasing contract that provides a discount schedule for purchases over the period of the contract.

applied research Research aimed at finding useful applications for new technologies.

arbitrary allocation Method of setting a promotional budget that picks a dollar amount without reference to other factors.

aspirational group Group that someone would like to join.

assumptive close Technique of ending a sales presentation that assumes the prospect is going to buy.

atmosphere Overall impression conveyed by a store's physical layout, decor, and surroundings.

attitude Learned tendency to respond consistently toward a given object.

attitudinal objective Promotional objective that seeks to improve or change the product's image by changing consumers' attitude toward it.

audience duplication Situation in which the same audience is reached by two different media vehicles.

audience selectivity Ability of an advertising medium to reach a precisely defined market.

audit Examination and verification of the sale of a product.

automatic identification (auto ID) Use of identification technology to mark and read products as they enter and leave the supplier's warehouse or as they are received by a manufacturer or retailer.

average total cost (ATC) Total costs divided by output.

average variable cost (AVC) Total variable costs divided by output.

awareness objective Promotional objective that seeks to increase consumers' knowledge of a product or brand.

B

backward integration Retailer's or wholesaler's acquisition of an intermediary closer to the manufacturing stage or performance of the functions formerly performed by an intermediary closer to the manufacturing stage.

bait pricing Price tactic that tries to get consumers into a store through false or misleading price advertising and then uses high-pressure selling to persuade consumers to buy more expensive merchandise.

balance of payments Difference between a country's total payments to other countries and its total receipts from other countries.

balance of trade Difference between the value of a country's exports and the value of its imports during a certain time.

base price General price level at which the company expects to sell the good or service.

basic research Scientific research aimed at discovering new technologies.

basing-point price Price that incorporates the freight cost from a given (basing) point, regardless of the city from which the goods are shipped.

behavioral objective Actions that marketing managers want target consumers to take; promotional objective that aims to change a buyer's behavior or prompt the buyer to take some action.

BehaviorScan Single-source research program that tracks the purchases of 3,000 households through store scanners.

belief Organized pattern of knowledge that an individual holds as true about his or her world.

benchmarking Rating a product against the world's best products of all types.

benefit segmentation Method of dividing markets based on the benefits customers seek from the product.

bid pricing Process in which potential sellers are invited to state, either orally or in writing, what they will charge to provide a good or service.

birdyback Form of intermodal transportation combining the use of truck and air freight to move containerized goods.

blanket purchasing contract Type of purchasing contract that requires the supplier to provide a certain amount of product at the same price each month during the course of a year.

boycott Exclusion of all products from certain countries or companies.

brainstorming Technique for generating new product ideas in which group members propose, without criticism or limitation, ways to vary a product or solve a problem.

brand Name, term, symbol, design, or combination thereof that identifies a seller's products and differentiates them from competitors' products.

brand equity Value of successful company and brand names.

brand loyalty Consumer's consistent preference for one brand over all others in its product category.

brand manager Person who is responsible for a single brand.

brand mark Elements of a brand that cannot be spoken, such as symbols.

brand name Part of a brand that can be spoken, including letters, words, and numbers.

break-even analysis Method of determining what sales volume must be reached for a product before the company breaks even (total costs equal total revenue) and no profits are earned.

broker Functional intermediary that brings buyers and sellers together.

business analysis Stage in the product development process where demand, cost, sales, and profitability estimates are made.

business product Product used to manufacture other goods or services, to facilitate an organization's operations, or to resell to other customers; also called industrial product.

business service Expense item obtained from an outside provider that does not become part of a final product, such as janitorial, advertising, legal, management consulting, marketing research, maintenance, and other services.

business-to-business marketing Marketing of goods and services to individuals and organizations for purposes other than personal consumption.

buyer Person who selects the merchandise for retail stores and may also be responsible for promotion and for personnel.

buyer for export Intermediary in the international market that assumes all ownership risks and sells internationally for its own account.

buying center Group within an organization consisting of all those who are involved in the purchase decision.

C

cannibalization Phenomenon in which sales of a new product cut into sales of a firm's existing products.

cash cow In the portfolio matrix, a business unit that generates more cash than it needs to maintain its market share.

cash discount Price reduction offered to a consumer, industrial user, or marketing intermediary in return for prompt payment of a bill.

cash-and-carry wholesaler Limited-service merchant wholesaler that sells for cash and usually carries a limited line of fast-moving merchandise.

category manager Person responsible for multiple product lines within a product category.

central-location telephone (CLT) facility Specially designed room used for conducting telephone interviews for survey research.

chain store Retail store that is one of a group owned and operated by a single corporation with central authority.

channel Medium of communication—such as a voice, radio, or newspaper—for transmitting a message.

channel conflict Clash of goals and methods between distribution channel members.

channel control Situation that occurs when one marketing channel member intentionally affects another member's behavior.

channel leader (channel captain) Institution in a vertical marketing system that coordinates the activities of the various channel members.

channel leadership Marketing channel member's exercise of authority and power over other channel members.

channel power Capacity of a particular marketing channel member to control or influence the behavior of other channel members.

closed-ended question Question that asks the respondent to make a selection from a limited list of responses.

code of ethics Guidelines developed by a company to help its employees make ethical decisions.

cognitive dissonance Inner tension that a consumer experiences after recognizing an inconsistency between behavior and values or opinions.

cold calling Form of lead generation in which the salesperson approaches potential buyers without any prior knowledge of the prospects' needs or financial status.

commercialization Final stage in the product development process, consisting of tasks necessary to begin marketing the product.

communication Process by which we exchange or share meanings through a common set of symbols.

company sales forecast Amount a company actually expects to sell in all segments in which it competes or plans to compete during a specified period.

company sales potential Amount an organization could possibly sell in all market segments in which it competes or plans to compete during a specified period.

comparative advertising Form of advertising that compares two or more specifically named or shown competing brands on one or more specific attributes.

competitive advertising Form of advertising designed to influence demand for a specific brand.

competitive parity Method of setting a promotional budget that matches a competitor's spending.

component part Finished item ready for assembly or product that needs very little processing before becoming part of some other product.

computer-assisted interviewing Interviewing method in which the interviewer reads the questions from a computer screen and enters the respondent's data directly into the computer.

concentrated targeting strategy (niche targeting strategy) Marketing approach based on appealing to a single segment of a market.

concept of exchange Idea that people give up something to receive something they would rather have.

concept test Evaluation of a new product idea, usually before any prototype has been created.

consumer behavior Processes a consumer uses to make purchase decisions, as well as to use and dispose of the purchased good or service; also includes factors that influence purchase decisions and the use of products.

consumer decision-making process Step-by-step process used by consumers when buying goods or services.

consumer product Product bought to satisfy an individual's personal wants.

Consumer Product Safety Commission (CPSC) Federal agency established to protect the health and safety of consumers in and around their homes.

consumerism Political and economic struggle to increase the rights and powers of buyers in relation to sellers.

container on flatcar (COFC) Form of intermodal transportation involving containers that can be transferred from rail or truck onto ship or barge.

containerization Putting large quantities of goods in sturdy containers that can be moved from ship to truck to airplane to train without repacking.

continuous improvement Commitment to constantly do things better.

continuous media schedule Media scheduling strategy, used for products in the latter stages of the product life cycle, in which advertising is run steadily throughout the advertising period.

contract logistics Use of an independent third party to buy and manage an entire subsystem of physical distribution, such as transportation or warehousing, for a manufacturer or supplier.

contract manufacturing Private-label manufacturing by a foreign company.

contract warehousing Agreement between a manufacturer and a public warehouse facility to provide storage space for a specified period.

contractual system Vertical marketing system composed of independent firms at different channel levels (manufacturer, wholesaler, retailer) coordinating their distribution activities by contractual agreement.

convenience product Relatively inexpensive item that merits little shopping effort.

convenience sample Nonprobability sample that uses respondents who are convenient or readily accessible to the researcher.

convenience store Miniature supermarket, carrying only a limited line of high-turnover convenience goods.

conventional channel Network of loosely aligned manufacturers, wholesalers, and retailers that bargain with each other at arm's length, negotiate aggressively over the terms of sale, and otherwise behave independently.

conventional morality Intermediate level of moral development, which is based on loyalty and obedience to the organization's or society's expectations.

cooperative advertising Arrangement in which the manufacturer and the retailer split the costs of advertising the manufacturer's brand.

corporate social responsibility Business's concern for society's welfare, demonstrated by managers who consider both the long-range best interests of the company and the company's relationship to the society within which it operates.

corporate system Vertical marketing system in which one firm owns successive stages in a channel of distribution.

corrective advertising Advertising that amends the false impressions left by previous advertisements.

cost per contact Cost of reaching one member of the target market.

cost per thousand (CPM) Standard criterion for comparing media, computed by dividing the price of a single ad by the audience size in thousands.

countertrade Form of trade in which all or part of the payment for goods or services is in the form of other goods or services.

coupon Certificate that entitles consumers to an immediate price reduction when they buy the product.

credence quality Characteristic that cannot easily be assessed even after purchase and experience.

crisis management Strategy used by public relations managers to handle the effects of unfavorable publicity.

cross-tabulation Type of data analysis that relates the responses to one question to the responses to one or more other questions.

culture Set of values, norms, attitudes, and other meaningful symbols that shape human behavior and the artifacts, or products, of that behavior as they are transmitted from one generation to the next.

cumulative quantity discount Deduction from list price that applies to the buyer's total purchases made during a specific period; it is intended to encourage customer loyalty.

cycle time Time between product inception and delivery.

D

database marketing Creation of a large computerized file of customers' and potential customers' profiles and purchase patterns as a tool for identifying target markets.

decision support system (DSS) Interactive, flexible information system that enables managers to obtain and manipulate information as they are making decisions.

decline stage Fourth and final stage of the product life cycle, in which sales drop and falling demand forces many competitors out of the market.

decoding Interpretation of the language and symbols sent by the source through a channel.

delayed-quotation pricing Pricing tactic used for industrial installations and many accessory items, in which a firm price is not set until the item is either finished or delivered.

deliverable Goods and services provided to the customer.

Delphi technique Sales forecasting technique that asks outside experts to express an anonymos opinion, review a summary of others' opinions, and express themselves again in order to reach consensus.

demand Quantity of a product that will be sold in the market at various prices for a specified period.

demographic segmentation Method of dividing markets based on demographic variables, such as age, gender, income, ethnic background, and family life cycle.

demography Study of people's vital statistics, such as their ages, births, deaths, and locations.

department store Retailer that carries a wide variety of shopping and specialty goods, including apparel, cosmetics, housewares, electronics, and sometimes furniture.

derived demand Demand that results from demand for another product.

development Stage in the product development process when a prototype is developed and a marketing strategy is outlined.

differential advantage One or more unique aspects of an organization that cause target consumers to patronize that firm rather than competitors; set of unique features of a company and its products that are perceived by the target market as significant and superior to the competition.

diffusion Process by which the adoption of an innovation spreads.

diffusion process Spread of a new idea from its source of invention or creation to its ultimate users or adopters.

direct channel Distribution channel in which producers sell directly to consumers.

direct foreign investment Active ownership of a foreign company or of overseas manufacturing or marketing facilities.

direct marketing Techniques used to get consumers to buy from their homes, including direct mail, catalogs and mail order, telemarketing, and electronic retailing.

direct-response advertising Advertising that calls for consumers' immediate action, or a direct response.

direct retailing Form of nonstore retailing that occurs in a home setting, such as door-to-door sales and party plan selling.

discount store Retail store that is one of a group competing on the basis of low prices, high turnover, and high volume.

discrepancy of assortment Lack of all the items needed to receive full satisfaction from a product or products.

discrepancy of quantity Difference between the amount of product produced and the amount an end user wants to buy.

discretionary income Income after taxes and necessities.

distribution center Type of warehouse that specializes in making bulk or breaking bulk and strives for rapid inventory turnover.

diversification Marketing strategy that increases sales by introducing new products into new markets.

dog In the portfolio matrix, a business unit that has low growth potential and a small market share.

downward extension Practice of adding to a product line a less-expensive product with fewer features or options and for a more price-sensitive segment of the market.

drop shipper Limited-service merchant wholesaler that places orders for its customers with the manufacturer but does not physically handle the products it sells.

dual distribution (multiple distribution) Use of two or more channels to distribute the same product to target markets.

dumping Practice of selling products either below cost or below their sale price in their domestic market.

E

early adopter Consumer among the second group to adopt a new idea or product; frequently an opinion leader.

early majority Third group of consumers to adopt a new idea or product, characterized by their deliberation.

economic order quantity (EOQ) Order volume that minimizes order processing costs and inventory carrying costs.

80/20 principle Idea that 20 percent of all customers generate 80 percent of the demand.

elastic demand Situation in which consumer demand is sensitive to price changes.

elasticity of demand Consumers' responsiveness or sensitivity to changes in price.

electronic data interchange (EDI) Computer technique that electronically transmits data about retail inventories to warehouses so orders can be filled more quickly and accurately.

empowerment Practice of giving employees expanded authority to solve customer problems as they arise.

encoding Conversion of the sender's ideas and thoughts into a message, usually in the form of words or signs.

environmental management Implementation of strategies that attempt to shape the external environment within which a firm operates.

environmental scanning Collection and interpretation of information about forces, events, and relationships that may affect the future of an organization.

equilibrium Price at which demand and supply are equal.

escalator pricing Pricing tactic in which the final selling price reflects cost increases incurred between the times when the order is placed and delivery is made.

ethics Moral principles or values that generally govern the conduct of an individual or a group.

everyday low price (EDLP) Pricing tactic of permanently reducing prices 10 to 15 percent below the traditional levels while eliminating trade discounts that create trade loading.

evoked set (consideration set) Group of brands, resulting from an information search, from which a buyer can choose.

exchange control Law compelling a company earning foreign exchange from its exports to sell it to a control agency, usually a central bank.

exclusive distribution Form of distribution that establishes one or a few dealers within a given area.

experience quality Characteristic that can be assessed only after purchase or use.

experiment Method of gathering primary data in which one or more variables are altered to measure their relative influence on another variable.

export agent Intermediary who either lives in a foreign country and performs the same functions as a domestic manufacturer's agent or lives in the manufacturer's country but represents foreign buyers.

export broker Broker who operates primarily in agriculture and raw materials.

exporting Practice of selling domestically produced products in another country.

express warranty Written guarantee that a good or service is fit for the purpose for which it was sold.

extensive decision making Most complex type of consumer decision making, used when buying an unfamiliar, expensive product or an infrequently bought item; requires use of several criteria for evaluating options and much time for seeking information.

external information search Process of seeking information in the outside environment.

external stimuli Sensory input stemming from sources outside the individual, such as packaging or advertising.

F

factory outlet Off-price retailer that is owned and operated by a manufacturer and that carries the manufacturer's own line of merchandise.

family brand Practice of using the same brand name to market several different products.

family life cycle (FLC) Series of life stages determined by a combination of age, marital status, and the presence or absence of children.

Federal Trade Commission (FTC) Federal agency empowered to prevent persons or corporations from using unfair methods of competition in commerce.

feedback Receiver's response to a message.

field order taker Someone who visits existing customers regularly, checks inventory, writes up new orders, and then delivers and stocks the product for the customers.

field service firm Firm that specializes in interviewing respondents on a subcontract basis.

fishbone diagram Visual tool resembling the skeleton of a fish that helps managers organize cause-and-effect relationships for problems.

fishyback Form of intermodal transportation combining the use of truck, rail, and ship or barge to move containerized goods.

fixed cost Cost that does not change as output is increased or decreased.

flexible pricing (variable pricing) Price tactic in which different customers pay different prices for essentially the same merchandise bought in equal quantities.

flighted media schedule Media scheduling strategy in which ads are run heavily every other month or every two weeks to achieve a greater impact with an increased frequency and reach at those times.

FOB origin pricing Price tactic that requires the buyer to absorb the freight costs from the shipping point.

focus group Group of seven to ten people with desired characteristics who participate in a group discussion about a subject of interest to a marketing organization.

follow-up Final step of the selling process, in which the salesperson ensures that delivery schedules are met, that the goods or services perform as promised, and that the buyers' employees are properly trained to use the products.

Food and Drug Administration (FDA) Federal agency charged with enforcing regulations against selling and distributing adulterated, misbranded, or hazardous food and drug products.

Foreign Corrupt Practices Act Legislation prohibiting U.S. corporations from making illegal payments to public officials of foreign governments in order to obtain business rights or enhance their business dealings in that country.

formal control Written, management-initiated mechanism that influences the probability that employees and systems will function in ways that support the stated marketing objectives.

formula pricing Pricing method in which a predetermined formula is used to set price.

forward buying Practice of purchasing in advance of needs to take advantage of promotional discounts offered by suppliers.

forward integration Manufacturer's or wholesaler's acquisition of an intermediary closer to the target market or performance of the functions of an intermediary closer to the target market.

four P's Product decisions, distribution (or place) decisions, promotion decisions, and pricing decisions, which together make up the marketing mix.

frame error Error that occurs when the sample drawn from a population differs from the target population.

franchise Right to operate a business or to sell a product.

franchise outlet Retail store owned and operated by an individual who is a licensee of a larger supporting organization.

franchisee Individual or business that is granted the right to sell another party's product.

franchisor Individual or business that grants operating rights to another party to sell its product.

free enterprise Economic system in which everyone has the right to engage in almost any business pursuit.

freight absorption pricing Price tactic in which the seller pays all or part of the actual freight charges and does not pass them on to the buyer.

freight forwarder Carrier that collects less-than-carload shipments from a number of shippers and consolidates them into carload lots.

frequency Number of times an individual is exposed to a given message during a specific period.

full-service merchant wholesaler Wholesaler that assembles an assortment of products, provides credit for clients, offers promotional help and technical advice, maintains a sales force to contact customers, and delivers merchandise and may offer research, planning, installation, and repair.

fully industrialized society Society that is an exporter of manufactured products, many of which are based on advanced technology.

functional discount (trade discount) Discount to wholesalers and retailers for performing channel functions.

functional modification Change in a product's versatility, effectiveness, convenience, or safety.

G

general merchandise wholesaler (full-line wholesaler) Wholesaler that stocks a full assortment of products within a product line.

generic product name Name that identifies a product by class or type and cannot be trademarked.

generic product No-frills, no–brand name, low-cost product.

geodemographic segmentation Method of dividing markets based on neighborhood lifestyle categories.

geographic segmentation Method of dividing markets based on region of the country or world, market size, market density, or climate.

geographic selectivity Ability of an advertising medium to cover a specific area.

global marketing Individuals and organizations using a global vision to effectively market goods and services across national boundaries.

global marketing standardization Production of uniform products that can be sold the same way all over the world.

global vision Ability to recognize and react to international marketing opportunities, awareness of threats from foreign competitors in all markets, and effective use of international distribution networks.

green marketing Marketing of products and packages that are less toxic than normal, are more durable, contain reusable materials, or are made of recyclable materials.

gross margin Difference between the price at which a product is actually sold and its cost; how much the retailer makes as a percentage of sales after the cost of goods sold is subtracted.

growth stage Second stage of the product life cycle, characterized by increasing sales, heightened competition, and healthy profits.

H

heterogeneity Characteristic of services that makes them less standardized and uniform than goods.

hierarchy of effects model Model that outlines the six-stage process by which consumers make purchase decisions: awareness, knowledge, liking, preference, conviction, and purchase.

high-involvement decision making Process of deliberately searching for information about products and brands in order to evaluate them thoroughly.

horizontal integration Distribution channel member's purchase of firms at the same level of the marketing channel.

horizontal marketing system (cooperative) Network of distribution channel members at the same level that pool their negotiating strength and achieve other economies of scale.

hypermarket Retail establishment that combines a supermarket and discount department store in one large building.

I

ideal self-image Way an individual would like to be.

implied warranty Unwritten guarantee that the good or service is fit for the purpose for which it was sold.

incremental productivity approach Method of determining sales force size in which salespeople are added as long as the total sales increase is greater than the increase in selling cost.

independent retailer Individual or partnership that owns one or several retail establishments not part of a larger retail organization.

individual branding Practice of using a different brand name for each product.

industrial distributor Full-service merchant wholesaler that sells to manufacturers rather than to retailers.

industrializing society Society characterized by the spread of technology to most sectors of the economy.

inelastic demand Demand that is not significantly affected by price changes; situation in which an increase or a decrease in price will not significantly affect demand for the product.

inflation General rise in prices resulting in decreased purchasing power.

infomercial Thirty-minute or longer advertisement that looks more like a TV talk show than a sales pitch.

informal control Unwritten, typically worker-initiated mechanism that influences individual or group behavior.

informational labeling Labeling designed to help consumers make a proper product selection and lower their cognitive dissonance after the purchase.

InfoScan Scanner-based, national sales-tracking service for the consumer packaged-goods industry, using data from purchases at retail stores.

innovation Product perceived as new by a potential adopter.

innovator Consumer among the small group who first adopts a new idea or product and is eager to try.

inseparability Characteristic of services that allows them to be produced and consumed simultaneously.

inside order taker Someone who takes orders from customers over the counter, on the sales floor, over the telephone, or by mail.

installation Capital good, such as a large or expensive machine, mainframe computer, blast furnace, generator, airplane, or building.

institutional advertising Form of advertising designed to enhance a company's image rather than promote a particular product.

intangibility Characteristic of services that prevents them from being touched, seen, tasted, heard, or felt in the same manner in which goods can be sensed.

intensive distribution Form of distribution aimed at having a product available in every outlet where target customers might want to buy it.

interaction Customer experience of the service process.

intermodal transportation Combination of two or more modes of moving freight.

internal information search Process of recalling past information stored in the memory.

internal marketing Treating employees as customers and developing systems and benefits that satisfy their needs.

internal stimuli Sensory input stemming from fundamental needs within the individual, such as hunger and thirst.

interpersonal communication Direct, face-to-face communication between two or more people.

introductory stage First stage of the product life cycle, which represents the full-scale launch of a new product into the marketplace.

inventory carrying cost Total of all expenses involved in maintaining inventory, including the cost of capital tied up in idle merchandise, the cost of obsolescence, space charges, handling charges, insurance costs, property taxes, losses due to depreciation and deterioration, and opportunity costs.

inventory control system Method of developing and maintaining an adequate assortment of products to meet customers' demands.

involvement Amount of time and effort a buyer invests in the search, evaluation, and decision processes of consumer behavior.

J

joint cost Cost that is shared in the manufacturing and marketing of more than one product in a product line.

joint demand Demand for two or more items that are used together in a final product.

joint venture Arrangement in which a domestic firm buys part of a foreign company or joins with a foreign company to create a new entity.

jury of executive opinion Sales forecasting technique that surveys a group of executive experts.

just-in-time (JIT) inventory management Redesigning and simplifying manufacturing by reducing inventory levels and delivering parts just when they are needed on the production line.

K

keh Asian-American cooperative of about twenty people who combine their money and award it to one member each month; when everyone has participated in the payout cycle, the *keh* disbands.

keiretsu Japanese societies of business, which take two main forms: bank-centered keiretsu, massive industrial combines centered around a bank, and supply keiretsu, groups of companies dominated by the major manufacturer they provide with supplies.

keystoning Practice of marking up prices by 100 percent, or to double the cost.

L

laggard Consumer among the final group to adopt a new idea or product, characterized by ties to tradition.

late majority Fourth group of consumers to adopt a new idea or product, characterized by their reliance on group norms.

lead generation Identification of those firms and people most likely to buy the seller's offerings.

lead qualification Determination of a sales prospect's authority to buy and ability to pay for the good or service.

lead time Time it takes to get parts from a supplier after an order has been placed; time that the customer has to wait before an order is filled.

leader pricing (loss-leader pricing) Price tactic in which a product is sold near or even below cost in the hope that shoppers will buy other items once they are in the store.

learning Process that creates changes in behavior, immediate or expected, through experience and practice.

licensing Legal process whereby a licensor agrees to let another firm use its manufacturing process, trademarks, patents, trade secrets, or other proprietary knowledge.

life cycle Orderly series of stages in which a person's attitudes and behavioral tendencies evolve, through maturity, experience, and changing income and status.

lifestyle Mode of living as identified by a person's activities, interests, and opinions.

limited decision making Type of decision making that requires a moderate amount of time for gathering information and deliberating about an unfamiliar brand in a familiar product category.

limited-service merchant wholesaler Wholesaler that performs only a few of the full-service merchant wholesaler's activities.

line extension Practice of adding products to a product line.

line filling Practice of increasing the depth of a product line by adding more items, in order to offer a complete product line.

logistics Procurement and management of raw materials for production.

logistics management Overseeing the movement of raw materials and finished products to intermediaries or end consumers.

low-involement decision making Process of deciding to buy a product in which the consumer experiences little perceived risk, low identification with the product, or little personal relevance.

M

macrosegmentation Method of dividing business markets based on such general characteristics as geographic location, type of organization, customer size, and product use.

mail-order wholesaler Limited-service merchant wholesaler that sells goods by catalog to businesses, institutions, government, and other organizations.

major equipment Capital goods, such as large or expensive machines, mainframe computers, blast furnaces, generators, airplanes, and buildings.

mall intercept interview Survey research method that involves interviewing people in the common areas of shopping malls.

manufacturer's brand Manufacturer's name used as a brand name.

manufacturers' agent Functional intermediary that represents one manufacturer or several manufacturers of complementary lines and follows the terms set by the manufacturer.

manufacturers' sales branch Manufacturer-owned and -controlled wholesale institution that carries inventory.

manufacturers' sales office Wholesale operation that performs a sales function and is owned, managed, and controlled by a manufacturer.

marginal cost (MC) Change in total costs associated with a one-unit change in output.

marginal revenue (MR) Extra revenue associated with selling an extra unit of output.

mark-on Initial markup.

market People or organizations with needs or wants and with the ability, and the willingness, to buy.

market development Marketing strategy that attracts new customers to existing products.

market grouping Common trade alliance in which several countries agree to work together to form a common trade area that enhances trade opportunities.

market opportunity analysis Description and estimation of the size and sales potential of market segments of interest to a firm and assessment of key competitors in these market segments.

market penetration Marketing strategy that increases market share among existing customers.

market sales potential Maximum amount of product that can be sold in a given industry with maximum marketing expenditures under existing marketing mixes within a specific external environment.

market segment Subgroup of people or organizations sharing one or more characteristics that cause them to have similar product needs.

market segment sales potential Maximum amount of a product that could be sold in a market segment during a specified period.

market segment size Number of potential customers in a market segment.

market segmentation Process of dividing a market into meaningful, relatively similar, and identifiable segments or groups.

market share Company's product sales as a percentage of total sales for that industry.

market share approach Method of setting a promotional budget that allocates the amount needed to maintain or win a certain market share.

marketing Process of planning and executing the conception, pricing, promotion, and distribution of ideas, goods, and services to create exchanges that satisfy individual and organizational objectives.

marketing audit Thorough, systematic, periodic evaluation of the goals, strategies, structure, and performance of the marketing organization.

marketing channel (channel of distribution) Set of interdependent organizations that ease the transfer of ownership as products move from producer to business user or consumer.

marketing concept Idea that the social and economic justification for an organization's existence is the satisfaction of customer wants and needs while meeting organizational objectives.

marketing-controlled information source Product information source that originates with marketers promoting the product.

marketing information system (MIS) System for continually gathering data from a variety of sources, synthesizing it, and funneling it to those responsible for meeting the marketplace's needs.

marketing intelligence Everyday information about developments in the marketing environment that managers use to prepare and adjust marketing plans.

marketing mix Unique blend of product, distribution, promotion, and pricing strategies designed to produce mutually satisfying exchanges with a target market.

marketing myopia Practice of defining a business in terms of goods and services rather than in terms of the benefits customers seek.

marketing objective Statement of what is to be accomplished through marketing activities.

marketing orientation Philosophy that assumes responsiveness to customer wants should be the central focus of all marketing activity.

marketing research Process of planning, collecting, and analyzing data relevant to marketing decision making.

marketing strategy Plan that involves selecting one or more target markets, setting marketing objectives, and developing and maintaining a marketing mix that will produce mutually satisfying exchanges with target markets.

markup pricing Pricing method that adds to the product cost an amount for profit and expenses not previously accounted for.

Maslow's hierarchy of needs Method of classifying human needs and motivations into five categories in ascending order of importance: physiological, safety, social, esteem, and self-actualization.

mass communication Communication to large audiences.

mass merchandising Retailing strategy of using moderate to low prices on most merchandise, coupled with big promotional budgets, to stimulate high turnover of products.

master brand Brand so dominant in consumers' minds that they think of it immediately when a product category, use situation, product attribute, or customer benefit is mentioned.

materials-handling system Method of moving inventory into, within, and out of the warehouse.

maturity stage Third stage of the product life cycle, in which sales begin to level off and the market approaches saturation.

measurement error Error that occurs when there is a difference between the information desired by the researcher and the information provided by the measurement process.

media mix Combination of media to be used for a promotional campaign.

media schedule Designation of the media, the specific publications or programs, and the insertion dates of advertising.

medium Channel used to convey a message to a target market.

merchant wholesaler Institution that buys goods from manufacturers and resells them to businesses, government agencies, and other wholesalers or retailers; also receives and takes title to goods, stores them in its own warehouses, and later reships them.

micromarketing Marketing program tailored to prospective buyers who live in small geographic regions, such as neighborhoods, or who have very specific lifestyle and demographic characteristics.

microsegmentation Method of dividing business markets based on the characteristics of decision-making units within a macrosegment.

missionary sales representative Someone who works for a manufacturer to stimulate goodwill within the channel of distribution and to support the company's sales efforts.

mixed economy Economy in which both the government and the private sector exercise economic control.

modified rebuy Situation in which the purchaser wants some change in the original good or service.

monopolistic competition Form of economic competition in which a relatively large number of suppliers offer similar but not identical products.

monopoly Form of economic competition in which one firm controls the output and price of a product for which there are no close substitutes.

morals Rules or habits that people develop as a result of cultural values and norms.

motive Driving force that causes a person to take action to satisfy specific needs.

moving average Sales forecasting technique that combines sales data from several of the most recent years and uses an average to obtain next year's forecast.

multiculturalism Phenomenon of all ethnic groups being roughly equally represented in an area.

multinational corporation (MNC) Company that moves resources, goods, services, and skills across national boundaries without regard to the country in which the headquarters is located.

multiplier effect (accelerator principle) Phenomenon in which a small increase or decrease in consumer demand produces a much larger change in demand for the facilities and equipment needed to make the consumer product.

multisegment targeting strategy Marketing approach based on serving two or more well-defined market segments, with a distinct marketing mix for each.

N

National Advertising Division (NAD) Complaint bureau for consumers and advertisers, part of the Council of Better Business Bureaus.

National Advertising Review Board (NARB) Appeals board for cases in which the National Advertising Division rules in favor of the complaining party.

need Anything an individual depends on to function efficiently; root of all human behavior.

need-satisfaction approach Sales pitch that focuses on satisfying a prospective buyer's particular needs.

negotiation (extra inducement close) Technique of withholding a special concession until the end of the selling process and using it to close a sale.

networking Finding out about potential clients from friends, business contacts, co-workers, acquaintances, and fellow members in professional and civic organizations.

new buy Situation requiring the purchase of a product for the first time.

new product Product new to the world, the market, the producer or seller, or some combination of these.

new product committee Ad hoc group whose members represent various functional interests and who manage the new product development process.

new product department Separate department that manages the new product development process on a full-time basis.

new product strategy Strategy that links the new product development process with the objectives of the marketing department, the business unit, and the corporation.

noise Anything that interferes with, distorts, or slows down the transmission of information.

nonaspirational reference group Group with which an individual does not want to associate.

nonbusiness marketing Marketing activities conducted by individuals and organizations to achieve some goal other than normal business goals (such as profit, market share, or return on investment).

noncumulative quantity discount Deduction from list price that applies to a single order rather than to the total volume of orders placed during a certain period.

nonmarketing-controlled information source Product information source that is not associated with advertising or promotion.

nonprobability sample Any sample in which little or no attempt is made to get a representative cross section of the population.

nonprofit organization marketing Effort by public and private nonprofit organizations to bring about mutually satisfying exchanges with target markets.

nonstore retailing Practice of selling goods and services to the ultimate consumer without setting up a store.

norm Value or attitude deemed acceptable by a group.

North American Free Trade Agreement (NAFTA) Treaty establishing the world's largest free-trade zone, which includes Canada, the United States, and Mexico.

O

objective and task approach Method of setting a promotional budget that begins with promotional objectives, defines the communication tools required to achieve those objectives, and then adds up the costs of the planned activities.

observation research Research method that relies on three types of observation: people watching people, people watching physical phenomena, and machines watching people.

odd-even pricing (psychological pricing) Price tactic that uses odd-numbered prices to denote bargains and even-numbered prices to imply quality.

off-price retailer Retailer that sells at prices 25 percent or more below traditional department store prices because it pays cash for its stock and usually doesn't ask for return privileges.

oligopoly Form of economic competition in which a small number of firms dominate the market for a good or service.

on-line data base Public information data base accessible by anyone with proper computer facilities.

on-line database vendor Intermediary that acquires data bases from database creators.

open-ended question Question worded to encourage unlimited answers phrased in the respondent's own words.

operations-oriented pricing Varying prices to coordinate supply and demand by encouraging maximum use of productive capacity.

opinion leader Individual who influences the opinions of others.

optimizer Type of business customer that considers numerous suppliers, both familiar and unfamiliar, solicits bids, and studies all proposals carefully before selecting one.

order entry First step in order processing in which a customer order is taken.

order getter Someone who actively seeks buyers for a product.

order handling Second step in order processing, in which the order is transmitted to the office, usually on a standardized order form, and then to the warehouse floor.

order lead time Expected time between the date an order is placed and the date the goods are received and made ready for resale to customers.

order processing cost Total of operating expenses for the ordering or purchasing department, costs of required follow-up, operating expenses for the receiving department, expenses incurred in paying invoices, and the portion of data-processing costs related to purchasing and acquiring inventory.

ordering cost Order processing cost divided by the number of orders placed per year, to arrive at an average cost per order.

P

packaging Container for protecting and promoting a product.

parallel engineering (simultaneous engineering, concurrent engineering) Product development process in which all relevant functional areas and outside suppliers participate at all stages, thereby streamlining the development process and reducing its cost.

Pareto analysis Method for identifying a company's biggest problems that uses a bar chart to rank causes of variation in production or service processes by the degree of their impact on quality.

patronage-oriented pricing Setting prices at a level that will maximize the number of customers using a service—for example, by pricing according to different market segments' ability to pay.

penetration pricing Pricing policy whereby a firm charges a relatively low price for a product as a way to reach the mass market in the early stages of the product life cycle.

percent of sales approach Method of setting a promotional budget that allocates an amount equal to a certain percentage of total sales.

perception Process by which people select, organize, and interpret stimuli into a meaningful and coherent picture.

perceptual mapping Means of displaying or graphing, in two or more dimensions, the location of products, brands, or groups of products in customers' minds.

perishability Characteristic of services that prevents them from being stored, warehoused, or inventoried.

personal selling Direct communication between a sales representative and one or more prospective buyers, for the purpose of making a sale; planned, face-to-face presentation to one or more prospective buyers for the purpose of making a sale.

personality Way of organizing and grouping the consistencies of an individual's reactions to situations.

persuasive labeling Labeling that focuses on a promotional theme or logo rather than on consumer information.

physical distribution Ingredient in the marketing mix that describes how products are moved and stored.

physical distribution service Interrelated activities performed by a supplier to ensure that the right product is in the right place at the right time.

piggyback (trailer on flatcar) (TOFC) Form of intermodal transportation combining the use of truck and rail to ship containerized goods.

pioneering advertising Form of advertising designed to stimulate primary demand for a new product or product category.

planned obsolescence Practice of changing a product's style so that it becomes outdated before it actually needs replacement.

point-of-purchase display Promotional display set up at the retailer's location to build traffic, advertise the product, or induce impulse buying.

poka-yoke Japanese concept that means finding ways to minimize human error by changing the design.

position Place that a product, brand, or group of products occupies in consumers' minds relative to competing offerings.

positioning Developing a specific marketing mix to influence potential customers' overall perception of a brand, product line, or organization in general.

postconventional morality Most advanced level of moral development, in which people are less concerned about how others might see them and more concerned about how they see and judge themselves over the long run.

poverty of time Lack of time to do anything but work, commute to work, handle family situations, do housework, shop, sleep, and eat.

preconventional morality Basic level of moral development, which is childlike, calculating, self-centered, and even selfish, based on what will be immediately punished or rewarded.

predatory pricing Practice of charging a very low price for a product with the intent of driving competitors out of business or out of a market.

preindustrial society Society characterized by economic and social change and the emergence of a rising middle class with an entrepreneurial spirit.

premium Extra item offered to the consumer, usually in exchange for some proof of purchase of the promoted product.

prepared sales presentation Structured, or canned, sales pitch.

price Perceived value of a good or service.

price bundling Marketing two or more products in a single package for a special price.

price discrimination Practice of charging different prices to different customers for the same product.

price fixing Agreement between two or more firms on the price they will charge for a product.

price lining Practice of offering a product line with several items at specific price points.

price policy Initial price for a product and the intended direction for price movements over the product life cycle.

price shading Use of discounts by salespeople to increase demand for one or more products in a line.

price skimming Pricing policy whereby a firm charges a high introductory price, often coupled with heavy promotion.

primary data Information collected for the first time and used to solve a particular problem.

primary membership group Reference group with which people interact regularly in an informal, face-to-face manner, such as family, friends, or fellow employees.

private brand Brand name that a wholesaler or a retailer uses for products it sells.

private warehouse Storage facility either leased or owned by a company that needs to store a large amount of its own merchandise.

proactive management Practice of altering the marketing mix to fit newly emerging economic, social, and competitive trends.

probability sample Sample drawn from a population characterized by every element having a known nonzero probability of being selected.

problem child (question mark) In the portfolio matrix, a business unit that shows rapid growth but poor profit margins.

problem recognition Result of an imbalance between actual and desired states.

processed material Good used directly in manufacturing other products.

producer segment That part of the business-to-business market consisting of individuals and organizations that buy goods and services to use in producing other products, incorporating into other products, or facilitating the organization's daily operations.

product Everything, both favorable and unfavorable, that a person receives in an exchange—for example, a good, a service, or an idea.

product advertising Form of advertising that touts the benefits of a specific good or service.

product category All brands that satisfy a particular type of need.

product development Marketing strategy that entails the creation of new products for present markets; process of converting applications for new technologies into marketable products.

product differentiation Marketing tactic designed to distinguish one firm's products from those of competitors.

product item Specific version of a product that can be designated as a distinct offering among an organization's products.

product life cycle Concept describing a product's acceptance in the marketplace over four stages: introduction, growth, maturity, and decline.

product line Group of closely related products offered by the organization.

product line depth Number of product items in a product line.

product line pricing Setting prices for an entire line of products.

product manager Person who is responsible for several brands within a product line or product group.

product mix All the products that an organization sells.

product mix consistency Extent to which product lines are similar in terms of end use, distribution outlets used, target markets, and price range.

product mix width Number of product lines that an organization offers.

product modification Change in one or more of a product's characteristics—for example, its quality, functional characteristics, or style.

product-review committee Group of high-level executives—representing the marketing, production, and finance departments—appointed to review products for elimination from a company's product line.

production orientation Philosophy that focuses on the internal capabilities of the firm rather than on the desires and needs of the marketplace.

promotion Communication by marketers that informs, persuades, and reminds potential buyers of a product to influence an opinion or elicit a response.

promotional allowance Payment to a dealer for promoting the manufacturer's products.

promotional mix Combination of promotional tools—including advertising, personal selling, sales promotion, and public relations—used to reach the target market and fulfill the organization's overall goals.

promotional plan Carefully arranged sequence of promotions designed around a common theme and geared to specific objectives.

promotional strategy Plan for the optimal use of the elements of promotion: advertising, personal selling, sales promotion, and public relations.

Protestant work ethic Set of principles that stress hard work, dedication to family, and frugality.

profit impact of market strategy (PIMS) Analyzing strategic alternatives by consulting a database program that summarizes the financial and market performance of 3,000 strategic business units of more than 450 firms.

profit maximization Pricing method that sets price where marginal revenue equals marginal cost.

profit Revenue minus expenses.

psychographic segmentation Method of dividing markets based on personality, motives, lifestyle, and geodemographics.

psychographics Analysis technique used to examine consumer lifestyles and to categorize consumers.

public relations Marketing function that evaluates public attitudes, identifies areas within the organization that the public may be interested in, and executes a program of action to earn public understanding and acceptance.

public service advertisement (PSA) Announcement that promotes programs, activities, or services of federal, state, or local governments or the programs, activities, or services of nonprofit organizations.

public warehouse Independently owned storage facility that stores merchandise for others; may specialize in certain types of products, such as furniture, refrigerated foods, or household goods.

publicity Public information about a company, good, or service appearing in the mass media as a news item.

pull strategy Marketing strategy that stimulates consumer demand to obtain product distribution.

pulsing media schedule Media scheduling strategy that uses continuous scheduling during the best sale periods and a flighted schedule at other times.

purchasing contract Agreement in which a business buyer promises to purchase a given amount of a product within a specified period.

purely competitive market Form of economic competition characterized by a large number of sellers marketing a standardized product to a group of buyers who are well informed about the marketplace.

push strategy Marketing strategy that uses aggressive personal selling and trade advertising to convince a wholesaler or a retailer to carry and sell particular merchandise.

pyramid of corporate social responsibility Theory that suggests corporate social responsibility is composed of economic, legal, ethical, and philanthropic responsibilities and that the firm's economic performance supports the entire structure.

Q

quality function deployment (QFD) Technique that helps companies translate customer requirements into product specifications by using a quality matrix that relates what customers want with how products will be designed.

quality modification Change in a product's dependability or durability.

quantity discount Price reduction offered to buyers buying in multiple units or above a specified dollar amount.

quota Limit on the amount of a specific product that can enter a country; statement of sales objectives, usually based on sales volume alone but sometimes including key accounts (those with greatest potential), new accounts, and specific products.

R

rack jobber Full-service wholesaler that performs the merchant wholesaler's functions and some usually carried out by the retailer, such as stocking shelves.

random error Error that occurs because the selected sample is an imperfect representation of the overall population.

random sample Type of probability sample in which every element of the population has an equal chance of being selected as part of the sample.

raw material Unprocessed extractive or agricultural product, such as mineral ore, lumber, wheat, corn, fruits, vegetables, and fish.

reach Number of target consumers exposed to a commercial at least once during a specific period, usually four weeks.

reactive management Practice of waiting for change to have a major impact on the firm before deciding to take action.

real self-image Way an individual actually perceives himself or herself.

rebate Cash refund given for the purchase of a product during a specific period.

recall objective Promotional objective aimed at increasing the percentage of the target market that can recall the campaign's message and the product.

receiver Person who decodes a message.

recession Period of economic activity when income, production, and employment tend to fall.

reciprocity Practice in which business purchasers choose to buy from their own customers.

reference group Group in society that influences an individual's purchasing behavior.

referral Recommendation from a customer or business associate.

regression Sales forecasting technique that defines a relationship between past sales (a dependent variable) and one or more independent variables.

relationship marketing Strategy of developing strong customer loyalty by creating satisfied customers who will buy additional services from the firm; strategy of forging long-term partnerships with customers.

reminder objective Promotional objective used to cue the consumer that the product is available.

reorder point Inventory level that signals when more inventory should be ordered.

repetition Promotional strategy in which advertising messages are spread over time, rather than clustered at one time, in order to increase learning.

repositioning Changing consumers' perceptions of a brand in relation to competing brands.

research design Outline of which research questions must be answered, where and when data will be gathered, and how the data will be analyzed.

reseller market That part of the business-to-business market consisting of retail and wholesale businesses that buy finished goods and resell them for a profit.

response function Graphed relationship between a marketing mix (or component of the mix) and sales to a specific market target.

retailer Firm that sells mainly to consumers.

retailing All activities directly related to the sale of goods and services to the ultimate consumer for personal, nonbusiness use or consumption.

retailing mix Combination of the six P's—price, place, product, promotion, personnel, and presentation—to sell goods and services to the ultimate customer.

revenue Price charged to customers multiplied by the number of units sold.

revenue-oriented pricing Setting prices at a level that will maximize the surplus of income over expenditures.

reverse channel Distribution channel in which products move from consumer back to producer.

routine response behavior Type of decision making exhibited by consumers buying frequently purchased, low-cost goods and services; requires little search and decision time.

S

safety stock Extra merchandise kept on hand to protect against running out of stock.

sales force composite Sales forecasting technique that surveys the sales force.

sales forecast Estimate of a firm's future sales or revenues for a specified period.

sales orientation Philosophy that assumes buyers resist purchasing items that are not essential.

sales presentation Face-to-face explanation of a product's benefits to a prospective buyer.

sales promotion Marketing activities—other than personal selling, advertising, and public relations—that stimulate consumer buying and dealer effectiveness; offer of a short-term incentive in order to induce the purchase of a particular good or service.

sales territory Particular geographic area assigned to a salesperson.

sample Subset for interviewing drawn from a larger population.

sampling error Error that occurs when a sample is not representative of the target population in some way.

satisficer Type of business customer that places an order with the first familiar supplier to satisfy product and delivery requirements.

scaled-response question Closed-ended question designed to measure the intensity of a respondent's answer.

scrambled merchandising Practice of offering a wide variety of nontraditional goods and services in one store.

screening Stage in the product development process that eliminates ideas inconsistent with the organization's new product strategy or obviously inappropriate for some other reason.

search quality Characteristic that can be easily assessed before purchase.

seasonal discount Price reduction offered to buyers purchasing merchandise out of season.

seasonal media schedule Media scheduling strategy that runs advertising only during times of the year when the product is most likely to be used.

secondary data Data previously collected for any purpose other than the one at hand.

secondary membership group Reference group with which people associate less consistently and more formally than a primary membership group, such as a club, professional group, or religious group.

segmentation base (variable) Characteristic of individuals, groups, or organizations used as a basis for dividing a market into segments.

selective distortion Process whereby a consumer changes or distorts information that conflicts with his or her feelings or beliefs.

selective distribution Form of distribution achieved by screening dealers to eliminate all but a few in any single area.

selective exposure Process whereby a consumer notices certain stimuli and ignores other stimuli.

selective retention Process whereby a consumer remembers only that information that supports his or her personal beliefs.

self-concept How a consumer perceives himself or herself in terms of attitudes, perceptions, beliefs, and self-evaluations.

selling agent Intermediary used mostly by small firms on a commission basis and contracted to sell the manufacturer's entire output.

sender Originator of the message in the communication process.

service Product in the form of an activity or a benefit provided to consumers, with four unique characteristics that distinguish it from a good: intangibility, inseparability, heterogeneity, and perishability.

service mark Trademark for a service.

shopping product Product that requires comparison shopping, because it is usually more expensive than a convenience product and found in fewer stores.

silent close Technique of ending a sales presention by saying nothing and waiting for the prospect to make a response.

simulated (laboratory) market test Presentation of advertising and other promotional materials for several products, including a test product, to members of the product's target market.

single-price tactic Policy of offering all goods and services at the same price.

single-source research System for gathering information from a single group of respondents by continuously monitoring the advertising, promotion, and pricing they are exposed to and the things they buy.

situation analysis Extensive background investigation into a particular marketing problem.

social class Group of people who are considered nearly equal in status or community esteem, who regularly socialize among themselves both formally and informally, and who share behavioral norms.

social cost Cost not directly paid for by individual consumers but borne by society as a whole.

social marketing Application of marketing methods to spread socially beneficial ideas or behaviors.

socialization process How cultural values and norms are passed down to children.

societal marketing concept Idea that an organization exists not only to satisfy customer wants and needs and to meet organizational objectives but also to preserve or enhance individuals' and society's long-term best interests.

spatial discrepancy Difference between the location of the producer and the location of widely scattered markets.

specialty merchandise wholesaler Wholesaler that offers part of a product line to target customers but in greater depth than general merchandise wholesalers offer.

specialty product Product for which consumers search extensively and are very reluctant to accept substitutes.

specialty store Retail store specializing in a given type of merchandise.

standard industrial classification (SIC) system Detailed numbering system developed by the U.S. government in order to classify business and government organizations by their main economic activity.

standing-room-only close Technique of ending a sales presention that urges customers to buy right away because the product is selling so well it may not be available later.

star In the portfolio matrix, a business unit that is a market leader and growing fast.

statistical quality control (SQC) Method of analyzing deviations in manufactured materials, parts, and products.

status quo pricing Pricing objective that seeks to maintain existing prices or simply meet the competition.

stimulus Any unit of input affecting the five senses: sight, smell, taste, touch, hearing.

stimulus discrimination Learned ability to differentiate among stimuli.

stimulus generalization Form of learning that occurs when one response is extended to a second stimulus similar to the first.

stimulus-response approach Sales pitch applying the concept that a given stimulus will produce a given response.

stitching niches Combining ethnic, age, income, and lifestyle markets on some common basis to form a mass market.

stockout cost Cost of being out of stock, which includes direct costs due to lost sales and indirect costs due to the loss of dissatisfied customers.

straight commission Method of compensation in which the salesperson is paid some percentage of sales.

straight rebuy Situation in which the purchaser reorders the same goods and/or services without looking for new information or investigating other suppliers.

straight salary Method of compensation in which the salesperson receives a salary regardless of sales productivity.

strategic alliance Cooperative agreement between business firms, taking the form of a licensing or distribution agreement, joint venture, research and development consortium, or partnership.

strategic business unit Subgroup in a larger organization, with a distinct mission and specific target market of its own, control over its resources, its own competitors, and plans independent of the other subgroups of the total organization.

strategic channel alliance Producers' agreement to jointly use one's already-established channel.

strategic planning Managerial process of creating and maintaining a fit between the organization's objectives and resources and evolving market opportunities.

style modification Aesthetic product change rather than a quality or functional change.

subculture Homogeneous group of people who share elements of the overall culture as well as unique elements of their own group.

summative close Technique of ending a sales presentation that summarizes the product's benefits and asks for the sale.

supermarket Large, departmentalized, self-service retailer that specializes in foodstuffs and a few nonfood items.

supply Consumable item that does not become part of the final product; quantity of a product that will be offered to the market by a supplier, or suppliers, at various prices for a specified period.

survey research Technique for gathering primary data in which a researcher interacts with people to obtain facts, opinions, and attitudes.

T

takeoff economy Period of transition from a developing to a developed nation, during which new industries arise.

target market Group of people or organizations for which an organization designs, implements, and maintains a marketing mix intended to meet the needs of that group or groups, resulting in mutually satisfying exchanges.

target return on investment (ROI) Profit objective calculated by dividing a firm's net profits after taxes by its total assets.

target return pricing Pricing method that sets price where revenues from sales of a targeted quantity yield the target return on investment.

tariff Tax levied on the goods entering a country.

team selling Practice of selling to business-to-business customers by assembling a team of experts who share the specialized knowledge of key buying influences within customer firms.

technical specialist Salesperson with a technical background who works out the details of custom-made products and communicates directly with the potential buyer's technical staff.

telemarketing Type of personal selling conducted over the telephone.

temporal discrepancy Difference between when a product is produced and when a consumer is ready to buy it.

test marketing Stage in the product development process during which a product is introduced in a limited way to determine the reactions of potential customers in a market situation.

time management Efficient allocation of time to tasks, based on their priority and urgency.

total quality management (TQM) Coordination, throughout the entire organization, of efforts to provide high-quality products, processes, and services in order to ensure customer satisfaction.

trade agreement Agreement to stimulate international trade.

trade allowance Price reduction offered by manufacturers to intermediaries, such as wholesalers and retailers.

trade deficit Excess of imports over exports.

trade loading Practice of temporarily lowering the price to induce wholesalers and retailers to buy more goods than can be sold in a reasonable time.

trademark Legal, exclusive right to use a product brand name or other identifying mark.

traditional society Largely agricultural society, with a social structure and value system that provide little opportunity for upward mobility.

truck jobber Limited-service merchant wholesaler that performs the functions of salesperson and delivery person.

two-part pricing Price tactic that charges two separate amounts to consume a single good or service.

U

unbundling Reducing the bundle of services that comes with the basic product.

undifferentiated targeting strategy Marketing approach based on the assumption that the market has no individual segments and thus requires a single marketing mix.

unfair trade practice act State law, passed in over half the states, that prohibits wholesalers and retailers from selling below cost.

uniform delivered pricing Price tactic in which the seller pays the actual freight charges and bills every purchaser an identical, flat freight charge.

unique selling proposition Desirable, exclusive, and believable advertising appeal selected as the theme for a campaign.

unitary elasticity Situation in which an increase in sales exactly offsets a decrease in price so that total revenue remains the same.

United Europe Agreement among members of the European Community to standardize business-related rules and reduce trade barriers.

unitization Increasing the efficiency of handling small packages by grouping boxes on a pallet or skid for movement from one place to another.

universal product code (UPC) Series of thick and thin vertical lines, readable by computerized optical scanners, that represent numbers used to track products; also called bar codes.

universe Population from which a sample is drawn.

unsought product Product unknown to the potential buyer or known product that the buyer does not actively seek.

upward extension Practice of adding to a product line a higher-quality product with more features and options and designed to sell at a higher price.

urgency close Technique of ending a sales presentation that suggests a reason for ordering soon, such as an impending price increase.

usage rate Rate at which a product is sold or consumed.

usage rate segmentation Method of dividing markets based on the amount of product bought or consumed.

V

value Enduring belief that a specific mode of conduct is personally or socially preferable to another mode of conduct; relationship between what customers get and what they give up in exchange.

value engineering Systematic search for less expensive substitute goods or services.

value marketing Offering the target market a high-quality product at a fair price and with good service.

Values and Lifestyles (VALS) program Consumer psychographic segmentation tool, developed by SRI International, that categorizes U.S. consumers by their values, beliefs, and lifestyles.

variable cost Cost that fluctuates with changes in the level of output.

vending Form of nonstore retailing that uses vending machines to offer products for sale.

vendor analysis Practice of comparing alternative suppliers in terms of attributes that the buying center views as important.

venture team Entrepreneurial, market-oriented group staffed by a small number of representatives from different disciplines.

vertical marketing system (VMS) Network of producers and intermediaries acting as a unified system.

W

want Recognition of an unfulfilled need and a product that will satisfy it.

warehouse club Limited-service merchant wholesaler that sells a limited selection of brand name appliances, household items, and groceries on a cash-and-carry basis to members, usually small businesses and groups.

warranty Guarantee of the quality or performance of a good or service.

wholesaler Firm that sells mainly to producers, resellers, governments, institutions, and retailers.

workload approach Method of determining sales force size based on dividing the total time required to cover the territory by the selling time available to one salesperson.

Z

zone pricing Modification of uniform delivered pricing that divides the United States (or the total market) into segments or zones and charges a flat freight rate to all customers in a given zone.

ENDNOTES

Chapter 1

1. Joyce Anne Oliver, "Xerox Marketing Exec Is Still a Sales Rep at Heart," *Marketing News,* 17 September 1990, p. 10; "The Rebirthing of Xerox," *Marketing Insights,* Summer 1992, pp. 73–80.
2. Peter D. Bennett, *Dictionary of Marketing Terms* (Chicago: American Marketing Association, 1988), p. 115.
3. Philip Kotler, *Marketing Management,* 7th ed. (Englewood Cliffs, NJ: Prentice-Hall, 1991), p. 7.
4. "Smart Selling: How Companies Are Winning Over Today's Tougher Customer," *Business Week,* 3 August 1992, pp. 46–48.
5. "Customers Must Be Pleased, Not Just Satisfied," *Business Week,* 3 August 1992, p. 52.
6. Amanda Bennett and Carol Hymowitz, "For Customers, More Than Lip Service," *Wall Street Journal,* 6 October 1989, p. B1.
7. Susan Caminiti, "The New Champs of Retailing," *Fortune,* 24 September 1990, p. 98.
8. "Smart Selling," p. 46.
9. Caminiti, "New Champs," p. 98.
10. "American Express: Service That Sells," *Fortune,* 20 November 1989, p. 84.
11. Sharyn Hunt and Ernest F. Cooke, "It's Basic but Necessary: Listen to the Customer," *Marketing News,* 5 March 1990, p. 23.
12. "Flexible Work Arrangements Continue to Find a Home at Companies," *Wall Street Journal,* 19 January 1993, p. A1.
13. "King Customer," *Business Week,* 12 March 1990, p. 9.
14. Bennett and Humowitz, p. B1.
15. Cyndee Miller, "Theaters Give 'Em More Than Goobers to Win Back Viewers," *Marketing News,* 1 October 1990, pp. 1, 20.
16. "King Customer," p. 89.
17. "Smart Selling," p. 48.
18. Susan Caminiti, "Finding New Ways to Sell More," *Fortune,* 27 July 1992, pp. 100–103.
19. Kotler, pp. 22–25.
20. "King Customer," p. 90.
21. Ajay K. Kohli and Bernard J. Jaworski, "Marketing Orientation: The Construct, Research Propositions, and Managerial Implications," *Journal of Marketing,* April 1990, pp. 1–18.
22. Francene Schwadel, "Nordstrom's Push East Will Test Its Renown for the Best in Science," *Wall Street Journal,* 1 August 1989, pp. A1, A4.
23. Cyndee Miller, "Nordstrom Is Tops in Survey," *Marketing News,* 15 February 1993, p. 12.
24. "The Rebirthing of Xerox," *Marketing Insights,* Summer 1992, pp. 73–80.
25. "King Customer," p. 91.
26. N. W. Pope, "More Mickey Mouse Marketing," *American Banker,* 12 September 1979, p. 54.
27. Thomas J. Watson, Jr., *A Business and Its Beliefs* (New York: McGraw-Hill, 1963), p. 3.

Chapter 2

1. William O'Hare, "In the Black," *American Demographics,* November 1989, pp. 25–29.
2. O'Hare, pp. 25–29.
3. "No 'Me Too' for These Two," *Marketing News,* 14 May 1990, pp. 1, 10.
4. "Welcome to the Age of 'Unpositioning,'" *Marketing News,* 16 April 1990, p. 11.
5. "The U.S. Mood: Ever Optimistic," *Fortune,* 26 March 1990, pp. 19–26.
6. Lynn Kahle, Basil Porilos, and Ajay Sukdial, "Changes in Social Values in the United States during the Past Decade," *Journal of Advertising Research,* February-March 1989, pp. 35–41.
7. "'90s Values: More Than Money, Less Than Perfect," *Money,* Fall 1988, p. 4.
8. "The Microwave Cooks Up a New Way of Life," *Wall Street Journal,* 19 September 1989, p. B1.
9. "How to Deal with Tough Customers," *Fortune,* 3 December 1990, pp. 38–48.
10. "Shades of Green," *Wall Street Journal,* 2 August 1991, pp. A1, A8.
11. "Will Consumers Ever Buy Again?" *Brand Week,* 27 July 1992, p. 36.
12. "Trading Fat Paychecks for Free Time," *Wall Street Journal,* 5 August 1991, p. B1.
13. "Working Hard at Play," *AdWeek's Marketing Week,* 20 January 1992, p. 12.
14. "Work Force 2005," *American Demographics,* May 1992, p. 59.
15. "This Bud's for You. No, Not You—Her," *Business Week,* 4 November 1991, p. 86.
16. "Snapshots of the Nation," *Wall Street Journal,* 9 March 1990, pp. R12–R13.
17. "Shrinking Markets," *Wall Street Journal,* 8 March 1990, p. R29.
18. "Shrinking Markets," p. R29.
19. Ruth Hamel, "Raging against Aging," *American Demographics,* March 1990, pp. 42–45.
20. Hamel, pp. 42–45; see also "New Study on Today's Maturity Market," *Service Marketing Newsletter,* Summer 1990, p. 3.

21. "How Big Will the Older Market Be?" *Marketing Demographics,* June 1990, pp. 30–36.
22. Michael Major, "Promoting to the Mature Market," *Promo,* November 1990, p. 7.
23. "Baby-Boomers May Seek Age-Friendly Stores," *Wall Street Journal,* 1 July 1992, p. B1.
24. "Changing Times," *Wall Street Journal,* 22 March 1991, p. B6.
25. "Home Alone—with $660 Billion," *Business Week,* 29 July 1991, pp. 76–77.
26. "Home Alone," pp. 76–77.
27. "Home Alone," pp. 76–77.
28. "Forever Single," *Adweek's Marketing Week,* 15 October 1991, p. 20.
29. "Americans on the Move," *American Demographics,* June 1990, pp. 46–48.
30. "Snapshots of the Nation," p. R12.
31. Louis Richman, "Why the Middle Class Is Anxious," *Fortune,* 21 May 1990, pp. 106–109.
32. "The Baby Boomlet Is for Real," *Fortune,* 10 February 1992, p. 104.
33. "The Incredible Shrinking Middle Class," *American Demographics,* May 1992, pp. 37–38.
34. Bob Arnold, "On Outfoxing Recessions," *Marketing Times,* January-February 1980, p. 11.
35. "Closing the Innovation Gap," *Fortune,* 2 December 1991, pp. 56–62.
36. "Report on R&D Spending Hints at Loss of U.S. Competitive Strength," *Marketing News,* 22 June 1992, pp. 1, 8.
37. "Report on R&D Spending," pp. 1, 8.
38. "Closing the Innovation Gap," p. 57.
39. "Report on R&D Spending," p. 8.
40. "Closing the Innovation Gap," p. 58; see also "On a Clear Day You Can See Progress," *Business Week,* 29 June 1992, pp. 104–105.
41. "Closing the Innovation Gap," p. 58.
42. Daniel Burrus, "A Glimpse of the Future," *Managing Your Career,* Spring 1991, pp. 6, 10.
43. "Procter & Gamble: On a Short Leash," *Business Week,* 22 July 1991, p. 76.
44. "Washington Cracks Another Whip against Misleading Claims," *Adweek's Marketing Week,* 20 May 1991, p. 7.
45. "Cereal Giants Battle over Market Share," *Wall Street Journal,* 16 December 1991, p. B1.
46. "Sindy vs. Barbie in Court: Are They Twins?" *WE/MBI,* 13–26 July 1992, p. 1.

Chapter 3

1. Michael Czinkota and Ilkka Ron Kainen, "Global Marketing 2000: A Marketing Survival Guide," *Marketing Management,* Winter 1992, pp. 37–43.
2. William J. Holstein, "The Stateless Corporation," *Business Week,* 14 May 1990, pp. 98–105.
3. Bruce Hager, "Can colgate Import Its Success from Overseas?" *Business Week,* 7 May 1990, pp. 114–116.
4. "International Experience Will Be Essential for Business Leaders of Tomorrow: Comentary by Lester Pullen," *Marketing News,* 10 December 1988, p. 14.
5. Edmund Faltermayer, "Is 'Made in the U.S.A.' Fading Away?" *Fortune,* 24 September 1990, pp. 62–73.
6. U.S. Department of Commerce, International Trade Administration, *U.S. Trade Performance in 1990, 1991* (Washington, DC: Government Printing Office, 1991).
7. U.S. Central Intelligence Agency, *The World Fact Book* (Washington, DC: Government Printing Office, 1990), p. 325; U.S. Department of Commerce, Bureau of the Census, *Statistical Abstract of the United States* (Washington, DC: Government Printing Office, 1991), p. 805.
8. U.S. Central Intelligence Agency, p. 325; U.S. Department of Commerce, p. 805.
9. U.S. Department of Commerce, p. 805.
10. Jeremy Main, "Manufacturing the Right Way," *Fortune,* 21 May 1990, p. 54–64.
11. Edward O. Wells, "Being There," *Inc.,* September 1990, pp. 143–145.
12. Neil Jacoby, "The Multinational Corporation," *Center Magazine,* May 1970, p. 37.
13. Robert Reich, "Who Is Them?" *Harvard Business Review,* March-April 1991, pp. 77–89.
14. "The Stateless Corporation," *Business Week,* 14 May 1990, pp. 98–105.
15. Theodore Levitt, "The Globalization of Markets," *Harvard Business Review,* May-June 1983, pp. 92–102.
16. Saeed Samiee and Kendall Roth, "The Influence of Global Marketing Standardization on Performance," *Journal of Marketing,* April 1992, pp. 1–17; see also James Willis, Coskun Samli, and Laurence Jacobs, "Developing Global Products and Marketing Strategies: A Construct and a Research Agenda," *Journal of the Academy of Marketing Science,* Winter 1991, pp. 1–10.
17. Adam Snyder, "Global Marketing: We Are the World," *Superbrands 1990: A Special Supplement to Adweek,* August 1990, pp. 59–68.
18. M. Katherine Glover, "Do's and Taboos: Cultural Aspects of International Business," *Business America,* 13 August 1990, pp. 2–6.
19. "How Motorola Took Asia by the Tail," *Business Week,* 11 November 1991, p. 68.
20. Fred S. Worthey, "A New Mass Market Emerges," *Fortune: Special Issue,* Fall 1990, pp. 51–57.
21. Igor Reichlin, "Crash Course in Capitalism for Ivan the Globetrotter," *Business Week,* 28 May 1990, pp. 42–44.
22. Kenneth Sheets, "Fields of Russian Dreams," *U.S. News & World Report,* 4 June 1990, p. 59.
23. Linda Robinson, "Daring to Be Different," *U.S. News & World Report,* 7 May 1990, pp. 38–43; see also "The Big Move to Free Markets in Latin America," *Business Week,* 15 June 1992, pp. 50–55.

24. "GATT Talks Résumé with France and India Calling Many of the Shots," *Wall Street Journal,* 13 January 1992, pp. A1, A13.
25. An excerpt from Marie Anchordoguy, "A Brief History of Japan's Keiretsu," *Harvard Business Review,* July-August 1990, pp. 58–59. Reprinted by permission of *Harvard Business Review.* Copyright © 1990 by the President and Fellows of Harvard College. All rights reserved.
26. Robert Cutts, "Capitalism in Japan: Cartels and Keiretsu," *Harvard Business Review,* July-August 1992, pp. 48–50.
27. "U.S. Sees Progress in Talks with Japan, but Seeks More Action on Trade Gap," *Wall Street Journal,* 31 July 1992, p. B2.
28. "Trade Pact Is Likely to Step Up Business Even before Approval," *Wall Street Journal,* 13 August 1992, pp. A1, A10.
29. "A Free-Trade Milestone, with Many More Miles to Go," *Business Week,* 24 August 1992, pp. 30, 31.
30. "Free Trade? They Can Hardly Wait," *Business Week,* 14 September 1992, pp. 24–25.
31. "Free Trade Isn't Painless," *Business Week,* 31 August 1992, pp. 38–39.
32. Bradley Schiller, *The Macro Economy Today,* 5th ed. (New York: McGraw-Hill, 1991), pp. 490–506; "The Global Economy: Who Gets Hurt?" *Business Week,* 10 August 1992, pp. 48–53; "Big Move to Free Markets in Latin America," pp. 50–55; Herbert Baum, "Borderless North America," *Marketing Management,* Winter 1992, pp. 46–48.
33. "Europe's New Populism Could Kill Unification," *Business Week,* 22 June 1992, p. 58; "EC Unity Pact Encounters Major Snags," *Wall Street Journal,* 23 September 1992, p. A12.
34. "In Pursuit of the Elusive Euroconsumer," *Wall Street Journal,* 23 April 1992, pp. B1, B3; "Europe 1992," *Fortune,* 10 August 1992, pp. 136–142.
35. "Making Global Alliances Work," *Fortune,* 17 December 1990, pp. 121–123.
36. Joel Bleeke and David Ernst, "The Way to Win in Cross-Border Alliances," *Harvard Business Review,* November-December 1991, p. 130.
37. "FedEx: Europe Nearly Killed the Messenger," *Business Week,* 25 May 1992, p. 124.
38. "Global Ad Campaigns, after Many Missteps, Finally Pay Dividends," *Wall Street Journal,* 27 August 1992, pp. A1, A8.
39. "Global Ad Campaigns," pp. A1, A8.
40. "When Slogans Go Wrong," *American Demographics,* February 1992, p. 14.
41. "Greeks Protest Coke's Use of Parthenon," *Dallas Morning News,* 17 August 1992, p. 4D.
42. "Now a Glamorous Barbie Heads to Japan," *Wall Street Journal,* 5 June 1991, pp. B1, B8.
43. "Why Countertrade Is Hot," *Fortune,* 29 June 1992, p. 25; Nathaniel Gilbert, "The Case for Countertrade," *Across the Board,* May 1992, pp. 43–45.

Chapter 4

1. Kathleen Deveny, "Reality of the 90's Hits Yuppie Brands," *Wall Street Journal,* 20 December 1990, pp. B1, B4; Janice Castro, "Hunkering Down," *Times,* 23 July 1990, pp. 56–57; Christina Duff, "Gardening Blooms as Baby Boomers Dig into an Environmentally Correct Hobby," *Wall Street Journal,* 11 March 1992, pp. B1, B5.
2. Charles D. Schewe, "Get in Position for the Older Market," *American Demographics,* June 1990, pp. 38–41, 61.
3. Patricia Braus, "The Spending Power of Puerto Rico," *American Demographics,* April 1991, pp. 46–49.
4. Narasimhan Srinivasan and Brian T. Ratchford, "An Empirical Test of a Model of External Search for Automobiles," *Journal of Consumer Research,* September 1991, pp. 223–242.
5. John R. Hauser and Birger Wernerfelt, "An Evaluation Cost Model of Consideration Sets," *Journal of Consumer Research,* March 1990, pp. 393–408.
6. Joe Schwartz, "Educated Consumers Are Suspicious," *American Demographics,* March 1992, p. 14.
7. This section based on Srinivasan and Ratchford, pp. 223–242; Peter D. Bennett and Gilbert Harrell, "The Role of Confidence in Understanding and Predicting Buyers' Attitudes and Purchase Intentions," *Journal of Consumer Research,* September 1975; pp. 110–117; Richard D. Johnson and Irwin Levin, "More Than Meets the Eye: The Effect of Missing Information on Purchase Evaluations," *Journal of Consumer Research,* September 1985, pp. 169–177.
8. William Mueller, "Who Reads the Label?" *American Demographics,* January 1991, pp. 36–41; Marjory Roberts, "Keeping Yogurt Honest," *U.S. News & World Report,* 5 November 1990, p. 76; Christine Moorman, "The Effects of Stimulus and Consumer Characteristics on the Utilization of Nutrition Information," *Journal of Consumer Research,* December 1990, pp. 362–374.
9. Joel Huber and Noreen M. Klein, "Adapting Cutoffs to the Choice Environment: The Effects of Attribute Correlation and Reliability," *Journal of Consumer Research,* December 1991, pp. 346–357.
10. Don Umphrey, "Consumer Costs: A Determinant of Upgrading or Downgrading of Cable Service," *Journalism Quarterly,* Winter 1991, pp. 698–708.
11. Wayne D. Hoyer and Steven P. Brown, "Effects of Brand Awareness on Choice for a Common, Repeat-Purchase Product," *Journal of Consumer Research,* September 1990, pp. 141–149.
12. Gail Tom, "Cueing the Consumer: The Role of Salient Cues in Consumer Perception," *Journal of Consumer Marketing,* Spring 1987, pp. 23–27.
13. Craig A. Kelley, William C. Gaidis, and Peter H. Reingen, "The Use of Vivid Stimuli to Enhance Comprehension of the Content of Product Warning

Messages," *Journal of Consumer Affairs,* Winter 1989, pp. 243–266.

14. Anita M. Busch, "Sexier the Better, Student Body Says," *Advertising Age: Special Report,* 5 February 1990, pp. S1–S2.
15. Tom, pp. 23–27.
16. Nancy Ten Kate, "Brand Names Can Be Prime Assets," *American Demographics,* December 1991, p. 20.
17. Ruth Hamel, "States of Mind," *American Demographics,* April 1992, pp. 40–43.
18. Elizabeth J. Wilson, "Using the Dollarmetric Scale to Establish the Just Meaningful Difference in Price," in *1987 AMA Educators' Proceedings,* ed. Susan Douglas et al. (Chicago: American Marketing Association, 1987), p. 107.
19. "A Precocious Little Beer," *Economist,* 15 June 1991, p. 62.
20. "Buyers Are Choosing Bags before Brakes," *Wall Street Journal,* 10 February 1992, p. B1; see also Steven Waldman, "The Selling of Safety," *Newsweek,* 12 March 1990, pp. 64–65; Joseph Bohn, "'Safety First' Ad Thinking No Longer a Crash Course," *Advertising Age,* 30 March 1992, p. S4.
21. David A. Aaker and Kevin Lane Keller, "Consumer Evaluations of Brand Extension," *Journal of Marketing,* January 1990, pp. 27–41.
22. Ellen R. Foxman, Darrel D. Muehling, and Phil W. Berger, "An Investigation of Factors Contributing to Consumer Brand Confusion," *Journal of Consumer Affairs,* Summer 1990, pp. 170–189; Damon Darlin, "Where Trademarks Are Up for Grabs," *Wall Street Journal,* 5 December 1989, pp. B1, B5.
23. Carrie Dolan, "Levi Tries to Round Up Counterfeiters," *Wall Street Journal,* 19 February 1992, pp. B1, B6.
24. Yumiko Ono, "Land of Rising Fun: With Careful Planning, Japan Sets Out to Be 'Life Style Superpower,'" *Wall Street Journal,* 2 October 1992, pp. A1, A11.
25. Leon G. Schiffman and Elaine Sherman, "Value Orientations of New-Age Elderly: The Coming of an Ageless Market," *Journal of Business Research,* March 1991, pp. 187–194.
26. David M. Gross and Sophfronia Scott, "Proceeding with Caution," *Time,* 16 July 1990, pp. 56–62.
27. Cyndee Miller, "Beef, Pork Industries Have Met the Enemy—and It Is Chicken," *Marketing News,* 5 August 1991, pp. 1, 7.
28. Mark M. Nelson, "Whirlpool Gives Pan-European Approach a Spin," *Wall Street Journal,* 23 April 1992, pp. B1, B3.
29. Beth A. Walker and Jerry C. Olsen, "Means-End Chains: Connecting Products with Self," *Journal of Business Research,* March 1991, pp. 111–118.
30. John W. Schouten, "Selves in Transition: Symbolic Consumption in Personal Rites of Passage and Identity Reconstruction," *Journal of Consumer Research,* March 1991, pp. 412–425.
31. Marc B. Rubner, "The Hearts of New-Car Buyers," *American Demographics,* August 1991, pp. 14–15.
32. Grant McCracken, "Who Is the Celebrity Endorser? Cultural Foundations of the Endorsement Process," *Journal of Consumer Research,* December 1989, pp. 310–321.
33. Diane Crispell, "The Brave New World of Men," *American Demographics,* January 1992, pp. 38–43.
34. Michael B. Menasco and David J. Curry, "Utility and Choice: An Empirical Study of Wife/Husband Decision Making," *Journal of Consumer Research,* June 1989, pp. 87–97.
35. Ellen R. Foxman, Patyria S. Tansuhaj, and Karin M. Ekstrom, "Family Members' Perception of Adolescents' Influence in Family Decision Making," *Journal of Consumer Research,* March 1989, pp. 482–491.
36. James U. McNeal, "The Littlest Consumers," *American Demographics,* February 1992, pp. 48–53; "The Littlest Advisors," *American Demographics,* April 1990, pp. 14–15.
37. Robin A. Douthitt and Joanne M. Fedyk, "Family Composition, Parental Time, and Market Goods: Life Cycle Trade-Offs," *Journal of Consumer Affairs,* Summer 1990, pp. 110–133; Robin a. Douthitt and Joanne M. Fedyk, "The Influence of Children on Family Life Cycle Spending Behavior: Theory and Applications," *Journal of Consumer Affairs,* Winter 1988, pp. 220–248.
38. Alix M. Freedman, "Amid Ghetto Hunger, Many More Suffer Eating Wrong Foods," *Wall Street Journal,* 18 December 1990, pp. A1, A8.
39. Richard Turner and Peter Gumbel, "Major Attraction: As Euro Disney Braces for Its Grand Opening, the French Go Goofy," *Wall Street Journal,* 10 April 1992, pp. A1, A8.
40. Martha Farnsworth Riche, "We're All Minorities Now," *American Demographics,* October 1991, pp. 26–34; William A. Henry III, "Beyond the Melting Pot," *Time,* 9 april 1990, pp. 28–31.
41. Jose de Cordoba, "One Newspaper Finds Way to Lure Readers: Publish in Spanish," *Wall Street Journal,* 23 April 1992, pp. A1, A8.
42. Cyndee Miller, "'Hot' Asian-American Market Not Starting Much of a Fire Yet," *Marketing News,* 21 January 1991, p. 12.

Chapter 5

1. Michael D. Hutt and Thomas W. Speh, *Business Marketing,* 4th Ed. (Fort Worth, TX: Dryden Press, 1992), p. 3.
2. U.S. Department of Commerce, Bureau of the Census, *Statistical Abstract of the United States* (Washington, DC: Government Printing Office, 1990), pp. 771, 772, 780.
3. *Selling to Government Markets: Local, State, and Federal* (Cleveland: Government Product News, 1991), p. 1.

4. Larry C. Giunipers, William Crittenden, and Vicky Crittenden, "Industrial Marketing in Non-Profit Organizations," *Industrial Marketing Management,* 19 (1990), p. 279.
5. Robert W. Haas, *Business Marketing Management* (Boston: PWS-Kent, 1992), p. 16.
6. Haas, p. 16.
7. Tom Stundza, "Metal Cans: Lusting for Market Share," *Purchasing,* 22 February 1990, pp. 61–64.
8. Jim Mele, "Leasing: Preparing for the 1990s," *Business Week,* 19 March 1990, pp. 23–32.
9. Frank G. Bingham, Jr., and Barney T. Raffield III, *Business to Business Marketing Management* (Homewood, IL: Richard D. Irwin, 1990), p. 12.
10. Bridget O'Brian, "Airlines' Ailments Give Most of Their Suppliers Big Headaches as Well," *Wall Street Journal,* 31 December 1991, p. A1.
11. Bradley Johnson, "The Preferred Chip," *Advertising Age,* 7 October 1991, p. 22.
12. "Body-Part Heat: Ford vs. the Independents," *Business Week,* 17 December 1990, p. 30.
13. Cited in Philip Kotler, *Marketing Management,* 7th ed. (Englewood Cliffs, NJ: Prentice-Hall, 1991), p. 201.
14. Haas, pp. 196–197.
15. Steven Volder Haas, "Contract Bold Step for EDS," *Fort Worth Star-Telegram,* 18 December 1991, p. 1.
16. Tom Hayes, "Using Customer Satisfaction Research to Get Closer to the Customers," *Marketing News,* 4 January 1993, p. 22.
17. James Brien Quinn, Thomas L. Doorley, and Penny C. Paquette, "Beyond Products: Services Based Strategy," *Harvard Business Review,* March-April 1990, pp. 58–60, 64–67.
18. Kevin T. Higgins, "Business Marketers Make Customer Service Job for All," *Marketing News,* 30 January 1989, pp. 1–2.
19. Kevin T. Higgins, "Service to Small Customers Builds Safety-Kleen into a Big Business," *Marketing News,* 30 January 1989, p. 2.
20. "Ford, Citibank Launch Card," *Marketing News,* 15 March 1993, p. 1; Terry Lefton, "Ford Forays into Citi Card Charge," *Brandweek,* 15 February 1993, p. 2.
21. Haas, p. 72.
22. Hutt and Speh, p. 265.
23. Paul Ingrassla and Asra Q. Nomani, "Some Fear a Backlash as Detroit Prepares Charges against Japan," *Wall Street Journal,* 8 February 1993, pp. A1, A4.
24. Karen Lowry Miller and James B. Treece, "The Partners," *Business Week,* 10 February 1992, p. 103.

Chapter 6

1. *Wall Street Journal,* 2 August 1990, p. A1.
2. John Morton, "How to Spot the Really Important Prospects," *Business Marketing,* January 1990, p. 62.
3. Subrata N. Chakravarty, "A Credit Card Is Not a Commodity," *Forbes,* 16 October 1989, pp. 128–130.
4. Dwight J. Shelton, "Regional Marketing Works and Is Here to Stay," *Marketing News,* 6 November 1987, pp. 1, 25.
5. Cara Appelbaum, "Forget about Global, Coke's Gone Texas," *Adweek's Marketing Week,* 9 March 1991, p. 10.
6. Kathy Thacker, "Coke Woos Texas with Major Push," *Adweek's Marketing Week,* 15 April 1991, pp. 1, 4.
7. "Getting 'Em while They're Young," *Business Week,* 9 September 1991, p. 94.
8. "Those Little Kids Have Big Pockets," *Wall Street Journal,* 26 August 1992, p. B1.
9. Carrie Goerne, "Marketers Try to Get More Creative in Reaching Teens," *Marketing News,* 15 August 1991, p. 2.
10. Fara Warner, "Kidfood," *Adweek's Marketing Week,* 16 December 1991, p. 20.
11. "How Spending Changes during Middle Age," *Wall Street Journal,* 14 January 1992, p. B1.
12. Geoffrey Smith, "Does Gillette Know How to Treat a Lady?" *Business Week,* 27 August 1990, p. 64.
13. Laura Zinn, "This Bud's for You. No, Not You—Her," *Business Week,* 4 November 1991, p. 86.
14. Cynthia Owens, "Citibank Assumes a Starring Role in Asia," *Wall Street Journal,* 2 August 1990, p. A8.
15. Jan Larson, "Reaching Downscale Markets," *American Demographics,* November 1991, pp. 38–40, 52.
16. Michael J. McCarthy, "Marketers Zero In on Their Consumers," *Wall Street Journal,* 18 March 1991, p. B1.
17. Raymond Serafin and Cleveland Horton, "Buick Ads Target ZIP Codes," *Advertising Age,* 1 April 1991, p. 1.
18. "Smoking Out the Elusive Smoker," *Business Week,* 16 March 1992, pp. 62–63.
19. *VALS 2: Your Marketing Edge for the 1990s* (Menlo Park, CA: SRI International).
20. Martha Farnsworth Riche, "Psychographics for the 1990s," *American Demographics,* July 1989, p. 30.
21. "Stalking the New Consumer," *Business Week,* 28 August 1989, p. 56.
22. Judith Waldrop, "More Toys for Girls and Boys," *American Demographics,* December 1991, p. 4.
23. Thomas Exter, "Boozing Boomers," *American Demographics,* December 1991, p. 6.
24. Bickley Townsend, "Market Research That Matters," *American Demographics,* August 1992, pp. 58–60.
25. "Hot Spots," *Business Week,* 19 October 1992, pp. 80–88.
26. "American Express Pulls Trigger with New Ads," *Marketing News,* 4 March 1991, p. 4.
27. Much of the material in this section based on Michael D. Hutt and Thomas W. Speh, *Business*

Marketing Management, 4th ed. (Hinsdale, IL: Dryden Press, 1992), pp. 170–180.

28. John H. Taylor, "Niche Player," *Forbes*, 1 April 1991, p. 70.
29. Jeffrey A. Tannenbaum, "Tiny Company Elevates an Idea to a Marketable Product, *Wall Street Journal*, 5 July 1990, p. B4.
30. "New Hershey Bar," *Wall Street Journal*, 27 February 1990, p. B1.
31. "Mr. Maybelline Gives Cover Girl the Edge," *Adweek's Marketing Week*, 22 October 1990, pp. 6–8.
32. Cyndee Miller, "Jeans Marketers Look for Good Fit with Older Men and Women," *Marketing News*, 16 September 1991, pp. 1, 6.
33. Bradley Johnson, "Carnival Cruise Line Beckons Hispanics," *Advertising Age*, 25 January 1993, p. 46.
34. David L. Rados, *Marketing for Nonprofit Organizations* (Boston: Auburn House, 1981), p. 93.
35. Richard Brunelli, "Data Prompts Coors to Cap Dry Beer Plans for Now," *Adweek*, 14 May 1990, p. 6.
36. Cyndee Miller, "Theaters Give 'Em More Than Goobers to Win Back Viewers," *Marketing News*, 1 October 1990, pp. 1, 20.
37. Laura Bird, "Major Brands Look for the Kosher Label," *Adweek's Marketing Week*, 1 April 1991, pp. 18–19.
38. Al Ries and Jack Trout, *Positioning: The Battle for Your Mind* (New York: McGraw-Hill, 1981), pp. 66–67.
39. Jesse Snyder, "4 GM Car Divisions Are Repositioned in Effort to Help Sales," *Automotive News*, 15 September 1986, p. 49.
40. "Shirley Young: Pushing GM's Humble-Pie Strategy," *Business Week*, 11 June 1990, p. 52.
41. These examples provided by David W. Cravens, Texas Christian University.
42. Pat Sloan, "New Toothpaste Ready," *Advertising Age*, 25 January 1993, p. 2.
43. James R. Healey, "Automaker Shifts Upscale," *USA Today*, 20 March 1993, pp. 9–10B.

Chapter 7

1. Martha Farnsworth Riche, "We're All Minorities Now," *American Demographics*, October 1991, pp. 26–33.
2. William Dunn, "The Move toward Ethnic Marketing," *Nation's Business*, July 1992, pp. 39–44.
3. "The Immigrants," *Business Week*, 13 July 1992, pp. 114–122; "Immigrant Tide Surges in '80s," *USA Today*, 29 May 1992, p. 1A.
4. "Immigrants," p. 114–122; "Immigrant Tide," p. 1A.
5. "Immigrants," p. 117.
6. Riche, p. 28.
7. James Allen and Eugene Turner, "Where Diversity Reigns," *American Demographics*, August 1990, pp. 24–38.
8. William O'Hare, "Reaching for the Dream," *American Demographics*, January 1992, pp. 32–36.
9. O'Hare, "Reaching," 32–36.
10. O'Hare, "Reaching," 32–36.
11. Riche, p. 28.
12. Riche, p. 28; "Beyond the Melting Pot," *Time*, 9 April 1990, pp. 28–32.
13. Dunn, p. 40.
14. Jon Berry, "An Empire of Niches," *Superbrands: A Special Supplement to Adweek's Marketing Week*, Fall 1991, pp. 17–22.
15. Berry, pp. 17–22.
16. William O'Hare, Kelvin Pollard, Taynia Mann, and Mary Kent, "African Americans in the 1990s," *Population Bulletin*, July 1991, pp. 2–22.
17. O'Hare, Pollard, Mann, and Kent, pp. 2–22.
18. Judith Waldrop, "Shades of Black," *American Demographics*, September 1990, pp. 30–34.
19. "Blacks' Family Incomes Grew during 1980s, Census Says," *Fort Worth Star-Telegram*, 25 July 1992, p. A3.
20. William O'Hare, "In the Black," *American Demographics*, November 1989, pp. 24–25, 27–29.
21. Brad Edmondson, "Targeting Black Enterprise," *American Demographics*, November 1989, pp. 26–27.
22. "Waking Up to a Major Market," *Business Week*, 23 March 1992, pp. 70–73.
23. Ronald Miller and Pepper Miller, "Trends Are Opportunities for Targeting African Americans," *Marketing News*, 20 January 1992, p. 9.
24. "Black-Owned Firms Are Catching an Afrocentric Wave," *Wall Street Journal*, 8 January 1992, p. B2.
25. "Fighting the Power," *Advertising Age*, 3 March 1991, p. 4; Thaddeus Spratlin, "The Controversy over Targeting Black Consumers in Cigarette Advertising," in *Developments in Marketing Science: Proceedings of the 1991 Academy of Marketing Science Annual Conference*, ed. Robert King, (Academy of Marketing Science, 1991), pp. 249–252; Kathleen Deveny, "Malt Liquor Makers Find Lucrative Market in the Urban Young," *Wall Street Journal*, 9 March 1992, pp. A1, A4.
26. "Fabrics Industry Makes a Fashion Statement Out of Africa," *Dallas Morning News*, 26 July 1992, p. 24.
27. Miller and Miller, p. 9.
28. "Six Myths about Black Consumers," *Adweek's Marketing Week*, 6 May 1991, pp. 16–19.
29. "African Americans," *Adweek's Marketing Week*, 21 January 1991, pp. 18–20.
30. Thelma Snuggs, "Minority Markets: Define the Consumer of the 21st Century," *Credit*, January-February 1992, pp. 8–11.
31. "African Americans," p. 19.
32. "African Americans," p. 19.
33. For articles on promotion stereotyping, see Robert Wilkes and Humberto Valencia, "Hispanics and Blacks in Television Commercials," *Journal of Advertising*, 18 (1989), pp. 19–25; Robert Pitts, D. Joel Whalen, Robert O'Keefe, and Vernon Murray, "Black and White Response to Culturally

Targeted Television Commercials: A Values-Based Approach," *Psychology and Marketing,* Winter 1989, pp. 311–328; Tommy Whittler and Joan DiMeo, "Viewers' Reactions to Racial Cues in Advertising Stimuli," *Journal of Advertising Research,* December 1991, pp. 37–46; William Qualls and David J. Moore, "Stereotyping Effects on Consumers' Evaluation of Advertising: Impact of Racial Differences between Actors and Viewers," *Psychology and Marketing,* Summer 1990, pp. 135–151; Richard Pollay, Jung Lee, and David Carter-Whitney, "Separate, but Not Equal: Racial Segmentation in Cigarette Advertising," *Journal of Advertising,* March 1992, pp. 45–57; David Strutton and Keith Tudor, "A Conceptually Based Discussion of Possible Antecedents and Societal Implications Associated with Marketing's Stereotypical Portrayal of Blacks," *Developments in Marketing Science: Proceedings of the 1991 Academy of Marketing Science Annual Conference,* ed. Robert King (Academy of Marketing Science, 1991), pp. 243–246; "What Role Do Ads Play in Racial Tension," *Advertising Age,* 10 August 1992, pp. 1, 35.

34. "Waking Up to a Major Market," p. 70.
35. "Advertisers Promote Racial Harmony; Nike Criticized," *Marketing News,* 6 July 1992, pp. 1, 10.
36. "Retailers Boost Efforts to Target African American Consumers," *Marketing News,* 22 June 1992, p. 2.
37. "Spiegel, Ebony Aim to Dress Black Women," *Wall Street Journal,* 18 September 1991, pp. B1, B7.
38. "Former Pizza Hut Official Takes Big Franchise Slice," *Wall Street Journal,* 24 March 1992, p. B1.
39. "After Demographic Shift, Atlanta Mall Restyles Itself as Black Shopping Center," *Wall Street Journal,* 26 February 1992, pp. B1, B5.
40. "After Demographic Shift," pp. B1, B5.
41. "After Demographic Shift," pp. B1, B5.
42. Students Attempt to Find: Do the Poor Really Pay More?" *Advancing the Consumer Interest,* Spring 1992, pp. 30–33.
43. "The Poor Pay More for Food in New York, Survey Finds," *Wall Street Journal,* 15 April 1991, pp. B1, B4.
44. Francine Schwadel, "Urban Consumers Pay More and Get Less, and Gap May Widen," *Wall Street Journal,* 2 July 1992, pp. A1, A4. Reprinted by permission of *The Wall Street Journal,* © 1992 Dow Jones & Company, Inc. All Rights Reserved Worldwide.
45. "One Million Hispanic Club," *American Demographics,* February 1991, p. 59.
46. "The Mexican Way," *American Demographics,* May 1992, p. 4.
47. "Mexican Way," p. 4.
48. "How to Speak to Hispanics," *American Demographics,* February 1990, pp. 40–41.
49. Snuggs, pp. 8–10.
50. Stuart Livingston, "Marketing to the Hispanic Community," *Journal of Business Strategy,* March-April 1992, pp. 54–57.
51. "Habla Español?" *Target Marketing,* October 1991, pp. 10–14.
52. "The United States of Miami," *Adweek's Marketing Week,* 15 July 1991, pp. 19–22.
53. "Hispanics' Tale of Two Cities," *U.S. News & World Report,* 25 May 1992, pp. 40–41.
54. "United States of Miami," p. 20.
55. "To Reach Minorities, Try Busting Myths," *American Demographics,* April 1992, pp. 14–15.
56. "Deposit-Hungry Consumer Banks Courting the Nation's Hispanics," *American Banker,* 2 May 1990, pp. 1, 6.
57. Elizabeth Roberts, "Different Strokes," *Adweek's Marketing Week,* 9 July 1990, p. 41.
58. "Mexican Way," p. 4.
59. "One Newspaper Finds Way to Lure Readers: Publish in Spanish," *Wall Street Journal,* 23 April 1992, pp. A1, A8.
60. "No Habla Español," *Forbes,* 23 December 1991, pp. 140–142.
61. "Targeting Hispanics: NutraSweet Educates while Coke Titillates," *Marketing News,* 11 November 1991, pp. 1, 2.
62. "The Challenge of the '90s: Pinning Down the Hispanic Market," *Progressive Grocer,* June 1990, pp. 69–74.
63. Livingston, p. 56.
64. Greg Muirhead, "Mexican-American Influx Offers Chance for Growth," *Progressive Grocer,* April 1992, p. 4.
65. "Asian Americans," *CQ Researcher,* 13 December 1991, pp. 947–964.
66. "Asian Americans Increase Rapidly," *Futurist,* September-October 1991, pp. 51–53.
67. This discussion adapted from William O'Hare, "A New Look at Asian Americans," *American Demographics,* October 1990, pp. 26–31. Reprinted with permission © American Demographics, October 1990. For subscription information, please call (800) 828-1131.
68. O'Hare, "New Look," pp. 26–31.
69. O'Hare, "New Look," pp. 26–31.
70. "Asian Americans," p. 953.
71. "Why Asians Can Prosper Where Blacks Fail," *Wall Street Journal,* 28 May 1992, p. A10.
72. "The California Asian Market," *American Demographics,* October 1990, pp. 34–37.
73. Jerry Goodbody, "Taking the Pulse of Asian Americans," *Adweek's Marketing Week,* 12 August 1991, p. 32. Used by permission of A/S/M Communications, Inc.
74. "Suddenly, Asian-Americans Are a Marketer's Dream," *Business Week,* 17 June 1991, pp. 54–55.
75. Goodbody, p. 32.
76. "Suddenly," p. 55.
77. "Marketers Say Budgets Hinder Targeting of Asian Americans," *Marketing News,* 30 March 1992, p. 2.
78. Nejdet Delener and James Neelankavil, "Informational Sources and Media Uses: A Comparison

between Asian and Hispanic Subcultures," *Journal of Advertising Research,* June-July 1990, pp. 45–52.

79. Keun Lee and Nejdet Delener, "Values of Minority Orientals: Subcultural Comparisons Using a Three Dimensional Approach to Values Measurement," in *Developments in Marketing Science: Proceedings of the 1991 Academy of Marketing Science Annual Conference,* ed. Robert King (Academy of Marketing Science, 1991), pp. 255–259.
80. "Suddenly," p. 54.
81. "American Dreams," *Wall Street Journal,* 16 June 1992, pp. A1, A5.
82. Richard DeSanta, "California's Oriental Stores: The Ultimate Niche Marketers," *Supermarket Business,* November 1991, pp. 25–30. Used by permission of the publisher.
83. "American Indians in the 1990s," *American Demographics,* December 1991, pp. 26–34.
84. Adapted from Leon Wynter, "Business and Race," *Wall Street Journal,* 16 November 1992, p. B1.

Chapter 8

1. Trish Baumann, "How Quaker Oats Transforms Information into Market Leadership," *Sales & Marketing Management,* June 1989, p. 79.
2. "More Marketers Are Going On Line for Decision Support," *Marketing News,* 12 November 1990, p. 14; Terrence O'Brien, "Decision Support Systems," *Marketing Research,* December 1990, pp. 51–55; "Database Is Nerve Center of Integrated Marketing Plan," *Marketing News,* 3 February 1992, p. 5.
3. "Hand-Held Computers Help Field Staff Cut Paper Work and Harvest More Data," *Wall Street Journal,* 30 January 1990, p. B1; "How Software Is Making Food Sales a Piece of Cake," *Business Week,* 2 July 1990, pp. 54–56.
4. "KGF Taps Database to Target Consumers," *Advertising Age,* 8 October 1990, pp. 3, 88.
5. "Databases Uncover Brands' Biggest Fans," *Advertising Age,* 19 February 1990, pp. 3, 73.
6. "Databases Uncover Brands' Biggest Fans," pp. 3, 73.
7. "Segments of One," *Wall Street Journal,* 22 March 1992, p. B4.
8. "The New Stars in Retailing," *Business Week,* 16 December 1991, p. 122.
9. Peter Pae, "American Express Company Discloses It Gives Merchants Data on Cardholders' Habits," *Wall Street Journal,* 14 May 1992, p. A3.
10. Ed Campbell, "CD-ROMs Bring Census Data In-House," *Marketing News,* 6 January 1992, pp. 12, 16.
11. "Latest Image Study Finds Mixed Results for Researchers," *Marketing News,* 14 September 1992, pp. 8–9.
12. Carl McDaniel and Roger Gates, *Contemporary Marketing Research,* 2nd ed. (Cincinnati: South-Western, 1993), pp. 223–226.
13. Diane Pyle, "How to Interview Your Customers," *American Demographics,* December 1990, pp. 44–45.
14. "King Customer," *Business Week,* 12 March 1990, p. 90.
15. "Network to Broadcast Live Focus Groups," *Marketing News,* 3 September 1990, pp. 10, 47.
16. "There's No Mystery in How to Retain Customers," *Marketing News,* 4 February 1991, p. 10.
17. "Real-World Device Sheds New Lights on Ad Readership Tests," *Marketing News,* 5 June 1987, pp. 1, 18.
18. "K Mart Testing Radar to Track Shopper Traffic," *Wall Street Journal,* 24 September 1991, pp. B1, B5.
19. "People Meter Rerun," *Marketing News,* 2 September 1991, pp. 1, 44; see also "Nielsen Rival to Unveil New Peoplemeter," *Wall Street Journal,* 4 December 1992, p. B8.
20. "Gadgets That Track Viewers," *Adweek,* 22 April 1991, p. 10.
21. Robert Levy, "Scanning for Dollars," *Dun's Business Month,* September 1986, p. 64.
22. "IRI, Nielsen Slug It Out in Scanning Wars," *Marketing News,* 2 September 1991, p. 1; for an excellent summary article on single-source systems, see "Futuristic Weaponry," *Advertising Age,* 11 June 1990, pp. 5–12.
23. Information Resources Incorporated, *1991 Annual Report.*
24. "Researchers Rev Up," *Advertising Age,* 13 January 1992, p. 34.
25. "Now Its Down to Two Equal Competitors," *Superbrands: A Special Supplement to Adweek's Marketing Week,* Fall 1991, p. 28.
26. "IRI, Nielsen Slug It Out," p. 47.
27. "Nielsen Weighs Assets," *Advertising Age,* 12 August 1991, p. 29.
28. "Information Resources Wires the Drugstores," *Adweek's Marketing Week,* 27 May 1991, p. 34.
29. "Researchers Rev Up," p. 34.
30. Laurence Gold, "New Technology Contributions to New Product and Advertising Strategy Testing: The ERIM Testsight System," speech by vice president of marketing, A.C. Nielsen Co.

Chapter 9

1. U.S. Department of Commerce, Bureau of the Census, *Statistical Abstract of the United States* (Washington, DC: Government Printing Office, 1989), p. 423.
2. J. Joseph Cronin and Steven A.Taylor, "Measuring Service Quality: A Reexamination and Extension," *Journal of Marketing,* July 1992, pp. 55–68.
3. Mark Robichaux, "Tabasco Sauce Market Remains Hot after 125 Years," *Wall Street Journal,* 11 May 1990, p. B2.
4. Mark Robichaux, "Avis Hit by Almost Every Obstacle in Franchise Book, *Wall Street Journal,* 3 May 1990, p. B2.

5. Marcy Magiera, "Levi's Dockers Look for Younger, Upscale Men with Authentics," *Advertising Age,* 18 January 1993, p. 4.
6. Christopher Power, "And Now, Finger-Lickin' Good for Ya?" *Business Week,* 18 February 1991, p. 60.
7. Barbara Holsomback, "F-L Takes Risk in Repositioning of Fritos Brand," *Adweek,* 25 February 1991, pp. 1, 4.
8. Terry Lefton, "Still Battling the Ozone Stigma," *Adweek's Marketing Week,* 16 March 1992, pp. 18–19.
9. Joanne Lipman, "Maxwell House, Folgers Clash over Coffee," *Wall Street Journal,* 20 February 1990, p. B6.
10. Carrie Goerne, "Coffee Consumption Down, but Sales of Exotic Blends Perk Up," *Marketing News,* 20 July 1992, pp., 1, 22.
11. "One Last Call for Fading Beer Brands," *Business Week,* 16 October 1989, p. 68.
12. Gerald Schoenfeld, "Treat Old Products Like New," *Marketing News,* 31 July 1990, p. 15.
13. Schoenfeld, p. 15.
14. Peg Masterson, "American Brand Names Gain Clout," *Advertising Age,* 30 March 1992, p. 47.
15. Mark Zandler, Zachary Schiller, and Lois Therrien, "What's in a Name? Less and Less," *Business Week,* 8 July 1991, pp. 66–67.
16. Zandler, Schiller, and Therrien, pp. 66–67.
17. Peter H. Farquhar, Julia Y. Han, Paul M. Herr, and Yuji Ijiri, "Strategies for Leveraging Master Brands," *Marketing Research,* September 1992, pp. 32–43.
18. Zandler, Schiller, and Therrien, pp. 66–67.
19. "Copying the Copycats," *Economist,* 12 September 1992, p. 78.
20. "The Dial Corp.: The New Name behind Some of the Best Names You Know," *Wall Street Journal,* 6 May 1991, p. R1.
21. Zandler, Schiller, and Therrien, p. 67.
22. "Private Label, Experts Predict, Will Reach 45% Market Share," *Brandweek,* 8 February 1993, p. 8.
23. "Retailers Hungry for Store Brands," *Advertising Age,* 11 January 1993, p. 20.
24. Jennifer Lawrence, "Wall-Mart Puts Its Own Spin on Private Label," *Advertising Age,* 16 December 1991, p. 26.
25. Betsy McKay, "Xerox Fights Trademark Battle," *Advertising Age,* 27 April 1992, p. 139.
26. Carrie Dolan, "Levi Tries to Round Up Counterfeiters," *Wall Street Journal,* 19 February 1992, pp. B1, B8; Damon Dorlin, "Coca-Cola's Sprite Enters South Korea; Local Sprint Follows," *Wall Street Journal,* 21 February 1992, p. B5.
27. "Another 15,000 New Products Expected for U.S. Supermarkets," *Marketing News,* 10 June 1991, p. 8.
28. "Economic Recovery Presages Packaging Explosion," *Marketing News,* February 1984, p. 1.
29. Howard Schlossberg, "Effective Packaging 'Talks' to Consumers," *Marketing News,* 6 August 1990, p. 6.
30. David Kiley, "For Schick's Tracer, Packaging Is Pivotal," *Adweek's Marketing Week,* 15 October 1990, p. 12.
31. Alison Fahey, "Fresca Freshens Up," *Advertising Age,* 6 January 1992, p. 23.
32. Fara Warner, "Safeguard's Risky Mission," *Adweek's Marketing Week,* 16 March 1992, pp. 36–37.
33. Dan Koeppel, "Spreckels Bags the Sack," *Adweek's Marketing Week,* 22 October 1990, p. 10.
34. Joe Schwaetz, "Americans Annoyed by Wasteful Packaging," *American Demographics,* April 1992, p. 13; Scott Hume, "Green Labels Good, but Confusing," *Advertising Age,* 9 December 1991, p. 43.
35. Robert McMath, "It's All in the Trigger," *Adweek's Marketing Week,* 6 January 1992, pp. 25–28; Robert McMath, "Green Packaging That Works," *Adweek's Marketing Week,* 2 December 1991, pp. 28–29.
36. John Calfee, "FDA's Ugly Package," *Advertising Age,* 16 March 1992, p. 25.

Chapter 10

1. Six category names and percentage of new products that each accounts for from *New Product Management in the 1980s* (New York: Booz, Allen and Hamilton, 1982), p. 8.
2. Judann Dagnoli and Julie Liesse, "Healthy Frozen Foods Launch Offensive," *Advertising Age,* 2 September 1991, p. 1.
3. Elaine Underwood, "Blue Collar Couture," *Adweek's Marketing Week,* 5 August 1991, p. 12.
4. Cara Appelbaum, "L'eggs Declares War on Baggy Pantyhose," *Adweek's Marketing Week,* 22 October 1991, p. 12.
5. Dan Koeppel, "Kingsford Achieves the Impossible," *Adweek's Marketing Week,* 2 September 1991, p. 6.
6. David Kiley, "Wilkinson Joins the Razor Frenzy," *Adweek's Marketing Week,* 29 October 1990, p. 14.
7. Fara Warner, "Kleenex Goes National with High-Tech Bathroom Roll," *Adweek's Marketing Week,* 25 November 1991, p. 7.
8. Brenton R. Schlender, "How Sony Keeps the Magic Going," *Fortune,* 24 February 1992, pp. 75–84.
9. Valerie Reitman, "Rubbermaid Turns Up Plenty of Profit in the Mundane," *Wall Street Journal,* 27 March 1992, p. B3.
10. Robin T. Peterson, "Speed Is Critical in New Product Introductions," *Marketing News,* 1 March 1993, p. 4.
11. John Bussey and Douglas R. Sease, "Manufacturers Strive to Slice Time Needed to Develop Products," *Wall Street Journal,* 23 February 1988, pp. 1, 13.
12. Joseph B. White, Gregory A. Patterson, and Paul Ingrassia, "American Auto Makers Need Major Overhaul to Match the Japanese," *Wall Street Journal,* 10 January 1992, pp. A1, A10.
13. David Woodruff, "The Racy Viper Is Already a Winner for Chrysler," *Business Week,* 4 November 1991, pp. 36–38.

14. Woodruff, pp. 36–38; White, Patterson, and Ingrassia, pp. A1, A10.
15. David Woodruff, "GM: All Charged Up over the Electric Car," *Business Week,* 21 October 1991, pp. 106–108.
16. B. G. Yovovich, "IBM's New-Product Design Approach Breaks the Mold," *Business Marketing,* July 1991, p. 32.
17. Bussey and Sease, p. 13.
18. *New Product Management,* p. 3.
19. *New Product Management,* pp. 10–11.
20. Julie Skur Hill, "Japan Hatches New Brands for Johnson," *Advertising Age,* 2 September 1991, p. 36.
21. Zachary Schiller, "At Rubbermaid, Little Things Mean a Lot," *Business Week,* 11 November 1991, p. 126.
22. Alix M. Freedman, "Western Union Plans Network to Cash Checks," *Wall Street Journal,* 27 September 1991, pp. B1, B6.
23. David W. Cravens, *Strategic Marketing,* 3rd ed. (Homewood, IL: Richard D. Irwin, 1991), p. 344.
24. Gerry Khermouch, "Seagram's Quest Aims Clearly at Canadian," *Brandweek,* 8 February 1993, p. 2.
25. Christopher Power, "Will It Sell in Podunk? Hard to Say," *Business Week,* 10 August 1992, pp. 46–47.
26. Cara Appelbaum, "Lever Rolls a New Deodorant Bar," *Adweek's Marketing Week,* 1 April 1991, p. 7.
27. Power, p. 46.
28. Power, p. 46.
29. Lawrence Ingrassia, "A Recovering Gillette Hopes for Vindication in a High-Tech Razor," *Wall Street Journal,* 29 September 1990, pp. A1, A4.
30. Richard Gibson, "Pinning Down Costs of Product Introductions," *Wall Street Journal,* 26 November 1990, p. B1.
31. Howard Schlossberg, "Fear of Failure Stifles Product Development," *Marketing News,* 14 May 1990, p. 1.
32. Michael R. Czinkota and Ilkka A. Ronkainen, *International Marketing* (Homewood, IL: Richard D. Irwin, 1990), p. 530.
33. "Category Management: Marketing for the '90s," *Marketing News,* 14 September 1992, pp. 12–13.
34. Gibson, p. B1.

Chapter 11

1. U.S. Department of Commerce, Bureau of the Census, *Statistical Abstract of the United States* (Washington, DC: Government Printing Office, 1989, p. 423.
2. James L. Heskett, "Lessons in the Service Sector," *Harvard Business Review,* March-April 1987, pp. 118–126.
3. James L. Heskett, "Thank Heaven for the Service Sector," *Business Week,* 26 January 1987, p. 22.
4. John G. Bateson, *Managing Services Marketing* (Hinsdale, IL: Dryden Press, 1989), p. 4.
5. "American Express: Service That Sells," *Fortune,* 20 November 1989, p. 80.
6. Paul N. Bloom and Torger Reve, "Transmitting Signals to Consumers for Competitive Advantage," *Business Horizons,* July-August 1990, pp. 58–66.
7. "Health Card for All in Clinton Plan 3 Officials Say," *Fort Worth Star-Telegram,* 10 April 1993, p. 1.
8. Reprinted with the permission of The Free Press, a Division of Macmillan, Inc., from *Marketing Services: Competing Through Quality,* by Leonard L. Berry and A. Parasuraman, p. 108. Copyright © 1991 by The Free Press.
9. George Leaming, "Demand Should Drive Services Too," *Marketing News,* 1 October 1990, p. 15.
10. Larry Armstrong and William C. Symonds, "Beyond 'May I Help You?'" *Business Week,* 25 October 1991, pp. 100–103.
11. Paul B. Carroll, "IBM, Seeking a Source of Renewal, Turns to Services," *Wall Street Journal,* 12 June 1990, p. B4.
12. Much of the material in this section based on Christopher H. Lovelock, *Services Marketing* (Englewood Cliffs, NJ: Prentice-Hall, 1991), pp. 13, 18–19.
13. Carlee R. Scott and Carrie Dolan, "Funeral Homes Hope to Attract Business by Offering Services after the Service," *Wall Street Journal,* 11 April 1991, pp. B1, B5.
14. Zachary Schiller, "Humana May Be Wearing Too Many Hats," *Business Week,* 8 June 1992, p. 31.
15. Kathy Brown, "A Burger and a Campaign to Go," *Adweek,* 14 January 1991, p. 6.
16. "Profiting from Nonprofits," *Business Week,* 26 March 1990, pp. 66–74.
17. Haim Oren, "Branding Financial Services Helps Consumers Find Order in Chaos," *Marketing News,* 29 March 1993, p. 6.
18. "Bar Restricts Lawyer Ads," *Marketing News,* 11 May 1992, p. 11.
19. Jonathan Dahl, "Airlines Use a Scalpel to Cut Fares in the Latest Round of Price Wars," *Wall Street Journal,* 26 November 1985, p. 31.
20. Lovelock, pp. 238–240.
21. This fact, along with much of the material in this section, based on Valarie A. Zeithaml, A. Parasuraman, and Leonard L. Berry, *Delivering Quality Service* (New York: Free Press).
22. Zeithaml, Parasuraman, and Berry.
23. Armstrong and Symonds, p. 100.
24. Dori Jones Yang, "Northern Hospitality," *Business Week,* 25 October 1991, p. 118.
25. "Quality Service Commitment," *Services Marketing Today* [American Marketing Association newsletter], January-February 1992, p. 3.
26. "Piety, Profits, and Productivity," *Fortune,* 29 June 1992, p. 84.
27. Barry and Parasuraman, p. 151.
28. Berry and Parasuraman, p. 152.
29. Armstrong and Symonds, p. 100.
30. Armstrong and Symonds, p. 100.
31. Berry and Parasuraman, p. 156.
32. Armstrong and Symonds, p. 102.

33. Much of the material in this section based on Berry and Parasuraman, pp. 132–150.
34. Otis Port and John Carey, "Questing for the Best," *Business Week,* 25 October 1991, p. 10.
35. Seymour H. Fine, *Social Marketing* (Boston: Allyn and Bacon, 1990), p. xiv.
36. "Profiting from the Nonprofits," p. 67.
37. Dori Jones Yang, "When City Hall Learns to Think Like a Business," *Business Week,* 25 October 1991, p. 136.
38. "Profiting from the Nonprofits," p. 69.
39. J. M. Prottas, "The Cost of Free Services: Organizational Impediments to Access to Public Services," *Public Administration Review,* September-October 1981, p. 526.

Chapter 12

1. *Morning Advocate,* 11 April 1993, p. D7.
2. Kyle Pope, "Compaq Plans a Mail-Order Operation, Putting It in Direct Rivalry with Dell," *Wall Street Journal,* 12 March 1993, p. B3.
3. Sunita Wadekar Bhargava and Stephanie Anderson Forest, "Computers by Mail: A Megabyte Business Boom," *Business Week,* 11 May 1992, pp. 93–96; Lois Therrien and Barbara Buell, "Whatever Happened to the Corner Computer Store?" *Business Week,* 20 May 1991, pp. 131–137; Stephanie Anderson Forest, "Attack of the Giant Discounters," *Business Week,* 20 May 1991, p. 132; Gary McWilliams, "Mail-Order Madness," *Business Week Special Edition: Quality 1991,* 25 October 1991, p. 128.
4. Three basic groupings of channel functions based in part on Eric Berkowitz, Roger Kerin, and William Rudelius, *Marketing* (Homewood, IL: Richard D. Irwin, 1992), p. 379.
5. Frank G. Bingham, Jr., and Barney T. Raffield III, *Business to Business Marketing Management* (Homewood, IL: Richard D. Irwin, 1990), p. 335.
6. Bingham and Raffield, p. 343.
7. Kate Fitzgerald, "Spiegel Adds Retail Outlets," *Advertising Age,* 15 July 1991, p. 12.
8. Allan J. Magrath, "Differentiating Yourself via Distribution," *Sales & Marketing Management,* March 1991, pp. 50–57.
9. Magrath, pp. 50–57.
10. Barbara Holsomback, "7-Eleven Follows Stop N Go in Search for C-Store of Future," *Adweek,* 11 November 1991, p. 3.
11. Magrath, pp. 50–57.
12. Jon Berry, "Ocean Spray Joins the Pepsi Generation," *Adweek's Marketing Week,* 9 March 1992, pp. 18–21.
13. Gabriella Stern, "Phar-Mor Forges Stronger Ties with Manufacturers," *Wall Street Journal,* 8 March 1993, p. B4.
14. Michael J. McCarthy and Richard Gibson, "General Mills, PepsiCo Plan Venture Abroad," *Wall Street Journal,* 13 May 1992, p. B1.
15. E. J. Muller, "The Quest for a Quality Environment," *Distribution,* January 1992, pp. 32–36.
16. Bert C. McCammon, Jr., "Perspectives for Distribution Programing," in *Vertical Marketing Systems,* ed. Louis P. Bucklin (Glenview, IL: Scott, Foresman, 1970), p. 43.
17. McCammon, p. 43.
18. Patricia Sellers, "Pepsi Keeps On Going After No. 1," *Fortune,* 11 March 1991, pp. 62–70.
19. Bill Saporito, "Is Wal-Mart Unstoppable?" *Fortune,* 6 May 1991, pp. 50–59.
20. Carla Rapoport, "Why Japan Keeps On Winning," *Fortune,* 15 July 1991, pp. 76–85.
21. Saul Klein, "Selection of International Marketing Channels," *Journal of Global Marketing,* 4 (1991), pp. 21–37; Erin Anderson and Anne T. Coughlan, "International Market Entry and Expansion via Independent or Integrated Channels of Distribution," *Journal of Marketing,* January 1987, pp. 71–82.
22. Anderson and Coughlan, p. 74.
23. Anderson and Coughlan, p. 72.
24. Roger E. Axtell, "Ten Common Mistakes of Potential Exporters," *Nation's Business,* June 1990, pp. 36–37.
25. Arieh Goldman, "Japan's Distribution System: Institutional Structure, Internal Political Economy, and Modernization," *Journal of Retailing,* Summer 1991, pp. 154–183.
26. Kenneth G. Hardy and Allan J. Magrath, *Marketing Channel Management: Strategic Planning and Tactics* (Glenview, IL: Scott, Foresman, 1988), p. 667.
27. Bert Rosenbloom, "Motivating Your International Channel Partners," *Business Horizons,* March-April 1990, pp. 53–57.
28. U.S. Department of Commerce, Bureau of the Census, *Statistical Abstract of the United States* (Washington, DC: Government Printing Office, 1991), p. 779.
29. Karen Blumenthal, "Wal-Mart Set to Eliminate Reps, Brokers," *Wall Street Journal,* 2 December 1991, pp. A3, A5.
30. Martin Everett, "When There's More Than One Route to the Customer," *Sales & Marketing Management,* August 1990, pp. 48–56.
31. Courtland L. Bovee and John V. Thill, *Marketing* (New York: McGraw-Hill, 1992), p. 401.
32. Mark Maremont, "They're All Screaming for Häagen-Dazs," *Business Week,* 14 October 1991, p. 121.
33. Allan J. Magrath and Kenneth G. Hardy, "Six Steps to Distribution Network Design," *Business Horizons,* January-February 1991, pp. 48–52.
34. Julia Flynn Siler, "OshKosh B'Gosh May Be Risking Its Upscale Image," *Business Week,* 15 July 1991, p. 140.
35. Magrath, p. 50.

36. Based on information contained in the case "Cantel, Inc.," prepared by Susan Fleming under the direction of Professors Terry H. Deutsher and Kenneth G. Hardy of the University of Western Ontario.
37. Bert Rosenbloom, *Marketing Channels,* 3rd ed. (Hinsdale, IL: Dryden Press, 1987), p. 166.
38. Eugene W. Lambert, "Financial Considerations in Choosing a Marketing Channel," *MSU Business Topics,* Winter 1966, pp. 17–26.
39. For an excellent review article, see Shelby Hunt, Nina Rayk, and Van Wood, "Behavioral Dimensions of Channels of Distribution: Review and Synthesis," *Journal of the Academy of Marketing Science,* Summer 1985, pp. 1–24.
40. For an excellent summary article on channel power, see John F. Gaski, "The Theory of Power and Conflict in Channels of Distribution," *Journal of Marketing Research,* Summer 1984, pp. 9–29; see also Jehoshua Eliashberg, "Multiple Business Goals Set as Determinants of Marketing Channel Conflict: An Empirical Study," *Journal of Marketing Research,* February 1984, pp. 75–88; Jean Johnson, Harold Koenig, and James R. Brown, "The Bases of Marketing Channel Power: An Exploration and Confirmation of Their Underlying Dimensions," in *1985 AMA Educators' Proceedings,* ed. Robert Lusch et al. (Chicago: American Marketing Association), pp. 160–165; Robert Lusch and Robert Ross," The Nature of Power in a Marketing Channel," *Journal of the Academy of Marketing Science,* Summer 1985, pp. 39–56.
41. Dana Milbank, "Independent Goodyear Dealers Rebel," *Wall Street Journal,* 8 July 1992, p. B2.
42. For an excellent discussion of how to measure power, see Gary L. Frazier, "On the Measurement of Interfirm Power in Channels of Distribution," *Journal of Marketing Research,* May 1983, pp. 158–166.
43. Arieh Goldman, "Evaluating the Performance of the Japanese Distribution System," *Journal of Retailing,* Spring 1992, pp. 11–39.
44. Bert Rosenbloom, "Motivating Channel Partners," p. 53.
45. Valerie Reitman, "Retail Resistance: Eliminated Discounts on P&G Goods Annoy Many Who Sell Them," *Wall Street Journal,* 11 August 1992, pp. A1, A6.
46. Robert F. Lusch and Patrick M. Dunne, *Retail Management* (Cincinnati, OH: South-Western, 1990), p. 94.
47. Reitman, pp. A1, A6.
48. Rajiv P. Dant and Patrick L. Schul, "Conflict Resolution Processes in Contractual Channels of Distribution," *Journal of Marketing,* January 1992, pp. 38–54.
49. Jeffrey A. Tannenbaum, "Dairy Queen Franchisees in the Lone Star State Revolt," *Wall Street Journal,* 1 November 1991, p. B2.

Chapter 13

1. Isadore Barmash, "The 'How' in Home Improvement," *New York Times,* 14 June 1992, p. F5; see also "Making a Splash in Elmont, L.I.," *New York Times,* 14 June 1922; p. F5; Roger Thompson, "There's No Place Like Home Depot," *Nation's Business,* February 1992, pp. 30–33.
2. U.S. Department of Commerce, Bureau of the Census, *Statistical Abstract of the United States* (Washington, DC: Government Printing Office, 1991).
3. Kevin Helliker, "Wal-Mart's Big Blitz into the Grocery Field Meets Stiff Resistance," *Wall Street Journal,* 9 October 1992, pp. A1, A7.
4. These four factors were taken from William Davidson, Albert Bates, and Stephen Bass, "The Retail Life Cycle," *Harvard Business Review,* 54 (November-December 1976), pp. 89–96.
5. Stephen Brown, "The Wheel of Retailing: Past and Future," *Journal of Retailing,* 66, 2 (Summer 1990), pp. 143–149.
6. Eleanor G. May, "A Retail Odyssey," *Journal of Retailing,* 65, 3 (Fall 1989), pp. 356–367.
7. "Huge Department Store Follows U.S. Example," *Wall Street Journal,* 21 April 1992, p. B1.
8. Francine Schwadel, "Sears Terms Retail Revenue Growth Its 'No. 1 Priority,'" *Wall Street Journal,* 3 April 1992, p. B3; Susan Caminiti, "Sears' Need: More Speed," *Fortune,* 15 July 1991, pp. 88–90.
9. Stephanie Anderson Forest, "Trapped Between the Up and Down Escalators," *Business Week,* 26 August 1991, pp. 49–50.
10. Mario Shao and Laura Zinn, "Everybody's Falling into The Gap," *Business Week,* 23 September 1991, p. 36; Francine Schwadel, "At Gap, Clothes make the Ads as Stars Fade," *Wall Street Journal,* 3 December 1990, p. B1.
11. Karen J. Sack, "Supermarkets: Outlook Good Despite Tough Operating Conditions," *Standard & Poor's Industry Surveys,* 4 June 1992, p. R86.
12. Sack, "Supermarkets: Outlook," p. R85.
13. Julie Liesse, "How Supermarket Chains Are Fighting Back—In Bulk," *Advertising Age,* 27 April 1992, p. S1.
14. Sack, "Supermarkets: Outlook," pp. R86–87.
15. Judith Waldrop, "Eating Out, Going Up?" *American Demographics,* January 1992, p. 55.
16. Sack, "Supermarkets: Outlook," p. R85.
17. Laurie Grossman, "Hypermarkets: A Sure-Fire Hit Bombs," *Wall Street Journal,* 25 June 1992, p. B1; Karen J. Sack, "Discount Stores: Less Hype about Hypermarkets," *Standard & Poor's Industry Surveys,* 19 April 1990, p. R84.
18. Barbara Holsomback, "7-Eleven Follows Stop N Go in Search for C-Store of Future," *Adweek,* 11 November 1991, p. 3.
19. Karen J. Sack, "The Outlook: Consumer Spending Machine Shifts Gears," *Standard & Poor's Industry Surveys,* 4 June 1992, p. R75.

20. Kevin Helliker, "Sam Walton, the Man Who Made Wal-Mart No. 1 Retailer, Dies," *Wall Street Journal,* 6 April 1992, pp. A1, A6; Wendy Zellner, "O.K., So He's Not Sam Walton," *Business Week,* 16 March 1992, pp. 56–58.
21. Jim Kirk and Cathy Madison, "Wal-Mart Prepares for Urban Assault," *Adweek,* 11 November 1991, p. 10; Bob Ortega, "Wal-Mart Plans to Enlarge Mexico Venture," *Wall Street Journal,* 1 June 1992, p. B3.
22. Laura Zinn and David Woodruff, "Attention, Shoppers: Kmart Is Fighting Back," *Business Week,* 7 October 1991, pp. 118–120.
23. Bill Saporito, "Ikea's Got 'Em Lining Up," *Fortune,* 11 March 1991, p. 72.
24. Robert Neff, "Guess Who's Selling Barbies in Japan Now?" *Business Week,* 9 December 1991, pp. 72–76.
25. Julie Skur Hill, "Toys 'R' Us Seeks Global Growth," *Advertising Age,* 30 March 1992, p. 33.
26. Kevin Cote, "Toys 'R' Us Grows in Europe," *Advertising Age,* 27 April 1992, pp. 1–16.
27. "Warehouse Clubs Have Big Impact on Grocers," *Wall Street Journal,* 6 April 1992, p. B2; Opinion Research Corp (1992).
28. Christina Duff, "Single-Price Stores' Formula for Success: Cheap Merchandise and a Lot of Clutter," *Wall Street Journal,* 30 June 1992, p. B1.
29. Gretchen Morgenson, "Cheapie Gucci," *Forbes,* 27 May 1991, pp. 43–44.
30. Andrew Tanzer, "War of the Sales Robots," *Forbes,* 7 January 1991, pp. 294–296.
31. Tanzer, pp. 294–296.
32. Laurie M. Grossman, "Families Have Changed but Tupperware Keeps Holding Its Parties," *Wall Street Journal,* 21 July 1992, pp. A1, A13.
33. Jeffrey A. Trachtenberg, "Catalogs Help Avon Get a Foot in the Door," *Wall Street Journal,* 28 February 1992, p. B1; Bruce Hagar, "Despite the Face-Lift, Avon Is Sagging," *Business Week,* 2 December 1991, pp. 101–102.
34. Wendy Zellner, "Mary Kay Is Singing 'I Feel Pretty,'" *Business Week,* 2 December 1991, p. 102.
35. James McGregor, "U.S. Companies in China Find Patience, Persistence, and Salesmanship Pay Off," *Wall Street Journal,* 3 April 1992, p. B1.
36. Jean C. Darian, "In-Home Shopping: Are There Consumer Segments?" *Journal of Retailing,* Summer 1987, pp. 163–187.
37. Judy Abel, "The Model Clutter-Buster," *Adweek's Marketing Week,* 27 January 1992, p. 26.
38. Timothy L. O'Brien, "Direct-Mail Scams Surge as Tele-Schemes Grow Stale," *Wall Street Journal,* 17 December 1992, p. B5.
39. Sunita Wadekar Bhargava and Stephanie Anderson Forest, "Computers by Mail: A Megabyte Business Boom," *Business Week,* 11 May 1992, pp. 93–94.
40. Elizabeth Fenner, "Buy a Computer by Mail and Save as Much as 20%," *Money,* April 1992, pp. 33–34.
41. Albert R. Karr, "Mailers, Address Problem of Postage Rise," *Wall Street Journal,* 23 January 1991, pp. B1, B5.
42. Eben Shapiro, "U.S. Mail-Order Merchants Try Japan," *New York Times,* 5 November 1991, p. D5.
43. William C. Moncrief, Shannon H. Shipp, Charles W. Lamb, Jr., and David Cravens, "Examining the Roles of Telemarketing in Selling Strategy," *Journal of Personal Selling & Sales Management,* Fall 1989, pp. 1–12.
44. Aimee L. Stern, "Telemarketing Polishes Its Image," *Sales & Marketing Management,* June 1991, pp. 107–110.
45. Junu Bryan Kim, "800/900: King of the Road in Marketing Value, Usage," *Advertising Age,* 17 February 1992, pp. S1-S6.
46. Johnnie L. Roberts and Mark Robichaux, "Diller Bets on Home Shopping's Future," *Wall Street Journal,* 11 December 1992, pp. B1, B4.
47. Stuart Elliot, "Prodigy Makes Pitch to Marketers," *New York Times,* 13 February 1992, p. D10.
48. Robert T. Justis and Richard Judd, *Franchising* (Cincinnati, OH: South-Western, 1989), p. 6.
49. Justis and Judd, p. 8.
50. Telephone conversation with Linda Gaudet at Popeye's Famous Fried Chicken and Biscuits, Inc., 14 September 1992.
51. Justis and Judd, pp. 35–55.
52. International Franchise Association, *Franchise Opportunities Guide,* Summer 1992, p. 38.
53. Justis and Judd, pp. 7–10.
54. Yumiko Ono, "Japan's Fast-Food Companies Cook Up Local Platters to Tempt Local Palates," *Wall Street Journal,* 29 May 1992, p. B1; John Labate, "Snapshot of the Pacific Rim," F*ortune,* 7 October 1991, pp. 128–129.
55. Karen J. Sack, "General Retailing: Productivity and Value Pricing Lure Customers," *Standard & Poor's Industry Surveys,* 9 January 1992, p. R64.
56. Gretchen Morgenson, "A Midas Touch," *Forbes,* 4 February 1991, p. 42.
57. Bruce Hager and Julia Flynn Siler, "Podunk Is Beckoning," *Business Week,* 23 December 1991, p. 76.
58. Richard Gibson, "Location, Luck, Service Can Make a Store Top Star," *Wall Street Journal,* 1 February 1993, p. B1.
59. Gibson, p. B1.
60. Kate Fitzgerald, "Built for the '90s, or the '80s?" *Advertising Age,* 27 January 1992, pp. S1, S8; "Nation's Largest Mall Seeks Big Niche," *Marketing News,* 27 April 1992, p. 2.
61. Chip Walker, "Strip Malls: Plain but Powerful," *American Demographics,* October 1991, pp. 48–51.
62. William C. Symonds, Marti Benedetti, and Doris Jones Yang, "Invasion of the Booty Snatchers," *Business Week,* 24 June 1991, pp. 66–69.
63. John Urquhart, "Canada Sets Tax to Curb Shopping across U.S. Border," *Wall Street Journal,* 13 February 1992, p. A13.

64. Christina Duff, "Megastores That Entertain and Educate May Signal the Future of Merchandising," *Wall Street Journal,* 11 March 1993, pp. B1, B3.
65. Gordon C. Bruner, "Music, Mood, and Marketing," *Journal of Marketing,* October 1990, pp. 94–103.
66. Cyndee Miller, "The Right Song in the Air Can Boost Retail Sales," *Marketing News,* 4 February 1991, p. 2.
67. Cyndee Miller, "Research Reveals How Marketers Can Win by a Nose," *Marketing News,* 4 February 1991, p. 1–2.
68. Joseph Bellizzi and Ayn Crowley, "The Effects of Color in Store Design," *Journal of Retailing,* Spring 1983, pp. 21–25.
69. This list taken from Patrick Dunne, Robert Lusch, Myron Gable, and Randall Gebhardt, *Retailing* (Cincinnati, OH: South-Western, 1992), pp. 316–321.
70. Christopher Power and Laura Zinn, "Their Wish Is Your Command," *Business Week Special Edition: Quality 1991,* 25 October 1991, pp. 126–127.
71. U.S. Department of Commerce.
72. Francine Schwadel, "Tony Chicago Shopping Area's Struggles Reflect Nationwide Glut of Store Space," *Wall Street Journal,* 19 December 1990, p. B1.
73. Karen J. Sack, "Retailers Vie for Elusive Consumer Dollars," *Standard & Poor's Industry Surveys,* 19 September 1991, pp. R61–R63.
74. Francesca Turchiano, "The (Un)Malling of America," *American Demographics,* April 1990, pp. 36–39; Francine Schwadel, "Shoppers' Blues: The Thrill Is Gone," *Wall Street Journal,* 13 October 1989, p. B1.
75. Karen J. Sack, "Supermarkets: Labor Costs Continue to Daunt Supermarkets," *Standard & Poor's Industry Surveys,* 2 May 1991, pp. R90–91.
76. Sack, "Supermarkets: Labor Costs," p. R90.
77. Lorne Manly, "Selling in the Stores of the Future," *Adweek,* 20 January 1992, pp. 12–13; Richard S. Teitelbaum, "Companies to Watch: Catalina Marketing," *Fortune,* 18 May 1992, p. 89.
78. This section adapted from Laurie Petersen, "21st Century Supermarket Shopping," *Adweek's Marketing Week,* 9 March 1992, p. 9; Howard Schlossberg, "Tomorrow's Retailing Technologies on Display Today at Smart Store," *Marketing News,* 20 January 1992, p. 2.
79. Matt Moffett, "U.S. Firms Yell Ole to Future in Mexico," *Wall Street Journal,* 8 March 1993, pp. B1, B5; Matt Moffett, "Chic Star of Mexican Retailing: Sears Roebuck," *Wall Street Journal,* 8 March 1993, pp. B1, B5.
80. Jeffrey A. Tannenbaum, "Plan to Aid Franchises in Emerging Nations Starts Slowly," *Wall Street Journal,* 13 February 1992, p. B2.
81. Roger Cohen, "Pizza and Persistence Win in Hungary," *New York Times,* 5 May 1992, pp. D1, D9.
82. Andrew Tanzer, "The Mountains Are High, the Emperor Is Far Away," *Forbes,* 5 August 1991, pp. 70–75.

Chapter 14

1. Elyse Tanouye, "Merck's 'River Blindness' Gift Hits Snags," *Wall Street Journal,* 23 September 1992, pp. B1, B4; Douglas Stanglin and Julie Corwin, "Making Sure Aid Is Delivered to the Needy, Not the Greedy," *U.S. News & World Report,* 20 January 1992, p. 36.
2. John T. Mentzer, Roger Gomes, and Robert E. Krapfel, Jr., "Physical Distribution Service: A Fundamental Marketing Concept," *Journal of the Academy of Marketing Science,* Winter 1989, pp. 53–62.
3. Mentzer, Gomes, and Krapfel, pp. 53–62.
4. E. J. Muller, "Climb Aboard the Quality Express," *Distribution,* February 1992, pp. 34–37.
5. Peter Bradley, "The Drive for Transportation Quality," *Purchasing,* 16 January 1992, p. 106.
6. Lisa H. Harrington, "Public Warehousing: The Original Third Party," *Distribution,* February 1993, pp. 47–52.
7. Kenneth B. Ackerman and Bernard T. LaLonde, "Making Warehousing More Efficient," *Harvard Business Review,* March-April 1980, p. 95.
8. "Casebook: Pro Fasteners," *Distribution,* May 1992, p. 56.
9. Jay Gordon, "Information Keys Warehouse Market," *Distribution,* July 1992, pp. 89–91.
10. Mark Alpert, "Building a Better Bar Code," *Fortune,* 15 June 1992, p. 101.
11. Ned Snell, "Bar Codes Break Out," *Datamation,* 1 April 1992, pp. 71–73.
12. William M. Bassin, "A Technique for Applying EOQ Models to Retail Cycle Stock Inventories," *Journal of Small Business Management,* January 1990, pp. 48–55.
13. Jay Gordon, "Bull's-Eye Computerization," *Distribution,* November 1991, pp. 62–64.
14. Benefits of JIT taken from Ernest Raia, "JIT in Purchasing: A Progress Report," *Purchasing,* 14 September 1989, pp. 58–77.
15. Thomas F. O'Boyle, "Firms' Newfound Skill in Managing Inventory May Soften Downturn," *Wall Street Journal,* 19 November 1990, pp. A1, A4.
16. Risks of JIT inventory management taken from Paul H. Zipkin, "Does Manufacturing Need a JIT Revolution?" *Harvard Business Review,* January-February 1991, pp. 40–50.
17. Joseph Weber, "It's Like Somebody Had Shot the Postman," *Business Week,* 13 January 1992, p. 82.
18. Karen J. Sack, "General Retailing: Productivity and Value Pricing Lure Customers," *Standard & Poor's Industry Surveys,* 9 January 1992, p. R63.
19. Leila Davis, "Instant Orders," *Nation's Business,* April 1990, pp. 34–36.
20. Adapted from William M. Pride and O.C. Ferrell, *Marketing,* 6th ed. (Boston: Houghton-Mifflin, 1989), pp. 412–417.
21. U.S. Department of Commerce, Bureau of the Census, *Statistical Abstract of the United States*

(Washington, DC: Government Printing Office, 1991), p. 622.
22. Stephen R. Klein, "Handful of Carriers Dominate Industry," *Standard & Poor's Industry Surveys,* 31 October 1991, p. R15.
23. Klein, "Handful of Carriers," pp. R15–16.
24. Stephen R. Klein, "Rail Traffic in Holding Pattern," *Standard & Poor's Industry Surveys,* 31 October 1991, p. R22.
25. U.S. Department of Commerce, p. 620.
26. Stephen R. Klein, "Trucks Dominate Freight Market," *Standard & Poor's Industry Surveys,* 31 October 1991, p. R50.
27. Klein, "Trucks," p. R47.
28. For another discussion on the undercharge crisis, see Thomas A. Foster, "Undercharges: Why There Is No Justice," *Distribution,* June 1992, pp. 26–32.
29. "Coming to a Truck Cab Near You: On-Board and Hand-Held Computers," *Distribution,* May 1992, p. 16.
30. U.S. Department of Commerce, p. 603.
31. Klein, "Rail Traffic," p. R20.
32. U.S. Department of Commerce, p. 603.
33. Kurt Hoffman, "Overnight Air Logistics: Tune In to How Cable Giant HBO Gets Its Products in and on the Air," *Distribution,* January 1993, pp. 57–59.
34. Thomas Canning, "Air Cargo: Continued Moderate Growth Ahead," *Standard & Poor's Industry Surveys,* 25 June 1992, p. A41.
35. Robert Selwitz, "No Longer an Uphill Haul," *Distribution,* April 1993, pp. 30–34.
36. Daniel Machalaba, "Railroads Getting in Better Shape for the Long Haul," *Wall Street Journal,* 26 February 1992, p. B4.
37. "Hunt Country," *Forbes,* 22 June 1992, p. 244.
38. "Union Pacific and J.B. Hunt Team Up on Mexican Intermodal Service," *Distribution,* May 1992, p. 18.
39. E. J. Muller, "Global Strategies for Small Shippers," *Distribution,* October 1991, pp. 28–34.
40. This section based on Jay Gordon, "Service Industry Logistics," *Distribution,* February 1992, pp. 27–31.
41. Jonn Harris, "Dinnerhouse Technology," *Forbes,* 8 July 1991, pp. 98–99.
42. Peter Bradley, "The World in a Computer Window," *Purchasing,* 16 July 1992, pp. 52–53.
43. Thomas A. Foster, "The Gospel of Green," *Distribution,* January 1992, pp. 27–28; Thomas A. Foster, "An Environmental Impact Statement," *Distribution,* January 1992, p. 4.
44. Foster, "Environmental Impact Statement," p. 4
45. Jay Gordon, "The Environmental Nitty Gritty," *Distribution,* May 1992, pp. 36–44.
46. Daniel J. McConville, "Tracking the Hazmat Express," *Distribution,* June 1992, pp. 51–56.
47. E. J. Muller, "Third Party Catches On," *Distribution,* July 1992, p. 60.
48. Muller, "Third Party," p. 60.
49. "Sorting Out the Complexities of a Global Logistics Contract," *Distribution,* May 1992, p. 24.
50. "It's Back to Basics for Carrier Quality," *Distribution,* August 1991, p. 57.
51. Peter Bradley, "The Drive for Transportation Quality," *Purchasing,* 16 January 1992, pp. 106–113.
52. Jay Gordon, "And Then There Was One," *Distribution,* May 1991, pp. 49–53.
53. Tan Miller, "The International Model Decision," *Distribution,* October 1991, pp. 82–84.
54. Muller, "Global Strategies," pp. 28–34.

Chapter 15

1. Valerie Reitman, "Buoyant Sales of Lever 2000 Soap Bring Sinking Sensation to Procter & Gamble," *Wall Street Journal,* 19 March 1992, pp. B1, B5.
2. Daniel M. Gold, "Reggie's Year in the Trenches," *Adweek's Marketing Week,* 9 March 1992, pp. 28–29.
3. E. S. Browning, "Helping Hands Promote Euro Disneyland," *Wall Street Journal,* 1 April 1992, p. B6.
4. William Keenan, Jr., "America's Best Sales Forces," *Sales & Marketing Management,* September 1992, pp. 46–52; "UPS Delivers More to Its Customers," *Sales & Marketing Management,* September 1992, p. 64.
5. Craig A. Kelley, William C. Gaidis, and Peter H. Reingen, "The Use of Vivid Stimuli to Enhance Comprehension of the Content of Product Warning Messages," *Journal of Consumer Affairs,* Winter 1989, pp. 243–266.
6. Jacob Jacoby and Wayne D. Hoyer, "The Comprehension/Miscomprehension of Print Communication: Selected Findings," *Journal of Consumer Research,* March 1989, pp. 434–443; "The Miscomprehension of Mass-Media Advertising Claims: A Reanalysis of Benchmark Data," *Journal of Advertising Research,* June-July 1990, pp. 9–16.
7. Gail Tom, "Cueing the Consumer: The Role of Salient Cues in Consumer Perception," *Journal of Consumer Marketing,* Spring 1987, pp. 23–27.
8. Helene Cooper, "Once Again, Ads Woo Teens with Slang," *Wall Street Journal,* 29 March 1993, pp. B1, B6.
9. Gabriella Stern, "Heinz Aims to Export Taste for Ketchup," *Wall Street Journal,* 20 November 1992, pp. B1, B9.
10. Thomas E. Barry and Daniel J. Howard, "A Review and Critique of the Hierarchy of Effects in Advertising," *International Journal of Advertising,* Spring 1990, pp. 121–135.
11. Terence O'Brien, "Stages in Consumer Decision Making," *Journal of Marketing Research,* August 1971, pp. 283–289.
12. Barry and Howard, pp. 124–125.
13. Kristian S. Palda, "The Hypothesis of a Hierarchy of Effects: A Partial Evaluation," *Journal of Marketing Research,* February 1966, pp. 13–24.

14. "G & R Research Links Recall, Buying Intent," *Advertising Age,* 16 August 1971, p. 3.
15. Regina Eisman, "Building Brand Loyalty," *Incentive,* September 1990, pp. 39–45.
16. John G. Udell, "The Perceived Importance of the Elements of Strategy," *Journal of Marketing,* January 1968, pp. 34–40; also see Thomas Petit and Martha McEnally, "Putting Strategy into Promotional Mix Decisions," *Journal of Consumer Marketing,* Winter 1985, pp. 41–47.
17. *Why Advertise? The Value of Advertising: Annual Supplement to The Wall Street Journal,* 1991.
18. James E. Lynch and Graham J. Hooley, "Increasing Sophistication in Advertising Budget Setting," *Journal of Advertising Research,* February-March 1990, pp. 67–75.
19. Nicolaos E. Synodinos, Charles F. Keown, and Laurence W. Jacobs, "Transnational Advertising Practices: A Survey of Leading Brand Advertisers in Fifteen Countries," *Journal of Advertising Research,* April-May 1989, pp. 43–50.
20. Lynch and Graham, p. 74.
21. Lynch and Graham, p. 68.

Chapter 16

1. Betsy Sharkey, "The New Coke," *Adweek,* 11 November 1991, pp. 30–38; Michael J. McCarthy, "Coca-Cola Plans New Slogan for Coke Classic," *Wall Street Journal,* 12 May 1992, pp. B1, B6; Pat Sloan and Melanie Wells, "Coke Closes In on a New Theme," *Advertising Age,* 29 June 1992, pp. 1, 50; Video Storyboard Tests, Inc., 1991.
2. "Total National Ad Spending by Media," *Advertising Age,* 6 January 1992, p. S11.
3. U.S. Department of Commerce, Bureau of the Census, *Statistical Abstract of the United States* (Washington, DC: Government Printing Office, 1990).
4. "Advertising-to-Sales Ratios," *Advertising Age,* 13 November 1989, p. 26.
5. "Radio and TV Broadcasting: Viewers Deluged with Ads," *Standard & Poor's Industry Surveys,* 13 February 1992, p. M26.
6. Amitava Chattopadhyay and Kunal Basu, "Humor in Advertising: The Moderating Role of Prior Brand Evaluation," *Journal of Marketing Research,* November 1990, pp. 466–476.
7. Marvin E. Goldberg and Jon Hartwick, "The Effects of Advertiser Reputation and Extremity of Advertising Claims on Advertising Effectiveness," *Journal of Consumer Research,* September 1990, pp. 172–179.
8. James C. Schroer, "Ad Spending: Growing Market Share," *Harvard Business Review,* January-February 1990, pp. 44–48.
9. Rajiv Grover and V. Srinivasan, "Evaluating the Multiple Effects of Retail Promotions on Brand Loyalty and Brand Switching Segments," *Journal of Marketing Research,* February 1992, pp. 76–89; S. P. Raj, "The Effects of Advertising on High and Low Loyalty Consumer Segments," *Journal of Consumer Research,* June 1982, pp. 77–89.
10. David W. Schumann, Jan M. Hathcote, and Susan West, "Corporate Advertising in America: A Review of Published Studies on Use, Measurement, and Effectiveness," *Journal of Advertising,* September 1991, pp. 35–56.
11. Alecia Swasy, "P{&G to Tout Name behind the Brands," *Wall Street Journal,* 12 December 1990, pp. B1, B6.
12. Bob D. Cutler and Darrel D. Muehling, "Advocacy Advertising and the Boundaries of Commercial Speech," *Journal of Advertising,* 18 (1989), pp. 40–50.
13. Ira Teinowitz, "Coors' Bud-Bashing Stays Regional," *Advertising Age,* 23 March 1992, p. 10.
14. Darrel D. Muehling, Jeffrey J. Stoltman, and Sanford Grossbart, "The Impact of Comparative Advertising on Levels of Message Involvement," *Journal of Advertising,* 4 (1990), pp. 41–50.
15. Cornelia Pechmann and David W. Stewart, "The Effects of Comparative Advertising on Attention, Memory, and Purchase Intentions," *Journal of Consumer Research,* September 1990, pp. 180-191.
16. Muehling, Stoltman, and Grossbart, pp. 41–50.
17. Jerry B. Gotlieb and Dan Sarel, "Comparative Advertising Effectiveness: The Role of Involvement and Source Credibility," *Journal of Advertising,* 1 (1991), pp. 38–45.
18. E. S. Browning, "Eastern Europe Poses Obstacles for Ads," *Wall Street Journal,* 30 July 1992, p. B6.
19. Cyndee Miller, "Babe-Based Beer Ads Likely to Flourish," *Marketing News,* 6 January 1992, pp. 1, 10–11; Joanne Lipman, "Beer Makers Brew Controversy with Ads Targeting Women," *Wall Street Journal,* 6 April 1992, pp. B1, B8.
20. Debra Goldman, "The French Style of Advertising," *Adweek,* 16 December 1991, p. 21.
21. "The Best Awards 1991: In Tough Year, Hottest Ads on TV Speak in Past Perfect," *Advertising Age,* 30 March 1992, pp. 18–25.
22. Kevin Goldman, "Barrage of Ads in Super Bowl Blurs Messages," *Wall Street Journal,* 3 February 1993, p. B6.
23. "Radio & TV Broadcasting: Radio Benefitting from Local Advertisers," *Standard & Poor's Industry Surveys,* 11 June 1992, p. M4.
24. "Television: Network's Dominance Still Slipping," *Standard & Poor's Industry Surveys,* 12 March 1992, p. L28.
25. "Radio & TV Broadcasting: TV Viewing Stabilizes," *Standard & Poor's Industry Surveys,* 13 February 1992, p. M23.
26. Joe Mandese, "Prime-Time Rates Take a Tumble," *Advertising Age,* 16 September 1991, p. 6.
27. Scot Hume and Alison Fahey, "McDonald's Readies Major Blast via Outdoor Boards," *Advertising Age,* 30 March 1992, p. 58.

28. Karen J. Marchetti, "Take a Direct Route for Cost-Effective Marketing," *Marketing News,* 22 July 1991, pp. 14–15.
29. David J. Jefferson and Thomas R. King, "Slice It, Dice It: 'Infomercials' Fill Up Air Time on Cable, Aim for Prime Time," *Wall Street Journal,* 22 October 1992, pp. A1, A4.
30. "Bush Signs Bill Aimed at Curbing Solicitation," *New York Times,* 22 December 1991, p. 14.
31. "Advertisers Take Cart," *Sales & Marketing Management,* March 1992, pp. 76–77.
32. Kevin Helliker, "For TV Giants, Big New Battle Is Still in Store," *Wall Street Journal,* 17 March 1992, pp. B1, B6.
33. Joanne Lipman, "ABC Tests 'Place-Based Media' at Penney," *Wall Street Journal,* 11 May 1992, p. B4.
34. Joshua Hammer, "A Golden Boy's Toughest Sell," *Newsweek,* 19 February 1990, pp. 52–53.
35. Christy Fisher, "Marketers Answer Interactive TV Call," *Advertising Age,* 30 March 1992, p. 36.
36. Laurie Petersen, "Wallboards for the Senior Set," *Adweek's Marketing Week,* 30 September 1991, p. 24.
37. Kevin Goldman, "Captive Paying Audiences Give Ads at the Cinema Mixed Reviews," *Wall Street Journal,* 18 February 1993, p. B10.
38. Gabriella Stern, "Tooth-Brushers Take a Shine to Baking Soda," *Wall Street Journal,* 2 March 1992, pp. B1, B5.
39. Pat Sloan and Cleveland Horton, "Costly Controversies: Nissan Turbo, Reebok Bungee Spots off the Air," *Advertising Age,* 26 March 1990, pp. 1, 52.
40. Jacob Jacoby and Wayne D. Hoyer, "The Miscomprehension of Mass-Media Advertising Claims: A Reanalysis of Benchmark Data," *Journal of Advertising Research,* June-July 1990, pp. 9–16.
41. Jeanne Saddler, "Ads for Diets Spark Inquiry by Regulators," *Wall Street Journal,* 26 March 1993, pp. B1, B5.
42. William Wilkie, Dennis McNeill, and Michael Mazis, "Marketing's 'Scarlet Letter': The Theory and Practice of Corrective Advertising," *Journal of Marketing,* Spring 1984, pp. 11–31.
43. Krystal Miller, "Such an Ad Was Almost Certain to Make Somebody Hit the Roof," *Wall Street Journal,* 8 November 1990, p. B1.
44. Eric Stoltz and Jack Torobin, "Public Relations by the Numbers," *American Demographics,* January 1991, pp. 42–46.
45. Philip Kotler and Gary Armstrong, *Marketing: An Introduction,* 2nd ed. (Englewood Cliffs, NJ: Prentice-Hall, 1990), p. 427.
46. Judith Waldrop, "Educating the Customer," *American Demographics,* September 1991, pp. 44–47.
47. Barbara Clark O'Hare, "Good Deeds Are Good Business," *American Demographics,* September 1992, pp. 38–42.
48. George Gruenwald, "Make a Good First Impression with PR," *Marketing News,* 6 November 1990, p. 9.
49. Alison Fahey, "Crystal Pepsi Sales Surge as Test Markets Clear Shelves," *Advertising Age,* 18 May 1992, pp. 3, 56.
50. Joanne Lipman, "Product Plugs Dot Olympic Landscape," *Wall Street Journal,* 11 February 1992, p. B8.
51. "Coke Plans Big European Push," *Marketing News,* 6 January 1992, p. 18.
52. Howard Schlossberg, "MasterCard Embarks on Tree-Planting Venture," *Marketing News,* 19 August 1991, p. 20.
53. Richard A. Truitt and Sheila S. Kelley, "Battling a Crisis in Advance," *Public Relations Quarterly,* Spring 1989, p. 6.
54. James E. Lukaszweski, "How Vulnerable Are You? The Lessons from Valdez," *Public Relations Quarterly,* Fall 1989, p.5.
55. E. Bruce Harrison andTom Prugh, "Assessing the Damage: Practitioners' Perspectives on the Valdez," *Public Relations Journal,* October 1989, p. 40.
56. Amy E. Gross, "How Popeye's and Reebok Confronted Product Rumors," *Adweek's Marketing Week,* 22 October 1990, pp. 27–30.

Chapter 17

1. Gary McWilliams and Marc Maremont, "Forget the Green Stamps—Give me a Ticket to Miami, *Business Week,* 24 February 1992, pp. 70–71; Kevin E. Collinane, "Incentive Plans Reward, Irk Consumers," *Wall Street Journal,* 2 September 1992, pp. B1, B5; "Air Miles Shuts U.S. Operations of Buying Plan," *Wall Street Journal,* 3 May 1993, p. B1.
2. Joe Mandese and Scott Donaton, "Media, Promotion Gap to Narrow," *Advertising Age,* 29 June 1992, p. 16.
3. Scott Hume, "Trade Promos Devour Half of All Marketing $," *Advertising Age,* 13 April 1992, pp. 3, 53.
4. Regina Eisman, "Building Brand Loyalty," *Incentive,* September 1990, pp. 39–45.
5. "Turning Coupon Flood into Guided Trickle," *Wall Street Journal,* 3 June 1992, p. B1.
6. "Global Coupon Use Up; U.K., Belgium Tops in Europe," *Marketing News,* 5 August 1991, p. 5.
7. Kamran Kashani and John A. Quelch, "Can Sales Promotion Go Global?" *Business Horizons,* May-June 1990, pp. 37–43.
8. Howard Schlossberg, "Frequent Mileage Club Sends Consumers Running to Shoe Stores," *Marketing News,* 3 August 1992, p. 12.
9. McWilliams and Maremont, pp. 70–71.
10. Jean J. Boddewyn and Monica Leardi, "Sales Promotion: Practice, Regulation and Self-Regulation around the World," *International Journal of Advertising,* August 1989, pp. 363–374.
11. Daniel M. Gold, "Reggie's Year in the Trenches," *Adweek's Marketing Week,* 9 March 1992, pp. 28–29.

12. John P. Cortez, "Pizza Pie Spies Heat Up Florida," *Advertising Age,* 20 April 1992, pp. 1, 48.
13. Kashani and Quelch, p. 38.
14. E. S. Browning, "Eastern Europe Poses Obstacles for Ads," *Wall Street Journal,* 30 July 1992, p. B6.
15. Douglas B. Leeds, "P-O-P Planning Especially Important during Recession," *Marketing News,* 1 April 1991, p. 11.
16. Cyndee Miller, "POP Gains Followers as 'Era of Retailing' Dawns," *Marketing News,* 14 May 1990, p. 2.
17. Bristol Voss, "Selling with Sentiment," *Sales & Marketing Management,* March 1993, pp. 60–65.
18. Miller, p. 2.
19. Kathleen Deveny, "Displays Pay Off for Grocery Marketers," *Wall Street Journal,* 15 October 1992, pp. B1, B5.
20. Kevin Higgins, "In-Store Merchandising Is Attracting More Marketing Dollars with Last Word in Sales," *Marketing News,* 19 August 1983, p. 1.
21. Deveny, p. B1.
22. Robert Black, "The Trade Show Industry: Management and Marketing Career Opportunities," lecture presented at Cornell University, 19 November 1986.
23. Daniel M. Gold, "A Shift in Direction? Trade Spending May Have Peaked in 1991," *Adweek's Marketing Week,* 13 April 1992, pp. 26–27.
24. Zachary Schiller, "Not Everyone Loves a Supermarket Special," *Business Week,* 17 February 1992, pp. 64–68.
25. Adapted from Douglas Dalrymple, *Sales Management: Concepts and Cases* (New York: Wiley, 1985), p. 12.
26. U.S. Department of Commerce, Bureau of the Census, *Statistical Abstract of the United States* (Washington, DC: Government Printing Office, 1991), p. 396.
27. "1992 Sales Manager's Budget Planner," *Sales & Marketing Management,* 22 June 1992, p. 70.
28. Bruce Hager and John Templeman, "Now, They're Selling BMW's Door-to-Door—Almost," *Business Week,* 14 May 1990, p. 65.
29. Cara M. Tuzzolino, "Dial 'M' for Motivation," *Incentive,* September 1991, pp. 88–90, 137.
30. Henry Holtzman, "Why Salespeople Don't Follow-Up Leads," *Implement & Tractor,* January 1990, p. 15.
31. Sue Kapp, "Prospects Stay Interested Six Months," *Business Marketing,* March 1990, p. 42.
32. Charles Greenburg, "Direct Response Can Become a Potent Sales Management Tool," *Marketing News,* 5 March 1990, p. 15.
33. "Hyatt Has No Reservations about Sales Excellence," *Sales & Marketing Management,* September 1991, p. 55.
34. Eric Hollreiser, "Drive, It Said," *Adweek's Marketing Week,* 23 March 1992, pp. 41, 44.
35. "1992 Sales Manager's Budget Planner," p. 73.
36. Rosann L. Spiro and Barton A. Weitz, "Adaptive Selling: Conceptualization, Measurement, and Nomological Validity," *Journal of Marketing Research,* February 1990, pp. 61–69.
37. "Hewlett-Packard Strives to Connect with Customers," *Sales & Marketing Management,* September 1991, p. 48.
38. "Eastman Kodak Brings Training into Sharper Focus," *Sales & Marketing Management,* September 1992, p. 62.
39. "1991 Sales Manager's Budget Planner," *Sales & Marketing Management,* 17 June 1991, p. 76; Dartnell Corporation, *26th Survey of Sales Force Compensation,* 1990.
40. Sergey Frank, "Global Negotiating: Vive Les Différences!" *Sales & Marketing Management,* May 1992, pp. 64–69.
41. This section adapted from Rolph E. Anderson, Joseph F. Hair, Jr., and Alan J. Bush, *Professional Sales Management,* 2nd Ed. (New York: McGraw-Hill, 1992), pp. 172–177.
42. Patricia Sellers, "How to Remake Your Sales Force," *Fortune,* 4 May 1992, pp. 98–103.
43. Anderson, Hair, and Bush, pp. 183–184.
44. Robert G. Head, "Restoring Balance to Sales Compensation," *Sales & Marketing Management,* August 1992, pp. 48–53.
45. Head, pp. 50–52.
46. "Progressive's Success Is No Accident," *Sales & Marketing Management,* September 1991, p. 57.
47. Robert G. Head, "Systematizing Salesperson Selection," *Sales & Marketing Management,* February 1992, pp. 65–68.
48. Tom Murray, "Starting a Sales Force from Scratch," *Sales & Marketing Management,* April 1991, pp. 51–59.
49. Robert P. DeGroot, "Desktop Guide to Sales Recruitment," *Sales & Marketing Management,* May 1990, p. 110.
50. "For Northwestern, Once Is Not Enough," *Sales & Marketing Management,* September 1992, p. 58.
51. "Eli Lilly Lauded for Its Bedside Manner," *Sales & Marketing Management,* September 1991, p. 56.
52. Head, "Systematizing Salesperson Selection," pp. 66–67.
53. John Swan, David Rink, G. E. Kiser, and Warren Martin, "Industrial Buyer Image of the Saleswoman," *Journal of Marketing,* Winter 1984, pp. 110–116.
54. Patrick L. Schul and Brent M. Wren, "The Emerging Role of Women in Industrial Selling: A Decade of Change," *Journal of Marketing,* July 1992, pp. 38–54.
55. Bill Kelley, "Selling in a Man's World," *Sales & Marketing Management,* January 1991, pp. 28–35.
56. "Dow Makes It Big by Thinking Small," *Sales & Marketing Management,* September 1991, p. 46.
57. Michael J. Major, "Sales Training Emphasizes Service and Quality," *Marketing News,* 5 March 1990, p. 5.

58. Bill Kelley, "Training: 'Just Plain Lousy' or 'Too Important to Ignore'?" *Sales & Marketing Management,* March 1993, pp. 66–70.
59. "Facts Survey: Sales Incentives," *Incentive,* September 1991, pp. 60–66.
60. Ajay Kohli, "Some Unexplored Supervisory Behaviors and Their Influence on Salespeople's Role Clarity, Specific Self Esteem, Job Satisfaction, and Motivations," *Journal of Marketing Research,* November 1985, pp. 424–433.
61. Thomas R. Wotroba and Michael L. Thurlow, "Sales Force Participation in Quota Selling and Sales Forecasting," *Journal of Marketing,* April 1976, pp. 11–16.
62. "Survey of Employee Motivation Practices," *Incentive,* 1991.
63. Christina Lovio-George, "What Motivates Best?" *Sales & Marketing Management,* April 1992, pp. 113–114.
64. "1991 Sales Manager's Budget Planner," p. 75.
65. George H. Lucas, Jr., A. Parasuraman, Robert A. Davis, and Ben M. Enis, "An Empirical Study of Salesforce Turnover," *Journal of Marketing,* July 1987, pp. 34–59.

Chapter 18

1. "The Big Brawl in Snack Food," *Adweek's Marketing Week,* 23 September 1992, pp. 4–5; Bill Saporito, "Why the Price Wars Never End," *Fortune,* 23 March 1992, pp. 68–78.
2. "A PC Price War Has Computer Buyers on a Shopping Spree," *Wall Street Journal,* 29 June 1992, pp. A1, A6.
3. "The Big Squeeze," *Adweek's Marketing Week,* 12 November 1990, p. 22.
4. Saporito, p. 69.
5. Saporito, p. 69.
6. "The Nonconformist," *Forbes,* 28 October 1991, p. 200.
7. "Egghead Scrambles Back," *Business Week,* 29 July 1991, pp. 70–71.
8. "Levi's Dockers Weigh into Casuals," *Adweek's Marketing Week,* 24 September 1990, pp. 26–27.
9. Akshay Rao and Kent Monroe, "The Effect of Price, Brand Name, and Store Name on Buyers' Perceptions of Product Quality: An Integrative Review," *Journal of Marketing Research,* August 1989, pp. 351–357; Gerard Tellis and Gary Gaeth, "Best Value, Price-Seeking, and Price Aversion: The Impact of Information and Learning on Consumer Choices," *Journal of Marketing,* April 1990, pp. 34–35.
10. William Dodds, Kent Monroe, and Dhruv Grewal, "Effects of Price, Brand, and Store Information on Buyers' Product Evaluations," *Journal of Marketing Research,* August 1991, pp. 307–319; see also Akshay Rao and Wanda Sieben, "The Effect of Prior Knowledge on Price Acceptability and the Type of Information Examined," *Journal of Consumer Research,* September 1992, pp. 256–270.
11. Michael Etgar and Naresh Malhotra, "Determinants of Price Dependency: Personal and Perceptual Factors," *Journal of Consumer Research,* September 1981, pp. 217–222; Jeen-Su Lim and Richard Olshavsky, "Impacts of Consumers' Familiarity and Product Class on Price Quality Inference and Product Evaluations," *Quarterly Journal of Business and Economics,* Summer 1988, pp. 130–141.
12. Donald Lichtenstein and Scott Burton, "The Relationship between Perceived and Objective Price-Quality," *Journal of Marketing Research,* November 1989, pp. 429–443.
13. "Store-Brand Pricing Has to Be Just Right," *Wall Street Journal,* 14 February 1992, p. B1.

Chapter 19

1. "Shaw Uses Price Cuts to Extend Its Rule over Carpet Business," *Wall Street Journal,* 12 June 1991, pp. A1, A8.
2. Partially adapted from "Value Pricing Is Hot as Shrewd Consumers Seek Low-Cost Quality," *Wall Street Journal,* 12 March 1991, pp. A1, A5; "Value Marketing: Quality, Service, and Fair Pricing Are the Keys to Selling in the '90s," *Business Week,* 11 November 1991, pp. 132–140.
3. *United States* v. *Sacony-Vacuum Oil Co.,* 310 U.S. 150 (1940).
4. Paul Barrett, "Nintendo's Latest Novelty Is a Price Fixing Settlement," *Wall Street Journal,* 11 April 1991, p. B1.
5. "U.S. Steps Up Probe on Fixing of Air Fares," *Wall Street Journal,* 18 March 1992, p. A3.
6. "FTC Broadens Trust Powers with Old Law," *Wall Street Journal,* 30 September 1992, pp. B1, B2.
7. Stephen Adler and Alix Freedman, "Tobacco Suit Exposes Ways Cigarette Firms Keep the Profits Fat," *Wall Street Journal,* 5 March 1990, pp. A1, A6. Reprinted by permission of The Wall Street Journal, © 1990 Dow Jones & Company, Inc. All rights reserved worldwide.
8. See James Wilcox, Roy Howell, Paul Kuzdrall, and Robert Britney, "Price Quantity Discounts: Some Implications for Buyers and Sellers," *Journal of Marketing,* July 1987, pp. 60–70.
9. George Day and Adrian Ryans, "Using Price Discounts for a Competitive Advantage," *Industrial Marketing Management,* February 1988, pp. 1–14.
10. Patricia Sellers, "The Dumbest Marketing Ploy," *Fortune,* 3 October 1992, pp. 88–94.
11. "Eliminated Discounts on P&G Goods Annoy Many Who Sell Them," *Wall Street Journal,* 11 August 1992, pp. A1, A6.
12. "Eliminated Discounts," pp. A1, A6.
13. Sellers, pp. 88–89. © 1992 Time Inc. All rights reserved.
14. "Eliminated Discounts," p. A6.

15. Ramon Avila, Joseph Chapman, and Teresa Avila, "An Exploratory Study on Consumers' Attitudes toward Rebates," in *Developments in Marketing Science,* ed. John Hawes and John Thanopoulos (Miami: Academy of Marketing Science, 1989), pp. 273–277.
16. "Single-Price Stores' Formula for Success: Cheap Merchandise and a Lot of Clutter," *Wall Street Journal,* 30 June 1992, pp. B1, B6.
17. "Ford Expands One-Price to Cougar," *Adweek's Brandweek,* 17 August 1992, p. 8; "Why Motown Is Going the Extra Mile in California," *Business Week,* 12 October 1992, pp. 70, 75.
18. Charles Quigley and Elaine Notarantonio, "An Exploratory Investigation of Perceptions of Odd and Even Pricing," in *Developments in Marketing Science,* ed. Victoria Crittenden (Miami: Academy of Marketing Science, 1992), pp. 306–309.
19. Francis Mulhern and Robert Leone, "Implicit Price Bundling of Retail Products: A Multiproduct Approach to Maximizing Store Profitability," *Journal of Marketing,* October 1991, pp. 63–76; Dorothy Paun, "Product Bundling: A Normative Model Based on an Orientation Perspective," in *Developments in Marketing Science,* ed. Victoria Crittenden (Miami: Academy of Marketing Science, 1992), pp. 301–305.
20. Myung-Soo Lee, "Two-Part Pricing in a Competitive Market: An Empirical Investigation of the Video Movie Rental Case," in *1988 AMA Educators' Proceedings: Efficiency and Effectiveness in Marketing,* ed. Gary Frazier and others (Chicago: American Marketing Association), pp. 195–199.
21. "Value Strategy to Battle Recession," *Advertising Age,* 7 January 1991, pp. 1, 44.
22. "How to Prosper in the Value Decade," *Fortune,* 30 November 1992, pp. 89–103.
23. "Cut Costs or Else," *Business Week,* 22 March 1993, pp. 28–29.
24. "Cut Costs," pp. 28–29.

Chapter 20

1. Suein L. Hwang, "Nicotine Patch Reignites Fight over Drug Ads," *Wall Street Journal,* 30 June 1992, pp. B1, B6.
2. Cynthia Crossen, "Baby Ads Spark Debate over Ethics," *Wall Street Journal,* 26 December 1990, p. 9.
3. Kathleen Deveny, "Strong Brew: Malt Liquor Makers Find Lucrative Market in the Urban Young," *Wall Street Journal,* 9 March 1992, pp. A1, A4.
4. Michael W. Miller, "Four Charities Charged by Two States with Fraudulent Fund-Raising Claims," *Wall Street Journal,* 4 August 1992, p. A4.
5. Francine Schwadel, "Poverty's Cost: Urban Consumers Pay More and Get Less, and Gap May Widen," *Wall Street Journal,* 2 July 1992, p. A1.
6. This concept taken from Frank Bingham, Jr., and Barney Raffield, "An Overview of Ethical Considerations in Industrial Marketing," in *Developments in Marketing Science,* vol. 12, ed. Jon Hawes and John Thanopoulous (Akron, OH: Academy of Marketing Science, 1989), pp. 244–248; see also Michael Mayo and Lawrence Marks, "An Empirical Investigation of a General Theory of Marketing Ethics," in *1989 AMA Educators' Proceedings: Enhancing Knowledge Development in Marketing,* ed. Paul Bloom and others (Chicago: American Marketing Association), p. 95.
7. Levels of moral development based on Edward Stevens, *Business Ethics* (New York: Paulist Press, 1979).
8. These points taken from Gene R. Laczniak and Patrick E. Murphy, "Fostering Ethical and Marketing Decisions," *Journal of Business Ethics,* April 1991, pp. 259–271.
9. L. B. Chonko, B. M. Enis, and J. F. Tanner, Jr., *Managing Salespeople* (Boston: Allyn and Bacon, 1992), p. 43.
10. Ishmael Akaah and Edward Riordan, "Judgments of Marketing Professionals about Ethical Issues in Marketing Research: A Replication and Extension," *Journal of Marketing Research,* February 1989, pp. 112–120.
11. This was also found to be true in an earlier study; see Shelby Hunt, Lawrence Chonko, and James Wilcox, "Ethical Problems of Marketing Researchers," *Journal of Marketing Research,* August 1984, pp. 309–324; see also Kenneth Andrews, "Ethics in Practice," *Harvard Business Review,* September-October 1989, pp. 99–104.
12. Adapted from Chonko, Enis, and Tanner, p. 43.
13. Michael R. Hyman, Robert Skipper, and Richard Tansey, "Ethical Codes Are Not Enough," *Business Horizons,* March-April 1990, p. 16.
14. John A. Byrne, "The Best-Laid Ethics Programs . . . ," *Business Week,* 9 March 1992, p. 67.
15. Joanne Lipman, "Surgeon General Says It's Time Joe Camel Quit," *Wall Street Journal,* 10 March 1992, pp. B1, B7; see also John P. Pierce, Elizabeth Gilpin, David M. Burns, Elizabeth Whalen, Bradley Rosbrook, Donald Shopland, and Michael Johnson, "Does Tobacco Advertising Target Young People to Start Smoking? Evidence from California," *Journal of the American Medical Association,* 11 December 1991, p. 3154.
16. Michael B. Mazis, Debra Jones Ringold, Elgin S. Perry, and Daniel W. Denman, "Perceived Age and Attractiveness of Models in Cigarette Advertisement," *Journal of Marketing,* January 1992, pp. 22–37.
17. Lipman, "Surgeon General Says," p. B1.
18. Janice Castro, "Volunteer Vice Squad," *Time,* 23 April 1990, pp. 60–61.
19. Eben Shapiro, "California Plans More Antismoking Ads," *Wall Street Journal,* 26 January 1993, p. B7.
20. Suein L. Hwang, "Some Stadiums Snuff Out Cigarette Ads," *Wall Street Journal,* 17 July 1992, p. B3.

21. Larry Dietz, "Who Enjoys the Right of Free Speech? Jane Fonda, Joe Camel, You, and Me," *Adweek Western Advertising News,* 20 April 1992, p. 44.
22. Paul M. Barrett, "Surprise Court Ruling Could Have Big Impact Far beyond Cigarettes," *Wall Street Journal,* 25 June 1992, pp. A1, A10.
23. Matthew Grimm, "Bud, Coors Mull 'Media' Strategy to Blunt Critics," *Adweek's Marketing Week,* 11 November 1991, p. 5.
24. Frank Rose, "If It Feels Good, It Must Be Bad," *Fortune,* 21 October 1991, pp. 91–100.
25. "Selling Sin to Blacks," *Fortune,* 21 October 1991, p. 100; Alix M. Freedman, "Heileman Tries a New Name for Strong Malt," *Wall Street Journal,* 11 May 1992, pp. B1, B5; Deveny, pp. A1, A4.
26. Joanne Lipman, "Why Activists Fume at Anti-Smoking Ads," *Wall Street Journal,* 20 February 1992, p. B3.
27. Julia Flynn Siler, "It Isn't Miller Time Yet, and This Bud's Not for You," *Business Week,* 24 June 1991, p. 52.
28. Lipman, "Why Activists Fume," p. B3; Siler, p. 52.
29. Joanne Lipman, Foes Claim Ad Bans Are Bad Business," *Wall Street Journal,* 27 February 1990, p. B1.
30. Terry Adams, "Tobacco Ad Ban in EC Nearer," *Advertising Age,* 17 February 1992, p. 59; "EC Panel Proposes Ban on Nearly All Tobacco Ads," *Marketing News,* 24 June 1991, p. 5; see also "The Tobacco Trade: The Search for El Dorado," *Economist,* 16 May 1992, p. 21.
31. Rosanna Tamburri and Christopher J. Chipello, "Court Upholds Canadian Ban on Tobacco Ads," *Wall Street Journal,* 18 January 1993, p. B5.
32. Deborah Schroeder, "Life, Liberty, and the Pursuit of Privacy," *American Demographics,* June 1992, p. 20.
33. Peter Pae, "American Express Co. Discloses It Gives Merchants Data on Cardholders' Habits," *Wall Street Journal,* 14 May 1992, p. A3.
34. "Blockbuster Video Says It Has No Plan to Sell Its Customer Lists," *Marketing News,* 4 February 1991, p. 2; see also the article that prompted the controversy, Michael W. Miller, "Coming Soon to Your Local Video Store: Big Brother," *Wall Street Journal,* 26 December 1990, p. 9.
35. "Equifax Says It Will Stop Giving Mailing Lists to Direct Marketers," *Marketing News,* 16 September 1991, p. 21.
36. Michael W. Miller, "How Drug Companies Get Medical Records of Individual Patients," *Wall Street Journal,* 27 February 1992, pp. A1, A4.
37. Evan I. Schwartz, "The Rush to Keep Mum," *Business Week,* 8 June 1992, pp. 36–38.
38. The first three points from Joe Schwartz and Thomas Miller, "The Earth's Best Friends," *American Demographics,* February 1991, pp. 26–35.
39. Joe Schwartz, "Americans Annoyed by Wasteful Packaging," *American Demographics,* April 1992, p. 13.
40. Schwartz and Miller, p. 28.
41. Terry Lefton, "Disposing of the Green Myth," *Adweek's Marketing Week,* 13 April 1992, pp. 20–21.
42. Terry Lefton, "Beating the Green Rap," *Adweek's Marketing Week,* 27 January 1992, p. 6.
43. Joe Schwartz, "Turtle Wax Shines Water, Too," *American Demographics,* April 1992, p. 14.
44. "L'eggs to Scrap Plastic 'Egg' Package," *Marketing News,* 19 August 1991, p. 20.
45. "Research Group Says Some Green Marketers Are Only Pretending," *Marketing News,* 20 January 1992, p. 3.
46. Arthur S. Hayes and Junda Woo, "'Green Marketing' Labeling Law Piques Food Industry Coalition," *Wall Street Journal,* 24 February 1992, p. B6.
47. Jeanne Saddler, "FTC Issues a 'Green-Marketing' Guide to Help Prevent Deceptive-Ad Charges," *Wall Street Journal,* 29 July 1992, p. B5.
48. "Free Trade's Green Hurdle," *Economist,* 15 June 1991, pp. 61–62.
49. "In the Market for a Better World," *Maclean's,* 11 May 1992, p. E1.
50. Paul F. Buller, John J. Kohls, and Kenneth S. Anderson, "The Challenge of Global Ethics," *Journal of Business Ethics,* October 1991, pp. 767–775.
51. See Russell Abratt, Deon Nel, and Nicola Susan Higgs, "An Examination of the Ethical Beliefs of Managers Using Selected Scenarios in a Cross-Cultural Environment," *Journal of Business Ethics,* January 1992, pp. 29–35.
52. John Tsalikis and Osita Nwachukwu, "A Comparison of Nigerian to American Views of Bribery and Extortion in International Commerce," *Journal of Business Ethics,* February 1991, pp. 85–98.
53. Daniel Treisman, "Korruptsia," *New Republic,* 11 May 1992, pp. 14–17.
54. Tsalikis and Nwachukwu, pp. 85–86.
55. Carla Rapoport, "Why Japan Keeps On Winning," *Fortune,* 15 July 1991, pp. 76–85; for more insight into Japanese attitudes toward business ethics, see Edwin Whenmouth, "A Matter of Ethics," *Industry Week,* 16 March 1992, pp. 57–62.
56. Tsalikis and Nwachukwu, p. 85.
57. John Dobson, "Ethics in the Transnational Corporation: The 'Moral Buck' Stops Where?" *Journal of Business Ethics,* January 1992, pp. 21–27.
58. "Tobacco Trade," pp. 21–23.
59. "Tobacco Trade," pp. 21–23.
60. Diana Solis and Sonia L. Nazario, "U.S., Mexico Take On Border Pollution," *Wall Street Journal,* 25 February 1992, pp. B1, B8; for more information on *maquiladoras* and the growth in the Mexican-American border population, see also Blayne Cutler, "Welcome to the Borderlands," *American Demographics,* February 1991, pp. 44–49, 57; see also Dan Koeppel, "The New Borderland," *Adweek's Marketing Week,* 17 February 1992, pp. 19–24.

61. Kenneth H. Bacon, "Round Two: With Free-Trade Pact About Wrapped Up, the Real Battle Begins," *Wall Street Journal,* 7 August 1992, pp. A1, A14.
62. Pros and cons of social responsibility adapted from Rogene Buchholz, *Business Environment and Public Policy,* 3rd ed. (Englewood Cliffs, NJ: Prentice-Hall, 1989).
63. Archie B. Carroll, "The Pyramid of Corporate Social Responsibility: Toward the Moral Management of Organizational Stakeholders," *Business Horizons,* July-August 1991, pp. 39–48.
64. Dan R. Dalton and Catherine M. Daily, "The Constituents of Corporate Responsibility: Separate, but Separable, Interests?" *Business Horizons,* July-August 1991, pp. 74–78.
65. This section based entirely on Carroll, pp. 39–48.
66. Leo Northart, "At Issue: Corporate Social Responsibility," *Public Relations Journal,* August 1983, p. 3.
67. "A Kinder, Gentler Generation of Executives?" *Business Week,* 23 April 1990, p. 86.
68. Barbara Clark O'Hare, "Good Deeds Are Good Business," *American Demographics,* September 1991, pp. 38–42.
69. Suzanne Alexander, "Life's Just a Bowl of Cherry Garcia for Ben & Jerry's," *Wall Street Journal,* 15 July 1992, p. B3.
70. Cara Appelbaum, "Jantzen to Pitch In for Clean Waters," *Adweek's Marketing Week,* 6 April 1992, p. 6.
71. Elyse Tanouye, "Drug Firms Start 'Compliance' Programs Reminding Patients to Take Their Pills," *Wall Street Journal,* 25 March 1992, pp. B1, B5.
72. Mzamo P. Mangaliso, "The Corporate Social Challenge for the Multinational Corporation," *Journal of Business Ethics,* July 1992, pp. 491–500.
73. Richard T. Hise, Peter L. Gillett, and J. Patrick Kelly, "The Corporate Consumer Affairs Effort," *MSU Business Topics,* Summer 1978, pp. 17–26.
74. Claes Fornell, "Increasing the Organizational Influence of Corporate Consumer Affairs Departments," *Journal of Consumer Affairs,* Winter 1981, p. 191.
75. Hise, Gillett, and Kelly, pp. 17–26.
76. Upton Sinclair, *The Jungle* (Garden City, NY: Doubleday, 1906), p. 41; see also Robert Hermann, "The Consumer Movement in Historical Perspective," in *Consumer: Search for the Consumer Interest,* 2nd ed., ed. David Aaker and Geroge Day (New York: Free Press, 1974), pp. 10–18.
77. "American Products: What Consumers Think," *Management Review,* May 1989, p. 14.
78. Barney Raffield, "Consumerism and Marketing Management Revisited: Enduring Implications for Marketing Managers," in *Developments in Marketing Science: Proceedings of the Academy of Marketing Science,* ed. Kenneth Bahn (Blacksburg, VA: Virginia Tech, 1988), pp. 242–246.
79. Les Carlson and Norman Kangun, "Demographic Discontinuity: Another Explanation for Consumerism?" *Journal of Consumer Affairs,* Summer 1988, pp. 55–73; see also Robert L. Egbert, Mary M. Kluender, Toni E. Santmire, and Richard G. Maybee, "Demographic Discontinuity: Social-Psychological Implications of Rapid Changes in the Size of Youth Populations," report prepared for the George A. Miller Lecture Series, University of Illinois at Champaign, 1982; see also Richard A. Easterlin, *Birth and Fortune: The Impact of Numbers on Personal Welfare* (New York: Basic Books, 1980).
80. Rajib N. Sanyal, "The Valdez Principles: Implications for Corporate Social Responsibility," *Journal of Business Ethics,* December 1991, pp. 883–890.
81. Quotes taken from Charles E. Watson, "Managing with Integrity: Social Responsibilities of Business as Seen by America's CEO's," *Business Horizons,* July-August 1991, pp. 99–109.

Chapter 21

1. Michael E. Porter, *Competitive Strategy: Techniques for Analyzing Industries and Competitors* (New York: Free Press, 1980).
2. Anheuser-Busch, *1991 Annual Report* (St. Louis: Anheuser-Busch).
3. Saturn Corporation, *Face to Face with the Future* (Detroit: Saturn Corporation).
4. "A Boring Brand Can Be Beautiful," *Fortune,* 18 November 1991, pp. 169–178.
5. "Dominant Brands Are Most Profitable Assets," *Conference Board's Management Briefing: Marketing,* October-November 1989, p. 6.
6. Michael Minor, "The Market Share Effect: A Review and Reconsideration," in *1989 AMA Educators' Proceedings: Enhancing Knowledge Development in Marketing,* ed. Paul Bloom and others (Chicago: American Marketing Association), pp. 121–125.
7. "Long-Term Thinking and Paternalistic Ways Carry Michelin to Top," *Wall Street Journal,* 5 January 1990, p. A1.
8. "Running the Biggest LBO," *Business Week,* 2 October 1989, p. 79; "How Long Can Nabisco Keep Doing More with Less?" *Business Week,* 23 April 1990, pp. 90–92.
9. "Getting Hot Ideas from Customers," *Fortune,* 18 May 1992, pp. 86–87.
10. Robert Buzzell and Bradley Gale, *The PIMS Principles* (New York: Free Press), 1987.
11. "Two Disparate Firms Find Keys to Success in Troubled Industries," *Wall Street Journal,* 29 May 1991, pp. A1, A9.
12. John Keller, "AT&T, MCI, Sprint Raise the Intensity of Their Endless War," *Wall Street Journal,* 20 October 1992, pp. A1, A6.
13. "Long-Term Thinking," pp. A1, A4.
14. McDonald's, *1991 Annual Report,* p. 4.
15. "McD Rewards, Researches Frequent Customers," *Nations' Restaurant News,* 1 June 1992, pp. 7, 89.
16. Kamron Kashani, *Managing Global Marketing* (Boston: PWS-Kent, 1992), pp. 5–6.

17. Kashani, p. 90.
18. Kashani, p. 90.

Chapter 22

1. Otis Port and John Carey, "Questing for the Best," *Business Week*, 25 October 1991, p. 10.
2. Keith H. Hammonds and Gail DeGeorge, "Where Did They Go Wrong?" *Business Week*, 25 October 1991, p. 35.
3. Jonathan B. Levine, "It's An Old World in More Ways Than One," *Business Week*, 25 October 1991, p. 28.
4. Cyndee Miller, "U.S. Firms Lag in Meeting Global Quality Standards," *Marketing News*, 15 February 1993, p. 1.
5. Arthur R. Tenner and Irving J. DeToro, *Total Quality Management* (Reading, MA: Addison-Wesley, 1992), p. 9.
6. David Woodruff, Karen L. Miller, Larry Armstrong, and Thane Peterson, "A New Era for Auto Quality," *Business Week*, 22 October 1990, p. 82.
7. "Total Quality Management," *Services Marketing Today* [American Marketing Association newsletter], January-February 1992, p. 4.
8. Tenner and DeToro, p. 60.
9. Allan J. Magrath, "Marching to a Different Drummer," in *Marketing Executive Report* [American Marketing Association], August 1992, p. 15.
10. Amanda Bennett, "Making the Grade with the Customer," *Wall Street Journal*, 12 November 1990, p. B1.
11. Laura Loro, "Customer Is Always Right," *Advertising Age*, 10 February 1992, p. 25.
12. Much of the material in this section adapted from Tenner and DeToro, pp. 61–66.
13. David A. Garvin, "Competing on the Eight Dimensions of Quality," *Harvard Business Review*, November-December 1987, pp. 101–109.
14. Christopher Power, Walecia Konrad, Alice Z. Cuneo, and James B. Treece, "Value Marketing," *Business Week*, 11 November 1991, p. 135.
15. Robert Neff, "No. 1—and Trying Harder," *Business Week*, 25 October 1991, p. 23.
16. Port and Carey, p. 10.
17. Port and Carey, p. 14.
18. Port and Carey, p. 14.
19. Kevin Kelly, "Motorola Wants to Light Up Another Market," *Business Week*, 14 October 1991, p. 50.
20. Chapman Wood, "The Prophets of Quality," *Quarterly Review* [American Society for Quality Control], Fall 1988.
21. Richard Colby, "Oldest Rule, Newest U.S. Trend: Customer Comes First," *Sunday Oregonian*, 22 March 1992, p. R1.
22. Tenner and DeToro, p. 118.
23. Levine, p. 27.
24. Hammonds and DeGeorge, p. 38.
25. Much of the discussion in this section adapted from Tenner and DeToro, pp. 179–180.
26. Port and Carey, p. 16.
27. Thane Peterson, Kevin Kelly, Joseph Weber, and Neil Gross, "Top Products for Less Than Top Dollar," *Business Week*, 25 October 1991, p. 68.
28. Naomi Freundlich and Michael Schroeder, "Getting Everybody into the Act," *Business Week*, 25 October 1991, p. 152.
29. David Woodruff and Jonathan B. Levine, "Miles Traveled, More to Go," *Business Week*, 25 October 1991, p. 71.
30. Magrath, p. 16.
31. Michael Barrier, "Small Firms Put Quality First," *Nation's Business*, May 1992, p. 30.
32. Barrier, p. 22.
33. Levine, p. 27.
34. Woodruff, Miller, Armstrong, and Peterson, p. 87.
35. Mike Vasilakes, "Wilson Oxygen Teams Up with Employees and Suppliers to Improve Quality," *Welding Distributor*, March-April 1993, pp. 65–70.
36. Diane H. Schmalensee, "Marketers Must Lead Quality Improvement or Risk Becoming Irrelevant," *Services Marketing* [American Marketing Association newsletter], Spring 1991, p. 1.
37. Eugene H. Fram and Martin L. Presburg, "TQM Is a Catalyst for New Marketing Applications," *Marketing News*, 9 November 1992, p. 17.
38. Much of the material in this section adapted from Elayne Cree, "Baldridge Award Proves That Customer Defines Quality," *Marketing News*, 6 January 1992, p. 30.
39. Bernard Jaworski, "Toward a Theory of Marketing Control: Environmental Context, Control Types, and Consequences," *Journal of Marketing*, July 1988, pp. 23–29.
40. "P&G Rewrites the Marketing Rules," *Fortune*, 6 November 1989, pp. 34–48.
41. Louis M. Copella and William S. Sekely, "The Marketing Audit: Usage and Application," in *1978 Southern Marketing Association Annual Conference Proceedings*, ed. Robert S. Franz, Robert M. Hawkins, and Al Toma (LaFayette, LA: University of Southern Louisiana Press, 1978), pp. 411–414; see also Philip Kotler, William Gregor, and William Rogers, "The Marketing Audit Comes of Age," *Sloan Management Review*, Winter 1989, pp. 49–62.
42. Philip Kotler, *Marketing Management*, 7th ed. (Englewood Cliffs, NJ: Prentice-Hall, 1991).
43. Michael P. Mokwa, "Marketing Control and Evaluation: A Framework for Strategic Arts Administration," in *Marketing the Arts*, ed. M. P. Mokwa, W. M. Dawson, and E. A. Price (New York: Praeger, 1980), p. 272.

Appendix A

1. C. F. Siegel and R. Powers, "FAB: A Useful Tool for the Job-Seeking Marketing Student," *Marketing Education Review*, Winter 1991, pp. 60–65.
2. Louisiana State University Placement Center, Baton Rouge, LA, 1993.
3. Louisiana State University Placement Center, Baton Rouge, LA, 1993.

Company/Product Index

Subject Index

N